UNITED STATES HISTORY

ISBN 978-0-544-45414-9

4 5 6 7 8 9 10   0868   24 23 22 21 20 19 18 17

4656573   B C D E F G

Educational Advisory Panel

The following educators provided ongoing review during the development of prototypes and key elements of this program.

Jose Colon

Berkeley High School
Berkeley, California

Bethany Copeland

Peach County High School
Fort Valley, Georgia

Darrel Dexter

Egyptian Community Unit School
Tamms, Illinois

Charles Dietz

Burnett Middle School
San Jose, California

John Hogan

Brevard High School
Brevard, North Carolina

Jeffrey Kaufman

Aspirations Diploma Plus High School
Brooklyn, New York

Beth E. Kuhlman

Queens Metropolitan High School
Forest Hills, New York

Beatrice Nudelman

Aptakisic Junior High School
Buffalo Grove, Illinois

Kyle Race

Greene High School
Greene, New York

Gretchen Ritter Varela

Northville High School
Northville, Michigan

Sharon Shirley

Branford High School
Branford, Connecticut

Yvette Snopkowski

Davis Junior High School
Sterling Heights, Michigan

La-Shanda West

Cutler Bay Senior High School
Cutler Bay, Florida

Contents

 Videos related to each module can be accessed through your digital Student Edition.

HISTORY. HISTORY® Partnership xviii

Reading Social Studies H2

Using This Book H6

Explore Online. H8

Module 1

America, Africa, and Europe before 1500,

Beginnings–AD 1500 2

Reading Social Studies Specialized Vocabulary

of Social Studies 4

Lesson 1   The Earliest Americans. 6

Lesson 2   Native American Cultures 11

Lesson 3   Trading Kingdoms of West Africa 19

Lesson 4   Europe before 1500 23

Social Studies Skills Interpret Diagrams 29

Module Assessment 30

Multimedia Connections
HISTORY. The Maya 31 MC1

Module 2

New Empires in the Americas, 1400–1700. 32

Reading Social Studies Outlining and History. 34

Lesson 1   Europeans Set Sail. 36

Lesson 2   Europeans Reach the Americas 41

Lesson 3   Spain Builds an Empire 46

Lesson 4   The Race for Empires. 53

Social Studies Skills Frame Historical Questions 61

Module Assessment 62

Multimedia Connections
HISTORY. Ponce de León 63 MC1

Module 3

★

The English Colonies, 1600–1770. 64

Reading Social Studies Vocabulary Clues. 66

Lesson 1   The Southern Colonies. 68
Lesson 2   The New England Colonies. 75
Lesson 3   The Middle Colonies. 84
Lesson 4   Life in the English Colonies 90

Social Studies Skills Interpret Timelines 99
Module Assessment 100

Module 4

★

The American Revolution, 1760–1785. 102

Reading Social Studies Main Ideas in Social Studies 104

Lesson 1   Conflict in the Colonies 106
Lesson 2   The Revolution Begins. 113
Lesson 3   Declaring Independence. 119

Historic Document The Declaration of Independence 124

Lesson 4   The Struggle for Liberty. 128
Lesson 5   Independence! 139

Social Studies Skills Understand Historical Interpretation. 145
Module Assessment 146

Multimedia Connections
HISTORY. The American Revolution. 147 MC1

Module 5

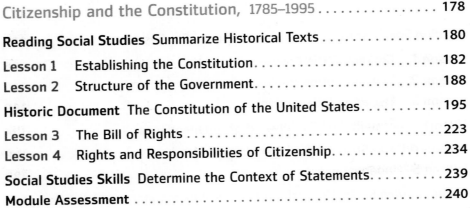

Forming a Government, 1775–1791 148

Reading Social Studies Understand Chronological Order 150

Lesson 1   The Articles of Confederation 152
Lesson 2   The New Nation Faces Challenges 158
Lesson 3   Creating the Constitution 164
Lesson 4   Ratifying the Constitution 170

Social Studies Skills Determine Different Points of View 175
Module Assessment 176

Module 6

Citizenship and the Constitution, 1785–1995 178

Reading Social Studies Summarize Historical Texts 180

Lesson 1   Establishing the Constitution 182
Lesson 2   Structure of the Government 188

Historic Document The Constitution of the United States 195

Lesson 3   The Bill of Rights 223
Lesson 4   Rights and Responsibilities of Citizenship 234

Social Studies Skills Determine the Context of Statements 239
Module Assessment 240

Module 7

★

Launching the Nation, 1785–1805 242

Reading Social Studies Inferences about History 244
Lesson 1　Washington Leads a New Nation 246
Lesson 2　Hamilton and National Finances 250
Lesson 3　Challenges for the New Nation 255
Lesson 4　John Adams's Presidency 263
Lesson 5　Jefferson Becomes President 268
Social Studies Skills Make Group Decisions 275
Module Assessment 276

Module 8

★

War and Expansion in the Americas, 1800–1820 278

Reading Social Studies Public Documents in History 280
Lesson 1　The Coming of War 282
Lesson 2　The War of 1812 288
Lesson 3　Settling International Issues 292
Social Studies Skills Work in a Group to Solve Issues 295
Module Assessment 296

Module 9

★

A New National Identity, 1810–1830 298

Reading Social Studies Bias and Historical Events 300
Lesson 1　American Foreign Policy 302
Lesson 2　Nationalism and Sectionalism 306
Lesson 3　American Culture 314
Social Studies Skills Identify Central Issues 321
Module Assessment 322

Module 10

★

The Age of Jackson, 1825–1845 324

Reading Social Studies Draw Conclusions about the Past 326

Lesson 1   Jacksonian Democracy 328
Lesson 2   Jackson's Administration 333
Lesson 3   Indian Removal 340

Social Studies Skills Solve Problems 345
Module Assessment 348

Module 11

★

Westward Expansion, 1800–1900 350

Reading Social Studies Ask Questions to Understand 352

Lesson 1   A Growing Nation 354
Lesson 2   Boom Times in the West 364
Lesson 3   Wars for the West 371
Lesson 4   Farming and Populism 378

Social Studies Skills Compare Migration Maps 385
Module Assessment 386

Multimedia Connections
HISTORY Lewis and Clark 387 MC1

Module 12

★

Expansion and Conflict, 1820–1855 388

Reading Social Studies Vocabulary in Context 390

Lesson 1   The Texas Revolution 392
Lesson 2   The Mexican-American War 397
Lesson 3   The California Gold Rush 408

Social Studies Skills Interpret Maps: Expansion 415
Module Assessment 418

Multimedia Connections
HISTORY The Real West: Rush for Gold 419 MC1

Module 13

---★---

The North, 1785–1860 . . . . **420**

Reading Social Studies Understand Causes and Effects
in History **422**

Lesson 1   The Industrial Revolution in America **424**
Lesson 2   Changes in Working Life **430**
Lesson 3   The Transportation Revolution **435**
Lesson 4   More Technological Advances **441**

Social Studies Skills Personal Conviction and Bias **445**
Module Assessment **446**

Module 14

---★---

The South, 1790–1860 . . . . **448**

Reading Social Studies Online Research **450**
Lesson 1   Growth of the Cotton Industry **452**
Lesson 2   Southern Society **459**
Lesson 3   Slavery in the South **463**

Social Studies Skills Interpret Graphs **469**
Module Assessment **470**

Module 15

★

Slavery in the United States, 1619–1852 472

Reading Social Studies Compare and Contrast
Historical Facts 474

Lesson 1   Beginnings of Slavery in the Americas 476
Lesson 2   The Slave System 482
Lesson 3   The Movement to End Slavery 489
Lesson 4   The Politics of Slavery 496

Social Studies Skills Conduct Internet Research 501
Module Assessment 502

Module 16

★

Reform Movements in the United States,
1815–1855 504

Reading Social Studies Information and Propaganda 506

Lesson 1   Immigrants and Urban Challenges 508
Lesson 2   American Arts 513
Lesson 3   Reforming Society 518
Lesson 4   Abolition 524
Lesson 5   Women's Rights 528

Social Studies Skills Accept Social Responsibility 535
Module Assessment 536

Module 17

★

A Divided Nation, 1845–1865 538

Reading Social Studies Fact, Opinions, and the Past 540

Lesson 1   The Debate over Slavery 542
Lesson 2   Trouble in Kansas 548
Lesson 3   Political Divisions 553
Lesson 4   The Nation Divides 558

Social Studies Skills Assess Primary and Secondary Sources 563
Module Assessment 564

Module 18

⭐

The Civil War, 1860–1866 566

Reading Social Studies Supporting Facts and Details 568

Lesson 1   The War Begins 570
Lesson 2   The War in the East 577
Lesson 3   The War in the West 583
Lesson 4   Daily Life during the War 590
Lesson 5   The Tide of War Turns 598

Social Studies Skills Interpret Political Cartoons 607
Module Assessment 608

Ⓗ **Multimedia Connections**
HISTORY Days of Darkness: The Gettysburg Civilians 609 MC1

Module 19

⭐

Reconstruction, 1860–1880 610

Reading Social Studies Analyze Historical Information 612

Lesson 1   Rebuilding the South 614
Lesson 2   The Fight over Reconstruction 620
Lesson 3   Reconstruction in the South 627

Social Studies Skills Chance, Oversight, and Error in History ... 635
Module Assessment 636

Module 20

⭐

The Industrial Age, 1870–1900 . . . . **638**

Reading Social Studies Identify Patterns of Organization **640**

Lesson 1 The Second Industrial Revolution **642**
Lesson 2 Big Business **648**
Lesson 3 Industrial Workers **652**

Social Studies Skills Analyze Costs and Benefits **657**
Module Assessment **658**

🏛 **Multimedia Connections**
HISTORY Henry Ford **659 MC1**

Module 21

⭐

Immigrants and Urban Life, 1870–1910 . . . . **660**

Reading Social Studies Understand Historical Fact versus
Historical Fiction **662**

Lesson 1 A New Wave of Immigration **664**
Lesson 2 The Growth of Cities **670**
Lesson 3 City Life **674**

Social Studies Skills Make Comparisons **679**
Module Assessment **680**

🏛 **Multimedia Connections**
HISTORY Ellis Island **681 MC1**

Module 22

⭐

The Progressive Spirit of Reform, 1865–1925 . . . . **682**

Reading Social Studies Evaluate Sources **684**

Lesson 1 The Gilded Age and the Progressive Movement **686**
Lesson 2 Reforming the Workplace **695**
Lesson 3 The Rights of Women and Minorities **701**
Lesson 4 The Progressive Presidents **707**

Social Studies Skills Short- and Long-term
Causal Relationships **711**
Module Assessment **712**

Module 23

★

America as a World Power, 1860–1920 714

Reading Social Studies Compare Historical Texts. 716

Lesson 1   The United States Gains Overseas Territories. 718
Lesson 2   The Spanish-American War 724
Lesson 3   The United States and Latin America 732

Social Studies Skills Understand Continuity and Change. 739
Module Assessment 740

Module 24

★

World War I, 1914–1920. 742

Reading Social Studies Recognize Fallacies in Reasoning 744

Lesson 1   The Road to War 746
Lesson 2   Americans Prepare for War 751
Lesson 3   Americans in World War I. 757
Lesson 4   Establishing Peace 763

Social Studies Skills Use Visual Resources. 769
Module Assessment 770

        Multimedia Connections
HISTORY Dear Home: Letters from WWI. 771 MC1

Module 25

★

The Roaring Twenties, 1918–1930 772

Reading Social Studies Synthesize Information 774

Lesson 1   Boom Times 776
Lesson 2   Life during the 1920s. 782
Lesson 3   The Jazz Age 790

Social Studies Skills Compare Graphs. 795
Module Assessment 796

Module 26

The Great Depression, 1925–1940 798

Reading Social Studies Recognize Implied Main Ideas 800

Lesson 1   The End of Prosperity 802
Lesson 2   Roosevelt's New Deal 809
Lesson 3   Americans Face Hard Times 816

Social Studies Skills Conduct a Debate 823
Module Assessment 824

Module 27

World War II, 1935–1950 826

Reading Social Studies Categorize 828

Lesson 1   The War Begins 830
Lesson 2   The Home Front 837
Lesson 3   War in Europe and North Africa 843
Lesson 4   War in the Pacific 849
Lesson 5   Victory and Consequences 855

Social Studies Skills Construct Timelines 861
Module Assessment 862

HISTORY **Multimedia Connections**
Memories of World War II 863 MC1

Module 28

★

The Cold War, 1945–1960. 864

Reading Social Studies Understand through Visualizing 866

Lesson 1   Adjusting to Peace. 868
Lesson 2   War in Korea and a New Red Scare. 876
Lesson 3   The Nation Prospers 882

Social Studies Skills Interpret Battle Maps. 887
Module Assessment 888

Module 29

★

The Vietnam War Years, 1960–1975 890

Reading Social Studies Set a Purpose 892

Lesson 1   Kennedy and Foreign Policy 894
Lesson 2   Escalation in Vietnam. 902
Lesson 3   The End of the War 910

Social Studies Skills Use Primary Sources: Oral Histories 917
Module Assessment 918

H **Multimedia Connections**
HISTORY October Fury: The Cuban Missile Crisis 919 MC1

Module 30

★

The Civil Rights Movement, 1950–1975 920

Reading Social Studies Use Context Clues: Synonyms. 922

Lesson 1   The Civil Rights Movement Takes Shape 924
Lesson 2   Kennedy, Johnson, and Civil Rights 931
Lesson 3   Rights for Other Americans 938

Social Studies Skills Make Speeches. 943
Module Assessment 944

Module 31

⭐

Searching for Order, 1968–2000 946

Reading Social Studies Summarize 948

Lesson 1   Nixon's Presidency and Watergate 950
Lesson 2   America in the 1970s 957
Lesson 3   The Reagan Presidency 964
Lesson 4   The End of the Twentieth Century 969

Social Studies Skills Determine the Strength of an Argument 975
Module Assessment 976

Module 32

⭐

The Twenty-First Century, 2000–Present 978

Reading Social Studies Predict 980

Lesson 1   Challenges for a New Millenium 982
Lesson 2   Domestic and Foreign Policy Issues 988
Lesson 3   Rapid Changes 994

Social Studies Skills Confront Controversial Issues 1001
Module Assessment 1004

References

Atlas R2

Writing Workshops R14

Symbols of the United States R36

English and Spanish Glossary R40

Index R80

Available Online

Reading Like a Historian

Historic Documents

Biographical Dictionary

Close-Read Screencasts

Facts About the States

Presidents of the United States

Supreme Court Decisions

Economics Handbook

Geography and Map Skills Handbook

Skillbuilder Handbook

 Multimedia Connections

▶ These online lessons feature award-winning content and include short video segments, maps and visual materials, primary source documents, and more.

The Maya

Ponce de León

The American Revolution

Lewis and Clark

The Real West: Rush for Gold

Days of Darkness: The Gettysburg Civilians

Henry Ford

Ellis Island

Dear Home: Letters from World War I

Memories of World War II

October Fury: The Cuban Missile Crisis

HISTORY programming greatly appeals to educators and young people who are drawn into the visual stories our documentaries tell. Our Education Department has a long-standing record in providing teachers and students with curriculum resources that bring the past to life in the classroom. Our content covers a diverse variety of subjects, including American and world history, government, economics, the natural and applied sciences, arts, literature and the humanities, health and guidance, and even pop culture.

The HISTORY website, located at **www.history.com**, is the definitive historical online source that delivers entertaining and informative content featuring broadband video, interactive timelines, maps, games, podcasts and more.

"We strive to engage, inspire and encourage the love of learning..."

Since its founding in 1995, HISTORY has demonstrated a commitment to providing the highest quality resources for educators. We develop multimedia resources for K–12 schools, two- and four-year colleges, government agencies, and other organizations by drawing on the award-winning documentary programming of A&E Television Networks. We strive to engage, inspire and encourage the love of learning by connecting with students in an informative and compelling manner. To help achieve this goal, we have formed a partnership with Houghton Mifflin Harcourt.

The Idea Book for Educators

Classroom resources that bring the past to life

Live webcasts

HISTORY Take a Veteran to School Day

In addition to premium video-based resources, **HISTORY** has extensive offerings for teachers, parents, and students to use in the classroom and in their in-home educational activities, including:

▶ *The Idea Book for Educators* is a biannual teacher's magazine, featuring guides and info on the latest happenings in history education to help keep teachers on the cutting edge.

▶ **HISTORY Classroom (www.history.com/classroom)** is an interactive website that serves as a portal for history educators nationwide. Streaming videos on topics ranging from the Roman aqueducts to the civil rights movement connect with classroom curricula.

▶ **HISTORY email newsletters** feature updates and supplements to our award-winning programming relevant to the classroom with links to teaching guides and video clips on a variety of topics, special offers, and more.

▶ **Live webcasts** are featured each year as schools tune in via streaming video.

▶ **HISTORY Take a Veteran to School Day** connects veterans with young people in our schools and communities nationwide.

In addition to **Houghton Mifflin Harcourt**, our partners include the *Library of Congress,* the *Smithsonian Institution, National History Day, The Gilder Lehrman Institute of American History,* the Organization of American Historians, and many more. HISTORY video is also featured in museums throughout America and in over 70 other historic sites worldwide.

Reading Social Studies

Did you ever think you would begin reading your social studies book by reading about reading? Actually, it makes better sense than you might think. You would probably make sure you learned soccer skills and strategies before playing in a game. Similarly, you need to learn reading skills and strategies before reading your social studies book. In other words, you need to make sure you know whatever you need to know in order to read this book successfully.

Tip #1

Use the Reading Social Studies Pages

Take advantage of the two pages on reading at the beginning of every module. Those pages introduce the module themes, explain a reading skill or strategy, and identify key terms and people.

Themes

Why are themes important? They help our minds organize facts and information. For example, when we talk about baseball, we may talk about types of pitches. When we talk about movies, we may discuss animation.

Historians are no different. When they discuss history or social studies, they tend to think about some common themes: Economics, Geography, Religion, Politics, Society and Culture, and Science and Technology.

Reading Skill or Strategy

Good readers use a number of skills and strategies to make sure they understand what they are reading. These lessons will give you the tools you need to read and understand social studies.

Key Terms and People

Before you read the module, review these words and think about them. Have you heard the word before? What do you already know about the people? Then watch for these words and their meanings as you read the module.

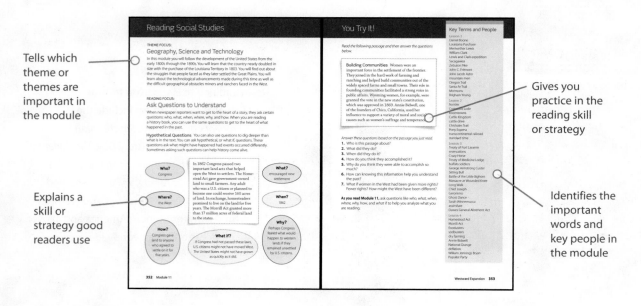

Tells which theme or themes are important in the module

Explains a skill or strategy good readers use

Gives you practice in the reading skill or strategy

Identifies the important words and key people in the module

Tip #2

Read like a Skilled Reader

You will never get better at reading your social studies book—or any book for that matter—unless you spend some time thinking about how to be a better reader.

Skilled readers do the following:

- They preview what they are supposed to read before they actually begin reading. They look for vocabulary words, titles of lessons, information in the margin, or maps or charts they should study.

- They divide their notebook paper into two columns. They title one column "Notes from the Lesson" and the other column "Questions or Comments I Have."

- They take notes in both columns as they read.

- They read like **active readers**. The Active Reading list below shows you what that means.

- They use clues in the text to help them figure out where the text is going. The best clues are called signal words.

    Chronological Order Signal Words: *first, second, third, before, after, later, next, following that, earlier, finally*

    Cause and Effect Signal Words: *because of, due to, as a result of, the reason for, therefore, consequently*

    Comparison/Contrast Signal Words: *likewise, also, as well as, similarly, on the other hand*

Active Reading

Successful readers are **active readers**. These readers know that it is up to them to figure out what the text means. Here are some steps you can take to become an active, and successful, reader.

Predict what will happen next based on what has already happened. When your predictions don't match what happens in the text, reread the confusing parts.

Question what is happening as you read. Constantly ask yourself why things have happened, what things mean, and what caused certain events.

Summarize what you are reading frequently. Do not try to summarize the entire module! Read a bit and then summarize it. Then read on.

Connect what is happening in the part you're reading to what you have already read.

Clarify your understanding. Stop occasionally to ask yourself whether you are confused by anything. You may need to reread to clarify, or you may need to read further and collect more information before you can understand.

Visualize what is happening in the text. Try to see the events or places in your mind by drawing maps, making charts, or jotting down notes about what you are reading.

Tip #3

Pay Attention to Vocabulary

It is no fun to read something when you don't know what the words mean, but you can't learn new words if you use or read only the words you already know. In this book, we know we probably have used some words you don't know. But, we have followed a pattern as we have used more difficult words.

Key Terms and People

At the beginning of each lesson you will find a list of key terms and people that you will need to know. Be on the lookout for those words as you read through the lesson.

Academic Vocabulary
facilitate to make easier

Academic Vocabulary

When the text uses a word that is important in all classes, not just social studies, we define it in the margin under the heading Academic Vocabulary. You will run into these academic words in other textbooks, so you should learn what they mean while reading this book.

Academic and Social Studies Words

As you read this social studies textbook, you will be more successful if you know or learn the meanings of the words on this page. Academic words are important in all classes, not just social studies. Social studies words are special to the study of U.S. history and other social studies topics.

Academic Words

abstract expressing a quality or idea without reference to an actual thing

acquire to get

advocate to plead in favor of

affect to change or influence

agreement a decision reached by two or more people or groups

aspects parts

authority power, right to rule

cause the reason something happens

circumstances surrounding situations

classical referring to the cultures of ancient Greece or Rome

complex difficult, not simple

concrete specific, real

consequences the effects of a particular event or events

contemporary existing at the same time

contract a binding legal agreement

criteria rules for defining

develop/development 1. to grow or improve; 2. the process of growing or improving

distinct separate

distribute to divide among a group of people

effect the result of an action or decision

efficient/efficiency 1. productive, not wasteful; 2. the quality of being efficient

element part

execute to perform, carry out

explicit fully revealed without vagueness

facilitate to bring about

factor cause

features characteristics

function use or purpose

impact effect, result

implement to put in place

implications effects of a decision

implicit understood though not clearly put into words

incentive something that leads people to follow a certain course of action

influence change or have an effect on

innovation a new idea or way of doing something

logic/logical 1. well-thought-out idea; 2. reasoned, well thought out

motive a reason for doing something

neutral unbiased, not favoring either side in a conflict

policy rule, course of action

primary main, most important

principle basic belief, rule, or law

procedure a series of steps taken to accomplish a task

process a series of steps by which a task is accomplished

reaction a response

role 1. a part or function; 2. assigned behavior

strategy a plan for fighting a battle or war

structure the way something is set up or organized

traditional customary, time-honored

values ideas that people hold dear and try to live by

vary/various 1. to be different; 2. of many types

Social Studies Words

AD refers to dates after the birth of Jesus of Nazareth

BC refers to dates before the birth of Jesus

BCE refers to "Before Common Era," dates before the birth of Jesus

CE refers to "Common Era," dates after the birth of Jesus

century a period of 100 years

civilization the culture of a particular time or place

climate the weather conditions in a certain area over a long period of time

culture the knowledge, beliefs, customs, and values of a group of people

custom a repeated practice, tradition

democracy governmental rule by the people, usually on a majority rule principle

economy the system in which people make and exchange goods and services

geography the study of the earth's physical and cultural features

independence freedom from forceful rule

monarchy governmental rule by one person, a king or queen

North the region of the United States sometimes defined by the states that did not secede from the Union during the Civil War

rebellion an organized resistance to the established government

society a group of people who share common traditions

South the region of the United States sometimes defined by the states that seceded from the Union to form the Confederate States of America

Using This Book

Studying U.S. history will be easy for you using this textbook. Take a few minutes to become familiar with the easy-to-use structure and special features of this history book. See how this U.S. history textbook will make history come alive for you!

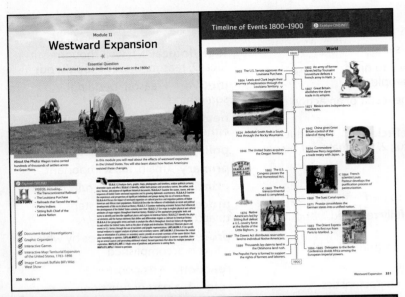

Module

Each module begins with an Essential Question and a Timeline of Events showing important dates in U.S. and world history, and ends with a Module Assessment.

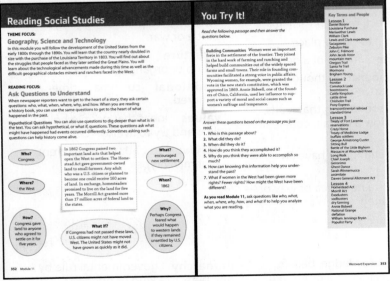

Reading Social Studies

These reading lessons teach you skills and provide opportunities for practice to help you read the textbook more successfully. There are questions in the Module Assessment to make sure you understand the reading skill.

Social Studies Skills

The Social Studies Skills lessons give you an opportunity to learn and use a skill you will most likely use again while in school. You will also be given a chance to make sure that you understand each skill by answering related questions in the Module Assessment activity.

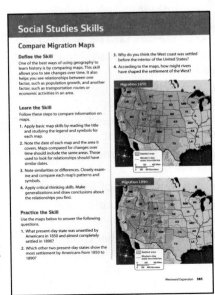

Lesson

The lesson opener includes an overarching Big Idea statement, Main Ideas, and Key Terms and People.

If YOU were there . . . introductions begin each lesson with a situation for you to respond to, placing you in the time period and in a situation related to the content you will be studying in the lesson.

Headings and subheadings organize the information into manageable chunks of text that will help you learn and understand the lesson's main ideas.

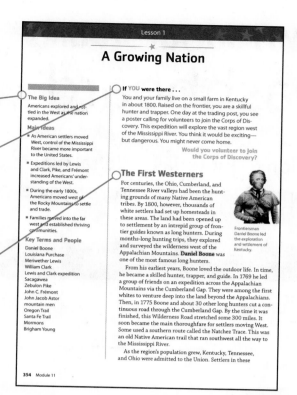

Lesson 1

★ A Growing Nation

The Big Idea
Americans explored and settled in the West as the nation expanded.

Main Ideas
- As American settlers moved West, control of the Mississippi River became more important to the United States.
- Expeditions led by Lewis and Clark, Pike, and Frémont increased Americans' understanding of the West.
- During the early 1800s, Americans moved west of the Rocky Mountains to settle and trade.
- Families moved into the far west and established thriving communities.

Key Terms and People
Daniel Boone
Louisiana Purchase
Meriwether Lewis
William Clark
Lewis and Clark expedition
Sacagawea
Zebulon Pike
John C. Frémont
John Jacob Astor
mountain men
Oregon Trail
Santa Fe Trail
Mormons
Brigham Young

If YOU were there . . .
You and your family live on a small farm in Kentucky in about 1800. Raised on the frontier, you are a skillful hunter and trapper. One day at the trading post, you see a poster calling for volunteers to join the Corps of Discovery. This expedition will explore the vast region west of the Mississippi River. You think it would be exciting—but dangerous. You might never come home.

Would you volunteer to join the Corps of Discovery?

The First Westerners
For centuries, the Ohio, Cumberland, and Tennessee River valleys had been the hunting grounds of many Native American tribes. By 1800, however, thousands of white settlers had set up homesteads in these areas. The land had been opened up to settlement by an intrepid group of frontier guides known as long hunters. During months-long hunting trips, they explored and surveyed the wilderness west of the Appalachian Mountains. **Daniel Boone** was one of the most famous long hunters.

Frontiersman Daniel Boone led the exploration and settlement of Kentucky.

From his earliest years, Boone loved the outdoor life. In time, he became a skilled hunter, trapper, and guide. In 1769 he led a group of friends on an expedition across the Appalachian Mountains via the Cumberland Gap. They were among the first whites to venture deep into the land beyond the Appalachians. Then, in 1775 Boone and about 30 other long hunters cut a continuous road through the Cumberland Gap. By the time it was finished, this Wilderness Road stretched some 300 miles. It soon became the main thoroughfare for settlers moving West. Some used a southern route called the Natchez Trace. This was an old Native American trail that ran southwest all the way to the Mississippi River.

As the region's population grew, Kentucky, Tennessee, and Ohio were admitted to the Union. Settlers in these

354 Module 11

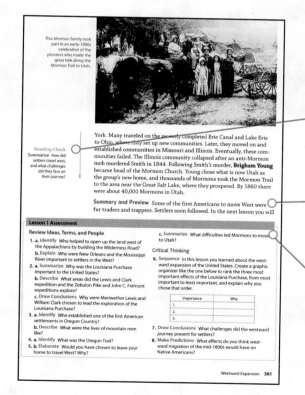

This Mormon family took part in an early-1900s celebration of the pioneers who made the great trek along the Mormon Trail to Utah.

Reading Check
Summarize How did settlers travel west, and what challenges did they face on their journey?

York. Many traveled on the recently completed Erie Canal and Lake Erie to Ohio, where they set up new communities. Later, they moved on and established communities in Missouri and Illinois. Eventually, these communities failed. The Illinois community collapsed after an anti-Mormon mob murdered Smith in 1844. Following Smith's murder, **Brigham Young** became head of the Mormon Church. Young chose what is now Utah as the group's new home, and thousands of Mormons took the Mormon Trail to the area near the Great Salt Lake, where they prospered. By 1860 there were about 40,000 Mormons in Utah.

Summary and Preview Some of the first Americans to move West were fur traders and trappers. Settlers soon followed. In the next lesson you will

Lesson 1 Assessment

Review Ideas, Terms, and People

1. **a. Identify** Who helped to open up the land west of the Appalachians by building the Wilderness Road?
   b. Explain Why were New Orleans and the Mississippi River important to settlers in the West?
2. **a. Summarize** Why was the Louisiana Purchase important to the United States?
   b. Describe What areas did the Lewis and Clark expedition and the Zebulon Pike and John C. Frémont expeditions explore?
   c. Draw Conclusions Why were Meriwether Lewis and William Clark chosen to lead the exploration of the Louisiana Purchase?
3. **a. Identify** Who established one of the first American settlements in Oregon Country?
   b. Describe What were the lives of mountain men like?
4. **a. Identify** What was the Oregon Trail?
5. **b. Elaborate** Would you have chosen to leave your home to travel West? Why?

c. Summarize What difficulties led Mormons to move to Utah?

Critical Thinking

6. **Sequence** In this lesson you learned about the westward expansion of the United States. Create a graphic organizer like the one below to rank the three most important effects of the Louisiana Purchase, from most important to least important, and explain why you chose that order.

Importance	Why
1.	
2.	
3.	

7. **Draw Conclusions** What challenges did the westward journey present for settlers?
8. **Make Predictions** What effects do you think westward migration of the mid-1800s would have on Native Americans?

Westward Expansion **361**

Reading Check questions are at the end of each main heading so you can test whether or not you understand what you have just studied.

Summary and Preview statements connect what you have just studied in the lesson to what you will study in the next lesson.

Lesson Assessment boxes provide an opportunity for you to make sure you understand the main ideas of the lesson.

HMH Social Studies
Dashboard

Designed for today's digital natives, **HMH® Social Studies** offers you an informative and exciting online experience.

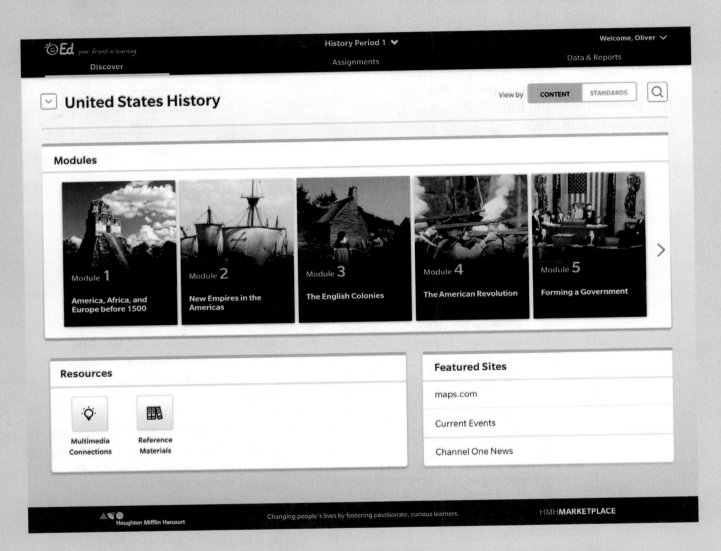

Your personalized Dashboard is organized into three main sections:

1. **Discover**—Quickly access content and search program resources

2. **Assignments**—Review your assignments and check your progress on them

3. **Data & Reports**—Monitor your progress on the course

Explore Online ⊙

to **Experience** the **Power** of
United States History

Houghton Mifflin Harcourt™ is changing
the way you **experience** social studies.

By delivering an immersive experience through compelling narratives
enriched with media, we're connecting you to history through experiences that are
energizing, inspiring, and memorable. The following pages highlight
some digital tools and instructional support that will help you
approach history through active inquiry, so you can connect to the past
while becoming active and informed citizens for the future.

The Student eBook is the primary learning portal.

More than just the digital version of a textbook, the Student eBook serves as the primary learning portal for you. The narrative is supported by a wealth of multimedia and learning resources to bring history to life and give you the tools you need to succeed.

Bringing Content to Life

HISTORY® videos and Multimedia Connections bring content to life through primary source footage, dramatic storytelling, and expert testimonials.

In-Depth Understanding

Close Read Screencasts model an analytical conversation about primary sources.

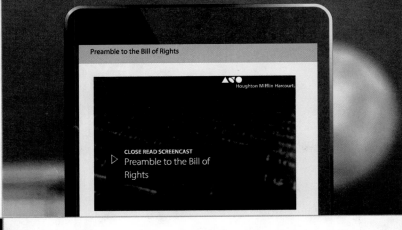

Content in a Fun Way

Interactive Features, Maps, and **Games** provide quick, entertaining activities and assessments that present important content in a fun way.

Investigate Like a Historian

Document-Based Investigations in every lesson build to end-of-module DBI performance tasks so you can examine and assess primary sources as historians do.

Full-Text Audio Support

You can listen while you read.

Skills Support

Point-of-use support is just a click away, providing instruction on critical reading and social studies skills.

Personalized Annotations

My Notes encourages you to take notes while you read and allows you to customize them to your study preferences. You can easily access them to review later as you prepare for exams.

Interactive Lesson Graphic Organizers

Graphic organizers help you process, summarize, and keep track of your learning for end-of-module performance tasks.

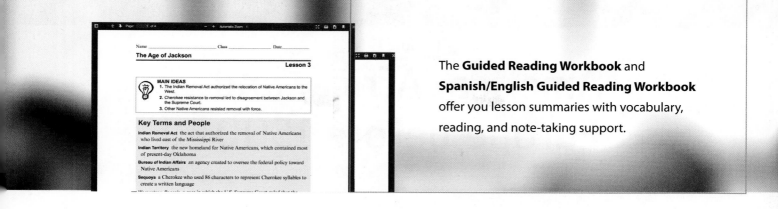

The **Guided Reading Workbook** and **Spanish/English Guided Reading Workbook** offer you lesson summaries with vocabulary, reading, and note-taking support.

Map Connections connects you with history and geography through interactive maps, games, and data.

Current Events features trustworthy articles on today's news that connect what you learn in class to the world around you.

No Wi-Fi®? No problem!

With the **HMH Player**® app, you can connect to content and resources by downloading when online and accessing when offline.

 HMH**PLAYER**® also allows you to:

Work Offline

Download lesson content and resources to work offline.

Communicate

"Raise a Hand" to ask or answer questions without having to be in the same room as your teacher.

Collaborate

Collaborate with your teacher via chat and in-lesson teamwork.

America, Africa, and Europe before 1500

Essential Question

Why might a U.S. historian study the Americas, Africa, and Europe before 1500?

About the Photo: American buffalo were a vital food source for many Native American groups.

Explore ONLINE!

HISTORY

VIDEOS, including...
- Mexico's Ancient Civilizations
- Corn
- Machu Picchu
- Salt
- Origins of Western Culture
- Rome Falls
- The First Crusade

✔ Document-Based Investigations

✔ Graphic Organizers

✔ Interactive Games

✔ Interactive Map: Migrations of Early People

✔ Image with Hotspots: The Chinook

✔ Image Carousel: Empires of Gold and Salt

In this module you will learn the histories of three regions—the Americas, West Africa, and Europe—whose people would come together and forever change North America.

What You Will Learn ...

Lesson 1: The Earliest Americans **6**
The Big Idea Native American societies developed across North and South America.

Lesson 2: Native American Cultures **11**
The Big Idea Many diverse Native American cultures developed across the different geographic regions of North America.

Lesson 3: Trading Kingdoms of West Africa **19**
The Big Idea Using trade to gain wealth, Ghana, Mali, and Songhai were West Africa's most powerful kingdoms.

Lesson 4: Europe before 1500 . . . . **23**
The Big Idea New ideas and trade changed Europeans' lives.

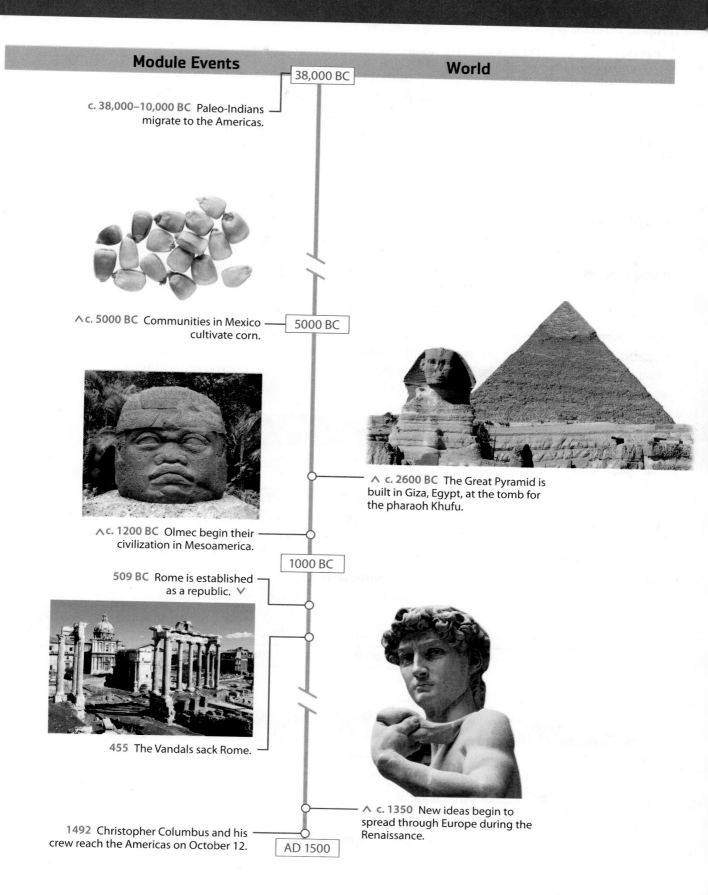

Module Events | 38,000 BC | **World**

c. 38,000–10,000 BC Paleo-Indians migrate to the Americas.

∧ c. 5000 BC Communities in Mexico cultivate corn. — 5000 BC

∧ c. 2600 BC The Great Pyramid is built in Giza, Egypt, at the tomb for the pharaoh Khufu.

∧ c. 1200 BC Olmec begin their civilization in Mesoamerica.

1000 BC

509 BC Rome is established as a republic. ∨

455 The Vandals sack Rome.

∧ c. 1350 New ideas begin to spread through Europe during the Renaissance.

1492 Christopher Columbus and his crew reach the Americas on October 12. AD 1500

Reading Social Studies

THEME FOCUS:

Economics, Geography

This module explains the development of major world regions before 1600. You will read about how, during the Ice Age, nomads made their way from Asia to North America. Over time they developed distinct cultures and built great civilizations. You will also read about the cultures and civilizations of Africa and Europe. As you read the module, you pay careful attention to how geography and economic issues affected the growth of cultures and civilizations.

READING FOCUS:

Specialized Vocabulary of Social Studies

If you flipped through the pages of this book, would you expect to see anything about square roots or formulas? How about petri dishes or hypotheses? Of course you wouldn't. Those are terms you see only in math and science books.

Specialized Vocabulary Like most subjects, social studies has its own specialized vocabulary. Included in it are words and phrases you will see over and over as you read social studies materials. The charts below list some terms you will encounter as you read this book.

Terms about Time	
decade	a period of 10 years
century	a period of 100 years
era	a long period marked by great events, developments, or figures
BC	a term used to identify dates that occurred long ago, before the birth of Jesus Christ, on whose teachings Christianity was founded; it means "before Christ." BC dates get smaller as time passes, so the larger the number, the earlier the date.
AD	a term used to identify dates that occurred after Jesus's birth; it comes from a Latin phrase that means "in the year of our Lord." Unlike BC dates, AD dates get larger as time passes, so the larger the number, the later the date.
BCE	another way to refer to BC dates; it stands for "before the common era"
CE	another way to refer to AD dates; it stands for "common era"

Terms about Government and Society	
politics	the art of creating government policies
economics	the study of the creation and use of goods and services
movement	a series of actions that bring about or try to bring about a change in society
campaign	an effort to win a political office, or a series of military actions
colony	a territory settled and controlled by a country

You Try It!

The following passage shows you how some specialized vocabulary is defined in context.

> **North and Northwest** Native Americans in the Pacific Northwest carved images of **totems**—ancestor or animal spirits—on tall, wooden poles. Totem poles held great religious and historical significance for Native Americans of the Northwest. Feasts called potlatches were another unique, or unusual, aspect of these Native Americans' culture.

Use the clues to understand meaning.

1. In the first sentence, find the word *totems*. Notice that the term is **highlighted** in yellow. Highlighted terms appear in a list under Key Terms and People on the first page of each lesson. Why do you think some specialized vocabulary terms are highlighted, while others are not?

2. Again, find the word *totems*. The phrase after the **dash** is the definition. Often in this book, specialized vocabulary words are defined after a dash. So be on the lookout for dashes.

3. The word *potlatches* is defined in the third sentence. The clue to finding this definition is the word **called**. Words like **called** and **known as** can indicate that a definition is coming up. In this case, the word *feasts* is a definition of potlatches.

4. The word *unique* is defined in the final sentence. The clue to finding this definition is the **comma** followed by the word **or**. So be on the lookout for commas followed by *or*.

As you read Module 1, keep track of the specialized vocabulary terms you learn.

Key Terms and People

Lesson 1
Bering Land Bridge
Paleo-Indians
migration
hunter-gatherers
environments
culture

Lesson 2
pueblos
kivas
totems
teepees
matrilineal
Iroquois League

Lesson 3
Berbers
Mansa Musa
hajj
mosques
Askia the Great

Lesson 4
Socrates
Plato
Aristotle
reason
democracy
knights
Black Death
Michelangelo
Leonardo da Vinci
Johannes Gutenberg
joint-stock companies

The Earliest Americans

The Big Idea
Native American societies developed across North and South America.

Main Ideas
- Climate changes allowed Paleo-Indians to migrate to the Americas.
- Major civilizations developed in Mesoamerica and South America.

Key Terms and People
Bering Land Bridge
Paleo-Indians
migration
hunter-gatherers
environments
culture

If YOU were there . . .

You are living in North America about 10,000 years ago, close to the end of the Ice Age. For weeks, your group has been following a herd of elk across a marshy landscape. This trip has taken you far from your usual hunting grounds. The air is warmer here. There are thick grasses and bushes full of berries. You decide to camp here for the summer and perhaps stay a while.

How would settling here change your way of life?

Early Migrations to the Americas

Many scientists believe that the first people arrived in North America during the last Ice Age. At the start of the Ice Age, Earth's climate became intensely cold. Large amounts of water froze into huge, moving sheets of ice called glaciers. As a result, ocean levels dropped more than 300 feet lower than they are today. When the sea level fell, a land bridge between northeastern Asia and present-day Alaska was exposed. Geographers call this strip of land the **Bering Land Bridge**. Although no one knows exactly when or how people crossed into North

Mammoths, such as the skeleton shown here, were present during the Ice Age and were hunted by early peoples in North America.

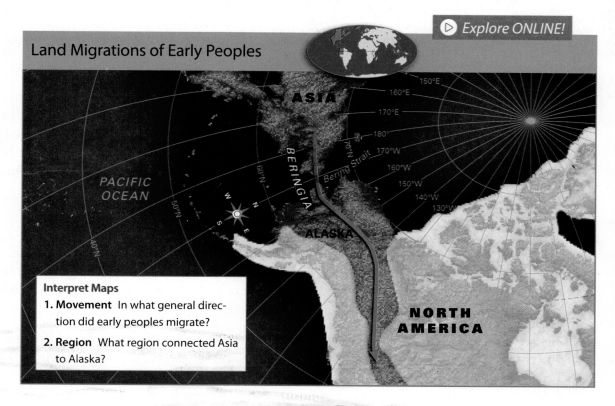

Land Migrations of Early Peoples

ASIA

BERINGIA

PACIFIC OCEAN

Bering Strait

ALASKA

NORTH AMERICA

150°E
160°E
170°E
180°
170°W
160°W
150°W
140°W
130°W
70°N
60°N
50°N
40°N

Interpret Maps

1. **Movement** In what general direction did early peoples migrate?

2. **Region** What region connected Asia to Alaska?

America, evidence suggests that people called **Paleo-Indians** crossed this bridge into Alaska between 38,000 and 10,000 BC.

This **migration**—a movement of people or animals from one region to another—took place over a long time. It is believed that Paleo-Indians traveled south into Canada, the United States, and Mexico following herds of animals. Over time, their descendants went as far as the southern tip of South America. These people were **hunter-gatherers**, people who hunted animals and gathered wild plants for food.

About 8000 BC Earth's climate grew warmer, and the Ice Age ended. Rising temperatures melted glaciers. Water levels in the oceans rose, and the Bering Land Bridge was covered with water.

Although most scholars agree that early peoples crossed the Bering Land Bridge into the Americas, some researchers have proposed other theories about the continents' settlement. Those scientists point to sites in South America that were occupied by humans long before people could have migrated to those places from Beringia, the area surrounding the Bering Land Bridge. One theory in particular provides an explanation. That theory says that people from East Asia came to the west coast of North and South America by boat. They could have stayed in sight of land as they traveled north and then south along the coast.

The warmer climate that developed at the end of the Ice Age created new **environments**—climates and landscapes that surround living things. Large herds of animals such as buffalo and deer ate new short grasses that thrived in the warm climate. As the number of these animals grew, Paleo-Indians hunted them for resources such as meat, hides, and bones.

Varied environments influenced the development of different Native American societies, or groups that share a culture. **Culture** is a group's set of common values and traditions, including language, government, and family relationships.

Like all societies, Native American groups changed over time. People planted seeds, and eventually they learned to breed animals, farm, and grow plants. Maize, or corn, was one of their most important early crops. Later, they learned to grow beans and squash. Farming allowed people to stop moving around looking for food and to settle in one place. With adequate food supplies, settlements could support larger populations. As populations grew, more advanced societies began to develop.

Reading Check
Draw Conclusions
How did climate change affect early peoples' migrations?

Early Mesoamerican and South American Societies

Some of the earliest American cultures arose in Mesoamerica, a region that includes the southern part of what is now Mexico and the northern parts of Central America.

Academic Vocabulary
develop the process of growing or improving

Olmec and Maya Around 1200 BC the Olmec **developed** the earliest-known civilization in Mesoamerica. The Olmec are known for their use of stone in architecture and sculpture. They built the first pyramids in the Americas, and they created sculptures of huge stone heads. When their civilization ended around 400 BC, trade had spread Olmec culture throughout the region.

Like the Olmec, the Maya grew maize and other crops and lived in small villages. These villages traded goods with each other, and by about AD 200, the Maya were building large cities.

Maya cities had pyramids, large stone temples, palaces, and bridges. The Maya also paved large plazas for public gatherings and built canals to control the flow of water through the cities.

In the 900s Maya civilization began to collapse. Historians are still not sure what caused this great civilization's decline. Theories include disease, soil exhaustion, and long-term drought, among others.

This pyramid is one of five that the Maya built in Tikal, Guatemala, which was an important Maya trading post.

Aztec The Aztec were fierce warriors, and their superior military ability was key to their success. Around the mid-1100s AD, the Aztec migrated south to central Mexico. There they settled down, conquered many towns, made alliances to build their empire, and controlled a huge trade network.

In AD 1325 the Aztec founded their capital, Tenochtitlán (tay-nawch-teet-LAHN), on an island in Lake Texcoco. Raised roads called causeways connected the island to the shore, making trade and travel easier. Tenochtitlán became the greatest city in the Americas and one of the world's largest cities.

Trade and tribute paid by conquered people in the form of cotton, gold, and food made the Aztec rich. By the early 1500s, they ruled the most powerful state in Mesoamerica.

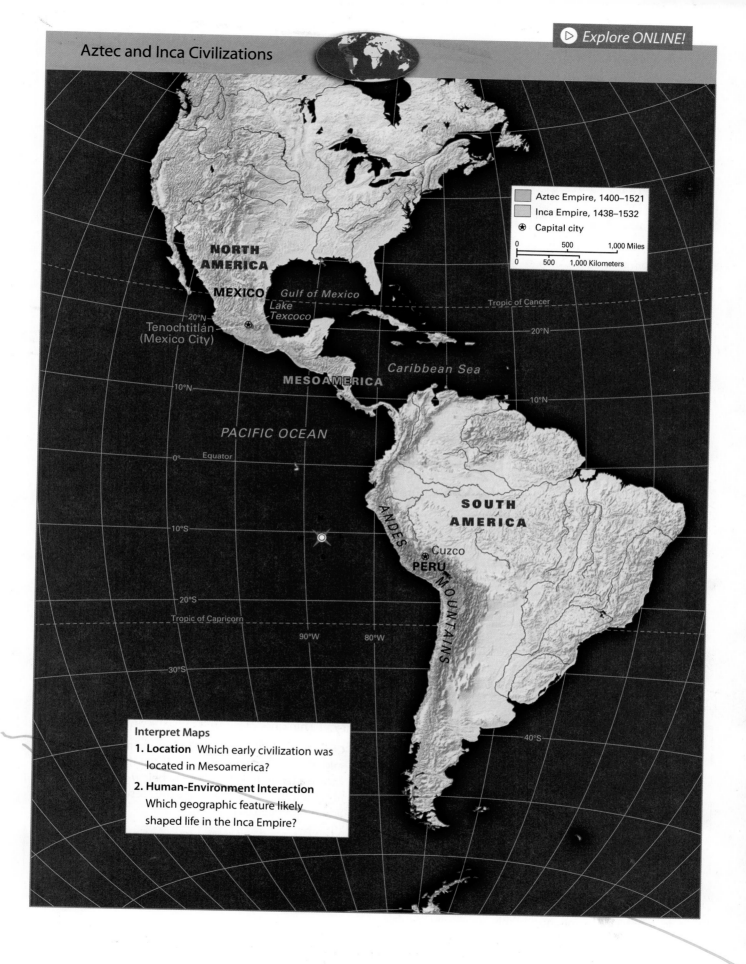

Aztec and Inca Civilizations

NORTH AMERICA

MEXICO

Gulf of Mexico

Lake Texcoco

Tenochtitlán (Mexico City)

20°N

Tropic of Cancer

20°N

Caribbean Sea

10°N

MESOAMERICA

10°N

PACIFIC OCEAN

0° Equator

SOUTH AMERICA

10°S

ANDES

Cuzco

PERU

MOUNTAINS

20°S

Tropic of Capricorn

90°W 80°W

30°S

40°S

Legend:
- Aztec Empire, 1400–1521
- Inca Empire, 1438–1532
- ⊛ Capital city

0   500   1,000 Miles
0   500   1,000 Kilometers

Interpret Maps

1. **Location** Which early civilization was located in Mesoamerica?

2. **Human-Environment Interaction** Which geographic feature likely shaped life in the Inca Empire?

Aztec Calendar of the World

This map is from an illustrated book of the Aztec calendar dating to the 1400s. The map shows the world in the shape of a cross. Each branch is a direction—east (top), west (bottom), north (left), and south (right).

The Aztec used mathematics and their observations of the heavens to create a calendar. The calendar was made up of two cycles that together formed a 52-year period. Among other Aztec achievements were jade and stone carvings, the use of medicinal herbs, and maintenance of a road system. They also had a writing system made up of signs and symbols. The Aztec spoke Nahuatl, a language that still has some 1.5 million speakers, most of whom live in Central Mexico.

Inca The Inca began as a small tribe in the Andes Mountains of South America. They named their capital city Cuzco (KOO-skoh). In the mid-1400s, the Inca began to expand their territory. By the 1500s the empire stretched along the Pacific coast from what is now northern Ecuador to central Chile. In time, the empire was home to about 12 million people. The Inca formed a strong central government with a king as ruler. The official language of the empire was Quechua.

Because they had no written language, the Inca kept records with a system of knotted strings called *quipu*. They also used *quipu* for mathematics. The knots and their positions on the string indicated numbers, while the strings' colors represented different types of information. For example, red strings may have been used to count warriors or yellow strings to count gold. The Inca also developed a device much like a calculator, allowing them to multiply, divide, and use fractions.

The Inca are known for building and for art. Massive buildings and forts were made of huge stone blocks. An advanced system of highways ran the length of the empire. Paved roads and rope bridges connected all parts of Inca territory. This enabled the Inca to communicate with and control their large empire.

Reading Check
Summarize
What early civilizations existed in Mesoamerica and South America?

Summary and Preview Early people migrated into North and South America and developed societies. In the next lesson you will learn about Native American cultures in North America.

Lesson 1 Assessment

Review Ideas, Terms, and People

1. a. **Recall** What was the Ice Age?

   b. **Summarize** Why were early peoples able to use the Bering Land Bridge?

   c. **Draw Conclusions** Why do you think the migration early peoples in the Americas flowed north to south?

2. a. **Identify** What was the earliest civilization in the Americas, and where was it located?

   b. **Analyze** How did the Aztec build such a powerful, rich state?

   c. **Evaluate** Which of the four civilizations discussed do you think was the most highly developed? Explain.

Critical Thinking

3. **Categorize** In this lesson you learned about the migration of early peoples and about their societies. Create a table similar to the one below and identify accomplishments of the four early Mesoamerican and South American civilizations.

	Significant Accomplishments
Olmec	
Maya	
Aztec	
Inca	

Native American Cultures

The Big Idea

Many diverse Native American cultures developed across the different geographic regions of North America.

Main Ideas

- Several early societies developed in North America long before Europeans explored the continent.
- Geographic areas influenced Native American cultures.
- Language united Native American groups and contributed to cultural diversity.
- Despite their differences, Native American cultures shared similar beliefs and practices.

Key Terms and People

pueblos
kivas
totems
teepees
matrilineal
Iroquois League

If YOU were there . . .

You live in the North American Southwest about 1,000 years ago. You've been working in the fields for several hours today. The maize crop looks good this summer, and you are hoping for a successful harvest. After finishing your work, you walk home. The opening to your house is in a cliff wall 30 feet above a canyon floor. You must use ladders to get to the opening.

Do you like the location of your home? Why?

Early Societies

The earliest people in North America were hunter-gatherers. After 5000 BC some of these people learned how to farm and settled in villages. In time, many diverse and complex societies developed throughout North America. Although they left no written record, historians have learned about them by studying artifacts, or the objects that they made and used.

Anasazi By 1500 BC the people who lived in the North American Southwest, like those who lived in Mesoamerica, were growing maize. One of the early farm cultures in the Southwest was the Anasazi (ah-nuh-SAH-zee). The Anasazi lived in the Four Corners region, where present-day Arizona, Colorado, New Mexico, and Utah meet. Anasazi farmers adapted to their dry environment and grew maize, beans, and squash. Over time, they began to use irrigation to increase food production. By the time the Anasazi settled in the area, they were already skilled basket makers. They wove straw, vines, and yucca to make containers for food and other items, and they eventually became skilled potters as well.

The early Anasazi lived in pit houses dug into the ground. After about AD 750 they built **pueblos**, or aboveground houses made of a heavy clay called adobe. The Anasazi built these houses on top of each other, creating large multistoried complexes. Some pueblos had several hundred rooms and

Anasazi Cliff Dwellings
Dwellings like these were built into cliffs for safety. Often, ladders were needed to reach the buildings. The ladders could be removed, keeping invaders from reaching the dwellings.

could house 1,000 people. The Anasazi often built their houses in canyon walls and had to use ladders to enter their homes. These cliff dwellings provided a strong defense against enemies. The Anasazi also built **kivas**, underground ceremonial chambers, at the center of each community. Kivas were sacred areas used for religious ceremonies. Some of these rituals focused on the life-giving forces of rain and maize.

The Anasazi thrived for hundreds of years. After AD 1300, however, they began to abandon their villages. Scholars believe that drought, disease, or raids by nomadic tribes from the north may have caused the Anasazi to move away from their pueblos.

Mound Builders Several farming societies developed in the eastern part of North America after 1000 BC. The Hopewell lived along the Mississippi, Ohio, and lower Missouri river valleys. They supported their large population with agriculture and trade. They built large burial mounds to honor their dead.

By AD 700 the Hopewell culture had declined and another culture, the Mississippian, began to thrive in the same area. Skilled farmers and traders, the Mississippian built large settlements. Their largest city, Cahokia, was located near present-day Saint Louis, Missouri. It had a population of 30,000.

The Mississippian people built hundreds of mounds for religious ceremonies. Cahokia alone had more than 100 temple and burial mounds. These mounds had flat tops, and temples were built on top of the mounds. Many of the mounds were gigantic. Monks Mound, near Collinsville, Illinois, for example, was 100 feet high and covered 16 acres.

Reading Check
Summarize
Why did some Native American groups build mounds?

Several other mound-building cultures thrived in eastern North America. More than 10,000 mounds have been found in the Ohio River valley alone. Some of these mounds are shaped like birds and snakes. The mound-building cultures had declined by the time European explorers reached the Southeast. Their societies no longer existed by the early 1700s.

Native American Culture Areas

Researchers use culture areas—the geographic locations that influenced societies—to help them describe ancient Native American peoples. North America is divided into several culture areas.

North and Northwest The far north of North America is divided into the Arctic and Subarctic culture areas. Few plants grow in the Arctic because the ground is always frozen beneath a thin top layer of soil. This harsh environment was home to two groups of people, the Inuit and the Aleut. The Inuit lived in present-day northern Alaska and Canada. Their homes were igloos, hide tents, and huts. The Aleut, whose home was in western and southern Alaska, lived in multifamily houses that were partially underground. The two groups shared many cultural features, including language. Both groups survived by fishing and hunting large mammals. The Aleut and Inuit also depended on dogs for many tasks, such as hunting and pulling sleds.

South of the Arctic lies the Subarctic, home to groups such as the Dogrib and Montagnais peoples. While they followed the seasonal migrations of deer, these peoples lived in shelters made of animal skins. At other times, they lived in villages made up of log houses. Farther south, the Kwakiutl and the Chinook thrived, thanks to the rich supply of game animals, fish, and wild plants that allowed large populations to increase without the need for farming.

Native Americans in the Pacific Northwest carved images of **totems**—ancestor or animal spirits—on tall, wooden poles. Totem poles held great religious and historical significance for Native Americans of the Northwest. Feasts called potlatches were another unique, or unusual, aspect of these Native Americans' culture. At these gatherings, hosts, usually chiefs or wealthy people, gave away most of their belongings as

People in different culture areas created unique artifacts. The bird-shaped pipe (left) is from the Northwest Coast culture area. The sewing tool (center) with a carved bone handle was used in the Great Plains. The human figure (right) was created by someone who lived in the Southwest culture area.

gifts. Those gifts would likely be distributed to friends or even neighboring tribes. By displaying their generosity, potlatch hosts increased their social status and power. Potlatches were also occasions for defining roles within the group and for granting economic privileges.

West and Southwest Farther south along the Pacific coast was the California region, which included the area between the Pacific and the Sierra Nevada mountain range. Food sources were plentiful, so farming was not necessary. One major plant food was acorns, which were ground into flour. People also fished and hunted deer and other game. Most Native Americans in the California region lived in groups of families of about 50 to 300. Among these groups, including the Hupa, Miwok, and Yokuts, more than 100 languages were spoken.

The area east of the Sierra Nevada, the Great Basin, received little rain. To survive, Native Americans adapted to the drier climate by gathering seeds, digging roots, and trapping small animals for food. Most groups in this area, including the Paiute, Shoshone, and Ute, spoke the same language.

The Southwest culture region included the present-day states of Arizona and New Mexico and parts of Colorado and Texas. Pueblo groups, such as the Hopi and Zuni, lived there. Like the Anasazi, these Native Americans also adapted to a dry climate. The Pueblo irrigated the land and grew maize, squash, and beans. These crops were vital to southwestern peoples. The Pueblo religion focused on two key areas of Pueblo life—rain and maize. The Pueblo performed religious rituals hoping to bring rain and a successful maize crop to their people.

Pueblo peoples were settled and built multistoried houses out of adobe bricks. Over time their towns grew larger, and some towns had more than 1,000 residents. Pueblo peoples made fine pottery that featured beautifully painted designs.

The Apache and Navajo also lived in the Southwest. These groups were nomadic—they moved from place to place hunting small animals and foraging for food. The Apache and Navajo also supported themselves by raiding the villages of the Pueblo and others.

Great Plains The huge Great Plains region stretches south from Canada into Texas. This culture area is bordered by the Mississippi Valley on the east and the Rocky Mountains on the west. The Plains were mainly grassland, home to millions of buffalo. Deer, elk, and other game also thrived there.

Most Great Plains peoples were nomadic hunters. Many groups hunted buffalo using bows and spears. Blackfoot and Arapaho hunters sometimes chased the animals over cliffs, drove them into corrals, or trapped them in a ring of fire. Native Americans on the Plains used buffalo skins for shields, clothing, and coverings for their **teepees**—cone-shaped shelters. Buffalo skins were also trade items.

Some Plains groups were farmers, while others depended more on gathering foods in addition to hunting. For example, some groups of Sioux

Pawnee Star Chart

The Pawnee carefully observed the night sky. This map of the night sky dates to the 1700s, but historians believe that Plains Indians used similar maps before 1500.

gathered wild rice and speared fish. The Mandan and Pawnee settled in villages and grew corn, beans, and squash. The Pawnee lived in round lodges made of dirt.

Like some other Native American groups, Pawnee society was **matrilineal**. This means that people traced their ancestry through their mothers, not their fathers. In some groups, such as the Sioux, women organized societies focused on the community's well-being. Men of the Sioux belonged to military societies that acted as a police force.

Northeast and Southeast Eastern North America was rich in sources of food and shelter. Animals, plant foods, fish, and wood for housing were plentiful in the region's woodlands and river valleys.

Most southeastern groups, including the Cherokee, Creek, and Seminole, lived in farming villages governed by village councils. In the Northeast, groups like the Algonquian survived by hunting and gathering plants. Those in the south farmed, hunted, gathered plants, and fished. Many tribes used strings of beads known as wampum for money.

To the east of the Algonquian lived the Iroquois (or Haudenosaunee). They were farmers, hunters, and traders. Among their crops were squash, corn, and beans. During the cold winters, the Iroquois cut holes in the ice over rivers and lakes to catch fish. In the spring, they tapped the region's maple trees to make syrup. The Iroquois lived in longhouses, or rectangular homes made from logs and bark, that housed eight to ten families.

Five Iroquois nations—the Cayuga, Mohawk, Oneida, Onondaga, and Seneca—formed a political alliance called the **Iroquois League**. This is also

Iroquois Longhouse

Northeastern Native Americans such as the Iroquois lived in longhouses made of tree bark. The drawing at right shows the longhouses in one Iroquois village.

Why do you think a fence was built around the longhouses?

Explore ONLINE!

Arctic	Northeast
Subarctic	Great Basin
Northwest Coast	California
Plateau	Southwest
Great Plains	Southeast

0   250   500 Miles
0   250   500 Kilometers

Interpret Maps

1. **Region** Why did some culture areas have fewer groups of people than other culture areas did?

2. **Human-Environment Interaction** What natural features served as boundaries between culture areas?

known as the Iroquois Confederation. In 1722, a sixth nation, the Tusca-rora, joined the league. The Confederation kept peace among its members and waged war to protect its territory from invasion.

Highly organized and extremely powerful, the Iroquois Confederation held strong for hundreds of years. Its government was founded in the Great Law of Peace, an oral constitution that emphasized the equality of all people. The confederation made decisions through representatives and consensus, or agreement. Some scholars propose that the constitution and structure of the Iroquois Confederation inspired the framers of the U.S. Constitution.

Reading Check
Generalize
How did environment influence Native American cultures in North America?

Native American Languages

As you can see on the "Native American Culture Areas" map, some cul-ture areas, such as the Arctic, occupied large regions, but had few distinct groups of people. By contrast, the California and Northwest Coast areas were home to many groups. Language played an important part in the cultural diversity of these regions.

At the time of European contact, about 300 languages were spoken in North America. Most could be grouped into 29 language families, or languages that descend from a common ancestor. Present-day California was home to more than 70 languages and 20 language families, some of which covered areas no larger than a modern county. Other language families occupied broader territory. One of the largest, the Uto-Aztecan language family, covered about a fourth of what is now the continental United States. Today the Shoshone in the Great Basin and the Hopi in the Southwest continue to speak Uto-Aztecan languages.

Reading Check
Make Inferences
How were Native American culture areas and languages connected?

Similar Beliefs and Practices

Despite their differences, Native American groups of North America shared a number of similar beliefs and practices. For example, Native Americans held similar spiritual and religious ideas. One was a spiri-tual connection to the natural world. A chief of a Wabanaki nation in the Northeast once described this idea by saying "The Great Spirit is our father, but the Earth is our mother."

In many belief systems, a tree stood at the center of the earth. For the Iroquois it was a white pine; for the Sioux, a mighty flowering tree. Animals, too, were thought to be powerful spirits. Hunters often carried out rituals to honor the spirit of an animal they were about to kill. Many groups chose an animal as their symbol and spirit guide.

Native Americans also had similar ideas about land ownership. Generally speaking, they did not believe that land could be bought, sold, or owned by individuals. Rather, land was held for the use of everyone in a group to hunt, fish, or gather and grow food as needed. Many believed that they should preserve the land and its resources for future generations. These beliefs contrasted sharply with those of Europeans, who believed that land and everything on it could be bought and owned by individuals. This difference would cause conflict for hundreds of years.

Though Native Americans did not own land, they did have other forms of private property. For example, in the Great Plains, women owned tepees and most household goods.

Among all the peoples of North America, women played essential roles in the groups' survival. Women performed many tasks, such as making baskets and clothing, cooking, hunting, child rearing, and gathering wild foods. Among the Inuit, women had to prepare meat obtained on a hunt before the cold air froze the meat. In farming societies, women were usually responsible for growing crops. In many North American groups, women owned property in their own right and held considerable power. For example, Iroquois clanmothers—older, respected women of the community—appointed the chief. The clanmothers could also fire the chief if he proved to be a poor leader.

Though they held similar traits in common, the diverse culture groups of North America generally did not join together into large political units. For most Native American peoples, respected elders and chiefs led local groups. Native Americans were, however, connected by thousands of miles of trade networks. Along with foodstuffs, raw materials, and exotic goods, trade networks carried ideas from place to place. One of the most famous routes began in Iroquois country and ran southward through mountain valleys to present-day North Carolina. It crossed the territory of the Shawnee, Choctaw, Cherokee, and other nations.

Summary and Preview People of North America formed many complex societies. In the next lesson you will read about societies in West Africa.

Reading Check
Identify Points of View What beliefs and practices did Native American groups share?

Lesson 2 Assessment

Review Ideas, Terms, and People

1. **a. Recall** Why did the Anasazi build kivas?

   b. Summarize What different types of housing were built by the Anasazi?

   c. Draw Conclusions Why do you think that some mounds were built in the shapes of birds and snakes?

2. **a. Identify** What are culture areas?

   b. Contrast How did food sources for Native Americans of the North and Northwest differ from those living in the West and Southwest?

   c. Elaborate Why was the formation of the Iroquois League considered to be a significant political development?

3. **a. Recall** About how many languages were spoken in North America at the time of European contact?

   b. Analyze What role did language have in the various regions of North America?

   c. Make Generalizations What generalization can you make about Native American languages in what is now California?

4. **a. Recall** How did Native Americans view land ownership?

   b. Analyze What role did nature play in the religious ideas of Native Americans?

   c. Explain Why do you think women held positions of power and influence in many Native American groups?

Critical Thinking

5. **Compare and Contrast** In this lesson you learned about early societies and culture areas. Create a graphic organizer like the one below to compare and contrast early Native American culture groups.

North and Northwest	
West and Southwest	
Great Plains	
Northeast and Southeast	

★
Trading Kingdoms of West Africa

The Big Idea

Using trade to gain wealth, Ghana, Mali, and Songhai were West Africa's most powerful kingdoms.

Main Ideas

- The Empire of Ghana was the first of three great West African trading kingdoms.
- Like Ghana, the empires of Mali and Songhai grew strong by controlling trade.

Key Terms and People

Berbers
Mansa Musa
hajj
mosques
Askia the Great

If YOU were there . . .

You are a trader's assistant from the Middle East, traveling in a caravan headed for West Africa. The caravan carries many goods, but the most precious is salt. Your job is to trade the salt for gold and return the gold to your employer immediately. Your boss never meets the traders face to face.

Why is your boss so secretive?

Empire of Ghana

By 1500 West Africa was well known for its trading kingdoms. Since ancient times, despite the dangers of the Sahara, trade routes crisscrossed West Africa. For many years, Berbers, a group of people from northern Africa, controlled these routes. In time, however, a series of three great trading empires arose thanks to the control of the salt and gold trades. Ghana (GAH-nuh) was the first of these empires.

The Rise of Ghana Historians think the first people in Ghana were farmers along the Niger River. Sometime after AD 300 these farmers, the Soninke (soh-NING-kee), were threatened by nomadic herders. The herders wanted to take the farmers' water and pastures. For protection, groups of Soninke families began to band together. This banding together was the beginning of Ghana.

Ghana was in an ideal position to become a trading center. To the north lay the vast Sahara, the source of much of the salt. Ghana itself was rich in gold. People wanted gold for its beauty, but they needed salt in their diets to survive. Salt, which could be used to preserve food, also made bland food tasty. These qualities made salt very valuable. In fact, Africans sometimes cut up slabs of salt and used the pieces as money.

As the gold and salt trade increased, Ghana's rulers gained power. Eventually, they built up armies equipped with iron weapons that were superior to the weapons of nearby people. Over time, Ghana conquered its neighbors and took control over trade in the region.

Ghana's rulers grew wealthy by controlling trade in salt and gold. Salt came from the north in large slabs, and gold came from the south.

By 800 Ghana was firmly in control of West Africa's trade routes. Nearly all trade between northern and southern Africa passed through Ghana. With so many traders passing through their lands, Ghana's rulers looked for ways to make money from them. One way they raised money was by forcing traders to pay taxes. All traders who entered Ghana had to pay a special tax on the goods they carried. Then they had to pay another tax on any goods they took with them when they left. Ghana's rulers gained incredible wealth from trade, taxes on traders and on the people of Ghana, and their own personal stores of gold. They used their wealth to build an army and an empire.

Islam in Ghana Extensive trade routes brought the people of Ghana into contact with people of many different cultures and beliefs. As the kingdom of Ghana extended into the Sahara, increased contact with Arab traders from the east brought the religion of Islam to Ghana.

Islam was founded in the 600s by an Arab man named Muhammad. Muslims, followers of Islam, believe that God had spoken to Muhammad through an angel and had made him a prophet, someone who tells of God's messages. After Muhammad's death, his followers wrote down his teachings to form the book known as the Qur'an. Islam spread quickly through the Arabian Peninsula.

In the 1060s a Muslim group called the Almoravids (al-muh-RAH-vuhdz) attacked Ghana in an effort to force its leaders to convert to Islam. The Almoravids weakened Ghana's empire and cut off many trade routes.

Without its trade, Ghana could not support its empire, and the empire eventually fell. The influence of Islam, however, remained strong. By the late 1400s Islam would become the most practiced religion in the region.

The Empires of Mali and Songhai

For about 150 years after Ghana's decline, no one kingdom controlled trade across the Sahara. Then two new trading empires rose to power in the region—Mali (MAH-lee) followed by Songhai (SAWNG-hy).

Kingdom of Mali Like Ghana, Mali lay along the upper Niger River. This area's fertile soil helped Mali grow. In addition, Mali's location on the Niger allowed its people to control trade on the river. Through this control of trade, the empire grew rich and powerful. According to legend, Mali's rise to power began under a ruler named Sundiata. Sundiata

Reading Check
Identify
How did Ghana become wealthy through trade?

Mansa Musa was a descendant of Sundiata, the first emperor to rule a united Mali.

won back his country's independence and conquered nearby kingdoms, including Ghana.

Mali's most famous ruler, however, was a Muslim king named **Mansa Musa** (MAHN-sah moo-SAH). Under his leadership, Mali reached the height of its wealth, power, and fame.

Mansa Musa ruled Mali for about 25 years, from 1312 to 1337. During that time, Mali added many important trade cities, including Timbuktu (tim-buhk-TOO), Djenné (je-NAY), and Gao (GOW), to its empire. Traders came to Timbuktu from the north and the south to trade for salt, gold, metals, shells, and many other goods.

Religion was also very important to Mansa Musa. In 1324 he left Mali on a **hajj**, or pilgrimage to Mecca. Making this journey once in their lives is the spiritual duty of all Muslims. As he traveled to Mecca, Mansa Musa introduced his empire to the world. The stories of Mali's wealth and religion spread far and wide. Because of Mansa Musa's influence, Islam spread through a large part of West Africa.

Mansa Musa wanted all Muslims to be able to read the Qur'an. Therefore, he stressed the importance of learning to read and write the Arabic language. He sent scholars to study in Morocco. These scholars later set up schools in Mali for studying the Qur'an.

To encourage the spread of Islam in West Africa, Mansa Musa brought back artists and architects from other Muslim countries to build **mosques**, or buildings for Muslim prayer, throughout his lands.

▷ *Explore ONLINE!*

Empires of West Africa, 800–1500

Interpret Maps

1. **Location** On what river are Timbuktu and Gao located?

2. **Region** Which empires ruled Timbuktu and Gao?

Legend:
- Ghana, 1000
- Mali, 1400
- Songhai, 1500
- • Settlement
- → Trade route
- → Trade goods

0 — 250 — 500 Miles
0 — 250 — 500 Kilometers

Askia the Great became ruler of Songhai when he was nearly 50 years old. He ruled Songhai for about 35 years.

Reading Check
Compare
What did Mali and Songhai have in common?

The architectural advances in cities like Timbuktu as well as an organized government, an emphasis on education, and an expansion of trade all combined to make Mansa Musa Mali's most successful ruler. Much of Mali's success depended on strong leaders. After Mansa Musa died, poor leadership weakened the empire. By 1500 nearly all of the lands the kingdom once ruled were lost. Only a small area of Mali remained.

Songhai Empire In the 1300s Mansa Musa had conquered a rival kingdom of people called the Songhai, who also lived along the Niger River. As the Mali Empire weakened in the 1400s, the Songhai grew wealthy by trading goods along the Niger. They took advantage of Mali's decline, regained their independence, and eventually conquered most of Mali.

One of Songhai's greatest rulers was Muhammad Ture, who chose the title *askia*, a title of military rank. He became known as **Askia the Great**. Like Mansa Musa, Askia the Great was a devout Muslim who supported education and learning. Under his rule, the cities of Gao and Timbuktu flourished. They contained great mosques, universities, schools, and libraries. People came from all parts of West Africa to study mathematics, science, medicine, grammar, and law.

Askia understood that an empire needed effective government. He created a professional army, and to improve the government, he set up five provinces within Songhai. He removed local leaders and appointed new governors who were loyal to him. He also created specialized departments to oversee various tasks, much like modern-day government offices do.

Soon after Askia the Great lost power, the empire of Songhai declined. Songhai was invaded by the Moroccans, the kingdom's northern neighbors. The Moroccans wanted to control the Saharan salt mines. They had superior military power and were able to take over Timbuktu and Gao. Changes in trade patterns completed Songhai's fall.

Summary and Preview Trade was important to the kingdoms of West Africa. In the next lesson you will learn about Europe before 1500.

Lesson 3 Assessment

Review Ideas, Terms, and People

1. **a. Identify** How did trade contribute to the rise of Ghana?

   b. Explain Why did Ghana's rulers tax traders passing through their kingdom?

   c. Evaluate Which resource do you think was more valuable to Ghana, gold or salt? Why?

2. **a. Describe** How did Mansa Musa introduce his empire to the world?

   b. Compare How did Islam affect the achievements of Mali and Songhai?

   c. Evaluate What do you think was the most important achievement of Askia the Great? Explain.

Critical Thinking

3. **Compare and Contrast** In this lesson you learned about African kingdoms and trade. Create a chart like the one below and identify the similarities and differences that led to the fall of the kingdoms of Ghana, Mali, and Songhai.

Fall of Ghana, Mali, and Songhai	Similarities	Differences

Europe before 1500

The Big Idea

New ideas and trade changed Europeans' lives.

Main Ideas

- The Greeks and Romans established new forms of government.

- During the Middle Ages, society eventually changed from a feudal system to a system with a middle class of artisans and merchants.

- The Renaissance was a time of rebirth in the arts and in learning.

Key Terms and People

Socrates
Plato
Aristotle
reason
democracy
knights
Black Death
Michelangelo
Leonardo da Vinci
Johannes Gutenberg
joint-stock companies

Academic Vocabulary
classical referring to the cultures of ancient Greece or Rome

If YOU were there . . .

You are a peasant in the Middle Ages, living on the land of a noble. Although you and your family work very hard from sunrise to sundown, much of the food you grow goes to the noble. Your house is very small and has a dirt floor. Your parents are tired and weak, and you wish you could do something to improve their lives.

Is there any way you could change your life?

Greek and Roman Influences

By 1500 European culture had been shaped by centuries of civilization and cultural development. Among the most significant and lasting contributions were those made by the ancient Greeks and Romans.

Greek Philosophers and Government Ancient Greeks valued human reason and believed in the power of the human mind to think, explain, and understand life. Three of the greatest Greek thinkers, or philosophers, were **Socrates**, **Plato**, and **Aristotle**. Socrates, a great teacher, wanted to make people think and question their own beliefs. Plato, a philosopher and teacher, wrote a work called *The Republic*. It describes an ideal society based on justice and fairness for everyone. Aristotle taught that people should live their lives based on **reason**, or clear and ordered thinking.

Greek scientists and mathematicians also gained fame for their contributions to geometry and for accurately calculating the size of Earth. Doctors studied the human body to understand how it worked. One Greek engineering invention that is still used today is a water screw, which brings water to farm fields.

One of the Greeks' most lasting contributions, however, is their political system. During the time known as the **Classical** Period, around the fifth and fourth centuries BC, Greece was organized into several hundred independent city-states, which became the foundation for Greek civilization. Athens was the first Greek city-state to establish **democracy**—a form of government in which people rule themselves. All male citizens in Athens had the right to participate in the assembly, a gathering of citizens, to debate and create the city's laws. Every citizen voted on every issue. Because all male citizens in Athens participated directly in government, we call the Greek form of government a direct democracy.

Roman Law and Government Later, Rome followed Greece's example by establishing a form of democratic government. The Roman Republic was created in 509 BC. Each year freeborn male citizens of Rome elected officials to rule the city. These officials acted on behalf of the citizens and debated ideas at an assembly of representatives. They had many powers, but stayed in power for only one year. Although this early republic was not a direct democracy, it did allow input from citizens. Later, the Romans changed their government into one with three parts. These three parts were made up of elected representatives who protected the city and its residents.

Roman laws were written and kept on public display so all people could know them. Roman concepts of equality before the law and innocent until proven guilty protected Roman citizens' rights.

The political ideas of Greece and Rome survived to influence governments around the world, including that of the United States. In the U.S. political system, citizens vote for representatives, making the nation a democratic republic.

Middle Ages

As the Roman Empire fell, groups from the north and east moved into former Roman lands. By the early 500s Europe was divided into many small kingdoms. This marked the beginning of the Middle Ages, a period that lasted about a thousand years.

Feudalism In the 480s a powerful group called the Franks conquered Gaul, the region we now call France. The Franks created a huge empire in

Reading Check
Analyze
How did Roman and Greek governments influence the United States?

The structure of feudal society has been likened to a pyramid, with kings sitting at the very top of society and peasants at the bottom.

Europe. When invaders began to attack European settlements in the 800s, the Frankish kings could not defend their empire. Nobles had to defend their own lands. As a result, the power of nobles grew, and kings became less powerful. Although loyal to the king, nobles ruled their lands as independent territories.

Nobles needed soldiers to defend their lands. Nobles gave **knights**, warriors who fought on horseback, land in exchange for military service. Nobles who gave land to knights so the knights would defend the land were called lords. A knight who promised to support the noble in battle was called a vassal. This system of promises between lords and vassals is known as feudalism.

Peasants owned no land, so they were not part of the feudal system. They did, however, need to grow food to live. As a result, a new economic system developed. Knights allowed peasants to farm land on their large estates, called manors. In return, the peasants had to give the knights food or other goods as payment.

Because of its structure, feudalism promoted the separation of territories and people. The Catholic Church, however, served as a strong unifying force among the states and people of Europe. During the Middle Ages, nearly everyone in Europe was Christian. Life revolved around the local church with markets, festivals, and religious ceremonies.

The Crusades In the late 1000s a long series of wars called the Crusades began between the European Christians and Muslims in Southwest Asia.

The Turks had captured Palestine, also known as the Holy Land because it was where Jesus had lived. Christians no longer felt safe to travel there on pilgrimages. Christians were called upon to go to war with the Turks to recapture Palestine.

Although the Crusades failed, they changed Europe forever. Trade between Europe and Asia began to grow, introducing Europeans to new products such as apricots, rice, and cotton cloth, as well as the ideas of Muslim thinkers.

Travel, Trade, and Towns In the Middle Ages, towns were small. After about 1000, this situation began to change. New technology meant farmers could produce larger harvests. As farmers grew more food, the population increased.

Travel became safer as increased protection from stronger rulers kept larger territories secure. Over time, kingdoms became nation-states—organized political units with central governments. This development provided even more protection to merchants.

The rulers of the Mongols made routes like the Silk Road (a caravan route that started in China and ended at the Mediterranean Sea) safe for travelers and traders. Among these traders was Marco Polo. In 1271 he journeyed from Europe to China along part of the old Silk Road. He spent 20 years living and traveling in Asia. When Marco Polo returned to Europe, he brought back stories of spices, coal, and paper money.

Timeline: Key Events in the Middle Ages

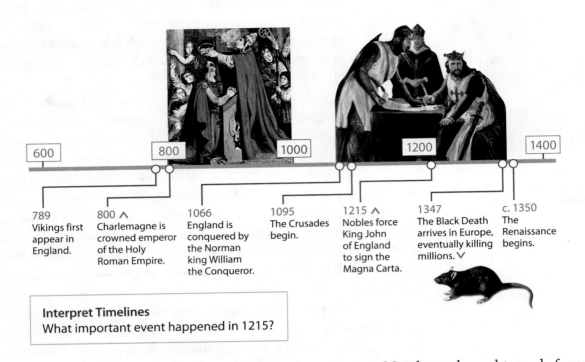

| 600 | 800 | 1000 | 1200 | 1400 |

789
Vikings first appear in England.

800 ∧
Charlemagne is crowned emperor of the Holy Roman Empire.

1066
England is conquered by the Norman king William the Conqueror.

1095
The Crusades begin.

1215 ∧
Nobles force King John of England to sign the Magna Carta.

1347
The Black Death arrives in Europe, eventually killing millions. ∨

c. 1350
The Renaissance begins.

> **Interpret Timelines**
> What important event happened in 1215?

Trade routes spread all across Europe. Merchants brought goods from Asia and Africa to sell in European markets. Their ships also brought back rats infected with the plague. The disease, known as the **Black Death**, spread across Europe, killing an estimated 25 million people. The European economy was dramatically affected by the shortage of workers. Peasants and serfs could now demand payment for their labor. They began to move to cities, which began to grow in size.

In time, the growth of trade led to the decline of feudalism and the manor system. A new middle class of artisans and merchants emerged, and trade cities became commercial centers. Trade associations called guilds became an influential part of European life.

Reading Check
Draw Conclusions
How did travel and trade affect the feudal system?

Renaissance

The Renaissance period brought new ways of thinking to Europe, weakening the old feudal system even more. The word *Renaissance* means "rebirth" and refers to the period that followed the Middle Ages in Europe. This movement began in Italy and eventually spread to other parts of Europe.

During the Renaissance, European rulers began to increase their power over the nobles in their countries. Fewer invasions from outside forces helped bring a period of order and stability to Europe.

Search for Knowledge Love of art and education was a key feature of the Renaissance. As Turks conquered much of the Byzantine Empire in the East, scholars fled to Italy. They brought ancient classical writings with them. Some of the works were by Greek thinkers like Plato.

Excited by the discoveries brought by Turkish scholars, European scholars went looking for ancient texts in Latin. They discovered many

Latin texts in monasteries, which had preserved works by Roman writers. As Italian scholars read these ancient texts, they rediscovered the glories of Greece and Rome.

The search for knowledge and learning spread to all fields, including art, literature, science, and political thought. The Renaissance emphasized the importance of people rather than focusing on religion. This new focus on human value and the study of humanities was called humanism. People's interest in the humanities led them to respect those who could write, create, or speak well. During the Middle Ages, most people had worked only to glorify God.

Italian artists created some of the most beautiful paintings and sculptures in the world. Their art reflected the basic Renaissance idea—the value of human beings. They rejected flat, two-dimensional images used in medieval art in favor of classical forms and techniques such as perspective. **Michelangelo** and **Leonardo da Vinci** are two of the greatest Renaissance artists. They are known for their work in the fields of painting, sculpture, and architecture. Leonardo was also an inventor, engineer, and mapmaker.

Italian writers also penned great works of literature. Dante Alighieri was a politician and poet. Before Dante, most authors wrote in Latin, the language of the church. But Dante chose to write in Italian, the common language of the people. This gave ordinary people the opportunity to read Dante's work.

Many texts that Europeans rediscovered in the 1300s dealt with science. After reading these works, Renaissance scholars went on to make their own scientific advances. They also studied ancient math texts and built on the ideas they read about. For example, they created symbols for the square root and for positive and negative numbers. Astronomers discovered that Earth moves around the sun. Other scientists used measurements and made calculations to create better, more accurate maps.

By 1450 Johannes Gutenberg had refined his invention of the printing press.

The development of the printing press was a giant step forward in spreading new ideas. In the mid-1400s, a German man, **Johannes Gutenberg** (GOOT-uhn-berk), developed a printing press that used movable type. This allowed an entire page to be printed at once. For the first time in history, thousands of people could read the same books and share ideas about them.

Economic Changes Affect Trade The growth in trade and services at the beginning of the Renaissance sparked a commercial revolution. This also brought a rise in mercantilism. Mercantilism is an economic system that unifies and increases the power and wealth of a nation.

Four northern Italian cities, Florence, Genoa, Milan, and Venice, developed into important trading centers. These cities played two major roles in trade. They served as ports along the Mediterranean Sea. They also served as manufacturing centers and specialized in certain crafts. This economic activity made some families in these cities very wealthy.

As trade and commerce grew, the need for banks arose. Bankers in Florence, Italy, kept money for merchants from all over Europe. The bankers also made money by charging interest on funds they loaned to merchants. The greatest bankers in Florence were from the Medici family. Although Florence was already wealthy from trade, banking increased that wealth.

During this time, merchants began to create **joint-stock companies**, or businesses in which a group of people invest together. In a joint-stock company, the investors share in the company's profits and losses. Forming joint-stock companies allowed investors to take fewer risks.

Summary and Preview Greek and Roman civilizations, the Middle Ages, and the Renaissance were major forces that shaped European history. In the next module you will read about how the Renaissance paved the way for exploration of the Americas.

Reading Check
Draw Conclusions
How did the Renaissance lead to trade and a commercial revolution?

Lesson 4 Assessment

Review Ideas, Terms, and People

1. **a. Identify** What is the difference between a direct democracy and a republic?
   b. Elaborate What is the importance of having a written law code?
2. **a. Describe** What was the relationship between knights and nobles?
   b. Elaborate How did the Crusades affect the feudal system?
3. **a. Identify** What does the term *Renaissance* mean?
   b. Analyze What is the relationship among trade, banking, and joint-stock companies?
   c. Elaborate What do you think was the greatest accomplishment of the Renaissance?

Critical Thinking

4. **Support a Point of View** You learned about the major changes that took place in Europe during the periods discussed in this lesson. Create a chart similar to the one below and identify which period you think was the most important and explain why.

Most Important	Why

Interpret Diagrams

Understand the Skill

Diagrams are drawings that use lines and labels to explain or illustrate something. Different types of diagrams have different purposes. *Pictorial diagrams* show an object in simple form, much like it would look if you were viewing it. *Cutaway diagrams* show the "insides" of an object. *Component diagrams* show how an object is organized by separating it into parts. Such diagrams are sometimes also called *schematic drawings*. The ability to interpret diagrams will help you to better understand a historical object, its function, and how it worked.

Learn the Skill

Use these basic steps to interpret a diagram:

1. Determine what type of diagram it is.

2. Read the diagram's title or caption to find out what the diagram represents.

3. Look for any labels and read them carefully. Most diagrams include text that identifies the object's parts or explains relationships among the parts.

4. If a legend is present, study it to identify and understand any symbols and colors that are used in the diagram.

5. Look for numbers or letters that might indicate a sequence of steps. Also, look for any arrows that might show direction or movement.

An Early Castle

Pulley · Oven · Chapel · Fireplaces · Windows · Drawbridge · Moat · Well

Practice and Apply

Interpret the diagram of an early castle and answer the following questions.

1. What type of diagram is this?

2. What labels in the diagram suggest how the castle was heated?

3. What was the purpose of the pulley?

4. Of what materials was the castle made?

5. What features of the castle helped make it secure against attack?

Review Vocabulary, Terms, and People

Complete each sentence by filling in the blank with the correct term or person.

1. During the Ice Age, a narrow strip of land called the _____ was exposed.

2. The _____ of Paleo-Indians from North to South America took thousands of years.

3. Native Americans living in the Pacific Northwest carved _____ on tall poles.

4. The first political confederation of Native Americans in North America was the _____.

5. The most famous ruler of Mali was _____.

6. While Mali's leader was on a _____, or pilgrimage to Mecca, he introduced his empire to the world.

7. The most famous ruler of Songhai took the name _____.

8. _____ describes an ideal society based on justice in *The Republic*.

Comprehension and Critical Thinking

Lesson 1

9. **a. Describe** How did early peoples in the Americas get their food?

   b. Analyze What led to the development of different culture groups in the Americas?

   c. Elaborate What features did the early civilizations of Mesoamerica and South America have in common?

Lesson 2

10. **a. Identify** Which early Native American society built cliff dwellings and which built mounds?

    b. Analyze How did Native Americans' religious beliefs affect their lives in North America?

    c. Evaluate Do you think it was easier for Native Americans to live in the dry climate of the Southwest, where rainfall was scarce, or in the North, where the cold climate presented a constant challenge?

Lesson 3

11. **a. Describe** Which two major trade goods made Ghana rich?

    b. Compare What characteristics did Mansa Musa and Askia the Great have in common?

    c. Elaborate How did geography contribute to the rise of Ghana, Mali, and Songhai?

Lesson 4

12. **a. Recall** What role did Greek and Roman traditions play in the development of the United States?

    b. Summarize How did the Crusades in Southwest Asia and the travels of Marco Polo in Asia contribute to the growth of trade in Europe?

    c. Evaluate Which do you think contributed the most to the advances in learning that occurred during the Renaissance—writing in the common language of a people or inventing the printing press?

Review Themes

13. Geography How did changes in climate lead to migration to the Americas?

14. Economics Describe the development of the European economy during the Middle Ages.

Reading Skills

Specialized Vocabulary of Social Studies *Use the Reading Skills taught in this module to answer the question about the reading selection below.*

> To encourage the spread of Islam in West Africa, Mansa Musa brought back artists and architects from other Muslim countries to build **mosques**, or buildings for Muslim prayer, throughout his lands.

15. What is the definition of the word *mosques* in the sentence above?

Social Studies Skills

Interpret Diagrams *Use the Social Studies Skills taught in this module to answer the question below.*

16. Look back at the diagram of a castle on the Social Studies Skills page. Which of the following is the main way to enter the castle?

   a. well

   b. moat

   c. drawbridge

   d. windows

Focus on Writing

17. Write a Travelogue In a travelogue, you describe a journey you have taken to an area. Someone who is not familiar with the area can learn about it from your descriptions. You have read about many cultures across a long span of history. Pick one area that you found the most interesting in the module. Organize your thoughts about the kinds of people you would have met, the sights and sounds you would have experienced, and the kind of things you would have done if you had traveled there during the time discussed.

Try to include information about a culture's history, customs, beliefs, practices, economies, political systems, and natural environments. Write a paragraph about what you might have liked or disliked about your trip. Be sure to include a main idea sentence and several sentences that support the main idea with evidence.

THE Maya

The Maya developed one of the most advanced civilizations in the Americas, but their story is shrouded in mystery. Around AD 250, the Maya began to build great cities in southern Mexico and Central America. They developed a writing system, practiced astronomy, and built magnificent palaces and pyramids with little more than stone tools. Around AD 900, however, the Maya abandoned their cities, leaving their monuments to be reclaimed by the jungle and, for a time, forgotten.

Explore some of the incredible monuments and cultural achievements of the ancient Maya online. You can find a wealth of information, video clips, primary sources, activities, and more through your online textbook.

"Thus let it be done! Let the emptiness be filled! Let the water recede and make a void, let the earth appear and become solid; let it be done . . . "Earth!" they said, and instantly it was made."

 The Popol Vuh
Read the document to learn how the Maya believed the world was created.

Destroying the Maya's Past
Watch the video to learn how the actions of one Spanish missionary nearly destroyed the written record of the Maya world.

Finding the City of Palenque
Watch the video to learn about the great Maya city of Palenque and the European discovery of the site in the eighteenth century.

Pakal's Tomb
Watch the video to explore how the discovery of the tomb of a great king helped archaeologists piece together the Maya past.

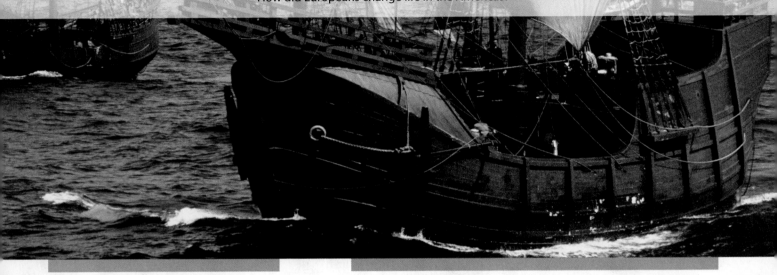

Module 2

New Empires in the Americas

★

Essential Question
How did Europeans change life in the Americas?

About the Photo: The ships of explorer Christopher Columbus sail again in the form of these replicas.

In this module you will learn about the Europeans who colonized the Americas.

What You Will Learn ...

Lesson 1: Europeans Set Sail 36
The Big Idea Europeans explored the world, searching for new lands and new trade routes.

Lesson 2: Europeans Reach the Americas. 41
The Big Idea Christopher Columbus's voyages led to new exchanges between Europe, Africa, and the Americas.

Lesson 3: Spain Builds an Empire 46
The Big Idea Spain established a large empire in the Americas.

Lesson 4 The Race for Empires. 53
The Big Idea Other European nations challenged Spain in the Americas.

▶ *Explore ONLINE!*

HISTORY

VIDEOS, including...
• Columbus Sails West

☑ Document-Based Investigations

☑ Graphic Organizers

☑ Interactive Games

☑ Interactive Map: Magellan's Voyage Around the World

☑ Image with Hotspots: Tenochtitlán

☑ Image Carousel: Key Events in Europe, 1450 – 1588

▶ *Explore ONLINE!*

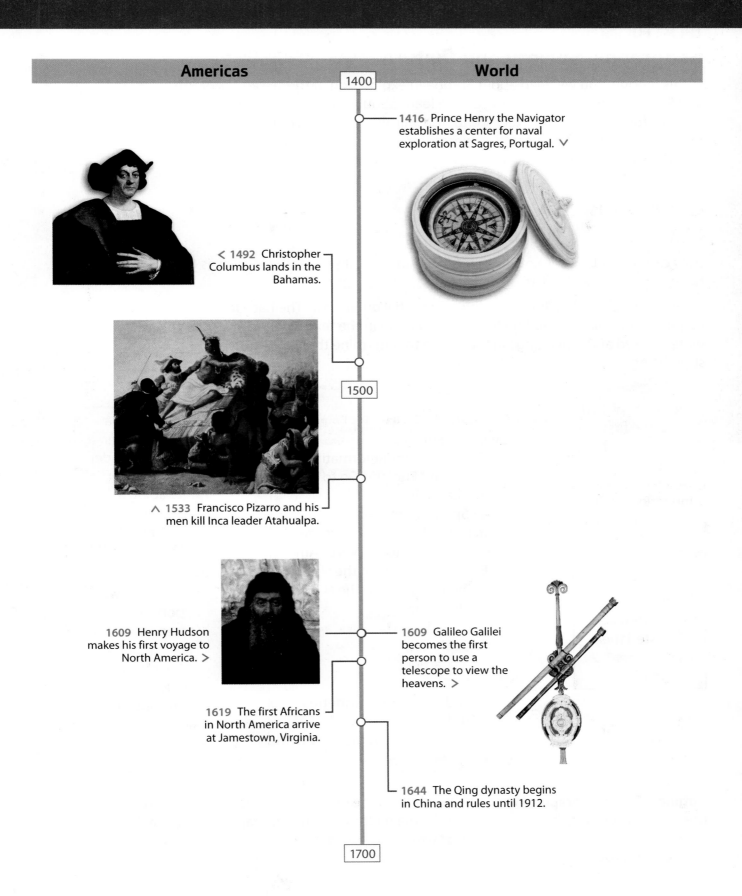

Americas | **World**

1400

1416 Prince Henry the Navigator establishes a center for naval exploration at Sagres, Portugal. ∨

< 1492 Christopher Columbus lands in the Bahamas.

1500

∧ 1533 Francisco Pizarro and his men kill Inca leader Atahualpa.

1609 Henry Hudson makes his first voyage to North America. >

1609 Galileo Galilei becomes the first person to use a telescope to view the heavens. >

1619 The first Africans in North America arrive at Jamestown, Virginia.

1644 The Qing dynasty begins in China and rules until 1912.

1700

Reading Social Studies

THEME FOCUS:

Geography, Society and Culture

In this module you will read about European exploration of the sea and of North and South America. As you read you will learn about how geography affected the race for empires in the New World. You will also read how, during journeys of exploration, society and culture were affected when Europeans and Native Americans encountered each other.

READING FOCUS:

Outlining and History

How can you make sense of all the facts and ideas that you read? One way is to take notes in the form of an outline.

Outline a Lesson Here is an example of a partial outline for "The Race for Empires." Compare the outline to the information in the text. Notice how the writer looked at the headings in the lesson to determine the main and supporting ideas.

> The writer picked up the first heading in the lesson as the first main idea. She identified it with Roman numeral I.

> The writer identified three facts that supported III.B. She listed them as numbers 1, 2, and 3.

Lesson 4: The Race for Empires

I. Events in Europe
    A. The Protestant Reformation
    B. Spain and England Go to War
        1. Sea dogs
        2. Spanish Armada
II. Search for a Northwest Passage
III. European Presence in North America
    A. English Presence in the New World
    B. French Presence in the New World
        1. Huguenots
        2. Canada
        3. Explorers
            a. Cartier
            b. Champlain
            c. Jolliet and Marquette
            d. La Salle
    C. Dutch Presence in the New World

> The writer saw two smaller headings under the bigger heading and listed them as A and B.

> The writer decided it was important to note some individual facts under B.3. That's why she added points a through d.

Outline a Few Paragraphs When you need to outline only a few paragraphs, you can use the same outline form. Just look for the main idea of each paragraph and give each one a Roman numeral. Supporting ideas within the paragraph can be listed with A, B, and so forth. You can use Arabic numbers for specific details and facts.

You Try It!

Read the following passage. Then fill in the blanks to complete the outline below.

Conquest of the Aztec Empire Moctezuma ruled the Aztec Empire, which was at the height of its power in the early 1500s. Moctezuma's capital, Tenochtitlán, was built in the middle of Lake Texcoco, near the present-day site of Mexico City. Tenochtitlán was a large city with temples, a palace, and buildings that were built on an island in the middle of the lake. The buildings and riches of the city impressed the Spaniards. They saw the Aztec Empire as a good source of gold and silver. They also wanted to convert the Aztec to Christianity.

The Aztec had thousands of warriors. In contrast, Cortés had only 508 soldiers, about 100 sailors, 16 horses, and some guns. Cortés hoped that his superior weapons would bring him victory.

Complete this outline based on the passage you just read.

I.   Moctezuma and the Aztec Empire were at the height of power in the early 1500s.
  A. Tenochtitlán was the capital
    1. Built in Lake Texcoco
    2. _____
  B. The buildings and riches impressed the Spaniards
    1. _____
    2. Christianity

II. _____
  A. Cortés had fewer soldiers
  B. _____

As you read Module 2, practice outlining a few paragraphs to help you make sense of the facts and ideas you have read.

Key Terms and People

Lesson 1
Leif Eriksson
Henry the Navigator
astrolabe
caravels

Lesson 2
Christopher Columbus
Line of Demarcation
Treaty of Tordesillas
Ferdinand Magellan
circumnavigate
Columbian Exchange

Lesson 3
conquistadors
Hernán Cortés
Moctezuma II
Francisco Pizarro
encomienda system
plantations
Bartolomé de Las Casas

Lesson 4
Protestant Reformation
Protestants
Spanish Armada
Northwest Passage
Jacques Cartier
charter

Europeans Set Sail

The Big Idea

Europeans explored the world, searching for new lands and new trade routes.

Main Ideas

- Vikings were skilled sailors, and they were the first Europeans to reach North America.

- Prince Henry the Navigator established a school for sailors and provided financial support that enabled the Portuguese to start exploring the oceans.

- Portuguese sailors sailed around Africa and found a sea route to Asia.

Key Terms and People

Leif Eriksson
Henry the Navigator
astrolabe
caravels

If YOU were there . . .

You are a sailor living in Portugal in the mid-1400s. Several of your friends are excited about joining an expedition to sail to new, unexplored lands. Although Portuguese navigators have made improvements to sailing ships and advancements in ocean travel, you have heard about the dangers other sailors have faced on the open seas.

Will you join the expedition or stay behind? Why?

Viking Sailors Reach North America

The Vikings were the first Europeans to make contact with North America. They came from Scandinavia, a peninsula that includes the present-day countries of Denmark, Norway, and Sweden. The Vikings were skilled sailors who developed a new style of ship, called the longship, which curved up at both ends. Viking vessels traveled the rough North Atlantic seas better than earlier ships because their designs were more stable.

The Vikings raided countries throughout Europe, but they also developed large trading networks. Viking ships sailed to the British Isles and the Mediterranean and Black seas. Eventually, the Vikings sailed west into the North Atlantic. There they founded a settlement on the island of Iceland in about 874. More than 100 years later, Viking Erik the Red, who had been convicted of crimes in Iceland, was sent away as punishment. He went to Greenland and brought settlers there.

Leif Eriksson, the son of Erik the Red, was also an adventurer. In the year 1000, he was sailing west from Norway to Greenland when strong winds blew his ship off course and carried it all the way to the North American coast.

Eriksson and his crew landed on the Labrador Peninsula in present-day Canada. The Vikings then sailed farther south to the island of Newfoundland, and perhaps to what is now

Norwegian explorer Leif Eriksson led a group of Vikings to North America in about 1000.

New England. According to their myths, Vikings saw forests, meadows, and rivers that held "larger salmon than they had ever seen."

Eriksson settled in a coastal area he called Vinland. The Vikings left after only a few years. Attacks by Native Americans posed a constant threat, and the area may have been too far from other Viking settlements to be supported.

After the Vikings left North America, Europeans did not return to the continent for centuries. In the 1400s, however, a growing interest in discovery and exploration spread across Europe.

Reading Check
Sequence List the stages of exploration that led to the Vikings' landing in North America.

Looking toward the Sea

Exploration was necessary for European trade. One reason was that European mines were running out of silver and gold. Merchants needed more of the precious metals to conduct business. In addition, new forms of production, such as spinning wheels and windmills, made manufacturing more efficient. As a result, workers needed more raw materials, and merchants needed new markets where they could sell the manufactured goods. Traders also sought products—from incense to silk—that could only be found in the East.

Since the 1200s Europeans had been traveling east by land. The Crusades had introduced them to knowledge, products, markets, and natural resources found across Asia. For a time, land routes to the east were relatively safe. The Mongols, who had conquered much of the continent, provided protection. When the Muslim Ottomans conquered Constantinople in 1453, however, they blocked the land trade routes to Asia. In response, the European powers began to compete in a race to find a sea route to Asia.

Riches and Religion During the 1400s Europeans had several reasons to explore the world. First, they wanted Asian spices. They hoped to bypass the merchants who had a monopoly on, or economic control of, the Asian products that reached the Mediterranean. If a sea route to Asia could be found, countries could buy spices and other items directly. Second, religion played a role in exploration. Christians in Europe wanted to convert more people to their faith. Third, many Europeans had become interested in Asian cultures. Explorer Marco Polo wrote a book about his travels throughout Asia. It remained popular in Europe long after his death in 1324. Many Europeans wanted to learn more about Asia and the money they could make by trading with Asians.

Portugal Leads the Way Portugal became a leader in world exploration. Prince **Henry the Navigator**, in particular, was responsible for advances that would make exploration more successful. Although he never set out on a voyage himself, Henry greatly advanced Portugal's exploration efforts.

In the early 1400s Prince Henry built an observatory and founded a school of navigation to teach better methods of sailing. He also financed research by mapmakers and shipbuilders. Finally, he paid for expeditions to explore the west coast of Africa.

The Caravel

A special type of ship called the caravel became the workhorse of many European explorers. Though small, caravels were sturdy. They could sail across huge oceans and up small rivers. Caravels featured important advances in sailing technology.

Triangular sails enabled the caravel to sail into the wind.

The smooth rounded hull handled high seas well.

Analyze Visuals
What features made the caravel an excellent sailing ship?

The large center rudder made quick turns possible.

Scientific and Technological Advances Scientific and geographical knowledge about the Earth had increased, thanks in part to rediscovery of Roman sources and to overland journeys by European merchants. This knowledge led to better maps. Sailors had more, although still incomplete, information about the sea and lands beyond it. New technology also played a major role in advancing world exploration. Sailors began to use tools such as the magnetic compass, which indicated all directions by always pointing north. In addition, sailors had the **astrolabe**, a device that enabled navigators to learn their ship's location by charting the position of the stars. Better instruments made it possible for sailors to travel the open seas without landmarks to guide them.

The Portuguese also made advances in shipbuilding. They began designing ships that were smaller, lighter, and easier to steer than the heavy galleons they had used before. These new ships, called **caravels** (KER-uh-velz), used triangular sails that, unlike traditional square sails, allowed ships to sail against the wind. By placing rudders at the back of the ship, the Portuguese also improved the steering of ships.

Reading Check
Summarize What factors led to increased exploration?

A Sea Route to Asia

By the 1400s Portugal had several motives, financial support, and the technology necessary for exploration. Portuguese explorers set out to find new lands.

Rounding Africa Even with new technology, travel on the open seas was dangerous and difficult. One person described the **effect** on sailors of a voyage south from Portugal.

Academic Vocabulary
effect the result of an action or decision

> "Those which survived could hardly be recognized as human. They had lost flesh and hair, the nails had gone from hands and feet. . . . They spoke of heat so incredible that it was a marvel that ships and crews were not burnt."
>
> —Sailor, quoted in *World Civilizations*, edited by Edward McNall Burns, et al.

In spite of the dangers, Portuguese explorers continued sailing south, setting up trading posts along the way.

In 1488 Portuguese navigator Bartolomeu Dias led an expedition from Portugal southward along the African coast. A storm blew his ships around the southern tip of Africa. This point became known as the Cape of Good Hope. Dias wanted to continue his voyage, but his men did not. Since supplies were very low, Dias decided to call off the voyage and return to Portugal.

Later, King Manuel of Portugal sent another explorer, Vasco da Gama, on an expedition around the Cape of Good Hope. Da Gama left Lisbon, Portugal, in July 1497 and arrived in southwestern India the next year. Portugal had won the European race for a sea route to Asia.

When da Gama reached the Indian port of Calicut, Muslim traders met him and his men. The Muslims surprised the sailors by speaking to them in Portuguese. Soon, da Gama and his crew learned that the people of India had been trading with Muslim and Italian merchants who knew Portuguese. Da Gama made two more trips back to India. He even governed a small colony there.

Results of Exploration Portugal's explorations would have major results, including the start of the Atlantic slave trade. As Portuguese sailors explored the west coast of Africa, they negotiated for gold, ivory, and slaves. The slave trade devastated African communities. It led to increased warfare among kingdoms and broke up many families. The Portuguese sent

Quick Facts

Causes and Effects of the Discovery of a Sea Route to Asia

Several factors led to the discovery of a sea route from Europe to Asia.

Causes

- Financial backing from Prince Henry the Navigator
- New technology (caravel and mariner's astrolabe)
- Seeking trade with Asia and financial gain
- Converting people to Christianity
- Curiosity

Effects

- Discovery of a sea route to Asia
- Face-to-face contact with traders in distant lands
- Awareness of different cultures and ways of life

Analyze Information
Why was trade with Asia so important to Europeans?

Portuguese Routes and Exploration

Explore ONLINE!

→ Dias 1487–1488
→ Da Gama 1497–1499

0   1,000   2,000 Miles
0   1,000   2,000 Kilometers

EUROPE

ASIA

PORTUGAL
40°N
SPAIN
Lisbon
Mediterranean Sea

INDIA
20°N
Calicut

AFRICA

Equator

Mombasa

INDIAN OCEAN

N
W   E
S

20°S

Cape of Good Hope

Interpret Maps

1. **Movement** How far east did Dias travel before turning back?

2. **Human-Environment Interaction** About how many miles was da Gama's 1497–1499 voyage?

ATLANTIC OCEAN
40°S

20°W   0°   20°E   40°E   60°E

many enslaved Africans to Europe and to islands in the Atlantic, where they lived and worked under brutal conditions.

The other nations of Europe watched as new trade routes brought increased wealth and power to Portugal. They soon launched voyages of exploration to find their own water routes to Asia.

Reading Check
Predict How would continued exploration affect Africans?

Summary and Preview In the 1400s the Portuguese started a new era of exploration. In the next lesson you will learn how Europeans reached the American continents.

Lesson 1 Assessment

Review Ideas, Terms, and People

1. a. **Identify** Who was Leif Eriksson?

   b. **Summarize** How did the Vikings eventually establish Vinland?

   c. **Draw Inferences** Why do you think the Vikings did not try to colonize the Americas?

2. a. **Identify** Who was Prince Henry the Navigator?

   b. **Summarize** Why were European merchants concerned about the supply of gold and silver?

3. a. **Recall** Who was the first explorer to find a sea route from Europe to Asia?

   b. **Explain** How did Muslims living in India learn Portuguese?

c. **Draw Conclusions** How did the slave trade affect African communities?

Critical Thinking

4. **Summarize** In this lesson you learned about European exploration. Create a chart similar to the one below and explain the reason for the explorations, the technology that made explorations possible, and the results of the explorations.

Reason

Technology → Results

Europeans Reach the Americas

The Big Idea

Christopher Columbus's voyages led to new exchanges between Europe, Africa, and the Americas.

Main Ideas

- Christopher Columbus sailed across the Atlantic Ocean and reached a continent that was previously unknown to him.

- After Columbus's voyages, other explorers sailed to the Americas.

Key Terms and People

Christopher Columbus
Line of Demarcation
Treaty of Tordesillas
Ferdinand Magellan
circumnavigate
Columbian Exchange

If YOU were there . . .

You are a European explorer who just returned to your homeland from the Americas. While you were gone, you tried new and different foods, including corn, potatoes, and cocoa. You have brought some of these foods back with you. You want your friends and family to sample these items, but they resist.

What will you say about these new foods?

Columbus Sails across the Atlantic

Stories of fabulous kingdoms and wealth in Asia captured the imagination of **Christopher Columbus**, a sailor from Genoa, Italy. Columbus was convinced that he could reach Asia by sailing west across the Atlantic Ocean.

Columbus knew that the Earth was round. In fact, the Earth's shape was well known among educated Westerners. Columbus's plans included errors, however. He thought the Earth was much smaller than it is. He also thought that Asia extended farther east and, therefore, that the lands he sought were closer to Europe.

The Journey Begins Columbus asked King Ferdinand and Queen Isabella of Spain to pay for an expedition across the Atlantic. He promised them great riches, new territory, and Catholic converts. It took Columbus several years to convince the king and queen, but they finally agreed to help finance the journey. Ferdinand and Isabella ordered Columbus to bring back any items of value and to claim for Spain any lands he explored.

On August 3, 1492, Columbus's three ships set sail. The *Niña* and the *Pinta* were caravels. Columbus sailed in the larger *Santa María*. The ships carried about 90 sailors and a year's worth of supplies. They made a stop in the Canary Islands, and then on September 6, they resumed their journey. Soon, they passed the limits of Columbus's maps and sailed into uncharted seas. After more than a month with no sight of land, the crew grew restless.

Soon the crew saw signs of land—birds and floating tree branches. Columbus promised a reward "to him who first sang out that he saw land." On October 12, 1492, a lookout cried, "Land! Land!" ending the long journey from the Canary Islands.

The ships landed on an island in the Bahamas. Columbus thought he had found a new route to Asia. Instead, he had reached another continent that was unknown to him. Columbus called the island San Salvador, which means "Holy Savior." Columbus also visited another island he called Hispaniola. There he met a group of native people called the Taino (TY-noh). At that time Europeans called Asia the Indies, so Columbus, believing he was in Asia, called these Native Americans Indians.

The Taino lived in small farming communities. In his journal, Columbus wrote that the Taino were "so generous . . . that no one would believe it who has not seen it." However, Columbus and his crew were not interested in Taino culture, but in gold. After three months of exploring, looking for gold, and collecting exotic plants and animals, Columbus returned to Spain.

▶ Explore ONLINE!

Columbus's Voyages, 1492–1504

Transatlantic Travel

Legend:
→ First voyage, 1492–1493
→ Second voyage, 1493–1496
→ Third voyage, 1498
→ Fourth voyage, 1502–1504
▨ Land seen by Columbus or crew members

0   250   500 Miles
0   250   500 Kilometers

Interpret Maps

1. **Place** Where did Columbus first land?

2. **Human-Environment Interaction** Why do you think Columbus saw only the coastal area of Mesoamerica?

Columbus made three more journeys to the Americas during his lifetime. In 1504 he returned to Spain in poor health. Columbus died two years later, still believing that he had reached Asia.

Impact of Columbus's Voyages The voyages of Columbus changed the way Europeans thought of the world and their place in it. A new era of interaction between Europe and the Americas had begun. Moreover, Columbus's voyages and the voyages of explorers who came after him would set in motion the development of American society.

Columbus's discovery also created conflict between European countries. Both Spain and Portugal wanted to add these lands to their growing empires. In 1493 Pope Alexander VI, originally from Spain, issued a decree that drew a new boundary for Spain and Portugal. This imaginary **Line of Demarcation** divided the Atlantic Ocean. Spain could claim all land west of the line.

The Portuguese king believed that this arrangement favored Spain. To prevent war, the two leaders signed the **Treaty of Tordesillas**, which moved the Line of Demarcation 800 miles farther west. This gave Portugal more opportunity to claim lands unexplored by other Europeans.

The pope's decree and the Treaty of Tordesillas helped establish the idea that a country that explored a newly found land was entitled to own and

---

DOCUMENT-BASED INVESTIGATION   Historical Source

Christopher Columbus's Letter, 1494

Two years after discovering the island of Hispaniola, Columbus wrote a letter to the Spanish king and queen outlining his ideas of its colonization.

Analyze Historical Sources
What were Columbus's main concerns in founding a colony on Hispaniola?

Most High and Mighty Sovereigns,

In the first place, as regards the Island of Espanola: Inasmuch as the numb colonists who desire to go thither [there] amounts to two thousand, owing to the land being safer and better for farming and trading. . . .

1. That in the said island there shall be founded three or four towns. . . .
2. That for the better and more speedy colonization of the said island, no one shall have liberty to collect gold in it except those who have taken out colonists' papers. . . .
3. That each town shall have its alcalde [mayor]. . . .
4. That there shall be a church, and parish priests or friars to administer the sacraments, to perform divine worship, and for the conversion of the Indians.

—Christopher Columbus, letter to the king and queen of Spain, 1494 rule it. This idea came to be known as the "Doctrine of Discovery." By this doctrine, native peoples who had lived on the land for generations were considered occupants, not owners with property rights. The policy would have a devastating effect on Native Americans for centuries to come.

Other Explorers Sail to the Americas

Columbus's discoveries inspired others to sail across the Atlantic Ocean. In 1501 explorer Amerigo Vespucci (vuh-SPOO-chee) led a Spanish fleet to the coast of present-day South America. He was convinced the land he reached was not Asia. Instead, Vespucci believed he had found a "new world." A German mapmaker labeled the continents across the ocean *America* in honor of Vespucci. Europeans began using the names North America and South America for these lands.

In a Spanish settlement in present-day Panama, another explorer, Vasco Núñez de Balboa (NOON-yays day bahl-BOH-uh), heard stories from local Native Americans about another ocean farther west. Balboa set out to find it. For weeks he and his men struggled through thick jungle and deadly swamps. In 1513 they reached the top of a mountain. From this spot Balboa saw a great blue sea—the Pacific Ocean—stretching out before him.

In 1519 **Ferdinand Magellan** (muh-JEHL-uhn), a Portuguese navigator, set out with a Spanish fleet to sail down the east coast of South America. After sailing around the southern tip of the continent, Magellan continued into the Pacific even though his ships were dangerously low on food and fresh water.

Portuguese navigator Ferdinand Magellan's ships were the first to sail full circle around the globe.

Magellan's fleet sailed across the Pacific Ocean. In the Philippines, Magellan was killed in a battle with native peoples. Down to three ships, the expedition continued sailing west into the Indian Ocean. In 1522 the voyage's only remaining ship returned to Spain. Only 18 members of Magellan's original crew survived. These sailors were the first people to **circumnavigate**, or go all the way around, the globe. Their entire journey was some 40,000 miles long.

European explorers and settlers took plants and animals with them to the Americas. They also brought back a variety of new plants and animals to Europe, Asia, and Africa. This transfer became known as the **Columbian Exchange** because it started with Columbus's explorations.

European explorers found many plants in the Americas that were unknown to them, including corn, potatoes, squash, tobacco, and cocoa. They brought these items to Europe, where they were highly valued. Turkeys, too, made the journey from the Americas to Europe. The explorers introduced horses, cattle, and pigs to the Americas. Native Americans came to use these animals for food and transportation. They also started to farm European grains such as wheat and barley. Citrus fruits and sugarcane were other plants that came from Europe. These became important crops over time.

Without intending to do so, the explorers also introduced deadly new diseases to the Americas. Native Americans had no natural resistance to European diseases. As a result, diseases such as smallpox killed from 80 to 95 percent of the native population within 150 years of Columbus's arrival. Not only did these deaths devastate Native American communities, they also had a terrible long-term effect. Soon after they established colonies, Europeans, especially the Spanish, forced Native Americans to work as laborers, raising food and mining for gold and silver. But because so many native people died from the new diseases, a labor shortage soon developed. The Europeans began looking for a new source of workers. They turned to Africa and began importing enslaved Africans. Over many years, Europeans shipped millions of slaves to the New World colonies.

The Columbian Exchange changed the world for all time. Environments, agriculture, trade relationships, and even entire cultures were affected in Europe, Africa, and the Americas. Some changes, such as the death of Native Americans from new diseases, happened very quickly. Others happened more gradually. For example, as some mountain-dwelling Native Americans acquired horses, which had come from Europe, they moved down to the Great Plains. There these peoples adopted lifestyles that depended on the buffalo herds.

Reading Check
Evaluate What were the negative aspects of the Columbian Exchange?

Over time, a trading pattern involving the exchange of raw materials, manufactured products, and slaves developed among Europe, Africa, and the Americas. This trading pattern would affect many aspects of history, both in the New World and the old.

Summary and Preview Columbus's voyages to America inspired other Europeans to explore the "New World." This led to new exchanges between both sides of the Atlantic. In the next lesson you will learn about Spain's empire in the Americas.

Lesson 2 Assessment

Review Ideas, Terms, and People

1. **a. Recall** What agreement did Christopher Columbus make with Queen Isabella and King Ferdinand of Spain?

   b. Explain Where did Columbus think he had landed when he reached the Bahamas?

   c. Evaluate How did Columbus's voyage lead to a dispute between Spain and Portugal?

2. **a. Identify** Who was the first European explorer to see the Pacific Ocean?

   b. Summarize What route did Ferdinand Magellan's ships take to circumnavigate the globe?

   c. Draw Conclusions How did the Columbian Exchange and the slave trade affect the economies and the people of Europe, Africa, and the Americas? Why would the people involved in the Columbian Exchange have had different perspectives on the events?

Critical Thinking

3. **Support a Point of View** In this lesson you learned about European exploration. Create a graphic organizer like the one below and rank, in order, the most important results of European voyages to the Americas. Explain your choices in the "Why" column. Add more rows as necessary.

Most Important	Why

Spain Builds an Empire

The Big Idea

Spain established a large empire in the Americas.

Main Ideas

- Spanish conquistadors conquered the Aztec and Inca empires.
- Spanish explorers traveled through the borderlands of New Spain, claiming more land.
- Spanish settlers treated Native Americans harshly, forcing them to work on plantations and in mines.

Key Terms and People

conquistadors
Hernán Cortés
Moctezuma II
Francisco Pizarro
encomienda system
plantations
Bartolomé de Las Casas

If YOU were there . . .

You are an Aztec warrior living in central Mexico in the 1500s. You are proud to serve your ruler, Moctezuma II. One day several hundred foreigners arrive on your shores. They are pale, bearded men, and they have strange animals and equipment.

From where do you think these strangers have come?

Spanish Conquistadors

The Spanish sent **conquistadors** (kahn-kees-tuh-DAWS), soldiers who led military expeditions in the Americas. Conquistador **Hernán Cortés** left the island of Cuba to sail to present-day Mexico in 1519. Cortés had heard of a wealthy land to the west ruled by a king named **Moctezuma II** (mawk-tay-SOO-mah).

Conquest of the Aztec Empire Moctezuma ruled the Aztec Empire, which was at the height of its power in the early 1500s. Moctezuma's capital, Tenochtitlán, was built in the middle of Lake Texcoco, near the present-day site of Mexico City. Tenochtitlán was a large city with temples, a palace, and buildings that were built on an island in the middle of the lake. The buildings and riches of the city impressed the Spaniards. They saw the Aztec Empire as a good source of gold and silver. They also wanted to convert the Aztec to Christianity.

The Aztec had thousands of warriors. In contrast, Cortés had only 508 soldiers, about 100 sailors, 16 horses, and some guns. Cortés hoped that his superior weapons would bring him victory. Cortés also sought help from enemies of the Aztec. An Indian woman named Malintzin (mah-LINT-suhn) helped Cortés win allies.

Spanish conquistadors (left), benefited from having stronger weapons and defenses than Aztec warriors (right).

At first Moctezuma believed Cortés to be a god and welcomed him. Cortés then took Moctezuma prisoner and seized control of Tenochtitlán. Eventually, Tenochtitlán was

Reasons for Spanish Victory

Several advantages helped the Spanish defeat the Aztec and Inca.

Causes of the Aztec and Inca Defeat
- Spanish steel armor and weapons
- Spanish horses
- European diseases
- Spanish alliances with Aztec and Inca enemies

Effects
- Reduced Native American population
- Spanish rule of the Americas
- Columbian Exchange

Analyze Information
Which cause do you think was most important to the Spanish victory?

destroyed and Moctezuma was killed. Smallpox and other diseases brought by the Spanish quickened the fall of the Aztec Empire.

Conquest of the Inca Empire Another Spanish conquistador, **Francisco Pizarro** (puh-ZAHR-oh), heard rumors of the Inca cities in the Andes of South America. The Inca ruled a large territory that stretched along the Pacific coast from present-day Chile to northern Ecuador.

Pizarro had fewer than 400 men in his army. But the Inca, like the Aztec, had no weapons to match the conquistadors' swords and guns. Though outnumbered, Pizarro's troops captured the great Inca capital at Cuzco in present-day Peru and killed the Inca leaders. By 1534 Pizarro and his Native American allies had conquered the entire Inca Empire.

In only a few years, the Spanish had conquered two great American empires. During the conquest, the Spanish and their allies killed thousands of Inca and Aztec and looted their settlements. Moreover, possibly more than three-quarters of the Aztec and Inca populations were killed by the diseases the Europeans brought.

Spanish Settlements The Spanish began to settle their vast empire, which they called New Spain. Spain's government wanted to control migration to the Americas. Most of the emigrants were Spanish, though a few non-Spanish subjects of the king also migrated. Jews, Muslims, and non-Christians were forbidden to settle in New Spain. At first, most emigrants were men. The government then encouraged families to migrate. Eventually, women comprised one-quarter of the total emigration from Spain.

Spain ruled its large American empire through a system of royal officials. At the top was the Council of the Indies, formed in 1524 to govern the Americas from Spain. The Council appointed two viceroys, or royal governors. The Viceroyalty of Peru governed most of South America. The Viceroyalty of New Spain governed all Spanish territories in Central America, Mexico, and the southern part of what is now the United States.

The Spanish established three kinds of settlements in New Spain. Pueblos served as trading posts and sometimes as centers of government. Priests started missions, where they converted local Native Americans to Catholicism. The Spanish also built presidios, or military bases, to protect towns and missions.

To connect some of the scattered communities of New Spain, Spanish settlers built *El Camino Real,* or "the Royal Road." This network of roads ran for hundreds of miles, from Mexico City to Santa Fe. The roads later stretched to settlements in California.

Exploring the Borderlands of New Spain

Spain's American empire was not limited to lands taken from the conquered Aztec and Inca empires. Many other Spanish explorers came to North America. They explored the borderlands of New Spain and claimed many new lands for the Spanish crown.

Exploring the Southeast In 1508 explorer Juan Ponce de León landed on the Caribbean island of Puerto Rico. By 1511 he had conquered the island for Spain and founded the city of San Juan. Ponce de León also discovered gold on Puerto Rico. Spanish officials appointed him governor of the colony.

In 1513 Ponce de León discovered the coast of present-day Florida. According to legend, Ponce de León heard that a Fountain of Youth, whose waters could make old people young again, could be found in Florida. However, this story did not appear until after his death. Whatever his goal might have been, Ponce de León set out to explore the area.

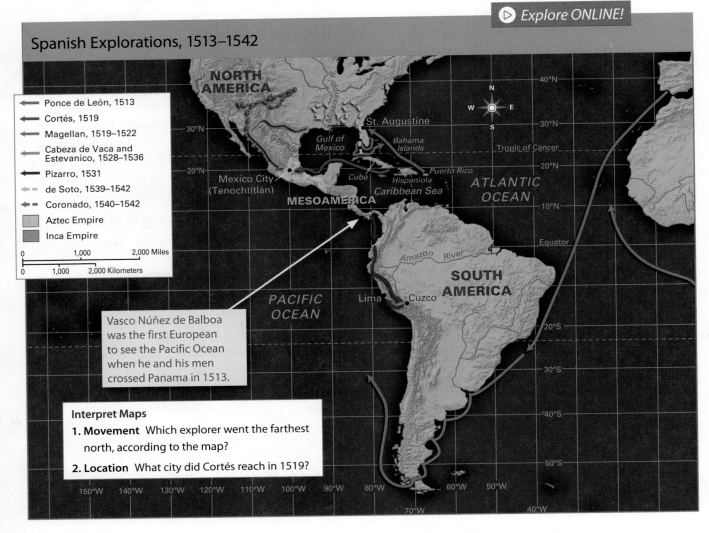

▶ *Explore ONLINE!*

Spanish Explorations, 1513–1542

Legend:
← Ponce de León, 1513
← Cortés, 1519
← Magellan, 1519–1522
← Cabeza de Vaca and Estevanico, 1528–1536
← Pizarro, 1531
←- de Soto, 1539–1542
←- Coronado, 1540–1542
▨ Aztec Empire
▨ Inca Empire

0   1,000   2,000 Miles
0   1,000   2,000 Kilometers

Vasco Núñez de Balboa was the first European to see the Pacific Ocean when he and his men crossed Panama in 1513.

Interpret Maps

1. **Movement** Which explorer went the farthest north, according to the map?

2. **Location** What city did Cortés reach in 1519?

Although he had royal permission to colonize Florida, he did not succeed in doing so.

Two decades later another explorer traveled through Florida. Royal officials gave Hernando de Soto permission to explore the coastal region of the Gulf of Mexico. In 1539 his expedition landed in an area near the present-day city of Tampa Bay, Florida. De Soto then led his men north through what is now Georgia and the Carolinas. In 1540, while in present-day Alabama, de Soto encountered the Muscogee peoples. De Soto took the Muscogee chief, Tuscaloosa, hostage as a way to gain supplies. Arguments between the Spaniards and the Muscogee led to a fierce battle. Several thousand Muscogee were killed. Although the Spaniards won the battle, they lost many men and almost all their supplies. Still, de Soto continued his journey, discovering the Mississippi River in 1541. The explorers then traveled west into present-day Oklahoma. De Soto died in 1542 on this journey.

Exploring the Southwest The Spanish also explored what is now the southwestern United States. In 1528 explorer Álvar Núñez Cabeza de Vaca joined conquistador Pánfilo de Narváez on an expedition to North America. Their group of 300 men first landed on the Florida coast. They faced many severe problems, including a shortage of food.

The group built boats, which made it possible for them to travel around the Florida panhandle. The explorers continued along the Gulf Coast and eventually reached the Mississippi River. Severe weather hit this group hard, and many members of the expedition died. Cabeza de Vaca's boat shipwrecked on what is now Galveston Island in Texas. Only Cabeza de Vaca and three other men survived. One of the survivors was a Moroccan-born slave named Estevanico. His Spanish slaveholder also survived.

Estevanico was an enslaved African who traveled with Cabeza de Vaca.

Each of the four survivors was captured and enslaved by local Native American groups. After six years of captivity, the men finally escaped. They journeyed on foot throughout the North American Southwest, receiving help from Native Americans they met along the way. In 1536, after turning south, the group reached Spanish settlements in Mexico.

Soon after their journey ended, Estevanico's slaveholder sold him to a Spanish viceroy. The viceroy assigned Estevanico to serve as a guide for a new expedition he was sending into the Southwest. Native Americans killed the enslaved African in 1539.

Cabeza de Vaca eventually returned to Spain, where he called for better treatment of Native Americans. He later wrote about his experiences in the first European book exclusively devoted to North America. Cabeza de Vaca's book increased Spanish interest in the New World. His writings fueled the rumors that riches could be found in North America.

> "For two thousand leagues did we travel, on land, and by sea in barges, besides ten months more after our rescue from captivity; untiringly did we walk across the land. . . . During all that time we crossed from one ocean to the other. . . . We heard that on the shores of the South there are pearls and great wealth, and that the richest and best is near there."
>
> —Cabeza de Vaca, *The Journey of Álvar Núñez Cabeza de Vaca*

Cabeza de Vaca's account inspired other explorers to travel to North America. In 1540 Francisco Vásquez de Coronado set out to explore the North American Southwest. He wanted to find the legendary Seven Cities of Gold that were rumored to exist there. His expedition went through present-day New Mexico and Arizona, where a group of his men discovered the Grand Canyon. Coronado trekked through Texas and Oklahoma, going as far north as Kansas before turning around. He never found the fabled cities of gold.

Reading Check
Compare How were the expeditions of Hernando de Soto and Francisco Vásquez de Coronado similar?

Explore ONLINE!

Spanish Viceroyalties, c. 1650

Viceroyalty of New Spain
Viceroyalty of Peru
⊛ Capital of viceroyalty

0   1,000   2,000 Miles
0   1,000   2,000 Kilometers

Interpret Maps

1. **Location** What was the capital city of the Viceroyalty of Peru?

2. **Place** Which viceroyalty included present-day Mexico?

The Devastation of the Indies: A Brief Account

Bartolomé de Las Casas, a Catholic priest in New Spain, wrote a book that encouraged better treatment of Native Americans.

"*When they [Spaniards] have slain all those who fought for their lives or to escape the tortures they would have to endure, that is to say, when they have slain all the native rulers and young men (since the Spaniards usually spare only the women and children, who are subjected to the hardest and bitterest servitude [slavery] ever suffered by man or beast), they enslave any survivors. With these infernal [devilish] methods of tyranny they debase and weaken countless numbers of those pitiful Indian nations.*"

—Bartolomé de Las Casas, from *The Devastation of the Indies: A Brief Account*

Analyze Historical Sources
How did Las Casas's view of the treatment of Native American groups differ from the views of other Spaniards?

Spanish Treatment of Native Americans

The journeys of the Spanish explorers allowed Spain to claim a huge empire in the Americas. Spain's American colonies helped make the country very wealthy. From 1503 to 1660, Spanish fleets loaded with treasure carried 200 tons of gold and 18,600 tons of silver from the former Aztec and Inca empires to Spain. Mexico and Peru also grew food to help support Spain's growing empire. However, these gains came with a price for Native Americans. Native peoples suffered greatly at the hands of the Spanish.

Forced Labor By 1650 the Spanish Empire in the Americas had grown to some 3 to 4 million people. Native Americans made up about 80 percent of the population. The rest were whites, Africans, and people of mixed racial background. Settlers who came from Spain were called *peninsulares* (pay-neen-soo-LAHR-ays) and usually held the highest government positions. To reward settlers for their service to the Crown, Spain established the **encomienda** (ayn-koh-mee-AYN-dah) **system**. It gave settlers the right to tax local Native Americans or to make them work. In exchange, these settlers were supposed to protect the Native American people and convert them to Christianity. Instead, most Spanish treated the Native Americans as slaves. Native Americans were forced to work in terrible conditions. They faced cruelty and desperate situations on a daily basis.

The Spanish operated many **plantations**, large farms that grew just one kind of crop. Plantations throughout the Caribbean colonies made huge profits for their owners. It took many workers to run a plantation, however, so colonists forced thousands of Native Americans to work in the fields. Indians who were taken to work on haciendas, the vast Spanish estates in Central and South America, had to raise and herd livestock. Other Native Americans were forced to endure the backbreaking work of mining gold and silver. The forced labor and harsh treatment killed many native people in New Spain.

The Role of the Catholic Church The Catholic Church played a major role in the interactions of the Spanish with Native Americans. The Spanish king commanded priests to convert the local people to the Christian faith. Some Native Americans combined Spanish customs with their own. Others rejected Spanish ideas completely.

Some European settlers in the Americas protested the terrible treatment of Native Americans. A priest named **Bartolomé de Las Casas** said that the Spanish should try to convert Native Americans to Christianity by showing them love, gentleness, and kindness. The Spanish monarchs agreed, but the colonists did not always follow their laws.

Reading Check
Find Main Ideas
How did the encomienda system strengthen Spanish rule?

Summary and Preview In the 1500s Spain built a vast empire in the Americas. The Spanish treated the Native Americans harshly in their new empire. In the next lesson you will learn about other European empires in the Americas.

Lesson 3 Assessment

Review Ideas, Terms, and People

1. **a. Identify** Who was Moctezuma II?
   b. Analyze How was Hernán Cortés able to conquer the Aztec Empire?
   c. Elaborate What advantages did the Spanish have over Native Americans?

2. **a. Recall** Which Spanish explorer received permission to colonize Florida?
   b. Analyze Why do you think Cabeza de Vaca wrote of great riches that could be found in the Americas?
   c. Evaluate Why do you think Cabeza de Vaca called for better treatment of Native Americans after having been held prisoner by them?

3. **a. Identify** What was the encomienda system?
   b. Analyze Why do you think the king of Spain commanded Catholic priests to teach Native Americans about Christianity?

Critical Thinking

4. **Categorize** In this lesson you learned about Spanish conquest and settlement in the Americas. Copy the graphic organizer below and use it to explain the impact Spain had on the Americas.

Spanish America	
government	
religion	
labor	

The Race for Empires

If YOU were there . . .

The people of your village in France have always belonged to the same church. Now, in the 1600s, your village is divided over religious beliefs. You have heard about the Dutch colony of New Netherland in America, where people can practice any religion freely. You would like to leave for America, but your parents are unwilling to leave their home.

How would you persuade your family to emigrate?

The Big Idea

Other European nations challenged Spain in the Americas.

Main Ideas

- Events in Europe affected settlement of North America.
- Several explorers searched for a Northwest Passage to the Pacific Ocean.
- European nations raced to establish empires in North America.

Key Terms and People

Protestant Reformation
Protestants
Spanish Armada
Northwest Passage
Jacques Cartier
charter

Events in Europe

Many significant events took place in Europe in the 1500s. Disagreements about religion threw Europe into turmoil. Some of these disagreements eventually led to wars. At the same time, several European nations began to compete for land and power overseas.

The Protestant Reformation In 1517 a German priest named Martin Luther publicly criticized the Roman Catholic Church. Luther charged that the church was too wealthy and that it abused its power. Criticisms like Luther's started the **Protestant Reformation**. This religious movement began in small German towns but quickly spread to much of Europe.

Martin Luther nailed his 95 theses to a church door in Wittenberg, Germany.

It became a part of many political disputes as well. The **Protestants** were reformers who protested some of the Catholic Church's practices. Many Protestants believed God meant for religion to be simple.

The printing press—a machine that produces printed copies using movable type—helped spread the ideas of the Reformation. Protestants printed large numbers of Bibles as well as short essays explaining their ideas. This allowed more people to read and think about the Bible on their own, rather than relying solely on the teachings of a priest.

Johannes Gutenberg developed a movable-type printing press around 1450.

Conflicts between Catholics and Protestants took place throughout Europe, often leading to civil war. In the late 1500s French Catholics fought with French Protestants, known as Huguenots (HYOO-guh-nahts). Many Huguenots eventually immigrated to the Americas in search of religious freedom.

In 1534 King Henry VIII founded the Church of England, or the Anglican Church. By making himself the head of the church, Henry challenged the authority of the pope and angered Catholics. Political issues soon became entangled with the religious struggles.

Spain and England Go to War In the late 1500s King Philip II used Spain's great wealth to lead a Catholic Reformation against the Protestant movement. He hoped to drive the Protestants out of England. Standing in his way was the Protestant English queen Elizabeth I and her sea dogs. Sea dogs was the name given to English sailors who raided Spanish treasure ships. The most successful and daring was Sir Francis Drake.

Philip was angered by English piracy. He began gathering the **Spanish Armada,** a huge fleet of warships meant to end English plans. The

In 1588 the Spanish Armada launched an attack on England.

Armada had about 130 ships and some 27,000 sailors and soldiers. This mighty fleet was launched to invade England and overthrow Queen Elizabeth and the Anglican Church. But in July 1588 the smaller, but faster, English fleet defeated the Armada in a huge battle.

The Armada's defeat shocked the Spanish. In addition to the naval defeat, Spain's economy was in trouble. The gold and silver that Spain received from the Americas caused high inflation. Inflation is a rise in the price of goods caused by an increase in the amount of money in use. Economic problems in Spain combined with the defeat of the Spanish Armada led countries such as England, France, and the Netherlands to challenge Spanish power overseas.

Reading Check
Analyze What led to the decline of the Spanish Empire?

Search for a Northwest Passage

Europeans wanted to find a **Northwest Passage**, a water route through North America that would allow ships to sail from the Atlantic to the Pacific. The English began sending explorers to find it.

Italian sailor John Cabot knew that the king of England wanted to find such a route. Cabot offered to pay for his own expedition, asking only that the king of England grant him a royal charter to any lands he found. The

Northwest Passage

Legend:
- Dutch exploration
- English exploration
- French exploration
- New Spain, 1492–1682

Interpret Maps

1. **Movement** According to the map, which explorers made two voyages to find a Northwest Passage?

2. **Place** Which explorer started farthest south in searching for a Northwest Passage?

king agreed, and Cabot made voyages to North America for England in 1497 and 1498.

Cabot sailed to North America, but he left very few records of his journeys. It is believed that he traveled along the coast of present-day Newfoundland in Canada. Although Cabot did not find a passage to the Pacific Ocean, his voyages were successful. They became the basis of England's claim to land in North America.

In 1524 France sent an Italian captain, Giovanni da Verrazano (vayr-ah-ZAH-noh), to seek a Northwest Passage. Verrazano sailed along the coast of North America from present-day North Carolina to Maine. **Jacques Cartier** (kahr-TYAY), a French sailor, led France's next major exploration of North America. He made two trips to what is now Canada. Cartier sailed into the Saint Lawrence River and traveled all the way to present-day Montreal, claiming the areas he explored for France.

The Dutch also entered the race. They hired English captain Henry Hudson to find a Northwest Passage. Hudson first sailed to present-day New York in 1609. The following year Hudson returned to North America, sailing under the English flag. He traveled far to the north. Eventually he reached a strait that he hoped would lead to the Pacific Ocean. Instead, it led into a huge bay, later named Hudson Bay.

None of these explorers ever found a Northwest Passage. Their explorations, however, led to increased European interest in North America.

European Presence in North America

The Spanish and the Portuguese were the early leaders in overseas exploration. They dominated the colonization of the New World through the 1500s. However, Spain and Portugal focused on Central America, the Caribbean, and South America. They left much of North America unexplored. The English, French, and Dutch explored North America. These nations then sought to expand their own empires there.

As their empires grew throughout the 1500s and into the 1600s, Europeans acquired a new tool for understanding their world. The Mercator projection map had been created especially for sailors. Although the far northern and southern regions were distorted on the map, the regions where Europeans wanted to explore and claim land were shown fairly well. This map would have helped explorers plan their journeys. It also showed the vast areas where they might find great riches and expand their presence.

English Presence in the New World In the late 1500s England decided to set up a permanent settlement in North America. This colony was to establish an English presence in the New World. Sir Walter Raleigh received a **charter**, a document giving him permission to start a colony. In 1584 he sent an expedition that landed in present-day Virginia and North Carolina. Raleigh named the entire area Virginia.

The following year, Raleigh sent another group to found a colony on Roanoke Island, off the coast of North Carolina. The English colonists at Roanoke found life hard. They fought with Native Americans and had

Reading Check
Find Main Ideas
Why did European explorers seek a Northwest Passage?

In 1584, England's Queen Elizabeth granted adventurer Sir Walter Raleigh permission to establish a permanent settlement in North America.

Explore ONLINE!

Hudson Bay

NORTH AMERICA

Great Lakes

CABOT 1497-98

CARTIER 1534-35

CARTIER 1534

Newfoundland

HUDSON 1610-11

CARTIER 1535-36

Quebec

Lake Champlain

CHAMPLAIN 1609

HUDSON 1609

Nova Scotia

CHAMPLAIN 1603-1615

Hudson's search for a Northwest Passage led him to the bay that still bears his name.

Mississippi River

La Salle sailed down the Mississippi to its mouth and claimed for France all the land along the river and its tributaries.

LA SALLE 1679-82

New York

ATLANTIC OCEAN

Colorado River

CORONADO 1540-42

DE SOTO 1539-42

Roanoke Island

Juan Ponce de León became the first European in Florida when he arrived in 1513,

CABEZA DE VACA AND ESTEVANICO 1528-36

Rio Grande

St. Augustine

PONCE DE LEON 1513

Gulf of Mexico

Bahama Islands

Tropic of Cancer

CORTÉS 1519

Cuba

Puerto Rico

Hispaniola

Mexico City (Tenochtitlán)

PACIFIC OCEAN

The Spanish gold coin bears the images of King Ferdinand and Queen Isabella.

Dutch exploration
English exploration
French exploration
Spanish exploration
New Spain, 1492–1682

0 150 300 Miles
0 150 300 Kilometers

60°N
50°N
50°W
40°N
60°W
20°N
10°W

Interpret Maps

1. **Movement** Why do you think European explorers traveled with cannons and armaments on their vessels?

2. **Region** In what regions did Spanish explorers travel?

trouble finding and growing food. After only a year, the remaining colonists returned to England.

John White, a talented artist, and 150 colonists resettled Roanoke in the spring of 1587. White's granddaughter, Virginia Dare, was the first English colonist born in North America. After a few months, White went back to England to get more supplies. War with Spain prevented White from returning for three years. When he came back, White found the colony deserted. The only clue he found to the fate of the colonists was the word *Croatoan,* the name of a nearby island, carved into a post. Did the colonists try to escape a Native American attack by fleeing to the island? Or did they intermarry and blend with the friendly Croatan tribe? White never found out. To this day, no one is certain what happened to the "lost colony" at Roanoke.

French Presence in the New World France built its first North American settlement in Florida, when Huguenots started a few small colonies there in 1564. The Spanish soon destroyed these settlements and drove out the French. Religious wars in France slowed further French efforts to colonize North America. When the religious conflicts ended, the French renewed efforts to settle present-day eastern Canada. The explorations of Jacques Cartier and Samuel de Champlain gave France a claim to this region.

Nearly 70 years after Cartier sailed up the Saint Lawrence, French sailor Samuel de Champlain began exploring North America. He recorded his ideas about European exploration in his journal.

"Through [exploration] we gain knowledge of different countries, regions and kingdoms; through it we attract and bring into our countries all kinds of riches; through it . . . Christianity [is spread] in all parts of the earth."

–Samuel de Champlain, quoted in *Voyages of Samuel de Champlain*

Champlain followed Cartier's old paths. Over the years he made many journeys along the Saint Lawrence River. He also visited the Great Lakes, led by Native American guides. During his travels Champlain met Native Americans called the Algonquin. Some Algonquins formed alliances with the French explorer.

In 1608 Champlain founded a small colony on the Saint Lawrence River. He named the colony Quebec. This trading post opened fur-trading routes for the French throughout the region. Champlain's explorations became the basis of France's claim to much of Canada.

In the late 1600s the French began spreading out from the Saint Lawrence River. Calling their North American territory New France, French fur traders, explorers, and missionaries were all on the move.

In the 1650s French missionaries told stories about "a beautiful river, large, broad, and deep." In 1673 explorer Louis Jolliet (jahl-ee-ET) and missionary Jacques Marquette set out to find this great river, the Mississippi. (Hernando de Soto was the first European to find the Mississippi

River, in 1541.) Jolliet and Marquette reached the river and traveled down it as far as present-day Arkansas.

Nine years later René-Robert de La Salle followed the Mississippi River to the Gulf of Mexico. He claimed the Mississippi Valley for King Louis XIV of France. To honor the king, La Salle named the region Louisiana.

Starting in the 1700s, the French built new outposts. These included Detroit on the Great Lakes and Saint Louis and New Orleans along the Mississippi River. Most towns in the French territory were small. As late as 1688 there were only about 12,000 French settlers in New France. Its small population and the value of the fur trade led French settlers to ally and trade with local Native American groups.

Because of their close trading relationships, the French treated the Native Americans with more respect than some other European settlers had done. Some Algonquins allied with French settlers against English settlers and the Iroquois. In turn, many French settlers learned Native American languages and even adopted their ways of life.

Dutch Presence in the New World The English and the French were not the only European powers to seek an empire in North America. The Dutch, who had merchant fleets around the world, came in search of trade. They claimed the land between the Delaware and Hudson rivers and called it New Netherland. This area included parts of what is now New York, New Jersey, Connecticut, and Delaware.

Dutch explorers and settlers encountered the Mahican, or Mohican, peoples, farmers who lived in large settlements of longhouses. At the center of the Mahican lands was the Hudson River. Conflicts with Dutch and other settlers pushed the Mahican eastward.

In 1624 the newly formed Dutch West India Company sent about

New Amsterdam

The Dutch settlement of New Amsterdam was built next to a harbor where the Hudson River flows into the Atlantic Ocean. By 1643 more than 400 people lived there.

Inside the fort at the center of New Amsterdam was a marketplace, a church, and a windmill.

Ships arrived at the public dock on the East River.

30 families to settle in New Netherland. Two years later Peter Minuit bought Manhattan Island from local Native Americans. He paid with goods that today would be worth less than $1,100. Minuit then founded the town of New Amsterdam, today called New York City. To attract colonists, the Dutch allowed members of all religions to settle in their colony.

Minuit also helped Swedish settlers found New Sweden along the Delaware River. The first settlement, Fort Christina, was begun in 1638. The Swedish settlement was small, but the Dutch felt that it threatened Dutch lands and fur trading. The two sides fought a series of battles. Finally, the governor of New Netherland, Peter Stuyvesant (STY-vuh-suhnt), conquered New Sweden in 1655. He allowed the Swedes to continue their colony, but he called it the "Swedish Nation."

Summary and Preview The English, French, Dutch, and Swedish explored the North American continent and later established colonies there. In the next module you will learn how all of those colonies became English possessions.

Reading Check
Draw Conclusions
Were the French explorers in North America successful? Explain.

Lesson 4 Assessment

Review Ideas, Terms, and People

1. **a. Identify** What was the Protestant Reformation?

   b. Explain What role did the printing press play in the Protestant Reformation?

   c. Summarize How did events that took place in Europe affect the relationships among the British, French, Spanish, and Dutch in their quests to explore North America?

2. **a. Identify** Who was the first European to search for the Northwest Passage?

   b. Describe Which French and Dutch explorers tried to find the Northwest Passage?

3. **a. Recall** What happened to the first English settlements in North America?

   b. Evaluate Which European empire in North America do you think was most successful? Why?

Critical Thinking

4. **Sequence** In this lesson you learned about European exploration and settlement of North America. Create a timeline like the one below and place the four events you think were most important to the development of European empires in North America on the timeline. Be sure to include the date of the event, as well as a description of it and its significance.

Frame Historical Questions

Define the Skill

One of the most valuable ways that people gain knowledge is by asking effective questions. An effective question is one that obtains the kind of information the person asking the question desires. The ability to frame, or construct, effective questions is an important life skill as well as a key to gaining a better understanding of history. Asking effective historical questions will aid you in studying history and in conducting historical research.

Learn the Skill

Effective questions are specific, straightforward, and directly related to the topic. When we do not obtain the information we want or need, often it is because we have asked the wrong questions. Asking effective questions is not as easy as it seems. It requires thought and preparation. The following guidelines will help you in framing effective questions.

1. Determine exactly what you want to know.

2. Decide what questions to ask and write them down. Having written questions is very important. They will help guide your study or research and keep you focused on your topic and goal.

3. Review each of your questions to make sure it is specific, straightforward, and directly related to your topic.

4. Rewrite any questions that are vague, too broad, or biased.

Questions that are vague or too broad are likely to produce information not directly related to what you want to know. For example, if you wanted to know more about trade and the voyages of exploration that you just read about, "What were the voyages of exploration?" may not be a good question to ask. It is too broad. Its answer would not give you the information you want.

Asking "Why was trade the most important cause of the voyages of exploration?" would not be an effective question either. This question is biased because it *assumes* trade was the main reason for the voyages, when that might not have been true. Good historical investigation assumes nothing that is not known to be fact. A more effective question, which would get the information you want, is "Were trade and the voyages of exploration connected, and, if so, in what ways?" Do you see now why wording is so important in asking effective questions and why you should write out and review your questions beforehand?

Practice the Skill

Re-read the information about Cortés and the Aztec, and then complete the activities below.

1. Suppose you wanted to learn more about Cortés's defeat of the Aztec. Decide whether each of the following would be an effective question to ask about this topic. Explain why or why not.

   a. What happened when the Aztec and the Spanish met?

   b. Why did other Indians betray the Aztec?

   c. What resources did Cortés have that helped him conquer the Aztec?

2. Frame five questions that would be effective in helping you to learn more about this topic.

Module 2 Assessment

Review Vocabulary, Terms, and People

1. The first Europeans to reach the east coast of North America were the _____.

2. _____ established a navigation school and financed expeditions to the west coast of Africa.

3. One of the most important European explorers was _____, who was the first person to claim lands in the Americas for Spain.

4. The first voyage that sailed completely around the world was headed by _____.

5. Sir Walter Raleigh founded the colony of Virginia after receiving a _____, a grant to set up a colony, from the queen of England.

6. Large farms, or _____, which specialize in growing one type of crop for profit, were common in Spanish America.

Comprehension and Critical Thinking

Lesson 1

7. a. **Recall** On which two islands did the Vikings establish settlements before coming to North America?

   b. **Analyze** What factors led Europeans to begin their voyages of exploration?

   c. **Evaluate** What do you think motivated sailors to sign on for voyages of exploration?

Lesson 2

8. a. **Recall** Why was Columbus's first voyage important?

   b. **Summarize** Explain the conflict that emerged between Spain and Portugal over their empires in the Americas and how it was resolved.

   c. **Evaluate** Do you think the Columbian Exchange improved life or made life worse in the Americas? Explain your answer.

Lesson 3

9. a. **Identify** What territories in the Americas did Spain control?

   b. **Analyze** What factors enabled the Spanish to defeat the Aztec and the Inca?

   c. **Elaborate** Why was the encomienda system important to Spanish settlers?

Lesson 4

10. a. **Describe** What were the results of the defeat of the Spanish Armada?

    b. **Contrast** How did French settlements and interactions with native peoples in the Americas differ from the English and Spanish settlements and interactions with native peoples?

    c. **Predict** What problems might arise among the different empires with settlements in North America?

Review Themes

11. **Geography** What geographic features in North America helped and hindered the exploration and colonization of the continent?

12. **Society and Culture** How did the Spanish interactions with the Muscogee, the English interactions with the native people at Roanoke, the French interactions with the Algonquins, and the Dutch interactions with the Mahican people compare?

13. **Economics** Refer to the gold coin that bears the images of King Ferdinand and Queen Isabella on the map titled European Exploration of the Americas, 1492–1682, in Lesson 4. What does this coin indicate about the monarchs' rule?

Reading Skills

Outlining and History *Use the Reading Skills taught in this module to complete the following activity.*

14. Make a short but complete outline of the text under the heading "Spanish Treatment of Native Americans."

Social Studies Skills

Frame Historical Questions *Use the Social Studies Skills taught in this module to complete the following activity.*

15. Write a historical question for each of the four lessons of this module.

Focus on Writing

16. **Write a Letter** In this module you learned about different groups that came to the Americas. Imagine that you are a member of one of these groups and write a letter home to tell your friends and family about the people you meet and the experiences you are having in the Americas. Which details will your friends and family be most interested in? Which do you find most important?

Ponce de León

The Spanish conquistador Juan Ponce de León was the first European to set foot on land that later became part of the United States. Ponce de León first sailed to the Americas with Christopher Columbus on his second voyage in 1493. Once in the Caribbean region, he helped conquer what is now Puerto Rico and was named ruler of the island. According to legend, Ponce de León learned about a Fountain of Youth, whose waters could make old people young again. He may have been searching for this fountain when, in 1513, he made landfall on the coast of what today is the southeastern United States. He named the area Florida and claimed it for Spain.

Explore important events in the life of Ponce de León online. You can find a wealth of information, video clips, primary sources, activities, and more through your online textbook.

📹 **Caribbean Island Encounters**

Watch the video to learn about the first encounters between Spanish explorers and the people of the Caribbean.

📹 **Claiming Florida for Spain**

Watch the video to learn about Ponce de León's first landing on the coast of what is now Florida.

🌎 **Ponce de León's 1513 Route**

Study the map to learn about the region of the Americas that Ponce de León explored in 1513.

Module 3

The English Colonies

★

Essential Question
How did the colonial experience shape America's political and social ideals?

About the Photo: Plymouth Colony thrives again in this highly accurate re-creation.

In this module you will learn about the English settlements that dotted the East Coast of North America.

What You Will Learn ...

Lesson 1: The Southern Colonies **68**
The Big Idea Despite a difficult beginning, the southern colonies soon flourished.

Lesson 2: The New England Colonies **75**
The Big Idea English colonists traveled to New England to gain religious freedom.

Lesson 3: The Middle Colonies. **84**
The Big Idea People from many nations settled in the middle colonies.

Lesson 4: Life in the English Colonies **90**
The Big Idea The English colonies continued to grow despite many challenges.

> ▶ *Explore ONLINE!*

HISTORY.

VIDEOS, including...
• Life in Jamestown

☑ Document-Based Investigations

☑ Graphic Organizers

☑ Interactive Games

☑ Image with Hotspots: Jamestown Fort

☑ Image with Hotspots: New England Town

☑ Interactive Graph: America's Population, 1760

Timeline of Events 1600–1770

▶ Explore ONLINE!

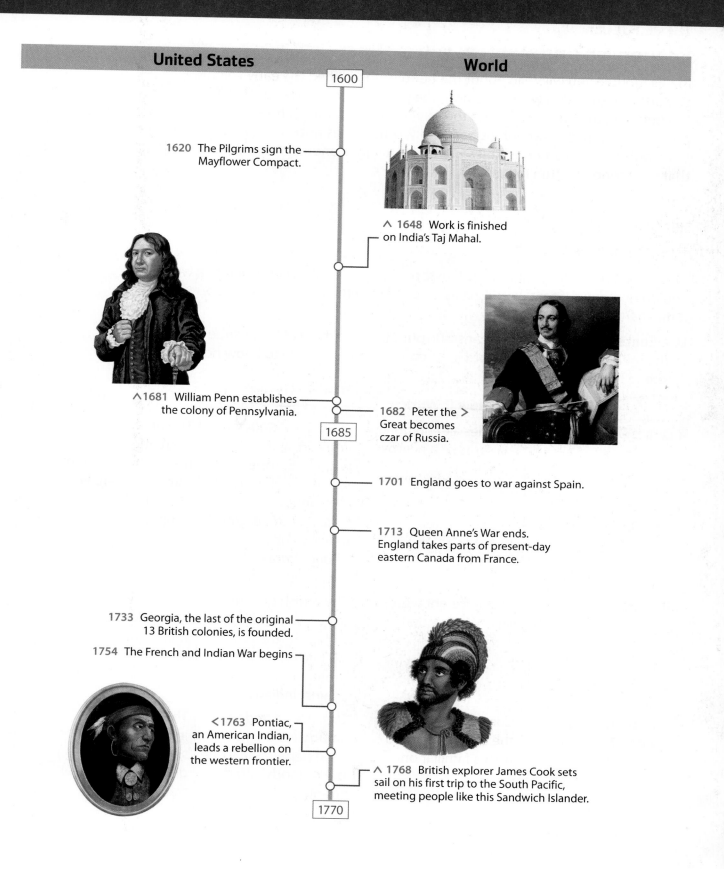

United States	World

1600

1620 The Pilgrims sign the Mayflower Compact.

∧ **1648** Work is finished on India's Taj Mahal.

∧**1681** William Penn establishes the colony of Pennsylvania.

1682 Peter the > Great becomes czar of Russia.

1685

1701 England goes to war against Spain.

1713 Queen Anne's War ends. England takes parts of present-day eastern Canada from France.

1733 Georgia, the last of the original 13 British colonies, is founded.

1754 The French and Indian War begins

<**1763** Pontiac, an American Indian, leads a rebellion on the western frontier.

∧ **1768** British explorer James Cook sets sail on his first trip to the South Pacific, meeting people like this Sandwich Islander.

1770

Reading Social Studies

THEME FOCUS:

Economics and Politics

In this module you will read about the people who settled the early colonies of North America. You will learn about the problems they faced as they felt the tug between their homeland and their new land. You will see how they settled political differences (sometimes peacefully, other times not) and learned how to trade goods and grow crops to establish a thriving economy. You will discover that the economy often influenced their politics.

READING FOCUS:

Vocabulary Clues

When you are reading your history textbook, you may often come across a word you do not know. If that word isn't listed as a key term, how do you find out what it means?

Use Context Clues *Context* means "surroundings." Authors often include clues to the meaning of a difficult word in its context. You just have to know how and where to look.

Clue	How It Works	Example	Explanation
Direct Definition	Includes a definition in the same or a nearby sentence	In the late 1600s England, like most western European nations, practiced mercantilism, *a system of creating and maintaining wealth through carefully controlled trade.*	The phrase "a system of creating and maintaining wealth through carefully controlled trade" defines *mercantilism*.
Restatement	Uses different words to say the same thing	The British continued to keep a standing, or *permanent*, army in North America to protect the colonists against Indian attacks.	The word *permanent* is another way to say *standing*.
Comparisons or Contrasts	Compares or contrasts the unfamiliar word with a familiar one	*Unlike legal traders,* smugglers did not have permission to bring goods into the country.	The word *unlike* indicates that smugglers are different from legal traders.

You Try It!

The following sentences are from this module. Each uses a definition or restatement clue to explain unfamiliar words. See if you can use the context to figure out the meaning of the words in italics.

> ## Context Clues Up Close
>
> **1.** In 1605 a company of English merchants asked King James I for the right to *found*, or establish, a settlement.
>
> **2.** The majority of workers were *indentured servants*. These servants signed a contract to work for four to seven years for those who paid for their journey to America.
>
> **3.** In New England, the center of politics was the *town meeting*. In town meetings people talked about and decided on issues of local interest, such as paying for schools.

Answer the questions about the sentences you read.

1. In example 1, what does the word *found* mean? What hints did you find in the sentence to figure that out?

2. In example 2, where do you find the meaning of *indentured servants*? What does this phrase mean?

3. In example 3, you learn the definition of *town meeting* in the second sentence. Can you combine these two sentences into one sentence? Try putting a dash after the word *meeting* and using "a place where" to replace "In town meetings."

As you read Module 3, look for context clues that can help you figure out the meanings of unfamiliar words or terms.

Key Terms and People

Lesson 1
Jamestown
John Smith
Pocahontas
indentured servants
Bacon's Rebellion
Toleration Act of 1649
Olaudah Equiano
slave codes

Lesson 2
Puritans
Pilgrims
immigrants
Mayflower Compact
Tisquantum
John Winthrop
Anne Hutchinson

Lesson 3
Peter Stuyvesant
Quakers
William Penn
staple crops

Lesson 4
town meeting
English Bill of Rights
triangular trade
Great Awakening
Jonathan Edwards
Enlightenment
John Locke
Pontiac
salutary neglect

The Southern Colonies

The Big Idea

Despite a difficult beginning, the southern colonies soon flourished.

Main Ideas

- Jamestown was the first permanent English settlement in America.
- Daily life in Virginia was challenging to the colonists.
- Religious freedom and economic opportunities were motives for founding other southern colonies, including Maryland, the Carolinas, and Georgia.
- Farming and slavery were important to the economies of the southern colonies.

Key Terms and People

Jamestown
John Smith
Pocahontas
indentured servants
Bacon's Rebellion
Toleration Act of 1649
Olaudah Equiano
slave codes

If YOU were there . . .

A year ago, in 1609, you moved to the colony of Virginia. Life here has been hard. During the winter many people died of cold or sickness. Food is always scarce. Now it is spring, and a ship has come from England bringing supplies. In a week it will sail home. Some of your neighbors are giving up and returning to England. They ask you to come, too.

Would you take the ship back to England?

Settlement in Jamestown

In 1605 a company of English merchants asked King James I for the right to found, or establish, a settlement. In 1606 the king issued the First Virginia Charter that gave the company permission to settle in a region called Virginia.

Founding a New Colony The investors in the new settlement formed a joint-stock company called the Virginia Company of London. This enabled the group to share the cost and risk of establishing the colony. Members of England's growing middle class purchased stock in the company, hoping to earn money from their investment. The middle class is a social class between the upper class and working class.

On April 26, 1607, the first 105 colonists sent by the Virginia Company arrived in America. On May 14, about 40 miles up the James River in Virginia, the colonists founded **Jamestown**, the first permanent English settlement in North America. Most of the colonists hoped to find gold and get rich. Others came looking for new opportunities in North America as cities in England were crowded and jobs were hard to find.

A lack of preparation cost a lot of the colonists their lives. Most of the men who came to Jamestown were adventurers with no farming experience or useful skills

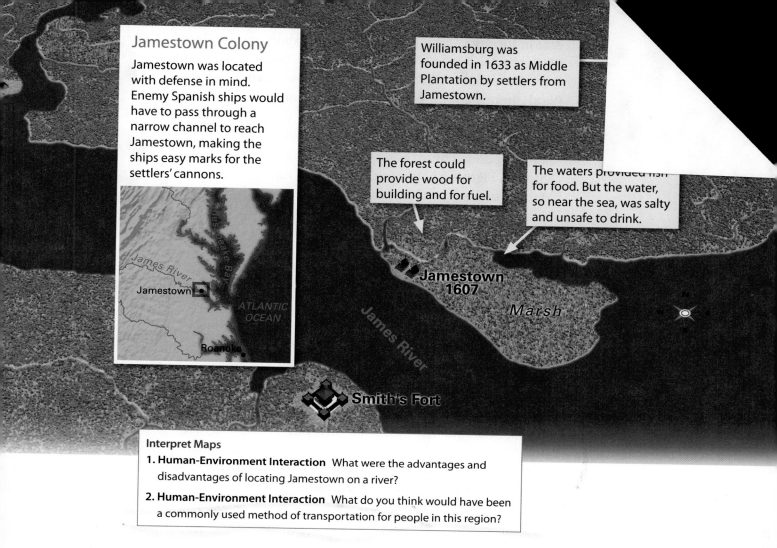

Jamestown Colony

Jamestown was located with defense in mind. Enemy Spanish ships would have to pass through a narrow channel to reach Jamestown, making the ships easy marks for the settlers' cannons.

Williamsburg was founded in 1633 as Middle Plantation by settlers from Jamestown.

The forest could provide wood for building and for fuel.

The waters provided fish for food. But the water, so near the sea, was salty and unsafe to drink.

Jamestown 1607

Marsh

James River

Smith's Fort

Chesapeake Bay

James River

Jamestown

ATLANTIC OCEAN

Roanoke

Interpret Maps

1. **Human-Environment Interaction** What were the advantages and disadvantages of locating Jamestown on a river?

2. **Human-Environment Interaction** What do you think would have been a commonly used method of transportation for people in this region?

such as carpentry. Jamestown was surrounded by marshes full of disease-carrying mosquitoes. By the time winter arrived, two-thirds of the original colonists had died.

Powhatan Confederacy Jamestown fared better under **John Smith**, who took control of the colony and built a fort in 1608. He forced the settlers to work harder and to build better housing by creating rules that rewarded harder workers with food. The colonists received help from the powerful Powhatan Confederacy of Native Americans after Smith made an agreement with them. The Powhatan traded food for tools and pots to help the colonists. They also taught the colonists how to grow corn.

In 1609 some 400 more settlers arrived in Jamestown. The Powhatan realized that the colony would continue to expand. They started to view the settlers as invaders who would take over their land. In the winter of 1609–1610, the Powhatan surrounded the Jamestown fort and killed anyone who tried to reach supplies outside.

That winter, disease and famine also hit the colony. The colonists called this period the starving time. By the spring of 1610, only 60 colonists were still alive. Jamestown failed to make a profit until colonist John Rolfe introduced a new type of tobacco that sold well in England.

Reading Check
Find Main Ideas
What problems
did the Jamestown
colonists face?

War in Virginia John Rolfe married **Pocahontas**, daughter of the Powhatan leader, in 1614. Their marriage helped the colonists form more peaceful relations with the Powhatan. However, Pocahontas died three years later in England, where she was visiting with Rolfe.

In 1622 colonists killed a Powhatan leader. The Powhatan responded by attacking the Virginia settlers later that year. Fighting between the colonists and the Powhatan continued for the next 20 years. Because the Virginia Company could not protect its colonists, the English Crown canceled the company's charter in 1624. Virginia became a royal colony and existed under the **authority** of a governor chosen by the king.

Pocahontas helped the English in Jamestown's early years.

Daily Life in Virginia

In early Virginia, people lived on scattered farms rather than in towns. Tobacco farmers established large farms called plantations. Tobacco was so valuable that it was sometimes used as money.

Headright System These plantations were made possible in part by the headright system, which was started by the Virginia Company. Under this system, colonists who paid their own way to Virginia received 50 acres of land. A colonist could earn another 50 acres for every additional person brought from England. Rich colonists who brought servants or relatives to Virginia gained large amounts of land.

Labor in Virginia Colonists in Virginia suffered very high death rates, which led to labor shortages. The majority of workers were **indentured servants**. These servants signed a contract to work for four to seven years for those who paid for their journey to America.

Expansion of Slavery Not all laborers in Virginia came from Europe. A Dutch ship brought the first Africans to Virginia in 1619. Some Africans were servants; others had been enslaved. Some African servants became successful farmers when their contracts ended.

Colonists overcame tough beginnings to create large and wealthy settlements like this one in Virginia. Churches were often the first major buildings in a growing town.

Colonial Williamsburg Foundation

The demand for workers was soon greater than the sup[ply] willing to work as indentured servants. Over time, the cos[t] These **factors** led some colonists to turn to slave labor. By most Africans in Virginia were being kept in lifelong slave[ry].

Academic Vocabulary
factors causes

Women and Children in Virginia Before 1619 most of Virgin[ia were] men. Only a few women and children lived in the colony. It was not until 1619 that the Virginia Company decided to send more women to the colony. The arrival of 90 English women in 1620 allowed more settlers to start families. As a result many settlers chose to make a permanent home in Virginia.

Women brought their skills in cooking, sewing, and making household items. Many could make and mend clothing. Others could make useful items for the home, such as soap and candles. As the Virginia colony grew, more women arrived. Many came as indentured servants.

Life was hard for children in colonial Virginia. They spent much of their time working. Boys who lived on farms helped take care of animals, plant crops, and chop firewood. Girls helped cook and clean. They also spun and wove cloth and helped make butter, soap, and candles.

Bacon's Rebellion As plantations grew, the economy of Jamestown began to expand. Soon, colonial officials began to ask for more taxes. During the mid-1600s poor colonists protested the higher taxes. They were also upset about the governor's policies toward Native Americans. They thought the colony was not well protected against attack. In 1676 a group of former indentured servants led by Nathaniel Bacon attacked some friendly American Indians. Bacon opposed the governor's policies promoting trade with American Indians. He also thought the colonists should be able to take the Indians' land. When the governor tried to stop him, Bacon and his followers attacked and burned Jamestown in an uprising known as **Bacon's Rebellion**.

At one point, Bacon controlled much of the colony. He died of fever, however, and the rebellion soon ended.

Reading Check
Analyze What factors led to the increased use of slave labor in Virginia?

Other Southern Colonies

As Jamestown was developing in Virginia, new groups of colonists began planning their move to America. Many English Catholics came to America to escape religious persecution. English Catholics had long been against England's separation from the Roman Catholic Church. For this reason they were not allowed by the Church of England to worship freely. English leaders also feared that English Catholics would ally with Catholic countries such as France and Spain in conflicts.

Maryland In the 1620s George Calvert, the first Lord Baltimore, asked King Charles I for a charter establishing a new colony in America for Catholics. In 1632 Charles issued the charter to Calvert's son, Cecilius, who took over the planning of the colony. Cecilius, known as the second Lord Baltimore, named the colony Maryland in honor of England's queen, Henrietta Maria. It was located just north of Virginia in the Chesapeake Bay area. Calvert intended for the colony to be a refuge for English

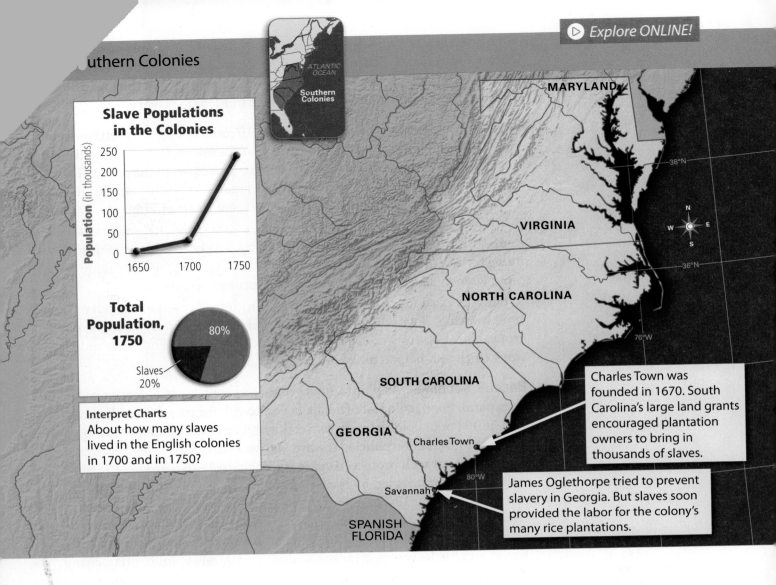

Slave Populations in the Colonies

Population (in thousands)

250
200
150
100
50
0

1650   1700   1750

Total Population, 1750

80%

Slaves 20%

Interpret Charts
About how many slaves lived in the English colonies in 1700 and in 1750?

MARYLAND

38°N

VIRGINIA

36°N

NORTH CAROLINA

76°W

SOUTH CAROLINA

Charles Town was founded in 1670. South Carolina's large land grants encouraged plantation owners to bring in thousands of slaves.

GEORGIA   Charles Town

80°W

James Oglethorpe tried to prevent slavery in Georgia. But slaves soon provided the labor for the colony's many rice plantations.

Savannah

SPANISH FLORIDA

Catholics. It would also be a proprietary colony. This meant that the colony's proprietors, or owners, controlled the government.

In 1634 a group of 200 English Catholics came to Maryland. Included in the group were wealthy landowners, servants, craftspeople, and farmers. Settlers in Maryland benefited from the lessons learned by the Jamestown colonists. They spent their time raising corn, cattle, and hogs so that they would have enough to eat. Before long, many colonists also began growing tobacco for profit.

Although Catholics founded Maryland, a growing number of Protestants began moving there in the 1640s. Soon, religious conflicts arose between Catholics and Protestants in the colony. To reduce tensions, Lord Baltimore presented a bill to the colonial assembly that became known as the **Toleration Act of 1649**. This bill made it a crime to restrict the religious rights of Christians. This was the first law supporting religious tolerance passed in the English colonies.

The Toleration Act did not stop all religious conflict. However, it did show that the government wanted to offer some religious freedom and protect the rights of minority groups.

The Carolinas and Georgia Colonies were also established s[...]
Virginia. In 1663 the English king, Charles II, gave much of [...]
between Virginia and Spanish Florida to eight of his suppor[...]
Carolina was a single colony. However, the settlements were [...]
it was hard to govern them. In 1712 the colony separated int[...]
South Carolina.

Most of the colonists in North Carolina were farmers who had migrated
south from Virginia. Among the earliest immigrants who settled North
Carolina were the Highland Scots, a group that came from northern
Scotland. Colonists primarily from Europe settled South Carolina. Those
who paid their own way received large grants of land, and some brought
enslaved Africans with them. By 1730 about 20,000 enslaved Africans
were living in the colony, compared to some 10,000 white settlers. Both
North and South Carolina had rice plantations on which enslaved Africans
did much of the work.

South Carolina's proprietors managed the colony poorly, and in 1719
the proprietary government was overthrown. The Crown then purchased North and South Carolina in 1729, making them royal colonies.

In 1732 King George II granted a charter to James Oglethorpe and
other trustees to found Georgia. The king hoped that Georgia would
act as a shield or buffer between Britain's other colonies and Spanish
Florida. In 1733 Oglethorpe and 120 colonists, mostly from England,
founded the city of Savannah.

Oglethorpe wanted the Georgia colony to be a place where debtors,
who had been jailed for their unpaid debts in England, could make a
new start. He offered settlers a bonus of 50 acres for every debtor they
brought along to help with the work on their farms. Oglethorpe hoped
that the debtors would better themselves through hard work instead
of spending time in prison. Only a few settlers were interested in his offer,
however, and his plan failed.

Oglethorpe did not want Georgia to have large plantations owned by a
few wealthy individuals. He wanted many small farmers. To reach this
goal, Oglethorpe outlawed slavery and limited the size of land grants.
Soon, however, the settlers grew unhappy with Oglethorpe's strict rules.
In 1752 the British government made Georgia a royal colony with new
laws. Coastal Georgia was soon filled with large rice plantations worked by
thousands of slaves.

Economies of the Southern Colonies

The economies of the southern colonies depended on agriculture. They
also exported materials for building ships, such as wood and tar. Some
colonies traded with local Indians for deerskins to sell.

The colonies had many small farms and some large plantations. Farms
did well because the southern colonies enjoyed a warm climate and a long
growing season. Many farms grew cash crops that were sold for profit.
Tobacco, rice, and indigo—a plant used to make blue dye—were the most
important cash crops.

James Oglethorpe
founded the colony of
Georgia in 1733.

Reading Check
Find Main Ideas
What were some of
the reasons colonists
came to the southern
colonies?

The southern colonies' cash crops required a great deal of difficult work to grow and harvest. This meant a large workforce was needed. By the 1700s enslaved Africans, rather than indentured servants, had become the main source of labor.

Slavery was a viciously brutal condition for many inhabitants of the southern colonies. One former slave named **Olaudah Equiano** recorded his experiences.

> "Tortures, murder, and every other imaginable barbarity . . . are practiced upon the poor slaves with impunity [no punishment]. I hope the slave-trade will be abolished."
>
> —Olaudah Equiano, from *The Interesting Narrative of the Life of Olaudah Equiano, or Gustavus Vassa, the African*

Reading Check
Summarize What role did slavery play in the southern plantation economy? How was it regulated?

Most of the southern colonies passed **slave codes**, or laws to control slaves. Colonies with large numbers of slaves had the strictest slave codes. For example, South Carolina's slaveholders feared that slaves would revolt. As a result, South Carolina's code said slaves could not hold meetings or own weapons. Some colonies did not allow slaveholders to free their slaves.

Summary and Preview In this lesson you read about life in the southern colonies. In the next lesson you will learn about the New England colonies.

Lesson 1 Assessment

Review Ideas, Terms, and People

1. a. **Describe** How did John Smith improve conditions in Jamestown?
   b. **Explain** What events led to a conflict between the Jamestown settlers and the Powhatan Confederacy?
2. a. **Recall** Why were indentured servants necessary in Virginia?
   b. **Evaluate** What do you think was the most serious problem faced by settlers in Virginia? Why?
3. a. **Identify** Which colony was the first to promote religious tolerance?
   b. **Analyze** Why did more enslaved Africans live in South Carolina than did white settlers?
   c. **Predict** How might the colony of Georgia have been different if Oglethorpe's plan had succeeded?
4. a. **Recall** What was the purpose of slave codes?
   b. **Analyze** Why were slaves in high demand in the southern colonies?

Critical Thinking

5. **Contrast** How did the want of natural resources result in cooperation between the Virginia colonists and Native Americans? How did it sometimes result in conflict?
6. **Summarize** In what ways did cultural and social influences help shape the southern colonies?
7. **Compare and Contrast** How were the experiences of indentured servants and enslaved people different from one another?
8. **Analyze** What does the idea of the Georgia colony acting as a shield from Spanish Florida tell you about England's relationship with Spain?
9. **Summarize** In this lesson you learned about the southern colonies. Create a chart similar to the one below and summarize the successes and/or failures of each colony.

Colony	Year	Why Founded	Successes/Failures

The New England Colonies

The Big Idea

English colonists traveled to New England to gain religious freedom.

Main Ideas

- The Pilgrims and Puritans came to America to avoid religious persecution.
- Religion and government were closely linked in the New England colonies.
- The New England economy was based on trade and farming.
- Education was important in the New England colonies.

Key Terms and People

Puritans
Pilgrims
immigrants
Mayflower Compact
Tisquantum
John Winthrop
Anne Hutchinson

If YOU were there . . .

You live in a town near London in the early 1700s. Some of your neighbors are starting new lives in the American colonies. You would like to go with them, but you cannot afford the cost of the trip. There is one way you can go, though. You can sign a paper promising to work as a servant for five years. After the five years, you would be free—and in a new country!

Would you sign the paper and go to America?

Pilgrims and Puritans

Religious tensions in England remained high after the Protestant Reformation. A Protestant group called the **Puritans** wanted to purify, or reform, the Anglican Church. The Puritans thought that bishops and priests had too much power over church members.

Pilgrims on the Move The most extreme English Protestants wanted to separate from the Church of England. These Separatists formed their own churches and cut all ties with the Church of England. In response, Anglican leaders began to punish Separatists.

The **Pilgrims** were one Separatist group that left England in the early 1600s to escape persecution. The Pilgrims moved to the Netherlands in 1608. The Pilgrims were **immigrants**—people who have left the country of their birth to live in another country.

The Pilgrims were glad to be able to practice their religion freely. They were not happy, however, that their children were learning the Dutch language and culture. The Pilgrims feared that their children would forget their English traditions. The Pilgrims decided to leave Europe altogether. They formed a joint-stock company with some merchants and then received permission from England to settle in the American colony of Virginia.

On September 16, 1620, a ship called the *Mayflower* left England with more than 100 men, women, and children aboard. Not all of these colonists were Pilgrims. However, Pilgrim leaders such as William Bradford sailed with the group.

The Mayflower Compact After two months of rough ocean travel, the Pilgrims sighted land far north of Virginia. The Pilgrims knew that they would thus be outside the authority of Virginia's colonial government when they landed. Their charter would not apply. So, they decided to establish their own basic laws and social rules to govern the colony they would found.

On November 21, 1620, 41 of the male passengers on the ship signed the **Mayflower Compact**, a legal contract in which they agreed to have fair laws to protect the general good. The Compact represents one of the first attempts at self-government in the English colonies.

In late 1620 the Pilgrims landed at Plymouth Rock in present-day Massachusetts. The colonists struggled through the winter to build the Plymouth settlement. Nearly half died during this first winter from sickness and the freezing weather.

DOCUMENT-BASED INVESTIGATION   Historical Source

The Mayflower Compact

In November 1620 Pilgrim leaders aboard the *Mayflower* drafted the Mayflower Compact. This excerpt from the Mayflower Compact describes the principles of the Pilgrim colony's government.

The Pilgrims describe the reasons they want to form a colony in North America.

The Pilgrims promise to obey laws that help the whole colony.

"*We whose names are underwritten . . . having undertaken, for the glory of God, and advancement of the Christian faith, and the honour of our King and country, a voyage to plant the first colony in the northern parts of Virginia, do by these* **presents**[1] *solemnly and mutually in the presence of God, and one of another,* **covenant**[2] *and combine ourselves together into a civil body* **politic**[3] *for our better ordering and preservation and furtherance of the ends* **aforesaid**[4]*; and by* **virtue**[5] *hereof, to enact, constitute, and frame such just and equal laws,* **ordinances**[6]*, acts, constitutions, and offices . . . as shall be thought most* **meet**[7] *and convenient for the general good of the colony unto which we promise all due . . . obedience.*"

[1]*by these presents:* by this document
[2]*covenant:* promise
[3]*civil body politic:* group organized to govern
[4]*aforesaid:* mentioned above
[5]*virtue:* authority
[6]*ordinances:* regulations
[7]*meet:* fitting

Analyze Historical Sources

1. Why do you think the colonists felt the need to establish a government for themselves?

2. How do you think the Mayflower Compact influenced later governments in America?

Tisquantum served as an interpreter, adviser, and friend to the Pilgrims who settled in Plymouth Colony.

Pilgrims and Native Americans In March 1621 a Native American named Samoset walked boldly into the colonists' settlement. He spoke in broken English. Samoset had learned some English from the crews of English fishing boats. He gave the Pilgrims useful information about the peoples and places of the area. He also introduced them to a Patuxet Indian named **Tisquantum**, or Squanto. Tisquantum had at one time lived in Europe and spoke English as well.

From Tisquantum the Pilgrims learned to fertilize the soil with fish remains. He also helped the Pilgrims establish relations with the local Wampanoag Indians. Conditions in Plymouth Colony soon began to improve.

In the fall of 1621 the Pilgrims gathered their first harvest. William Bradford, governor of Plymouth Colony, decided they should have a celebration so that people could give thanks to God. He invited Wampanoag chief Massasoit and 90 other guests to celebrate their harvest. This is what many people today think of as the first Thanksgiving. However, Thanksgiving celebrations, such as the Green Corn Ceremony, have been held by Native Americans for thousands of years. The Pilgrims' Thanksgiving feast included wild turkeys, fish, and lobsters. This event marked the survival of the Pilgrims in the new colony.

Pilgrim Community Although the Pilgrims overcame many problems, their small settlement still struggled. Most Pilgrims became farmers, but the farmland around their settlement was poor. They had hoped to make money by trading furs and by fishing. Unfortunately, fishing and hunting conditions were not good in the area. Some colonists traded corn with American Indians for beaver furs. The Pilgrims made little money but were able to form a strong community. The colony began to grow stronger in the mid-1620s after new settlers arrived and, as in Jamestown, colonists began to have more rights to farm their own land.

The Pilgrims' settlement was different from Virginia's in that it had many families. The Pilgrims taught their children to read and offered some education to their indentured servants. Families served as centers of religious life, health care, and community well-being.

All family members worked together to survive during the early years of the colony. Women generally cooked, spun and wove wool, and sewed clothing. They also made soap and butter, carried water, dried fruit, and cared for livestock. Men spent most of their time repairing tools and working in the fields. They also chopped wood and built shelters.

Women in the Colony In Plymouth, women had more legal rights than they did in England. In England, women were not allowed to make contracts, to sue, or to own property. In America, Pilgrim women had the right to sign contracts and to bring some cases before local courts. Widows could also own property. From time to time, local courts recognized the ways women helped the business community. Widow Naomi Silvester received a large share of her husband's estate. The court called her "a frugal [thrifty] and laborious [hardworking] woman."

Plymouth Colony

New England Colonies

ATLANTIC OCEAN

Several years later, the second colony, Duxbury, was founded.

Plymouth Bay

The Pilgrims landed in a region of forests, streams, and rocky soil.

INDIAN TRAIL

Plymouth Colony was surrounded by stakes that formed a wall of protection. Outside the wall were colonists' crop fields.

Abandoned Indian Village

Plymouth Colony (1620)

Analyze Visuals
In what ways were Plymouth Colony and the Indian village similar and different?

Puritans Leave England During the 1620s England's economy suffered. Many people lost their jobs. The English king, Charles I, made the situation worse by raising taxes. This unpopular act led to a political crisis. At the same time, the Church of England began to punish Puritans because they were dissenters, or people who disagree with official opinions. King Charles refused to allow Puritans to criticize church actions.

Great Migration These economic, political, and religious problems in England led to the Great Migration. Between 1629 and 1640 many thousands of English men, women, and children left England. More than 40,000 of these people moved to English colonies in New England and the Caribbean. In 1629 Charles granted a group of Puritans and merchants a charter to settle in New England. The group formed the Massachusetts Bay Company.

In 1630 a group of Puritan colonists seeking religious freedom sailed on a fleet of ships from England to Massachusetts. They were led by **John Winthrop**. The Puritans believed that they had made a covenant, or promise, with God to build an ideal Christian community.

Puritan leader John Winthrop was the first governor of Massachussetts Bay Colony.

A New Colony The Puritans arrived in New England well prepared to start their colony. They brought large amounts of tools and livestock with them. Like the Pilgrims, the Puritans faced little resistance from local American Indians. Trade with Plymouth Colony helped them, too. In addition, the region around Boston had a fairly healthful climate. Thus, few Puritans died from sickness. All of these things helped Massachusetts Bay Colony do well. By 1691 Massachusetts Bay Colony had expanded to include the Pilgrims' Plymouth Colony.

Religion and Government in New England

Massachusetts Bay Colony had to obey English laws. However, the colony's charter provided more independence than did the royal charter of Virginia. For example, it created a General Court to help run the Massachusetts colony.

The Puritan colonists turned this court into a type of self-government to represent the needs of the people. Each town sent two or three delegates to the Court. After John Winthrop served as the colony's first governor, the General Court elected the governor and his assistants. In 1644 the General Court became a two-house, or bicameral, legislature.

Politics and religion were closely linked in Puritan New England. Government leaders were also church members, and ministers often had a great deal of power in Puritan communities. Male church members were the only colonists who could vote. Colonists became full members in the church by becoming what the Puritans called God's "elect," or chosen. Reaching this status was a difficult process. Individuals had to pass a public test to prove that their faith was strong.

In 1636 minister Thomas Hooker and his followers left Massachusetts to help found Connecticut, another New England colony. In 1639 Hooker wrote the Fundamental Orders of Connecticut. This set of principles made Connecticut's government more democratic. For example, the Orders allowed men who were not church members to vote. As a result, some historians call Hooker the father of American democracy. The Fundamental Orders of Connecticut also outlined the powers of the general courts.

Not all Puritans shared the same religious views. Minister Roger Williams did not agree with the leadership of Massachusetts. He called for his church to separate completely from the other New England congregations. Williams also criticized the General Court for taking land from American Indians without paying them.

Puritan leaders worried that Williams's ideas might hurt the unity of the colony. They made him leave Massachusetts. Williams took his supporters to southern New England. They formed a new settlement called Providence. This settlement later developed into the colony of Rhode

Reading Check
Summarize What role did religion play in the establishment of the Massachusetts Bay Colony?

Anne Hutchinson 1591–1643

In 1634 Anne Hutchinson emigrated with her family from England to Massachusetts Bay Colony. After settling in Boston, she worked as a nurse and midwife. She also hosted a Bible-study class that met in her home. Over time, Hutchinson began to question the teachings of the local ministers. Meanwhile, her popularity grew.

After being banished from the colony, Hutchinson settled in Rhode Island and, later, Long Island. She died in an American Indian attack. Today, we remember her as a symbol of the struggle for religious freedom.

Draw Conclusions
Why do you think church leaders disliked Hutchinson's ideas?

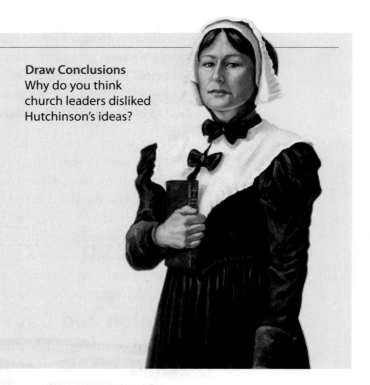

Island. In Providence, Williams supported the separation of the church from the state. He also believed in religious tolerance for all members of the community.

In Boston an outspoken woman also angered Puritan church leaders. **Anne Hutchinson** publicly discussed religious ideas that some leaders thought were radical. For example, Hutchinson believed that people's relationship with God did not need guidance from ministers.

Hutchinson's views alarmed Puritans such as John Winthrop. Puritan leaders did not believe that women should be religious leaders. Puritan leaders put Hutchinson on trial for her ideas. The court decided to force her out of the colony. With a group of followers, Hutchinson helped found the new colony of Portsmouth, later a part of the colony of Rhode Island.

In 1643 the New England colonies made an early move toward unity. Several of the colonies formed the United Colonies of New England. This union was established by the New England Articles of Confederation. The articles were an important document in the development of self-government in the English colonies.

Perhaps the worst community conflicts in New England involved the witchcraft trials of the early 1690s. The largest number of trials were held in Salem, Massachusetts. In Salem a group of girls had accused people of casting

Quick Facts

Church and State

Religion Affected Government
- Government leaders were church members.
- Ministers had great authority.

Government Affected Religion
- Government leaders outlawed certain religious views.
- Government leaders punished dissenters.

spells on them. The community formed a special court to judge the witch-craft cases. The court often pressured the suspected witches to confess. Before the trials had ended, the Salem witch trials led to 19 people being put to death.

The growth of the New England colonies caused conflicts with Native Americans. As colonists spread across New England, they settled where Native Americans already lived and hunted. Each group had different ideas about land ownership. The Wampanoag and other tribes believed that no one person could own land. The English, however, believed that if they claimed an area, the land was theirs. The colonists expected the Native American tribes to leave the land. Arguments over land sometimes led to wars between the colonists and Native Americans.

Reading Check
Identify Cause and Effect What led to religious disagreements among the Puritans, and what was the result?

New England Economy

Connecticut, Massachusetts, New Hampshire, and Rhode Island were very different from the southern colonies. The often harsh climate and rocky soil meant that few New England farms could grow cash crops. Most farming families grew crops and raised animals for their own use. There was thus little demand for farm laborers. Although some people held slaves, slavery did not become as important to this region.

Merchants Trade was vital to New England's economy. New England merchants traded goods locally, with other colonies, and overseas. Many of them traded local products such as furs, pickled beef, and pork. Many merchants grew in power and wealth, becoming leading members of the New England colonies.

Fishing Fishing became one of the region's leading industries. The rich waters off New England's coast served as home to many fish, including cod, mackerel, and halibut. Merchants exported dried fish. Colonists also began hunting for whales that swam close to shore. Whales were captured with harpoons, or spears, and dragged to shore. Whaling provided valuable oil for lighting.

Shipbuilding Shipbuilding became an important industry in New England for several reasons. The area had plenty of forests that provided materials for shipbuilding. As trade—particularly in slaves—in the New England seaports grew, more merchant ships were built. The fishing industry also needed ships. New England shipyards made high-quality, valuable vessels. Ship owners sometimes even told their captains to sell the ship along with the cargo when they reached their destination.

Skilled Craftspeople The northern economy needed skilled crafts-people. Families often sent younger sons to learn skilled trades such as blacksmithing, weaving, shipbuilding, and printing. The young boys who learned skilled trades were known as apprentices.

Apprentices lived with a master craftsman and learned from him. In exchange, the boys performed simple tasks. Apprentices promised to work for a master craftsman for a set number of years. They learned trades that were essential to the survival of the colonies. Apprentices received food and often clothing from the craftsmen. Gabriel Ginings, for example, was an apprentice in Portsmouth, Rhode Island. He received "sufficient food and raiment [clothing] suitable for such an apprentice," as his 1663 contract stated.

After a certain amount of time had passed, apprentices became journeymen. They usually traveled and learned new skills in their trade. Eventually, they would become a master of the trade themselves.

Reading Check
Categorize What types of jobs were common in the New England colonies?

Education in the Colonies

Education was important in colonial New England. Mothers and fathers wanted their children to be able to read the Bible. Massachusetts Bay Colony passed some of the first laws requiring parents to provide instruction for their children.

Public Education To be sure that future generations would have educated ministers, communities established town schools. In 1647 the General Court of Massachusetts issued an order that a school be founded in every township of 50 families.

Schoolchildren often used the *New England Primer*, which had characters and stories from the Bible. They learned to read at the same time that they learned about the community's religious values.

The availability of schooling varied in the colonies. There were more schools in New England than in the other colonies, where most children lived far from towns. These children had to be taught by their parents or by private tutors. Most colonial children stopped their education after the elementary grades. Many went to work, either on their family farm or away from home.

A meeting house and a school were located at the center of most New England towns.

Higher Education Higher education was also important to the colonists. In 1636 John Harvard and the General Court founded Harvard College. Harvard taught ministers and met the colony's need for higher education. The second college founded in the colonies, William and Mary, was established in Virginia in 1693.

By 1700 about 70 percent of men and 45 percent of women in New England could read and write. These figures were much lower in Virginia, where Jamestown was the only major settlement.

Reading Check
Analyze Why was education important to the New England colonies?

Summary and Preview In this lesson you learned about the role that religion played in the New England colonies. In the next lesson you'll learn about New York, New Jersey, and Pennsylvania.

Lesson 2 Assessment

Review Ideas, Terms, and People

1. **a. Recall** Why did the Pilgrims and Puritans leave Europe for the Americas?

   b. Elaborate Do you think the Pilgrims could have survived without the assistance of Tisquantum and Massasoit? Explain your answer.

   c. Analyze How did political problems in England encourage the Puritans to start a colony in North America?

2. **a. Describe** What role did the church play in Massachusetts?

   b. Analyze Why did some colonists disagree with the leaders of Massachusetts?

3. **a. Identify** Describe the economy in the New England colonies.

   b. Analyze Why do you think New England merchants became leading members of society?

4. **a. Describe** What are some of the steps Massachusetts Bay Colony took to promote education?

   b. Predict What are some possible benefits that New England's emphasis on education might bring?

Critical Thinking

5. **Analyze** What impact do you think the Mayflower Compact and the Fundamental Orders of Connecticut had on the creation of the United States government?

6. **Contrast** How did New England colonists and Native Americans share natural resources? How did the want of natural resources sometimes result in conflict?

7. **Identify Cause and Effect** In this lesson you learned about the reasons English colonists came to New England. Create a diagram like the one below and show how the colonists' experiences caused them to build certain types of colonies.

Causes → Effects

The Middle Colonies

The Big Idea

People from many nations settled in the middle colonies.

Main Ideas

- The English created New York and New Jersey from former Dutch territory.

- William Penn established the colony of Pennsylvania.

- The economy of the middle colonies was supported by trade and staple crops.

Key Terms and People

Peter Stuyvesant
Quakers
William Penn
staple crops

If YOU were there . . .

You are a farmer in southern Germany in 1730. Religious wars have torn your country apart for many years. Now you hear stories about a place in America where people of all religions are welcome. But the leaders of the colony—and many of its people—are English. You would not know their language or customs. Still, you would be free to live and worship as you like.

How would you feel about moving to a country full of strangers?

New York and New Jersey

The Dutch founded New Netherland in 1613 as a trading post for exchanging furs with the Iroquois and other Native American groups. The center of the fur trade in New Netherland was the town of New Amsterdam on Manhattan Island. The colonists traded Dutch goods with the Native Americans for furs and land.

Generous land grants to patroons, or lords, and religious tolerance soon brought Jews, French Huguenots, Puritans, and others to New Netherland. The patroons brought at least 50 new settlers to the colony. Following the Dutch patroon system, the settlers farmed the patroon's land and paid him rent. Director-general **Peter Stuyvesant** (STY-vuh-suhnt) led the New Netherland colony beginning in 1647.

Peter Stuyvesant was forced to surrender New Netherland to the English in 1664.

Characteristics of the Middle Colonies

Social
- New York: Dutch influence
- New Jersey: diverse population
- Pennsylvania: founded by Quakers

Economic
- successful farming of staple crops
- workforce of slaves and indentured servants
- active trade with Britain and West Indies

The first enslaved Africans were brought to New Netherland in 1626 by the Dutch West India Company. Over time, the population of enslaved Africans increased in the colony. Many were forced to work on farms, in shops, and in homes. Others had to help build ships and work on loading docks. The Dutch West India Company freed some enslaved Africans. Others were able to buy their freedom.

King Charles II of England wanted to take over the growing colony of New Netherland so England could control the entire Atlantic coast of North America. In 1664 an English fleet captured the undefended colony without firing a single shot. New Netherland was renamed New York, and New Amsterdam became New York City.

Soon after the English conquest in 1664, the Duke of York made Sir George Carteret and Lord John Berkeley proprietors of New Jersey. This colony occupied lands between the Hudson and Delaware rivers. It had a diverse population, including Dutch, Swedes, Finns, and Scots. The fur trade was important to the economies of New York and New Jersey through the end of the 1600s.

In the early 1700s New York's African population grew. By 1723 more than 6,000 Africans—both free and enslaved—lived in the colony. However, free and enslaved Africans had fewer rights under English rule than under the Dutch. It was difficult for enslaved Africans to earn their freedom under English laws. Because they were mistreated and lived under harsh conditions, some resisted slavery.

In 1712 a group of enslaved Africans led an armed revolt to escape from slavery. This uprising became known as the New York Slave Revolt of 1712. The resistors failed to gain their freedom, however. As a result, harsher laws were passed to prevent future revolts.

Reading Check
Compare How were New York and New Jersey similar?

Penn's Colony

The Society of Friends, or the **Quakers**, made up one of the largest religious groups in New Jersey. Quakers did not follow formal religious practices and dressed plainly. They believed in the equality of men and women before God. They also supported nonviolence and religious tolerance for all people. At the time, many Quaker beliefs and practices shocked most Christians. As a result, Quakers were persecuted in both England and America.

William Penn 1644–1718

William Penn was born in London as the son of a wealthy admiral. Penn joined the Quakers in 1666 and became an active preacher and writer of religious works. He supported toleration of dissenters.

In 1681 he received a charter to establish a new colony called Pennsylvania. There, Penn put his beliefs into practice. He insisted on fair dealings with local American Indians, welcomed immigrants, and promised religious toleration.

Make Generalizations
How did Penn's ideas influence the rules of the colony?

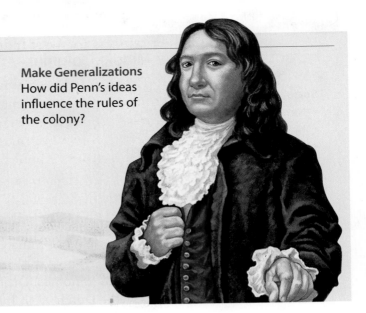

One proprietor of the New Jersey colony was a Quaker named **William Penn**. Penn wished to found a larger colony under his own control that would provide a safe home for Quakers. In 1681 King Charles II agreed to grant Penn a charter to begin a colony west of New Jersey.

Penn's colony, known as Pennsylvania, grew rapidly. Penn limited his own power and established an elected assembly. He also promised religious freedom to all Christians. His work made Pennsylvania an important example of representative self-government—a government that reflects its citizens' will—in the colonies.

Penn named the capital of his colony Philadelphia, which means "the city of brotherly love." In 1682 the Duke of York sold Penn a region to the south of Pennsylvania. This area, called Delaware, remained part of Pennsylvania until 1776.

Reading Check
Find Main Ideas
Why did William Penn establish Pennsylvania, and how did he influence its government?

Economy of the Middle Colonies

The middle colonies combined characteristics of the New England and southern colonies. With a good climate and rich land, farmers there could grow large amounts of **staple crops**—crops that are always needed. These crops included wheat, barley, and oats. Farmers also raised livestock.

Slaves were somewhat more important to the middle colonies than they were to New England. They worked in cities as skilled laborers, such as blacksmiths and carpenters. Other slaves worked on farms, onboard ships, and in the growing shipbuilding industry. However, indentured servants largely filled the middle colonies' growing labor needs. Between 1700 and 1775 about 135,000 indentured servants came to the middle colonies. About half of them moved to Pennsylvania. By 1760 Philadelphia had become the largest British colonial city. Other cities in the middle colonies, such as New York City, also grew quickly.

Trade was important to the economy of the middle colonies. Merchants in Philadelphia and New York City exported colonial goods to markets in

Britain and the West Indies. These products included wheat from New York, Pennsylvania, and New Jersey.

Throughout the colonies, women made important contributions to the economy. They ran farms and businesses such as clothing and grocery stores, bakeries, and drugstores. Some women also practiced medicine and worked as nurses and midwives. However, colonial laws and customs limited women's economic opportunities.

Most colonial women worked primarily in the home. Married women managed households and raised children. Sometimes they earned money for their families by selling products like butter. They also provided paid services such as washing clothes.

Summary and Preview In this lesson you learned about the middle colonies. In the next lesson you will read about colonial government, the slave trade, and conflicts that arose in the English colonies.

Reading Check
Find the Main Idea
On what were the economies of the middle colonies based?

Lesson 3 Assessment

Review Ideas, Terms, and People

1. **a. Describe** Name the middle colonies. Where were they located?

   b. Draw Inferences What led to the diverse populations of New York and New Jersey?

2. **a. Identify** Who are the Quakers?

   b. Analyze How did William Penn attempt to create a colonial government that would be fair to all?

3. **a. Describe** What different types of jobs did slaves in the middle colonies hold?

   b. Evaluate In what ways were women essential to the middle colonies?

Critical Thinking

4. **Analyze** What does England's capturing of the New Netherland colony tell you about its relationship with the Dutch?

5. **Compare and Contrast** In what ways was the development of the English colonies similar to the development of the Dutch colonies in North America? In what ways was it different?

6. **Analyze** What impact do you think William Penn's elected assembly had on the creation of the United States government?

7. **Sequence** In this lesson you learned about the nations that founded the middle colonies. Create a timeline like the one below and list the event that occurred on each of the dates on the timeline.

1613   1647   1664   1681

America's Growth by 1760

The English colonies in 1760 were located between the Atlantic Ocean and the Appalachian Mountains. The total population of the colonies was around 1.8 million. Soon, however, the colonies began to grow both in size and in population.

In 1763 Great Britain and France signed the Treaty of Paris, giving Britain control over all lands east of the Mississippi River. With the stroke of a pen, the colonies increased enormously in size. The westward expansion of the English colonies—soon to be the United States—had begun.

America's Population, 1760: 1.8 million

Ethnic Groups, 1760
- White/European
- African American
- Native American
- Other

1%
11%
18%
70%

Religions, 1760
- Protestant
- Catholic
- Jewish
- Other

>1%
2%
5%
92%

A Wall of Mountains The 1,500-mile-long Appalachian Mountain range formed a natural barrier to westward expansion. The Appalachians' dense forests and steep terrain made passage on foot or by horse difficult.

- New England colonies
- Middle colonies
- Southern colonies

0   150   300 Miles
0   150   300 Kilometers

Natural Harbors The largest cities in the colonies, such as Philadelphia, New York, and Boston, grew where the best natural ports were. Ships were vital to the colonies: for the growing fishing industry, for overseas trade, and to bring more settlers to the new land.

Boston Harbor provided natural protection for ships.

ME
(part of MA)

NH

NY

MA

CT

RI

Boston, population 16,000

PA

DE
(part of PA)

NJ

New York, population 25,000

MD

Philadelphia, population 25,000

40°N

VA

ATLANTIC OCEAN

APPALACHIAN MOUNTAINS

NC

A Flood of People The colonial population doubled between 1750 and 1770. Roughly half of the immigrants to the colonies were English. But the second-largest group of immigrants had no choice in the matter— they were enslaved people from Africa.

SC

GA

Mississippi River

30°N

Interpret Maps

1. **Location** Where were the colonies' largest cities located at this time?

2. **Human-Environment Interaction** How did mountains and seas influence the location of the colonies?

Tropic of Cancer

90°W

70°W

Life in the English Colonies

The Big Idea

The English colonies continued to grow despite many challenges.

Main Ideas

- Colonial governments were influenced by political changes in England.

- English trade laws limited free trade in the colonies.

- The Great Awakening and the Enlightenment led to ideas of political equality among many colonists.

- The French and Indian War gave England control of more land in North America.

Key Terms and People

town meeting
English Bill of Rights
triangular trade
Great Awakening
Jonathan Edwards
Enlightenment
John Locke
Pontiac
salutary neglect

If YOU were there . . .

Your family migrated to America in the 1700s and started a small farm in western Pennsylvania. Now, more and more people are moving in. You would like to move farther west, into the Ohio River valley. But a new law says you cannot move west of the mountains because it is too dangerous. Still, you are restless and want more land and more freedom.

Why might you decide to break the law and move west?

Colonial Governments

The English colonies in North America all had their own governments. Each government was given power by a charter. The English monarch had ultimate authority over all of the colonies. A group of royal advisers called the Privy Council set English colonial policies.

Colonial Governors and Legislatures Each colony had a governor who served as head of the government. Most governors were assisted by an advisory council. In royal colonies the English king or queen selected the governor and the council members. In proprietary colonies the proprietors chose all of these officials. In a few colonies, such as Connecticut, the people elected the governor.

In some colonies the people also elected representatives to help make laws and set policy. These officials served on assemblies. Each colonial assembly passed laws that had to be approved first by the advisory council and then by the governor.

Established in 1619, Virginia's assembly was the first colonial legislature in North America. At first it met as a single body, but it was later split into two houses. The first house was known as the Council of State. The governor's advisory council and the Virginia Company selected its

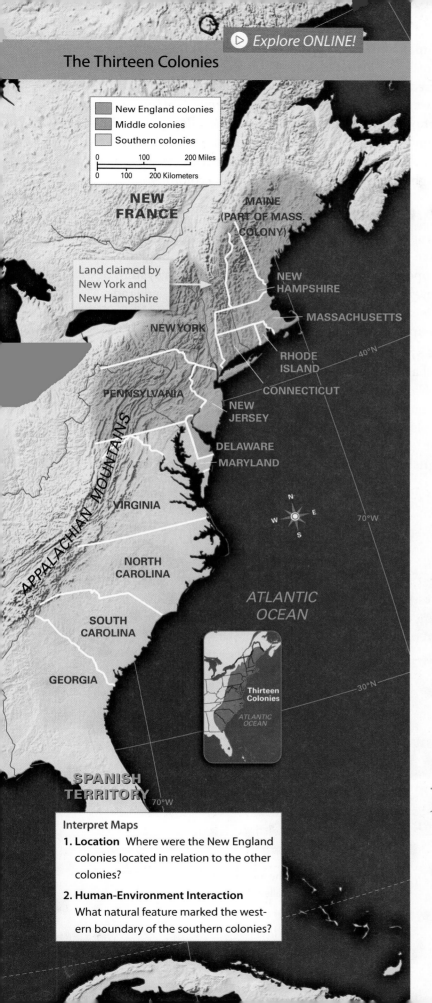

The Thirteen Colonies

▶ Explore ONLINE!

Legend:
- New England colonies
- Middle colonies
- Southern colonies

0   100   200 Miles
0   100   200 Kilometers

NEW FRANCE

MAINE (PART OF MASS. COLONY)

Land claimed by New York and New Hampshire

NEW HAMPSHIRE

MASSACHUSETTS

NEW YORK

RHODE ISLAND

CONNECTICUT

PENNSYLVANIA

NEW JERSEY

DELAWARE

MARYLAND

APPALACHIAN MOUNTAINS

VIRGINIA

NORTH CAROLINA

ATLANTIC OCEAN

SOUTH CAROLINA

GEORGIA

Thirteen Colonies

ATLANTIC OCEAN

SPANISH TERRITORY

40°N
70°W
70°W
30°N

Interpret Maps

1. **Location** Where were the New England colonies located in relation to the other colonies?

2. **Human-Environment Interaction** What natural feature marked the western boundary of the southern colonies?

members. The House of Burgesses was the assembly's second house. The members were elected by colonists.

In New England the center of politics was the **town meeting**. In town meetings people talked about and decided on issues of local interest, such as paying for schools.

In the southern colonies people typically lived farther away from one another. Therefore, many decisions were made at the county level. The middle colonies used both county meetings and town meetings to make laws.

Political Change in England In 1685 James II became king of England. He was determined to take more control over the English government, both in England and in the colonies.

James believed that the colonies were too independent. In 1686 he united the northern colonies under one government called the Dominion of New England. James named Sir Edmund Andros royal governor of the Dominion. The colonists disliked Andros because he used his authority to limit the powers of town meetings.

English Bill of Rights Parliament replaced the unpopular King James and passed the **English Bill of Rights** in 1689. This act reduced the powers of the English monarch. At the same time, Parliament gained power. As time went on, the colonists valued their own right to elect representatives to decide local issues. Following these changes, the colonies in the Dominion quickly formed new assemblies and charters.

Colonial Courts Colonial courts made up another important part of colonial governments. Whenever possible, colonists used the courts to control local affairs. In general, the courts reflected the beliefs of their local communities. For example, many laws in Massachusetts enforced the Puritans' religious beliefs. Laws based on the Bible set the standard for the community's conduct.

Sometimes colonial courts also protected individual freedoms. For example, in 1733 officials arrested John Peter Zenger for printing statements that criticized the governor of New York. The governor claimed that these statements were false. Andrew Hamilton, Zenger's attorney, argued that the statements were true and that he should be allowed to publish his opinions. Jury members believed that colonists had a right to voice their ideas openly and found him not guilty. The Zenger trial was important in establishing the right to freedom of the press in the colonies.

English Trade Laws

One of England's main reasons for founding and controlling its American colonies was to earn money from trade. In the late 1600s England, like most western European nations, practiced mercantilism, a system of creating and maintaining wealth through carefully controlled trade. A country gained wealth if it had fewer imports—goods bought from other countries—than exports—goods sold to other countries.

To support this system of mercantilism, between 1650 and 1696 Parliament passed a series of Navigation Acts limiting colonial trade. For example, the Navigation Act of 1660 forbade colonists from trading specific items such as sugar and cotton with any country other than England. The act also required colonists to use English ships to transport goods. Parliament later passed other acts that required all trade goods to pass through English ports, where duties, or import taxes, were added to the items.

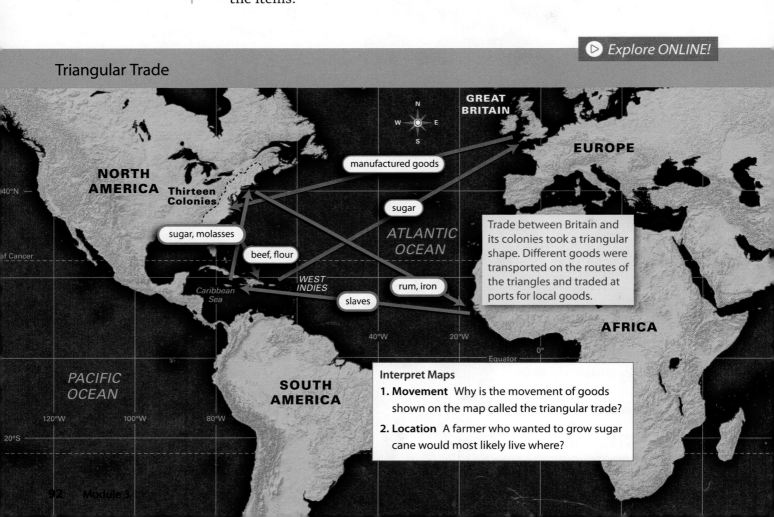

▷ Explore ONLINE!

Triangular Trade

Trade between Britain and its colonies took a triangular shape. Different goods were transported on the routes of the triangles and traded at ports for local goods.

Interpret Maps
1. **Movement** Why is the movement of goods shown on the map called the triangular trade?
2. **Location** A farmer who wanted to grow sugar cane would most likely live where?

England claimed that the Navigation Acts were good for the colonies. After all, the colonies had a steady market in England for their goods. But not all colonists agreed. Many colonists wanted more freedom to buy or sell goods wherever they could get the best price. Local demand for colonial goods was small compared to foreign demand.

Despite colonial complaints, the trade restrictions continued into the 1700s. Some traders turned to smuggling, or illegal trading. They often smuggled sugar, molasses, and rum into the colonies from non-English islands in the Caribbean. Parliament responded with the Molasses Act of 1733, which placed duties on these items. British officials, however, rarely carried out this law.

By the early 1700s English merchants were trading around the world. Most American merchants traded directly with Great Britain or the West Indies. By importing and exporting goods such as sugar and tobacco, some American merchants became wealthy.

Triangular Trade Trade between the American colonies and Great Britain was not direct. Rather, it generally took the form of **triangular trade**—a system in which goods and slaves were traded among the Americas, Britain, and Africa. There were several routes of the triangular trade. In one route colonists exchanged goods like beef and flour with plantation owners in the West Indies for sugar, some of which they shipped to Britain. The sugar was then exchanged for manufactured products to be sold in the colonies. Colonial merchants traveled great distances to find the best markets for their goods.

Middle Passage One version of the triangular trade began with traders exchanging rum for slaves on the West African coast. The traders then sold the enslaved Africans in the West Indies for molasses or brought them to sell in the mainland American colonies.

BIOGRAPHY

Olaudah Equiano 1745–1797

Olaudah Equiano claimed to have been born in Africa in present-day Nigeria. His autobiography told the story of his enslavement. According to his autobiography, Equiano survived the Middle Passage, traveling in a slave ship across the Atlantic. After he arrived in the colonies, a Virginia planter purchased him and again sold him to a British naval officer. While working as a sailor, Equiano eventually earned enough money to purchase his own freedom in 1766.

Equiano later settled in England and devoted much of his life to ending slavery.

Analyze Information
How did Equiano gain his freedom?

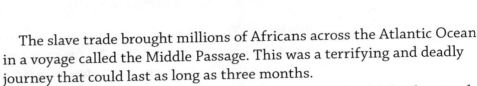

"I received such a salutation [smell] in my nostrils, as I had never experienced in my life; . . . I became so sick and low that I was not able to eat . . .

The groans of the dying, rendered [made] the whole a scene of horror almost inconceivable [unbelievable]."

—Olaudah Equiano, from *The Interesting Narrative of the Life of Olaudah Equiano, or Gustavus Vassa, the African*

Enslaved Africans endured a long, terrifying trip in overcrowded ships.

The slave trade brought millions of Africans across the Atlantic Ocean in a voyage called the Middle Passage. This was a terrifying and deadly journey that could last as long as three months.

Enslaved Africans lived in a space not even three feet high. Slave traders fit as many slaves as possible on board so they could earn greater profits. Thousands of captives died on slave ships during the Middle Passage. In many cases, they died from diseases such as smallpox. As farmers began to use fewer indentured servants, slaves became even more valuable.

Enslaved Africans in the English colonies tried to deal with their hardships by keeping their culture alive. They told stories and sang songs about their African homelands. By the late 1700s the Christian religion also became a source of strength for many enslaved Africans. Some enslaved Africans resisted slavery. They rebelled by breaking tools, pretending to be sick, or working slowly.

Great Awakening and Enlightenment

In the early 1700s revolutions in both religious and nonreligious thought transformed the Western world. These movements began in Europe and affected life in the American colonies.

Great Awakening After years of population growth, religious leaders wanted to spread religious feeling throughout the colonies. In the late 1730s these ministers began holding revivals, emotional gatherings where people came together to hear sermons.

Many American colonists experienced "a great awakening" in their religious lives. This **Great Awakening**—a religious movement that swept through the colonies in the 1730s and 1740s—changed colonial religion. It also affected social and political life. **Jonathan Edwards** of Massachusetts was one of the most important leaders of the Great Awakening. His dramatic sermons told sinners to seek forgiveness for their sins or face punishment in Hell forever. British minister George Whitefield held revivals from Georgia to New England.

Reading Check
Identify Cause and Effect What factors caused the slave trade to grow? How did this affect conditions on the Middle Passage?

The Great Awakening drew people of different regions, classes, and races. Women, members of minority groups, and poor people often took part in services. Ministers from different colonies met and shared ideas with one another. This represented one of the few exchanges between people from different colonies.

The Great Awakening promoted ideas and virtues that may also have affected colonial politics. Sermons about the spiritual equality of all people led some colonists to begin demanding more political equality. Revivals became popular places to talk about political and social issues. People from those colonies with less political freedom were thus introduced to more democratic systems used in other colonies.

Enlightenment During the 1600s Europeans began to reexamine their world. Scientists began to better understand the basic laws that govern nature. Their new ideas about the universe began the Scientific Revolution. The revolution changed how people thought of the world.

Many colonists were also influenced by the **Enlightenment**. This movement, which took place during the 1700s, spread the idea that reason and logic could improve society. Enlightenment thinkers also formed ideas about how government should work.

Some Enlightenment thinkers believed that there was a social contract between government and citizens. Philosophers such as **John Locke** thought that people had natural rights such as equality and liberty. Ideas of the Scientific Revolution and the Enlightenment eventually influenced colonial leaders.

French and Indian War

By the 1670s tensions had arisen between New England colonists and the Wampanoag. Metacomet, a Wampanoag leader also known as King Philip, opposed the colonists' efforts to take his people's lands. In 1675 these tensions finally erupted in a conflict known as King Philip's War. The colonial militia—civilians serving as soldiers—fought American Indian warriors. Both sides attacked each other's settlements, killing men, women, and children. The fighting finally ended in 1676, but only after about 600 colonists and some 3,000 Indians had been killed, including Metacomet.

Native American Allies Some Native Americans allied with the colonists to fight against Metacomet and his forces. These Indians had developed trade relations with colonists. They wanted tools, weapons, and other goods that Europeans could provide. In exchange, the colonists wanted furs, which they sold for large profits in Europe. As a result, each side came to depend upon the other.

French colonists traded and allied with the Algonquian and Huron. English colonists traded and allied with the Iroquois League, in the New York colony. This powerful group united American Indians from six different groups. Many American Indians trusted the French more than they did the English. The smaller French settlements were less threatening than the rapidly growing English colonies. No matter who their allies were,

Reading Check
Summarize How did the Great Awakening and the Enlightenment influence colonial society?

In King Philip's War, Wampanoag leader Metacomet led a coalition force of Native Americans against the colonial militia.

North American Empires before and after the Treaty of Paris

▶ *Explore ONLINE!*

1754

Legend:
- British
- Spanish
- French
- Russian
- Boundary of the Iroquois League
- Disputed by Britain and France
- Disputed by Britain and Spain
- Disputed by Britain, Spain and Russia
- 13 Colonies boundary

0 500 1,000 Miles
0 500 1,000 Kilometers

1763

Interpret Maps

1. **Regions** Which countries gained North American territory between 1754 and 1763?

2. **Human-Environment Interaction** What natural feature helped form the boundary between British and Spanish territory in 1763?

many Indian leaders took care to protect their people's independence. As one leader said:

> "We are born free. We neither depend upon [the governor of New France] nor [the governor of New York]. We may go where we please . . . and buy and sell what we please."
>
> —Garangula, quoted in *A Complete History of the United States of America*, by Frederick Butler

War Erupts Until the mid-1700s France and Great Britain struggled for control of territory in North America. British colonists wanted to settle in the Ohio River valley, where they could take advantage of the valuable fur trade. The French believed this settlement would hurt their fur trade profits. A standoff developed in the Ohio River valley where the French had built three forts. Fighting erupted in 1753 as the British military moved to take over the valley.

When a young Virginian named George Washington arrived with more soldiers, he found the area under French control. Washington and his troops built a small, simple fort that he named Fort Necessity. After his troops suffered many casualties—captured, injured, or killed soldiers—Washington finally surrendered. His defeat in 1754 was the start of the French and Indian War.

Colonial leaders, such as Benjamin Franklin, met to discuss defense. The convention produced a plan called the Albany Plan of Union, based on Franklin's idea for uniting the colonies. The Iroquois tribes, or Haudenosaunee as they called themselves, took part in the convention. They may have helped shape the Albany Plan with their ideas about government. Franklin published his famous "Join, or Die" political cartoon to help convince the colonies to unite. Meanwhile, in 1756 fighting began in Europe, starting what became known as the Seven Years' War.

Treaty of Paris The turning point of the war came in 1759. That year British general James Wolfe captured Quebec, gaining the advantage in the war. However, the war dragged on for four more years. Finally, in 1763 Britain and France signed the Treaty of Paris, officially ending the war.

The terms of the treaty gave Canada to Britain. Britain also gained all French lands east of the Mississippi River except the city of New Orleans and two small islands in the Gulf of St. Lawrence. From Spain, which had allied with France in 1762, Britain received Florida. In an earlier treaty, Spain had received Louisiana, the land that France had claimed west of the Mississippi River. The Treaty of Paris changed the balance of power in North America. Soon, British settlers began moving west to settle new lands.

Western Frontier In the late 1600s and early 1700s, most colonial settlements were located along the Atlantic coast. At that time few colonists had settled the backcountry. Thick forests, steep hills, and few roads made it hard to settle. By the mid-1700s, however, many colonial settlers, or pioneers, were slowly moving into the Virginia and Carolina backcountry and the Ohio River valley. Many of these settlers were Scots-Irish immigrants. The Scots-Irish were people whose ancestors had migrated from Scotland to Ireland. A group of German immigrants called Moravians settled in the foothills of North Carolina's backcountry mountains. They were a religious group who saw themselves as a large "family."

Indian leaders like Chief **Pontiac** opposed British settlement of this new land. Pontiac's Rebellion began in May 1763, when his forces attacked British forts on the frontier. Within one month they had destroyed or captured seven forts. Pontiac then led an attack on Fort Detroit. The British held out for months.

British leaders feared that more fighting would take place on the frontier if colonists kept moving onto American Indian lands. To avoid more conflict, King George III issued the Proclamation of 1763. This law banned British settlement west of the Appalachian Mountains. The law also ordered settlers to leave the upper Ohio River valley. The right to settle and claim ownership of land was important to the colonists, so the proclamation angered them.

BIOGRAPHY

Pontiac 1720–1769

Pontiac, an Ottawa chief who had fought for France, tried to resist British settlement west of the Appalachians. Calling them "dogs dressed in red who have come to rob us," he attacked the British in the Ohio country in 1763. Pontiac's Rebellion was put down, and he surrendered in 1766.

Analyze Information
How did Pontiac try to stop the British?

Most colonists ignored the king's proclamation. They believed they had fought the war to keep the French from blocking their settlement of the western frontier. They did not like the British government telling them to stay out of those lands. As a result, fighting between the settlers and the American Indians continued.

The colonists were not used to laws being strictly enforced in the colonies. Before 1763 Britain interfered very little in colonial affairs. This hands-off policy was known as **salutary neglect**. The British Parliament passed laws to help govern the colonies, but governors rarely enforced these laws. The practice of salutary neglect encouraged individualism and self-reliance in the colonies. The colonists got accustomed to acting on their own. Soon new laws would be passed by Parliament that would further anger the colonists.

Reading Check
Summarize Why did George III issue the Proclamation of 1763?

Summary and Preview In this lesson you read about colonial governments, the slave trade, and the conflicts with foreign countries and with Native Americans that the colonies faced as they grew. In the next lesson you'll learn about the increasing tension between the colonies and Great Britain that led to independence.

Lesson 4 Assessment

Review Ideas, Terms, and People

1. a. **Describe** How were colonial governments organized?
   b. **Analyze** How did political change in England affect colonial governments?
2. a. **Explain** What is mercantilism?
   b. **Analyze** How did the Navigation Acts support the system of mercantilism?
   c. **Evaluate** Did the colonies benefit from mercantilism? Why or why not?
3. a. **Identify** What was the Great Awakening?
   b. **Compare** How was the Enlightenment similar to the Great Awakening?
4. a. **Explain** What caused the French and Indian War?
   b. **Examine** What were some of the outcomes of the French and Indian War?
   c. **Evaluate** Defend the British decision to ban colonists from settling on the western frontier.

Critical Thinking

5. **Analyze** What impact did colonial governments have on American politics and institutions?
6. **Summarize** In this lesson you learned about developments in the colonies during the late 1600s to mid-1700s. Create a chart like the one below to explain the effects of these developments. Then add a box to the bottom of your chart in which you briefly summarize how the colonies grew, changed, and faced challenges during the period.

Development	Effects
Establishment of local government	
Political change in England	
Trade laws	
Great Awakening/ Enlightenment	
French and Indian War	

How the colonies grew, changed, and faced challenges

Social Studies Skills

Interpret Timelines

Define the Skill

Knowing the sequence, or order, in which historical events took place is important to understanding these events. Timelines visually display the sequence of events during a particular period of time. They also let you easily see time spans between events, such as how long after one event a related event took place—and what events occurred in between. In addition, comparing timelines for different places makes relationships between distant events easier to identify and understand.

Learn the Skill

Follow these guidelines to read, interpret, and compare timelines.

1. Determine each timeline's framework. Note the years it covers and the periods of time into which it is divided. Be aware that a pair of timelines may not have the same framework.

2. Study the order of events on each timeline. Note the length of time between events. Compare what was taking place on different timelines around the same time period.

3. Look for relationships between events. Pay particular attention to how an event on one timeline might relate to an event on another.

Practice the Skill

Interpret the timelines below to answer the following questions.

1. What is each timeline's framework?

2. How long was England without a king?

3. What event in England allowed the colonists to get rid of the Dominion of New England in 1689?

4. Massachusetts's independence had troubled English officials for many years. What do the timelines suggest about why this colony was allowed to remain independent until 1686?

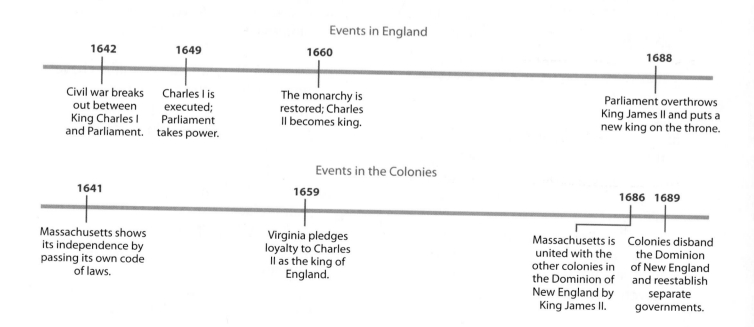

Events in England

1642	1649	1660	1688
Civil war breaks out between King Charles I and Parliament.	Charles I is executed; Parliament takes power.	The monarchy is restored; Charles II becomes king.	Parliament overthrows King James II and puts a new king on the throne.

Events in the Colonies

1641	1659	1686	1689
Massachusetts shows its independence by passing its own code of laws.	Virginia pledges loyalty to Charles II as the king of England.	Massachusetts is united with the other colonies in the Dominion of New England by King James II.	Colonies disband the Dominion of New England and reestablish separate governments.

Module 3 Assessment

Review Vocabulary, Terms, and People

Match the words in the left column with the correct definition in the right column.

1. salutary neglect
2. Jonathan Edwards
3. mercantilism
4. immigrants
5. indentured servants
6. William Penn
7. Pocahontas
8. Quakers
9. staple crops
10. town meeting

a. colonists who received free passage to North America in exchange for working without pay for a certain number of years
b. a hands-off policy under which Britain interfered very little in colonial affairs
c. crops that are continuously in demand
d. daughter of Powhatan chief whose marriage to colonist John Rolfe eased tensions between the Powhatan and the colonists
e. one of the leaders of the Great Awakening, he urged sinners to seek forgiveness
f. Protestant sect founded in England that believed salvation was available to all people
g. people who move to another country after leaving their homeland
h. political gathering at which people make decisions on local issues
i. Quaker leader who established a colony with the goal of fair government for all
j. system of creating and maintaining wealth through controlled trade

Comprehension and Critical Thinking

Lesson 1

11. a. **Explain** What problems did the settlers of Virginia face?
     b. **Draw Conclusions** Why was Maryland's Toleration Act of 1649 important?
     c. **Predict** How might the southern colonies' reliance on slave labor eventually cause problems?

Lesson 2

12. a. **Describe** On what was the economy of the New England colonies based?
     b. **Compare and Contrast** How were the Pilgrim and Puritan colonies similar and different?
     c. **Evaluate** Explain why you think the close ties between church and state in Massachusetts helped or hurt its government.

Lesson 3

13. a. **Identify** What types of crops were grown in the middle colonies?
     b. **Draw Conclusions** Why did the middle colonies have a more diverse population than either New England or the South?
     c. **Elaborate** Why would immigrants have chosen to live in the middle colonies?
     d. **Compare and Contrast** How did cultural and social influences help shape the middle colonies?

Lesson 4

14. a. **Identify** What challenges did the English colonies face?
     b. **Analyze** What effect did the Great Awakening and the Enlightenment have on the colonies?
     c. **Evaluate** Explain which you think had a greater impact on colonial government—the passage of the English Bill of Rights or the Great Awakening.

Review Themes

15. **Politics** What political influences shaped the governments of the British colonies?

16. **Economics** How did mercantilism affect the economies of Great Britain and the colonies?

17. **Economics** In what ways were the economies of the southern, New England, and middle colonies similar to one another? In what ways were they different?

Reading Skills

Vocabulary Clues *Use the Reading Skills taught in this module to answer the question about the reading selection below.*

> King James I issued a charter, which gave the Virginia Company permission to settle Virginia.

18. According to the reading selection above, what is the best definition of *charter*?
    a. a chart that showed Virginia's location
    b. an instruction manual on how to sail a ship
    c. a contract setting a limit on the number of indentured servants
    d. a document that gives permission to start a colony

Social Studies Skills

Interpret Timelines *Use the Social Studies Skills taught in this module to answer the questions about the "Events in England" and "Events in the Colonies" timelines shown on the Social Studies Skills page.*

19. How many years after the start of the English Civil War did Parliament overthrow King James II?

20. How many years did the Dominion of New England last?
    a. 41
    b. 18
    c. 3
    d. 6

Focus on Writing

21. **Write an Infomercial** What if television had been invented during the time the English colonies were being founded in North America? Instead of relying on printed flyers and word of mouth to attract settlers, the founders of colonies might have made infomercials. Choose a colony and time period and make a list of reasons why English citizens might want to settle there. Then write an infomercial with at least four scenes. Each scene should have video and a voice-over telling one of the reasons for immigrating.

Module 4

The American Revolution

Essential Question
Why were the American Patriots willing to risk their lives for independence?

About the Photo: Soldiers fight with single-shot muskets in this reenactment of a battle during the Revolutionary War.

▶ *Explore ONLINE!*

HISTORY.

VIDEOS, including...
- American Revolution: One Word
- Jefferson Writes the Declaration of Independence
- George Washington: Yorktown

☑ Document-Based Investigations

☑ Graphic Organizers

☑ Interactive Games

☑ Image with Hotspots: Battle of Bunker Hill

☑ Image with Hotspots: Winter at Valley Forge

☑ Interactive Map: Battle of Yorktown

In this module you will learn about the American War for Independence.

What You Will Learn ...

Lesson 1: Conflict in the Colonies 106
The Big Idea Tensions developed as the British government placed tax after tax on the colonies.

Lesson 2: The Revolution Begins 113
The Big Idea The tensions between the colonies and Great Britain led to armed conflict in 1775.

Lesson 3: Declaring Independence 119
The Big Idea The colonies formally declared their independence from Great Britain.

The Declaration of Independence 124

Lesson 4: The Struggle for Liberty 128
The Big Idea Patriot forces faced many obstacles in the war against Britain.

Lesson 5: Independence! 139
The Big Idea The war spread to the southern colonies, where the British were finally defeated.

Timeline of Events 1760–1785

▶ Explore ONLINE!

| United States | 1760 | World |

1763 The Seven Years' War ends with a British victory over France.

1765

∧ **1765** Great Britain's Parliament passes the Stamp Act, establishing new taxes for the American colonists.

1770

1774 The First Continental Congress meets.

1775 The Revolutionary War begins with the fighting at Lexington and Concord.

1775

<**1776** On July 4 the thirteen colonies issue the Declaration of Independence and break away from Great Britain.

∧ **1778** France allies with the Americans and joins the war against Great Britain.

1779 Spain declares war against Great Britain.

1781 The British surrender to George Washington at Yorktown. ∨

1780

1783 Simon Bolívar is born in present-day Venezuela. >

1783 The Treaty of Paris is signed, ending the war.

1785

Reading Social Studies

Geography, Politics

In this module you will read about the events of the Revolutionary War, the war by which the United States won its independence. You will learn about some of the major battles that occurred between the American colonists and the British army and how geography sometimes affected their outcomes. You will also read the Declaration of Independence, one of the most important political documents in all of American history.

READING FOCUS:

Main Ideas in Social Studies

When you are reading, it is not always necessary to remember every tiny detail of the text. Instead, what you want to remember are the main ideas, the most important concepts around which the text is based.

Identify Main Ideas Most paragraphs in history books include main ideas. Sometimes the main idea is stated clearly in a single sentence. At other times, the main idea is suggested, not stated. However, that idea still shapes the paragraph's content and the meaning of all of the facts and details in it.

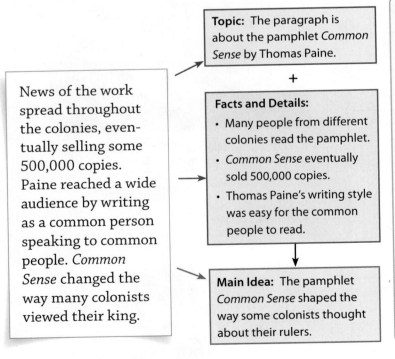

News of the work spread throughout the colonies, eventually selling some 500,000 copies. Paine reached a wide audience by writing as a common person speaking to common people. *Common Sense* changed the way many colonists viewed their king.

Topic: The paragraph is about the pamphlet *Common Sense* by Thomas Paine.

+

Facts and Details:
- Many people from different colonies read the pamphlet.
- *Common Sense* eventually sold 500,000 copies.
- Thomas Paine's writing style was easy for the common people to read.

Main Idea: The pamphlet *Common Sense* shaped the way some colonists thought about their rulers.

Steps in Identifying Main Ideas

1. Read the paragraph. Ask yourself, "What is this paragraph mostly about?" This will be the topic of this paragraph.

2. List the important facts and details that relate to that topic.

3. Ask yourself, "What seems to be the most important point the writer is making about the topic?" Or ask, "If the writer could say only one thing about this paragraph, what would it be?" This is the **main idea** of the paragraph.

You Try It!

The following passage is from the module you are about to read. Read it and then answer the questions below.

The Treaty of Paris

After Yorktown, only a few small battles took place. Lacking the money to pay for a new army, Great Britain entered into peace talks with America. Benjamin Franklin had a key role in the negotiations.

Delegates took more than two years to come to a peace agreement. In the Treaty of Paris of 1783, Great Britain recognized the independence of the United States. The treaty also set America's borders. A separate treaty between Britain and Spain returned Florida to the Spanish. British leaders also accepted American rights to settle and trade west of the original thirteen colonies.

Answer these questions based on the passage you just read.

1. The main idea of the second paragraph is stated in a sentence. Which sentence expresses the main idea?

2. What is the first paragraph about? What facts and details are included in the paragraph? Based on your answers to these questions, what is the main idea of the first paragraph?

As you read Module 4, identify the main ideas of the paragraphs you are reading.

Key Terms and People

Lesson 1
Samuel Adams
Committees of Correspondence
Stamp Act of 1765
Mercy Otis Warren
Boston Massacre
Tea Act
Boston Tea Party
Intolerable Acts
Quartering Act

Lesson 2
First Continental Congress
Patriots
minutemen
Redcoats
Second Continental Congress
Continental army
George Washington
Battle of Bunker Hill

Lesson 3
Common Sense
Thomas Paine
Declaration of Independence
Thomas Jefferson
Loyalists

Lesson 4
Haym Salomon
mercenaries
Battle of Trenton
Battle of Saratoga
Marquis de Lafayette
Baron Friedrich von Steuben
Bernardo de Gálvez
John Paul Jones
George Rogers Clark

Lesson 5
Francis Marion
James Armistead
Comte de Rochambeau
Battle of Yorktown
Treaty of Paris of 1783

Conflict in the Colonies

The Big Idea

Tensions developed as the British government placed tax after tax on the colonies.

Main Ideas

- British efforts to raise taxes on colonists sparked protest.
- The Boston Massacre caused colonial resentment toward Great Britain.
- Colonists protested the British tax on tea with the Boston Tea Party.
- Great Britain responded to colonial actions by passing the Intolerable Acts.

Key Terms and People

Samuel Adams
Committees of Correspondence
Stamp Act of 1765
Mercy Otis Warren
Boston Massacre
Tea Act
Boston Tea Party
Intolerable Acts
Quartering Act

If YOU were there . . .

You live in the New England colonies in the 1700s. Recently, British officials have placed new taxes on tea—your favorite beverage. You've never been very interested in politics, but you're beginning to think that people far across the ocean in Britain shouldn't be able to tell you what to do. Some of your friends have joined a group that refuses to buy British tea.

Would you give up your favorite drink to join the boycott?

Great Britain Raises Taxes

Great Britain had won the French and Indian War, but Parliament still had to pay for it. The British continued to keep a standing, or permanent, army in North America to protect the colonists against Indian attacks. To help pay for this army, Prime Minister George Grenville asked Parliament to tax the colonists. In 1764 Parliament passed the Sugar Act, which set duties on molasses and sugar imported by colonists. This was the first act passed specifically to raise money in the colonies.

British officials also tried harder to arrest smugglers. Colonial merchants were required to list all the trade goods they carried aboard their ships. These lists had to be approved before ships could leave colonial ports. This made it difficult for traders to avoid paying duties. The British navy also began to stop and search ships for smuggled goods.

Parliament also changed the colonies' legal system by giving greater powers to the vice-admiralty courts. These courts had no juries, and the judges treated suspected smugglers as guilty until proven innocent. In regular British courts, accused persons were treated as innocent until proven guilty.

Taxation without Representation Parliament's actions upset many colonists who had grown used to being independent and governing themselves. The Parliament's longtime

Voice of Protest

Leaders like Patrick Henry made speeches that encouraged colonists to protest the British government. Here, Henry is shown protesting the Crown's control of religion in front of a Virginia court.

Why were public speeches so important to protesting British rule?

practice of salutary neglect, or not enforcing most laws governing the colonies, had fostered individualism among the colonists. The government's previous hands-off approach made these actions seem even harsher to the colonists. The rising merchant class thought the taxes were unfair and hurt business. Many believed that Great Britain had no right to tax the colonies at all without popular consent.

James Otis, a colonial lawyer, argued that the power of the Crown and Parliament was limited. Otis said they could not "take from any man any part of his property, without his consent in person or by representation." Colonial assemblies had little influence on Parliament's decisions. In addition, the colonists had no direct representatives in Parliament. The colonists were subjects of the Crown instead of citizens of England.

At a Boston town meeting in May 1764, local leader **Samuel Adams** agreed with Otis. He believed that Parliament could not tax the colonists without their permission. The ideas of Otis and Adams were summed up in the slogan "No Taxation without Representation," which spread throughout the colonies.

Adams helped found the **Committees of Correspondence**. Each committee got in touch with other towns and colonies. Its members shared ideas and information about the new British laws and ways to challenge them.

A popular method of protest was the boycott, in which people refused to buy British goods. The first colonial boycott started in New York in 1765. It soon spread to other colonies. Colonists hoped that their efforts would hurt the British economy and might convince Parliament to end the new taxes.

Stamp Act The British government continued to search for new ways to tax the American colonies, further angering many colonists. For example, Prime Minister Grenville proposed the **Stamp Act of 1765**. This act required colonists to pay for an official stamp, or seal, when they bought

Colonists had to pay for a stamp, such as this halfpenny stamp, when purchasing any paper item.

paper items. The tax had to be paid on legal documents, licenses, newspapers, pamphlets, and even playing cards. Colonists who refused to buy stamps could be fined or sent to jail.

Grenville did not expect this tax to spark protest. After all, in Britain people already paid similar taxes. But colonists saw it differently. The Stamp Act was Parliament's first attempt to raise money by taxing the colonists directly, rather than by taxing imported goods. **Mercy Otis Warren**, a writer in the Massachusetts colony, disagreed with the new tax. She began writing plays that accused British leaders of being greedy.

Protests against the Stamp Act began almost immediately. Colonists formed a secret society called the Sons of Liberty. Samuel Adams helped organize the group in Boston. This group sometimes used violence to frighten tax collectors. Many colonial courts shut down because people refused to buy the stamps required for legal documents. Businesses openly ignored the law by refusing to buy stamps.

In May 1765 a Virginia lawyer named Patrick Henry presented a series of resolutions to the Virginia House of Burgesses. These resolutions stated that the Stamp Act violated colonists' rights. In addition to taxation without representation, the Stamp Act denied the accused a trial by jury. Henry's speech in support of the resolutions convinced the assembly to support some of his ideas.

Repealing the Stamp Act In Boston the members of the Massachusetts legislature called for a Stamp Act Congress. In October 1765 delegates from nine colonies met in New York. They issued a declaration that the Stamp Act was a violation of their rights and liberties.

Pressure on Parliament to repeal, or do away with, the Stamp Act grew quickly. A group of London merchants complained that their trade suffered from the colonial boycott. Parliament repealed the Stamp Act in 1766.

Members of Parliament were upset that colonists had challenged their authority. Thus, Parliament issued the Declaratory Act, which stated that Parliament had the power to make laws for the colonies "in all cases whatsoever." The Declaratory Act further worried the colonists. The act stripped away much of their independence.

Townshend Acts In June 1767 Parliament passed the Townshend Acts. These acts placed duties on glass, lead, paint, paper, and tea. To enforce the Townshend Acts, British officials used writs of assistance. These allowed tax collectors to search for smuggled goods. Colonists hated the new laws because they took power away from colonial governments.

The colonists responded to the Townshend Acts by once again boycotting many British goods. Women calling themselves the Daughters of Liberty supported the boycott. In February 1768 Samuel Adams wrote a letter arguing that the laws violated the legal rights of the colonists. The Massachusetts legislature sent the letter to other colonies' legislatures, who voted to join the protest.

Reading Check
Sequence What series of events led to the arrival of British troops in Boston in 1768?

At the same time, tax collectors in Massachusetts seized the ship *Liberty* on suspicion of smuggling. This action angered the ship's owner and the Sons of Liberty. They attacked the houses of customs officials in protest. In response, the governor broke up the Massachusetts legislature. He also asked troops to restore order. British soldiers arrived in Boston in October 1768.

Boston Massacre

Many Bostonians saw the presence of British troops as a threat by the British government against its critics in Massachusetts. Some colonists agreed with Samuel Adams, who said, "I look upon [British soldiers] as foreign enemies." The soldiers knew that they were not welcome. Both sides resented each other, and name-calling, arguments, and fights between Bostonians and the soldiers were common.

The tension exploded on March 5, 1770. A lone British soldier standing guard had an argument with a colonist and struck him. A crowd gathered around the soldier, throwing snowballs and shouting insults. Soon a small number of troops arrived. The crowd grew louder and angrier by the moment. Some yelled, "Come on you rascals . . . Fire if you dare!" Suddenly, the soldiers fired into the crowd, instantly killing three men, including African American sailor Crispus Attucks. Attucks is the best-remembered casualty of the incident. Two others died within a few days.

Samuel Adams and other protesters quickly spread the story of the shootings. They used it as propaganda—a story giving only one side in an argument—against the British. Colonists called the shootings the **Boston Massacre**. Paul Revere created an elaborate color print titled "The Bloody Massacre perpetrated in King Street."

The soldiers and their officer, Thomas Preston, were charged with murder. Two Boston lawyers, Josiah Quincy and John Adams—Samuel

Paul Revere's engraving of the Boston Massacre became an effective piece of propaganda. It stirred up anti-British feelings among the colonists.

The Boston Massacre

An account of the Boston Massacre appeared in the *Boston Gazette and Country Journal* soon after the event.

Analyze Historical Sources
Why do you think the people described were not intimidated by the soldiers?

"*The People were immediately alarmed with the Report of this horrid Massacre, the Bells were set a Ringing, and great Numbers soon assembled at the Place where this tragical Scene had been acted; their Feelings may be better conceived than expressed; and while some were taking Care of the Dead and Wounded, the Rest were in Consultation what to do in these dreadful Circumstances.*

But so little intimidated were they [Bostonians], notwithstanding their being within a few Yards of the Main Guard, and seeing the 29th Regiment under Arms, and drawn up in King street; that they kept their Station and appeared, as an Officer of Rank expressed it, ready to run upon the very Muzzles of their Muskets."

—*Boston Gazette and Country Journal,*
March 12, 1770

Adams's cousin—agreed to defend the soldiers. The British soldiers claimed that they acted in self-defense. Quincy and Adams argued this point in the trial. The Boston jury agreed, finding Preston and six soldiers not guilty. Two soldiers were convicted of killing people in the crowd by accident. These men were branded on the hand and released. The trial helped calm people down, but many were still angry at the British.

Reading Check
Analyze What was the significance of the Boston Massacre?

The Boston Tea Party

To reduce tensions in the colonies, Parliament repealed almost all of the Townshend Acts. However, it kept the tax on tea. British officials knew that the colonial demand for tea was high despite the boycott. But colonial merchants were smuggling most of this imported tea and paying no duty on it.

The British East India Company offered Parliament a solution. The company had huge amounts of tea but was not allowed to sell it directly to the colonists. If the company could sell directly to the colonists, it could charge low prices and still make money. Cheaper tea might encourage colonists to stop smuggling. Less smuggling would result in more tax money.

Parliament agreed and passed the **Tea Act** in 1773, which allowed the British East India Company to sell tea directly to the colonists. Many colonial merchants and smugglers feared that the British East India Company's cheap tea would put them out of business.

Three ships loaded with tea from the British East India Company arrived in Boston Harbor in 1773. Members of the Sons of Liberty

Angered by the passage of the Tea Act, colonists in Boston dumped chests of British tea into the harbor before it could be unloaded.

demanded that the ships leave. But the governor of Massachusetts would not let the ships leave without paying the duty. Unsure of what to do, the captains waited in the harbor.

On the night of December 16, 1773, colonists disguised as Native Americans sneaked onto the three tea-filled ships and dumped over 340 tea chests into Boston Harbor. This event became known as the **Boston Tea Party**. Soon the streets echoed with shouts of "Boston harbor is a teapot tonight!"

Reading Check
Summarize What factors led to the Boston Tea Party?

Quick Facts

The Road to Revolution

Colonists reacted to British laws with anger and violence. The British Parliament continued to pass tax after tax.

	British Actions	Colonists' Reactions
1764 The Sugar Act	The Sugar Act is passed to raise money from the colonies for Britain.	Samuel Adams founds the Committees of Correspondence to improve communication among the colonies.
1765 The Stamp Act	The Stamp Act taxes newspapers, licenses, and colonial paper products.	A series of resolutions is published, stating that the Stamp Act violates the rights of the colonists.
1770 The Boston Massacre	British soldiers fire into a crowd of colonists, killing five men.	Colonists protest and bring the soldiers to trial.
1773 The Sugar Act	The Tea Act is passed, making British tea cheaper than colonial tea.	Colonists protest by dumping chests of British tea into Boston Harbor.
1774 The Intolerable Acts	Boston Harbor is closed, and British troops are quartered in colonists' homes.	Colonists' resentment toward Britain builds.

Analyze Visuals
In what year did the conflict between Britain and the colonists turn violent?

The Intolerable Acts

Lord North, the new British prime minister, was furious when he heard the news. Parliament decided to punish Boston. In the spring of 1774 it passed the Coercive Acts. Colonists called these laws the **Intolerable Acts**. The acts had several effects.

1. Boston Harbor was closed until Boston paid for the ruined tea.
2. Massachusetts's charter was canceled. The governor decided if and when the legislature could meet.
3. Royal officials accused of crimes were sent to Britain for trial. This let them face a friendlier judge and jury.
4. A new **Quartering Act** required colonists to house British soldiers.
5. The Quebec Act gave a large amount of land to the colony of Quebec.
6. General Thomas Gage became the new governor of Massachusetts.

The British hoped that these steps would bring back order in the colonies. Instead, they simply increased people's anger at Britain.

Reading Check
Analyze What was the purpose of the Intolerable Acts?

Summary and Preview In this lesson you learned about the increasing dissatisfaction between the colonists and Great Britain. In the next lesson you'll learn about the events that started the American Revolution.

Lesson 1 Assessment

Review Ideas, Terms, and People

1. a. Explain Why did Great Britain raise taxes in its American colonies?

b. Evaluate Which method of protesting taxes do you think was most successful for the colonists? Why?

2. a. Describe What events led to the Boston Massacre?

b. Elaborate Why do you think John Adams and Josiah Quincy agreed to defend the British soldiers who were involved in the Boston Massacre?

c. Explain How did the colonists' and the British soldiers' viewpoints differ about the Boston Massacre?

3. a. Recall What was the purpose of the Tea Act?

b. Draw Conclusions What message did the Boston Tea Party send to the British government?

4. a. Explain Why did Parliament pass the Intolerable Acts?

b. Draw Conclusions Why do you think the colonists believed that these laws were "intolerable"?

Critical Thinking

5. Identify Cause and Effect In this lesson you learned about laws passed by the British government that impacted the American colonies. Create a chart similar to the one below to identify these laws and their results.

Law	Result
1.	
2.	
3.	
4.	
5.	

The Revolution Begins

The Big Idea

The tensions between the colonies and Great Britain led to armed conflict in 1775.

Main Ideas

- The First Continental Congress demanded certain rights from Great Britain.
- Armed conflict between British soldiers and colonists broke out with the "shot heard 'round the world."
- The Second Continental Congress created the Continental army to fight the British.
- In two early battles, the army lost control of Boston but then regained it.

Key Terms and People

First Continental Congress
Patriots
minutemen
Redcoats
Second Continental Congress
Continental army
George Washington
Battle of Bunker Hill

If YOU were there . . .

You are a member of the British Parliament in the 1770s. Some members say that the Americans are defying the king. Others point out that the colonists are British citizens who have certain rights. Now the king must decide to punish the rebellious colonists or listen to their complaints.

What advice would you give the king?

First Continental Congress

To many colonists the closing of Boston Harbor was the final insult in a long list of abuses. In response to the mounting crisis, all the colonies except Georgia sent representatives to a meeting in October 1774. This meeting, known as the **First Continental Congress**, was a gathering of colonial leaders who were deeply troubled about the relationship between Great Britain and its colonies in America. At Carpenters' Hall in Philadelphia, the leaders remained locked in weeks of intense debate. Patrick Henry and others believed that violence was unavoidable. On the other hand, delegates from Pennsylvania and New York had strict orders to seek peace.

Wisely, the delegates compromised. They encouraged colonists to continue boycotting British goods but told colonial militias to prepare for war. Meanwhile, they drafted the Declaration of Rights, a list of ten resolutions to be presented to King George III. Included was the colonists' right to "life, liberty, and property."

The First Continental Congress did not seek a separation from Britain. Its goal was to state the colonists' concerns and ask the king to correct the problems. But before they left Philadelphia, the delegates agreed to meet in 1775 if the king refused their petition.

Patrick Henry returned from the Congress and reported to his fellow Virginians. To encourage them to support the Patriot cause, Henry voiced these famous words:

Reading Check
Identify Cause and Effect Why did the delegates attend the First Continental Congress? What were the results?

"They tell us, Sir, that we are weak; unable to cope with so formidable an adversary. But when will we be stronger? Gentlemen may cry, Peace, Peace—but there is no peace. I know not what course others may take; but as for me, give me liberty or give me death."

—Patrick Henry, quoted in *Eyewitnesses and Others*

In time many colonists came to agree with Henry. They became known as **Patriots**—colonists who chose to fight for independence from Great Britain.

"Shot Heard 'round the World"

The Continental Congress planned to meet again in 1775. Before it could, the situation in the colonies had changed—for the worse.

The Ride of Paul Revere British military leaders in the colonies grew uneasy when local militias seemed to be preparing for action. The governor of Massachusetts, Thomas Gage, learned that a stockpile of weapons was stored in Concord, about 20 miles from Boston. He also heard that colonial leaders Samuel Adams and John Hancock were meeting in nearby Lexington. In April 1775 he decided to seize the supplies and arrest the two leaders.

Gage thought he had kept his plan a secret. However, Boston was full of spies for the Patriot cause. They noticed the British were preparing for action and quickly informed the Patriots. Unsure of how the British would strike, Sons of Liberty member Paul Revere enlisted the aid of Robert Newman. Newman was to climb into the steeple of the Old North Church and watch for British soldiers. If they advanced across land, Newman would display one lantern from the steeple. If they rowed across the Charles River, Newman would display two lanterns.

When Revere and fellow Patriot William Dawes saw two lights shine, they set off on horseback. Using two different routes out of Boston, they

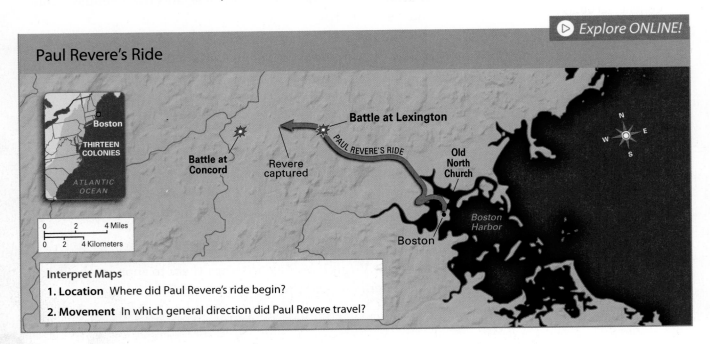

▶ Explore ONLINE!

Paul Revere's Ride

Battle at Lexington

Battle at Concord

Revere captured

PAUL REVERE'S RIDE

Old North Church

Boston

Boston Harbor

Boston

THIRTEEN COLONIES

ATLANTIC OCEAN

0   2   4 Miles
0   2   4 Kilometers

Interpret Maps

1. **Location** Where did Paul Revere's ride begin?

2. **Movement** In which general direction did Paul Revere travel?

sounded the alert. As the riders advanced, drums and church bells called out the local militia, or **minutemen**—who got their name because they were ready to fight at a minute's notice. Many minutemen were rural farmers. Others were craftsmen who lived in towns and cities.

Battles at Lexington and Concord At dawn on April 19, the British troops arrived at the town of Lexington, near Concord, where 70 armed minutemen waited. Patriot captain John Parker yelled to his troops, "Don't fire unless fired upon." Suddenly a shot rang out. To this day, no one knows who fired this "shot heard 'round the world."

The battle at Lexington ended in minutes, with only a few volleys fired. When the smoke cleared, eight of the badly outnumbered minutemen lay dead, and ten were wounded. The British, with only one soldier wounded, marched on to Concord.

Although Revere had been arrested, the citizens of Concord were warned by another rider, Samuel Prescott. Most of the weapons in Concord had already been hidden, but the few that were left were now concealed. Some of the British troops, frustrated because the stockpile had disappeared, set fire to a few buildings. In **reaction** the minutemen charged forward.

For the skilled colonial marksmen of Concord, the British soldiers made an easy target. They were wearing the British military uniform with its bright red jacket. For some time the colonists had called the British soldiers **Redcoats** because of these jackets. The British were forced to retreat to Boston, suffering many casualties along the way.

Academic
Vocabulary
reaction response

Reading Check
Draw Inferences
Why did the Patriots
need several riders?
Why did they take
different routes?

Battle of Lexington
The Battle of Lexington was the first battle of the Revolutionary War.

Second Continental Congress

King George III had refused to address the concerns listed in the Declaration of Rights. In May 1775 delegates from 12 colonies met again in Philadelphia for the **Second Continental Congress**. This second group of delegates from the colonies was still far from unified, but represented the first attempt at a Republican government in the colonies.

Some of the delegates called for a war, others for peace. Once again they compromised. Although the Congress did not openly revolt, delegates showed their growing dissatisfaction. They sent word to colonial authorities asking for new state constitutions. States set up conventions to write them. They also authorized the Massachusetts militia to become the **Continental army**. This force would soon include soldiers from all colonies and would carry out the fight against Britain. Congress named a Virginian, **George Washington**, to command the army.

As Washington prepared for war, the Congress pursued peace. On July 5 the delegates signed the Olive Branch Petition as a final attempt to restore harmony. King George refused to read it. Instead, he looked for new ways to punish the colonies.

Reading Check
Summarize
What did the Second Continental Congress accomplish?

— BIOGRAPHY —

George Washington
1732–1799

George Washington was a true American, born in the Virginia colony. Although he was a wealthy farmer, he spent most of his life in the military and in politics. In 1775 he served in the Second Continental Congress and was selected to be the commander of the Continental army. Leading the colonial forces to victory in the Revolutionary War, he then helped shape the new government of the United States.

On April 30, 1789, Washington was sworn in as the first president of the United States. As president, he lived in New York City and Philadelphia, the nation's first two capitals. Washington served two terms as president.

Washington inspired Americans and helped to unite them. One of his greatest accomplishments as president was to keep the peace with Britain and France. Upon leaving the presidency in 1796, he urged Americans to avoid becoming politically divided. When he retired, he returned to his plantation home at Mount Vernon, in Virginia.

Draw Conclusions
How might Washington's leadership in the Revolutionary War have prepared him for his role as president?

Early Battles

While the Congress discussed peace, the Massachusetts militia began to fight. Boston was a key city in the early days of the war. Both Patriots and the British fought to hold it.

Bunker Hill Desperate for supplies, leaders in Boston sent Benedict Arnold and a force of 400 men to New York State. Their objective was to attack the British at Fort Ticonderoga. In May 1775 Arnold captured the fort and its large supply of weapons.

Meanwhile, the poorly supplied Patriots kept the British pinned down inside Boston. Although British leaders were trying to form a battle plan, they awoke on June 17 to a stunning sight. The colonial forces had quietly dug in at Breed's Hill, a point overlooking north Boston. The Redcoats would have to cross Boston Harbor and fight their way uphill.

As the British force of 2,400 advanced, 1,600 militia members waited. Low on gunpowder, the commander ordered his troops not to fire "until you see the whites of their eyes." As they climbed the exposed hillside with their heavy packs, the British soldiers were cut down. Twice they retreated. Stepping over the dead and wounded, they returned for a third try. The colonists were now out of ammunition, and eventually they had to retreat.

This famous conflict is now known as the **Battle of Bunker Hill**, although it was actually launched from Breed's Hill. While the Patriots lost, they proved they could take on the Redcoats. For the British, the

Battles for Boston, 1775–1776

Explore ONLINE!

THIRTEEN COLONIES

ATLANTIC OCEAN

Boston

The colonists were forced to retreat from Breed's Hill, but the British suffered heavy losses during the battle.

- American advance
- American retreat
- American troops
- British advance
- British retreat
- British troops
- British victory

0   .5   1 Mile
0   .5   1 Kilometer

Bunker Hill

Breed's Hill

HOWE JUNE 1775

Charles River

Boston

42°22'N

71°06'W

71°04'W

Boston Harbor

General Washington arrived two weeks later and took command of 14,000 troops. In 1776 they drove the British from Boston.

Nook's Hill

Dorchester Heights

Interpret Maps

1. **Place** What geographic advantage did control of Boston provide?

2. **Movement** How did British troops retreat from Boston? How can you tell?

71°02'W   71°00'W   70°

battle was a tragic victory. To win, they had sacrificed about double the number of Patriot soldiers.

Dorchester Heights Shortly after the Battle of Bunker Hill, General Washington arrived in Boston to command the Continental army. Washington knew that he would need heavier guns to drive the British out of Boston, and he knew where to get them—Fort Ticonderoga. Colonel Henry Knox was assigned to transport the captured cannons from Fort Ticonderoga to Boston. He successfully brought the heavy guns over 300 miles of rough terrain in the middle of winter. When Knox delivered the cannons, Washington was ready to regain control of Boston.

On March 4, 1776, Washington moved his army to Dorchester Heights, an area that overlooked Boston from the south. He stationed the cannons and his troops on Nook's Hill overlooking British general William Howe's position. When Howe awoke the next morning and saw the Patriots' well-positioned artillery, he knew he would have to retreat. "The Rebels have done more in one night than my whole army could do in months," Howe declared. On March 7 Howe retreated from Boston to Canada. The birthplace of the rebellion was now in Patriot hands.

Summary and Preview Some colonial leaders became convinced that they could not avoid war with Great Britain. In the next lesson you will read about another step toward war—the writing of the Declaration of Independence.

Reading Check
Draw Inferences
Why was the geography of the Boston area important in forming a battle plan?

Lesson 2 Assessment

Review Ideas, Terms, and People

1. **a. Identify** What was the First Continental Congress?

   b. Make Inferences Why did the First Continental Congress send the Declaration of Rights to the king?

   c. Elaborate Why did King George III refuse to consider the colonists' declaration?

2. **a. Identify** Who warned the colonists of the British advance toward Lexington and Concord?

   b. Analyze Why did the British army march on Lexington and Concord?

   c. Elaborate What is meant by the expression "shot heard 'round the world"?

3. **a. Describe** What was the purpose of the Second Continental Congress?

   b. Draw Conclusions Were the delegates to the Second Continental Congress ready to revolt against George III? Explain.

   c. Evaluate Defend George III's response to the Declaration of Rights and the Olive Branch Petition.

4. **a. Identify** What leader captured Fort Ticonderoga?

   b. Draw Conclusions How was the Continental army able to drive British forces out of Boston?

   c. Evaluate How would you evaluate the performance of the Continental army in the early battles of the war? Explain.

Critical Thinking

5. **Categorize** In this lesson you learned about the early battles of the Revolution. Create a graphic organizer similar to the one below and categorize events in the early days of the Revolution. Some events will be attempts at peace; others will be movement toward war.

Attempts at Peace	Movement toward War

Declaring Independence

The Big Idea

The colonies formally declared their independence from Great Britain.

Main Ideas

- Thomas Paine's *Common Sense* led many colonists to support independence.

- Colonists had to choose sides when independence was declared.

- The Declaration of Independence did not address the rights of all colonists.

Key Terms and People

Common Sense
Thomas Paine
Declaration of Independence
Thomas Jefferson
Loyalists

Reading Check
Support a Point of View Would you have agreed with Thomas Paine? Explain.

If YOU were there . . .

You live on a farm in New York in 1776. The conflicts with the British have torn your family apart. Your father is loyal to King George and wants to remain British. But your mother is a fierce Patriot, and your brother wants to join the Continental army. Your father and others who feel the same way are moving to British-held Canada. Now you must decide what you will do.

Would you go to Canada or support the Patriots?

Paine's *Common Sense*

"[There] is something very absurd in supporting a continent to be perpetually [forever] governed by an island." This plain-spoken argument against British rule over America appeared in *Common Sense*, a 47-page pamphlet that was distributed in Philadelphia in January 1776. *Common Sense* was published anonymously—that is, without the author's name. The author, **Thomas Paine**, had recently emigrated to the colonies from Great Britain. He argued that citizens, not kings and queens, should make laws. At a time when monarchs ruled much of the world, this was a bold idea.

News of the work spread throughout the colonies, eventually selling some 500,000 copies. Paine reached a wide audience by writing as a common person speaking to common people. He used loaded language to influence people's opinions. Loaded language is powerful words and phrases used to persuade people by appealing to their emotions. *Common Sense* changed the way many colonists viewed their king. It made a strong case for economic freedom in the colonies and for the right to military self-defense. It cried out against tyranny—that is, the abuse of government power. Thomas Paine's words rang out in his time, and they have echoed throughout American history.

In *Common Sense,* Thomas Paine argued that the colonies should claim their independence.

Independence Is Declared

Many colonists agreed with Paine. In April 1776 more than 90 percent of adult males in New Hampshire signed a document called the Association Test. Signers of this document swore to take up arms and resist British rule. Among the signers was Wentworth Cheswell, an African American teacher and government leader.

In June 1776 the Second Continental Congress formed a committee to write a document declaring the colonies' independence. A committee also created a seal for the new country with the Latin motto "*E pluribus unum*" or "out of many, one." This motto recognized the new union of states.

A New Philosophy of Government The **Declaration of Independence** formally announced the colonies' break from Great Britain. In the Preamble, **Thomas Jefferson**, the document's main author, stated why the members of the Continental Congress believed the colonies had the right to become a free nation. The Declaration of Independence expressed three main ideas. First, Jefferson argued that all people possess unalienable rights, including the rights of "life, liberty, and the pursuit of happiness." Jefferson's eloquent argument reflected the English Bill of Rights of 1689 and the ideas of philosopher John Locke and English lawyer William Blackstone about natural rights.

Next, Jefferson asserted that King George III had violated the colonists' rights by taxing them without their consent. Jefferson accused the king of passing unfair laws and interfering with colonial governments. Jefferson also believed that stationing a large British army within the colonies was a burden.

Third, Jefferson stated that the colonies had the right to break from Britain. Influenced by the Enlightenment ideal of the social contract that came from philosophers such as John Locke, Jefferson maintained that governments and rulers must protect the rights of citizens. In exchange, the people agree to be governed. Jefferson argued that King George III had broken the social contract.

On July 4, 1776, the Continental Congress approved the Declaration of Independence. This act broke all ties to the British crown. The United States of America was born. Today, the key principles of the Declaration of Independence are part of the unifying ideas of American democracy.

Choosing Sides The signing of the Declaration made the rebellion a full-scale revolt against Britain. Those who supported it would be considered traitors. Colonists who chose to side with the British were known as **Loyalists**—often called Tories. Historians estimate that 40 to 45 percent of Americans were Patriots, while 20 to 30 percent were Loyalists. The rest were neutral. In every colony there were more Patriots than Loyalists.

Because of persecution by Patriots, more than 50,000 Loyalists fled the colonies during the Revolution. Most went to Canada, where Britain allowed them more self-rule after the Revolution. In doing so, they abandoned their homes and property. Divided allegiances tore apart families and friendships—even Benjamin Franklin became separated from his

Patriot Benjamin Franklin was a printer, author, scientist, inventor, and musician. He would soon become one of America's founders.

Choosing Sides

When Ben Franklin's son William was a child, he helped his father experiment with lightning. But by the time William had grown and the Revolution started, the two men viewed the conflict differently. They exchanged letters on the subject.

In a letter to his father, William Franklin expressed his opinion that all British laws governing the American colonies should be obeyed unless legal action was taken to repeal them. He also said it was the responsibility of executive members of government to enforce these laws. Benjamin Franklin had a very different opinion about the laws that the British Parliament made for the colonies.

"I am indeed of the opinion, that the parliament has no right to make any law whatever, binding on the colonies . . . I know your sentiments differ from mine on these subjects. You are a thorough government man, which I do not wonder at, nor do I aim at converting you. I only wish you to act uprightly and steadily."

—Benjamin Franklin, quoted in *The Private Correspondence of Benjamin Franklin*

Analyze Historical Sources
How did the two men view the British government differently?

Loyalist son William. Benjamin Franklin wrote about his political beliefs and his scientific experiments in his *Autobiography*, which was first published in 1791.

Native Americans were at first encouraged by both sides to remain neutral. By the summer of 1776, however, both Patriots and the British were aggressively recruiting Indian fighters. Many Native Americans, particularly in the South, sided with the British because the British promised to give them guns and other European goods if they agreed to help them. In northern New York, four of the six Iroquois nations fought for the British. However, the Oneida and Tuscarora helped the Patriots, even delivering food to the soldiers at Valley Forge. Other Native American groups stayed out of the fighting.

Reading Check
Draw Conclusions
Why would Native Americans have lost out no matter who won the war?

Unfinished Business

Today we recognize that the Declaration of Independence excluded many colonists. While it declared that "all men are created equal," the document failed to mention women, enslaved Africans, or Native Americans. The rights of these minorities would be subject to the rule of the majority.

Signing the Declaration of Independence
The Declaration of Independence was adopted on July 4, 1776. This painting shows 47 of the 56 signers of the document. The man sitting on the right is John Hancock, who was the president of the Second Continental Congress. He is accepting the Declaration from the committee that wrote it.

How realistic do you think this painting is?

1 John Adams	5 Benjamin Franklin
2 Roger Sherman	6 Charles Thomson
3 Robert Livingston	7 John Hancock
4 Thomas Jefferson	

Women Although many colonial women were Patriots, the Declaration of Independence did not address their rights. At least one delegate's wife, Abigail Adams, tried to influence her husband, John Adams, to include women's rights in the Declaration. In a failed effort, she expressed her concerns:

> "Remember the Ladies, and be more generous and favorable to them than your ancestors. Do not put such unlimited power into the hands of the Husbands . . . If particular care and attention is not paid to the Ladies we are and will not hold ourselves bound by Laws in which we have no voice, or Representation."
>
> —Abigail Adams, from a letter from Abigail Adams to John Adams

African Americans and Native Americans The Declaration did not recognize the rights of enslaved Africans, either. The authors had compared life under British rule to living as an enslaved people. The obvious question arose: Why did any form of slavery exist in a land that valued personal freedom? Even Thomas Jefferson, the main author of the Declaration, was a slaveholder.

In July 1776 slavery was legal in all the colonies. By the 1780s the New England colonies were taking steps to end slavery. Even so, the conflict over slavery continued long after the Revolutionary War.

The Declaration of Independence also did not address the rights of Native Americans to life, liberty, or property. Despite the Proclamation of 1763, American colonists had been quietly settling on lands that belonged to Native Americans. This tendency to disregard the rights of Native Americans would develop into a pattern after the colonists won their independence from Great Britain.

Reading Check
Find Main Ideas
What groups were unrepresented in the Declaration of Independence?

Summary and Preview In 1776 the colonists declared their independence. To achieve their goal, however, they would have to win a war against the British army. In the next lesson you will learn about some of the battles of the Revolutionary War. For a time, it seemed as if the British would defeat the colonists.

Lesson 3 Assessment

Review Ideas, Terms, and People

1. **a. Identify** Who was Thomas Paine?

   b. Make Inferences Why do you think Thomas Paine originally published *Common Sense* anonymously?

   c. Elaborate Do you think that most colonists would have supported independence from Britain without Thomas Paine's publication of *Common Sense*? Explain.

2. **a. Identify** What two sides emerged in response to the Declaration of Independence? What did each side favor?

   b. Explain What arguments did the authors of the Declaration of Independence give for declaring the colonies free from British control?

   c. Predict How might some groups use the Declaration of Independence in the future to gain rights?

3. **a. Identify** Who urged her husband to "remember the ladies"?

   b. Make Inferences Why did the authors of the Declaration of Independence fail to address the rights of women, African Americans, and Native Americans in the document?

Critical Thinking

4. **Evaluate** Think about the main ideas expressed in the Declaration of Independence. In what ways are these ideas important in today's world?

5. **Compare and Contrast** Create a chart that compares the points of view of Patriots and Loyalists.

6. **Analyze** In this lesson you learned about the Declaration of Independence. Create a graphic organizer like the one below and identify three results of the Declaration of Independence.

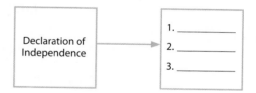

Declaration of Independence → 1. _____ 2. _____ 3. _____

The Declaration of Independence

EXPLORE THE DOCUMENT

Thomas Jefferson wrote the first draft of the Declaration in a little more than two weeks. *How is the Declaration's idea about why governments are formed still important to our country today?*

Vocabulary

[1] **impel** force

[2] **endowed** provided

[3] **usurpations** wrongful seizures of power

[4] **evinces** clearly displays

[5] **despotism** unlimited power

[6] **tyranny** oppressive power exerted by a government or ruler

[7] **candid** fair

[8] **relinquish** release, yield

EXPLORE THE DOCUMENT

Here the Declaration lists the charges that the colonists had against King George III. *How does the language in the list appeal to people's emotions?*

In Congress, July 4, 1776
The unanimous Declaration of the thirteen united States of America,

When in the Course of human events, it becomes necessary for one people to dissolve the political bands which have connected them with another, and to assume among the Powers of the earth, the separate and equal station to which the Laws of Nature and of Nature's God entitle them, a decent respect to the opinions of mankind requires that they should declare the causes which **impel**[1] them to the separation.

We hold these truths to be self-evident, that all men are created equal, that they are **endowed**[2] by their Creator with certain unalienable Rights, that among these are Life, Liberty, and the pursuit of Happiness. That to secure these rights, Governments are instituted among Men, deriving their just powers from the consent of the governed, That whenever any Form of Government becomes destructive of these ends, it is the Right of the People to alter or to abolish it, and to institute new Government, laying its foundation on such principles and organizing its powers in such form, as to them shall seem most likely to effect their Safety and Happiness. Prudence, indeed, will dictate that Governments long established should not be changed for light and transient causes; and accordingly all experience hath shown, that mankind are more disposed to suffer, while evils are sufferable, than to right themselves by abolishing the forms to which they are accustomed. But when a long train of abuses and **usurpations**[3], pursuing invariably the same Object **evinces**[4] a design to reduce them under absolute **Despotism**[5], it is their right, it is their duty, to throw off such Government, and to provide new Guards for their future security.—Such has been the patient sufferance of these Colonies; and such is now the necessity which constrains them to alter their former Systems of Government. The history of the present King of Great Britain is a history of repeated injuries and usurpations, all having in direct object the establishment of an absolute **Tyranny**[6] over these States. To prove this, let Facts be submitted to a **candid**[7] world.

He has refused his Assent to Laws, the most wholesome and necessary for the public good.

He has forbidden his Governors to pass Laws of immediate and pressing importance, unless suspended in their operation till his Assent should be obtained; and when so suspended, he has utterly neglected to attend to them.

He has refused to pass other Laws for the accommodation of large districts of people, unless those people would **relinquish**[8] the right of

Vocabulary

[9] **inestimable**
priceless

[10] **formidable**
causing dread

[11] **annihilation**
destruction

[12] **convulsions**
violent disturbances

[13] **naturalization
of foreigners** the
process by which
foreign-born persons
become citizens

[14] **appropriations of
lands** setting aside
land for settlement

[15] **tenure** term

[16] **a multitude of**
many

Representation in the Legislature, a right **inestimable**[9] to them and **formidable**[10] to tyrants only.

He has called together legislative bodies at places unusual, uncomfortable, and distant from the depository of their Public Records, for the sole purpose of fatiguing them into compliance with his measures.

He has dissolved Representative Houses repeatedly, for opposing with manly firmness his invasions on the rights of the people.

He has refused for a long time, after such dissolutions, to cause others to be elected; whereby the Legislative Powers, incapable of **Annihilation**[11], have returned to the People at large for their exercise; the State remaining in the mean time exposed to all the dangers of invasion from without, and **convulsions**[12] within.

He has endeavored to prevent the population of these States; for that purpose obstructing the Laws of **Naturalization of Foreigners**[13]; refusing to pass others to encourage their migration hither, and raising the conditions of new **Appropriations of Lands**[14].

He has obstructed the Administration of Justice, by refusing his Assent to Laws for establishing Judiciary Powers.

He has made Judges dependent on his Will alone, for the **tenure**[15] of their offices, and the amount and payment of their salaries.

He has erected **a multitude of**[16] New Offices, and sent hither swarms of Officers to harass our people, and eat out their substance.

He has kept among us, in times of peace, Standing Armies without the Consent of our legislature.

He has affected to render the Military independent of and superior to the Civil Power.

Mum Bett, a Massachusetts slave, believed that the words "all men are created equal" should apply to her and other enslaved Africans. She successfully sued for her freedom in 1781.

[17] **quartering** lodging, housing

[18] **arbitrary** not based on law

[19] **render** make

[20] **abdicated** given up

[21] **foreign mercenaies** soldiers hired to fight for a country not their own

[22] **perfidy** violation of trust

[23] **insurrections** rebellions

[24] **petitioned for redress** asked formally for a correction of wrongs

[25] **unwarrantable jurisdiction** unjustified authority

[26] **magnanimity** generous spirit

[27] **conjured** urgently called upon

EXPLORE THE DOCUMENT
Here the Declaration calls the king a tyrant. *What do you think* tyrant *means in this passage?*

He has combined with others to subject us to a jurisdiction foreign to our constitution, and unacknowledged by our laws; giving his Assent to their Acts of pretended legislation:

For **quartering**[17] large bodies of armed troops among us:

For protecting them, by a mock Trial, from Punishment for any Murders which they should commit on the Inhabitants of these States:

For cutting off our Trade with all parts of the world:

For imposing taxes on us without our Consent:

For depriving us in many cases, of the benefits of Trial by Jury:

For transporting us beyond Seas to be tried for pretended offences:

For abolishing the free System of English Laws in a neighboring Province, establishing therein an **Arbitrary**[18] government, and enlarging its Boundaries so as to **render**[19] it at once an example and fit instrument for introducing the same absolute rule into these Colonies:

For taking away our Charters, abolishing our most valuable Laws, and altering fundamentally the Forms of our Governments:

For suspending our own Legislature, and declaring themselves invested with Power to legislate for us in all cases whatsoever.

He has **abdicated**[20] Government here, by declaring us out of his Protection and waging War against us.

He has plundered our seas, ravaged our Coasts, burnt our towns, and destroyed the lives of our people.

He is at this time transporting large armies of **foreign mercenaries**[21] to complete the works of death, desolation and tyranny, already begun with circumstances of Cruelty & **perfidy**[22] scarcely paralleled in the most barbarous ages, and totally unworthy the Head of a civilized nation.

He has constrained our fellow Citizens taken Captive on the high Seas to bear Arms against their Country, to become the executioners of their friends and Brethren, or to fall themselves by their Hands.

He has excited domestic **insurrections**[23] amongst us, and has endeavored to bring on the inhabitants of our frontiers, the merciless Indian Savages, whose known rule of warfare, is an undistinguished destruction of all ages, sexes and conditions.

In every stage of these Oppressions We have **Petitioned for Redress**[24] in the most humble terms: Our repeated Petitions have been answered only by repeated injury. A Prince, whose character is thus marked by every act which may define a Tyrant, is unfit to be the ruler of a free People.

Nor have We been wanting in attention to our British brethren. We have warned them from time to time of attempts by their legislature to extend an **unwarrantable jurisdiction**[25] over us. We have reminded them of the circumstances of our emigration and settlement here. We have appealed to their native justice and **magnanimity**[26], and we have **conjured**[27] them by the ties of our common kindred to disavow these

Vocabulary

[28] **consanguinity**
common ancestry

[29] **acquiesce**
consent to

[30] **rectitude**
rightness

EXPLORE THE DOCUMENT
Here is where the document declares the independence of the colonies. *Whose authority does the Congress use to declare independence?*

EXPLORE THE DOCUMENT
The Congress adopted the final draft of the Declaration of Independence on July 4, 1776. A formal copy, written on parchment paper, was signed on August 2, 1776. *From whom did the Declaration's signers receive their authority to declare independence?*

EXPLORE THE DOCUMENT
The following is part of a passage that the Congress removed from Jefferson's original draft: "He has waged cruel war against human nature itself, violating its most sacred rights of life and liberty in the persons of a distant people who never offended him, captivating and carrying them into slavery in another hemisphere, or to incur miserable death in their transportation thither." *Why do you think the Congress deleted this passage?*

usurpations, which, would inevitably interrupt our connections and correspondence. They too have been deaf to the voice of justice and of **consanguinity**[28]. We must, therefore, **acquiesce**[29] in the necessity, which denounces our Separation, and hold them, as we hold the rest of mankind, Enemies in War, in Peace Friends.

We, therefore, the Representatives of the united States of America, in General Congress, Assembled, appealing to the Supreme Judge of the world for the **rectitude**[30] of our intentions, do, in the Name, and by Authority of the good People of these Colonies, solemnly publish and declare, That these United Colonies are, and of Right ought to be Free and Independent States; that they are Absolved from all Allegiance to the British Crown, and that all political connection between them and the State of Great Britain, is and ought to be totally dissolved; and that as Free and Independent States, they have full Power to levy War, conclude Peace, contract Alliances, establish Commerce, and to do all other Acts and Things which Independent States may of right do. And for the support of this Declaration, with a firm reliance on the Protection of Divine Providence, we mutually pledge to each other our Lives, our Fortunes and our sacred Honor.

John Hancock	Benjamin Harrison	Lewis Morris
Button Gwinnett	Thomas Nelson, Jr.	Richard Stockton
Lyman Hall	Francis Lightfoot Lee	John Witherspoon
George Walton	Carter Braxton	Francis Hopkinson
William Hooper	Robert Morris	John Hart
Joseph Hewes	Benjamin Rush	Abraham Clark
John Penn	Benjamin Franklin	Josiah Bartlett
Edward Rutledge	John Morton	William Whipple
Thomas Heyward, Jr.	George Clymer	Samuel Adams
Thomas Lynch, Jr.	James Smith	John Adams
Arthur Middleton	George Taylor	Robert Treat Paine
Samuel Chase	James Wilson	Elbridge Gerry
William Paca	George Ross	Stephen Hopkins
Thomas Stone	Caesar Rodney	William Ellery
Charles Carroll of Carrollton	George Read	Roger Sherman
George Wythe	Thomas McKean	Samuel Huntington
Richard Henry Lee	William Floyd	William Williams
Thomas Jefferson	Philip Livingston	Oliver Wolcott
	Francis Lewis	Matthew Thornton

The Struggle for Liberty

The Big Idea

Patriot forces faced many obstacles in the war against Britain.

Main Ideas

- Many Americans supported the war effort.
- The Patriots both won and lost battles during the years 1775–1777.
- France and Spain helped the Patriots fight the British.
- The winter at Valley Forge tested the strength of Patriot troops.
- The war continued at sea and in the West.

Key Terms and People

Haym Salomon
mercenaries
Battle of Trenton
Battle of Saratoga
Marquis de Lafayette
Baron Friedrich von Steuben
Bernardo de Gálvez
John Paul Jones
George Rogers Clark

If YOU were there . . .

You are a serving maid at an inn in New York City. British soldiers often stop at the inn for a meal. You sometimes overhear their conversations, though they don't notice that you do. Now a Patriot militia officer has asked you to bring him any information that you hear. You want to help the Patriot cause. Yet, you are worried about what will happen to you if you are caught spying.

Would you agree to spy for the Patriots?

Supporting the War Effort

George Washington's chief task as the Continental army's Commander in Chief was to raise troops. During the war, more than 230,000 soldiers served in the Continental army, and another 145,000 enlisted in local militias. The typical soldier was young, often under the legal age of 16, and had little money or property. The army offered low pay, harsh conditions, and a big chance of becoming a casualty. Yet the Patriots knew they were fighting for their homes and their freedom.

Finding and keeping dedicated soldiers would be a constant challenge throughout the war. In time, the Continental Congress required states to supply soldiers. Men who could afford it often paid others, such as slaves or apprentices, to fight in their places.

One question facing General Washington was whether to recruit African Americans. Many white southerners, particularly wealthy planters, were against the idea, and at first Washington banned African Americans from serving. When the British promised freedom to any enslaved person who fought on their side, however, thousands of African Americans joined the British army. In response, the Continental army began to recruit free African Americans to fight on their side.

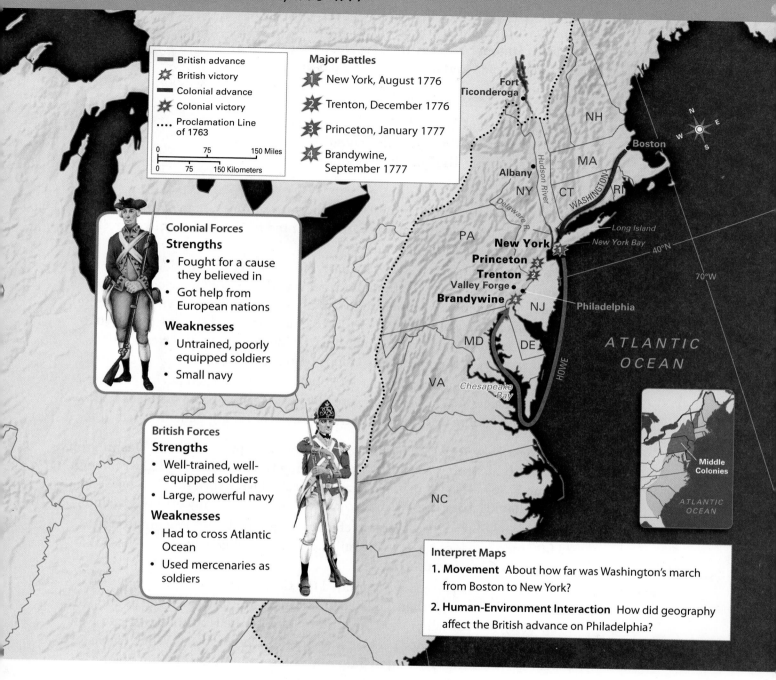

Battles in the Middle Colonies, 1776–1777

Explore ONLINE!

Legend
- British advance
- ✴ British victory
- Colonial advance
- ✴ Colonial victory
- •••• Proclamation Line of 1763

0 75 150 Miles
0 75 150 Kilometers

Major Battles
1. New York, August 1776
2. Trenton, December 1776
3. Princeton, January 1777
4. Brandywine, September 1777

Colonial Forces

Strengths
- Fought for a cause they believed in
- Got help from European nations

Weaknesses
- Untrained, poorly equipped soldiers
- Small navy

British Forces

Strengths
- Well-trained, well-equipped soldiers
- Large, powerful navy

Weaknesses
- Had to cross Atlantic Ocean
- Used mercenaries as soldiers

Fort Ticonderoga · NH · Boston · MA · Albany · NY · Hudson River · CT · RI · WASHINGTON · Delaware R. · PA · New York · Princeton · Trenton · Long Island · New York Bay · 40°N · 70°W · Valley Forge · Brandywine · NJ · Philadelphia · MD · DE · HOWE · VA · Chesapeake Bay · ATLANTIC OCEAN · NC

Middle Colonies · ATLANTIC OCEAN

Interpret Maps
1. **Movement** About how far was Washington's march from Boston to New York?
2. **Human-Environment Interaction** How did geography affect the British advance on Philadelphia?

While men served as soldiers, many women ran farms and businesses. Others helped the Continental army by raising money for supplies or making clothing. Women served as messengers, nurses, and spies. A man from Massachusetts noted:

"At every house Women and children [are] making Cartridges, running Bullets . . . and at the same time animating [encouraging] their Husbands and Sons to fight."

—Anonymous, quoted in *The Literary Diary of Ezra Stiles*

Reading Check
Summarize How
did various groups
contribute to the
war effort?

Perhaps the best-known woman to fight in the war was Mary Ludwig Hays. She was called Molly Pitcher because she brought water to the troops. When her husband was wounded in a 1778 battle, she took his place loading cannons. Another woman, Deborah Sampson, dressed as a man and fought in several battles.

Mary Ludwig Hays, better known as Molly Pitcher, loaded cannons during the Battle of Monmouth after her husband fell in battle.

Defeats and Victories

As the Revolution gathered steam, it became more deadly. At first the Continental army suffered a number of defeats. In time, though, the Patriots' patience began to pay off.

Canada In part because the army was short on supplies, many Patriot leaders favored fighting a defensive war. Others wanted to invade British-controlled Canada and make it the "14th colony."

Patriot troops led by General Richard Montgomery captured Montreal in November 1775. The next major target was the city of Quebec. Benedict Arnold, now a general, led his troops north on a remarkable trek through the rough backcountry of Maine. He reached Quebec around the same time that Montreal fell to Montgomery. Since his first attempt to take the city failed, Arnold waited for Montgomery's troops to join his.

Taking an immense chance, the combined armies attacked during a fierce blizzard on New Year's Eve. They were quickly defeated. The Americans had suffered a crushing loss, and the Patriots' hopes of taking Canada faded.

New York New York City became the next battleground. General Washington had moved his troops to New York, expecting the British arrival. Sure enough, in June 1776, a fleet of British ships approached New York Bay. Led by General William Howe, the British forced the Continental army off Long Island.

Howe's 32,000 soldiers were much better equipped than Washington's 23,000 men, most of whom were militia. The Patriot general had to use all of his skills just to save his army.

In a series of battles, Howe pounded the Continental army, forcing it to retreat farther and farther. The Redcoats captured Patriots as well as supplies. Eventually, the British pushed Washington across the Hudson River into New Jersey. Howe's revenge for his defeat at Boston was complete. When Howe captured New York City, **Haym Salomon**, a recent immigrant from Poland, stayed there and spied for the Patriots. He later used his skills as a banker to help fund the American Revolution.

During the New York campaigns, a young Connecticut officer named Nathan Hale went behind British lines to get secret information. Seized by the British with documents hidden in the soles of his shoes, Hale was ordered to be hanged. Before his execution, he is said to have declared, "I regret that I have but one life to lose for my country."

After the British gained control of New York City and Long Island, some Patriots left those areas and the Loyalist population grew. Many of these Loyalists fled from other colonies. In the inland part of the New York colony, however, the Patriots still greatly outnumbered the Loyalists.

check
word
pass

Crossing the Delaware

George Washington and his troops crossed the partially frozen Delaware River on the night of December 25, 1776. This daring act led to a key Patriot victory at the Battle of Trenton. German American artist Emanuel Leutze created this famous painting in 1851. A version of Leutze's *Washington Crossing the Delaware* hangs in the Metropolitan Museum of Art in New York City.

What feelings do you think Leutze wanted to inspire with this painting?

New Jersey In November 1776 the tattered Continental army was on the run. Washington's remaining 6,000 men were tired and discouraged. The one-year contract for many of them would end on December 31. Who would reenlist in this losing army, and who would replace the soldiers who left? Washington's army was in danger of vanishing.

Thinking the rebellion would end soon, Howe left New Jersey in the hands of soldiers from the German state of Hesse. The Hessians were **mercenaries**—foreign soldiers who fought not out of loyalty, but for pay.

On December 7 Washington retreated across the Delaware River into Pennsylvania. Even with 2,000 fresh troops, the Patriots were near the end. "These are the times that try men's souls," wrote Thomas Paine in *The American Crisis*, a series of pamphlets he began publishing in late 1776. Paine wrote *The American Crisis* to inspire the Patriots. He used loaded language—words that appeal to people's emotions—to help strengthen the American soldiers' morale.

Without a convincing victory, Washington knew he would lose his army. He decided to take a big chance and go on the offensive. The Americans would attack the Hessians at Trenton, New Jersey.

On Christmas night, 1776, with a winter storm lashing about them, Washington and 2,400 soldiers silently rowed across the ice-clogged Delaware River. As morning broke, the men, short on supplies and many with no shoes, marched through the snow to reach the enemy camp at Trenton.

The Hessians, having celebrated the holiday the night before, were fast asleep when the Patriots sprang upon them. The **Battle of Trenton** was an important Patriot victory. American soldiers took more than 900 prisoners.

British general Charles Cornwallis rushed to stop Washington as he marched northeast to Princeton. On the night of January 2, 1777, the Patriots left their campfires burning, then slipped into the darkness and circled behind the British troops. In the morning, Washington attacked. A local resident witnessed it:

> "The battle was plainly seen from our door . . . and the guns went off so quick and many together that they could not be numbered . . . Almost as soon as the firing was over, our house was filled and surrounded with General Washington's men."
>
> —Anonymous, quoted in *A Brief Narrative of the Ravages of the British and Hessians at Princeton*

As Washington watched the Redcoats flee Princeton, he cheered, "It is a fine fox chase, my boys!" Now, new soldiers joined the chase. Others reenlisted. The army—and the Revolution—was saved.

Saratoga The two quick defeats stung the British. In the spring of 1777, they wanted a victory.

British general John Burgoyne decided to push through New York State and cut off New England from the other colonies. The **strategy** required perfect timing. According to the plan, Burgoyne's army would invade from Canada, recapture Fort Ticonderoga, and sweep south to Albany. General Howe, in New York City, would sail up the Hudson River to meet him, strangling New England.

Indeed, Burgoyne took Ticonderoga in early July and headed toward Albany. Here, the timing went wrong for the British. Unknown to Burgoyne, Howe had left New York, sailed up the Chesapeake Bay, and captured Philadelphia. Delegates to the Continental Congress were forced to flee.

Meanwhile, Burgoyne's army was bogged down in thick forests. The Patriots had chopped down large trees and dammed rivers to create obstacles. All along the route, the militia swarmed out of nowhere to attack the Redcoats. As Burgoyne neared Saratoga, New York, he found himself surrounded. On October 17, 1777, he was forced to surrender his entire army to General Horatio Gates.

The **Battle of Saratoga** in New York was the turning point of the Revolutionary War. It was the greatest victory yet for the American forces. Morale soared. Patriot James Thacher wrote, "This event will make one of the most brilliant pages of American history."

Battle of Saratoga

Legend:
→ British advance
✶ British victory
→ Patriot advance
✶ Patriot victory

0 50 100 Miles
0 50 100 Kilometers

QUÉBEC
Montréal
BURGOYNE
Fort Ticonderoga
NH
Saratoga
NY Albany
MA
RI
CT
Hudson River
PA
NJ

Interpret Maps

1. Location From which city did the Patriot troops march into battle?

2. Movement In which direction did the British soldiers march to meet the Patriots?

Help from Europe

The French and Indian War had drastically changed the balance of power in North America. The French and Spanish had lost a large expanse of valuable land to the British. Both countries were delighted to see their powerful rival experiencing trouble in its American colonies.

The victory at Saratoga gave the Patriots something they had been desperately seeking: foreign help. Not surprisingly, it came from Britain's enemies, France and Spain. Even Britain's old ally, Holland, joined the fight on the side of the Patriots.

Two Remarkable Europeans "The welfare of America is closely bound up with the welfare of mankind," declared a wealthy young Frenchman, the **Marquis de Lafayette**. Inspired by the ideas of the Revolution, Lafayette bought his own ship and arrived in America in 1777. He brought with him a group of well-trained soldiers and volunteered to serve in the Continental army himself without pay.

Lafayette spoke little English and had never seen battle. However, he quickly became a skillful commander, earning the title of major general. Lafayette led 2,000 Patriots to successfully pursue 6,000 Redcoats throughout Virginia during 1780–81. He gave $200,000 of his own money to support the Revolution and wrote many letters home to powerful friends and family asking their aid for the Patriot cause.

The Patriots Gain Ground

1776 — 1780

December 26, 1776
Patriots win the Battle of Trenton.

January 3, 1777
Patriots win the Battle of Princeton.

July 27, 1777 ∧
Marquis de Lafayette arrives in Philadelphia to offer his assistance to the Patriot cause.

October 17, 1777
Patriots win the Battle of Saratoga.

February 1778
Baron Friedrich von Steuben begins training Patriot soldiers.

May 1778
France joins the Patriots in an alliance.

June 21, 1779
Spain declares war against Britain.

March 14, 1780 ∧
Bernardo de Gálvez, the governor of Spanish Louisiana, captures the British stronghold of Fort Charlotte at present-day Mobile, Alabama.

Interpret Timelines
Which nations joined the Patriot cause?

In February 1778 another European came to serve heroically under Washington. **Baron Friedrich von Steuben**, an experienced military officer from Prussia, led with a combination of respect and fear. He started training the American troops, focusing on basic military drills. Soon he turned the Continental army into a finely tuned fighting force. A historian called von Steuben's feat "perhaps the most remarkable achievement in rapid military training in the history of the world."

Help from France Benjamin Franklin, a skilled and experienced diplomat, had gone to France in 1776 to ask for support from King Louis XVI. Finally, the Battle of Saratoga in 1777 persuaded the French king that the colonists could win the war. Not until then did the king agree to an alliance with the Patriots.

In May 1778 the Continental Congress ratified the treaty of support with France. The French had been helping the Patriots all along with supplies and ammunition. After the treaty became official, the French increased the level of supplies and agreed to provide soldiers and ships. The French naval support would be a key strategic ingredient in defeating the British.

Help from Spain Spain, also a bitter enemy of Britain, joined the war in 1779. **Bernardo de Gálvez**, the governor of Spanish Louisiana, became a key ally to the Patriots. Gálvez gathered a small army of Spanish soldiers, French Americans, colonists, and Native Americans. Together they made their way east from Louisiana. Gálvez seized British posts all the way to Pensacola, Florida.

Reading Check
Summarize How did France and Spain help the Patriots?

Winter at Valley Forge

The entry of France and Spain into the war came at a crucial moment. The Continental army was running very low on food and clothing. In December 1777 Washington settled his 12,000 men at Valley Forge, north of Philadelphia.

To this day, the name of Valley Forge brings to mind suffering—and courage. Yet no battles took place here. The only enemy was the brutal winter of 1777–78.

Washington's men lacked even the most basic protections against shin-deep snows. In spite of the general's repeated requests for supplies, conflicts over funding between state authorities and Congress kept supplies from coming. Washington wrote in a letter:

> "To see men without clothes . . . without blankets to lie upon, without shoes . . . without a house or hut to cover them until those could be built, and submitting without a murmur, is a proof of patience and obedience which, in my opinion, can scarcely be paralleled [matched]."
>
> —George Washington, from *The Writings of George Washington,*
> edited by Worthington Chauncey Ford

As winter roared in, soldiers quickly built crude shelters that offered little protection against the weather. Some soldiers had no shirts. Others had marched the shoes off their feet. At their guard posts, they stood on their hats to keep their feet from touching the freezing ground. One soldier wrote that getting food was the "business that usually employed us."

Historical Source

Valley Forge

A surgeon at Valley Forge, Albigence Waldo kept a journal of what he saw during the winter of 1777–78.

> "The Army which has been surprisingly healthy hitherto, now begins to grow sickly from the continued fatigues they have suffered this Campaign. Yet they still show a spirit of Alacrity [cheerful readiness] and Contentment not to be expected from so young Troops. I am Sick—discontented—and out of humour. Poor food—hard lodging—Cold Weather—fatigue—Nasty Cloaths [clothes]—nasty Cookery . . . smoke and Cold—hunger and filthyness—A pox on my bad luck."
>
> —Albigence Waldo, from
> *The Pennsylvania Magazine
> of History and Biography,* Volume 21

Analyze Historical Sources
Why did Waldo seem surprised by the soldiers' attitude?

During that terrible winter at Valley Forge, some 2,000 soldiers died of disease and malnutrition. Amazingly, those who survived not only stayed—they drilled and marched to the orders of Baron von Steuben and became better soldiers.

While the soldiers suffered through the winter at Valley Forge, the British lived a life of luxury in Philadelphia. Most of the Patriots had fled the city, leaving only Loyalists and British soldiers. Together they enjoyed the city's houses, taverns, and theaters, and held parties and balls.

War at Sea and in the West

While some Americans struggled against the British on land in the former colonies, others fought at sea and on the western frontier. Each area posed tough challenges.

War at Sea The entry of the French navy into the war greatly aided the colonists. Many people had thought that the mighty British navy would crush the much smaller American fleet. However, the British failed to use their powerful navy effectively during the war.

In the fall of 1775, the Continental Congress made plans to build four American warships. Soon afterward the Congress formally established the marines and the Continental navy. By adapting merchant vessels, the navy had eight fighting ships ready for combat by February 1776.

That month the tiny American navy launched a major offensive to damage the operating ability of the British fleet located off the Carolina coast. Rather than attack the fleet directly, the Patriots went after the British supply base on Nassau, in the Bahamas.

The American troops seized the main supply fort on the island. They then raised the newly created flag of the American Revolution over Nassau. After that campaign, the American navy focused on seizing British supply ships and weakening Britain's naval forces in the West Indies.

John Paul Jones The Patriots owed much of their success on the seas to naval hero **John Paul Jones**. Jones had once been considered an outlaw. He was born John Paul in Scotland and began working on ships at a young age. After accidentally killing the leader of a mutiny, he fled to America and added Jones to his name.

When the war broke out, Jones volunteered his services to the newly created navy. He quickly established himself as a brave and clever sailor. Considered a pirate by the British, Jones captured many British supply ships. The French greatly admired Jones. When France entered the war in 1778, French leaders presented him with a small fleet of seven vessels to command. He named his flagship *Bonhomme Richard* ("Gentleman Richard") in honor of Benjamin Franklin's *Poor Richard's Almanac*. Among the almanac's stories, jokes, and wise sayings were weather forecasts for the year and other practical scientific information.

One of Jones's most famous victories was the capture of the British warship *Serapis* on September 23, 1779. Early in the battle, the British knocked out the heaviest artillery on the *Bonhomme Richard*. Captain

Reading Check
Find Main Ideas What challenges did the Continental army face at Valley Forge?

On July 27, 1778, French and British fleets fought each other in the Battle of Ushant near the mouth of the English Channel. It was the first major naval battle between the two powers after France formed an alliance with the Patriots.

War in the West, 1778–1779

▶ Explore ONLINE!

THIRTEEN COLONIES

Lake Michigan

Fort Detroit

Lake Erie

BRITISH

Fort Pitt

PA

Wabash River

Vincennes (Ft. Sackville)

CLARK

Ohio River

VA

Cahokia

Kaskaskia

Fort Massac

Mississippi River

APPALACHIAN MOUNTAINS

NC

Tennessee River

British forces
Patriot forces
✷ **Patriot victory**

0   50   100 Miles
0   50   100 Kilometers

Interpret Maps

1. **Movement** How far did the Patriots march to get to Vincennes?

2. **Human-Environment Interaction** Why did military forces follow river routes?

American Revolutionary war hero and frontiersman George Rogers Clark helped defeat British forces in the West.

Richard Pearson of the *Serapis* then called out to Jones, "Has your ship struck [surrendered]?" Jones replied, "I have not yet begun to fight!" The battle continued for more than two hours. Finally, the Americans wore down the British, who surrendered at 10:30 P.M.

The Continental navy used fewer than 100 ships over the course of the war. Yet the British lost more than 200 ships to the small but effective American naval force.

War in the West The lands west of the Appalachian Mountains were controlled by Native American nations. Both the British and the Patriots tried to enlist these groups in their cause.

George Rogers Clark volunteered to lead the western campaign. Clark had been a surveyor along the Ohio and Kentucky rivers. By the time the war broke out, he knew the lands of the Ohio River valley well. Clark created an army from the scattered settlements in the area. One of the best-known groups was the Over Mountain Men, a band of settlers from present-day Tennessee.

Determined to weaken British support systems, Clark targeted trading villages. Following the Ohio River to the Tennessee, Clark's force set out on a 120-mile overland trek to Kaskaskia, in present-day Illinois. The village's leaders learned of the attack and surrendered. Other Patriots took Cahokia without a fight.

In February 1779 Clark launched a surprise attack on Fort Sackville near the town of Vincennes. The attack was unexpected because the nearby Wabash River was icy and flooded. Despite overflowing riverbanks, Clark's force of 150 men endured an 18-day march through freezing water. They also managed to bring enough Patriot flags for an army of hundreds. The flags were displayed near the fort, and the skilled pioneers sustained enough musket fire to indicate a much larger army. Falling for the ruse, the commander of Fort Sackville surrendered.

In general the British were more successful at winning over the Native Americans. But Clark's many campaigns undermined British support in the West.

Summary and Preview The Patriots faced hardships as the war continued. In the next lesson you will see how they finally achieved their goal of independence.

Reading Check
Find Main Ideas
How did Jones and Clark help the Patriots' war effort?

Lesson 4 Assessment

Review Ideas, Terms, and People

1. **a. Identify** What groups supported the Patriot war effort? How did each group contribute?

   b. Analyze Why was it difficult to find and keep soldiers in the Continental army?

2. **a. Describe** What early defeats did the Patriots face?

   b. Elaborate Was it a mistake for the British to use mercenaries to help them fight the war? Why or why not?

   c. Explain How did New Jersey's location play an important role in the American Revolution?

3. **a. Elaborate** Why do you think European nations supported the colonists rather than Great Britain?

   b. Evaluate Do you think that the Patriots would have won the war without help from France and Spain? Why or why not?

4. **a. Describe** What difficulties did the Patriots face at Valley Forge?

   b. Elaborate How might weather conditions affect the outcome of a battle?

5. **a. Identify** Who was John Paul Jones?

   b. Compare In what ways was Jones's naval strategy like that of the Continental army?

Critical Thinking

6. **Draw Conclusions** In this lesson you learned about the war for American independence. Create a chart similar to the one below and identify the region in which major wartime events took place and how the events reflected the Patriots' successes and failures.

Region	Patriot Problems	Patriot Successes

Independence!

The Big Idea

The war spread to the southern colonies, where the British were finally defeated.

Main Ideas

- Patriot forces faced many problems in the war in the South.
- The American Patriots finally defeated the British at the Battle of Yorktown.
- The British and the Americans officially ended the war by signing the Treaty of Paris of 1783.

Key Terms and People

Francis Marion
James Armistead
Comte de Rochambeau
Battle of Yorktown
Treaty of Paris of 1783

If YOU were there . . .

You have grown up on a farm in South Carolina. You know every inch of the woods and marshes around your home. You are too young to join the Continental army, but you have heard stories about a brave group of soldiers who carry out quick raids on the British, then disappear into the woods. These fighters get no pay and live in constant danger.

Would you consider joining the fighters? Why?

War in the South

The war across the ocean was not going the way the British government in London had planned. The northern colonies, with their ragged, scrappy fighters, proved to be tough to tame. So the British switched strategies and set their sights on the South.

The British hoped to find support from the large Loyalist populations living in Georgia, the Carolinas, and Virginia. As they moved across the South, the British also planned to free enslaved Africans and enlist them as British soldiers. Under the leadership of a new commander, General Henry Clinton, the strategy paid off—for a while.

Brutal Fighting The southern war was particularly brutal. Much more than in the North, this phase of the war pitted Americans—Patriots versus Loyalists—against one another in direct combat. The British also destroyed crops, farm animals, and other property as they marched through the South. One British officer, Banastre Tarleton, sowed fear throughout the South by refusing to take prisoners and killing soldiers who tried to surrender.

Georgia, the last colony to join the Revolution, was the first to fall to the British. A force of 3,500 Redcoats easily took Savannah in 1778 and soon put in place a new colonial government.

Britain's next major target was Charleston, South Carolina. In early 1780 General Clinton landed a force of 14,000 troops around the port city. With a minimal cost of about 250 casualties, the British scored one of their biggest victories of the war. The Patriots surrendered Charleston in May, handing over four ships and some 5,400 prisoners.

A Failed Attack and an Important Victory In August 1780 Patriot forces led by Horatio Gates tried to drive the British out of Camden, South Carolina. The attack was poorly executed, however. Gates had only half as many soldiers as he had planned for, and most were tired and hungry. In the heat of battle, many panicked and ran. The Patriot attack quickly fell apart. Of some 4,000 American troops, only about 700 escaped.

General Nathanael Greene arrived to reorganize the army. As he rode through the southern countryside, he was discouraged by the devastation. He later wrote, "I have never witnessed such scenes."

On October 7, 1780, a group of Patriot militias won an important battle against a group of Loyalist militias in what is today York County, South Carolina. It became known as the Battle of Kings Mountain. The victory boosted the Patriots' morale and kept the British from further invading the Carolinas.

Guerrilla Warfare The southern Patriots switched to swift hit-and-run attacks known as guerrilla warfare. No Patriot was better at this style of fighting than **Francis Marion**. He organized Marion's Brigade, a group of guerrilla soldiers.

Marion's Brigade used surprise attacks to disrupt British communication and supply lines. Despite their great efforts, the British could not catch Marion and his men. One frustrated general claimed, "As for this . . . old fox, the devil himself could not catch him." From that point on, Marion was known as the Swamp Fox.

Reading Check Sequence List the events of the war in the South in chronological order.

Swamp Fox

Francis Marion leads his soldiers down a river in South Carolina. Marion built a hideout on one of the river's islands. From there, he would lead lightning-fast raids against British communication and supply lines.

Which figure do you think is Francis Marion? Why?

The British scuttled, or purposely sank, dozens of their ships. This formed a barrier that kept the French ships from coming too close.

Battle of Yorktown

In October 1781 American and French troops surrounded British forces and defeated them in the Battle of Yorktown.

THIRTEEN COLONIES
Yorktown

ATLANTIC OCEAN

American troop positions
French troop positions
British troop positions
British defensive lines

0   0.5   1 Mile
0   0.5   1 Kilometer

Analyze Visuals
Human-Environment Interaction How did American and French forces trap the British at Yorktown?

Battle of Yorktown

In early 1781 the war was going badly for the Patriots. They were low on money to pay soldiers and buy supplies. The help of their foreign allies had not brought the war to a quick end as they had hoped. The British held most of the South, plus Philadelphia and New York City. The Patriots' morale took another blow when Benedict Arnold, one of America's most gifted officers, turned traitor.

Regrouped under Nathanael Greene, the Continental army began harassing British general Charles Cornwallis in the Carolinas. Hoping to stay in communication with the British naval fleet, Cornwallis moved his force of 7,200 men to Yorktown, Virginia. It was a fatal mistake.

An enslaved African named **James Armistead** worked as a spy for the Marquis de Lafayette. The information Armistead collected for Lafayette gave the Continental army an advantage over the British at Yorktown. General Washington saw a chance to trap Cornwallis there. He ordered Lafayette to block Cornwallis's escape by land. Then he combined his 2,500 troops with 4,000 French troops commanded by the **Comte de Rochambeau** (raw-shahn-BOH). Washington led the French-American force on a swift march to Virginia to cut off the other escape routes. The Patriots surrounded Cornwallis with some 16,000 soldiers. Meanwhile, a French naval fleet seized control of the Chesapeake Bay, preventing British ships from rescuing Cornwallis's stranded army.

The siege began. For weeks, the fighting steadily wore down the British defenses. Alexander Hamilton, who later became America's first secretary of the treasury, took part in the Battle of Yorktown. He commanded an infantry battalion under General Washington. In early October, Washington prepared for a major attack on the weakened British troops.

Facing near-certain defeat, on October 19, 1781, Cornwallis sent a drummer and a soldier with a white flag of surrender to Washington's camp. The Patriots took some 8,000 British prisoners—the largest British army in America.

The **Battle of Yorktown** was the last major battle of the American Revolution. Prime Minister Lord North received word of the Yorktown surrender in November. In shock he declared, "It is all over!"

The Treaty of Paris

After Yorktown, only a few small battles took place. Lacking the money to pay for a new army, Great Britain entered into peace talks with America. Benjamin Franklin had a key role in the negotiations.

Reading Check
Draw Conclusions
Why did the victory at Yorktown end the fighting?

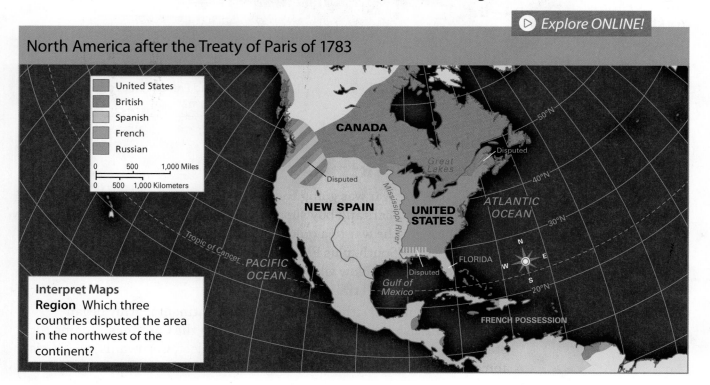

▶ Explore ONLINE!

North America after the Treaty of Paris of 1783

Legend:
- United States
- British
- Spanish
- French
- Russian

0   500   1,000 Miles
0   500   1,000 Kilometers

CANADA
Disputed
Great Lakes
Disputed
NEW SPAIN
Mississippi River
UNITED STATES
ATLANTIC OCEAN
50°N
40°N
30°N
20°N
Tropic of Cancer
PACIFIC OCEAN
Disputed
FLORIDA
Gulf of Mexico
FRENCH POSSESSION

Interpret Maps
Region Which three countries disputed the area in the northwest of the continent?

Sentiments of an American Woman

The Continental army received aid from female Patriots led by Esther DeBerdt Reed and Sarah Franklin Bache, the daughter of Benjamin Franklin. In 1780 these women organized a campaign that raised $300,000 for soldiers' clothing. The following pamphlet, written by the campaign's leaders, announced the campaign. In it, the authors used images of women helping with war efforts of the past to gain support for their cause.

The women declare that they would fight if they were allowed.

The authors list ways in which women have helped fight wars in the past.

In this phrase, the women link themselves to great women rulers of the past.

"On the **commencement**[1] of actual war, the Women of America **manifested**[2] a firm resolution to contribute . . . to the deliverance of their country. Animated by the purest patriotism they are sensible of sorrow at this day, in not offering more than barren wishes for the success of so glorious a Revolution. They aspire to **render**[3] themselves more really useful; and this sentiment is universal from the north to the south of the Thirteen United States. Our ambition is kindled by the fame of those heroines of **antiquity**[4], who . . . have proved to the universe, that . . . if opinion and manners did not forbid us to march to glory by the same paths as the Men, we should at least equal, and sometimes surpass them in our love for the public good. I glory in all that which my sex has done great and **commendable**[5]. I call to mind with enthusiasm and with admiration, all those acts of courage, of constancy and patriotism, which history has transmitted to us. . . ."

"So many famous sieges where the Women have been seen . . . building new walls, digging trenches with their feeble hands, furnishing arms to their defenders, they themselves darting the missile weapons of the enemy, resigning the ornaments of their apparel, and their fortune, to fill the public treasury, and to hasten the deliverance of their country; burying themselves under its ruins; throwing themselves into the flames rather than submit to the disgrace of humiliation before a proud enemy."

"Born for liberty, **disdaining**[6] to bear the irons of a **tyrannic**[7] Government, we associate ourselves . . . [with those rulers] who have extended the empire of liberty, and **contented**[8] to reign by sweetness and justice, have broken the chains of slavery, forged by tyrants."

Analyze Historical Sources
1. What do the writers "call to mind" in asking women to join the Patriot cause?
2. With whom do the writers associate themselves?

[1] commencement start
[2] manifested presented
[3] render make
[4] antiquity ancient times
[5] commendable praiseworthy
[6] disdaining refusing
[7] tyrannic unjust
[8] contented determined

Delegates took more than two years to come to a peace agreement. In the **Treaty of Paris of 1783**, Great Britain recognized the independence of the United States. The treaty also set America's borders. A separate treaty between Britain and Spain returned Florida to the Spanish. British leaders also accepted American rights to settle and trade west of the original thirteen colonies.

At the war's end, many members of the Iroquois nations who had fought on the side of the British moved to Canada. Those who did not were ordered to live on reservations in the northern, central, and western parts of New York. Otherwise, when the terms of the Treaty of Paris were negotiated, the concerns of Native Americans were largely ignored.

Now that the war was over, Patriot soldiers returned to their homes and families. The courage of soldiers and civilians had made America's victory possible. As they returned home, George Washington thanked his troops for their devotion. "I . . . wish that your latter days be as prosperous as your former ones have been glorious."

Summary and Preview Americans won their independence from Great Britain in 1783. In the next module you will learn how the new nation formed its first government.

Reading Check
Summarize
Explain how the War for Independence finally came to an end.

Lesson 5 Assessment

Review Ideas, Terms, and People

1. a. **Describe** What problems did the Patriots experience in the war in the South?
   b. **Analyze** What advantages did the southern Patriots have over the British in the South?
2. a. **Describe** What was the Patriots' strategy for defeating the British at Yorktown?
   b. **Elaborate** Why do you think General Cornwallis decided to surrender at the Battle of Yorktown?
3. a. **Identify** Who helped to negotiate the Treaty of Paris of 1783 for the Americans?
   b. **Predict** How might relations between Great Britain and its former colonies be affected by the war?

Critical Thinking

4. **Evaluate** In this lesson you learned about the events that led to the end of the war. Create a graphic organizer like the one below and then identify and describe the most important event in turning the war in the Patriots' favor.

Event	Importance to end of war

Social Studies Skills

Understand Historical Interpretation

Define the Skill

Historical interpretations are ways of explaining the past. They are based on what is known about the people, ideas, and actions that make up history. Two historians can look at the same set of facts about a person or event of the past and see things in different ways. Their explanations of the person or event, and the conclusions they reach, can be very different. The ability to recognize, understand, and evaluate historical interpretations is a valuable skill in the study of history.

Learn the Skill

When people study the past, they decide which facts are the most important in explaining why something happened. One person may believe certain facts to be important, while other people may believe other facts are more important. Therefore, their explanation of the topic, and the conclusions they draw about it, may not be the same. In addition, if new facts are uncovered about the topic, still more interpretations of it may result.

Asking the following questions will help you to understand and evaluate historical interpretations.

1. What is the main idea in the way the topic is explained? What conclusions are reached? Be aware that these may not be directly stated but only hinted at in the information provided.

2. On what facts has the writer or speaker relied? Do these facts seem to support his or her explanation and conclusions?

3. Is there important information about the topic that the writer or speaker has dismissed or ignored? If so, you should suspect that the interpretation may be inaccurate or deliberately slanted to prove a particular point of view.

Just because interpretations differ, one is not necessarily "right" and others "wrong." As long as a person considers all the evidence and draws conclusions based on a fair evaluation of that evidence, his or her interpretation is probably acceptable.

Remember, however, that trained historians let the facts *lead* them to conclusions. People who *start* with a conclusion, select only facts that support it, and ignore opposing evidence produce interpretations that have little value for understanding history.

Practice the Skill

Two widely accepted interpretations exist of the causes of the American Revolution. One holds that the Revolution was a struggle by freedom-loving Americans to be free from harsh British rule. In this view the colonists were used to self-government and resisted British efforts to take rights they claimed. The other interpretation is that a clash of economic interests caused the Revolution. In this view, the war resulted from a struggle between British and colonial merchants over control of America's economy.

Review Lessons 1, 2, and 3 of Module 4. Then answer the following questions.

1. What facts in the text support the economic interpretation of the Revolution? What evidence supports the political interpretation?

2. Which interpretation seems more convincing? Explain why.

Module 4 Assessment

Review Vocabulary, Terms, and People

1. What were American colonists who remained loyal to Great Britain called?
   a. Whigs
   b. Loyalists
   c. Royalists
   d. Democrats

2. What was the name of the battle in which the Patriots finally defeated the British?
   a. Battle of Saratoga
   b. Battle of New Jersey
   c. Battle of Yorktown
   d. Battle of Valley Forge

3. What was the name for the colonial military force created to fight the British?
   a. mercenaries
   b. Redcoats
   c. Hessians
   d. Continental army

4. Who was the French nobleman who helped the Patriots fight the British?
   a. Bernardo de Gálvez
   b. Marquis de Lafayette
   c. Baron von Steuben
   d. Lord Dunmore

Comprehension and Critical Thinking

Lesson 1

5. a. Recall Why did the British believe it was necessary to raise taxes on the American colonists?
    b. Draw Conclusions How did the Boston Massacre and the Boston Tea Party affect relations between Great Britain and the colonies?
    c. Evaluate Did the British government overreact to colonial protests by issuing the Intolerable Acts? Why or why not?

Lesson 2

6. a. Recall What actions did the First and Second Continental Congresses take?
    b. Analyze How did the events at Lexington and Concord change the conflict between Great Britain and the colonies?
    c. Elaborate Why do you think that control of Boston early in the Revolutionary War was important?

Lesson 3

7. a. Identify Why is July 4, 1776, a significant date?
    b. Draw Conclusions What effect did

Common Sense have on colonial attitudes toward Great Britain?
    c. Predict How might the content of the Declaration of Independence lead to questions over the issue of slavery?

Lesson 4

8. a. Describe What difficulties did the Patriots experience in the early years of the war?
    b. Analyze How did the Patriots turn the tide of the war?
    c. Elaborate Could the Patriots have succeeded in the war without foreign help? Explain.

Lesson 5

9. a. Recall Why did the British think they might find support in the southern colonies?
    b. Make Inferences Why did it take more than two years for the British and the Americans to agree to the terms of the Treaty of Paris?
    c. Evaluate In your opinion, what was the most important reason for the Patriot defeat of the British?

Social Studies Skills

Understand Historical Interpretation *Use the Social Studies Skills taught in this module to answer the questions about the reading selection below.*

> In a series of battles, Howe pounded the Continental army, forcing it to retreat farther and farther. The Redcoats captured Patriots as well as supplies. Eventually, the British pushed Washington across the Hudson River into New Jersey. Howe's revenge for his defeat at Boston was complete.

10. Which statement from the passage is an interpretation of historical facts?

   a. The Redcoats captured Patriots as well as supplies.

   b. Eventually, the British pushed Washington across the Hudson River into New Jersey.

   c. Howe's revenge for his defeat at Boston was complete.

11. What might a different interpretation of the facts be?

Review Themes

12. Politics What are three important rights listed in the Declaration of Independence?

13. Geography What role did geography play in the fighting that took place in the West?

Reading Skills

Main Ideas in Social Studies *Use the Reading Skills taught at the beginning of the module to answer the question about the reading selection below.*

> (1) Native Americans were at first encouraged by both sides to remain neutral. (2) By the summer of 1776, however, both Patriots and the British were aggressively recruiting Indian fighters. (3) Many Native Americans sided with the British. (4) In northern New York, four of the six Iroquois nations fought for the British.

14. Which sentence contains the main idea of the paragraph?

   a. Sentence 1

   b. Sentence 2

   c. Sentence 3

   d. Sentence 4

Map Skills

15. Draw a Map Using the map of North America in Lesson 5 as reference, draw a map that shows the boundary that was set for the United States by the Treaty of Paris of 1783. Illustrate also the areas in North America that were controlled by the British, Spanish, French, and Russians.

Focus on Speaking

16. Prepare an Oral Report In this module you learned about great events, courageous deeds, and heroic people in the Revolutionary War. Begin preparations for an oral report by identifying one or two important ideas, events, or people for each period of the war. Next, write a one-sentence introduction to your talk. Then write a sentence or two about each period of the war. Write a concluding sentence that makes a quick connection between the Revolutionary War and our lives today. Practice your talk until you can give it with only a glance or two at your notes.

THE *American* REVOLUTION

The American Revolution led to the formation of the United States of America in 1776. Beginning in the 1760s, tensions grew between American colonists and their British rulers when Britain started passing a series of new laws and taxes for the colonies. With no representation in the British government, however, colonists had no say in these laws, which led to growing discontent. After fighting broke out in 1775, colonial leaders met to decide what to do. They approved the Declaration of Independence, announcing that the American colonies were free from British rule. In reality, however, freedom would not come until after years of fighting.

Explore some of the people and events of the American Revolution online. You can find a wealth of information, video clips, primary sources, activities, and more through your online textbook.

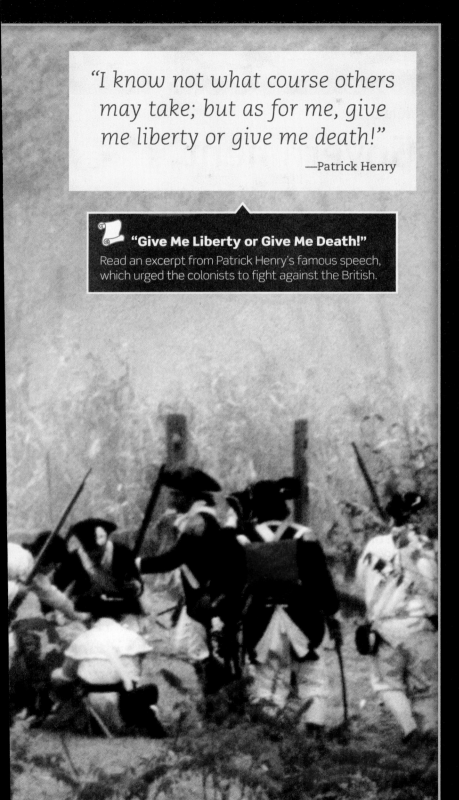

> "I know not what course others may take; but as for me, give me liberty or give me death!"
>
> —Patrick Henry

"Give Me Liberty or Give Me Death!"
Read an excerpt from Patrick Henry's famous speech, which urged the colonists to fight against the British.

Seeds of Revolution
Watch the video to learn about colonial discontent in the years before the Revolutionary War.

Independence!
Watch the video to learn about the origins of the Declaration of Independence.

Victory!
Watch the video to learn how the American colonists won the Revolutionary War.

Module 5

Forming a Government

★

Essential Question
Did compromise make the U.S. Constitution stronger or weaker?

About the Photo: Speaker of the House Nancy Pelosi swears in the members of the 111th Congress of the United States.

In this module you will learn about the nation's earliest government, the Articles of Confederation, and its failure to achieve national unity. You will also read about the writing of the Constitution and how it attempted to solve the problems of the Articles by creating a new system of government.

What You Will Learn ...

Lesson 1: The Articles of Confederation. **152**
The Big Idea The Articles of Confederation provided a framework for a national government.

Lesson 2: The New Nation Faces Challenges **158**
The Big Idea Problems faced by the young nation made it clear that a new constitution was needed.

Lesson 3: Creating the Constitution **164**
The Big Idea A new constitution provided a framework for a stronger national government.

Lesson 4: Ratifying the Constitution **170**
The Big Idea Americans carried on a vigorous debate before ratifying the Constitution.

▶ *Explore ONLINE!*

HISTORY

VIDEOS, including...
- America Gets a Constitution
- Shays's Rebellion

☑ Document-Based Investigations

☑ Graphic Organizers

☑ Interactive Games

☑ Interactive Map: Land Ordinances of 1785 and 1787

☑ Image with Hotspots: Signing the Constitution

☑ Image Carousel: Federalist Leaders

Timeline of Events 1775–1791

▶ Explore ONLINE!

United States 1775 **World**

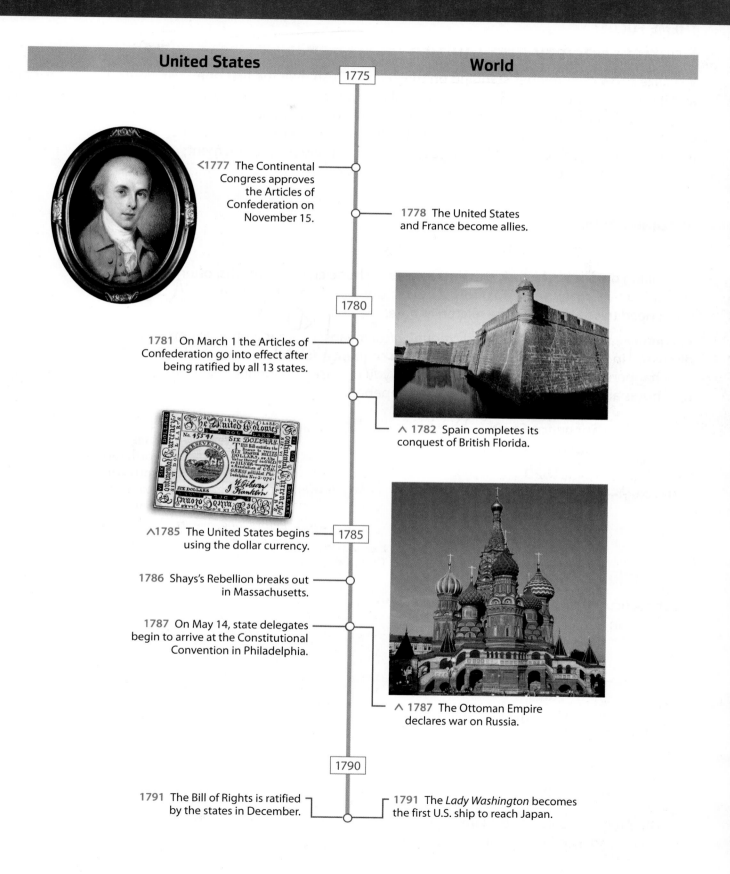

<1777 The Continental Congress approves the Articles of Confederation on November 15.

1778 The United States and France become allies.

1780

1781 On March 1 the Articles of Confederation go into effect after being ratified by all 13 states.

∧ **1782** Spain completes its conquest of British Florida.

∧**1785** The United States begins using the dollar currency. 1785

1786 Shays's Rebellion breaks out in Massachusetts.

1787 On May 14, state delegates begin to arrive at the Constitutional Convention in Philadelphia.

∧ **1787** The Ottoman Empire declares war on Russia.

1790

1791 The Bill of Rights is ratified by the states in December.

1791 The *Lady Washington* becomes the first U.S. ship to reach Japan.

Reading Social Studies

THEME FOCUS:

Politics, Society and Culture

Visualize a row of dominoes standing on their edges. Push over the first one, and it knocks over the second, and so on, until they all fall down. In a way, the events in this module are like a row of dominoes falling down in order. These events, one after another, eventually led to the formation of a new government and a new society. If you read closely, you will see that political disagreements started the entire process.

READING FOCUS:

Understand Chronological Order

Like falling dominoes, historical events can create huge chains of results, often stretching over many years. To understand history and events, therefore, we often need to see how they are related in time.

Putting Events in Order The word *chronological* means "related to time." Events discussed in this history book are discussed in sequence, in the order in which they happened. To understand history better, you can use a sequence chain to take notes about events in the order they happened.

Sequence Chain

1620
The Pilgrims sign the Mayflower Compact.

↓

1639
Connecticut creates the first constitution in the English colonies.

↓

1689
The English Bill of Rights is passed.

↓

1776
The American colonies declare their independence from Great Britain.

> **Tip:** Writers sometimes signal chronological order, or sequence, by using words or phrases like these: *first, before, then, later, soon, after, next, before long, eventually, finally.*

You Try It!

Read the following passage and answer the questions that follow.

Farmers Rebel In August 1786, farmers in three western counties began a revolt. Bands of angry citizens closed down courts in western Massachusetts. Their reasoning was simple—with the courts shut down, no one's property could be taken. In September a poor farmer and Revolutionary War veteran, Daniel Shays, led hundreds of men in a forced shutdown of the Supreme Court in Springfield, Massachusetts. The state government ordered the farmers to stop the revolt under threat of capture and death. These threats only made Shays and his followers more determined. The uprising of farmers to protest high taxes and heavy debt became known as Shays's Rebellion.

Shays's forces were defeated by state troops in January 1787. By February many of the rebels were in prison. During their trials, 14 leaders were sentenced to death. However, the state soon freed most of the rebels, including Shays. State officials knew that many citizens of the state agreed with the rebels and their cause.

After you have read the passage, answer the following questions.

1. Which happened first—citizens closing courts in western Massachusetts or Shays shutting down the Supreme Court? How can you tell?

2. What happened after Shays's forces were defeated by state troops?

3. Draw a sequence chain that shows the effects of Shays's Rebellion in the order in which they occurred.

As you read Module 5, look for clues that signal the order in which events occurred.

Key Terms and People

Lesson 1
Magna Carta
constitution
Virginia Statute for Religious Freedom
suffrage
Articles of Confederation
ratification
Land Ordinance of 1785
Northwest Ordinance of 1787
Northwest Territory

Lesson 2
tariffs
interstate commerce
inflation
depression
Daniel Shays
Shays's Rebellion

Lesson 3
Constitutional Convention
James Madison
Virginia Plan
New Jersey Plan
Great Compromise
Three-Fifths Compromise
popular sovereignty
legislative branch
executive branch
judicial branch
checks and balances
federalism

Lesson 4
Antifederalists
George Mason
Federalists
Federalist Papers
amendments
Bill of Rights

The Articles of Confederation

The Big Idea

The Articles of Confederation provided a framework for a national government.

Main Ideas

- The American people examined many ideas about government.
- The Articles of Confederation laid the base for the first national government of the United States.
- The Confederation Congress established the Northwest Territory.

Key Terms and People

Magna Carta
constitution
Virginia Statute for Religious Freedom
suffrage
Articles of Confederation
ratification
Land Ordinance of 1785
Northwest Ordinance of 1787
Northwest Territory

If YOU were there . . .

You live in a town in New England during the 1770s. In the town meeting, people are hotly debating about who will have the right to vote. Most think that only men who own property should be able to vote. Some think that all property owners—men and women—should have that right. A few others want all free men to have the vote. Now it is time for the meeting to decide.

How would you have voted on this issue?

Ideas about Government

The American colonies had taken a bold step in declaring their independence from Great Britain in July 1776. Their next political goal was to form a new government. To do so, the American people drew from a wide range of political ideas.

English Laws and the Enlightenment England had limited the power of its kings and queens in two documents. These were the Magna Carta and the English Bill of Rights. **Magna Carta**, a document signed by King John in 1215, made the king subject to law. The English Bill of Rights, passed in 1689, declared the supremacy of Parliament. It kept the king or queen from changing laws without Parliament's consent. As a result, the people's representatives had a strong voice in England's government.

Many Americans of this period were also influenced by the Enlightenment—a philosophical movement that emphasized the use of reason to examine old ideas and traditions. Philosopher John Locke believed that a social contract existed between political rulers and the people they ruled. Baron de Montesquieu argued that the only way to achieve liberty was through the separation of governmental powers.

American Models of Government Americans had their own models of self-government to follow, like town meetings, the Virginia House of Burgesses, and the Mayflower Compact. In 1639 the people of Connecticut drew

Women's Suffrage

New Jersey allowed women to vote when it first joined the United States. This right was taken away by 1807.

up the English colonies' first written **constitution**. A constitution is a set of basic principles and laws that states the powers and duties of the government. In addition, the Declaration of Independence clearly set forth the beliefs on which Americans thought government should be based, such as the importance of laws to protect individual rights.

To keep individual leaders from gaining too much power, the new state constitutions created limited governments by restricting the power of government officials to take certain actions. The constitutions also supported the principle known as the *rule of law*, which requires that every citizen obey the laws, including political leaders. Most state constitutions had rules to protect the rights of citizens or those accused of crimes. Some banned slavery. The Massachusetts Constitution of 1780 is the oldest state constitution still in effect.

Thomas Jefferson's ideas about religious freedom were included in the **Virginia Statute for Religious Freedom**. This document declared that no person could be forced to attend a particular church or be required to pay for a church with tax money.

Right to Vote Under British rule, only free, white men who owned land could vote. Many states' constitutions expanded **suffrage**, or the right to vote, by allowing any white man who paid taxes to vote. In every state, however, only landowners could hold public office. Although some states originally allowed women and free African Americans to vote, these rights were soon taken away. Suffrage would not be restored to these groups for many decades to come.

Articles of Confederation

The Second Continental Congress was organized to create a national government. The Continental Congress appointed a Committee of Thirteen, with one member from each colony. This group was assigned to discuss and draft a national constitution.

Reading Check
Compare What two principles were common to state constitutions written during the Revolutionary War?

Under their plan, called the **Articles of Confederation**, ~~Congress~~ became the single branch of the national government. Congress's powers were limited to protect the individual liberties promoted in the Declaration of Independence. Each state had one vote in Congress. Congress could settle conflicts among the states, issue coins, borrow money, and make treaties with other countries and with Native Americans. Congress could also ask the states for money and soldiers. However, states had the power to refuse these requests. The government did not have a president or a national court system. Despite these limitations, the Articles provided a basis for uniting the colonies into one nation.

The Second Continental Congress passed the Articles of Confederation on November 15, 1777. Then it sent the Articles to each state legislature for **ratification**, or official approval, before the new national government could take effect.

Conflicts over claims to western lands slowed the process, but by 1779 every state except Maryland had ratified the Articles. Maryland's leaders refused to ratify until other states gave up their western land claims. Thomas Jefferson assured Maryland that western lands would be made into new states, rather than increasing territory for existing states. Satisfied with this condition, Maryland ratified the Articles in March 1781. This put the first national government of the United States into effect.

Reading Check
Summarize What were two weaknesses of the new national government?

The Land Ordinances of 1785 and 1787

▷ Explore ONLINE!

CANADA

Lake Superior

Lake Michigan

Lake Huron

Lake Ontario

Lake Erie

Mississippi River

WISCONSIN
1848

MICHIGAN
1837

NORTHWEST TERRITORY

ILLINOIS
1818

INDIANA
1816

OHIO
1803

Area of first survey

Ohio River

One section = 1 square mile

| Half section 320 acres | |
| Quarter section 160 acres | |

6	5	4	3	2	1
7	8	9	10	11	12
18	17	16	15	14	13
19	20	21	22	23	24
30	29	28	27	26	25
31	32	33	34	35	36

One township = 36 square miles

0   100   200 Miles
0   100   200 Kilometers

Interpret Maps
1. Location Which states were formed out of the Northwest Territory?
2. Region Into how many sections was a township divided?

Northwest Territory

Congress had to decide what to do with the western lands now under its control and how to raise money to pay debts. It tried to solve both problems by selling the western lands. Congress passed the **Land Ordinance of 1785**, which set up a system for surveying and dividing western lands. The land was split into townships, which were 36 square miles divided into 36 lots of 640 acres each. One lot was reserved for a public school, and four lots were given to veterans. The remaining lots were sold to the public.

To form a political system for the region, Congress passed the **Northwest Ordinance of 1787**. The ordinance established the **Northwest Territory**, which included areas that are now in Illinois, Indiana, Michigan, Ohio, Minnesota, and Wisconsin. The Northwest Ordinance created a system for bringing new states into the Union. Congress agreed that the Northwest Territory would be divided into several smaller territories with a governor appointed by Congress. When the population of a territory reached 60,000, its settlers could draft their own constitution and ask to join the Union.

In addition, the law protected civil liberties and required that public education be provided. Finally, the ordinance stated that "there shall be neither slavery nor involuntary servitude [forced labor] in the . . . territory." This last condition banned slavery in the Territory and set the standard for future territories. However, slavery would continue to be a controversial issue.

Reading Check
Analyze Information How did the Northwest Ordinance of 1787 affect the United States?

Summary and Preview The Northwest Ordinance settled the future of the Northwest Territory. In the next lesson you will read about other challenges the new government faced.

Lesson 1 Assessment

Review Ideas, Terms, and People

1. a. Identify What documents influenced ideas about government in the United States?

b. Draw Conclusions What impact did the Virginia Statute for Religious Freedom and the Declaration of Independence have on the U.S. government?

c. Make Inferences How did the experience of living under British rule influence the attitude of Americans toward limited government and the rule of law?

d. Identify Which groups of people were left out of the debate over the formation of a new American government?

2. a. Identify What was the Articles of Confederation?

b. Summarize What powers were granted to Congress by the Articles of Confederation?

c. Predict What are some possible problems that might result from the lack of a national court system?

3. a. Describe How were public lands in the West divided by the Land Ordinance of 1785?

b. Evaluate In your opinion, what was the most important element of the Northwest Ordinance of 1787? Why?

c. Elaborate What does the assignment of township lots reveal about values of Americans at this time?

Critical Thinking

4. Categorize In this lesson you learned about the Articles of Confederation. Create a chart similar to the one below and use it to show the strengths and weaknesses of the new government.

Articles of Confederation

Strengths	Weaknesses

History and Geography

Origins of the Constitution

The U.S. Constitution created a republican form of government based on the consent of the people. The framers of the Constitution blended ideas and examples from both the American colonies and England to write this lasting document.

THE MAYFLOWER COMPACT, 1620

The *Mayflower*, shown here in an illustration, sailed to America in 1620. Aboard the ship, 41 men signed the Mayflower Compact, the first document in the colonies to establish guidelines for self-government. The signers agreed that they and their families would combine to form a "civil body politic," or community.

COLONIAL ASSEMBLIES

The British Parliament's two-chamber structure also influenced colonial governments. In Article I, Section 1, of the Constitution, the framers continued the practice of a two-chamber legislature.

"All legislative powers . . . shall be vested in a Congress of the United States, which shall consist of a Senate and House of Representatives."

—Article I, Section 1, U.S. Constitution

VIRGINIA STATUTE FOR RELIGIOUS FREEDOM, 1786

Classical liberal principles, such as the written protection of citizens' personal liberties, were reflected in the addition of the Bill of Rights. The First Amendment's freedom of religion clauses were based on Thomas Jefferson's Virginia Statute for Religious Freedom. The document, which was accepted by the Virginia legislature in 1786, ensured the separation of church and state in Virginia.

"Congress shall make no law respecting an establishment of religion, or prohibiting the free exercise thereof . . ."

—First Amendment, U.S. Constitution

American colonies

MAGNA CARTA, 1215

In this painting King John of England is signing the Magna Carta, or the Great Charter, which established that the king was subject to the law just like everyone else. It also declared that people could not be deprived of their lives, liberty, or property "except by the lawful judgment of [their] peers, or by the law of the land." Compare this language to that of the Fifth Amendment to the Constitution.

"No person shall be . . . deprived of life, liberty, or property, without due process of law . . . "

—Fifth Amendment, U.S. Constitution

THE ENGLISH BILL OF RIGHTS, 1689

This painting shows King William and Queen Mary of England. Before taking the throne, William and Mary had to accept the English Bill of Rights. The English Bill of Rights took even more power away from the monarch than did the Magna Carta. It also protected the rights of English citizens. These ideas would later influence the U.S. Constitution.

"Excessive bail ought not be required, nor excessive fines imposed; nor cruel and unusual punishments inflicted."

—English Bill of Rights

THE ENLIGHTENMENT, 1700s

Enlightenment thinkers such as English philosopher John Locke supported the movement toward self-government. Locke argued in his writings that government could exist only with "the consent of the governed." The framers of the Constitution looked to Locke for inspiration when writing the Constitution, as you can see from its very first words.

"We the people of the United States, . . . "

—Preamble, U.S. Constitution

Analyze Information

1. What documents did the framers look to when writing the Constitution?

2. How did the English Parliamentary system affect the kind of government the framers created?

England

The New Nation Faces Challenges

The Big Idea
Problems faced by the young nation made it clear that a new constitution was needed.

Main Ideas
- The United States had difficulties with other nations.
- Internal economic problems plagued the new nation.
- Shays's Rebellion pointed out weaknesses in the Articles of Confederation.
- Many Americans called for changes in the national government.

Key Terms and People
tariffs
interstate commerce
inflation
depression
Daniel Shays
Shays's Rebellion

If YOU were there . . .

You own an orchard in Maryland in the 1780s. When you sell apples and apple pies in the market, people pay you with paper money. But now the tax collector says you must pay your taxes in gold or silver coins, not paper money. You and the other farmers are furious. Is this the liberty you fought a war for?

What would you do to protest these taxes?

Relations with Other Countries

Under the Articles of Confederation, Congress could not force states to provide soldiers for an army. The Continental Army had disbanded, or dissolved, soon after the signing of the Treaty of Paris of 1783. Without an army, the national government found it difficult to protect its citizens against foreign threats.

Trouble with Britain It was also difficult to enforce international treaties such as the Treaty of Paris of 1783. The United States found it especially hard to force the British to turn over "with all convenient speed" their forts on the American side of the Great Lakes. The United States wanted to gain control of these forts because they protected valuable land and fur-trade routes. Still, Britain was slow to withdraw from the area. A British official warned against the United States trying to seize the forts by force. He said that any attempt to do so would be opposed by the thousands of British soldiers who had settled in Canada after the Revolution and "are ready to fly to arms at a moment's warning."

Trade with Britain The United States also faced problems trading with Great Britain. After the signing of the Treaty of Paris, Britain closed many of its ports to American ships. Before the Revolutionary War, colonial ships had traded a

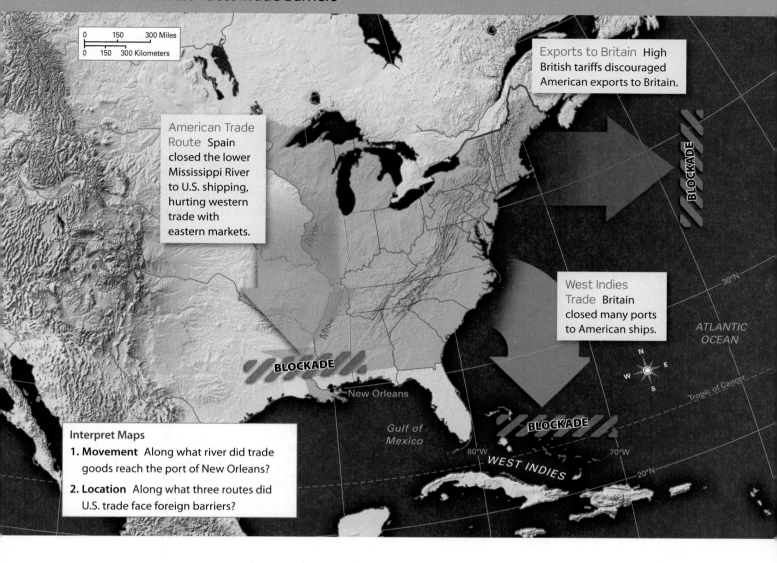

Explore ONLINE!

Exports to Britain High British tariffs discouraged American exports to Britain.

American Trade Route Spain closed the lower Mississippi River to U.S. shipping, hurting western trade with eastern markets.

West Indies Trade Britain closed many ports to American ships.

BLOCKADE

BLOCKADE

BLOCKADE

New Orleans

Gulf of Mexico

ATLANTIC OCEAN

Tropic of Cancer

WEST INDIES

30°N

20°N

80°W

70°W

Interpret Maps

1. **Movement** Along what river did trade goods reach the port of New Orleans?

2. **Location** Along what three routes did U.S. trade face foreign barriers?

great deal with the British West Indies and stopped there on their way to other destinations. This travel and trading stopped after 1783.

In addition, Britain forced American merchants to pay high **tariffs**—taxes on imports or exports. The tariffs applied to goods such as rice, tobacco, tar, and oil that were grown or mined in the United States and then sold in Britain. Merchants had to raise prices to cover the tariffs. Ultimately, the costs would be passed on to customers, who had to pay higher prices for the goods. The economic condition of the country was getting worse by the day.

Trade with Spain In 1784 Spanish officials closed the lower Mississippi River to U.S. shipping. Western farmers and merchants were furious because they used the Mississippi to send goods to eastern and foreign markets. Congress tried to work out an agreement with Spain, but the plan did not receive a majority vote in Congress. The plan could not be passed. As a result, Spain broke off the negotiations.

Many state leaders began to criticize the national government. Rhode Island's representatives wrote, "Our federal government is but a name; a mere shadow without substance [power]." Critics believed that Spain might have continued to negotiate if the United States had possessed a strong military. These leaders believed that the national government needed to be more powerful.

Impact of Closed Markets The closing of markets in the British West Indies seriously affected the U.S. economy. James Madison of Virginia wrote about the crisis.

> "The Revolution has robbed us of our trade with the West Indies . . . without opening any other channels to compensate [make up for] it. In every point of view, indeed, the trade of this country is in a deplorable [terrible] condition."
>
> —James Madison, quoted in *The Writings of James Madison,* edited by Gaillard Hunt

Farmers could no longer export their goods to the British West Indies. They also had to hire British ships to carry their goods to British markets, which was very expensive. American exports dropped while British goods flowed freely into the United States.

This unequal trade caused serious economic problems for the new nation. British merchants could sell manufactured products in the United States at much lower prices than locally made goods. This difference in prices hurt American businesses.

The Confederation Congress could not correct the problem because it did not have the authority either to pass tariffs or to order the states to pass tariffs. The states could offer little help. If one state passed a tariff, the British could simply sell their goods in another state. Most states did not cooperate in trade matters. Instead, states worked only to increase their own trade rather than working to improve the trade situation for the whole country.

In 1785 the situation led a British magazine to call the new nation the Dis-United States. As a result of the trade problems with Britain, American merchants began looking for other markets such as China, France, and the Netherlands. Despite such attempts, Britain remained the most important trading partner of the United States.

Economic Problems

In addition to international trade issues, other challenges soon appeared. Trade problems among the states, war debts, and a weak economy plagued the states.

Trade among States Because the Confederation Congress had no power to regulate **interstate commerce**—trade between two or more states—states followed their own trade interests. As a result, trade laws differed from state to state. The laws governing trade in one state could be very different from the laws in a neighboring state. This situation made trade difficult for merchants whose businesses crossed state lines.

Reading Check
Analyze Information
Why was the Confederation Congress unable to solve America's international trade problems?

This five-shilling note was issued by Rhode Island. Paper money printed by state governments helped fuel inflation.

Reading Check
Summarize What economic problems did the new nation face?

Inflation After the Revolutionary War, most states had a hard time paying off war debts and struggled to collect overdue taxes. To ease this hardship, some states began printing large amounts of paper money. The result was inflation. This money had little or no real value because states did not have gold or silver reserves to back it up. **Inflation** occurs when there are increased prices for goods and services combined with the reduced value of money. Because there was no common currency, Congress had no power to stop states from issuing more paper money and thus stop inflation.

Weak Economy In Rhode Island the state legislature printed large amounts of paper money worth very little. This made debtors—people who owe money—quite happy. They could pay back their debts with paper money worth less than the coins they had borrowed. However, creditors—people who lend money—were upset. Hundreds of creditors fled Rhode Island to avoid being paid back with worthless money.

The loss of trade with Britain combined with inflation created a **depression**. A depression is a period of low economic activity combined with a rise in unemployment.

Shays's Rebellion

Each state handled its economic problems differently. Massachusetts refused to print worthless paper money. It tried to pay its war debts by collecting taxes on land.

Heavy Debts for Farmers Massachusetts's tax policy hit farmers hard. As landowners, they had to pay the new taxes. However, farmers had trouble paying their debts. The courts began forcing them to sell their property. Some farmers had to serve terms in debtors' prison; others had to sell their labor.

Many government leaders in the state did not care about the problems of poor farmers, however. In some cases, farmers actually owed these political leaders money.

Farmers Rebel In August 1786 farmers in three western counties began a revolt. Bands of angry citizens closed down courts in western Massachusetts. Their reasoning was simple—with the courts shut down, no one's property could be taken. In September a poor farmer and Revolutionary War veteran, **Daniel Shays**, led hundreds of men in a forced shutdown of the Supreme Court in Springfield, Massachusetts. The state government ordered the farmers to stop the revolt under threat of capture and death. These threats only made Shays and his followers more determined. The uprising of farmers to protest high taxes and heavy debt became known as **Shays's Rebellion**.

Shays's Defeat Shays's forces were defeated by state troops in January 1787. By February many of the rebels were in prison. During their trials, 14 leaders were sentenced to death. However, the state soon freed most of

Daniel Shays, at the top of the steps, stands firm in the face of demands that he leave the courthouse in Springfield, Massachusetts. By shutting down the courts, farmers hoped to stop the government from selling their land.

Reading Check Find Main Ideas What led to Shays's Rebellion?

the rebels, including Shays. State officials knew that many citizens of the state agreed with the rebels and their cause.

Calls for Change

In the end, Shays's Rebellion showed the weakness of the Confederation government. It led some Americans to admit that the Articles of Confederation had failed to protect the ideals of liberty set forth in the Declaration of Independence. When Massachusetts had asked the national government to help put down Shays's Rebellion, Congress could offer little help. More Americans began calling for a stronger central government. They wanted leaders who would be able to protect the nation in times of crisis.

Earlier in 1786 the Virginia legislature had called for a national conference. It wanted to talk about economic problems and ways to change the Articles of Confederation. The meeting took place in Annapolis, Maryland, in September 1786.

Nine states decided to send delegates to the Annapolis Convention, but some of their delegates were late and missed the meeting. Connecticut, Georgia, Maryland, and South Carolina did not respond to the request at all and sent no delegates.

Because of the poor attendance, the participants, including James Madison and Alexander Hamilton, called on all 13 states to send delegates to a Constitutional Convention in Philadelphia in May 1787. They planned to revise the Articles of Confederation to better meet the needs of the nation.

Reading Check
Find Main Ideas
Why did some people believe the national government needed to change?

Summary and Preview Many Americans believed that Shays's Rebellion was final proof that the national government needed to be changed. In the next lesson you will read about the Constitutional Convention.

Quick Facts

Weaknesses of the Articles of Confederation

- Most power held by states
- One branch of government
- Legislative branch has few powers
- No executive branch
- No judicial system
- No system of checks and balances

Lesson 2 Assessment

Review Ideas, Terms, and People

1. **a. Summarize** What problems did the United States experience with Spain and Great Britain after the Revolutionary War?

   b. Explain Why did Congress's inability to tax goods hurt American merchants?

   c. Predict What are some possible results of the growing problems between the United States and Great Britain? Why?

2. **a. Describe** What difficulties were involved with interstate commerce?

   b. Analyze What was the cause of inflation in the new nation, and how could it have been prevented?

3. **a. Explain** How did Massachusetts's tax policy affect poor farmers?

   b. Evaluate Defend the actions of Daniel Shays and the other rebels.

4. **a. Recall** Why did Madison and Hamilton call for a Constitutional Convention?

   b. Analyze How did Shays's Rebellion lead to a call for change in the United States?

Critical Thinking

5. **Categorize** In this lesson you learned about the problems faced by the new nation. Create a chart similar to the one below and identify those problems as either domestic or international.

Domestic Problems	International Problems

Creating the Constitution

The Big Idea

A new constitution provided a framework for a stronger national government.

Main Ideas

■ The Constitutional Convention met to improve the government of the United States.

■ The issue of representation led to the Great Compromise.

■ Regional debate over slavery led to the Three-Fifths Compromise.

■ The U.S. Constitution created federalism and a balance of power.

Key Terms and People

Constitutional Convention
James Madison
Virginia Plan
New Jersey Plan
Great Compromise
Three-Fifths Compromise
popular sovereignty
legislative branch
executive branch
judicial branch
checks and balances
federalism

If YOU were there . . .

You are a merchant in Connecticut in 1787. You have been a member of your state legislature for several years. This spring, the legislature is choosing delegates to a convention to revise the Articles of Confederation. Delegates will meet in Philadelphia. It means leaving your business in others' hands for most of the summer. Still, you hope to be chosen.

Why would you want to go to the Constitutional Convention?

Constitutional Convention

In February 1787 the Confederation Congress invited each state to send delegates to a convention in Philadelphia. The goal of the meeting was to improve the Articles of Confederation.

The **Constitutional Convention** was held in May 1787 in Philadelphia's Independence Hall to improve the Articles of Confederation. However, delegates would leave with an entirely new U.S. Constitution. This decision angered some of the participants.

Most delegates were well educated, and many had served in state legislatures or Congress. Benjamin Franklin and **James Madison** were there. Revolutionary War hero George Washington was elected president of the Convention.

Several important voices were absent. John Adams and Thomas Jefferson could not attend. Patrick Henry chose not to attend because he did not want a stronger central government. Women, African Americans, and Native Americans did not take part because they did not yet have the rights of citizens.

James Madison

Reading Check
Summarize What was the purpose of the Constitutional Convention?

Signing of the Constitution

This painting shows the signing of the Constitution on September 17, 1787. James Madison, number 4 on the diagram, became known as the "Father of the Constitution" for his ideas about government and his ability to lead the delegates to agreement.

1 Roger Sherman   4 James Madison
2 Alexander Hamilton   5 George Washington
3 Benjamin Franklin   6 James Wilson

Great Compromise

Several issues divided the delegates to the Constitutional Convention. Some members wanted only small changes to the Articles of Confederation, while others wanted to rewrite the Articles completely.

Those delegates who wanted major changes to the Articles had different goals. For example, small and large states had different ideas about representation, economic concerns such as tariffs, and slavery. In addition, delegates disagreed over how strong to make the national government.

Virginia Plan After the delegates had met for four days, Edmund Randolph of Virginia presented the **Virginia Plan**. He proposed a new federal constitution that would give sovereignty, or supreme power, to the central government. The legislature would be bicameral—made up of two houses, or groups of representatives—and chosen on the basis of state populations. Larger states would thus have more representatives than would smaller states. Delegates from the smaller states believed that it would give too much power to the larger states.

Virginia Plan	Great Compromise	New Jersey Plan
• Gave more power to national government • Bicameral legislature • Number in both houses based on population	• Bicameral legislature • Number of representatives based on state populations in lower house • Number of representatives equal from each state in upper house	• Gave more power to state governments • Unicameral legislature • Number of representatives equal from each state

New Jersey Plan The smaller states came up with a plan to stop the larger states from getting too much power. New Jersey delegate William Paterson presented the small-state or **New Jersey Plan**, which called for a unicameral, or one-house, legislature. The plan gave each state an equal number of votes, and thus an equal voice, in the federal government. The plan gave the federal government the power to tax citizens in all states, and it allowed the government to regulate commerce.

Compromise Is Reached After a month of debate, the delegates were unable to agree on how states should be represented. The convention reached a deadlock.

Finally, Roger Sherman of Connecticut proposed a compromise plan. The legislative branch would have two houses. Each state, regardless of its size, would have two representatives in the Senate, or upper house. This would give each state an equal voice, pleasing the smaller states. In the House of Representatives, or lower house, the number of representatives for each state would be determined by the state's population. This pleased the larger states. The agreement to create a two-house legislature became known as the **Great Compromise**. James Wilson, a great speaker, saw his dream of a strong national government come true.

Roger Sherman

James Wilson

Three-Fifths Compromise

The debate over representation also involved regional differences. Southern delegates wanted enslaved Africans to be counted as part of their state populations. This way they would have more representatives, and more power, in Congress. Northerners disagreed. They wanted the number of slaves to determine taxes but not representation.

To resolve this problem, some delegates thought of a compromise. They wanted to count three-fifths of the slaves in each state as part of that state's population to decide how many representatives a state would have.

Reading Check
Contrast How did the Virginia Plan and New Jersey Plan differ?

After much debate, the delegates voted to accept the proposal, called the **Three-Fifths Compromise**. Under this agreement only three-fifths of a state's slave population would count when determining representation.

Another major issue was the foreign slave trade. Some of the delegates believed slavery was wrong and wanted the federal government to ban the slave trade. Others said that the southern states' economies needed the slave trade. Many southern delegates said they would leave the Union if the Constitution immediately ended the slave trade. Also at issue was Congress's ability to tax imports and exports.

Worried delegates reached another compromise. The Commerce Compromises allowed Congress to levy tariffs on imports, but not exports, and allowed the importation of slaves until the end of 1807. The delegates omitted, or left out, the words *slavery* and *slave* in the Constitution. They referred instead to "free Persons" and "all other Persons."

Reading Check
Summarize What compromise was reached over the issue of the slave trade?

A New System of Government

Most of the delegates to the Convention wanted a stronger central government than the Articles of Confederation could provide. They believed it was necessary for the protection and administration of the group of states. But delegates also wanted to protect the individual rights that had been won in the Revolution. They wanted the new system of government to support the ideals stated in the Declaration of Independence.

The rights of citizens to "life, liberty, and the pursuit of happiness" are supported by the idea of **popular sovereignty**. This is the idea that political authority is in the hands of the people. In the new nation, people would express this power through their votes. The power of government is limited by the power of voters. In a republic, or representative democracy, the government consists of people elected by voters to represent them. This system requires government to depend on the consent of the governed. Voters can limit the actions of government by removing representatives who do not truly work for their goals.

Checks and Balances The delegates divided the power of the central government among three branches, each having specific roles. This arrangement is known as the separation of powers. The **legislative branch**, called Congress, is responsible for proposing and passing laws. It is made up of two houses, as created in the Great Compromise. The Senate and the House of Representatives have different rules governing how many members represent each state, which helps balance the power between large and small states. The **executive branch** includes the president and the departments that help run the government. The executive branch makes sure that laws are carried out. The **judicial branch** is made up of all the national courts. This branch is responsible for interpreting laws, punishing criminals, and settling disputes between states.

The framers of the Constitution created a system of **checks and balances** that keeps any branch of government from becoming too

As the home and office of the president, the White House is today a well-known symbol of the executive branch of government.

powerful. For example, Congress has the power to pass bills into law. The president has the power to veto, or reject, laws that Congress passes. However, Congress can override the president's veto with a two-thirds majority vote. The Supreme Court has the power to review laws passed by Congress and strike down any law that violates the Constitution.

Federalism Even though many of the delegates wanted a stronger central government, they did not want to destroy state governments. State governments can be more sensitive to local concerns and traditions, and they can serve as laboratories for new ideas. To balance the power between these two types of government, the delegates created the system of **federalism**. Federalism divides the powers of government between a central government and the states that make up a nation. Under the previous confederal system, states were only loosely joined together.

The Constitution requires each state to obey the authority of the federal, or national, government. States have control over government functions not specifically assigned to the federal government. These include control of local government, education, the chartering of corporations, and the supervision of religious bodies. States also have the power to create and oversee civil and criminal law. States must protect the welfare of their citizens.

Amending the Constitution One of the most important decisions the framers made was to include a method for changing or adding to the Constitution. They wanted the government to be able to adapt as changes were needed. The process for amending the Constitution was made difficult, however, so that major changes to the government would require the support of a large majority of voters. Two-thirds of each house of Congress and three-fourths of states must approve a change before it can take effect. Although many amendments, or changes to the Constitution, have been suggested, only twenty-seven have been approved. The purposes of these amendments have usually focused on protecting civil and voting rights, and on procedures for administering the government.

Quick Facts

The Constitution Strengthens the National Government

Strengths of the Constitution
- ✓ most power held by national government
- ✓ three branches of government
- ✓ legislative branch has many powers
- ✓ executive branch led by president
- ✓ judicial branch to review the laws
- ✓ firm system of checks and balances

Weaknesses of the Articles of Confederation
- most power held by states
- one branch of government
- legislative branch has few powers
- no executive branch
- no judicial system
- no system of checks and balances

Reading Check
Explain How does the constitutional system of government prevent government power from becoming too concentrated?

Even though the final draft of the Constitution was adopted by the Convention, many disagreements still existed among the delegates. Debates continued around the power of state governments and the role of each branch. Almost as soon as the document was adopted, different interpretations of its language began to appear. Some of the disagreements affect the views of lawmakers even today, but the Constitution is still the guiding blueprint for the nation's government.

Summary and Preview The Constitution balanced power among three branches of the federal government but was only written after many compromises. In the next lesson you will read about Antifederalist and Federalist views of the Constitution, and the struggle to get it approved by the states.

Lesson 3 Assessment

Review Ideas, Terms, and People

1. **a. Recall** Why did the Confederation Congress call for a Constitutional Convention?

   b. Elaborate Why do you think it was important that most delegates had served in state legislatures?

   c. Make Inferences Why did the delegates elect Washington as president of the Convention?

2. **a. Identify** What was the Great Compromise?

   b. Draw Conclusions How did state issues lead to debate over structure of the legislature?

3. **a. Recall** How did the delegates resolve their debate on tariffs in the Commerce Compromise?

   b. Explain What was the debate between North and South over counting slave populations?

   c. Contrast How did delegates' views differ on the issue of the foreign slave trade?

4. **a. Recall** Why did the framers of the Constitution create a system of checks and balances through the separation of powers?

   b. Analyze How did federalism limit the power of the central government?

   c. Evaluate Did the Constitution resolve the weaknesses in the Articles of Confederation? Explain your answer.

Critical Thinking

5. **Evaluate** What circumstances justified the decision of the delegates to draft a new constitution instead of revising the Articles of Confederation, as was originally planned?

6. **Identify Cause and Effect** In this lesson you learned about several issues that were resolved by compromise during the Constitutional Convention. Create a graphic organizer like the one below and use it to show how the compromises affected the framework of the new government.

Compromise		Effect

7. **Compare and Contrast** How do the Articles of the Confederation and the Constitution each carry out democratic ideals?

8. **Draw Conclusions** Why is limited government important for maintaining popular sovereignty in a republic or representative democracy?

Ratifying the Constitution

The Big Idea

Americans carried on a vigorous debate before ratifying the Constitution.

Main Ideas

- Federalists and Antifederalists engaged in debate over the new Constitution.

- The *Federalist Papers* played an important role in the fight for ratification of the Constitution.

- Ten amendments were added to the Constitution to provide a Bill of Rights to protect citizens.

Key Terms and People

Antifederalists
George Mason
Federalists
Federalist Papers
amendments
Bill of Rights

If YOU were there . . .

You are a newspaper editor in Philadelphia. During colonial rule, officials sometimes closed down your newspaper because you had criticized the governor. Now you are one of many Americans who want to be sure the new Constitution will guarantee individual rights. You are writing an editorial in your paper explaining what you want.

What rights would you want the Constitution to protect?

Federalists and Antifederalists

When the Constitution was made public, a huge debate began among many Americans. Some **Antifederalists**—people who opposed the Constitution—thought that the Constitutional Convention should not have created a new government. Others, such as James Monroe, thought the Constitution weakened states' rights by giving too much power to the central government. For some Antifederalists, including **George Mason**, the main problem was that the Constitution did not have a section that guaranteed individual rights. Thomas Jefferson, who was otherwise in favor of the Constitution, wrote to Madison from Paris to argue that a bill of rights was needed.

Many Antifederalists were small farmers and debtors. Some Patriots, including Samuel Adams and Patrick Henry, were also strong Antifederalists. At the Virginia ratifying convention, Henry spoke out against the lack of protection of individual freedoms, saying that he valued American liberty over American union.

Antifederalists were challenged by those who believed that the United States needed a stronger central government. **Federalists**—supporters of the Constitution—included James Madison, George Washington, Benjamin Franklin, and Alexander Hamilton. Most Federalists believed that through compromise, the delegates had created a

Federalists vs. Antifederalists

Alexander Hamilton
Federalist

- Supported the Constitution as an excellent plan for government
- Defended his views in the *Federalist Papers*

George Mason
Antifederalist

- Opposed the Constitution
- Believed the Constitution needed a section guaranteeing individual rights

Constitution that offered a good balance of power between various political views. Many Federalists were wealthy planters, farmers, and lawyers. However, others were workers and craftspeople.

Federalists and Antifederalists debated whether the new Constitution should be approved. They made speeches and printed pamphlets **advocating** their views. Mercy Otis Warren, an ardent Patriot during the war, wrote a pamphlet entitled *Observations on the New Constitution*, in which she criticized the lack of individual rights it provided. The Federalists had to convince people that a change in the structure of government was needed. To do this, they had to overcome people's fears that the Constitution would make the government too powerful.

Federalist Papers

One of the most important defenses of the Constitution appeared in a series of essays that became known as the *Federalist Papers*. These essays supporting the Constitution were written anonymously under the name Publius. They were actually written by Alexander Hamilton, James Madison, and John Jay.

Academic Vocabulary
advocate to plead in favor of

Reading Check
Compare and Contrast Explain the similarities and differences between the Antifederalists and the Federalists.

Federalist Papers
Nos. 10 and 51

These essays are part of a series called the Federalist Papers, *written between 1787 and 1788 to support ratification of the Constitution. They discuss how the new system of government will overcome disagreements within society and prevent abuses of power.*

Madison believes that lawmakers are responsible for regulating the many competing concerns that make up society.

The federal government will handle issues affecting the nation as a whole; state and local governments will handle local issues.

The Constitution creates a national government that will be strong but limited in power.

The federalist system provides checks and balances on the power of the national government.

"*A landed interest, a manufacturing interest, a mercantile [trading] interest, a moneyed interest, with many lesser interests, grow up of necessity in civilized nations, and divide them into different classes, actuated [moved] by different sentiments and views. The regulation of these various and interfering interests [opinions] forms the principal task of modern legislation, and involves the spirit of party and faction [group] in the necessary and ordinary operations of the government. . . .*

The federal Constitution forms a happy combination . . . the great . . . interests being referred to the national [legislature], the local and particular to the State legislatures. . . . The influence of factious leaders may kindle [start] a flame within their particular States, but will be unable to spread a general conflagration [large fire] through the other States.

—James Madison, from "Federalist No 10"

If men were angels, no government would be necessary. If angels were to govern men, neither external nor internal controls on government would be necessary. In framing a government which is to be administered by men over men, the great difficulty lies in this: you must first enable the government to control the governed; and in the next place oblige it to control itself. A dependence on the people is, no doubt, the primary control on the government; but experience has taught mankind the necessity of auxiliary precautions. . . . We see it particularly displayed in all the subordinate distributions of power, where the constant aim is to divide and arrange the several offices in such a manner as that each may be a check on the other that the private interest of every individual may be a sentinel over the public rights.

—Alexander Hamilton or James Madison, from "Federalist No 51"

Analyze Historical Sources
According to the excerpts from the essays, what will prevent the national government from becoming oppressive?

After serving a leading role in the Constitutional Convention, James Madison went on to defend the Constitution in essays he wrote for the *Federalist Papers*.

Reading Check
Draw Conclusions
Why were Virginia and New York important to the ratification of the Constitution?

The authors of the *Federalist Papers* tried to reassure Americans that the new federal government would not overpower the newly created states. In Federalist Paper No. 10, Madison argued that the diversity of the United States would prevent any single group from dominating the government.

The *Federalist Papers* were widely reprinted in newspapers around the country as the debate over the Constitution continued. Finally, they were collected and published in book form in 1788.

The Constitution needed only nine states to pass it. However, to establish and preserve national unity, each state needed to ratify it. Every state except Rhode Island held special state conventions that gave citizens the chance to discuss and vote on the Constitution.

Paul Revere served on a committee supporting ratification. He wrote of the Constitution, "The proposed . . . government, is well calculated [planned] to secure the liberties, protect the property, and guard the rights of the citizens of America." Antifederalists also spoke out in state conventions, and wrote articles and pamphlets that became known as the Antifederalist Papers. In New York, one citizen said, "It appears that the government will fall into the hands of the few and the great."

On December 7, 1787, Delaware became the first state to ratify the Constitution. It went into effect in June 1788 after New Hampshire became the ninth state to ratify it.

Political leaders across America knew the new government needed the support of the large states of Virginia and New York, where debate still raged. Finally, Madison and fellow Virginia Federalists convinced Virginia to ratify it in mid-1788. In New York, riots had occurred when the draft of the Constitution was made public. At the state convention in Poughkeepsie to discuss ratification, Hamilton and Jay argued convincingly against the Antifederalists led by DeWitt Clinton. When news arrived of Virginia's ratification, New York ratified it as well. Rhode Island was the last state to ratify the Constitution in May 1790.

Bill of Rights

Several states ratified the Constitution only after they were promised that a bill protecting individual rights would be added to it. Many Antifederalists did not think that the Constitution would protect personal freedoms.

Some Federalists said that the nation did not need a federal bill of rights because the Constitution itself was a bill of rights. It was, they argued, written to protect the liberty of all U.S. citizens.

James Madison wanted to make a bill of rights one of the new government's first priorities. In Congress's first session, Madison encouraged the legislators to put together a bill of rights. The rights would then be added to the Constitution as **amendments**, or official changes. In Article V of the Constitution, the founders had provided a way to change the document when necessary in order to reflect the will of the people. The process requires that proposed amendments must be approved by a two-thirds majority of both houses of Congress and then ratified by three-fourths of the states before taking effect.

In this document, Congress proposed 12 amendments to the U.S. Constitution. Articles III to XII became the 10 amendments known as the Bill of Rights.

Legislators took ideas from the state ratifying conventions, the Virginia Declaration of Rights, the English Bill of Rights, and the Declaration of Independence to make sure that the abuses listed in the Declaration of Independence would be illegal under the new government. In September 1789 Congress proposed 12 amendments and sent them to the states for ratification. By December 1791 the states had ratified the **Bill of Rights**— ten of the proposed amendments intended to protect citizens' rights.

These ten amendments set a clear example of how to amend the Constitution to fit the needs of a changing nation. The flexibility of the U.S. Constitution has allowed it to survive as a living document for more than two hundred years.

Reading Check
Summarize Why is being able to amend the Constitution important?

Summary and Preview Early disagreements over individual rights resulted in the Bill of Rights. In the next module you will learn about the structure of the Constitution.

Lesson 4 Assessment

Review Ideas, Terms, and People

1. a. Identify Who were the Federalists and the Antifederalists?

b. Explain Why did Antifederalists such as George Mason, James Monroe, and Patrick Henry object to the Constitution?

c. Draw Conclusions What position did Thomas Jefferson take in the debate over the Constitution?

2. a. Recall When did the Constitution go into effect?

b. Draw Conclusions Why was it important that all 13 states ratify the Constitution?

c. Elaborate Do you think that the *Federalist Papers* played an essential role in the ratification of the Constitution? Explain your answer.

3. a. Recall Why did Congress add the Bill of Rights?

b. Explain From where did legislators' ideas for the Bill of Rights come?

c. Evaluate Do you think the process for amending the Constitution is too difficult? Explain your position.

Critical Thinking

4. Analyze In this lesson you learned about the debate between Federalists and Antifederalists about the Constitution. Create a graphic organizer similar to the one below, and identify the outcome of the debate. Be sure to mention the Bill of Rights.

Social Studies Skills

Determine Different Points of View

Define the Skill

A *point of view* is a person's outlook or attitude. It is the way he or she looks at a topic or thing. Each person's point of view is shaped by his or her background. Because people's backgrounds are different, their points of view differ too. Since a person's point of view shapes his or her opinions, knowing that point of view helps you understand and evaluate those opinions. It also helps you understand why people in history think and act differently.

Learn the Skill

When you encounter someone's beliefs, opinions, or actions in your study of history, use the following guidelines to determine his or her point of view.

1. Look for information about the person's background.

2. Ask yourself what factors in the person's background might have influenced his or her opinion or action concerning the topic or event.

3. Be aware that sometimes the person's opinions or actions themselves will provide clues to his or her point of view.

Benjamin Lincoln led the troops that put down Shays's Rebellion in Massachusetts. He was also a state politician and a general during the Revolution. Lincoln offered this explanation of Shays's uprising.

"Among [the main causes] I rank the ease with which . . . credit was obtained . . . in the time of [the Revolution]. . . . The moment the day arrived when all discovered that things were fast returning [to normal], . . . and that the indolent [lazy persons] and improvident [unwise persons] would soon experience the evils of their idleness and sloth, many startled [panicked] . . . and . . . complained . . . of the weight of public taxes . . . and at the cruelty of . . . creditors [those to whom money is owed] to call for their just dues [rightful payment]. . . . The disaffected [unhappy people] . . . attempted . . . to stop the courts of law, and to suspend the operations of government. This they hoped to do until . . . an end should thereby be put to public and private debts."

Lincoln's background as a general, state official, and leader against the rebels likely gave him a negative point of view on the revolt. His reference to the rebels as lazy and unwise also provides clues to his attitude. You should weigh such factors when evaluating the accuracy of his statement.

Practice the Skill

The following statement about Shays's Rebellion came from a Massachusetts farmer. Read it and apply the guidelines to answer the questions.

"I've labored hard all my days. . . . I have been . . . obliged to do more than my part in the [Revolutionary] war; been loaded with . . . rates [taxes], . . . been . . . [abused] by sheriffs . . . and [debt] collectors. . . . I have lost a great deal. . . . [T]he great men are going to get all we have, and I think it is time for us to . . . put a stop to it."

1. From what point of view is this person commenting on the revolt? What is his opinion of it?

2. How does his view of himself differ from Lincoln's view of people like him?

3. Is this view of the revolt likely to be more accurate than Lincoln's view? Why or why not?

Review Vocabulary, Terms, and People

Match the numbered person or term with the correct lettered definition.

1. Bill of Rights
2. checks and balances
3. constitution
4. Constitutional Convention
5. *Federalist Papers*
6. inflation
7. Northwest Territory
8. George Mason
9. tariffs
10. Three-Fifths Compromise

a. agreement that stated that each slave would be counted as three-fifths of a person when determining representation

b. delegate to the Constitutional Convention who became an Antifederalist

c. increased prices for goods and services combined with the reduced value of money

d. area including present-day Illinois, Indiana, Michigan, Ohio, Wisconsin, and part of Minnesota

e. meetings held in Philadelphia at which delegates from the states attempted to improve the existing government

f. series of essays in support of the Constitution

g. set of basic principles that determines the powers and duties of a government

h. system that prevents any branch of government from becoming too powerful

i. taxes on imports or exports

j. the first 10 amendments to the Constitution

Comprehension and Critical Thinking

Lesson 1

11. a. Describe What powers did the Articles of Confederation give the national government?
    b. Summarize What did the Confederation Congress do to strengthen the United States?
    c. Evaluate Which document or institution do you think had the greatest influence on the development of the United States? Why?

Lesson 2

12. a. Recall What was Shays's Rebellion?
    b. Draw Conclusions What was the general attitude of foreign nations toward the new government of the United States? Why?

    c. Evaluate Of the problems experienced by the Confederation Congress, which do you think was the most harmful? Why?

Lesson 3

13. a. Describe In what ways did the Constitution strengthen the central government?
    b. Explain How does federalism limit the power of the central government?
    c. Explain How did the two compromises reached during the Constitutional Convention satisfy competing groups?
    d. Elaborate Which decisions made in the Constitutional Convention gave the national government greater decision-making powers than it had under the Articles of Confederation?
    e. Evaluate In your opinion were there any weaknesses in the Constitution? Explain your answer.

Lesson 4

14. **a.** Recall What was the purpose of the Bill of Rights?

b. Explain Why were some Americans opposed to the Constitution?

c. Draw Conclusions How did the compromises in the Constitutional Convention affect the results of the ratification process?

d. Evaluate Would you have supported the Federalists or the Antifederalists? Explain your answer.

Review Themes

15. **Politics** What political problems resulted from a weak central government under the Articles of Confederation?

16. **Politics** How did political disagreements lead to important compromises in the creation of the Constitution?

Reading Skills

Understand Chronological Order *Use the Reading Skills taught in this module to answer the question below.*

17. Organize the following events chronologically according to the module.

a. The *Federalist Papers* are published.

b. The Constitution is ratified.

c. The Articles of Confederation is ratified.

d. Shays's Rebellion occurs.

e. The Constitutional Convention meets in Philadelphia.

Social Studies Skills

Determine Different Points of View *Use the Social Studies Skills taught in this module to answer the question below.*

18. List three differences between the Virginia Plan and the New Jersey Plan.

Focus on Writing

19. **Write an Editorial** It is 1788 and you are writing an editorial to a local newspaper. You want to convince your readers that the new Constitution will be much better than the old Articles of Confederation. You should start your editorial with a strong statement of your opinion about the Constitution. Then write two sentences about each of your main points of support—a weakness of the Articles of Confederation and/or a strength of the Constitution. End your editorial with a call to action: Ask the delegates to the Constitutional Convention to ratify the Constitution. Remember that you are trying to convince people to make a very important decision for our country—be persuasive.

Module 6

Citizenship and the Constitution

Essential Question

Which ideas in the Constitution are most important for preserving freedom?

About the Photo: Citizens like these must fulfill the duties and responsibilities of citizenship.

 Explore ONLINE!

VIDEOS, including...
• Could You Pass the U.S. Citizenship Test?

HISTORY.

☑ Document-Based Investigations

☑ Graphic Organizers

☑ Interactive Games

☑ Image Carousel: The Federal Government

☑ Interactive Chart: How a Bill Becomes a Law

☑ Interactive Chart: The Pathway to Citizenship

In this module you will learn about the Constitution of the United States, the Bill of Rights, and what it means to be an American citizen. You will also be able to read the full text of the Constitution.

What You Will Learn ...

Lesson 1: Establishing the Constitution. **182**
The Big Idea   A new Constitution strengthened the national government.

Lesson 2: Structure of the Government **188**
The Big Idea   The U.S. Constitution balances the powers of the federal government among the legislative, executive, and judicial branches.

The Constitution of the United States **195**

Lesson 3: The Bill of Rights **223**
The Big Idea   The Bill of Rights was added to the Constitution to define clearly the rights and freedoms of citizens.

Lesson 4: Rights and Responsibilities of Citizenship. **234**
The Big Idea   American citizenship involves great privileges and serious responsibilities.

United States

1785

1787 On May 14, state delegates begin to arrive at the Constitutional Convention in Philadelphia.

1791 The Bill of Rights becomes part of the Constitution on December 15.

1788 The Constitution goes into effect after New Hampshire becomes the ninth state to ratify it.

1910

< 1920 The Nineteenth Amendment gives all American women the right to vote.

1942 The Fair Employment Act bans discrimination in the workplace.

1950

∧ 1954 In *Brown* v. *Board of Education*, the Supreme Court declares segregation in public schools to be unconstitutional.

< 1971 The Twenty-Sixth Amendment is ratified, giving the right to vote to all U.S. citizens 18 years or older.

1990 The Americans with Disabilities Act is passed.

1995

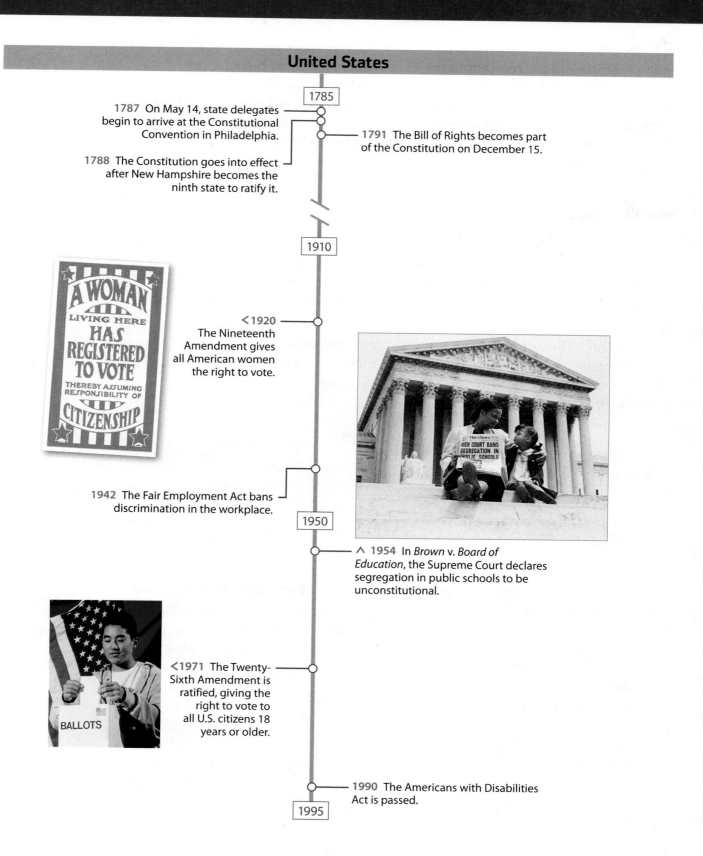

Reading Social Studies

Politics

In this module you will read about the Constitution, the three branches of government, the Bill of Rights, and the duties and responsibilities of a United States citizen. As you read about each of these topics, you will see the American political system at work—not only in the Bill of Rights, but also through the responsibilities U.S. citizens have as they vote for leaders and work to help their communities and nation.

READING FOCUS:

Summarize Historical Texts

History books are full of information. Sometimes the sheer amount of information they contain can make processing what you read difficult. In those cases, it may be helpful to stop for a moment and summarize what you've read.

Write a Summary A summary is a short restatement of the most important ideas in a text. The example below shows three steps used in writing a summary. First, underline important details. Then, write a short summary of each paragraph. Finally, combine these paragraph summaries into a short summary of the whole passage.

The Constitution
Article II, Section 1

1. The <u>executive Power</u> shall be vested in a <u>President of the United States of America</u>. He shall hold his Office during the Term of <u>four Years</u>, and, together with the <u>Vice President</u>, chosen for the same Term, be <u>elected</u>, as follows:

2. Each state shall <u>appoint</u>, in such Manner as the Legislature thereof may direct, a Number of <u>Electors</u>, equal to the whole <u>Number of Senators and Representatives</u> to which the State may be entitled in the Congress; but no Senator or Representative, or Person holding an Office of Trust or Profit under the United States, shall be appointed an Elector.

Summary of Paragraph 1
The executive branch is headed by a president and vice president, each elected for four-year terms.

Summary of Paragraph 2
The electors who choose the president and vice president are appointed. Each state has the same number of electors as it has members of Congress.

Combined Summary
The president and vice president, who run the executive branch, are elected every four years by state-appointed electors.

You Try It!

The following passage is from the U.S. Constitution. As you read it, decide which facts you would include in a summary of the passage.

The Constitution
Article I, Section 2

1. The House of Representatives shall be composed of Members chosen every second Year by the People of the several States, and the Electors in each State shall have the Qualifications requisite for Electors of the most numerous branch of the State Legislature.

2. No person shall be a Representative who shall not have attained to the Age of twenty five years, and been seven Years a Citizen of the United States, and who shall not, when elected, be an Inhabitant of the State in which he shall be chosen.

After you read the passage, answer the following questions.

1. Which of the following statements best summarizes the first paragraph of this passage?
   a. Congress has a House of Representatives.
   b. Members of the House of Representatives are elected every two years by state electors.

2. Using the steps described on the previous page, write a summary of the second paragraph of this passage.

3. Combine the summary statement you chose in Question 1 with the summary statement you wrote in Question 2 to create a single summary of this entire passage.

As you read Module 6, think about what details you would include in a summary of each paragraph.

Key Terms and People

Lesson 1
Constitutional Convention
James Madison
Virginia Plan
New Jersey Plan
Great Compromise
Three-Fifths Compromise
popular sovereignty
legislative branch
executive branch
judicial branch
checks and balances
federalism
amendments
Federalists
Federalist Papers
Antifederalists
Bill of Rights

Lesson 2
federal system
impeach
veto
executive orders
pardons
Thurgood Marshall
Sandra Day O'Connor
Sonia Sotomayor

Lesson 3
majority rule
petition
search warrant
due process
indict
double jeopardy
eminent domain

Lesson 4
naturalized citizens
deport
draft
interest groups
political action committees

Establishing the Constitution

The Big Idea
A new Constitution strengthened the national government.

Main Ideas
- Delegates met at the Constitutional Convention to improve the government.
- The Great Compromise and the Three-Fifths Compromise resolved controversial issues.
- The new government was based on popular sovereignty, balance of power, and federalism.
- Federalists and Antifederalists debated the Constitution.
- The Constitution was ratified.

Key Terms and People
Constitutional Convention
James Madison
Virginia Plan
New Jersey Plan
Great Compromise
Three-Fifths Compromise
popular sovereignty
legislative branch
executive branch
judicial branch
checks and balances
federalism
amendments
Federalists
Federalist Papers
Antifederalists
Bill of Rights

If YOU were there . . .

You are representing your county at the New York Convention in 1788. You will be voting on the new Constitution. The majority of delegates oppose the new Constitution. They think it will give the national government too much power. You have read that the Constitution proposes a government that is shared between a federal government and the states. By the time you arrive in Poughkeepsie for the convention, eight states have already ratified the Constitution.

What do you want to know before you vote?

Constitutional Convention
The Confederation Congress invited each state to send delegates to a convention with the goal of improving the Articles of Confederation. The Convention opened on May 25, 1787, in Philadelphia. The first order of business was to nominate a president for the Convention. Every delegate voted for the hero of the Revolution, George Washington.

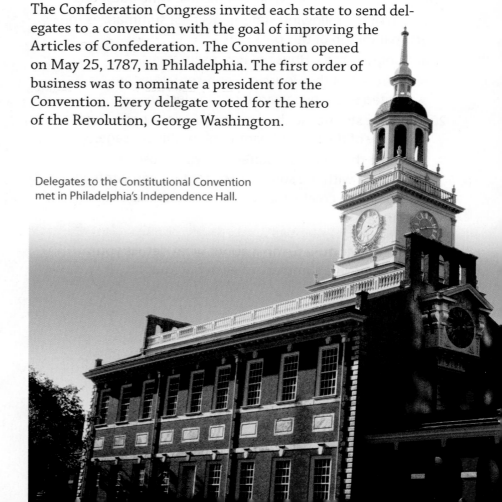

Delegates to the Constitutional Convention met in Philadelphia's Independence Hall.

The 55 delegates to the **Constitutional Convention**, as the Philadelphia meeting became known, were a very impressive group. Many had been members of their state legislatures and had helped write their state constitutions. Roger Sherman, a Connecticut delegate, was a signer of the Declaration of Independence and the Articles of Confederation. Pennsylvania's Gouverneur Morris had also signed the Articles of Confederation. Pennsylvania delegate James Wilson was known for his brilliant legal mind. Virginia delegate **James Madison** contributed many ideas that shaped the Constitution.

Some key people did not attend. Thomas Jefferson and John Adams were overseas at their diplomatic posts. Others had political objections. For example, Patrick Henry, who had been elected as a delegate from Virginia, refused to go. He said he "smelled a rat . . . tending toward monarchy."

Also, the Convention did not reflect the diverse U.S. population of the 1780s. There were no Native Americans, African Americans, or women among the delegates. These groups of people were not recognized as citizens and were not invited to attend.

Reading Check
Summarize Why did the Confederation Congress call for the Constitutional Convention?

Great Compromise

By 1787, many Americans realized that the nation needed a government that could keep order. They wanted a government that was strong enough to protect individual rights but not so strong that it would oppress them.

As the Convention began, the delegates disagreed about what form the new government would take. Edmund Randolph of Virginia presented the **Virginia Plan**. He proposed a new federal constitution that would give supreme power to the central government. The legislature would be made up of two houses of representatives. States with larger populations would have more representatives than would smaller states. Delegates from the small states feared that this plan would give large states too much power.

New Jersey delegate William Paterson presented an alternative plan. The **New Jersey Plan** called for a one-house legislature. According to this plan, each state would have an equal number of votes in the federal government. The plan gave the federal government the power to tax citizens, and it allowed the government to regulate commerce.

Connecticut delegate Roger Sherman proposed the Great Compromise on June 30, 1787. The compromise combined features of the Virginia and New Jersey plans.

The delegates struggled to solve the problem of representation in the legislature. In early July, a committee led by Roger Sherman and other delegates from Connecticut offered a deal known as the **Great Compromise**. The legislative branch would have two houses. To satisfy the smaller states, each state would have an equal number of votes in the Senate. To satisfy the larger states, representation in the House of Representatives was set according to state populations.

Reading Check
Describe What were the major challenges at the Convention in creating a stronger national government?

Compromises on Slavery

Because representation in the House of Representatives would be based on the population of each state, the delegates had to decide who would be counted in that population.

Compromise and the Slave Trade

The issue of slavery highlighted the growing division between the North and the South. Gouverneur Morris, representing Pennsylvania, spoke with much emotion against the Three-Fifths Compromise. Also, the idea of banning the foreign slave trade prompted southerners such as John Rutledge of South Carolina to defend the practice.

"If the Convention thinks that North Carolina, South Carolina, and Georgia will ever agree to the plan [to prohibit the slave trade], unless their right to import slaves be untouched, the expectation is vain [useless]."

—John Rutledge, quoted in *The Atlantic Monthly,* February 1891, by Frank Gaylord Cook

"The admission of slaves into the Representation . . . comes to this: that the inhabitant of [a state] who goes to the coast of Africa and . . . tears away his fellow creatures from their dearest connections and damns them to the most cruel bondage [slavery], shall have more votes in a Government [established] for protection of the rights of mankind."

—Gouverneur Morris, quoted in *The Constitution: A Pro-Slavery Compact,* edited by Wendell Phillips

Analyze Historical Sources
How did these two views of slavery differ?

Representation based on population raised the question of whether slaves should be counted as people. The southern states had many more slaves than the northern states. Southerners wanted the slaves to be counted as part of the population for representation but not for taxation. Northerners, whose states had few slaves, argued that slaves were not citizens and should not be counted for representation but should be counted for taxation.

The delegates reached an agreement, known as the **Three-Fifths Compromise**. Three-fifths of the slave population would be counted for both purposes: representation in the legislature and taxation.

The delegates had another point of disagreement. Some of the delegates believed slavery was wrong and wanted the federal government to ban the slave trade. Others said that the southern states' economies needed the slave trade. The delegates from South Carolina and Georgia stated that they would never accept any plan "unless their right to import slaves be untouched." Again, the delegates settled on a compromise. On August 29, they agreed that Congress could not ban the slave trade until 1808.

Reading Check
Analyze Point of View How did the Constitutional Convention compromise on the issue of slavery?

A New System of Government

Most Convention delegates wanted a strong national government. At the same time, they hoped to protect **popular sovereignty**, the idea that political authority belongs to the people. Americans had boldly declared this idea in the Declaration of Independence.

The framers of the Constitution divided the national government into three branches. The **legislative branch** is responsible for proposing and passing laws. It is made up of the Senate and the House of Representatives. The **executive branch** includes the president and the departments that help run the government. The executive branch makes sure that laws are carried out. The **judicial branch** is made up of all the national courts. This branch interprets laws, punishes criminals, and settles disputes between states.

The Constitution also includes a system of **checks and balances**, which keeps any branch of the government from becoming too powerful. For example, Congress has the power to pass bills into law. The president has the power to veto laws that Congress passes. Congress can then override the president's veto with a two-thirds majority vote. The Supreme Court has the power to review laws passed by Congress and strike down any laws that violate the Constitution.

To balance the power between the national and state governments, the delegates created the system of **federalism**. Federalism is the sharing of power between a central government and the states that make up a country. The Constitution requires each state to obey the authority of the federal, or national, government. States have control over government functions not specifically assigned to the federal government.

The framers of the Constitution also included a method for changing or adding to the Constitution. They wanted the government to be able to adapt as changes were needed. The process for amending, or adding **amendments** to, the Constitution was made difficult. Major changes to the government would require the approval of two-thirds of each house of Congress and three-fourths of states before it could take effect.

On September 17, 1787, the delegates passed the Constitution. All but three of the 42 delegates present signed the Constitution. Even though the Constitution was adopted by the Convention, delegates continued to debate the power of state governments and the role of each branch of the national government.

The legislative branch consists of the Senate and the House of Representatives. Members of both bodies meet at the U.S. Capitol in Washington, DC, to discuss, debate, and craft national policies and laws.

Reading Check
Explain How did the concept of popular sovereignty influence the new system of government?

Federalists and Antifederalists

The framers of the Constitution knew that the document would cause controversy. At once they began to campaign for ratification, or approval, of the Constitution.

Concerns of the Federalists The framers suspected that people might be afraid that the Constitution would take too much power away from the states. To address this fear, the framers explained that the Constitution was based on federalism. Linking themselves to the idea of federalism, the people who supported the Constitution took the name **Federalists**.

The Federalists promoted their views and answered their critics in a series of essays known as the **Federalist Papers**. Three well-known politicians wrote the *Federalist Papers*—James Madison, Alexander Hamilton, and John Jay. These essays first appeared as letters in New York newspapers. Calling for ratification of the Constitution, the *Federalist Papers* appealed both to reason and emotion.

Concerns of the Antifederalists The **Antifederalists**, people who opposed the Constitution, thought the Constitution took too much power away from the states and did not guarantee rights for the people. Some feared that a strong president might be declared king. Others feared the Senate might become a powerful ruling class. In either case, they thought, the liberties fiercely won during the Revolution might be lost.

Antifederalists received support from rural areas, where people feared a strong government that might add to their tax burden. Large states and those with strong economies, such as New York, also were unsupportive of the Constitution at first.

Reading Check
Compare and Contrast Describe the disagreements between Federalists and Antifederalists.

Ratifying the Constitution

The proposed U.S. Constitution contained no guarantee that the government would protect the rights of the people or of the states. Some supporters of the Constitution, including Thomas Jefferson, wanted to add a bill of rights—a formal summary of citizens' rights and freedoms—as a set of amendments to the Constitution.

Ratification Process Antifederalists wanted written guarantees that the people would have their individual freedoms protected. In the end, Federalists yielded to the people's demands and promised to add a bill of rights if the states ratified the Constitution.

In December 1787, Delaware, New Jersey, and Pennsylvania voted for ratification. In January 1788, Georgia and Connecticut ratified the Constitution, followed by Massachusetts in early February. By late June, nine states had ratified. The Constitution was officially ratified with nine votes.

It was vital, however, to get the support of Virginia, the largest state. James Madison recommended that Virginia ratify the Constitution, with the addition of a bill of rights. After bitter debate, at the end of June, Virginia narrowly ratified the Constitution with 89 in favor and 79 opposed.

The news of Virginia's vote arrived while the New York convention was in debate. Until then, the Antifederalists had outnumbered the Federalists. But with Virginia's ratification, New Yorkers decided to join the Union. New York also called for a bill of rights. It would be another year before North Carolina ratified the Constitution, followed by Rhode Island in 1790. By then, the new Congress had already written a bill of rights and submitted it to the states for approval.

Bill of Rights Madison, who took office in the first Congress in the winter of 1789, took up the cause of the bill of rights. In September 1789 Congress

Virginian James Madison is often called the Father of the Constitution. He played a key role in writing the document, and then rallied support for its adoption along with the Bill of Rights.

proposed 12 amendments and sent them to the states for ratification. By December 1791 the states had ratified the **Bill of Rights**—ten of the proposed amendments intended to protect citizens' rights.

Of these amendments to the Constitution, the first nine guarantee basic individual freedoms, including freedom of religion, of speech, and of the press. Taken as a whole, the Bill of Rights creates an invisible but powerful shield that protects people from government abuse.

But the Bill of Rights was more than that. It was the first step in making the Constitution a living document, one that can be amended to reflect changes in society. The Constitutional Convention provided for such changes. Two-thirds of each house of Congress or two-thirds of the state legislatures can propose an amendment. To become law, an amendment then needs the approval of three-fourths of the states. By this process, the Bill of Rights became the first ten amendments.

Summary and Preview In this lesson you learned how the Constitution was created, developed, debated, and finally ratified. In the next lesson you will learn more details about the structure of the U.S. government.

Reading Check
Evaluate Explain how the lack of a bill of rights made ratification of the Constitution more difficult.

Lesson 1 Assessment

Review Ideas, Terms, and People

1. **a. Summarize** What was the purpose of the Constitutional Convention?

   b. Describe Who attended the Constitutional Convention?

   c. Explain Why did the Convention not reflect the diverse U.S. population at that time?

2. **a. Contrast** How did the Virginia Plan and New Jersey Plan differ?

   b. Analyze Which plan appealed more to the smaller states? Explain why.

   c. Summarize How did the Great Compromise resolve the issue over representation?

3. **a. Recall** Under the Three-Fifths Compromise, what was decided about how each state's population would be counted?

   b. Describe Under what conditions did southern states agree to consider a ban on the slave trade?

   c. Summarize What were the main points of disagreement on the issue of slavery?

4. **a. Recall** Why did the framers of the Constitution create the ability to add amendments?

   b. Explain What is popular sovereignty?

   c. Analyze What power did federalism give to state governments?

5. **a. Recall** How did Federalists get their name?

   b. Summarize What arguments did the Antifederalists use to convince people to reject the Constitution?

   c. Explain Why were the *Federalist Papers* important?

6. **a. Recall** When was the Constitution officially ratified?

   b. Explain Why was the ratification of the Constitution in Virginia especially important?

   c. Analyze Why did the Antifederalists demand the Bill of Rights?

Critical Thinking

7. **Summarize** In this lesson you learned how the Constitution was developed and established. Create a web diagram similar to the one below and use it to summarize the important achievements of the Constitution.

Creating the Constitution

Structure of the Government

The Big Idea

The U.S. Constitution balances the powers of the federal government among the legislative, executive, and judicial branches.

Main Ideas

- The framers of the Constitution devised the federal system.

- The legislative branch makes the nation's laws.

- The executive branch enforces the nation's laws.

- The judicial branch determines whether or not laws are constitutional.

Key Terms and People

federal system
impeach
veto
executive orders
pardons
Thurgood Marshall
Sandra Day O'Connor
Sonia Sotomayor

If YOU were there . . .

You have just been elected to the U.S. House of Representatives. You know that committees do much of the work in Congress. They deal with many different fields such as foreign policy, agriculture, national security, science, and education. You would like to ask for a spot on a committee whose work interests you.

Which committee would you ask to serve on?

The Federal System

The framers of the Constitution wanted to create a government powerful enough to protect the rights of citizens and defend the country against its enemies. To do so, they set up a **federal system** of government, a system that divides powers between the states and the federal government.

The Constitution assigns certain powers to the national government. These are called delegated powers. Among them are the right to coin and regulate money, regulate trade among the states and with other nations, make treaties with foreign nations, declare war, and make any laws necessary to carry out these powers. National powers are designed to promote the general welfare, or common good—the needs and interests of the people as a whole. For example, by regulating trade and developing a uniform monetary system, the government creates conditions that allow businesses throughout the nation to prosper.

Reserved powers are those kept by the states. These powers include creating local governments and holding elections. Concurrent powers are those shared by the federal and state governments. They include taxing, borrowing money, and enforcing laws.

Sometimes, Congress has had to stretch its delegated powers to deal with new or unexpected issues. A clause in the Constitution states that Congress may "make all

Compare Landmark Documents

Magna Carta (1215)
- set limits to the king's power
- guaranteed fair legal proceedings for all free English citizens

Declaration of Independence (1776)
- declared that citizens have natural rights that cannot be taken away
- argued that a government's power comes from the consent of the governed

Articles of Confederation (1777)
- created a democratic republic
- established a national government while preserving most state powers

U.S. Constitution (1787)
- created a federal system with a strong national government
- balanced power among three branches of the national government

Federalist Papers (1787–1788)
- defended the Constitution against critics
- explained how checks and balances and other features of the Constitution limited authority and preserved liberty

Bill of Rights (1789)
- guaranteed basic individual freedoms such as freedom of speech and the right to due process for all free Americans
- set an example of how to change the Constitution through amendments

The original copy of the U.S. Constitution is housed in the National Archives in Washington, DC.

Reading Check
Summarize How is power divided between the federal and state governments?

Academic Vocabulary
distinct separate

Laws which shall be necessary and proper" for carrying out its duties. This clause, called the elastic clause—because it can be stretched (like elastic)—provides flexibility for the government. The federal government has used this clause to provide public services such as funding for the arts and humanities.

Legislative Branch

The federal government has three branches, each with <u>distinct</u> responsibilities and powers. This separation balances the branches and keeps any one of them from growing too powerful. The first branch of government

Separation of Powers

U.S. Constitution

Legislative Branch (Congress)	Executive Branch (President)	Judicial Branch (Supreme Court)
• Writes the laws • Confirms presidential appointments • Approves treaties • Grants money • Declares war	• Proposes laws • Administers the laws • Commands armed forces • Appoints ambassadors and other officials • Conducts foreign policy • Makes treaties	• Interprets the Constitution and other laws • Reviews lower-court decisions

is the legislative branch, or Congress. The legislators elected to Congress make the nation's laws. Article I of the Constitution divides Congress into the House of Representatives and the Senate.

With 435 members, the House of Representatives is the larger congressional house. The U.S. Census, a population count made every ten years, determines how many members represent each state. A system called apportionment keeps total membership at 435. If one state gains a member, another state loses one. Members must be at least 25 years old, live in the state where they were elected, and have been U.S. citizens for seven years. They serve two-year terms.

The Senate has two members, or senators, per state. Senators represent the interests of the whole state, not just a district. They must be at least 30 years old, have been U.S. citizens for nine years, and live in the state they represent. They serve six-year terms. The senior senator of a state is the one who has served the longer of the two. Members of Congress can serve an unlimited number of terms in office.

The political party with more members in each house is the majority party. The one with fewer members is the minority party. The leader of the House of Representatives, or Speaker of the House, is elected by House members from the majority party.

The U.S. vice president serves as president of the Senate. He takes no part in Senate debates but can vote to break ties. If the vice president is absent, the president pro tempore (pro tem for short) leads the Senate. There is no law for how the Senate must choose this position, but it traditionally goes to the majority party's senator who has served the longest.

Congress begins sessions, or meetings, each year in the first week of January. Both houses do most of their work in committees. Each committee studies certain types of bills, or suggested laws. For example, all bills about taxes begin in the House Ways and Means Committee.

Reading Check
Compare and Contrast What are the similarities in requirements for members of the House of Representatives and the Senate? What are the differences?

Executive Branch

Article II of the Constitution lists the powers of the executive branch. This branch enforces the laws passed by Congress.

President and Vice President As head of the executive branch, the president is the most powerful elected leader in the United States. To qualify for the presidency or vice presidency, one must be a native-born U.S. citizen at least 35 years old. The president must also have been a U.S. resident for 14 years.

Americans elect a president and vice president every four years. Franklin D. Roosevelt, who won four times, was the only president to serve more than two terms. Now, the Twenty-Second Amendment limits presidents to two terms. If a president dies, resigns, or is removed from office, the vice president becomes president for the rest of the term.

The House of Representatives can **impeach**, or vote to bring charges of serious crimes against, a president. Impeachment cases are tried in the Senate. If a president is found guilty, Congress can remove him from office. In 1868 Andrew Johnson was the first president to be impeached. President Bill Clinton was impeached in 1998. However, in each instance, the Senate found the president not guilty.

Quick Facts

Checks and Balances

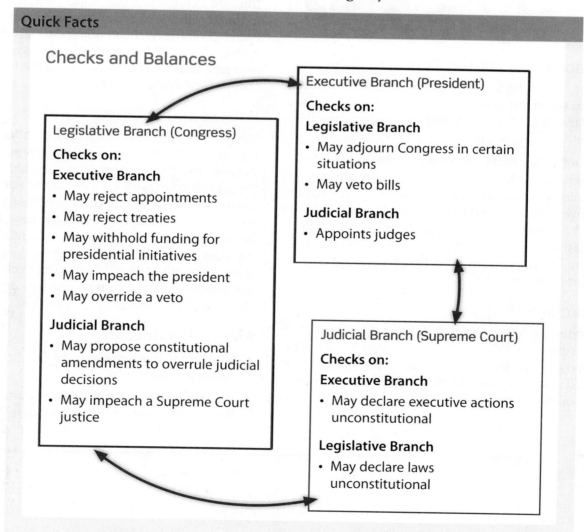

Legislative Branch (Congress)

Checks on:

Executive Branch
- May reject appointments
- May reject treaties
- May withhold funding for presidential initiatives
- May impeach the president
- May override a veto

Judicial Branch
- May propose constitutional amendments to overrule judicial decisions
- May impeach a Supreme Court justice

Executive Branch (President)

Checks on:

Legislative Branch
- May adjourn Congress in certain situations
- May veto bills

Judicial Branch
- Appoints judges

Judicial Branch (Supreme Court)

Checks on:

Executive Branch
- May declare executive actions unconstitutional

Legislative Branch
- May declare laws unconstitutional

Working with Congress The president and Congress are often on different sides of an issue. However, they must still work together.

Congress passes laws. The president, however, can ask Congress to pass or reject bills. The president also can **veto**, or cancel, laws Congress has passed. Congress can try to override, or undo, the veto. However, this is difficult since it takes a two-thirds majority vote. To carry out laws affecting the Constitution, treaties, and statutes, the president issues **executive orders**. These commands have the power of law. The president also may grant **pardons**, or freedom from punishment, to persons convicted of federal crimes or facing criminal charges.

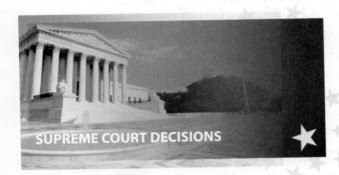

SUPREME COURT DECISIONS

Background of the Court

The rest of the Supreme Court Decisions features you see in this book will highlight important cases of the Court. But in this first one, we'll discuss the history of the Court.

The first Supreme Court met in 1790 at the Royal Exchange in New York City. The ground floor of this building was an open-air market. When the national government moved to Philadelphia, the Court met in basement rooms in Independence Hall. Once in Washington, the Court heard cases in the Capitol until the present Supreme Court building was completed in 1932.

Circuit Riding

Today the Supreme Court holds court only in Washington, DC. In the past, however, the justices had to travel through assigned circuits, hearing cases together with a district judge in a practice known as circuit riding.

The justices complained bitterly about the inconvenience of travel, which was often over unpaved roads and in bad weather. This system was not just inconvenient to the justices, however. Some people worried about the fairness of a system that required justices who had heard cases at trial to rule on them again on appeal. Other people, however, thought that the practice helped keep the justices in touch with the needs and feelings of the average citizen. Eventually, circuit riding interfered so much with the increased amount of business of the Supreme Court that Congress passed a law ending the practice in the late 1800s.

Path to the Supreme Court

When a case is decided by a state or federal court, the losing side may have a chance to appeal the decision to a higher court. Under the federal system, this higher court is called the court of appeals. A person who loses in that court may then appeal to the Supreme Court to review the case. But the Supreme Court does not have to accept all appeals. It usually chooses to hear only cases in which there is an important legal principle to be decided or if two federal courts of appeals disagree on how an issue should be decided.

Analyze Information

1. What are two reasons why the practice of circuit riding ended?

2. Why do you think the Supreme Court does not hear every case that is appealed to it?

The president also commands the armed forces. In emergencies, the president can call on U.S. troops. Only Congress, however, can declare war. Other executive duties include conducting foreign relations and creating treaties.

Reading Check
Analyze How does the veto help balance power between the president and Congress?

Executive departments do most of the executive branch work. As of 2014 there were 15 such departments. The president chooses department heads, who are called secretaries, and the Senate approves them. The heads make up the cabinet, which advises the president. The Office of Homeland Security was established in 2002 to address the increased threat of terrorism following September 11, 2001. In 2003 the office became the Department of Homeland Security, the newest executive department.

Judicial Branch

The third branch of government, the judicial branch, is made up of a system of federal courts headed by the U.S. Supreme Court. The Constitution created the Supreme Court, but the Judiciary Act of 1789 created the system of lower district and circuit courts.

Article III generally outlines the courts' duties. Federal courts can strike down a state or federal law if the court finds a law unconstitutional. Congress can then try to revise the law to make it constitutional.

District Courts The president makes appointments to federal courts. In an effort to keep federal judges free of party influence, the judges are given life appointments. The lower federal courts are divided according to cases over which they have jurisdiction, or authority. Each state has at least one of the 94 district courts.

Sonia Sotomayor is the first Hispanic American and the third woman to serve on the Supreme Court.

Courts of Appeals If someone convicted of a crime believes the trial was unfair, he or she may take the case to the court of appeals. There are 13 courts of appeals. Each has a panel of judges to decide if cases heard in the lower courts were tried appropriately. If the judges uphold, or accept, the original decision, the original outcome stands. Otherwise, the case may be retried in the lower court.

Supreme Court After a case is decided by the court of appeals, the losing side may appeal the decision to the Supreme Court. Thousands of cases go to the Supreme Court yearly in the hope of a hearing, but the Court has time to hear only about 100. Generally, the cases heard involve important constitutional or public-interest issues. If the Court declines to hear a case, the court of appeals decision is final.

Nine justices sit on the Supreme Court. The chief justice of the United States leads the Court. Unlike the president and members of Congress, there are no specific constitutional requirements for becoming a justice.

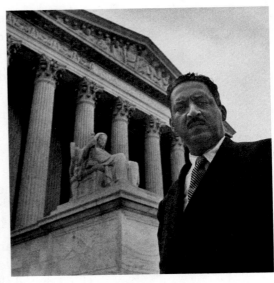

In recent decades, the Supreme Court has become more diverse. In 1967 **Thurgood Marshall** became the first African American justice. **Sandra Day O'Connor** became the first female Court justice after her 1981 appointment by President Ronald Reagan. In 2009 President Barack Obama appointed the first Hispanic American justice, **Sonia Sotomayor**.

As a lawyer, Thurgood Marshall challenged racial discrimination in the courts, arguing thirty-two cases before the Supreme Court. In 1967, he became the Court's first African American justice.

Reading Check
Summarize
Describe the structure and responsibilities of the judicial branch.

Summary and Preview In this lesson you learned about the balance between the different branches of the federal government. In the next lesson you will learn about the Bill of Rights.

Lesson 2 Assessment

Review Ideas, Terms, and People

1. **a. Describe** What type of government did the Constitution establish for the United States?
   b. Contrast What is the difference between delegated, reserved, and concurrent (shared) powers?
   c. Draw Conclusions In what circumstances are national laws and rules better suited for promoting the common good than laws and rules of individual states?

2. **a. Compare and Contrast** In what ways are the Senate and the House of Representatives similar and different?
   b. Elaborate Why do you think the requirements for serving in the Senate are stricter than those for serving in the House of Representatives?
   c. Evaluate How important is the role of legislator in a representative democracy? Explain.

3. **a. Describe** What powers are granted to the president?
   b. Make Generalizations Why is it important that the president and Congress work together in resolving governmental issues?
   c. Evaluate What do you think is the most important power granted to the president? Why?

4. **a. Explain** What is the main power of the judicial branch?
   b. Summarize What are the roles of the different levels in the federal court system?
   c. Evaluate Which branch of government do you feel is most important? Explain your answer.

Critical Thinking

5. **Categorize** In this lesson you learned about the branches of government. Create a web diagram similar to the one below and use it to show two powers of each branch of government.

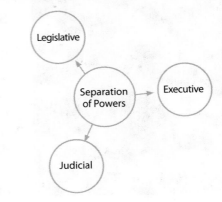

The Constitution
of the United States

Preamble

The preamble states the main purposes of the new government under the Constitution. The government will strengthen the relationship between the states, create a fair legal system, maintain order within the country, defend the nation against foreign enemies, promote the public's well-being, and protect individual liberties. The phrase "We the People" emphasizes that the government's power and legitimacy come from the American people as a whole, not from the individual states.

We the People of the United States, in Order to form a more perfect Union, establish Justice, insure domestic Tranquility, provide for the common defence, promote the general Welfare, and secure the Blessings of Liberty to ourselves and our Posterity, do ordain and establish this Constitution for the United States of America.

Note: The parts of the Constitution that have been lined through are no longer in force or no longer apply because of later amendments. The titles of the sections and articles are added for easier reference.

Legislative
Branch Article
I explains how the
legislative branch,
called Congress,
is organized. The
chief purpose of the
legislative branch is to
make laws. Congress
is made up of the Sen-
ate and the House of
Representatives.

**The House of
Representatives**
The number of mem-
bers each state has
in the House is based
on the population of
the individual state.
In 1929 Congress
permanently fixed the
size of the House at
435 members.

Vocabulary

[1] **those bound to
Service** indentured
servants

[2] **all other Persons**
slaves

[3] **Enumeration**
census or official
population count

ARTICLE I THE LEGISLATURE

Section 1. Congress

All legislative Powers herein granted shall be vested in a Congress
of the United States, which shall consist of a Senate and House of
Representatives.

Section 2. The House of Representatives

1. Elections The House of Representatives shall be composed of Members
chosen every second Year by the People of the several States, and the Electors in each State shall have the Qualifications requisite for Electors of the
most numerous Branch of the State Legislature.

2. Qualifications No Person shall be a Representative who shall not have
attained to the Age of twenty five Years, and been seven Years a Citizen
of the United States, and who shall not, when elected, be an Inhabitant of
that State in which he shall be chosen.

3. Number of Representatives Representatives and direct Taxes shall be
apportioned among the several States which may be included within this
Union, according to their respective Numbers, which shall be determined
by adding to the whole Number of free Persons, including **those bound to
Service**[1] for a Term of Years, and excluding Indians not taxed, three fifths
of all other Persons.[2] The actual **Enumeration**[3] shall be made within
three Years after the first Meeting of the Congress of the United States,
and within every subsequent Term of ten Years, in such Manner as they
shall by Law direct. The Number of Representatives shall not exceed one
for every thirty Thousand, but each State shall have at Least one Representative; and until such enumeration shall be made, the State of New Hampshire shall be entitled to choose three, Massachusetts eight, Rhode Island
and Providence Plantations one, Connecticut five, New York six, New
Jersey four, Pennsylvania eight, Delaware one, Maryland six, Virginia ten,
North Carolina five, South Carolina five, and Georgia three.

4. Vacancies When vacancies happen in the Representation from any
State, the Executive Authority thereof shall issue Writs of Election to fill
such Vacancies.

5. Officers and Impeachment The House of Representatives shall
choose their Speaker and other Officers; and shall have the sole Power of
impeachment.

Section 3. The Senate

1. Number of Senators The Senate of the United States shall be composed
of two Senators from each State, chosen by the Legislature thereof, for six
Years; and each Senator shall have one Vote.

The Vice President The only duty that the Constitution assigns to the vice president is to preside over meetings of the Senate. Modern presidents have usually given their vice presidents more responsibilities.

EXPLORE THE DOCUMENT
If the House of Representatives charges a government official with wrongdoing, the Senate acts as a court to decide if the official is guilty. *How does the power of impeachment represent part of the system of checks and balances?*

Vocabulary

[4] **pro tempore** temporarily

[5] **Impeachments** official accusations of federal wrongdoing

2. Classifying Terms Immediately after they shall be assembled in Consequence of the first Election, they shall be divided as equally as may be into three Classes. The Seats of the Senators of the first Class shall be vacated at the Expiration of the second Year, of the second Class at the Expiration of the fourth Year, and of the third Class at the Expiration of the sixth Year, so that one third may be chosen every second Year; ~~and if Vacancies happen by Resignation, or otherwise, during the Recess of the Legislature of any State, the Executive thereof may make temporary Appointments until the next Meeting of the Legislature, which shall then fill such Vacancies.~~

3. Qualifications No Person shall be a Senator who shall not have attained to the Age of thirty Years, and been nine Years a Citizen of the United States, and who shall not, when elected, be an Inhabitant of that State for which he shall be chosen.

4. Role of Vice President The Vice President of the United States shall be President of the Senate, but shall have no Vote, unless they be equally divided.

5. Officers The Senate shall choose their other Officers, and also a President **pro tempore**,[4] in the Absence of the Vice President, or when he shall exercise the Office of President of the United States.

6. Impeachment Trials The Senate shall have the sole Power to try all **Impeachments**.[5] When sitting for that Purpose, they shall be on Oath or Affirmation. When the President of the United States is tried, the Chief Justice shall preside: And no Person shall be convicted without the Concurrence of two thirds of the Members present.

7. Punishment for Impeachment Judgment in Cases of Impeachment shall not extend further than to removal from Office, and disqualification to hold and enjoy any Office of honor, Trust or Profit under the United States: but the Party convicted shall nevertheless be liable and subject to Indictment, Trial, Judgment and Punishment, according to Law.

Quick Facts

Federal Office Terms and Requirements

Position	Term	Minimum Age	Residency	Citizenship
President	4 years	35	14 years in the U.S.	natural-born
Vice President	4 years	35	14 years in the U.S.	natural-born
Supreme Court Justice	unlimited	none	none	none
Senator	6 years	30	state in which elected	9 years
Representative	2 years	25	state in which elected	7 years

Section 4. Congressional Elections

1. Regulations The Times, Places and Manner of holding Elections for Senators and Representatives, shall be prescribed in each State by the Legislature thereof; but the Congress may at any time by Law make or alter such Regulations, except as to the Places of choosing Senators.

2. Sessions ~~The Congress shall assemble at least once in every Year, and such Meeting shall be on the first Monday in December, unless they shall by Law appoint a different Day.~~

Section 5. Rules/Procedures

1. Quorum Each House shall be the Judge of the Elections, Returns and Qualifications of its own Members, and a Majority of each shall constitute a **Quorum**[6] to do Business; but a smaller Number may **adjourn**[7] from day to day, and may be authorized to compel the Attendance of absent Members, in such Manner, and under such Penalties as each House may provide.

2. Rules and Conduct Each House may determine the Rules of its Proceedings, punish its Members for disorderly Behaviour, and, with the Concurrence of two thirds, expel a Member.

3. Records Each House shall keep a Journal of its Proceedings, and from time to time publish the same, excepting such Parts as may in their Judgment require Secrecy; and the Yeas and Nays of the Members of either House on any question shall, at the Desire of one fifth of those Present, be entered on the Journal.

4. Adjournment Neither House, during the Session of Congress, shall, without the Consent of the other, adjourn for more than three days, nor to any other Place than that in which the two Houses shall be sitting.

Section 6. Payment

1. Salary The Senators and Representatives shall receive a Compensation for their Services, to be ascertained by Law, and paid out of the Treasury of the United States. They shall in all Cases, except Treason, Felony and Breach of the Peace, be privileged from Arrest during their Attendance at the Session of their respective Houses, and in going to and returning from the same; and for any Speech or Debate in either House, they shall not be questioned in any other Place.

2. Restrictions No Senator or Representative shall, during the Time for which he was elected, be appointed to any civil Office under the Authority of the United States, which shall have been created, or the **Emoluments**[8] whereof shall have been increased during such time; and no Person holding any Office under the United States, shall be a Member of either House during his **Continuance**[9] in Office.

Vocabulary

[6] **Quorum** the minimum number of people needed to conduct business

[7] **adjourn** to stop indefinitely

[8] **Emoluments** salary

[9] **Continuance** term

Section 7. How a Bill Becomes a Law

1. Tax Bills All **Bills**[10] for raising Revenue shall originate in the House of Representatives; but the Senate may propose or concur with Amendments as on other Bills.

2. Lawmaking Every Bill which shall have passed the House of Representatives and the Senate, shall, before it become a Law, be presented to the President of the United States: If he approve he shall sign it, but if not he shall return it, with his Objections to that House in which it shall have originated, who shall enter the Objections at large on their Journal, and proceed to reconsider it. If after such Reconsideration two thirds of that House shall agree to pass the Bill, it shall be sent, together with the Objections, to the other House, by which it shall likewise be reconsidered, and if approved by two thirds of that House, it shall become a Law. But in all such Cases the Votes of both Houses shall be determined by Yeas and Nays, and the Names of the Persons voting for and against the Bill shall be entered on the Journal of each House respectively. If any Bill shall not be returned

How a Bill Becomes a Law

❶ A member of the House or the Senate introduces a bill and refers it to a committee.

❷ The House or Senate Committee may approve, rewrite, or kill the bill.

❸ The House or the Senate debates and votes on its version of the bill.

❹ House and Senate conference committee members work out the differences between the two versions.

❺ Both houses of Congress pass the revised bill.

❻ The president signs or vetoes the bill.

❼ Two-thirds majority vote of Congress is needed to approve a vetoed bill. Bill becomes a law.

Analyze Information
Why do you think the framers created this complex system for adopting laws?

by the President within ten Days (Sundays excepted) after it shall have been presented to him, the Same shall be a Law, in like Manner as if he had signed it, unless the Congress by their Adjournment prevent its Return, in which Case it shall not be a Law.

3. Role of the President Every Order, Resolution, or Vote to which the Concurrence of the Senate and House of Representatives may be necessary (except on a question of Adjournment) shall be presented to the President of the United States; and before the Same shall take Effect, shall be approved by him, or being disapproved by him, shall be repassed by two thirds of the Senate and House of Representatives, according to the Rules and Limitations prescribed in the Case of a Bill.

Section 8. Powers Granted to Congress

1. Taxation The Congress shall have Power To lay and collect Taxes, **Duties**,[11] **Imposts**[12] and **Excises**,[13] to pay the Debts and provide for the common Defense and general Welfare of the United States; but all Duties, Imposts and Excises shall be uniform throughout the United States;

2. Credit To borrow Money on the credit of the United States;

3. Commerce To regulate Commerce with foreign Nations, and among the several States, and with the Indian Tribes;

4. Naturalization and Bankruptcy To establish an uniform **Rule of Naturalization**,[14] and uniform Laws on the subject of Bankruptcies throughout the United States;

5. Money To coin Money, regulate the Value thereof, and of foreign Coin, and fix the Standard of Weights and Measures;

6. Counterfeiting To provide for the Punishment of counterfeiting the **Securities**[15] and current Coin of the United States;

7. Post Office To establish Post Offices and post Roads;

EXPLORE THE DOCUMENT
The veto power of the president is one of the important checks and balances in the Constitution. *Why do you think the framers included the ability of Congress to override a veto?*

Vocabulary

[11] **Duties** tariffs

[12] **Imposts** taxes

[13] **Excises** internal taxes on the manufacture, sale, or consumption of a commodity

[14] **Rule of Naturalization** a law by which a foreign-born person becomes a citizen

[15] **Securities** bonds

Link to Today

Native Americans and the Commerce Clause

The commerce clause gives Congress the power to "regulate Commerce with . . . the Indian Tribes." The clause has been interpreted to mean that the states cannot tax or interfere with businesses on Indian reservations, but that the federal government can. It also allows American Indian nations to develop their own governments and laws. These laws, however, can be challenged in federal court. Although reservation land usually belongs to the government of the Indian group, it is administered by the U.S. government.

Draw Conclusions
How would you describe the status of American Indian nations under the commerce clause?

Vocabulary

[16] **Letters of Marque and Reprisal** documents issued by governments allowing merchant ships to arm themselves and attack ships of an enemy nation

The Elastic Clause The framers of the Constitution wanted a national government that was strong enough to be effective. This section lists the powers given to Congress. The last portion of Section 8 contains the so-called elastic clause.

8. Patents and Copyrights To promote the Progress of Science and useful Arts, by securing for limited Times to Authors and Inventors the exclusive Right to their respective Writings and Discoveries;

9. Courts To constitute Tribunals inferior to the supreme Court;

10. International Law To define and punish Piracies and Felonies committed on the high Seas, and Offences against the Law of Nations;

11. War To declare War, grant **Letters of Marque and Reprisal**,[16] and make Rules concerning Captures on Land and Water;

12. Army To raise and support Armies, but no Appropriation of Money to that Use shall be for a longer Term than two Years;

13. Navy To provide and maintain a Navy;

14. Regulation of the Military To make Rules for the Government and Regulation of the land and naval Forces;

15. Militia To provide for calling forth the Militia to execute the Laws of the Union, suppress Insurrections and repel Invasions;

16. Regulation of the Militia To provide for organizing, arming, and disciplining, the Militia, and for governing such Part of them as may be employed in the Service of the United States, reserving to the States respectively, the Appointment of the Officers, and the Authority of training the Militia according to the discipline prescribed by Congress;

17. District of Columbia To exercise exclusive Legislation in all Cases whatsoever, over such District (not exceeding ten Miles square) as may, by Cession of particular States, and the Acceptance of Congress, become the Seat of the Government of the United States, and to exercise like Authority over all Places purchased by the Consent of the Legislature of the State in which the Same shall be, for the Erection of Forts, Magazines, Arsenals, dock-Yards, and other needful Buildings;—And

18. Necessary and Proper Clause To make all Laws which shall be necessary and proper for carrying into Execution the foregoing Powers, and all other Powers vested by this Constitution in the Government of the United States, or in any Department or Officer thereof.

Vocabulary

[17] **Writ of Habeas Corpus** a court order that requires the government to bring a prisoner to court and explain why he or she is being held

[18] **Bill of Attainder** a law declaring that a person is guilty of a particular crime

[19] **ex post facto Law** a law that is made effective prior to the date that it was passed and therefore punishes people for acts that were not illegal at the time

[20] **Capitation** a direct uniform tax imposed on each head, or person

Section 9. Powers Denied Congress

1. **Slave Trade** ~~The Migration or Importation of such Persons as any of the States now existing shall think proper to admit, shall not be prohibited by the Congress prior to the Year one thousand eight hundred and eight, but a Tax or duty may be imposed on such Importation, not exceeding ten dollars for each Person.~~

2. **Habeas Corpus** The Privilege of the **Writ of Habeas Corpus**[17] shall not be suspended, unless when in Cases of Rebellion or Invasion the public Safety may require it.

3. **Illegal Punishment** No **Bill of Attainder**[18] or **ex post facto Law**[19] shall be passed.

4. **Direct Taxes** No **Capitation**,[20] or other direct, Tax shall be laid, unless in Proportion to the Census or enumeration herein before directed to be taken.

5. **Export Taxes** No Tax or Duty shall be laid on Articles exported from any State.

6. **No Favorites** No Preference shall be given by any Regulation of Commerce or Revenue to the Ports of one State over those of another; nor shall Vessels bound to, or from, one State, be obliged to enter, clear, or pay Duties in another.

7. **Public Money** No Money shall be drawn from the Treasury, but in Consequence of Appropriations made by Law; and a regular Statement and Account of the Receipts and Expenditures of all public Money shall be published from time to time.

8. **Titles of Nobility** No Title of Nobility shall be granted by the United States: And no Person holding any Office of Profit or Trust under them, shall, without the Consent of the Congress, accept of any present, Emolument, Office, or Title, of any kind whatever, from any King, Prince, or foreign State.

Section 10. Powers Denied the States

1. **Restrictions** No State shall enter into any Treaty, Alliance, or Confederation; grant Letters of Marque and Reprisal; coin Money; emit Bills of Credit; make any Thing but gold and silver Coin a Tender in Payment of Debts; pass any Bill of Attainder, ex post facto Law, or Law impairing the Obligation of Contracts, or grant any Title of Nobility.

2. **Import and Export Taxes** No State shall, without the Consent of the Congress, lay any Imposts or Duties on Imports or Exports, except what may be absolutely necessary for executing it's inspection Laws: and the net Produce of all Duties and Imposts, laid by any State on Imports or Exports, shall be for the Use of the Treasury of the United States; and all such Laws shall be subject to the Revision and Control of the Congress.

Executive Branch The president is the chief of the executive branch. It is the job of the president to enforce the laws. The framers wanted the president's and vice president's terms of office and manner of selection to be different from those of members of Congress. They decided on four-year terms, but they had a difficult time agreeing on how to select the president and vice president. The framers finally set up an electoral system, which varies greatly from our electoral process today.

Presidential Elections In 1845 Congress set the Tuesday following the first Monday in November of every fourth year as the general election date for selecting presidential electors.

3. Peacetime and War Restraints No State shall, without the Consent of Congress, lay any Duty of Tonnage, keep Troops, or Ships of War in time of Peace, enter into any Agreement or Compact with another State, or with a foreign Power, or engage in War, unless actually invaded, or in such imminent Danger as will not admit of delay.

ARTICLE II. THE EXECUTIVE

Section 1. The Presidency

1. Terms of Office The executive Power shall be vested in a President of the United States of America. He shall hold his Office during the Term of four Years, and, together with the Vice President, chosen for the same Term, be elected, as follows:

2. Electoral College Each State shall appoint, in such Manner as the Legislature thereof may direct, a Number of Electors, equal to the whole Number of Senators and Representatives to which the State may be entitled in the Congress: but no Senator or Representative, or Person holding an Office of Trust or Profit under the United States, shall be appointed an Elector.

3. Former Method of Electing President The Electors shall meet in their respective States, and vote by Ballot for two Persons, of whom one at least shall not be an Inhabitant of the same State with themselves. And they shall make a List of all the Persons voted for, and of the Number

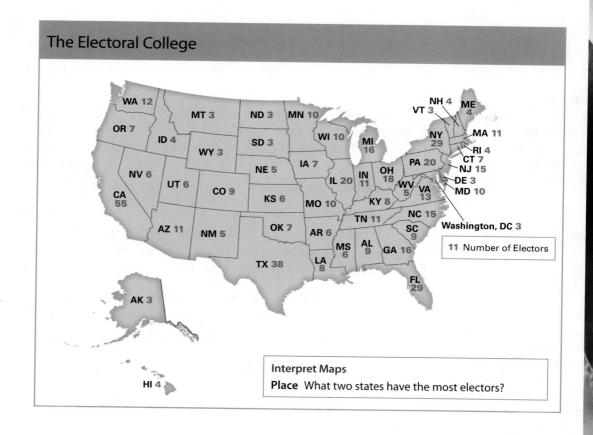

The Electoral College

Interpret Maps
Place What two states have the most electors?

of Votes for each; which List they shall sign and certify, and transmit sealed to the Seat of the Government of the United States, directed to the President of the Senate. The President of the Senate shall, in the Presence of the Senate and House of Representatives, open all the Certificates, and the Votes shall then be counted. The Person having the greatest Number of Votes shall be the President, if such Number be a Majority of the whole Number of Electors appointed; and if there be more than one who have such Majority, and have an equal Number of Votes, then the House of Representatives shall immediately choose by Ballot one of them for President; and if no Person have a Majority, then from the five highest on the List the said House shall in like Manner choose the President. But in choosing the President, the Votes shall be taken by States, the Representation from each State having one Vote; A quorum for this purpose shall consist of a Member or Members from two thirds of the States, and a Majority of all the States shall be necessary to a Choice. In every Case, after the Choice of the President, the Person having the greatest Number of Votes of the Electors shall be the Vice President. But if there should remain two or more who have equal Votes, the Senate shall choose from them by Ballot the Vice President.

4. Election Day The Congress may determine the Time of choosing the Electors, and the Day on which they shall give their Votes; which Day shall be the same throughout the United States.

5. Qualifications No Person except a natural born Citizen, or a Citizen of the United States, at the time of the Adoption of this Constitution, shall be eligible to the Office of President; neither shall any Person be eligible to that Office who shall not have attained to the Age of thirty five Years, and been fourteen Years a Resident within the United States.

6. Succession In Case of the Removal of the President from Office, or of his Death, Resignation, or Inability to discharge the Powers and Duties of the said Office, the Same shall devolve on the Vice President, and the Congress may by Law provide for the Case of Removal, Death, Resignation or Inability, both of the President and Vice President, declaring what Officer shall then act as President, and such Officer shall act accordingly, until the Disability be removed, or a President shall be elected.

7. Salary The President shall, at stated Times, receive for his Services, a Compensation, which shall neither be increased nor diminished during the Period for which he shall have been elected, and he shall not receive within that Period any other Emolument from the United States, or any of them.

8. Oath of Office Before he enter on the Execution of his Office, he shall take the following Oath or Affirmation:—"I do solemnly swear (or affirm) that I will faithfully execute the Office of President of the United States, and will to the best of my Ability, preserve, protect and defend the Constitution of the United States."

Commander in Chief Today the president is in charge of the army, navy, air force, marines, and coast guard. Only Congress, however, can decide if the United States will declare war.

Appointments Most of the president's appointments to office must be approved by the Senate.

Vocabulary

[21] **Reprieves** delays of punishment

[22] **Pardons** releases from the legal penalties associated with a crime

The State of the Union Every year the president presents to Congress a State of the Union message. In this message, the president introduces and explains a legislative plan for the coming year.

Section 2. Powers of Presidency

1. Military Powers The President shall be Commander in Chief of the Army and Navy of the United States, and of the Militia of the several States, when called into the actual Service of the United States; he may require the Opinion, in writing, of the principal Officer in each of the executive Departments, upon any Subject relating to the Duties of their respective Offices, and he shall have Power to grant **Reprieves**[21] and **Pardons**[22] for Offences against the United States, except in Cases of Impeachment.

2. Treaties and Appointments He shall have Power, by and with the Advice and Consent of the Senate, to make Treaties, provided two thirds of the Senators present concur; and he shall nominate, and by and with the Advice and Consent of the Senate, shall appoint Ambassadors, other public Ministers and Consuls, Judges of the supreme Court, and all other Officers of the United States, whose Appointments are not herein otherwise provided for, and which shall be established by Law: but the Congress may by Law vest the Appointment of such inferior Officers, as they think proper, in the President alone, in the Courts of Law, or in the Heads of Departments.

3. Vacancies The President shall have Power to fill up all Vacancies that may happen during the Recess of the Senate, by granting Commissions which shall expire at the End of their next Session.

Section 3. Presidential Duties

He shall from time to time give to the Congress Information of the State of the Union, and recommend to their Consideration such Measures as he shall judge necessary and expedient; he may, on extraordinary Occasions, convene both Houses, or either of them, and in Case of Disagreement between them, with Respect to the Time of Adjournment, he may adjourn them to such Time as he shall think proper; he shall receive Ambassadors and other public Ministers; he shall take Care that the Laws be faithfully executed, and shall Commission all the Officers of the United States.

Section 4. Impeachment

The President, Vice President and all civil Officers of the United States, shall be removed from Office on Impeachment for, and Conviction of, Treason, Bribery, or other high Crimes and Misdemeanors.

ARTICLE III THE JUDICIARY

Section 1. Federal Courts and Judges

The judicial Power of the United States shall be vested in one supreme Court, and in such inferior Courts as the Congress may from time to time ordain and establish. The Judges, both of the supreme and inferior Courts, shall hold their Offices during good Behavior, and shall, at stated Times, receive for their Services a Compensation, which shall not be diminished during their Continuance in Office.

Section 2. Authority of the Courts

1. General Authority The judicial Power shall extend to all Cases, in Law and Equity, arising under this Constitution, the Laws of the United States, and Treaties made, or which shall be made, under their Authority;—to all Cases affecting Ambassadors, other public Ministers and Consuls;—to all Cases of admiralty and maritime Jurisdiction;—to Controversies to which the United States shall be a Party;—to Controversies between two or more States —between a State and Citizens of another State; —between Citizens of different States;—between Citizens of the same State claiming Lands under Grants of different States, and between a State, or the Citizens thereof, and foreign States, Citizens or Subjects.

2. Supreme Authority In all Cases affecting Ambassadors, other public Ministers and Consuls, and those in which a State shall be Party, the supreme Court shall have original Jurisdiction. In all the other Cases before mentioned, the supreme Court shall have appellate Jurisdiction, both as to Law and Fact, with such Exceptions, and under such Regulations as the Congress shall make.

3. Trial by Jury The Trial of all Crimes, except in Cases of Impeachment, shall be by Jury; and such Trial shall be held in the State where the said Crimes shall have been committed; but when not committed within any State, the Trial shall be at such Place or Places as the Congress may by Law have directed.

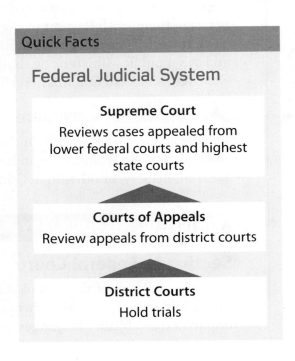

Quick Facts

Federal Judicial System

Supreme Court
Reviews cases appealed from lower federal courts and highest state courts

Courts of Appeals
Review appeals from district courts

District Courts
Hold trials

Section 3. Treason

1. Definition Treason against the United States, shall consist only in levying War against them, or in adhering to their Enemies, giving them Aid and Comfort. No Person shall be convicted of Treason unless on the Testimony of two Witnesses to the same overt Act, or on Confession in open Court.

2. Punishment The Congress shall have Power to declare the Punishment of Treason, but no Attainder of Treason shall work **Corruption of Blood**,[23] or Forfeiture except during the Life of the Person attainted.

ARTICLE IV RELATIONS AMONG STATES

Section 1. State Acts and Records

Full Faith and Credit shall be given in each State to the public Acts, Records, and judicial Proceedings of every other State. And the Congress may by general Laws prescribe the Manner in which such Acts, Records and Proceedings shall be proved, and the Effect thereof.

Section 2. Rights of Citizens

1. Citizenship The Citizens of each State shall be entitled to all Privileges and Immunities of Citizens in the several States.

2. Extradition A Person charged in any State with Treason, Felony, or other Crime, who shall flee from Justice, and be found in another State, shall on Demand of the executive Authority of the State from which he fled, be delivered up, to be removed to the State having Jurisdiction of the Crime.

3. Fugitive Slaves ~~No Person held to Service or Labour in one State, under the Laws thereof, escaping into another, shall, in Consequence of any Law or Regulation therein, be discharged from such Service or Labour, but shall be delivered up on Claim of the Party to whom such Service or Labour may be due.~~

Section 3. New States

1. Admission New States may be admitted by the Congress into this Union; but no new State shall be formed or erected within the Jurisdiction of any other State; nor any State be formed by the Junction of two or more States, or Parts of States, without the Consent of the Legislatures of the States concerned as well as of the Congress.

2. Congressional Authority The Congress shall have Power to dispose of and make all needful Rules and Regulations respecting the Territory or other Property belonging to the United States; and nothing in this Constitution shall be so construed as to Prejudice any Claims of the United States, or of any particular State.

Vocabulary

[23] **Corruption of Blood** punishing the family of a person convicted of treason

The States States must honor the laws, records, and court decisions of other states. A person cannot escape a legal obligation by moving from one state to another.

EXPLORE THE DOCUMENT

The framers wanted to ensure that citizens could determine how state governments would operate. *How does the need to respect the laws of each state support the principle of popular sovereignty?*

Federalism

National

- Declare war
- Maintain armed forces
- Regulate interstate and foreign trade
- Admit new states
- Establish post offices
- Set standard weights and measures
- Coin money
- Establish foreign policy
- Make all laws necessary and proper for carrying out delegated powers

Shared

- Maintain law and order
- Levy taxes
- Borrow money
- Charter banks
- Establish courts
- Provide for public welfare

State

- Establish and maintain schools
- Establish local governments
- Regulate business within the state
- Make marriage laws
- Provide for public safety
- Assume other powers not delegated to the national government nor prohibited to the states

Analyze Information
Why does the power to declare war belong only to the national government?

EXPLORE THE DOCUMENT
In a republic, voters elect representatives to act in their best interest. *How does Article IV protect the practice of republicanism in the United States?*

EXPLORE THE DOCUMENT
America's founders may not have realized how long the Constitution would last, but they did set up a system for changing or adding to it. They did not want to make it easy to change the Constitution. *By what methods may the Constitution be amended? Under what sorts of circumstances do you think an amendment might be necessary?*

Section 4. Guarantees to the States

The United States shall guarantee to every State in this Union a Republican Form of Government, and shall protect each of them against Invasion; and on Application of the Legislature, or of the Executive (when the Legislature cannot be convened), against domestic Violence.

ARTICLE V AMENDING THE CONSTITUTION

The Congress, whenever two thirds of both Houses shall deem it necessary, shall propose Amendments to this Constitution, or, on the Application of the Legislatures of two thirds of the several States, shall call a Convention for proposing Amendments, which, in either Case, shall be valid to all Intents and Purposes, as Part of this Constitution, when ratified by the Legislatures of three fourths of the several States, or by Conventions in three fourths thereof, as the one or the other Mode of Ratification may be proposed by the Congress; Provided that no Amendment which may be made prior to the Year One thousand eight hundred and eight shall in any Manner affect the first and fourth Clauses in the Ninth Section of the first Article; and that no State, without its Consent, shall be deprived of its equal Suffrage in the Senate.

ARTICLE VI SUPREMACY OF NATIONAL GOVERNMENT

All Debts contracted and Engagements entered into, before the Adoption of this Constitution, shall be as valid against the United States under this Constitution, as under the Confederation.

This Constitution, and the Laws of the United States which shall be made in Pursuance thereof; and all Treaties made, or which shall be made, under the Authority of the United States, shall be the supreme Law of the Land; and the Judges in every State shall be bound thereby, any Thing in the Constitution or Laws of any State to the Contrary notwithstanding.

The Senators and Representatives before mentioned, and the Members of the several State Legislatures, and all executive and judicial Officers, both of the United States and of the several States, shall be bound by Oath or Affirmation, to support this Constitution; but no religious Test shall ever be required as a Qualification to any Office or public Trust under the United States.

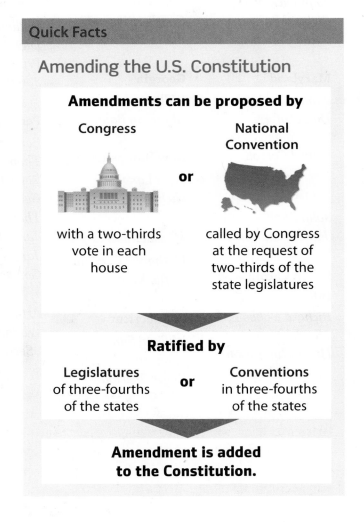

Quick Facts

Amending the U.S. Constitution

Amendments can be proposed by

Congress
with a two-thirds vote in each house

or

National Convention
called by Congress at the request of two-thirds of the state legislatures

Ratified by

Legislatures of three-fourths of the states

or

Conventions in three-fourths of the states

Amendment is added to the Constitution.

ARTICLE VII RATIFICATION

The Ratification of the Conventions of nine States, shall be sufficient for the Establishment of this Constitution between the States so ratifying the Same.

Done in Convention by the Unanimous Consent of the States present the Seventeenth Day of September in the Year of our Lord one thousand seven hundred and Eighty seven and of the Independence of the United States of America the Twelfth In witness whereof We have hereunto subscribed our Names,

George Washington— President and deputy from Virginia

Delaware

George Read
Gunning Bedford Jr.
John Dickinson
Richard Bassett
Jacob Broom

Maryland

James McHenry
*Daniel of
   St. Thomas Jenifer*
Daniel Carroll

Virginia

John Blair
James Madison Jr.

North Carolina

William Blount
*Richard Dobbs
   Spaight*
Hugh Williamson

South Carolina

John Rutledge
*Charles Cotesworth
   Pinckney*
Charles Pinckney
Pierce Butler

Georgia

William Few
Abraham Baldwin

New Hampshire

John Langdon
Nicholas Gilman

Massachusetts

Nathaniel Gorham
Rufus King

Connecticut

*William Samuel
   Johnson*
Roger Sherman

New York

Alexander Hamilton

New Jersey

William Livingston
David Brearley
William Paterson
Jonathan Dayton

Pennsylvania

Benjamin Franklin
Thomas Mifflin
Robert Morris
George Clymer
Thomas FitzSimons
Jared Ingersoll
James Wilson
Gouverneur Morris

Attest:
*William Jackson,
   Secretary*

Constitutional Amendments

Note: The first ten amendments to the Constitution were ratified on December 15, 1791, and form what is known as the Bill of Rights.

Bill of Rights
One of the conditions set by several states for ratifying the Constitution was the inclusion of a bill of rights. Many people feared that a stronger central government might take away basic rights of the people that had been guaranteed in state constitutions.

EXPLORE THE DOCUMENT
The First Amendment forbids Congress from making any "law respecting an establishment of religion" or restraining the freedom to practice religion as one chooses. *Why is freedom of religion an important right?*

Rights of the Accused The Fifth, Sixth, and Seventh Amendments describe the procedures that courts must follow when trying people accused of crimes.

Vocabulary
[24] **quartered** housed

[25] **Warrants** written orders authorizing a person to make an arrest, a seizure, or a search

[26] **infamous** disgraceful

[27] **indictment** the act of charging with a crime

AMENDMENTS 1–10. THE BILL OF RIGHTS

Amendment I

Congress shall make no law respecting an establishment of religion, or prohibiting the free exercise thereof; or abridging the freedom of speech, or of the press; or the right of the people peaceably to assemble, and to petition the Government for a redress of grievances.

Amendment II

A well regulated Militia, being necessary to the security of a free State, the right of the people to keep and bear Arms, shall not be infringed.

Amendment III

No Soldier shall, in time of peace be **quartered**[24] in any house, without the consent of the Owner, nor in time of war, but in a manner to be prescribed by law.

Amendment IV

The right of the people to be secure in their persons, houses, papers, and effects, against unreasonable searches and seizures, shall not be violated, and no **Warrants**[25] shall issue, but upon probable cause, supported by Oath or affirmation, and particularly describing the place to be searched, and the persons or things to be seized.

Amendment V

No person shall be held to answer for a capital, or otherwise **infamous**[26] crime, unless on a presentment or **indictment**[27] of a Grand Jury, except in cases arising in the land or naval forces, or in the Militia, when in actual service in time of War or public danger; nor shall any person be subject for the same offence to be twice put in jeopardy of life or limb; nor shall be compelled in any criminal case to be a witness against himself, nor be deprived of life, liberty, or property, without due process of law; nor shall private property be taken for public use, without just compensation.

Fundamental Liberties

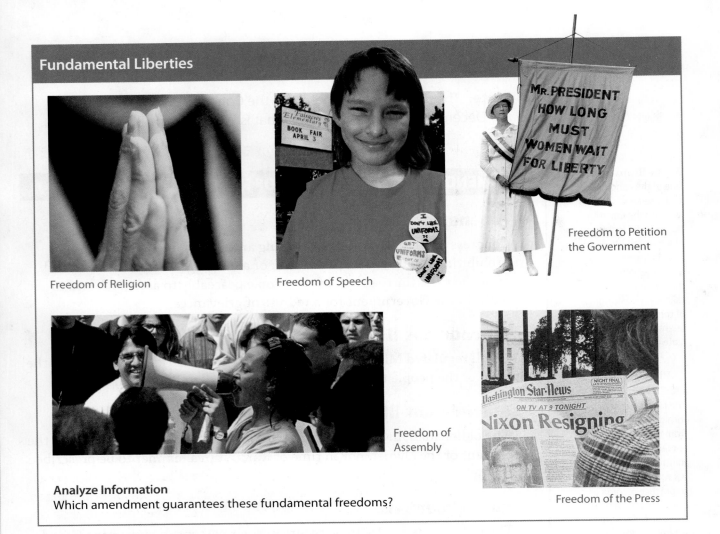

Freedom of Religion

Freedom of Speech

Freedom to Petition the Government

Freedom of Assembly

Freedom of the Press

Analyze Information
Which amendment guarantees these fundamental freedoms?

Trials The Sixth Amendment makes several guarantees, including a prompt trial and a trial by a jury chosen from the state and district in which the crime was committed.

Vocabulary

[28] **ascertained** found out

Amendment VI

In all criminal prosecutions, the accused shall enjoy the right to a speedy and public trial, by an impartial jury of the State and district wherein the crime shall have been committed, which district shall have been previously **ascertained**[28] by law, and to be informed of the nature and cause of the accusation; to be confronted with the witnesses against him; to have compulsory process for obtaining witnesses in his favor, and to have the Assistance of Counsel for his defence.

Amendment VII

In suits at common law, where the value in controversy shall exceed twenty dollars, the right of trial by jury shall be preserved, and no fact tried by a jury, shall be otherwise reexamined in any Court of the United States, than according to the rules of the common law.

Amendment VIII

Excessive bail shall not be required, nor excessive fines imposed, nor cruel and unusual punishments inflicted.

EXPLORE THE DOCUMENT

The Ninth and Tenth Amendments were added because not every right of the people or of the states could be listed in the Constitution. *How do the Ninth and Tenth Amendments limit the power of the federal government?*

Vocabulary

[29] **construed**
explained or interpreted

President and Vice President
The Twelfth Amendment changed the election procedure for president and vice president.

Amendment IX

The enumeration in the Constitution, of certain rights, shall not be construed to deny or disparage others retained by the people.

Amendment X

The powers not delegated to the United States by the Constitution, nor prohibited by it to the States, are reserved to the States respectively, or to the people.

AMENDMENTS 11–27

Amendment XI

PASSED BY CONGRESS MARCH 4, 1794. RATIFIED FEBRUARY 7, 1795.

The Judicial power of the United States shall not be **construed**[29] to extend to any suit in law or equity, commenced or prosecuted against one of the United States by Citizens of another State, or by Citizens or Subjects of any Foreign State.

Amendment XII

PASSED BY CONGRESS DECEMBER 9, 1803. RATIFIED JUNE 15, 1804.

The Electors shall meet in their respective states and vote by ballot for President and Vice-President, one of whom, at least, shall not be an inhabitant of the same state with themselves; they shall name in their ballots the person voted for as President, and in distinct ballots the person voted for as Vice-President, and they shall make distinct lists of all persons voted for as President, and of all persons voted for as Vice-President, and of the number of votes for each, which lists they shall sign and certify, and transmit sealed to the seat of the government of the United States, directed to the President of the Senate;—the President of the Senate shall, in the presence of the Senate and House of Representatives, open all the certificates and the votes shall then be counted;—The person having the greatest number of votes for President, shall be the President, if such number be a majority of the whole number of Electors appointed; and if no person have such majority, then from the persons having the highest numbers not exceeding three on the list of those voted for as President, the House of Representatives shall choose immediately, by ballot, the President. But in choosing the President, the votes shall be taken by states, the representation from each state having one vote; a quorum for this purpose shall consist of a member or members from two-thirds of the states, and a majority of all the states shall be necessary to a choice. And if the House of Representatives shall not choose a President whenever the right of choice shall devolve upon them, before the fourth day of March next following, then the Vice-President shall act as President, as in case of the death or other constitutional disability of the President.—The person having the greatest number of votes as Vice-President, shall be the Vice-President, if such number be a majority of the whole number of Electors appointed, and if no person have a majority, then from the two highest numbers on the list, the Senate shall choose the Vice-President; a quorum for the purpose shall consist of two-thirds of the whole number of Senators, and a majority of the whole number shall be necessary to a choice. But no person constitutionally ineligible to the office of President shall be eligible to that of Vice-President of the United States.

Amendment XIII

PASSED BY CONGRESS JANUARY 31, 1865. RATIFIED DECEMBER 6, 1865.

1. Slavery Banned Neither slavery nor **involuntary servitude**,[30] except as a punishment for crime whereof the party shall have been duly convicted, shall exist within the United States, or any place subject to their jurisdiction.

2. Enforcement Congress shall have power to enforce this article by appropriate legislation.

Amendment XIV

PASSED BY CONGRESS JUNE 13, 1866. RATIFIED JULY 9, 1868.

1. Citizenship Defined All persons born or naturalized in the United States, and subject to the jurisdiction thereof, are citizens of the United

Abolishing Slavery Although some slaves had been freed during the Civil War, slavery was not abolished until the Thirteenth Amendment took effect.

Vocabulary
[30] **involuntary servitude**
being forced to work against one's will

The Reconstruction Amendments

The Thirteenth, Fourteenth, and Fifteenth Amendments are often called the Reconstruction Amendments. This is because they arose during Reconstruction, the period of American history following the Civil War. A key aspect of Reconstruction was extending the rights of citizenship to former slaves.

The Thirteenth Amendment banned slavery. The Fourteenth Amendment defined citizenship to include former slaves. It also required states to follow established rules (due process) when subjecting anyone to legal procedures and to provide all people with equal protection of their rights. The Fifteenth Amendment gave African American men the right to vote.

African Americans participate in an election.

Analyze Information
Why was the "equal protection" clause of Section 1 of the Fourteenth Amendment important for the goals of Reconstruction?

**Protecting
the Rights of
Citizens** In 1833
the Supreme Court
ruled that the Bill of
Rights limited the fed-
eral government but
not the state govern-
ments. This ruling was
interpreted to mean
that states were able
to keep African Ameri-
cans from becoming
state citizens and keep
the Bill of Rights from
protecting them. The
Fourteenth Amend-
ment defines citizen-
ship and prevents
states from interfering
in the rights of citizens
of the United States.

States and of the State wherein they reside. No State shall make or enforce any law which shall abridge the privileges or immunities of citizens of the United States; nor shall any State deprive any person of life, liberty, or property, without due process of law; nor deny to any person within its jurisdiction the equal protection of the laws.

2. Voting Rights Representatives shall be apportioned among the several States according to their respective numbers, counting the whole number of persons in each State, ~~excluding Indians not taxed~~. But when the right to vote at any election for the choice of electors for President and Vice-President of the United States, Representatives in Congress, the Executive and Judicial officers of a State, or the members of the Legislature thereof, is denied to any of the ~~male~~ inhabitants of such State, ~~being twenty-one years of age~~, and citizens of the United States, or in any way abridged, except for participation in rebellion, or other crime, the basis of representation therein shall be reduced in the proportion which the number of such ~~male~~ citizens shall bear to the whole number of ~~male~~ citizens ~~twenty-one years of age~~ in such State.

3. Rebels Banned from Government No person shall be a Senator or Representative in Congress, or elector of President and Vice-President, or hold any office, civil or military, under the United States, or under any State, who, having previously taken an oath, as a member of Congress, or as an officer of the United States, or as a member of any State legislature, or as an executive or judicial officer of any State, to support the Constitution of the United States, shall have engaged in insurrection or rebellion against the same, or given aid or comfort to the enemies thereof. But Congress may by a vote of two-thirds of each House, remove such disability.

4. Payment of Debts The validity of the public debt of the United States, authorized by law, including debts incurred for payment of pensions and bounties for services in suppressing insurrection or rebellion, shall not be questioned. But neither the United States nor any State shall assume or pay any debt or obligation incurred in aid of insurrection or rebellion against the United States, or any claim for the loss or emancipation of any slave; but all such debts, obligations and claims shall be held illegal and void.

5. Enforcement The Congress shall have the power to enforce, by appropriate legislation, the provisions of this article.

Amendment XV

PASSED BY CONGRESS FEBRUARY 26, 1869. RATIFIED FEBRUARY 3, 1870.

1. Voting Rights The right of citizens of the United States to vote shall not be denied or abridged by the United States or by any State on account of race, color, or previous condition of servitude.

2. Enforcement The Congress shall have the power to enforce this article by appropriate legislation.

Timeline: Amendments to the U.S. Constitution

The Constitution has been amended only 27 times since it was ratified more than 200 years ago. Amendments help the structure of the government change along with the values of the nation's people. Read the timeline below to learn how each amendment changed the government.

1790

1791
Bill of Rights
Amendments 1–10

1795
Amendment 11
Protects the states from lawsuits filed by citizens of other states or countries

1804
Amendment 12
Requires separate ballots for the offices of president and vice president

1820

1865
Amendment 13
Bans slavery

1870
Amendment 15
Prohibits national and state governments from denying the vote based on race

1870

1868
Amendment 14
Defines citizenship and citizens' rights

1913
Amendment 16
Allows Congress to tax incomes

1919
Amendment 18
Bans the making, selling, and shipping of alcoholic beverages

Amendment 17
Establishes the direct election of U.S. senators

1920

1920
Amendment 19
Extends the right to vote to women

1933
Amendment 20
Changes the date for starting a new congressional term and inaugurating a new president

Amendment 21
Repeals Amendment 18

1951
Amendment 22
Limits terms a president can serve to two

1961
Amendment 23
Gives citizens of Washington, DC, the right to vote in presidential elections

1964
Amendment 24
Bans poll taxes

1970

1967
Amendment 25
Establishes procedures for presidential succession

1971
Amendment 26
Gives 18-year-olds the right to vote in federal and state elections

1992
Amendment 27
Limits the ability of Congress to increase its pay

2000

Analyze Timelines

1. How are the Eighteenth and Twenty-First Amendments related?

2. Which amendments relate to the right to vote?

Amendment XVI

PASSED BY CONGRESS JULY 2, 1909. RATIFIED FEBRUARY 3, 1913.

The Congress shall have power to lay and collect taxes on incomes, from whatever source derived, without apportionment among the several States, and without regard to any census or enumeration.

Amendment XVII

PASSED BY CONGRESS MAY 13, 1912. RATIFIED APRIL 8, 1913.

EXPLORE THE DOCUMENT
The Seventeenth Amendment requires that senators be elected directly by the people instead of by the state legislatures. *What principle of our government does the Seventeenth Amendment protect?*

1. Senators Elected by Citizens The Senate of the United States shall be composed of two Senators from each State, elected by the people thereof, for six years; and each Senator shall have one vote. The electors in each State shall have the qualifications requisite for electors of the most numerous branch of the State legislatures.

2. Vacancies When vacancies happen in the representation of any State in the Senate, the executive authority of such State shall issue writs of election to fill such vacancies: *Provided*, That the legislature of any State may empower the executive thereof to make temporary appointments until the people fill the vacancies by election as the legislature may direct.

3. Future Elections ~~This amendment shall not be so construed as to affect the election or term of any Senator chosen before it becomes valid as part of the Constitution.~~

Amendment XVIII

PASSED BY CONGRESS DECEMBER 18, 1917. RATIFIED JANUARY 16, 1919. REPEALED BY AMENDMENT XXI.

Prohibition
Although many people believed that the Eighteenth Amendment was good for the health and welfare of the American people, it was repealed 14 years later.

1. Liquor Banned ~~After one year from the ratification of this article the manufacture, sale, or transportation of intoxicating liquors within, the importation thereof into, or the exportation thereof from the United States and all territory subject to the jurisdiction thereof for beverage purposes is hereby prohibited.~~

2. Enforcement ~~The Congress and the several States shall have concurrent power to enforce this article by appropriate legislation.~~

3. Ratification ~~This article shall be inoperative unless it shall have been ratified as an amendment to the Constitution by the legislatures of the several States, as provided in the Constitution, within seven years from the date of the submission hereof to the States by the Congress.~~

Women's Suffrage Abigail Adams and others were disappointed that the Declaration of Independence and the Constitution did not specifically include women. It took many years and much campaigning before suffrage for women was finally achieved.

Amendment XIX

PASSED BY CONGRESS JUNE 4, 1919. RATIFIED AUGUST 18, 1920.

1. Voting Rights The right of citizens of the United States to vote shall not be denied or abridged by the United States or by any State on account of sex.

Women Fight for the Vote

To become part of the Constitution, a proposed amendment must be ratified by three-fourths of the states. Here, suffragists witness Kentucky governor Edwin P. Morrow signing the Nineteenth Amendment in January 1920. By June of that year, enough states had ratified the amendment to make it part of the Constitution. American women, after generations of struggle, had finally won the right to vote.

Analyze Information
What right did the Nineteenth Amendment grant?

Taking Office
In the original Constitution, a newly elected president and Congress did not take office until March 4, which was four months after the November election. The officials who were leaving office were called lame ducks because they had little influence during those four months. The Twentieth Amendment changed the date that the new president and Congress take office. Members of Congress now take office during the first week of January, and the president takes office on January 20.

2. Enforcement Congress shall have power to enforce this article by appropriate legislation.

Amendment XX

PASSED BY CONGRESS MARCH 2, 1932. RATIFIED JANUARY 23, 1933.

1. Presidential Terms The terms of the President and the Vice President shall end at noon on the 20th day of January, and the terms of Senators and Representatives at noon on the 3d day of January, of the years in which such terms would have ended if this article had not been ratified; and the terms of their successors shall then begin.

2. Meeting of Congress The Congress shall assemble at least once in every year, and such meeting shall begin at noon on the 3d day of January, unless they shall by law appoint a different day.

3. Succession of Vice President If, at the time fixed for the beginning of the term of the President, the President elect shall have died, the Vice President elect shall become President. If a President shall not have been chosen before the time fixed for the beginning of his term, or if the President elect shall have failed to qualify, then the Vice President elect shall act as President until a President shall have qualified; and the Congress may by law provide for the case wherein neither a President elect nor a Vice President shall have qualified, declaring who shall then act as President, or the manner in which one who is to act shall be selected, and such person shall act accordingly until a President or Vice President shall have qualified.

4. Succession by Vote of Congress The Congress may by law provide for the case of the death of any of the persons from whom the House of Representatives may choose a President whenever the right of choice shall have devolved upon them, and for the case of the death of any of the persons from whom the Senate may choose a Vice President whenever the right of choice shall have devolved upon them.

5. Ratification ~~Sections 1 and 2 shall take effect on the 15th day of October following the ratification of this article.~~

6. Ratification ~~This article shall be inoperative unless it shall have been ratified as an amendment to the Constitution by the legislatures of three-fourths of the several States within seven years from the date of its submission.~~

Amendment XXI
PASSED BY CONGRESS FEBRUARY 20, 1933. RATIFIED DECEMBER 5, 1933.

1. 18th Amendment Repealed The eighteenth article of amendment to the Constitution of the United States is hereby repealed.

2. Liquor Allowed by Law The transportation or importation into any State, Territory, or Possession of the United States for delivery or use therein of intoxicating liquors, in violation of the laws thereof, is hereby prohibited.

3. Ratification ~~This article shall be inoperative unless it shall have been ratified as an amendment to the Constitution by conventions in the several States, as provided in the Constitution, within seven years from the date of the submission hereof to the States by the Congress.~~

Amendment XXII
PASSED BY CONGRESS MARCH 21, 1947. RATIFIED FEBRUARY 27, 1951.

1. Term Limits No person shall be elected to the office of the President more than twice, and no person who has held the office of President, or acted as President, for more than two years of a term to which some other person was elected President shall be elected to the office of President more than once. ~~But this Article shall not apply to any person holding the office of President when this Article was proposed by Congress, and shall not prevent any person who may be holding the office of President, or acting as President, during the term within which this Article becomes operative from holding the office of President or acting as President during the remainder of such term.~~

EXPLORE THE DOCUMENT
From the time of President George Washington's administration, it was a custom for presidents to serve no more than two terms in office. Franklin D. Roosevelt, however, was elected to four terms. The Twenty-Second Amendment restricted presidents to no more than two terms in office. *Why do you think citizens chose to limit the power of the president in this way?*

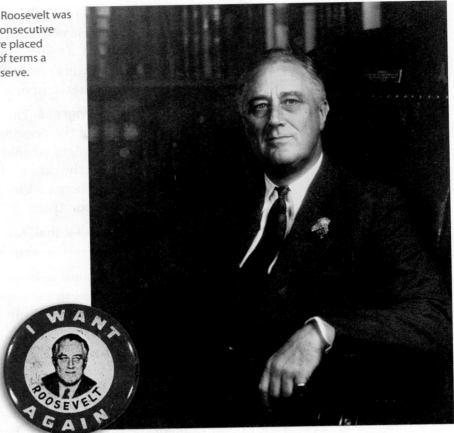

After Franklin D. Roosevelt was elected to four consecutive terms, limits were placed on the number of terms a president could serve.

2. Ratification ~~This article shall be inoperative unless it shall have been ratified as an amendment to the Constitution by the legislatures of three-fourths of the several States within seven years from the date of its submission to the States by the Congress.~~

Amendment XXIII

PASSED BY CONGRESS JUNE 16, 1960. RATIFIED MARCH 29, 1961.

1. District of Columbia Represented The District constituting the seat of Government of the United States shall appoint in such manner as Congress may direct:

A number of electors of President and Vice President equal to the whole number of Senators and Representatives in Congress to which the District would be entitled if it were a State, but in no event more than the least populous State; they shall be in addition to those appointed by the States, but they shall be considered, for the purposes of the election of President and Vice President, to be electors appointed by a State; and they shall meet in the District and perform such duties as provided by the twelfth article of amendment.

2. Enforcement The Congress shall have power to enforce this article by appropriate legislation.

Voting Rights
Until the ratification of the Twenty-Third Amendment, the people of Washington, DC, could not vote in presidential elections.

Poll Tax Amendment

Poll taxes were used to deny many poor Americans, including African Americans and Hispanic Americans, their right to vote. These taxes were made unconstitutional by the Twenty-Fourth Amendment. Above, an African American woman in Alabama votes for the first time.

Analyze Information
How did poll taxes deny poor Americans the opportunity to vote?

Presidential Disability The illness of President Eisenhower in the 1950s and the assassination of President Kennedy in 1963 were the events behind the Twenty-Fifth Amendment. The Constitution did not provide a clear-cut method for a vice president to take over for a disabled president or upon the death of a president. This amendment provides for filling the office of the vice president if a vacancy occurs, and it provides a way for the vice president—or someone else in the line of succession—to take over if the president is unable to perform the duties of that office.

Amendment XXIV
PASSED BY CONGRESS AUGUST 27, 1962. RATIFIED JANUARY 23, 1964.

1. Voting Rights The right of citizens of the United States to vote in any primary or other election for President or Vice President, for electors for President or Vice President, or for Senator or Representative in Congress, shall not be denied or abridged by the United States or any State by reason of failure to pay poll tax or other tax.

2. Enforcement The Congress shall have power to enforce this article by appropriate legislation.

Amendment XXV
PASSED BY CONGRESS JULY 6, 1965. RATIFIED FEBRUARY 10, 1967.

1. Succession of Vice President In case of the removal of the President from office or of his death or resignation, the Vice President shall become President.

2. Vacancy of Vice President Whenever there is a vacancy in the office of the Vice President, the President shall nominate a Vice President who shall take office upon confirmation by a majority vote of both Houses of Congress.

3. Written Declaration Whenever the President transmits to the President pro tempore of the Senate and the Speaker of the House of Representatives his written declaration that he is unable to discharge the powers and duties of his office, and until he transmits to them a written declaration to the contrary, such powers and duties shall be discharged by the Vice President as Acting President.

4. Removing the President Whenever the Vice President and a majority of either the principal officers of the executive departments or of such other body as Congress may by law provide, transmit to the President pro tempore of the Senate and the Speaker of the House of Representatives their written declaration that the President is unable to discharge the powers and duties of his office, the Vice President shall immediately assume the powers and duties of the office as Acting President.

Thereafter, when the President transmits to the President pro tempore of the Senate and the Speaker of the House of Representatives his written declaration that no inability exists, he shall resume the powers and duties of his office unless the Vice President and a majority of either the principal officers of the executive department or of such other body as Congress may by law provide, transmit within four days to the President pro tempore of the Senate and the Speaker of the House of Representatives their written declaration that the President is unable to discharge the powers and duties of his office. Thereupon Congress shall decide the issue, assembling within forty-eight hours for that purpose if not in session. If the Congress, within twenty-one days after receipt of the latter written declaration, or, if Congress is not in session, within twenty-one days after Congress is required to assemble, determines by two-thirds vote of both Houses that the President is unable to discharge the powers and duties of his office, the Vice President shall continue to discharge the same as Acting President; otherwise, the President shall resume the powers and duties of his office.

Amendment XXVI
PASSED BY CONGRESS MARCH 23, 1971. RATIFIED JULY 1, 1971.

1. Voting Rights The right of citizens of the United States, who are eighteen years of age or older, to vote shall not be denied or abridged by the United States or by any State on account of age.

2. Enforcement The Congress shall have power to enforce this article by appropriate legislation.

Amendment XXVII
ORIGINALLY PROPOSED SEPTEMBER 25, 1789. RATIFIED MAY 7, 1992.

No law, varying the compensation for the services of the Senators and Representatives, shall take effect, until an election of representatives shall have intervened.

Expanded Suffrage The Voting Rights Act of 1970 tried to set the voting age at 18. However, the Supreme Court ruled that the act set the voting age for national elections only, not for state or local elections. The Twenty-Sixth Amendment gave 18-year-old citizens the right to vote in all elections.

★ The Bill of Rights

The Big Idea

The Bill of Rights was added to the Constitution to define clearly the rights and freedoms of citizens.

Main Ideas

- The First Amendment guarantees basic freedoms to individuals.
- Other amendments focus on protecting citizens from certain abuses.
- The rights of the accused are an important part of the Bill of Rights.
- The rights of states and citizens are protected by the Bill of Rights.

Key Terms and People

majority rule
petition
search warrant
due process
indict
double jeopardy
eminent domain

If YOU were there . . .

Your father runs a bookshop in colonial Boston in 1770. Your family lives in a very small brick house. You and your sisters must share one small bedroom. One day, a red-coated British officer knocks on your front door and strides into the parlor. He says that your family will have to provide a room and meals for two British soldiers. "We're already crowded!" you protest, but he insists.

Would you support the British government's requirement that colonists provide food and shelter for troops? Why?

First Amendment

Federalist James Madison promised that a bill of rights would be added to the Constitution. This promise allowed the Constitution to pass. In 1789 Madison began writing down a huge list of proposed amendments. He then presented a shorter list to the House of Representatives. Of those, the House approved 12. The states ratified ten, which took effect December 15, 1791. Those ten amendments, called the Bill of Rights, protect U.S. citizens' individual liberties.

The protection of individual liberties is important in a representative democracy. Without safeguards, people's rights would not always be protected because of **majority rule**. This is the idea that the greatest number of people in society can make policies for everyone. While this means that most people agree on what the law should be, it also means that smaller groups, or minorities, might lose their rights. The Bill of Rights ensures that the rights of all citizens are protected.

The ideas spelled out in the First Amendment form the most basic rights of all U.S. citizens. These rights include freedom of religion, freedom of the press, freedom of speech, freedom of assembly, and the right to petition.

Amendment I

Congress shall make no law respecting an establishment of religion, or prohibiting the free exercise thereof; or abridging the freedom of speech, or of the press; or the right of the people peaceably to assemble, and to petition the Government for a redress of grievances.

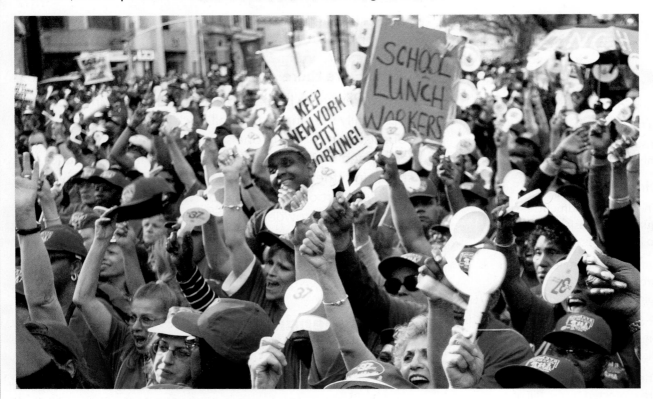

Workers use the right of assembly to protest a proposed budget in New York City.

In the spirit of Thomas Jefferson's Virginia Statute for Religious Freedom, the First Amendment begins, "Congress shall make no law respecting an establishment of religion, or prohibiting the free exercise thereof." In other words, the government cannot support or interfere with the practice of a religion. This amendment keeps the government from favoring one religion over any other or establishing an official religion.

The First Amendment also guarantees freedom of speech and of the press. This means that Americans have the right to express their own ideas and views. They also have the right to hear the ideas and views of others. Former senator Margaret Chase Smith discussed why these freedoms are important. "The key to security," she once said, "is public information."

The right to free speech and a free press does not mean that people can say or print anything they want to, however. The Constitution does not protect slander—false statements meant to damage someone's reputation. Libel, or intentionally writing a lie that harms another person, is not protected, either. The Supreme Court has also ruled that speech that endangers public safety is not protected. For example, Justice Oliver Wendell Holmes declared in 1919 that falsely shouting "Fire" in a crowded theater is not protected as free speech. The government can also restrict speech or printed material that is considered obscene or poses a danger to national security.

Americans also have freedom of assembly, or of holding meetings. Any group may gather to discuss issues or conduct business. If people gather peacefully and do not engage in illegal activities, the government cannot interfere. The right to **petition**, or make a request of the government, is another right of the American people. Any American can present a petition to a government official. This right lets Americans show dissatisfaction with a law. They can also suggest new laws.

Protecting Citizens

The Second, Third, and Fourth Amendments relate to colonial disputes with Britain and reflect many of the ideals outlined in the Declaration of Independence. The Second Amendment deals with state militias and the right to bear arms. Colonial militias played a big role in the Revolutionary War. The framers of the Constitution thought that the states needed their militias for emergencies. Today the National Guard has largely replaced organized state militias.

Supporters of gun-control laws have generally argued that the Second Amendment was intended to protect the collective right of states to maintain well-regulated militia units. Opponents hold that the amendment was meant to protect an individual's right of self-defense. The meaning of the amendment continues to be debated.

The Third Amendment prevents the military from forcing citizens to house soldiers. Before the Revolution, the British pressured colonists to shelter and feed British soldiers. British leaders also forced colonists to submit to having their property searched for illegal goods. Anger over such actions led to the Fourth Amendment rule against "unreasonable searches and seizures." Before a citizen's property can be searched, authorities must now get a **search warrant**. This order gives authorities permission to search someone's property. A judge issues this order only when it seems likely that a search might uncover evidence relating to a crime. In emergencies, however, police can make an emergency search. This may preserve evidence needed to prove possible illegal activity.

Reading Check
Summarize What rights does the First Amendment guarantee to Americans?

Reading Check
Find Main Ideas Why were the Third and Fourth Amendments matters of great importance to Americans when the Bill of Rights was written?

Amendment II

A well regulated Militia, being necessary to the security of a free State, the right of the people to keep and bear Arms, shall not be infringed.

Amendment III

No Soldier shall, in time of peace be quartered in any house, without the consent of the Owner, nor in time of war, but in a manner to be prescribed by law.

Amendment IV

The right of the people to be secure in their persons, houses, papers, and effects, against unreasonable searches and seizures, shall not be violated, and no Warrants shall issue, but upon probable cause, supported by Oath or affirmation, and particularly describing the place to be searched, and the persons or things to be seized.

Rights of the Accused

The Fifth, Sixth, Seventh, and Eighth Amendments provide guidelines for protecting the rights of the accused. According to the Fifth Amendment, the government cannot punish anyone without **due process** of law. This means that the law must be fairly applied. A grand jury decides if there is enough evidence to **indict** (en–DYT), or formally accuse, a person. Without an indictment, the court cannot try anyone for a serious crime. The Fifth Amendment also protects people from having to testify at their own criminal trial. To keep from testifying, a person need only "take the Fifth." In addition, anyone found not guilty in a criminal trial cannot face **double jeopardy**. In other words, he or she cannot be tried again for the same crime.

The final clause of the Fifth Amendment states that no one can have property taken without due process of law. There is one exception: the government's power of **eminent domain**. This is the power to take personal property to benefit the public. One example would be taking private land to build a public road. However, the government must pay the owners a fair price for the property. If the property was gained illegally, then the owners are not paid.

The Sixth Amendment protects the rights of a person who has been indicted. It guarantees that person a speedy public trial. Public trials ensure that laws are being followed by allowing the public to witness the proceedings. Accused people have the right to know the charges against them and can hear and question witnesses testifying against them. Accused people

Amendment V

No person shall be held to answer for a capital, or otherwise infamous crime, unless on a presentment or indictment of a Grand Jury, except in cases arising in the land or naval forces, or in the Militia, when in actual service in time of War or public danger; nor shall any person be subject for the same offence to be twice put in jeopardy of life or limb; nor shall be compelled in any criminal case to be a witness against himself, nor be deprived of life, liberty, or property, without due process of law; nor shall private property be taken for public use, without just compensation.

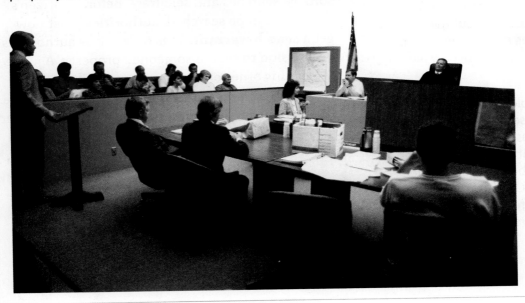

A judge and jury listen to a witness in a courtroom in Orange County, California.

Amendment VI

In all criminal prosecutions, the accused shall enjoy the right to a speedy and public trial, by an impartial jury of the State and district wherein the crime shall have been committed, which district shall have been previously ascertained by law, and to be informed of the nature and cause of the accusation; to be confronted with the witnesses against him; to have compulsory process for obtaining witnesses in his favor, and to have the Assistance of Counsel for his defence.

Amendment VII

In suits at common law, where the value in controversy shall exceed twenty dollars, the right of trial by jury shall be preserved, and no fact tried by a jury, shall be otherwise reexamined in any Court of the United States, than according to the rules of the common law.

Amendment VIII

Excessive bail shall not be required, nor excessive fines imposed, nor cruel and unusual punishments inflicted.

have the right to an attorney. If they cannot pay for legal service, the government must provide it. Sometimes accused persons refuse their Sixth Amendment rights. For example, some defendants refuse the services of an attorney, while others choose to have a trial in front of a judge alone instead of before a jury. In many cases, defendants can forgo trial and agree to a plea bargain. This means that a defendant pleads guilty to a lesser charge and avoids risking conviction for a crime with a greater sentence.

The Seventh Amendment states that juries can decide civil cases. It is possible to harm another person without committing a crime. In such cases, the injured party may sue, or seek justice, in a civil court. Civil cases usually involve disputes over money or property. For example, someone might bring a civil suit against a person who refuses to repay a debt.

A Right to Bail The Eighth Amendment allows for bail. Bail is a set amount of money that defendants promise to pay the court if they fail to appear in court at the proper time.

By posting, or paying, bail, a defendant can avoid staying in jail before and during a trial. If a defendant does not show up in court for trial, the court demands the bail money be paid and issues a warrant for arrest.

The Eighth Amendment keeps courts from setting unfairly high bail. However, in cases of very serious crimes, a judge may refuse to set bail altogether. This can be the case, for example, if the court regards a defendant as being potentially dangerous to the public by being left free. A judge can also deny bail if he or she thinks the defendant will not show up for trial. In such cases the defendant must remain in jail throughout the trial.

"Cruel and Unusual Punishments"

The Eighth Amendment also bans "cruel and unusual punishments" against a person convicted of a crime. For many years, Americans have debated the question of what exactly constitutes cruel and unusual punishment. The debate has often centered on the issue of capital punishment. In 1972 the Supreme Court ruled that the way in which most states carried out the death penalty was cruel and unusual. The Court also found that the ways in which many states sentenced people to death were unfair. However, a few years later, the Court ruled that not all executions were in themselves cruel and unusual.

Amendment IX

The enumeration in the Constitution, of certain rights, shall not be construed to deny or disparage others retained by the people.

Amendment X

The powers not delegated to the United States by the Constitution, nor prohibited by it to the States, are reserved to the States respectively, or to the people.

Students learn about the rights and responsibilities of being a U.S. citizen.

Reading Check Summarize What is the purpose of the Eighth Amendment?

Most states still allow the death penalty. Those that do must follow the Supreme Court's rules. To do so, many states have changed the ways in which they carry out the death penalty.

Rights of States and Citizens

The final two amendments in the Bill of Rights give a general protection for other rights not addressed by the first eight amendments. These amendments also reserve some governmental powers for the states and the people.

Ninth Amendment The Ninth Amendment says that the rights listed in the Constitution are not the only rights that citizens have. This amendment has allowed the courts and Congress to decide other basic rights of citizens.

The Constitution does not address the question of education. However, most Americans believe that it is a basic and essential right. This seems especially true in view of the fact that American citizens must be able to vote for the people who represent them in government. "Education is not just another consumer item. It is the bedrock [foundation] of our democracy," explained educational leader Mary Hatwood Futrell. Today state governments offer free education from elementary through high school—to all citizens.

Tenth Amendment The Tenth Amendment recognizes that the states and the people have additional powers. These powers are any ones that the Constitution does not specifically give to Congress—the delegated powers. The Tenth Amendment makes it clear that any powers not either delegated to the federal government or prohibited to the states belong to the states and the people. Thus, the last amendment in the Bill of Rights protects citizens' rights and helps keep the balance of power between the federal and state governments.

Summary and Preview In this lesson you learned about the Bill of Rights. In the next lesson you will learn about the responsibilities of citizenship.

Reading Check
Summarize How does the Tenth Amendment protect the rights of citizens?

Lesson 3 Assessment

Review Ideas, Terms, and People

1. **a. Identify** What basic rights are protected by the First Amendment?

   b. Recall What are two ways in which the First Amendment protects the religious rights of minority groups?

   c. Explain What does the right to petition the government mean?

   d. Elaborate Why is freedom of the press an important right?

   e. Draw Conclusions Why is it important that citizens behave responsibly when using their First Amendment rights?

2. **a. Describe** How are citizens protected under the Third and Fourth Amendments?

   b. Draw Conclusions In what ways did British actions before the Revolution lead to the Second, Third, and Fourth Amendments?

3. **a. Recall** What responsibilities do the Fifth and Sixth Amendments require of the government?

   b. Identify What protections does the Eighth Amendment provide for people accused of crimes?

   c. Elaborate Why is it important that the Bill of Rights protects people accused of crimes?

4. **a. Recall** What is the purpose of the final two amendments in the Bill of Rights?

   b. Analyze How does the Tenth Amendment balance power between national and state governments?

Critical Thinking

5. **Summarize** In this lesson you learned about the Bill of Rights. Create a chart similar to the one below. Use it to summarize the rights guaranteed to citizens by each amendment in the Bill of Rights.

Amendment	Guaranteed Rights
1	
2	
3	
4	
5	
6	
7	
8	
9	
10	

On September 17, Constitution Day, Americans celebrate the signing of the United States Constitution in 1787.

Around this time, many social studies classrooms also observe Celebrate Freedom Week. This important celebration focuses on the meaning and significance of the two foundational documents in U.S. history—the Declaration of Independence and the U.S. Constitution.

The Declaration of Independence

One of the most eloquent and influential documents ever written, the Declaration of Independence gave the reasons the American colonies were willing to fight for independence. Thomas Jefferson, the main author of the document, began by explaining the purpose of government. Part of this first section, known as the Preamble, is perhaps the most famous statement from the document:

> "We hold these Truths to be self-evident, that all Men are created equal, that they are endowed by their Creator with certain unalienable Rights, that among these are Life, Liberty, and the Pursuit of Happiness. That to secure these Rights, Governments are instituted among Men, deriving their just Powers from the Consent of the Governed."
>
> —Declaration of Independence

These powerful words established the idea that governments exist to serve their citizens, and that people have basic natural rights that government cannot take away. Throughout our history, these words have inspired Americans to fight for and expand the definitions of freedom, equality, and basic rights. For example, women's rights advocates echoed the language of the Declaration of Independence in 1848 when they demanded the right to vote by declaring that "all men and women are created equal." Abolitionists and civil rights leaders also looked to the Declaration of Independence in their struggles to end slavery and ensure that African Americans were guaranteed equal rights. Even beyond America, the Declaration of Independence has inspired independence and pro-democracy movements around the world. It continues to inspire us today.

Key Facts

Declaration of Independence

Date

- Adopted July 4, 1776, by the Continental Congress

Key Author

- Thomas Jefferson

Intent

- To announce formally that the 13 American colonies considered themselves independent states no longer part of the British Empire
- To explain and justify the reasons for independence

Meaning and Importance

- Established in writing the principle that all people have certain fundamental rights that no government can take away
- Explained that the purpose of government is to serve citizens
- Influenced the U.S. Constitution and Bill of Rights
- Has inspired people throughout history in the struggle for equality, justice, and basic human rights

The U.S. Constitution

Building on the Declaration of Independence, the U.S. Constitution established the system of government that is still in effect today. Another truly ground-breaking document, the Constitution established the rule of law and made clear that no one, including the highest government official, is above it. The document's opening words, the Preamble, elegantly state its purpose:

> "We the People of the United States, in Order to form a more perfect Union, establish Justice, insure domestic Tranquility, provide for the common defense, promote the general Welfare, and secure the Blessings of Liberty to ourselves and our Posterity, do ordain and establish this Constitution for the United States of America."

> —United States Constitution

The three opening words, *We the People*, which were written so much larger than the others, announced dramatically that in the United States the people are the source of all government power and authority.

To protect people's rights and to balance power, the Constitution set up a system that divides power among federal and state governments. Federal power is supreme, and certain powers are shared or reserved for the states. A system of checks and balances further divides power among three equal branches of government—legislative, executive, and judicial.

The Constitution also includes a process by which it can be amended, or changed. It is sometimes referred to as "a living document" for this reason; it can be added to and improved by the people to reflect changes in society. Since it was adopted in 1787, the Constitution has been amended 27 times. These amendments have abolished slavery, guaranteed women and minorities the right to vote and to receive equal treatment under the law, changed voting and election procedures, and made other improvements to our government.

One of the most important parts of the Constitution is the Bill of Rights—the first ten amendments. The Bill of Rights helps protect the rights described in the Declaration of Independence. For example, the Bill of Rights protects such basic rights as freedom of speech, press, and religion as well as due process rights such as the right to a fair trial. The Bill of Rights was an important early addition to the Constitution because it stated in writing some of the specific individual rights and protections guaranteed for all Americans.

Key Facts

The Constitution

Date
- Adopted September 17, 1787, by the Constitutional Convention

Key Author
- James Madison

Intent
- To establish a new national government of the United States
- To replace the Articles of Confederation
- To safeguard the freedoms of all Americans, present and future

Meaning and Importance
- Establishes the supreme law of the land for the United States that is still in effect today
- Identifies the people as the ultimate source of government power
- Sets up a system of power sharing among the federal and state government
- Divides power into three equal branches of government
- Includes an amendment process
- Includes the Bill of Rights and other amendments that have protected and expanded individual rights and freedoms

Bill of Rights

Amendment	Protection
1st Amendment	Protects freedom of religion, speech, press, assembly, petition
2nd Amendment	Protects the right to keep and bear arms
3rd Amendment	Provides restrictions on quartering soldiers in citizens' homes
4th Amendment	Bans unreasonable searches or seizures
5th Amendment	Protects citizens against self-incrimination and being tried twice for the same crime; prohibits government from depriving citizens of life, liberty, or property without due process of law
6th Amendment	Protects citizens' right to a swift and fair trial
7th Amendment	Guarantees right to trial by jury
8th Amendment	Protects citizens against cruel and unusual punishment
9th Amendment	States that citizens have rights beyond those specifically written in the Constitution
10th Amendment	States that powers not given to the government are reserved to the states or to the people

Research Activity

As part of Celebrate Freedom Week, conduct research on the two most influential documents in U.S. history. First, read the Declaration of Independence and explore how it influenced subsequent American history and has inspired people for generations. In your own words, explain how the Declaration of Independence is still relevant in our lives today. Then, review a copy of the U.S. Constitution to explore how it has been amended throughout our nation's history. Give an example of how the Constitution or Bill of Rights protects your rights and the rights of others.

Rights and Responsibilities of Citizenship

The Big Idea

American citizenship involves great privileges and serious responsibilities.

Main Ideas

- Citizenship in the United States is determined in several ways.
- Citizens are expected to fulfill a number of important duties.
- Active citizen involvement in government and the community is encouraged.

Key Terms

naturalized citizens
deport
draft
interest groups
political action committees

If YOU were there . . .

Your older brother and his friends have just turned 18. That means they must register with selective service. But it also means that they are old enough to vote in national elections. You are interested in the upcoming elections and think it would be exciting to have a real voice in politics. But your brother and his friends don't even plan to register to vote.

How would you persuade your brother that voting is important?

Gaining U.S. Citizenship

People become U.S. citizens in several ways. First, anyone born in the United States or a territory it controls is a citizen. People born in a foreign country are U.S. citizens if at least one parent is a U.S. citizen. Foreign-born people whose parents are not citizens must move to the United States to become **naturalized citizens**. Once in the United States, they go through a long process before applying for citizenship. If they succeed, they become naturalized citizens, giving them most of the rights and responsibilities of other citizens.

In the United States, legal immigrants have many of the rights and responsibilities of citizens but cannot vote or hold public office. The U.S. government can **deport**, or return to the country of origin, immigrants who break the law.

Legal immigrants over age 18 may request naturalization after living in the United States for five years. All legal immigrants have to support themselves financially. If not, someone must assume financial responsibility for them. Immigrants must be law-abiding and support the U.S. Constitution. They must demonstrate understanding of written and spoken English. They also must show basic knowledge of U.S. history and government.

When this is done, candidates go before a naturalization court and take an oath of allegiance to the United States. They then get certificates of naturalization.

Only two differences between naturalized and native-born citizens exist. Naturalized citizens can lose their citizenship, and they cannot become president or vice president. Many famous Americans have been naturalized citizens, including German Jewish scientist Albert Einstein and former secretary of state Madeleine Albright, originally from Czechoslovakia.

Responsibilities of Citizenship

For a representative democracy to work, Americans need to fulfill their civic duties. "The stakes . . . are too high for government to be a spectator sport," former Texas congresswoman Barbara Jordan once said.

Civic Duties Citizens elect officials to make laws for them. In turn, citizens must obey those laws and respect the authorities who enforce them. Obeying laws includes knowing what they are and staying informed about any changes to the law. Ignorance of a law will not prevent a person from being punished for breaking it.

Another duty is paying taxes for services such as public roads, police, and public schools. People pay sales taxes, property taxes, and tariffs. Many Americans also pay a tax on their income to the federal, and sometimes state, government.

Citizens have the duty to defend the nation. Men 18 years or older must register with selective service. In the event of a **draft**, or required military

Reading Check
Draw Conclusions
Why does U.S. law have such demanding requirements for people to become naturalized citizens?

Becoming a Citizen

For many people around the world, becoming a citizen of the United States is a lifelong dream. The highlight of the naturalization process is the ceremony, where candidates promise to "support and defend the Constitution and laws of the United States of America."

service, those able to fight are already registered. Although women do not register, many serve in the armed forces.

Americans have the right to a trial by jury under the Sixth Amendment. To protect this right, citizens should be willing to serve on a jury when they are called. Otherwise, fulfilling each person's Sixth Amendment rights would be difficult.

Civic Responsibilities In addition to duties, which are required by law, citizens also have responsibilities to fulfill. Although voluntary, these responsibilities are necessary for American democracy to work. The most important civic responsibility is voting. Representatives respond to the opinions of the voters who elect them. If only a small portion of constituents vote, the policies of a representative may not reflect the true opinions of the people he or she represents.

Military Service
By serving in the military, men and women help protect the nation from foreign threats. In addition to conducting combat and peace-keeping operations, the U.S. military may provide humanitarian assistance in overseas disasters.

Voting is closely tied to participation in political parties, because people often vote for the candidate of their own party. A majority of Americans are members of either the Democratic or the Republican Party. Others belong to smaller parties or consider themselves to be independent voters. The U.S. government has generally been dominated by two major parties, but smaller parties focused on single issues may influence public opinion. Citizens can support political parties through donations or by working on election campaigns.

Voting
A representative democracy needs its citizens to vote regularly. This responsibility involves not only casting votes in elections but also becoming educated about candidates and issues.

To make the best choices in voting, people have a responsibility to stay informed on public issues and candidates. Information is available from many sources: the Internet, newspapers, television, other media, and from attending public meetings or listening to speeches. However, voters should also be aware that some material may be deliberately biased to help or harm a particular candidate or cause. Comparing many sources of information and opinions can help voters make decisions that reflect their interests.

Citizens and Society

Participation of ordinary citizens in public groups is part of our national identity. When French writer Alexis de Tocqueville visited the United States in 1831 to study American democracy, he was amazed at the number and variety of groups that had formed to tackle problems great and small. He wrote about them:

> "What political power could ever carry on the vast multitude [large number] of lesser undertakings which the American citizens perform every day, with the assistance of the principle of association [joining a group]? . . . Nothing, in my opinion, is more deserving of our attention than the intellectual and moral associations of America."
> —Alexis de Tocqueville, *Democracy in America*

Influencing Government Even after an election, citizens can <u>influence</u> officials. The tradition of people joining together to present views to political leaders dates back to the colonial period. U.S. citizens sometimes work with **interest groups**. These groups of people share a common interest that motivates them to take political action. Interest groups organize speeches and rallies to support their cause. Sometimes they hire lobbyists, people whose job involves trying to influence the thinking of legislators or government officials. However, citizens need not join a group to influence government. They can write letters to leaders of government or attend city council meetings. Active political participation is an important responsibility for U.S. citizens and immigrants alike.

In addition to voting, many Americans choose to campaign for candidates or issues. Anyone can help a campaign, even if he or she is not eligible to vote. Many people also help campaigns by giving money directly or through **political action committees (PACs)**, groups that collect money for candidates who support certain issues.

Environmental volunteers may plant trees or clear trails in nature preserves.

Helping the Community Volunteering is another important tradition in our society. Some small communities rely on volunteer groups for essential services such as fire protection and law enforcement. In larger communities, volunteers may walk through neighborhoods and alert police if they observe criminal activity. The American Red Cross helps people cope with natural disasters and other emergencies. The Boy Scouts and Girl Scouts plan many projects such as planting trees to improve the environment. Even simple acts such as picking up trash in parks or serving food in homeless shelters will improve a community.

Community Service
Serving as a part of a volunteer group is another way to be involved in a community.

Reading Check
Summarize In what ways do volunteer groups benefit a community?

Today, social media is increasingly used to connect volunteers with organizations that can use their help. Volunteerism reduces the strain on government to provide social services, and it strengthens the bonds between members of a community.

Summary and Preview In this lesson you learned about citizens' duties toward their nation and their communities. In the next module you will learn about the first government formed under the Constitution.

Lesson 4 Assessment

Review Ideas, Terms, and People

1. a. **Identify** What are the different ways in which a person can become a U.S. citizen?
   b. **Make Inferences** Why do you think the law requires an immigrant to live in the United States at least five years before he or she can apply to become a naturalized citizen?

2. a. **Describe** What are three duties required of U.S. citizens?
   b. **Evaluate** In your opinion, which duty required of citizens is the most important? Why?

3. a. **Identify** In what ways can citizens participate in the election process?
   b. **Draw Conclusions** Why do you think it is important that citizens participate in the political process?

Critical Thinking

4. **Categorize** In this lesson you learned about becoming a U.S. citizen. Create a graphic organizer similar to the one below. List the ways a person becomes a citizen and then add the duties and responsibilities of citizenship.

Social Studies Skills

Determine the Context of Statements

Define the Skill

A *context* is the circumstances under which something happens. *Historical context* includes values, beliefs, conditions, and practices that were common in the past. At times, some of these were quite different from what they are today. To truly understand a historical statement or event, you have to take its context into account. It is not right to judge what people in history did or said based on present-day values alone. To be fair, you must also consider the historical context of the statement or event.

Learn the Skill

To better understand something a historical figure said or wrote, use the following guidelines to determine the context of the statement.

1. Identify the speaker or writer, the date, and the topic and main idea of the statement.

2. Determine the speaker's or writer's attitude and point of view about the topic.

3. Review what you know about beliefs, conditions, or practices related to the topic that were common at the time. Find out more about the times in which the statement was made, if you need to.

4. Decide how well the statement reflects the values, attitudes, and practices of people living at that time. Then, determine how well it reflects values, attitudes, and practices related to the topic today.

Applying these guidelines will give you a better understanding of statements made by the Constitution's framers. You read in Module 6 that the Constitution created a representative democracy. However, the original Constitution gave most Americans little voice in choosing their leaders. Only the House of Representatives was elected by the voters. Alexander Hamilton, one of the Constitutional Convention's leaders, told the delegates:

"The people are turbulent and changing; they seldom judge or determine right. Give therefore to the first [upper] class a distinct, permanent share in government. They will check the unsteadiness of the second [the masses]."

By modern standards, Hamilton's remark is undemocratic. But think about the times in which it was made. Shays's Rebellion had recently occurred. In addition, in those days most Americans had little or no education. Many could not even read or write. When its historical context is considered, the statement seems less harsh and extreme.

Practice the Skill

Read the following statement made by Patrick Henry in 1788. Then answer the questions to determine its context and better understand it.

"The Constitution is said to have beautiful features, but . . . they appear to me horribly frightful. . . . Your dearest rights may be sacrificed by what may be a small minority . . . [that] . . . may continue forever unchangeably this government, although horribly defective."

1. What was Henry's opinion of the Constitution?

2. How might Americans' recent experience in the Revolution have caused him to feel that way?

Module 6 Assessment

Review Vocabulary, Terms, and People

1. What proposal for the structure of the U.S. Congress was created at the Constitutional Convention?
   a. Virginia Plan
   b. Great Compromise
   c. New Jersey Plan
   d. Three-Fifths Compromise

2. Who promised to add a bill of rights to the U.S. Constitution?
   a. Benjamin Franklin
   b. Thomas Jefferson
   c. Alexander Hamilton
   d. James Madison

3. What is the term for a person born in another country who becomes a citizen of the United States?
   a. immigrant
   b. partial citizen
   c. naturalized citizen
   d. separatist

4. What are powers granted to the states called?
   a. reserved powers
   b. concurrent powers
   c. stately powers
   d. delegated powers

5. What is the permission to look for evidence of a crime in a particular location called?
   a. petition
   b. impeachment
   c. indictment
   d. search warrant

6. Who was the first female Supreme Court justice?
   a. Abigail Adams
   b. Sonia Sotomayor
   c. Barbara Jordan
   d. Sandra Day O'Connor

Comprehension and Critical Thinking

Lesson 1

7. a. **Draw Conclusions** How was the purpose of the Constitutional Convention different from the final outcome?
    b. **Analyze** Why did the framers of the Constitution create a system of checks and balances?
    c. **Explain** What was the process for ratifying the Constitution?

Lesson 2

8. a. **Describe** Name each branch of government, and explain the duties of each.
    b. **Analyze** What checks and balances exist between the branches of government?
    c. **Evaluate** Do you think the three branches of government share their power equally? Explain your answer.

Lesson 3

9. a. **Identify** What is the Bill of Rights, and why was it added to the Constitution?
    b. **Compare and Contrast** The Bill of Rights and the Constitution both deal with issues of government power. How does their focus on this topic differ?
    c. **Analyze** In what ways does the Bill of Rights protect individuals from the power of government?
    d. **Elaborate** Which of the amendments in the Bill of Rights do you think is the most important? Why?

Lesson 4

10. a. **Describe** What are the ways in which a person can gain U.S. citizenship?
    b. **Analyze** How are citizens able to influence their government?

Reading Skills

Summarize Historical Texts *Use the Reading Skills taught in this module to answer the question about the reading selection below.*

> "The judicial power of the United States shall be vested in one supreme Court, and in such inferior Courts as the Congress may from time to time . . . establish. The Judges, both of the supreme and inferior Courts, shall hold their Offices during good Behavior, and . . . receive for their Services a Compensation. . . ."

11. Which of the following is the best summary of the selection?
  a. The U.S. judiciary consists of the Supreme Court and lower courts, and judges are paid.
  b. Congress creates lower courts.

Review Themes

12. **Politics** What important ideas has the U.S. Constitution contributed to government?

13. **Politics** Why is active political participation an important responsibility for people in the United States?

Social Studies Skills

Determine the Context of Statements *Use the Social Studies Skills taught in this module to answer the questions about the quotation below.*

> "What political power could ever carry on the vast multitude [large number] of lesser undertakings which the American citizens perform every day, with the assistance of the principle of association [joining a group]? . . . Nothing, in my opinion, is more deserving of our attention than the intellectual and moral associations of America."
>
> —Alexis de Tocqueville, *Democracy in America*

14. De Tocqueville wrote this about his trip to the United States in 1831. What is his main idea?
  a. Governments can fill every need of citizens.
  b. American organizations cannot accomplish much.
  c. American organizations get too much attention.
  d. American organizations fill important needs of citizens that government cannot.

15. Do you think that de Tocqueville's statement accurately describes modern America? Why or why not?

Focus on Writing

16. **Create a Pamphlet** Everyone in the United States benefits from our Constitution. However, many people don't know the Constitution as well as they should. Use the information you have learned about the Constitution, the Bill of Rights, and citizenship to create a four-page pamphlet. On the first page, write a title and a phrase that will get your audience's attention. On each of the following pages, you can use this format: (1) a heading and sentence at the top of the page identifying the topic of the page, and (2) the list of the most important points for that topic. Develop your pamphlet so that page 2 is on the Constitution, page 3 is on the Bill of Rights, and page 4 is on citizenship. On page 3, choose the right that you think is most important, and explain why it is important to individuals or groups. Use the Bill of Rights and modern sources to support your opinion.

Module 7
Launching the Nation

★

Essential Question
How did challenges and disagreements help shape the new nation?

About the Photo: The Washington Monument in the nation's capital is one of many tributes to George Washington.

In this module you will learn about the important events of the first three presidencies and how they affected the country. You will also learn about the beginnings of many traditions that still exist today.

What You Will Learn ...

Lesson 1: Washington Leads a New Nation. **246**
The Big Idea President Washington and members of Congress established a new national government.

Lesson 2: Hamilton and National Finances. **250**
The Big Idea Treasury secretary Alexander Hamilton developed a financial plan for the national government.

Lesson 3: Challenges for the New Nation. **255**
The Big Idea The United States faced significant foreign and domestic challenges under Washington.

Lesson 4: John Adams's Presidency **263**
The Big Idea The development of political parties in the United States contributed to differing ideas about the role of the federal government.

Lesson 5: Jefferson Becomes President **268**
The Big Idea Thomas Jefferson's election began a new era in American government.

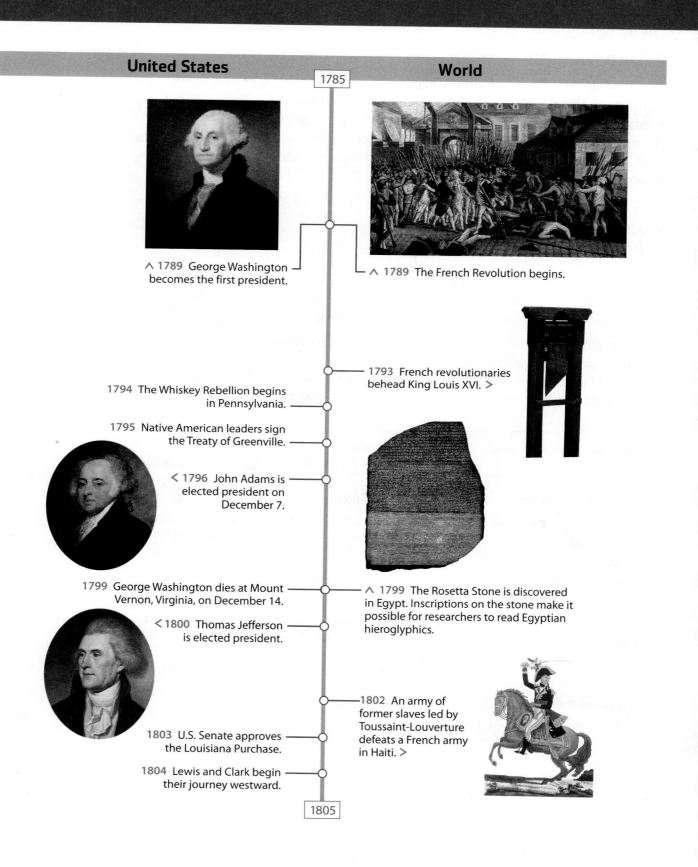

| United States | 1785 | World |

1789 George Washington becomes the first president.

1789 The French Revolution begins.

1793 French revolutionaries behead King Louis XVI. >

1794 The Whiskey Rebellion begins in Pennsylvania.

1795 Native American leaders sign the Treaty of Greenville.

< 1796 John Adams is elected president on December 7.

1799 George Washington dies at Mount Vernon, Virginia, on December 14.

1799 The Rosetta Stone is discovered in Egypt. Inscriptions on the stone make it possible for researchers to read Egyptian hieroglyphics.

<1800 Thomas Jefferson is elected president.

1802 An army of former slaves led by Toussaint-Louverture defeats a French army in Haiti. >

1803 U.S. Senate approves the Louisiana Purchase.

1804 Lewis and Clark begin their journey westward.

1805

Reading Social Studies

Economics and Politics

This module, titled "Launching the Nation," describes how the early leaders established this nation's political and economic systems. You will read about Washington's presidency, Hamilton's plan for financial security for the nation, the establishment of two parties to elect the president, and Jefferson's struggles with both Washington and Hamilton. Throughout the module you will see that disagreement often defined these early days.

READING FOCUS:

Inferences about History

What's the difference between a good guess and a weak guess? A good guess is an *educated* guess. In other words, the guess is based on some knowledge or information. That's what an **inference** is, an educated guess.

Make Inferences about What You Read To make an inference, combine information from your reading with what you already know, and make an educated guess about what it all means. Once you have made several inferences, you may be able to draw a conclusion that ties them all together.

Question What kind of person was Alexander Hamilton?

Inside the Text

- Hamilton ran a company when he was just a teenager.
- He had a career as a lawyer.
- He became the secretary of the treasury under Washington.

Outside the Text

- Running a company takes intelligence and cleverness.
- Becoming a lawyer takes dedication.
- Washington probably wanted someone clever and capable.

Inference Alexander Hamilton was an intelligent, clever, and dedicated man.

Steps for Making Inferences

1. Ask a question.
2. Note information "Inside the Text."
3. Note information "Outside the Text."
4. Use both sets of information to make an educated guess, or inference.

You Try It!

Read the following passage and answer the questions that follow.

Economic Differences Hamilton wanted new forms of economic growth. He wanted to promote manufacturing and business. He even suggested that the government award a prize to companies that made excellent products.

In addition, Hamilton wanted to pass higher tariffs. Known as protective tariffs, these taxes would raise the prices of foreign products. Hamilton hoped this would cause Americans to buy U.S. goods. As a result, American manufacturing would be protected from foreign competition.

Jefferson worried about depending too much on business and manufacturing. He believed that farmers were the most independent voters . . . Jefferson wanted to help farmers by keeping the costs of the goods they bought low. Lower tariffs would help keep prices low.

Answer these questions based on the passage you just read.

1. Which two questions can be answered directly from the text above and which one requires that you make an inference?

   a. Who wanted higher tariffs—Hamilton or Jefferson?

   b. Why do you think Hamilton and Jefferson had different views on the importance of manufacturing?

   c. Which man wanted to help the farmers?

2. To answer question b, it might help to know that Hamilton lived in New York City and Jefferson was from the more rural area of Virginia. Use that information and information in the passage to explain why one man might have valued manufacturing more than the other.

As you read Module 7, remember that you need to combine what you already know with the information in the module to make inferences.

Key Terms and People

Lesson 1
George Washington
electoral college
Martha Washington
precedent
Judiciary Act of 1789

Lesson 2
Alexander Hamilton
national debt
bonds
speculators
Thomas Jefferson
loose construction
strict construction
Bank of the United States

Lesson 3
French Revolution
Neutrality Proclamation
privateers
Jay's Treaty
Pinckney's Treaty
Little Turtle
Battle of Fallen Timbers
Treaty of Greenville
Whiskey Rebellion

Lesson 4
political parties
Federalist Party
Democratic-Republican Party
XYZ affair
Alien and Sedition Acts
Kentucky and Virginia
   Resolutions

Lesson 5
John Adams
Louisiana Purchase
Meriwether Lewis
William Clark
Sacagawea
John Marshall
Marbury v. *Madison*
judicial review

Washington Leads a New Nation

The Big Idea

President Washington and members of Congress established a new national government.

Main Ideas

- In 1789 George Washington became the first president of the United States.

- Congress and the president organized the executive and judicial branches of government.

- Americans had high expectations for their new nation.

Key Terms and People

George Washington
electoral college
Martha Washington
precedent
Judiciary Act of 1789

If YOU were there . . .

You are a seamstress in New York City in 1789. You've joined the excited crowd in the streets for Inauguration Day. Church bells are ringing, and people are cheering. Even though you were just a young child during the Revolution, Washington is your hero. Now you watch as he takes the oath of office. You are proud to see that he is wearing a suit of American-made cloth.

What do you think America's future will be like under President Washington?

The First President

Americans believed in **George Washington**. They saw him as an honest leader and a hero of the Revolution. Many believed he should be the first U.S. president. Washington had been looking forward to retirement and a quiet life on his Virginia farm. When he hesitated at becoming a candidate for the presidency, his friends convinced him to run. Fellow politician Gouverneur Morris told him, "Should the idea prevail [win] that you would not accept the presidency, it should prove fatal . . . to the new government." Morris concluded confidently, "Of all men, you are the best fitted to fill that office."

In January 1789 each of the 11 states that had passed the Constitution sent electors to choose the first president. These delegates formed a group called the **electoral college**. The electoral college is a body of electors who represent the people's vote in choosing the president. The electoral college selected Washington unanimously, and John Adams became his vice president.

Martha Washington

Washington's wife, First Lady **Martha Washington**, entertained guests and attended social events with her husband. She described the scene to her niece: "I have not had one half-hour to myself since the day of my arrival." She ran the presidential household with style.

Other women of the time period, such as author Judith Sargent Murray, believed that women needed to play a greater role in the new nation than Martha Washington did. Murray, Abigail Adams, and others believed in Republican Motherhood, the idea that women played an important role in teaching their children to be good citizens.

Some promoters of Republican Motherhood did not expect women to participate in politics or business. Other people, however, hoped that Republican Motherhood would lead to greater opportunities for women. They hoped more women would receive an education. Only a few families were willing to provide much education for their daughters, and adult women rarely had the time or money to get an education later in life. Most women in the early republic faced long days managing their households and working hard inside or outside the home to support their families.

Reading Check
Analyze Information Why was Washington selected to be president?

Organizing the Government

Hard work also lay ahead for members of the new government. The new federal government had to create policies and procedures that would determine the future of the country. As President Washington noted in a letter to James Madison, "The first of everything in our situation will serve to establish a precedent." A **precedent** is an action or decision that later serves as an example.

The First Congress created departments in the executive branch for different areas of national policy. Washington met with the department heads, or cabinet members, who advised him.

Today we know that presidents have cabinet meetings with their top advisers. This practice started during Washington's presidency and was common by 1792.

For two of his most important cabinet positions, Washington chose carefully. He picked Alexander Hamilton as secretary of the treasury and Thomas Jefferson as secretary of state. Henry Knox served as secretary of war, and Samuel Osgood was chosen as postmaster general. Hamilton was a gifted economic planner, and Jefferson had served as ambassador to France. Knox had helped Washington run the Continental army, and Osgood had government experience.

The First Cabinet

Washington's cabinet members kept him informed on political matters and debated important issues with one another. Each of the men chosen had experience that made him a wise choice to advise the nation's first president. By 1792 cabinet meetings were a common practice.

1 Henry Knox, secretary of war
2 Thomas Jefferson, secretary of state
3 Edmund Randolph, attorney general
4 Alexander Hamilton, secretary of the treasury
5 George Washington, president

To set up the federal court system and the courts' locations, Congress passed the **Judiciary Act of 1789**. This act created three levels of federal courts and defined their powers and relationship to the state courts. It set up federal district courts and circuit courts of appeals. The president nominated candidates for federal judgeships. Those candidates then had to be approved or rejected by the Senate. Washington wrote about the importance of these duties:

"I have always been persuaded that the stability and success of the national government . . . would depend in a considerable degree on the interpretation and execution of its laws. In my opinion, therefore, it is important that the judiciary system should not only be independent in its operations, but as perfect as possible in its formation."

—George Washington to the Justices of the Supreme Court, April 3, 1790

The basic parts of the federal government were now in place. Leaders began to face the challenges of the new nation. Hard work lay ahead.

Reading Check
Find Main Ideas
What two important precedents were established for the federal government?

Americans' Expectations for the Nation

Most Americans had high expectations for the new country. They wanted improved trade, free from too many restrictions. But they also expected the government to protect them and to keep the economy stable. However, the idea of belonging to one united nation was new to them.

In 1790 the United States was home to almost 4 million people. Most Americans lived in the countryside and worked on farms. Farmers wanted fair tax laws and the right to settle western lands. They did not want the government to interfere with their daily lives.

Other Americans worked in towns as craftspeople, laborers, or merchants. These people looked to the government to help their businesses. Most merchants wanted simpler trade laws established. Manufacturers wanted laws to protect them from foreign competitors.

A Rural Nation

Some Americans lived in growing cities like New York City, shown here. However, the new republic was overwhelmingly rural. Most Americans lived and worked on farms.

Why might rural Americans and urban Americans want different things from their new government?

Urban vs. Rural Population, 1790

Urban 5%

Rural 95%

Most cities were small. Only New York City and Philadelphia had populations larger than 25,000. New York City was the first capital of the United States, and it represented the spirit of the new nation. Although badly damaged during the Revolution, the city had already begun to recover. Citizens got rid of many signs of British rule.

New York City had a bustling economy. International trade and business became more active. A French visitor to New York City noted the city's energy.

"Everything in the city is in motion; everywhere the shops resound [ring out] with the noise of workers . . . one sees vessels arriving from every part of the world."
—A French visitor to New York City, quoted in *Travels Through the Two Louisianas and Among the Savage Nations of the Missouri* by Perrin du Lac and Francois Marie

In 1792 some 24 stockbrokers signed an **agreement** under a buttonwood tree on Wall Street. This agreement was the foundation for what later became the New York Stock Exchange. It cemented Wall Street's image as the economic hub of the United States and eventually the world. Today, the New York Stock Exchange is the largest market for securities, or stocks, in the world.

By 1790 the city's population had topped 33,000 and was growing rapidly. To many officials, this vibrant city reflected the potential future of the new nation. It was thus a fitting place for the capital.

Summary and Preview Americans, led by President George Washington, set up their new government. In the next lesson you will read about Alexander Hamilton's economic plan.

Academic Vocabulary
agreement a decision reached by two or more people or groups

Reading Check
Analyze Information Why was New York City chosen as the first capital of the United States?

Lesson 1 Assessment

Review Ideas, Terms, and People

1. **a. Describe** What role did the electoral college play in George Washington's election to the presidency?

   b. Summarize What were some of Martha Washington's duties as First Lady?

2. **a. Describe** What precedent did President Washington and Congress establish regarding the executive branch?

   b. Explain What was the purpose of the Judiciary Act of 1789?

   c. Evaluate What do you think was the most important element of the Judiciary Act of 1789? Why?

3. **a. Recall** What city served as the first capital of the United States? Why?

   b. Draw Conclusions What expectations did most Americans have for the new nation?

   c. Make Judgments Do you think New York City should still be the capital city of the United States? Explain your answer.

Critical Thinking

4. **Compare** In this lesson you learned about the presidency of George Washington. Create a chart similar to the one below and use it to compare how Washington and Congress organized the new government.

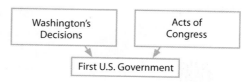

Hamilton and National Finances

The Big Idea

Treasury secretary Alexander Hamilton developed a financial plan for the national government.

Main Ideas

- Hamilton tackled the problem of settling national and state debt.
- Thomas Jefferson opposed Hamilton's views on government and the economy.
- Hamilton created a national bank to strengthen the U.S. economy.

Key Terms and People

Alexander Hamilton
national debt
bonds
speculators
Thomas Jefferson
loose construction
strict construction
Bank of the United States

If YOU were there . . .

You live on a plantation in North Carolina in the 1790s. You have just heard that the federal government plans to pay most of the northern states' debts from the war. Your neighbors are outraged about this idea. It means more taxes and tariffs! New York and Massachusetts are far away, they say. Why should North Carolina farmers have to pay northern debts?

Would you pay other states' war debts? Why?

Settling the Debt

Alexander Hamilton seemed born with a head for economics. While still in his teens, he helped run a shipping company in his native British West Indies. Family friends then sent him to the American colonies for an education. Hamilton eventually married into a wealthy New York family and began practicing law. He served as Washington's aide and as a delegate to four Continental Congresses.

National Debt As secretary of the treasury, Hamilton's biggest challenge was paying off the **national debt**—money owed by the United States—from the Revolutionary War. The United States owed about $11.7 million to foreign countries and about $40.4 million to U.S. citizens. During the war the government raised money with bonds. **Bonds** are certificates of debt that carry a promise to buy back the bonds at a higher price. The new government could not afford to keep this promise. Bondholders who needed money sold their bonds for less than the original value to **speculators**, or people who buy items at low prices in the hope that the value will rise and they can sell the items for a profit.

Hamilton wanted to pay the foreign debt immediately and gradually repay the total value of all bonds. The second part of his plan caused disagreements because paying full value would allow speculators to make a profit. Hamilton thought

Hamilton's Economic Plan

Alexander Hamilton developed a three-point plan to solve the nation's financial problems.

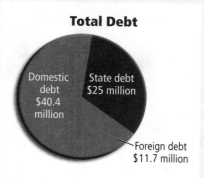

Total Debt

Domestic debt $40.4 million

State debt $25 million

Foreign debt $11.7 million

❶ **Deal with the Debt**
- Take on the foreign and domestic debt by replacing creditors' old, low-value bonds with new, interest-bearing bonds
- Take over most of the states' $25 million Revolutionary War debts

❷ **Gain Revenue**
- Pass a tariff to both bring in revenue and help American manufacturers

❸ **Stabilize the Banking System**
- Create a national bank
- Create a national mint

would build investor confidence in the stability of the new nation

would free up state money for business and trade

---

this was fair. He said, "He [the speculator] paid what the commodity [bond] was worth . . . and took the risks."

Thomas Jefferson disagreed. He thought the idea cheated bondholders who had sold their bonds at low prices. Jefferson wrote, "Immense sums were thus filched [stolen] from the poor and ignorant." But more politicians agreed with Hamilton. In 1790 the government exchanged old bonds for new, more reliable ones that were guaranteed.

States' Debts The states owed $25 million for Revolutionary War expenses. Hamilton wanted the federal government to pay for $21.5 million of this debt. Hamilton believed that this action would help the federal government. He thought that paying the states' debts would help the national economy. Debtor states would not have to spend so much on repayment and would have money to develop business and trade. Increased business and trade would put more money back into the national economy.

The South, however, did not want to help the federal government pay the debts of other states. States such as Virginia and North Carolina did not have many war debts. They thought Hamilton's idea was unfair. Patrick Henry said he did not believe that the Constitution gave Congress the power to pay state debts. Hamilton knew that he needed the help of southern representatives to get his plan approved.

Moving the Capital Hamilton also knew that he had something to bargain with. Officials from the southern states wanted to change the location of the nation's capital. Many southerners thought that having the capital in New York gave the northern states too much influence over national policy. Hamilton, Jefferson, and James Madison met in June 1790. Hamilton promised to convince northern members of Congress to move the capital. Jefferson and Madison then agreed to gather support in the South for Hamilton's debt plan.

Benjamin Banneker 1731–1806

Benjamin Banneker was born to a free African American family in rural Maryland. He attended a Quaker school but was largely self-educated. He was a skilled mathematician and scientist. His mathematical skills prompted Thomas Jefferson to give him a job surveying the land for the new national capital.

Draw Conclusions
How was Benjamin Banneker's life different from most African Americans' of the time?

The compromise worked. The national capital was moved to Philadelphia in 1791 for ten years. For the capital's permanent location, Washington chose a place on the Potomac River that included part of both Maryland and Virginia. The land was made up of swamps and farms. This site would eventually become the city of Washington, DC.

Jefferson Opposes Hamilton

Hamilton and Jefferson did not cooperate for long. Instead, they began to disagree about how to define the authority of the central government. Hamilton believed in a strong federal government. Jefferson wanted to protect the powers of the states. Their conflict reflected basic differences in their opinions about democracy. Hamilton had little faith in the average individual. He once said that "the people . . . seldom judge or determine [decide] right."

Differing Views Hamilton wanted a strong central government that balanced power between the "mass of the people" and wealthier citizens. He believed that his approach would protect everyone's liberties while keeping the people from having too much power.

Jefferson disagreed strongly with Hamilton's views of the average citizen's ability to make decisions for the country. He admitted that "the people can not be all, and always, well informed." However, Jefferson believed that it was the right of the people to rule the country.

Economic Differences Hamilton and Jefferson also fought over how the country's economy should grow. Hamilton wanted new forms of economic growth. He wanted to promote manufacturing and business. He even suggested that the government award a prize to companies that made excellent products.

In addition, Hamilton wanted to pass higher tariffs. Known as protective tariffs, these taxes would raise the prices of foreign products. Hamilton hoped this would cause Americans to buy U.S. goods. As a result, American manufacturing would be protected from foreign competition.

Reading Check
Identify Points of View How did southerners feel about the federal government paying state war debts, and how did Hamilton change their minds?

Role of a Citizen

Alexander Hamilton thought that the average citizen had no interest in public affairs.

> "We must take man as we find him, and if we expect him to serve the public, [we] must interest his passions in doing so. A reliance on pure patriotism has been the source of many of our errors."
>
> —Alexander Hamilton, from *The Works of Alexander Hamilton*, ed. Henry Cabot Lodge

Thomas Jefferson believed that each citizen could work to better society.

> "It is my principle that the will of the Majority should always prevail [win] . . . Above all things I hope the education of the common people will be attended to; [I am] convinced that on their good sense we may rely with the most security for the preservation of a due degree of liberty."
>
> —Thomas Jefferson, from a letter to John Adams, December 1787

Analyze Historical Sources
How did the views of Hamilton and Jefferson differ?

Reading Check
Summarize What were the main differences between Hamilton and Jefferson concerning the power of the nation's government?

Jefferson worried about depending too much on business and manufacturing. He believed that farmers were the most independent voters. They did not depend on other people's work to make a living.

Jefferson wrote, "Our governments will remain virtuous [pure] for many centuries; as long as they are chiefly agricultural." Jefferson wanted to help farmers by keeping the costs of the goods they bought low. Lower tariffs would help keep prices low.

A National Bank

Hamilton's and Jefferson's differences became more and more public in early 1791. The two men had very different opinions about how the government should approach its economic problems.

Hamilton's Plan for a National Bank Hamilton wanted to start a national bank where the government could safely deposit its money. The bank would also make loans to the government and businesses. Hamilton also thought that the United States should build a national mint, a place to make coins. Then the country could begin issuing its own currency.

Hamilton knew that people who wanted to protect states' rights might have a strong reaction to the idea of a national bank, so he suggested limiting it to a 20-year charter. After that time Congress could decide whether to extend the charter. Hamilton also asked each state to start its own bank so the national bank would not have a monopoly.

Jefferson Opposes the Bank Both Jefferson and Madison believed that Hamilton's plans for the economy gave too much power to the federal government. They also thought the U.S. Constitution did not give Congress the power to create a bank. But Hamilton quoted the elastic clause, which states that Congress can "make all laws which shall be necessary and proper" to govern the nation.

Hamilton declared that the clause allowed the government to create a national bank. Hamilton believed in **loose construction** of the Constitution. Loose construction means that the federal government can take reasonable actions that the Constitution does not specifically forbid.

Jefferson thought that the elastic clause should be used only in special cases. He wrote to President Washington, "The Constitution allows only the means which are 'necessary,' not those which are merely 'convenient.'" Jefferson believed in strict construction of the Constitution. People who favor **strict construction** think that the federal government should do only what the Constitution specifically says it can do.

Reading Check
Draw Conclusions
Why did Congress and the president agree to create a national bank?

President Washington and Congress agreed with Hamilton. They hoped a bank would offer stability for the U.S. economy. In February 1791 Congress enacted the charter for the **Bank of the United States**—the country's first national bank. The bank played an important role in making the U.S. economy more stable.

Summary and Preview Washington and Hamilton developed plans for paying the national debt. In the next lesson you will read about the U.S. neutrality policy.

Lesson 2 Assessment

Review Ideas, Terms, and People

1. **a. Describe** What economic problems did the new government face?

   b. Summarize What compromise did Alexander Hamilton, Thomas Jefferson, and James Madison reach regarding repayment of state debts?

2. **a. Identify** What disagreement did Jefferson and Hamilton have over the central government?

   b. Draw Conclusions Hamilton was a New Yorker, while Jefferson was from Virginia. How do you think that affected their views on the economy?

   c. Elaborate Do you agree with Hamilton or Jefferson regarding the average citizen's ability to make decisions for the country? Explain your answer.

3. **a. Recall** Why did Jefferson oppose the creation of the Bank of the United States?

   b. Contrast What is the difference between loose construction and strict construction of the Constitution?

   c. Elaborate Defend Alexander Hamilton's stance in favor of the creation of a national bank.

Critical Thinking

4. **Identify Solutions** In this lesson you learned about U.S. economic problems and Hamilton's solutions. Create a chart similar to the one below and use it to show how Hamilton's views on the economy differed from those of Thomas Jefferson.

	Hamilton	Jefferson
Bonds		
Economy		
Tariffs		
National Bank		

Challenges for the New Nation

The Big Idea

The United States faced significant foreign and domestic challenges under Washington.

Main Ideas

- The United States tried to remain neutral regarding events in Europe.
- The United States and Native Americans came into conflict in the Northwest Territory.
- The Whiskey Rebellion tested Washington's administration.
- In his Farewell Address, Washington advised the nation.

Key Terms and People

French Revolution
Neutrality Proclamation
privateers
Jay's Treaty
Pinckney's Treaty
Little Turtle
Battle of Fallen Timbers
Treaty of Greenville
Whiskey Rebellion

Academic Vocabulary
neutral unbiased, not favoring either side in a conflict

If YOU were there . . .

You are the captain of an American merchant ship in the 1790s. Your ship has just picked up cargo in the French West Indies. You are headed back to your home port of Philadelphia. Suddenly, a British warship pulls alongside your ship. Marines swarm aboard. They order you into the nearest harbor and seize your goods.

How would this incident affect your views of Great Britain?

Remaining Neutral

Tensions between France and Great Britain began to build after the French people rebelled against their king. On July 14, 1789, citizens of Paris attacked and captured the Bastille, a hated fortress and prison that stood as a mighty symbol of royal power.

The storming of the Bastille was one of the first acts of the **French Revolution**—a rebellion of French people against their king in 1789. The French people overthrew their king and created a republican government.

Many French citizens had been inspired to take action by the American Revolution. Many Americans, in turn, supported the French Revolution. They thought that France was creating the same kind of democracy as the United States.

Some Americans worried about the French Revolution's violent riots and attacks on traditional authority. Revolutionaries shocked many Americans by beheading King Louis XVI in January 1793 and Queen Marie-Antoinette later that year.

A few years after the French Revolution started, France and Great Britain went to war. Some Americans supported the French, while others backed the British. Some wanted to remain **neutral**.

The Neutrality Proclamation The debate divided Congress and Washington's cabinet. Washington presented his opinion to Congress on April 22, 1793:

"The duty and interest of the United States require that they should with sincerity and good faith adopt and pursue a conduct friendly and impartial [unbiased] towards the belligerent [fighting] powers."

—George Washington, from *The Writings of George Washington*

This **Neutrality Proclamation** stated that the United States would not take sides with any European countries that were at war. Washington believed his plan was the safest for the long run, but not everyone agreed.

Some members of Congress criticized Washington's ideas. James Madison believed that the president had gone beyond his authority. He questioned Washington's right to issue the proclamation without the approval of Congress.

The French Question France's new representative to the United States, Edmond Genet (zhuh-NAY), asked American sailors to help France fight England by commanding **privateers**. Privateers were private ships hired by a country to attack its enemies. Washington told Genet that using American privateers violated U.S. neutrality. Jefferson wanted the French revolutionaries to succeed, but even he agreed that allowing France to use American privateers against England was a bad idea.

Jefferson was still upset by U.S. policy toward France. He believed that the United States should back France because France had supported the United States during the Revolutionary War. Hamilton, on the other hand, was pro-British. He hoped to strengthen trading ties with Britain—the most powerful trading nation in the world at the time. Jefferson thought

Timeline: The Struggle for Neutrality

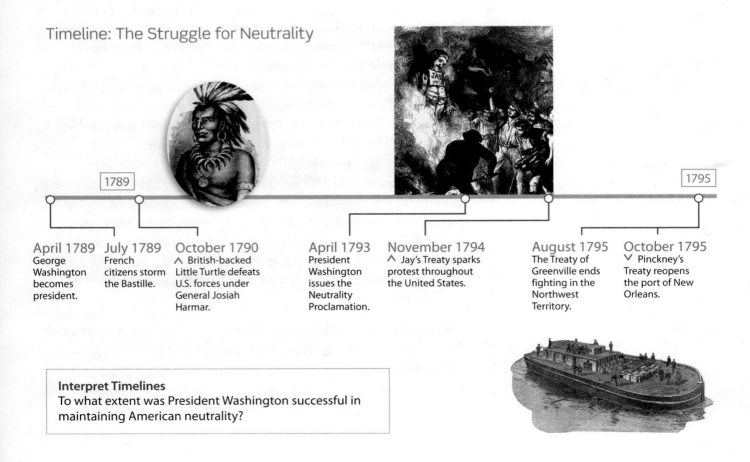

1789

1795

April 1789
George Washington becomes president.

July 1789
French citizens storm the Bastille.

October 1790
∧ British-backed Little Turtle defeats U.S. forces under General Josiah Harmar.

April 1793
President Washington issues the Neutrality Proclamation.

November 1794
∧ Jay's Treaty sparks protest throughout the United States.

August 1795
The Treaty of Greenville ends fighting in the Northwest Territory.

October 1795
∨ Pinckney's Treaty reopens the port of New Orleans.

Interpret Timelines
To what extent was President Washington successful in maintaining American neutrality?

that Hamilton had too much influence on the president's foreign policy and that Hamilton interfered with Jefferson's role as secretary of state. Jefferson decided to resign from Washington's cabinet in 1793.

Jay's Treaty There were other threats to U.S. neutrality. In late 1793 the British seized ships carrying food to the French West Indies. Hundreds of the ships were neutral American merchant ships. Also, British officers were helping Native Americans fight settlers.

Washington wanted to prevent another war with the British. He sent Chief Justice John Jay to London to work out a compromise. The British knew the United States lacked a strong navy and that U.S. businesses relied heavily on British trade. However, the British did not want to fight another war in America.

In November 1794 the two sides signed **Jay's Treaty**. Jay's Treaty settled the disputes that had arisen between the United States and Great Britain in the early 1790s. The British would pay damages on seized American ships and abandon their forts on the northwestern frontier. The United States agreed to pay debts it owed the British.

The treaty was unpopular and sparked violent protests. Citizens and congressional leaders thought the treaty hurt trade and did not punish Britain enough for some of its actions. Southerners were especially angry that the treaty did not ask Britain to repay them for slaves that Britain had set free during the Revolutionary War. Washington did not like the treaty but believed it was the most that could be done. At his urging the Senate approved the treaty.

Pinckney's Treaty American businesses faced problems as well. The Spanish disputed the border between the United States and Florida. Spain closed the port of New Orleans to U.S. trade in 1784. This hurt the American economy because all goods moving down the Mississippi to places in the East or overseas had to pass through New Orleans.

Washington asked Ambassador Thomas Pinckney to meet with Spanish officials to discuss the problem. He asked the Spaniards to reopen New Orleans to U.S. trade. Pinckney also asked for the right of deposit in New Orleans. This right would allow American boats to transfer goods in New Orleans without paying cargo fees.

Spanish minister Manuel de Godoy (goh•THOY) tried to delay reaching an agreement, hoping Pinckney would become desperate and sign a treaty that favored the Spanish. He was worried that the United States and Great Britain might join against Spain after signing Jay's Treaty. Pinckney was patient, however, and his patience was rewarded.

In October 1795 Godoy agreed to **Pinckney's Treaty**, which settled the border and trade disputes with Spain. Under the treaty Spain agreed to recognize the U.S. southern boundary as 31° north latitude. Spain's government also reopened the port at New Orleans to American ships and gave them the right of deposit. Because it opened the frontier to more expansion, Washington and most other Americans believed that Pinckney's Treaty was a successful compromise.

Reading Check
Summarize Why did President Washington want the United States to remain neutral?

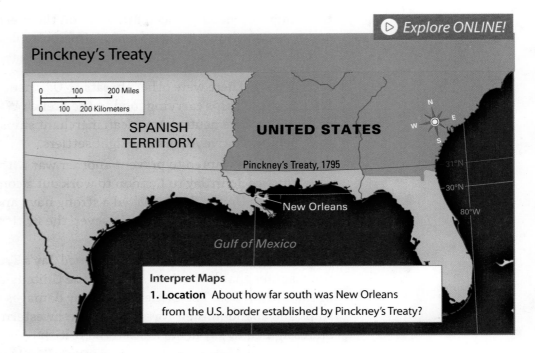

Pinckney's Treaty

0 100 200 Miles
0 100 200 Kilometers

SPANISH TERRITORY

UNITED STATES

Pinckney's Treaty, 1795

New Orleans

31°N
30°N
80°W

Gulf of Mexico

Interpret Maps

1. Location About how far south was New Orleans from the U.S. border established by Pinckney's Treaty?

Conflict in the Northwest Territory

As the United States dealt with international conflicts, trouble was also brewing at home. Americans continued to settle the Northwest Territory despite Native Americans' protests. Supplied by British traders with guns, Native Americans went to war. In 1790 a Native American alliance under the command of Miami chief **Little Turtle** defeated U.S. forces under General Josiah Harmar. Then, in 1791 Native Americans defeated General Arthur St. Clair's troops.

General Wayne Takes Command In 1792 President Washington gave command of the army in the West to General Anthony Wayne. Wayne's task was to bring troops to the frontier to fight against the Indians. In 1793 General Wayne arrived in Ohio. Many of his men were ill from smallpox and influenza, so they were unable to fight well.

Wayne's troops moved north and built Fort Greenville, where they remained during the winter. They built additional forts for protection and to have supplies at hand.

As the summer of 1794 neared, several Native American groups led by Little Turtle attacked a supply train near the fort. Wayne and his men responded. They attacked Native American towns and burned crops.

The British no longer aided the Native Americans after this defeat, and Little Turtle realized that he was outmatched. He urged his people to seek peace.

"The trail has been long and bloody; it has no end. The [whites] . . . are many. They are like the leaves of the trees. When the frost comes they fall and are blown away. But when the sunshine comes again they come back more plentiful than ever before."

—Little Turtle, quoted in *The Ohio Frontier* by Douglas Hurt

Little Turtle, also known as Michikinikwa, was a Miami chief who won many battles against the United States, but eventually called for peace.

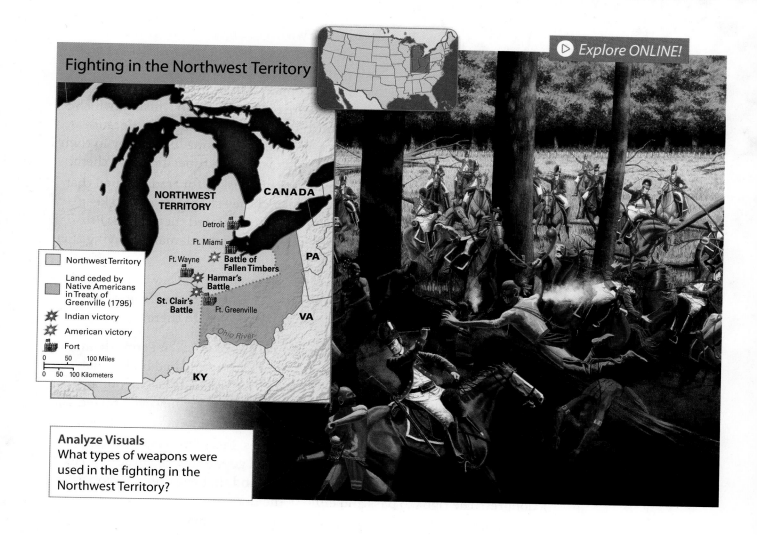

Fighting in the Northwest Territory

▶ Explore ONLINE!

NORTHWEST TERRITORY

CANADA

Detroit

Ft. Miami

Ft. Wayne ☆ **Battle of Fallen Timbers**

☆ **Harmar's Battle**

PA

St. Clair's Battle ☆ Ft. Greenville

VA

Ohio River

KY

Map legend:
- Northwest Territory
- Land ceded by Native Americans in Treaty of Greenville (1795)
- ☆ Indian victory
- ☆ American victory
- Fort

0 50 100 Miles
0 50 100 Kilometers

Analyze Visuals
What types of weapons were used in the fighting in the Northwest Territory?

The End of Conflict On August 20, 1794, Native Americans fought Wayne's troops in the **Battle of Fallen Timbers** and were defeated. The battle was named for an area where many trees had been destroyed by a tornado. Wayne's forces burned Indians' villages and fields. The strength of Indian forces in the region was broken.

The frontier war soon ended. In August 1795 Native American leaders signed the **Treaty of Greenville**, which gave the United States claim to most Indian lands in the Northwest Territory. The treaty also guaranteed the safety of citizens there. In exchange, Native Americans received $20,000 worth of goods and an acknowledgment of their claim to the lands they still held.

Reading Check
Find Main Ideas
What conflicts did the United States face in the late 1700s?

The Whiskey Rebellion

Other conflicts were happening on the frontier. Congress passed a tax on American-made whiskey in March 1791. The tax was part of Hamilton's plan to raise money to help pay the federal debt. He was also testing the power of the federal government to control the states' actions.

Reaction in the West People in the western parts of states such as Pennsylvania, Virginia, and North Carolina were bitter about the tax. They were

Protesters tar and feather a tax collector during the Whiskey Rebellion in Pennsylvania.

already angry with the federal government, which they believed did not protect settlers from Native American attacks and did not allow settlers enough opportunities for trade. The farmers' corn crops were often made into whiskey, which was easier to transport than the corn. Because cash was rare, whiskey became like money in their region. The farmers believed that the tax was aimed specifically at them.

Farmers who produced small amounts of whiskey for trade argued that they could not afford the tax. They believed they should be able to keep the money they had made from a product they created themselves. Protests in 1792 led President Washington to issue a proclamation saying that people had to obey the law.

Westerners also disliked the fact that cases about the law were to be tried in a district court. These courts were usually far away from the people they affected and were a great inconvenience to them.

Whiskey Rebellion Is Crushed The complaints of western Pennsylvanians were at first expressed peacefully. But by 1794 fighting had broken out. In what became known as the **Whiskey Rebellion**, farmers lashed out against the tax on whiskey. Protesters refused to pay the tax. They even tarred and feathered tax collectors. Some called themselves the new Sons of Liberty.

Incidents of violence spread to other states. President Washington feared that the rebels threatened the federal government's authority. He believed he needed to make people understand that the Constitution gave Congress the right to pass and enforce the tax.

Washington declared that he could "no longer remain a passive [inactive] spectator" in the event. He personally led the army in military action against the rebellion—the first and only time an American president has done so. The army of about 13,000 men approached western Pennsylvania in November 1794. By this time most of the rebels had fled. The Whiskey Rebellion ended without a battle.

Washington Says Farewell

In 1796 Washington decided not to run for a third presidential term. He wrote that he was "tired of public life" and "devoutly [strongly] wished for retirement." He also wanted to remind Americans that the people were the country's true leaders. His decision to serve for only two terms set an example for future presidents.

With the help of Alexander Hamilton and James Madison, Washington wrote his Farewell Address. In it he spoke about what he believed were the greatest dangers to the American republic. Among these were the dangers of foreign ties and political conflicts at home. Washington warned against forming permanent ties with other countries because choosing sides could draw the United States into war.

Washington also worried about growing political conflicts within the nation. He believed that the disagreements between political groups weakened government. Political unity, he said, was a key to national success.

Reading Check
Support Points of View Defend the viewpoint of the Pennsylvania farmers who did not want to pay the whiskey tax.

Washington's Farewell Address

On September 19, 1796, President George Washington's Farewell Address first appeared in a Philadelphia newspaper. In it, Washington wrote about the nation's economy, political parties, and foreign policy.

While, then, every part of our country . . . feels an immediate and particular interest in union, all the parts combined cannot fail to find in the united mass . . . greater strength, greater resource, proportionally greater security from external danger, [and] a less frequent interruption of their peace by foreign nations; . . .

I have already intimated[1] to you the danger of [political] parties in the state, with particular reference to the founding of them on geographical discriminations[2]. Let me now take a more comprehensive[3] view, and warn you in the most solemn manner against the baneful[4] effects of the spirit of party, generally.

If, in the opinion of the people, the distribution or modification[5] of the constitutional powers be in any particular wrong, let it be corrected by an amendment . . .

Promote, then, as an object of primary importance, institutions for the general diffusion[6] of knowledge . . . As the structure of a government gives force to public opinion, it is essential that public opinion should be enlightened . . .

[Avoid] likewise the accumulation of debt, . . . not ungenerously throwing upon posterity[7] the burden, which we ourselves ought to bear . . .

Observe good faith and justice toward all nations; cultivate[8] peace and harmony with all . . .

The great rule of conduct for us, in regard to foreign nations, is . . . to have with them as little political connection as possible.

It is our true policy to steer clear of permanent alliances with any portion of the foreign world . . . There can be no greater error than to expect, or calculate[9] upon real favors from nation to nation. It is an illusion, which experience must cure, which a just pride ought to discard.

The duty of holding a neutral conduct may be inferred . . . from the obligation which justice and humanity impose on every nation . . . to maintain inviolate[10] the relations of peace and amity[11] towards other nations.

Washington lists the benefits of uniting the states under one government.

In this phrase, Washington emphasizes his warning against the dangers of political parties.

Washington points out the need for education.

This is Washington's advice to the new nation about foreign policy.

[1] *intimated:* told
[2] *discriminations:* differences
[3] *comprehensive:* complete
[4] *baneful:* destructive
[5] *modification:* change
[6] *diffusion:* spreading
[7] *posterity:* future generations
[8] *cultivate:* seek
[9] *calculate:* plan
[10] *inviolate:* unchanging
[11] *amity:* friendship

Analyze Historical Sources

1. What events happened that might have led to Washington's warning against political parties?

2. Why did Washington suggest neutrality as a foreign policy?

Washington left office warning the nation to work out its differences and protect its independence. Washington also warned against too much public debt. He thought the government should try not to borrow money. He wanted future generations to be protected from debt.

He concluded his speech by looking forward to his retirement and praising his country. "I anticipate . . . the sweet enjoyment . . . of good laws under a free government, the ever favorite object of my heart."

Summary and Preview Americans responded to foreign and domestic conflict during Washington's presidency. In the next lesson you will read about the formation of political parties in the United States and the presidency of John Adams.

Reading Check
Find Main Ideas
What issues did Washington believe were most dangerous to the future of the new nation?

Lesson 3 Assessment

Review Ideas, Terms, and People

1. a. **Describe** What did Washington's Neutrality Proclamation state?

   b. **Compare and Contrast** In what ways were Jay's Treaty and Pinckney's Treaty similar and different?

2. a. **Identify** Who were the leaders of American Indian and U.S. forces in the conflict in the Northwest Territory?

   b. **Predict** What are some possible consequences of the Treaty of Greenville for American Indians in the Northwest Territory?

3. a. **Recall** Why did Congress tax American-made whiskey?

   b. **Explain** How did the tax lead to the Whiskey Rebellion?

   c. **Elaborate** Why do you think that President Washington personally led the army against westerners in the Whiskey Rebellion?

4. a. **Describe** What warnings did Washington give the nation in his Farewell Address?

   b. **Draw Conclusions** Why did Washington not run for a third term as president?

Critical Thinking

5. **Categorize** In this lesson you learned about the challenges the young United States faced. Create a chart similar to the one below and then categorize those challenges as either foreign or domestic.

Challenges	
Foreign	
Domestic	

John Adams's Presidency

The Big Idea

The development of political parties in the United States contributed to differing ideas about the role of the federal government.

Main Ideas

- The rise of political parties created competition in the election of 1796.

- The XYZ affair caused problems for President John Adams.

- Controversy broke out over the Alien and Sedition Acts.

Key Terms and People

political parties
Federalist Party
Democratic-Republican Party
XYZ affair
Alien and Sedition Acts
Kentucky and Virginia
 Resolutions

If YOU were there . . .

You are a newspaper editor in Virginia in 1798. You've joined Jefferson's political party, which opposes the new president. In fact, your paper has printed many articles that criticize him, calling him greedy and foolish. You believe that's your right in a free country. But now Congress has passed a law that makes it illegal to criticize the government. You could be arrested for your articles!

Would you stop criticizing the government? Why?

The Election of 1796

The election of 1796 began a new era in U.S. politics. For the first time, more than one candidate ran for president. **Political parties**, groups that help elect people and shape policies, had begun to form during Washington's presidency. Despite Washington's warnings about political parties, the rivalry between two parties dominated the 1796 election.

Alexander Hamilton helped found the **Federalist Party**, which wanted a strong federal government and supported industry and trade. The Federalists chose John Adams and Thomas Pinckney as candidates. Adams knew he was not well liked in the South or the West, but he hoped people would support him after they thought about his years of loyal public service.

The Federalists, who wanted a strong federal government, were more popular in the North.

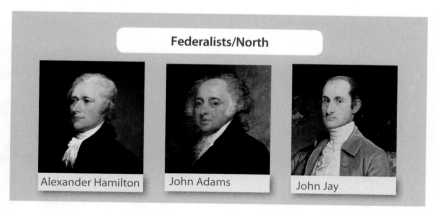

Federalists/North

Alexander Hamilton   John Adams   John Jay

The First Political Parties, 1796

Interpret Maps
Region Which political party had more electoral votes in 1796?

Thomas Jefferson and James Madison founded the **Democratic-Republican Party**. Its members, called Republicans, wanted to limit the federal government's power. (This party is not related to today's Republican Party.) They chose Thomas Jefferson and Aaron Burr as their candidates.

Party differences were based partly on where and how people lived. Businesspeople in the cities tended to support the Federalists. Farmers in more isolated areas generally favored the Democratic-Republicans. Both sides attacked each other. Republicans called Adams a royalist—an insult to a man so involved in the Revolution. The Federalists accused the Republicans of favoring the French.

The Republicans, who wanted to limit the federal government's power, were more popular in the South.

Republicans/South

Thomas Jefferson

James Madison

Albert Gallatin

In the end, Adams defeated Jefferson. At the time, the person who came in second in a presidential election became vice president. So, after months of campaigning against one another, Adams and Jefferson took office together.

Reading Check
Find Main Ideas
How did the election of 1796 change the nature of politics in the United States?

President Adams and the XYZ Affair

John Adams had the challenging task of following Washington as president. The people had adored Washington. Adams would have to work hard to win the people's trust.

A New President At first glance, John Adams did not appear well suited for the presidency. Although Adams had been a leading Patriot during the American Revolution and had later served as a foreign diplomat, he lacked Washington's dignity, and most people saw him as a cold and distant person. Still, many people—even those who opposed him—respected Adams. They recognized his hard work, honesty, and intelligence.

The United States and France One of Adams's first goals as president was to improve the relationship between the United States and France. With Great Britain and France still at war, the French had begun harassing and seizing U.S. ships. Adams sent U.S. diplomats to Paris to smooth over the conflict and to negotiate a treaty to protect U.S. shipping.

When the diplomats arrived in France, they learned that French foreign minister Talleyrand would not speak to them. Instead, they had a strange and secret visit from three French agents. Shockingly, the agents said that Talleyrand would discuss a treaty only in exchange for a $250,000 bribe. The French government also wanted a loan of $12 million. The amazed diplomats refused these demands.

In March 1798 President Adams told Congress that the peace-seeking mission had failed. He described the French terms, substituting the letters X, Y, and Z for the names of the French agents. Upon hearing the disgraceful news, Federalists in Congress called for war with France.

The **XYZ affair**, as the French demand for a bribe came to be called, outraged the American public. "Millions for defense, but not one cent for tribute!" became the rallying cry of the American people.

Preparations for War Fearing war, Adams asked Congress to expand the navy to a fleet of more than 30 ships. He thought war with France might be unavoidable. He also decided the United States should keep a peacetime army. Congress approved both measures.

Although Adams had asked Congress for military support, he did not want to go to war with France. He was worried about its cost. Therefore, he did not ask Congress to declare war. Instead, he tried to reopen peace talks with France.

Peace Efforts Adams's decision not to declare war stunned Federalists. Despite intense pressure from members of his own party, Adams refused to change his mind.

The XYZ Affair

After the XYZ affair, French ships continued to attack American ships. In this political cartoon, the United States is represented by the woman. The men, representing the French, are taking valuables from her. The people in the distance are other European nations.

Why do you think this man is encouraging the woman to look away?

These people aren't helping the woman. What do you think the cartoon is suggesting by this?

Analyze Historical Sources
How does the political cartoon show that America is being preyed upon by the French?

Reading Check
Identify Points of View What did Americans mean when they said "Millions for defense, but not one cent for tribute"?

American and French ships, however, began fighting each other in the Caribbean. Adams sent a representative to France to engage in talks to try to end the fighting. The United States and France eventually signed a treaty. Adams then forced two members of his cabinet to resign for trying to block his peace efforts.

The Alien and Sedition Acts

Many Democratic-Republicans continued to sympathize with France. Federalists, angered by their stand, called them "democrats, mobocrats, and all other kinds of rats."

In 1798 the Federalist-controlled Congress passed four laws known together as the **Alien and Sedition Acts**. These laws were said to protect the United States, but the Federalists intended them to crush opposition to war. The most controversial of these laws was the Sedition Act, which forbade anyone from publishing or voicing criticism of the federal government. In effect, this canceled basic protections of freedom of speech and freedom of the press.

The two main Democratic-Republican leaders, Thomas Jefferson and James Madison, viewed these acts as a misuse of the government's power. Attacking the problem at the state level, they wrote resolutions passed by the Kentucky legislature in 1798 and by Virginia in 1799. Known as the

Kentucky and Virginia Resolutions, these documents argued that the Alien and Sedition Acts were unconstitutional. They stated that the federal government could not pass these acts because they interfered with state government. Madison and Jefferson pressured Congress to repeal the Alien and Sedition Acts. Congress did not, although it allowed the acts to expire within a few years.

The Kentucky and Virginia Resolutions did not have the force of national law, but they supported the idea that states could challenge the federal government. This idea would grow to have a tremendous impact on American history later in the 1800s.

Summary and Preview Political parties formed to reflect different viewpoints. In the next lesson you will read about Thomas Jefferson's presidency.

Reading Check
Analyze Information How did the Kentucky and Virginia Resolutions support the rights of states?

Lesson 4 Assessment

Review Ideas, Terms, and People

1. **a. Recall** What two political parties emerged before the election of 1796? Who were the founders of each party?

   b. Analyze What effect did political parties have on the election of 1796?

   c. Elaborate Do you think it was difficult for Adams and Jefferson to serve together as president and vice president? Explain your answer.

2. **a. Recall** What was one of Adams's first goals as president?

   b. Make Inferences Why were Federalists shocked by Adams's decision to resume peace talks with the French?

3. **a. Identify** What did the Alien and Sedition Acts state?

   b. Explain What idea regarding states' rights did the Kentucky and Virginia Resolutions support?

   c. Elaborate Would you have supported the Alien and Sedition Acts? Explain your answer.

Critical Thinking

4. **Contrast** In this lesson you learned about the election of 1796 and the formation of political parties. Create a chart similar to the one below and then identify how each of the terms listed below reflected party disagreements.

XYZ Affair	
Alien and Sedition Acts	
Kentucky and Virginia Resolutions	

Jefferson Becomes President

The Big Idea

Thomas Jefferson's election began a new era in American government.

Main Ideas

- The election of 1800 marked the first peaceful transition in power from one political party to another.

- President Jefferson's beliefs about the federal government were reflected in his policies.

- *Marbury* v. *Madison* increased the power of the judicial branch of government.

Key Terms and People

John Adams
Louisiana Purchase
Meriwether Lewis
William Clark
Sacagawea
John Marshall
Marbury v. *Madison*
judicial review

If YOU were there . . .

You are a Maryland voter from a frontier district—and you are tired! For days, you and your friends have been wrangling over the presidential election. Who shall it be—John Adams or Thomas Jefferson? Your vote depends on your personal judgment.

Which candidate would you choose for president?

The Election of 1800

In the presidential election of 1800, Federalists **John Adams** and Charles C. Pinckney ran against Democratic-Republicans Thomas Jefferson and Aaron Burr. Each party believed that the American republic's survival depended upon the success of their candidates. With so much at stake, the election was hotly contested.

Unlike today, candidates did not travel around giving speeches. Instead, the candidates' supporters made their arguments in letters and newspaper editorials. Adams's supporters claimed that Jefferson was a pro-French radical. Put Jefferson in office, they warned, and the violence and chaos of the French Revolution would surely follow in the United States. In addition, Federalists argued that Jefferson's interest in science and philosophy proved that he wanted to destroy organized religion.

Democratic-Republican newspapers responded that Adams wanted to crown himself king. What else, they asked, could be the purpose of the Alien and Sedition Acts? Republicans also hinted that Adams would use the newly created permanent army to limit Americans' rights.

When the election results came in, Jefferson and Burr had won 73 electoral votes each to 65 for Adams and 64 for Pinckney. The Democratic-Republicans had won the election, but the tie between Jefferson and Burr caused a problem. Under the Constitution at that time, the two candidates with

The Election of 1800

**John Adams
and the Federalists**

- Rule by wealthy class
- Strong federal government
- Emphasis on manufacturing
- Loose interpretation of the Constitution
- British alliance

**Thomas Jefferson and the
Democratic-Republicans**

- Rule by the people
- Strong state governments
- Emphasis on agriculture
- Strict interpretation of the Constitution
- French alliance

Adams receives 65 votes and Pinckney receives 64 votes.

Election Results

Jefferson and running mate Burr receive 73 votes each.

- Peaceful change of political power from one party to another
- The tied race led to the Twelfth Amendment (1804), which created a separate ballot for president and vice president.

the most votes became president and vice-president. The decision went to the House of Representatives, as called for in the Constitution.

The House, like the electoral college, also deadlocked. Days went by as vote after vote was called, each ending in ties. Exhausted lawmakers put their heads on their desks and slept between votes. Some napped on the House floor.

Jefferson finally won on the 36th vote. The election marked the first time that one party had replaced another in power in the United States.

The problems with the voting system led Congress to propose the Twelfth Amendment. This amendment created a separate ballot for president and vice president.

**Reading Check
Analyze
Information** What was significant about Jefferson's victory?

Jefferson in Office

When Jefferson took office, he brought with him a style and political ideas different from those of Adams and Washington. Jefferson was less formal than his predecessors, and he wanted to limit the powers of government.

Jefferson Is Inaugurated Americans looked forward with excitement to Jefferson's first speech as president. People from across the nation gathered in the new capital, Washington, DC, to hear him. Curious travelers looked with pride at the partially completed Capitol and at the executive mansion (not yet called the White House). The two buildings dominated the surrounding homes and forests.

Small businesses dotted the landscape. At one of these, a modest boardinghouse, the president-elect was putting the finishing touches on his speech. On the morning of March 4, 1801, he left the boardinghouse and walked to the Capitol. The leader of a republic, Jefferson believed, should not ride in fancy carriages.

Jefferson read his speech in a quiet voice. He wanted to make it clear that he supported the will of the majority. He also stressed the need for a limited government and the protection of civil liberties.

From these humble surroundings in which Jefferson delivered his speech, Washington eventually grew into a large and impressive city. Over the years, the Capitol and the executive mansion were joined by other state buildings and monuments. Jefferson, who had long dreamed of a new national capital that would be independent of the interests of any one state, was pleased to be a part of this process of building a federal city.

DOCUMENT-BASED INVESTIGATION   Historical Source

Jefferson's Inaugural Address

On March 4, 1801, Thomas Jefferson gave his first inaugural address. In the following excerpt, Jefferson describes his thoughts on the nation's future.

> "Let us, then, fellow citizens, unite with one heart and one mind . . . [E]very difference of opinion is not a difference of principle. We have called by different names **brethren**[1] of the same principle. We are all republicans; we are all federalists."

> "Still one thing more, fellow citizens, a wise and **frugal**[2] Government, which shall restrain men from injuring one another, shall leave them otherwise free to regulate their own pursuits of industry and improvement, and shall not take from the mouth of labor the bread it has earned. This is the sum of good government . . ."

By using phrases like these, Jefferson tries to reassure his political opponents.

Here Jefferson states his opinion of what is essential to good government.

[1] *brethren:* brothers
[2] *frugal:* thrifty

This phrase shows Jefferson's determination to keep government small.

Analyze Historical Sources
What words and phrases indicate Jefferson's support for a small national government?

Jefferson Makes Changes President Jefferson faced the task of putting his Republican ideas into practice. One of his first actions was to select the members of his cabinet. His choices included James Madison as secretary of state and Albert Gallatin as secretary of the treasury.

Jefferson would also benefit from the Democratic-Republican Party's newly won control of both houses of Congress. At Jefferson's urging, Congress allowed the hated Alien and Sedition Acts to expire. Jefferson lowered military spending and reduced the size of the army. The navy was cut to seven active ships. Jefferson and Gallatin hoped that saving this money would allow the government to repay the national debt. Jefferson also asked Gallatin to find ways to get rid of domestic taxes, like the tax on whiskey. The Democratic-Republican–led Congress passed the laws needed to carry out these policies.

The entire national government in 1801 consisted of only several hundred people. Jefferson preferred to keep it that way. He believed that the primary **functions** of the federal government were to protect the nation from foreign threats, deliver the mail, and collect customs duties.

Jefferson did recognize that some of the Federalist policies—such as the creation of the Bank of the United States—should be kept. Although Jefferson had battled Hamilton over the Bank, as president, he agreed to leave it in place.

The Louisiana Purchase

Jefferson wanted to expand the borders of the United States. One problem that the young nation faced was that it had no ports on the Gulf of Mexico. Farmers in western areas had to ship their crops on boats down the Mississippi River to the port of New Orleans. The port of New Orleans was controlled by Spain. In 1801 in a secret treaty, Spain gave the Louisiana Territory back to France. The Louisiana Territory was a huge area to the west of the Mississippi that included New Orleans.

Jefferson feared that France would close New Orleans to American trade. So he sent James Monroe to Paris to try to purchase New Orleans. The French, however, offered to sell all of the Louisiana Territory to the United States for just $15 million. Monroe quickly agreed. Finalized in 1803, the **Louisiana Purchase** more than doubled the size of the United States.

The Louisiana Purchase was a remarkable bargain. However, it raised many questions. The U.S. Constitution made no mention of buying foreign lands. As a strict constructionist, Jefferson was troubled that he might be overstepping his power. However, common sense told him the purchase was a good idea. He and his advisers decided that the right to acquire territory was part of the president's constitutional power to make treaties. Some Federalists in Congress, however, called the Louisiana Purchase unconstitutional. Yet even Hamilton agreed that the purchase was good for the country. Congress quickly gave its approval.

Jefferson wanted Americans to learn more about the lands of the Louisiana Purchase. He asked his secretary, **Meriwether Lewis**, to lead an expedition to gather information about the territory. Lewis invited experienced frontiersman **William Clark** to join him as co-leader. In May 1804

Academic Vocabulary **functions** uses or purposes

Reading Check Summarize What policy changes did Democratic-Republicans introduce, and which Federalist policies did Jefferson keep?

Thomas Jefferson 1743–1826

Thomas Jefferson was born in Virginia, where he inherited a large estate from his father. At age 26 he began building his elegant lifetime home, Monticello, but he spent much of his life away from home.

Jefferson's powerful words in the Declaration of Independence have inspired people throughout the world to seek freedom, equality, and self-rule. One of his most celebrated achievements as president (1801–1809) was the purchase of the Louisiana Territory from France.

Jefferson died at Monticello on July 4, 1826, within hours of the death of President John Adams, his rival and friend. The date was also the 50th anniversary of the Declaration of Independence. Jefferson wanted only three of his accomplishments listed on his tomb: author of the Declaration of American Independence, author of the Virginia Statute for Religious Freedom, and Father of the

University of Virginia. Yet, he had many other accomplishments—governor of Virginia, lawyer, Revolutionary leader, writer, inventor, architect, musician, astronomer, ambassador, secretary of state, and, of course, president of the United States.

Evaluate
Why has Thomas Jefferson been a hero to generations of Americans?

Lewis and Clark led about 30 frontier soldiers from their camp in St. Louis northwest up the Missouri River. By October the group, called the Corps of Discovery, had reached what is now North Dakota. One member of the Corps was York, an enslaved African owned by William Clark. York was a very skilled hunter.

A Shoshone Indian woman named **Sacagawea** (sak-uh-juh-WEE -uh) agreed to guide the expedition when it reached Shoshone land near the Rocky Mountains. In November 1805, after traveling more than 3,000 miles, the Corps of Discovery reached the Pacific Ocean. They finally got back to St. Louis in September 1806. Newspaper reports of their journey and the detailed journals they published made many Americans want to travel west.

The Supreme Court

Although Republicans controlled the presidency and Congress, Federalists dominated the federal judiciary. In an effort to continue their control over the judiciary, Federalist legislators passed the Judiciary Act of 1801 shortly before their terms of office ended. This act created 16 new federal judgeships that President Adams filled with Federalists before leaving office. The Republican press referred to these people as midnight judges.

Reading Check
Draw Conclusions
Why did the Louisiana Purchase trouble Jefferson?

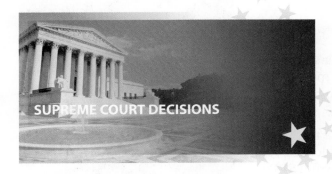

SUPREME COURT DECISIONS

Marbury v. *Madison* (1803)

Background of the Case

Shortly before Thomas Jefferson took office, John Adams had appointed William Marbury to be a justice of the peace. Adams had signed Marbury's commission, but it was never delivered. Marbury sued to force Madison to give him the commission.

The Court's Ruling

The Court ruled that the law Marbury based his claim on was unconstitutional.

The Court's Reasoning

The Judiciary Act of 1789 gave the Supreme Court the authority to hear a wide variety of cases, including those like Marbury's. But the Supreme Court ruled that Congress did not have the power to make such a law. Why? Because the Constitution limits the types of cases the Supreme Court can hear. Thus, the law was in conflict with the Constitution and had to be struck down.

Why It Matters

Marbury v. *Madison* was important for several reasons. It confirmed the Supreme Court's power to declare acts of Congress unconstitutional. By doing so, it established the Court as the final authority on the Constitution. This helped make the judicial branch of government equal to the other two branches. Chief Justice John Marshall and later federal judges would use this power of judicial review as a check on the legislative and executive branches.

Analyze Information

1. What do you think it means to be the final authority on the Constitution?
2. How did *Marbury* v. *Madison* affect the Constitution's system of checks and balances?

They argued that Adams had packed the judiciary with Federalists the night before he left office.

Some of these appointments were made so late that the documents that authorized them had not been delivered by the time Adams left office. This led to controversy once Jefferson took office. William Marbury, named as a justice of the peace by President Adams, did not receive his documents before Adams left office. When Jefferson took office, Marbury demanded the documents. On Jefferson's advice, however, the new secretary of state, James Madison, refused to deliver them. Jefferson argued that the appointment of the midnight judges was not valid.

Marbury brought suit, asking the Supreme Court to order Madison to deliver the appointment papers. Marbury claimed that the Judiciary Act of 1789 gave the Supreme Court the power to do so.

John Marshall, a Federalist appointed by John Adams, was the chief justice of the United States. Chief Justice Marshall and President Jefferson disagreed about many political issues. When Marshall agreed to hear Marbury's case, Jefferson protested. He said that the Federalists "have retired into the judiciary as a stronghold." Marshall wrote the Court's opinion in ***Marbury v. Madison***. This case helped establish the Supreme Court's power to check the power of the other branches of government.

John Marshall (1755–1835)

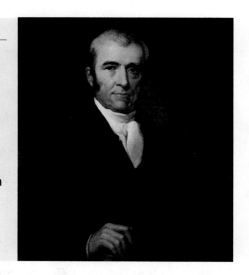

John Marshall was born, the first of 15 children, in Virginia's backcountry. He had little formal schooling. He received most of his education from his parents and a minister who lived with the family one year.

Even so, the lasting strength of the U.S. Constitution is partly due to Marshall's brilliant legal mind. In his long tenure as Chief Justice, John Marshall participated in more than 1,000 decisions and wrote 519 of them himself.

The Constitution, Chief Justice Marshall noted, gave the Supreme Court authority to hear only certain types of cases. A request like Marbury's was not one of them. The law that Marbury's case depended upon was, therefore, unconstitutional.

In denying Marbury's request in this way, the Court avoided a direct confrontation with Jefferson's administration. But more importantly, it established the Court's power of **judicial review**, the power to declare an act of Congress unconstitutional. Marshall and later federal judges would use this power of judicial review to make the judiciary a much stronger part of the national government.

Reading Check
Analyze Information Why was *Marbury* v. *Madison* an important ruling?

Summary and Preview A peaceful transfer of power took place in Washington after the election of 1800. In this module you learned about the early years of the new nation, the United States.

Lesson 5 Assessment

Review Ideas, Terms, and People

1. a. **Identify** What were the political parties in the election of 1800, and who were their candidates?
   b. **Analyze** Why was the election of 1800 significant?

2. a. **Describe** What ideas for government did Thomas Jefferson stress in his inaugural address?
   b. **Compare and Contrast** What similarities and differences did Jefferson's Republican government have with the previous Federalist one?
   c. **Elaborate** Defend Jefferson's preference for keeping the national government small.

3. a. **Identify** Who was John Marshall?
   b. **Draw Conclusions** Why is the power of judicial review important?
   c. **Predict** How might the *Marbury* v. *Madison* ruling affect future actions by Congress?

Critical Thinking

4. **Categorize** In this lesson you learned about Thomas Jefferson's beliefs and policies. Create a chart similar to the one below and show how Jefferson brought change through his policies.

Jefferson as President

Federalist Policies	Republican Policies

Social Studies Skills

Make Group Decisions

Define the Skill

Democracy is one of the most valued principles of American society. It is based on the idea that the members of society, or representatives they choose, make the decisions that affect society. Decision making would be much more efficient if just one person decided what to do and how to do it. However, that method is not at all democratic.

Making decisions as a group is a complicated and difficult skill. However, it is an important one at all levels of society—from governing the nation to making group decisions at school, in the community, and with your friends. At every level, the skill is based on the ability of the group to interact in effective and cooperative ways.

Learn the Skill

Think about the job the first Congress faced after the Constitution was ratified. The nation was still millions of dollars in debt from the Revolutionary War. Congress had to find a way to pay these debts as well as raise money to run the government.

Leaders like Jefferson and Hamilton had ideas about how to accomplish these goals. However, neither man could act alone. In a democracy, a group such as Congress must make the decisions and take action.

This task was complicated by the fact that Jefferson and Hamilton disagreed on what to do. Each man's supporters in Congress pushed his point of view. Fortunately, its members were able to overcome their differences, compromise on goals and actions, and accept group decisions they might not have agreed with personally. Had they not possessed this ability and skill, the nation's early years might have been even more difficult than they were.

Like that first Congress, being part of an effective group requires that you behave in certain ways.

1. **Be an active member.** Take part in setting the group's goals and in making its decisions. Participate in planning and taking group action.

2. **Take a position.** State your views and work to persuade other members to accept them. However, also be open to negotiating and compromising to settle differences within the group.

3. **Be willing to take charge if leadership is needed.** But also be willing to follow the leadership of other members.

Practice the Skill

Suppose that you are a member of the first Congress. With a group of classmates, you must decide what and who should be taxed to raise the money the government needs. Remember that you are an elected official. If you do something to upset the people, you could lose your job. When your group has finished, answer the following questions.

1. Did your group have a plan for completing its task? Did it discuss what taxes to pass? Compared to other members, how much did you take part in those activities?

2. How well did your group work together? What role did you play in that? Was it a positive contribution or a negative one? Explain.

3. Was your group able to make a decision? If not, why? If so, was compromise involved? Do you support the decision? Explain why or why not.

Module 7 Assessment

Review Vocabulary, Terms, and People

Complete each sentence by filling in the blank with the correct term or person.

1. The _____ established the structure of the federal court system and its relationship to state courts.

2. Federalists angered many Republicans when they passed the _____ to protect the United States from traitors.

3. As president, Washington was able to establish several _____, or decisions that serve as examples for later action.

4. Farmers in western Pennsylvania protested taxes in the _____.

5. The _____ was created in order to strengthen the U.S. economy.

Comprehension and Critical Thinking

Lesson 1

6. a. Recall What precedents did President Washington and Congress establish for the executive and judicial branches?

    b. Draw Conclusions Why did Americans select George Washington as their first president?

    c. Evaluate Do you think the newly established government met the expectations of its citizens? Why or why not?

Lesson 2

7. a. Identify What changes did Alexander Hamilton make to the national economy?

    b. Contrast In what ways did Hamilton and Jefferson disagree on the economy?

    c. Evaluate Which of Hamilton's economic plans do you think was the most important to the new nation? Why?

Lesson 3

8. a. Describe What challenges did the nation face during Washington's presidency?

    b. Make Inferences Why did Washington believe that it was important for the United States to remain neutral in foreign conflicts?

    c. Evaluate Rate the success of Washington's presidency. Explain the reasons for your rating.

Lesson 4

9. a. Describe What role did political parties play in the election of 1796?

    b. Analyze How did the Alien and Sedition Acts create division among some Americans?

    c. Predict How might the political attacks between the Federalist and Democratic-Republican parties lead to problems in the future?

Lesson 5

10. a. Recall What were the key issues in the election of 1800?

    b. Analyze In what ways did *Marbury* v. *Madison* affect the power of the judicial branch?

    c. Evaluate Which of Jefferson's new policies do you think was most important? Why?

Review Themes

11. Economics What economic problems troubled the nation at the beginning of Washington's presidency? How were they solved?

12. Politics How did the creation of political parties change politics in the United States?

Reading Skills

Inferences about History *Use the Reading Skills taught in this module to answer the question about the reading selection below.*

> Party differences were based partly on where and how people lived. Businesspeople in the cities tended to support the Federalists. Farmers in more isolated areas generally favored the Democratic-Republicans.

13. Which of the following statements can be inferred from the selection?
   a. Farmers wanted a large federal government.
   b. Urban Americans were usually Republicans.
   c. Merchants supported John Adams.
   d. People in the cities had different concerns than did the rural population.

Social Studies Skills

Make Group Decisions *Use the Social Studies Skills taught in this module to complete the activity below.*

Get together with a group of three or four students and discuss the Alien and Sedition Acts. Answer the following questions individually and as a group.

14. Do you think that limits should have been put on Americans' speeches and printed articles?

15. What other ideas might Congress have considered to resolve the tensions over the issue?

Focus on Writing

16. Write a Nobel Nomination The Nobel Prize is a prestigious world prize that was established in 1901, long after the four American leaders discussed in this module lived. But if the Nobel Prize had existed when Washington, Hamilton, Adams, and Jefferson were alive, which person would you choose to nominate for the Nobel Prize? Make your selection from one of these four people and write your nomination. Begin with a sentence that identifies the person you are nominating. Then give at least three reasons for your nomination. Each reason should include a specific achievement or contribution of this person. End your nomination with a sentence that sums up your reasons for nominating this person for the Nobel Prize. Be persuasive. You need to convince the Nobel Prize committee that this person deserves the prize more than anyone else in the world.

War and Expansion in the Americas

Essential Question

How should the War of 1812 be remembered?

About the Painting: General Andrew Jackson, on horseback, commands his troops against the British during the Battle of New Orleans.

 Explore ONLINE!

VIDEOS, including...
- War of 1812: Madison Declares War

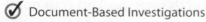 **HISTORY**

☑ Document-Based Investigations

☑ Graphic Organizers

☑ Interactive Games

☑ Image with Hotspots: The USS *Constitution*

☑ Interactive Map: The War of 1812

☑ Interactive Map: U.S. Boundary Changes 1818–1819

In this module you will learn about events and issues surrounding the War of 1812.

What You Will Learn ...

Lesson 1: The Coming of War. 282
The Big Idea Challenges at home and abroad led the United States to declare war on Great Britain.

Lesson 2: The War of 1812 288
The Big Idea Great Britain and the United States went to battle in the War of 1812.

Lesson 3: Settling International Issues 292
The Big Idea The Monroe administration secured and expanded its borders by settling issues with other nations.

| United States | 1800 | World |

∧ **1807** Congress passes the Embargo Act, banning foreign trade.

∧ **1807** The slave trade is abolished in the British Empire.

1810

∧ **1812** Congress declares war against Great Britain.

1814 Kurozumi Munetada founds an influential Shinto religious sect that stresses patriotism in Japan.

< **1815** The Battle of New Orleans is fought.

1815 Napoléon returns to power in France but is defeated at the Battle of Waterloo.

1816 James Monroe is elected president. >

1820

Reading Social Studies

Geography, Politics

In this module you will learn about the War of 1812, challenges that led up to the war, and international issues that came as a result of the war. During Thomas Jefferson's second term, America found itself at war with Great Britain, and James Madison, Jefferson's successor, carried out that war. You will also learn how the United States was able to settle some international issues peacefully. You will see how America's expanding geography and politics were intertwined.

READING FOCUS:

Public Documents in History

Historians use many types of documents to learn about the past. These documents can often be divided into two types—private and public. Private documents are those written for a person's own use, such as letters, journals, or notebooks. Public documents, on the other hand, are available for everyone to read and examine. They include such things as laws, tax codes, and treaties.

Studying Public Documents Studying public documents from the past can tell us a great deal about the politics and society of the time. However, public documents can often be confusing or difficult to understand. When you read such a document, you may want to use a list of questions like the one below to be sure you understand what you're reading.

You can often figure out the topic of a public document from the title and introduction.

Public documents often use unfamiliar words or use familiar words in unfamiliar ways. For example, the document on the next page uses the word *augmented*. Do you know what the word means in this context? If not, you should look it up.

Many public documents deal with several issues and will therefore have several main ideas.

Questions Sheet for Public Documents

1. What is the topic of the document?
2. Do I understand what I'm reading?
3. Is there any vocabulary in the document that I do not understand?
4. What parts of the document should I re-read?
5. What are the main ideas and details of the document?
6. What have I learned from reading this document?

You Try It!

The passage below was taken from a Post Office notice from 1815. Read the passage and then answer the questions that follow.

Rates of Postage Postmasters will take notice, that by an act of Congress, passed on the 23d instant, the several rates of postage are augmented fifty per cent; and that after the first of February next, the Rates of Postage for single Letters will be,

For any distance not exceeding 40 miles, 12 cents

  Over 40 miles and not exceeding 90 miles, 15 cents

  Over 90 miles and not exceeding 150 miles,
    18 1/2 cents

  Over 150 miles and not exceeding 300 miles,
    25 1/2 cents

  Over 300 miles and not exceeding 500 miles, 30 cents

  Over 500 miles, 37 1/2 cents

  Double letters, or those composed of two pieces
    of paper, double those rates.

  Triple letters, or those composed of three pieces
    of paper, triple those rates.

  Packets, or letters composed of four or more
    pieces of paper, and weighing one ounce or
    more, avoirdupois, are to be rated equal to one
    single letter for each quarter ounce.

After reading the document above, answer the following questions.

1. What is this document about?

2. What was the main idea or ideas of this document? What supporting details were included?

3. Look at the word *packets* in the last paragraph of the document. The word is not used here in the same way we usually use *packets* today. What does the word mean in this case? How can you tell?

4. Are there any other words in this passage with which you are unfamiliar? How might not knowing those words hinder your understanding of the passage?

As you read Module 8, look for passages from other public documents. What can these documents teach you about the past?

Key Terms and People

Lesson 1
USS *Constitution*
impressment
embargo
Embargo Act
Non-Intercourse Act
Tecumseh
Battle of Tippecanoe
War Hawks
James Madison

Lesson 2
Oliver Hazard Perry
Battle of Lake Erie
Andrew Jackson
Treaty of Fort Jackson
Battle of New Orleans
Hartford Convention
Treaty of Ghent

Lesson 3
James Monroe
Rush-Bagot Agreement
Convention of 1818
Adams-Onís Treaty

The Coming of War

The Big Idea

Challenges at home and abroad led the United States to declare war on Great Britain.

Main Ideas

- Violations of U.S. neutrality led Congress to enact a ban on trade.
- Native Americans, Great Britain, and the United States came into conflict in the West.
- The War Hawks led a growing call for war with Great Britain.

Key Terms and People

USS Constitution
impressment
embargo
Embargo Act
Non-Intercourse Act
Tecumseh
Battle of Tippecanoe
War Hawks
James Madison

If YOU were there . . .

You are a tea merchant in Boston in 1807, but right now your business is at a standstill. A new law forbids trading with European nations. Now Boston Harbor is full of empty ships. It seems to you that the law is hurting American merchants more than European ones! You know that some merchants are breaking the law and smuggling goods, just to stay in business.

Would you obey the law or turn to smuggling?

Violations of Neutrality

During the late 1700s and early 1800s, American merchant ships fanned out across the oceans. The overseas trade, while profitable, was also risky. Ships had to travel vast distances, often through violent storms. Merchant ships sailing in the Mediterranean risked capture by pirates from the Barbary States of North Africa, who would steal cargo and hold ships' crews for ransom. Attacks continued until the United States sent the **USS Constitution**, a large warship, and other ships to end them.

The Barbary pirates were a serious problem, but an even larger threat soon loomed. When Great Britain and France went to war in 1803, each country wanted to stop the United States from supplying goods to the other. Each government passed laws designed to prevent American merchants from trading with the other. In addition, the British and French navies captured many American merchant ships, searching for war supplies.

The real trouble, however, started when Britain began stopping and searching American ships for sailors who had run away from the British navy, forcing the sailors to return to British ships. Sometimes U.S. citizens were captured by accident. This **impressment**, or the practice of kidnapping and forcing people to serve in the army or navy, continued despite American protests.

The USS Constitution

Connect to Science and Technology In the early years of the republic, foreign trade was critical for the nation's survival. In 1797 Congress decided to create a navy to protect American merchant ships. The powerful warship USS *Constitution* was a key part of the new navy and was undefeated in battle. It is the oldest commissioned warship in the world.

The main mast is 220 feet high.

Copper sheathing supplied by Paul Revere protected the hull.

Most of the ship's cannons were located on the gun deck.

The crew slept and ate on the berth deck.

Boys called "powder monkeys" carried gunpowder from the orlop, or lowest deck, up to the gunners.

Analyze Visuals
Why do you think gunpowder was stored on the bottom deck?

Soon Britain was even targeting American navy ships. In June 1807, for example, the British ship *Leopard* stopped the U.S. Navy ship *Chesapeake* and tried to remove sailors. When the captain of the *Chesapeake* refused, the British took the sailors by force. The brazen attack on the *Chesapeake* stunned Americans.

The Embargo Act Great Britain's violations of U.S. neutrality sparked intense debate in America about how to respond. Some people wanted to go to war. Others favored an **embargo**, or the banning of trade, against Britain.

President Thomas Jefferson, who had easily won re-election in 1804, supported an embargo. At his urging, in late 1807 Congress passed the **Embargo Act**. The law essentially banned trade with all foreign countries. American ships could not sail to foreign ports. American ports were also closed to British ships. Congress hoped that the embargo would punish Britain and France and protect American merchant ships from capture.

The effect of the law was devastating to American merchants. Without foreign trade, they lost enormous amounts of money. Northern states that

The Embargo Act

The unpopularity of the Embargo Act prompted political cartoonists to show visually how the act was hurting American trade.

What do you think the turtle represents?

What is the turtle preventing this man from doing?

Analyze Historical Sources
How does the cartoonist emphasize the unpopularity of the Embargo Act?

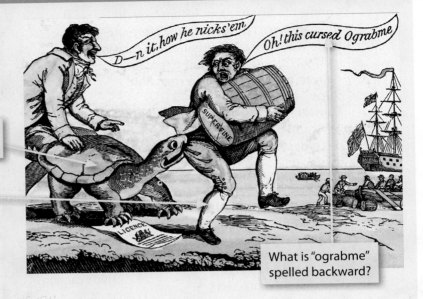

What is "ograbme" spelled backward?

relied heavily on trade were especially hard hit by the embargo. Congressman Josiah Quincy of Massachusetts, in a speech before Congress, described the situation. "All the business of the nation is in disorder. All the nation's industry is at a standstill," he said.

The embargo damaged Jefferson's popularity and strengthened the Federalist Party. Angry merchants sent Jefferson hundreds of petitions demanding the Embargo Act's repeal. One New Englander said the embargo was like "cutting one's throat to stop the nose-bleed." Even worse, the embargo had little effect on Britain and France.

Non-Intercourse Act In 1809 Congress tried to revive the nation's trade by replacing the unpopular act with the **Non-Intercourse Act**. This new law banned trade only with Britain, France, and their colonies. It also stated that the United States would resume trading with the first side that stopped violating U.S. neutrality. In time, however, the law was no more successful than the Embargo Act.

Conflict in the West

Disagreements between Great Britain and the United States went beyond the neutrality issue. In the West, the British and Native Americans again clashed with American settlers over land.

The Conflict over Land In the early 1800s, Native Americans in the old Northwest Territory continued to lose land as thousands of settlers poured into the region. The United States had gained this land in the Treaty of Greenville, but American Indian leaders who had not agreed to the treaty protested the settlers' arrival. Frustrated American Indian groups considered what to do. In the meantime, Britain saw an opportunity to slow America's westward growth. British agents from Canada began to arm Native Americans who were living along the western frontier. Rumors

Reading Check
Compare and Contrast In what ways were the Embargo Act and the Non-Intercourse Act similar and different?

of British activity in the old Northwest Territory quickly spread, filling American settlers with fear and anger.

Tecumseh Resists U.S. Settlers Soon an American Indian leader emerged who seemed capable of halting the American settlers. **Tecumseh** (tuh-KUHM-suh), a Shawnee chief, had watched angrily as Native Americans were pushed off their land. A brilliant speaker, he warned other American Indians about the dangers they faced from settlers. He believed that the Native Americans had to do what white Americans had done: unite.

Tecumseh hoped to unite the Native Americans of the northwestern frontier, the South, and the eastern Mississippi Valley. He was helped by his brother, a religious leader called "the Prophet." They founded a village called Prophetstown for their followers near the Wabash and Tippecanoe rivers.

The Battle of Tippecanoe The governor of the Indiana Territory, William Henry Harrison, watched Tecumseh's activities with alarm. Harrison called him "one of those uncommon geniuses which spring up occasionally to . . . overturn the established order." The governor was convinced that Tecumseh had British backing. If true, Tecumseh could be a serious threat to American power in the West.

In 1810 Tecumseh met face to face with Harrison. The governor urged him to follow the Treaty of Greenville, which had been signed in 1795. Tecumseh replied, "The white people have no right to take the land from the Indians, because the Indians had it first." No single chief, he insisted, could sell land belonging to all American Indians who used it. In response, Harrison warned Tecumseh not to resist the power of the United States.

Tecumseh traveled south to ask the Creek nation to join his forces. In his absence, Harrison attacked. Harrison raised an army and marched his troops close to Prophetstown. Fighting broke out when the Prophet ordered an attack on Harrison's camp on November 7, 1811.

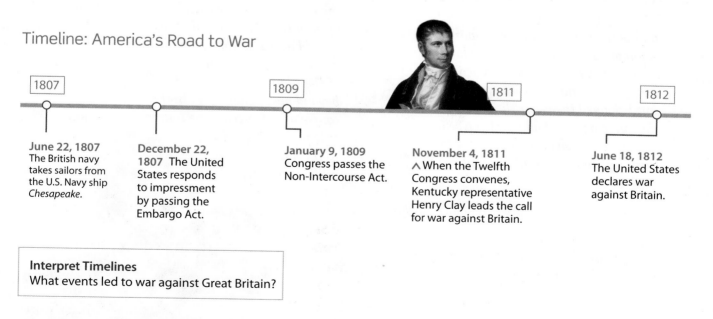

Timeline: America's Road to War

1807

June 22, 1807 The British navy takes sailors from the U.S. Navy ship *Chesapeake*.

December 22, 1807 The United States responds to impressment by passing the Embargo Act.

1809

January 9, 1809 Congress passes the Non-Intercourse Act.

1811

November 4, 1811 ∧ When the Twelfth Congress convenes, Kentucky representative Henry Clay leads the call for war against Britain.

1812

June 18, 1812 The United States declares war against Britain.

Interpret Timelines
What events led to war against Great Britain?

The American Indians broke through army lines, but Harrison kept a "calm, cool, and collected" manner, according to one observer. During the all-day battle, Harrison's soldiers forced the American Indian warriors to retreat and then destroyed Tecumseh's village. Said Chief Shabbona, "With the smoke of that town and loss of that battle, I lost all hope." Although Tecumseh was safe, U.S. forces defeated Tecumseh and his followers in the **Battle of Tippecanoe**. The defeat destroyed Tecumseh's dream of a great American Indian confederation. He fled to Canada.

Reading Check
Find Main Ideas
Why were U.S. officials worried about Tecumseh's actions?

Call for War

The evidence of British support for Tecumseh further inflamed Americans. A Democratic-Republican newspaper declared, "The war on the Wabash [River] is purely BRITISH." Many Americans felt that Britain had encouraged Tecumseh to attack settlers in the West.

The War Hawks Several young members of Congress—called **War Hawks** by their opponents—took the lead in calling for war against Britain. These legislators, most of whom were from the South and West, were led by Henry Clay of Kentucky, John C. Calhoun of South Carolina, and Felix Grundy of Tennessee. They saw war as the only answer to British insults. "If we submit," Calhoun warned, "the independence of this nation is lost." Calls for war grew. Leaders wanted to put a stop to British influence among Native Americans. They also wanted to invade Canada and gain more land

DOCUMENT-BASED INVESTIGATION   Historical Source

Views of War

Tecumseh urged Native Americans to unite to oppose what he called the "evil" of white settlement.

> "The only way to stop this evil is for all the red men to unite in claiming a common and equal right to the land, as it was at first, and should be yet. Before, the land never was divided, but belonged to all, for the use of each person. No group had a right to sell, not even to each other, much less to strangers who want all and will not do with less."
>
> —Tecumseh

William Henry Harrison was proud of his efforts to obtain land for settlers.

> "By my own exertions in securing the friendship of the chiefs . . . by admitting them at all times to my house and table, my propositions for the purchase of their lands were successful beyond my . . . hopes . . . In the course of seven years the Indian title was extinguished to the amount of fifty millions of acres."
>
> —William Henry Harrison

Analyze Historical Sources
How did Harrison's and Tecumseh's views on western settlement differ?

for settlement. Others were angered by British trade restrictions that hurt southern planters and western farmers. The War Hawks gave emotional speeches urging Americans to stand up to Great Britain.

The Opposition The strongest opponents of the War Hawks were New England Federalists. British trade restrictions and impressment had hurt New England's economy. People there wanted to renew friendly business ties with Britain instead of fighting another war.

Other politicians argued that war with Great Britain would be foolish. They feared that the United States was not yet ready to fight powerful Britain. America's army and navy were small and poorly equipped compared to Britain's military. In addition, Americans could produce only a fraction of the military supplies Britain could. Senator Obadiah German of New York pleaded with the War Hawks to be patient: "Prior to any declaration of war . . . my plan would be, and my first wish is, to prepare for it—to put the country in complete armor."

Declaring War Republican **James Madison** was elected president in 1808. He faced the difficulty of continuing an unpopular trade war begun by Jefferson. He also felt growing pressure from the War Hawks. By 1812 he decided that Congress must vote on war. Speaking to Congress, Madison blasted Great Britain's conduct. He asked Congress to decide how the nation should respond.

When Congress voted a few days later, the War Hawks won. For the first time in the nation's brief history, Congress had declared war. Months later, Americans elected Madison to a second term. He would serve as commander in chief during the War of 1812.

Summary and Preview Conflicts on the frontier and with Great Britain dominated U.S. foreign policy under Jefferson and Madison. In the next lesson you will read about the War of 1812.

New Hampshire congressman Daniel Webster was a leading Federalist. He openly criticized war against the British and the violation of New England's shipping rights.

Reading Check
Summarize Why did the United States declare war in 1812?

Lesson 1 Assessment

Review Ideas, Terms, and People

1. **a. Describe** In what ways did the war between France and Britain cause problems for the United States?

   b. Make Inferences What were the reasons for the failure of the Embargo Act?

   c. Elaborate Why do you think embargoes against Britain and France failed?

2. **a. Identify** What was Tecumseh's goal?

   b. Explain What role did Great Britain play in the conflict between the United States and American Indians on the western frontier?

3. **a. Identify** Who were the War Hawks? Why did they support war with Britain?

   b. Elaborate Would you have supported going to war against Great Britain? Explain your answer.

Critical Thinking

4. **Categorize** In this lesson you learned about the challenges that led to the War of 1812. Were most challenges foreign or domestic? Categorize them in a chart like the one below.

Foreign	Domestic

The War of 1812

The Big Idea

Great Britain and the United States went to battle in the War of 1812.

Main Ideas

- American forces held their own against the British in the early battles of the war.

- U.S. forces stopped British offensives in the East and South.

- The effects of the war included prosperity and national pride.

Key Terms and People

Oliver Hazard Perry
Battle of Lake Erie
Andrew Jackson
Treaty of Fort Jackson
Battle of New Orleans
Hartford Convention
Treaty of Ghent

If YOU were there . . .

It's 1812, and the United States and Great Britain are at war. You are a sailor on an American merchant ship that has been licensed as a privateer. Your ship's mission will be to chase and capture ships of the mighty British navy. Even with the help of merchant ships like yours, the American navy is badly outnumbered. You know you face danger and may not survive.

Do you think your mission will succeed?

Early Battles

In the summer of 1812, the United States was at war with one of the world's most powerful nations. Despite claims by the War Hawks, the War of 1812 would not be an easy fight.

War at Sea When the war began, the British navy had hundreds of ships. In contrast, the U.S. Navy had fewer than 20 ships. None of them was as powerful as the greatest British warships.

Most of the British navy's ships, however, were scattered around the globe. Although small, the U.S. Navy had well-trained sailors and powerful new warships such as the USS *Constitution*. American vessels defeated British ships several times in one-on-one duels. Such victories embarrassed the British and raised American morale. Eventually the British ships blockaded America's seaports.

Battles Along the Canadian Border American leaders hoped to follow up victories at sea with an overland invasion of Canada. Three attacks were planned—from Detroit, from Niagara Falls, and from up the Hudson River valley toward Montreal.

The attack from Detroit failed when British soldiers and American Indians led by Tecumseh captured Fort Detroit. The other American attacks failed when state militia troops refused to cross the Canadian border, arguing that they did not have to fight in a foreign country.

The War of 1812

Disputed

BRITISH TERRITORY

ME
(PART OF MA)

Lake Superior

Montreal

Plattsburg · VT

ILLINOIS
TERRITORY

Lake Huron

NH

Lake
Ontario

Boston

York

Thames

Fort Niagara

NY

MA

MICHIGAN
TERR.

Lake Erie

CT

RI

Fort
Detroit

PERRY

PA

New York
City

40°N

HARRISON

Philadelphia

NJ

Lake Michigan

Fort
Dearborn

HULL

Lake
Erie

Baltimore

DE

MISSOURI
TERRITORY

INDIANA
TERRITORY

OH

Washington,
D.C.

MD

VA

KY

35°N

NC

TN

JACKSON

Tallapoosa
River

SC

MISSISSIPPI
TERRITORY

Horseshoe Bend

Alabama
River

GA

30°N

SPANISH
TERRITORY

LA

Fort
Mims

ATLANTIC
OCEAN

Legend:
- ▬ American forces
- ✦ American victories
- ▬ British forces
- ✦ British victories
- ||| British blockades
- ✦ Creek victory

Disputed

New Orleans

SPANISH
TERRITORY

80°W

0   150   300 Miles
0   150   300 Kilometers

95°W   90°W

Gulf of
Mexico

85°W

75°W

25°N

N
W · E
S

Interpret Maps

1. **Location** According to the map, what major southern port was affected by the British blockade?

2. **Region** Which battles took place in the Great Lakes region?

In 1813 the United States went on the attack again. A key goal was to break Britain's control of Lake Erie. The navy gave the task to Commodore **Oliver Hazard Perry**. After building a small fleet, Perry sailed out to meet the British on September 10, beginning the **Battle of Lake Erie**. The battle ended when the British surrendered. Perry sent a message to General William Henry Harrison: "We have met the enemy and they are ours." Perry's brilliant victory forced the British to withdraw, giving the U.S. Army control of the lake and new hope.

With American control of Lake Erie established, General Harrison marched his army into Canada. At the Battle of the Thames River in

October 1813, he defeated a combined force of British troops and Native Americans. Harrison's victory ended British power in the Northwest. Tecumseh's death during the fighting also dealt a blow to the British alliance with Native Americans in the region.

The Creek War Meanwhile, war with American Indians erupted in the South. Creek Indians, angry at American settlers for pushing into their lands, took up arms in 1813. A large force attacked Fort Mims on the Alabama River, destroying the fort and killing close to 250 of its defenders. In response, the commander of the Tennessee militia, **Andrew Jackson**, gathered about 2,000 volunteers to move against the Creek nation.

In the spring of 1814, Jackson attacked the Creek along the Tallapoosa River in Alabama. Jackson's troops won this battle, the Battle of Horseshoe Bend. The **Treaty of Fort Jackson**, signed late in 1814, ended the Creek War and forced the Creek to give up millions of acres of their land.

Great Britain on the Offensive

Despite U.S. success on the western and southern frontiers, the situation in the East grew worse. After defeating France in April 1814, the British sent more troops to America.

British Attacks in the East Now reinforced, the British attacked Washington, DC. President Madison was forced to flee when the British broke through U.S. defenses. The British set fire to the White House, the Capitol, and other government buildings.

The British sailed on to Baltimore, Maryland, which was guarded by Fort McHenry. They shelled the fort for 25 hours. The Americans refused to surrender Fort McHenry. The British chose to retreat instead of continuing to fight.

The Battle of New Orleans After the attack on Washington, the British moved against New Orleans. British commanders hoped to capture the city and thus take control of the Mississippi River.

Reading Check
Compare What advantages did Great Britain and the United States have at the start of the war?

When the British attacked Washington, DC, First Lady Dolley Madison refused to leave until a famous portrait of George Washington was safely taken away from the White House.

Reading Check
Find Main Ideas
What happened at
the Battle of New
Orleans?

Andrew Jackson commanded the U.S. forces around New Orleans. His troops were a mix of regular soldiers, including two battalions of free African Americans, a group of Choctaw Indians, state militia, and pirates led by Jean Lafitte.

The battle began on the morning of January 8, 1815. Some 5,300 British troops attacked Jackson's force of about 4,500. The British began marching toward the U.S. defenses, but they were caught on an open field. The British were cut down with frightening speed. More than 2,000 British soldiers were killed or wounded. The Americans, for their part, had suffered about 70 casualties. The **Battle of New Orleans** made Andrew Jackson a hero and was the last major conflict of the War of 1812.

Effects of the War

Before the Battle of New Orleans, a group of New England Federalists gathered secretly at Hartford, Connecticut. At the **Hartford Convention**, Federalists agreed to oppose the war and send delegates to meet with Congress. Before the delegates reached Washington, however, news arrived that the war had ended. Some critics now laughed at the Federalists, and the party lost much of its political power.

Academic
Vocabulary
consequences the
effects of a particular
event or events

Reading Check
Analyze
Information
What were the
main effects of the
War of 1812?

Slow communications at the time meant that neither the Federalists nor Jackson knew about the **Treaty of Ghent**. The treaty, which had been signed in Belgium on December 24, 1814, ended the War of 1812.

Though each nation returned the territory it had conquered, the fighting did have several underlineconsequences. The war produced feelings of patriotism in Americans for having stood up to the mighty British. Some even called it the second war for independence. The war also broke the power of many Native American groups. Finally, a lack of goods caused by the interruption in trade boosted American manufacturing.

Summary and Preview The War of 1812 showed Americans that the nation would survive. In the next lesson you will see how the United States continued to grow.

Lesson 2 Assessment

Review Ideas, Terms, and People

1. **a. Identify** What losses did American forces face in the early battles of the War of 1812? What victories did they win?

   b. Make Generalizations What role did American Indians play in the war?

2. **a. Describe** What attacks did the British lead against American forces?

   b. Evaluate What do you think were the two most important battles of the war? Why?

3. **a. Identify** What was the purpose of the Hartford Convention?

   b. Draw Conclusions How did the War of 1812 positively affect the United States?

Critical Thinking

4. **Compare and Contrast** In this lesson you learned about the battles of the War of 1812. Compare and contrast the details of the major battles during the War of 1812 in a chart like the one below.

Battle	Details (Winner, Location, Effects)

Settling International Issues

The Big Idea

The Monroe administration secured and expanded its borders by settling issues with other nations.

Main Ideas

- The United States and Great Britain settled their disputes over boundaries and control of waterways.

- The United States gained Florida in an agreement with Spain.

Key Terms and People

James Monroe
Rush-Bagot Agreement
Convention of 1818
Adams-Onís Treaty

If YOU were there . . .

You are a Spanish settler living in West Florida in 1820. Your family has lived in Florida for many years. Only a few years ago, people in Spanish Florida were furious when American soldiers occupied the town of Pensacola. Now you hear that Spain has signed a treaty with the United States—Florida is no longer Spanish territory but rather part of the United States.

How would you feel about living under a new government?

Settling Disputes with Great Britain

In 1816 voters elected **James Monroe** to the presidency. From 1817 to 1825, Monroe's administration achieved a series of brilliant diplomatic successes. These successes settled long-standing disputes and helped secure and expand the borders of the United States.

For example, although the War of 1812 was over, there were still issues between Britain and the United States. Tensions remained high along the United States' northern border with British Canada. Both nations kept armed naval fleets in the Great Lakes to protect their interests.

On April 20, 1817, the two sides signed the **Rush-Bagot Agreement**, which limited naval power on the Great Lakes. In effect, the agreement demilitarized the border. Each nation agreed to keep only one military ship and one cannon on Lake Ontario and Lake Champlain. For the other Great Lakes, each nation was permitted two ships.

Another treaty with Britain gave the United States fishing rights off parts of the Newfoundland and Labrador coasts. This treaty, known as the **Convention of 1818**, also set the border between the United States and Canada at 49°N latitude as far west as the Rocky Mountains. Interest in the valuable fur trade in the Oregon Country was another issue resolved by this treaty. Both countries agreed to occupy the Pacific Northwest together, an agreement that would be tested in the years to come.

Reading Check
Summarize
What were the main disputes between the United States and Britain?

U.S. Boundary Changes, 1818–1819

Legend:
- U.S.–Canadian border, Convention of 1818
- U.S.–Spanish territory border, Adams-Onís Treaty of 1819
- From Britain to United States, 1818
- From Spain to United States, 1819
- Disputed by United States and Great Britain, 1818

0   200   400 Miles
0   200   400 Kilometers

Map Labels: BRITISH TERRITORY, OREGON COUNTRY, 49th Parallel, 42nd Parallel, ROCKY MOUNTAINS, UNORGANIZED TERRITORY, Mississippi River, MICHIGAN TERRITORY, Great Lakes, ME, VT, NH, MA, NY, RI, CT, PA, NJ, DE, MD, OH, IN, IL, VA, APPALACHIAN MOUNTAINS, MISSOURI TERRITORY, KY, NC, TN, Arkansas River, ARKANSAS TERRITORY, SC, GA, SPANISH TERRITORY, Red River, MS, AL, Sabine River, LA, UNORGANIZED TERRITORY (FLORIDA), ATLANTIC OCEAN, Gulf of Mexico, PACIFIC OCEAN, 70°W, 110°W

Interpret Maps

1. **Place** What territory did the United States acquire from Spain in 1819?

2. **Region** What western region was claimed by both the United States and Great Britain?

United States Gains Florida

The United States also had disputes along its southern border with Spanish Florida. After the War of 1812, the Seminoles in Florida continued to welcome runaway slaves from the United States. In turn, Americans continued to enter Florida. Some came as settlers, and others came to capture escaped slaves. Encounters between these Americans and the Seminoles were unfriendly. From 1817 to 1818, the Seminoles and their African American allies fought against Americans in a series of small battles that came to be known as the First Seminole War.

In April 1818, under General Andrew Jackson, U.S. troops invaded Florida. They drove out the Seminoles living in East Florida near the Georgia border, as well as those living west of the Suwannee River. Jackson wrote to the United States government that "the possession of Florida would be desirable [good] . . . and in sixty days it will be accomplished."

Then, believing that he had the permission of the U.S. government, Jackson seized the Spanish forts at St. Marks and Pensacola. Spain objected to Jackson's actions. The United States said that Jackson had acted without authority and returned to Spain the forts that Jackson had captured. Still, Jackson's campaign showed that Spain's hold on Florida was loosening.

Jackson's presence in Florida convinced Spain to negotiate with the United States over the ownership of Florida. On February 22, 1819, U.S. Secretary of State John Quincy Adams, son of John and Abigail Adams, and Spanish diplomat Luis de Onís signed the **Adams-Onís Treaty**, which settled all border disputes between Spain and the United States. Spain agreed to give Florida to the United States. In return, the United States gave up its claims to what is now Texas and agreed to pay up to $5 million of U.S. citizens' claims against Spain.

Andrew Jackson earned the nickname "Old Hickory" during the War of 1812. Soldiers called him that because he was strict. They said he was as tough as the wood of a hickory tree.

Reading Check
Summarize
How were the disagreements between the United States and Spanish Florida settled?

Summary and Preview In this lesson you learned that compromise was one characteristic of U.S. foreign policy in the years following the War of 1812. In the next lesson you will learn about strong U.S. leadership and the Monroe Doctrine.

Lesson 3 Assessment

Review Ideas, Terms, and People

1. **a. Identify** What issues were settled between the United States and Great Britain in 1817 and 1818?

   b. Make Inferences Why would the United States and Britain agree to occupy the Pacific Northwest together?

   c. Elaborate Why were the Rush-Bagot Agreement and the Convention of 1818 compromises?

2. **a. Recall** What problems existed between Spain and the United States?

   b. Analyze Why was the Adams-Onís Treaty important?

   c. Evaluate Do you think that Andrew Jackson was right to act without orders? Explain your answer.

Critical Thinking

3. **Identify Cause and Effect** In this lesson you learned about U.S. foreign policy issues. Create a new chart and, for each issue, identify the nations involved, the agreement or treaty, and the effects.

Issue	Nations	Agreement/Treaty	Effects

Social Studies Skills

Work in a Group to Solve Issues

Define the Skill

You already know that the decision-making process is more complex in a group than it is if just one person makes the decisions. However, group decision-making becomes an even greater challenge when controversial issues are involved.

Group members must have additional skills for the group to function effectively when conflict exists within it. These include respect for differing views, the arts of persuasion and negotiation, and an ability to compromise. A group may not be able to find solutions to controversial problems unless its members have these skills.

Learn the Skill

Some of the biggest challenges Congress faced in the early 1800s were related to the war between Great Britain and France. Some Americans supported the British, while others favored the French. Both countries hoped for American help. When the United States would not take sides, they each began interfering with U.S. ships on the open seas.

As you read in this module, Congress tried to solve this problem by passing the Embargo Act. That solution was controversial, however. The northern states were hard hit by the law's ban on overseas trade. Their representatives in Congress demanded a less extreme action. The result was the Non-Intercourse Act. This law was a compromise between members who wanted to lift the trade ban and those who wanted to continue it. Congress was able to solve this problem because its members were able to work around their differences.

The skills Congress needed to reach its solution are valuable ones for any group that must make decisions involving controversial issues. They include the following attitudes and behaviors.

1. **Willingness to take a position.** If an issue is controversial, it is likely that group members will have differing opinions about it. You have a right to state your views and try to persuade others that you are correct.

2. **Willingness to listen to differing views.** Every other member has the same right you do. You have a duty to listen to their views, even if you do not agree. Disrespect for those whose views differ from yours makes it more difficult for the group to reach a solution.

3. **Willingness to debate.** Debate is a form of "healthy" argument because it defends and attacks ideas instead of the people who hold them. Debating the group's differences of opinion is an important step in reaching a solution.

4. **Willingness to negotiate and compromise.** If debate does not produce agreement, a compromise may be needed. Often it is better to have a solution that members may not like but can accept, than to have no agreement at all.

Practice the Skill

Check your understanding of the skill by answering the following questions.

1. Why would refusing to listen to other members make group decision-making more difficult?

2. Why is compromise often a better solution than forcing a decision on members who disagree?

Module 8 Assessment

Review Vocabulary, Terms, and People

Complete each sentence by filling in the blank with the correct term or person.

1. The British practice of capturing American sailors and forcing them to serve in the British navy, or _____, was one of the issues that led to the War of 1812.

2. After U.S. neutrality was violated, the United States issued an _____ against trade with foreign nations.

3. The War of 1812 ended soon after the U.S. victory over the British at the _____.

4. As commander of the Tennessee militia, _____ led his troops in battle against the Creek nation.

5. The border between the United States and Canada was settled in a treaty known as the _____.

6. Spain gave East Florida to the United States and the United States gave up its claims to what is now Texas when the two countries signed the _____.

Comprehension and Critical Thinking

Lesson 1

7. a. **Identify** What group, led by Congressman Henry Clay, called for war with Great Britain?

   b. **Contrast** What arguments were given in favor of war with Great Britain? What arguments were given against war with Britain?

   c. **Elaborate** In your opinion, why were the Embargo Act and the Non-Intercourse Act unsuccessful?

Lesson 2

8. a. **Identify** What roles did Andrew Jackson and William Henry Harrison play in the War of 1812?

   b. **Make Inferences** Why did the British want to capture the cities of Washington and New Orleans in the War of 1812?

   c. **Predict** In what ways might the U.S. victory over Great Britain in the War of 1812 affect the status of the United States in the world?

Lesson 3

9. a. **Identify** What issues did the Convention of 1818 resolve for the United States and Britain?

   b. **Predict** How might the decision that both countries occupy the Oregon Country be tested in the future?

   c. **Identify Cause and Effect** How did the First Seminole War begin? What effect did the war have on border disputes between Spain and the United States?

Review Themes

10. **Geography** In which bodies of water did the British set up blockades during the War of 1812?

11. **Politics** What impact did the Hartford Convention have on American politics?

Reading Skills

Public Documents in History *Use the Reading Skills taught in this module to answer the question below.*

12. Which of the following is an example of a public document?

    a. the Constitution

    b. the current president's journal

    c. a tax return

    d. an ambassador's letter to the president

Social Studies Skills

Work in a Group to Solve Issues *Use the Social Studies Skills taught in this module to answer the question below.*

13. Organize into groups of two or three students. Decide which of the following reasons for the War of 1812 you think might have been most important in Congress's decision to declare war.

    a. impressment of American sailors

    b. trade barriers with Britain and France

    c. battles with Native Americans on the frontier

    d. gaining land in Canada

Focus on Writing

14. **Write a Résumé for Andrew Jackson** A résumé lists a person's qualifications and work experience. It can also include a person's abilities and leadership experience. Review the information about Andrew Jackson's actions during the War of 1812 and in Florida during the First Seminole War. Choose three or four actions you think are the most important to show what kind of leader Jackson was. Write a sentence on each of those actions. Conclude with one or two sentences that summarize Andrew Jackson's leadership ability.

Module 9

A New National Identity

★

Essential Question
Why did America's national identity change in the early 1800s?

About the Photo: The Erie Canal, completed in 1825, improved travel between cities and helped to unify the country.

▶ *Explore ONLINE!*

VIDEOS, including...
- James Monroe
- Building the Erie Canal

HISTORY

☑ Document-Based Investigations

☑ Graphic Organizers

☑ Interactive Games

☑ Image with Hotspots: We Owe Allegiance to No Crown, 1814

☑ Image Carousel: Key Features of the American System

☑ Image with Hotspots: The Oxbow

☑ Image Carousel: Portraying America

In this module you will learn about the factors that contributed to the emergence of a distinctly American identity.

What You Will Learn ...

Lesson 1: American Foreign Policy 302
The Big Idea Nationalism helped guide American foreign policy in the early 1800s.

Lesson 2: Nationalism and Sectionalism 306
The Big Idea A rising sense of national unity allowed some regional differences to be set aside and national interests to be served.

Lesson 3: American Culture 314
The Big Idea As the United States grew, developments in many cultural areas contributed to the creation of a new American identity.

Timeline of Events 1810–1830

▶ Explore ONLINE!

United States | **World**

1810

1812 Congress declares war against Great Britain.

1815 Napoléon returns to power in France but is defeated at the Battle of Waterloo.

< **1816** James Monroe is elected president.

1820 The Missouri Compromise allows Maine and Missouri to become states.

1820

∧ **1821** Mexico and Peru gain their independence from Spain.

1823 The Monroe Doctrine is issued.

1824 John Quincy Adams is elected president. ∨

1824 Liberia is founded by freed American slaves. >

1829 The Ottoman Empire recognizes the independence of Greece.

1830

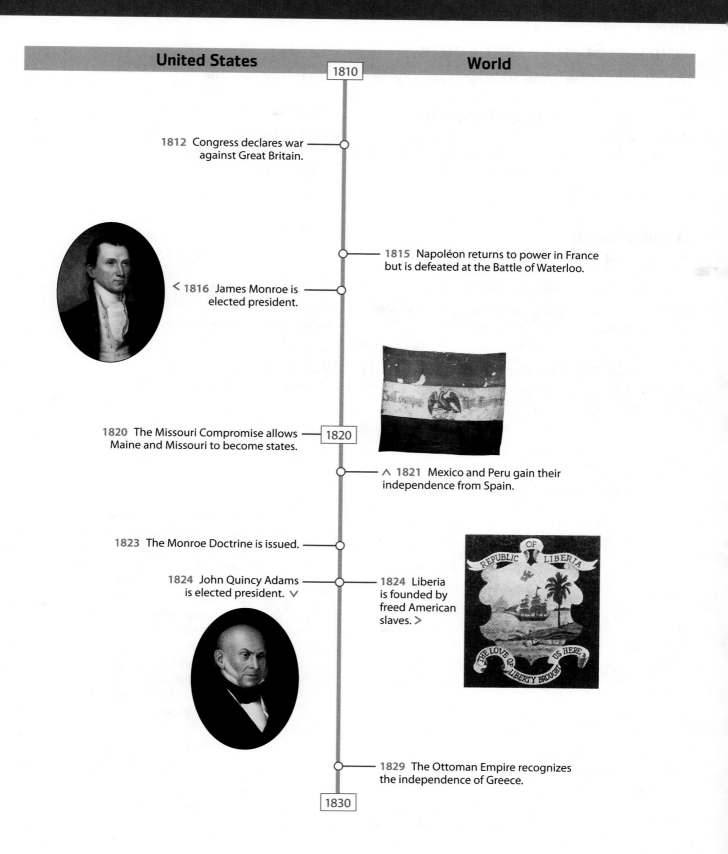

Reading Social Studies

Politics, Society and Culture

This module is titled "A New National Identity" because it explains how the United States government established relations with European powers and how Americans developed a strong sense of national pride even as they struggled with important state issues. You will learn about the Monroe Doctrine, the Missouri Compromise, the Cumberland Road project, and the rise of American music, literature, and public schools—events that changed the country's culture and politics.

READING FOCUS:

Bias and Historical Events

As you read this module, you will find that some people supported the idea of using federal dollars to create new and better roads. Others, however, did not think federal dollars should be used that way. People who can only see one side of an issue or situation may become biased, or prejudiced against the opposite view.

Recognizing Bias To understand the events and people in history, you have to be able to recognize a speaker's or writer's bias. Here are some steps you can take to do that.

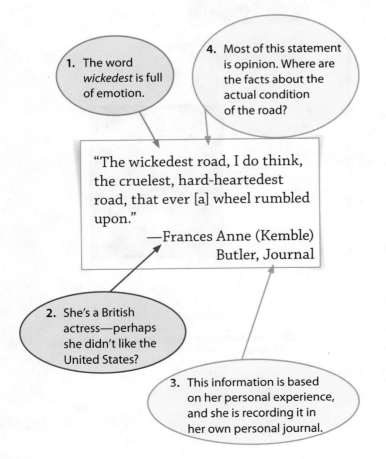

1. The word *wickedest* is full of emotion.

4. Most of this statement is opinion. Where are the facts about the actual condition of the road?

"The wickedest road, I do think, the cruelest, hard-heartedest road, that ever [a] wheel rumbled upon."
—Frances Anne (Kemble) Butler, Journal

2. She's a British actress—perhaps she didn't like the United States?

3. This information is based on her personal experience, and she is recording it in her own personal journal.

Steps to Recognize Bias

1. **Look at the words and images.** Are they emotionally charged? Do they present only one side or one point of view?

2. **Look at the writer.** What's the writer's background and what does that tell you about the writer's point of view?

3. **Look at the writer's sources.** Where does the writer get his or her information? Does the writer rely on sources who only support one point of view?

4. **Look at the information.** How much is fact and how much is opinion? Remember, facts can be proven. Opinions are personal beliefs—they can easily be biased.

You Try It!

Key Terms and People

Lesson 1
nationalism
Era of Good Feelings
Simon Bolívar
Monroe Doctrine

Lesson 2
Henry Clay
American System
Cumberland Road
Erie Canal
sectionalism
Missouri Compromise
John Quincy Adams

Lesson 3
Washington Irving
James Fenimore Cooper
Hudson River school
Thomas Cole
George Caleb Bingham

The following passage is from the module you are getting ready to read. As you read the passage, think about living during the early to mid-1800s when there were no public schools.

Architecture and Education Americans also embraced educational progress. Several early American political leaders expressed a belief that democracy would only succeed in a country of educated and enlightened people. But there was no general agreement on who should provide that education.

Eventually, the idea of a state-funded public school gathered support. In 1837, Massachusetts lawmakers created a state board of education. Other states followed this example, and the number of public schools slowly grew.

After you read the passage, answer the following questions.

1. You are the editor of your town's newspaper in the year 1835. You think schools should be financed by the state government rather than the federal government. You decide to write an editorial to express your opinion. Which of the phrases below would reveal your personal bias to your readers? Why? What words in each statement create bias?

   a. overbearing federal government

   b. protecting state interests

   c. powerful federal government

   d. concerned state citizens

2. If you were going to write the editorial described in question 1, how could you avoid biased statements? How do you think this might affect people's reactions to your writing?

As you read Module 9, study the historical documents carefully. Do you see any examples of bias?

American Foreign Policy

The Big Idea

Nationalism helped guide American foreign policy in the early 1800s.

Main Ideas

- Success in foreign affairs contributed to a growing sense of American nationalism.
- The Monroe Doctrine was a major shift in American Foreign Policy.

Key Terms and People

nationalism
Era of Good Feelings
Simon Bolívar
Monroe Doctrine

If YOU were there . . .

You are a fur trader living in the Pacific Northwest in 1817. You have been extremely successful in your trade for many years. Now you hear that Great Britain and the United States have signed a treaty agreeing to occupy the Pacific Northwest together, opening the region to more settlers. Recently, you have discovered that several new fur traders are trapping on the lands you consider your hunting area.

What effect will this treaty have on your livelihood?

Growing Nationalism

American foreign policy in the early 1800s reflected a growing spirit of nationalism. **Nationalism** is a feeling of pride and loyalty to a nation. It is the belief that the interests of the nation as a whole are more important than regional interests or the interests of other countries.

In 1817 James Monroe took office as the fifth president of the United States. His presidency lasted two terms, from 1817 to 1825. During this time, the economy grew rapidly, and a spirit of nationalism and optimism prevailed. One Boston newspaper called the time the "**Era of Good Feelings**."

The good feelings at home were boosted by successes in foreign affairs. Americans were proud of their victory in the War of 1812. It made them confident in the strength of their young but growing country. Moreover, Monroe's administration achieved a series of diplomatic successes. With the Rush-Bagot Treaty and the Convention of 1818, the United States secured its northern border and convinced Britain to share territory in the Pacific Northwest. With the Adams-Onís Treaty, Monroe secured Florida for the United States.

Settled and secure at home, Americans were ready to take their place on the world stage. Nationalist feelings would soon drive a major shift in U.S. foreign policy.

Reading Check
Summarize
What events contributed to a growing sense of nationalism among Americans?

We Owe Allegiance to No Crown, 1814

After the United States won the War of 1812, American artist John Archibald Woodside painted this image.

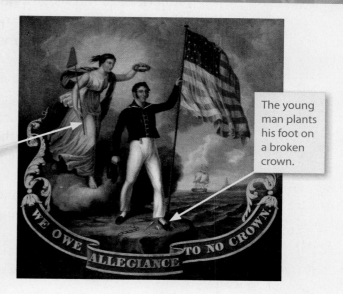

Lady Liberty carries a liberty pole and crown.

The young man plants his foot on a broken crown.

WE OWE ALLEGIANCE TO NO CROWN

Analyze Historical Sources
How does Woodside's painting express national pride?

Monroe Doctrine

Despite Monroe's skillfully won agreements with Britain and Spain, the United States still faced foreign policy issues. These issues focused on the nation's neighbors to the south in Central and South America.

Spain had colonized Central and South America in the 1600s and 1700s. By the early 1820s, however, most of the Spanish colonies in the Americas had declared independence. Revolutionary fighter **Simon Bolívar**, called "the Liberator," led many of these struggles for independence. The political **circumstances** surrounding the revolutions reminded most American leaders of the American Revolution. As a result, they supported these struggles.

After Mexico broke free from Spain in 1821, President Monroe grew worried. He feared that rival European powers might try to take control of newly independent Latin American countries. He was also concerned about Russia's interest in the northwest coast of North America.

Secretary of State Adams shared President Monroe's concerns. In a Fourth of July speech before Congress, Adams said that the United States had always been friendly with European powers, and that the country did not want to be involved in wars with them. He implied that he supported the newly independent countries but said the United States would not fight their battles.

Great Britain was also interested in restraining the influence of other European nations in the Americas. This was because

Academic Vocabulary
circumstances
surrounding situation

President from 1817–1825, James Monroe helped shape U.S. foreign policy for the next century.

Britain had formed close trading ties with most of the independent Latin American countries. Britain wanted to issue a joint statement with the United States to warn the rest of Europe not to interfere in Latin America.

Instead, President Monroe and Secretary of State John Quincy Adams responded by declaring a new foreign policy for the United States. The policy was designed to protect American interests. In time, it would be called the Monroe Doctrine.

The **Monroe Doctrine** stated that the United States would view any European attempts to further colonize the Americas "as dangerous to our peace and safety." On December 2, 1823, Monroe issued the doctrine during his annual message to Congress.

The Monroe Doctrine had four basic points.
1. The United States would not interfere in the affairs of European nations.
2. The United States would recognize, and not interfere with, European colonies that already existed in North and South America.

DOCUMENT-BASED INVESTIGATION   Historical Source

The Monroe Doctrine

President James Monroe established the foundation for U.S. foreign policy in Latin America in the Monroe Doctrine of 1823.

In this phrase, Monroe warns European nations against trying to influence events in the Western Hemisphere.

Monroe notes here the difference between existing colonies and newly independent countries.

The occasion has been judged proper for asserting . . . that the American continents . . . are henceforth not to be considered as subjects for future colonization by any European powers . . .

The political system of the allied powers is essentially different . . . from that of America. We . . . declare that we should consider any attempt on their part to extend their system to any portion of this hemisphere as dangerous to our peace and safety . . .

With the existing colonies . . . we have not interfered and shall not interfere. But with the governments who have declared their independence and maintained it, and whose independence we have . . . acknowledged, we could not view any **interposition**[1] *for the purpose of oppressing them . . . by any European power in any other light than as the* **manifestation**[2] *of an unfriendly* **disposition**[3] *toward the United States.*

[1] *interposition:* interference
[2] *manifestation:* evidence
[3] *disposition:* attitude

Analyze Historical Sources
1. What warning did President Monroe give to European powers in the Monroe Doctrine?
2. How does Monroe say the United States will treat existing European colonies?

This political cartoon depicts the Monroe Doctrine, which forbade European powers from interfering with the nations of the Western Hemisphere.

How does the cartoon depict the United States in relation to the nations of Europe and Latin America?

3. The Western Hemisphere was to be off-limits to future colonization by any foreign power.
4. The United States would consider any European power's attempt to colonize or interfere with nations in the Western Hemisphere to be a hostile act.

The Monroe Doctrine was a bold statement to the great powers of Europe. It declared the Americas closed to any future European colonization. The United States would stay out of European affairs, but it would serve as leader and protector of the Americas. Some Europeans strongly criticized the Monroe Doctrine, but few European nations challenged it.

Over the next century, the Monroe Doctrine would guide American foreign policy. It was used to justify the westward expansion of the United States as well as expansionist foreign policies in Central and South America. The United States had taken its first steps toward becoming a world power.

Reading Check
Analyze What effect did the revolutions in Latin America have on U.S. foreign policy?

Summary and Preview In this lesson you learned how a growing sense of nationalism guided a major shift in U.S. foreign policy. In the next lesson you will learn how national pride shaped domestic policy.

Lesson 1 Assessment

Review Ideas, Terms, and People

1. a. **Identify** What is nationalism?
   b. **Describe** What circumstances characterized the Era of Good Feelings?
   c. **Predict** How might the Era of Good Feelings have been different if Americans had lost the War of 1812?
2. a. **Describe** What were the main points of the Monroe Doctrine?
   b. **Contrast** How did the Monroe Doctrine differ from Adams's Fourth of July Address?
   c. **Draw Conclusions** How did the Monroe Doctrine likely impact U.S. foreign policy?
   d. **Elaborate** What do you think the newly independent Latin American countries thought of the Monroe Doctrine?

Critical Thinking

3. **Identify Cause and Effect** In this lesson, you learned about nationalism and changes in U.S. foreign policy. Create a chart like the one below and use it to identify the causes and effects of foreign policy changes.

U.S. Foreign Policy

Causes	Effects

Nationalism and Sectionalism

The Big Idea

A rising sense of national unity allowed some regional differences to be set aside and national interests to be served.

Main Ideas

- Growing nationalism led to improvements in the nation's transportation systems.

- The Missouri Compromise settled an important regional conflict.

- The outcome of the election of 1824 led to controversy.

Key Terms and People

Henry Clay
American System
Cumberland Road
Erie Canal
National Road
sectionalism
Missouri Compromise
John Quincy Adams

If YOU were there . . .

You live near the western end of the newly completed Erie Canal in New York State in 1831. In fact, your older brothers helped build the canal. Every day you watch as mules pull the canal boats along the still water of the canal. Sometimes the boats carry passengers traveling from city to city. You have never been far from your home, and you are curious about their journey.

What would you like to ask the travelers on the canal boat?

Nationalism Guides Domestic Policy

The swell in nationalist feelings that arose in the early 1800s soon found its way into government policies. This new pride in the nation found a strong supporter in U.S. representative **Henry Clay** from Kentucky.

Clay believed that the nation's unity and future depended upon a strong national economy. He developed a plan eventually known as the **American System**—a series of measures intended to make the United States economically self-sufficient. The three main measures of the plan were:

1. **Establish a protective tariff,** a tax on imported goods that would protect American businesses from foreign competition. Congress passed such a tariff in 1816. By making European goods more expensive, the tariff encouraged Americans to buy less expensive American-made products.

2. **Establish a national bank** that would promote a single currency, making trade easier. At the time, most regional banks issued their own money. In 1816, Congress set up the second Bank of the United States.

3. **Improve the country's transportation systems,** which were essential for a strong economy. Poor roads, great distances, and geography slowed the movement of goods and made trade difficult and costly.

Henry Clay 1777–1852

Known as the silver-tongued Kentuckian, Henry Clay was a gifted speaker. He became involved in local politics early in his life, and by age 29 he was appointed to the U.S. Senate. Throughout his career in the Senate, he was dedicated to preserving the Union. The Missouri Compromise and a later agreement, the Compromise of 1850, helped to ease sectional tensions, at least temporarily.

Analyze
Why did Henry Clay work for compromises between regions?

Clay also proposed that the national government could spend the money it raised from a protective tariff and from selling public lands in the West to improve roads and canals. These improvements would strengthen the economy and unite North, South, East, and West.

However, some members of Congress opposed the plan. They argued that there was nothing in the Constitution granting the national government power to spend money on internal improvements. Still, Clay argued that the possible gains for the country justified federal action.

Roads and Canals In the early 1800s most roads in the United States were made of dirt, making travel difficult. British actress Frances Kemble described one New York road she had struggled along during a visit in the 1830s.

"The wickedest road, I do think, the cruellest, hard-heartedest road, that ever [a] wheel rumbled upon."

—Frances Anne (Kemble) Butler, *Journal*

Great distances and the lack of good roads made travel, trade, and communication difficult between North and South, East and West. Those settlers living in states west of the Appalachians found it especially difficult to ship goods east across the mountains.

To improve the nation's roads, Congress agreed with Clay and invested in road building. The **Cumberland Road** was the first road built by the federal government. It ran from Cumberland, Maryland, to Wheeling, a town on the Ohio River in present-day West Virginia. Construction began in 1815. Workers had to cut a 66-foot-wide band, sometimes through forest,

U.S. Roads and Canals, 1850

Americans used flatboats like this one to travel the country's canals.

Travelers on the National Road stopped at inns to eat and rest from a long day's journey.

Interpret Maps

1. **Place** What physical and human features likely made Buffalo, New York, a center of trade?

2. **Human-Environment Interaction** How did people modify the environment to improve transportation between Albany and Buffalo, New York?

to make way for the road. Then they had to use shovels and pickaxes to dig a 12- to 18-inch roadbed, which they filled with crushed stone. All of the work had to be done without the benefit of today's bulldozers and steamrollers.

By 1818 the road reached Wheeling. By 1833 the **National Road**, as the expansion was called, stretched to Columbus, Ohio. By 1850 it reached all the way to Illinois. The National Road and smaller roads allowed people to travel and transport goods more easily, but land transportation remained slow and costly.

Boats offered faster and cheaper transportation, but geographic features could also be a challenge along water routes. Many rivers had changes in elevation and, in some places, rapids and waterfalls made boat travel impossible. To help solve these problems, Americans built canals, human-made waterways that connected bodies of water.

In fact, the **incentive** for canal building caused so many to be built that the period from 1825 to 1850 is often called the Age of Canals. The most notable was the **Erie Canal**, a canal that created a waterway in New York between Albany and Buffalo, connecting the Hudson River with Lake Erie. Construction on the canal began in 1817 and was completed in 1825. It was 40 feet wide, 4 feet deep, and crossed 363 miles of wilderness and hilly terrain. Most of the laborers were American-born, but some were British, German, and Irish immigrants. With the help of hand tools, oxen, horses, and mules, they dug mile after mile through forests, fields, and swampland.

The opening of the Erie Canal sparked Americans' first major westward migration. It gave settlers and industries access to the fertile land and resources in the upper Ohio Valley and the Great Lakes region. People and manufactured goods moved west along the canal. In turn, farm products, timber, and other raw materials flowed east from the Great Lakes region to factories and mills in New York City.

Construction of the Erie Canal topped $7 million, but it proved a quick success and dramatically changed trade and settlement patterns. It cut the time and cost of shipping a ton of goods from Buffalo to New York City from 20 days to 6 days and from about $100 to less than $10. This helped establish New York City as a great city for industry and trade. Located where the Hudson River meets the Atlantic Ocean, New York was at the perfect geographic location to serve as a gateway between domestic and foreign trade. Smaller cities and towns sprouted up along the course of the Erie Canal and in the Great Lakes region. Trade and passenger traffic boosted local economies.

The Erie Canal also functioned as a communication highway. News and ideas travelled the waterway along with people and products. Ideas about women's rights and the abolition of slavery flourished in canal communities, as did new religious groups such as the Latter-Day Saints, or Mormons. Their ideas spread along the canal. Moreover, settlers bound for western lands brought with them different languages, customs, and religions. At a time of rising nationalist feelings, this flow of ideas helped create a bond between East and West.

Supreme Court Rulings From 1801 until 1835, John Marshall served as Chief Justice of the Supreme Court. Marshall was a firm believer in a strong national government. His Court made two key rulings that reflected nationalist feelings and strengthened the national government.

The emphasis on national unity was strengthened by two Supreme Court case decisions that reinforced the power of the federal government. In the 1819 case *McCulloch* v. *Maryland*, the Court asserted the implied powers of Congress in allowing for the creation of a national bank. In the 1824 case *Gibbons* v. *Ogden*, the Court said that the states could not interfere with the power of Congress to regulate interstate commerce.

Missouri Compromise

At the same time nationalism was unifying the country, sectionalism threatened to drive it apart. **Sectionalism** is loyalty to the interests of one region of a country over the interests of the country as a whole. Regional economic and cultural differences had created some political divisions within the United States. For instance, white southerners developed an economy and culture based on cotton production and slavery. In the Northeast, wealth was based on manufacturing and trade. In the West, settlers wanted cheap land and strong transportation systems. At the level of national government, sectional interests based on regional differences often led to disagreements.

One such disagreement arose in 1819 when Congress considered Missouri's application to enter the Union as a slave state. At the time, the Union had 11 free states and 11 slave states. Adding a new slave state would have tipped the balance in the Senate in favor of the South.

To protect the power of the free states, the House passed a special amendment. It declared that the United States would accept Missouri as a slave state, but importing enslaved Africans into Missouri would be illegal. The amendment also set free the children of Missouri slaves. Southern politicians angrily opposed this plan.

North Carolina senator Nathaniel Macon wanted to continue adding slave states. "Why depart from the good old way, which has kept us in quiet, peace, and harmony?" he asked. Eventually, the Senate rejected the amendment. Missouri was still not a state.

Henry Clay convinced Congress to agree to the **Missouri Compromise**, which settled the conflict that had arisen from Missouri's application for statehood. This compromise had three main conditions:

▶ Explore ONLINE!

The Missouri Compromise, 1820

Interpret Maps

1. **Region** Which part of the United States permitted slavery?

2. **Location** What line of latitude separated free territories from territories that allowed slavery?

1. Missouri would enter the Union as a slave state.
2. Maine would join the Union as a free state, keeping the number of slave and free states equal.
3. Slavery would be prohibited in any new territories or states formed north of 36°30' latitude—Missouri's southern border.

Congress passed the Missouri Compromise in 1820. Despite the success of the compromise, there were still strong disagreements between the North and South over the expansion of slavery.

Reading Check
Draw Conclusions
Why did Henry Clay propose the Missouri Compromise to resolve the issue of Missouri statehood?

The Election of 1824

Soon, a presidential election also brought controversy. Andrew Jackson won the most popular votes in 1824. However, he did not have enough electoral votes to win office. Under the Constitution, the House of Representatives had to choose the winner. When the House chose **John Quincy Adams** as president, Jackson's supporters claimed that Adams had made a corrupt bargain with Henry Clay. These accusations grew after Adams chose Clay to be secretary of state. The controversy weakened Adams's support.

Reading Check
Draw Inferences
Why did Adams have weak support during his presidency?

Summary and Preview In this lesson you learned how strong nationalistic feelings guided government policies, and how feelings of sectionalism challenged national unity. In the next lesson you will read about the development of a new national culture.

From 1825 to 1829, John Quincy Adams, son of John and Abigail Adams, served as the sixth president of the United States.

Lesson 2 Assessment

Review Ideas, Terms, and People

1. a. **Describe** How did national interests shape the policies related to regional commerce in the American System?

   b. **Analyze** Explain the impact the *McCulloch* v. *Maryland* and *Gibbons* v. *Ogden* decisions had on the federal government.

   c. **Predict** How would the National Road and the Erie Canal eventually contribute to the U.S. economy? to the westward expansion of trade and settlement?

   d. **Make Inferences** How did national goals, interests, and advances in transportation change perceptions of places and regions in the early 1800s?

2. a. **Describe** How was American society affected by sectionalism?

   b. **Recall** What role did Henry Clay play in the debate over Missouri's statehood?

   c. **Explain** What problem did Missouri's request for statehood cause?

   d. **Elaborate** Was the Missouri Compromise a good solution to the debate between free states and slave states? Explain your answer.

3. a. **Identify** Who were the candidates in the presidential election of 1824? How was the winner determined?

   b. **Draw Conclusions** Why did John Quincy Adams lose popular support following the election of 1824?

Critical Thinking

4. **Evaluate** In this lesson you learned about how nationalism and sectionalism affected national unity. Create a chart like the one below and use it to identify how the Missouri Compromise resolved threats to nationalism.

Sectional differences → Missouri Compromise → Outcome 1. 2. 3.

The Erie Canal

In 1825 New York opened the Erie Canal, which connected Buffalo on Lake Erie to Albany on the Hudson River. With the new canal, boats and barges could travel from New York Harbor in the east to the Great Lakes region in the west. Trade boomed, new cities formed, and settlers moved farther west as the Erie Canal helped open up the Midwest region to farming and settlement.

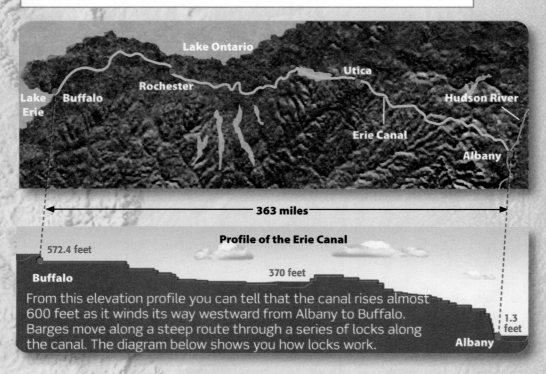

Lake Ontario

Utica

Rochester

Lake Erie Buffalo

Hudson River

Erie Canal

Albany

363 miles

Profile of the Erie Canal

572.4 feet

Buffalo

370 feet

From this elevation profile you can tell that the canal rises almost 600 feet as it winds its way westward from Albany to Buffalo. Barges move along a steep route through a series of locks along the canal. The diagram below shows you how locks work.

1.3 feet

Albany

①

Tow path   Lock

Main gate ②

Sluice gate

③

How a Canal Lock Works

1. A barge enters the lock through the main gate.
2. Water flows into the lock through the sluice gate to raise the boat to the next level.
3. The barge leaves the lock as mules help pull it across the water.

Lake Superior

Lake Huron

Lake Michigan

WI

Lake Ontario

ME

VT

NH

MA

RI

NY

CT

Hudson River

New York

Later canals extended west into Ohio and Indiana.

MI

Buffalo

Lake Erie

Toledo

Cleveland

Chicago

IL

Settlers and goods moved west.

OH

Agricultural products moved east.

FLOUR FLOUR

IN

PA

NJ

ATLANTIC OCEAN

Trade through New York Harbor boomed as goods flowed along the Erie Canal to overseas markets and back to settlers and cities in the West.

VA

KY

NC

EFFECTS OF THE CANAL

Thanks to the canal, the cost of shipping dropped. Lower costs led to increases in shipping and in city populations.

Cost of Shipping

1824: $100 per ton by road

1825: $10 per ton by canal

Population Growth

Population (Thousands)

40

30

20

10

0

Albany

Buffalo

Chicago

Cleveland

1820   1830   1840

Year

SC

GA

FL

Interpret Maps

1. **Location** What effect do you think the Erie Canal had on New York City?

2. **Place** How were changes brought about by the Erie Canal similar and different for people living in the Great Lakes region and in New York City?

3. **Movement** Use the map of the Erie Canal to write a paragraph about how the canal supported cultural diffusion, or the spread of people, ideas, and goods. Be sure to describe the resources in each region, tell how the canal changed the regions it connected, and use geographic terms such as migration, place of origin, and destination.

American Culture

The Big Idea

As the United States grew, developments in many cultural areas contributed to the creation of a new American identity.

Main Ideas

- American writers created a new style of literature.

- A new style of art showcased the beauty of America and its people.

- American ideals influenced other aspects of culture, including religion and music.

- Architecture and education were affected by cultural ideals.

Key Terms and People

Washington Irving
James Fenimore Cooper
Hudson River school
Thomas Cole
George Caleb Bingham

If YOU were there . . .

You live in Philadelphia in 1830. Though you've lived in the city all your life, you dream about the West and the frontier. Now you've discovered a wonderful writer whose stories tell about frontier life and events in American history. You can't wait to read his next exciting adventure. You think that perhaps someday you could be a frontier hero, too.

Why would the frontier seem so exciting?

American Writers

Like many people the world over, Americans expressed their thoughts and feelings in literature and art and sought spiritual comfort in religion and music. Writers and artists were inspired by American history and the American landscape.

One of the first American writers to gain international fame was **Washington Irving**. Born in 1783, he was named after George Washington. Irving's works often told about American history. Through a humorous form of writing called satire, Irving warned that Americans should learn from the past and be cautious about the future.

Irving shared this idea in one of his best-known short stories, "Rip Van Winkle." This story describes a man who falls asleep during the time of the American Revolution. He wakes up 20 years later to a society he does not recognize. Irving published this and another well-known tale, "The Legend of Sleepy Hollow," in an 1819–1820 collection.

In some of his most popular works, Irving combined European influences with American settings and characters. His work served as a bridge between European literary traditions and a new type of writer who focused on authentically American characters and society.

Perhaps the best known of these new writers was **James Fenimore Cooper**. Cooper was born to a wealthy

New Jersey family in 1789. Stories about the West and the Native Americans who lived on the frontier fascinated him. These subjects became the focus of his best-known works.

Cooper's first book was not very successful, but his next novel, *The Spy*, was a huge success. Published in 1821, it was an adventure story set during the American Revolution. It appealed to American readers' patriotism and desire for an exciting, action-filled story.

In 1823 Cooper published *The Pioneers*, the first of five novels featuring the heroic character Natty Bumppo. Cooper's novels told of settling the western frontier and included historical events. For example, his novel *The Last of the Mohicans* takes place during the French and Indian War. By placing fictional characters in a real historical setting, Cooper popularized a type of writing called historical fiction.

Some critics said that Cooper's characters were not interesting. They particularly criticized the women in his stories; one writer labeled them "flat as a prairie." Other authors of historical fiction, such as Catharine Maria Sedgwick, wrote about interesting heroines. Sedgwick's characters were inspired by the people of the Berkshire Hills region of Massachusetts, where she lived. Her works include *A New-England Tale* and *Hope Leslie*.

Reading Check
Analyze How did American writers such as Irving and Cooper help create a new cultural identity in the United States?

A New Style of Art

The writings of Irving and Cooper inspired painters. These artists began to paint landscapes that showed the history of America and the beauty of the land. Earlier American painters had mainly painted portraits. By the 1830s, the Hudson River school had emerged. The artists of the **Hudson River school** created paintings that reflected national pride and an appreciation of the American landscape. They took their name from the subject of many of their paintings—the Hudson River valley.

Painters of the Hudson River school proved American landscapes were worthy of art. (Thomas Cole's *The Oxbow*, 1836)

In 1827 John Audubon began publishing *The Birds of America*, which was highly admired in England.

George Catlin traveled widely to paint images of Native American ways of life before they were lost.

Landscape painter **Thomas Cole** was a founder of the Hudson River school. He had moved to the United States from Britain in 1819. He soon recognized the unique qualities of the American landscape. As his work gained fame, he encouraged other American artists to show the beauty of nature. "To walk with nature as a poet is the necessary condition of a perfect artist," Cole once said.

Artists devoted themselves to other distinctly American subjects, too. John James Audubon began studying and drawing birds in the United States at the age of 18. Audubon's *The Birds of America* is a collection of 435 types of American birds.

By the 1840s the style of American painting was changing. More artists were trying to combine images of the American landscape with scenes from people's daily lives. Painters like **George Caleb Bingham** and Alfred Jacob Miller travelled west to paint scenes of the American frontier, including trappers, traders, settlers, and Native Americans.

Religion and Music

Through the early and mid-1800s, several waves of religious revivalism swept the United States. During periods of revivalism, meetings were held for the purpose of reawakening religious faith. These meetings sometimes lasted for days and included large sing-alongs.

At many revival meetings people sang songs called spirituals. Spirituals are a type of folk hymn found in both white and African American

Reading Check
Find Main Ideas
How did the style of American art change to reflect the American way of life in the early 1800s?

folk-music traditions. This type of song developed from the practice of calling out text from the Bible. A leader would call out the text one line at a time, and the congregation would sing the words using a familiar tune. Each singer added his or her own style to the tune. The congregation of singers sang freely as inspiration led them.

While spirituals reflected the religious nature of some Americans, popular folk music of the period reflected the unique views of the growing nation in a different way. One of the most popular songs of the era was "Hunters of Kentucky," which celebrated the Battle of New Orleans. It became an anthem for the spirit of nationalism in the United States and was used successfully in Andrew Jackson's campaign for the presidency in 1828.

Reading Check
Summarize How did music reflect American interests in the early to mid-1800s?

Architecture and Education

American creativity extended to the ways in which people designed buildings. Before the American Revolution, most architects followed the style used in Great Britain. After the Revolution, leaders such as Thomas Jefferson called for Americans to model their architecture after the styles used in ancient Greece and Rome. Many Americans admired the ancient civilization of Greece and the Roman Republic because they contained some of the same democratic and republican ideals as the new American nation did.

As time went by, more architects followed Jefferson's ideas. Growing American cities soon had distinctive new buildings designed in the Greek and Roman styles. These buildings were usually made of marble or other stone and featured large, stately columns.

In the early to mid-1800s, American architects were inspired by ancient Greece and Rome.

Americans also embraced educational progress. Noah Webster, well known for his dictionary of American English published in 1828, spent much of his life working to provide children with a distinctly American education.

Several early American political leaders expressed a belief that democracy would only succeed in a country of educated and enlightened people. But there was no general agreement on who should provide that education.

Noah Webster publishes *The American Spelling Book* in 1783 in an effort to promote American education.

Eventually, the idea of a state-funded public school gathered support. In 1837 Massachusetts lawmakers created a state board of education. Other states followed this example, and the number of public schools slowly grew.

Summary and Preview As the United States grew, so did a unique national identity. In Module 10 you will read about the changing face of American democracy.

Reading Check
Identify Points of View Why did some Americans call for new architectural styles and more education after the American Revolution?

Lesson 3 Assessment

Review Ideas, Terms, and People

1. a. **Describe** What topics interested American writers in the early 1800s?
   b. **Explain** Why is Washington Irving considered an important American writer?
2. a. **Identify** What influence did Thomas Cole have on American painters?
   b. **Describe** How did American painting styles change from the early period to the mid-1800s?
3. a. **Describe** What effect did religious revivalism have on American music?
   b. **Elaborate** Why do you think folk songs like "Hunters of Kentucky" were popular?
4. a. **Identify** On what historical examples did many American architects model their buildings? Why?
   b. **Predict** What might be some possible results of the growing interest in education in the United States?

Critical Thinking

5. **Categorize** In this lesson, you learned about new developments in American culture in the early 1800s. Create a graphic organizer similar to the one below and use it to show how cultural traits, beliefs, and characteristics reflected a new American identity.

Cultural Development	→	New Identity
Cultural Development	→	New Identity
Cultural Development	→	New Identity
Cultural Development	→	New Identity
Cultural Development	→	New Identity

Literature in History

Literature of the American Frontier

WORD HELP

accoutrements dress and gear

rude crude; rough

attenuated made thin

indurated hardened

unremitted ongoing

gartered fastened

ingenious clever

❶ *What do you learn about Natty Bumppo in the first paragraph?*

❷ *A "girdle of wampum" is a belt strung with beads. Wampum were used by Native Americans for both money and decoration.*

Make a list of the items Bumppo wears and carries. What does each item suggest about him?

About the Reading *The Last of the Mohicans* is one of five novels known as the Leatherstocking Tales. These novels follow the life and adventures of American pioneer Natty Bumppo (also known as Leatherstocking, Hawkeye, and the Deerslayer). Bumppo is the perfect woodsman: resourceful, honest, kind to both his friends and his enemies, but always a loner at heart.

As You Read Try to imagine what Natty Bumppo looks like.

From *The Last of the Mohicans*
by James Fenimore Cooper (1789–1851)

On that day, two men were lingering on the banks of a small but rapid stream . . . While one of these loiterers showed the red skin and wild accoutrements of a native of the woods, the other exhibited, through the mask of his rude and nearly savage equipments, the brighter though sunburnt and long-faded complexion of one who might claim descent from a European parentage. ❶

The frame of the white man, judging by such parts as were not concealed by his clothes, was like that of one who had known hardships and exertion from his earliest youth. His person, though muscular, was rather attenuated than full; but every nerve and muscle appeared strung and indurated by unremitted exposure and toil. He wore a hunting shirt of forest green, fringed with faded yellow, and a summer cap of skins which had been shorn of their fur. He also bore a knife in a girdle of wampum, ❷ like that which confined the scanty garments of the Indian, but no tomahawk. His moccasins were ornamented after the . . . fashion of the natives, while the only part of his underdress which appeared below the hunting frock was a pair of buckskin leggings that laced at the sides, and which were gartered above the knees with the sinews of a deer. A pouch and horn completed his personal accoutrements, though a rifle of great length, which the theory of the more ingenious whites had taught them was the most dangerous of all firearms, leaned against a neighboring sapling.

Literature in History, continued

WORD HELP

WORD HELP

dominant prevailing; ruling

apparition a ghostlike form that appears suddenly

collating comparing

spectre ghost

allege to firmly state

purport sense; gist

❶ A Hessian trooper is a German mercenary soldier from the American Revolution. *How and when is the horseman said to have died?*

❷ *Why does the horseman ride forth each night?*

❸ *What is happening "at all the country firesides"? What does this suggest about how early Americans entertained themselves?*

About the Reading "The Legend of Sleepy Hollow" has been called one of the first American short stories. Even though it is based on an old German folktale, its setting—a small village in the Hudson River valley—is American through and through. Irving's knack for capturing the look and feel of the region made the story instantly popular—as did the tale's eerie central character, a horseman without a head.

As You Read Try to picture both the ghost and the setting.

From "The Legend of Sleepy Hollow"
by Washington Irving (1783–1859)

The dominant spirit, however, that haunts this enchanted region, and seems to be commander in chief of all the powers of the air, is the apparition of a figure on horseback without a head. It is said by some to be the ghost of a Hessian trooper, ❶ whose head had been carried away by a cannon ball, in some nameless battle during the revolutionary war, and who is ever and anon seen by the country folk, hurrying along in the gloom of night, as if on the wings of the wind. His haunts are not confined to the valley, but extend at times to the adjacent roads, and especially to the vicinity of a church at no great distance. Indeed, certain of the most authentic historians of those parts, who have been careful in collecting and collating the floating facts concerning this spectre, allege, that the body of the trooper having been buried in the church yard, the ghost rides forth to the scene of battle in nightly quest of his head, ❷ and that the rushing speed with which he sometimes passes along the hollow, like a midnight blast, is owing to his being belated, and in a hurry to get back to the church yard before day break.

Such is the general purport of this legendary superstition, which has furnished materials for many a wild story in that region of shadows; and the spectre is known, at all the country firesides, by the name of The Headless Horseman of Sleepy Hollow. ❸

Connect Literature to History

1. **Draw Inferences** The writing of the period reflects a new national culture and identity. What do these passages suggest about the thoughts, feelings, or lives of early Americans?

2. **Make Predictions** *The Last of the Mohicans* takes place during the French and Indian War. Whose side do you think Natty Bumppo would most likely take—that of the French and Indians, that of the English, or neither? Explain your answer.

3. **Draw Conclusions** Both of these stories were very popular in their time. Why do you think these stories were so popular? What is it about the stories that makes them entertaining?

Social Studies Skills

Identify Central Issues

Define the Skill

The reasons for historical events are often complex and difficult to determine. An accurate understanding of them requires the ability to identify the central issues involved. A *central issue* is the main topic of concern in a discussion or dispute. In history, these issues are usually matters of public debate or concern. They generally involve political, social, moral, economic, or territorial matters.

Being able to identify central issues lets you go beyond what the participants in an event said and gain a more accurate understanding of it. The skill is also useful for understanding issues today and for evaluating the statements of those involved.

Learn the Skill

In this module you learned about the dispute that arose over Missouri's admission to the Union. Yet that was not what this controversy was really about. Recognizing the central issue in this dispute helps you understand why each side fought so hard over just one state.

Use the following steps to identify central issues when you read about historical events.

1. Identify the main subject of the information.

2. Determine the nature and purpose of what you are reading. Is it a primary source or a secondary one? Why has the information been provided?

3. Find the strongest or most forceful phrases or statements in the material. These are often clues to the issues or ideas the speaker or writer thinks most central or important.

4. Determine how the information might be connected to the major events or controversies of the time.

Practice the Skill

Soon after the Missouri Compromise passed, Secretary of State John Quincy Adams wrote:

"The impression produced upon my mind by the progress of this discussion [the dispute over Missouri] is that the bargain between freedom and slavery contained in the Constitution . . . is morally and politically vicious, . . . cruel and oppressive. . . . I have favored this Missouri Compromise, believing it to be all that can be effected [accomplished] under the present Constitution, and from an extreme unwillingness to put the Union at hazard [risk]. But perhaps it would have been a . . . bolder course to have persisted in the restriction upon Missouri till it should have terminated [ended] in a convention of the states to . . . amend the Constitution. This would have produced a new Union of thirteen or fourteen states unpolluted with slavery. . . . If the Union must be dissolved, slavery is precisely the question upon which it ought to break. For the present, however, this contest [issue] is laid to sleep."

Identify the central issues in the quote from Adams and answer the following questions:

1. What is Adams's subject? What is his reason for making these remarks?

2. What did Adams believe was the most important issue in the dispute? What strong language does he use to indicate this?

3. What evidence suggests Adams did not think the breakup of the Union was the central issue?

Module 9 Assessment

Review Vocabulary, Terms, and People

Match the word in the left column with the correct definition in the right column.

1. American System
2. George Caleb Bingham
3. Simon Bolívar
4. Henry Clay
5. Erie Canal
6. Hudson River school
7. James Monroe
8. Monroe Doctrine
9. nationalism
10. sectionalism

a. loyalty to the interests of one region of a country over the interests of the country as a whole

b. American artist known for his focus on the American landscape and people

c. sense of pride and devotion to a nation

d. a group of American artists in the mid-1800s who focused on the American landscape

e. a leader of independence movements in Latin America, known as "the Liberator"

f. the plan to raise tariffs in order to finance internal improvements such as roads and canals

g. president who promoted the acquisition of Florida, closer ties to Latin America, and presided during the Era of Good Feelings

h. project that connected the Hudson River to Lake Erie and improved trade and transportation

i. representative from Kentucky who promoted improvements in transportation and the Missouri Compromise

j. U.S. declaration that any attempt by a foreign nation to establish colonies in the Americas would be viewed as a hostile act

Comprehension and Critical Thinking

Lesson 1

11. a. **Identify** What were the four main points of the Monroe Doctrine?

    b. **Summarize** How did nationalism guide foreign policy in the early 1800s?

    c. **Draw Conclusions** Why do you think the Monroe Doctrine had such a lasting impact on U.S. foreign policy?

Lesson 2

12. a. **Recall** What developments helped strengthen national unity in this period?

    b. **Summarize** Under the American System, how did the national government use taxing and spending to influence the economy?

    c. **Analyze** How was the disagreement over Missouri's statehood an example of sectionalism? How was the disagreement resolved by Congress?

    d. **Predict** What effect might the election of 1824 have on national unity? Why?

Lesson 3

13. a. **Describe** How did popular music show the interests of Americans in the early 1800s?

    b. **Make Inferences** Why do you think new American styles of art and literature emerged?

    c. **Elaborate** Which element of American culture of the early 1800s do you find most appealing? Why?

Review Themes

14. Politics How did the relations of the United States with foreign nations lead to a rise in nationalism?

15. Society and Culture What led to the creation of a uniquely American culture?

Reading Skills 21ST CENTURY

Bias and Historical Events *Use the Reading Skills taught in this module to answer the question about the reading selection below.*

> When the House chose John Quincy Adams as president, Jackson's supporters claimed that Adams had made a corrupt bargain with Henry Clay. These accusations grew after Adams chose Clay to be secretary of state.

16. Which of the following used a biased definition, according to the above selection?
   a. Andrew Jackson
   b. Henry Clay
   c. supporters of Jackson
   d. John Quincy Adams

Social Studies Skills

Identify Central Issues *Use the Social Studies Skills taught in this module to answer the question about the reading selection below.*

> [Henry Clay] developed a plan eventually known as the American System—a series of measures intended to make the United States economically self-sufficient. To build the economy, he pushed for a national bank that would provide a single currency, making interstate trade easier. Clay wanted the money from a protective tariff to be used to improve roads and canals.

17. Which of the following is the central issue addressed by the American System?
   a. economic unity
   b. protective tariff
   c. national bank
   d. improving roads and canals

Focus on Writing

18. Write a Character Sketch Nations, like people, have characters. For example, a nation might be described as peaceful or aggressive, prosperous or struggling. Write a paragraph describing your overall impression of the nation's character. Write one sentence describing each of these aspects of the United States: its relationships with others, its feelings about itself, and its values.

Module 10
The Age of Jackson

★

Essential Question
Did Andrew Jackson advance the cause of democracy?

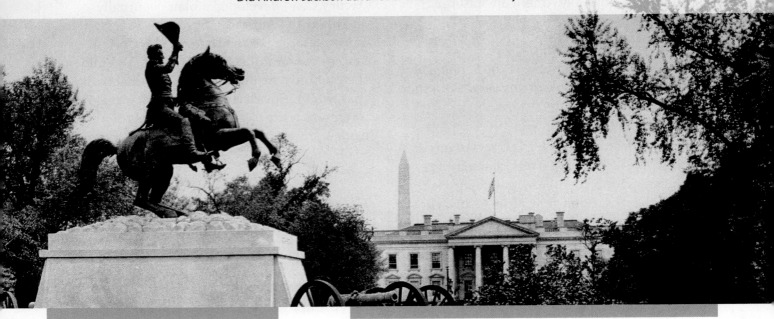

About the Photo: This statue of Andrew Jackson has stood in Washington, DC, for more than 150 years and captures the drive and spirit of the seventh president of the United States.

▷ Explore ONLINE!

VIDEOS, including...
- Jackson: Cherokees, Tariffs, and Nullification
- Jackson's Personality and Legacy
- Jackson Censured in Bank War

HISTORY.

- ✔ Document-Based Investigations
- ✔ Graphic Organizers
- ✔ Interactive Games
- ✔ Image Slider: Dirty Politics in the 1828 Campaign
- ✔ Image Carousel: Regions of the United States
- ✔ Image Carousel: Native American Groups

In this module you will learn about President Andrew Jackson and why historians refer to his time in office as the Age of Jackson.

What You Will Learn ...

Lesson 1: Jacksonian Democracy 328
The Big Idea The expansion of voting rights and the election of Andrew Jackson signaled the growing power of the American people.

Lesson 2: Jackson's Administration 333
The Big Idea Andrew Jackson's presidency was marked by political conflicts.

Lesson 3: Indian Removal. 340
The Big Idea President Jackson supported a policy of Indian removal.

Timeline of Events 1825–1845

▶ Explore ONLINE!

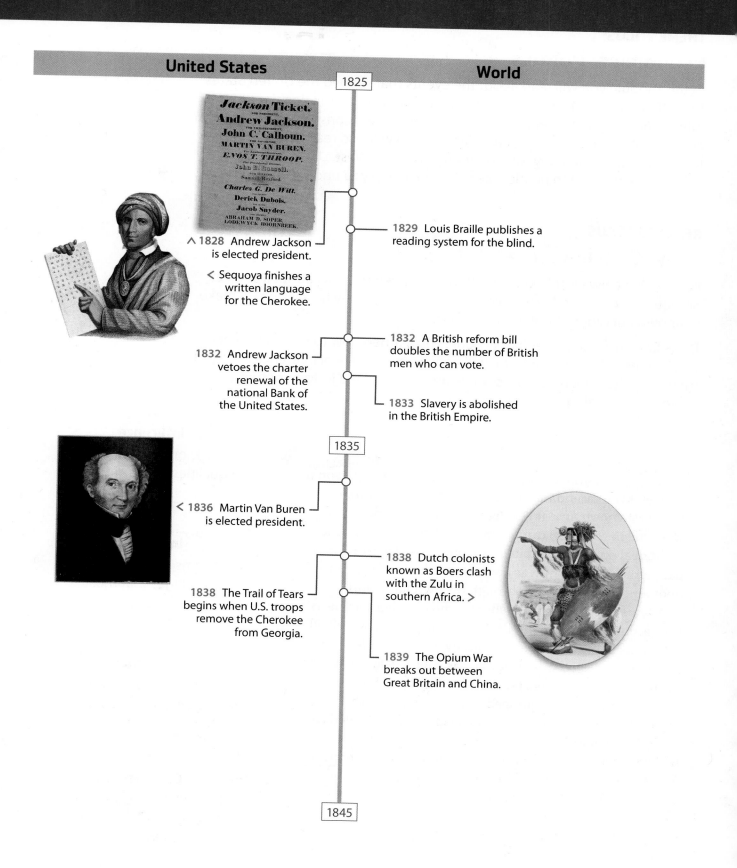

United States

World

1825

Jackson Ticket.
FOR PRESIDENT,
Andrew Jackson.
FOR VICE-PRESIDENT,
John C. Calhoun.
FOR GOVERNOR,
MARTIN VAN BUREN.
For Lieutenant-Governor,
ENOS T. THROOP.
For Presidential Electors,
John B. Russell.
FOR SENATOR,
Samuel Roxford.
FOR ASSEMBLY,
Charles G. De Witt.
FOR SHERIFF,
Derick Dubois.
FOR CLERK,
Jacob Snyder.
AND OTHERS,
ABRAHAM D. SOPER,
LODEWYCK HOORNBEEK.

∧ **1828** Andrew Jackson is elected president.

< Sequoya finishes a written language for the Cherokee.

1829 Louis Braille publishes a reading system for the blind.

1832 Andrew Jackson vetoes the charter renewal of the national Bank of the United States.

1832 A British reform bill doubles the number of British men who can vote.

1833 Slavery is abolished in the British Empire.

1835

< **1836** Martin Van Buren is elected president.

1838 Dutch colonists known as Boers clash with the Zulu in southern Africa. >

1838 The Trail of Tears begins when U.S. troops remove the Cherokee from Georgia.

1839 The Opium War breaks out between Great Britain and China.

1845

Reading Social Studies

Economics, Politics

In this module you will read about the events that shaped the United States from 1828 to 1838. You will see how political and economic decisions were intertwined. For instance, you will read about the tensions between southern and northern states over tariff regulations. You will also read about the forced relocation of many Native Americans to the West. Understanding how economic issues led to political decisions will help you understand this time.

READING FOCUS:
Draw Conclusions about the Past

Writers don't always tell you everything you need to know about a subject. Sometimes you need to think critically about what they have said and make your own decisions about what you've read.

Draw Conclusions Earlier in this book, you learned how to make inferences. Sometimes when you read, you will need to make several inferences and put them together. The result is a **conclusion**, an informed judgment that you make by combining information.

Election of 1828

Today, presidential campaigns often focus on the personal image of the candidates—labeling them strong versus weak, or a government insider versus a newcomer. That was true in the 1828 campaign as well, which focused a great deal on the candidates' personalities. Jackson's campaigners described him as a war hero who had <u>been born poor and rose to success through his own hard work.</u>

<u>Adams was a Harvard graduate whose father had been the second U.S. president.</u> Jackson's supporters described Adams as being out of touch with everyday people. Even a fan of Adams agreed that he was "as cold as a lump of ice." In turn, Adams's supporters said Jackson was hot tempered, crude, and ill-equipped to be president of the United States. Still Jackson was a strong leader who appealed to everyday people. When the ballots were counted, <u>Jackson had defeated Adams, winning a record number of popular votes.</u> The time period of Jackson's presidency is sometimes called the "Age of Jackson."

Inference
Jackson shared many qualities with American voters.

+

Inference
Adams enjoyed many privileges that most Americans did not.

+

Inference
Jackson easily won the election by a huge majority.

Conclusion
In 1828 Americans chose a president to whom they could relate.

You Try It!

The following passage is from the module you are getting ready to read. As you read the passage, look for the facts of the situation.

> **The Election of 1834** In 1834 a new political party had formed to oppose Jackson. Its members called themselves Whigs, after an English political party that opposed the monarchy, to make the point that Jackson was using his power like a king. The Whig Party favored the idea of a weak president and a strong Congress. Unable to agree on a candidate, the Whigs chose four men to run against Van Buren. Because of this indecision, and with backing from Jackson, Van Buren won the election.

After you read the passage, answer the following questions.

1. From this passage, what can you infer about President Jackson's popularity with the Whig Party?

2. The Whigs could not choose a single presidential candidate, so they nominated four men. Based on what you know about elections from your studies and your past experiences, how do you think this affected the votes each man received?

3. Jackson's backing helped Van Buren win the presidency. From this, what can you infer about Jackson's popularity with the American people as a whole?

4. Using the inferences you made answering questions 1 through 3, draw a conclusion about why Van Buren won the election of 1834.

As you read Module 10, use your personal background knowledge and experience to draw conclusions about what you are reading.

Key Terms and People

Lesson 1
nominating conventions
Jacksonian Democracy
Democratic Party
John C. Calhoun
spoils system
Martin Van Buren
Kitchen Cabinet

Lesson 2
Tariff of Abominations
states' rights doctrine
nullification crisis
Daniel Webster
McCulloch v. *Maryland*
Whig Party
Panic of 1837
William Henry Harrison

Lesson 3
Indian Removal Act
Indian Territory
Bureau of Indian Affairs
Sequoya
Worcester v. *Georgia*
Trail of Tears
Black Hawk
Osceola

Jacksonian Democracy

The Big Idea

The expansion of voting rights and the election of Andrew Jackson signaled the growing power of the American people.

Main Ideas

- Democracy expanded in the 1820s as more Americans held the right to vote.

- Jackson's victory in the election of 1828 marked a change in American politics.

Key Terms and People

nominating conventions
Jacksonian Democracy
Democratic Party
John C. Calhoun
spoils system
Martin Van Buren
Kitchen Cabinet

If YOU were there . . .

It's 1829 and you live in Washington, D.C. You've come with a friend to the party for Andrew Jackson's inauguration as president. Your friend admires Jackson as a man of the people. You are less sure about his ability. Jackson's inauguration soon turns into a rowdy party, as mobs crowd into the White House. They break glasses and overturn the furniture.

How would you feel about having Jackson as your president?

Expansion of Democracy

America in the early 1800s was changing fast. In the North, workshops run by the craftspeople who owned them were being replaced by large-scale factories owned by businesspeople and staffed by hired workers. In the South, small family farms began to give way to large cotton plantations, owned by wealthy white people and worked by enslaved African Americans. Wealth seemed to be concentrating into fewer hands. Many ordinary Americans felt left behind.

These same people also began to believe they were losing power in their government. In the late 1700s some Americans thought that government was best managed by wealthy, property-owning men. Government policies seemed targeted to help build their power. The result was a growing belief that the wealthy were tightening their grip on power.

Hoping for change, small farmers, frontier settlers, and slaveholders rallied behind reformer Andrew Jackson, the popular hero of the War of 1812 and presidential candidate in the 1824 election. Even though he was a political leader, they believed Jackson would defend the rights of the common people and the slave states. They had been disappointed in the way Jackson had lost the 1824 election because of a decision in the House of Representatives. Jackson's supporters felt his policies and philosophies represented a move toward greater democratization.

In 1824 four men hoped to replace James Monroe as president. They were John Quincy Adams, William Crawford, Henry Clay, and Andrew Jackson. Jackson won the popular vote, but he did not receive a majority of electoral votes. According to the Constitution, if no person wins a majority of the electoral votes, the House of Representatives must choose the president. The selection was made from the top three vote-getters. Clay came in fourth and was out of the running. In the House vote, he threw his support to Adams, who then won. Because Adams later named Clay as his secretary of state, Jackson's supporters claimed that Adams gained the presidency by making a deal with Clay. Charges of a "corrupt bargain" followed Adams throughout his term. Adams had many plans for his presidency. But Congress, led by Jackson supporters, defeated his proposals.

During the time of Jackson's popularity, many democratic reforms were made. Some states changed their qualifications for voters to grant

Link to Today

Democracy in Action

Democracy spread in the early 1800s as more people became active in politics. Many of these people lived in the new western states. In these mostly rural areas, a political rally could be as simple as neighboring farmers meeting to talk about the issues of the day.

During the early 1800s democracy and demonstrations blossomed in the United States. The demonstrators of today owe much to the Americans of Andrew Jackson's time. Today, political rallies are a familiar sight in communities all over the country. The influence of Jackson is still seen in the U.S. political system today.

Analyze Information
How are the people in both pictures practicing democracy?

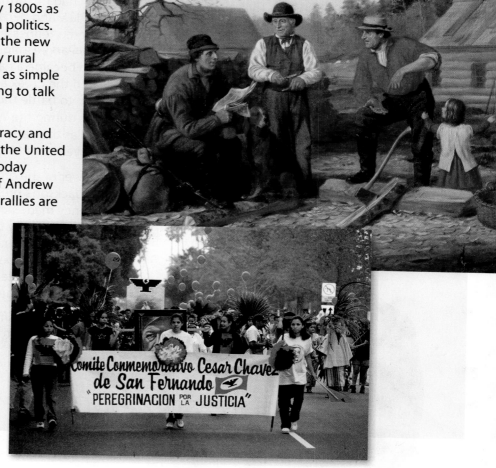

more white males suffrage. The revised rules, although they extended the franchise of voting to more white men, usually excluded free blacks from voting as they had been allowed under original state constitutions. Political parties began holding public **nominating conventions**, where party members choose the party's candidates instead of the party leaders. This period of expanding democracy, its ideas, and influences, in the 1820s and 1830s later became known as **Jacksonian Democracy**.

Reading Check
Find Main Ideas
How did voting rights change in the early 1800s?

Election of 1828

Jackson supporters were determined that their candidate would win the 1828 election. They formed the **Democratic Party** to support Jackson's candidacy. Many people who backed President Adams began calling themselves National Republicans.

The 1828 presidential contest was a rematch of the 1824 election. Once again, John Quincy Adams faced Andrew Jackson. Jackson chose **John C. Calhoun** as his vice presidential running mate.

The Campaign Today, presidential campaigns often focus on the personal image of the candidates—labeling them strong versus weak,

---

— BIOGRAPHY —

Andrew Jackson 1767–1845

Jackson was born in Waxhaw, a region along the border of the North and South Carolina colonies. In 1788 he moved to Nashville, Tennessee, which was still a part of North Carolina. There he built a mansion called the Hermitage. He lived in Washington as president, then retired to the Hermitage, where he died.

Jackson had no formal education, but he taught himself law and became a successful lawyer. He became Tennessee's first representative to the U.S. Congress and also served in the Senate. Jackson became a national hero when his forces defeated the Creek and Seminole Indians. He went on to battle the British in the Battle of New Orleans during the War of 1812. Jackson was elected as the nation's seventh president in 1828 and served until 1837.

The power of the office became more powerful during Jackson's presidency. His belief in a strong presidency made him both loved and hated. He vetoed as many bills as the six previous presidents together. Jackson also believed in a strong Union. When South Carolina tried to nullify, or reject, a federal tariff, he threatened to send troops into the state to force it to obey.

Identify Cause and Effect
Why did Jackson gain loyal friends and fierce enemies?

People's President

Washington resident Margaret Bayard Smith was surprised by the chaos surrounding Jackson's inauguration.

> *"What a scene did we witness! . . . a rabble, a mob, of boys, . . . women, children, scrambling, fighting, romping. . . . Cut glass and china to the amount of several thousand dollars had been broken. . . . But it was the people's day, and the people's President, and the people would rule."*
>
> —Margaret Bayard Smith, letter to Mrs. Kirkpatrick
> March 11, 1829

Analyze Historical Sources
How does the author view the people who support Jackson?

or a government insider versus a newcomer. That was true in the 1828 campaign as well, which focused a great deal on the candidates' personalities. Jackson's campaigners described him as a war hero who had been born poor and rose to success through his own hard work.

Adams was a Harvard graduate whose father had been the second U.S. president. Jackson's supporters described Adams as being out of touch with everyday people. Even a fan of Adams agreed that he was "as cold as a lump of ice." In turn, Adams's supporters said Jackson was hot-tempered, crude, and ill-equipped to be president of the United States. Still, Jackson was a strong leader who appealed to everyday people. When the ballots were counted, Jackson had defeated Adams, winning a record number of popular votes. The time period of Jackson's presidency is sometimes called the "Age of Jackson."

Quick Facts

Views of Democracy

Jackson's presidency marked a dramatic shift in American politics. Although Jackson's Democrats had grown out of Jefferson's Democratic-Republican Party, ideas of democracy had changed.

Jeffersonian Democracy	Jacksonian Democracy
Government by an educated few	More public involvement in government
Voting restricted to property owners	Voting expanded to all white males
Limited government	Limited government with a stronger executive branch

Interpret Charts
What ideas did Jeffersonians and Jacksonians share in common?

Jackson's Inauguration Jackson's supporters saw his victory as a win for the common people. A crowd cheered outside the Capitol as he took his oath of office. The massive crowd followed Jackson to a huge party on the White House lawn. The few police officers on hand had difficulty controlling the partygoers.

As president, Jackson rewarded some of his supporters with government jobs. This **spoils system**—the practice of giving government jobs to political backers—comes from the saying "to the victor belong the spoils [valued goods] of the enemy."

Secretary of State **Martin Van Buren** was one of Jackson's strongest allies in his official cabinet. President Jackson also relied a great deal on his **Kitchen Cabinet**, an informal group of trusted advisers who sometimes met in the White House kitchen.

Summary and Preview The expansion of democracy swept Andrew Jackson into office. In the next lesson you will read about the increasing regional tensions that occurred during Jackson's presidency.

Reading Check
Analyze Information
How might the spoils system cause disputes?

Lesson 1 Assessment

Review Ideas, Terms, and People

1. a. **Recall** What changes did the new western states make that allowed more people to vote?

   b. **Draw Conclusions** How did nominating conventions allow the people more say in politics?

   c. **Explain** How did the policies and philosophies of the Jacksonian Era represent a move toward greater democratization? How were voting rights expanded during the Jacksonian period?

   d. **Predict** How might changes to the voting process brought about by Jacksonian Democracy affect politics in the future? What were the key ideas and influences of Jacksonian Democracy?

2. a. **Recall** What two new political parties faced off in the election of 1828? Which candidate did each party support?

   b. **Make Inferences** Why did Andrew Jackson have more popular support than did Adams?

   c. **Analyze** What leadership qualities helped Andrew Jackson become president of the United States?

   d. **Evaluate** Do you think the spoils system was an acceptable practice? Explain your answer.

Critical Thinking

3. **Identify Effect** In this lesson you learned about the election of Andrew Jackson to the presidency. Use a cause-and-effect chart like this one to show the ways in which Jacksonian Democracy increased Americans' political power.

Jacksonian Democracy	increased Americans' political power	

★
Jackson's Administration

The Big Idea

Andrew Jackson's presidency was marked by political conflicts.

Main Ideas

■ Regional differences grew during Jackson's presidency.

■ The rights of the states were debated amid arguments about a national tariff.

■ Jackson's attack on the Bank sparked controversy.

■ Jackson's policies led to the Panic of 1837.

Key Terms and People

Tariff of Abominations
states' rights doctrine
nullification crisis
Daniel Webster
McCulloch v. *Maryland*
Whig Party
Panic of 1837
William Henry Harrison

If YOU were there . . .

You live on a small farm in South Carolina in 1829. Your family grows corn and cotton to sell, as well as vegetables for your own table. Although you grow your own food, you also depend on imported wool, flax, iron, and hemp to make ropes. But the government has just put new taxes on these products from Europe. Now they're too expensive for you to buy!

How would you feel about the new taxes on imports?

Sectional Differences Increase

Regional differences had a major effect on Andrew Jackson's presidency. Americans' views of Jackson's policies were based on where they lived and the economy of those regions.

Three Regions Emerge There were three main U.S. regions in the early 1800s. Different viewpoints in these regions led to debate about what was the best for the nation. The North, first of all, had an economy based on trade and on manufacturing. Northerners supported tariffs because tariffs helped them compete with British factories. Northerners also opposed the federal government's sale of public land at cheap prices. Cheap land encouraged potential laborers to move from northern factory towns to the West.

The second region was the South. Its economy was based on farming. Southern farmers raised all types of crops, but the most popular were the cash crops of cotton and tobacco. Southerners sold a large portion of their crops to foreign nations.

Southerners imported their manufactured goods. Tariffs made imported goods more expensive for southern farmers. In addition, high tariffs angered some of the South's European trading partners. These trading partners would likely raise their own tariffs in retaliation. To avoid this situation, southerners called for low tariffs.

south Afer turnps

3 re gions
re con omic
sed tions

if a rule
its num
it's not
have to
be

Southerners also relied on enslaved African Americans to work the plantations. The issue of slavery would become increasingly controversial between the North and South.

Political parties also developed along these regional lines. They were influenced by the tariff policy. Tariffs, sometimes called protective tariffs, were favored by Republicans, mostly northerners, because they protected northern manufacturing. Democrats, mostly southerners, were against tariffs because they made goods they needed to import much more expensive.

In the third region, the West, the frontier economy was just emerging. Settlers favored policies that boosted their farming economy and encouraged further settlement. Western farmers grew a wide variety of crops. Their biggest priority was cheap land and internal improvements such as better roads and water transportation.

Tariff of Abominations Tariffs became one of the first issues of debate that President Jackson faced. In 1827, the year before Jackson's election, northern manufacturers began to demand a tariff on imported woolen goods. Northerners wanted the tariff to protect their industries from foreign competition, especially from Great Britain. For them the tariff helped meet economic challenges.

British companies were driving American ones out of business with their inexpensive manufactured goods. The tariff northerners supported, however, was so high that importing wool would be impossible. Southerners opposed the tariff, saying it would hurt their economy. *south*

Before Andrew Jackson took office, Congress placed a high tariff on imports. Angry southerners called it the **Tariff of Abominations**. *hat g* (An abomination is a hateful thing.) Southern voters were outraged. *this*

President John Quincy Adams signed the tariff legislation, though he did not fully support it. In early U.S. history, presidents tended to reserve veto power for legislation that they believed violated the Constitution. Signing the tariff bill meant Adams would surely be defeated in his re-election bid. The new tariff added fuel to the growing sectional differences plaguing the young nation. Citing states' rights, some southerners said that the states could nullify laws they felt were not authorized by the Constitution. Most northerners opposed nullification.

Reading Check
Summarize
Describe the sectional economic differences in the United States during the early 1800s.

States' Rights Debate

When Andrew Jackson took office in 1829, he was forced to respond to the growing conflict over tariffs. At the core of the dispute was the question of an individual state's right to disregard a law that had been passed by the U.S. Congress. This led to growing sectionalism, or sectional differences.

Nullification Crisis Early in his political career, Vice President John C. Calhoun had supported the **criteria** of a strong central government. But in 1828 when Congress passed the Tariff of Abominations, Calhoun joined his fellow southerners in protest. Economic depression and previous tariffs had severely damaged the economy of his home state, South Carolina. It was only beginning to recover in 1828. Some leaders in the state even

Academic Vocabulary
criteria basic requirements

Regions of the United States, Early 1800s

North
- Economy based on manufacturing
- Support for tariffs—American goods could be sold at lower prices than could British goods

South
- Economy based on agriculture
- Opposition to tariffs, which increased the cost of imported goods

West
- Emerging economy
- Support for internal improvements and the sale of public lands

spoke of leaving, or secession from, the Union over the issue of tariffs. Calhoun understood the problems of South Carolina's farmers because he was one himself. But he wanted to find a way to keep South Carolina from leaving the Union. The answer he arrived at was the doctrine of nullification. A state, Calhoun said, had the right to nullify, or reject, a federal law that it considers unconstitutional.

In response to the tariff, Calhoun drafted the *South Carolina Exposition and Protest*. It said that Congress should not favor one state or region over another. Calhoun used the *Protest* to advance the **states' rights doctrine**, which said that since the states had formed the national government, state power should be greater than federal power. He believed states had the right to nullify, or reject, any federal law they judged to be unconstitutional. The debate about the importance of states' rights increased sectional tensions that would further divide the nation.

Calhoun's theory was controversial, and it drew some fierce challengers. Many of them were from the northern states that had benefited from increased tariffs. These opponents believed that the American people, not the individual states, made up the Union. Conflict between the supporters and the opponents of nullification deepened. The dispute became known as the **nullification crisis**.

Although he chose not to put his name on his *Exposition and Protest*, Calhoun did resign from the vice presidency. He was then elected to the Senate, where he continued his arguments in favor of nullification. Martin Van Buren replaced Calhoun as vice president when Jackson was re-elected president.

The Hayne-Webster Debate The debate about states' rights began, or originated, early in our nation's history. This resulted in constitutional issues arising regarding states' rights. Calhoun was not the first person to propose the doctrine of nullification. Thomas Jefferson and James Madison supported the states' power to disagree with the federal government in the Virginia and Kentucky Resolutions of 1798–99. Some of the delegates at the Hartford Convention supported states' rights. But Calhoun's theory went further. He believed that states could judge whether a law was or was not constitutional. This put the power of the Supreme Court in question.

The issue of nullification was intensely debated on the floor of the Senate in 1830. Robert Y. Hayne, senator from South Carolina, defended states' rights. He argued that nullification gave states a way to lawfully protest federal legislation. **Daniel Webster** of Massachusetts argued that the United States was one nation, not a pact among independent states. He believed that the welfare of the nation should override that of individual states.

Jackson Responds Although deeply opposed to nullification, Jackson was concerned about economic problems in the southern states. In 1832 he urged Congress to pass another tariff that lowered the previous rate. South Carolina thought the slight change was inadequate. The state legislature took a monumental step; it decided to test the doctrine of states' rights.

South Carolina's first action was to pass the Nullification Act, which declared the 1828 and 1832 tariffs "null, void . . . [and not] binding upon this State, its officers or citizens." South Carolina threatened to withdraw from the Union if federal troops were used to collect duties. The legislature also voted to form its own army. Jackson was enraged.

The president sternly condemned nullification. Jackson declared that he would enforce the law in South Carolina. At his request, Congress passed the Force Bill, approving use of the army if necessary. In light of Jackson's determined position, no other state chose to support South Carolina.

Early in 1833 Henry Clay of Kentucky had proposed a compromise that would gradually lower the tariff over several years. As Jackson's intentions became clear, both the U.S. Congress and South Carolina moved quickly to approve the compromise. The Congress would decrease the tariff, and South Carolina's leaders would enforce the law.

The tariff policy prompted sectional differences. Despite the provisions of this compromise, neither side changed its beliefs about states' rights. The argument continued for years, ending in the huge conflict known as the Civil War.

Jackson Attacks the Bank

Jackson upheld federal authority in the nullification crisis. He did not, however, always support greater federal power. For example, he opposed the Second Bank of the United States, founded by Congress in 1816.

The Second Bank of the United States was given a 20-year charter. This charter gave it the power to act exclusively as the federal government's financial agent. The Bank held federal deposits, made transfers of federal funds between states, and dealt with any payments or receipts involving the federal government. It also issued bank notes, or paper currency. Some 80 percent of the Bank was privately owned, but its operations were supervised by Congress and the president.

In the 1830 Hayne-Webster debate, Daniel Webster (above) staunchly championed the Constitution and national unity.

Reading Check
Summarize
What led to the nullification crisis, and why was it important?

States' Rights vs. the Union

The framers of the Constitution created a document that was remarkable in its scope. But a few issues were unresolved. One of the most controversial was the matter of states' rights versus the authority of the federal government. **Daniel Webster** (left) insisted that the interests of the Union should prevail. **John C. Calhoun** (right) believed that the powers of the states were greater.

Analyze Historical Sources
How did the views of Calhoun and Webster differ?

> "While the Union lasts we have high, exciting, gratifying [rewarding] prospects spread out before us, for us and our children. God grant that in my day . . . my eyes shall be turned to behold the gorgeous ensign [flag] of the republic . . . bearing for its motto . . . Liberty and Union, now and forever one and inseparable."
>
> —Daniel Webster from the Hayne-Webster debate, 1830

> "If there be no protective power in the reserved rights of the states, they must in the end be forced to rebel. . . ."
>
> —John C. Calhoun from a letter to Virgil Maxcy, September 11, 1830

There was debate about the Bank. Many states, particularly in the South, had opposed the Bank. Small farmers believed that the Bank only helped wealthy businesspeople. Jackson also questioned the legality of the Bank. He believed it was an unconstitutional extension of the power of Congress. The states, he thought, should have the power to control the banking system.

Some states decided to take action. Maryland tried to pass a tax that would limit the Bank's operations. James McCulloch, cashier of the Bank's branch in Maryland, refused to pay this tax. The state took him to court, and the resulting case went all the way to the U.S. Supreme Court. In the landmark case *McCulloch v. Maryland*, the Court decision was that the national bank was constitutional.

Nicholas Biddle, the Bank's director, decided to push for a bill to renew the Bank's charter in 1832. Jackson campaigned for the bill's defeat. "I will kill it," he promised. True to his word, Jackson vetoed the legislation when Congress sent it to him.

Congress could not get the two-thirds majority needed to override Jackson's veto. Jackson also weakened the Bank's power by moving most of its funds to state banks. In many cases, these banks used the funds to offer easy credit terms to people buying land. While this practice helped expansion in the West, it also led to inflation.

In the summer of 1836 Jackson tried to slow this inflation. He ordered Americans to use only gold or silver—instead of paper state-bank notes—to buy government-owned land. This policy did not help the national

Jackson against the Bank

Andrew Jackson's fight with the Bank was the subject of many political cartoons, like this one.

In this scene, Jackson is shown fighting a hydra that represents the national bank. The hydra is a mythological monster whose heads grow back when cut off. The heads of the hydra are portraits of politicians who opposed Jackson's policies.

Analyze Historical Sources
How does this image show the difficulty Jackson had politically?

Andrew Jackson fights the hydra with a cane labeled "veto."

Nicholas Biddle is at the center of the hydra.

Reading Check
Analyze Information
Why did critics of the Second Bank of the United States oppose it?

economy as Jackson had hoped. Jackson did improve the economy and met economic challenges by lowering the national debt. However, his policies opened the door for approaching economic troubles.

Panic of 1837

Jackson was still very popular with voters in 1836. He chose not to run in 1836, however, and the Democrats nominated Vice President Martin Van Buren.

Timeline: The Supreme Court and Capitalism

Connect to Economics During the early 1800s, the Supreme Court made several rulings that helped define federal power over contracts and commerce. These rulings reinforced capitalism as the ruling economic system in the United States.

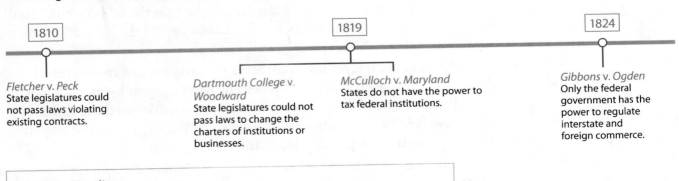

1810

Fletcher v. *Peck*
State legislatures could not pass laws violating existing contracts.

1819

Dartmouth College v. *Woodward*
State legislatures could not pass laws to change the charters of institutions or businesses.

McCulloch v. *Maryland*
States do not have the power to tax federal institutions.

1824

Gibbons v. *Ogden*
Only the federal government has the power to regulate interstate and foreign commerce.

Interpret Timelines
What effect did the Supreme Court have on economic development?

In 1834 a new political party had formed to oppose Jackson. Its members called themselves Whigs, after an English political party that opposed the monarchy, to make the point that Jackson was using his power like a king. The **Whig Party** favored the idea of a weak president and a strong Congress. Unable to agree on a candidate, the Whigs chose four men to run against Van Buren. Because of this indecision, and with backing from Jackson, Van Buren won the election.

Shortly after Van Buren took office, the country experienced the **Panic of 1837**, a severe economic depression. Jackson's banking policies and his unsuccessful plan to curb inflation contributed to the panic. But people blamed Van Buren.

In 1840 the Whigs united against the weakened Van Buren to stand behind one candidate, **William Henry Harrison**, an army general. Harrison won in an electoral landslide. The Whigs had achieved their goal of winning the presidency.

Reading Check
Identify Cause and Effect What contributed to the Panic of 1837, and how did it affect the 1840 election?

Summary and Preview The states' rights debate dominated much of Jackson's presidency. In the next lesson you will learn about the removal of American Indians from the southeastern United States.

Lesson 2 Assessment

Review Ideas, Terms, and People

1. **a. Recall** On what were the economies of the northern, southern, and western states, or regions, based? What were the causes and effects of their economic differences?

   b. Analyze What was the impact of tariff policies on sections of the United States during this time period?

   c. Summarize What were the arguments for and against protective tariffs?

   d. Predict How might the sectional issues involved in the dispute over the Tariff of Abominations lead to future problems between the North and South? What issues were debated?

2. **a. Describe** What roles did Daniel Webster and John C. Calhoun play in the nullification crisis?

   b. Summarize What idea did supporters of the states' rights doctrine promote?

   c. Compare and Contrast How do the effects of congressional conflicts and compromises compare? Include examples of the roles of John C. Calhoun, Henry Clay, and Daniel Webster. Identify the provisions of these compromises.

3. **a. Describe** What problems resulted from weakening the Bank? Specifically, how did the absence of a national banking system affect economic stability?

   b. Draw Conclusions Why did Jackson veto the bill to renew the Second Bank of the United States?

   c. Analyze What different viewpoints resulted in debate about the Second Bank of the United States?

4. **a. Recall** What caused the Panic of 1837?

   b. Summarize How did the Whig Party win the election of 1840?

   c. Elaborate Why do you think Jackson chose not to run for the presidency in 1836? Do you think he made the right decision? Why?

Critical Thinking

5. **Identify Cause and Effect** In this lesson you learned about the political conflicts during Jackson's administration. Use a graphic organizer like the one below to show how some of Jackson's policies dealing with conflicts led to the Panic of 1837.

Indian Removal

The Big Idea

President Jackson supported a policy of Indian removal.

Main Ideas

- The Indian Removal Act authorized the relocation of Native Americans to the West.

- Cherokee resistance to removal led to disagreement between Jackson and the Supreme Court.

- Other Native Americans resisted removal with force.

Key Terms and People

Indian Removal Act
Indian Territory
Bureau of Indian Affairs
Sequoya
Worcester v. *Georgia*
Trail of Tears
Black Hawk
Osceola

If YOU were there . . .

You belong to the Cherokee nation. Your family has farmed rich lands in Georgia for as long as anyone can remember. You've learned some new ways from white settlers, too. At school you've learned to read both English and Cherokee. But now that doesn't seem important. The U.S. government is sending you and your people far away to unknown places in the West.

How would you feel about being taken away from your home?

Indian Removal Act

Native Americans had long lived in settlements stretching from Georgia to Mississippi. However, President Jackson and other political leaders wanted to open this land to settlement by American farmers. Opening new land to white settlement would also increase economic development. Under pressure from Jackson, Congress passed the **Indian Removal Act** in 1830. This policy toward American Indian nations authorized the removal of Native Americans who lived east of the Mississippi River to lands in the West.

Congress then established **Indian Territory**—U.S. land in what is now Oklahoma—and planned to move Native Americans there. Some supporters of this plan, like John C. Calhoun, argued that removal to Indian Territory would protect Indians from further conflicts with American settlers. "One of the greatest evils to which they are subject is that incessant [constant] pressure of our population," he noted. "To guard against this evil . . . there ought to be the strongest . . . assurance that the country given [to] them should be theirs." To manage Indian removal to western lands, Congress approved the creation of a new government agency, the **Bureau of Indian Affairs**.

The Choctaw were the first Indians sent to Indian Territory. The Mississippi legislature abolished the Choctaw

Indian Removal

During the Trail of Tears, thousands of Cherokee died from conditions such as disease, starvation, and harsh weather. They were forced to walk hundreds of miles to their new land in the West. Other Native Americans were also moved, with similar results.

Reading Check
Find Main Ideas
What major changes did President Jackson make to U.S. policy regarding Native Americans?

Academic Vocabulary
contemporary
existing at the same time

government and then forced the Choctaw leaders to sign the Treaty of Dancing Rabbit Creek. This treaty gave more than 7.5 million acres of their land to the state. The Choctaw moved to Indian Territory during a disastrous winter trip. Federal officials did not provide enough food or supplies to the Choctaw, most of whom were on foot. About one-fourth of the Choctaw died of cold, disease, or starvation.

News of the Choctaw's hardships caused other Indians to resist removal. When the Creek resisted in 1836, federal troops resolved this conflict by moving in and capturing some 14,500 of them. They led the Creek, many in chains, to Indian Territory. One Creek woman remembered the trip being filled with "the awful silence that showed the heartaches and sorrow at being taken from the homes and even separation from loved ones." The Chickasaw, who lived in upper Mississippi, negotiated a treaty for better supplies on their trip to Indian Territory. Nevertheless, many Chickasaw lives were also lost during removal.

Cherokee Resistance

Many Cherokee had believed that they could prevent conflicts and avoid removal by adopting the **contemporary** culture of white people. In the early 1800s they invited missionaries to set up schools where Cherokee children learned how to read and write in English. The Cherokee developed their own government modeled after the U.S. Constitution with an

Trail of Tears

The Cherokee knew that they would be forced to march West, but they did not know that so many of their people would die on the way. Here is an account of the Trail of Tears, written before it started, by a Cherokee girl who made the trip.

> "March 10, 1838
> Beloved Martha, I have delayed writing to you so long. . . . If we Cherokees are to be driven to the west by the cruel hand of oppression to seek a new home in the west, it will be impossible. . . . It is thus all our rights are invaded."
>
> —Letter from Jenny, a Cherokee girl, just before her removal

Analyze Historical Sources
What is the concern of the Cherokee girl before the Trail of Tears? What do you think her concerns were after the trip?

election system, a bicameral council, and a court system. All of these were headed by a principal chief.

A Cherokee named **Sequoya** used 86 characters to represent Cherokee syllables to create a writing system for their own complex language. In 1828 his contribution led the Cherokee to begin publishing a newspaper printed in both English and Cherokee.

The adoption of white culture did not protect the Cherokee. After gold was discovered on their land in Georgia, their treaty rights were ignored. Georgia leaders began preparing for the Cherokee's removal. When they refused to move, the Georgia militia began attacking Cherokee towns. Instead of responding with force, the Cherokee fought in the American court, or judicial, system. They sued the federal government, claiming that they had sovereignty, or the right to be respected as a foreign country. The case, the *Cherokee Nation* v. *Georgia* reached the Supreme Court in 1831. Chief Justice John Marshall, however, refused to hear the case. He ruled that the Cherokee had no right to bring suit since they were neither citizens nor a foreign country.

The Cherokee, however, had another plan of attack. Samuel Austin Worcester was a white man, a teacher, and a friend to the Cherokee. The state of Georgia, carrying out the Indian Removal Act, ordered Worcester to leave Cherokee land. He refused and brought suit on behalf of himself and the Cherokee. In the suit, the Cherokee said that they were an independent, or sovereign, nation and claimed that the government of Georgia had no legal power over their lands.

In 1832 the Supreme Court, under the leadership of Chief Justice John Marshall, agreed. In **Worcester v. Georgia** the Court ruled that the Cherokee nation was a distinct community in which the laws of Georgia had no force. The Court also stated that only the federal government, not the states, had authority over Native Americans.

Georgia, however, ignored the Court's ruling, and President Jackson's response was to take no action to make Georgia follow the ruling. "John Marshall has made his decision; now let him enforce it," Jackson supposedly said. By not enforcing the Court's decision, Jackson violated his presidential oath to uphold the laws of the land. However, most members of Congress and American citizens did not protest the ways Jackson removed Native Americans. This contributed to the struggle between the Cherokee nation and the United States government.

In the spring of 1838, U.S. troops began to remove all Cherokee and resettle them in Indian Territory. A few were able to escape and hide in the mountains of North Carolina. After the Cherokee were removed, Georgia took their businesses, farms, and property.

The Cherokee's 800-mile forced march became known as the **Trail of Tears**. During the march, the Cherokee suffered from disease, hunger, and harsh weather. Almost one-fourth of the 18,000 Cherokee died on the march.

Today, members of the Cherokee nation of northeastern Oklahoma are descendants of the Cherokee who were removed to Indian Territory. The group's population is about 70,000. Members of the Eastern Band of Cherokee Indians are the descendants of the Cherokee who escaped removal. The 8,100 members of this group live mostly in western North Carolina.

Reading Check
Find Main Ideas
What was the *Worcester* v. *Georgia* ruling, and what was Jackson's response?

Other Native Americans Resist

Other Native Americans decided to fight U.S. troops to avoid removal. Chief **Black Hawk**, a leader of the Fox and the Sauk Indians, led his people in a struggle to protect their lands in Illinois. By 1832, however, the Sauk forces

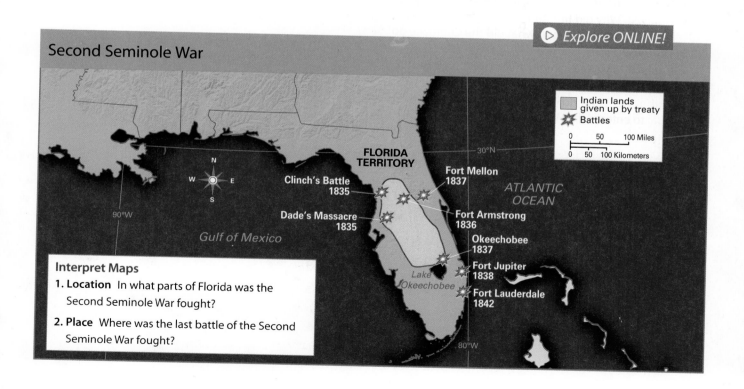

Second Seminole War

> ▷ Explore ONLINE!

FLORIDA TERRITORY

Clinch's Battle 1835

Fort Mellon 1837

ATLANTIC OCEAN

Dade's Massacre 1835

Fort Armstrong 1836

Gulf of Mexico

Okeechobee 1837

Lake Okeechobee

Fort Jupiter 1838

Fort Lauderdale 1842

Indian lands given up by treaty
✷ Battles

0   50   100 Miles
0   50   100 Kilometers

30°N
90°W
80°W

Interpret Maps

1. **Location** In what parts of Florida was the Second Seminole War fought?

2. **Place** Where was the last battle of the Second Seminole War fought?

were running out of food and supplies, and by 1850 they had been forced to leave.

In Florida, Seminole leaders were forced to sign a removal treaty that their followers decided to ignore. A leader named **Osceola** called upon his people to resist with force, and the Second Seminole War began. Osceola was captured and soon died in prison. His followers, however, continued to fight. Some 4,000 Seminole were removed and hundreds of others killed. Eventually, U.S. officials decided to give up the fight. Small groups of Seminole had resisted removal, and their descendants live in Florida today. In this way the conflict between the Seminoles and United States officials was resolved. Chief Black Hawk and Osceola were social leaders because they worked for better living conditions for their people.

Reading Check
Analyze Information
How effective was Native American resistance to removal?

Summary and Preview President Jackson supported the removal of thousands of Native Americans from their traditional lands to the federal territory in the West. In the next module you will learn about the westward growth of the nation as farmers, ranchers, and other settlers moved West.

Lesson 3 Assessment

Review Ideas, Terms, and People

1. a. **Identify** What Native American groups were affected by the Indian Removal Act? Where were they relocated?
   b. **Explain** Why did government officials want to relocate Native Americans to the West?
   c. **Predict** What are some possible effects that the Indian Removal Act might have on Native Americans already living in the West?
2. a. **Identify** What was the Trail of Tears?
   b. **Analyze** Why did the state of Georgia want to relocate the Cherokee, and what did the Cherokee do in response?
   c. **Analyze** Give an example of Jackson's presidential response to the Court ruling. How did he handle it?
   d. **Elaborate** What do you think of President Jackson's refusal to enforce the *Worcester* v. *Georgia* ruling?

3. a. **Describe** What led to the Second Seminole War?
   b. **Compare and Contrast** How were the Seminole and the Sauk resistance efforts similar and different?

Critical Thinking

4. **Compare and Contrast** In this lesson you learned about Indian removal. Copy the chart below and use it to identify the Native American groups and their responses to removal.

Native American Group	Response to Removal

Social Studies Skills

Solve Problems

Define the Skill

Problem solving is a process for finding workable solutions to difficult situations. The process involves asking questions, identifying and evaluating information, comparing and contrasting, and making judgments. Problem solving is useful in studying history because it helps you better understand problems people faced at certain points in time and how they dealt with those difficulties.

The ability to understand and evaluate how people solved problems in the past can help in solving similar problems today. The skill can also be applied to many other kinds of difficulties besides historical ones. It is a method for thinking through almost any situation.

Learn the Skill

Using the following steps will enable you to better understand and solve problems.

1. **Identify the problem.** Ask questions of yourself and others to make sure you know exactly what the situation is and understand why it is a problem.

2. **Gather information.** Ask questions and conduct research to learn more about the problem, such as its history, what caused it, what contributes to it, and other factors.

3. **List options.** Based on the information you have gathered, identify possible options for solving the problem that you might consider. Be aware that your final solution will probably be better and easier to reach if you have as many options as possible to consider.

4. **Evaluate the options.** Weigh each option you are considering. Think of and list the advantages it has as a solution, as well as its potential disadvantages.

5. **Choose and implement a solution.** After comparing the advantages and disadvantages of each solution, choose the one that seems best and apply it.

6. **Evaluate the solution.** Once the solution has been tried, evaluate its effectiveness in solving the problem. This step will tell you if the solution was a good one, or if another of the possible solutions should be tried instead.

Practice the Skill

One of the most challenging situations that President Jackson faced was the nullification crisis. You can use the problem-solving skills to better understand this problem and to evaluate his solution for it. Review the information about the nullification crisis in this module. Then answer the questions below.

1. What was the specific problem that Jackson faced? Why was it a problem?

2. What event led to the problem? What earlier circumstances and conditions contributed to it?

3. List possible solutions to the problem that you would have considered if you had been president, along with advantages and disadvantages.

4. Jackson threatened to send troops to South Carolina to enforce federal law. Do you think his solution was the best one? Explain why, or if not, what solution would have been better.

The Indian Removal Treaties

In 1830 President Andrew Jackson signed the Indian Removal Act into law. As its name implies, the purpose of the act was to remove Native Americans from land that white settlers wanted for themselves. The impact of this act was that five tribes were forced to leave their traditional lands and walk to a territory west of the Mississippi River. The land in the new Indian Territory was land white settlers did not want. It was poor and not good for farming. The poor land made life very difficult for newly arrived Indians. Many died from malnutrition and disease. Within ten years, about 60,000 Indians had been relocated.

MO

KS

Trail of Tears, 1838–39

Cherokee

Creek

AR

Seminole

OK

Chickasaw

Choctaw

TX

LA

95°W

Treaty	Date	Indian Group	Results for United States	Results for Indian Groups	Outcome
Treaty of Greenville	1795	12 Groups	Ended battles in Northwest Territory	Payment of $20,000; acknowledgment of lands	Indian land claims disregarded by American settlers
Treaty at Holston River	1798	Cherokee	Received land promised to Cherokee	Payment of $5,000 followed by annual payments	Cherokee lands reduced
Treaty at St. Louis	1804	Sauk, Fox	Received land from the Sauk and the Fox	Annual payments of $1,000	Indians claimed their leaders acted without permission; conflicts arose as settlers moved to Sauk and Fox lands
Treaty at Fort Jackson	1814	Creek	Ended battles with Red Eagle; received 23 million acres of land in Georgia	Later receives small amount of land in Indian Territory	Conflicts between settlers and Creek led to removal of Creek to Indian Territory
Treaty of Dancing Rabbit Creek	1830	Choctaw	Received all Choctaw lands east of Mississippi River	Received land in Indian Territory	Choctaw became first tribe moved from southeast to land in Indian Territory

The Cherokee For generations, the Cherokee had called the southern Appalachian Mountain region home. But when they were forced off their land in the Trail of Tears, thousands died.

The Creek The Creek had to leave a land rich in variety. It stretched from the ridges and valleys of the Appalachian Mountains in the north, through a region of low hills and valleys, to a flat area of pine forest in the south.

The Seminole Many Seminole Indians refused to leave Florida. They hid in the swamps, battling American soldiers. Many of their descendants still live in Florida today.

The Chickasaw The Chickasaw lived in a land of rich, black prairie soil. They would find the soil west of the Mississippi much less suited for farming.

The Choctaw The Choctaw were forced to leave behind the low, rolling hills and plains of their homeland. For generations they had farmed the rich soil there.

KY

TN

Cherokee

Chickasaw

Choctaw

AL

Creek

GA

MS

FL

Seminole

75°W

30°

ATLANTIC OCEAN

80°W

Gulf of Mexico

85°W

90°W

25°N

N
W E
S

Interpret Maps

1. **Place** How did land in the Indian Territory compare to the land in the Indians' homelands?

2. **Movement** How do you think being forced to leave their homelands impacted the Indians' way of life?

Module 10 Assessment

Review Vocabulary, Terms, and People

Complete each sentence by filling in the blank with the correct term or person.

1. In the Supreme Court case of _____, the Court ruled that the federal government, not the states, had authority over the Cherokee.

2. President Jackson's group of advisers was known as the _____ because of where its members met in the White House.

3. _____ served as Andrew Jackson's vice president until he resigned due to the dispute over nullification.

4. The _____ supported the power of the states over the power of the federal government.

5. The practice of rewarding supporters with positions in government is known as the _____.

Comprehension and Critical Thinking

Lesson 1

6. a. **Identify** What changes took place in the early 1800s that broadened democracy in the United States?

   b. **Analyze** How was Jackson's victory in the election of 1828 a reflection of a change in American politics?

   c. **Evaluate** Do you think the changes brought about by Jacksonian Democracy went far enough in expanding democracy? Why or why not?

Lesson 2

7. a. **Describe** What conflicts troubled the Jackson administration?

   b. **Draw Conclusions** What were the results of the conflict over the Second Bank of the United States?

   c. **Analyze** How did the Second Bank and tariffs help meet economic challenges?

   d. **Compare and Contrast** Compare and contrast how economic factors, such as tariffs, led to sectionalism. What was the impact of tariff policies on different parts of the country in this time period?

   e. **Summarize** What were the arguments for and against the banking system?

   f. **Predict** How might sectional differences and the debate over states' rights lead to future problems for the United States?

Lesson 3

8. a. **Identify** Who was Sequoya? What important contribution did he make?

   b. **Identify** What are some ways conflicts between Native Americans and government officials were solved?

   c. **Describe** What were the successes and failures of the reforms of the Age of Jackson, including Indian Removal and the Trail of Tears?

   d. **Contrast** In what different ways did the Cherokee and the Seminole attempt to resist removal to Indian Territory?

   e. **Elaborate** Do you agree with Jackson's refusal to enforce the *Worcester* v. *Georgia* ruling? Why or why not?

Module 10 Assessment, continued

Review Themes

9. **Politics** What new political party rose in opposition to President Andrew Jackson? What was the party's attitude toward the power of the president?

10. **Economics** What economic factors influenced the policy of Indian removal?

11. **Politics** Make a list of both the events and impacts of Andrew Jackson's presidency. Then write a paragraph explaining the events and their impact.

12. **Politics** What were some contributions of significant political and social leaders of this time period?

Reading Skills

Draw Conclusions about the Past *Use the Reading Skills taught in this module to answer the question about the reading selection below.*

> Native Americans had long lived in settlements stretching from Georgia to Mississippi. However, President Jackson and other political leaders wanted to open this land to settlement by American farmers.

13. Which statement below can you conclude from the passage above?
- **a.** Farmers moved onto the Native Americans' land after removal.
- **b.** Native Americans wanted to move from their lands.
- **c.** Native Americans resisted removal.
- **d.** Government officials had to use force to remove Native Americans from their land.

Social Studies Skills

Solve Problems *Use the Social Studies Skills taught in this module to answer the question about the reading selection below.*

> Northerners wanted the tariff to protect their industries from foreign competition, especially from Great Britain.
>
> British companies were driving American ones out of business with their inexpensive manufactured goods . . . Southerners opposed the tariff, saying it would hurt their economy.

14. Which of the following might be a reasonable solution to the problem discussed above?
- **a.** passing a low tariff
- **b.** passing a high tariff only in the South
- **c.** Britain passing a tariff
- **d.** selling northern and British goods for a higher price

Focus on Writing

15. **Write Interview Questions** You are a reporter for a large city newspaper in the year 1837. Andrew Jackson has just left office, and you have been given the assignment of interviewing him about his presidency and his role in American politics. Review what you have learned about Jackson's political significance, the conflicts he was involved in, and the causes and effects of his policies toward Indians. Then begin writing questions for your interview with Jackson. What will the readers of your newspaper want to learn more about? Write at least ten interview questions that your readers will want answered.

Module 11
Westward Expansion

★

Essential Question
Was the United States truly destined to expand west in the 1800s?

About the Photo: Wagon trains carried hundreds of thousands of settlers across the Great Plains.

In this module you will read about the effects of westward expansion in the United States. You will also learn about how Native Americans resisted these changes.

What You Will Learn ...

Lesson 1: A Growing Nation **354**
The Big Idea Americans explored and settled in the West as the nation expanded.

Lesson 2: Boom Times in the West **364**
The Big Idea American settlers dramatically changed the western frontier as they began to tame the land.

Lesson 3: Wars for the West. **371**
The Big Idea Native Americans and the U.S. government came into conflict over land in the West.

Lesson 4: Farming and Populism **378**
The Big Idea Settlers on the Great Plains created new communities and a unique political movement.

▶ Explore ONLINE!

HISTORY.

VIDEOS, including...
- The Transcontinental Railroad
- The Louisiana Purchase
- Railroads that Tamed the West
- Plains Indians
- Sitting Bull: Chief of the Lakota Nation

✓ Document-Based Investigations

✓ Graphic Organizers

✓ Interactive Games

✓ Interactive Map: Territorial Expansion of the United States, 1783–1898

✓ Image Carousel: Buffalo Bill's Wild West Show

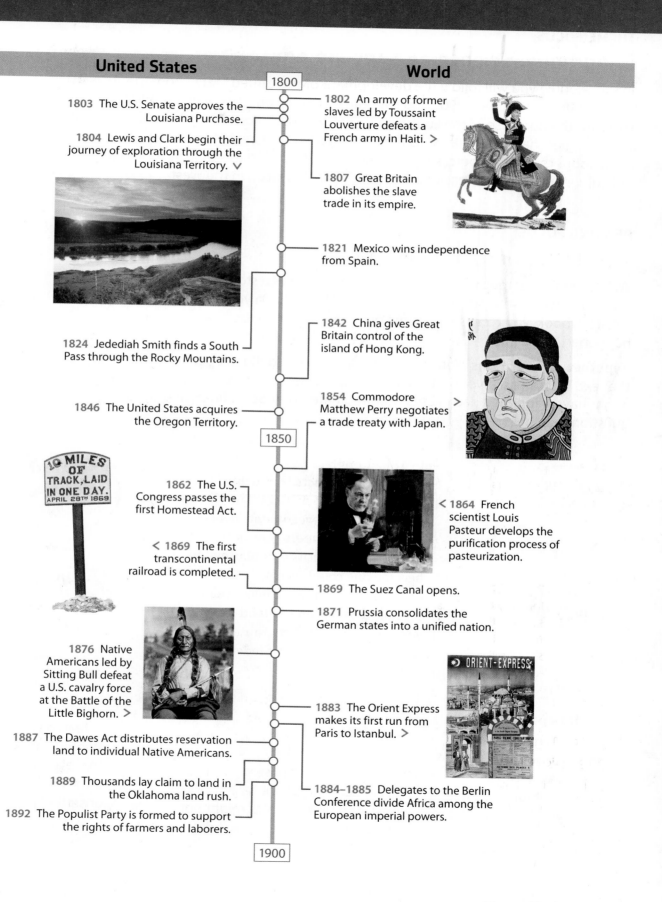

United States

World

1800

1803 The U.S. Senate approves the Louisiana Purchase.

1804 Lewis and Clark begin their journey of exploration through the Louisiana Territory. ∨

1802 An army of former slaves led by Toussaint Louverture defeats a French army in Haiti. >

1807 Great Britain abolishes the slave trade in its empire.

1821 Mexico wins independence from Spain.

1824 Jedediah Smith finds a South Pass through the Rocky Mountains.

1842 China gives Great Britain control of the island of Hong Kong.

1846 The United States acquires the Oregon Territory.

1854 Commodore Matthew Perry negotiates a trade treaty with Japan.

1850

10 MILES OF TRACK, LAID IN ONE DAY. APRIL 28TH 1869

1862 The U.S. Congress passes the first Homestead Act.

< 1864 French scientist Louis Pasteur develops the purification process of pasteurization.

< 1869 The first transcontinental railroad is completed.

1869 The Suez Canal opens.

1871 Prussia consolidates the German states into a unified nation.

1876 Native Americans led by Sitting Bull defeat a U.S. cavalry force at the Battle of the Little Bighorn. >

1883 The Orient Express makes its first run from Paris to Istanbul. >

1887 The Dawes Act distributes reservation land to individual Native Americans.

1889 Thousands lay claim to land in the Oklahoma land rush.

1884–1885 Delegates to the Berlin Conference divide Africa among the European imperial powers.

1892 The Populist Party is formed to support the rights of farmers and laborers.

1900

Reading Social Studies

THEME FOCUS:

Geography, Science and Technology

In this module you will follow the development of the United States from the early 1800s through the 1890s. You will learn that the country nearly doubled in size with the purchase of the Louisiana Territory in 1803. You will find out about the struggles that people faced as they later settled the Great Plains. You will learn about the technological advancements made during this time as well as the difficult geographical obstacles miners and ranchers faced in the West.

READING FOCUS:

Ask Questions to Understand

When newspaper reporters want to get to the heart of a story, they ask certain questions: who, what, when, where, why, and how. When you are reading a history book, you can use the same questions to get to the heart of what happened in the past.

Hypothetical Questions You can also use questions to dig deeper than what is in the text. You can ask hypothetical, or what if, questions. These questions ask what might have happened had events occurred differently. Sometimes asking such questions can help history come alive.

Who?
Congress

Where?
the West

How?
Congress gave land to anyone who agreed to settle on it for five years.

In 1862 Congress passed two important land acts that helped open the West to settlers. The Homestead Act gave government-owned land to small farmers. Any adult who was a U.S. citizen or planned to become one could receive 160 acres of land. In exchange, homesteaders promised to live on the land for five years. The Morrill Act granted more than 17 million acres of federal land to the states.

What?
encouraged new settlement

When?
1862

Why?
Perhaps Congress feared what would happen to western lands if they remained unsettled by U.S. citizens.

What if?
If Congress had not passed these laws, U.S. citizens might not have moved West. The United States might not have grown as quickly as it did.

You Try It!

Read the following passage and then answer the questions below.

Building Communities Women were an important force in the settlement of the frontier. They joined in the hard work of farming and ranching and helped build communities out of the widely spaced farms and small towns. Their role in founding communities facilitated a strong voice in public affairs. Wyoming women, for example, were granted the vote in the new state's constitution, which was approved in 1869. Annie Bidwell, one of the founders of Chico, California, used her influence to support a variety of moral and social causes such as women's suffrage and temperance.

Answer these questions based on the passage you just read.

1. Who is this passage about?
2. What did they do?
3. When did they do it?
4. How do you think they accomplished it?
5. Why do you think they were able to accomplish so much?
6. How can knowing this information help you understand the past?
7. What if women in the West had been given more rights? Fewer rights? How might the West have been different?

As you read Module 11, ask questions like *who, what, when, where, why, how,* and *what* if to help you analyze what you are reading.

Key Terms and People

Lesson 1
Daniel Boone
Louisiana Purchase
Meriwether Lewis
William Clark
Lewis and Clark expedition
Sacagawea
Zebulon Pike
John C. Frémont
John Jacob Astor
mountain men
Oregon Trail
Santa Fe Trail
Mormons
Brigham Young

Lesson 2
frontier
Comstock Lode
boomtowns
Cattle Kingdom
cattle drive
Chisholm Trail
Pony Express
transcontinental railroad
standard time

Lesson 3
Treaty of Fort Laramie
reservations
Crazy Horse
Treaty of Medicine Lodge
buffalo soldiers
George Armstrong Custer
Sitting Bull
Battle of the Little Bighorn
Massacre at Wounded Knee
Long Walk
Chief Joseph
Geronimo
Ghost Dance
Sarah Winnemucca
assimilate
Dawes General Allotment Act

Lesson 4
Homestead Act
Morrill Act
Exodusters
sodbusters
dry farming
Annie Bidwell
National Grange
deflation
William Jennings Bryan
Populist Party

A Growing Nation

The Big Idea

Americans explored and settled in the West as the nation expanded.

Main Ideas

- As American settlers moved West, control of the Mississippi River became more important to the United States.

- Expeditions led by Lewis and Clark, Pike, and Frémont increased Americans' understanding of the West.

- During the early 1800s, Americans moved west of the Rocky Mountains to settle and trade.

- Families moved into the far west and established thriving communities.

Key Terms and People

Daniel Boone
Louisiana Purchase
Meriwether Lewis
William Clark
Lewis and Clark expedition
Sacagawea
Zebulon Pike
John C. Frémont
John Jacob Astor
mountain men
Oregon Trail
Santa Fe Trail
Mormons
Brigham Young

If YOU were there . . .

You and your family live on a small farm in Kentucky in about 1800. Raised on the frontier, you are a skillful hunter and trapper. One day at the trading post, you see a poster calling for volunteers to join the Corps of Discovery. This expedition will explore the vast region west of the Mississippi River. You think it would be exciting—but dangerous. You might never come home.

Would you volunteer to join the Corps of Discovery?

The First Westerners

For centuries, the Ohio, Cumberland, and Tennessee River valleys had been the hunting grounds of many Native American tribes. By 1800, however, thousands of white settlers had set up homesteads in these areas. The land had been opened up to settlement by an intrepid group of frontier guides known as long hunters. During months-long hunting trips, they explored and surveyed the wilderness west of the Appalachian Mountains. **Daniel Boone** was one of the most famous long hunters.

Frontiersman Daniel Boone led the exploration and settlement of Kentucky.

From his earliest years, Boone loved the outdoor life. In time, he became a skilled hunter, trapper, and guide. In 1769 he led a group of friends on an expedition across the Appalachian Mountains via the Cumberland Gap. They were among the first whites to venture deep into the land beyond the Appalachians. Then, in 1775 Boone and about 30 other long hunters cut a continuous road through the Cumberland Gap. By the time it was finished, this Wilderness Road stretched some 300 miles. It soon became the main thoroughfare for settlers moving West. Some used a southern route called the Natchez Trace. This was an old Native American trail that ran southwest all the way to the Mississippi River.

As the region's population grew, Kentucky, Tennessee, and Ohio were admitted to the Union. Settlers in these states depended upon the Mississippi and Ohio rivers to move their products to eastern markets. New Orleans, located at the mouth of the Mississippi, was a very important port. Its busy docks were filled with settlers' farm products and valuable furs bought from American Indians. Many of these cargoes were then sent to Europe. At the same time, manufactured goods passed through the port on their way upriver. As American dependence on the river grew, President Thomas Jefferson began to worry that a foreign power might shut down access to New Orleans.

Spain controlled both New Orleans and the Louisiana Territory. This region stretched west from the Mississippi River to the Rocky Mountains. Although Spain owned Louisiana, Spanish officials found it impossible to keep Americans out of the territory. "You can't put doors on open country," the foreign minister said in despair. Years of effort failed to improve Spain's position. Under a secret treaty, Spain agreed to trade Louisiana to France, passing the problem on to someone else. One Spanish officer expressed his relief. "I can hardly wait to leave them [the Americans] behind me," he said.

Reading Check
Analyze Information
Why was New Orleans important to settlers in the western regions of the United States?

The Louisiana Purchase and Western Expeditions

▶ Explore ONLINE!

Interpret Maps

1. **Location** What major port city was located at the southern tip of the Louisiana Territory?

2. **Human-Environment Interaction** Why might Lewis and Clark have followed the Missouri River?

Louisiana and Western Explorers

In 1802, just before handing over Louisiana to France, Spain closed New Orleans to American shipping. Angry farmers worried about what this would do to the economy. President Jefferson asked the U.S. ambassador to France, Robert R. Livingston, to try to buy New Orleans. Jefferson sent James Monroe to help Livingston.

Napoléon and Louisiana France was led by Napoléon (nuh-POH-lay-uhn) Bonaparte, a powerful ruler who had conquered most of Europe. He wished to rebuild France's empire in North America. Napoléon's strategy was to use the French colony of Haiti, in the Caribbean, as a supply base. From there he could send troops to Louisiana. However, in the 1790s enslaved Africans, led by Toussaint Louverture (too-SAN loo-vehr-TOOR), revolted and freed themselves from French rule. Napoléon sent troops to try to regain control of the island, but they were defeated in 1802. This defeat ended his hopes of rebuilding a North American empire.

Jefferson Buys Louisiana Livingston and Monroe got a surprising offer during their negotiations with French foreign minister Charles Talleyrand. When the Americans tried to buy New Orleans, Talleyrand offered to sell all of Louisiana. With his hopes for a North American empire dashed, Napoléon had turned his attention back to Europe. France was at war with Great Britain, and Napoléon needed money for military supplies. He also hoped that a larger United States would challenge British power.

Livingston and Monroe knew a bargain when they saw one. They quickly accepted the French offer to sell Louisiana for $15 million, and Jefferson agreed to the purchase. On October 20, 1803, the Senate approved the **Louisiana Purchase** agreement, which roughly doubled the size of the United States.

Explorers Head West President Jefferson wanted to learn more about the West and the Native Americans who lived there. He also wanted to see if there was a river route that could be taken to the Pacific Ocean. So, in 1803 Jefferson asked Congress to fund an expedition to explore the West. To lead it, he chose former army captain **Meriwether Lewis**. Lewis then chose his friend Lieutenant **William Clark** to be the co-leader of the expedition. With Clark, Lewis carefully selected about 50 skilled frontiersmen to join the Corps of Discovery, as they called their group.

In May 1804 the **Lewis and Clark expedition** began its long journey to explore the Louisiana Purchase. Lewis and Clark used the Missouri River as their highway through the unknown lands. By late October the Corps of Discovery had pushed more than 1,600 miles upriver. They spent the winter among the Mandan people. At this time, the Corps also came into contact with British and Canadian trappers and traders, who were not happy to see them. The traders feared American competition in the trade in beaver fur—and they would be proved right.

The Lewis and Clark expedition followed the Missouri River for most of the journey across the Great Plains.

Meriwether Lewis's Journal Entry

On September 17, 1804, while traveling across the Great Plains, Meriwether Lewis marveled at the richness of the land.

Analyze Historical Sources
What did Lewis find so impressive about the Great Plains?

> "*The shortness . . . of grass gave the plain the appearance throughout its whole extent of beautiful bowling-green in fine order . . . this scenery, already rich, pleasing, and beautiful was still farther heightened by immense herds of Buffaloe, deer Elk and Antelopes which we saw in every direction feeding on the hills and plains. I do not think I exaggerate when I estimate the number of Buffalo which could be compre[hend]ed at one view to amount to 3000.*"
>
> —Meriwether Lewis, quoted in *Original Journals of the Lewis and Clark Expedition*, edited by Reuben Bold Theraites

Sacagawea, whose name is believed to mean "bird woman," contributed greatly to the success of the Lewis and Clark expedition.

In the spring of 1805, the expedition set out again. They were joined by **Sacagawea** (sak-uh-guh-WEE-uh), a Shoshone from the Rocky Mountains. Her language skills—she knew several Native American languages—and her knowledge of the geography of the region proved very useful to Lewis and Clark. Sacagawea also helped the expedition by naming plants and by gathering edible fruits and vegetables for the group. At one point, the group met with Sacagawea's brother, who provided horses and a guide to lead the expedition across the mountains.

After crossing the Rockies, Lewis and Clark followed the Columbia River. Along the way they met the powerful Nez Percé. Like the Shoshone, the Nez Percé provided the expedition with supplies. At last, in November 1805 Lewis and Clark reached the Pacific Ocean. The explorers stayed in the Pacific Northwest during the rough winter. In March 1806 Lewis and Clark set out on the long trip home.

Lewis and Clark had not found a river route across the West to the Pacific Ocean. But they had learned much about western lands and paths across the Rockies. They used this knowledge to produce the first accurate maps of the Louisiana Territory. The explorers also established contact with many Native American groups and collected much valuable information about western plants and animals.

Other Explorations In 1806 a young army officer named **Zebulon Pike** was sent on another mission to the West. He was ordered to find the starting point of the Red River. This was important because the United States considered the Red River to be a part of the Louisiana Territory's western border with New Spain.

Heading into the Rocky Mountains, in present-day Colorado, Pike tried to reach the summit of the mountain now known as Pikes Peak. In 1807 he traveled into Spanish-held lands until Spanish cavalry arrested him. They suspected Pike of being a spy. When he was finally released, he returned to the United States and reported on his trip. This report offered many Americans their first description of the Southwest. Not all of Pike's information was accurate, however. For example, he described the treeless Great Plains as a desert. This led many Americans to believe, mistakenly, that the Plains region was useless for farming.

Another explorer, **John C. Frémont**, led an expedition to the Rocky Mountains in May 1842. Upon his return, Frémont compiled a report of his journey, which became a guide for future travelers to the West. It detailed the geology, botany, and climate of the region. It also crushed the mistaken belief that the West was a vast desert, attracting more settlers as a result. Buoyed by the success of his first effort, Frémont led several more surveys of the American West in the 1840s and 1850s.

Mountain Men Go West

In the early 1800s, Americans pushed steadily westward, moving even beyond the territory of the United States. They traveled by canoe and flat-boat, on horseback, and by wagon train. Some even walked much of the way.

The rush to the West occurred, in part, because of a hat. The "high hat," made of water-repellent beaver fur, was popular in the United States and Europe. While acquiring fur for the hats, French, British, and American companies gradually killed off the beaver population in the East. Companies moved West in search of more beavers. Most of the first non-Native Americans who traveled to the Rocky Mountains and the Pacific North-west were fur traders and trappers.

American merchant **John Jacob Astor** created one of the largest fur businesses, the American Fur Company. His company bought skins from western fur traders and trappers, who became known as **mountain men**. These adventurers were among the first to explore the Rocky Mountains and lands west of them. The knowledge they acquired helped settlers who made the westward journey. Mountain men lived lonely and often danger-ous lives. They trapped animals on their own, far from towns and settle-ments. Mountain men such as Jedediah Smith, Manuel Lisa, Jim Bridger, and Jim Beckwourth survived many hardships during their search for wealth and adventure. To survive on the frontier, mountain men adopted Native American customs and clothing. In addition, they often married Native American women. The Indian wives of trappers often worked hard to contribute to their success.

Pioneer William Ashley saw that frequently bringing furs out of the Rocky Mountains was expensive. He asked his traders to stay in the mountains and meet once a year to trade and socialize. This practice helped make the fur trade more profitable. The yearly meeting was known as the rendezvous. At the rendezvous, mountain men and Native American trappers sold their fur to fur-company agents. One trapper described the people at a typical rendezvous in 1837. He saw Americans, Canadian French, some Europeans, and "Indians, of nearly every tribe in the Rocky Mountains." The rendezvous was filled with celebrating and storytelling. At the same time, the meeting was also about conducting business.

**Reading Check
Compare** What did the expeditions of Lewis and Clark, Pike, and Frémont reveal about the West?

Jim Beckwourth was an African American fur trapper and explorer of the West in the early 1800s.

In 1811 John Jacob Astor founded a fur-trading post called Astoria at the mouth of the Columbia River. Astoria was one of the first American settlements in what became known as Oregon Country. American Indians occupied the region, which was rich in forests, rivers, and wildlife. However, Britain, Russia, Spain, and the United States all claimed the land. Recognizing the huge economic value of the Pacific Northwest, the United States made treaties in which Spain and Russia gave up their claims to various areas. The United States also signed treaties with Britain allowing both countries to occupy Oregon Country, the Columbia River, and its surrounding lands.

By the 1840s the era of American fur trading in the Pacific Northwest was drawing to a close. The demand for beaver furs had fallen because fashions had changed. Too much trapping had also greatly reduced the number of beavers. Some mountain men gave up their work and moved back East. Their daring stories, however, along with the treaties made by the U.S. government, fired the imagination of many Americans.

Reading Check
Draw Conclusions
How did the mountain men help to open up the West for future settlement?

Settling the West

The success of early pioneers convinced thousands of families and individuals to make the dangerous journey west. They traveled along a series of routes that led to New Mexico, Oregon, and Utah. Once in these places, the new pioneers claimed the land and established settlements.

The Oregon Trail Many settlers moving to Oregon Country and other western areas followed the 2,000-mile-long **Oregon Trail**, which stretched from places such as Independence, Missouri, and Council Bluffs, Iowa, west into Oregon Country. The trail followed the Platte and Sweetwater Rivers over the Plains. After it crossed the Rocky Mountains, the trail forked. The northern branch led to the Willamette Valley in Oregon. The other branch went to California and became known as the California Trail.

Traveling the trail challenged the strength and determination of pioneer families. The journey usually began after the rainy season ended in late spring and lasted about six months. The cost, about $600 for a family of four, was high at a time when a typical worker usually made about $1.50 per day. Young families made up most groups of settlers. They gathered in wagon trains for the trip. There could be as few as ten wagons or as many as several dozen in a wagon train. Some pioneers brought small herds of cattle with them on the trail.

Oxen, mules, or horses pulled the wagons. Pioneers often walked to save their animals' strength. They kept up a tiring pace, traveling from dawn until dusk. They faced severe hardships, including shortages of food, supplies, and water. Rough weather and geographic barriers, such as rivers and mountains, sometimes forced large numbers of pioneers to abandon their wagons. In the early days of the Oregon Trail, many Native Americans helped the pioneers, acting as guides. They also traded goods for food. Although newspapers sometimes reported Native American "massacres" of pioneers, few settlers died from Indian attacks. The settlers who arrived safely in Oregon and California found generally healthy and pleasant climates. By 1845 some 5,000 settlers occupied the Willamette Valley.

Explore ONLINE!

Trails, Distances, and Travel Times

- California 2,000 miles, 6 months
- Santa Fe 1,200 miles, 2 months
- Mormon 1,300 miles, 4 months
- Old Spanish 700 miles, 7 weeks
- Oregon 2,000 miles, 6 months
- Fort or trading post

0   200   400 Miles
0   200   400 Kilometers

Interpret Maps

1. **Movement** Which trails took the longest to travel?

2. **Human-Environment Interaction** What difficulties do you think travelers on the trails faced?

The Santa Fe Trail The **Santa Fe Trail** was another important path west. It led from Independence, Missouri, to Santa Fe, New Mexico. It followed an ancient trading route first used by Native Americans. American traders loaded their wagon trains with cloth and other manufactured goods to exchange for horses, mules, and silver from Mexican traders in Santa Fe.

The long trip across blazing deserts and rough mountains was dangerous. But the lure of high profits encouraged traders to take to the trail. One trader reported a 2,000 percent profit on his cargo. The U.S. government helped protect traders by sending troops to ensure that Native Americans were not a threat.

Mormons Travel West One large group of settlers traveled to the West in search of religious freedom. In 1830 a young man named Joseph Smith founded the Church of Jesus Christ of Latter-day Saints in western New York. The members of his church became known as **Mormons**. Smith told his followers that he had found and translated a set of golden tablets containing religious teachings. The writings were called the *Book of Mormon*.

Church membership grew rapidly, but certain beliefs and practices caused Mormons to be persecuted. For example, beginning in the 1850s some Mormon men practiced polygamy—a practice in which one man is married to several women at the same time. The church outlawed this practice in 1890.

In the early 1830s Smith and his growing number of converts left New York. Many traveled on the recently completed Erie Canal and Lake Erie to Ohio, where they set up new communities. Later, they moved on and

This Mormon family took part in an early-1900s celebration of the pioneers who made the great trek along the Mormon Trail to Utah.

established communities in Missouri and Illinois. Eventually, these communities failed. The Illinois community collapsed after an anti-Mormon mob murdered Smith in 1844. Following Smith's murder, **Brigham Young** became head of the Mormon Church. Young chose what is now Utah as the group's new home, and thousands of Mormons took the Mormon Trail to the area near the Great Salt Lake, where they prospered. By 1860 there were about 40,000 Mormons in Utah.

Summary and Preview Some of the first Americans to move West were fur traders and trappers. Settlers soon followed. In the next lesson you will learn about America's continued westward expansion.

Reading Check
Summarize How did settlers travel west, and what challenges did they face on their journey?

Lesson 1 Assessment

Review Ideas, Terms, and People

1. a. Identify Who helped to open up the land west of the Appalachians by building the Wilderness Road?

b. Explain Why were New Orleans and the Mississippi River important to settlers in the West?

2. a. Summarize Why was the Louisiana Purchase important to the United States?

b. Describe What areas did the Lewis and Clark expedition and the Zebulon Pike and John C. Frémont expeditions explore?

c. Draw Conclusions Why were Meriwether Lewis and William Clark chosen to lead the exploration of the Louisiana Purchase?

3. a. Identify Who established one of the first American settlements in Oregon Country?

b. Describe What were the lives of mountain men like?

4. a. Identify What was the Oregon Trail?

b. Elaborate Would you have chosen to leave your home to travel West? Why?

c. Summarize What difficulties led Mormons to move to Utah?

Critical Thinking

5. Sequence In this lesson you learned about the westward expansion of the United States. Create a graphic organizer like the one below to rank the three most important effects of the Louisiana Purchase, from most important to least important, and explain why you chose that order.

Importance	Why
1.	
2.	
3.	

6. Draw Conclusions What challenges did the westward journey present for settlers?

7. Make Predictions What effects do you think westward migration of the mid-1800s would have on Native Americans?

America's Growth by 1820

In 1803 the United States made the biggest land purchase in its history—the Louisiana Purchase. With this purchase, the country stretched west all the way to the Rocky Mountains. In 1819 the United States acquired Florida from Spain, gaining even more new territory. By 1820 the young American republic had roughly doubled in size, as you can see on the map. Explorers, traders, and settlers began to pour into the new lands in search of wealth, land, and a place to call home.

—50°N

British Territory

Claimed by United States, ceded to Great Britain in 1818

49th Parallel

R O C K Y   M O U N T A I N S

Oregon Country Both the United States and Great Britain claimed Oregon Country.

Oregon Country

42nd Parallel

PACIFIC OCEAN

Spanish Territory

—30°N

America's Population, 1820: 10.1 million

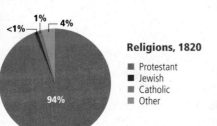

4%   1%
18%
77%

Ethnic Groups, 1820
- White/European
- African American
- Native American
- Other

1%   4%
<1%
94%

Religions, 1820
- Protestant
- Jewish
- Catholic
- Other

- Louisiana Purchase, 1803
- Claimed by United States and Great Britain, 1818
- Convention of 1818
- From Britain to United States, 1818
- Adams-Onís Treaty of 1819
- From Spain to United States, 1819

0	150	300 Miles
0	150	300 Kilometers

130°W   120°W   110°W

Early Traders Soon after Lewis and Clark explored the Louisiana Territory, American fur traders and trappers began setting up trading posts there. Many of these posts later became towns as more settlers arrived.

Through the Gaps Settlers crossed the Appalachians through valleys called gaps. In time, roads were built through the gaps, making it easier for settlers to head West.

ATLANTIC OCEAN

40°N

Unorganized Territory

Missouri River

Missouri Territory

Delaware Gap

APPALACHIAN MTS

Cumberland Gap

Arkansas Territory

Red River

Mississippi River

The Mighty Mississippi The Mississippi River was the great highway of the United States. Americans west of the Appalachians shipped farm goods and supplies up and down the Mississippi and to its major port, New Orleans.

Louisiana   New Orleans

Gulf of Mexico

Unorganized Territory (Florida)

70°W

Interpret Maps

1. **Movement** In which directions did the United States expand before 1820?

2. **Region** Based on the map, why do you think the United States was interested in claiming Oregon Country?

Boom Times in the West

The Big Idea
American settlers dramatically changed the western frontier as they began to tame the land.

Main Ideas
- Valuable deposits of gold and silver in the West created opportunities for wealth and brought more settlers to the region.
- The cattle industry thrived on the Great Plains, supplying beef to the East.
- The transcontinental railroad succeeded in linking the eastern and western United States.

Key Terms
frontier
Comstock Lode
boomtowns
Cattle Kingdom
cattle drive
Chisholm Trail
Pony Express
transcontinental railroad
standard time

Hydraulic Mining
Miners used high-powered water jets to blast earth from a hillside in order to expose the gold in the rock.

If YOU were there . . .

You are a cowboy in Texas in 1875. You love life on the open range, the quiet nights, and the freedom. You even like the hard work of the long cattle drives to Kansas. But you know that times are changing. Homesteaders are moving in and fencing off their lands. Some of the older cowboys say it's time to settle down and buy a small ranch. You hope that they're not right.

What would make you give up a cowboy's life?

Mining Boom Brings Growth

During the years surrounding the Civil War, most Americans had thought of the Great Plains and other western lands as the Great American Desert. In the years following the Civil War, Americans witnessed the rapid growth of the U.S. population and the spread of settlements throughout the West. With the admission of the state of California to the Union in 1850, the western boundary of the American **frontier**—an undeveloped area—had reached the Pacific Ocean.

The frontier changed dramatically as more and more people moved westward. Settlers built homes, fenced off land, and laid out ranches and farms. Miners, ranchers, and farmers remade the landscape of the West as they adapted to their new surroundings. The geography of the West was further changed by the development and expansion of a large and successful railroad industry that moved the West's natural resources to eastern markets. Gold and silver were the most valuable natural resources, and mining companies used the growing railroad network to bring these precious metals to the East.

Big Business Most of the precious metals were located in western Nevada. In 1859 miner Henry Comstock discovered a huge deposit of gold and silver in Nevada that became called the **Comstock Lode**. The deposit was incredibly rich

Posters like this one were designed to persuade people to move West.

and deep. In just the first year after its discovery, the Comstock Lode lured thousands of California miners to Nevada. Over the next 20 years, the Comstock Lode produced more than $500 million worth of gold and silver.

Expensive equipment was needed to remove the silver and gold that were trapped within quartz rock. Larger mining companies bought up land claims from miners who could not afford this machinery. As a result, mining became a big business in the West.

As companies dug bigger and deeper mines, the work became more dangerous. Miners had to use unsafe equipment, such as elevator platforms without protective walls. They worked in dark tunnels and breathed hot, stuffy air. They suffered from lung disease caused by dusty air. Miners often were injured or killed by poorly planned explosions or by cave-ins. Fire was also a great danger. Mining was therefore one of the most dangerous jobs in the country. In the West, worries about safety and pay led miners to form several unions in the 1860s.

Settlers People from all over the world came to work in the western mines. Some miners came from the eastern United States. Others emigrated from Europe, Central and South America, and Asia. Many Mexican immigrants and Mexican Americans were experienced miners. They were skilled in assaying, or testing, the contents of valuable ore. One newspaper reporter wrote, "Here were congregated the most varied elements of humanity . . . belonging to almost every nationality and every status of life."

New Towns Mining booms also produced **boomtowns**, communities that grew suddenly when a mine opened. They disappeared just as quickly when the mine closed. The California town of Bodie, located just southeast of Lake Tahoe, provides a vivid illustration of a mining boomtown. In the early 1870s it was a mining camp with just a handful of inhabitants. The discovery of a rich vein of gold in the late 1870s drew thousands. Within months, Bodie had become a bustling town of some 8,000 people. It had a railroad station, a school, two banks, three newspapers, two churches, and dozens of saloons. Once the gold in the mine was worked out, however, Bodie went into an equally rapid decline. By 1900 the population was less than 1,000.

Few women or families lived in even the most bustling boomtowns. "I was never so lonely and homesick in all my life," wrote one young woman. The women who did settle there washed, cooked, made clothes, and chopped wood. They also raised families, established schools, and wrote for newspapers. Their work helped turn some boomtowns into successful, permanent towns.

Reading Check
Summarize What risks did miners face?

Cattle Ranching in the West

The cattle industry was another area of rapid growth. Following the Civil War, a growing economy and population created a greater demand for beef in the East. Cattle worth $3 to $6 each in Texas could be sold for $38 each in Kansas. In New York, they could be sold for $80 each. The most popular breed of cattle was the longhorn. The longhorn breed spread quickly throughout western Texas. Because these animals needed very little water and could survive harsh weather, they were well suited to the dry, desert-like environment of western Texas. But how could Texas ranchers move the longhorns to eastern markets?

In 1867 businessman Joseph McCoy discovered a solution. He built pens for cattle in the small town of Abilene, Kansas. The Kansas Pacific Railroad line went through Abilene. As a result, cattle could be shipped by rail from there. Soon, countless Texas ranchers were making the trip north to Abilene to sell their herds of cattle.

Around the same time, cattle ranching began to expand in the Midwest. The vast open range of the Great Plains from Texas to Canada, where many ranchers raised cattle in the late 1800s, became known as the **Cattle Kingdom**. Ranchers grazed huge herds on public land called the open range. The land had once been occupied by Plains Indians and buffalo herds.

Importance of Cowboys The workers who took care of the ranchers' cattle were known as cowhands or cowboys. They adopted many techniques and tools from vaqueros (bah-KER-ohs), Mexican ranch hands who cared for cattle and horses. From vaqueros came the western saddle and the lariat, a rope used for lassoing cattle. The cowboys also borrowed the vaqueros' boot. Its narrow toe fit easily into the riding stirrup, and the high heel hooked the stirrup for stability. Cowboys adopted and changed the vaqueros' broad felt hat, turning it into the familiar high-peaked cowboy hat.

One of the cowboy's most important and dangerous duties was the **cattle drive**. On these long journeys, cowboys herded cattle to the market or to the northern Plains for grazing. These long drives usually lasted several months and covered hundreds of miles. Workdays on the drive were long—often up to 15 hours—and sometimes very dull. Excitement came with events such as stampedes. Frightened by a sudden noise such as a thunderclap, the whole herd would take off running wildly. Bringing the herd under control was dangerous and hard work. The **Chisholm Trail**, which ran from San Antonio, Texas, to the cattle town of Abilene, Kansas, was one of the earliest and most popular routes for cattle drives. It was blazed, or marked, by Texas cowboy Jesse Chisholm in the late 1860s.

At times, rowdy cowboys made life in cattle towns rough and violent. There were rarely shoot-outs in the street, but there often was disorderly behavior. Law officials such as Wyatt Earp became famous for keeping the peace in cattle towns.

End of the Open Range As the cattle business boomed, ranchers faced more competition for use of the open range. Farmers began to buy range

Myth and Reality in the Wild West

No episode in American history has given rise to as many myths as the Wild West. Writers of dime novels, popular in the East, helped create the myths in the years after the Civil War. Even today, popular books, television shows, and movies continue to portray the West in ways that are more myth than reality.

Myth: The cowboy was a free-spirited individual.

Reality: Most cowboys were employees. Many joined labor unions and even went on strike.

Myth: Western cow towns were wild places where cowboys had gunfights, and there was little law and order.

Reality: Most were orderly places with active law enforcement. Showdowns rarely, if ever, occurred.

Myth: Almost all cowboys were Anglo Americans.

Reality: About 25 percent of cowboys were African Americans, and 12 percent were Hispanic. Some Native Americans also worked as cowhands.

African American cowboy Nat Love (above); Marshal Wyatt Earp (left)

land on the Great Plains, where cattle had once grazed. Small ranchers also began competing with large ranchers for land. Then in 1874, Joseph Glidden's invention of barbed wire allowed westerners to fence off large amounts of land cheaply. The competition between farmers, large ranchers, and small ranchers increased. This competition led to range wars, or fights for access to land.

Making matters worse, in 1885 and 1886, disaster struck the Cattle Kingdom. The huge cattle herds on the Plains had eaten most of the prairie grass. Unusually severe winters in both years made the ranching situation even worse. Thousands of cattle died, and many ranchers were ruined financially. The Cattle Kingdom had come to an end.

Reading Check
Draw Conclusions
Why did the Cattle Kingdom come to an end?

The Transcontinental Railroad

As more Americans began moving West, the need to send goods and information between the East and West increased. Americans searched for ways to improve communication and travel across the country.

In 1860 a system of messengers on horseback called the **Pony Express** began to carry the mail West. The Pony Express operated from St. Joseph, Missouri, to Sacramento, California, a route of almost 2,000 miles. The business purchased over 400 horses, and riders used a relay system, switching horses at stations 10 to 15 miles apart. The Pony Express cut mail delivery time in half, from three weeks to ten days. The completion of a telegraph line to California in 1861, which sent messages much faster, quickly put the Pony Express out of business.

The Pony Express mail system helped speed up communication across the United States.

Routes West, 1870

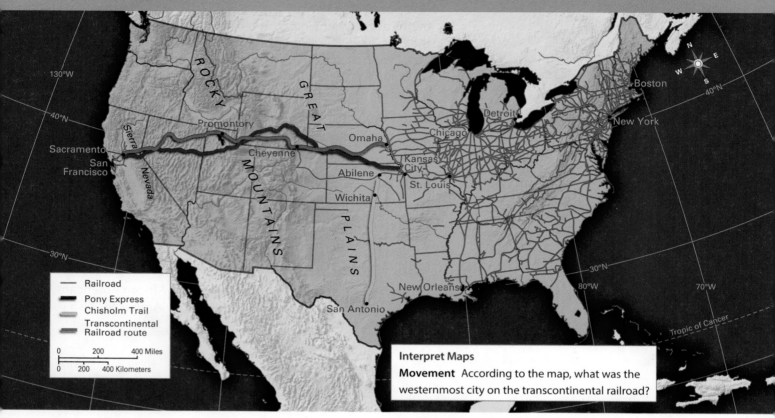

Interpret Maps

Movement According to the map, what was the westernmost city on the transcontinental railroad?

Map Legend:
- Railroad
- Pony Express
- Chisholm Trail
- Transcontinental Railroad route

0   200   400 Miles
0   200   400 Kilometers

Some Americans wanted to build a **transcontinental railroad**—a railroad that would cross the continent and connect the East to the West. The federal government, therefore, passed the Pacific Railway Acts in 1862 and in 1864. These acts gave railroad companies loans and large land grants that could be sold to pay for construction costs. Congress had granted more than 131 million acres of public land to railroad companies. In exchange, the government asked the railroads to carry U.S. mail and troops at a lower cost. Many railroad companies were inspired to begin laying miles of track.

Great Race Two companies, the Central Pacific and the Union Pacific, led the race to complete the transcontinental railroad. In February 1863 the Central Pacific began building east from Sacramento, California. At the end of the year, the Union Pacific started building west from Omaha, Nebraska.

The Union Pacific hired thousands of railroad workers, particularly Irish immigrants. Chinese immigrants made up some 85 percent of the Central Pacific workforce. The railroad's part-owner Leland Stanford praised them, but he paid them less than other laborers. Chinese crews also were given the most dangerous tasks and had to work longer hours than other railroad laborers. They took the job, however, because the $30 a month that the Central Pacific paid was as much as ten times what they could earn in China.

Railroad companies faced many geographic challenges. For example, workers for Central Pacific struggled to cross the Sierra Nevada mountain range in California. Breaking apart its rock formations required setting carefully controlled explosions using large amounts of blasting powder and the explosive nitroglycerin. And in the winter of 1866, snowdrifts more than 60 feet high trapped and killed dozens of workers. Faced with these obstacles, the Central Pacific took four years to lay the first 115 miles of track.

Meanwhile, Union Pacific workers faced harsh weather on the Great Plains. In addition, the company pressured them to work at a rapid pace—at times laying 250 miles of track in six months.

For both railroad companies, providing food and supplies for workers was vital. This job became more difficult in remote areas. The railroad companies consequently often relied on local resources. Professional hunters, such as William "Buffalo Bill" Cody, shot thousands of buffalo to feed Union Pacific workers.

Golden Spike Congress required the two completed rail lines to connect at Promontory, Utah. On May 10, 1869, a golden spike was used to connect the railroad tie joining the two tracks. Alexander Toponce witnessed the event.

> "Governor Stanford, president of the Central Pacific, took the sledge [hammer], and the first time he struck he missed the spike and hit the rail. What a howl went up! Irish, Chinese, Mexicans, and everybody yelled with delight. 'He missed it' . . . Then Stanford tried it again and tapped the spike."
>
> —Alexander Toponce, from *Reminiscences of Alexander Toponce, Written by Himself*

The railroad companies were not finished, though. Following completion of the transcontinental railroad, they continued building railroads until the West was crisscrossed with rail lines.

The Central Pacific and Union Pacific connected their tracks at Promontory, Utah, in 1869, completing the transcontinental railroad.

Results of the Railroad The transcontinental railroad increased both economic growth and the population in the West. Railroad companies provided better transportation for people and goods. They also sold land to settlers, which encouraged people to move West. The development of the West brought about the railroad; however, it also would prove to be the beginning of the end of the Plains Indians' way of life.

New railroads helped businesses. Western timber companies, miners, ranchers, and farmers shipped wood, metals, meat, and grain East by railroad. In exchange, eastern businesses shipped manufactured goods to the West. As trade between regions increased, the idea that the U.S. economy was interdependent became more widespread.

Even perceptions of time became more formal as railroad schedules began to unite areas that before had existed under different times. Before the railroads, each community determined its own time, based on calculations about the sun's travels. This system, called "solar time," caused problems for people who scheduled trains crossing a long distance. The railroad companies addressed the issue by setting up **standard time**. This system divided the United States into four time zones.

Railroad companies encouraged people to invest in the railroads, which they did—sometimes unwisely. Speculation and the collapse of railroad owner Jay Cooke's banking firm helped start the Panic of 1873. Despite such setbacks, Americans remained interested in railroad investments. By 1890 there were about 164,000 more miles of track than in 1865. Railroads had become one of the biggest industries in the United States.

Summary and Preview In this lesson you learned about the increased settlement of the West. In the next lesson you will learn about conflicts with Native Americans.

Reading Check
Find Main Ideas
How did the railroad affect the development of the West?

Lesson 2 Assessment

Review Ideas, Terms, and People

1. **a. Recall** Why did Americans move West in the years following the Civil War?

   b. Draw Conclusions What effect did the discovery of the Comstock Lode have on the West?

   c. Evaluate Do you think women were important to the success of mining towns? Why or why not?

2. **a. Recall** What led to the cattle boom in the West?

   b. Analyze Why was there competition between ranchers and farmers to settle in the Great Plains?

   c. Evaluate What played the biggest role in ending the Cattle Kingdom? Why?

3. **a. Recall** When and where did the Union Pacific and Central Pacific lines meet?

   b. Describe What role did Irish and Chinese immigrants play in opening up the West?

   c. Make Generalizations How do you think the transcontinental railroad improved people's lives?

Critical Thinking

4. **Identify Cause and Effect** In this lesson you learned about the kinds of economic opportunities that people found in the West. Create a graphic organizer similar to the one below to list these opportunities and their effects.

Opportunity	Effect

Wars for the West

The Big Idea

Native Americans and the U.S. government came into conflict over land in the West.

Main Ideas

- As settlers moved to the Great Plains, they encountered the Plains Indians.

- Native Americans attempted to keep their lands through treaties with the U.S. government.

- Continued pressure from white settlement and government legislation brought the Plains Indians' traditional way of life to an end.

Key Terms and People

Treaty of Fort Laramie
reservations
Crazy Horse
Treaty of Medicine Lodge
buffalo soldiers
George Armstrong Custer
Sitting Bull
Battle of the Little Bighorn
Massacre at Wounded Knee
Long Walk
Chief Joseph
Geronimo
Ghost Dance
Sarah Winnemucca
assimilate
Dawes General Allotment Act

If YOU were there . . .

You are a member of the Sioux nation, living in Dakota Territory in 1875. These lands are sacred to your people, and the U.S. government has promised them to you. But now gold has been found here, and the government has ordered you to give up your land. Some Sioux leaders want to fight. Others say that it is of no use, that the soldiers will win.

Would you fight to keep your lands? Why?

Settlers Encounter the Plains Indians

As miners and settlers began crossing the Great Plains in the mid-1800s, they pressured the federal government for more access to western lands. To protect these travelers, U.S. officials sent agents to negotiate treaties with the Plains Indians.

Crazy Horse (Tashunka Witco) was a Sioux chief who fought to defend his people's way of life and resisted attempts to force the Sioux onto reservations.

The Plains Indians lived in the Great Plains, which stretch north into Canada and south into Texas. Indian groups such as the Apache and the Comanche lived in and around Texas and what is now Oklahoma. The Cheyenne and the Arapaho lived in different regions across the central Plains. The Pawnee lived in parts of Nebraska. To the north were the Sioux. These groups spoke many different languages. However, they used a common sign language to communicate and they shared a similar lifestyle.

Hunting Buffalo For survival, the Plains Indians depended on two animals—the horse and the buffalo. The Spanish brought horses to America in the 1500s. The Plains Indians learned to ride horses, and hunters used them to follow buffalo herds year-round. While on horseback, most Plains Indian hunters used a short bow and arrows to shoot buffalo from close range.

The Plains Indians used buffalo for food, shelter, clothing, utensils, and tools. Women dried buffalo meat to make

The Plains Indians depended on two animals—the horse and the buffalo.

jerky. They made tepees and clothing from buffalo hides, and cups and tools from buffalo horns. As one Sioux explained, "When our people killed a buffalo, all of the animal was utilized [used] in some manner; nothing was wasted." The Plains Indians prospered. By 1850 some 75,000 Native Americans lived on the Plains.

Struggle to Keep Land Miners and settlers were also increasing in numbers—and they wanted the Indians' land. The U.S. government tried to avoid disputes by negotiating the **Treaty of Fort Laramie**, the first major treaty between the U.S. government and Plains Indians. Two years later, several southern Plains nations signed a treaty at Fort Atkinson in Nebraska. These treaties recognized Indian claims to most of the Great Plains. They also allowed the United States to build forts and roads and to travel across Indian homelands. The U.S. government promised to pay for any damages to Indian lands.

The treaties did not keep the peace for long. In 1858 the discovery of gold in what is now Colorado brought thousands of miners to the West. They soon clashed with the Cheyenne and the Arapaho. In 1861 the U.S. government negotiated new treaties with Plains Indians. These treaties created **reservations**, areas of federal land set aside for Native Americans. The government expected Indians to stay on the reservations, which made hunting buffalo almost impossible.

Pioneers and miners continued to cross the Great Plains. Many miners used the Bozeman Trail. To protect them, the U.S. Army built forts along the trail, which ran through favored Sioux hunting grounds. The Sioux responded with war. In late 1866 a group led by **Crazy Horse**, an Oglala Sioux chief, ambushed and killed 81 cavalry troops.

In 1868, under the Second Treaty of Fort Laramie, the U.S. government agreed to close the Bozeman Trail, abandon the forts, and provide reservation land to the Sioux.

Reading Check
Summarize What
was the federal policy
toward the Plains
Indians in the 1860s
and 1870s?

The U.S. government also negotiated for southern Plains Indians to move off their land. In the 1867 **Treaty of Medicine Lodge**, most southern Plains Indians agreed to live on reservations. However, many Indians did not want to give up their hunting grounds. Fighting soon broke out between the Comanche and Texans. The U.S. Army and the Texas Rangers were unable to defeat the Comanche, so they cut off the Comanche's access to food and water. In 1875 the last of the Comanche war leaders surrendered.

Fighting on the Plains

In the northern Plains, Southwest, and Far West, Native Americans continued to resist being moved to and confined on reservations. The U.S. government sent troops into the area to force the Indians to leave. These troops included African American cavalry, who the Indians called **buffalo soldiers**—a term of honor, inspired by their short, curly hair, that compared their fighting spirit to that of the buffalo.

Battles on the Northern Plains As fighting on the southern Plains came to an end, new trouble started in the north. In 1874 Lieutenant Colonel

▶ *Explore ONLINE!*

Native American Land Loss in the West, 1850–1890

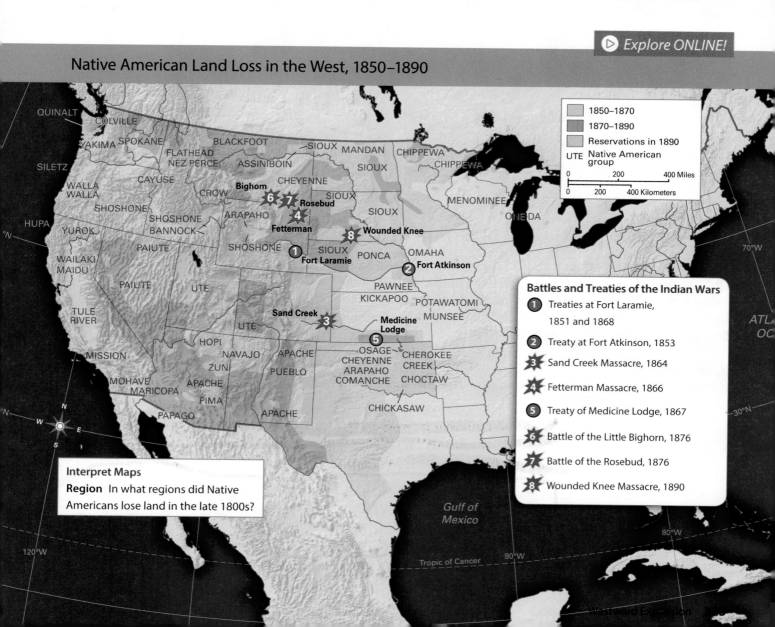

Interpret Maps

Region In what regions did Native Americans lose land in the late 1800s?

The Native Americans are shown surrounding a small force of U.S. soldiers.

Custer is shown standing among his men as he fires.

The U.S. Army is shown on horseback in this drawing.

These horses have been captured by the Native Americans.

Two Views of a Historic Battle

Art historians have identified about 1,000 paintings of the Battle of the Little Bighorn. The painting at the top was painted in 1899. The drawing below it is one of the many colored-pencil drawings of the battle done by Amos Bad Heart Buffalo, who based his drawing on memories from Sioux warriors who participated in the battle.

Analyze Visuals
How do these paintings show the influences of different cultures?

George Armstrong Custer's soldiers discovered gold in the Black Hills of the Dakotas. **Sitting Bull**, a leader of the Lakota Sioux, protested U.S. demands for the land.

"What treaty that the whites have kept has the red man broken? Not one. What treaty that the white man ever made with us have they kept? Not one."

—Sitting Bull, quoted in *Life of Sitting Bull and the History of the Indian Wars of 1890–1891* by W. Fletcher Johnson

Apache leader Geronimo fought settlers on his land for more than 25 years—all the while avoiding permanent capture.

Other Sioux leaders listened to Sitting Bull and refused to give up land. During late 1875 and early 1876, many Sioux and Cheyenne warriors left their reservations. They united under the leadership of Sitting Bull and Crazy Horse. Their plan was to drive the intruders from the Black Hills. Custer was sent to force the Native Americans back onto their reservations.

On June 25, 1876, Custer's scouts found a large Sioux camp along the Little Bighorn River in Montana Territory. Leading about 200 of his soldiers, Custer raced ahead without waiting for any supporting forces. In the **Battle of the Little Bighorn**, Sioux and Cheyenne forces led by Crazy Horse surrounded and defeated Custer and his troops. Newspapers called the battle "Custer's Last Stand" because his entire command was killed. It was the worst defeat the U.S. Army suffered in the West. The Battle of the Little Bighorn was also the Sioux's last major victory in the Sioux Wars.

In 1881 Sitting Bull and a few followers returned from Canada where they had fled after Little Bighorn. They had run out of food during the hard winter. They joined the Sioux on Standing Rock Reservation in Dakota Territory.

Almost a decade later, in 1890, while following orders to arrest Sitting Bull, reservation police killed him. Many Sioux left the reservation in protest. Later that year, the U.S. Army shot and killed about 150 Sioux near Wounded Knee Creek in South Dakota. This **Massacre at Wounded Knee** was the last major military incident on the Great Plains.

Southwest The Navajo lived in what became Arizona and New Mexico. In 1863 the Navajo refused to settle on a reservation. In response, U.S. troops made raids on the Navajo's fields, homes, and livestock.

When the Navajo ran out of food and shelter, they started surrendering to the U.S. Army. In 1864 the army led Navajo captives on the **Long Walk**. On this brutal 300-mile march, the Navajo were forced to walk across the desert to a reservation in Bosque Redondo, New Mexico. Along the way, countless Navajo died.

Far West The United States had promised to let the peaceful Nez Percé keep their land in Oregon. Within a few years, however, the government ordered the Nez Percé to a reservation in what is now Idaho. A group of Nez Percé led by **Chief Joseph** resisted, and in 1877 left to seek refuge in Canada. For four months, they crossed more than 1,000 miles with army troops in pursuit. Near the border, U.S. troops overtook them and sent them to a reservation in what is now Oklahoma.

Final Battles By the 1880s, most Native Americans had stopped fighting. The Apache of the Southwest, however, continued to battle the U.S. Army. A Chiricahua Apache named **Geronimo** and his band led raids on both sides of the Arizona–Mexico border, avoiding capture for many years. In September 1886 Geronimo surrendered and was sent to an Apache internment camp in Florida. This ended the Apache armed resistance in the Southwest.

Reading Check
Contrast How did the Apache resistance differ from that of the Navajo?

A Way of Life Ends

By the 1870s many Native Americans lived on reservations, where land was usually not useful for farming or buffalo hunting. Many were starving.

A Paiute Indian named Wovoka began a religious movement, the **Ghost Dance**, that predicted the arrival of paradise for Native Americans. In this paradise, the buffalo herds would return and the settlers would disappear.

U.S. officials did not understand the meaning of the Ghost Dance. They feared it would lead to rebellion, so they tried to end the movement, which had spread to other groups, including the Sioux. After the massacre in 1890 at Wounded Knee, the Ghost Dance movement gradually died out.

In the late 1870s a Paiute Indian named **Sarah Winnemucca** called for reform—particularly of the reservation system. A writer, educator, and interpreter, she toured the country speaking on behalf of Native Americans. Her 1883 autobiography *Life Among the Paiutes* is one of the

BIOGRAPHY

Chief Joseph c. 1840–1904

Chief Joseph became leader of the Nez Percé in 1871. He led his people in an effort to hold onto their homeland and to avoid war with the United States. In 1877, when the U.S. government ordered the Nez Percé to relocate to a reservation, Chief Joseph at first agreed, but then was forced to flee. He attempted to escape into Canada with about 750 of his people. On a courageous journey across Idaho, Montana, Oregon, and Washington, they defeated pursuing troops who greatly outnumbered them. Traveling with families, and low on supplies, the Nez Percé managed to evade the U.S. Army for four months. Ultimately though, Chief Joseph saw that resistance was futile. Upon his surrender, he gave a speech that has become one of the most famous in American history.

"I am tired of fighting. Our chiefs are killed. . . . The old men are all dead. . . . It is cold, and we have no blankets. The little children are freezing to death. My people, some of them, have run away to the hills, and have no blankets, no food. No one knows where they are—perhaps freezing to death. I want to have time to look for my children, and see how many of them I can find. Maybe I shall find them among the dead. Hear me, my chiefs! I am tired. My heart is sick and sad. From where the sun now stands I will fight no more forever."

—Chief Joseph, October 5, 1877

Identify Cause and Effect
What brought suffering to Chief Joseph and his people?

Sarah Winnemucca spoke out for the fair treatment of her people.

most significant accounts of traditional Native American culture. Writer Helen Hunt Jackson published a book in 1881 that pushed for reform of U.S. Indian policy. Titled *A Century of Dishonor*, it described the mistreatment of many Native American groups in an attempt to force the government to establish fairer policies.

Some reformers believed that Native Americans should **assimilate** by giving up traditional ways and adopting the ways of white people. The **Dawes General Allotment Act** of 1887 tried to lessen traditional influences on Indian society by making land ownership private rather than shared. The act also promised—but failed to deliver—U.S. citizenship to Native Americans. After breaking up reservation land, the government sold the acreage remaining. The act took about two-thirds of Indian land.

The U.S. government also sent many Native American children to boarding schools in an effort to "Americanize" them. The children were dressed in European-style clothes, learned English, and often spent part of the day farming or doing other work. They were discouraged from practicing their own culture or speaking their own language. Many were separated from their families for years at a time.

Reading Check
Summarize
How did reformers try to influence Native Americans' lives?

Summary and Preview In this lesson you read about conflict in the settlement of the West. In the next lesson you will learn more about Great Plains settlers.

Lesson 3 Assessment

Review Ideas, Terms, and People

1. **a. Describe** What animals did Plains Indians depend on, and how did they use those animals?

   b. Analyze How did U.S. policy toward the Plains Indians change in the late 1850s?

   c. Elaborate Would you have agreed to move to a reservation? Why or why not?

2. **a. Describe** What events led to the Battle of the Little Bighorn?

   b. Elaborate Why do you think most Indian groups eventually stopped resisting the United States?

3. **a. Describe** How did the Dawes General Allotment Act affect American Indians?

   b. Predict What effect do you think the Massacre at Wounded Knee would have on relations between Plains Indians and the United States?

Critical Thinking

4. **Sequence** In this lesson you learned about the major events surrounding the loss of land rights of Native Americans. Create a timeline similar to the one below to organize the events in sequence.

1851   1864 1867   1887

Farming and Populism

The Big Idea

Settlers on the Great Plains created new communities and a unique political movement.

Main Ideas

- Many Americans started new lives on the Great Plains.
- Economic challenges led to the creation of farmers' political groups.
- By the 1890s the western frontier had come to an end.

Key Terms and People

Homestead Act
Morrill Act
Exodusters
sodbusters
dry farming
Annie Bidwell
National Grange
deflation
William Jennings Bryan
Populist Party

If YOU were there . . .

You are a female schoolteacher in Wisconsin in 1880. You live and teach in a small town, but you grew up on a farm and are used to hard work. Now you are thinking about moving West to claim free land from the government. You could teach in a school there, too. You think it would be an exciting adventure, but your family is horrified that a single woman would move West on her own.

Would you decide to become a homesteader?

New Lives on the Plains

In 1862 Congress passed two important land grant acts that helped open the West to settlers. The **Homestead Act** gave government-owned land to small farmers. Any adult who was a U.S. citizen or planned to become one could receive 160 acres of land. In exchange, homesteaders promised to live on the land for five years. The **Morrill Act** granted more than 17 million acres of federal land to the states. The act required each state to sell this land and to use the money to build colleges to teach agriculture and engineering.

Pioneers like this family often lived in houses made of sod because there were few trees for lumber on the Plains.

This family of African Americans moved to the West in order to build new lives after the Civil War.

Settling the Plains People from all over the country moved West. Many farming families moved from areas where farmland was becoming scarce or expensive, such as New England. Many single women moved West. The Homestead Act granted land to unmarried women, which was unusual for the time.

In the late 1870s, large numbers of African Americans began to move West. Some fled the South because of violence and repression. The end of Reconstruction in 1877 led to harsh new segregation laws. Also, the withdrawal of federal troops left African Americans unprotected from attacks by such groups as the Ku Klux Klan. Benjamin "Pap" Singleton, a former slave from Tennessee, inspired others. Born in Nashville in 1809, Singleton fled slavery several times. Eventually he got to the North and settled in Detroit. There, he helped runaway slaves escape to Canada. After the Civil War, he returned to Tennessee. He wanted to help freed African Americans buy farmland. However, white landowners refused to sell. So he urged African Americans to leave the South and build their own communities in Kansas and elsewhere in the West.

By 1879 some 20,000 southern African Americans had moved to Kansas. Many others settled in Missouri, Indiana, and Illinois. These African American migrants were known as **Exodusters** because they had made a mass exodus, or departure, from the South.

The promise of free land also drew thousands of Europeans to the West. Scandinavians from Norway, Sweden, Denmark, and Finland came to the northern Great Plains in the 1870s. Many Irish who had helped to build the railroads decided to settle on the Plains. Russians also came to the Plains, bringing with them their experience of farming on the vast steppes, or grasslands, of their homeland. Germans and Czechs created many small farming communities on the Plains, especially in Texas.

Letter from the Plains, 1863

In a letter to her family in Norway, immigrant Gro Svendsen describes her new life as a farmer on the plains of Iowa.

"I remember I used to wonder when I heard that it would be impossible to keep the milk here as we did at home. Now I have learned that it is indeed impossible because of the heat here in the summertime . . . It's difficult, too, to preserve the butter. One must pour brine [salt water] over it or salt it.

The thunderstorms are so violent that one might think it was the end of the world . . . Quite often the lightning strikes down both cattle and people, damages property, and splinters sturdy oak trees into many pieces."

—quoted in *Frontier Mother: The Letters of Gro Svendsen*

Analyze Historical Sources
What might be some of the differences between Norway and Svendsen's new home in Iowa?

Laura Ingalls Wilder (right) wrote the *Little House on the Prairie* series based on her childhood in a settler family.

Academic Vocabulary
facilitate to make easier

Farming the Plains Plains farmers had many unique challenges. The seasons were extreme. Weather could be harsh. Also, the root-filled sod, or dirt, beneath the Plains grass was very tough. The hard work of breaking up the sod earned Plains farmers the nickname **sodbusters**.

In the 1890s western Plains farmers began **dry farming**, a new method of farming that shifted the focus away from water-dependent crops such as corn. Instead, farmers grew more hardy crops like red wheat. In addition, new inventions helped Plains farmers meet some of the challenges of frontier life. A steel plow invented by John Deere in 1837 and improved upon by James Oliver in 1868 sliced through the tough sod of the prairie. Windmills adapted to the Plains pumped water from deep wells to the surface. Barbed wire allowed farmers to fence in land and livestock. Reapers made the harvesting of crops much easier, and threshers helped farmers to separate grain or seed from straw.

These inventions also made farm work more efficient. During the late 1800s, farmers greatly increased their crop production. They shipped their harvest east by train. From there, crops were shipped overseas. The Great Plains soon became known as the breadbasket of the world.

Building Communities Women were an important force in the settlement of the frontier. They joined in the hard work of farming and ranching and helped build communities out of the widely spaced farms and small towns. Their role in founding communities **facilitated** a strong voice in public affairs. Wyoming women, for example, were granted the vote in the new state's constitution, which was approved in 1869. **Annie Bidwell**, one of the founders of Chico, California, used her influence to support a variety of moral and social causes such as women's suffrage and temperance.

Reading Check
Compare and Contrast How were settlers' lives alike and different from their lives in the East?

Many early settlers found life on their remote farms to be extremely difficult. Farmers formed communities so that they could assist one another in times of need. One of the first things that many pioneer communities did was establish a local church and school.

Children helped with many chores around the farm. Author Laura Ingalls Wilder was one of four children in a pioneer family. Wilder's books about settlers' lives on the prairie are still popular today.

Farmers' Political Groups

From 1860 to 1900, the U.S. population more than doubled. To feed this growing population, the number of farms tripled. With modern machines, farmers in 1900 could harvest a bushel of wheat almost 20 times faster than they could in 1830.

Farm Incomes Fall The combination of more farms and greater productivity, however, led to overproduction. Overproduction resulted in lower prices for crops. As their incomes decreased, many farmers found it difficult to pay bills. Farmers who could not make their mortgage payments lost their farms and homes. Many of these homeless farmers became tenant farmers who worked land owned by others. By 1880 one-fourth of all farms were rented by tenants, and the number continued to grow.

The National Grange Many farmers blamed businesspeople—wholesalers, brokers, grain buyers, and especially railroad owners—for making money at their expense. As economic conditions worsened, farmers began to follow the example of other workers. They formed associations to protect and help their interests.

Explore ONLINE!

Agricultural Supply and Demand

Connect to Economics The amount of goods available for sale is the supply. The willingness and ability of consumers to buy goods is called demand. The law of supply and demand says that when supply increases or demand decreases, prices fall. By contrast, when supply decreases or demand rises, prices rise.

What happened to the price of wheat as the supply increased?

Wheat Production, 1866–1880

Wheat Prices, 1866–1880

After the founding of the National Grange, other groups, including the Farmers' Alliance, formed to advance the interests of farmers.

One such organization was founded by Oliver Hudson Kelley, who toured the South in 1866 for the U.S. Department of Agriculture. Kelley saw firsthand how the country's farmers suffered. Afterward, Kelley and several government clerks formed the National Grange of the Patrons of Husbandry in 1867. The **National Grange** was a social and educational organization for farmers. (*Grange* is an old word for "granary.") Local chapters were quickly founded, and membership grew rapidly.

The Grange campaigned for political candidates who supported farmers' goals. The organization also called for laws that regulated rates charged by railroads. The U.S. Supreme Court ruled in 1877 that the government could regulate railroads because they affected the public interest. In 1886 the Court said that the federal government could only regulate companies doing business across state lines. Rate regulation for railroad lines within states fell to the state governments.

In February 1887 Congress passed the Interstate Commerce Act, providing national regulations over trade between states and creating the Interstate Commerce Commission to ensure fair railroad rates. However, the commission lacked power to enforce its regulations.

Free Silver Debate Money issues also caused problems for farmers. Many farmers hoped that help would come from new laws affecting the money supply.

Since 1873 the United States had been on the gold standard, meaning that all paper money had to be backed by gold in the treasury. As a result, the money supply grew more slowly than the nation's population and led to **deflation**—a decrease in the money supply and overall lower prices. One solution was to allow the unlimited coining of silver and to back paper currency with silver. This was the position of those in the Free Silver movement.

During the late 1870s, there was a great deal of support for the Free Silver movement. Many farmers began backing political candidates who favored free silver coinage. One such candidate was **William Jennings Bryan** of Nebraska.

The two major political parties, however, largely ignored the money issue. After the election of 1888, the Republican-controlled Congress passed the Sherman Silver Purchase Act. The act increased the amount of silver purchased for coinage. However, this did not help farmers as much as they had hoped.

Populist Party To have greater power, many farmers organized to elect candidates who would help them. These political organizations became known as the Farmers' Alliances.

In the 1890 elections the Alliances were a strong political force. State and local wins raised farmers' political hopes. At a conference in Cincinnati, Ohio, in 1891, Alliance leaders met with labor and reform groups. Then, at a convention in St. Louis in February 1892, the Alliances formed a new national political party.

William Jennings Bryan
1860–1925

William Jennings Bryan was born in Illinois but moved to Nebraska when he finished law school. He was elected Nebraska's first Democratic Congress member in 1890. Through his political campaigns and work as a newspaper editor, he became one of the best-known supporters of Populist ideas. After a dramatic speech at the 1896 Democratic National Convention, Bryan was nominated for the presidency. He was the youngest presidential candidate up to that time. Although he lost the election, he continued to be an influential speaker and political leader. Many of the reforms that he fought for in the late 1800s, such as an eight-hour workday and woman suffrage, later became law.

Make Inferences
Why was Bryan's support of Populist ideas important?

The new party was called the **Populist Party**, and it called for the government to own railroads and telephone and telegraph systems. It also favored the "free and unlimited coinage of silver." To gain the votes of workers, the Populists backed an eight-hour workday and limits on immigration.

The concerns of the Populists were soon put in the national spotlight. During the Panic of 1893, the U.S. economy experienced a crisis that some critics blamed on the shortage of gold. The failure of several major railroad companies also contributed to the economic problems.

The Panic of 1893 led more people to back the Populist call for economic reform. In 1896 the Republicans nominated William McKinley for president. McKinley was firmly against free coinage of silver. The Democrats nominated William Jennings Bryan, a strong supporter of the Free Silver movement.

The Populists had to decide between running their own candidate, and thus splitting the silver vote, or supporting Bryan. They decided to support Bryan. The Republicans had a well-financed campaign, and they won the election. McKinley's victory in 1896 marked the end of both the Populist Party and the Farmers' Alliances.

Reading Check
Summarize Why did farmers, laborers, and reformers join to form the Populist Party?

End of the Frontier

By 1870 only small portions of the Great Plains remained unsettled. For most of the next two decades, this land remained open range.

In March 1889, government officials announced that homesteaders could file claims on land in what is now the state of Oklahoma. This land had belonged to Creek and Seminole Indians. Within a month, about 50,000 people rushed to Oklahoma to stake their claims.

In all, settlers claimed more than 11 million acres of former Indian land in the famous Oklahoma land rush. This huge wave of pioneers was the

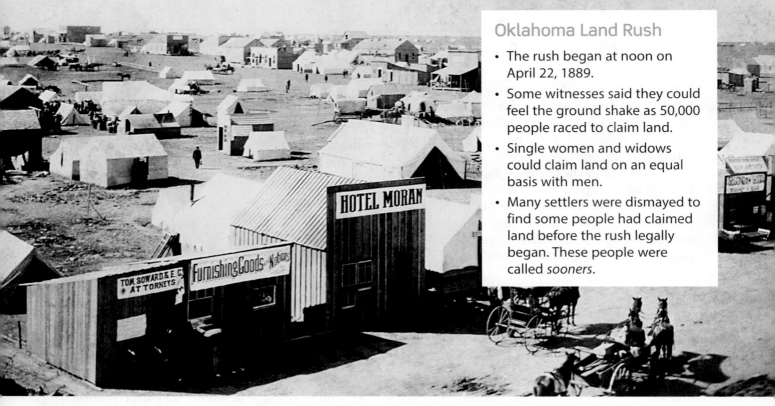

Oklahoma Land Rush

- The rush began at noon on April 22, 1889.
- Some witnesses said they could feel the ground shake as 50,000 people raced to claim land.
- Single women and widows could claim land on an equal basis with men.
- Many settlers were dismayed to find some people had claimed land before the rush legally began. These people were called *sooners*.

Guthrie, Oklahoma

Reading Check
Find Main Ideas
What event signaled the closing of the frontier?

last chapter of the westward movement. From the time it began gathering information, the U.S. Census Bureau had mapped a "frontier line" along the edge of western population. The 1890 census showed that more than 20 million people lived between the Mississippi River and the Pacific coast. "There can hardly be said to be a frontier line," a Bureau report stated. The disappearance of the "line" is considered the closing of the frontier.

Summary and Preview In this lesson you read about the challenges settlers in the West faced. Despite these difficulties, the promise of open land and a fresh start continued to lure Americans westward.

Lesson 4 Assessment

Review Ideas, Terms, and People

1. a. Describe What groups settled in the Great Plains?

b. Explain How did the U.S. government make lands available to western settlers?

c. Elaborate Would you have chosen to settle on the frontier? Why or why not?

2. a. Recall What was the goal of the National Grange?

b. Make Inferences Why did the Populist Party want the government to own railroads and telegraph and telephone systems?

c. Evaluate Do you think farmers were successful in bringing about economic and political change? Explain.

3. a. Recall What was the Oklahoma land rush?

b. Explain Why did the frontier cease to exist in the United States?

Critical Thinking

4. Compare and Contrast In this lesson you learned about the reasons for the rise of populism in the United States. Create a table similar to the one below to explain why Populists sought the changes they did.

Change sought	Reason why

Social Studies Skills

Compare Migration Maps

Define the Skill

One of the best ways of using geography to learn history is by comparing maps. This skill allows you to see changes over time. It also helps you see relationships between one factor, such as population growth, and another factor, such as transportation routes or economic activities in an area.

Learn the Skill

Follow these steps to compare information on maps.

1. Apply basic map skills by reading the title and studying the legend and symbols for each map.

2. Note the date of each map and the area it covers. Maps compared for changes over time should include the same areas. Those used to look for relationships should have similar dates.

3. Note similarities or differences. Closely examine and compare each map's patterns and symbols.

4. Apply critical thinking skills. Make generalizations and draw conclusions about the relationships you find.

Practice the Skill

Use the maps below to answer the following questions.

1. What present-day state was unsettled by Americans in 1850 and almost completely settled in 1890?

2. Which other two present-day states show the most settlement by Americans from 1850 to 1890?

3. Why do you think the West coast was settled before the interior of the United States?

4. According to the maps, how might rivers have shaped the settlement of the West?

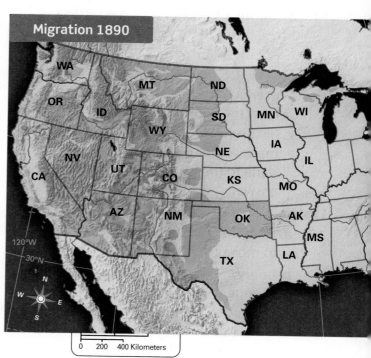

Module 11 Assessment

Review Vocabulary, Terms, and People

Complete each sentence by filling in the blank with the correct term or person.

1. In 1803 Congress approved the _____, which added former French territory in the West to the United States.

2. Members of the Church of Jesus Christ of Latter-day Saints were known as _____.

3. _____ were fur traders and trappers who lived west of the Rocky Mountains and in the Pacific Northwest.

4. The _____ Trail, which ran from Missouri to New Mexico, was an important route for trade between American and Mexican merchants.

5. _____ lead the 7th Cavalry in the Battle of the Little Bighorn.

6. The _____ gave government-owned land to small farmers. In return the farmers had to live on the land for at least five years.

7. A Paiute Indian named _____ worked hard to reform the reservation system.

8. The _____ Trail was one of the most popular routes for cattle drives.

9. The huge deposit of gold and silver found in Nevada in 1859 was known as the _____.

10. Formed in 1867, the _____ was a social and educational organization for farmers.

Comprehension and Critical Thinking

Lesson 1

11. a. **Identify** Which routes did settlers use to move into the land west of the Appalachians?

    b. **Draw Conclusions** What are three ways in which the United States benefited from the Louisiana Purchase?

    c. **Evaluate** Do you think that Napoléon made a wise decision when he sold Louisiana to the United States? Explain your answer.

Lesson 2

12. a. **Recall** Why were many Americans eager to move to the western frontier?

    b. **Analyze** How did railroads and ranching change the landscape of the West?

    c. **Elaborate** In your opinion, which made the greatest changes to the West—mining, ranching, or railroads? Explain your answer.

Lesson 3

13. a. **Describe** What was life like for the Plains Indians before and after the arrival of large numbers of American settlers?

    b. **Draw Conclusions** Why did the spread of the Ghost Dance movement cause concern for U.S. officials?

    c. **Elaborate** What do you think about the reservation system established by the United States?

Lesson 4

14. a. **Identify** What political organizations did western farmers create? Why did farmers create these organizations?

    b. **Analyze** How did women participate in the settling of the American frontier?

    c. **Predict** How might the end of the frontier in the United States affect the nation?

Module 11 Assessment, continued

Review Themes

15. **Geography** Through what geographic regions did the Lewis and Clark expedition travel?

16. **Geography** What geographic obstacles did miners, ranchers, and railroad workers face in the West?

17. **Science and Technology** What types of technology did farmers on the Great Plains use, and how did it benefit them?

Reading Skills

Ask Questions to Understand *Use the Reading Skills taught in this module to answer the question about the reading selection below.*

> For survival, Plains Indians depended on two animals—the horse and the buffalo. The Spanish brought horses to America in the 1500s. Plains Indians learned to ride horses, and hunters used them to follow buffalo herds year-round.

18. Write two or three questions you have about the information in the passage above. Remember to use the five Ws—Who? What? When? Where? and Why?

Social Studies Skills

Compare Migration Maps *Use the Social Studies Skills taught in this module to answer the question about the map below.*

19. According to the map above, for what reasons did settlers migrate to the West?
   a. for mining, ranching, and farming
   b. for jobs in manufacturing
   c. for the homes in the major cities there
   d. for the fishing industry

Focus on Writing

20. **Write a Job Description** Write a job description for a cowboy. Note the skills required for the job and the equipment needed. Also outline a typical workday for a cowboy. To add interest to your description, include appropriate visual materials.

Lewis and Clark

In 1804, Meriwether Lewis, William Clark, and the 33-man Corps of Discovery began an 8,000-mile journey across uncharted territory. Under orders from President Thomas Jefferson, the expedition mapped a route across the Louisiana Purchase to the Pacific Ocean. From St. Louis, Missouri, they traveled west up the Missouri River, then across the Rocky Mountains, and to the Pacific. They met Native American peoples and cataloged geography, plants, and animals. Not only was their mission one of history's greatest explorations; it also secured an American claim to the Pacific coast and helped inspire millions to migrate west.

Explore entries from Lewis's journal and other primary sources online. You can find a wealth of information, video clips, activities, and more through your online textbook.

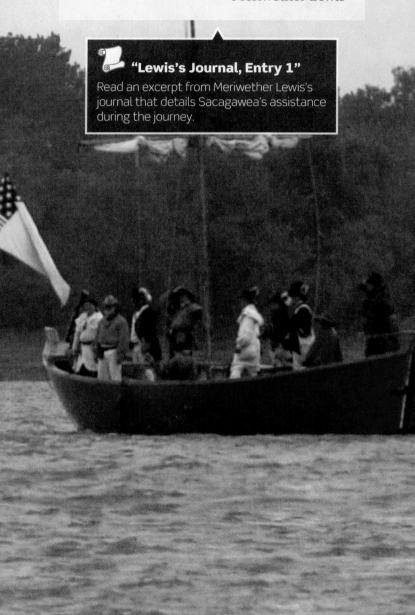

> "... the Indian woman recognized the point of a high plain to our right which she informed us was not very distant from the summer retreat of her nation on a river beyond the mountains which runs to the west."
>
> — Meriwether Lewis

"Lewis's Journal, Entry 1"

Read an excerpt from Meriwether Lewis's journal that details Sacagawea's assistance during the journey.

Go online to view these and other **HISTORY**® resources.

Underway on the Missouri

Watch the video to see how the Corps of Discovery sailed up the Missouri River to begin their expedition.

Making Friends Upriver

Watch the video to see which Native American peoples the Corps met and traded with as they made their journey west.

The Shores of the Pacific

Watch the video to see how the Corps tried to adapt to a different climate and the new peoples that they met along the Pacific coast.

Module 12
Expansion and Conflict

★

Essential Question

What was gained and lost as Americans expanded into the Southwest?

About the Photo: This Spanish mission in San Antonio was the site of the Battle of the Alamo, which was fought in March 1836 during the Texas Revolution. After losing this battle, "Remember the Alamo!" became a rallying cry for Texans during the battle that followed.

In this module you will learn about how the United States acquired lands in the Southwest.

What You Will Learn ...

Lesson 1: The Texas Revolution **392**
The Big Idea In 1836 Texas gained its independence from Mexico.

Lesson 2: The Mexican-American War **397**
The Big Idea The ideals of manifest destiny and the outcome of the Mexican-American War led to U.S. expansion to the Pacific Ocean.

Lesson 3: The California Gold Rush. **408**
The Big Idea The California gold rush changed the future of the West.

 Explore ONLINE!

VIDEOS, including...
- Heading West
- Independence for Texas
- The Mexican-American War
- The Gold Rush
- Search for the Mother Lode
- Statehood

☑ Document-Based Investigations

☑ Graphic Organizers

☑ Interactive Games

☑ Image Carousel: Texas Settlers

☑ Image with Hotpots: Ranch Life

Timeline of Events 1820–1855

 Explore ONLINE!

United States	World

1820

1821 Mexico wins its independence from Spain.

1827 The United States and Great Britain agree to continue joint occupation of Oregon Country.

1830

1833 Antonio López de Santa Anna is elected president of Mexico.

1835 The Texas Revolution breaks out at Gonzales.

1838 Californios revolt unsuccessfully against the Mexican government.

1840 Pioneers begin traveling West along the Oregon Trail.

1840

1842 China gives Great Britain control of the island of Hong Kong.

1846 The United States declares war against Mexico.

1848 Gold is discovered in California on January 24. ∨

1850

∧ **1854** Commodore Matthew Perry negotiates a trade treaty with Japan.

1855

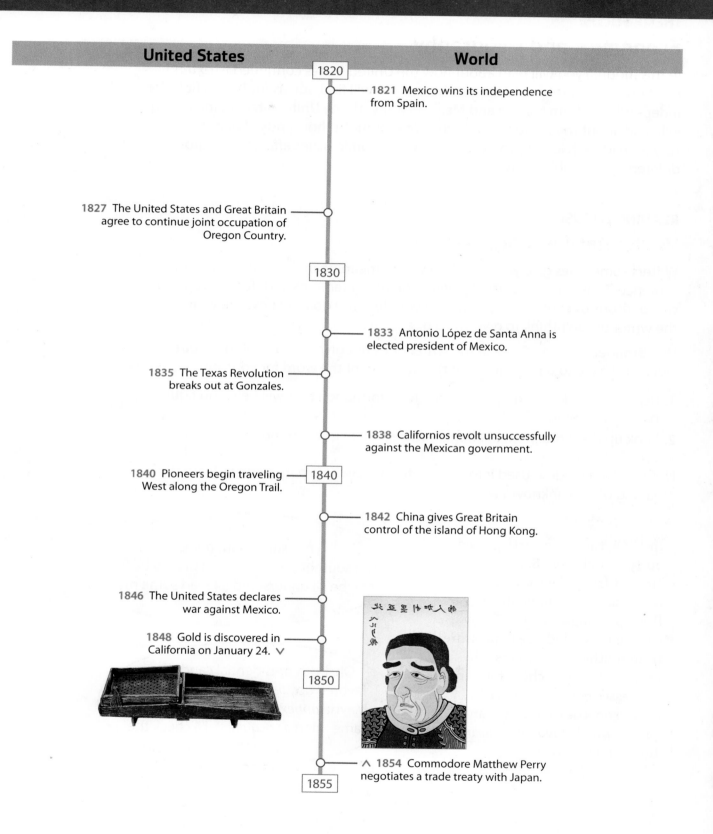

Reading Social Studies

Economics and Geography

In this module you will read about how the United States continued to extend its boundaries, this time to the southwest. You will find out about Texas's fight for independence from Mexico and Mexico's war with the United States. Finally, you will read about the California gold rush that brought thousands of people west. As you read each lesson, you will see how economic issues affected the growth of different geographic areas.

READING FOCUS:

Vocabulary in Context

Writers sometimes give you clues to a word's meaning in the same or a nearby sentence. Those clues are usually definitions, restatements in different words, or comparisons or contrasts. But what do you do if you do not know the word and the writer doesn't think to give you a direct clue?

Use Broader Context Clues If the writer does not give you one of those direct clues, you have to try to figure out the meaning of the word for yourself.

1. Read the whole paragraph and look for information that will help you figure out the meaning.
2. Look up the word in the dictionary to be sure of its meaning.

Notice how a student used information from the whole paragraph to learn the meaning of two unknown words.

In 1844, the Whig Party passed up Tyler and chose Senator Henry Clay of Kentucky as its presidential candidate. At first opposing *annexation*, Clay changed his mind due to pressure from southern politicians. The Democratic Party chose former Tennessee governor James K. Polk to oppose Clay. Both candidates strongly favored *acquiring* Texas and Oregon.

I'm not sure about *annexation*. The southerners convinced Clay to be for it. Maybe I'll understand if I read some more.

Oh, both presidential candidates favored *acquiring* Texas and Oregon. Maybe *annexation* means almost the same thing as *acquiring*. I'll check the dictionary.

You Try It!

The following passage is from the module you are about to read. Read the passage and then answer the questions.

American Settlement in the Mexican Cession The war ended after Scott took Mexico City. In February 1848, the United States and Mexico signed the Treaty of Guadalupe Hidalgo, which officially ended the war and forced Mexico to turn over much of its northern territory to the United States. Known as the Mexican Cession, this land included the present-day states of California, Nevada, and Utah. . . .

In exchange for this vast territory, the United States agreed to pay Mexico $15 million. In addition, the United States assumed claims of more than $3 million held by American citizens against the Mexican government.

Refer to the passage to answer the following questions.

1. Do you know what the word *cession* means? What clues in the first paragraph can help you figure out what the word might mean? Use those clues to write a definition of cession.

2. Look up *cession* in a dictionary. How does your definition compare to the dictionary definition?

3. In your experience, what does the word *assume* usually mean? Do you think that meaning is the one used in the second paragraph? If not, what do you think *assume* means in this case?

4. Look up *assume* in a dictionary. Does one of its meanings match the one you came up with?

As you read Module 12, use context clues to figure out the meanings of unfamiliar words. Check yourself by looking the words up in a dictionary.

Key Terms and People

Lesson 1
Father Miguel Hidalgo y Costilla
empresarios
Stephen F. Austin
Antonio López de Santa Anna
Alamo
Battle of San Jacinto

Lesson 2
manifest destiny
James K. Polk
vaqueros
Californios
Bear Flag Revolt
Treaty of Guadalupe Hidalgo
Gadsden Purchase

Lesson 3
John Sutter
Donner party
forty-niners
prospect
placer miners

The Texas Revolution

The Big Idea

In 1836 Texas gained its independence from Mexico.

Main Ideas

- Many American settlers moved to Texas after Mexico achieved independence from Spain.

- Texans revolted against Mexican rule and established an independent nation.

Key Terms and People

Father Miguel Hidalgo y Costilla
empresarios
Stephen F. Austin
Antonio López de Santa Anna
Alamo
Battle of San Jacinto

If YOU were there . . .

You are the father of a large farm family in Missouri. There is not enough land for everyone, so you're looking for another opportunity. One day, a land agent comes to town. He is looking for people to settle in Texas. The Mexican government is offering generous tracts of land to colonists. However, you have to become a citizen of Mexico and follow Mexican laws.

Would you decide to move your family to Texas? Why or why not?

American Settlers Move to Texas

By the early 1700s Spain's colony in Mexico was thriving. However, in the territories to the north—which included the modern states of California, Arizona, New Mexico, and Texas—the situation was very different. Few Spaniards lived in these largely barren territories. The Spanish government, though, feared losing territory to attacks by neighbors. They wanted to establish settlements that would secure the Spanish claim to what we now call the Southwest.

However, the Spanish did not form colonies like the English had on the East Coast. Instead, they established small individual settlements. Among them were three major types of settlements. Missions were religious settlements. Each mission housed a small number of priests and others who worked to teach local Native Americans about Christianity and the Spanish way of life. The Native Americans also grew crops to feed themselves and the priests. To protect the missions from attacks, the Spanish built presidios, or forts. The soldiers based at a presidio could ride out to defend the priests at any nearby missions. Finally, the Spanish also created towns, sometimes called pueblos, near some missions. In these towns, Spanish citizens would live, grow crops, and raise cattle. Although missions, presidios, and towns were often located near each other, each had to be able to support

Settling Texas
Stephen F. Austin (standing, in black coat) and other settlers were empresarios—they contracted with the Mexican government to bring settlers to Texas in exchange for land of their own.

itself. No one could depend entirely on support from others or from Spain to guarantee its survival.

The political situation in the Southwest changed when Mexicans moved to overthrow Spanish rule in the early 1800s. In September 1810 **Father Miguel Hidalgo y Costilla**, a Mexican priest, led a rebellion of about 80,000 poor Indians and mestizos, or people of Indian and Spanish ancestry. They hoped that if Mexico became independent from the Spanish monarchy, their lives would improve.

Hidalgo's revolt failed, but the rebellion he started grew. In 1821 Mexico became independent. In 1824 it adopted a republican constitution that declared rights for all Mexicans. The new Mexican government contracted with **empresarios**, or agents, to bring settlers to Texas. They paid the agents in land.

In 1821 one young agent, **Stephen F. Austin**, started a Texas colony on the lower Colorado River. The first 300 families became known as the Old Three Hundred. Austin's successful colony attracted other agents, and American settlers flocked to the region. These Anglo-American settlers, most of them Protestant, became known as Texians. The Mexican residents of Texas, the Tejanos, were Catholic. The two groups generally lived in separate communities. Over time, Texas developed a culture that was distinct from the rest of Mexico and from the United States.

In exchange for cheap land, settlers had to obey Mexican laws. But some settlers often **explicitly** ignored these laws. For example, despite restrictions on slavery, many brought slaves. Concerned that it was losing control of the growing American population, Mexico responded. In 1830 it banned further settlement by Americans. Angry about the new law, many Texans, as they came to be known, began to think of gaining independence from Mexico.

Academic Vocabulary
explicit fully revealed without vagueness

Reading Check
Find Main Ideas
Why did settlers
move to Texas?

By 1834 Mexico came under the rule of General **Antonio López de Santa Anna**. He soon suspended Mexico's republican constitution and gave himself more power. To the already unhappy Texans, this was too much. They felt the time had come to fight for independence.

Texans Revolt against Mexico

In October 1835 the Mexican army tried to remove a cannon from the town of Gonzales, Texas. Rebels stood next to the cannon with a flag reading "Come and take it." After a short battle, the rebels drove the Mexican force away, keeping the cannon. Within a few months, the Texas rebels formed an army and captured the key settlements of Goliad and San Antonio. The Texas Revolution, also known as the Texas War for Independence, had begun.

In 1836, when American settlers in Texas rebelled, Mexican president General Santa Anna personally marched his army into San Antonio.

Texas Independence On March 2, 1836, Texans declared their independence from Mexico. The new Republic of Texas was born. Both the declaration and the constitution that shortly followed were modeled after the U.S. documents. The Texas constitution, however, made slavery legal.

Delegates to the new Texas government chose politician David Burnet as president and Lorenzo de Zavala as vice president. Another revolutionary, Sam Houston, was named to head the Texas army. Austin went to the United States to seek money and troops.

Battle at the Alamo The Texans' actions angered Santa Anna. He began assembling a force of thousands to stop the rebellion.

A hastily created army of Texas volunteers had been clashing with Mexican troops for months. Near San Antonio, the Texans occupied and fortified the **Alamo**, a former mission that became an important battle site in the Texas Revolution. Volunteers from the United States, including frontiersman Davy Crockett, joined Texans such as Colonel Jim Bowie in the Alamo's defense.

The rebels, numbering about 200, hoped for reinforcement from other parts of Texas. For almost two weeks, from February 23 to March 6, 1836, the Texans held out. Colonel William Travis managed to get a message to other Texans through enemy lines:

> "I call on you in the name of Liberty, of patriotism, and everything dear to the American character, to come to our aid with all dispatch [speed] . . . VICTORY OR DEATH."
>
> —William Travis, from a letter written at the Alamo, 1836

Before dawn on March 6, the Mexican army attacked. Despite heavy losses, the army overcame the Texans. All the defenders of the Alamo were killed, though some civilians survived. Following a later battle at Goliad, Santa Anna ordered the execution of 350 prisoners who had surrendered. Texans were enraged by the massacres. Mexican leaders hoped that these terrible defeats would convince the Texans to stop fighting. However, the battles had the opposite effect. Outraged by the harsh treatment Texan soldiers had received, the people of Texas vowed to fight on.

Battle of San Jacinto Santa Anna now chased the untrained forces of Sam Houston. Outnumbered, the Texans fled east. Finally, they reorganized at the San Jacinto River, near Galveston Bay. There, the Texans took a stand.

Santa Anna was confident of victory, but he was careless in choosing the site for his camp. On the afternoon of April 21, 1836, while Mexican troops were resting, Houston launched a surprise attack. The Texan forces swarmed over the camp, shouting, "Remember the Alamo!" and "Remember Goliad!"

The fighting ended swiftly. In fewer than 20 minutes, Santa Anna's army was all but destroyed. In the **Battle of San Jacinto**, the Texans captured Santa Anna and forced him to sign a treaty giving Texas its independence.

An Independent Nation Sam Houston was the hero of the new independent nation of Texas. The republic created a new town named Houston and made it the capital. Voters elected Sam Houston as president. Stephen F. Austin became secretary of state, but died shortly after his election.

To increase the population, Texas offered land grants. American settlers came from nearby southern states, often bringing slaves with them to help grow and harvest cotton.

Most Texans hoped that the United States would annex, or take control of, Texas, making it a state. Some Southerners in Congress wanted to

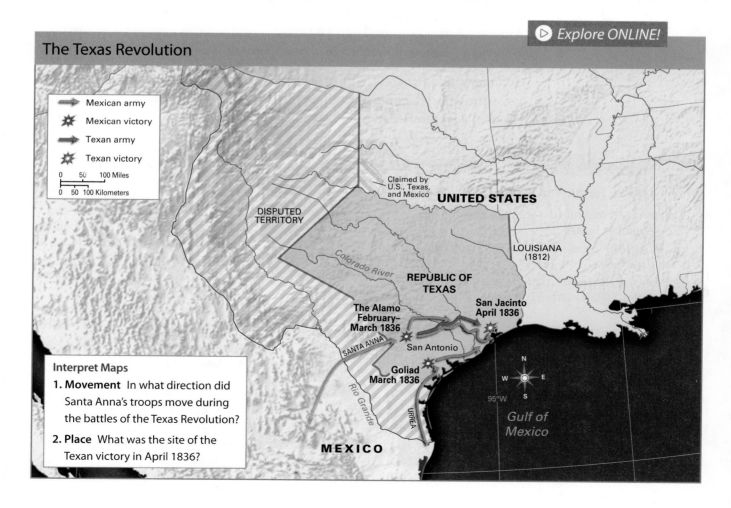

The Texas Revolution

Explore ONLINE!

- → Mexican army
- ✴ Mexican victory
- → Texan army
- ✴ Texan victory

0   50   100 Miles
0   50 100 Kilometers

DISPUTED TERRITORY

Claimed by U.S., Texas, and Mexico

UNITED STATES

Colorado River

LOUISIANA (1812)

REPUBLIC OF TEXAS

The Alamo February–March 1836

San Jacinto April 1836

SANTA ANNA

San Antonio

Goliad March 1836

Rio Grande

URREA

95°W

Gulf of Mexico

MEXICO

Interpret Maps

1. **Movement** In what direction did Santa Anna's troops move during the battles of the Texas Revolution?

2. **Place** What was the site of the Texan victory in April 1836?

The single star of the flag represents the Republic of Texas, also called the Lone Star Republic.

annex Texas, but President Andrew Jackson did not pursue the issue. He was concerned that admitting Texas as a slave state would upset the fragile balance of free and slave states. The president also did not want to have a war with Mexico over Texas.

Finally, Jackson did recognize Texas as an independent nation. France did so in 1839. Britain, which wanted to halt U.S. expansion, recognized Texas in 1840.

The Mexican government, however, did not recognize Santa Anna's forced handover of Texas. For this reason, in 1837 the republic organized the Texas Rangers to guard its long frontier from Mexican and Native American attacks. Finally, in 1844 Texas and Mexico signed an armistice. However, Mexico refused to recognize Texas's independence.

Reading Check
Find Main Ideas
What issues did the new nation of Texas face?

Summary and Preview American settlers in Texas challenged the Mexican government and won their independence. In the next lesson you will learn about the war between Mexico and the United States.

Lesson 1 Assessment

Review Ideas, Terms, and People

1. a. **Identify** What role did Stephen F. Austin play in the settlement of Texas?

   b. **Make Inferences** Why did Mexican officials want to bring more settlers to Texas?

   c. **Contrast** How was Spanish settlement in the Southwest different from English settlement on the East Coast?

   d. **Evaluate** Do you think Mexico's requirements for foreign immigrants were reasonable or unreasonable? Explain.

2. a. **Describe** What were the important battles in the Texas War for Independence? Why was each important?

   b. **Make Inferences** Why did Texas offer land grants to settlers?

   c. **Predict** What problems might the Republic of Texas face?

Critical Thinking

3. **Sequence** In this lesson you learned about American settlement in Texas. Create a chart similar to the one below and use it to show the significant events that led to the formation of the Republic of Texas.

Significant Events
1.
2.
3.
4.
5.
6. Houston is founded and made the capital.

The Mexican-American War

The Big Idea

The ideals of manifest destiny and the outcome of the Mexican-American War led to U.S. expansion to the Pacific Ocean.

Main Ideas

- Many Americans believed that the nation had a manifest destiny to claim new lands in the West.

- As a result of the Mexican-American War, the United States added territory in the Southwest.

- American settlement in the Mexican Cession produced conflict and a blending of cultures.

Key Terms and People

manifest destiny
James K. Polk
vaqueros
Californios
Bear Flag Revolt
Treaty of Guadalupe Hidalgo
Gadsden Purchase

If YOU were there . . .

Your family are Californios, Spanish settlers who have lived in California for many years. You raise horses on your ranch. So far, you have gotten along with American settlers. But it has become clear that the American government wants to take over California. You hear that fighting has already started between American and Mexican troops.

How might life change under American rule?

Manifest Destiny

"We have it in our power to start the world over again."
—Thomas Paine, from his pamphlet *Common Sense*

Americans had always believed they could build a new, better society founded on democratic principles. In 1839 writer John O'Sullivan noted, "We are the nation of human progress, and who will, what can, set limits to our onward march?"

Actually, there was one limit: land. By the 1840s the United States had a booming economy and population. Barely 70 years old, the nation already needed more room for farms, ranches, businesses, and ever-growing families. Americans looked West to what they saw as a vast wilderness, ready to be taken. With American settlers already living in Oregon, New Mexico, and Texas, many believed that the country should annex those lands to the United States, giving Americans more lands into which they could spread.

Some people believed it was America's **manifest destiny**, or obvious fate, to settle land all the way to the Pacific Ocean in order to spread American ideals. O'Sullivan coined the term in 1845. He wrote that it was America's "manifest destiny to overspread and to possess the whole continent which Providence [God] has given us for the development of the great experiment of liberty. . . ."

The woman represents America, moving west and bringing sunlight, settlers, and telegraph wires to the new lands.

The Mississippi River is in the background as settlers push farther west.

Native Americans and buffalo are pushed away by the approaching settlers.

Manifest Destiny

John Gast's 1872 painting *American Progress* shows the spirit of manifest destiny leading settlers westward.

In the 1840s and 1850s, manifest destiny was tied up with the slavery issue. If America expanded, would slavery be allowed in the new territories? Several presidents became involved in the difficult issue, including President John Tyler. A pro-slavery Whig, Tyler wanted to increase the power of the southern slave states by annexing Texas. His fellow Whigs disagreed.

In 1844 the Whig Party passed up Tyler and chose Senator Henry Clay of Kentucky as its presidential candidate. At first opposing annexation, Clay changed his mind due to pressure from southern politicians. The Democratic Party chose former Tennessee governor **James K. Polk** to oppose Clay. Both candidates strongly favored acquiring Texas and Oregon.

Southerners feared the loss of Texas, a possible new slave state. Others worried that Texas might become an ally of Britain. These concerns helped Polk narrowly defeat Clay.

Acquiring New Territory President Polk quickly set out to fulfill his campaign promise to annex Oregon and Texas. By the 1820s Russia and Spain had given up their claims to Oregon Country. Britain and the United States had agreed to occupy the territory together.

As more Americans settled there, they began to ask that Oregon become part of the United States. Polk wanted to protect these settlers' interests. Some politicians noted that Oregon Country would provide a Pacific port for the growing U.S. trade with China.

Meanwhile, Britain and the United States disagreed over how to draw the United States–Canadian border. American expansionists cried, "Fifty-four forty or fight!" This slogan referred to 54°40' north latitude, the line to which Americans wanted their northern territory to extend.

Neither side really wanted a war, though. In 1846 Great Britain and the United States signed a treaty that gave the United States all Oregon land south of the forty-ninth parallel. This treaty drew the border that still exists today. Oregon became an organized U.S. territory in February 1848.

The Texas question was also coming to a head. By March 1845 Congress had approved annexation and needed only the support of the Republic of Texas. Texas politicians hoped that joining the United States would help solve the republic's financial and military problems. The Texas Congress approved annexation in June 1845. Texas became part of the United States in December. This action angered the Mexican government, which considered Texas to be a "stolen province."

The Mexican Borderlands Though it had lost Texas, Mexico still had settlements in other areas of the present-day Southwest to govern. New Mexico was the oldest settled area, with its capital at Santa Fe. Mexico also had settlements in present-day Arizona, Nevada, and California.

During early Spanish rule, the mission system had dominated much of the present-day Southwest. Over time, it had become less important there, especially in New Mexico, where settlers lived in small villages. In California, however, missions remained the focus of everyday life. Missions under later Spanish rule carried out huge farming and ranching operations using the labor of Native Americans. Some of the Native Americans came willingly to the missions. Others were brought by force. Usually, they were not allowed to leave the mission once they had arrived. They had to adopt the clothing, food, and religion of the Spaniards.

Missions often sold their goods to local pueblos, or towns, that arose near the missions and presidios. One wealthy California settler, Mariano Guadalupe Vallejo, remembered the early days.

> "We were the pioneers of the Pacific coast, building towns and missions while General [George] Washington was carrying on the war of the Revolution."
>
> —Mariano Guadalupe Vallejo, "Ranch and Mission Days in Alta California," *The Century Magazine*

After winning independence from Spain in 1821, Mexico began to change old Spanish policies toward California and Texas. In 1833, for example, Mexico ended the mission system in California. Mission lands were broken up, and huge grants were given to some of the wealthiest California settlers, including Vallejo. They created vast ranchos, or ranches, with tens of thousands of acres of land. *Vaqueros*, or cowboys, managed the large herds of cattle and sheep. Cowhides were so valuable that they were called "California banknotes." Hides were traded for household items and luxury goods from the eastern United States. Some settlers also made wine and grew citrus fruits.

Ranch Life

Spanish and Mexican *vaqueros*, or cowboys, were expert horse riders. They used their horses to herd cattle on the ranches of the Spanish Southwest.

Vaqueros were known for their specially designed hats.

Saddles like these were highly prized by *vaqueros*.

Leather chaps protected riders from dust and scrapes.

Analyze Visuals
What features of the *vaqueros'* life are shown in the painting?

Academic Vocabulary
element a basic part of an individual's surroundings

Although they had been freed from the missions, for most California Indians the **elements** of life changed very little. They continued to herd animals and do much of the hard physical labor on ranches and farms. Some, however, ran away into the wilderness or to the nearby towns of San Diego and Los Angeles.

The Californios Because of the great distance between California and the center of Mexico's government, by the early 1820s California had only around 3,200 colonists. These early California settlers, called **Californios**, felt little connection to their faraway government.

Californios developed a lasting reputation for hospitality and skilled horse riding. In *Two Years Before the Mast*, American novelist Richard Henry Dana Jr. wrote about his encounters with Californio culture. He described, for example, what happened after a Californio served a feast to Dana and a friend.

> "We took out some money and asked him how much we were to pay. He shook his head and crossed himself, saying that it was charity—that the Lord gave it to us."
>
> —Richard Henry Dana Jr., from *Two Years Before the Mast*

Reading Check
Draw Inferences
How did manifest destiny affect Mexican rule in California?

In addition to traders and travelers, a small number of settlers also arrived from the United States. They were called Anglos by the Californios. Although there were few Anglo settlers in California, their calls for independence increased tensions between Mexico and the United States.

Mexican-American War

Although diplomacy helped the United States resolve territorial disputes in the Pacific Northwest, diplomats working in the Southwest faced more challenges. Faced with an unstable and uncooperative Mexican government, the U.S. government found it necessary to become more aggressive in its diplomatic overtures. As a result, diplomatic relations between Mexico and the United States became increasingly strained. U.S. involvement in California and Texas contributed to this tension.

Conflict Breaks Out Mexico had long insisted that its northern border in Texas lay along the Nueces River and refused to accept Texas annexation as legitimate. The United States said the border was farther south, along the Rio Grande. In June 1845 President Polk ordered General Zachary Taylor to lead an army into the disputed region.

Polk sent diplomat John Slidell to Mexico City to try to settle the border dispute. Slidell came with an offer to buy New Mexico and California for $30 million. Mexican officials refused to speak to him.

In March 1846 General Taylor led his troops to the Rio Grande. He camped across from Mexican forces stationed near the town of Matamoros, Mexico. In April, the Mexican commander told Taylor to withdraw from Mexican territory. Taylor refused. The two sides clashed, and several U.S. soldiers were killed.

In response, President Polk said to Congress:

"Mexico has passed the boundary of the United States, has invaded our territory, and shed American blood upon the American soil. . . . The two nations are now at war."

—James K. Polk, from his address to Congress, May 11, 1846

Polk's war message was persuasive. Two days later, Congress declared war on Mexico.

War Begins At the beginning of the war with Mexico, the U.S. Army had better weapons and equipment. Yet it was greatly outnumbered and poorly prepared. The government put out a call for 50,000 volunteers. About 200,000 responded. Many were young men who thought the war would be a grand adventure in a foreign land.

On the home front, many Americans supported the war. However, many Whigs thought the war was unjustified and avoidable. Northern abolitionists also opposed the conflict. They feared the spread of slavery into southwestern lands.

While Americans debated the war, fighting proceeded. General Taylor's soldiers won battles south of the Nueces River. Taylor then crossed the Rio Grande and occupied Matamoros, Mexico. While Taylor waited for more men, Polk ordered General Stephen Kearny to attack New Mexico. On August 18, 1846, Kearny took Santa Fe, the capital city, without a fight. He claimed the entire province of New Mexico for the United States and marched west to California, where another conflict with Mexico was already under way.

Explore ONLINE!

	American forces
	American victory
	Mexican forces
	Mexican victory
	Fort
	Modern-day state boundaries

0   100   200 Miles

0   100   200 Kilometers

OREGON COUNTRY

Great Salt Lake

UNORGANIZED TERRITORY

Bear Flag Revolt, June 1846

Sutter's Fort

Sonoma
San Francisco
Monterey

SIERRA NEVADA

FRÉMONT

CA

San Gabriel, Jan. 1847

Los Angeles

San Pasqual, Dec. 1846

STOCKTON

San Diego

KEARNY

Gila River

Colorado River

Bent's Fort

NEW MEXICO
Santa Fe

KEARNY

DISPUTED TERRITORY

Fort Leavenworth

KEARNY

UNITED STATES

Arkansas River

Red River

Mississippi River

TEXAS

San Antonio

New Orleans

DONIPHAN

Rio Grande

Chihuahua

Nueces River

WOOL

Corpus Christi

Palo Alto, May 1846

TAYLOR

Resaca de la Palma, May 1846

Matamoros

SCOTT

PACIFIC OCEAN

SLOAT

Monterrey, Sept. 1846

Buena Vista, Feb. 1847

SANTA ANNA

Gulf of Mexico

Tropic of Cancer

MEXICO

Mazatlán

Tampico

SCOTT

Mexico City, Sept. 1847

SCOTT

Veracruz, Mar. 1847

SANTA ANNA

Cerro Gordo, April 1847

120°W

30°N

110°W

90°W

20°N

10°N

N W E S

Interpret Maps

1. **Location** What Mexican city did Scott's forces attack in March 1847?

2. **Movement** Which U.S. commander led forces from Santa Fe to San Diego?

The Bear Flag Revolt
American settlers took over Sonoma, the regional headquarters of the Mexican general Mariano Vallejo, and declared California a new country: the California Republic.

The Bear Flag Revolt In 1846 only about 500 Americans lived in the huge province of California, in contrast to about 12,000 Californios. Yet, in the spirit of manifest destiny, a small group of American settlers seized the town of Sonoma, north of San Francisco, on June 14. Hostilities began between the two sides when the Americans took some horses that were intended for the Mexican militia. In what became known as the **Bear Flag Revolt**, the Americans declared California to be an independent nation. Above the town, the rebels hoisted a hastily made flag of a grizzly bear facing a red star. Californios laughed at the roughly made bear, thinking it "looked more like a pig than a bear."

John C. Frémont, a U.S. Army captain, was leading a mapping expedition across the Sierra Nevada when he heard of the possible war with Mexico. Frémont went to Sonoma and quickly joined the American settlers in their revolt against the Californios. Because war had already broken out between the United States and Mexico, Frémont's actions were seen as beneficial to the American cause in the region. His stated goal, however, was Californian independence, not to annex California to the United States. During the revolt, several important Californios were taken prisoner, including Mariano Vallejo. Governor Vallejo and his brother were held at an Anglo settlement for two months without any formal charges being brought against them. Long after his release, Vallejo wrote a history of California that included an account of his time as a bear flag prisoner.

But the bear flag was quick to fall. In July, naval forces from the United States—which never recognized Californian independence—came ashore in California and raised the stars and stripes. Kearny's army arrived from the East. The towns of San Diego, Los Angeles, and San Francisco fell rapidly. In August, U.S. Navy commodore Robert Stockton claimed California for the United States. Some Californios continued to resist until early 1847, when they surrendered.

War's End In Mexico General Taylor finally got the reinforcements he needed. He drove his forces deep into enemy lands. Santa Anna, who had been removed from office and exiled the previous year, returned to power in Mexico in September 1846. He quickly came after Taylor.

The two armies clashed at Buena Vista in February 1847. After a close battle with heavy casualties on both sides, the Mexican Army retreated. The next morning, the cry went up: "The enemy has fled! The field is ours!"

Taylor's success made him a war hero back home. The general's popularity troubled President Polk, and when Taylor's progress stalled, Polk gave the command to General Winfield Scott. A beloved leader, Scott was known by his troops as "Old Fuss and Feathers" because of his strict military discipline.

Scott sailed to the port of Veracruz, a major port and the site of the strongest fortress in Mexico. On March 29, after an 88-hour artillery attack, Veracruz fell. Scott moved on to the final goal, Mexico City, the capital. Taking a route similar to one followed by Spanish conquistador Hernán Cortés in 1519, the Americans pushed 200 or so miles inland. Santa Anna tried to stop the U.S. forces at Cerro Gordo in mid-April, but failed. By August 1847 U.S. troops were at the edge of Mexico City.

After a truce failed, Scott ordered a massive attack on Mexico City. Mexican soldiers and civilians fought fierce battles in and around the capital. At a military school atop the steep, fortified hill of Chapultepec, young Mexican cadets bravely defended their hopeless position. At least one soldier jumped to his death rather than surrender to the invading forces. Finally, on September 14, 1847, Mexico City fell. Santa Anna soon fled the country. Scott's capture of the Mexican capital led to the end of the war.

Reading Check
Sequence In chronological order, list the key battles of the Mexican-American War.

American soldier

Battle of Buena Vista
After the two-day Battle of Buena Vista, the American army gained control of northern Mexico. At the beginning of the battle, Mexican forces outnumbered the Americans. But the Mexicans suffered more than twice as many casualties.

American Settlement in the Mexican Cession

The war ended after Scott took Mexico City. In February 1848 the United States and Mexico signed the **Treaty of Guadalupe Hidalgo**, which officially ended the war and forced Mexico to turn over much of its northern territory to the United States. Known as the Mexican Cession, this land included the present-day states of California, Nevada, and Utah. In addition, it included most of Arizona and New Mexico and parts of Colorado and Wyoming. The United States also won the area claimed by Texas north of the Rio Grande. The Mexican Cession totaled more than 500,000 square miles and increased the size of the United States by almost 25 percent.

Diplomatic Agreements and Payments In exchange for this vast territory, the United States agreed to pay Mexico $15 million. In addition, the United States assumed claims of more than $3 million held by American citizens against the Mexican government. The treaty also addressed the status of Mexicans in the Mexican Cession. The treaty provided that they would be "protected in the free enjoyment of their liberty and property, and secured in the free exercise of their religion." The Senate passed the treaty in March 1848.

After the war with Mexico, some Americans wanted to guarantee that any southern railroad to California would be built completely on American soil. James Gadsden, U.S. minister to Mexico, negotiated an important diplomatic agreement with Mexico in December 1853. Under the terms of the **Gadsden Purchase**, the U.S. government paid Mexico $10 million. In exchange, the United States received the southern parts of what are now Arizona and New Mexico. With this purchase, the existing boundary with Mexico was finally fixed.

Surge of American Settlers After the Mexican-American War, a flood of Americans moved to the Southwest. Their movement sparked a new debate about slavery in the United States. Many southerners who moved west wanted to bring slaves with them into the new territories. Northerners who opposed slavery wanted to ban the practice in the new lands. Even before the war had ended, northern Senator David Wilmot proposed a policy, called the Wilmot Proviso. His policy would have banned slavery in all lands gained from Mexico. The proviso was defeated in Congress, but debates about slavery in the Mexican Cession continued for several years.

American newcomers struggled against longtime residents to control the land and other valuable resources, such as water and minerals. Most Mexicans, Mexican Americans, and Native Americans faced legal, economic, and social discrimination. As a result, they found it difficult to protect their rights.

The Treaty of Guadalupe Hidalgo promised full U.S. citizenship to all Mexicans who wished to stay in the new American lands. However, many of those who stayed faced discrimination. Even Mexican Americans who

Mexican Americans Today

Today Mexican Americans make up a little over 10 percent of the U.S. population, or about 33 million people. Mexican Americans live in all 50 states, although most live in the South and Southwest. Many Mexican Americans in these areas are descended from people who lived there long before the region became part of the United States.

Top Ten States by Mexican American Population

Rank	State	Mexican American Population
1	California	11,423,146
2	Texas	7,951,193
3	Arizona	1,657,668
4	Illinois	1,602,403
5	New Mexico	837,171
6	Colorado	757,181
7	Florida	629,718
8	Washington	601,768
9	Nevada	540,978
10	Georgia	519,502

Source: U.S. Census Bureau (2010)

were already living in Texas, some of whom had fought against Mexico, faced challenges. For example, differences between Mexican and U.S. land laws led to great confusion. The U.S. government often made Mexican American landowners go to court to prove that they had titles to their land. Landowners had to pay their own travel costs as well as those of witnesses and interpreters. They also had to pay attorneys' and interpreters' fees. These legal battles often bankrupted landowners. New settlers also tended to ignore Mexican legal concepts, such as community property or community water rights.

White settlers also battled with Native Americans over property rights. In some areas, for example, new white settlers soon outnumbered southwestern Native Americans. The Anglo settlers often tried to take control of valuable water resources and grazing lands. In addition, settlers rarely respected Native American holy places. Native American peoples such as the Navajo and the Apache tried to protect their land and livestock from the settlers. Settlers and Native Americans alike attacked one another to protect their interests.

Cultural Encounters Despite conflicts, different cultures shaped one another in the Southwest. In settlements with large Mexican populations, laws were often printed in both English and Spanish. Names of places—such as San Antonio, San Diego, and Santa Barbara—show Hispanic heritage. Other place-names, such as Taos and Tesuque, are derived from Native American words. Communities throughout the Southwest regularly celebrated both Mexican and American holidays.

Mexican and Native American knowledge and traditions also shaped many local economies. Mexican Americans taught Anglo settlers about mining in the mountains. Many ranching communities were first started by Mexican settlers. In addition, Mexican Americans introduced new types of saddles and other equipment to American ranchers. Adobe, developed by the Anasazi Indians, was adopted from the Pueblo people by the Spanish. It is still commonly used by American residents in New Mexico, Arizona, and California.

Trade also changed the Southwest. For example, the Navajo created handwoven woolen blankets to sell to Americans. Americans in turn brought manufactured goods and money to the Southwest. The city of El

Paso became an important regional trading center. As trade increased after the Mexican-American War, the economies of many Mexican American and Native American communities in the Southwest began to change.

Water Rights Eastern water-use laws commonly required owners whose land bordered streams or rivers to maintain a free flow of water. These restrictions generally prevented landowners from constructing dams because doing so would infringe upon the water rights of neighbors downstream.

In the typically dry climate of the West, large-scale agriculture was not possible without irrigation. Dams and canals were required to direct scarce water to fields. This need conflicted with the accepted eastern tradition of equal access to water.

Brigham Young established a strict code regulating water rights for the Mormon community. In any dispute over water use, the good of the community would outweigh the interests of individuals. Young's approach stood as an example for modern water laws throughout the West.

Summary and Preview America's westward expansion continued rapidly after the Mexican-American War. In the next lesson you will learn about the California gold rush.

Reading Check
Summarize What were some of the early important agreements between the United States and Mexico, and why were they significant?

Lesson 2 Assessment

Review Ideas, Terms, and People

1. **a. Define** What was manifest destiny?

   b. Make Inferences Why was westward expansion such an important issue in the election of 1844?

   c. Identify Cause and Effect How did Mexican independence affect California?

2. **a. Recall** Why did the United States declare war on Mexico?

   b. Explain Why did American diplomacy with Mexico become more aggressive, and what was the result?

   c. Summarize What was General Winfield Scott's strategy for winning the war with Mexico?

   d. Elaborate Would you have sided with those who opposed the war with Mexico or with those who supported it? Why?

3. **a. Describe** What conflicts did American settlers, Native Americans, and Mexican Americans in the Mexican Cession experience?

   b. Draw Conclusions Why were water rights so important in the American Southwest?

   c. Evaluate In your opinion, what was the most important effect of the annexation of the Mexican Cession?

Critical Thinking

4. **Identify Cause and Effect** In this lesson you learned about manifest destiny and U.S. territorial expansion. Create a graphic organizer like the one shown below. Identify how Americans' expansion into California caused the war with Mexico as well as the effects of the war.

The California Gold Rush

If YOU were there . . .

You are a low-paid bank clerk in New England in early 1849. Local newspaper headlines are shouting exciting news: "Gold Is Discovered in California! Thousands Are on Their Way West." You enjoy having a steady job. However, some of your friends are planning to go west, and you are being influenced by their excitement. Your friends are even buying pickaxes and other mining equipment. They urge you to go with them.

Would you go west to seek your fortune in California? Why?

Discovery of Gold Brings Settlers

In the 1830s and 1840s, Americans who wanted to move to California started up the Oregon Trail. At the Snake River in present-day Idaho, the trail split. People bound for California took the southern route, which became known as the California Trail. This path ran through the Sierra Nevada mountain range. American emigrants and traders on the California Trail tried to cross these mountains before the season's first snows.

Although many Americans traveled along the California Trail, few actually settled in California. American merchants were usually more interested in trading goods made in factories than in establishing settlements. They traded for gold and silver coins, hides, and tallow (animal fat used to make soap and candles) from Mexico. California became a meeting ground for traders from Mexico and the United States.

Before the Mexican-American War, California's population consisted mostly of Mexicans and Native Americans. When Mexico controlled California, Mexican officials did not want many Americans to settle there. However, in 1839 they did give Swiss immigrant **John Sutter** permission to start a colony. Sutter's Fort, located near the Sacramento River, soon became a popular rest stop for many American emigrants. These new arrivals praised Sutter's hospitality

The Big Idea

The California gold rush changed the future of the West.

Main Ideas

- The discovery of gold brought settlers to California.
- The gold rush had a lasting impact on California's population and economy.

Key Terms and People

John Sutter
Donner party
forty-niners
prospect
placer miners

and helpfulness. By the mid-1840s some Anglo Californians were publishing newspaper advertisements and guidebooks encouraging other settlers to move to the West.

The **Donner party** was a group of western-bound travelers who went to California but were stranded in the Sierra Nevada Mountains during winter. The party began its journey west in the spring of 1846. Trying to find a shortcut, the group left the main trail and got lost. When the Donner party reached the Sierra Nevada Mountains, they became trapped by heavy snows. They were stuck and had almost no food.

A rescue party found the starving and freezing group in February 1847. Of the original 87 travelers, 42 had died.

Gold in California In January 1848 Sutter sent a carpenter named James Marshall to build a sawmill beside a nearby river. While working near Sutter's Mill, Marshall glanced at the ground. "I reached my hand down and picked it up; it made my heart thump, for I was certain it was gold."

Sutter and Marshall agreed to keep the discovery a secret. However, when they examined the work site the next day, they met a Spanish-speaking Native American worker holding a nugget and shouting, "Oro [gold]! Oro! Oro!"

Sutter's workers soon quit to search for gold. Stories of the discovery rapidly spread across the country. President Polk added to the national excitement by confirming the California gold strike in his farewell message to Congress in December 1848. In 1849 about 80,000 gold-seekers came to California, hoping to strike it rich. These gold-seeking migrants to California were called **forty-niners**. As one Iowa woman who left to find gold recalled, "At that time the 'gold fever' was contagious, and few, old or young, escaped the malady [sickness]." Nearly 80 percent of the forty-niners were Americans, while the rest came from all over the world.

"Gold Fever"

"Gold fever" brought 80,000 people, like this miner, to California in 1849 alone. One California newspaper captured the excitement: "The whole country, from San Francisco to Los Angeles, and from the sea shore to the base of the Sierra Nevadas, resounds with the cry of 'gold, GOLD, GOLD!' while the field is left half planted, the house half built, and everything neglected but the manufacture of shovels and pickaxes."

Most forty-niners braved long and often dangerous journeys to reach California. Many easterners and Europeans arrived via sea routes. Midwestern gold-seekers usually traveled west in wagon trains. Most forty-niners first arrived in San Francisco. This port town became a convenient trade center and stopping point for travelers. As a result, its population increased from around 800 in March 1848 to more than 25,000 by 1850.

Staking a Claim Few of the forty-niners had any previous gold-mining experience. The work was difficult and time-consuming. The forty-niners would **prospect**, or search for gold, along the banks of streams or in shallow surface mines. The early forty-niners worked an area that ran for 70 miles along rivers in northern California.

The first person to arrive at a site would "stake a claim." Early miners frequently banded together to prospect for gold. The miners agreed that each would keep a share of whatever gold was discovered. When one group abandoned a claim, more recent arrivals often took it over, hoping for success. Sometimes two or more groups arrived in an area at the same time. In the early gold-rush days, before courts were established, this competition often led to conflict. Occasionally, violent disputes arose over competing claims.

Mining methods varied according to the location. The most popular method, placer (PLA-suhr) mining, was done along rivers and streams. **Placer miners** used pans or other devices to wash gold nuggets out of loose rock and gravel. To reach gold deposits buried in the hills, miners had to dig shafts and tunnels. These tasks were usually pursued by mining companies, rather than by individuals.

Miners came to California from around the world to make their fortune. In the photo, Anglo and Chinese miners work together in Auburn Ravine in 1852.

In 1853 California's yearly gold production peaked at more than $60 million. Individual success stories inspired many miners. One lucky man found two and a half pounds of gold after only 15 minutes of work. Two African American miners found a rich gold deposit that became known as Negro Hill in honor of their discovery. The vast majority of miners, however, did not become rich. Forty-niner Alonzo Delano commented that the "lean, meager [thin], worn-out and woebegone [sorrowful] miner . . . might daily be seen at almost every point in the upper mines."

Life in the Mining Camps

Mining camps sprang up wherever enough people gathered to look for gold. These camps had colorful names, such as Hangtown or Poker Flat. The mining camps usually began as a row of tents along the streams flowing out of the Sierra Nevada. In time the tents gave way to rough wooden houses, stores, and saloons.

Miners in the camps came from many cultures and backgrounds. Most miners were young, unmarried men in search of adventure. Only around 5 percent of gold-rush immigrants were women or children. The hardworking women generally made good money by cooking meals, washing clothes, and operating boardinghouses. One such woman, Catherine Haun, recalled her first home in California—a wooden shed that was built in a day. The building next door was a saloon. However, she quite liked her new home and neighbors.

Haun's husband was a lawyer. He concluded that he could make more money practicing law than he could panning for gold. He was one of many people who made a good living supplying miners with food, clothing, equipment, and other services. Miners paid high prices for basic necessities because the large amounts of gold in circulation caused severe inflation in California. A loaf of bread, for example, might cost 5 cents in the East, but would sell for 50 to 75 cents in San Francisco. Eggs sometimes sold for $1 apiece.

Some settlers took full advantage of these conditions for free enterprise. Biddy Mason and her family, for instance, had arrived in California

A woman joins men to look for gold. Fewer women than men moved west to search for gold, but the ones who did often found greater social and economic opportunity than they had in the east.

as slaves. A Georgia slaveholder had brought them during the gold-rush years. Mason quickly discovered that most Californians opposed slavery, particularly in the gold mines. She and her family gained their freedom and moved to the small village of Los Angeles. There she saved money until she could purchase some land. Over time, Mason's property increased in value from $250 to $200,000. She became one of the wealthiest land-owners in California, a community leader, and a well-known supporter of charities.

Immigrants to California The lure of gold in California attracted miners from around the world. Many were from countries that had seen few immigrants to the United States in the past. They were drawn to California by the lure of wealth. For example, famine and economic hard-ship in southeastern China caused many Chinese men to leave China for America. Most hoped to find great wealth, and then return home to China. These immigrants were known in Chinese as *gam saan haak*, or "travelers to Gold Mountain." Between 1849 and 1853, about 24,000 Chinese men moved to California. "From far and near we came and were pleased," wrote merchant Lai Chun-chuen in 1855.

Chinese immigrants soon discovered that many Americans did not welcome them, however. In 1852 California placed a tax of $20 a month on all foreign miners. This was more than many of the Chinese miners could afford. However, they had no choice but to find a way to pay this tax if they wanted to prospect for gold. Some Chinese workers were the targets of violent attacks. If the Chinese miners dared to protest the attacks, the legal system favored Americans over immigrants.

Despite such treatment, many Chinese immigrants still worked in the gold mines. Some looked for other jobs. Others opened their own businesses. A newspaper reported Chinese working as "ploughmen, laundry-men, placer miners, woolen spinners and weavers, domestic servants, cigar makers, [and] shoemakers." So many Chinese owned busi-nesses in San Francisco that their neighborhood became known as China-town, as it still is today.

In 1849 alone, about 20,000 immigrants arrived in California not only from China but also from Europe, Mexico, and South America. Like most Americans who sought gold, these new arrivals intended to return home after they had made their fortunes. However, many decided to stay. Some began businesses. For example, Levi Strauss, a German immigrant, earned a fortune by making tough denim pants for miners.

Impact on California

During the Spanish and Mexican periods of settlement, California's population grew slowly. The arrival of the forty-niners changed this dramatically.

Population Boom By 1849 California was home to more than 100,000 people, including Americans and immigrants. Also included in this num-ber were slaves, although a state constitution written in 1849 outlawed

Reading Check
Categorize
What types of people came to California hoping to benefit from the gold rush?

Westward Movement in the United States

Causes

- Americans believe in the idea of manifest destiny.
- The United States acquires vast new lands in the West.
- Pathfinders open trails to new territories.
- Gold is discovered in California.

Effects

- Native Americans are forced off lands.
- Americans travel west to settle new areas.
- The United States stretches to the Pacific Ocean.
- California experiences a population boom.

slavery. California's population explosion made it eligible for statehood only two years after being acquired by the United States. In 1850 California became the 31st state.

However, fast population growth had negative consequences for many Californios and California Native Americans. One early observer of the gold rush described why.

> "The Yankee regarded every man but [his own kind] as an interloper [trespasser], who had no right to come to California and pick up the gold of 'free and enlightened citizens.'"
>
> —W. Kelly, *An Excursion to California*

Economic Growth In addition to rapid population growth, a flood of new businesses and industries transformed California's economy. Gold mining remained an important part of its early economy. But Californians soon discovered other ways to make a living. Farming and ranching became industries for those willing to do the necessary hard labor. The California farming industry quickly took off, with Sacramento as its business center. Soon crops from the state were being shipped to markets around the United States and the world. In addition, lumber mills and factories were established to provide for the needs of miners and city dwellers.

Perhaps the most successful industry during the gold rush, however, was retail trade. Miners wanted to spend their time looking for gold, not growing crops or making products. Instead, they chose to buy the food and supplies they needed from merchants. However, the prices they paid were often very high. California could not supply all the food and materials its new population demanded, and materials had to be imported. Food and lumber were shipped from the eastern United States and from other parts of the world in return for gold. Merchants, in turn, sold these goods for inflated prices. Many successful merchants made huge fortunes in California. Some of them took their money back east to create new companies of their own. Among the entrepreneurs who owed their fortunes to gold rush sales were railroad tycoon Leland Stanford and blue jeans manufacturer Levi Strauss.

San Francisco Population, 1847–1850

San Francisco Grows

San Francisco boomed in the early years of the gold rush.

What factors led to San Francisco's population growth?

Reading Check
Analyze Information
What political effect resulted from California's rapid population growth?

California faced an obstacle to growth, though. The state was isolated from the rest of the country. It was difficult to bring in and ship out goods. The answer to the isolation problem was to bring the railroad all the way to California. Although Californians would have to wait almost 20 years for that, the gold rush did inspire the development of the American railroad industry. Completion of the transcontinental railroad in 1869 at last gave Californians the means to grow a stronger economy.

Summary and Preview Americans moved west to create new lives and seize new opportunities. In the next module you will learn about the Industrial Revolution in America.

Lesson 3 Assessment

Review Ideas, Terms, and People

1. **a. Recall** Why was Sutter's Mill important?

    b. Summarize What types of people participated in the California gold rush, and how did they take part in it?

    c. Elaborate What are some possible problems caused by the arrival of so many new settlers to California?

2. **a. Describe** How did some people hope to solve the problem of California's isolation from the rest of the country?

    b. Draw Inferences What effect did California's rapid population growth have on Californios and Native Americans?

    c. Evaluate Overall, do you think that the gold rush had a positive or negative effect on California? Explain.

Critical Thinking

3. **Evaluate** In this lesson you learned about the California gold rush. Create a concept web like the one shown below. Use it to show how the discovery of gold changed California.

Discovery of Gold

Social Studies Skills

Interpret Maps: Expansion

Define the Skill

Maps show features on Earth's surface. These can be physical features, such as mountains and rivers, or human features, such as roads and settlements. Historical maps show an area as it was in the past. Some show how a nation's boundaries changed over time. Interpreting maps can answer questions about history as well as geography.

Learn the Skill

Follow these steps to gain information from a map.

1. Read the title to determine what the map is about and the time period it covers.

2. Study the legend or key to understand what the colors or symbols on the map mean. Note the map scale, which is used to measure distances.

3. Note the map's other features. Maps often contain labels and other information in addition to what is explained in the legend or key.

Practice the Skill

Interpret the map below to answer the following questions about the expansion of the United States.

1. The addition of which territory almost doubled the size of the United States?

2. What was the last expansion that completed the establishment of the northern U.S. border, and when did it take place?

3. According to the map, when did California become part of the United States?

4. What choice of overland routes did a traveler have for getting to California?

5. What physical obstacles does the map show that such a traveler would face?

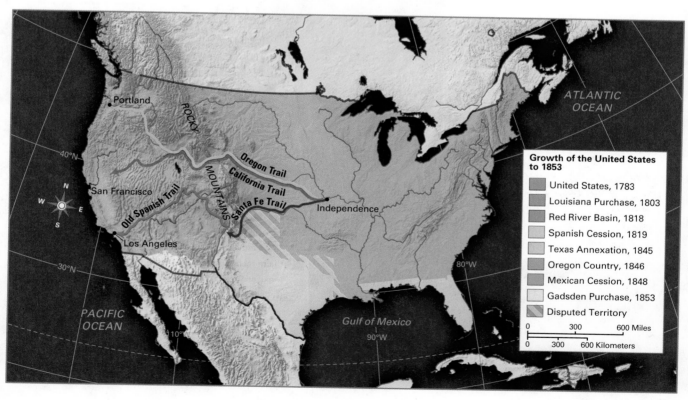

Growth of the United States to 1853

- United States, 1783
- Louisiana Purchase, 1803
- Red River Basin, 1818
- Spanish Cession, 1819
- Texas Annexation, 1845
- Oregon Country, 1846
- Mexican Cession, 1848
- Gadsden Purchase, 1853
- Disputed Territory

0   300   600 Miles

0   300   600 Kilometers

America's Growth by 1850

In the 1830s a new dream began to shape the American mind—manifest destiny. Manifest destiny was the belief that the United States should extend all the way to the Pacific Ocean. By 1850 that dream had become a reality. In 1845 the United States annexed Texas. In 1848 it acquired Oregon and the huge Mexican Cession. By 1853, with the Gadsden Purchase, the United States had taken the basic shape it still has today.

America's Population, 1850: 23.6 million

Ethnic Groups, 1850

2%, <1%, <1%, 16%, 80%

- White/European
- African American
- Native American
- Asian
- Mexican American

Religions, 1850

1%, 3%, 5%, 91%

- Protestant
- Catholic
- Jewish
- Other

CANADA

Washington Territory

ROCKY MOUNTAINS

Oregon Territory

California

Utah Territory

San Francisco

New Mexico Territory

MEXICO

Gold Fever The discovery of gold in California in 1848 set off a massive migration. In 1849 some 80,000 forty-niners headed toward California. San Francisco, located on an excellent natural port, grew quickly as a result.

PACIFIC OCEAN

- Texas annexation, 1845
- Claim recognized in Oregon Treaty, 1848
- Mexican Cession, 1848
- Gadsden Purchase, 1853

0   150   300 Miles

0   150   300 Kilometers

40°N

Tropic of Cancer

130°W   120°W   110°W

Water Rights Water was critical in the dry West. Bitter disputes arose over who had the water rights to streams. Gold rush miners developed a simple system: whoever used the water first owned the rights to it. In other parts of the West, the community as a whole had a right to use the water source.

Manifest Destiny Supporters of manifest destiny believed it was God's will that the United States should expand and spread democracy across North America. Huge numbers of settlers headed west to tame new lands.

The Rocky Mountains The Rocky Mountains were a gigantic obstacle to settlers on their way west. Pathfinders like Lt. John C. Frémont traveled widely in the region, making maps and noting possible trails. The South Pass, through which the Oregon Trail ran, was one of the few easy ways through the great chain of mountains.

GREAT PLAINS

Oregon Trail

Missouri River

Mississippi River

Unorganized Territory

Indian Territory

Claimed by Texas

Texas

Gulf of Mexico

ATLANTIC OCEAN

70°W

90°W

N
W E
S

Interpret Maps

1. **Movement** Why did San Francisco grow so rapidly?

2. **Human-Environment Interaction** Why was water so important in the West?

Module 12 Assessment

Review Vocabulary, Terms, and People

Identify the correct term or person from the module that best fits each of the following descriptions.

1. Mexican priest who led a rebellion for independence from Spain
2. Early settlers in California
3. A group of pioneers who were stranded in the Sierra Nevada Mountains and struggled to survive the winter
4. Agents hired by the Mexican government to attract settlers to Texas
5. The belief that the United States was meant to expand across the continent to the Pacific Ocean
6. Mexican ruler who fought to keep Texas from gaining independence
7. Swiss immigrant who received permission from Mexico to start a colony in California

Comprehension and Critical Thinking

Lesson 1

8. a. **Identify** Who were Stephen F. Austin and Antonio López de Santa Anna?
    b. **Draw Conclusions** Why did settlers in Texas rebel against Mexican rule?
    c. **Elaborate** In what ways was the Texas struggle for independence similar to that of the United States?

Lesson 2

9. a. **Recall** Why were some Americans opposed to the annexation of new territories?
    b. **Draw Conclusions** What economic and cultural influences did Native Americans and Mexican Americans have on American settlers in the Mexican Cession?
    c. **Predict** What are some possible problems the acquisition of so much territory might cause the United States?

Lesson 3

10. a. **Identify** What roles did women and immigrants play in the California gold rush?
    b. **Make Inferences** Why were most gold-rush settlers young, unmarried men?
    c. **Predict** What long-term effects might the gold rush have on California's future?

Review Themes

11. **Economics** What impact did the gold rush have on the economy in California?
12. **Geography** Why did many Americans in the 1840s believe the United States should annex the territories of Oregon, New Mexico, and Texas?

Reading Skills

Vocabulary in Context *Use the Reading Skills taught in this module to answer the question about the reading selection below.*

> Texas politicians hoped that joining the United States would help solve the republic's financial and military problems. The Texas Congress approved annexation in June 1845. Texas became part of the United States in December.

13. Determine the definition of *annexation* using context clues.

Module 12 Assessment, continued

Social Studies Skills

Interpret Maps: Expansion *Use the Social Studies Skills taught in this module to answer the question about the map below.*

14. Place the expansions in the order in which they were acquired by the United States, according to the map.

Focus on Writing

15. **Write an Outline for a Documentary Film** Choose one topic from this module that you think would make a good 10-minute documentary. Your outline should be organized by scene (no more than three scenes) and in chronological order. For each scene, give the following information: main idea of scene, costumes and images to be used, audio to be used, and length of scene. As you plan, remember that the audience will be students your own age.

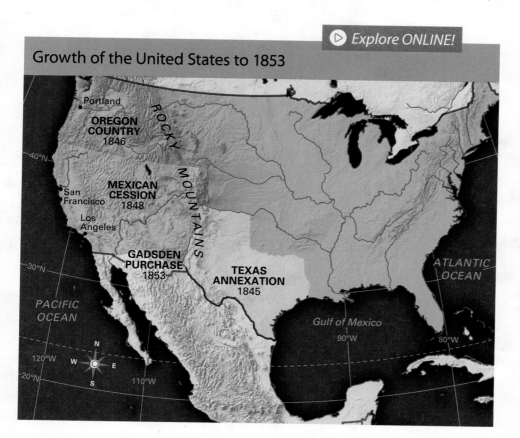

Growth of the United States to 1853

The Real West: Rush for Gold

When gold was discovered in northern California in 1848, it caused a sensation. Gold seekers from the United States and the rest of the world rushed to California to find their fortunes. The conditions of the trip were difficult, as was the labor required to extract the gold from rivers and mines. Although some people became wealthy, many more never found the riches they had expected. So many people arrived so quickly that California became a state within three years of gold being discovered.

Explore some of the history and documents of the California gold rush online. You can find a wealth of information, video clips, primary sources, activities, and more through your online textbook.

CALIFORNIA!
Mutual Protection
Trading & Mining Co.

"If any man has his health &
will work, he can make more
than ten times as much here
as he can in the states in
the same length of time. But
many, very many, that come
here meet with bad success
& thousands will leave their
bones here."

—S. Shufelt

A Miner's Letter Home
Read the document to learn about
one miner's opinion on the possibility
of becoming rich in California.

Go online to view these and
other HISTORY® resources.

Heading West
Watch the video to learn about the dangers that
overland travelers faced when trying to get to
California from the eastern United States.

Search for the Mother Lode
Watch the video to see the various methods that
forty-niners used to mine the gold in California.

Statehood
Watch the video to discover the political issues
surrounding the admission of California as a free
state and its implication for the rest of the nation.

Module 13
The North

★

Essential Question
How did the Industrial Revolution help shape life in the North?

About the Photo: New machinery like this textile mill helped fuel the Industrial Revolution.

Explore ONLINE!

VIDEOS, including...
• Industrial Revolution
• Train Technology

HISTORY

☑ Document-Based Investigations

☑ Graphic Organizers

☑ Interactive Games

☑ Image Carousel: Elements of Mass Production

☑ Image with Hotspots: Life of a Mill Girl

☑ Image with Hotspots: The Steam Train

In this module you will read about the changes that occurred in the lives of Americans in the North as the result of rapid industrialization. You will also learn about some of the new inventions of the period.

What You Will Learn ...

Lesson 1: The Industrial Revolution in America **424**
The Big Idea The Industrial Revolution transformed the way goods were produced in the United States.

Lesson 2: Changes in Working Life **430**
The Big Idea The introduction of factories changed working life for many Americans.

Lesson 3: The Transportation Revolution **435**
The Big Idea New forms of transportation improved business, travel, and communication in the United States.

Lesson 4: More Technological Advances **441**
The Big Idea Advances in technology led to new inventions that continued to change daily life and work.

Timeline of Events 1785–1860

United States		World
	1785	

1790 The first steam-powered mill opens in Great Britain.

< **1807** Robert Fulton's *Clermont* becomes the first commercially successful steamboat.

1800

1815

∧ **1830** The *Tom Thumb* becomes the first locomotive in the United States to carry passengers.

1830

1838 The *Sirius* becomes the first ship to cross the Atlantic Ocean entirely on steam power.

1840 Federal government employees receive a 10-hour workday.

1846 German astronomer Johann Galle observes that Neptune is a planet. >

1845 Sarah G. Bagley is appointed secretary of the New England Working Men's Association.

1845

< **1856** Gail Borden patents a method of condensing milk so that it can safely be stored in cans.

1851 London's Great Exhibition displays inventions from around the world in the Crystal Palace. >

1860

Reading Social Studies

THEME FOCUS:

Science and Technology, Economics

As you read this module, you will learn about how developments in science and technology brought about what is called the Industrial Revolution. As a result of the Industrial Revolution, you will see how American economic patterns changed. Next, you will read about how family life changed as more and more people went to work in factories. Finally, you will see how new methods of transportation changed where people lived and how new inventions affected daily life and work.

READING FOCUS:

Understand Causes and Effects in History

Have you heard the saying, "We have to understand the past to avoid repeating it."? That is one reason we look for causes and effects in history.

Cause and Effect Chains You might say that all of history is one long chain of causes and effects. It may help you to understand the course of history better if you draw out such a chain as you read.

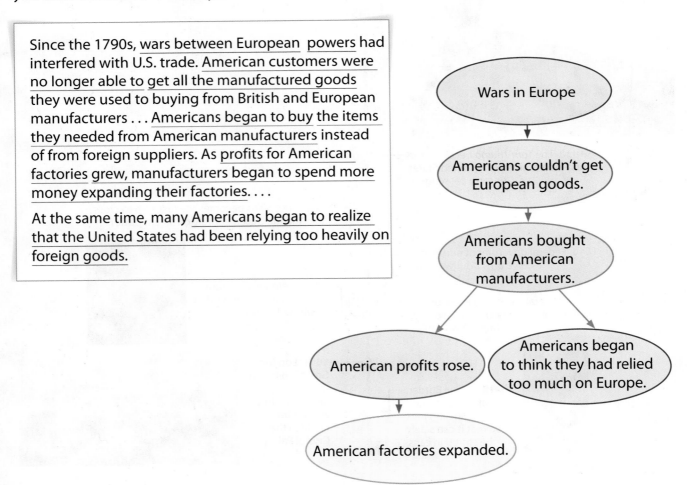

Since the 1790s, wars between European powers had interfered with U.S. trade. American customers were no longer able to get all the manufactured goods they were used to buying from British and European manufacturers . . . Americans began to buy the items they needed from American manufacturers instead of from foreign suppliers. As profits for American factories grew, manufacturers began to spend more money expanding their factories. . . .

At the same time, many Americans began to realize that the United States had been relying too heavily on foreign goods.

Wars in Europe

Americans couldn't get European goods.

Americans bought from American manufacturers.

American profits rose.

Americans began to think they had relied too much on Europe.

American factories expanded.

You Try It!

The following passage is from the module you are about to read. As you read each paragraph, ask yourself what is the cause and what is the effect of what is being discussed.

Workers Organize Factories continued to spread in the 1800s. Craftspeople, who made goods by hand, felt threatened. Factories quickly produced low-priced goods. To compete with factories, shop owners had to hire more workers and pay them less. . . .

The wages of factory workers also went down as people competed for jobs. A wave of immigration in the 1840s brought people from other, poorer countries. They were willing to work for low pay. More immigrants came to the Northeast, where the mills were located, than to the South. Competition for jobs also came from people unemployed during the financial Panic of 1837.

After you have read the passage, answer the following questions.

1. What cause is being discussed in the first paragraph? What were its effects?

2. Draw a cause and effect chain that shows the events described in the first paragraph.

3. What main effect is discussed in the second paragraph? How many causes are given for it?

4. Draw a cause and effect chain that shows the events described in the second paragraph.

As you read Module 13, look for words that signal causes or effects. Picture these causes and effects as the links in a cause and effect chain.

Key Terms and People

Lesson 1
Industrial Revolution
textiles
Richard Arkwright
Samuel Slater
technology
Eli Whitney
interchangeable parts
mass production

Lesson 2
Rhode Island system
Francis Cabot Lowell
Lowell system
trade unions
strikes
Sarah G. Bagley

Lesson 3
Transportation Revolution
Robert Fulton
Clermont
Gibbons v. *Ogden*
Peter Cooper

Lesson 4
Samuel F. B. Morse
telegraph
Morse code
John Deere
Cyrus McCormick
Isaac Singer

The Industrial Revolution in America

The Big Idea

The Industrial Revolution transformed the way goods were produced in the United States.

Main Ideas

- The invention of new machines in Great Britain led to the beginning of the Industrial Revolution.
- The development of new machines and processes brought the Industrial Revolution to the United States.
- Despite a slow start in manufacturing, the United States made rapid improvements during the War of 1812.

Key Terms and People

Industrial Revolution
textiles
Richard Arkwright
Samuel Slater
technology
Eli Whitney
interchangeable parts
mass production

Academic
Vocabulary
efficient productive
and not wasteful

If YOU were there . . .

You live in a small Pennsylvania town in the 1780s. You earn money for your family by raising sheep and spinning their wool into yarn. Your sisters knit the yarn into gloves and mittens that you sell to city merchants. But now you hear that someone has invented machines that can spin thread and make cloth.

Would you still be able to earn the same amount of money for your family? Why?

The Industrial Revolution

At the start of the 1700s, the majority of people in Europe and the United States were farmers. They made most of what they needed by hand. For example, female family members usually made clothing. First, they used a spinning wheel to spin raw materials, such as cotton or wool, into thread. Then they used a hand loom to weave the thread into cloth.

Some families produced extra cloth to sell to merchants, who sold it for a profit. In towns, a few skilled craftspeople made goods by hand in their own shops. Workers including blacksmiths, carpenters, and shoemakers specialized in their work and the goods that they produced. Their ways of life had stayed the same for generations.

A Need for Change By the mid-1700s, however, changes in Great Britain led to a greater demand for manufactured goods. As agriculture and roads improved, cities and populations grew. Overseas trade also expanded. Traditional manufacturing methods did not produce enough goods to meet everyone's needs.

People began using machines to create processes that made goods in more **efficient** ways. They also discovered new power resources to fuel the machines. These developments led to the **Industrial Revolution**, a period of rapid growth in using machines for manufacturing and production that began in the mid-1700s.

Women workers in a textile mill

Textile Industry The first important breakthrough of the Industrial Revolution took place in how **textiles**, or cloth items, were made. Before the Industrial Revolution, spinning thread took much more time than making cloth. Several skilled workers were needed to spin enough thread to supply a single weaver.

In 1769 British entrepreneur **Richard Arkwright** invented a large spinning machine called a water frame. The water frame could produce dozens of cotton threads at the same time. It lowered the cost of cotton cloth and increased the speed of textile production.

The water frame used flowing water as its source of power. Merchants began to build large textile mills, or factories, near rivers and streams. The mills were filled with spinning machines. Merchants began hiring people to work in the mills.

Reading Check
Draw Conclusions
How did machines speed up textile manufacturing?

Additional improvements also speeded up the spinning process. Britain soon had the world's most productive textile manufacturing industry.

New Machines and Processes

New machines encouraged the rise of new processes in business and manufacturing. As the machines used to make products became more efficient, the processes involved changed dramatically.

Slater and His Secrets The new textile machines allowed Great Britain to produce cloth more quickly and inexpensively than other countries could. To protect British industry, the British Parliament had made it illegal for skilled mechanics or machine plans to leave the country. Disguised as a farmer, **Samuel Slater**, a skilled British mechanic, immigrated to the United States after carefully memorizing the designs of textile mill machines. Soon after arriving, he sent a letter to Moses Brown, who owned a textile business in New England. Slater claimed he could improve the way textiles were manufactured in the United States.

Brown had one of his workers test Slater's knowledge of machinery. Slater passed. Brown's son, Smith Brown, and son-in-law, William Almy, formed a partnership with Slater. Economic freedom in the United States allowed entrepreneurs such as Slater, Brown, and Almy to take risks by using their money and talents to launch new ventures. In 1793 they opened their first mill in Pawtucket, Rhode Island. The production of cotton thread by American machines had begun. Slater ran the mill and the machinery. He was confident that his new machines would work well.

> "If I do not make as good yarn as they do in England, I will have nothing for my services, but will throw the whole of what I have attempted over the bridge."
>
> —Samuel Slater, from *Memoir of Samuel Slater*

Slater could have lost all of his investment, but his machines worked and the Pawtucket mill became a success. Slater's wife also invented a new cotton thread for sewing. In 1798 Slater formed his own company to build a mill. By the time he died in 1835, he owned all or part of 13 textile mills.

Other Americans began building textile mills. Most were located in the Northeast. In New England, in particular, merchants had the money to invest in new mills. More importantly, the physical environment in this region was made up of many rivers and streams that provided a reliable supply of power. Fewer mills were built in the South, partly because investors in the South concentrated on expanding agriculture. There, agriculture was seen as an easier way to make money. The expansion of industrialization in the North and the South's concentration on agriculture caused the two regions to develop significant economic and cultural differences.

A Manufacturing Breakthrough Despite these great changes in machines and processes, most manufacturing was still done by hand. In the late 1790s the U.S. government worried about a possible war with France, so it wanted more muskets for the army. Skilled workers made the parts for each weapon by hand. No two parts were exactly alike, and carefully fitting all the pieces together took much time and skill.

As a result, American gunmakers could not produce the muskets quickly enough to satisfy the government's demand. Factories needed better **technology**, the tools used to produce items or to do work.

In 1798 inventor **Eli Whitney** tried to address some of these problems. Whitney gave officials a proposal for mass-producing guns for the U.S. government using water-powered machinery. Whitney explained the benefits of his ideas.

> "I am persuaded that machinery moved by water [and] adapted to this business would greatly reduce the labor and facilitate [ease] the manufacture of this article."
>
> —Eli Whitney to Secretary of the Treasury Oliver Wolcott

Whitney also came up with the idea of using **interchangeable parts**—parts of a machine that are identical. Interchangeable parts became important because each part does not have to be custom-made by hand, so it saves production time. Using interchangeable parts made machines easier to assemble and broken parts easier to replace. Whitney promised to build 10,000 muskets in two years. The federal government gave him money to build his factory, and in 1801 he was called to Washington, DC, to give a demonstration.

Eli Whitney developed the idea of using interchangeable parts. Interchangeable, or identical, parts are needed so each part does not have to be custom-made by hand.

Elements of Mass Production

Mass production requires the use of interchangeable parts, machine tools, and the division of labor. Machine tools like the one at bottom left make parts that are identical and therefore interchangeable. Mass production uses a division of labor in which the work is divided among several people. Each worker performs a specific task, like the workers below who change the spools of wire. The end result is goods that have been mass-produced. These techniques were used to build items such as the firearms at bottom right.

Why are interchangeable parts important?

Machine Tools

Division of Labor

Mass-Produced Goods

Whitney stood before President John Adams and his secretary of war. He had an assortment of parts for ten guns. He then randomly chose parts and quickly assembled them into muskets. To the audience's amazement, he repeated the process several times.

Whitney's ideas helped businesses in the manufacturing industry determine the best way to produce the goods that consumers in the American market needed. He had proven that American inventors could improve upon the new British technology. Machines that produced matching parts soon became the standard in industry. Interchangeable parts sped up **mass production**, the efficient production of large numbers of identical goods. Mass-production techniques allowed manufacturers to efficiently create more goods for the marketplace.

Reading Check
Summarize How did Eli Whitney influence American manufacturing?

Manufacturing Grows Slowly

Despite the hard work of people such as Samuel Slater and Eli Whitney, manufacturing in the United States grew slowly. In 1810 Secretary of the Treasury Albert Gallatin described some of the obstacles faced by potential factory owners in the United States.

"[The reasons include] . . . the superior attractions of agricultural pursuits [farming], . . . the abundance of land compared with the population, the high price of labor, and the want [lack] of sufficient capital [investment]."

—Albert Gallatin, from *The Writings of Albert Gallatin*

Gallatin and others believed that few people would choose to work in a factory if they could own their own farm instead. In Great Britain, on the other hand, land was more scarce and more expensive than in the United

Modern Manufacturing

The word *manufacture* comes from Latin words that mean "to make by hand." Yet in modern manufacturing, machines—not human hands—do most of the work.

A key feature of modern manufacturing is the assembly line. An assembly line is a long conveyer belt. As the product moves along the belt, or "down the line," workers assemble it. Often, the workers use machines to help them. On a growing number of assembly lines, there are no workers at all: the product is assembled by computer-controlled robots.

Although a far cry from Eli Whitney's factory, modern factories use the same elements of mass production that Whitney did more than 200 years ago.

Analyze Information
How do interchangeable parts help the modern assembly line work?

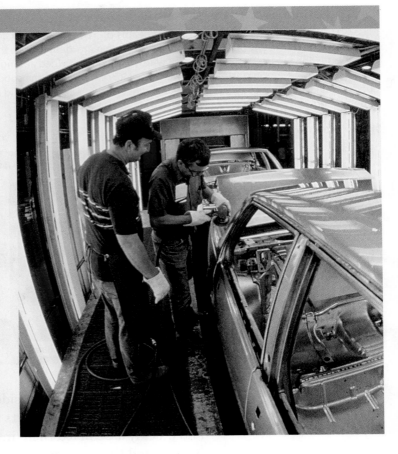

States. As a result, fewer people were able to own farms. British factory workers generally were willing to work for lower wages than factory workers in the United States were.

Because British manufacturers had plenty of factory workers with technical skills, they could produce large amounts of goods less expensively than most American businesses could. As a result, they could charge lower prices for the goods. Lower British prices made it difficult for many American manufacturers to compete with British companies. This situation in turn discouraged American investors from spending the money needed to build new factories and machinery. As a result, only a few industries had found a place to compete in the American market economy. These included cotton goods, flour milling, weapons, and iron production.

These circumstances began to change around the time of the War of 1812. Since the 1790s, conflict and wars between European powers had interfered with U.S. trade. Some goods became scarce, as American consumers were no longer able to get all the manufactured goods they were used to buying from British and European manufacturers. Then, during the War of 1812, British ships blockaded eastern seaports, preventing foreign ships from delivering goods. Americans began to buy the items they needed from American manufacturers instead of from foreign suppliers. As profits for American factories grew, manufacturers began to spend more money expanding their factories. State banks and private investors began to lend money to manufacturers for their businesses.

At the same time, many Americans began to realize that the United States had been relying too heavily on foreign goods. If the United States could not meet its own needs, it might be weak and open to attack. Former president Thomas Jefferson, who had once opposed manufacturing, changed his mind. He, too, realized that the United States was too dependent on imports.

> "To be independent for the comforts of life we must fabricate [make] them ourselves. We must now place the manufacturer by the side of the agriculturalist [farmer]."
>
> —Thomas Jefferson, from *Memoir, Correspondence, and Miscellanies from the Papers of Thomas Jefferson*

In February 1815, New Yorkers celebrated the end of the War of 1812 and the return of free trade. The streets were decorated and filled with merchants whose ships were loaded with goods. "With Peace and Commerce, America Prospers," declared one display. Eager businesspeople prepared to lead the United States into a period of industrial and economic growth. These merchants and industrialists urged northern politicians to pass higher tariffs on foreign goods to protect American companies.

Summary and Preview The Industrial Revolution started with the textile industry in England but soon spread to the United States. In the next lesson you will learn about how the spread of factories changed the working lives of many Americans.

Reading Check
Analyze Information How did the War of 1812 aid the growth of American manufacturing?

Lesson 1 Assessment

Review Ideas, Terms, and People

1. a. **Identify** What was the first industry to begin to use machines to manufacture goods?

   b. **Analyze** What were some causes of the Industrial Revolution, and what effect did it have on the way products were made?

   c. **Predict** In what ways might life for workers change as a result of the Industrial Revolution?

2. a. **Recall** In what part of the United States were most mills located? Why?

   b. **Draw Conclusions** How did the ideas of Samuel Slater and Eli Whitney affect manufacturing in the United States?

   c. **Evaluate** Whose contributions do you think were more important—Slater's textile machines or Whitney's interchangeable parts? Why?

3. a. **Explain** How did conflict in Europe influence economic growth in America?

   b. **Contrast** Why was manufacturing in Great Britain in the early years more successful than that in the United States?

Critical Thinking

4. **Draw Conclusions** In this lesson you learned about the changes in manufacturing and the effect those changes had in the early 1800s. Create a chart similar to the one below and use it to show how each contribution affected manufacturing.

Invention/ Improvement	Effect on Manufacturing

★ Changes in Working Life

The Big Idea

The introduction of factories changed working life for many Americans.

Main Ideas

- The spread of mills in the Northeast changed workers' lives.
- The Lowell system revolutionized the textile industry in the Northeast.
- Workers organized to reform working conditions.

Key Terms and People

Rhode Island system
Francis Cabot Lowell
Lowell system
trade unions
strikes
Sarah G. Bagley

If YOU were there . . .

You live on a dairy farm in Massachusetts in about 1820. On the farm, you get up at dawn to milk the cows, and your work goes on until nighttime. But now you have a chance at a different life. A nearby textile mill is hiring young people. You would leave the farm and live with other workers. You could go to classes. Most importantly, you could earn money of your own.

Would you go to work in the textile mill? Why?

Mills Change Workers' Lives

Workers no longer needed the specific skills of craftspeople to run the machines of the new mills. The lives of workers changed along with their jobs. Resistance to these changes sometimes sparked protests.

Many mill owners in the United States could not find enough people to work in factories because other jobs were available. At first, Samuel Slater and his two partners used apprentices—young men who worked for several years to learn the trade. However, they often were given only simple work. For example, their jobs might include feeding cotton into the machines and cleaning the mill equipment. They grew tired of this work and frequently left. Apprentice James Horton, for example, ran away from Slater's mill. "Mr. Slater . . . keep me always at one thing . . . ," Horton complained. "I might have stayed there until this time and never knew nothing."

Eventually, Slater began to hire entire families who moved to Pawtucket to work in the mills. This practice allowed Slater to fill his labor needs at a low cost. Children as well as adults worked in the mills.

On most farms children worked to help their families. Therefore, few people complained about the hiring of children to work in factories. H. Humphrey, an author of books on raising children, told parents that children needed to be useful. Humphrey wrote, "If he [a child] will not study, put him on to a farm, or send him into the shop, or in some other way provide regular employment for him." The machines made many tasks in the mill simple enough for children to do. Mill owners profited because they paid children low wages. Adults usually earned as much in a day as most children did in a week.

To attract families to his mill, Slater built housing for the workers. He also provided them with a company store where they could buy necessities. In addition, he started the practice of paying workers with credit at the company store. Instead of paying the full price for an item all at once, small payments could be made over a period of time. This practice allowed Slater to reinvest his money in his business.

Slater's strategy of hiring families and dividing factory work into simple tasks became known as the **Rhode Island system**. Mill owners throughout the Northeast copied Slater's methods. Owners advertised with "Men with growing families wanted." They also sent recruiters to poor communities to find new workers. For many people, the chance to work in a factory was a welcome opportunity to earn money and to learn a new skill.

Entire families worked at Slater's mill in Pawtucket, Rhode Island. The mill's machinery was powered by the Blackstone River.

Reading Check
Summarize What problem did Slater have in his mills, and how did he solve it?

One of the earliest of the mill towns, Slatersville, was named after Samuel Slater. The town was built by Slater and his brother John. It included two houses for workers and their families, the owner's house, the company store, and the Slatersville Mill. The mill was the largest and most modern industrial building of its time.

The mills employed not only the textile workers who operated the machinery but also machine part makers and dam builders. Although the company store sold food and necessary items to workers, mill towns supported the same variety of businesses any other town needed to thrive. These included tailors and dressmakers, butchers, and other small workshops.

The Lowell System

Not all mill owners followed this system. **Francis Cabot Lowell**, an entrepreneur from New England, developed a very different approach. His ideas completely changed the textile industry in the Northeast.

The **Lowell system** was based on water-powered textile mills that employed young, unmarried women from local farms. The system included a loom that could both spin thread and weave cloth in the same mill. Lowell constructed boardinghouses for the women. Boardinghouse residents were given a room and meals along with their jobs.

With financial support from investors of the Boston Manufacturing Company, Lowell's first textile mill opened in Waltham, Massachusetts, in 1814. "From the first starting of the first power loom there was not . . . doubt about the success," wrote one investor. In 1822 the company built a larger mill in a Massachusetts town later named Lowell. Visitors to Lowell were amazed by the clean factories and neatly kept boardinghouses as well as the new machinery.

Life of a Mill Girl

No record exists today of the name of this girl, who worked in a mill around 1850. Judging from the photograph, if she were in school today, she would probably be in the seventh or eighth grade. Although hard to see in this photograph, her hands and arms are scratched and swollen—telltale signs of the hard labor required of young girls who worked up to 14 hours a day.

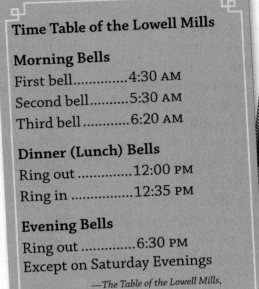

Time Table of the Lowell Mills

Morning Bells

First bell..............4:30 AM

Second bell..........5:30 AM

Third bell............6:20 AM

Dinner (Lunch) Bells

Ring out ....12:00 PM

Ring in ....12:35 PM

Evening Bells

Ring out ....6:30 PM
Except on Saturday Evenings

—*The Table of the Lowell Mills,*
October 21, 1851

The young women working in the mills soon became known as Lowell girls. The mills paid them between $2 and $4 each week. The workers were required to pay $1.25 for room and board. These wages were much better than the wages women could earn per week in other available jobs, such as domestic work.

Many young women came to Lowell from different parts of New England. They wanted the chance to earn money instead of working on the family farm. Working in the Lowell mills gave young women the opportunity to achieve economic independence. "I must of course have something of my own before many more years have passed over my head," wrote one young woman. The typical Lowell girl worked at the mills for about four years.

The Lowell system aimed to overcome the perception that factory workers had a lower social status. Unlike other factory workers, the Lowell girls were encouraged to use their free time to take classes and form women's clubs. They even wrote their own magazine, the *Lowell Offering.* Lucy Larcom, who started working in the Lowell mills at age 11, later praised her fellow workers:

> "I regard it as one of the privileges [advantages] of my youth that I . . . [grew] up among those active, interesting girls, whose lives . . . had principle [ideals] and purpose distinctly their own."
>
> —Lucy Larcom, from *A New England Girlhood*

Reading Check
Contrast How was the Lowell system different from the Rhode Island system?

Mill life was hard, however. The workday was between 12 and 14 hours long, and daily life was carefully controlled. Ringing bells ordered workers to breakfast or lunch. Employees had to work harder and faster to keep up with new equipment. Cotton dust also began to cause health problems, such as chronic cough, for workers.

Workers Organize

Factories continued to spread in the 1800s. Craftspeople, who made goods by hand, felt threatened because factories were able to produce low-priced goods more quickly. To compete with factories, shop owners had to hire more workers and pay them less. Shoemaker William Frazier complained about the situation in the mid-1840s. "We have to sit on our seats from twelve to sixteen hours per day, to earn one dollar."

The wages of factory workers also went down as people competed for jobs. A wave of immigration in the 1840s brought people from other, poorer countries. They were willing to work for low pay. More immigrants came to the Northeast, where the mills were located, than to the South. Competition for jobs also came from people unemployed during the financial Panic of 1837. For example, about 50,000 workers in New York City alone lost their jobs.

The Beginning of Trade Unions Facing low wages and the fear of losing their jobs, skilled workers formed **trade unions**, groups that tried to improve pay and working conditions. Eventually, unskilled factory workers also formed trade unions, seeking economic equity. Most employers did not want to hire union workers. Employers believed that the higher cost of union employees prevented competition with other manufacturers.

Sometimes, labor unions staged protests called **strikes**. Workers on strike refuse to work until employers meet their demands. Most early strikes were not successful, however. Courts and police usually supported companies, not striking union members.

Labor Reform Efforts A strong voice in the union movement was that of millworker **Sarah G. Bagley**. She wrote magazine articles and made speeches about working in the mills. She organized workers to help change conditions. Bagley founded the Lowell Female Labor Reform Association in 1844 and publicized the struggles of factory laborers. The association's two main goals were to influence an investigation of working conditions by the Massachusetts state legislature and to obtain a ten-hour workday. Members of the association passed out pamphlets and circulated petitions.

President Martin Van Buren had granted a ten-hour workday in 1840 for many federal employees. Bagley wanted this rule to apply to employees of private businesses. These men and women often worked 12 to 14 hours per day, six days per week.

Many working men and women supported the ten-hour-workday campaign, despite the opposition of business owners. In 1845 Sarah G. Bagley was elected vice president of the New England Working Men's Association. She was the first woman to hold such a high-ranking position in the American labor movement.

Over time, the unions achieved some **concrete** legal victories. Connecticut, Maine, New Hampshire, Ohio, Pennsylvania, and a few other states passed ten-hour-workday laws.

Reading Check
Find Main Ideas
Why did workers form unions, and what were the main goals of union reformers?

For factory workers in other states, long hours remained common. One witness described how children were "summoned by the factory bell before daylight" and worked until eight o'clock at night "with nothing but [a] recess of forty-five minutes to get their dinner." Union supporters continued to fight for work reforms such as an end to child labor in factories during the 1800s.

Summary and Preview With the growth of factories, workers faced new opportunities and challenges. In the next lesson you will learn about how the Transportation Revolution brought changes to commerce and the daily lives of Americans.

Lesson 2 Assessment

Review Ideas, Terms, and People

1. a. **Identify** What problems did many mill owners have in finding workers?
   b. **Analyze** How did Samuel Slater's Rhode Island system change employment practices in mills?
2. a. **Describe** What was life like for mill workers in the Lowell system?
   b. **Make Inferences** Why would young women have wanted to go to work in the Lowell mills?
3. a. **Recall** Why did workers form trade unions?
   b. **Predict** What are some possible problems that might arise between factory owners and trade unions?

Critical Thinking

4. **Draw Conclusions** In this lesson you learned about mill life and the effect conditions had on workers. Create a chart similar to the one below to show how Samuel Slater, Francis Cabot Lowell, and Sarah G. Bagley affected workers' lives.

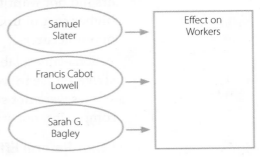

The Transportation Revolution

The Big Idea
New forms of transportation improved business, travel, and communication in the United States.

Main Ideas
- The Transportation Revolution affected trade and daily life.
- The steamboat was one of the first developments of the Transportation Revolution.
- Railroads were a vital part of the Transportation Revolution.
- The Transportation Revolution brought many changes to American life and industry.

Key Terms and People
Transportation Revolution
Robert Fulton
Clermont
Gibbons v. *Ogden*
Peter Cooper

Reading Check
Find Main Ideas
What benefits did the Transportation Revolution bring to trade and daily life?

If YOU were there . . .
You live in a small town in Iowa in the 1860s. You've never been more than 30 miles from home and have always traveled by wagon or on horseback. Now there are plans to build a railroad westward from Chicago, 200 miles to the east. The tracks will come through your town! Twice a week, trains will bring goods from the city and take people farther west.

How would the coming of the railroad change your life?

Trade and Daily Life

During the 1800s the United States was transformed by a **Transportation Revolution**—a period of rapid growth in the speed and convenience of travel because of new methods of transportation. The Transportation Revolution created a boom in business across the country, particularly by reducing shipping time and costs. As one foreign observer declared in 1835, "The Americans . . . have joined the Hudson to the Mississippi, and made the Atlantic Ocean communicate with the Gulf of Mexico."

These improvements were made possible largely by the invention of two new forms of transportation: steamboats and steam-powered trains. They enabled goods, people, and information to travel rapidly and efficiently across the United States.

Steamboats

American and European inventors had developed steam-powered boats in the late 1700s. However, they were not in wide use until the early 1800s.

Steamboat Era In 1803 American **Robert Fulton** tested his first steamboat design in France. Several years later, he tested the first full-sized commercial steamboat, called the ***Clermont***, in the United States. On August 9, 1807,

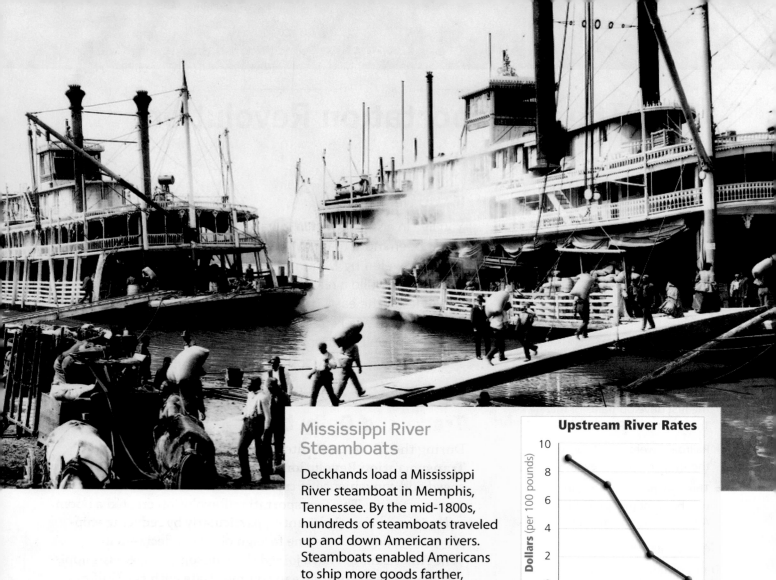

Mississippi River Steamboats

Deckhands load a Mississippi River steamboat in Memphis, Tennessee. By the mid-1800s, hundreds of steamboats traveled up and down American rivers. Steamboats enabled Americans to ship more goods farther, faster, and for less money than ever before.

Upstream River Rates

Dollars (per 100 pounds)

Year

the *Clermont* traveled against the current up the Hudson River without trouble. Demand for steamboat ferry service soon arose.

The steamboat was well suited for river travel. It could move upriver and did not rely on wind power. Steamboats and the location of rivers in the United States created new economic opportunities during the 1800s. Steamboats increased trade and profits because goods could be moved quickly and thus more cheaply. More than 500 steamboats were in use in the United States by 1840. By the 1850s steamboats were also being used to carry people and goods across the Atlantic Ocean, creating more opportunities for international trade.

Gibbons v. Ogden Increased steamboat shipping led to conflict over waterway rights. In 1819 Aaron Ogden sued Thomas Gibbons for operating steamboats in New York waters that Ogden said he owned. Gibbons did not have a license to operate in New York, but argued that his federal license gave him the right to use New York waterways.

Reading Check
Summarize Explain the effects of the *Gibbons* v. *Ogden* ruling.

In the case of **Gibbons v. Ogden**, which reached the Supreme Court in 1824, Chief Justice John Marshall reinforced the federal government's authority to regulate trade between the states by ending monopolistic control over waterways in several states. At the same time, it strengthened the idea that national interests should be placed ahead of regional concerns. The ruling freed up waters to even greater trade and competition within the shipping industry.

American Railroads

What the steamboat did for water travel, the train did for overland travel. Steam-powered trains had first been developed in Great Britain in the early 1800s. However, they did not become popular in the United States until the 1830s. In 1830 **Peter Cooper** built a small but powerful locomotive called the *Tom Thumb*. He raced the locomotive against a horse-drawn railcar.

The *Tom Thumb* was made famous in a race against a horse-drawn carriage. The locomotive was small, but powerful for its day.

Eyewitness John Latrobe later described the race, in which *Tom Thumb* had a slow start and fell behind. Latrobe wrote, "The pace increased, the passengers shouted, the engine gained on the horse . . . then the engine passes the horse, and a great hurrah hailed the victory." Unfortunately for Cooper, victory was spoiled when *Tom Thumb* broke down and lost the race near the end.

Despite the defeat, the contest showed the power and speed of even a small locomotive. Railroad fever soon spread. By 1840 railroad companies had laid about 2,800 miles of tracks—more than existed in all of Europe. French economist Michel Chevalier described Americans as having "a perfect passion for railroads."

As more railroads were built, engineers and mechanics overcame many tough challenges. Most British railroads, for example, ran on straight tracks across flat ground. In the United States, however, many railroads had to run up and down steep mountains, around tight curves, and over swift rivers. Railroad companies also built the tracks quickly and often with the least expensive materials available. As time went on, engineers and mechanics built heavier, faster, and more powerful steam locomotives.

By 1860 about 30,000 miles of tracks linked almost every major city in the eastern United States. As a result, the economy surged forward. For example, American locomotives hauled more freight than those in any other country. The railroad companies quickly became some of the most powerful businesses in the nation. As the railroad system grew, manufacturers and farmers could send their goods to distant markets.

In addition to their tremendous economic impact, the railroads made a powerful impression on the senses of many passengers and observers. Trains were the fastest form of transportation that most people had ever experienced. While wagons often traveled less than 2 miles per hour, locomotives averaged about 20 miles per hour. Writer George Templeton Strong of New York City described the thrill of a steam train passing by in the night:

"Whizzing and rattling and panting, with its fiery furnace gleaming in front, its chimney vomiting fiery smoke above, and its long train of cars rushing along behind like the body and tail of a gigantic dragon— . . . and all darting forward at the rate of twenty miles an hour. Whew!"

—George Templeton Strong, from *The Diary of George Templeton Strong*

Riding on the early trains was often an adventure, but it could also be quite dangerous. Engineers trying to stay on time sometimes traveled too fast. English citizen Charles Richard Weld was on a railroad car that flew off the tracks. To his amazement, the other passengers did not complain about the accident. Instead, they praised the engineer for trying to keep on schedule!

Passengers accepted such risks because the railroads reduced travel time dramatically. The development of the railroads changed people's perceptions of distance. What was once considered to be a long distance to travel suddenly became just a short train ride away. Railroads also helped tie communities together. In 1847 Senator Daniel Webster spoke for many people in the United States when he declared that the railroad "towers above all other inventions of this or the preceding age."

Reading Check
Make Inferences
In what ways did railroads affect the economy of the United States?

Transportation Revolution Brings Changes

The Transportation Revolution brought many changes to America. Steamboats and railroads made getting goods to distant markets much easier and less costly. People in all areas of the nation now had access to products made and grown far away. More than ever before, there was a national economy. The wealth, however, was centered in the North.

Railroads contributed to the expansion of the borders of the nation and guided population growth. Towns sprang up at railroad junctions as people migrated from rural areas. Those towns that did not have railroads nearby suffered and began to decline. Cities grew as trains brought new residents and raw materials for industry and construction. By linking previously isolated cities, towns, and settlements, the railroads promoted trade and interdependence. The growing prosperity of the nation, especially in the North, encouraged Americans to take pride in their country.

A New Fuel The Transportation Revolution also increased the use of certain natural resources that had not been important until then. Throughout the early Transportation Revolution, wood was the primary source of fuel for trains and steamboats, as well as for cooking, light, and heat. As faster locomotives were built, new power resources were used to fuel them. Coal replaced wood as the main source of power. A half ton of coal produced as much energy as two tons of wood but at half the cost. Coal also became popular for heating homes. Railroads transported the coal from mines to towns and cities.

As the demand for coal increased, a coal-mining industry developed in many states, including Pennsylvania, western Virginia, and Illinois. Coal mining changed the landscape in a number of ways. New towns, such as

Transportation Routes, 1850

▶ Explore ONLINE!

By 1850 the United States already had about 9,000 miles of railroad tracks. Timber was needed for railroad ties, cars, and bridges and as fuel for steam locomotives.

Interpret Maps

1. **Region** Where were most railroads located in 1850?

2. **Human-Environment Interaction** How does this map suggest that people modified the landscape?

Coal City and Carbondale in Illinois, sprang up in places where coal deposits could be mined. Miners made deep gashes in the earth removing the coal.

Later, in the 1870s, the demand for coal increased as the demand for steel grew. Many steel mills were built where there was an abundance of coal and iron ore. Steel is made through a smelting process—heating iron ore to very high temperatures. Coal was used to fire the furnaces. Steel, which is much stronger than iron, was increasingly used to build factories and the machines they produced.

Cooperation among the steel and railroad industries helped the economy grow. Steel was used to make the rails that trains ride on and the growing market for steel helped fuel the need for more railroads. Railroads transported steel to places where new factories were being built. Railroads also brought new steel farming tools and machines to farmers in the Midwest. Using the new equipment, farmers produced more crops. Railroads then transported their harvests to markets.

Effects of Railroads The development of railroads helped establish new markets and offered more opportunities for entrepreneurs to start their own businesses. The railroads also played a role in the growth of existing businesses. The logging industry expanded as people in the growing towns and cities needed wood for houses and furniture. As newspaper publishing increased, demand for paper grew. Lumber items became the primary product of New England. Sometimes there were unintended environmental consequences. Settlers spreading out across the Midwest cut down trees and plowed up prairies to make farmland. Deforestation, or cutting down and removing trees, took place on a large scale.

Railroads also caused cities to grow. Some cities became transportation hubs. Chicago was one such city. Its location on Lake Michigan made it an ideal transportation hub, linking the Midwest to the East and South.

Summary and Preview The Transportation Revolution changed the way business was done. In the next lesson you will learn about more technological advances.

Reading Check
Analyze Information
What role did railroads play in the growth of the coal industry?

Lesson 3 Assessment

Review Ideas, Terms, and People

1. a. **Identify** What forms of transportation were improved or invented at this time?

   b. **Analyze** What effect did the Transportation Revolution have on the United States?

2. a. **Describe** What were the benefits of steamboat travel?

   b. **Analyze** What effect did the ruling in the *Gibbons* v. *Ogden* case have on federal government?

3. a. **Describe** What event showed the power and speed of locomotives?

   b. **Draw Conclusions** How did railroads affect trade and business in the United States?

   c. **Elaborate** Why do you think Americans were fascinated by railroads?

4. a. **Describe** What physical obstacles did railroad construction in the United States face?

   b. **Analyze** What effects did the Transportation Revolution have on the U.S. economy?

   c. **Identify** What kind of changes did humans make to the environment during the Transportation Revolution?

Critical Thinking

5. **Identify Effects** In this lesson you learned about the steamboat and the locomotive. Create a chart similar to the one below and use it to show how they affected business, travel, and communication in the United States.

★ More Technological Advances

The Big Idea

Advances in technology led to new inventions that continued to change daily life and work.

Main Ideas

- The telegraph made swift communication possible from coast to coast.
- With the shift to steam power, businesses built new factories closer to cities and transportation centers.
- Improved farm equipment and other labor-saving devices made life easier for many Americans.
- New inventions changed lives in American homes.

Key Terms and People

Samuel F. B. Morse
telegraph
Morse code
John Deere
Cyrus McCormick
Isaac Singer

If YOU were there . . .

You own a small shop in Chicago, Illinois, in the 1850s. You sell ladies' hats and gowns. When you need more hats, you send a letter to the manufacturer in New York. Sometimes it takes weeks for the letter to get there. One day, the owner of the shop next door tells you about a wonderful new machine. It can send orders from Chicago to New York in just minutes!

How would a machine like this change your business?

Telegraph Speeds Communication

In 1832 **Samuel F. B. Morse** perfected the **telegraph**—a device that could send information over wires across great distances. To develop the telegraph, Morse studied electricity and magnetism. In time, Morse put the work of other scientists together in a practical machine.

The telegraph sent pulses, or surges, of electric current through a wire. The telegraph operator tapped a bar, called a telegraph key, that controlled the length of each pulse. At the other end of the wire, these pulses were changed into clicking sounds. A short click was called a dot. A long click was called a dash. Morse's partner, Alfred Lewis Vail, developed a system known as **Morse code**—different combinations of dots and dashes that represent each letter of the alphabet. For example, *dot dot dot, dash dash dash, dot dot dot* is the distress signal called SOS. Skilled telegraph operators could send and receive many words per minute.

Several years passed before Morse was able to connect two locations with telegraph wires. Despite that achievement, people doubted his machine. Some people did not think that he was reading messages sent from miles away. They claimed that he was making lucky guesses.

Morse's break came during the 1844 Democratic National Convention in Baltimore, Maryland. A telegraph wired news of the presidential candidate's nomination to politicians

Samuel F. B. Morse 1791–1872

Like steamboat creator Robert Fulton, Samuel F. B. Morse began his career as a painter rather than as an inventor. In 1832 Morse was a widower struggling to raise his three children alone. He became interested in the idea of sending messages electrically. Morse hoped he could invent a device that would earn him enough money to support his family. Eventually, earnings from the telegraph made Morse extremely wealthy.

Draw Conclusions
What motivated Morse to invent the telegraph?

in Washington. The waiting politicians responded, "Three cheers for the telegraph!" Telegraphs were soon sending and receiving information for businesses, the government, and newspapers. This new tool helped businesses become more efficient by speeding up their communication. Private citizens also began using the telegraph to communicate socially.

The telegraph grew with the railroad. Telegraph companies strung their wires on poles along railroads across the country. They established telegraph offices in many train stations. Thousands of miles of telegraph line were added every year in the 1850s. The first transcontinental line was finished in 1861. By the time he died in 1872, Morse was famous across the United States.

Reading Check
Identify Cause and Effect
What event led to the widespread use of the telegraph, and what effect did the telegraph have on cross-country communications?

Steam Power and New Factories

At the start of the Industrial Revolution, most factories ran on water-power. In time, however, factory owners began using steam power. This shift brought major changes to the nation's industries. Water-powered factories had to be built near streams or waterfalls. In contrast, steam power allowed business owners to build factories almost anywhere. Yet the Northeast was still home to most of the nation's industries. By 1860 New England alone had as many factories as the entire South did.

Some companies decided to build their factories closer to cities and transportation centers. This provided easier access to workers, allowing businesses to lower wages. Being closer to cities also reduced shipping costs. Cities soon became the center of industrial growth. People from rural areas as well as foreign countries flocked to the cities for factory jobs.

Reading Check
Find Main Ideas
What changes resulted from the shift to steam power?

Factory workers improved the designs of many kinds of machines. Mechanics invented tools that could cut and shape metal, stone, and wood with great precision. By the 1840s this new machinery was able to produce interchangeable parts. Within a short period of time, the growing machine-tool industry was even making customized equipment.

Timeline: American Inventions

1830

1855

1831
Cyrus McCormick invents the mechanical reaper and harvesting grain becomes much more efficient.

1832 ∨
Samuel Morse invents the telegraph making long-distance communication almost instantaneous.

1837 ∧
John Deere invents the steel plow that makes plowing the tough prairie soil easier.

1849
Walter Hunt invents the safety pin.

1851
Isaac Singer improves the sewing machine. The production and repair of clothing becomes much easier.

Improved Farm Equipment

During the 1830s technology began transforming the farm as well as the factory. In 1837 blacksmith **John Deere** saw that friends in Illinois had difficulty plowing thick soil with iron plows. He thought a steel blade might work better. His design for a steel plow was a success. By 1846 Deere was selling 1,000 plows per year.

In 1831 **Cyrus McCormick** developed a new harvesting machine, the mechanical reaper, which quickly and efficiently cut down wheat. He began mass-producing his reapers in a Chicago factory. McCormick used new methods to encourage sales. His company advertised, gave demonstrations, and provided a repair and spare parts department. He also let customers buy on credit.

The combination of Deere's plow and McCormick's reaper allowed Midwestern farmers to plant and harvest huge crop fields. By 1860 U.S. farmers were producing more than 170 million bushels of wheat and more than 800 million bushels of corn per year.

Improvements in farming technology made farming more efficient, but it also meant fewer laborers were needed to work the land. As a result, many people moved from rural areas to cities to find work.

Changing Life at Home

Many inventions of the Industrial Revolution simply made life easier. When Alexis de Tocqueville of France visited the United States in the early 1830s, he identified what he called a very American quality.

"[Americans want] to be always making life more comfortable and convenient, to avoid trouble, and to satisfy the smallest wants [desires] without effort and almost without cost."

—Alexis de Tocqueville, from *Democracy in America*

Reading Check
Summarize
What marketing methods did McCormick use to help sell his farm equipment?

The sewing machine was one of these conveniences. It was first invented by Elias Howe, a factory apprentice in Lowell, Massachusetts. **Isaac Singer** then made improvements to Howe's design. Like McCormick, Singer allowed customers to buy his machines on credit and provided a repair service. By 1860 Singer's company was the world's largest maker of sewing machines.

Other advances improved on everyday items. In the 1830s iceboxes cooled by large blocks of ice became available. Iceboxes stored fresh food safely for longer periods. Iron cookstoves began replacing cooking fires and stone hearths.

Companies also began to mass-produce earlier inventions. This allowed many families to buy household items, such as clocks, that they could not afford in the past. For example, a clock that cost $50 in 1800 was selling for only $1.50 by the 1850s. Additional useful items created during this period include matches, introduced in the 1830s, and the safety pin, invented in 1849. All of these inventions helped make life at home more convenient for an increasing number of Americans.

Summary and Preview New machines and inventions changed the way Americans lived and did business in the early 1800s. A market economy developed as people began to buy and sell goods rather than making goods for their own use. In the next module you will learn how agricultural changes affected the South.

Reading Check
Analyze How did labor-saving inventions affect daily life?

Lesson 4 Assessment

Review Ideas, Terms, and People

1. **a. Describe** How did the telegraph work?

   b. Predict What impact might the telegraph have on the future of the United States?

2. **a. Describe** How did water-powered factories differ from steam-powered factories?

   b. Explain How did the shift to steam power lead to the growth of cities?

3. **a. Identify** What contributions did John Deere and Cyrus McCormick make to farming?

   b. Analyze What effect did new inventions have on agriculture in the United States?

4. **a. Identify** What inventions improved life at home?

   b. Evaluate Which invention do you think had the greatest effect on the daily lives of Americans? Why?

Critical Thinking

5. **Support a Point of View** In this lesson you learned about more technological advances and their effects. Create a table like the one below that shows the three advances you think are most important and why.

Most Important	Why

Social Studies Skills

Personal Conviction and Bias

Define the Skill

Everyone has *convictions*, or firmly held beliefs. However, when we let our beliefs automatically slant or shape our point of view on topics, we may be showing bias. *Bias* is a fixed idea or opinion about someone or something. Some bias is based on a set of ideas about a group to which the person or thing belongs. This type of bias is called a *stereotype*. If the group is defined by race, religion, age, gender, or similar characteristics, the bias is known as *prejudice*.

Bias, stereotypes, and prejudice are not always negative in nature. They include favorable opinions, too. For example, the belief that a student is good at math because that person is male is a bias that shows both stereotyping and prejudice.

We should always be on guard for the presence of personal bias. Eliminating stereotyping and prejudice is particularly important. However, even "good" biases can slant how we view, judge, and communicate information. Honest and accurate communication requires that the information and ideas we express be as free of bias as possible.

Learn the Skill

Not all beliefs are biases, even if those beliefs are strongly held. Biases are beliefs that have little or no evidence to support them. The more unreasonable a person's view is in light of facts and evidence, the more likely it is that the belief is a bias.

Another characteristic of bias is the person's reluctance to question his or her belief if it is challenged by evidence. Sometimes people stubbornly cling to views that overwhelming

evidence proves wrong. This is why bias is defined as a "fixed" idea or opinion. One of the most damaging effects of bias, and a good reason for trying to avoid it, is that it can prevent us from learning new things.

The following precautions can help you reduce the amount of bias you express.

1. When discussing a topic, keep in mind beliefs and experiences in your own background that might affect how you feel about the topic.

2. Try to not mix statements of fact with statements of opinion. Clearly separate and indicate what you *know* to be true from what you *believe* to be true.

3. Avoid using emotional, positive, or negative words when communicating factual information.

Practice the Skill

In 1834 Tennessee congressman Davy Crockett visited the textile mills at Lowell, Massachusetts. Read his account of the "Lowell girls" who worked in the factory and complete the activity below.

"Here are thousands [of young women], useful to others, . . . with the prospect before them of future comfort and respectability. . . . There are more than five thousand females employed in Lowell; and when you come to see the amount of labour performed by them, in superintending [operating] the different machinery, you will be astonished."

Suppose that you were a "Lowell girl" who has just read this account of Crockett's visit. Write a letter to the editor of the *Lowell Offering* reacting to the biases and stereotypes about women that Crockett shows in his account.

Module 13 Assessment

Review Vocabulary, Terms, and People

Complete each sentence below by filling in the blank with the correct term or person from the module.

1. The system of _____ was developed to represent letters of the alphabet when sending telegraph messages.

2. The first American woman to hold a high-ranking position in the labor movement was _____.

3. The _____ was a period of rapid growth in the use of machines and manufacturing.

4. The first locomotive in the United States was built by _____.

5. Workers would sometimes go on _____ to force factory owners to meet their demands for better pay and working conditions.

6. The _____ industry, which produced cloth items, was the first to use machines for manufacturing.

Comprehension and Critical Thinking

Lesson 1

7. **a. Identify** What ideas did Eli Whitney want to apply to the manufacture of guns?

   b. Analyze How did the War of 1812 lead to a boom in manufacturing in the United States?

   c. Elaborate Why do you think the Industrial Revolution began in Great Britain rather than in the United States?

Lesson 2

8. **a. Describe** What was mill life like?

   b. Draw Conclusions How did the Rhode Island system and the Lowell system change the lives of American workers?

   c. Evaluate Were reformers such as Sarah G. Bagley effective in improving labor conditions? Why?

Lesson 3

9. **a. Describe** How were Americans affected by the introduction of steamboats?

   b. Make Inferences How did railroad companies become some of the most powerful businesses in the country?

   c. Elaborate What was the most important result of the Transportation Revolution? Why?

Lesson 4

10. **a. Recall** What important change took place in how factories were powered?

    b. Draw Conclusions How did the telegraph affect communication in the United States?

    c. Evaluate Do you think moving factories close to cities helped or hurt working life? Explain.

Module 13 Assessment, continued

Review Themes

11. **Science and Technology** What are the three most important inventions of the Industrial Revolution? Why?

12. **Economics** What was the overall effect of the Industrial Revolution on the U.S. economy?

Reading Skills

Understand Causes and Effects in History *Use the Reading Skills taught in this module to answer the question about the reading selection below.*

> Many young women came to Lowell from different parts of New England. They wanted the chance to earn money instead of working on the family farm.

13. According to the passage above, what was a cause for moving to Lowell?

    a. working long hours

    b. earning money

    c. meeting people

    d. working on a farm

Social Studies Skills

Personal Conviction and Bias *Use the Social Studies Skills taught in this module to answer the question about the reading selection below.*

> "Is anyone such a fool as to suppose that out of six thousand factory girls in Lowell, sixty would be there if they could help it?"
>
> —Sarah G. Bagley, quoted in *Voice of Industry*, September 18, 1845

14. Do you think that Bagley's opposition to the Lowell system was unfairly biased? Why or why not?

Focus on Writing

15. **Write a Newspaper Advertisement** Review the inventions discussed in the module. Choose one invention for which you will create an advertisement. Then answer these questions to help you plan your advertisement: Who is your audience? Who will buy this invention? How will the invention benefit this audience? What words or phrases will best persuade this audience? Once you have answered these questions, design your advertisement. To draw readers' attention to your ad, include an illustration, a catchy heading, and a few lines of text.

The South

★

Essential Question

How important was slavery for the economy and society of the South?

About the Photo: Slaves processing sugarcane on a Georgia plantation

▶ Explore ONLINE!

HISTORY.

VIDEOS, including...
• Growth of the Cotton Industry

☑ Document-Based Investigations

☑ Graphic Organizers

☑ Interactive Games

☑ Animation: The Cotton Gin

☑ Image with Hotspots: A Southern Plantation

☑ Image Carousel: Images of Slavery

In this module you will learn how the South developed an agricultural economy and how that economy was dependent on the labor of enslaved people. You will also read about the role of slavery in Southern society.

What You Will Learn ...

Lesson 1: Growth of the Cotton Industry **452**
The Big Idea The invention of the cotton gin made the South a one-crop economy and increased the need for slave labor.
Lesson 2: Southern Society. **459**
The Big Idea Southern society centered around agriculture.
Lesson 3: Slavery in the South. **463**
The Big Idea Enslaved people faced cruel treatment and difficult lives, which led them to resist the slave system and sometimes rebel.

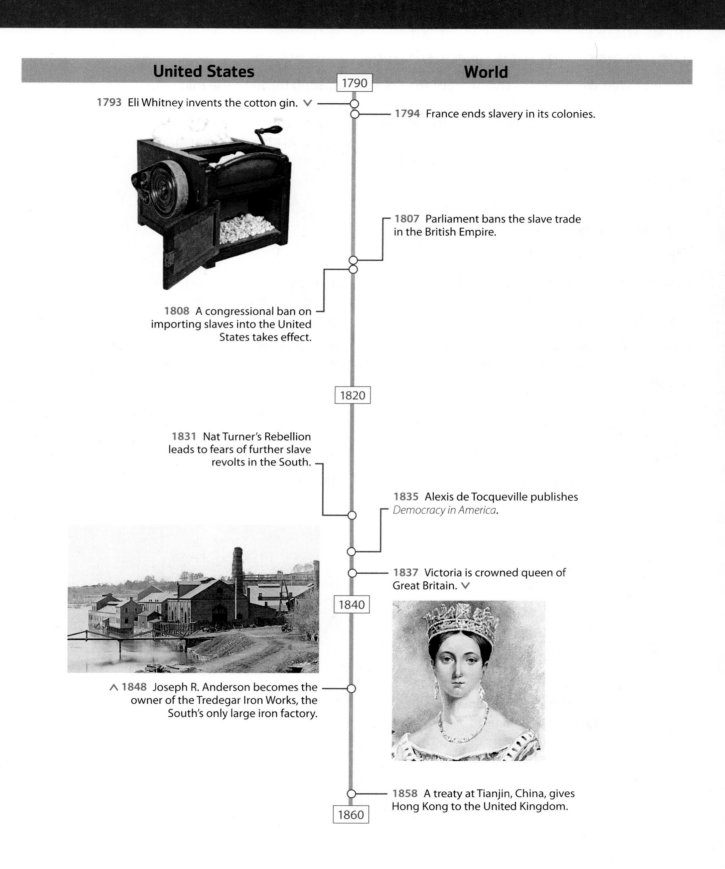

United States	World

1790

1793 Eli Whitney invents the cotton gin. ∨

1794 France ends slavery in its colonies.

1807 Parliament bans the slave trade in the British Empire.

1808 A congressional ban on importing slaves into the United States takes effect.

1820

1831 Nat Turner's Rebellion leads to fears of further slave revolts in the South.

1835 Alexis de Tocqueville publishes *Democracy in America*.

1837 Victoria is crowned queen of Great Britain. ∨

1840

∧ **1848** Joseph R. Anderson becomes the owner of the Tredegar Iron Works, the South's only large iron factory.

1858 A treaty at Tianjin, China, gives Hong Kong to the United Kingdom.

1860

Reading Social Studies

Economics, Society and Culture

This module takes you into the heart of the South from 1800 through the mid-1800s. As you read, you will discover that the South depended on cotton as its economic backbone, especially after the invention of the cotton gin. You will also read about the slave system in the South during this time and about the harsh living conditions slaves endured. As you will see, the South was home to a variety of societies and cultures.

READING FOCUS:

Online Research

Researching history topics on the World Wide Web can give you access to valuable information. However, just because the information is on the web doesn't mean it is automatically valuable.

Evaluate Websites Before you use information you find online, you need to evaluate the website it comes from. The checklist below can help you determine if the site is worth your time.

Evaluate Websites

Site: _____ URL: _____ Date of access: _____

Rate each item on this 1–3 scale. Then add up the total score.

	No	Some	Yes
I. Authority			
a. Authors are clearly identified by name.	1	2	3
b. Contact information is provided for authors.	1	2	3
c. Authors' qualifications are clearly stated.	1	2	3
d. Site has been updated recently.	1	2	3
II. Content			
a. Site's information is useful to your project.	1	2	3
b. Information is clear and well organized.	1	2	3
c. Information appears to be at the right level.	1	2	3
d. Links to additional important information are provided.	1	2	3
e. Information can be verified in other sources.	1	2	3
f. Graphics are helpful, not just decorative.	1	2	3
III. Design and Technical Elements			
a. Pages are readable and easy to navigate.	1	2	3
b. Links to other sites work.	1	2	3

Total Score _____

36–28 = very good site   27–20 = average site below 20 = poor site

---

You Try It!

Key Terms and People

Lesson 1
cotton gin
planters
cotton belt
factors
Tredegar Iron Works
Lesson 2
yeomen
Lesson 3
overseers
spirituals
oral tradition
folktales
Nat Turner

The passage below is from the module you are about to read.

Cotton Becomes Profitable Cotton had been grown in the New World for centuries, but it had not been a very profitable crop. Before cotton could be spun into thread for weaving into cloth, the seeds had to be removed from the cotton fibers.

Long-staple cotton, also called black-seed cotton, was fairly easy to process. Workers could pick the seeds from the cotton with relative ease. But long-staple cotton grew well in only a few places in the South. More common was short-staple cotton, which was also known as green-seed cotton. Removing the seeds from this cotton was difficult and time consuming. A worker could spend an entire day picking the seeds from a single pound of short-staple cotton.

After you read the passage, complete the following activity.

Suppose that after reading this passage you decide to do some research on cotton growing. You use a search engine that directs you to a website. At that site, you find the information described below. Using the evaluation criteria listed on the previous page, decide if this is a site you would recommend to others.

a. The authors of the site are listed as "Bob and Mack, good friends who enjoy working together."

b. The site was last updated on "the last time we got together."

c. The title of the site is "Cotton Pickin'." There are few headings.

d. This ten-page site includes nine pages about the authors' childhood on a cotton farm. No illustrations are included.

e. Pages are very long, but they load quickly, as there are no graphics. There is one link to a site selling cotton clothing.

As you read Module 14, think about what topics would be interesting to research on the web. If you do some research on the web, remember to use the evaluation list to analyze websites.

Growth of the Cotton Industry

The Big Idea
The invention of the cotton gin made the South a one-crop economy and increased the need for slave labor.

Main Ideas
- The invention of the cotton gin revived the economy of the South.
- The cotton gin created a cotton boom in which farmers grew little else.
- Some people encouraged southerners to focus on other crops and industries.

Key Terms and People
cotton gin
planters
cotton belt
factors
Tredegar Iron Works

If YOU were there . . .

You are a field-worker on a cotton farm in the South in about 1800. Your job is to separate the seeds from the cotton fibers. It is dull, tiring work because the tiny seeds are tangled in the fibers. Sometimes it takes you a whole day just to clean one pound of cotton! Now you hear that someone has invented a machine that can clean cotton 50 times faster than by hand.

How might this machine change your life?

Reviving the South's Economy

Sectional differences had always existed between different regions of the United States. The geographic features of each region contributed to the development of differing economic activities. Revolutionary changes in industry and transportation deepened the differences between North and South. While the North began to focus on industrialization, the South remained mainly agricultural.

Before the American Revolution, three crops dominated southern agriculture—tobacco, rice, and indigo. These crops played a central role in the southern economy and culture. They were produced mostly by enslaved African Americans.

After the American Revolution, however, prices for tobacco, rice, and indigo dropped. When crop prices fell, the demand for and the price of slaves also went down. In an effort to protect their incomes, many farmers tried, with little success, to grow other crops that needed less labor. Soon, however, cotton would transform the southern economy and greatly increase the demand for slave labor.

Cotton Becomes Profitable Cotton had been grown in the New World for centuries, but it had not been a very profitable crop. Before cotton could be spun into thread for weaving into cloth, the seeds had to be removed from the cotton fibers.

Cotton Gin

Connect to Science and Technology Eli Whitney's cotton gin enabled workers to easily remove seeds from cotton fibers. The result was a dramatic increase in cotton production in the South.

How did the cotton gin remove seeds from cotton fibers?

1. The operator turned the crank.
2. The crank turned a roller with teeth that stripped the seeds away from the cotton fiber.
3. Brushes on a second roller lifted the seedless cotton off the teeth of the first cylinder and dropped it out of the machine.
4. A belt connected the rollers so that they would both turn when the crank was turned.

Long-staple cotton, also called black-seed cotton, was fairly easy to process. Workers could pick the seeds from the cotton with relative ease. But long-staple cotton grew well in only a few places in the South. More common was short-staple cotton, which was also known as green-seed cotton. Removing the seeds from this cotton was difficult and time consuming. A worker could spend an entire day picking the seeds from a single pound of short-staple cotton.

By the early 1790s the demand for American cotton began increasing rapidly. For instance, in Great Britain, new textile factories needed raw cotton that could be used for making cloth. American cotton producers could not keep up with the high demand for their cotton. These producers of cotton needed a machine that could remove the seeds from the cotton more rapidly.

Eli Whitney's Cotton Gin Northerner Eli Whitney finally patented such a machine in 1793. The year before, Whitney had visited a Georgia plantation owned by Catherine Greene. Workers there were using a machine that removed seeds from long-staple cotton. This machine did not work well on short-staple cotton. Greene asked Whitney if he could improve it. By the next spring, Whitney had perfected his design for the **cotton gin**, a machine that removes seeds from short-staple cotton. (*Gin* is short for "engine.") The cotton gin used a hand-cranked cylinder with wire teeth to pull cotton fibers from the seeds.

Whitney hoped to keep the design of the gin a secret, but the machine was very useful. His patent was often ignored by other manufacturers. Whitney described how his invention would improve the cotton business.

"One man will clean ten times as much cotton as he can in any other way before known and also clean it much better than in the usual mode [method]. This machine may be turned by water or with a horse, with the greatest ease, and one man and a horse will do more than fifty men with the old machines."

—Eli Whitney, quoted in "Correspondence of Eli Whitney Relative to the Invention of the Cotton Gin," *The American Historical Review* Vol. 3

Reading Check
Draw Conclusions
What effects did the cotton gin have on the southern economy?

Whitney's cotton gin revolutionized the cotton industry for **planters**. Planters were large-scale farmers who held more than 20 slaves. They built cotton gins that could process tons of cotton much faster than hand processing. A healthy crop almost guaranteed financial success because of high demand from the textile industry.

The Cotton Boom

Whitney's invention of the cotton gin made cotton so profitable that southern farmers abandoned other crops in favor of growing cotton. The removal of Native Americans opened up more land. The development of new types of cotton plants helped spread cotton production throughout the South from Virginia and North Carolina to as far west as Texas. This area of high cotton production became known as the **cotton belt**.

Production increased rapidly—from about 2 million pounds in 1791 to roughly a billion pounds by 1860. As early as 1840, the United States was producing more than half of the cotton grown in the entire world. The economic boom attracted new settlers and built up wealth among wealthy white southerners. The cotton economy firmly put in place the institution of slavery in the South.

Cotton Belt Cotton had many advantages as a cash crop. It cost little to market. Unlike food staples, harvested cotton could be stored for a long time. Because cotton was lighter than other staple crops, it also cost less to transport long distances.

Farmers eager to profit from growing cotton headed west to find land. Farmers also began to apply scientific methods to improve crop production. Cotton had one disadvantage as a crop—it rapidly used up the nutrients in the soil. After a few years, cotton could make the land useless for growing anything. Some agricultural scientists recommended crop rotation—changing the crop grown on a particular plot of land every few years. Different crops needed different nutrients, so crop rotation would keep the land fertile longer. Other agricultural scientists began to study soil chemistry, in an effort to keep the land rich and productive.

As the cotton belt grew, farmers continued trying to improve the crop. Agricultural scientists worked at crossbreeding short-staple cotton with other varieties. As a result, new stronger types of cotton were soon growing throughout the cotton belt. This led to expansion of the cotton industry through the 1860s.

The cotton boom involved much more than growing and harvesting cotton. Harvested cotton had to be ginned, pressed into bales, and then

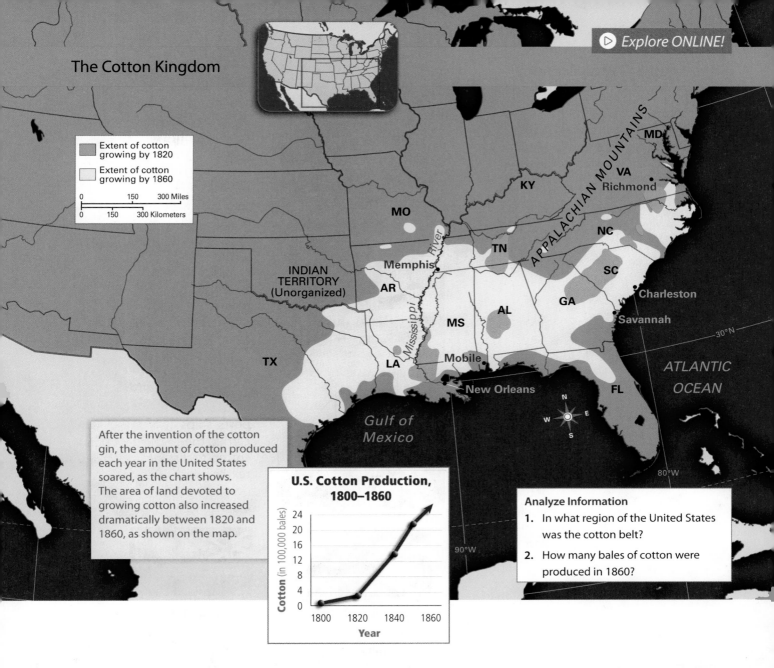

The Cotton Kingdom

Explore ONLINE!

Extent of cotton growing by 1820

Extent of cotton growing by 1860

0   150   300 Miles

0   150   300 Kilometers

MD

APPALACHIAN MOUNTAINS

VA

Richmond

KY

MO

NC

TN

SC

Memphis

Charleston

INDIAN TERRITORY (Unorganized)

AR

GA

Savannah

Mississippi River

AL

30°N

MS

Mobile

TX

LA

New Orleans

FL

ATLANTIC OCEAN

Gulf of Mexico

80°W

N W E S

After the invention of the cotton gin, the amount of cotton produced each year in the United States soared, as the chart shows. The area of land devoted to growing cotton also increased dramatically between 1820 and 1860, as shown on the map.

U.S. Cotton Production, 1800–1860

Cotton (in 100,000 bales)

24
20
16
12
8
4
0

1800   1820   1840   1860

Year

90°W

Analyze Information

1. In what region of the United States was the cotton belt?

2. How many bales of cotton were produced in 1860?

shipped to market or to warehouses. Special agents helped do everything. They helped market cotton to customers and also insured crops against loss or damage. Factories were built to produce items needed by cotton farmers, such as ropes to bale cotton.

Growing and harvesting cotton required many field hands. Rather than pay wages to free workers, planters began to use more slave labor. Congress had made bringing slaves into the United States illegal in 1808. However, the growing demand for slaves led to an increase in the slave trade within the United States.

Cotton Trade In an 1858 speech before the U.S. Senate, South Carolina politician James Henry Hammond declared, "Cotton is King!" Without cotton, Hammond claimed, the global economy would fail. He believed that southern cotton was one of the most valuable resources in the world.

The South's Cotton Economy

Eli Whitney's cotton gin began the cotton boom. Soon, the Cotton Kingdom stretched across the South. For the cotton planters to succeed, they had to get their cotton to market.

Enslaved African Americans did most of the planting, harvesting, and processing of cotton.

Cotton was shipped on river steamboats to major ports such as Charleston.

From southern ports, ships carried the cotton to distant textile mills.

A large amount of cotton was sold to textile mills in the northeastern United States.

Textile mills in Great Britain were the largest foreign buyers of southern cotton.

Draw Conclusions
Why do you think cotton was so important to the South's economy?

Southern cotton was used to make cloth in England and the North. Many southerners shared Hammond's viewpoints about cotton. Southerner David Christy declared, "King cotton is a profound [learned] statesman, and knows what measures will best sustain [protect] his throne."

The cotton boom made the South a major player in world trade. Great Britain became the South's most valued foreign trading partner. Southerners also sold tons of cotton to the growing textile industry in the northeastern United States. This increased trade led to the growth of major port cities in the South, including Charleston, South Carolina; Savannah, Georgia; and New Orleans, Louisiana.

Reading Check
Identify Cause and Effect What effect did the cotton boom have on the slave trade within the United States?

Academic Vocabulary
primary main, most important

In these cities, crop brokers called **factors** managed the cotton trade. Farmers sold their cotton to merchants, who then made deals with the factors. Merchants and factors also arranged loans for farmers who needed to buy supplies. They often advised farmers on how to invest profits. Once farmers got their cotton to the port cities, factors arranged for transportation aboard trading ships.

However, shipping cotton by land to port cities was very difficult in the South. The few major road projects at the time were limited to the Southeast. Most southern farmers had to ship their goods on the region's rivers. On the Ohio and Mississippi rivers, flatboats and steamboats carried cotton and other products to port. Eventually, hundreds of steamboats traveled up and down the mighty Mississippi River each day.

Other Crops and Industries

While industrialization continued to grow in the North, some leaders worried that the South was depending too much on cotton. They wanted southerners to try a variety of cash crops and investments.

Food and Cash Crops One such crop was corn, the **primary** southern food crop. By the late 1830s the top three corn-growing states in the nation were all in the South. The South's other successful food crops included rice, sweet potatoes, wheat, and sugarcane.

Production of tobacco, the South's first major cash crop, was very time consuming. Tobacco leaves had to be cured, or dried, before they could be shipped to market. In 1839 a slave discovered a way to improve the drying process by using heat from burning charcoal. This new, faster curing process increased tobacco production.

Partly as a result of the cotton boom, hemp and flax also became major cash crops. Their fibers were used to make rope and sackcloth. Farmers used the rope and sackcloth to bundle cotton into bales.

Industry Many of the first factories in the South were built to serve farmers' needs by processing crops such as sugarcane. In 1803 the nation's first steam-powered sawmill was built in Donaldsonville, Louisiana. This new technology enabled lumber companies to cut, sort, and clean wood quickly.

By the 1840s entrepreneurs in Georgia began investing in cotton mills. In 1840 there were 14 cotton mills. By the mid-1850s there were more than 50. A few mill owners followed the model established by Francis Cabot Lowell. However, most built small-scale factories on the falls of a river for waterpower. A few steam-powered mills were built in towns without enough waterpower.

Southerners such as Hinton Rowan Helper encouraged industrial growth in the South.

"We should . . . keep pace with the progress of the age. We must expand our energies, and acquire habits of enterprise and industry; we should rouse ourselves from the couch of lassitude [laziness] and inure [set] our minds to thought and our bodies to action."
—Hinton Rowan Helper, *The Impending Crisis of the South: How to Meet It*

Tredegar Iron Works
After Joseph Anderson took over the Tredegar Iron Works in 1848, it became the largest manufacturer of iron products in the South.

Joseph R. Anderson followed Helper's advice. In 1848 Anderson became the owner of the **Tredegar Iron Works** in Richmond, Virginia. It was one of the most productive ironworks in the nation. It was the only factory in the South to produce products such as cannons, steam engines, and bridge materials.

Unlike in the North, however, industry remained a small part of the southern economy. Southern industry faced stiff competition from the North and from England, both of which could produce many goods more cheaply. And as long as agricultural profits remained high, southern investors preferred to invest in land.

Reading Check
Make Inferences
Why were there fewer industries in the South?

Summary and Preview You have read about how southern farmers worked to improve farming methods. In the next lesson you will read about the structure of southern society.

Lesson 1 Assessment

Review Ideas, Terms, and People

1. a. Describe How did the cotton gin make processing cotton easier?

b. Draw Conclusions Why had slavery been on the decline before the invention of the cotton gin? How did slavery change as a result of the cotton gin?

c. Predict How might the rise of cotton production and slavery affect southern society?

2. a. Identify What areas of the United States made up the cotton belt?

b. Evaluate Do you think the South should have paid more attention to its industrial growth? Why?

3. a. Describe What other crops and industries were encouraged in the South?

b. Make Inferences Why were some southern leaders worried about the South's reliance on cotton?

Critical Thinking

4. Identify Cause and Effect In this lesson you learned about the causes of the cotton boom. Create a graphic organizer similar to the one below and add to it to identify the effects of the cotton boom on the South.

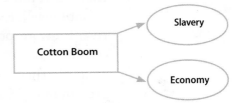

Southern Society

The Big Idea

Southern society centered around agriculture.

Main Ideas

■ Southern society and culture consisted of four main groups.

■ Free African Americans in the South faced a great deal of discrimination.

Key Terms and People

yeomen

If YOU were there . . .

Your family owns a small farm in Georgia in the 1840s. Sometimes you work in the fields, but more often you tend the vegetable garden and peach orchard. Since you have no close neighbors, you look forward to Sundays. Going to church gives you a chance to socialize with other young people. Sometimes you wonder what it would be like to live in a city like Savannah.

How would life be different if you left the farm for the city?

Southern Society and Culture

Although the South had some industry, the economy was not primarily industrial as it was in the North. Agriculture was the heart of the southern economy, and cotton was king.

Popular fiction often made it seem that all white southerners had many slaves and lived on large plantations. Many fiction writers wrote about wealthy southern families who had frequent, grand parties. The ideal image of the Antebellum (before the war) South included hospitality and well-treated slaves on beautiful plantations that almost ran themselves.

This romantic view was far from the reality. During the first half of the 1800s, only about one-third of white southern families had slaves. Fewer families had plantations. Despite their small numbers, these planters had a powerful influence over the South. Many served as political leaders. They led a society made up of many different kinds of people, including yeoman farmers, poor whites, slaves, and free African Americans. Each of these segments of society contributed to the economic success of the South.

Planters As the wealthiest members of southern society, planters also greatly influenced the economy. Some showed off their wealth by living in beautiful mansions. Many others chose to live more simply. A visitor described wealthy planter

Alexander Stephens's estate as "an old wooden house" surrounded by weeds. Some planters saved all of their money to buy more land and slaves.

Male planters were primarily concerned with raising crops and supervising slave laborers. They left the running of the plantation household to their wives. The planter's wife oversaw the raising of the children and supervised the work of all slaves within the household. Slave women typically cooked, cleaned, and helped care for the planter's children. Wives also took on the important social duties of the family. For example, many southern leaders discussed political issues at the dances and dinners hosted by their wives.

Planters often arranged their children's marriages based on business interests. Lucy Breckinridge, the daughter of a wealthy Virginia planter, was married by arrangement in 1865. Three years earlier, she had described in her journal how she dreaded the very thought of marriage. "A woman's life after she is married, unless there is an immense amount of love, is nothing but suffering and hard work." How Breckinridge's life in her own arranged marriage would have turned out cannot be known. She died of typhoid fever just months after her wedding.

A Southern Plantation

A typical plantation had fields as well as many buildings where different work was done. This picture shows some of the more important buildings that were a part of the plantation system.

Slave Cabins Slaves lived crowded together in small cabins. Cabins were crude, wooden structures with dirt floors.

Fields

Barn

Warehouse

Cotton-Ginning Shed This sizable plantation had several large cotton gins. The vital machines were housed in a shed to protect them from the weather.

Smokehouse

Overseer's House

Stable

Plantation House The planter and his family lived in the plantation house. The planter's wife was in charge of running the household.

Analyze Visuals
How can you tell that the owner of this plantation was wealthy?

Yeomen and Poor Whites Most white southerners were **yeomen**, owners of small farms. Yeomen owned few slaves or none at all. The typical farm averaged 100 acres. Yeomen took great pride in their work. In 1849 a young Georgia man wrote, "I desire above all things to be a 'Farmer.' It is the most honest, upright, and sure way of securing all the comforts of life."

Yeoman families, including women and children, typically worked long days at a variety of tasks. Some yeomen held a few slaves but worked alongside them.

The poorest of white southerners lived on land that could not grow cash crops. They survived by hunting, fishing, raising small gardens, and doing odd jobs for money.

Religion and Society Most white southerners shared similar religious beliefs. Because of the long distances between farms, families often saw their neighbors only at church events, such as revivals or socials. Rural women often played volunteer roles in their churches. Wealthy white southerners thought that their religion justified their position in society and the institution of slavery. They argued that God created some people, like themselves, to rule others. This belief opposed many northern Christians' belief that God was against slavery.

Urban Life Many of the largest and most important cities in the South were strung along the Atlantic coast and had begun as shipping centers. Although fewer in number, the southern cities were similar to northern cities. City governments built public water systems and provided well-maintained streets. Public education was available in a few places. Wealthy residents occasionally gave large sums of money to charities, such as orphanages and public libraries. Southern urban leaders wanted their cities to appear as modern as possible.

As on plantations, slaves did much of the work in southern cities. Slaves worked as domestic servants, in mills, in shipyards, and at skilled jobs. Many business leaders held slaves or hired them from nearby plantations.

Reading Check
Summarize
What different groups made up southern society?

Free African Americans and Discrimination

Although the vast majority of African Americans in the South were enslaved, more than 250,000 free African Americans lived in the region by 1860. Some were descendants of slaves who were freed after the American Revolution. Others were descendants of refugees from the Haitian Revolution led by Toussaint Louverture in the late 1790s. Still others were former slaves who had run away, been freed by their slaveholder, or earned enough money to buy their freedom.

Free African Americans lived in both rural and urban areas. Most lived in the countryside and worked as paid laborers on plantations or farms. Free African Americans in cities often worked a variety of jobs, mostly as skilled artisans. Some, like barber William Johnson of Natchez, Mississippi, became quite successful in their businesses. Frequently, free African Americans, especially those in the cities, formed social and economic ties with one another. Churches often served as the center of their social lives.

Free African Americans in the South

In 1860 about 1 out of 50 African Americans in the South was free. Many worked in skilled trades, like this barber in Richmond, Virginia. In Charleston, South Carolina, a system of badges was set up to distinguish between free African Americans and slaves.

How would the work of the free African American in this picture be different from that of slaves in the South?

Free African Americans faced constant discrimination from white southerners. Many governments passed laws limiting the rights of free African Americans. Most free African Americans could not vote, travel freely, or hold certain jobs. In some places, free African Americans had to have a white person represent them in any business transaction. In others, laws restricted where they were allowed to live or conduct business.

Many white southerners argued that free African Americans did not have the ability to take care of themselves. Southerners used this belief to justify the institution of slavery. "The status of slavery is the only one for which the African is adapted," wrote one white Mississippian. To many white southerners, the very existence of free African Americans threatened the institution of slavery.

Reading Check
Find Main Ideas What challenges did free African Americans face in the South?

Summary and Preview Southern society was led by rich planters but included groups of small farmers, slaves, and free African Americans as well. These groups each had their own culture. In the next lesson you will read about life under slavery.

Lesson 2 Assessment

Review Ideas, Terms, and People

1. **a. Identify** What was the largest social group in the South? How did its members make a living?

   b. Compare In what ways were southern cities similar to northern cities?

   c. Elaborate Which southern social class do you think had the most difficult life? Why?

2. **a. Describe** What jobs were available to free African Americans in the South? Why were these jobs the only ones available?

   b. Analyze Why did many white southerners fear free African Americans?

   c. Elaborate Why do you think that discrimination against free African Americans was harsher in the South than in the North?

Critical Thinking

3. **Compare and Contrast** In this lesson you learned about the different groups of people who lived in the South. Create a graphic organizer similar to the one below to identify the similarities and differences of the lives of planters, yeomen, and free African Americans.

	Similarities	Differences
Planters		
Free African Americans		
Yeomen		

★ Slavery in the South

The Big Idea

Enslaved people faced cruel treatment and difficult lives, which led them to resist the slave system and sometimes rebel.

Main Ideas

- Slaves faced harsh living conditions in the South.

- A common African American culture developed in the South, which helped slaves to survive the cruelties of slavery.

- Slave rebellions drew a harsh response from white southerners.

Key Terms and People

overseers
spirituals
oral tradition
folktales
Nat Turner

If YOU were there . . .

You are an enslaved person living on a large cotton plantation in the South in the 1850s. You work in the hot sun all day long picking cotton. After working in the fields, your body aches from bending over, your hands hurt from picking the cotton, and you're hungry from having little to eat. To take your mind off of your harsh life and to bring you comfort, you make up stories and poems. Your family and friends love to gather round to hear you tell these stories.

What is a story you think you would tell?

Living Under Slavery

Eli Whitney's cotton gin made cotton growing very profitable. Soon, cotton farming spread across the South. Since it required a lot of labor to grow cotton, the need for enslaved people grew as the number of cotton farms increased. By the mid-1800s, enslaved African Americans accounted for about one-third of the population of the South.

Differences existed in the lives of enslaved people. Where they lived, the work they did, and how they were treated all affected their day-to-day lives.

Working Life Work was the dominant feature of the lives of enslaved people. Men, women, and children were forced to work whenever their slaveholders demanded. For most slaves this meant every day of their lives from sunrise to sunset. Even sickness and poor weather rarely served as reasons to stop working.

Enslaved African American house servants often cared for the children of slaveholders.

The majority of enslaved people lived and worked on farms or large plantations in the South, where cotton was the leading crop. The majority of slaves worked as field hands. They planted, tended, picked, and processed cotton. They also cleared land, repaired buildings and fences, and performed many of the other tasks needed to keep the farms and plantations running. Slaves who worked outside were supervised by **overseers**. These were men that farmers and planters hired to watch over and direct the work of slaves. Other slaves worked in the plantation owners' homes. They performed a wide variety of servant duties, such as cooking, cleaning, and child care. Some enslaved people had learned a trade. They worked as bricklayers, blacksmiths, and carpenters.

Not all enslaved people worked on plantations. In cities, some worked as domestic servants, skilled craftspeople, factory hands, and day laborers. Some were hired out and allowed to keep part of their earnings. But they were still enslaved—under the law, they were considered property.

Living Conditions Enslaved African Americans who worked in the fields on plantations usually lived in terrible conditions. They were housed in tiny cabins with leaky roofs and dirt floors. The food and clothing they were given were equally as poor. When they were sick, they rarely, if ever, received medical care.

Some slaveholders provided better living conditions than others. Generally, they did this to gain obedience, not out of a sense of compassion. Most slaveholders, however, treated their slaves harshly. They used a wide variety of punishments to ensure obedience, including beatings, withholding food, and threatening family members. Wes Brady recalled the punishments faced by field hands:

"The overseer was 'straddle his big horse at three o'clock in the mornin', roustin' the hands off to the field. . . . The rows was a mile long and no matter how much grass was in them, if you [left] one sprig on your row they [beat] you nearly to death."

—Wes Brady, quoted in *Born in Slavery: Slave Narratives from the Federal Writers' Project, 1936–1938*

Enslaved people often lived in small cabins with dirt floors.

An African American father is sold away from his family.

Perhaps the cruelest part of slavery was the sale of family members away from one another. Although some slaveholders would not separate mothers from children, many did, causing unforgettable grief. When enslaved families could manage to be together, they took comfort in family life. Enslaved people did marry each other, although their marriages were not legally recognized. They tried to raise children while knowing that their children could be taken from them and sold at any time. Abolitionist Frederick Douglass, who was born into slavery, recalled visits from his mother, who lived 12 miles away.

"I do not recollect [remember] ever seeing my mother by the light of day. She was with me in the night. She would lie down with me, and get me to sleep, but long before I waked she was gone."

—Frederick Douglass, *Narrative of the Life of Frederick Douglass, an American Slave*

Reading Check
Summarize How did slaveholders treat enslaved people?

Douglass's mother resisted slavery by the simple act of visiting her child. Douglass later rebelled by escaping to the North. By and large, the vast majority of enslaved people resisted slavery in one way or another.

A Common Culture

By the early 1800s, a distinctive African American culture had emerged in the South. This common culture was based on strong religious convictions, close personal bonds, and music that accompanied almost every part of life. It helped enslaved African Americans to endure the hardships of plantation life.

Finding Strength in Religion Religion was a cornerstone of African American culture in the South. By the early 1800s, a large number of slaves practiced Christianity. Some slaveholders tried to use religion to force enslaved people to accept mistreatment. They emphasized such Bible passages as "Servants, obey your masters." But slaves took their own messages from the Bible. They were particularly inspired by the book of Exodus, which tells of Moses leading the Hebrews out of bondage in Egypt. Many enslaved African Americans believed that this story offered a message of hope for their own people.

Slaves developed their own form of Christianity, which mixed in features of their traditional African religions. The practice of religion became a way for slaves to resist the power and control that slaveholders wielded over them. So, they worshipped in secret, often at night under the cover of darkness.

Enslaved African Americans often expressed their beliefs in **spirituals**—folk songs that mixed African and European music and were often religious in nature. Singing spirituals offered comfort for pain, eased the drudgery of daily work, and bound people together at religious meetings. Many spirituals voiced the desire for freedom:

Plantation Burial
The English artist John Antrobus painted this work in 1860. Antrobus lived in the United States for about eight years. *Plantation Burial* was part of a series of paintings he planned to create about life in rural Louisiana.

"Dear Lord! dear Lord! when slavery'll cease,
  Then we poor souls can have our peace;
  There's a better day coming, will you go along with me?
  There's a better day coming, go sound the jubilee."

—from *The Anti-Slavery Harp*, compiled by William W. Brown

Sometimes, spirituals contained coded messages about a planned escape or a plantation owner's unexpected return. African American spirituals had a strong influence on later developments in American music, such as gospel, blues, and jazz.

An Oral Tradition Another feature of African American culture was **oral tradition**—the passing on of stories, poems, and songs by word of mouth. In this way enslaved African Americans kept their heritage alive by passing down family histories and African traditions and customs. **Folktales**, or stories with a moral, also were part of this oral tradition. These tales usually included animals with human characteristics. Most often a smaller animal, such as a rabbit, would defeat a bigger, stronger animal, such as a bear, fox, or wolf, by outwitting it.

The rabbit represented slaves. The moral of the folktales was that slaves could survive by outsmarting the slaveholder, who was represented by the more powerful animal. In some tales, however, the bigger animal outsmarted the rabbit. This reflected how slaveholders sometimes lied to and deceived slaves. Such stories served as a warning that slaves should be very careful about trusting slaveholders.

Other Challenges to Slavery In small ways, and on a daily basis, slaves resisted the slave system and tried to gain a measure of control over their lives. Some worked slowly or damaged equipment or crops to protest

Reading Check
Make Inferences
Why might slaves
be inspired by
the biblical story
of Moses?

increased hours in the fields. Others ran away for a few days to visit family members or to avoid an angry slaveholder. Sometimes, slaves tried to escape to the North. But this journey to freedom was long and difficult. If they were captured, the punishment was flogging or, sometimes, death. Even so, thousands of enslaved people succeeded in getting to the North.

Slave Rebellions

Armed rebellion by enslaved persons was the most extreme form of resistance to slavery. Gabriel Prosser planned an attack on Richmond, Virginia, in 1800. In 1822 Denmark Vesey planned a revolt in Charleston, South Carolina. Both plots were betrayed, and the leaders, as well as numerous followers, were hanged.

The most famous rebellion was led by **Nat Turner** in Southampton County, Virginia, in 1831. Turner planned to gain freedom by killing slaveholders and their families. On August 21, Turner gathered about 70 followers and encouraged them with these words:

"We do not go forth for the sake of blood and carnage; . . . Remember that ours is not a war for robbery, . . . it is a struggle for freedom."
—Nat Turner, quoted in *History of the Negro Race in America, 1619–1880*, by George Washington Williams

— BIOGRAPHY —

Nat Turner 1800–1831

Nat Turner was born into slavery in Virginia. As a child, he learned to read and write and became an enthusiastic reader of the Bible. He soon gained a reputation in the local slave community for his religious beliefs. Enslaved people regularly gathered in forest clearings to listen to his powerful sermons.

Turner believed that he had been called by God to free the slaves, by armed rebellion if necessary. When a solar eclipse took place in August 1831, he interpreted it as a sign that it was time to revolt. In an account of events that he dictated to a white lawyer before his execution, Turner defended the justice of his cause. He was a "prophet," he claimed, called by God to commit his violent acts.

Analyze Points of View
How did Turner justify his rebellion?

Nat Turner meets with a group of followers in the woods.

Turner and his followers killed about 55 white men, women, and children. The rebellion was quickly put down. Most of Turner's men were captured when their ammunition ran out, and some were killed. Dozens of innocent slaves who played no part in the uprising also were put to death. Turner managed to evade capture for six weeks. After he was caught, he was tried and hanged.

Turner's rebellion spread fear throughout the South. Whites killed hundreds of African Americans in revenge. The state of Virginia even considered ending slavery because of the upheaval, but the proposal was narrowly defeated. Most southern state legislatures, however, passed harsh laws that further restricted the limited freedoms of both enslaved and free African Americans. For African Americans in the South, the grip of slavery grew ever tighter.

Summary and Preview Enslaved African Americans adopted many ways to adapt to and resist the harsh conditions of slavery. Some attempted to end slavery by rebellion, but they failed. In the next module you will review the origins and development of slavery in the United States.

Reading Check
Find Main Ideas
How did white southerners respond to Nat Turner's Rebellion?

Lesson 3 Assessment

Review Ideas, Terms, and People

1. **a. Identify** What types of work did enslaved people in cities do?

   b. Summarize What challenges did enslaved families face?

2. **a. Recall** What forms did resistance to slavery take?

   b. Explain How were enslaved African Americans able to keep their African heritage alive?

3. **a. Describe** Who was Nat Turner, and how did he resist slavery?

   b. Make Inferences How do you think the actions of Nat Turner affected the lives of enslaved African Americans who did not join his cause?

Critical Thinking

4. **Categorize** In this lesson you learned about the hardships faced by enslaved people. Create a graphic organizer similar to the one below to identify how the following characteristics of their culture helped them respond to their conditions and endure their hardships.

Religion	
Spirituals	
Oral Tradition	

Social Studies Skills

Interpret Graphs

Define the Skill

Graphs are drawings that classify and display data in a clear, visual format. There are three basic types of graphs. *Line graphs* and *bar graphs* plot changes in quantities over time. Bar graphs are also used to compare quantities within a category at a particular time. *Circle graphs*, also called *pie graphs*, have a similar use. The circle represents the whole of something, and the slices show what proportion of the whole is made by each part.

Graphs allow you to see and understand patterns and relationships more easily than you can in information delivered in tables or text. This is especially true if the information is detailed or the relationships are complicated.

Learn the Skill

The following guidelines will help you interpret data that is presented as a graph.

1. Read the title to identify the subject and purpose of the graph. Note the type of graph, remembering what each type is designed to indicate. Also note how the graph's subject relates to any printed material that accompanies it.

2. Study the graph's parts. Pay close attention to the labels that define each axis. Note the units of measure. Identify the categories used. If there are different colors on bars or lines in the graph, determine what those differences mean.

3. Analyze the data in the graph. Note any increases or decreases in quantities. Look for trends, changes, and other relationships in the data.

4. Apply the information in the graph. Use the results of your analysis to draw conclusions. Ask yourself what generalizations can be made about the trends, changes, or relationships shown in the graph.

Practice the Skill

The graph below is a double-line graph. It shows both changes and relationships over time. This type of graph allows you to see how changes in one thing compare with changes in something else. Apply the guidelines to interpret the graph and answer the questions that follow.

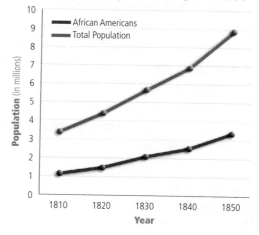

Population of the South, 1810–1850

1. What is shown on each axis of this graph? What are the units of measure on each axis?

2. What does each of the lines represent?

3. What was the total population of the South in 1810? in 1850? By how much did the African American population grow during that period?

4. Was the white population or the African American population growing faster? Explain how you know.

Module 14 Assessment

Review Vocabulary, Terms, and People

Match the definition in the left column with the correct term in the right column.

1. A region of cotton-producing areas that stretched from South Carolina to Texas
2. Emotional songs that mixed African and European music and expressed religious beliefs
3. Owners of small farms who made up the largest social class in the South
4. Crop brokers who often managed the cotton trade in the South
5. Wealthy farmers and plantation owners

a. cotton belt
b. factors
c. planters
d. spirituals
e. yeomen

Comprehension and Critical Thinking

Lesson 1

6. a. **Describe** How did the cotton gin lead to a cotton boom in the South?
    b. **Analyze** What were the positive and negative results of the cotton boom?
    c. **Evaluate** Do you think that the South suffered as a result of its reliance on cotton? Why or why not?

Lesson 2

7. a. **Describe** What three groups made up white southern society?
    b. **Compare and Contrast** In what ways were the lives of free African Americans and white southerners similar and different?
    c. **Predict** What might have been the attitude of yeomen and poor white southerners toward slavery? Why?

Lesson 3

8. a. **Identify** What are some small ways in which enslaved people tried to challenge the slave system?
    b. **Analyze Information** What were some ways that enslaved people sent messages or warnings to one another?
    c. **Make Inferences** How did religion and family help enslaved people cope with their lives?

Reading Skills

Online Research *Use the Reading Skills taught in this module to answer the question below.*

9. Which of the following would be the best website to find information about life in the South before the Civil War?
    a. a Civil War historian's homepage
    b. a collection of autobiographies written by slaves
    c. a site with information about how to grow cotton
    d. a collection of biographies of inventors

Review Themes

10. **Society and Culture** How were the different social classes in the South affected by the cotton boom?
11. **Economics** How did the cotton boom affect the economy of the South?

Social Studies Skills

Interpret Graphs *Use the Social Studies Skills taught in this module to answer the questions about the graph below.*

U.S. Cotton Production, 1800–1860

12. What span of time saw the largest increase in cotton production?

a. 1800 to 1820

b. 1820 to 1840

c. 1840 to 1860

d. after 1860

13. About what year did cotton production reach 1.2 million bales per year?

a. 1800

b. 1820

c. 1840

d. 1860

Focus on Writing

14. **Write a Biographical Sketch** In this module you learned about life in the South during the first half of the 1800s. List what you learned about living on a large cotton farm in the South and then choose an imaginary person to write about. Think about what life would have been like for this person. What might he or she have looked like? How might he or she have spoken? What might a typical day have been like? Once you have answered these questions, write two paragraphs about a day in the life of this person.

Module 15
Slavery in the United States

★

Essential Question
How did slavery shape life in the United States?

About the Painting: In the painting *A Ride for Liberty—The Fugitive Slaves*, artist Eastman Johnson depicts a family of slaves attempting an escape toward freedom.

> ▶ *Explore ONLINE!*

VIDEOS, including...
- Freedom's Road: Slavery and the Opposition
- The Sale of Josiah Henson

✓ Document-Based Investigations

✓ Graphic Organizers

✓ Interactive Games

✓ Image Carousel: Plantation Work

✓ Interactive Map: Growth of the United States to 1848

✓ Image Carousel: Resistance to the Fugitive Slave Act

In this module you will read about slavery in the United States. You will learn about how it began, what life as a slave was like, and how the issue of slavery affected American politics and society.

What You Will Learn ...

Lesson 1: Beginnings of Slavery in the Americas **476**
The Big Idea Europeans forced millions of African slaves to work in their colonies.

Lesson 2: The Slave System. **482**
The Big Idea The slave system in the South produced harsh living conditions and occasional rebellions.

Lesson 3: The Movement to End Slavery **489**
The Big Idea In the mid-1800s, debate over slavery increased as abolitionists organized to challenge slavery in the United States.

Lesson 4: The Politics of Slavery. **496**
The Big Idea The acquisition of new lands and antislavery writings intensified the debate over slavery.

Timeline of Events 1619–1852

 Explore ONLINE!

United States	World
	1600

1619 The first Africans in North America arrive at Jamestown, Virginia. ∨

1644 The Qing dynasty begins in China and rules until 1912.

1700

1763 Treaty of Paris ends French and Indian War.

1769 Scotland's James Watt patents a steam engine capable of running other machines.

1776 Congress approves the Declaration of Independence.

1776 Tukolor empire arises in the former Songhai region of West Africa.

1794 France ends slavery in its colonies.

1800

1808 A congressional ban on importing slaves in the United States takes effect.

1807 Parliament bans the slave trade in the British Empire.

1831 Nat Turner's Rebellion leads to fears of further slave revolts in the South.

1848 Revolutionary movements sweep across Europe.

1850 Congress passes the Fugitive Slave Act.

< **1852** *Uncle Tom's Cabin* is published.

1900

Reading Social Studies

THEME FOCUS:

Politics, Society and Culture

Since colonial times, the issue of slavery divided Americans. By the mid-1800s, the slavery debate reached its greatest height, nearly breaking the nation in two. The issue deeply affected American politics as Congress worked hard to ensure that the differing views and stances of the North and the South were met on an equal basis. Religious beliefs, American values, and economic concerns surrounded the slavery issue and helped shape and change the nation's society and culture. This module discusses the nation's complex struggle with this issue.

READING FOCUS:

Compare and Contrast Historical Facts

Comparing and contrasting are good ways to learn. That is one reason historians use comparison and contrast to explain people and events in history.

Understand Comparison and Contrast To **compare** is to look for likenesses, or similarities. To **contrast** is to look for differences. Sometimes writers point out similarities and differences. Other times you have to look for them yourself. You can use a diagram like this one to keep track of similarities and differences as you read.

Viewpoints on Slavery

The South

Differences
- Part of the southern way of life
- A state's political right

Similarities
- Necessary to keep the economy stable
- Required to keep the Union together

The North

Differences
- Morally wrong
- Cruel and inhumane
- Against American belief of equality

Clues for Comparison—Contrast

Writers sometimes signal comparisons or contrasts with words like these:

Comparison—similarly, like, in the same way, too

Contrast—however, unlike, but, while, although, in contrast

You Try It!

The following passage is from the module you are getting ready to read. As you read the passage, look for word clues about similarities and differences.

Abolitionists came from many different backgrounds and opposed slavery for various reasons. The Quakers were among the first groups to challenge slavery on religious grounds. Elihu Embree, the son of a Quaker minister, published the first newspapers in the country devoted to the abolitionist cause.

Other religious leaders gave speeches and published pamphlets that moved many Americans to support abolition. In one of these, abolitionist Theodore Weld wrote that "everyman knows that slavery is a curse." Other abolitionists referred to the Declaration of Independence. They reminded people that the American Revolution had been fought in the name of liberty.

Antislavery reformers did not always agree on the details, however. They differed over how much equality they thought African Americans should have. Some believed that African Americans should receive the same treatment as white Americans, whereas other abolitionists were against full political and social equality.

Key Terms and People

Lesson 1
immune
Middle Passage
African Diaspora

Lesson 2
folktales
spirituals
Nat Turner's Rebellion
Nat Turner

Lesson 3
abolition
Elihu Embree
William Lloyd Garrison
American Anti-Slavery Society
Angelina and Sarah Grimké
Frederick Douglass
Sojourner Truth
Underground Railroad
Harriet Tubman

Lesson 4
Wilmot Proviso
sectionalism
Free-Soil Party
secede
Compromise of 1850
Fugitive Slave Act
Anthony Burns
Harriet Beecher Stowe
Uncle Tom's Cabin

After you read the passage, answer the following questions.

1. What does the word *whereas* (in the last sentence of the passage) compare or contrast?

2. On what issue did abolitionists disagree? What comparison or contrast signal word helped you answer this question?

3. What other comparison or contrast words do you find in the passage? How do these words or phrases help you understand the passage?

As you read Module 15, keep an eye out for compare and contrast signal words. How do they help you understand the content?

Beginnings of Slavery in the Americas

The Big Idea
Europeans forced millions of African slaves to work in their colonies.

Main Ideas
- European diseases wiped out much of the Native American population, causing colonists to look for a new labor force.
- Europeans enslaved millions of Africans and sent them to work in their colonies.
- Slaves in the Americas created distinct cultures.

Key Terms and People
immune
Middle Passage
African Diaspora

Academic
Vocabulary
structure the way something is set up or organized

If YOU were there . . .

You are an enslaved African living in North America. Your family is all that you have. You help each other, and your family provides some relief from the forced labor and harsh life on the plantation. Still, you long for your freedom. A fellow slave has told you of a plan to escape.

Will you stay with your family or try to flee?

The Need for a New Labor Force

European diseases had a devastating effect on the Native American population. Measles, smallpox, and typhus were common in Europe. As a result, most adult Europeans were **immune**, or had a natural resistance, to them. Native Americans, however, had never been exposed to such diseases and had no immunity to them. As a result, many Native Americans became terribly sick after their first encounters with Europeans. Millions of them died in the years after Columbus reached the New World.

No one knows exactly how many Native Americans died from European diseases, but the loss of life was staggering. Spanish author Fernández de Oviedo reported in 1548 about the destruction of the Native Americans of Hispaniola. He reported that, of the estimated 1 million Indians who had lived on the island in 1492, "there are not now believed to be at the present time . . . five hundred persons [left]." In North America the Native American population north of Mexico was about 10 million when Columbus arrived. This number would drop to less than a million. The drop in the native population played a major role in the emerging need for an alternative labor force.

Plantation agriculture was a mainstay of the colonial economic **structure**. Spain and Portugal established sugar plantations that relied on large numbers of native laborers.

In the 1600s English tobacco farmers in North America also needed workers for their plantations. With a lack of Native American workers, they, too, needed another source of labor. Plantation owners in both North and South America wanted a cheap work force.

Some colonists, including Spanish priest Bartolomé de Las Casas, suggested using enslaved Africans as workers. Africans had already developed immunity to European diseases. The colonists soon agreed that slaves from West Africa could be the solution to their labor needs.

Reading Check
Analyze
How did disease contribute to the slave trade?

Native Americans had no resistance to European diseases. As a result, throughout the Americas, millions suffered and died. This illustration from a Spanish missionary account of 16th-century Mexico shows victims of smallpox.

The Slave Trade

The practice of slavery had existed in Africa and in many parts of the world for centuries. Traditionally, slavery in West Africa mostly involved only black Africans, who were both slaveholders and slaves. This changed in the 600s when Arab Muslims, and later Europeans, became slave traders. Though Europeans had long traded resources with Africa, they became more interested in the growing slave trade.

In 1510 the Spanish government legalized the sale of slaves in its colonies. The first full cargo ship of Africans arrived in the Americas eight years later. Over the next century, more than a million enslaved Africans were brought to the Spanish and Portuguese colonies in the New World. The Dutch and English also became active in the slave trade.

Middle Passage Enslavement was a horrible experience for the slaves. Most enslaved people had been captured in the interior of Africa, often by Africans who profited from selling slaves to Europeans. The captives were chained around the neck and then marched to the coast. This journey could be as long as 1,000 miles.

The **Middle Passage** was the voyage across the Atlantic Ocean that enslaved Africans were forced to endure. Africans were packed like cargo in the lower decks of the slave ships. The slaves were chained together and crammed into spaces about the size of coffins. The height between the decks was sometimes only 18 inches.

In this confinement, disease spread quickly, killing many Africans. Others suffocated or died from malnutrition. Some slaves took their own lives to end their suffering. It is estimated that one out of every six Africans died during the Middle Passage.

African Diaspora Between the 1520s and 1860s, about 12 million Africans were shipped across the Atlantic as slaves. More than 10 million of these captives survived the voyage and reached the Americas. The slave trade led to the **African Diaspora**. (A diaspora is the scattering of a people.) Enslaved Africans were sent all across the New World.

More than a third of the enslaved Africans, nearly 4 million people, were sent to work in Brazil. Most of these people were forced to labor on Portuguese sugar plantations. Nearly 2 million enslaved people were sent to the colonies of New Spain. Some worked on plantations in the Caribbean, while others were taken to toil in the mines of Peru and Mexico.

King Afonso of Kongo (seated) wrote the king of Portugal in 1526 asking him to do what he could to stop the practice of taking African slaves from his kingdom.

Some 3 million slaves worked in British and French colonies in the Caribbean and Latin America. More than 600,000 slaves went to Britain's North American colonies, which later became the United States.

Colonial leaders across the Americas developed laws that regulated slave treatment and behavior. Slaves were given few rights in the colonies. The law considered enslaved Africans to be property. In some colonies, a slaveholder was not charged with murder if he killed a slave while punishing him. Enslaved Africans, on the other hand, received harsh penalties for minor offenses, such as breaking a tool. Runaways were often tortured and sometimes killed.

The treatment of enslaved Africans varied from slaveholder to slaveholder. To protect their investment, some slaveholders provided adequate food, clothing, and shelter for their slaves. However, severe treatment was more common. Whippings, brandings, and even worse torture were all part of American slavery.

The Enslaved Fight Back Although they were in bondage, people of African origin found ways to resist their enslavement. They sometimes worked slowly, damaged goods, or deliberately carried out orders the wrong way.

In South Carolina, enslaved people vastly outnumbered whites, who lived in fear of slave rebellions. Their fears came true in the late 1730s when a revolt occurred in South Carolina. In September 1739, an uprising known as the Stono Rebellion took place. The revolt began when about 20 slaves gathered at the Stono River just southwest of Charles Town. Wielding weapons, they killed whites and marched south, beating drums and chanting "Liberty!" They called out for others to join them in their plan to seek freedom in Spanish-held Florida. Many joined, and their numbers grew until there were perhaps 100 in open rebellion. Seven plantations were burned along their route and 20 whites were killed. By late that afternoon, however, a white militia had surrounded the escaping slaves. The two sides clashed, and many slaves died in the fighting. Those captured were executed.

Stono and similar revolts led planters to make slave codes even stricter. Slaves were now forbidden from leaving plantations without written permission. The laws also made it illegal for slaves to meet with free blacks. Such laws made the conditions of slavery even more inhumane.

Slave Culture in the Americas

Slaves in the Americas came from many different parts of Africa. They spoke different languages and had different cultural backgrounds. But enslaved Africans also shared many customs and viewpoints. They built upon what they had in common to create new African American cultures.

Families were a vital part of slave culture. Families provided a refuge—a relationship not fully under the slaveholders' control. However, slave families faced many challenges. Families were often broken apart when a family member was sold to another owner. In Latin America, there were many more enslaved males than females. This made it difficult for slaves there to form stable families.

Religion was a second refuge for slaves. It gave enslaved Africans a form of expression that was partially free from their slaveholders' control. Slave religion was primarily Christian, but it included traditional elements from African religions as well. Religion gave slaves a sense of self-worth and a hope for salvation in this life and the next. Spirituals were a common form of religious expression among slaves. Slaves also used songs and folktales to tell their stories of sorrow, hope, agony, and joy.

Many slaves expressed themselves through art and dance. Dances were important social events in slave communities. Like most elements of slave culture, art and dance were heavily influenced by African traditions.

Summary and Preview After disease wiped out much of the Native American population, colonists turned to African slave labor. In the next lesson you will learn what life was like under slavery and how some tried to rebel against it.

Reading Check
Generalize
How were enslaved Africans treated in the Americas?

Reading Check
Identify Points of View Why was religion important to slaves in the Americas?

Lesson 1 Assessment

Review Ideas, Terms, and People

1. a. **Recall** Why did so many Native Americans die after coming into contact with Europeans?

   b. **Summarize** Why did plantation owners turn to enslaved Africans as a labor force?

2. a. **Identify** What was the Middle Passage?

   b. **Describe** Explain how enslaved Africans were treated after they reached the colonies in the Americas.

3. a. **Explain** What are spirituals?

   b. **Analyze** How did religion and family provide a refuge from the harsh life enslaved Africans were forced to endure?

Critical Thinking

4. **Identify Cause and Effect** In this lesson you learned about the slave trade. Create a chart similar to the one below and identify the causes and effects of the slave trade.

The Atlantic Slave Trade

The slave system that arose in the American colonies was strongly influenced by geographic forces. The climate of the southern colonies was suited to growing certain crops, like cotton, tobacco, and sugarcane. These crops required a great deal of labor to grow and to process. To meet this great demand for labor, the colonists looked to one main source—enslaved Africans.

Colonial Slave Ports Slave ships sailed to slave ports, where they unloaded their human cargo. Slave ports like Boston, Newport, and Charleston were located near farming areas and the mouths of rivers.

The West Indies Africans were brought to the West Indies to work on large sugar plantations. Sugarcane thrived in the West Indies, but it required huge amounts of labor to grow.

The Middle Passage The terrifying and deadly voyage across the Atlantic was known as the Middle Passage. Enslaved Africans were chained and crowded together under ships' decks on this long voyage, as the drawing shows.

MIDDLE PASSAGE

Boston
Newport
NORTH AMERICA
Charleston
ATLANTIC OCEAN
40°N
Tropic of Cancer
20°N
WEST INDIES
SOUTH AMERICA
Equator
20°S
Tropic of Capricorn
40°S
60°S

160°W   140°W   120°W   100°W   80°W   0°

Slave forts began as trading posts. They were built near river mouths to provide easy access to both the sea and inland areas.

AFRICA

St. Luis de Senegal

James Fort

Accra

Elmina

Whydah

Assinie

Elmina slave fort, Ghana

New England traders exchanged goods for slaves on the West African coast and then transported the slaves to the American colonies or to the West Indies.

20°N

AFRICA

Kidnapped and Taken to a Slave Ship

Mahommah G. Baquaqua was captured and sold into slavery as a young man. In this 1854 account, he recalls being taken to the African coast to board a slave ship.

"I was taken down to the river and placed on board a boat; the river was very large and branched off in two different directions, previous to emptying itself into the sea. . . . We were two nights and one day on this river, when we came to a . . . place . . . [where] the slaves were all put into a pen, and placed with our backs to the fire. . . . When all were ready to go aboard, we were chained together, and tied with ropes round about our necks, and were thus drawn down to the sea shore."

Slaves Brought to the Americas, 1493–1810

Number of slaves (in millions)

Years	
1493–1600	0.1
1601–1700	1.3
1701–1810	6.1

40°S

20°E   40°E   60°E   80°E   100°E

Interpret Maps

Human-Environment Interaction What geographic factors influenced the development of the Atlantic slave trade?

60°S

The Slave System

The Big Idea
The slave system in the South produced harsh living conditions and occasional rebellions.

Main Ideas
- Slaves worked at a variety of jobs on plantations.
- Life under slavery was difficult and dehumanizing.
- Slave culture centered around family, community, and religion.
- Slave uprisings led to stricter slave codes in many states.

Key Terms and People
folktales
spirituals
Nat Turner's Rebellion
Nat Turner

If YOU were there . . .

You are a reporter for a newspaper in Philadelphia in the 1850s. You are writing a series of articles about the slave system in the South. To get background for your stories, you are planning to interview some former slaves who now live in Philadelphia. Some have bought their freedom, while others have successfully escaped from slavery.

What questions will you ask in your interviews?

Slaves and Work

Most enslaved African Americans lived in rural areas where they worked on farms and plantations. Enslaved people on small farms usually did a variety of jobs. On large plantations, most slaves were assigned to specific jobs, and most worked in the fields. Most slaveholders demanded that slaves work as much as possible. Supervisors known as drivers, who were sometimes slaves themselves, made sure that slaves followed orders. Drivers also carried out punishments.

Working in the Field Most plantation owners used the gang-labor system. In this system, all field hands worked on the same task at the same time. They usually worked from sunup to sundown. Former slave Harry McMillan had worked on a plantation in South Carolina. He recalled that the field hands usually did not even get a break to eat lunch. "You had to get your victuals [food] standing at your hoe," he remembered.

Men, women, and even children older than about 10 usually did the same tasks. Sickness and poor weather rarely stopped the work. "The times I hated most was picking cotton when the frost was on the bolls [seed pods]," recalled former Louisiana slave Mary Reynolds. "My hands git sore and crack open and bleed."

Working in the Planter's Home Some slaves worked as butlers, cooks, or nurses in the planter's home. These slaves

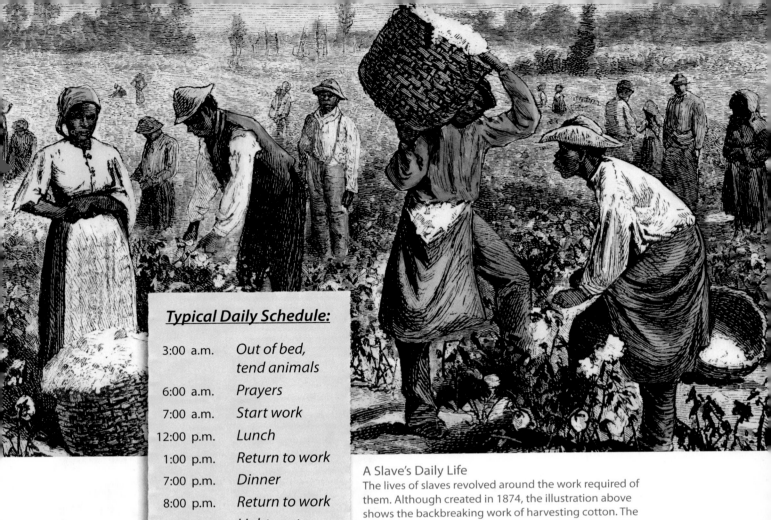

Typical Daily Schedule:

3:00 a.m.	Out of bed, tend animals
6:00 a.m.	Prayers
7:00 a.m.	Start work
12:00 p.m.	Lunch
1:00 p.m.	Return to work
7:00 p.m.	Dinner
8:00 p.m.	Return to work
11:00 p.m.	Lights out

A Slave's Daily Life
The lives of slaves revolved around the work required of them. Although created in 1874, the illustration above shows the backbreaking work of harvesting cotton. The schedule at left details how a slave might have spent his or her day.

often had better food, clothing, and shelter than field hands did, but they often worked longer hours. They had to serve the planter's family 24 hours a day.

Working at Skilled Jobs On larger plantations, some enslaved African Americans worked at skilled jobs, such as blacksmithing or carpentry. Sometimes planters let these slaves sell their services to other people. Often planters collected a portion of what was earned but allowed slaves to keep the rest. In this way, some skilled slaves earned enough money to buy their freedom from their slaveholders. For example, William Ellison earned his freedom in South Carolina by working for wages as a cotton gin maker. For years he worked late at night and on Sundays. He bought his freedom with the money he earned. Eventually he was also able to buy the freedom of his wife and daughter.

Life Under Slavery

Generally, slaveholders viewed slaves as property, not as people. Slaveholders bought and sold slaves to make a profit. The most common method of sale was at an auction. The auction itself determined whether families would be kept together or separated. Sometimes a buyer wanted a slave to

Reading Check
Summarize
What were some types of work done by enslaved people on plantations?

A Nurse's Work
Slaveholders' children were often cared for by enslaved women. At the time, women who looked after children were called nurses. This nurse is posing with her slaveholder's child in about 1850.

fill a specific position, such as heavy laborer, carpenter, or blacksmith. The buyer might be willing to pay for the slave who could do the work, but not for that slave's family. Families would then be separated, with little hope of ever getting back together.

Slave traders sometimes even kidnapped free African Americans and then sold them into slavery. For example, Solomon Northup, a free African American, was kidnapped in Washington, DC. He spent 12 years as a slave until he finally proved his identity and gained his release.

Living Conditions Enslaved people often endured poor living conditions. Planters housed them in dirt-floor cabins with few furnishings and often leaky roofs. The clothing given to them was usually simple and made of cheap, coarse fabric. Some slaves tried to brighten up their clothing by sewing on designs from discarded scraps of material. In this way, they expressed their individuality and personalized the clothing assigned to them by the planters.

Likewise, many slaves did what they could to improve their small food rations. Some planters allowed slaves to keep their own gardens for vegetables and chickens for eggs. Other slaves were able to add a little variety to their diet by fishing or picking wild berries.

Punishment and Slave Codes Some planters offered more food or better living conditions to encourage slaves' obedience. However, most slave-holders used punishment instead. Some would punish one slave in front of others as a warning to them all. Harry McMillan recalled some of the punishments he had witnessed.

> "The punishments were whipping, putting you in the stocks [wooden frames to lock people in] and making you wear irons and a chain at work. Then they had a collar to put round your neck with two horns, like cows' horns, so that you could not lie down. . . . Sometimes they dug a hole like a well with a door on top. This they called a dungeon keeping you in it two or three weeks or a month, or sometimes till you died in there."
>
> —Harry McMillan, quoted in *Major Problems in the History of the American South, Volume I*, edited by Paul D. Escott and David R. Goldfield

To further control slaves' actions, many states passed strict laws called slave codes. Some laws prohibited slaves from traveling far from their homes. Literacy laws in most southern states prohibited the education of slaves. Alabama, Virginia, and Georgia had laws that allowed the fining and whipping of anyone caught teaching enslaved people to read and write.

Reading Check
Summarize
How did slaveholders control slaves?

Slave Culture

Many enslaved Africans found comfort in their community and culture. They made time for social activity, even after exhausting workdays, in order to relieve the hardship of their lives.

Academic Vocabulary
aspect part

Family and Community Family was the most important **aspect** of slave communities, and many slaves feared separation more than they feared punishment. Josiah Henson never forgot the day that he and his family were auctioned. His mother begged the slaveholder who bought her to buy Josiah, too. The slaveholder refused, and Henson's entire family was separated. "I must have been then between five or six years old," he recalled years later. "I seem to see and hear my poor weeping mother now."

Enslaved parents kept their heritage alive by passing down family histories as well as African customs and traditions. They also told **folktales**, or traditional stories that often had a moral, to teach lessons about how to survive under slavery. These folktales often included a clever animal character called a trickster. The trickster—which often represented slaves—defeated a stronger animal by outwitting it. Folktales reassured slaves that they could survive by outsmarting more powerful slaveholders.

Religion Religion also played an important part in slave culture. By the early 1800s, many slaves were Christians. They came to see themselves, like the slaves in the Old Testament, as God's chosen people, much like the Hebrew slaves in ancient Egypt who had faith that they would someday live in freedom.

Some slaves sang **spirituals**, emotional Christian songs that blended African and European music, to express their deeply held religious beliefs.

Most slaves found hope and a short escape from their daily misery in Sunday church services. Others sought to escape permanently and ran away, hoping to reach the freedom of the North. A failed escape attempt, however, could result in a cruel whipping—or worse.

For example, "The Heavenly Road" reflected slaves' belief in their equality in the eyes of God.

> "Come, my brother, if you never did pray,
>   I hope you pray tonight;
>   For I really believe I am a child of God
>   As I walk on the heavenly road."
>
> —Anonymous, quoted in *Afro-American Religious History*, edited by Milton C. Sernett

Slaves blended some aspects of their traditional African religions with those of the Christianity that the slaveholders followed. They worshipped in secret, out of sight of slaveholders. Some historians have called slave religion the invisible institution.

Seeds of Rebellion Maintaining their own religious beliefs and practices was only one way in which enslaved people resisted slaveholders' attempts to control them completely. In small ways, slaves rebelled against the system daily. Sometimes they worked slower to protest long hours in the fields. Other times they ran away for a few days to avoid an angry slaveholder. Some slaves tried to escape permanently, but most left only for short periods, often to go and visit relatives.

Gaining freedom by escaping to the North was hard. If discovered, slaves were captured and sent back to their slaveholders, where they faced certain punishment or death. However, thousands of enslaved people succeeded in escaping.

Slave Uprisings

Although violent slave revolts were relatively rare, white southerners lived in fear of them. Two planned rebellions were stopped before they began. Gabriel Prosser planned a rebellion near Richmond, Virginia, in 1800. Denmark Vesey planned one in Charleston, South Carolina, in 1822. Local authorities executed most of those involved in planning these rebellions. Though Vesey was executed as the leader of the Charleston conspiracy, several accounts written after his death by antislavery writers claimed he was a hero.

Reading Check
Summarize
How did slaves' religious beliefs affect their attitudes toward slavery?

The most violent slave revolt in the country occurred in 1831 and is known as **Nat Turner's Rebellion**. **Nat Turner**, a slave from Southampton County, Virginia, believed that God had told him to end slavery. On an August night in 1831, Turner led a group of slaves in a plan to kill all of the slaveholders and their families in the county. First they attacked the family who held Turner as a slave. Soon they had killed about 60 white people in the community.

More than 100 innocent slaves who were not part of Turner's group were killed in an attempt to stop the rebellion. Turner himself led authorities on a chase around the countryside for six weeks. He hid in caves and in the woods before he was caught and brought to trial. Before his trial, Turner made a confession. He expressed his belief that the revolt was justified and

Enslaved Nat Turner led a revolt against white slaveholders in 1831. The map shows his route. The image depicts his capture.

▷ *Explore ONLINE!*

Nat Turner's Rebellion

VIRGINIA

August 23, 1831 Most rebels are captured, but Turner escapes.

October 30, 1831 Turner is captured

Cypress Bridge

Nottoway River

August 21, 1831 Turner and others begin the revolt.

SOUTHAMPTON COUNTY

ATLANTIC OCEAN

Meherrin River

NORTH CAROLINA

→ Nat Turner's route
○ House or plantation
◉ Hiding place

0   3   6 Miles
0   3   6 Kilometers

Interpret Maps

1. **Movement** Why do you think Nat Turner followed the route shown as he prepared his rebellion?

2. **Movement** How many days did it take to capture Nat Turner?

Nat Turner's Rebellion

In 1831 a white southerner who had escaped the rebellion wrote a letter describing the mood of the area where Nat Turner's group had killed slaveholders and their families.

> The author believes no one in the county has been through a worse event.

> The author says that many people went into hiding when the rebellion began.

"The oldest inhabitants of our county have never experienced such a distressing [terrible] time, as we have had since Sunday night last. The [slaves], about fifteen miles from this place, have massacred from 50 to 75 women and children, and some 8 or 10 men. Every house, room and corner in this place is full of women and children, driven from home, who had to take to the woods, until they could get to this place. We are worn out with fatigue [tiredness]."

—Richmond Enquirer, quoted in *The Southampton Slave Revolt of 1831* by Henry I. Tragle

Analyze Historical Sources
What emotions do you think the author of this letter was feeling?

Reading Check
Find Main Ideas
What was Nat Turner's Rebellion, and what happened as a result?

worth his death: "I am willing to suffer the fate that awaits me." Turner was executed on November 11, 1831. After the rebellion, many states strengthened their slave codes. The new codes placed stricter control on enslaved people. Despite resistance, slavery continued to spread.

Summary and Preview Several groups of African Americans attempted to end slavery by rebellion. All of the attempts failed. In the next lesson, you will read about the reform-minded people who opposed the practice of slavery.

Lesson 2 Assessment

Review Ideas, Terms, and People

1. a. **Identify** What different types of work were done by slaves on plantations?

   b. **Elaborate** Do you think that skilled slaves had advantages over other slaves? Why or why not?

2. a. **Describe** What were living conditions like for most slaves?

   b. **Summarize** In what different ways did slaveholders encourage obedience from their slaves?

3. a. **Recall** What was the purpose of African American folktales?

   b. **Explain** How did slaves try to maintain a sense of community?

4. a. **Describe** What was the outcome of Nat Turner's Rebellion?

   b. **Elaborate** What do you think were some reasons why slaves rebelled?

Critical Thinking

5. **Evaluate** In this lesson you learned about the slavery system. Create a graphic organizer like the one shown below to identify the two most important reasons why enslaved people challenged the system as well as how they did so.

Reasons for Challenging Slavery	→	Ways of Challenging Slavery

The Movement to End Slavery

The Big Idea

In the mid-1800s, debate over slavery increased as abolitionists organized to challenge slavery in the United States.

Main Ideas

- Americans from a variety of backgrounds actively opposed slavery.

- Abolitionists organized the Underground Railroad to help enslaved Africans escape.

- Despite efforts of abolitionists, many Americans remained opposed to ending slavery.

Key Terms and People

abolition
Elihu Embree
William Lloyd Garrison
American Anti-Slavery Society
Angelina and Sarah Grimké
Frederick Douglass
Sojourner Truth
Underground Railroad
Harriet Tubman

If YOU were there . . .

You live in southern Ohio in the 1850s. A friend who lives across the river in Kentucky has asked you to join a network that helps escaping slaves. She reminds you that your house has a secret cellar where you could easily hide fugitives for a few days. You are opposed to slavery. But you know this might get you in trouble with your neighbors—and with the law.

Would you become an agent for the Underground Railroad? Why?

Americans Oppose Slavery

Some Americans had opposed slavery since before the country was founded. Benjamin Franklin was the president of the first antislavery society in America, the Pennsylvania Society for Promoting the Abolition of Slavery. In the 1830s Americans took more organized action to support **abolition**, or a complete end to slavery.

Differences among Abolitionists Abolitionists came from many different backgrounds and opposed slavery for various reasons. The Quakers were among the first groups to challenge slavery on religious grounds. **Elihu Embree**, the son of a Quaker minister, published the first newspapers in the country devoted to the abolitionist cause. One newspaper was called *The Emancipator*. Embree proclaimed that "freedom is the inalienable right of *all men*."

Other religious leaders gave speeches and published pamphlets that moved many Americans to support abolition. In one of these, abolitionist Theodore Weld wrote that "everyman knows that slavery is a curse." Other abolitionists referred to the Declaration of Independence. They reminded people that the American Revolution had been fought in the name of liberty.

Antislavery reformers did not always agree on the details, however. They differed over how much equality they thought

African Americans should have. Some believed that African Americans should receive the same treatment as white Americans. In contrast, other abolitionists were against full political and social equality.

Some abolitionists wanted to send freed African Americans to Africa to start new colonies. They thought that this would prevent conflicts between the races in the United States. In 1817 a minister named Robert Finley started the American Colonization Society, an organization dedicated to establishing colonies of freed slaves in Africa. Five years later, the society founded the colony of Liberia on the west coast of Africa. About 12,000 African Americans eventually settled in Liberia. However, many abolitionists who once favored colonization later opposed it. Some African Americans also opposed it. David Walker was one such person. In his 1829 essay, "Appeal to the Colored Citizens of the World," Walker explained his opposition to colonization.

> "The greatest riches in all America have arisen from our blood and tears: and they [whites] will drive us from our property and homes, which we have earned with our blood."
>
> —David Walker, quoted in *From Slavery to Freedom* by John Hope Franklin and Alfred A. Moss Jr.

Spreading the Abolitionist Message Abolitionists found many ways to further their cause. Some went on speaking tours or wrote pamphlets and newspaper articles. John Greenleaf Whittier wrote abolitionist poetry and literature. **William Lloyd Garrison** published an abolitionist newspaper, the *Liberator,* beginning in 1831. In 1833 he also helped found the **American Anti-Slavery Society**. Its members wanted immediate emancipation and racial equality for African Americans. Garrison later became its president.

Both the *Liberator* and the Anti-Slavery Society relied on support from free African Americans. Society members distributed antislavery literature and petitioned Congress to end federal support of slavery. In 1840 the American Anti-Slavery Society split. One group wanted immediate freedom for enslaved African Americans and a bigger role for women. The others wanted gradual emancipation and for women to play only minor roles in the movement.

Angelina and Sarah Grimké, two white southern women, were prominent antislavery activists of the 1830s. They came from a South Carolina slaveholding family but disagreed with their parents' support of slavery. Angelina Grimké tried to recruit other white southern women in a pamphlet called *Appeal to the Christian Women of the South* in 1836.

William Lloyd Garrison proclaimed in 1853, "Wherever there is a human being, I see God-given rights. . . ."

"I know you do not make the laws, but . . . if you really suppose you can do nothing to overthrow slavery, you are greatly mistaken. . . . Try to persuade your husband, father, brothers, and sons that slavery is a crime against God and man."

—Angelina Grimké, quoted in *The Grimké Sisters from South Carolina*, edited by Gerda Lerner

This essay was very popular in the North. In 1839 the Grimké sisters wrote *American Slavery As It Is*. The book was one of the most important antislavery works of its time.

African American Abolitionists Many former slaves were active in the antislavery cause. **Frederick Douglass** escaped from slavery when he was 20 and went on to become one of the most important African American leaders of the 1800s. Douglass secretly learned to read and write as a boy, despite a law against it. His public-speaking skills impressed members of the Anti-Slavery Society. In 1841 they asked him to give regular lectures.

At a Fourth of July celebration in 1852, he captured the audience's attention with his powerful voice.

"The blessings in which you, this day, rejoice, are not enjoyed in common. . . . This Fourth of July is *yours*, not *mine*. You may rejoice, I must mourn."

—Frederick Douglass, quoted in *From Slavery to Freedom* by John Hope Franklin and Alfred A. Moss Jr.

--- BIOGRAPHY ---

Frederick Douglass 1817–1895

Frederick Douglass was born in rural Maryland. At age six he was sent to live in Baltimore, and at age 20 he escaped to New York City. For most of his life, Douglass lived in Rochester, New York, making his home into a stop along the Underground Railroad. Douglass became the most famous African American in the 1800s.

After hearing the abolitionist William Lloyd Garrison speak in 1841, Douglass began his own speaking tours about his experiences as a slave. He traveled often, giving powerful antislavery speeches to audiences throughout the North and in Europe. His personal stories and elegant speaking style helped the abolitionist movement to grow.

In midlife he wrote an autobiography and started an abolitionist newspaper called the *North Star*. During the Civil War, Douglass persuaded black soldiers to fight for the North. His words remain an inspiration to this day.

Draw Conclusions
What made Frederick Douglass's speeches and writings so powerful?

Sojourner Truth was a former slave who became a leading abolitionist as well as an active supporter of women's rights.

In addition to his many speaking tours in the United States and Europe, Douglass published a newspaper called the *North Star* and wrote several autobiographies. His autobiographies were intended to show the injustices of slavery.

Another former slave, **Sojourner Truth**, also contributed to the abolitionist cause. She claimed God had called her to travel through the United States and preach the truth about slavery and women's rights. With her deep voice and quick wit, Truth became legendary in the antislavery movement for her fiery and dramatic speeches.

Other African Americans wrote narratives about their experiences as slaves to expose the cruelties that many slaves faced. In 1861 Harriet Jacobs published *Incidents in the Life of a Slave Girl*, one of the few slave narratives by a woman. William Wells Brown wrote an antislavery play as well as a personal narrative in the form of a novel called *Clotel*.

Reading Check
Find Main Ideas In what ways did African Americans participate in the abolition movement?

The Underground Railroad

By the 1830s, a loosely organized group had begun helping slaves escape from the South. Free African Americans, former slaves, and a few white abolitionists worked together. They created what became known as the **Underground Railroad**. The organization was not an actual railroad but was a network of people who arranged transportation and hiding places for fugitives, or escaped slaves.

Fugitives would travel along "freedom trails" that led them to northern states or sometimes into Canada. At no time did the Railroad have a central leadership. No one person, or group of people, was ever officially in charge. Despite the lack of any real structure, the Underground Railroad managed to achieve dramatic results.

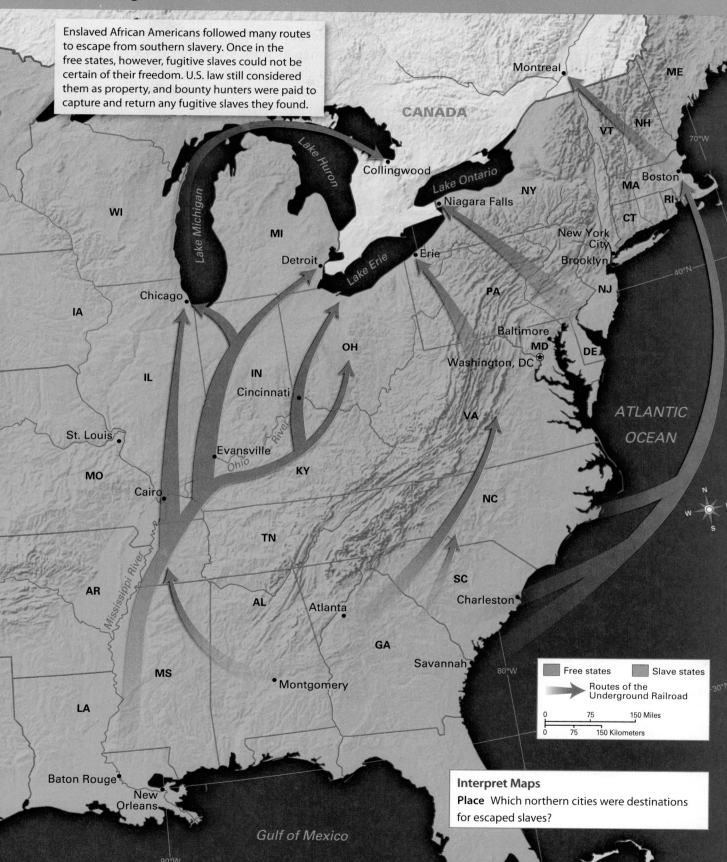

The Underground Railroad

▶ Explore ONLINE!

Enslaved African Americans followed many routes to escape from southern slavery. Once in the free states, however, fugitive slaves could not be certain of their freedom. U.S. law still considered them as property, and bounty hunters were paid to capture and return any fugitive slaves they found.

CANADA

Montreal

ME

VT

NH

Collingwood

Lake Ontario

Boston

Niagara Falls

NY

MA

RI

WI

Lake Huron

Lake Michigan

MI

Detroit

Lake Erie

Erie

New York City

CT

Chicago

OH

Brooklyn

PA

NJ

IA

IN

Baltimore

MD

DE

IL

Cincinnati

Washington, DC

St. Louis

Ohio River

KY

VA

ATLANTIC OCEAN

MO

Evansville

Cairo

NC

TN

Mississippi River

AR

AL

Atlanta

SC

Charleston

MS

GA

Montgomery

Savannah

LA

Baton Rouge

New Orleans

Gulf of Mexico

Free states   **Slave states**

➤ Routes of the Underground Railroad

0   75   150 Miles

0   75   150 Kilometers

Interpret Maps

Place Which northern cities were destinations for escaped slaves?

Often wearing disguises, fugitives moved along the "railroad" at night, led by people known as conductors. Many times, the fugitives had no other guideposts but the stars. They stopped to rest during the day at "stations," often barns, attics, or other places on property owned by abolitionists known as station masters. The station masters hid and fed the fugitives.

The most famous and daring conductor on the Underground Railroad was **Harriet Tubman**. When Tubman escaped slavery in 1849, she left behind her family. She swore that she would return and lead her whole family to freedom in the North. Tubman returned to the South 19 times, successfully leading her family and more than 300 other slaves to freedom. At one time, the reward for Tubman's capture reportedly climbed to $40,000, a huge amount of money at that time.

Reading Check
Draw Inferences
Why were the operations of the Underground Railroad kept secret?

Opposition to Ending Slavery

Although the North was the center of the abolitionist movement, many white northerners agreed with the South and supported slavery. Others disliked slavery but opposed equality for African Americans.

Newspaper editors and politicians warned that freed slaves would move north and take jobs from white workers. Some workers feared losing jobs to newly freed African Americans, whom they believed would accept lower wages. Abolitionist leaders were threatened with violence as some northerners joined mobs. Such a mob killed abolitionist Elijah Lovejoy in 1837 in Alton, Illinois.

The federal government also obstructed abolitionists. Between 1836 and 1844, the U.S. House of Representatives used what was called a gag rule. Congress had received thousands of antislavery petitions. Yet the gag rule forbade members of Congress from discussing them. This rule

DOCUMENT-BASED INVESTIGATION Historical Source

Anti-Abolitionist Rally

Members of an anti-abolitionist group used this flyer to call people together in order to disrupt a meeting of abolitionists in 1837.

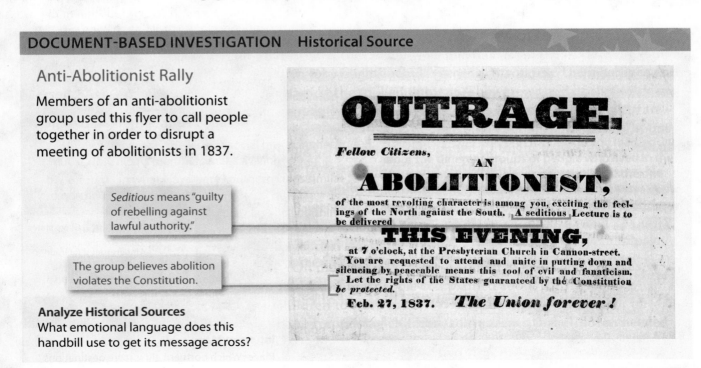

Seditious means "guilty of rebelling against lawful authority."

The group believes abolition violates the Constitution.

Analyze Historical Sources
What emotional language does this handbill use to get its message across?

OUTRAGE.

Fellow Citizens,

AN

ABOLITIONIST,

of the most revolting character is among you, exciting the feelings of the North against the South. A seditious Lecture is to be delivered

THIS EVENING,

at 7 o'clock, at the Presbyterian Church in Cannon-street. You are requested to attend and unite in putting down and silencing by peaceable means this tool of evil and fanaticism, Let the rights of the States guaranteed by the Constitution be protected.

Feb. 27, 1837. *The Union forever!*

violated the First Amendment right of citizens to petition the government. But southern members of Congress did not want to debate slavery. Many northern members of Congress preferred to avoid the issue.

Eventually, representative and former president John Quincy Adams was able to get the gag rule overturned. His resolution to enact a constitutional amendment halting the expansion of slavery never passed, however.

Many white southerners saw slavery as vital to the South's economy and culture. They also felt that outsiders should not interfere with their way of life. After Nat Turner's Rebellion in 1831, when Turner led some slaves to kill slaveholders, open talk about slavery disappeared in the South. It became dangerous to voice antislavery sentiments in southern states. Abolitionists like the Grimké sisters left rather than air unpopular views to hostile neighbors. Racism, fear, and economic dependence on slavery made emancipation all but impossible in the South.

Summary and Preview The issue of slavery grew more controversial in the United States during the first half of the nineteenth century. In the next lesson you will learn how slavery affected politics in the United States.

Reading Check
Draw Conclusions
Why did many northern workers oppose the abolition movement?

Lesson 3 Assessment

Review Ideas, Terms, and People

1. a. Identify What contributions did William Lloyd Garrison make to the abolition movement?

b. Draw Conclusions In what ways did contributions from African Americans aid the struggle for abolition?

c. Elaborate What do you think about the American Colonization Society's plan to send free African Americans to Liberia?

2. a. Describe How did the Underground Railroad work?

b. Explain Why did Harriet Tubman first become involved with the Underground Railroad?

c. Evaluate Do you think the Underground Railroad was a success? Why or why not?

3. a. Describe What action did Congress take to block abolitionists?

b. Analyze Why did some Americans oppose equality for African Americans?

c. Predict How might the debate over slavery lead to conflict in the future?

Critical Thinking

4. Identify Cause and Effect In this lesson, you learned about the abolitionist movement of the early and mid-1800s. Create a graphic organizer similar to the one below to show the reasons for opposition to the movement and the effects of that opposition.

| Reasons for Opposing the End of Slavery | → | Effects of Opposition to the Movement |

The Politics of Slavery

The Big Idea

The acquisition of new lands and antislavery writings intensified the debate over slavery.

Main Ideas

- The gaining of new territory in the West renewed disputes over the issue of slavery.

- The Compromise of 1850 tried to solve the disputes over slavery.

- The Fugitive Slave Act caused controversy and led to the growth of antislavery leanings.

Key Terms and People

Wilmot Proviso
sectionalism
Free-Soil Party
secede
Compromise of 1850
Fugitive Slave Act
Anthony Burns
Harriet Beecher Stowe
Uncle Tom's Cabin

If YOU were there . . .

You are a member of Congress from the North in 1850. You have just taken part in a heated floor debate about whether or not California should be accepted into the Union as a free or slave state. Several members from the South have threatened that their states will leave the Union if California enters as a free state. The nation is on the verge of splitting up.

What can you do to keep the nation united?

Slavery and Territorial Expansion

By the mid-1800s the nation was divided into two societies— the North, where workers labored for wages, and the South, where a large number of workers were enslaved. The developing debate over slavery was largely one of property rights versus human rights. Many Americans at the time thought that the property rights of slaveholders were more important that the human rights of slaves.

After winning the Mexican-American War, the United States added more than 500,000 square miles of new territory through the Mexican Cession. Eventually, new states would be formed out of this vast area. The key question became whether these states would ban or allow slavery. The Missouri Compromise of 1820 had banned slavery in most of the northern part of the Louisiana Purchase. Antislavery supporters wanted to do something similar with this new territory. On the other hand, some Americans wanted to allow slavery in the new lands.

During the Mexican-American War, Representative David Wilmot offered the **Wilmot Proviso**, a document stating that "neither slavery nor involuntary servitude shall ever exist in any part of [the] territory." Although the document was passed in the northern-controlled House, it was not passed by the southern-dominated Senate. Politicians formerly supported their party's ideas, but the Wilmot Proviso spurred a

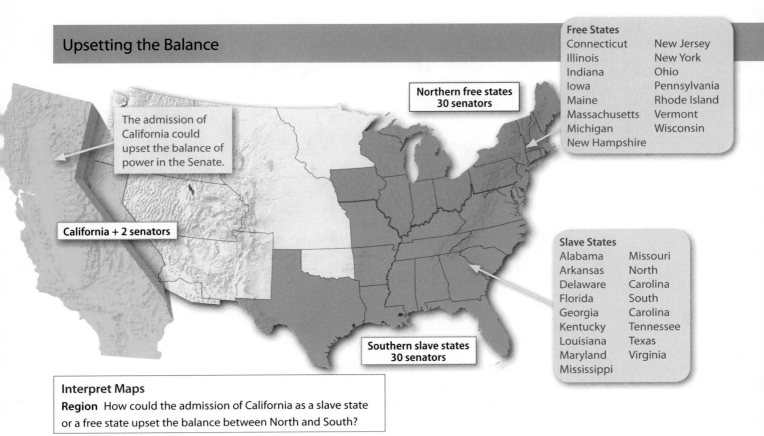

Upsetting the Balance

The admission of California could upset the balance of power in the Senate.

California + 2 senators

Northern free states
30 senators

Free States

Connecticut	New Jersey
Illinois	New York
Indiana	Ohio
Iowa	Pennsylvania
Maine	Rhode Island
Massachusetts	Vermont
Michigan	Wisconsin
New Hampshire	

Slave States

Alabama	Missouri
Arkansas	North
Delaware	Carolina
Florida	South
Georgia	Carolina
Kentucky	Tennessee
Louisiana	Texas
Maryland	Virginia
Mississippi	

Southern slave states
30 senators

Interpret Maps

Region How could the admission of California as a slave state or a free state upset the balance between North and South?

debate that showed growing **sectionalism**, or favoring the interests of one section or region over the interests of the entire country.

In response to the unwillingness of the Democrats and Whigs to take a clear position on slavery, a new political party developed during the presidential campaign of 1848. Antislavery northerners formed the **Free-Soil Party**, which supported the Wilmot Proviso. They chose former president Martin Van Buren as their candidate. Their candidate did not win, but the votes he received helped Democrat Lewis Cass, who opposed the Wilmot Proviso, to lose to Whig candidate Zachary Taylor. The Wilmot Proviso, however, never was passed.

Reading Check
Draw Inferences
How did the mixed results of the passage of the Wilmot Proviso illustrate the growth of sectionalism?

Another Attempt at Compromise

By 1850 the population in California had grown so much because of the gold rush that it applied to join the Union as a state instead of as a territory. This request brought the issue of slavery to the surface. If California entered the Union as a free state, the balance between free and slave states would change, favoring the free states. This was unacceptable to the South.

Kentucky Senator Henry Clay introduced a plan that proposed several compromises on the slavery issue. Clay's plan drew attack from representatives from the North and the South. Senator John C. Calhoun of South Carolina argued that letting California enter as a free state would destroy the nation's balance. He asked that the slave states be allowed to **secede**, or formally withdraw, from the Union.

The Great Compromiser
Henry Clay was nicknamed "the Great Compromiser" for his success in negotiating agreements that balanced the interests of slave-owning states and the rest of the country. He was instrumental in achieving the Compromise of 1820, the Compromise Tariff of 1833, and the Compromise of 1850.

Reading Check
Analyze
Which element of the Compromise of 1850 could be considered a "win" by both northerners and southerners?

After months of debate, the Senate finally passed five laws based on Clay's resolutions. Together, these laws formed what became known as the **Compromise of 1850**. California was able to enter the Union as a free state. The rest of the Mexican Cession was divided into two territories—Utah and New Mexico—where the question of whether to allow slavery would be decided by popular sovereignty. Texas agreed to give up its land claims in New Mexico in exchange for financial aid from the federal government. Lastly, the compromise outlawed the slave trade in the District of Columbia and established a new fugitive slave law.

The Crisis Deepens

The issues the Compromise of 1850 seemed to solve were soon replaced by others. One part of the compromise itself was very controversial.

The Fugitive Slave Act The **Fugitive Slave Act** made it a crime to help runaway slaves and allowed officials to arrest those slaves in free areas. People accused of being escaped slaves had to prove that they were not, which was often difficult or impossible. Also, escaped slaves who had lived in the North for years were returned to slavery if caught.

The law was openly resisted by people in the North. Many northerners who had previously been quiet on slavery issues were now furious. Mobs rescued enslaved people from northern police stations. They threatened slave catchers. In 1854 **Anthony Burns**, a fugitive slave from Virginia, was arrested in Boston. Abolitionists used force while trying to rescue him from jail, killing a deputy marshal. A federal ship was ordered to return Burns to Virginia after his trial. Many people in the North, particularly in Massachusetts, were outraged.

The event persuaded many to join the abolitionist cause. At the same time, angered by these reactions of the northerners, some southern leaders began again to talk of seceding from the Union.

Outrage over the Act Abolitionists in the North used the stories of fugitive slaves like Anthony Burns to gain sympathy for their cause. These slave narratives also educated people about their hardships.

Harriet Beecher Stowe, a magazine writer in Maine, had once lived in Cincinnati, Ohio, an important stop on the Underground Railroad. There she heard tales of slavery's cruelty and horror. Angered by the Fugitive Slave Act, she wrote a series of short stories about slave life for an anti-slavery newspaper in 1851. A year later these stories were published as an antislavery novel entitled *Uncle Tom's Cabin*.

Uncle Tom's Cabin was published by Harriet Beecher Stowe in 1852.

Although Stowe had little firsthand knowledge of slavery or the South, her novel became an enormous success, selling more than two million copies around the United States. Its popularity caused one northerner to claim that the book had created "two millions of abolitionists." However, the book outraged many southerners. They accused Stowe of writing lies about plantation life. *Uncle Tom's Cabin* raised tensions over slavery to new heights.

Reading Check
Identify Cause and Effect What effect did the Fugitive Slave Act have on the antislavery movement?

Summary and Preview The United States experienced increasing disagreement over the issue of slavery. The Compromise of 1850 and the Fugitive Slave Act tried to address these disagreements with legislation. In the next module you will read about several reform movements in the United States that arose from issues, including that of slavery.

Lesson 4 Assessment

Reviewing Ideas, Terms, and People

1. **a. Recall** What caused the creation of the Free-Soil Party?

   b. Predict What do you think might result from the growing sectionalism in Congress?

2. **a. Make Inferences** Why might the Compromise of 1850 have been controversial in both the North and the South?

   b. Evaluate Was the Compromise of 1850 a good solution to the conflict over slavery?

3. **a. Identify** What were the effects of the Fugitive Slave Act?

   b. Elaborate Do you think slave narratives such as *Uncle Tom's Cabin* were an effective tool in the fight against slavery? Why or why not?

Critical Thinking

4. **Sequence** In this lesson, you learned about the sequence of events surrounding the debate over slavery during the mid-1800s. Create a graphic organizer like the one below to illustrate the chain of events explaining how each event led to the next. Add boxes as necessary.

Literature in History

Antislavery Literature

WORD HELP

conceive imagine

desolate alone

forlorn unhappy

slacking slowing
down

thither there

❶ What detail tells
you how long Eliza has
walked up to this point?

❷ Why do you think
she chooses that escape
route?

About the Reading Harriet Beecher Stowe came from a family of abolitionists. While Stowe and her family were living in Cincinnati, Ohio, they bravely sheltered slaves fleeing from the neighboring slave state of Kentucky. Outrage at the Fugitive Slave Act of 1850 led Stowe to write *Uncle Tom's Cabin*. This novel, published in 1852, revealed the cruelties of slavery. But it also went a step further—and showed the evil effects that slavery had on slaveholders themselves.

Uncle Tom's Cabin made Stowe famous. It was translated into more than 20 languages. Because of its popularity, it drew the world's attention to the injustice of slavery in the South. Published nine years before the outbreak of the Civil War, *Uncle Tom's Cabin* focused the nation's attention on the cruelties of slavery. In the following section, Stowe describes how a slave named Eliza is trying to escape to save her son from being sold.

As You Read Look for details that appeal to your feelings.

From *Uncle Tom's Cabin*
by Harriet Beecher Stowe (1811–1896)

It is impossible to conceive of a human creature more wholly desolate and forlorn than Eliza when she turned her footsteps from Uncle Tom's cabin. . . .
The boundaries of the farm, the grove, the wood lot passed by her dizzily as she walked on; and still she went, leaving one familiar object after another, slacking not, pausing not, till reddening daylight found her many a long mile from all traces of any familiar objects upon the open highway. ❶
She had often been, with her mistress, to visit some connections in the little town of T—, not far from the Ohio River, and knew the road well. ❷ To go thither, to escape across the Ohio River, were the first hurried outlines of her plan of escape; beyond that she could only hope in God. . . .

Connect Literature to History

1. **Analyze** Slaves had no legal rights. They were considered to be property, not human beings. How do the actions and description in this passage contradict these ideas about slaves?

2. **Compare and Contrast** Frederick Douglass, Sojourner Truth, and other former slaves wrote narratives about their experiences. Yet these true stories did not have as much impact as Stowe's novel. Why do you think this fictional story about slavery had more impact than true slave narratives?

Social Studies Skills

Conduct Internet Research

Define the Skill

The Internet is a huge network of computers that are linked together. You can connect to this network from a personal computer or from a computer at a public library or school. Once connected, you can go to places called websites, which consist of one or more web pages. Each page contains information that you can view on the computer screen. Governments, businesses, individuals, and many different types of organizations, such as universities, news organizations, and libraries, have websites.

The Internet can be a very good reference source. It allows you to gather information on almost any topic without ever having to leave your chair. However, finding the information you need can sometimes be difficult. Having the skill to use the Internet efficiently increases its usefulness.

Learn the Skill

There are millions of websites on the Internet. This can make it hard to locate specific information. The following steps will help you in doing research on the Internet.

1. **Use a search engine.** This is a website that searches other sites. Type a word or phrase related to your topic into the search engine. It will list web pages that might contain information on your topic. Clicking on an entry in this list will bring that page to your screen.

2. **Study the web page.** Read the information to see if it is useful. You can print the page on the computer's printer or take notes. If you take notes, be sure to include the page's URL. This is its location or "address" on the Internet. You need this as the source of the information.

3. **Use hyperlinks.** Many web pages have connections, called hyperlinks, to related information on the site or on other websites. Clicking on these links will take you to those pages. You can follow their links to even more pages, collecting information as you go.

4. **Return to your results list.** If the information or a hyperlink on a web page is not useful, return to the list of pages that your search engine produced and repeat the process.

The Internet is a useful tool. But remember that information on the Internet is no different than printed resources. It must be evaluated with the same care and critical thinking as other sources.

Practice the Skill

Apply the guidelines to explore slavery in the United States during the 1800s and answer the following questions.

1. How would you begin if you wanted information about the abolition movement from the Internet?

2. What words might you type into a search engine to find out about life as a plantation slave?

3. Use a computer to research the Fugitive Slave Act. What kinds of pages did your research produce? Evaluate the usefulness of each type.

Module 15 Assessment

Review Vocabulary, Terms, and People

Match the word in the left column with the correct definition in the right column.

1. Middle Passage
2. Frederick Douglass
3. secede
4. Free-Soil Party
5. sectionalism
6. Fugitive Slave Act
7. Harriet Beecher Stowe
8. Nat Turner
9. Underground Railroad
10. abolition

a. a network of people who arranged transportation and hiding places for escaped slaves
b. leader of the most violent slave revolt in the country
c. group formed by antislavery northerners to promote and support the Wilmot Proviso
d. author of the antislavery novel, *Uncle Tom's Cabin*
e. favoring the interests of one region over the interests of the entire country
f. provision within the Compromise of 1850 that made it a crime to help runaway slaves
g. the complete end to slavery
h. the voyage across the Atlantic Ocean that enslaved Africans were forced to endure
i. formally withdraw
j. an escaped slave who became an important leader in the abolition movement

Comprehension and Critical Thinking

Lesson 1

11. a. **Identify** What was the main reason the Spanish could not continue to use Native Americans for slave labor?
    b. **Make Inferences** How might the African Diaspora have affected the societies and cultures within Africa?
    c. **Analyze** What role did religion play in the American slave culture?

Lesson 2

12. a. **Recall** How were slaves viewed in the South?
    b. **Make Inferences** What types of jobs were assigned to slaves, and why do you think this was the case?
    c. **Analyze** How might the slave codes have helped prevent revolts by slaves?

Lesson 3

13. a. **Identify** What were the methods use by members of the abolition movement to gain support for their cause?
    b. **Describe** How did the Underground Railroad work?
    c. **Draw Conclusions** Why do you think members of Congress refused to address petitions from abolitionists?

Lesson 4

14. a. **Identify** What was the main reason members of Congress were concerned about accepting California as a free state?
    b. **Analyze** Why was the Fugitive Slave Act so controversial for northerners?
    c. **Draw Conclusions** Why might slave narratives and other forms of literature have helped the abolitionists' cause?

Review Themes

15. Politics How did the issue of slavery affect the actions of Congress during the 1800s?

16. Society and Culture What effect did their belief in abolition have on southern abolitionists?

Reading Skills

Compare and Contrast Historical Facts *Use the Reading Skills taught in this module to answer the question about the reading selection below.*

> The Missouri Compromise of 1820 had banned slavery in most of the northern part of the Louisiana Purchase. Antislavery supporters wanted to do something similar with this new territory. On the other hand, some Americans wanted to allow slavery in the new lands.

17. Based on the reading selection above, which of the following phrases signals a contrast?
   a. banned slavery
   b. on the other hand
   c. antislavery supporters
   d. something similar

Social Studies Skills

Conduct Internet Research *Use the Social Studies Skills taught in this module to answer the question below.*

18. Which of the following terms would be a useful search term when researching the Compromise of 1850?
   a. Wilmot Proviso
   b. Anthony Burns
   c. *Uncle Tom's Cabin*
   d. Henry Clay

Focus on Writing

19. Write a Biographical Sketch Review the content in the text relating to what life was like for slaves who worked on plantations. Then choose an imaginary person to write about. Think about what their life was like. Who were they and what did they look like? What did they wear? What job did they perform? How difficult was it to perform? Where did they live? Who did they interact with? What might a typical day have been like? Take your answers to these questions and write two paragraphs about a day in the life of this person from their perspective.

Module 16

Reform Movements in the United States

★

Essential Question

How successful were reformers at improving living conditions for Americans in the early 1800s?

About the Photo: Busy port cities brought goods and people across the Atlantic.

In this module you will read about changes in American society and the goals of social reformers. You will also learn about the leaders of social reform movements.

▶ *Explore ONLINE!*

VIDEOS, including...
• Abolitionists and the Underground Railroad
• Frederick Douglass

☑ Document-Based Investigations

☑ Graphic Organizers

☑ Interactive Games

☑ Image with Hotspots: New York City, Mid-1800s

☑ Image Carousel: Transcendentalists

☑ Image Carousel: Abolitionist Leaders

What You Will Learn ...

Lesson 1: Immigrants and Urban Challenges **508**
The Big Idea The population of the United States grew rapidly in the early 1800s with the arrival of millions of immigrants.

Lesson 2: American Arts. **513**
The Big Idea New movements in art and literature influenced many Americans in the early 1800s.

Lesson 3: Reforming Society. **518**
The Big Idea Reform movements in the early 1800s affected religion, education, and society.

Lesson 4: Abolition **524**
The Big Idea The movement to end slavery was the most prominent and divisive effort of reform in the United States in the mid-1800s.

Lesson 5: Women's Rights. **528**
The Big Idea Reformers sought to improve women's rights in American society.

United States	World

1815

1817 Thomas Gallaudet founds a school for people who have hearing impairments.

1824 British laws making trade unions illegal are repealed.

∧ **1829** French educator Louis Braille creates a writing system of raised dots for people who are blind.

∧ **1831** William Lloyd Garrison begins publishing the abolitionist newspaper *The Liberator*.

1835

<**1848** A major meeting for women's rights—the Seneca Falls Convention—is held in New York.

∧ **1845** A potato famine in Ireland increases Irish immigration to the United States.

1848 Revolutionaries attempt to unify German-speaking peoples in central Europe.

1850 Nathaniel Hawthorne publishes *The Scarlet Letter*.

1855

Reading Social Studies

THEME FOCUS:

Society and Culture

The mid-1800s was a time of change in America. Society and culture changed for several reasons: thousands of immigrants arrived in America; women began to work hard for equal rights; and the North and South debated more and more over the slavery issue. Religious beliefs helped shape people's views toward abolition—the move to end slavery—and women's suffrage—the move to give women the right to vote. This module discusses these issues.

READING FOCUS:

Information and Propaganda

Where do you get information about historical events and people? One source is this textbook and others like it. You can expect the authors of your textbook to do their best to present the facts objectively and fairly. But some sources of historical information may have a totally different purpose in mind. For example, advertisements in political campaigns may contain information, but their main purpose is to persuade people to act or think in a certain way.

Recognize Propaganda Techniques Propaganda is created to change people's opinions or get them to act in a certain way. Learn to recognize propaganda techniques, and you will be able to separate propaganda from the facts.

"People who don't support public education are greedy monsters who don't care about children!"

→ **Name Calling** Using loaded words, words that create strong positive or negative emotions, to make someone else's ideas seem inappropriate or wrong

"People all around the country are opening free public schools. It's obviously the right thing to do."

→ **Bandwagon** Encouraging people to do something because "everyone else is doing it"

"If we provide free education for all children, everyone will be able to get jobs. Poverty and unemployment will disappear."

→ **Oversimplification** Making a complex situation seem simple; a complex problem easy to solve

You Try It!

The flyer below was published in 1837.

Flyer from 1837

> # OUTRAGE.
>
> *Fellow Citizens,*
>
> AN
>
> # ABOLITIONIST,
>
> of the most revolting character is among you, exciting the feelings of the North against the South. A seditious Lecture is to be delivered
>
> ## THIS EVENING,
>
> at 7 o'clock, at the Presbyterian Church in Cannon-street. You are requested to attend and unite in putting down and silencing by peaceable means this tool of evil and fanaticism. Let the rights of the States guaranteed by the Constitution be protected.
>
> Feb. 27, 1837.   *The Union forever!*

After studying the flyer, answer the following questions.

1. What is the purpose of this flyer?
2. Who do you think distributed this flyer?
3. Do you think this flyer is an example of propaganda? Why or why not? If you think it is propaganda, what kind is it?
4. If you were the subject of this flyer, how would you feel? How might you respond to it?

As you read Module 16, look carefully at all the primary sources. Do any of them include examples of propaganda?

Key Terms and People

Lesson 1
nativists
Know-Nothing Party
middle class
tenements

Lesson 2
transcendentalism
Ralph Waldo Emerson
Margaret Fuller
Henry David Thoreau
utopian communities
Nathaniel Hawthorne
Edgar Allan Poe
Emily Dickinson
Henry Wadsworth Longfellow
Walt Whitman

Lesson 3
Second Great Awakening
Charles Grandison Finney
Lyman Beecher
temperance movement
Dorothea Dix
common-school movement
Horace Mann
Catharine Beecher
Thomas Gallaudet

Lesson 4
abolition movement
Lucretia Mott
William Lloyd Garrison
American Anti-Slavery Society
Angelina and Sarah Grimké
Frederick Douglass
Sojourner Truth
Underground Railroad
Harriet Tubman

Lesson 5
Elizabeth Cady Stanton
Seneca Falls Convention
Declaration of Sentiments
Lucy Stone
Susan B. Anthony
Matilda Joslyn Gage

Immigrants and Urban Challenges

The Big Idea

The population of the United States grew rapidly in the early 1800s with the arrival of millions of immigrants.

Main Ideas

- Millions of immigrants, mostly German and Irish, arrived in the United States despite anti-immigrant movements.

- Industrialization led to the growth of cities.

- American cities experienced urban problems due to rapid growth.

Key Terms

nativists
Know-Nothing Party
middle class
tenements

If YOU were there . . .

It is 1850, and you are a German immigrant standing on the deck of a steamboat, crossing Lake Erie. Other immigrants are on board, but they are strangers to you. Soon, you will arrive at your new home in Cleveland, Ohio. You've been told that other Germans have settled there. You hope to find friends and work as a baker. Right now, America seems very big and very strange.

What would you expect from your new life in America?

Millions of Immigrants Arrive

In the mid-1800s, large numbers of immigrants crossed the Atlantic Ocean to begin new lives in the United States. More than 4 million of them settled in the United States between 1840 and 1860, most from Europe. More than 3 million of these immigrants arrived from Ireland and Germany. Many of them were fleeing economic troubles in their native countries. Some were seeking political or religious freedom.

Fleeing the Irish Potato Famine Most immigrants from the British Isles during that period were Irish. In the mid-1840s, potato blight, a disease that causes rot in potatoes, left many families in Ireland with little food. More than a million Irish people died of starvation and disease. Even more fled to the United States.

Most Irish immigrants were very poor and settled in northeastern cities to look for work. By 1850 the Irish made up one-fifth of the population in seven major cities, including New York, Philadelphia, and Boston. They worked at unskilled jobs in the cities or on building canals and railroads. Irish women often worked as domestic servants for wealthy families, laboring 16 or more hours per day. In 1849 a Boston health committee reported that low wages forced most Irish immigrants to live in poor housing.

An Irish immigrant family could expect hardships in their adopted country, but they could also find greater opportunities for a new and better life.

Still, many immigrants enjoyed a new feeling of equality. Patrick Dunny wrote home to his family about this situation.

"People that cuts a great dash [style] at home . . . think it strange [in the United States] for the humble class of people to get as much respect as themselves."

—Patrick Dunny, quoted in *Who Built America?* by Bruce Levine et al.

A Failed German Revolution Many Germans also came to the United States during this time. In the early 1800s, many Germans were attracted by the First Amendment protection of religious freedom and came to the United States to escape religious persecution. In 1848 some Germans had staged a revolution against harsh rule. Some educated Germans fled to the United States to escape persecution caused by their political activities. Most German immigrants, however, were working class, and they came for economic reasons. The United States seemed to offer both greater economic opportunity and more freedom from government control. While most Irish immigrants were Catholics, German immigrant groups included Catholics, Jews, and Protestants.

German immigrants were more likely than the Irish to become farmers and live in rural areas. They moved to midwestern states where more land was available. Unlike the Irish, a high percentage of German immigrants arrived in the United States with money. Despite their funds and skills, German immigrants often had to take low-paying jobs. Many German immigrants worked as tailors, seamstresses, bricklayers, servants, clerks, cabinetmakers, bakers, and food merchants.

Anti-Immigration Movements Industrialization and the waves of people from Europe greatly changed the American labor force. While many immigrants went to the Midwest to get farmland, other immigrants filled the need for cheap labor in towns and cities. Industrial jobs in the Northeast attracted many people.

Pull Factors
- Jobs
- Greater freedom and equality
- Abundant land

Push Factors
- Starvation
- Poverty
- Lack of political freedom

Push-Pull Factors of Immigration

Starvation and poverty pushed many Irish families from their homes, while economic opportunities pulled them toward the United States.

Analyze Visuals
How was freedom a push factor and a pull factor?

Academic Vocabulary
implicit understood though not clearly put into words

Yet a great deal of native-born Americans feared losing their jobs to immigrants who might work for lower wages. Some felt **implicitly** threatened by the new immigrants' cultures and religions. For example, before Catholic immigrants arrived, most Americans were Protestants. Conflicts between Catholics and Protestants in Europe caused American Protestants to mistrust Catholic immigrants. Some Protestants believed that Catholics threatened democracy. Those Protestants feared that the pope, the head of the Roman Catholic Church, was plotting to overthrow democracy in America. Those Americans and others who opposed immigration were called **nativists**. In cities such as New York and Boston, nativists formed a secret society. Members promised not to vote for Catholics or immigrants running for political office.

In the 1840s and 1850s some nativists became politically active. An 1844 election flyer gave Americans this warning.

"Look at the . . . thieves and vagabonds [tramps] roaming our streets . . . monopolizing [taking] the business which properly belongs to our own native and true-born citizens."

—Election flyer, quoted in *Who Built America?*, by Bruce Levine et al.

In 1849 nativists founded a political organization, the **Know-Nothing Party**, that supported measures making it difficult for foreigners to become citizens or hold office. Its members wanted to keep Catholics and immigrants out of public office. They also wanted to require immigrants to live in the United States for 21 years before becoming citizens. Know-Nothing politicians had some success getting elected during the 1850s. Later, disagreements over the issue of slavery caused the party to fall apart. Immigrants continued to come to the United States, and the resulting mix of ethnicities and religions continued to influence American society and culture.

Reading Check
Identify Cause and Effect Why did the Know-Nothing Party try to limit the rights of immigrants?

Rapid Growth of Cities

The Industrial Revolution led to the creation of many new jobs in American cities. These city jobs drew immigrants from many nations as well as migrants from rural parts of the United States. The Transportation Revolution helped connect cities and made it easier for people to move to them. As a result of these two trends, American cities grew rapidly in number and population during the mid-1800s. Cities in the northeastern and Middle Atlantic states grew the most. By the mid-1800s, three-quarters of the country's manufacturing jobs were in these areas.

The rise of industry and the growth of cities changed American life. Those who owned their own businesses or worked in skilled jobs benefited most from those changes. The families of these merchants, manufacturers, professionals, and master craftspeople made up a growing social class. This new **middle class** was a social and economic level between the wealthy and the poor. Those in the new middle class built large, dignified homes that demonstrated their place in society.

In the growing cities, people found entertainment and an enriched cultural life. Many enjoyed visiting places such as libraries and clubs or attending concerts or lectures. In the mid-1800s people also attended urban theaters. Favorite pastimes included bowling, boxing, and playing cards. The rules of baseball were formalized in 1845, and the game became increasingly popular.

Cities during this time were compact and crowded. Many people lived close enough to their jobs that they could walk to work. Wagons carried goods down streets paved with stones, making a noisy, busy scene. One observer noted that the professionals in New York City always had a "hurried walk."

Reading Check
Summarize
How did the Industrial Revolution affect life in American cities?

Urban Problems

American cities in the mid-1800s faced many challenges due to rapid growth. Because public and private transportation was limited, city residents had to live near their workplaces. In addition, there was a lack of safe housing. Many city dwellers, particularly immigrants, could afford to live only in **tenements**—poorly designed apartment buildings that housed large numbers of people. These structures were often dirty, overcrowded, and unsafe.

Public services were also poor. The majority of cities did not have clean water, public health regulations, or healthful ways to get rid of garbage and human and animal waste. Under these conditions, diseases spread easily and epidemics were common. In 1832 and 1849, for example, New York City suffered cholera epidemics that killed thousands.

City life held other dangers. As urban areas grew, they became centers of criminal activity. Most cities—including New York, Boston, and Philadelphia—had no permanent or organized force to fight crime and violence. Instead, they relied on volunteer night watches, which offered little protection. The violence was often between various ethnic or racial groups, who had different economic and social goals. Immigrants often

In the mid-1800s, cities such as New York City lured thousands of people in search of jobs and a better life. Many city dwellers found living in crowded urban conditions difficult.

came from a mix of social classes, which led to cultural conflicts among groups. Differences in political goals and opinions also led to disagreements between groups.

Fire was another constant and serious danger in crowded cities. There was little organized fire protection. Most cities were served by volunteer fire companies. Firefighters used hand pumps and buckets to put out fires. In addition, there were not enough sanitation workers and road maintenance crews. These shortages and flaws caused health and safety problems for many city residents.

Reading Check
Analyze Information
Why did so many American cities have problems in the mid-1800s?

Summary and Preview Immigrants expected a better life in America, but not all Americans welcomed newcomers. The rapid growth of cities caused many problems. In the next lesson you will read about how America developed its own style of art and literature.

Lesson 1 Assessment

Review Ideas, Terms, and People

1. **a. Identify** Who were the nativists?

   b. Identify What were the most common religious groups among the Irish and German immigrants?

   c. Compare and Contrast In what ways were Irish and German immigrants to the United States similar and different?

   d. Analyze How did the First Amendment's guarantee of religious freedom help change the ethnic and religious makeup of the United States?

   e. Predict How might the rise of anti-immigrant groups lead to problems in the United States?

2. **a. Describe** What led to the growth of cities?

   b. Analyze How did the rise of industrialization and the growth of cities change American society?

3. **a. Describe** What were tenements?

   b. Summarize What problems affected American cities in the mid-1800s?

   c. Explain How did religion, social class, and political beliefs cause conflicts between immigrant groups? How were these conflicts resolved?

   d. Evaluate What do you think was the biggest problem facing cities in the United States? Why?

Critical Thinking

4. **Identify Cause and Effect** In this lesson you learned about the causes and effects of immigration and urban growth. Create a graphic organizer similar to the ones below, identifying the causes and effects of each.

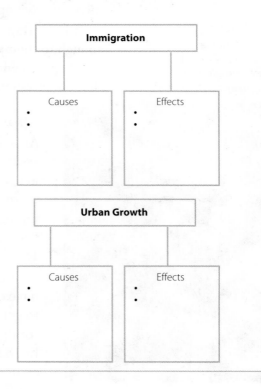

American Arts

The Big Idea

New movements in art and literature influenced many Americans in the early 1800s.

Main Ideas

- Transcendentalists and utopian communities withdrew from American society.
- American Romantic painters and writers made important contributions to art and literature.

Key Terms and People

transcendentalism
Ralph Waldo Emerson
Margaret Fuller
Henry David Thoreau
utopian communities
Nathaniel Hawthorne
Edgar Allan Poe
Emily Dickinson
Henry Wadsworth Longfellow
Walt Whitman

If YOU were there . . .

You are a teacher living in Massachusetts in the 1840s. Some of your neighbors have started an experimental community. They want to live more simply than present-day society allows. They hope to have time to write and think, while still sharing the work. Some people will teach; others will raise food. You think this might be an interesting place to live.

What would you ask the leaders of the community?

Transcendentalists

Some New England writers and philosophers found spiritual wisdom in **transcendentalism**, the belief that people could transcend, or rise above, material things in life. Transcendentalists also believed that people should depend on themselves and their own insights, rather than on outside authorities. Important transcendentalists included **Ralph Waldo Emerson**, **Margaret Fuller**, and **Henry David Thoreau**.

Walden Pond, where Thoreau lived for two years

The First Harvest in the Wilderness painted by Asher Durand is an example of how artists of the Romantic movement celebrated nature in their dramatic paintings.

Academic Vocabulary
abstract expressing a quality or idea without reference to an actual thing

Reading Check
Make Inferences
Why did utopian communities only last a short time?

Emerson was a popular writer and thinker who argued that Americans should disregard institutions and follow their own beliefs. "What I must do is all that concerns me, not what the people think," he wrote in an essay called "Self-Reliance." Fuller edited the famous transcendentalist publication *The Dial*. Thoreau advised even stronger self-reliance and simple living away from society in natural settings. He wrote his book *Walden* after he lived for two years at Walden Pond.

Some transcendentalists formed a community at Brook Farm, Massachusetts, in the 1840s. It was one of many experiments with **utopian communities**, groups of people who tried to form a perfect society. People in utopian communities pursued **abstract** spirituality and cooperative lifestyles. Communities sprang up in New Harmony, Oneida, and many other places. However, few communities lasted for long.

American Romanticism

Ideas about the simple life and nature also inspired painters and writers in the early and mid-1800s. Some joined the Romantic movement that had begun in Europe. Romanticism involved a great interest in nature, an emphasis on individual expression, and a rejection of many established rules. These painters and writers felt that each person brings a unique view to the world. They believed in using emotion to guide their creative output. Some Romantic artists, like Thomas Cole, painted the American landscape. Their works showed the beauty and wonder of nature in the United States.

Nathaniel Hawthorne was born in Salem, Massachusetts. Much of his writing is set in New England and expresses themes of evil and sin.

Their images contrasted with the huge cities and corruption of nature that many Americans saw as typical of Europe.

Many female writers, like Ann Sophia Stephens, wrote historical fiction that was popular in the mid-1800s. New England writer **Nathaniel Hawthorne** wrote *The Scarlet Letter* during that period. One of the greatest classics of Romantic literature, it explored Puritan life in the 1600s. Hawthorne's friend Herman Melville, a writer and former sailor, wrote novels about the sea, such as *Moby-Dick* and *Billy Budd*. Many people believe that *Moby-Dick* is one of the finest American novels ever written.

American Romantic authors also wrote a great deal of poetry. The poet **Edgar Allan Poe**, also a short-story writer, became famous for a haunting poem called "The Raven." Other gifted American poets included **Emily Dickinson**, **Henry Wadsworth Longfellow**, and **Walt Whitman**. Most of Dickinson's short, thoughtful poems were not published until after her death. Longfellow, the best-known poet of the mid-1800s, wrote popular story-poems, like *The Song of Hiawatha*. Whitman praised American individualism and democracy in his simple, unrhymed poetry. In his poetry collection *Leaves of Grass*, he wrote, "The United States themselves are essentially the greatest poem."

Reading Check
Summarize
Who were some American Romantic authors, and why were they important?

Summary and Preview American Romantic artists and authors were inspired by ideas about the simple life, nature, and spirituality. In the next lesson you will learn about ideas that changed American society.

Lesson 2 Assessment

Review Ideas, Terms, and People

1. **a. Identify** What were the main teachings of transcendentalism?

   b. Summarize What was one of the utopian communities established in the United States, and what was its goal?

   c. Elaborate Do you agree with transcendentalists that Americans put too much emphasis on institutions and traditions? Explain your answer.

2. **a. Recall** Who were some important American authors and poets at this time?

   b. Explain What ideas did artists in the Romantic movement express?

   c. Evaluate Do you think the Romantic movement was important to American culture? Explain.

Critical Thinking

3. **Compare and Contrast** In this lesson you learned about new movements in art and literature in the mid-1800s. Create a graphic organizer similar to the one below and use it to show the similarities and differences between the two movements.

Transcendentalism | Similarities | Romanticism

Literature in History

Literature of the Young Nation: Romanticism and Realism

About the Reading "Paul Revere's Ride" was published in a book called *Tales of a Wayside Inn*. The book is a collection of poems that tell well-known stories from history and mythology. By including the story of Paul Revere with other famous stories, Longfellow helped increase the importance of Paul Revere's ride.

As You Read Notice how Longfellow describes Revere as a hero.

From "Paul Revere's Ride" from *Tales of a Wayside Inn*
by Henry Wadsworth Longfellow (1807–1882)

Listen my children and you shall hear
Of the midnight ride of Paul Revere,
On the eighteenth of April, in Seventy-five;
Hardly a man is now alive
Who remembers that famous day and year. ❶

He said to his friend, "If the British march
By land or sea from the town to-night,
Hang a lantern aloft in the belfry arch
Of the North Church tower as a signal light,—
One if by land, and two if by sea;
And I on the opposite shore will be,
Ready to ride and spread the alarm
Through every . . . village and farm,
For the country folk to be up and to arm." ❷

Meanwhile, his friend, through alley and street
Wanders and watches with eager ears,
Till in the silence around him he hears
The muster of men at the barrack door,
The sound of arms, and the tramp of feet,
And the measured tread of the grenadiers,
Marching down to their boats on the shore. ❸

Word Help

lame disabled

irascible difficult

bliss happiness

ambition hope for the future

affliction problem

pathetic very sad

perpetual constant

❶ Some women kept companions to help entertain them and perform small chores. *Why might Jo not want to be a companion?*

❷ *How was Jo different from most women in the 1880s?*

❸ *What might Jo be able to do for work in the 1800s?*

About the Reading *Little Women* is a novel about four sisters living in a small New England town before the Civil War. Still popular with young people today, *Little Women* describes a family much like the one Louisa May Alcott grew up in. Alcott based the main character, Jo March, on herself. Like Alcott, Jo was different from most women of her time. She was outspoken, eager for adventure, and in conflict with the role her society expected her to play.

As You Read Try to understand how Jo is different from Aunt March.

From *Little Women*
by Louisa May Alcott (1832–1888)

Jo happened to suit Aunt March, who was lame and needed an active person to wait upon her. The childless old lady had offered to adopt one of the girls when the troubles came, and was much offended because her offer was declined . . .

The old lady wouldn't speak to them for a time, but happening to meet Jo at a friend's, . . . she proposed to take her for a companion. ❶ This did not suit Jo at all, but she accepted the place since nothing better appeared, and to everyone's surprise, got on remarkably well with her irascible relative . . .

I suspect that the real attraction was a large library of fine books, which was left to dust and spiders since Uncle March died . . . The dim, dusty room, with the busts staring down from the tall bookcases, the cozy chairs, the globes, and, best of all, the wilderness of books, in which she could wander where she liked, made the library a region of bliss to her . . . ❷

Jo's ambition was to do something very splendid. What it was she had no idea, as yet, but left it for time to tell her, and, meanwhile, found her greatest affliction in the fact that she couldn't read, run, and ride as much as she liked. ❸ A quick temper, sharp tongue, and restless spirit were always getting her into scrapes, and her life was a series of ups and downs, which were both comic and pathetic. But the training she received at Aunt March's was just what she needed, and the thought that she was doing something to support herself made her happy in spite of the perpetual "Josy-phine!"

Connect Literature to History

1. **Draw Conclusions** Henry Wadsworth Longfellow was the most popular American poet of his time. How does his version of Paul Revere's ride increase the importance of the story?

2. **Compare and Contrast** The lives of women in the 1800s were very different from the lives of women today. How does this excerpt of *Little Women* show some similarities and differences between now and then?

Image Credits:

Reforming Society

The Big Idea

Reform movements in the early 1800s affected religion, education, and society.

Main Ideas

- The Second Great Awakening sparked interest in religion.
- Social reformers began to speak out about temperance and prison reform.
- Improvements in education reform affected many segments of the population.
- Northern African American communities became involved in reform efforts.

Key Terms and People

Second Great Awakening
Charles Grandison Finney
Lyman Beecher
temperance movement
Dorothea Dix
common-school movement
Horace Mann
Catharine Beecher
Thomas Gallaudet

If YOU were there . . .

You live in New York State in the 1850s. You are the oldest daughter in your family. Since childhood you have loved mathematics, which puzzles your family. Your sisters are happy learning to sew and cook and run a household. You want more. You know that there is a female seminary nearby, where you could study and learn much more. But your parents are undecided.

How might you persuade your parents to send you to the school?

Second Great Awakening

During the 1790s and early 1800s, some Americans felt there was a strong need for religious reform and took part in a Christian renewal movement called the **Second Great Awakening**. It swept through towns across upstate New York and through the frontier regions of Kentucky, Ohio, Tennessee, and South Carolina. By the 1820s and 1830s, this new interest in religion had spread to New England and the South.

Charles Grandison Finney was one of the most important leaders of the Second Great Awakening. After experiencing a dramatic religious conversion in 1821, Finney left his career as a lawyer and began preaching. He challenged some traditional Protestant beliefs, telling congregations that each individual was responsible for his or her own salvation. He also believed that sin was avoidable. Finney held revivals, emotional prayer meetings that lasted for days. Many people converted to Christianity during these revivals. Finney told new converts to prove their faith by doing good deeds.

Finney's style of preaching and his ideas angered some traditional ministers, like Boston's **Lyman Beecher**. Beecher wanted to prevent Finney from holding revivals in his city. "You mean to carry a streak of fire to Boston. If you attempt it, as the Lord liveth, I'll meet you . . . and fight every inch of the way." Despite the opposition of Beecher and other traditional

The Second Great Awakening saw the growth of revivals such as the one shown here. Revivals were designed to reawaken religious feelings.

ministers, Finney's appeal remained powerful. Also, the First Amendment guarantee of freedom of religion prevented the government from passing laws banning the new religious practices. Ministers were therefore free to spread their message of faith and salvation to whoever wished to listen.

Due to the efforts of Finney and his followers, church membership across the country grew a great deal during the Second Great Awakening. Many new church members were women and African Americans. The African Methodist Episcopal Church was formed and spread across the Middle Atlantic states. Although the movement had begun in the Northeast and on the frontier, the Second Great Awakening renewed some people's religious faith throughout America.

Reading Check
Draw Conclusions
What impact did the Second Great Awakening have on religion in America?

Social Reformers Speak Out

Renewed religious faith often led to involvement in movements to fix the problems created by urban growth. One solution was political action. For example, in 1844 New York City created the first city police force.

Members of the growing middle class, especially women, often led the efforts. Many of the women did not work outside the home and had servants to care for their households. This gave them time to work in reform groups.

Temperance Movement Many social reformers worked to prevent alcohol abuse. They believed that Americans drank too much. In the 1830s, on average, an American consumed seven gallons of alcohol per year. Countless Americans thought that alcohol abuse caused social problems, such as family violence, poverty, and criminal behavior.

The temperance movement, an effort to convince people to avoid drinking alcohol, promoted abstinence with posters like the one shown here.

Americans' worries about the effects of alcohol on people led to the growth of a **temperance movement**. This reform effort urged people to use self-discipline to stop drinking hard liquor.

Reformers asked people to limit themselves to beer and wine in small amounts. Groups like the American Temperance Society and the American Temperance Union helped to spread the message. Minister Lyman Beecher spoke widely about the evils of alcohol. He claimed that people who drank alcohol were "neglecting the education of their families—and corrupting their morals." As a result of the temperance movement, the legislators of the state of Maine outlawed alcohol in 1851. Over the next several years, the legislators of 12 other states outlawed it as well.

Prison Reform Another target of reform was the prison system. **Dorothea Dix** was a middle-class reformer who visited prisons throughout Massachusetts beginning in 1841. Dix reported that mentally ill people frequently were jailed with criminals. They were sometimes left in dark cells without clothes or heat and were chained to the walls and beaten. Dix spoke of what she saw to the state legislature.

In response, the Massachusetts government built facilities for the mentally ill. Dix's work had a nationwide effect. Eventually, more than 100 state hospitals were built to give mentally ill people professional care.

Prisons also held runaway children and orphans. Some had survived only by begging or stealing, and they got the same punishment as adult criminals. Boston mayor Josiah Quincy asked that young offenders receive different punishments than adults. In the 1820s several state and local governments founded reform schools for children who had been housed in prisons. There, children lived under strict rules and learned useful skills.

Some reformers also tried to end the overcrowding and cruel conditions in prisons. Their efforts led to the creation of houses of correction. These institutions did not use punishment alone to change behavior. They also offered prisoners education.

Reading Check
Summarize How did reformers change the punishment of criminals?

Improvements in Education

Another challenge facing America in the early 1800s was poor public education. During this era, childhood was beginning to be viewed as a separate stage of life in which education was of the utmost importance in creating responsible citizens. However, many children worked in factories or on farms to help support their families. If children could read the Bible, write, and do simple math, that was often considered to be enough.

Education in the Early 1800s The availability of education varied widely. New England had the most schools, while the South and the West had the fewest. Few teachers were trained. Schoolhouses were small, and students of all ages and levels worked in one room.

McGuffey's Readers were the most popular textbooks. William Holmes McGuffey, an educator and minister, put selections from British and American literature in them as well as instruction in moral and social values.

Social background and wealth affected the quality of education. Rich families sent children to private schools or hired tutors. However, poor children had only public schools. Girls could go to school, but parents usually thought that girls needed little education and kept them home. Therefore, few girls learned to read.

This photograph shows a Washington, DC, classroom inspired by the ideas of Horace Mann.

Common-School Movement People in the **common-school movement** wanted all children taught in a common place, regardless of background. **Horace Mann** was a leader of this movement.

In 1837 Mann became Massachusetts's first secretary of education. He convinced the state to double its school budget and raise teachers' salaries. He lengthened the school year and began the first school for teacher training. Mann's success set a standard for education reform throughout the country.

Women's Education Education reform created greater opportunities for women. **Catharine Beecher** started an all-female academy in Hartford, Connecticut. The first college-level educational institution available to women was the Troy Female Seminary, opened by Emma Willard in 1821. Several other women's colleges opened during the 1830s, including Mount Holyoke College. The first medical college for women, who were barred from men's medical schools, opened in Boston in 1848.

BIOGRAPHY

Horace Mann 1796–1859

Born in Franklin, Massachusetts, Mann had little schooling, but he educated himself well enough at the local library to get into Brown University and attend law school. Despite a busy law practice, he served in the Massachusetts legislature for ten years. He was also an outspoken advocate for public education. In 1837 the state created the post of secretary of education for him. His achievements in that office made him famous. He later served in the U.S. House of Representatives and as president of Antioch College in Ohio.

His influence on education is reflected by the fact that many American schools are named for him.

Analyze Information
How do you think Mann's own education influenced his desire for public schools?

Reading Check
Summarize
What were Horace
Mann's achievements?

Teaching People with Special Needs Efforts to improve education also helped people with special needs. In 1831 Samuel Gridley Howe opened the Perkins School for the Blind in Massachusetts. Howe traveled widely, talking about teaching people with visual impairment. **Thomas Gallaudet** improved the education and lives of people with hearing impairments. He founded the first free American school for hearing-impaired people in 1817.

African American Communities

Free African Americans usually lived in segregated, or separate, communities in the North. Most of them lived in cities such as New York, Boston, and Philadelphia. Community leaders were often influenced by the Second Great Awakening and its spirit of reform.

Founded by former slave Richard Allen, the Free African Religious Society became a model for other groups that pressed for racial equality and the education of blacks. In 1816 Allen became the first bishop of the African Methodist Episcopal Church, or AME Church. This church broke away from white Methodist churches after African Americans were treated poorly in some white congregations.

Other influential African Americans of the time, such as Alexander Crummel, pushed for the creation of schools for black Americans. The New York African Free School in New York City educated hundreds of children, many of whom became brilliant scholars and important African American leaders. Philadelphia also had a long history of educating African Americans. This was largely because Philadelphia was a center of Quaker influence, and the Quakers believed strongly in equality. The city ran seven schools for African American students by the year 1800. In 1820 Boston followed Philadelphia's lead and opened a separate

This photograph of the Oberlin College class of 1855 shows the expansion of education for women as well as the slow integration of African Americans into previously white colleges.

elementary school for African American children. The city began allowing them to attend school with whites in 1855.

African Americans rarely attended college because few colleges would accept them. In 1835 Oberlin College became the first to do so. Harvard University soon admitted African Americans, too. Several African American colleges were founded beginning in the 1840s. In 1842 the Institute for Colored Youth opened in Philadelphia. Avery College, also in Pennsylvania, was founded in 1849.

While free African Americans had some opportunities to attend school in the North and Midwest, few had this chance in the South. Laws in the South barred most enslaved people from getting any education, even at the primary school level. While some slaves learned to read on their own, they almost always did so in secret. Slaveholders were fearful that education and knowledge in general might encourage a spirit of revolt among enslaved African Americans.

Summary and Preview The efforts of reformers led to improvements in many aspects of American life in the early to mid-1800s. In the next lesson you will learn about reform-minded people who opposed the practice of slavery.

Reading Check
Draw Conclusions
Why was it difficult for African Americans to get an education in the South in the early 1800s?

Lesson 3 Assessment

Review Ideas, Terms, and People

1. **a. Identify** What was the Second Great Awakening, and who was one of its leaders?

   b. Identify What was one cause of the Second Great Awakening?

   c. Summarize What effects did the Second Great Awakening have on religion in the United States?

2. **a. Identify** What role did Dorothea Dix play in social reforms of the early 1800s?

   b. Summarize What different reforms helped improve the U.S. prison system?

   c. Elaborate How might the Second Great Awakening have led to the growth of social reform movements?

3. **a. Identify** What was the common-school movement, and who was one of its leaders?

   b. Analyze Why did reformers set out to improve education in the United States?

   c. Evaluate Do you think Horace Mann's ideas for educational reform were good ones? Explain.

4. **a. Recall** In what cities were the first public schools for African Americans located?

   b. Draw Conclusions How did free African Americans benefit from educational reforms?

Critical Thinking

5. **Categorize** In this lesson you learned about key reform movements in the early to mid-1800s. Create a chart similar to the one below to identify the leaders and accomplishments of each reform movement.

Movement	Leaders	Accomplishments
Prison and Mental Health Reform		
Temperance		
Education		

★
Abolition

The Big Idea

The movement to end slavery was the most prominent and divisive effort of reform in the United States in the mid-1800s.

Main Ideas

- Abolitionist leaders used a variety of methods in their campaign against slavery in the United States.

- The Underground Railroad was an informal network that helped enslaved Africans escape to freedom.

- Even as the movement grew, many Americans remained opposed to ending slavery.

Key Terms and People

abolition movement
Lucretia Mott
William Lloyd Garrison
American Anti-Slavery Society
Angelina and Sarah Grimké
Frederick Douglass
Sojourner Truth
Underground Railroad
Harriet Tubman

If YOU were there . . .

You live in South Carolina in the 1850s. You are invited by a friend to hear Angelina and Sarah Grimké, two southerners fighting to abolish slavery, speak at your friend's house. Your father is a slaveholder, and you know he disapproves of abolition and the Grimké sisters. You are interested in hearing what they have to say. But you know this might get you in trouble with your father and other family members.

Would you attend the meeting? Why?

Demanding an End to Slavery

Since the beginning of slavery in the United States, enslaved people made efforts to escape their difficult lives. However, the number of escape attempts increased sharply during the 1830s. These courageous slaves may have been encouraged by a small movement that was gaining support in the North. The **abolition movement** was a campaign to abolish, or end, slavery. This movement grew into one of the largest reform movements of the mid-1800s. No other movement attracted as many followers or had such an impact on the history of the United States. Supporters of the abolition movement were called abolitionists, and they included men and women as well as blacks and whites from both the North and the South.

Religious Roots The abolition movement had deep roots in religion. Since the colonial period, the Quakers were among the first groups to challenge slavery on religious grounds, believing it to be immoral. Pennsylvania, with many Quaker residents, was a center of activity, with the Pennsylvania Abolition Society established in 1775. Other religious leaders published pamphlets and gave speeches that encouraged many Americans to support the cause.

The rebirth of religious fervor in the Second Great Awakening also contributed to the rise of the abolition movement.

This engraving highlighted the connections between the antislavery movement and the women's rights movement in the mid-1800s.

Many religious people in the North saw slavery as a clear moral wrong that went directly against their beliefs. Many joined reform societies to campaign against slavery. By 1836 more than 500 of these groups existed.

However, antislavery reformers did not always agree on the details. They differed over how much equality they thought African Americans should have. Some believed that African Americans should be treated as equal to white Americans, while others were against full political and social equality. **Lucretia Mott** founded the Philadelphia Female Anti-Slavery Society in 1833, when women were prohibited from joining the American Anti-Slavery Society. This organization, unlike some others, had both white and black members from its beginnings.

Abolitionist Leaders One of the most outspoken abolitionists was a Philadelphia journalist named **William Lloyd Garrison**. In 1828 he was convinced by a Quaker friend to join the abolition movement and soon became its leading spokesperson. Although many abolitionists favored a gradual abolition of slavery, Garrison demanded that it be abolished immediately. In 1831 he began publishing an abolitionist newspaper called the *Liberator*. He continued to publish the paper until slavery was abolished 35 years later.

In 1833 he helped found the **American Anti-Slavery Society**, the most influential abolitionist group to call for the immediate end to slavery in the United States. By 1840 the society's membership was almost 200,000. In the same year, however, the society split into two groups. One wanted immediate freedom for enslaved African Americans and a bigger role for women. The other wanted gradual emancipation and for women to play a minor role in the movement.

As in other reform movements of the time, however, women played a major role in the abolition campaign. Two outspoken campaigners for the movement were **Angelina and Sarah Grimké**. Daughters of a South Carolina plantation owner, the Grimké sisters witnessed the suffering of slaves firsthand. Angelina Grimké wrote a pamphlet trying to recruit other white southern women to the cause. Their vocal and public support of the movement earned them the disapproval of their community. They eventually moved to the North, where they not only fought against slavery but also for the rights of women. After moving to Philadelphia, the sisters wrote *American Slavery As It Is*. This book was considered to be one of the most important antislavery works of its time.

Like the Grimkés, **Frederick Douglass** supported women's rights. He was a featured speaker at the Seneca Falls Convention. But he is most remembered for his work as an abolitionist. Born into slavery in Maryland, Douglass escaped when he was 20. His intelligence and speech-making skills eventually earned him a place as a popular speaker to antislavery audiences. In 1845 he published his autobiography, *Narrative of the Life of Frederick Douglass*. In writing about his quest to escape slavery, Douglass stated, "You have seen how a man was made a slave, you shall now see how a slave was made a man." Douglass went on to publish an abolitionist newspaper called *The North Star*. His firsthand experience, his writings, and his powerful speeches made Douglass one of the most influential abolitionists in the United States.

Another former slave, **Sojourner Truth**, also contributed to the abolitionist cause. She believed God had called her to travel around the United States and preach the truth about slavery as well as about women's rights. With her deep voice and quick wit, Truth became legendary in the antislavery movement for her fiery and dramatic speeches, especially her "Ain't I a Woman" speech given in 1851.

Escape to the North

In their attempt to escape their enslavement, many enslaved people tried to reach the free states of the North or get as far as Canada or Mexico, where slavery was illegal. Over the years an informal, constantly changing network of escape routes developed. By the 1830s a loosely organized group had begun helping slaves escape from the South. Known as the **Underground Railroad**, the organization was not an actual railroad but a network of people who arranged transportation and hiding places for fugitives, or escaped slaves.

Reading Check
Find Main Ideas
What methods did abolitionists use to gain support for their cause?

Frederick Douglass began publishing *The North Star,* an abolitionist newspaper, in 1847.

Harriet Tubman was a courageous conductor on the Underground Railroad.

Reading Check
Make Inferences
Why do you think the routes of the Underground Railroad constantly changed?

Sympathetic white people and free blacks provided escapees with food, hiding places, and directions to their next destination, closer to free territory. Despite the lack of any real structure, the Underground Railroad managed to achieve dramatic results. The most famous conductor on the Underground Railroad was **Harriet Tubman**. Tubman had escaped slavery herself, and she helped many others on their journey to freedom. She returned to the South nearly 20 times, successfully leading her family and more than 300 other slaves to freedom.

Opposing Abolition

The majority of white southerners did not own slaves. To those who were slaveholders, the abolition movement was an outrage. They viewed the movement as an attack on their livelihood, their way of life, and even their religion.

Southern ministers built arguments attempting to justify slavery in biblical terms. Slaveholders and politicians argued that slavery was essential to the production of cotton and the health of the economy. Even in the North, to many this was a powerful argument.

Reading Check
Summarize
What arguments were used against the abolishment of slavery?

In fact, there was support for, and toleration of, slavery in the North. To northern workers, freedom for slaves meant more competition for jobs. Even Congress obstructed the efforts of abolitionists by establishing a gag rule that forbade members of Congress from discussing antislavery petitions. Still the pressure to abolish slavery was undeniable. Frederick Douglass said the issue of slavery was "the great, paramount, imperative, and all-commanding question for this age and nation to solve." This proved all too true, as the tensions regarding slavery soon would rip the nation apart.

Summary and Preview The abolition movement led to increased tensions and conflict among Americans during the mid-1800s. In the next lesson you will learn about women's rights.

Lesson 4 Assessment

Review Ideas, Terms, and People

1. **a. Identify** Who was William Lloyd Garrison?

   b. Draw Conclusions Why do you think it was necessary for Angelina and Sarah Grimké to move to the North?

   c. Elaborate What do you think made Frederick Douglass such an effective abolitionist?

2. **a. Describe** What was the Underground Railroad, and how did it work?

   b. Draw Conclusions Why do you think Harriet Tubman was willing to risk her freedom by helping others escape on the Underground Railroad?

   c. Evaluate What words would best describe the experiences of traveling on the Underground Railroad?

3. **a. Describe** How did Congress restrict progress of the abolition movement?

   b. Analyze Why did some Americans oppose equality for African Americans?

   c. Predict How might the conflicting opinions over slavery lead to conflict in the future?

Critical Thinking

4. **Identify Cause and Effect** In this lesson you learned about the abolition movement and its leaders. Create a graphic organizer similar to the one below to list each key individual of the movement and their contribution.

Individual	Contribution to Abolition

Women's Rights

The Big Idea
Reformers sought to improve women's rights in American society.

Main Ideas
- Influenced by the abolition movement, many women struggled to gain equal rights for themselves.
- Calls for women's rights met opposition from men and women.
- The Seneca Falls Convention launched the first organized women's rights movement in the United States.

Key Terms and People
Elizabeth Cady Stanton
Seneca Falls Convention
Declaration of Sentiments
Lucy Stone
Susan B. Anthony
Matilda Joslyn Gage

If YOU were there . . .

You are a schoolteacher in New York State in 1848. Although you earn a small salary, you still live at home. Your father does not believe that unmarried women should live alone or look after their own money. One day in a shop, you see a poster about a public meeting to discuss women's rights. You know your father will be angry if you go to the meeting. But you are very curious.

Would you attend the meeting? Why?

Women's Struggle for Equal Rights

Fighting for the rights of African Americans led many female abolitionists to fight for women's rights. In the mid-1800s, these women found that they had to defend their right to speak in public, particularly when a woman addressed both men and women. For example, members of the press, the clergy, and even some male abolitionists criticized the Grimké sisters. These critics thought that the sisters should not give public speeches. They did not want women to leave their traditional female roles. The Grimkés protested that women had a moral duty to lead the antislavery movement.

The Grimké sisters, Sarah and Angelina, fought for rights for African Americans and women.

Early Writings for Women's Rights In 1838 Sarah Grimké published a pamphlet arguing for equal rights for women. She titled it *Letters on the Equality of the Sexes and the Condition of Women*.

> "I ask no favors for my sex . . . All I ask our brethren [brothers] is that they will take their feet from off our necks, and permit us to stand upright on that ground which God designed us to occupy."
>
> —Sarah Grimké, *Letter on the Equality of the Sexes and the Condition of Women*
> Addressed to Mary S. Parker

Sarah Grimké also argued for equal educational opportunities. She pointed out laws that negatively affected women. In addition, she demanded equal pay for equal work.

Sarah Grimké never married. She explained that the government did not protect the rights of women. The laws of the day gave a husband complete control of his wife's property. Therefore, she feared that by marrying, she would become more like a slave than a wife. Her sister, Angelina, did marry, but she refused to promise to obey her husband during their marriage ceremony. She married Theodore Weld, an abolitionist. Weld agreed to give up his legal right to control her property after they married. For the Grimkés, the abolitionist principles and women's rights principles were identical.

In 1845 the famous transcendentalist Margaret Fuller published *Woman in the Nineteenth Century*. This book used well-known sayings to explain the role of women in American society. Fuller used democratic and transcendentalist principles to stress the importance of individualism to all people, especially women. The book influenced many leaders of the women's rights movement.

Sojourner Truth Sojourner Truth was another powerful supporter of both abolition and women's rights. She had been born into slavery in about 1797. Her birth name was Isabella Baumfree. She took the name Sojourner Truth because she felt that her mission was to be a sojourner, or traveler, and spread the truth. Though she never learned to read or write, she impressed many well-educated people. One person who thought highly of her was the author Harriet Beecher Stowe. Stowe said that she had never spoken "with anyone who had more . . . personal presence than this woman." Truth stood six feet tall and was a confident speaker.

In 1851 Truth gave a speech that is often quoted to this day.

> "That man over here says that women need to be helped into carriages and lifted over ditches, and to have the best place everywhere. Nobody ever helps me into carriages or over mud puddles, or gives me any best place . . . Look at me! I have ploughed and planted and . . . no man could head [outwork] me. And ain't I a woman?"
>
> —Sojourner Truth, Delivered at the 1851 Women's Convention, Akron, Ohio

Truth, the Grimké sisters, and other supporters of the women's movement were determined to be heard.

Reading Check
Make Inferences
Why would reformers link the issues of abolition and women's rights?

Antisuffragists
As the suffrage movement picked up speed, opponents to women's suffrage also began to organize. Antisuffragists argued that women's suffrage would distract women from building strong families and improving communities.

Opposing the Call for Women's Rights

Publications about women's rights first appeared in the United States shortly after the American Revolution. However, women's concerns did not become a national issue with strong opposition for many more years.

The Movement Grows The change took place when women took a more active and leading role in reform and abolition. Other social changes also led to the rise of the women's movement. Women took advantage of better educational opportunities in the early 1800s. Their efforts on behalf of reform groups helped them learn how to organize more effectively and to work together.

Another benefit of reform-group work was that some men began to fight for women's rights. Many activists, both men and women, found it unacceptable that women were denied the democratic right to vote or sit on juries. They were also upset that married women in many states had little or no control over their own property.

Opposition to Women's Rights Like the abolitionist movement, the struggle for women's rights faced opposition. Many people did not agree with some of the goals of the women's rights movement. Some women believed that they did not need new rights. They said that women were not unequal to men, only different. Some critics believed that women should not try to work in public for social changes. Women were welcome to work for social change, but only from within their homes. "Let her not look away from her own little family circle for the means of producing moral and social reforms," wrote T. S. Arthur. His advice appeared in a popular women's magazine called *The Lady at Home*.

Reading Check
Draw Conclusions
Why did some men and women think that the women's rights movement was misguided?

Some people also thought that women lacked the physical or mental strength to survive without men's protection. They believed that a woman should go from the protection of her father's home to that of her husband's. They also thought that women could not cope with the outside world; therefore, a husband should control his wife's property. Despite opposition, women continued to pursue their goal of greater rights.

Seneca Falls Convention

In 1840 **Elizabeth Cady Stanton** attended the World's Anti-Slavery Convention in London, England, while on her honeymoon. She discovered that, unlike her husband, she was not allowed to participate. All women in attendance had to sit behind a curtain in a separate gallery of the convention hall. William Lloyd Garrison, who had helped found the American Anti-Slavery Society, sat with them in protest.

The treatment of women abolitionists at the convention angered Stanton and her new friend, Lucretia Mott, a Quaker, abolitionist, and women's rights advocate from Massachusetts. Apparently, even many abolitionists did not think that women were equal to men. Stanton and Mott wanted to change this, so they planned to "form a society to advance the rights of

--- BIOGRAPHY ---

Elizabeth Cady Stanton 1815–1902

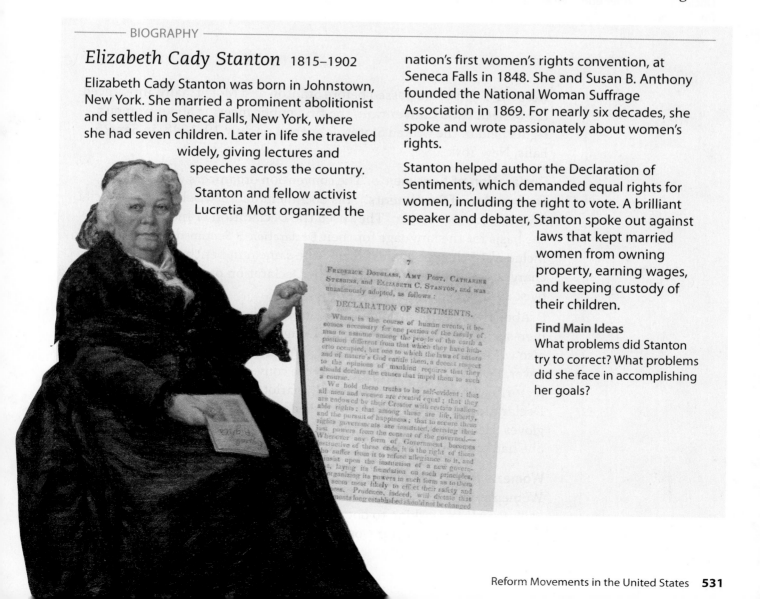

Elizabeth Cady Stanton was born in Johnstown, New York. She married a prominent abolitionist and settled in Seneca Falls, New York, where she had seven children. Later in life she traveled widely, giving lectures and speeches across the country.

Stanton and fellow activist Lucretia Mott organized the

nation's first women's rights convention, at Seneca Falls in 1848. She and Susan B. Anthony founded the National Woman Suffrage Association in 1869. For nearly six decades, she spoke and wrote passionately about women's rights.

Stanton helped author the Declaration of Sentiments, which demanded equal rights for women, including the right to vote. A brilliant speaker and debater, Stanton spoke out against laws that kept married women from owning property, earning wages, and keeping custody of their children.

Find Main Ideas
What problems did Stanton try to correct? What problems did she face in accomplishing her goals?

Declaration of Sentiments

At the 1848 Seneca Falls Convention, 100 people signed the Declaration of Sentiments, a document declaring the rights of women. The wording of the document purposely echoed the Declaration of Independence.

The authors use the same words that are in the Declaration of Independence, but include women.

Here the women demand that they become a part of government.

*We hold these truths to be self-evident: that all men and women are created equal; that they are endowed by their Creator with certain **inalienable**[1] rights; that among these are life, liberty, and the pursuit of happiness; that to secure these rights governments are instituted, deriving their just powers from the consent of the governed. Whenever any form of government becomes destructive of these ends, it is the right of those who suffer from it to refuse **allegiance**[2] to it, and to insist upon the institution of a new government, laying its foundation on such principles, and organizing its powers in such form, as to them shall seem most likely to effect their safety and happiness.*

[1] *inalienable* not able to be taken away   [2] *allegiance* loyalty

Analyze Historical Sources
Why would women want to use the Declaration of Independence as a source for their own declaration?

women." Eight years passed before Stanton and Mott finally announced the **Seneca Falls Convention**, the first public meeting about women's rights held in the United States. It opened on July 19, 1848, in Seneca Falls, New York.

Declaration of Sentiments The convention organizers wrote a **Declaration of Sentiments**. This document detailed beliefs about social injustice toward women. They used the Declaration of Independence as the basis for the language for their Declaration of Sentiments. The authors included 18 charges against men—the same number that had been charged against King George III. The Declaration of Sentiments was signed by some 100 people.

About 240 people attended the Seneca Falls Convention, including men such as abolitionist Frederick Douglass. Many other reformers who also worked in the temperance and abolitionist movements were present. Several women who participated in the convention worked in nearby factories. One of them, 19-year-old Charlotte Woodward, signed the Declaration of Sentiments. She worked long hours in a factory, making gloves. Her wages were very low, and she could not even keep her earnings. She had to turn her wages over to her father.

Women's Rights Leaders After the convention, the struggle continued. Women's rights activists battled many difficulties and much opposition. Still, they kept working to obtain greater equality for women. Among the many women working for women's rights, four became important leaders:

Lucy Stone, Susan B. Anthony, Matilda Joslyn Gage, and Elizabeth Cady Stanton. Each brought different strengths to the fight for women's rights.

Lucy Stone was a well-known spokesperson for the Anti-Slavery Society. In the early years of the women's rights movement, Stone became known as a gifted speaker. Elizabeth Cady Stanton called her "the first who really stirred the nation's heart on the subject of women's wrongs."

Susan B. Anthony brought strong organizational skills to the women's rights movement. She did much to turn the fight for women's rights into a political movement. Anthony argued that women and men should receive equal pay for equal work. She also believed that women should be allowed to enter traditionally male professions, such as religion and law. Anthony was especially concerned with laws that affected women's control of money and property.

Anthony led a campaign to change laws regarding the property rights of women. She wrote in her diary that no woman could ever be free without "a purse of her own." After forming a network to cover the entire state of New York, she collected more than 6,000 signatures to petition

Lucy Stone worked for equal rights for women and African Americans.

Timeline: Women's Rights

1776

1920

1776
Abigail Adams asks her husband, John Adams, to "remember the ladies" and their rights in the Declaration of Independence.

1848
The Seneca Falls Convention is held, and the Declaration of Sentiments is written.

1872
Susan B. Anthony is arrested while trying to vote in New York.

1890
Wyoming's new state constitution includes women's suffrage.

1911
The National Association Opposed to Woman Suffrage is formed.

1920
On August 26, the Nineteenth Amendment is declared ratified by Congress, recognizing women's right to vote.

Analyze Timelines
How many years after women in Wyoming gained the right to vote did women in the rest of the country gain the right?

for a new property-rights law. In 1860, due largely to the efforts of Anthony, New York finally gave married women ownership of their wages and property. Other states in the Northeast and Midwest soon created similar laws.

Elizabeth Cady Stanton wrote many of the documents and speeches of the movement, which were often delivered by Anthony. Along with Lucy Stone and **Matilda Joslyn Gage**, Stanton founded the National Woman Suffrage Association (NWSA) in 1869. This organization was considered one of the more radical groups because of its position that abolition was not a more important cause than women's rights.

Matilda Joslyn Gage was a writer and an advocate in New York. After cofounding the NWSA, she became the publisher of its official newspaper, the *National Citizen and Ballot Box*. She also worked with Stanton and Anthony to write and edit *History of Woman Suffrage*.

Not every battle was won. Other major reforms, such as women's right to vote, were not achieved at this time. Still, more women than ever before became actively involved in women's rights issues. Leaders such as Stanton, Anthony, Stone, and Gage continued to fight for equal treatment and recognition. This increased activity was one of the movement's greatest accomplishments.

Summary and Preview Women's rights became a major issue in the mid-1800s, as women began to demand a greater degree of equality. In the next module you will read about western expansion.

Reading Check
Draw Conclusions
What did Susan B. Anthony mean when she said that no woman could be free without "a purse of her own"?

Lesson 5 Assessment

Review Ideas, Terms, and People

1. **a. Identify** What role did Sojourner Truth play in both the abolition and women's rights movements?

   b. Analyze How did the abolition movement influence women to demand equal rights?

2. **a. Identify** What limitations on women's rights did many activists find unacceptable?

   b. Summarize Why did many Americans oppose equal rights for women?

   c. Elaborate What arguments might you use to counter the arguments of men and women who opposed equal rights for women?

3. **a. Recall** Who were the four main leaders of the women's rights movement, and how did they each contribute to the movement?

   b. Draw Conclusions Why might working-class women like Charlotte Woodward have supported the Seneca Falls Convention and the Declaration of Sentiments?

   c. Evaluate Do you agree with Susan B. Anthony that women should receive equal pay for equal work? Explain your answer.

Critical Thinking

4. **Analyze** In this lesson you learned about the challenges women faced in their struggle for equal rights. Create a graphic organizer similar to the one shown below and use it to show the goals of the movement, as well as the arguments against it.

Goals	Opponents' Arguments

Social Studies Skills

Accept Social Responsibility

Define the Skill

A *society* is an organized group of people who share a common set of activities, traditions, and goals. You are part of many societies— your school, community, and nation are just three. Every society's strength depends on the support and contributions of its members. *Social responsibility* is the obligation that every person has to the societies of which he or she is a member.

Learn the Skill

As a part of your school, community, and nation, you have obligations to the people around you. The most obvious is to do nothing to harm your society. You also have a duty to take part in it. At the very least, this means exercising the rights and responsibilities of membership. These include being informed about issues in your society.

Another level of social responsibility is support of change to benefit society. This level of involvement goes beyond being informed about issues to trying to do something about them. If you take this important step, here are some points to consider.

1. Few efforts to change society have everyone's support. Some people will want things to stay the same. They may treat you badly if you work for change. You must be prepared for this possibility.

2. Sometimes, efforts to improve things involve opposing laws or rules that need to be changed. No matter how just your cause is, if you break laws or rules, you must be willing to accept the consequences of your behavior.

3. Remember that violence is *never* an acceptable method for change. People who use force in seeking change are not behaving in a socially responsible manner, even if their cause is good.

This module was filled with the stories of socially responsible people. Many of them devoted their lives to changing society for the better. Some did so at great personal risk. Boston abolitionist William Lloyd Garrison barely escaped with his life from a local mob that tried to lynch him because of his views.

Garrison and the other reformers you read about demonstrated the highest level of social responsibility. They saw an issue they believed to be a problem in society, and they worked tirelessly to make changes.

Practice the Skill

Review the "If you were there" scene in Lesson 4. Imagine yourself as that South Carolinian. You believe slavery to be wrong. However, you also respect your father. In addition, you know that most of your neighbors do not feel as you do about slavery. They might harm you or your property if you take this stand against it.

1. Would listening to the Grimké sisters' speak help benefit society? Explain why or why not.

2. Are you willing to risk the anger of your neighbors? Why or why not?

3. Would helping the Grimké sisters be a socially responsible thing to do? Explain why or why not.

Module 16 Assessment

Review Vocabulary, Terms, and People

1. Which of the following authors wrote about Puritan life in *The Scarlet Letter*?
   a. Emily Dickinson
   b. Herman Melville
   c. Thomas Gallaudet
   d. Nathaniel Hawthorne

2. Which document expressed the complaints of supporters of women's rights?
   a. Declaration of the Rights of Women
   b. Declaration of Sentiments
   c. Letters on Women's Rights
   d. Seneca Falls Convention

3. As leader of the common-school movement, who worked to improve free public education?
   a. Walt Whitman
   b. Horace Mann
   c. Lyman Beecher
   d. Sojourner Truth

Comprehension and Critical Thinking

Lesson 1

4. a. Identify What political party was founded by nativists, and what policies did it support?
   b. Analyze What factors caused U.S. cities to grow so fast?
   c. Evaluate Do you think that the benefits of city life outweighed its drawbacks? Explain.

Lesson 2

5. a. Describe Who were some important transcendentalists, and what ideas did they promote?
   b. Compare and Contrast In what ways were transcendentalists and Romantics similar and different?
   c. Elaborate Which movement appeals to you more—American transcendentalism or Romanticism? Why?

Lesson 3

6. a. Identify What important reform movements became popular in the early 1800s?
   b. Analyze Why did education become an important topic for reformers in the 1800s?

   c. Evaluate Which reform movement do you think had the greatest effect on the United States? Why?

Lesson 4

7. a. Recall What caused some Americans to support the abolition movement?
   b. Make Inferences How did northerners and southerners use the economy to support their reason for opposing abolition?
   c. Evaluate Which of the methods used by leaders of the abolition movement do you think was most successful? Why?

Lesson 5

8. a. Recall What led many women to question their place in American society?
   b. Make Inferences Why did female factory workers like Charlotte Woodward support the women's rights movement?
   c. Evaluate Do you think the women's movement was successful by 1860? Explain your answer.

Review Themes

9. **Society and Culture** What social and cultural changes took place from 1800 to the mid-1800s?

Reading Skills

Information and Propaganda *Use the Reading Skills taught in this module to answer the question below.*

10. Which of the following is *not* an example of propaganda?

a. a flyer protesting new tax laws

b. an ad about a political candidate

c. a radio announcement sponsored by an interest group

d. a list of camping rules from a park

Social Studies Skills

Accept Social Responsibility *Use the Social Studies Skills taught in this module to fill in the chart below.*

11.

Action	Is it socially responsible?	Why or why not?
Remove litter from a park		
Vote		
Read a political magazine		
Run a red light		

Focus on Writing

12. **Write a Persuasive Letter** In this module you have learned about a number of important events and political, religious, and artistic movements of the early 1800s. Choose the one you consider most important. Think about how it changed life for people in the United States. Then write a two-paragraph persuasive letter to the newspaper, arguing for the event or movement you chose. In the first paragraph, identify the event or movement you chose as well as a thesis explaining why it is important. In the second paragraph, include details about the event or movement that support your thesis. Close with one or two sentences that sum up your points.

A Divided Nation

★

Essential Question
Could the Civil War have been avoided?

About the Photo:

About the Photo: Historical photos and artifacts, such as these in the Charles H. Wright Museum of African American History, allow us to explore our nation's history.

> ▶ *Explore ONLINE!*

VIDEOS, including...
- The Debate Over Slavery
- John Brown's War
- Lincoln's Road Toward Emancipation

☑ Document-Based Investigations

☑ Graphic Organizers

☑ Interactive Games

☑ Image Carousel: Debating the Compromise of 1850

☑ Interactive Chart: *Dred Scott* v. *Sandford* (1857)

☑ Image with Hotspots: Rebel Government

In this module you will learn about how the debate over slavery increasingly divided Americans during the mid-1800s. You will also read about the major events that preceded the Civil War.

What You Will Learn ...

Lesson 1: The Debate over Slavery **542**
The Big Idea Antislavery literature and the annexation of new lands intensified the debate over slavery.

Lesson 2: Trouble in Kansas **548**
The Big Idea The Kansas-Nebraska Act heightened tensions in the conflict over slavery.

Lesson 3: Political Divisions **553**
The Big Idea The split over the issue of slavery intensified due to political division and judicial decisions.

Lesson 4: The Nation Divides **558**
The Big Idea The United States broke apart due to the growing conflict over slavery.

Timeline of Events 1845–1865

United States

World

1845

1848 The Free-Soil Party is formed on August 9.

1848 Revolutionary movements sweep across Europe.

1850

1850 Congress passes the Fugitive Slave Act on September 18.

< **1852** *Uncle Tom's Cabin* by Harriet Beecher Stowe is published.

1852 Louis-Napoléon declares himself Emperor Napoléon III of France. >

1855

1856 British and French forces defeat Russia in the Crimean War.

1856 In the Sack of Lawrence, pro-slavery forces attack the town of Lawrence, Kansas, on May 21.

< **1857** Indian soldiers in the British army begin the Sepoy Mutiny against British control of India.

1859 John Brown takes control of the federal arsenal at Harpers Ferry, Virginia.

1860 On December 20, South Carolina votes to secede from the United States. ∨

1860

CHARLESTON
MERCURY
EXTRA:

THE
UNION
IS
DISSOLVED!

1865

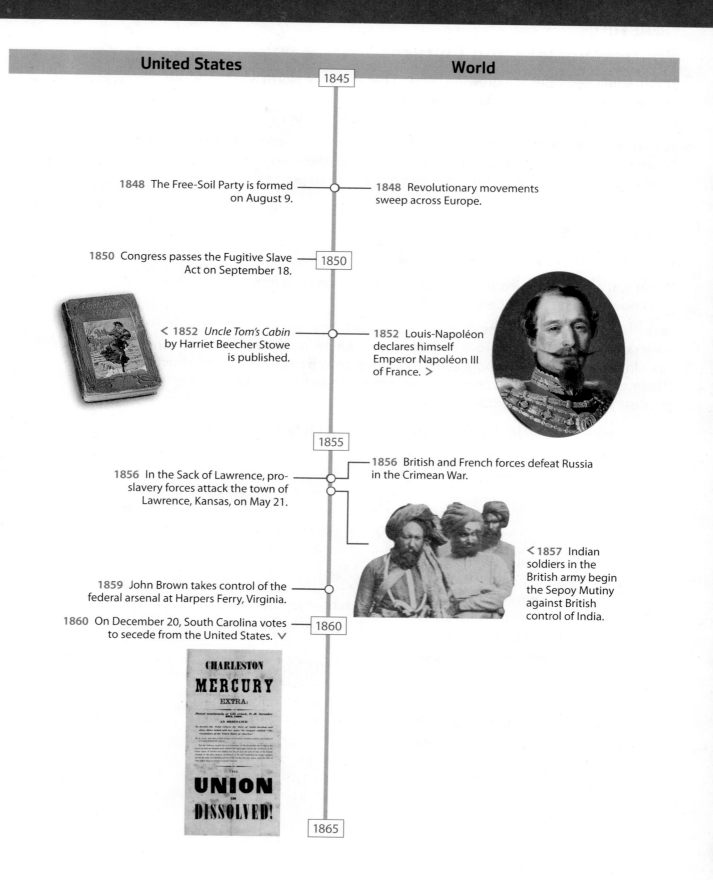

Reading Social Studies

THEME FOCUS:

Politics, Society and Culture

This module describes the growing tension between the North and the South over the slavery issue. You will read what happened as more states were admitted to the Union and people argued if they should be slave states or not.

You will read about events that widened the division between the North and the South so that the South finally chose to secede from the Union. Throughout the module you will see that cultural differences influenced political decisions.

READING FOCUS:

Facts, Opinions, and the Past

When you are trying to learn about history, separating facts from opinions helps you know what really happened.

Identify Facts and Opinions Something is a **fact** if there is a way to prove it. For example, research can prove or disprove the following statement: "Abraham Lincoln belonged to the Republican Party." But research can't prove the following statement because it is just an **opinion**, or someone's belief: "Lincoln was the greatest president in American history."

Use the process below to decide whether a statement is fact or opinion.

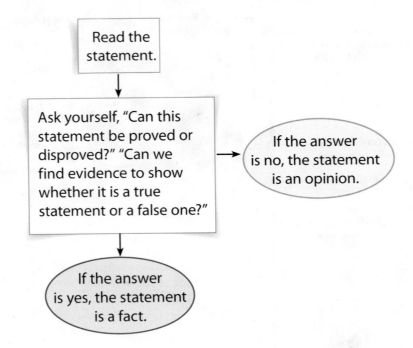

You Try It!

The following passage tells about the debates that Abraham Lincoln had with Stephen Douglas. All the statements in this passage are facts. What makes them facts and not opinions?

> **The Lincoln-Douglas Debates** In 1858 Illinois Republicans nominated Abraham Lincoln for the U.S. Senate. His opponent was Democrat Stephen Douglas, who had represented Illinois in the Senate since 1847. Lincoln challenged Douglas in what became the historic Lincoln-Douglas debates.
>
> In each debate, Lincoln stressed that the central issue of the campaign was the spread of slavery in the West. He said that the Democrats were trying to spread slavery across the nation.
>
> Lincoln talked about the *Dred Scott* decision. He said that African Americans were "entitled to all the natural rights" listed in the Declaration of Independence, specifically mentioning "the right to life, liberty, and the pursuit of happiness."

Identify each of the following as a fact or an opinion and then explain your choice.

1. Lincoln accused the Democrats of trying to spread slavery across the nation.
2. The Lincoln-Douglas debates were the most important debates in the history of the nation.
3. Stephen Douglas was a U.S. senator from Illinois.
4. Abraham Lincoln ran against Douglas in the 1858 Senate election.
5. Most Americans believed that the *Dred Scott* decision was a good one.
6. Lincoln was the best debater people from Illinois had ever heard.

As you read Module 17, look closely at quotes from historical figures. Are these quotes showing you facts or opinions?

Key Terms and People

Lesson 1
popular sovereignty
Wilmot Proviso
sectionalism
Free-Soil Party
secede
Compromise of 1850
Fugitive Slave Act
Anthony Burns
Uncle Tom's Cabin
Harriet Beecher Stowe

Lesson 2
Franklin Pierce
Stephen Douglas
Kansas-Nebraska Act
Pottawatomie Massacre
Charles Sumner
Preston Brooks

Lesson 3
Republican Party
James Buchanan
John C. Frémont
Dred Scott
Roger B. Taney
Abraham Lincoln
Lincoln-Douglas debates
Freeport Doctrine

Lesson 4
John Brown's raid
John C. Breckinridge
Constitutional Union Party
John Bell
John J. Crittenden
Confederate States of America
Jefferson Davis

The Debate over Slavery

The Big Idea

Antislavery literature and the annexation of new lands intensified the debate over slavery.

Main Ideas

- The addition of new land in the West renewed disputes over the expansion of slavery.
- The Compromise of 1850 tried to solve the disputes over slavery.
- The Fugitive Slave Act caused more controversy.
- Abolitionists used antislavery literature to promote opposition.

Key Terms and People

popular sovereignty
Wilmot Proviso
sectionalism
Free-Soil Party
secede
Compromise of 1850
Fugitive Slave Act
Anthony Burns
Uncle Tom's Cabin
Harriet Beecher Stowe

If YOU were there . . .

You live in a crowded neighborhood in New York City in 1854. Your apartment building is home to a variety of people—long-time residents, Irish immigrants, and free African Americans. One day federal marshals knock on your door. They claim that one of your neighbors is a fugitive slave. The marshals say you must help them find her. If you don't, you will be fined or even sent to jail.

What would you tell the federal marshals?

New Land Renews Slavery Disputes

The United States added more than 500,000 square miles of land as a result of winning the Mexican-American War in 1848. The additional land caused bitter debate about slavery. The Missouri Compromise of 1820 had divided the Louisiana Purchase into either free or slave regions. It prohibited slavery north of latitude 36°30' but let Missouri become a slave state. In the 1840s President James K. Polk wanted to extend the 36°30' line to the West coast, dividing the Mexican Cession into two parts—one free and one enslaved. Some leaders, including Senator Lewis Cass of Michigan, encouraged **popular sovereignty**, the idea that political power belongs to the people, who should decide on banning or allowing slavery.

Regional Differences about Slavery Some northerners wanted to outlaw slavery in all parts of the Mexican Cession. During the war, Representative David Wilmot offered the **Wilmot Proviso**, a document stating that "neither slavery nor involuntary servitude shall ever exist in any part of [the] territory."

The northern-controlled House passed the document, but in the Senate, the South had more power. The Wilmot

Whig candidate Zachary Taylor is shown here on an 1848 presidential campaign banner with his running mate, Millard Fillmore.

Proviso did not pass. Before this time, politicians had usually supported the ideas of their political parties. However, the Wilmot Proviso spurred a debate that showed growing **sectionalism**, or favoring the interests of one section or region over the interests of the entire country.

To attract voters, the Democrats and the Whigs did not take a clear position on slavery in the presidential campaign of 1848. In response, antislavery northerners formed a new party, the **Free-Soil Party**, which supported the Wilmot Proviso. They worried that slave labor would mean fewer jobs for white workers. Party members chose former president Martin Van Buren as their candidate. The new party won 10 percent of the popular vote, drawing away votes from Democrat Lewis Cass. Whig candidate Zachary Taylor won a narrow victory.

The California Question The California gold rush caused such rapid population growth that California applied to join the Union as a state instead of as a territory. But would California enter the Union as a free state or a slave state?

Most Californians opposed slavery, which had been illegal when the state was part of Mexico. Also, many forty-niners had come from free states. But if California became a free state, the balance between free and slave states would change, favoring the free states.

In the South, an imbalance was unacceptable. "We are about permanently to destroy the balance of power between the sections," said Senator Jefferson Davis of Mississippi. He and many other southerners did not want California to enter the Union as a free state.

Reading Check
Make Inferences
Why did sectionalism in the United States increase in the late 1840s?

Compromise of 1850

Senator Henry Clay of Kentucky had helped to settle the Missouri crisis of 1819–20 and the nullification crisis of 1832–33 by proposing compromises. He now had another plan to help the nation maintain peace. His ideas were designed to give both sides things that they wanted:

1. California would enter the Union as a free state.
2. The rest of the Mexican Cession would be federal land. In this territory, popular sovereignty would decide on slavery.
3. Texas would give up land east of the upper Rio Grande. In return, the government would pay Texas's debts from when it was an independent republic.
4. The slave trade—but not slavery—would end in the nation's capital.
5. A more effective fugitive slave law would be passed.

Clay's plan drew attack, especially regarding California. Senator William Seward of New York defended antislavery views and wanted California admitted "directly, without conditions, without qualifications, and without compromise." However, Senator John C. Calhoun of South Carolina argued that letting California enter as a free state would destroy the nation's balance. He warned people of issues that would later start the Civil War. Calhoun asked that the slave states be allowed to **secede**—formally withdraw—from the Union.

In contrast, Senator Daniel Webster of Massachusetts favored Clay's plan:

> "I wish to speak today, not as a Massachusetts man, nor as a Northern man, but as an American . . . I speak today for the preservation of the Union. Hear me for my cause."
>
> —from the Seventh of March Speech, March 7, 1850

Webster criticized northern abolitionists and southerners who talked of secession.

A compromise was enacted that year and seemed to settle most disputes between free and slave states. It achieved the majority of Clay's proposals. With the **Compromise of 1850**, California was able to enter the Union

Historical Source

The Seventh of March Speech

On March 7, 1850, Daniel Webster spoke on the floor of the Senate in favor of the Compromise of 1850.

Webster is upset by talk of secession.

Webster is saying that just as it is impossible to move water in the ocean without making waves, it is impossible for states to peacefully secede.

> *I hear with pain and anguish, and distress, the word secession. . . . Secession! Peaceable secession! Sir, your eyes and mine are never destined to see that miracle. The dismemberment [taking apart] of this vast country without convulsion! The breaking up of the fountains of the great deep without ruffling the surface! Who is so foolish— I beg everybody's pardon—as to expect to see any such thing? . . . There can be no such thing as a peaceable secession.*
>
> —from the Seventh of March Speech, March 7, 1850

Analyze Historical Sources
Why did Webster support the Compromise of 1850?

Southern View of the Compromise of 1850

John C. Calhoun from South Carolina wrote a speech saying that the proposed compromise did not go far enough to satisfy the South.

> *I have, senators, believed from the first that the agitation [unrest] of the subject of slavery would, if not prevented by some timely and effective measure, end in disunion. . . . The South asks for justice, simple justice, and less she ought not to take. She has no compromise to offer but the Constitution, and no concession or surrender to make."*
>
> —from Speech on the Slavery Question, delivered in the Senate, March 4, 1850

Analyze Historical Sources
Why did Calhoun urge southern senators to vote against the compromise?

Calhoun believes the South's position was supported by the Constitution.

Henry Clay introduced the Compromise of 1850 on the Senate floor.

Daniel Webster spoke eloquently in support of the compromise.

John C. Calhoun was weak and near death. He had his speech in support of slavery read to the Senate for him.

as a free state. The rest of the Mexican Cession was divided into two territories—Utah and New Mexico—where the question of whether to allow slavery would be decided by popular sovereignty.

Texas agreed to give up its land claims in New Mexico in exchange for financial aid from the federal government. The compromise outlawed the slave trade in the District of Columbia and established a new fugitive slave law.

Reading Check
Analyze Information
How was Texas affected by the Compromise of 1850?

Fugitive Slave Act

The newly passed **Fugitive Slave Act** made it a crime to help runaway slaves and allowed officials to arrest those slaves in free areas. Slaveholders were permitted to take suspected fugitives to U.S. commissioners, who decided their fate.

Details of the Fugitive Slave Act Slaveholders could use testimony from white witnesses, but enslaved African Americans accused of being fugitives could not testify. Nor could people who hid or helped a runaway slave—they faced six months in jail and a $1,000 fine. Commissioners who rejected a slaveholder's claim earned $5, while those who returned suspected fugitives to slaveholders earned $10. Clearly, the commissioners benefited from helping slaveholders.

Reactions to the Fugitive Slave Act Enforcement of the Fugitive Slave Act began immediately. In September 1850—the same month the law was passed—federal marshals arrested African American James Hamlet.

Public rallies denouncing the Fugitive Slave Act often included speeches from key abolitionists such as Frederick Douglass (seated at the table on the left).

They returned him to a slaveholder in Maryland, although he had lived in New York City for three years.

Thousands of northern African Americans fled to Canada in fear. In the ten years after Congress passed the Fugitive Slave Act, some 343 fugitive slave cases were reviewed. The accused fugitives were declared free in only 11 cases.

The Fugitive Slave Act upset northerners, who were uncomfortable with the commissioners' power. Northerners disliked the idea of a trial without a jury. They also disapproved of commissioners' higher fees for returning slaves. Most were horrified that some free African Americans had been captured and sent to the South.

Most northerners opposed to the act peacefully resisted, but violence did erupt. In 1854 **Anthony Burns**, a fugitive slave from Virginia, was arrested in Boston. Abolitionists used force while trying to rescue him from jail, killing a deputy marshal. A federal ship was ordered to return Burns to Virginia after his trial. Many people in the North, particularly in Massachusetts, were outraged. The event persuaded many to join the abolitionist cause.

Antislavery Literature

Abolitionists in the North used the stories of fugitive slaves like James Hamlet and Anthony Burns to gain sympathy for their cause. Slave narratives also educated people about their hardships.

Fiction also informed people about the evils of slavery. *Uncle Tom's Cabin*, the antislavery novel written by **Harriet Beecher Stowe**, spoke out powerfully against slavery. Stowe, the daughter of Connecticut minister

Reading Check
Draw Conclusions
What concerns did northerners have about the Fugitive Slave Act?

Lyman Beecher, moved to Ohio when she was 21. There she met fugitive slaves and learned about the cruelties of slavery. The Fugitive Slave Act greatly angered Stowe. She decided to write a book that would educate northerners about the realities of slavery.

Uncle Tom's Cabin was published in 1852. The main character, a kindly enslaved African American named Tom, is taken from his wife and sold "down the river" in Louisiana. Tom becomes the slave of cruel Simon Legree. In a rage, Legree has Tom beaten to death.

The novel electrified the nation and sparked outrage in the South. Louisa McCord, a famous southern writer, questioned the "foul imagination which could invent such scenes."

Within a decade, more than 2 million copies of *Uncle Tom's Cabin* had been sold in the United States. The book's popularity caused one northerner to remark that Stowe and her book had created "two millions of abolitionists." Stowe later wrote *A Key to Uncle Tom's Cabin* to answer those who had criticized her book.

The impact of Stowe's book is suggested by her reported meeting with Abraham Lincoln in 1862, a year after the start of the Civil War. Lincoln supposedly said to Stowe that she was "the little lady who made this big war." Her book is still widely read today as a source of information about the harsh realities of slavery.

Summary and Preview The United States experienced increasing disagreement over the issue of slavery. The Compromise of 1850 and the Fugitive Slave Act tried to address these disagreements with legislation. In the next lesson you will read about another disputed law concerning slavery—the Kansas-Nebraska Act—and the violence it sparked.

Reading Check
Identify Cause and Effect Why did abolitionists use antislavery literature to promote their cause, and what effect did it have on the slavery debate?

Lesson 1 Assessment

Review Ideas, Terms, and People

1. **a. Describe** What ideas did the Free-Soil Party promote?

   b. Predict What are some possible results of the growing sectional debate over slavery?

2. **a. Describe** What were the major points of the Compromise of 1850?

   b. Contrast What differing opinions emerged toward Henry Clay's proposed compromise?

3. **a. Identify** What were the effects of the Fugitive Slave Act?

   b. Draw Conclusions Why did some Americans believe the Fugitive Slave Act was unfair?

4. **a. Identify** What are three examples of antislavery literature?

   b. Elaborate Do you think literature was an effective tool against slavery? Why or why not?

Critical Thinking

5. **Evaluate** In this lesson you learned about the sequence of events in the debate over slavery and the effects of each. Create a graphic organizer similar to the one below to evaluate how the Compromise of 1850, the Fugitive Slave Act, and antislavery literature affected the slavery debate.

| Compromise of 1850 | Fugitive Slave Act | Antislavery Literature |

Slavery Debate

Trouble in Kansas

The Big Idea

The Kansas-Nebraska Act heightened tensions in the conflict over slavery.

Main Ideas

- The debate over the expansion of slavery influenced the election of 1852.

- The Kansas-Nebraska Act gave voters the choice to allow or prohibit slavery.

- Pro-slavery and antislavery groups clashed violently in what became known as "Bleeding Kansas."

Key Terms and People

Franklin Pierce
Stephen Douglas
Kansas-Nebraska Act
Pottawatomie Massacre
Charles Sumner
Preston Brooks

If YOU were there . . .

You live on a New England farm in 1855. You often think about moving West. But the last few harvests have been bad, and you can't afford to have another bad harvest. Now the Emigrant Aid Society offers to help you move to Kansas. To bring in antislavery voters like you, they'll give you a wagon, livestock, and farm machines. Still, you know that Kansas might be dangerous.

Would you decide to risk settling in Kansas?

Election of 1852

Four leading candidates for the Democratic presidential nomination emerged in 1852. It became clear that none of them would win a majority of votes. Frustrated delegates at the Democratic National Convention turned to **Franklin Pierce**, a little-known politician from New Hampshire. Pierce promised to honor the Compromise of 1850 and the Fugitive Slave Act. Therefore, southerners trusted Pierce on the issue of slavery.

Franklin Pierce

The opposing Whigs also held their convention in 1852. In other presidential elections, they had nominated well-known former generals such as William Henry Harrison and Zachary Taylor. This had been a good strategy, as both men had won. The Whigs decided to choose another war hero. They passed over the current president, Millard Fillmore, because they believed that his strict enforcement of the Fugitive Slave Act would cost votes. Instead, they chose Winfield Scott, a Mexican War hero. Southerners did not trust Scott, however, because he had not fully supported the Compromise of 1850.

Pierce won the election of 1852 by a large margin. Many Whigs viewed the election as a painful defeat not just for their candidate but also for their party.

Reading Check
Draw Conclusions
What issues determined the outcome of the presidential election of 1852?

The Kansas-Nebraska Act

In his inaugural address, President Pierce expressed his hope that the slavery issue had been put to rest "and that no sectional . . . excitement may again threaten the durability [stability] of our institutions." Less than a year later, however, a proposal to build a railroad to the West coast helped revive the slavery controversy and opened a new period of sectional conflict.

Douglas and the Railroad Ever since entering Congress in the mid-1840s, **Stephen Douglas** had supported the idea of building a railroad to the Pacific Ocean. Douglas favored a line running from Chicago. The first step toward building such a railroad would be organizing what remained of the Louisiana Purchase into a federal territory. The Missouri Compromise required that this land be free territory and eventually free states.

Southerners in Congress did not support Douglas's plan, recommending a southern route for the railroad. Their preferred line ran from New Orleans, across Texas and New Mexico Territory, to southern California. Determined to have the railroad start in Chicago, Douglas asked a few key southern senators to support his plan. They agreed to do so if the new territory west of Missouri was opened to slavery.

Two New Territories In January 1854 Douglas introduced what became the **Kansas-Nebraska Act**, a plan that would divide the remainder of the Louisiana Purchase into two territories—Kansas and Nebraska—and allow the people in each territory to decide on the question of slavery. The act would eliminate the Missouri Compromise's restriction on slavery north of the 36°30' line.

Antislavery northerners were outraged by the **implications**. Some believed the proposal was part of a terrible plot to turn free territory into a "dreary region . . . inhabited by masters and slaves." All across the North, citizens attended protest meetings and sent anti-Nebraska petitions to Congress.

Even so, with strong southern support—and with Douglas and President Pierce pressuring their fellow Democrats to vote for it—the measure passed both houses of Congress and was signed into law on May 30, 1854. Lost amid all the controversy over the territorial bill was Douglas's proposed railroad to the Pacific Ocean. Congress would not approve the construction of such a railroad until 1862.

Kansas Divided Antislavery and pro-slavery groups rushed their supporters to Kansas. One of the people who spoke out strongly against slavery in Kansas was Senator Seward.

> "Gentlemen of the Slave States . . . I accept [your challenge] in . . . the cause of freedom. We will engage in competition for . . . Kansas, and God give the victory to the side which is stronger in numbers as it is in right."
>
> —from Speech of William Henry Seward on the Kansas and Nebraska Bill, delivered in the Senate, May 26, 1854

Academic Vocabulary
implications things that are inferred or deduced

From Compromise to Conflict

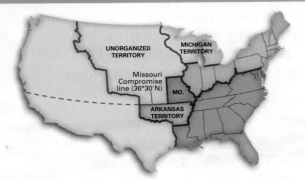

The Missouri Compromise, 1820

Under the Missouri Compromise of 1820, there are an equal number of free states (orange) and slave states (green).

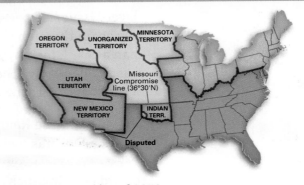

The Compromise of 1850

The Compromise of 1850 allowed for one more free state (California) than slave state, but also passed a strict fugitive slave law.

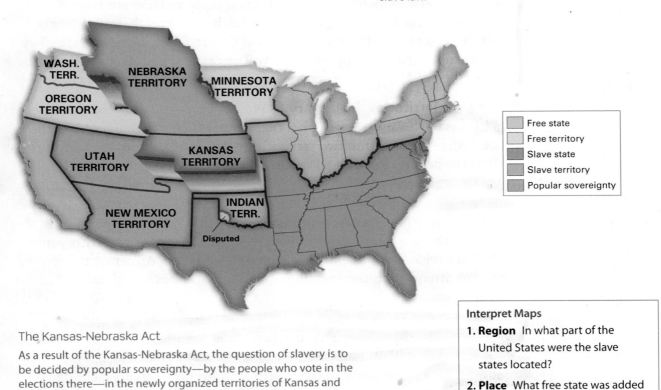

The Kansas-Nebraska Act

As a result of the Kansas-Nebraska Act, the question of slavery is to be decided by popular sovereignty—by the people who vote in the elections there—in the newly organized territories of Kansas and Nebraska. The act sparked violent conflict between pro-slavery and antislavery groups.

Interpret Maps

1. **Region** In what part of the United States were the slave states located?

2. **Place** What free state was added with the Compromise of 1850?

Elections for the Kansas territorial legislature were held in March 1855. Almost 5,000 pro-slavery voters crossed the border from Missouri, voted in Kansas, and then returned home. As a result, the new legislature had a huge pro-slavery majority. The members of the legislature passed strict laws that made it a crime to question slaveholders' rights and said that those who helped fugitive slaves could be put to death. In protest, antislavery Kansans formed their own legislature 25 miles away in Topeka. President Pierce, however, only recognized the pro-slavery legislature.

Reading Check
Analyze Information
Why did northerners dislike the Kansas-Nebraska Act?

Bleeding Kansas

By early 1856 Kansas had two opposing governments, and the population was angry. Settlers had moved to Kansas to homestead in peace, but the controversy over slavery began to affect everyone.

In April 1856 a congressional committee arrived in Kansas to decide which government was legitimate. Although committee members declared the election of the pro-slavery legislature to be unfair, the federal government did not agree.

Attack on Lawrence The new pro-slavery settlers owned guns, and anti-slavery settlers received weapons shipments from friends in the East. Then, violence broke out. In May 1856 a pro-slavery grand jury in Kansas charged leaders of the antislavery government with treason. About 800 men rode to the city of Lawrence to arrest the antislavery leaders, but they had fled. The posse took its anger out on Lawrence by setting fires, looting buildings, and destroying presses used to print antislavery newspapers. One man was killed in the pro-slavery attack that became known as the Sack of Lawrence.

John Brown's Response Abolitionist John Brown was from New England, but he and some of his sons had moved to Kansas in 1855. The Sack of Lawrence made him determined to "fight fire with fire" and to "strike terror in the hearts of the pro-slavery people." On the night of May 24, 1856, along Pottawatomie Creek, Brown and his men killed five pro-slavery men in Kansas in what became known as the **Pottawatomie Massacre**. Brown and his men dragged the pro-slavery men out of their cabins and killed them with swords. The abolitionist band managed to escape capture. Brown declared that his actions had been ordered by God.

Kansas collapsed into civil war, and about 200 people were killed. The events in "Bleeding Kansas" became national front-page news stories. In September 1856 a new territorial governor arrived and began to restore order.

This group of abolitionists took the law into their own hands to free one of their comrades from prison.

This cartoon shows Preston Brooks beating Charles Sumner with his cane. Sumner's only protection is a quill pen, symbolically representing the law.

Brooks Attacks Sumner Congress also reacted to the violence of the Sack of Lawrence. Senator **Charles Sumner** of Massachusetts criticized pro-slavery people in Kansas and personally insulted Andrew Pickens Butler, a pro-slavery senator from South Carolina. Representative **Preston Brooks**, a relative of Butler's, responded strongly.

On May 22, 1856, Brooks used a walking cane to beat Sumner unconscious in the Senate chambers. Dozens of southerners sent Brooks new canes, but northerners were outraged and called the attacker "Bully Brooks." Brooks only had to pay a $300 fine to the federal court. It took Sumner three years before he was well enough to return to the Senate.

Summary and Preview The Kansas-Nebraska Act produced a national uproar. In the next lesson you will read about divisions in political parties.

Reading Check
Summarize
What were some of the results of the intense division in Kansas?

Lesson 2 Assessment

Review Ideas, Terms, and People

1. a. **Identify** What issues influenced the outcome of the election of 1852?

   b. **Draw Conclusions** Why did northern and southern Democrats support Franklin Pierce?

2. a. **Recall** What did the Kansas-Nebraska Act do?

   b. **Explain** Why did antislavery and pro-slavery groups encourage people to move to Kansas?

   c. **Evaluate** Would you have supported or opposed the Kansas-Nebraska Act? Why?

3. a. **Describe** What was the Pottawatomie Massacre?

   b. **Analyze** How did Charles Sumner's views on "Bleeding Kansas" lead to conflict?

   c. **Elaborate** Do you think Preston Brooks's punishment was reasonable? Why or why not?

Critical Thinking

4. **Sequence** In this lesson you learned about the railroad construction plan of Stephen Douglas and how it led to the Kansas-Nebraska Act. Create a graphic organizer like the one shown below and use it to show the sequence of events that led to violence in Kansas.

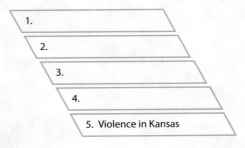

1.

2.

3.

4.

5. Violence in Kansas

Political Divisions

The Big Idea

The split over the issue of slavery intensified due to political division and judicial decisions.

Main Ideas

- Political parties in the United States underwent change due to the movement to expand slavery.

- The *Dred Scott* decision created further division over the issue of slavery.

- The Lincoln-Douglas debates brought much attention to the conflict over slavery.

Key Terms and People

Republican Party
James Buchanan
John C. Frémont
Dred Scott
Roger B. Taney
Abraham Lincoln
Lincoln-Douglas debates
Freeport Doctrine

If YOU were there . . .

You are traveling through Michigan in July 1854. As you pass through the town of Jackson, you see a crowd of several hundred people gathered under the trees. You join them and find that it is a political rally. Antislavery supporters from different parties are meeting to form a new political party. Speakers promise to fight slavery "until the contest be terminated."

How do you think this new party will affect American politics?

Political Parties Undergo Change

Democrat Stephen Douglas had predicted that the Kansas-Nebraska Act would "raise a . . . storm." He was right. The Kansas-Nebraska Act brought the slavery issue back into the national spotlight. Some Whigs, Democrats, Free-Soilers, and abolitionists joined in 1854 to form the **Republican Party**, a political party united against the spread of slavery in the West.

Democrats were in trouble. Those who supported the Kansas-Nebraska Act were not re-elected. The Whig Party also fell apart when northern and southern Whigs refused to work together. A senator from Connecticut complained, "The Whig Party has been killed off . . . by that miserable Nebraska business." Some Whigs and Democrats joined the American Party, also known as the Know-Nothing Party. At the party's convention, delegates argued over slavery, then chose former president Millard Fillmore as their candidate for the election of 1856.

The Democrats knew they could not choose a strong supporter of the Kansas-Nebraska Act, such as President Pierce or Senator Douglas. They nominated **James Buchanan** of Pennsylvania. Buchanan had a great deal of political experience as Polk's secretary of state. Most importantly, he had been in Great Britain as ambassador during the Kansas-Nebraska Act dispute and had not been involved in the debate.

At their first nominating convention, the Republicans chose explorer **John C. Frémont** as their candidate. He had little political experience, but he stood against the spread of slavery. The public saw Republicans as a single-issue party. They had almost no supporters outside of the free states.

On election day, Buchanan won 14 of the 15 slave states and became the new president. Frémont won 11 of the 16 free states. Fillmore won only one state—Maryland. Buchanan had won the election.

Dred Scott Decision

Just two days after Buchanan became president, the Supreme Court issued a historic ruling about slavery. News of the decision threw the country back into crisis. The Court reviewed and decided the **complex** case involving an enslaved man named **Dred Scott**.

Dred Scott Sues for Freedom Dred Scott was the slave of Dr. John Emerson, an army surgeon who lived in St. Louis, Missouri. In the 1830s Emerson had taken Scott on tours of duty in Illinois and the Wisconsin Territory. After they returned to Missouri, the doctor died, and Scott became the slave of Emerson's widow. In 1846 Scott sued for his freedom in the Missouri state courts, arguing that he had become free when he lived in free territory. Though a lower court ruled in his favor, the Missouri Supreme Court overturned this ruling.

Scott's case reached the U.S. Supreme Court 11 years later, in 1857. The justices—a majority of whom were from the South—had three key issues before them. First, the Court had to rule on whether Scott was a citizen. Only citizens could sue in federal court. Second, the Court had to decide if his time living on free soil made him free. Third, the Court had to determine the constitutionality of prohibiting slavery in parts of the Louisiana Purchase.

The Supreme Court's Ruling Chief Justice **Roger B. Taney** (TAW•nee), himself from a slaveholding family in Maryland, wrote the majority opinion in the *Dred Scott* decision in March 1857. First, he addressed the issue of Dred Scott's citizenship. Taney said the nation's founders believed that African Americans "had no rights which a white man was bound to respect." He therefore concluded that all African Americans, whether slave or free, were not citizens under the U.S. Constitution. Thus, Dred Scott did not have the right to file suit in federal court.

Reading Check Summarize What were the major political parties in the election of 1856, and who was the candidate for each party?

Academic Vocabulary **complex** difficult, not simple

The Supreme Court's decision against Dred Scott (seen here) was a severe setback for abolitionists.

Taney also ruled on the other issues before the Court. As to whether Scott's residence on free soil made him free, Taney flatly said it did not. Because Scott had returned to the slave state of Missouri, the chief justice said, "his *status*, as free or slave, depended on the laws of Missouri."

Finally, Taney declared the Missouri Compromise restriction on slavery north of 36°30' to be unconstitutional. He pointed out that the Fifth Amendment said no one could "be deprived of life, liberty, or property without due process of law." Because slaves were considered property, Congress could not prohibit someone from taking slaves into a federal territory. Under this ruling, Congress had no right to ban slavery in any federal territory.

Most white southerners cheered this decision. It "covers every question regarding slavery and settles it in favor of the South," reported a Georgia newspaper. Another newspaper, the New Orleans *Picayune*, assured its readers that the ruling put "the whole basis of the . . . Republican organization under the ban of law."

The ruling stunned many northerners. The Republicans were particularly upset because their platform in 1856 had argued that Congress held the right to ban slavery in the federal territories. Now the nation's highest court had ruled that Congress did not have this right.

Indeed, some northerners feared that the spread of slavery would not stop with the federal territories. Illinois lawyer **Abraham Lincoln** warned that a future Court ruling, or what he called "the next *Dred Scott* decision," would prohibit states from banning slavery.

> "We shall *lie down* pleasantly dreaming that the people of *Missouri* are on the verge of [close to] making their state *free*; and we shall *awake* to the *reality*, instead, that the Supreme Court has made *Illinois* a *slave state.*"
>
> —Abraham Lincoln, quoted in *Speeches and Letters of Abraham Lincoln 1832–1865*, edited by Merwin Roe

Reading Check
Summarize
What were the major rulings of the *Dred Scott* decision?

Lincoln-Douglas Debates

In 1858 Illinois Republicans nominated Abraham Lincoln for the U.S. Senate. His opponent was Democrat Stephen Douglas, who had represented Illinois in the Senate since 1847. Lincoln challenged Douglas in what became the historic **Lincoln-Douglas debates**.

In each debate, Lincoln stressed that the central issue of the campaign was the spread of slavery in the West. He said that the Democrats were trying to spread slavery across the nation.

Lincoln talked about the *Dred Scott* decision. He said that African Americans were "entitled to all the natural rights" listed in the Declaration of Independence, specifically mentioning "the right to life, liberty, and the pursuit of happiness." However, Lincoln believed that African Americans were not necessarily the social or political equals of whites. Hoping to cost Lincoln votes, Douglas charged that Lincoln "thinks that the Negro is his brother . . ."

A House Divided

In 1858 Abraham Lincoln gave a passionate speech to Illinois Republicans about the dangers of the disagreement over slavery. Some considered it a call for war.

This line is a paraphrase of a line in the Bible.

Lincoln expresses confidence that the Union will survive.

"In my opinion, it [disagreement over slavery] will not cease [stop], until a crisis shall have been reached and passed. "A house divided against itself cannot stand." I believe this government cannot endure permanently half slave and half free. I do not expect the Union to be dissolved—I do not expect the house to fall—but I do expect it will cease to be divided."

—Abraham Lincoln, quoted in *Speeches and Letters of Abraham Lincoln 1832–1865*, edited by Merwin Roe

Analyze Historical Sources
What do you think Lincoln meant by "crisis"?

Quick Facts

A Growing Conflict

Causes of Conflict
- Failure of Missouri Compromise
- Failure of Compromise of 1850
- Kansas-Nebraska Act
- *Dred Scott* decision

Short-Term Effects
- Political battles
- Sectional diffearences
- "Bleeding Kansas"
- Lincoln-Douglas debates

Long-Term Effect
- Civil War

Douglas also criticized Lincoln for saying that the nation could not remain "half slave and half free." Douglas said that the statement revealed a Republican desire to make every state a free state. This, he warned, would only lead to "a dissolution [destruction] of the Union" and "warfare between the North and the South."

At the second debate, in the northern Illinois town of Freeport, Lincoln pressed Douglas on the apparent contradiction between the Democrats' belief in popular sovereignty and the *Dred Scott* decision. Lincoln asked Douglas to explain how, if Congress could not ban slavery from a federal territory, Congress could allow the citizens of that territory to ban it.

Douglas responded that it did not matter what the Supreme Court decided about slavery. He argued that "the people have the lawful means to introduce it or exclude it as they please, for the reason that slavery cannot exist a day or an hour anywhere, unless it is supported by local police regulations."

This notion that the police would enforce the voters' decision if it contradicted the Supreme Court's decision in the *Dred Scott* case became known as the **Freeport Doctrine**.

The Freeport Doctrine put the slavery question back in the hands of American citizens. It helped Douglas win the Senate seat. Lincoln, while not victorious, became a strong, important leader of the Republican Party.

Summary and Preview The *Dred Scott* decision and the Lincoln-Douglas debates dealt with the conflict over slavery in the western territories. In the next lesson you will read about how the conflict broke apart the Union.

Stephen Douglas (seen here) debated with Abraham Lincoln seven times during their 1858 election campaign.

Reading Check
Make Inferences
Why did Abraham Lincoln make slavery's expansion the central issue of the Lincoln-Douglas debates?

Lesson 3 Assessment

Review Ideas, Terms, and People

1. **a. Identify** What was the major issue of the newly formed Republican Party?

   b. Draw Conclusions How did the Kansas-Nebraska Act affect political parties?

   c. Elaborate Why do you think James Buchanan won the election of 1856?

2. **a. Identify** Who was Roger B. Taney, and why was he important?

   b. Draw Conclusions How did the *Dred Scott* decision affect the Missouri Compromise and the expansion of slavery?

   c. Predict What problems might result from the Supreme Court's ruling in the *Dred Scott* case?

3. **a. Recall** What was the major issue of the Lincoln-Douglas debates?

   b. Make Inferences Despite his loss in the election, how did Lincoln become the leader of the Republican Party?

Critical Thinking

4. **Identify Points of View** In this lesson you learned about the effects the political divisions and the *Dred Scott* decision had on the slavery debate. Create a graphic organizer like the one below and identify the views of Abraham Lincoln and Stephen Douglas on the issue of slavery.

Lincoln		Douglas
	vs.	

The Nation Divides

The Big Idea
The United States broke apart due to the growing conflict over slavery.

Main Ideas
- John Brown's raid on Harpers Ferry intensified the disagreement between free states and slave states.

- The outcome of the election of 1860 divided the United States.

- The dispute over slavery led the South to secede.

Key Terms and People
John Brown's raid
John C. Breckinridge
Constitutional Union Party
John Bell
John J. Crittenden
Confederate States of America
Jefferson Davis

If YOU were there . . .

You work for the weekly newspaper in Harpers Ferry, Virginia. You strongly oppose slavery, but you think the question ought to be resolved by laws, not bloodshed. Now your newspaper has sent you to interview the famous abolitionist John Brown in prison. His raids in "Bleeding Kansas" killed several people. Now he is in jail for attacking a federal arsenal and taking weapons.

What questions would you ask John Brown?

Raid on Harpers Ferry

In 1858 John Brown tried to start an uprising. He wanted to attack the federal arsenal in Virginia and seize weapons there. He planned to arm local slaves. Brown expected to kill or take hostage white southerners who stood in his way. He urged abolitionists to give him money so that he could support a small army. But after nearly two years, Brown's army had only about 20 men.

On the night of October 16, 1859, **John Brown's raid** began when he and his men took over the arsenal in Harpers Ferry, Virginia, in hopes of starting a slave rebellion. He sent several of his men into the countryside to get slaves to join him. However, enslaved African Americans did not come to Harpers Ferry, fearing punishment if they took part. Instead, local white southerners attacked Brown. Eight of his men and three local men were killed. Brown and some followers retreated to a firehouse.

Federal troops arrived in Harpers Ferry the following night. The next morning, Colonel Robert E. Lee ordered a squad of marines to storm the firehouse. In a matter of seconds, the marines killed two more of Brown's men and captured the rest—including Brown.

Brown was quickly convicted of treason, murder, and conspiracy. Some of his men received death sentences. John A. Copeland, a fugitive slave, defended his actions:

"If I am dying for freedom, I could not die for a better cause." Convinced that he also would be sentenced to death, Brown delivered a memorable speech.

> "Now, if it is deemed [thought] necessary that I should forfeit [give up] my life for the furtherance of the ends of justice, and mingle [mix] my blood . . . with the blood of millions in this slave country whose rights are disregarded by wicked, cruel, and unjust enactments, I say, let it be done."
>
> —John Brown, quoted in *John Brown, 1800–1859* by Oswald Garrison Villard

As expected, the judge ordered Brown to be hanged. The sentence was carried out one month later on December 2, 1859.

Many northerners mourned John Brown's death, but some abolitionists criticized his extreme actions. Abraham Lincoln said Brown "agreed with us in thinking slavery wrong." However, Lincoln continued, "That cannot excuse violence, bloodshed, and treason."

Most southern whites—both slaveholders and non-slaveholders—felt threatened by the actions of John Brown. They worried that a "John Brown the Second" might attack. One South Carolina newspaper voiced these fears: "We are convinced the safety of the South lies only outside the present Union." Another newspaper stated that "the sooner we get out of the Union, the better."

Reading Check
Draw Conclusions
Why did John Brown's raid lead some southerners to talk about leaving the Union?

DOCUMENT-BASED INVESTIGATION   Historical Source

John Brown's Last Speech

At his trial, after being pronounced guilty, John Brown spoke in his own defense about his plan to free slaves.

Brown says he never meant to start a rebellion.

By *His*, Brown means "God's."

> "I intended certainly to have made a clean thing of that matter [freeing slaves]. . . . I never did intend murder or treason, or the destruction of property, or to excite or incite the slaves to rebellion, or to make insurrection [revolt]. . . . Had I interfered in the manner which I admit . . . in behalf of the rich, the powerful, the intelligent, the so-called great . . . it would have been all right, and every man in this Court would have deemed it an act worthy of reward rather than punishment. . . . I believe that to have interfered as I have done . . . in behalf of His despised poor, is no wrong, but right."
>
> —John Brown, quoted in *The Life, Trial and Execution of Captain John Brown*

Analyze Historical Sources
How does Brown contrast his ideas with the Court's ideas?

Election of 1860

In this climate of distrust, Americans prepared for another presidential election in 1860. The northern and southern Democrats could not agree on a candidate. Northern Democrats chose Senator Stephen Douglas. Southern Democrats backed the current vice president, **John C. Breckinridge** of Kentucky, who supported slavery in the territories.

Meanwhile, a new political party emerged. The **Constitutional Union Party** recognized "no political principle other than the Constitution of the country, the Union of the states, and the enforcement of the laws." Members of this new party met in Baltimore, Maryland, and selected **John Bell** of Tennessee as their candidate. Bell was a slaveholder, but he had opposed the Kansas-Nebraska Act in 1854.

Senator William Seward of New York was the Republicans' leading candidate at the start of their convention. But it turned out that Lincoln appealed to more party members. A moderate who was against the spread of slavery, Lincoln promised not to abolish slavery where it already existed.

Douglas, Breckinridge, and Bell each knew he might not win the election. They hoped to win enough electoral votes to prevent Lincoln from winning in the electoral college. But with a unified Republican Party behind him, Lincoln won. Although he received the highest number of votes, he won only about 40 percent of the overall popular vote.

▶ Explore ONLINE!

Election of 1860

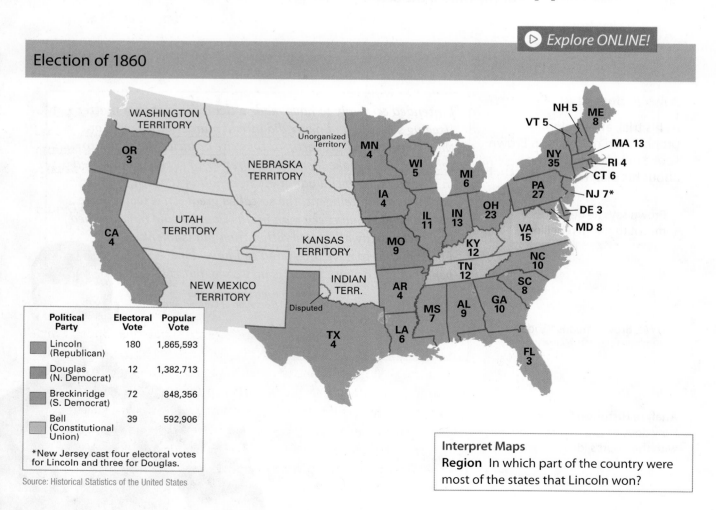

Political Party	Electoral Vote	Popular Vote
Lincoln (Republican)	180	1,865,593
Douglas (N. Democrat)	12	1,382,713
Breckinridge (S. Democrat)	72	848,356
Bell (Constitutional Union)	39	592,906

*New Jersey cast four electoral votes for Lincoln and three for Douglas.

Source: Historical Statistics of the United States

Interpret Maps
Region In which part of the country were most of the states that Lincoln won?

Reading Check
Analyze Information Why was Lincoln viewed by many as a moderate candidate during his campaign for the presidency?

Lincoln won 180 of 183 electoral votes in free states. Douglas had the second-highest number of popular votes, but he won only one state. He earned just 12 electoral votes. Breckinridge and Bell split electoral votes in other slave states.

The election results angered southerners. Lincoln did not campaign in their region and did not carry any southern states, but he became the next president. The election signaled that the South was losing its national political power.

The South Secedes

Lincoln insisted that he would not change slavery in the South. However, he said that slavery could not expand and thus would eventually die out completely. That idea angered many southerners.

Southerners' Reactions People in the South believed their economy and way of life would be destroyed without slave labor. They reacted immediately. Within a week of Lincoln's election, South Carolina's legislature called for a special convention. The delegates considered secession. Southern secessionists believed that they had a right to leave the Union. They pointed out that each of the original states had voluntarily joined the Union by holding a special convention that had ratified the Constitution. Surely, they reasoned, states could leave the Union by the same process.

Critics of secession thought this argument was ridiculous. President Buchanan said the Union was not "a mere voluntary association of States, to be dissolved at pleasure by any one of the contracting parties." President-elect Abraham Lincoln agreed, saying, "No State, upon its own mere motion, can lawfully get out of the Union." Lincoln added, "They can only do so against [the] law, and by revolution."

While South Carolina representatives were meeting in Charleston to discuss secession, Congress examined a plan to save the Union. Senator **John J. Crittenden** of Kentucky proposed a series of constitutional amendments that he believed would satisfy the South by protecting slavery. Crittenden hoped the country could avoid secession and a civil war.

Lincoln disagreed with Crittenden's plan. He believed there could be no compromise about the extension of slavery. Lincoln wrote, "The tug has to come and better now than later." A Senate committee voted on Crittenden's plan, and every Republican rejected it, as Lincoln had requested.

The Confederate States of America South Carolina elected to dissolve "the union now subsisting [existing] between South Carolina and other States" on December 20, 1860. Mississippi, Florida, Alabama, Georgia, Louisiana, and Texas also seceded to form the **Confederate States of America**, also called the Confederacy. Its new constitution guaranteed citizens the right to own slaves.

Delegates from seceded states elected **Jefferson Davis** of Mississippi as president of the Confederacy. Davis had hoped to be the commanding general of Mississippi's troops. He responded to the news of his election with reluctance.

Rebel Government
This photograph shows a crowd gathered at the inauguration of Jefferson Davis. The ceremony took place on February 18, 1861 on the steps of the state capitol in Montgomery, Alabama.

When the southern states seceded, the question of who owned federal property in the South arose. For instance, the forts in the harbor of Charleston, South Carolina, were federal property. However, Confederate president Davis and the Confederacy were ready to prevent the federal army from controlling the property.

Lincoln Takes Office President Lincoln was inaugurated on March 4, 1861. In writing his inaugural address, Lincoln looked to many of the nation's founding documents. Referring to the idea that governments receive "their just powers from the consent of the governed," a line from the Declaration of Independence, Lincoln stated, "This country, with its institutions, belongs to the people who inhabit it. Whenever they shall grow weary of the existing Government, they can exercise their *constitutional* right of amending it or their *revolutionary* right to dismember [take apart] or overthrow it. I can not be ignorant of the fact that many worthy and patriotic citizens are desirous [wanting] of having the National Constitution amended . . ."

While he believed that U.S. citizens had the power to change their government through majority consent, he opposed the idea that southern states could leave the Union because they were unhappy with the government's position on slavery.

He announced in his inaugural address that he would keep all government property in the seceding states. However, he also tried to convince southerners that his government would not provoke a war. He hoped that, given time, southern states would return to the Union.

Summary and Preview The secession of the southern states hinted at the violence to come. In the next module you will read about the Civil War.

Reading Check
Draw Conclusions
Why did some southern states secede from the Union?

Lesson 4 Assessment

Review Ideas, Terms, and People

1. **a. Recall** Why did John Brown want to seize the federal arsenal at Harpers Ferry?

   b. Explain Why did some abolitionists disagree with Brown's actions?

2. **a. Identify** List the candidates in the presidential election of 1860, and identify what party each supported.

   b. Predict How might Abraham Lincoln's victory in the election of 1860 lead to future problems?

3. **a. Identify** What states made up the Confederate States of America?

   b. Explain Why did Lincoln disagree with John J. Crittenden's plan to keep the Union together?

   c. Elaborate Do you believe that the southern states had the right to secede? Why or why not?

Critical Thinking

4. **Summarize** In this lesson you learned about key people and events that led to secession. Create a graphic organizer similar to the one below and use it to summarize the causes of secession.

Assess Primary and Secondary Sources

Define the Skill

All historical information comes from primary and secondary sources. *Primary sources* are documents written by someone who witnessed or took part in an event. They include diaries, letters, autobiographies, and newspaper reports. *Secondary sources* are accounts of events written after the events have occurred by someone who did not witness or take part in them. They retell, interpret, and summarize information from primary sources. History books and biographies are examples of secondary sources.

Historical sources often disagree. One writer's version of an event may be different from another writer's version. You must assess the reliability of a primary or secondary source in order to weigh its value to you as a source of accurate information.

Learn the Skill

Use these guidelines to analyze and evaluate primary and secondary sources.

1. Identify the nature of the material. Is it a first-hand, eyewitness account or is it based on information provided by others?

2. Evaluate the author. If the material is a secondary source, what qualifications does the author have to interpret the sources from which it came? If the material is a primary source, what was the author's connection to the event he or she is writing about?

3. Determine the audience. Was the source meant to be seen by the public? Was it meant for a friend, or for the writer alone? The intended audience can influence a source's content.

4. Determine the purpose. Even authors of primary sources can have reasons to distort the truth to suit their own purposes. Look for evidence of emotion, exaggeration, opinion, or bias that may have influenced the account.

5. Look for documentation. Look for other information or evidence that supports the source's account. Compare sources whenever possible.

Practice the Skill

The passage below concerns the attack on Lawrence, Kansas, that you read about in this module. The passage contains both a primary and a secondary source. The secondary account was written by John A. Garraty, a well-known historian. Review the information on the attack, analyze the passage, and answer the questions that follow.

"Sheriff Jones, at the head of an army of Missourians, marched into Lawrence. In broad daylight they threw the printing presses of two newspapers into a river. They burned down the Free State Hotel and other buildings. Antislavery Kansans seethed with rage. Here is how one eyewitness described the attack:

'Sheriff Jones, after looking at the flames rising from the hotel and saying that it was 'the happiest day of his life,' dismissed the troops and they began their lawless destruction.'"

1. Did the author of the primary source likely support the attackers or the people of Lawrence? What clues in the passage suggest this?

2. For whom was the primary source likely written?

3. Which source is more reliable for information about this incident? Explain why.

Module 17 Assessment

Review Vocabulary, Terms, and People

Identify the correct term or person from the module that best fits each of the following descriptions.

1. belief that voters should be given the right to decide if slavery would be permitted or banned

2. chief justice of the Supreme Court who wrote the majority opinion for the *Dred Scott* decision

3. Democratic candidate for president in 1852 who promised to enforce the Compromise of 1850 and the Fugitive Slave Act

4. a fugitive slave whose arrest led to violence between government officials and abolitionists

5. Republican candidate for the presidency in 1856 who opposed the spread of slavery in the West

6. slave who sued for freedom, claiming that by living in free territory, he had earned his freedom

7. Stephen Douglas's bill leaving states and territories to determine the issue of slavery through popular sovereignty

Comprehension and Critical Thinking

Lesson 1

8.
   a. **Describe** How did literature aid the anti-slavery movement?
   b. **Draw Conclusions** How did the issue of slavery promote sectionalism?
   c. **Evaluate** Do you think the Compromise of 1850 was a good solution? Explain your answer.

Lesson 2

9.
   a. **Identify** Who were the candidates in the presidential election of 1852, and what issues did each support?
   b. **Analyze** How did the Kansas-Nebraska Act lead to growing hostility between pro-slavery and antislavery supporters?
   c. **Elaborate** Why do you think "Bleeding Kansas" produced intense controversy among many Americans?

Lesson 3

10.
   a. **Identify** Who was Dred Scott, and why was his case important?
   b. **Analyze** How were political parties affected by the debate over slavery?
   c. **Elaborate** Why do you think Republicans challenged Stephen Douglas's run for the Senate?

Lesson 4

11.
   a. **Recall** Why did John Brown's raid on Harpers Ferry fail?
   b. **Explain** Why did the results of the election of 1860 anger southerners?
   c. **Draw Conclusions** Do you think that Lincoln could have avoided losing southern states to the Confederacy after he was elected in 1861? Explain why or why not.

Review Themes

12. Politics Copy the graphic organizer below. List the five most important events that led to the Civil War, and explain how each event increased conflict between the North and the South.

Events	Effect on Conflict

13. Politics How did sectionalism affect American politics?

14. Society and Culture What effect did Harriet Beecher Stowe's book *Uncle Tom's Cabin* have on the debate over slavery?

Reading Skills

Facts, Opinions, and the Past *Use the Reading Skills taught in this module to answer the question about the reading selection below.*

> In 1858 John Brown tried to start an uprising. He wanted to attack the federal arsenal in Virginia and seize weapons there. He planned to arm local slaves. Brown expected to kill or take hostage white southerners who stood in his way.

15. Based on the reading selection above, which of the following statements is an opinion?
 a. John Brown's raid was in 1858.
 b. John Brown hated all slaveholders.
 c. John Brown's raid took place in Virginia.
 d. Local slaves helped John Brown.

Social Studies Skills

Assess Primary and Secondary Sources *Use the Social Studies Skills taught in this module to answer the question below.*

16. Which of the following is *not* an example of a primary source used in this module?
 a. *A People's History of the United States* by Howard Zinn
 b. the "Seventh of March" speech by Daniel Webster
 c. Abraham Lincoln's "A House Divided" speech
 d. John Brown's last speech

Focus on Writing

17. Write an Autobiography When you read about history, it can be difficult to imagine how events you read about affected ordinary people. Write an autobiography of a fictional character, telling how the events covered in this module affected him or her. As you write the autobiography, be sure to mention each of the events and how your character heard about them, what he or she was doing at the time, how he or she felt about the event, and how it affected him or her. What are your character's hopes and fears for the future?

Module 18
The Civil War

Essential Question
How did the Civil War transform the nation?

About the Photo: Among those who marched off to war were these drummer boys of the Union army.

▷ Explore ONLINE!

HISTORY

VIDEOS, including...
- Emancipation Proclamation
- Battle of Antietam
- Indian Warriors
- 54th Regiment
- The Civil War: Gettysburg
- Sherman's March to the Sea

☑ Document-Based Investigations

☑ Graphic Organizers

☑ Interactive Games

☑ Animation: Ironclad Technology

☑ Image with Hotspots: Copperhead Political Cartoon

☑ Image Carousel: Civil War Families

In this module you will learn how the resources of the North enabled it to defeat the South in the Civil War.

What You Will Learn ...

Lesson 1: The War Begins **570**
The Big Idea Civil war broke out between the North and the South in 1861.

Lesson 2: The War in the East. **577**
The Big Idea Confederate and Union forces faced off in Virginia and at sea.

Lesson 3: The War in the West **583**
The Big Idea Fighting in the Civil War spread to the western United States.

Lesson 4: Daily Life during the War. **590**
The Big Idea The lives of many Americans were affected by the Civil War.

Lesson 5: The Tide of War Turns **598**
The Big Idea Union victories in 1863, 1864, and 1865 ended the Civil War.

United States		World
	1860	

1861 Confederate guns open fire on Fort Sumter on April 12. Confederates win the first battle of the Civil War on July 21 at Bull Run in Virginia. — **1861** — **1861** Great Britain and France decide to buy cotton from Egypt instead of from the Confederacy.

1862 The *Monitor* fights the *Virginia* on March 9. — **1862** — **1862** An imperial decree expels foreigners from Japan.

1863 The Emancipation Proclamation is issued on January 1. ∨ — **1863**

1864 With the support of French troops Archduke Maximilian of Austria becomes emperor of Mexico. >

— **1864** —

1864 The Taiping Rebellion in China ends after the capture of Nanjing in July.

1865 General Robert E. Lee surrenders to General Ulysses S. Grant on April 9. ∨ — **1865**

| | 1866 | |

Reading Social Studies

THEME FOCUS:

Politics, Society and Culture

As you read this module about the Civil War, you will see that this was a time in our history dominated by two major concerns: politics and society and culture. You will not only read about the political decisions made during this war, but also you will see how the war affected all of American society. You will read about the causes and the key events during the war and the many consequences of this war. This module tells of one of the most important events in our history.

READING FOCUS:

Supporting Facts and Details

Main ideas and big ideas are just that, ideas. How do we know what those ideas really mean?

Understand Ideas and Their Support A main idea or big idea may be a kind of summary statement or it may be a statement of the author's opinion. Either way, a good reader looks to see what support—facts and various kinds of details—the writer provides. If the writer doesn't provide good support, the ideas may not be trustworthy.

Notice how the passage below uses facts and details to support the main idea.

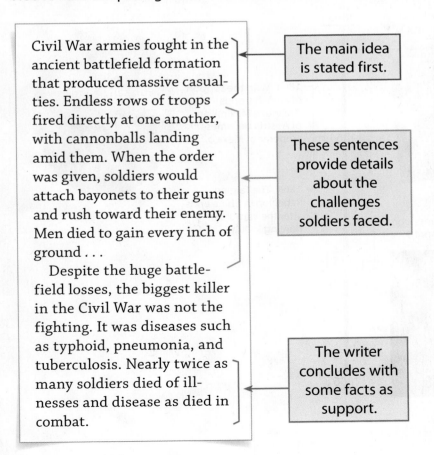

Civil War armies fought in the ancient battlefield formation that produced massive casualties. Endless rows of troops fired directly at one another, with cannonballs landing amid them. When the order was given, soldiers would attach bayonets to their guns and rush toward their enemy. Men died to gain every inch of ground . . .

Despite the huge battlefield losses, the biggest killer in the Civil War was not the fighting. It was diseases such as typhoid, pneumonia, and tuberculosis. Nearly twice as many soldiers died of illnesses and disease as died in combat.

The main idea is stated first.

These sentences provide details about the challenges soldiers faced.

The writer concludes with some facts as support.

Writers support propositions with . . .

1. **Facts and statistics—** statements that can be proved; facts in number form

2. **Examples—**specific instances that illustrate the facts

3. **Anecdotes—**brief stories that help explain the facts

4. **Definitions—**explanation of unusual terms or words

5. **Comments from the experts or eyewitnesses—** statements from reliable sources

You Try It!

The following passage is from the module you are about to read. As you read it, look for the writer's main idea and support.

> In February 1862 Grant led an assault force into Tennessee. With help from navy gunboats, Grant's Army of the Tennessee took two outposts on key rivers in the West. On February 6 he captured Fort Henry on the Tennessee River. Several days later he took Fort Donelson on the Cumberland River.
>
> Fort Donelson's commander asked for the terms of surrender. Grant replied, "No terms except an unconditional and immediate surrender can be accepted." The fort surrendered. The North gave a new name to Grant's initials: "Unconditional Surrender" Grant.

After you read the passage, answer the following questions.

1. Which sentence best states the writer's main idea?
   a. The fort surrendered.
   b. In February 1862 Grant led an assault force into Tennessee.
   c. Fort Donelson's commander asked for the terms of surrender.

2. Which method of support is not used to support the main idea?
   a. facts
   b. comments from experts or eyewitnesses
   c. anecdotes

3. Which sentence in this passage provides a comment from an expert or eyewitness?

As you read Module 18, pay attention to the details that the writers have chosen to support their main ideas.

Key Terms and People

Lesson 1
Fort Sumter
border states
Winfield Scott
cotton diplomacy

Lesson 2
Thomas "Stonewall" Jackson
First Battle of Bull Run
George B. McClellan
Robert E. Lee
Seven Days' Battles
Second Battle of Bull Run
Battle of Antietam
ironclads

Lesson 3
Ulysses S. Grant
Battle of Shiloh
David Farragut
Siege of Vicksburg

Lesson 4
emancipation
Emancipation Proclamation
contrabands
54th Massachusetts Infantry
Copperheads
habeas corpus
Clara Barton

Lesson 5
Battle of Gettysburg
George Pickett
Pickett's Charge
Gettysburg Address
Wilderness Campaign
William Tecumseh Sherman
total war
Appomattox Courthouse

The War Begins

You are a college student in Charleston in early 1861. Seven southern states have left the Union and formed their own government. All-out war seems unavoidable. Your friends have begun to volunteer for either the Union or the Confederate forces. You are torn between loyalty to your home state and to the United States.

Would you join the Union or the Confederate army?

The Big Idea

Civil war broke out between the North and the South in 1861.

Main Ideas

- Following the outbreak of war at Fort Sumter, Americans chose sides.
- The Union and the Confederacy prepared for war.

Key Terms and People

Fort Sumter
border states
Winfield Scott
cotton diplomacy

Americans Choose Sides

Furious at Lincoln's election and fearing a federal invasion, seven southern states had seceded. The new Commander in Chief tried desperately to save the Union.

In his inaugural address, Lincoln promised not to end slavery where it existed. The federal government "will not assail [attack] you. You can have no conflict without being yourselves the aggressors," he said, trying to calm southerners' fears. However, Lincoln also stated his intention to preserve the Union. He believed that saving the Union would help to save democracy. If the Union and its government failed, then monarchs could say that people were unable to rule themselves. As a result, Lincoln refused to recognize secession, declaring the Union to be "unbroken."

In fact, after decades of painful compromises, the Union was badly broken. From the Lower South, a battle cry was arising, born out of fear, rage—and excitement. Confederate officials began seizing branches of the federal mint, arsenals, and military outposts. In a last-ditch effort to avoid war between the states, Secretary of State Seward suggested a united effort of threatening war against Spain and France for interfering in Mexico and the Caribbean. In the highly charged atmosphere, it would take only a spark to unleash the heat of war.

In 1861 that spark occurred at **Fort Sumter**, a federal outpost in Charleston, South Carolina, that was attacked by

In Charleston all activity came to a complete stop. Citizens crowded rooftops to watch the battle.

Charleston

Castle Pinckney

The first shot fired on Fort Sumter was fired from Fort Johnson.

Charleston Harbor

Shots fired at the ironclad battery did little damage.

Fort Johnson

Fort Sumter

Fort Sumter was strategically placed to control Charleston Harbor.

Cummings Point

Fort Moultrie

Atlantic Ocean

Charleston

ATLANTIC OCEAN

Fort Sumter

The first shots of the Civil War were fired at Fort Sumter, South Carolina. Although no one was killed there, the bloodiest war in the country's history had begun.

Interpret Maps

1. **Human-Environment Interaction** Why would the Union army need to resupply Fort Sumter?

2. **Place** What advantages would a floating battery have?

Confederate troops, beginning the Civil War. Determined to seize the fortress—which controlled the entrance to Charleston Harbor—the Confederates ringed the harbor with heavy guns. Instead of surrendering the fort, Lincoln decided to send in ships to provide badly needed supplies to defend the fort. Confederate officials demanded that the federal troops evacuate. The fort's commander, Major Robert Anderson, refused.

Now it was Jefferson Davis who faced a dilemma. If he did nothing, he would damage the image of the Confederacy as a sovereign, independent nation. On the other hand, if Davis ordered an attack on Fort Sumter, he would turn peaceful secession into war. Davis chose war. Before sunrise on April 12, 1861, Confederate guns opened fire on Fort Sumter. A witness wrote that the first shots brought "every soldier in the harbor to his feet, and every man, woman, and child in the city of Charleston from their beds." The Civil War had begun.

The fort, although massive, stood little chance. Its heavy guns faced the Atlantic Ocean, not the shore. After 34 hours of cannon blasts, Fort Sumter surrendered. "The last ray of hope for preserving the Union has expired at the assault upon Fort Sumter . . ." Lincoln wrote.

Reaction to Lincoln's Call The fall of Fort Sumter stunned the North. Lincoln declared the South to be in a state of rebellion and asked state governors for 75,000 militiamen to put down the rebellion. States now had to choose: Would they secede, or would they stay in the Union? Democratic senator Stephen Douglas, speaking in support of Lincoln's call for troops, declared, "There can be no neutrals in this war, *only patriots—or traitors*."

Pennsylvania, New Jersey, and the states north of them rallied to the president's call. The crucial slave states of the Upper South—North Carolina, Tennessee, Virginia, and Arkansas—seceded and joined the Confederate States of Texas, Louisiana, Mississippi, Alabama, Georgia, Florida, and South Carolina. The slave states of the Upper South provided soldiers and supplies to the rest of the South. The western territories were disputed between the Union and the Confederacy. Mary Boykin Chesnut, whose husband became a Confederate congressman, wrote in her diary:

"I did not know that one could live in such days of excitement. . . . Everybody tells you half of something, and then rushes off . . . to hear the last news."

—Mary Boykin Chesnut, quoted in *Mary Chesnut's Civil War*, edited by C. Vann Woodward

Recruitment posters like this one made use of eye-catching symbols and colors to entice Pennsylvanians to fight for the Union.

Wedged between the North and the South were the key **border states** of Delaware, Kentucky, Maryland, and Missouri—slave states that did not join the Confederacy. Kentucky and Missouri controlled parts of important rivers. Maryland separated the Union capital, Washington, DC, from the North.

People in the border states were deeply divided on the war. The president's own wife, Mary Todd Lincoln, had four brothers from Kentucky who fought for the Confederacy. Lincoln sent federal troops into the border states to help keep them in the Union. He also sent soldiers into western Virginia, where Union loyalties were strong. West Virginia set up its own state government in 1863.

Northern Resources Numbers tell an important story about the Civil War. Consider the North's advantages. It could draw soldiers and workers from a population of 22 million. The South had only 5.5 million people to draw from. One of the greatest advantages in the North was the region's network of roads, canals, and railroads. Some 22,000 miles of railroad track could move soldiers and supplies throughout the North. The South had only about 9,000 miles of track.

In the North, the Civil War stimulated economic growth. To supply the military, the production of coal, iron, wheat, and wool increased. Also, the export of corn, wheat, beef, and pork to Europe doubled. In the South, the export of resources decreased because of the Union blockade.

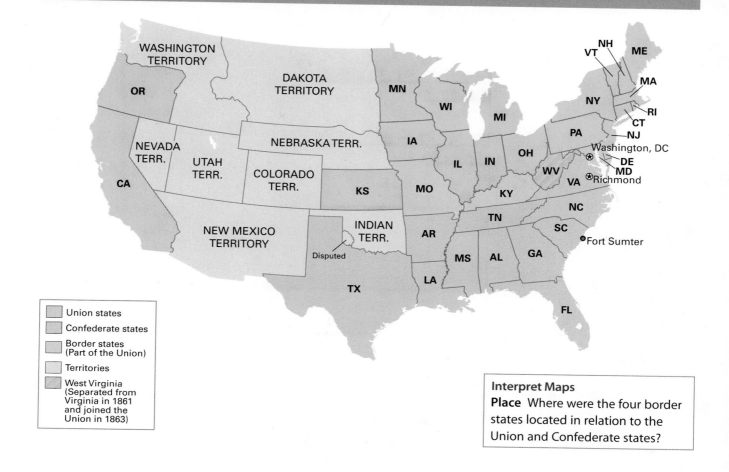

Union states
Confederate states
Border states (Part of the Union)
Territories
West Virginia (Separated from Virginia in 1861 and joined the Union in 1863)

Interpret Maps
Place Where were the four border states located in relation to the Union and Confederate states?

Finally, the Union had money. It had a more developed economy, banking system, and a currency called greenbacks. The South had to start printing its own Confederate dollars. Some states printed their own money, too. This led to financial chaos.

Taking advantage of the Union's strengths, General **Winfield Scott** developed a two-part strategy: (1) destroy the South's economy with a naval blockade of southern ports; (2) gain control of the Mississippi River to divide the South. Other leaders urged an attack on Richmond, Virginia, the Confederate capital.

Southern Resources The Confederacy had advantages as well. With its strong military tradition, the South put many brilliant officers into battle. Southern farms provided food for its armies. The South's best advantage, however, was strategic. It needed only to defend itself until the North grew tired of fighting.

The North had to invade and control the South. To accomplish this, the Union army had to travel huge distances. For example, the distance from northern Virginia to central Georgia is about the length of Scotland and England combined. Because of distances such as this, the North had to maintain long supply lines.

Resources of the North and South

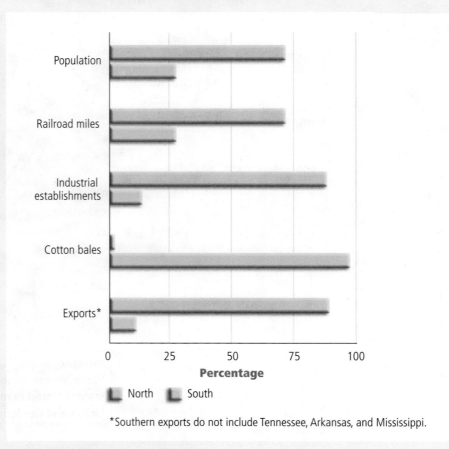

*Southern exports do not include Tennessee, Arkansas, and Mississippi.

Analyze Visuals
1. Do you think the North or the South could maintain better supply lines for their troops? Explain.
2. Do you think the North or the South could provide more weapons for their troops? Explain.

In addition, wilderness covered much of the South. Armies found this land difficult to cross. Also, in Virginia many of the rivers ran from east to west. Because of this, they formed a natural defense against an army that attacked from the north to the south. As a result, northern generals were often forced to attack Confederate troops from the side rather than from the front. Furthermore, because southerners fought mostly on their home soil, they were often familiar with the area.

The South hoped to wear down the North and to capture Washington, DC. Confederate president Jefferson Davis also tried to win foreign allies through **cotton diplomacy**. This was the idea that Great Britain would support the Confederacy because it needed the South's raw cotton to supply its booming textile industry. Cotton diplomacy did not work as the South had hoped. Britain had large supplies of cotton, and it got more from India and Egypt.

Reading Check
Compare What advantages did the North and South have leading up to the war?

Union and Confederate Soldiers

Early in the war, uniforms differed greatly, especially in the Confederate army. Uniforms became simpler and more standard as the war dragged on.

The soldiers carried food, extra ammunition, and other items in their haversacks.

Each soldier was armed with a bayonet, a knife that can be attached to the barrel of a rifle. The bayonets were stored in scabbards on their belts.

Confederate Soldier

Both soldiers were also armed with single-shot, muzzle-loading rifles.

Union Soldier

Analyze Visuals
How are the Union and Confederate uniforms and equipment similar and different?

Preparing for War

The North and the South now rushed to war. Neither side was prepared for the tragedy to come.

Volunteer Armies Volunteer militias had sparked the revolution that created the United States. Now they would battle for its future. At the start of the war, the Union army had only 16,000 soldiers. Within months that number had swelled to a half million soldiers. Southern men rose up to defend their land and their ways of life. Virginian Thomas Webber came to fight "against the invading foe [enemy] who now pollute the sacred soil of my beloved native state." When Union soldiers asked one captured rebel why he was fighting, he replied, "I'm fighting because you're down here."

Helping the Troops Civilians on both sides helped those in uniform. They raised money, provided aid for soldiers and their families, and ran emergency hospitals. Dr. Elizabeth Blackwell, the first woman to receive a license to practice medicine, organized a group that pressured President Lincoln to form the U.S. Sanitary Commission in June 1861. The Sanitary, as it was called, was run by clergyman Henry Bellows. Tens of thousands of volunteers worked with the U.S. Sanitary Commission to send bandages, medicines, and food to Union army camps and hospitals. Some 3,000 women served as nurses in the Union army.

Training the Soldiers Both the Union and Confederate armies faced shortages of clothing, food, and even rifles. While the U.S. Army troops had standard issue uniforms, volunteer militias frequently had their own uniforms and individual volunteers often simply wore their own clothes. Eventually, each side chose a color for their uniforms. The Union chose blue. The Confederates wore gray.

The problem with volunteers was that many of them had no idea how to fight. Schoolteachers, farmers, and laborers all had to learn the combat basics of marching, shooting, and using bayonets.

Days in camp were long and boring. They typically began at 5 a.m. in summer and 6 a.m. in winter. After breakfast, the men took part in up to five daily drills. During these two-hour sessions they learned and practiced battlefield maneuvers. Between drills, the troops cleaned the camp, gathered firewood, wrote letters home, and played games. With visions of glory and action, many young soldiers were eager to fight. They would not have to wait long.

Discipline and drill were used to turn raw volunteers into an efficient fighting machine. During a battle, the success or failure of a regiment often depended on its discipline—how well it responded to orders.

Volunteers also learned how to use rifles. Eventually, soldiers were expected to be able to load, aim, and fire their rifles three times in one minute. The quality of the weapons provided varied greatly. Most soldiers favored the Springfield and Enfield rifles for their accuracy. On the other hand, soldiers often complained about their Austrian and Belgian rifles. A soldier remarked, "I don't believe one could hit the broadside of a barn with them."

On average, soldiers spent about 75 percent of their time in camp. In wet weather, camps were a sea of mud. In dry weather, they were filled with clouds of dust. The Union army provided the infantry with two-person tents. However, soldiers often discarded these tents in favor of more portable ones. The Confederate army did not usually issue tents. Instead, Confederates often used tents that were captured from the Union army.

Reading Check
Summarize
How did soldiers and civilians prepare for war?

Summary and Preview As citizens chose sides in the Civil War, civilians and soldiers alike became involved in the war effort. In the next lesson you will learn about some early battles in the war, both on land and at sea.

Lesson 1 Assessment

Review Ideas, Terms, and People

1. a. **Identify** What event triggered the war between the Union and the Confederacy?

   b. **Contrast** How did the Union's strategy differ from that of the Confederacy?

   c. **Evaluate** Which side do you believe was better prepared for war? Explain your answer.

2. a. **Describe** How did women take part in the war?

   b. **Summarize** In what ways were the armies of the North and South unprepared for war?

   c. **Elaborate** Why did men volunteer to fight in the war?

Critical Thinking

3. **Compare and Contrast** In this lesson you learned about the preparations for war by the North and the South. Create a chart similar to the one below and use it to show the strengths and weaknesses of each side in the war.

	Union	Confederacy
Strengths		
Weaknesses		

The War in the East

The Big Idea

Confederate and Union forces faced off in Virginia and at sea.

Main Ideas

- Union and Confederate forces fought for control of the war in Virginia.
- The Battle of Antietam gave the North a slight advantage.
- The Confederacy attempted to break the Union naval blockade.

Key Terms and People

Thomas "Stonewall" Jackson
First Battle of Bull Run
George B. McClellan
Robert E. Lee
Seven Days' Battles
Second Battle of Bull Run
Battle of Antietam
ironclads

If YOU were there . . .

You live in Washington, DC, in July 1861. You and your friends are on your way to Manassas, near Washington, to watch the battle there. Everyone expects a quick Union victory. Your wagon is loaded with food for a picnic, and people are in a holiday mood. You see some members of Congress riding toward Manassas, too. Maybe this battle will end the war!

Why would you want to watch this battle?

War in Virginia

The troops that met in the first major battle of the Civil War found that it was no picnic. In July 1861 Lincoln ordered General Irvin McDowell to lead his 35,000-man army from the Union capital, Washington, to the Confederate capital, Richmond. The soldiers were barely trained. McDowell complained that they "stopped every moment to pick blackberries or get water; they would not keep in the ranks." The first day's march covered only five miles.

Bull Run/Manassas McDowell's army was headed to Manassas, Virginia, an important railroad junction. If McDowell could seize Manassas, he would control the best route to the Confederate capital. Some 22,000 Confederate troops under the command of General Pierre G. T. Beauregard were waiting for McDowell and his troops along a creek called Bull Run. For two days Union troops tried to find a way around the Confederates. During that time, Beauregard requested assistance, and General Joseph E. Johnston headed toward Manassas with another 10,000 Confederate troops. By July 21, 1861, they had all arrived.

In this painting of the First Battle of Bull Run, Confederate general Thomas "Stonewall" Jackson looks over the battlefield.

That morning, Union troops managed to cross the creek and drive back the left side of the Confederate line. Yet one unit held firmly in place.

"There is Jackson standing like a stone wall!" cried one southern officer. "Rally behind the Virginians!" At that moment General **Thomas "Stonewall" Jackson** earned his famous nickname.

A steady stream of Virginia volunteers arrived to counter the attack. The Confederates surged forward. One eyewitness described the scene.

> "There is smoke, dust, wild talking, shouting; hissings, howlings, explosions. It is a new, strange, unanticipated experience to the soldiers of both armies, far different from what they thought it would be."
>
> —Charles Coffin, quoted in *Voices of the Civil War* by Richard Wheeler

The battle raged through the day, with rebel soldiers still arriving. Finally, the weary Union troops gave out. They tried to make an orderly retreat back across the creek, but the roads were clogged with the fancy carriages of panicked spectators. The Union army scattered in the chaos.

The Confederates lacked the strength to push north and capture Washington, DC. But clearly, the rebels had won the day. The **First Battle of Bull Run** was the first major battle of the Civil War and the Confederates' victory. The battle is also known as the First Battle of Manassas. It shattered the North's hopes of winning the war quickly.

More Battles in Virginia The shock at Bull Run persuaded Lincoln of the need for a better-trained army. He put his hopes in General **George B. McClellan**. The general assembled a highly disciplined force of 100,000 soldiers called the Army of the Potomac. The careful McClellan spent

Explore ONLINE!

Battles in the East

Antietam
Sep. 1862

MARYLAND

WEST VIRGINIA

Shenandoah Valley

Potomac River

Washington, DC

Manassas Junction

Bull Run
July 1861 &
Aug. 1862

Fair Oaks
May–June
1862

Richmond

James River

Seven Days
June 1862

Yorktown

VIRGINIA

Chesapeake Bay

York R.

ATLANTIC OCEAN

Union state

West Virginia (Separated from Virginia in 1861 and joined the Union in 1863)

Confederate state

Union forces

Union victory

Confederate forces

Confederate victory

0   15   30 Miles

0   15   30 Kilometers

Interpret Maps

1. **Location** Which battle was fought in Maryland?

2. **Human-Environment Interaction** How did geography influence the movement of forces?

Robert E. Lee 1807–1870

Robert E. Lee was born into a wealthy Virginia family and graduated second in his class from West Point, the U.S. military academy. He fought in the Mexican-American War of 1846, helping to capture Veracruz. When the Civil War began, President Lincoln asked Lee to lead the Union army. Although Lee opposed secession, he declined Lincoln's offer and resigned from the U.S. Army to become a general in the Confederate army. As a general, Lee was brilliant, but a lack of supplies from civilian leaders weakened his position. His soldiers—some of whom called him

Uncle Robert—almost worshiped him because he insisted on sharing their hardships. After the war ended, Lee became president of Washington College in Virginia, now known as Washington and Lee University. Lee swore renewed allegiance to the United States, but Congress accidentally neglected to restore his citizenship. Still, Lee never spoke bitterly of northerners or the Union, and many southerners saw Lee as a war hero.

Draw Conclusions
How did Lee's choice reflect the division of the states?

months training. However, because he overestimated the size of the Confederate army, McClellan hesitated to attack. Lincoln grew impatient. Finally, in the spring of 1862 McClellan launched an effort to capture Richmond, called the "Peninsular Campaign." Instead of marching south for a direct assault, McClellan slowly brought his force through the peninsula between the James and York rivers. More time slipped away.

The South feared that McClellan would receive reinforcements from Washington. To prevent this, Stonewall Jackson launched an attack toward Washington. Although the attack was pushed back, it prevented the Union from sending reinforcements to McClellan.

In June 1862, with McClellan's force poised outside Richmond, the Confederate army in Virginia came under the command of General **Robert E. Lee**. A graduate of the U.S. Military Academy at West Point, Lee had served in the Mexican War and had led federal troops at Harpers Ferry. Lee was willing to take risks and make unpredictable moves to throw Union forces off balance.

During the summer of 1862, Lee strengthened his positions. On June 26 he launched a series of clashes known as the **Seven Days' Battles** that forced the Union army to retreat from near Richmond. Confederate general D. H. Hill described one failed attack. "It was not war—it was murder," he said. Lee saved Richmond and forced McClellan to retreat. A frustrated Lincoln ordered General John Pope to march directly on Richmond.

Jackson wanted to defeat Pope's army before it could join up with McClellan's larger Army of the Potomac. Jackson's troops met Pope's Union forces on the battlefield in August 1862. The three-day battle became known as the **Second Battle of Bull Run**, or the Second Battle of Manassas.

The first day's fighting was savage. Captain George Fairfield of the 7th Wisconsin regiment later recalled, "What a slaughter! No one appeared to know the object of the fight, and there we stood for one hour, the men falling all around." The fighting ended in a stalemate.

On the second day, Pope found Jackson's troops along an unfinished railroad grade. Pope hurled his men against the Confederates. But the attacks were pushed back with heavy casualties on both sides.

On the third day, the Confederates crushed the Union army's assault and forced it to retreat in defeat. The Confederates had won a major victory, and General Robert E. Lee decided it was time to take the war to the North.

Battle of Antietam

Confederate leaders hoped to follow up Lee's successes in Virginia with a major victory on northern soil. On September 4, 1862, some 40,000 Confederate soldiers began crossing into Maryland. General Robert E. Lee decided to divide his army. He sent about half of his troops, under the command of Stonewall Jackson, to Harpers Ferry. There they defeated a Union force and captured the town. Meanwhile, Lee arrived in the town of Frederick and issued a Proclamation to the People of Maryland, urging them to join the Confederates. However, his words would not be enough to convince Marylanders to abandon the Union. Union soldiers, however, found a copy of Lee's battle plan, which had been left at an abandoned Confederate camp. General McClellan learned that Lee had divided his army in order to attack Harpers Ferry. However, McClellan hesitated to attack. As a result, the Confederates had time to reunite.

The two armies met along Antietam Creek in Maryland on September 17, 1862. The battle lasted for hours. By the end of the day, the Union had

Reading Check
Sequence List in order the events that forced Union troops out of Virginia.

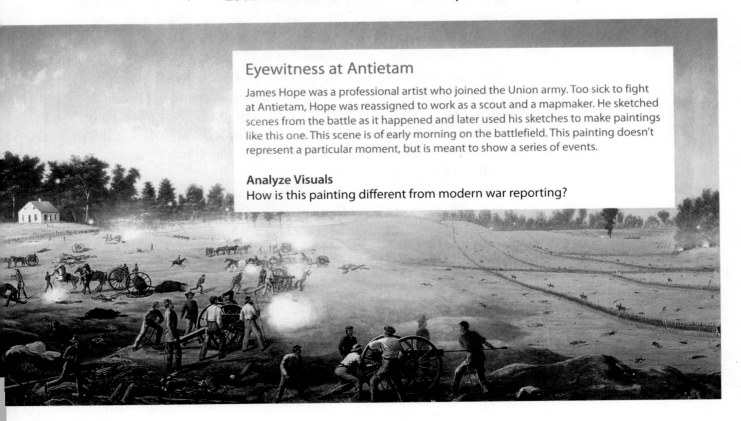

Eyewitness at Antietam

James Hope was a professional artist who joined the Union army. Too sick to fight at Antietam, Hope was reassigned to work as a scout and a mapmaker. He sketched scenes from the battle as it happened and later used his sketches to make paintings like this one. This scene is of early morning on the battlefield. This painting doesn't represent a particular moment, but is meant to show a series of events.

Analyze Visuals
How is this painting different from modern war reporting?

suffered more than 12,000 casualties. The Confederates endured more than 13,000 casualties. Union officer A. H. Nickerson later recalled, "It seemed that everybody near me was killed." The **Battle of Antietam**, also known as the Battle of Sharpsburg, was the bloodiest single-day battle of the Civil War—and of U.S. history. More soldiers were killed and wounded at the Battle of Antietam than the deaths of all Americans in the American Revolution, War of 1812, and Mexican-American War combined.

During the battle, McClellan kept four divisions of soldiers in reserve and refused to use them to attack Lee's devastated army. McClellan was convinced that Lee was massing reserves for a counterattack. Those reserves did not exist. Despite this blunder, Antietam was an important victory. Lee's northward advance had been stopped.

Reading Check
Analyze Why was the Battle of Antietam significant?

Breaking the Union's Blockade

While the two armies fought for control of the land, the Union navy controlled the sea. The North had most of the U.S. Navy's small fleet, and many experienced naval officers had remained loyal to the Union. The North also had enough industry to build more ships. The Confederacy turned to British companies for new ships.

The Union's Naval Strategy The Union navy quickly mobilized to set up a blockade of southern ports. The blockade largely prevented the South from selling or receiving goods, and it seriously damaged the southern economy.

The blockade was hard to maintain because the Union navy had to patrol thousands of miles of coastline from Virginia to Texas. The South used small, fast ships to outrun the larger Union warships. Most of these blockade runners traveled to the Bahamas or Nassau to buy supplies for the Confederacy. These ships, however, could not make up for the South's

Historical Source

Anaconda Plan

This cartoon shows visually the North's plan to cut off supplies to the South through naval blockades, a strategy called the Anaconda Plan.

Why is the snake's head red, white, and blue?

How does the cartoonist show what the snake represents?

Analyze Historical Sources
Why do you think the plan was called the Anaconda Plan?

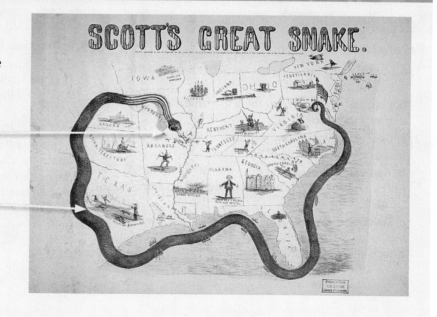

SCOTT'S GREAT SNAKE.

loss of trade. The Union blockade reduced the number of ships entering southern ports from 6,000 to 800 per year.

Clash of the Ironclads Hoping to take away the Union's advantage at sea, the Confederacy turned to a new type of warship—**ironclads**, or ships heavily armored with iron. The British government neglected to stop these ships from being delivered, in violation of its pledge of neutrality. The Confederates had captured a Union steamship, the *Merrimack*, and turned it into an ironclad, renamed the *Virginia*. One Union sailor described the **innovation** as "a huge half-submerged crocodile." In early March 1862 the ironclad sailed into Hampton Roads, Virginia, an important waterway guarded by Union ships. Before nightfall, the *Virginia* easily sank two of the Union's wooden warships, while it received minor damage.

Academic Vocabulary
innovation a new idea or way of doing something

The Union navy had already built its own ironclad, the *Monitor*, designed by Swedish-born engineer John Ericsson. Ericsson's ship had unusual new features, such as a revolving gun tower. One Confederate soldier called the *Monitor* "a tin can on a shingle!" Although small, the *Monitor* carried powerful guns and had thick plating.

When the *Virginia* returned to Hampton Roads later that month, the *Monitor* was waiting. After several hours of fighting, neither ship was seriously damaged, but the *Monitor* forced the *Virginia* to withdraw. This success saved the Union fleet and continued the blockade. The clash of the ironclads also signaled a revolution in naval warfare. The days of wooden warships powered by wind and sails were drawing to a close.

Reading Check
Evaluate How effective was the Union blockade?

The *Monitor* sank in North Carolina in the winter of 1862. Scientists located the shipwreck in 1973, and remains of the ship are part of the exhibit at the USS *Monitor* Center, which opened in 2007.

Summary and Preview The early battles of the Civil War were centered in the East. In the next lesson you will read about battles in the West.

Lesson 2 Assessment

Review Ideas, Terms, and People

1. **a. Identify** List the early battles in the East and the outcome of each battle.

   b. Elaborate Why do you think the Union lost the First Battle of Bull Run?

2. **a. Describe** What costly mistake did the Confederacy make before the Battle of Antietam?

   b. Analyze What was the outcome of the Battle of Antietam, and what effect did it have on both the North and the South?

   c. Elaborate Why do you think General George B. McClellan did not finish off General Robert E. Lee's troops when he had the chance?

3. **a. Describe** What was the Union's strategy in the war at sea?

   b. Draw Conclusions Why were ironclads more successful than older, wooden ships?

Critical Thinking

4. **Support a Point of View** In this lesson you learned about the Civil War battles in the East and at sea. Create a chart similar to the one below and use it to show which three conflicts you think were the most significant and why.

Most Significant	Why

The War in the West

The Big Idea

Fighting in the Civil War spread to the western United States.

Main Ideas

- Union strategy in the West centered on control of the Mississippi River.

- Confederate and Union troops struggled for dominance in the Far West.

Key Terms and People

Ulysses S. Grant
Battle of Shiloh
David Farragut
Siege of Vicksburg

If YOU were there . . .

You live in the city of Vicksburg, set on high bluffs above the Mississippi River. Vicksburg is vital to the control of the river, and Confederate defenses are strong. But the Union general is determined to take the town. For weeks you have been surrounded and besieged. Cannon shells burst overhead, day and night. Some have fallen on nearby homes. Supplies of food are running low.

How would you survive this siege?

Union Strategy in the West

While Lincoln fumed over the cautious, hesitant General McClellan, he had no such problems with **Ulysses S. Grant**. Bold and restless, Grant grew impatient when he was asked to lead defensive military maneuvers. He wanted to be on the attack. As a commander of forces in the Union's western campaign, he would get his wish.

The western campaign focused on taking control of the Mississippi River. This strategy would cut off the eastern part of the Confederacy from sources of food production in Arkansas, Louisiana, and Texas. From bases on the Mississippi, the Union army could attack southern communication and transportation networks.

In February 1862 Grant led an assault force into Tennessee. With help from navy gunboats, Grant's Army of the Tennessee took two outposts on key rivers in the West. On February 6 he captured Fort Henry on the Tennessee River. Several days later he took Fort Donelson on the Cumberland River.

Fort Donelson's commander asked for the terms of surrender. Grant replied, "No terms except an unconditional and immediate surrender can be accepted." The fort surrendered. The North gave a new name to Grant's initials: "Unconditional Surrender" Grant.

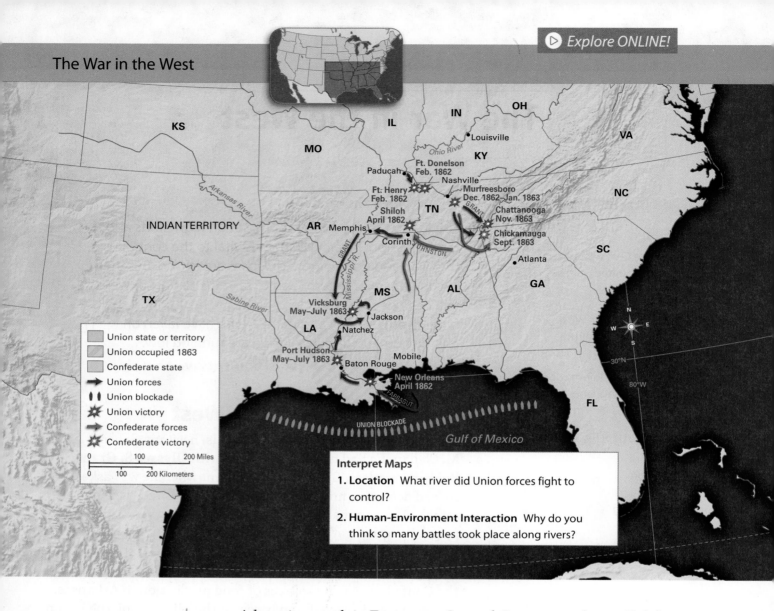

Map labels:

KS

MO

IL

IN

OH

Louisville

VA

KY

Ohio River

Paducah

Ft. Donelson
Feb. 1862

Nashville

Murfreesboro
Dec. 1862–Jan. 1863

NC

Ft. Henry
Feb. 1862

Shiloh
April 1862

TN

GRANT

Chattanooga
Nov. 1863

Arkansas River

INDIAN TERRITORY

AR

Memphis

Corinth

JOHNSTON

Chickamauga
Sept. 1863

SC

Atlanta

GRANT

Mississippi R.

Vicksburg
May–July 1863

MS

AL

GA

TX

Sabine River

Jackson

LA

Natchez

Port Hudson
May–July 1863

Baton Rouge

Mobile

New Orleans
April 1862

FARRAGUT

30°N

80°W

FL

UNION BLOCKADE

Gulf of Mexico

Legend:

- Union state or territory
- Union occupied 1863
- Confederate state
- Union forces
- Union blockade
- Union victory
- Confederate forces
- Confederate victory

0   100   200 Miles
0   100   200 Kilometers

Interpret Maps

1. **Location** What river did Union forces fight to control?

2. **Human-Environment Interaction** Why do you think so many battles took place along rivers?

Advancing south in Tennessee, General Grant paused near Shiloh Church to await the arrival of the Army of the Ohio. Grant knew that the large rebel army of General A. S. Johnston was nearby in Corinth, Mississippi, but he did not expect an attack. Instead of setting up defenses, he worked on drilling his new recruits.

In the early morning of April 6, 1862, the rebels sprang on Grant's sleepy camp. This began the **Battle of Shiloh**, in which the Union army gained greater control of the Mississippi River valley.

During the bloody two-day battle, each side gained and lost ground. Johnston was killed on the first day. The arrival of the Ohio force helped Grant regain territory and push the enemy back into Mississippi. The armies finally gave out, each with about 10,000 casualties. Both sides claimed victory, but, in fact, the victor was Grant.

The Fall of New Orleans As Grant battled his way down the Mississippi, the Union navy prepared to blast its way upriver to meet him. The first obstacle was the port of New Orleans, the largest city in the Confederacy and the gateway to the Mississippi River.

David Farragut 1801–1870

David Farragut was born in Tennessee to a Spanish father and an American mother. At age seven Farragut was adopted by a family friend who agreed to train the young boy for the navy. Farragut received his first navy position—midshipman at large—at age nine and commanded his first vessel at 12. He spent the rest of his life in the U.S. Navy. Farragut helped the war effort of the North by leading key attacks on the southern ports of Vicksburg and New Orleans.

Draw Inferences
How did Farragut help the war effort of the North?

With 18 ships and 700 men, Admiral **David Farragut** approached the two forts that guarded the entrance to New Orleans from the Gulf of Mexico. Unable to destroy the forts, Farragut decided to race past them.

The risky operation would take place at night. Farragut had his wooden ships wrapped in heavy chains to protect them like ironclads. Sailors slapped Mississippi mud on the ships' hulls to make them hard to see. Trees were tied to the masts to make the ships look like the forested shore.

Before dawn on April 24, 1862, the warships made their daring dash. The Confederates fired at Farragut's ships from the shore and from gunboats. They launched burning rafts, one of which scorched Farragut's own ship. But his fleet slipped by the twin forts and made it to New Orleans. The city fell on April 29.

Farragut sailed up the Mississippi River, taking Baton Rouge, Louisiana, and Natchez, Mississippi. He then approached the city of Vicksburg, Mississippi.

The Siege of Vicksburg Vicksburg's geography made invasion all but impossible. Perched on 200-foot-high cliffs above the Mississippi River, the city could rain down firepower on enemy ships or on soldiers trying to scale the cliffs. Deep gorges surrounded the city, turning back land assaults. Nevertheless, Farragut ordered Vicksburg to surrender.

> "Mississippians don't know, and refuse to learn, how to surrender . . . If Commodore Farragut . . . can teach them, let [him] come and try."
> —Colonel James L. Autry, military commander of Vicksburg

Farragut's guns had trouble reaching the city above. It was up to General Grant. His solution was to starve the city into surrender.

General Grant's troops began the **Siege of Vicksburg** in mid-May 1863, cutting off the city and shelling it repeatedly. As food ran out, residents and soldiers survived by eating horses, dogs, and rats. "We are utterly cut off from the world, surrounded by a circle of fire," wrote one woman. "People do nothing but eat what they can get, sleep when they can, and dodge the shells."

The Confederate soldiers were also sick and hungry. In late June a group of soldiers sent their commander a warning.

"If you can't feed us, you had better surrender us, horrible as the idea is. . . . This army is now ripe for mutiny [rebellion], unless it can be fed."

—Confederate soldiers at Vicksburg to General John C. Pemberton, 1863

On July 4 Pemberton surrendered. Grant immediately sent food to the soldiers and civilians. He later claimed that "the fate of the Confederacy was sealed when Vicksburg fell."

Reading Check
Summarize
How did the Union gain control of the Mississippi River?

Struggle for the Far West

Early on in the war, the Union halted several attempts by Confederate armies to control lands west of the Mississippi. In August 1861 a Union detachment from Colorado turned back a Confederate force at Glorieta Pass. Union volunteers also defeated rebel forces at Arizona's Pichaco Pass.

Confederate attempts to take the border state of Missouri also collapsed. Failing to seize the federal arsenal at St. Louis in mid-1861, the rebels fell back to Pea Ridge in northwest Arkansas. There, in March 1862 they attacked again, aided by some 800 Cherokee. The Union defense of Missouri held.

The Union navy played an important part in the Civil War. Besides blockading and raiding southern ports, the navy joined battles along the Mississippi River, as in this painting of Vicksburg.

DOCUMENT-BASED INVESTIGATION
Historical Source

Response to Farragut

The mayor of New Orleans considered the surrender of the city to the Union navy:

"We yield to physical force alone and maintain allegiance to the Confederate States; beyond this, a due respect for our dignity, our rights and the flag of our contry does not, I think, permit us to go."

—Mayor John T. Monroe quoted in *Confederate Military History*, Vol. 10

Analyze Historical Sources
How does Monroe's statement reveal his attitude about surrender?

Although the Union army won the battle, Indian troops commanded by Cherokee leader Stand Watie fought bravely. Watie was later promoted to general, the only Native American on either side to hold this rank in the war.

More than 10,000 Native Americans took part in the Civil War. Many Cherokee fought for the Confederacy, but the war bitterly divided the Cherokee—and other nations as well—over issues of loyalty and slavery.

Some nations saw the transfer of soldiers from western forts to eastern battlefields as a chance to take back land they had lost. The Indians also hoped the Confederates would give them greater freedom. In addition, slavery was legal in Indian Territory, and some Native Americans who were slaveholders supported the Confederacy. Pro-Confederate forces remained active in the region throughout the war. They attacked Union forts and raided towns in Missouri and Kansas, forcing Union commanders to keep valuable troops stationed in the area.

Reading Check
Analyze What was the importance of the fighting in the Far West?

Summary and Preview The North and the South continued their struggle with battles in the West. A number of key battles took place in the Western theater, and several important Union leaders emerged from these battles. One, Ulysses S. Grant, would soon become even more important to the Union army. In the next lesson you will learn about the lives of civilians, enslaved African Americans, and soldiers during the war.

Lesson 3 Assessment

Review Ideas, Terms, and People

1. a. Identify What role did Ulysses S. Grant play in the war in the West?

b. Explain Why was the Battle of Shiloh important?

c. Elaborate Do you think President Lincoln would have approved of Grant's actions in the West? Why or why not?

2. a. Describe How did the Union take New Orleans, and why was it an important victory?

b. Draw Conclusions How were civilians affected by the Siege of Vicksburg?

c. Predict What might be some possible results of the Union victory at Vicksburg?

Critical Thinking

3. Identify Cause and Effect In this lesson you learned about the Union's military strategy in the West. Create a graphic organizer similar to the one below and use it to show the causes and effects of each battle.

The Vicksburg Strategy

"Vicksburg is the key!"
President Abraham Lincoln declared. "The war can never be brought to a close until that key is in our pocket." Vicksburg was so important because of its location on the Mississippi River, a vital trade route and supply line. Union ships couldn't get past the Confederate guns mounted on the high bluffs of Vicksburg. Capturing Vicksburg would give the Union control of the Mississippi, stealing a vital supply line and splitting the Confederacy in two. The task fell to General Ulysses S. Grant.

Grant Crosses into Louisiana General Grant planned to attack Vicksburg from the north, but the swampy land made attack from that direction difficult. So, Grant crossed the Mississippi River into Louisiana and marched south.

5 **The Siege of Vicksburg** Grant now had 30,000 Confederate troops trapped in Vicksburg. After two assaults on the city failed, Grant was forced to lay siege. After six weeks of bombardment, the Confederate surrendered on July 4, 1863. Grant's bold campaign had given the Union control of the Mississippi River.

Vicksburg

2 **Grant Moves East** Grant's troops met up with their supply boats here and crossed back into Mississippi. In a daring gamble, Grant decided to move without a supply line, allowing the army to move quickly.

Port Gibson

3 **Port Gibson** A skirmish at Port Gibson proved that the Confederates could not defend the Mississippi line.

Jackson

④ **The Battle of Jackson** Grant defeated a Confederate army at Jackson and then moved on to Vicksburg. This prevented Confederate forces from reinforcing Vicksburg.

Ironclads Union ironclads were vital to the Vicksburg campaign. These gunboats protected Grant's troops when they crossed the Mississippi. Later, they bombarded Vicksburg during the siege of the city.

Map legend:
- UNION CONTROL
- CONFEDERATE CONTROL

States on map: Missouri, Kentucky, Virginia, Arkansas, Tennessee, North Carolina, South Carolina, Alabama, Georgia, Mississippi, VICKSBURG, Louisiana, GULF OF MEXICO

--- BIOGRAPHY ---

Ulysses S. Grant 1822–1885

Ulysses S. Grant was born in April 1822 in Ohio. Grant attended West Point in New York and fought in the Mexican-American War. He resigned in 1854 and worked at various jobs in farming, real estate, and retail. When the Civil War started, he joined the Union army and was quickly promoted to general. After the Civil War, Grant rode a wave of popularity to become president of the United States.

Interpret Maps

1. **Location** Why was Vicksburg's location so important?

2. **Place** What natural features made Vicksburg difficult to attack?

Daily Life during the War

The Big Idea

The lives of many Americans were affected by the Civil War.

Main Ideas

- The Emancipation Proclamation freed slaves in Confederate states.
- African Americans participated in the war in a variety of ways.
- President Lincoln faced opposition to the war.
- Life was difficult for soldiers and civilians alike.

Key Terms and People

emancipation
Emancipation Proclamation
contrabands
54th Massachusetts Infantry
Copperheads
habeas corpus
Clara Barton

If YOU were there . . .

You live in Maryland in 1864. Your father and brothers are in the Union army, and you want to do your part in the war. You hear that a woman in Washington, DC, is supplying medicines and caring for wounded soldiers on the battlefield. She is looking for volunteers. You know the work will be dangerous, for you'll be in the line of fire. You might be shot or even killed.

Would you join the nurses on the battlefield?

Emancipation Proclamation

At the heart of the nation's bloody struggle were millions of enslaved African Americans. Abolitionists urged President Lincoln to free them.

In an 1858 speech, Lincoln declared, "There is no reason in the world why the negro is not entitled to all the natural rights numerated in the Declaration of Independence—the right to life, liberty, and the pursuit of happiness." Yet as president, Lincoln found **emancipation**, or the freeing of slaves, to be a difficult issue. He did not believe he had the constitutional power. He also worried about the effects of emancipation.

Lincoln Issues the Proclamation Northerners had a range of opinions about abolishing slavery.

- The Democratic Party, which included many laborers, opposed emancipation. Laborers feared that freed slaves would come north and take their jobs at lower wages.
- Abolitionists argued that the war was pointless if it did not win freedom for African Americans. They warned that the Union would remain divided until the problem was resolved.

- Lincoln worried about losing support for the war. Previous wartime Confiscation Acts that had attempted to free the slaves had been unpopular in the border states.
- Others, including Secretary of War Edwin Stanton, agreed with Lincoln that the use of slave labor was helping the Confederacy make war. Therefore, as commander in chief, the president could free the slaves in all rebellious states. Freed African Americans could then be recruited into the Union army.

For several weeks in 1862, Lincoln worked intensely, thinking, writing, and rewriting. He finally wrote the **Emancipation Proclamation**, the order to free the Confederate slaves. The proclamation declared that:

". . . all persons held as slaves within any State or designated part of a State the people whereof shall then be in rebellion against the United States shall be then, thenceforward, and forever free."

—Emancipation Proclamation, 1862

Confederates reacted to the Proclamation with outrage. Jefferson Davis called it the "most execrable [hateful] measure recorded in the history of guilty man." As some northern Democrats had predicted, the Proclamation had made the Confederacy more determined than ever to fight to preserve its way of life.

The Emancipation Proclamation was a military order that freed slaves only in areas controlled by the Confederacy. In fact, the proclamation had little immediate effect. It was impossible for the federal government to enforce the proclamation in the areas where it actually applied—the states in rebellion that were not under federal control. The proclamation did not

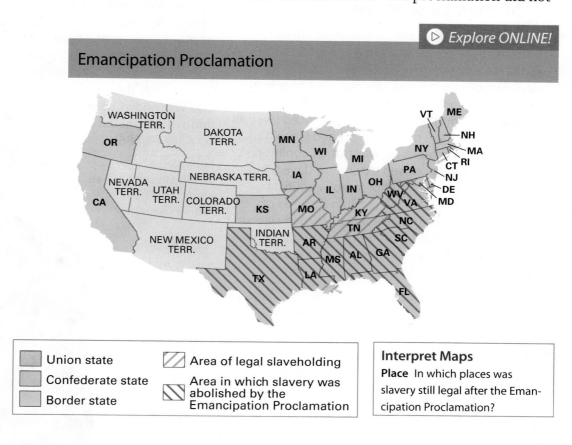

Explore ONLINE!

Emancipation Proclamation

Legend:
- Union state
- Confederate state
- Border state
- Area of legal slaveholding
- Area in which slavery was abolished by the Emancipation Proclamation

Interpret Maps

Place In which places was slavery still legal after the Emancipation Proclamation?

stop slavery in the border states, where the federal government would have had the power to enforce it. The words written in the Emancipation Proclamation were powerful, but the impact of the document was more symbolic than real. It defined what the Union was fighting against and discouraged Britain from aiding the Confederacy.

Lincoln wanted to be in a strong position in the war before announcing his plan. The Battle of Antietam gave him the victory he needed. He issued the Emancipation Proclamation on September 22, 1862. The proclamation went into effect on January 1, 1863. As one of the first civil rights documents in United States history, the Emancipation Proclamation continues to impact Americans today as a symbol of equal rights for all Americans. The historic document paved the way for future civil rights legislation, which gave minorities and women more equal rights.

Reaction to the Proclamation New Year's Eve, December 31, 1862: In "night watch" meetings at many African American churches, worshippers prayed, sang, and gave thanks. When the clocks struck midnight, millions were free. Abolitionists rejoiced. Frederick Douglass called January 1, 1863, "the great day which is to determine the destiny not only of the American Republic, but that of the American Continent."

William Lloyd Garrison was quick to note, however, that "slavery, as a system" continued to exist in the loyal slave states. Yet where slavery

Abraham Lincoln 1809–1865

Abraham Lincoln is one of the great symbols of American democracy. He was born in a log cabin to a poor family in Kentucky and grew-up in Kentucky and Illinois. Lincoln went to school for less than a year, but taught himself law and settled in Springfield, where he practiced law and politics. The issue of slavery defined Lincoln's entire political career. He was not an abolitionist, but he strongly opposed extending slavery into the territories. In a series of famous political debates against Senator Stephen Douglas of Illinois, Lincoln championed his views on slavery and made a brilliant defense of democracy and the Union. "A house divided against itself cannot stand," he declared in a debate with Douglas.

Elected president in 1860, Lincoln led the nation through the Civil War and worked constantly to preserve a unified nation. In 1863, he issued the Emancipation Proclamation. His address to commemorate the bloody battlefield at Gettysburg is considered to be one of the best political speeches in American history. Only days after the Civil War ended, John Wilkes Booth assassinated Lincoln on April 14, 1865.

Summarize
Why is Lincoln such an important figure in American history?

remained, the proclamation encouraged many enslaved African Americans to escape when the Union troops came near. They flocked to the Union camps and followed them for protection. The loss of slaves crippled the South's ability to wage war.

African Americans Participate in the War

As the war casualties climbed, the Union needed even more troops. African Americans were ready to volunteer. Not all white northerners were ready to accept them, but eventually they had to. Frederick Douglass believed that military service would help African Americans gain rights.

> "Once let the black man get upon his person the brass letters, U.S.; . . . and a musket on his shoulder and bullets in his pocket, and there is no power on earth which can deny that he has earned the right to citizenship."

—Frederick Douglass, quoted in *The Life and Writings of Frederick Douglass, Vol. 3*

Congress began allowing the army to sign up African American volunteers as laborers in July 1862. The War Department also gave **contrabands**, or escaped slaves, the right to join the Union army in South Carolina. Free African Americans in Louisiana and Kansas also formed their own units in the Union army. By the spring of 1863, African American army units were proving themselves in combat. They took part in a Union attack on Port Hudson, Louisiana, in May.

One unit stood out above the others. The **54th Massachusetts Infantry** consisted mostly of free African Americans. In July 1863 this regiment led a heroic charge on South Carolina's Fort Wagner. The 54th took heavy fire and suffered huge casualties in the failed operation. About half the regiment was killed, wounded, or captured. Edward L. Pierce, a

Reading Check
Find Main Ideas
How did northerners view the Emancipation Proclamation?

DOCUMENT-BASED INVESTIGATION   Historical Source

Letter from a Union Soldier

On June 23, 1863, Joseph E. Williams, an African American soldier and recruiter from Pennsylvania, wrote this letter describing why African Americans fought for the Union.

Analyze Historical Sources
Why did Williams think being soldiers was so important for African Americans?

> "We are now determined to hold every step that has been offered to us as citizens of the United States for our elevation [benefit], which represent justice, the purity, the truth, the aspiration [hope] of heaven. We must learn deeply to realize the duty, the moral and practical necessity for the benefit of our race . . . Every consideration of honor, of interest, and of duty to God and man, requires that we should be true to our trust."

—quoted in *A Grand Army of Black Men*, edited by Edwin S. Redkey

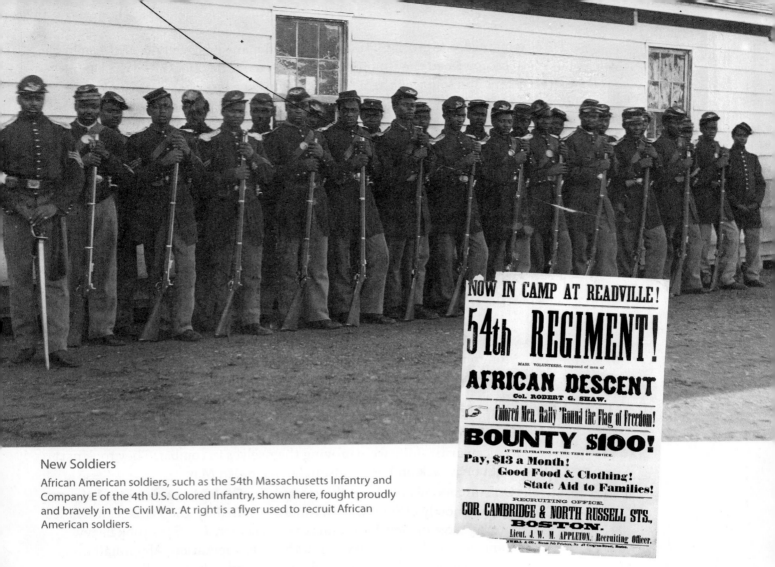

New Soldiers

African American soldiers, such as the 54th Massachusetts Infantry and Company E of the 4th U.S. Colored Infantry, shown here, fought proudly and bravely in the Civil War. At right is a flyer used to recruit African American soldiers.

NOW IN CAMP AT READVILLE!

54th REGIMENT!

MASS. VOLUNTEERS, composed of men of

AFRICAN DESCENT

Col. ROBERT G. SHAW.

Colored Men, Rally 'Round the Flag of Freedom!

BOUNTY $100!

AT THE EXPIRATION OF THE TERM OF SERVICE.

Pay, $13 a Month!
Good Food & Clothing!
State Aid to Families!

RECRUITING OFFICE.

COR. CAMBRIDGE & NORTH RUSSELL STS.,

BOSTON.

Lieut. J. W. M. APPLETON, Recruiting Officer.

correspondent for the *New York Tribune*, wrote, "The Fifty-fourth did well and nobly . . . They moved up as gallantly as any troops could, and with their enthusiasm they deserved a better fate." The bravery of the 54th regiment made it the most celebrated African American unit of the war.

About 180,000 African Americans served with the Union army. They initially received $10 a month, while white soldiers got $13. In June 1864 Congress passed a bill granting African American soldiers equal pay.

African Americans faced special horrors on the battlefield. Confederates often killed their black captives or sold them into slavery. In the 1864 election, Lincoln suggested rewarding African American soldiers by giving them the right to vote.

Reading Check
Analyze Information How did African Americans support the Union?

Growing Opposition

The deepening shadows in Lincoln's face reflected the huge responsibilities he carried. Besides running the war, he had to deal with growing tensions in the North.

Copperheads As the months rolled on and the number of dead continued to increase, a group of northern Democrats began speaking out against

The Copperheads
This political cartoon pokes fun at Copperhead northerners who want peace. The cartoon implies that the Copperheads plan is to bore the Confederate states into rejoining the Union.

the war. Led by U.S. representative Clement L. Vallandigham of Ohio, they called themselves Peace Democrats. Their enemies called them Copperheads, comparing them to a poisonous snake. The name stuck.

Many **Copperheads** were midwesterners who sympathized with the South and opposed abolition. They believed the war was not necessary and called for its end. Vallandigham asked what the war had gained and then said, "Let the dead at Fredericksburg and Vicksburg answer."

Lincoln saw the Copperheads as a threat to support of the war effort. To silence them, he suspended the right of habeas corpus. **Habeas corpus** is a constitutional protection against unlawful imprisonment. Ignoring this protection, Union officials jailed their enemies, including some Copperheads, without evidence or trial. Lincoln's action greatly angered Democrats and some Republicans.

Northern Draft In March 1863 war critics erupted again when Congress approved a draft, or forced military service. For $300, men were allowed to buy their way out of military service. For an unskilled laborer, however, that was nearly a year's wages. Critics of the draft called the Civil War a "rich man's war and a poor man's fight."

In July 1863 riots broke out when African Americans were brought into New York City to replace striking Irish dockworkers. The city happened to be holding a war draft at the same time. The two events enraged rioters, who attacked African Americans and draft offices. More than 100 people died.

In this tense situation, the northern Democrats nominated former general George McClellan for president in 1864. They called for an immediate end to the war. Lincoln defeated McClellan in the popular vote, winning by about 400,000 votes out of 4 million cast. The electoral vote was not even close. Lincoln won 212 to 21.

Life for Soldiers and Civilians

Young, fresh recruits in both armies were generally eager to fight. Experienced troops, however, knew better.

On the Battlefield Civil War armies fought in the ancient battlefield formation that produced massive casualties. Endless rows of troops fired directly at one another, with cannonballs landing amid them. When the order was given, soldiers would attach bayonets to their guns and rush toward their enemy. Men died to gain every inch of ground.

Doctors and nurses in the field saved many lives. Yet they had no medicines to stop infections that developed after soldiers were wounded. Many soldiers endured the horror of having infected legs and arms amputated without painkillers. Infections from minor injuries caused many deaths.

Despite the huge battlefield losses, the biggest killer in the Civil War was not the fighting. It was diseases such as typhoid, pneumonia, and tuberculosis. Nearly twice as many soldiers died of illnesses and disease as died in combat.

Reading Check
Identify Cause and Effect Who opposed the war, and how did Lincoln respond to the conflict?

Prisoners of War As hard as army life was, conditions for prisoners of war were much worse. At first, neither North nor South kept large numbers of captured soldiers. Many prisoners were released if they promised to go home instead of back to their army. Others were exchanged for prisoners held by the other side. Military prisoners on both sides lived in unimaginable misery. In prison camps, such as Andersonville, Georgia, and Elmira, New York, soldiers were packed into camps designed to hold only a fraction of their number. Soldiers had little shelter, food, or clothing. Starvation and disease killed thousands of prisoners.

Life as a Civilian The war effort involved all levels of society. Women as well as people too young or too old for military service worked in factories and on farms. Economy in the North boomed as production and prices soared. The lack of workers caused wages to rise by 43 percent between 1860 and 1865.

Women were the backbone of civilian life and took over farms, plantations, stores, and other businesses while their fathers, husbands, and sons served in armies. On the farms, women and children performed the daily chores usually done by men. One visitor to Iowa in 1862 reported that he "met more women . . . at work in the fields than men." Southern women also managed farms and plantations.

The need for clothes, shoes, and other supplies created about 100,000 jobs for women in northern factories. Women also worked in the South's few factories, and women on both sides performed dangerous work making ammunition for the troops.

Many women found new occupations. Hundreds were hired by the Union government as clerks. They became the first women to hold federal government jobs. Women also staffed government offices in the South. Like clerical work, nursing was a man's job before the war. During the war, however, about 3,000 women served the Union army as paid nurses.

One woman brought strength and comfort to countless wounded Union soldiers. Volunteer **Clara Barton** organized the collection of medicine and supplies for delivery to the battlefield. At the field hospitals, the "angel of the battlefield" soothed the wounded and dying and assisted doctors as bullets flew around her. Barton's work formed the basis for the future American Red Cross.

In the South, Sally Louisa Tompkins established a small hospital in Richmond, Virginia. By the end of the war, it had grown into a major army hospital. Jefferson Davis recognized her value to the war effort by making her a captain in the Confederate army.

Clara Barton founded the American Red Cross.

Reading Check
Analyze How did women help the war effort on both sides?

Summary and Preview Many lives were changed by the war. In the next lesson you will learn about the end of the war.

Lesson 4 Assessment

Review Ideas, Terms, and People

1. **a. Recall** Why did some Americans want to end slavery?

   b. Contrast How did reactions to the Emancipation Proclamation differ?

   c. Elaborate How and why does the Emancipation Proclamation continue to impact American life? Explain your answer.

2. **a. Recall** Why did some northerners want to recruit African Americans into the Union army?

   b. Contrast In what ways did African American soldiers face more difficulties than white soldiers did?

3. **a. Identify** Who were Copperheads, and why did they oppose the war?

   b. Evaluate Should President Lincoln have suspended the right to habeas corpus? Why?

4. **a. Describe** What were conditions like in military camps?

   b. Draw Conclusions How did the war change life on the home front?

Critical Thinking

5. **Identify Effects** In this lesson you learned about the Emancipation Proclamation. Create a chart similar to the one below and use it to summarize the reasons for the Emancipation Proclamation, its main points, and its effects on different people.

Reasons for the Emancipation Proclamation
↓
Main Points of the Proclamation
↓
Effect on People's Lives
↓

The Tide of War Turns

The Big Idea

Union victories in 1863, 1864, and 1865 ended the Civil War.

Main Ideas

- The Union tried to divide the Confederate army at Fredericksburg, but the attempt failed.

- The Battle of Gettysburg in 1863 was a major turning point in the war.

- During 1864, Union campaigns in the East and South dealt crippling blows to the Confederacy.

- Union troops forced the South to surrender in 1865, ending the Civil War.

Key Terms and People

Battle of Gettysburg
George Pickett
Pickett's Charge
Gettysburg Address
Wilderness Campaign
William Tecumseh Sherman
total war
Appomattox Courthouse

If YOU were there . . .

You live in southern Pennsylvania in 1863, near a battlefield where thousands died. Now people have come from miles around to dedicate a cemetery here. You are near the front of the crowd. The first speaker impresses everyone with two hours of dramatic words and gestures. Then President Lincoln speaks—just a few minutes of simple words. Many people are disappointed.

Why do you think the president's speech was so short?

Fredericksburg and Chancellorsville

Frustrated by McClellan's lack of aggression, Lincoln replaced him with General Ambrose E. Burnside as leader of the Army of the Potomac. Burnside favored a swift, decisive attack on Richmond by way of Fredericksburg. In November 1862 he set out with 120,000 troops.

Burnside's tactics surprised General Lee. The Confederate commander had divided his force of 78,000 men. Neither section of the Confederate army was in a good position to defend Fredericksburg. However, Burnside's army experienced delays in crossing the Rappahannock River. These delays allowed Lee's army to reunite and entrench themselves around Fredericksburg. Finally, the Union army crossed the Rappahannock and launched a series of charges. These attacks had heavy casualties and failed to break the Confederate line. Eventually, after suffering about 12,600 casualties, Burnside ordered a retreat. The Confederates had about 5,300 casualties.

Soon Burnside stepped down from his position. Lincoln made General Joseph Hooker the commander of the Army of the Potomac. At the end of April 1863, Hooker and his army of about 138,000 men launched a frontal attack on Fredericksburg. Then Hooker ordered about 115,000 of his troops to split off and approach the Confederate's flank, or side. Hooker's strategy seemed about to work. But for some reason he hesitated and had his flanking troops take a defensive position at Chancellorsville. This town was located a few miles west of Fredericksburg.

The following day, Lee used most of his army (about 60,000 men) to attack Hooker's troops at Chancellorsville. Stonewall Jackson led an attack on Hooker's flank while Lee commanded an assault on the Union front. The Union army was almost cut in two. They managed to form a defensive line, which they held for three days. Then Hooker ordered a retreat.

Lee's army won a major victory. But this victory had severe casualties. During the battle, Lee's trusted general, Stonewall Jackson, was accidentally shot by his own troops. He died a few days later.

Battle of Gettysburg

General Lee launched more attacks within Union territory. As before, his goal was to break the North's will to fight. He also hoped that a victory would convince other nations to recognize the Confederacy. The three-day battle at Gettysburg was the largest and bloodiest battle of the Civil War. In three days, more than 51,000 soldiers were killed, wounded, captured, or went missing. It was an important victory for the Union, and it stopped Lee's plan of invading the North.

First Day In early June 1863 Lee cut across northern Maryland into southern Pennsylvania. His forces gathered west of a small town called Gettysburg. Lee was unaware that Union soldiers were encamped closer to town. He had been suffering from a lack of enemy information for three days because his cavalry chief "Jeb" Stuart was not performing his duties. Stuart and his cavalry had gone off on their own raiding party, disobeying Lee's orders.

Reading Check
Compare What did generals McClellan, Burnside, and Hooker have in common?

Day One:
July 1, 1863
Artillery played a key role in the Battle of Gettysburg on July 1, 1863.

Another Confederate raiding party went to Gettysburg for boots and other supplies. There, Lee's troops ran right into Union general George G. Meade's cavalry, triggering the **Battle of Gettysburg**, a key battle that finally turned the tide against the Confederates. The battle began on July 1, 1863, when the Confederate raiding party and the Union forces began exchanging fire. The larger Confederate forces began to push the Union troops back through Gettysburg.

The Union soldiers regrouped along the high ground of Cemetery Ridge and Culp's Hill. General Lee wanted to prevent the Union forces from entrenching themselves. He therefore ordered General Ewell to attack immediately. However, Ewell hesitated and thereby gave the Federals time to establish an excellent defensive position.

In fact, Confederate general James Longstreet thought that the Union position was almost impossible to overrun. Instead of attacking, he felt that the Confederate army should move east, take a strong defensive position, and wait for the Union forces to attack them. However, General Lee was not convinced. He believed that his troops were invincible.

The Confederates camped at Seminary Ridge, which ran parallel to the Union forces. Both camps called for their main forces to reinforce them and prepare for combat the next day.

Second Day On July 2, Lee ordered an attack on the left side of the Union line. Lee knew that he could win the battle if his troops captured Little Round Top from the Union forces. From this hill, Lee's troops could easily fire down on the line of Union forces. Union forces and Confederate troops fought viciously for control of Little Round Top. The fighting was particularly fierce on the south side of the hill. There, the 20th Maine led by Colonel Joshua Chamberlain battled the 15th Alabama led by Colonel

Day Two: July 2, 1863, 10 a.m.

Union soldiers desperately defended Little Round Top from a fierce Confederate charge.

William Oates. Later, when describing the conflict, Oates said, "The blood stood in puddles in some places in the rocks." Eventually, the Union soldiers forced the Confederates to pull back from Little Round Top.

Then, the Confederates attacked Cemetery Hill and Culp's Hill. The fighting lasted until nightfall. The assault on Cemetery Hill was unsuccessful. The Confederates did manage to take a few trenches on Culp's Hill. Even so, the Union forces still held a strong defensive position by the day's end.

Pickett's Charge On the third day of battle, Longstreet again tried to convince Lee not to attack. But Lee thought that the Union forces were severely battered and ready to break. Because of this, he planned to attack the center of the Union line on Cemetery Ridge. Such a tactic, he felt, would not be expected. Indeed, General Meade left only about 5,750 troops to defend the center.

For over an hour, the Confederates shelled Cemetery Ridge with cannon fire. For a while, the Union cannons fired back. Then they slacked off. The Confederates assumed that they had seriously damaged the Union artillery. In reality, the Confederate barrage did little damage.

The task of charging the Union center fell to three divisions of Confederate soldiers. General **George Pickett** commanded the largest unit. In late afternoon nearly 15,000 men took part in **Pickett's Charge**. For one mile the Confederates marched slowly up toward Cemetery Ridge.

Pickett's Charge, July 3, 1863

PENNSYLVANIA
Gettysburg

Washington, DC

Explore ONLINE!

Day Three:
General George Pickett led his troops across Emmitsburg Road to attack the Union position. He lost more than half of his men in the 50-minute battle.

Union positions
Confederate troop movements
Confederate positions
Roads

0   0.5   1 Mile
0   0.5   1 Kilometer

Hagerstown Road
Gettysburg
Willoughby's Run
Seminary Ridge
Pitzer's Run
Pickett's Charge
Emmitsburg Road
Plum Run
Little Round Top
Big Round Top
Cemetery Ridge
Taneytown Road
Baltimore Pike
Culp's Hill
Cemetery Hill
Hanover Road
Rock Creek

N W E S

Interpret Maps
1. **Human-Environment Interaction** How do you think geography affected Pickett's Charge?
2. **Movement** In which direction did Pickett's soldiers charge?

Showered with cannon and rifle fire, they suffered severe losses. But eventually, some of them almost reached their destination. Then Union reinforcements added to the barrage on the rebels. Soon the Confederates retreated, leaving about 7,500 casualties on the field of battle. Distressed by this defeat, General Lee rode among the survivors and told them, "It is all my fault."

On the fourth day, Lee began to retreat to Virginia. In all, nearly 75,000 Confederate soldiers and 90,000 Union troops had fought during the Battle of Gettysburg.

General Meade decided not to follow Lee's army. This decision angered Lincoln. He felt that Meade had missed an opportunity to crush the Confederates and possibly end the war.

Aftermath of Gettysburg Gettysburg was a turning point in the war. Lee's troops would never again launch an attack in the North. The Union victory at Gettysburg took place on the day before Grant's capture of Vicksburg, Mississippi. These victories made northerners believe that the war could be won.

In addition, the Union win at Gettysburg helped to end the South's search for foreign influence in the war. After Gettysburg, Great Britain and France refused to provide aid to the Confederacy. The South's attempt at cotton diplomacy failed.

The Gettysburg Address On November 19, 1863, at the dedicating ceremony of the Gettysburg battlefield cemetery, President Lincoln gave a speech called the **Gettysburg Address**, in which he praised the bravery of Union soldiers and renewed his commitment to winning the Civil War. This short but moving speech is one of the most famous in American history. In one of its frequently quoted lines, Lincoln referenced the Declaration of Independence and its ideals of liberty, equality, and

Lincoln's address at the dedication of the Gettysburg National Cemetery democracy—ideals that still impact Americans today. He reminded listeners that the war was being fought for those reasons.

Lincoln rededicated himself to winning the war and preserving the Union. A difficult road still lay ahead.

Union Campaigns Cripple the Confederacy

Lincoln had been impressed with General Grant's successes in capturing Vicksburg. He transferred Grant to the East and gave him command of the Union army. In early 1864 Grant forced Lee to fight a series of battles in Virginia that stretched Confederate soldiers and supplies to their limits.

Wilderness Campaign in the East From May through June, the armies fought in northern and central Virginia. Union troops launched the **Wilderness Campaign**—a series of battles designed to capture the Confederate capital at Richmond, Virginia. The first battle took place in early May, in woods about 50 miles outside of Richmond. Grant then ordered General Meade to Spotsylvania, where the fighting raged for five days.

Over the next month Union soldiers moved the Confederate troops back toward Richmond. However, Grant experienced his worst defeat at the Battle of Cold Harbor in early June, just 10 miles northeast of Richmond. In only a few hours the Union army suffered 7,000 casualties. The battle delayed Grant's plans to take the Confederate capital.

Union forces had suffered twice as many casualties as the Confederates had, yet Grant continued his strategy. He knew he would be getting additional soldiers, and Lee could not. Grant slowly but surely advanced his troops through Virginia. He told another officer, "I propose to fight it out on this line if it takes all summer."

After Cold Harbor, General Grant moved south of Richmond. He had hoped to take control of the key railroad junction at Petersburg, Virginia. Lee's army, however, formed a solid defense, and Grant could not **execute** his attack. Grant was winning the war, but he still had not captured Richmond. Facing re-election, Lincoln was especially discouraged by this failure.

Sherman Strikes the South Lincoln needed a victory for the Union army to help him win re-election in 1864. The bold campaign of General **William Tecumseh Sherman** provided this key victory. Sherman carried out the Union plan to destroy southern railroads and industries.

In the spring of 1864 Sherman marched south from Tennessee with 100,000 troops. His goal was to take Atlanta, Georgia, and knock out an important railroad link. From May through August, Sherman's army moved steadily through the Appalachians toward Atlanta. Several times, Sherman avoided defenses set up by Confederate general Joseph Johnston.

In July Sherman was within sight of Atlanta. Confederate president Jefferson Davis gave General John Hood command of Confederate forces in the region. Hood repeatedly attacked Sherman in a final attempt to save Atlanta, but the Union troops proved stronger. The Confederate troops retreated as Sherman held Atlanta under siege.

Explore ONLINE!

Union state
Union occupied, 1865
Confederate state
Union forces
Union victory
Confederate forces
Confederate victory

Interpret Maps

1. **Movement** About how long was Sherman's March to the Sea from Atlanta to Savannah?

2. **Movement** What challenges do you think Sherman faced on his southern attacks?

Atlanta fell to Sherman's troops on September 2, 1864. Much of the city was destroyed by artillery and fire. Sherman ordered the residents who still remained to leave. Responding to his critics, Sherman later wrote, "War is war, and not popularity-seeking." The loss of Atlanta cost the South an important railroad link and its center of industry.

Many people in the North had been upset with the length of the war. However, the capture of Atlanta showed that progress was being made in defeating the South. This success helped to convince Union voters to re-elect Lincoln in a landslide.

Sherman did not wait long to begin his next campaign. His goal was the port city of Savannah, Georgia. In mid-November 1864, Sherman left Atlanta with a force of about 60,000 men. He said he would "make Georgia howl!"

During his March to the Sea, Sherman practiced **total war**—destroying civilian and economic resources. Sherman believed that total war would ruin the South's economy and its ability to fight. He ordered his troops to destroy railways, bridges, crops, livestock, and other resources. They burned plantations and freed slaves.

Reading Check
Draw Conclusions
How did Sherman
hope to help the
Union with his total-
war strategy?

Sherman's army reached Savannah on December 10, 1864. They left behind a path of destruction 60 miles wide. Sherman believed that this march would speed the end of the war. He wanted to break the South's will to fight by marching Union troops through the heart of the Confederacy. In the end Sherman's destruction of the South led to anger and resentment toward the people of the North that would last for generations.

The South Surrenders

In early April Sherman closed in on the last Confederate defenders in North Carolina. At the same time, Grant finally broke through the Confederate defenses at Petersburg. On April 2 Lee was forced to retreat from Richmond.

Fighting Ends By the second week of April 1865, Grant had surrounded Lee's army and demanded the soldiers' surrender. Lee hoped to join other Confederates in fighting in North Carolina, but Grant cut off his escape just west of Richmond. Lee tried some last-minute attacks but could not break the Union line. Lee's forces were running low on supplies. General James Longstreet told about the condition of Confederate troops. "Many weary soldiers were picked up . . . some with, many without, arms [weapons],—all asking for food."

Trapped by the Union army, Lee recognized that the situation was hopeless. "There is nothing left for me to do but go and see General Grant," Lee said, "and I would rather die a thousand deaths."

On April 9, 1865, the Union and Confederate leaders met at a home in the small town of **Appomattox Courthouse** where Lee surrendered to Grant, thus ending the Civil War.

During the meeting, Grant assured Lee that his troops would be fed and allowed to keep their horses, and they would not be tried for treason. Then

Surrender at Appomattox
Union general Grant rose to shake hands with Confederate general Lee after the surrender. Grant allowed Lee to keep his sword and Lee's men to keep their horses.

Was it important for Grant and Lee to shake hands? Why or why not?

Quick Facts

Causes and Effects of the Civil War

Causes
- Disagreement over the institution of slavery
- Economic differences
- Political differences

▼

Effects
- Slavery ends
- 620,000 Americans killed
- Military districts created
- Southern economy in ruins

Interpret Charts
How important was slavery to the Civil War?

Reading Check
Predict What problems might the Union face following the Civil War?

Lee signed the surrender documents. The long, bloody war had finally ended. Grant later wrote that he found the scene at Appomattox Court-house more tragic than joyful.

"I felt . . . sad and depressed at the downfall of a foe [enemy] who had fought so long and valiantly [bravely], and had suffered so much for a cause, though that cause was, I believe, one of the worst for which a people ever fought."

—Ulysses S. Grant, *Battle Cry of Freedom*

As General Lee returned to his troops, General Grant stopped Union forces from cheering their victory. "The war is over," Grant said with relief. "The rebels are our countrymen again."

The Civil War had deep and long-lasting effects. Almost 620,000 Americans lost their lives during the four years of fighting.

The defeat of the South ended slavery there. The majority of former slaves, however, had no homes or jobs. The southern economy was in ruins. A tremendous amount of hostility remained, even after the fighting had ceased. The war was over, but the question remained: How could the United States be united once more?

Summary and Preview After four long years of battles, the Civil War ended with General Lee's surrender at Appomattox Courthouse. In the next module you will read about the consequences of the war in the South.

Lesson 5 Assessment

Review Ideas, Terms, and People

1. **a. Identify** What Confederate general died from his wounds at Chancellorsville?
   b. Draw Conclusions Why was the Union army defeated at Chancellorsville?
2. **a. Identify** What was the Gettysburg Address?
   b. Analyze Why was geography important to the outcome of the Battle of Gettysburg?
   Recall What was the purpose of the Wilderness   paign?
   Conclusions In what way was the capture of   important victory for President Lincoln?

4. **a. Identify** What events led to Lee's surrender at Appomattox Courthouse?
   b. Summarize How did the military conflict of the Civil War impact the United States?

Critical Thinking

5. **Support a Point of View** In this lesson you learned about the end of the Civil War. Create a similar triangle to the one below and use it to show the three events in this lesson that you think contributed most to the end of the Civil War and explain why.

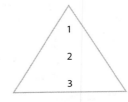

Social Studies Skills

Interpret Political Cartoons

Define the Skill

Political cartoons are drawings that express views on important issues. They have been used throughout history to influence public opinion. The ability to interpret political cartoons will help you understand issues and people's attitudes about them.

Learn the Skill

Political cartoons use both words and images to convey their message. They often contain caricatures or symbolism. A caricature is a drawing that exaggerates the features of a person or object. Symbolism is the use of one thing to represent something else. Cartoonists use these techniques to help make their point clear. They also use titles, labels, and captions to get their message across.

Use these steps to interpret political cartoons.

1. Read any title, labels, and caption to identify the cartoon's general topic.

2. Identify the people and objects. Determine if they are exaggerated and, if so, why. Identify any symbols and analyze their meaning.

3. Draw conclusions about the message the cartoonist is trying to convey.

The following cartoon was published in the North in 1863. The cartoonist has used symbols to make his point. Lady Liberty, representing the Union, is being threatened by the Copperheads. The cartoonist has expressed his opinion of these people by drawing them as the poisonous snake for which they were named. This cartoon clearly supports the Union's continuing to fight the war.

Practice the Skill

Apply the guidelines to interpret the cartoon below and answer the questions that follow.

1. What do the two men on either side of Lincoln represent?

2. What message do you think the artist was trying to convey?

b. Draw
Union le
West?

c. Evaluate Which
most valuable to th

Module 18 Assessment

Review Vocabulary, Terms, and People

Match the numbered definitions with the correct terms from the list below.

a. contrabands

b. cotton diplomacy

c. Second Battle of Bull Run

d. Siege of Vicksburg

e. Thomas "Stonewall" Jackson

1. Attack by Union general Ulysses S. Grant that gave the North control of the Mississippi River

2. Confederate general who held off Union attacks and helped the South win the First Battle of Bull Run

3. Important Confederate victory in which General Robert E. Lee defeated Union troops and pushed into Union territory for the first time

4. Southern strategy of using cotton exports to gain Britain's support in the Civil War

5. Term given to escaped slaves from the South

Comprehension and Critical Thinking

Lesson 1

6. **a. Identify** When and where did fighting in the U.S. Civil War begin?

   b. Analyze How did civilians help the war effort in both the North and the South?

   c. Elaborate Why do you think the border states chose to remain in the Union despite their support of slavery?

Lesson 2

7. **a. Identify** What was the first major battle of the war? What was the outcome of the battle?

   b. Analyze What was the Union army hoping to accomplish when it marched into Virginia at the start of the war?

   c. Evaluate Was the Union's naval blockade of the South successful? Why or why not?

Lesson 3

8. **a. Identify** Which side did the Cherokee support in the fighting at Pea Ridge? Why?

   b. Conclusions What progress did _____ders make in the war in the _____

   _____ victory in the West was _____ Union? Why?

Lesson 4

9. **a. Describe** What responsibilities did women take on during the war?

   b. Analyze What opposition to the war did President Lincoln face, and how did he deal with that opposition?

   c. Predict What might be some possible problems that the newly freed slaves in the South might face?

Lesson 5

10. **a. Recall** When and where did the war finally end?

    b. Compare and Contrast How were the efforts of generals Grant and Sherman at the end of the war similar and different?

    c. Elaborate What do you think led to the South's defeat in the Civil War? Explain.

Social Studies Skills

Interpret Political Cartoons *Use the Social Studies Skills taught in this module to answer the question about the political cartoon below.*

11. What do you think the artist is saying about politicians with this cartoon?

Reading Skills

Supporting Facts and Details *Use the Reading Skills taught in this module to answer the question about the reading selection below.*

> Lee was unaware that Union soldiers were encamped closer to town. He had been suffering from a lack of enemy information for three days because his cavalry chief "Jeb" Stuart was not performing his duties. Stuart and his cavalry had gone off on their own raiding party, disobeying Lee's orders.

12. What is the main idea of the reading selection?

    a. "Jeb" Stuart was not performing his duties.

    b. Stuart and his cavalry had gone off on their own.

    c. Stuart and his cavalry disobeyed Lee's orders.

    d. Lee was suffering from a lack of enemy information.

Review Themes

13. **Society and Culture** What effects did the Civil War have on American society?

14. **Politics** What political difficulties did the Emancipation Proclamation cause for President Lincoln?

Focus on Writing

15. **Write a Newspaper Article** Consider all the Civil War events discussed in this module. Then choose one of those events to write about in a newspaper article. Write an attention-grabbing headline. Then write the news article, describing the event and giving as many facts as possible about the event. Be sure to use proper grammar, punctuation, spelling, and capitalization.

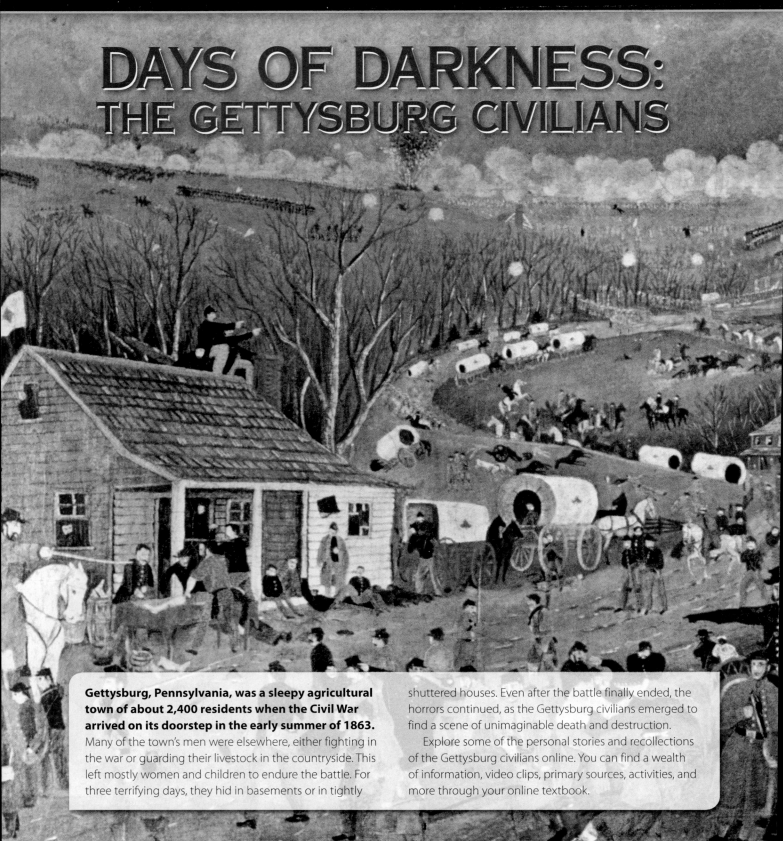

DAYS OF DARKNESS:
THE GETTYSBURG CIVILIANS

Gettysburg, Pennsylvania, was a sleepy agricultural town of about 2,400 residents when the Civil War arrived on its doorstep in the early summer of 1863. Many of the town's men were elsewhere, either fighting in the war or guarding their livestock in the countryside. This left mostly women and children to endure the battle. For three terrifying days, they hid in basements or in tightly shuttered houses. Even after the battle finally ended, the horrors continued, as the Gettysburg civilians emerged to find a scene of unimaginable death and destruction.

Explore some of the personal stories and recollections of the Gettysburg civilians online. You can find a wealth of information, video clips, primary sources, activities, and more through your online textbook.

> "I had scarcely reached the front door, when, on looking up the street, I saw some of the men on horseback. . . . What a horrible sight! . . .
> I was fully persuaded that the Rebels had actually come at last. What they would do with us was a fearful question to my young mind. . . ."
>
> —Tillie Pierce, age 15

 A Young Woman's Account

Read the document to witness the arrival of Confederate troops through the eyes of a Gettysburg teenager.

 HISTORY

Go online to view these and other **HISTORY**® resources.

A Citizen-Soldier

Watch the video to meet John Burns, the man who would come to be called the "Citizen Hero of Gettysburg."

A Family's Story

Watch the video to discover the story of courage and commitment exhibited by one Gettysburg family.

The National Cemetery

Watch the video to learn about the Soldiers' National Cemetery and the speech President Lincoln gave there.

Reconstruction

★

Essential Question

To what extent did Reconstruction achieve its goals?

About the Photo: The ruins of this southern plantation stand as a bleak reminder of the changes brought to the South by the Civil War.

 Explore ONLINE!

VIDEOS, including...
- Lincoln's Legacy
- The Fall of Richmond
- After the Assassination
- Johnson's Impeachment

 Document-Based Investigations

 Graphic Organizers

 Interactive Games

 Image Carousel: Testing Freedoms

 Image with Hotspots: *The First Vote*

In this module you will learn about the challenges that faced the nation after the Civil War and the attempts to meet those challenges.

What You Will Learn ...

Lesson 1: Rebuilding the South 614
The Big Idea The nation faced many problems in rebuilding the Union.

Lesson 2: The Fight over Reconstruction 620
The Big Idea The return to power of the pre-war southern leadership led Republicans in Congress to take control of Reconstruction.

Lesson 3: Reconstruction in the South 627
The Big Idea As Reconstruction ended, African Americans faced new hurdles and the South attempted to rebuild.

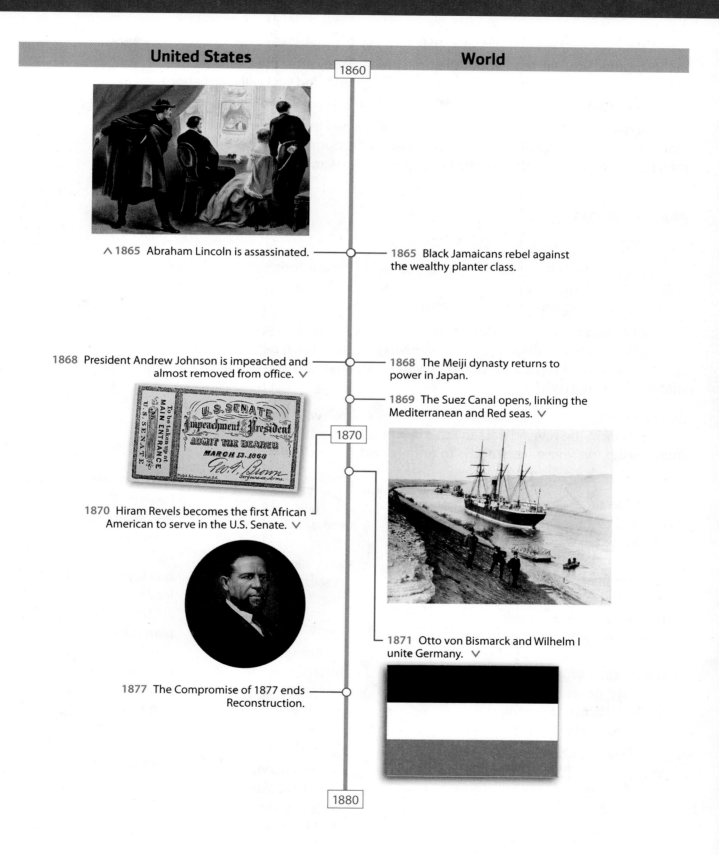

United States

World

1860

∧ **1865** Abraham Lincoln is assassinated.

1865 Black Jamaicans rebel against the wealthy planter class.

1868 President Andrew Johnson is impeached and almost removed from office. ∨

1868 The Meiji dynasty returns to power in Japan.

1869 The Suez Canal opens, linking the Mediterranean and Red seas. ∨

1870

1870 Hiram Revels becomes the first African American to serve in the U.S. Senate. ∨

1871 Otto von Bismarck and Wilhelm I unite Germany. ∨

1877 The Compromise of 1877 ends Reconstruction.

1880

Reading Social Studies

THEME FOCUS:

Politics, Society and Culture

In this module you will read about the time immediately after the Civil War. You will see how the government tried to rebuild the South and you will learn about how life changed for African Americans after slavery was declared illegal.

You will read about the political conflicts that emerged as southern leadership worked to gain control of Reconstruction efforts. Throughout the module you will read how the culture of the South changed after the war.

READING FOCUS:

Analyze Historical Information

History books are full of information. As you read, you are confronted with names, dates, places, terms, and descriptions on every page. You don't want to have to deal with anything unimportant or untrue.

Identify Relevant and Essential Information Information in a history book should be relevant to the topic you're studying. It should also be essential to understanding the topic and should be verifiable. Anything else distracts from the material you are studying.

The first passage below includes several pieces of irrelevant and nonessential information. In the revised passage this information has been removed. Note how much easier the revised passage is to understand.

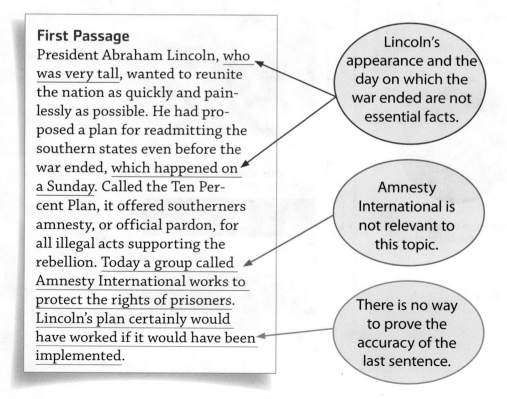

First Passage
President Abraham Lincoln, <u>who was very tall</u>, wanted to reunite the nation as quickly and painlessly as possible. He had proposed a plan for readmitting the southern states even before the war ended, <u>which happened on a Sunday</u>. Called the Ten Percent Plan, it offered southerners amnesty, or official pardon, for all illegal acts supporting the rebellion. <u>Today a group called Amnesty International works to protect the rights of prisoners.</u> <u>Lincoln's plan certainly would have worked if it would have been implemented.</u>

Lincoln's appearance and the day on which the war ended are not essential facts.

Amnesty International is not relevant to this topic.

There is no way to prove the accuracy of the last sentence.

Revised Passage
President Abraham Lincoln wanted to reunite the nation as quickly and painlessly as possible. He had proposed a plan for readmitting the southern states even before the war ended. Called the Ten Percent Plan, it offered southerners amnesty, or official pardon, for all illegal acts supporting the rebellion.

You Try It!

The following passage is adapted from the module you are about to read. As you read the passage, look for irrelevant, nonessential, or unverifiable information.

> **Freedmen's Bureau** In 1865 Congress established the Freedmen's Bureau, an agency providing relief for freedpeople and certain poor people in the South. The Bureau had a difficult job. It may have been one of the most difficult jobs ever. At its high point, about 900 agents served the entire South. All 900 people could fit into one hotel ballroom today. Bureau commissioner Oliver O. Howard eventually decided to use the Bureau's limited budget to distribute food to the poor and to provide education and legal help for freedpeople. One common food in the South at that time was salted meat. The Bureau also helped African American war veterans. Today the Department of Veterans' Affairs assists American war veterans.

After you read the passage, answer the following questions.

1. Which sentence in this passage is unverifiable and should be cut?

2. Find two sentences in this passage that are irrelevant to the discussion of the Freedmen's Bureau. What makes those sentences irrelevant?

3. Look at the last sentence of the passage. Do you think this sentence is essential to the discussion? Why or why not?

As you read Module 19, ask yourself what makes the information you are reading essential to a study of Reconstruction.

Key Terms and People

Lesson 1
Reconstruction
Ten Percent Plan
Thirteenth Amendment
Freedmen's Bureau
Andrew Johnson

Lesson 2
Black Codes
Radical Republicans
Civil Rights Act of 1866
Fourteenth Amendment
Reconstruction Acts
impeachment
Fifteenth Amendment

Lesson 3
Hiram Revels
Ku Klux Klan
Enforcement Acts
Compromise of 1877
poll tax
segregation
Jim Crow laws
Plessy v. *Ferguson*
sharecropping

Rebuilding the South

The Big Idea

The nation faced many problems in rebuilding the Union.

Main Ideas

- President Lincoln and Congress differed in their views as Reconstruction began.

- The end of the Civil War meant freedom for African Americans in the South.

- President Johnson's plan began the process of Reconstruction.

Key Terms and People

Reconstruction
Ten Percent Plan
Thirteenth Amendment
Freedmen's Bureau
Andrew Johnson

If YOU were there . . .

You are a young soldier who has been fighting in the Civil War for many months. Now that the war is over, you are on your way home. During your journey, you pass plantation manor homes, houses, and barns that have been burned down. No one is doing spring planting in the fields. As you near your family's farm, you see that fences and sheds have been destroyed. You wonder what is left of your home and family.

What would you think your future on the farm would be like?

Reconstruction Begins

After the Civil War ended in 1865, the U.S. government faced the problem of dealing with the defeated southern states. The challenges of **Reconstruction**, the process of readmitting the former Confederate states to the Union, lasted from 1865 to 1877.

Damaged South Tired southern soldiers returned home to find that the world they had known before the war was gone. Cities, towns, and farms had been ruined. Because of high food prices and widespread crop failures, many southerners faced starvation. The Confederate money most southerners held was now worthless. Banks failed, and merchants had gone bankrupt because people could not pay their debts.

Former Confederate general Braxton Bragg was one of many southerners who faced economic hardship. He found that "*all, all* was lost, except my debts." In South Carolina, Mary Boykin Chesnut wrote in her diary about the isolation she experienced after the war. "We are shut in here. . . . All RR's [railroads] destroyed—bridges gone. We are cut off from the world."

Lincoln's Plan President Abraham Lincoln wanted to reunite the nation as quickly and painlessly as possible. He had proposed a plan for readmitting the southern states even before the war ended. Called the **Ten Percent Plan**, it offered southerners amnesty, or official pardon, for all illegal acts supporting the rebellion. To receive amnesty, southerners had to do two things. They had to swear an oath of loyalty to the United States. They also had to agree that slavery was illegal. Once 10 percent of voters in a state made these pledges, they could form a new government. The state then could be readmitted to the Union.

Louisiana quickly elected a new state legislature under the Ten Percent Plan. Other southern states that had been occupied by Union troops soon followed Louisiana back into the United States.

Wade-Davis Bill Some politicians argued that Congress, not the president, should control the southern states' return to the Union. They believed that Congress had the power to admit new states. Also, many Republican members of Congress thought the Ten Percent Plan did not go far enough. A senator from Michigan expressed their views.

> "The people of the North are not such fools as to . . . turn around and say to the traitors, 'all you have to do [to return] is . . . take an oath that henceforth you will be true to the Government.'"
>
> —Senator Jacob Howard, quoted in *Reconstruction: America's Unfinished Revolution, 1863–1877*, by Eric Foner

Academic Vocabulary
procedure a series of steps taken to accomplish a task

Two Republicans—Senator Benjamin Wade and Representative Henry Davis—had an alternative to Lincoln's plan. Following **procedures** of the Wade-Davis bill, a state had to meet two conditions before it could rejoin the Union. First, it had to ban slavery. Second, a majority of adult males in the state had to take the loyalty oath.

Under the Wade-Davis bill, only southerners who swore that they had never supported the Confederacy could vote or hold office. In general, the bill was much stricter than the Ten Percent Plan. Its provisions would make it harder for southern states to rejoin the Union quickly.

President Lincoln therefore refused to sign the bill into law. He thought that few southern states would agree to meet its requirements. He believed that his plan would help restore order more quickly.

Reading Check
Contrast How was the Ten Percent Plan different from the Wade-Davis bill?

Freedom for African Americans

One thing Republicans agreed on was abolishing slavery. The Emancipation Proclamation had freed slaves only in areas that had not been occupied by Union forces, not in the border states. Many people feared that the federal courts might someday declare the proclamation unconstitutional.

Slavery Ends On January 31, 1865, at President Lincoln's urging, Congress proposed the **Thirteenth Amendment**. This amendment made slavery illegal throughout the United States.

The amendment was ratified and took effect on December 18, 1865. When abolitionist William Lloyd Garrison heard the news, he declared that his work was now finished. He called for the American Anti-Slavery Society to break up. Not all abolitionists agreed that their work was done,

These freedpeople have packed their household belongings and are leaving Richmond. Many people traveled in search of relatives. Others placed newspaper advertisements looking for long-lost relatives.

In what ways did former slaves react to freedom?

however. Frederick Douglass insisted that "slavery is not abolished until the black man has the ballot [vote]."

Freedom brought important changes to newly freed slaves. Many couples held ceremonies to legalize marriages that had not been recognized under slavery. Many freedpeople searched for relatives who had been sold away from their families years earlier. Others placed newspaper ads seeking information about their children. Many women began to work at home instead of in the fields. Still others adopted children of dead relatives to keep families together. Church members established voluntary associations and mutual-aid societies to help those in need.

Now that they could travel without a pass, many freedpeople moved from mostly white counties to places with more African Americans. Other freedpeople traveled simply to test their new freedom of movement. Northern migration, while not as extensive as the coming World War I Great Migration beginning in 1910, significantly increased the urban black population of the North. Detroit's African American population, for instance, more than doubled during the 1860s with the vast majority of its new arrivals coming from the South. A South Carolina woman explained this need. "I must go, if I stay here I'll never know I'm free."

For this couple, freedom brought the right to marry.

For most former slaves, freedom to travel was just the first step on a long road toward equal rights and new ways of life. Adults took new last names and began to insist on being called Mr. or Mrs. as a sign of respect, rather than by their first names or by nicknames. Freedpeople began to demand the same economic and political rights as white citizens. Henry Adams, a former slave, argued that "if I cannot do like a white man I am not free."

Forty Acres to Farm? Many former slaves wanted their own land to farm. Near the end of the Civil War, Union general William Tecumseh Sherman had issued an order to break up plantations in coastal South Carolina and Georgia. He wanted to divide the land into 40-acre plots and give them to former slaves as compensation for their forced labor before the war.

Many white planters refused to surrender their land. Some freedpeople pointed out that it was only fair that they receive some of this land because their labor had made the plantations prosper. In the end, the U.S. government returned the land to its original owners. At this time, many freedpeople were unsure about where they would live, what kind of work they would do, and what rights they had. Freedoms that were theirs by law were difficult to enforce.

Freedmen's Bureau In 1865 Congress established the **Freedmen's Bureau**, an agency providing relief for freedpeople and certain poor people in the South. The Bureau had a difficult job. At its high point, about 900 agents served the entire South. Bureau commissioner Oliver O. Howard eventually decided to use the Bureau's limited budget to distribute food to the poor and to provide education and legal help for freedpeople. The Bureau also helped African American war veterans.

The Freedmen's Bureau played an important role in establishing more schools in the South. Laws against educating slaves meant that most freedpeople had never learned to read or write. Before the war ended, however, northern groups, such as the American Missionary Association, began providing books and teachers to African Americans. The teachers were mostly women who were committed to helping freedpeople. One teacher said of her students, "I never before saw children so eager to learn. . . . It is wonderful how [they] . . . can have so great a desire for knowledge, and such a capacity for attaining [reaching] it."

After the war, some freedpeople organized their own education efforts. For example, Freedmen's Bureau agents found that some African Americans had opened schools in abandoned buildings. Many white southerners continued to believe that African Americans should not be educated. Despite

African American students and teachers outside the Freedmen's Bureau school in Beaufort, South Carolina

Reading Check
Analyze How did the Freedmen's Bureau help reform education in the South?

Helping the Freedpeople

Congress created the Freedmen's Bureau to help freedpeople and poor southerners recover from the Civil War. The Bureau assisted people by:

- providing supplies and medical services.
- establishing schools.
- supervising contracts between freedpeople and employers.
- taking care of lands abandoned or captured during the war.

What role did the Freedmen's Bureau play during Reconstruction?

opposition, by 1869 more than 150,000 African American students were attending more than 3,000 schools. The Freedmen's Bureau also helped establish a number of universities for African Americans, including Howard and Fisk universities.

Students quickly filled the new classrooms. Working adults attended classes in the evening. African Americans hoped that education would help them to understand and protect their rights and to enable them to find better jobs. Both black and white southerners benefited from the effort to provide greater access to education in the South.

President Johnson's Reconstruction Plan

While the Freedmen's Bureau was helping African Americans, the issue of how the South would politically rejoin the Union remained unresolved. Soon, however, a tragic event ended Lincoln's dream of peacefully reuniting the country.

A New President On the evening of April 14, 1865, President Lincoln and his wife attended a play at Ford's Theater in Washington, DC. During the play, John Wilkes Booth, a southerner who opposed Lincoln's policies, sneaked into the president's theater box and shot him. Lincoln was rushed to a boardinghouse across the street, where he died early the next morning. Lincoln, his leadership remembered for its honesty, deep intelligence, and high morals, became a symbol for the nation of the struggle of the Civil War.

Vice President **Andrew Johnson** was sworn into office quickly. Reconstruction had now become his responsibility. He would have to win the trust of a nation shocked at its leader's death. Johnson's plan for bringing southern states back into the Union was similar to Lincoln's plan. However, he decided that wealthy southerners and former Confederate officials would need a presidential pardon to receive amnesty. Johnson shocked Radical Republicans by eventually pardoning more than 7,000 people by 1866.

New State Governments Johnson was a Democrat whom Republicans had put on the ticket in 1864 to appeal to the border states. A former slaveholder, he was a stubborn man who would soon face a hostile Congress.

Johnson offered a mild program for setting up new southern state governments. First, he appointed a temporary governor for each state. Then, he required that the states revise their constitutions. Next, voters elected state and federal representatives. The new state government had to declare that secession was illegal. It also had to ratify the Thirteenth Amendment and refuse to pay Confederate debts.

By the end of 1865, all the southern states except Texas had created new governments. Johnson approved them all and declared that the United States was restored. Newly elected representatives came to Washington from each reconstructed southern state. However, Republicans complained that many new representatives had been leaders of the Confederacy. Congress therefore refused to readmit the southern states into the Union. Clearly, the nation was still divided.

Summary and Preview In this lesson you learned about early plans for Reconstruction. In the next lesson you will learn that disagreements about Reconstruction became so serious that the president was almost removed from office.

Reading Check
Summarize What was President Johnson's plan for Reconstruction?

Lesson 1 Assessment

Review Ideas, Terms, and People

1. **a. Identify** What does Reconstruction mean?
   b. Summarize What was President Lincoln's plan for Reconstruction?
2. **a. Recall** What is the Thirteenth Amendment?
   b. Elaborate In your opinion, what was the most important accomplishment of the Freedmen's Bureau? Explain.
3. **a. Recall** Why was President Lincoln killed?
   b. Analyze Why did some Americans oppose President Johnson's Reconstruction plan?

Critical Thinking

4. **Summarize** In this lesson you learned about Reconstruction. Create a graphic organizer similar to the one below and show how African Americans were affected by the end of the war.

African Americans and Reconstruction — Marriages are legalized.

The Fight over Reconstruction

The Big Idea

The return to power of the pre-war southern leadership led Republicans in Congress to take control of Reconstruction.

Main Ideas

- Black Codes led to opposition to President Johnson's plan for Reconstruction.
- The Fourteenth Amendment ensured citizenship for African Americans.
- Radical Republicans in Congress took charge of Reconstruction.
- The Fifteenth Amendment gave African Americans the right to vote.

Key Terms and People

Black Codes
Radical Republicans
Civil Rights Act of 1866
Fourteenth Amendment
Reconstruction Acts
impeachment
Fifteenth Amendment

If YOU were there . . .

A member of Congress, you belong to the same political party as the president. But you strongly disagree with his ideas about Reconstruction and civil rights for African Americans. Now some of the president's opponents are trying to remove him from office. You do not think he is a good president. On the other hand, you think removing him would be bad for the unity of the country.

Will you vote to remove the president?

Opposition to President Johnson

In 1866 Congress continued to debate the rules for restoring the Union. Meanwhile, new state legislatures approved by President Johnson had already begun passing laws to deny African Americans' civil rights. "This is a white man's government, and intended for white men only," declared Governor Benjamin F. Perry of South Carolina.

Black Codes Soon, every southern state passed **Black Codes**, or laws that greatly limited the freedom of African Americans. They required African Americans to sign work contracts, creating working conditions similar to those under slavery. In most southern states, any African Americans who could not prove they were employed could be arrested. Their punishment might be one year of work without pay. African Americans were also prevented from owning guns. In addition, they were not allowed to rent property except in cities.

Black Codes in Mississippi and South Carolina also included Apprentice Laws. These laws required law enforcement officials to semiannually report to the Probate Court orphaned children or children of parents deemed unfit. The Probate Court was then required to find work for the minor as an apprentice. The former owner had priority in choosing the minor as his apprentice.

"Provided, that said apprentice shall be bound by indenture, in case of males until they are twenty-one years old, and in case of females until they are eighteen years old."

—Laws of the State of Mississippi, Passed at a Regular Session of the Mississippi Legislature, Jackson, 1865

Masters had the right to inflict moderate punishment on their apprentices and to recapture runaways. But the codes also required masters to provide food and clothing to their apprentices, teach them a trade, and send them to school.

The Black Codes alarmed many Americans. As one Civil War veteran asked, "If you call this freedom, what do you call slavery?" African Americans organized to oppose the codes. One group sent a petition to officials in South Carolina.

"We simply ask . . . that the same laws which govern *white men* shall govern *black men* . . . that, in short, we be dealt with as others are—in equity [equality] and justice."

—Petition from an African American convention held in South Carolina, quoted in *There Is a River: The Black Struggle for Freedom in America* by Vincent Harding

Radical Republicans The Black Codes angered many Republicans. They thought the South was returning to its old ways. Most Republicans were moderates who wanted the South to have loyal state governments. They also believed that African Americans should have rights as citizens. They

DOCUMENT-BASED INVESTIGATION   Historical Source

Johnson vs. Stevens

President **Andrew Johnson**, a southern Democrat from Tennessee and former slaveholder, argued that the South should not be placed under military control.

Thaddeus Stevens, a Pennsylvanian Radical Republican and champion of equal rights for African Americans, believed that Congress had the power to treat the South as conquered territory.

Analyze Historical Sources
How did Johnson's and Stevens's views on the South differ? What role do you think their personal backgrounds played in shaping their views?

"*Military governments . . . established for an indefinite period, would have divided the people into the vanquishers and the vanquished, and would have envenomed [made poisonous] hatred rather than have restored affection.*"

—Andrew Johnson

"*The future condition of the conquered power depends on the will of the conqueror. They must come in as new states or remain as conquered provinces. Congress . . . is the only power that can act in the matter.*"

—Thaddeus Stevens

hoped that the government would not have to force the South to follow federal laws.

Radical Republicans, on the other hand, took a harsher stance. They wanted the federal government to force change in the South. Like the moderates, they thought the Black Codes were cruel and unjust. The Radicals, however, wanted the federal government to be much more involved in Reconstruction. They feared that too many southern leaders remained loyal to the former Confederacy and would not enforce the new laws. Thaddeus Stevens of Pennsylvania and Charles Sumner of Massachusetts were the leaders of the Radical Republicans.

A harsh critic of President Johnson, Stevens was known for his honesty and sharp tongue. He wanted economic and political justice for both African Americans and poor white southerners. Sumner had been a strong opponent of slavery before the Civil War. He continued to argue tirelessly for African Americans' civil rights, including the right to vote and the right to fair laws.

Both Stevens and Sumner believed that, like Lincoln's proposed Ten Percent Plan, President Johnson's Reconstruction plan was too lenient toward the South, thereby making it a failure. Although the Radicals did not control Congress, they began to gain support among moderates when President Johnson ignored criticism of the Black Codes. Stevens believed the federal government could not allow racial inequality to survive.

Reading Check
Compare and Contrast How were Radical Republicans and moderate Republicans similar and different?

Fourteenth Amendment

Urged on by the Radicals in 1866, Congress proposed a new bill. It would give the Freedmen's Bureau more powers. The law would allow the Freedmen's Bureau to use military courts to try people accused of violating African Americans' rights. The bill's supporters hoped that these courts would be fairer than local courts in the South.

Johnson versus Congress Surprising many members of Congress, Johnson vetoed the Freedmen's Bureau bill. He insisted that Congress could not pass any new laws until the southern states were represented in Congress. Johnson also argued that the Freedmen's Bureau was unconstitutional.

Republicans responded with the **Civil Rights Act of 1866**. This act provided African Americans with the same legal rights as white Americans. President Johnson once again used his veto power. He argued that the act gave too much power to the federal government. He also rejected the **principle** of equal rights for African Americans. Congress, however, overrode Johnson's veto.

Many Republicans worried about what would happen when the southern states were readmitted. Fearing that the Civil Rights Act might be overturned, the Republicans proposed the **Fourteenth Amendment** in the summer of 1866. The Fourteenth Amendment included the following provisions:

1. It defined all people born or naturalized within the United States, except Native Americans, as citizens.

Academic Vocabulary
principle basic belief, rule, or law

2. It guaranteed citizens the equal protection of the laws.
3. It said that states could not "deprive any person of life, liberty, or property, without due process of law."
4. It banned many former Confederate officials from holding state or federal offices.
5. It made state laws subject to federal court review.
6. It gave Congress the power to pass any laws needed to enforce it.

1866 Elections President Johnson and most Democrats opposed the Fourteenth Amendment. As a result, civil rights for African Americans became a key issue in the 1866 congressional elections. To help the Democrats, Johnson traveled around the country defending his Reconstruction plan. Johnson's speaking tour was a disaster. It did little to win votes for the Democratic Party. Johnson even got into arguments with people in the audiences of some of his speaking engagements.

Two major riots in the South also hurt Johnson's campaign. On May 1, 1866, a dispute in Memphis, Tennessee, took place between local police and black Union soldiers. The dispute turned into a three-day wave of violence against African Americans. About three months later, another riot took place during a political demonstration in New Orleans. During that dispute, 34 African Americans and three white Republicans were killed.

Reading Check
Summarize What issue did the Fourteenth Amendment address, and how did it affect the congressional elections of 1866?

Congress Takes Control of Reconstruction

The 1866 elections gave the Republican Party a commanding two-thirds majority in both the House and the Senate. This majority gave the Republicans the power to override any presidential veto. In addition, the Republicans became united as the moderates joined with the Radicals. Together, they called for a new form of Reconstruction.

Reconstruction Acts In March 1867, Congress passed the first of several **Reconstruction Acts**. These laws divided the South into five districts. A U.S. military commander controlled each district.

The military would remain in control of the South until the southern states rejoined the Union. To be readmitted, a state had to write a new state constitution supporting the Fourteenth Amendment. Finally, the state had to give African American men the right to vote.

Thaddeus Stevens was one of the new Reconstruction Acts' most enthusiastic supporters. He spoke in Congress to defend the acts.

> "Have not loyal blacks quite as good a right to choose rulers and make laws as rebel whites? Every man, no matter what his race or color . . . has an equal right to justice, honesty, and fair play with every other man; and the law should secure him those rights."
>
> –Thaddeus Stevens, quoted in *Sources of the American Republic*, edited by Marvin Meyers et al.

President on Trial President Johnson strongly disagreed with Stevens. He argued that African Americans did not deserve the same treatment as white people. The Reconstruction Acts, he said, used "powers not granted

The Reconstruction Amendments

Thirteenth Amendment (1865)

"Neither slavery nor involuntary servitude, except as a punishment for crime whereof the party shall have been duly convicted, shall exist within the United States, or any place subject to their jurisdiction."

This amendment legally banned slavery throughout the United States but it was not without fault. A loophole, or an ambiguity of a law, existed. "Involuntary servitude," according to this amendment, could be enforced as punishment for a crime. The amendment also failed to specify what the legal status of freedpeople would be or if they would be fully entitled to the rights of American citizens.

How might the loophole in the Thirteenth Amendment have been exploited by opponents of the amendment's ratification?

Fourteenth Amendment (1868)

"All persons born or naturalized in the United States, and subject to the jurisdiction thereof, are citizens of the United States and the State wherein they reside. No State shall make or enforce any law which shall abridge the privileges or immunities of citizens of the United States; nor shall any State deprive any person of life, liberty, or property, without due process of law; nor deny to any person within its jurisdiction the equal protection of the laws."

Most notably, this amendment overturned the *Dred Scott* case by granting citizenship to all people born in the United States (except for Native Americans).

What role do you think Black Codes played in the drafting of this amendment?

Fifteenth Amendment (1870)

"The right of citizens of the United States to vote shall not be denied or abridged by the United States or by any State on account of race, color, or previous condition of servitude."

This amendment, for all intents and purposes, gave African American men the right to vote.

According to the language of this amendment, what group of citizens was not granted voting rights? How would you change the language to include all citizens?

---

to the federal government or any one of its branches." Knowing that Johnson did not support its Reconstruction policies, Congress passed a law limiting his power. This law prevented the president from removing cabinet officials without Senate approval. Johnson quickly broke the law by firing Edwin Stanton, the secretary of war.

For the first time in United States history, the House of Representatives responded by voting to impeach the president. **Impeachment** is the process used by a legislative body to bring charges of wrongdoing against a public official. The next step, under Article I of the Constitution, was a trial in the Senate. A two-thirds majority was required to find Johnson guilty and remove him from office.

Although Johnson was unpopular with Republicans, some of them believed he was being judged unfairly. Others did not trust the president

This Reconstruction-era painting shows African American men voting after passage of the Fifteenth Amendment.

What right did the Fifteenth Amendment protect?

pro tempore of the Senate, Benjamin Wade. He would become president if Johnson were removed from office. By a single vote, Senate Republicans failed to convict Johnson. Even so, the trial weakened his power as president.

Election of 1868 Johnson did not run for another term in 1868. The Democrats chose former New York governor Horatio Seymour as their presidential candidate. The Republicans chose Ulysses S. Grant. As a war hero, Grant appealed to many northern voters. He had no political experience but supported the congressional Reconstruction plan. He ran under the slogan "Let Us Have Peace."

Shortly after Grant was nominated, Congress readmitted seven southern states—Alabama, Arkansas, Florida, Georgia, Louisiana, North Carolina, and South Carolina. (Tennessee had already been readmitted in 1866.) Under the terms of readmission, these seven states approved the Fourteenth Amendment. They also agreed to let African American men vote. However, white southerners used violence to try to keep African Americans away from the polls.

Despite such tactics, thousands of African Americans voted for Grant and the "party of Lincoln." The *New Orleans Tribune* reported that many former slaves "see clearly enough that the Republican party [is] their political life boat." African American votes helped Grant to win a narrow victory.

Reading Check
Analyze Information
To which voters did Grant appeal in the presidential election of 1868?

Fifteenth Amendment

After Grant's victory, Congressional Republicans wanted to protect their Reconstruction plan. They worried that the southern states might try to keep black voters from the polls in future elections. Also, some Radical Republicans argued that it was not fair that many northern states still had laws preventing African Americans from voting. After all, every southern state was required to grant suffrage to African American men.

In 1869 Congress proposed the **Fifteenth Amendment**, which gave African American men the right to vote. Abolitionist William Lloyd Garrison praised what he saw as "this wonderful, quiet, sudden transformation of four millions of human beings from . . . the auction block to the ballot-box." The amendment went into effect in 1870 as one of the last Reconstruction laws passed at the federal level.

The Fifteenth Amendment did not please every reformer, however. Many women were angry because the amendment did not also grant them the right to vote.

Summary and Preview In this lesson you learned that Congress took control of Reconstruction and took steps to protect the rights of African Americans. In the next lesson you will learn about increasing opposition to Reconstruction.

Reading Check
Find Main Ideas
How did Radical Republicans take control of Reconstruction?

Lesson 2 Assessment

Review Ideas, Terms, and People

1. **a. Describe** What were Black Codes?
   b. Make Inferences Why did Republicans think Johnson's Reconstruction plan was a failure?

2. **a. Recall** What was the Civil Rights Act of 1866?
   b. Summarize Why was the Fourteenth Amendment important?

3. **a. Recall** Why was President Johnson impeached?
   b. Evaluate Which element of the Reconstruction Acts do you believe was most important? Why?

4. **a. Recall** What does the Fifteenth Amendment state?
   b. Elaborate Do you think that women should have been included in the Fifteenth Amendment? Explain.

Critical Thinking

5. **Identify** In this lesson you learned about the issues that led Republicans to take over Reconstruction. Create a graphic organizer similar to the one below and identify the main provisions of the Fourteenth Amendment and their effects.

Provisions	Effects

Reconstruction in the South

The Big Idea

As Reconstruction ended, African Americans faced new hurdles and the South attempted to rebuild.

Main Ideas

- Reconstruction governments helped reform the South.

- The Ku Klux Klan was organized as African Americans moved into positions of power.

- As Reconstruction ended, the rights of African Americans were restricted.

- Southern business leaders relied on industry to rebuild the South.

Key Terms and People

Hiram Revels
Ku Klux Klan
Enforcement Acts
Compromise of 1877
poll tax
segregation
Jim Crow laws
Plessy v. *Ferguson*
sharecropping

If YOU were there . . .

You live on a farm in the South in the 1870s. Times are hard because you do not own your farm. Instead, you and your family work in a landowner's cotton fields. You never seem to earn enough to buy land of your own. Some of your neighbors have decided to give up farming and move to the city. Others are going to work in the textile mills. But you have always been a farmer.

Will you decide to change your way of life?

Reconstruction Governments

After Grant became president in 1869, the Republicans seemed stronger than ever. They controlled most southern governments, partly because of the support of African American voters. However, most of the Republican officeholders were unpopular with white southerners.

Carpetbaggers and Scalawags Some of these office-holders were northern-born Republicans who had moved to the South after the war. Many white southerners called them carpetbaggers. Supposedly, they had rushed there carrying all their possessions in bags made from carpeting. Many southerners resented these northerners, accusing them—often unfairly—of trying to profit from Reconstruction. Because the South needed both physical and economic rebuilding, there were many business opportunities. Northerners who had not been devastated by the war had more money to invest and could therefore profit from these opportunities.

Southern Democrats cared even less for white southern Republicans. They referred to them as scalawags, or greedy rascals. Democrats believed that these southerners had betrayed the South by voting for the Republican Party. Many southern Republicans were small farmers who had supported the Union during the war. Others, like Mississippi governor James Alcorn, were former members of the Whig Party. They preferred to become Republicans rather than join the Democrats.

African American Leaders African Americans were the largest group of southern Republican voters. During Reconstruction, more than 600 African Americans won election to state legislatures. Some 16 of these politicians were elected to Congress. Other African Americans held local offices in counties throughout the South.

African American politicians came from many backgrounds. **Hiram Revels** was born free in North Carolina and went to college in Illinois. He became a Methodist minister and served as a chaplain in the Union army. In 1870 Revels became the first African American in the U.S. Senate. He took over the seat previously held by Confederate president Jefferson Davis. Revels held a moderate view of the readmission of former Confederates. Education and employment for African Americans were two of his top priorities. Revels exemplified the ability of African Americans to take part in governing. After completing his term, he became the first president of Alcorn University.

Unlike Revels, Blanche K. Bruce grew up in slavery in Virginia. Bruce became an important Republican in Mississippi and served one term as a U.S. senator. He worked to integrate the military while in office.

State Governments Change Direction The new Reconstruction state governments made policies that increased civil and voting rights for African Americans. They passed laws that ensured African Americans were allowed to vote in every community. In many places, however, there was still resistance by whites. Because former Confederates usually could not vote, they struggled to maintain political influence.

Reconstruction governments provided money for many new programs and organizations in the South. They helped to establish some of the first state-funded public school systems in the South. They also built new hospitals, prisons, and orphanages and passed laws prohibiting discrimination against African Americans. Many of these programs improved the lives of African Americans and whites in the South and gave people economic opportunities and access to political offices. However, racism and the dramatically different culture of groups led to conflicting expectations, and sometimes tensions led to violence.

Southern states under Republican control spent large amounts of money. They aided the construction of railroads, bridges, and public buildings. These improvements were intended to help the southern economy recover from the war. To get the money for these projects, the Reconstruction governments raised taxes and issued bonds. Although some people protested the increased taxes, the improved infrastructure helped the South to increase its trade and production capabilities.

Ku Klux Klan

As more African Americans took office, resistance to Reconstruction increased among white southerners. Democrats claimed that the Reconstruction governments were corrupt, illegal, and unjust. They also disliked having federal soldiers stationed in their states. Many white southerners disapproved of African American officeholders. One Democrat

Clergyman and educator Hiram Revels was the first African American elected to the U.S. Senate in 1870.

Reading Check
Summarize What reforms did Reconstruction state governments carry out?

The Ku Klux Klan

Members of the Ku Klux Klan often attacked under cover of darkness to hide their identities. This Klan member, shown on the left, even disguised his horse.

Why do you think Klan members disguised themselves?

noted, "'A white man's government' [is] the most popular rallying cry we have." In 1866 a group of white southerners in Tennessee created the **Ku Klux Klan**. This secret society opposed civil rights, particularly suffrage, for African Americans. The Klan used violence and terror against African Americans. The group's membership grew rapidly as it spread throughout the South. Klan members wore robes and disguises to hide their identities. They attacked—and even murdered—African Americans, white Republican voters, and public officials, usually at night.

Local governments did little to stop the violence. Many officials feared the Klan or were sympathetic to its activities. In 1870 and 1871 the federal government took action. In an affirmation of federal authority, Congress passed laws, called the **Enforcement Acts**, that made it a federal crime to interfere with elections or to deny citizens equal protection under the law.

Within a few years, the Klan was no longer an organized threat. But groups of white vigilantes, including the White League in Louisiana and the Red Shirts in Mississippi, North and South Carolina, continued to assault African Americans and Republicans throughout the 1870s. Unlike the Ku Klux Klan, the White League and the Red Shirts operated openly.

Reconstruction Ends

The violence of the Ku Klux Klan was not the only challenge to Reconstruction. Republicans slowly lost control of southern state governments to the Democratic Party. The General Amnesty Act of 1872 allowed former Confederates, except those who had held high ranks, to serve in public office. Many of these former Confederates, most of whom were Democrats, were soon elected to southern governments.

The Republican Party also began losing its power in the North. Although President Grant was re-elected in 1872, financial and political scandals in his administration upset voters. In his first term, a gold-buying

Reading Check
Draw Conclusions
Why did southerners join the Ku Klux Klan or other vigilante groups?

scheme involving Grant's cousin led to a brief crisis on the stock market called Black Friday. During his second term, his personal secretary was involved in the Whiskey Ring scandal, in which whiskey distillers and public officials worked together to steal liquor taxes from the federal government. Also, people blamed Republican policies for the Panic of 1873.

Panic of 1873 This severe economic downturn began in September 1873 when Jay Cooke and Company, a major investor in railroads and the largest financier of the Union's Civil War effort, declared bankruptcy. The company had lied about the value of land along the side of the Northern Pacific Railroad that it owned and was trying to sell. When the truth leaked out, the company failed.

The failure of such an important business sent panic through the stock market, and investors began selling shares of stock more rapidly than people wanted to buy them. Soon, 89 of the nation's 364 railroads had failed as well. The failure of almost 18,000 other businesses followed within two years. By 1876 unemployment had risen to 14 percent, with an estimated two million people out of work. The high unemployment rate set off numerous strikes and protests, many involving railroad workers. In 1874 the Democrats gained control of the House of Representatives. Northerners were becoming less concerned about southern racism and more concerned about their financial well-being.

Election of 1876 Republicans could tell that northern support for Reconstruction was fading. Voters' attention was shifting to economic problems. In 1874 the Republican Party lost control of the House of Representatives to the Democrats. The Republicans in Congress managed to pass one last civil rights law. The Civil Rights Act of 1875 guaranteed African Americans equal rights in public places, such as theaters and public transportation. But as Americans became increasingly worried about economic problems and government corruption, the Republican Party began to abandon Reconstruction.

Republicans selected Ohio governor Rutherford B. Hayes as their 1876 presidential candidate. He believed in ending federal support of the Reconstruction governments. The Democrats nominated New York governor Samuel J. Tilden. During the election, Democrats in the South again used violence at the polls to keep Republican voters away.

The election between Hayes and Tilden was close. Tilden appeared to have won. Republicans challenged the electoral votes in Oregon and three southern states. A special commission of members of Congress and Supreme Court justices was appointed to settle the issue.

The commission narrowly decided to give all the disputed votes to Hayes. Hayes thus won the presidency by one electoral vote. In the **Compromise of 1877**, the Democrats agreed to accept Hayes's victory. In return, they wanted all remaining federal troops removed from the South. They also asked for funding for internal improvements in the South and the appointment of a southern Democrat to the president's cabinet. Shortly after he took office in 1877, President Hayes removed the last of the federal troops from the South.

Redeemers Gradually, Democrats regained control of state governments in the South. In each state, they moved quickly to get rid of the Reconstruction reforms.

Democrats who brought their party back to power in the South were called Redeemers. They came from a variety of backgrounds. For instance, U.S. senator John T. Morgan of Alabama was a former general in the Confederate army. Newspaper editor Henry Grady of Georgia was interested in promoting southern industry.

Redeemers wanted to reduce the size of state government and limit the rights of African Americans. They lowered state budgets and got rid of a variety of social programs. The Redeemers cut property taxes and cut public funding for schools. They also succeeded in limiting African Americans' civil rights.

Jim Crow Laws
This 1913 illustration shows the segregation of society caused by Jim Crow laws. After Reconstruction ended, the U.S. court system upheld legalized segregation for nearly eighty years. The Civil Rights Act of 1964 finally put an end to all state and local laws requiring segregation.

African Americans' Rights Restricted Redeemers set up the poll tax in an effort to deny the vote to African Americans. The **poll tax** was a special tax people had to pay before they could vote.

Some states also targeted African American voters by requiring them to pass a literacy test. A so-called grandfather clause written into law affected men whose fathers or grandfathers could vote before 1867. In those cases, a voter did not have to pay a poll tax or pass a literacy test. As a result, almost every white man could escape the voting restrictions.

Redeemer governments also introduced legal **segregation**, the forced separation of whites and African Americans in public places. **Jim Crow laws**—laws that enforced segregation—became common in southern states in the 1880s.

African Americans challenged Jim Crow laws in court. In 1883, however, the U.S. Supreme Court ruled that the Civil Rights Act of 1875 was unconstitutional. The Court also ruled that the Fourteenth Amendment applied only to the actions of state governments. This ruling allowed private individuals and businesses to practice segregation.

Plessy v. Ferguson In 1896 the U.S. Supreme Court returned to the issue of segregation. When Homer Plessy, an African American, refused to leave the whites-only Louisiana train car he was riding on, he was arrested and accused of breaking Louisiana's Separate Car Act of 1890. This Jim Crow law stated that:

> "all railway companies carrying passengers in their coaches in this state, shall provide equal but separate accommodations for the white, and colored races, by providing two or more passenger coaches for each passenger train, or by dividing the passenger coaches by a partition so as to secure separate accommodations. . . ."
> —Separate Car Act of 1890, Louisiana state law

Plessy sued the railroad company and lost. His lawyers argued that the law violated his right to equal treatment under the Fourteenth Amendment. He then appealed to the U.S. Supreme Court. The Supreme Court ruled against Plessy in *Plessy v. Ferguson.* Segregation was allowed, said the Court, if "separate-but-equal" facilities were provided. Among the justices, only John Marshall Harlan disagreed with the Court's decision.

Segregation became widespread across the country. African Americans were forced to use separate public schools, libraries, and parks. When they existed, these facilities were usually of poorer quality than those created for whites. In practice, these so-called separate-but-equal facilities were separate and unequal. Neither Congress nor the president would make significant actions to overturn the doctrine until the 1900s.

Farming in the South Few African Americans in the South could afford to buy or even rent farms. Many African Americans therefore remained on plantations. Others tried to make a living in the cities.

African Americans who stayed on plantations often became part of a system known as **sharecropping**, or sharing the crop. Landowners provided the land, tools, and supplies, and sharecroppers provided the labor. At harvest time, the sharecropper usually had to give most of the crop to the landowner. Whatever remained belonged to the sharecropper. In theory, "croppers" who saved a little might even rent land for cash and keep their full harvest in a system known as tenant farming.

Instead, most sharecroppers lived in a cycle of debt. When they needed food, clothing, or supplies, most families had to buy goods on credit because they had little cash. When sharecroppers sold their crops, they hoped to be able to pay off these debts. However, bad weather, poor harvests, or low crop prices often made this dream impossible.

Sharecroppers usually grew cotton, one of the South's most important cash crops. When too many farmers planted cotton, however, the supply became excessive. As a result, the price per bale of cotton dropped. Many farmers understood the drawbacks of planting cotton. However, farmers felt pressure from banks and others to keep raising cotton.

Reading Check
Find Main Ideas How were African Americans' rights restricted?

Rebuilding Southern Industry

The southern economy suffered through cycles of good and bad years as cotton prices went up and down. Some business leaders hoped industry would strengthen the southern economy and create a New South.

Southern Industry Henry Grady, an Atlanta newspaper editor, was a leader of the New South movement. Grady and his supporters felt that with its cheap and abundant labor, the South could build factories and provide a workforce for them.

The most successful industrial development in the South involved textile production. Businesspeople built textile mills in many small towns to produce cotton fabric. Many people from rural areas came to work in the mills, but African Americans were not allowed to work in most of them.

Southern Mill Life Work in the cotton mills appealed to farm families who had trouble making ends meet. Recruiters sent out by the mills promised good wages and steady work. Mills employed large numbers of women and children. Women did most of the spinning and were valued workers. However, few women had the opportunity to advance within the company.

The New South

Atlanta rebuilt quickly after the war, becoming a leading railroad and industrial center. Newspaper editor Henry Grady gave stirring speeches about the need for industry in the South. He became one of the best-known spokesmen of the "New South."

Why might Grady point to Atlanta as a model for economic change?

"The New South . . . is stirred with the breath of a new life."

—Henry Grady

Reading Check
Find Main Ideas
What did southern business leaders hope industry would do?

Many mill workers were proud of the skills they used, but they did not enjoy their work. Workers often labored 12 hours a day, six days a week. Cotton dust and lint filled the air, causing asthma and an illness known as brown-lung disease. Fast-moving machinery caused injuries and even deaths. Despite the long hours and dangerous working conditions, wages remained low. However, mill work did offer an alternative to farming.

Reconstruction in the North

Although most federal Reconstruction policies were designed to reform the South, they affected groups in the North as well. There were many groups that worked to advance their own rights and interests during this time.

Women and Northern African Americans The Radical Republicans passed many federal laws that required southern states to allow African American men to vote. They based their cause on the ideal of equality found in the Declaration of Independence and the Constitution. Women's suffragists began using these same arguments to support their own suffrage. Wyoming and Utah granted women the vote in 1869, but their motivations were not just to ensure equal rights for women. Wyoming leaders hoped to attract more women residents, while Utahans hoped to counteract the rising number of non-Mormon voters.

African Americans in the North faced less social discrimination than they did in the South but still faced racism and segregation. In response, some state governments passed laws that made segregation illegal. Some integrated their school systems. Still, most states upheld the principle of separate-but-equal facilities.

A Changing Economy During the war and Reconstruction, the economy of the North and the West grew rapidly. Manufacturing, commerce, and rail transportation generated tremendous fortunes. Large companies grew by buying smaller companies, and railroads made huge profits transporting goods and people. Tax revenue increased as well, and governments were able to provide more services and make more investments.

Between 1865 and 1873, more than 2 million immigrants arrived in the United States. They provided a new pool of labor for the growing industrial economy. The number of labor unions increased, and they began to push for policies that protected workers. Reformers pressed for eight-hour-workday and fair-pay laws. In addition, the increase in commercial and trading businesses led to a shift in the makeup of the working class. It now included a majority of professionals and white-collar workers.

Eventually the focus of the Republican Party began to move away from civil rights for African Americans and toward reducing government corruption. The acceptance of the Compromise of 1877 signaled the end of the Republican focus on reforming racial politics in the South.

Summary and Preview In this lesson you learned about the end of Reconstruction. In the years that followed, the South continued to rebuild, but the gains made by African Americans were reversed.

Reading Check
Compare and Contrast How was Reconstruction in the North similar to and different from Reconstruction in the South?

Lesson 3 Assessment

Review Ideas, Terms, and People

1. a. Identify Who were some prominent African American leaders during Reconstruction? Why was the election of Hiram Revels significant?

b. Evaluate What do you think was the most important change made by Reconstruction state governments? Explain your answer.

2. a. Recall For what reasons did some local governments not stop the Ku Klux Klan?

b. Draw Conclusions How did the Ku Klux Klan's use of terror interfere with elections in the South?

3. a. Summarize What was the Compromise of 1877?

b. Evaluate How did *Plessy* v. *Ferguson* affect life in the United States?

c. Explain What was the relationship between Jim Crow laws and segregation?

4. a. Identify Who was Henry Grady, and why was he important?

b. Predict What are some possible results of the rise of the "New South"?

Critical Thinking

5. Identify Causes and Effects In this lesson you learned about Reconstruction governments. Create a graphic organizer similar to the one below and show why Reconstruction ended, as well as the results of its end.

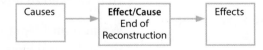

Causes → Effect/Cause End of Reconstruction → Effects

Social Studies Skills

Chance, Oversight, and Error in History

Understand the Skill

Sometimes, history can seem very routine. One event leads to others which, in turn, lead to still others. You learn to look for cause-and-effect relationships among events. You learn how point of view and bias can influence decisions and actions. These approaches to the study of history imply that the events of the past are orderly and predictable.

In fact, many of the events of the past *are* orderly and predictable. They may seem even more so since they're over and done with, and we know how things turned out. Yet, predictable patterns of behavior *do* exist throughout history. Recognizing them is one of the great values and rewards of studying the past. As the philosopher George Santayana once famously said, "Those who cannot remember the past are condemned to repeat it."

At its most basic level, however, history is people, and people are "human." They make mistakes. Unexpected things happen to them, both good things and bad. This is the unpredictable element of history. The current phrase "stuff happens" is just as true of the past as it is today. Mistakes, oversights, and just plain "dumb luck" have shaped the course of history—and have helped to make the study of it so exciting.

Learn the Skill

California merchant John Sutter decided to build a sawmill along a nearby American river in 1848. He planned to sell the lumber it produced to settlers who were moving into the area. Sutter put James W. Marshall to work building the mill. To install the large waterwheel that would power the saw, Marshall first had to deepen the riverbed next to the mill. During his digging, he noticed some shiny bits of yellow metal in the water. The result of this accidental find was the California gold rush, which sent thousands of Americans to California, and speeded settlement of the West.

In 1863 the army of Confederate general Robert E. Lee invaded Maryland. The Civil War had been going well for the South. Lee hoped a southern victory on Union soil would convince the British to aid the South in the war. However, a Confederate officer forgot his cigars as his unit left its camp in the Maryland countryside. Wrapped around the cigars was a copy of Lee's battle plans. When a Union soldier came upon the abandoned camp, he spotted the cigars. This chance discovery enabled the Union army to defeat Lee at the Battle of Antietam. The Union victory helped keep the British out of the war. More importantly, it allowed President Lincoln to issue the Emancipation Proclamation and begin the process of ending slavery in the United States.

Practice the Skill

In April 1865 President Lincoln was assassinated while attending the theater in Washington, DC. Bodyguard John Parker was stationed outside the door of the president's box. However, Parker left his post to find a seat from which he could watch the play. This allowed the killer to enter the box and shoot the unprotected president.

Write an essay about how this chance event altered the course of history. How might Reconstruction, North–South relations, and African Americans' struggle for equality have been different had Lincoln lived?

Module 19 Assessment

Review Vocabulary, Terms, and People

Complete each sentence by filling in the blank with the correct term or person from the module.

1. _____ were laws that allowed racial segregation in public places.

2. The Radical Republicans were led by _____, a member of Congress from Pennsylvania.

3. The period from 1865 to 1877 that focused on reuniting the nation is known as _____.

4. Following the Civil War, many African Americans in the South made a living by participating in the _____ system.

5. After opposing Congress, Andrew Johnson became the first president to face _____ proceedings.

6. The _____ Amendment made slavery in the United States illegal.

7. In 1870 _____ became the first African American to serve in the U.S. Senate.

Comprehension and Critical Thinking

Lesson 1

8. a. **Describe** How did the lives of African Americans change after the Civil War?

   b. **Compare and Contrast** How was President Johnson's Reconstruction plan similar and different from President Lincoln's Ten Percent Plan?

   c. **Evaluate** Which of the three Reconstruction plans that were originally proposed do you think would have been the most successful? Why?

Lesson 2

9. a. **Identify** Who were the Radical Republicans, and how did they change Reconstruction?

   b. **Analyze** How did the debate over the Fourteenth Amendment affect the election of 1866?

   c. **Elaborate** Do you think Congress was right to impeach President Andrew Johnson? Explain.

Lesson 3

10. a. **Describe** What reforms did Reconstruction governments in the South support?

    b. **Draw Conclusions** In what ways did southern governments attempt to reverse the accomplishments of Reconstruction?

    c. **Evaluate** Do you think the South was successful or unsuccessful in its rebuilding efforts? Explain your answer.

Module 19 Assessment, continued

Review Themes

11. **Politics** Explain the political struggles that took place during Reconstruction.

12. **Society and Culture** How were the lives of ordinary southerners affected in the years after Reconstruction?

Reading Skills

Analyze Historical Information *Use the Reading Skills taught in this module to answer the question about the reading selection below.*

> Radical Republicans, on the other hand, took a harsher stance. They wanted the federal government to force change in the South. Like the moderates, they thought the Black Codes were cruel and unjust.

13. Which of the following is relevant information for the passage above?
    a. Thaddeus Stevens was a Radical Republican.
    b. Andrew Johnson was a Democrat.
    c. Radical Republicans wanted the federal government to make major changes in the South.
    d. Radical Republicans were eventually removed from power.

Social Studies Skills

Chance, Oversight, and Error in History *Use the Social Studies Skills taught in this module to answer the question about the reading selection below.*

> Johnson's speaking tour was a disaster. It did little to win votes for the Democratic Party. Johnson even got into arguments with people in the audiences of some of his speaking engagements.

14. Which of the following is an example of chance, oversight, or error that affected history?
    a. Johnson got into arguments with audiences.
    b. The tour was a disaster.
    c. The tour did not win votes.
    d. Johnson spoke for the Democratic Party.

Focus on Writing

15. **Write a Job History** In this module you read about the changing job scene during Reconstruction. Put yourself in the shoes of a person living then. It could be anyone—a returning soldier, a shopkeeper, a schoolteacher, or a politician. What jobs would that person seek? Why would he or she leave one job for another? Write a brief job history for that person during Reconstruction. Include at least four jobs. Make each job description two to four sentences long. End each one with a sentence or two about why the person left that job. Add one sentence explaining why he or she took the next job. Be sure to include specific historical details.

Module 20

The Industrial Age

★

Essential Question

How revolutionary was the Second Industrial Revolution?

About the Photo: Technological advances changed city life in the United States.

In this module you will learn about the new inventions of the late 1800s. You will also read about how life and business changed because of these inventions.

What You Will Learn ...

Lesson 1: The Second Industrial Revolution **642**
The Big Idea The Second Industrial Revolution led to new sources of power and advances in transportation and communication.
Lesson 2: Big Business **648**
The Big Idea The growth of big business in the late 1800s led to the creation of monopolies.
Lesson 3: Industrial Workers **652**
The Big Idea Changes in the workplace led to a rise in labor unions and workers' strikes.

▷ *Explore ONLINE!*

HISTORY

VIDEOS, including...
- Skyscrapers
- The Steel Industry
- Henry Ford and the Model T
- The Wright Brothers Controversy
- John D. Rockefeller: The Standard Oil Trust
- Homestead Strike

☑ Document-Based Investigations

☑ Graphic Organizers

☑ Interactive Games

☑ Animation: Early Refrigerated Railroad Cars

☑ Image Carousel: The Age of Inventions

☑ Interactive Map: Major Labor Strikes, Late 1800s

Timeline of Events 1870–1900

United States	World

1870

‹ **1876** Alexander Graham Bell invents the telephone.

1876 German engineer Nikolaus A. Otto perfects a gasoline-powered engine.

1879 Thomas Edison invents the first lightbulb.

1883 The island volcano of Krakatau in the Pacific Ocean erupts in one of the world's greatest natural disasters.

∧ **1886** The American Federation of Labor is formed on December 8.

∧ **1889** The Eiffel Tower is built in Paris.

1890 Congress passes the Sherman Antitrust Act.

1892 On June 29 the Homestead strike begins. Carnegie Steel Company refuses to negotiate with the union.

∧ **1898** French scientists Pierre and Marie Curie discover radium.

1900

Reading Social Studies

THEME FOCUS:

Economics, Society and Culture

In this module you will read about the advancements in transportation and communication made during what is called the Second Industrial Revolution. You will learn about the rise of powerful corporations. You will also read about the workers who organized in the late 1800s and will see what happened as unions began demanding better treatment for workers. Throughout the module you will see how society was affected by the changing economy.

READING FOCUS:

Identify Patterns of Organization

How are clothes organized in a department store? How are files arranged in a file cabinet? Clear organization helps us find the product we need, and it also helps us find facts and information.

Understand Structural Patterns Writers use structural patterns to organize information in sentences or paragraphs. What's a structural pattern? It's simply a way of organizing information. Learning to recognize those patterns will make it easier for you to read and understand social studies texts.

Patterns of Organization		
Pattern	**Clue Words**	**Graphic Organizer**
Cause-effect shows how one thing leads to another.	as a result, therefore, because, this led to	Cause → Effect, Effect, Effect → Effect
Chronological order shows the sequence of events or actions.	after, before, first, then, not long after, finally	First → Next → Last
Comparison-contrast points out similarities and/or differences.	although, but, however, on the other hand, similarly, also	Differences / Similarities
Listing presents information in categories such as size, location, or importance.	also, most important, for example, in fact	Category • Fact • Fact • Fact

To use text structure to improve your understanding, follow these steps:
1. Look for the main idea of the passage you are reading.
2. Then look for clues that signal a specific pattern.
3. Look for other important ideas and think about how the ideas connect. Is there any obvious pattern?
4. Use a graphic organizer to map the relationships among the facts and details.

You Try It!

The following passages are from the module you are about to read. As you read each set of sentences, ask yourself what structural pattern the writer used to organize the information.

(A) Great advances in communication technologies took place in the late 1800s. By 1861 telegraph wires connected the East and West coasts. Five years later, a telegraph cable on the floor of the Atlantic Ocean connected the United States and Great Britain.

(B) Many business leaders justified their business methods through their belief in social Darwinism. . . . Other business leaders, however, believed that the rich had a duty to aid the poor.

(C) During the late 1800s, several factors led to a decline in the quality of working conditions. Machines run by unskilled workers were eliminating the jobs of many skilled craftspeople. These low-paid workers could be replaced easily.

After you read the passages, answer the following questions:

1. Re-read passage A. What structural pattern did the writer use to organize this information? How can you tell?

2. Re-read passage B. What structural pattern did the writer use to organize this information? How can you tell? Why do you think the writer chose this pattern?

3. Re-read passage C. What structural pattern did the writer use to organize this information? How can you tell? Why do you think the writer chose this pattern?

As you read Module 20, think about the organization of the ideas. Ask yourself why the writer chose to organize the information in this way.

Key Terms and People

Lesson 1
Second Industrial Revolution
Bessemer process
Thomas Edison
patents
Alexander Graham Bell
Henry Ford
moving assembly line
Wilbur and Orville Wright

Lesson 2
corporations
Andrew Carnegie
vertical integration
John D. Rockefeller
horizontal integration
trust
Leland Stanford
social Darwinism
monopoly
Sherman Antitrust Act

Lesson 3
Frederick W. Taylor
collective bargaining
Knights of Labor
Terence V. Powderly
American Federation
   of Labor (AFL)
Samuel Gompers
Mary Harris Jones
Haymarket Riot
Homestead strike
Pullman strike

The Second Industrial Revolution

The Big Idea

The Second Industrial Revolution led to new sources of power and advances in transportation and communication.

Main Ideas

- Breakthroughs in steel processing led to a boom in railroad construction.

- Advances in the use of oil and electricity improved communication and transportation.

- A rush of inventions changed Americans' lives.

Key Terms and People

Second Industrial Revolution
Bessemer process
Thomas Edison
patents
Alexander Graham Bell
Henry Ford
moving assembly line
Wilbur and Orville Wright

If YOU were there . . .

You live in a small town but are visiting an aunt in the city in the 1890s. You are amazed when your aunt pushes a button on the wall to turn on electric lights. At home you still use kerosene lamps. You hear a clatter outside and see an electric streetcar traveling down the street. You are shocked when a telephone rings and your aunt speaks to someone miles away!

Which of these inventions would you find most amazing?

Breakthroughs Fuel Industrialization

In the late 1800s, new technologies helped industry grow at a staggering pace. Electrical power replaced steam and water power. Factories became larger and produced more and more goods. Faster transportation helped move people and goods more cheaply. These advances and others fueled the **Second Industrial Revolution**, a period of rapid growth in U.S. manufacturing in the late 1800s. By the mid-1890s the United States had become the world's industrial leader.

Bessemer Steel Process Some of the most important advances in technology happened in the steel industry. Steel is iron that has been made stronger by heat and the addition of other metals. In the mid-1850s Henry Bessemer invented the **Bessemer process**, a way to manufacture steel quickly and cheaply by blasting hot air through melted iron to quickly remove impurities. Before, turning several tons of iron ore into steel took a day or more. The Bessemer process took only 10 to 20 minutes.

New Use for Steel The Bessemer process cut the time and the cost required to produce steel. Factories began to make many products out of steel, including barbed wire, nails, and beams for buildings. To meet demand for these products, the nation's steel production rose dramatically, from 77,000 tons in 1870 to more than 1 million tons in 1879.

Steel made innovative construction possible. One of the most remarkable structures was the Brooklyn Bridge. Completed in 1883 it spanned 1,595 feet across the East River in New York City. Not only was it the longest suspension bridge in the world, it was the first to use steel cables.

Riding the Rails Steel was also used for rails to expand the railroads. As steel prices dropped, so too did the cost of railroad construction. Companies built thousands of miles of new steel track. The design of elegant passenger and sleeping cars improved passenger service. Manufacturers and farmers sent products to market faster than ever by rail in newly invented refrigerated shipping cars. Cities where major rail lines crossed, such as Chicago, grew rapidly. Railroads also increased western growth by offering free tickets to settlers. Finally, as rail travel and shipping increased, railroads and related industries began employing more people.

Use of Oil and Electricity

The Second Industrial Revolution was characterized by dramatic developments in the use and distribution of oil and electricity. These power sources fueled other changes.

Oil as a Power Source Other important technological breakthroughs in the late 1800s led to the widespread use of petroleum, or oil, as a power

Reading Check
Identify Cause and Effect
How did steel processing change in the 1850s, and how did this affect the United States?

Homestead Steel Mill

Steel mills like this one in Homestead, Pennsylvania, were the center of the new steel industry that led to advancements in rail travel. Workers used the Bessemer process to make steel more quickly.

How do you think mills like this one affected the surrounding area?

Quick Facts

Factors Affecting Industrial Growth

- Greater ability to use natural resources
- A growing population
- Transportation advances
- Rising immigration
- Inventions and innovations
- Increasing business investment
- Government policies assisting business, such as protective tariffs

source. In the 1850s scientists discovered an inexpensive way to convert crude, or unprocessed, oil into a fuel called kerosene that could be used to light lamps. Because kerosene was so affordable, people quickly put it to good use lighting their homes and businesses.

Not surprisingly, demand for oil skyrocketed and companies set out to discover new oil sources. Until this time, people had collected oil from seeps, places where oil naturally oozes from the ground. However, oil from seeps couldn't keep up with demand. One company hired Edwin L. Drake, who believed he could access oil by drilling into the ground in Pennsylvania. At first people mocked Drake's drilling efforts as "Drake's Folly." Then, in 1859 his crew hit an underground spring deep in the rock. The next day, oil seeped up and the crew scrambled to collect it in buckets, tubs, and barrels. Edwin Drake had drilled the first commercial oil well. He was soon steadily pumping "black gold" to the surface.

The output from Drake's well was modest, but it drew plenty of wildcatters, or oil prospectors, to Ohio, Pennsylvania, and West Virginia. Oil became a big business as these states began producing millions of barrels per year. Oil companies built refineries to turn the crude oil into finished products like kerosene. One oil company supervisor referred to oil workers as "men who are supplying light for the world."

Electricity Spreads In addition to kerosene, electricity became a critical source of light and power during the Second Industrial Revolution. The possible uses of electricity interested inventors like **Thomas Edison**. His

Timeline: The Spirit of Innovation

Improvements in steel production and the use of oil and electricity as power sources led to inventions that changed the ways Americans communicated, traveled, worked, and lived.

1850

1903

1852 Elisha Otis invents the elevator safety brake, making elevators safe for people.

1854 Henry Bessemer patents a method for making cast steel.

1869 John Roebling begins work on the Brooklyn Bridge.

1872 Elijah McCoy receives the patent for his device that oiled machine engines.

1876 Alexander Graham Bell invents the telephone.

1879 Thomas Edison creates a durable electric lightbulb.

1887 Harriet Strong receives a patent for her advances in dam and reservoir construction.

1890 J. Frank and Charles Duryea successfully test their first gasoline-powered automobile.

1893 George Ferris displays the first Ferris wheel at the World's Columbian Exposition in Chicago.

1903 Orville Wright makes the first flight in a motorized airplane.

Analyze Timelines
Which inventions improved transportation and communication?

research center in Menlo Park, New Jersey, was called an invention factory. Edison explained his practical approach to science.

> "I do not regard myself as a pure scientist, as so many persons have insisted that I am. I do not search for the laws of nature . . . for the purpose of learning truth. I am only a professional inventor . . . with the object [goal] of inventing that which will have commercial utility [use]."
>
> —Thomas Edison, quoted in *Scientific American*, July 8, 1893

Edison eventually held more than 1,000 **patents**, exclusive rights to make or sell inventions. Patents allowed inventors to protect their inventions from being manufactured by others.

In 1878 Edison announced that he would soon invent a practical electric light. By the end of 1879 Edison and his team of inventors had created the electric lightbulb. The public was excited. However, Edison had a problem. At the time, few homes or businesses could get electricity. Edison therefore built a power plant that began supplying electricity to dozens of New York City buildings in September 1882. The *New York Times* reported that with electric lighting in the newspaper offices, "it seemed almost like writing by daylight." However, Edison's equipment could not send electricity over long distances. As a result, his power company, Edison Electric, provided electricity mainly to central cities.

In the late 1880s George Westinghouse built a power system that could send electricity across many miles. As Edison and Westinghouse competed, the use of electricity spread rapidly in the nation's cities. After a while, electricity soon lit homes and businesses and powered city factories. Electricity also was used to power streetcars in cities across the nation.

Reading Check
Draw Conclusions
Why did people begin to pump oil from the ground?

Rush of Inventions

In the late 1800s inventors focused on finding solutions to practical problems. Communication and transportation took the lead.

Advances in Communication Great advances in communication technologies took place in the late 1800s. By 1861 telegraph wires connected the East and West coasts. Five years later, a telegraph cable on the floor of the Atlantic Ocean connected the United States and Great Britain.

However, the telegraph carried only written messages and was difficult for untrained people to use. These problems were solved in March 1876, when inventor **Alexander Graham Bell** patented the telephone. Bell was a Scottish-born speech teacher who studied the science of sound. He called the telephone a "talking telegraph."

Companies quickly found telephones to be an essential business tool. People wanted them in their homes, too. Telephone companies raced to lay thousands of miles of phone lines. By 1880 there were about 55,000 telephones

Alexander Graham Bell opened the telephone line that connected New York and Chicago in 1892.

J. Frank and Charles Duryea designed and invented the first gasoline-powered automobile in America.

Academic Vocabulary
implement to put in place

in the United States. By 1900 about 1.5 million telephones had been installed in homes and offices across the nation.

Automobiles and Planes In 1876 a German engineer invented an engine powered by gasoline, another fuel made from oil. In 1893 two brothers, Charles and J. Frank Duryea, used a gasoline engine to build the first practical motorcar in the United States. By the early 1900s, thousands of cars were being built in the United States.

At first, cars were luxury items that only the wealthy could buy. That changed when a young entrepreneur, **Henry Ford**, introduced the Model T in 1908. Ford aimed to make "a motor car for the great multitude." At first, Ford's mechanics built Model Ts one car at a time, but this soon changed.

Ford started by simplifying his design and making all of his cars identical. This brought the cost down, but not enough to make cars affordable to ordinary people. So Ford studied manufacturing processes that would reduce costs by increasing productivity and efficiency, such as using interchangeable parts and the assembly line.

Ford became the first to **implement** a large-scale **moving assembly line** to make cars. On Ford's assembly line, each car that was being built moved along a conveyor belt to workers at various workstations. The work of building the car was broken down into 84 steps. Each worker was trained to do just one job, requiring simple skills and interchangeable parts. This process allowed Ford to produce more cars at a lower cost. In its first year, the Ford assembly line produced a car every hour and a half. The cars sold for under $500, about half the cost of the first Model Ts and a price that many people could afford.

New engine technology helped make another breakthrough in transportation possible—air flight. Brothers **Wilbur and Orville Wright** built a lightweight airplane that used a small, gas-powered engine. On December 17, 1903, the Wright brothers tried out their airplane at Kitty Hawk, North Carolina. In freezing temperatures and a strong wind, Orville climbed into the pilot's seat and the plane took off across the beach. It flew just inches above the ground and landed 120 feet from where it had started. This short trip—12 seconds in all—was the first true flight in an airplane. The Wright brothers quickly followed this success with even longer flights.

Airplanes would soon give Americans another transportation option. Passenger airlines first flew through American skies in the 1920s. Early flights offered little comfort—some passengers wore goggles and helmets for protection. Moreover, planes couldn't fly over mountains or at night. In

Wilbur and Orville Wright invented the first power-driven airplane in 1903.

Reading Check
Compare What new inventions excited the public in the 1800s, and how were they used?

fact, for cross-country travel, trains were more comfortable, faster, and less expensive option. Still, for a handful of Americans, the thrill of air travel outweighed the early discomfort.

Summary and Preview The Second Industrial Revolution led to advances in energy sources, communication, and transportation. In the next lesson you will learn about the growth of big business.

Lesson 1 Assessment

Review Ideas, Terms, and People

1. **a. Describe** What was the Bessemer process?

   b. Summarize How did improvements to railroads affect the economy and transportation in the United States?

   c. Elaborate What was the most important effect of the Bessemer process? Why?

2. **a. Describe** How does the paragraph about Edwin L. Drake and oil drilling show the cause and effect structure?

   b. Describe Using technology related to oil production, explain how technological innovations impact how people modify the physical environment.

   c. Explain What problem did Thomas Edison face regarding the use of electricity, and how did he solve it?

3. **a. Recall** What contribution did Wilbur and Orville Wright make to transportation?

   b. Draw Conclusions How did Alexander Graham Bell's invention improve life in the United States?

   c. Elaborate Why do you think there was a rush of inventions in the late 1800s?

Critical Thinking

4. **Analyze** In this lesson you learned about inventors. Complete a table like the one below about inventors, their inventions, and their impact on Americans.

Inventor	Invention	Impact

Big Business

The Big Idea

The growth of big business in the late 1800s led to the creation of monopolies.

Main Ideas

- The rise of corporations and powerful business leaders led to the dominance of big business in the United States.
- People and the government began to question the methods of big business.

Key Terms and People

corporations
Andrew Carnegie
vertical integration
John D. Rockefeller
horizontal integration
trust
Leland Stanford
social Darwinism
monopoly
Sherman Antitrust Act

If YOU were there . . .

It is 1895, and your town is home to a large corporation. The company's founder and owner, a wealthy man, lives in a mansion on a hill. He is a fair employer but not especially generous. Many townspeople work in his factory. You and other town leaders feel that he should contribute more to local charities and community organizations.

How could this business leader help the town more?

Dominance of Big Business

In the late 1800s many entrepreneurs formed their businesses as **corporations**, or businesses that sell portions of ownership called stock shares. The leaders of these corporations were some of the richest and most influential members of American society in the late 1800s. Political leaders praised prosperous businesspeople as examples of American hard work, talent, and success.

Corporations Generate Wealth Successful corporations reward not only the people who found them but also investors who hold stock. Stockholders in a corporation typically get a percentage of profits based on the amount of stock they own. Although stockholders actually own the corporation, they do not run its day-to-day business. Instead, they elect a board of directors that chooses the corporation's main leaders, such as the president.

New sales techniques like those taught by John H. Patterson helped change business practices.

The Rise of Investing

Investors purchased stock in corporations in record numbers in the late 1800s. They received stock certificates, like the one shown here, to document their part ownership in corporations. Corporations used the money raised by selling stocks to expand. Standard Oil Company financed the building of this refinery in Richmond, California, by selling stock.

Why did investors buy stock?

Corporations provided several important advantages over earlier business forms. Stockholders in a corporation are not responsible for business debts. If a corporation fails financially, the stockholders lose only the money that they invested. Stockholders are also usually free to sell their stock to whomever they want, whenever they want. As a result, corporations encouraged more investment in businesses. By 1900 more than 100 million shares per year were being traded on the New York Stock Exchange.

Business Leaders Some business leaders became wealthy, powerful, and famous because of the business boom. **Andrew Carnegie** was one of the most admired businesspeople of the time. Born in Scotland, Carnegie came to the United States as a poor immigrant. As a teenager he took a job with a railroad company and quickly worked his way up to the position of railroad superintendent.

In 1873 he focused his efforts on steelmaking. Carnegie expanded his business by buying out competitors when steel prices were low. By 1901 Carnegie's mills were producing more steel than all of Great Britain's mills combined. Carnegie's businesses succeeded largely through **vertical integration**, or ownership of businesses involved in each step of a manufacturing process. For example, to lower production costs, Carnegie **acquired** the iron ore mines, coalfields, and railroads needed to supply and support his steel mills.

John D. Rockefeller was also successful in consolidating, or combining, businesses. By age 21, while a partner in a wholesale business, he decided to start an oil-refining company. In only ten years Rockefeller's Standard Oil Company was the country's largest oil refiner. Like Carnegie, Rockefeller used vertical integration. For example, the company controlled most of the pipelines it used.

Academic Vocabulary
acquire to get

Rockefeller's company also developed **horizontal integration**, or owning all businesses in a certain field. By 1880 Rockefeller's companies controlled about 90 percent of the oil refining business in the United States. Rockefeller also formed a **trust**, a legal arrangement grouping together a number of companies under a single board of directors. To earn more money, trusts often tried to get rid of competition and to control production.

Reading Check
Compare and Contrast Why did Andrew Carnegie use vertical integration?

Leland Stanford was another important business leader of the late 1800s. He made a fortune selling equipment to miners. While governor of California, he became one of the founders of the state's Central Pacific Railroad. He also founded Stanford University. Late in life, Stanford argued that industries should be owned and managed cooperatively by workers. He believed this would be the fulfillment of democracy.

Leland Stanford moved to California during the Gold Rush and made his fortune in the railroad industry.

Questioning the Methods of Big Business

In the late 1800s many Americans admired business tycoons as natural leaders and "captains of industry." However, other people and the government began to see the tough tactics of big business as a problem.

Social Darwinism Many business leaders justified their business methods through their belief in **social Darwinism**, a view of society based on scientist Charles Darwin's theory of natural selection. Social Darwinists thought that Darwin's "survival of the fittest" theory decided which human beings would succeed in business and in life in general.

Other business leaders, however, believed that the rich had a duty to aid the poor. These leaders tried to help the less fortunate through philanthropy, or giving money to charities. Carnegie, Rockefeller, Stanford, and other business leaders gave away large sums. Carnegie gave away more than $350 million to charities, about $60 million of which went to fund public libraries to expand access to books. By the late 1800s various charities had received millions of dollars from philanthropists.

The Antitrust Movement Critics of big business said that many business leaders earned their fortunes through unfair business practices. These criticisms grew stronger in the 1880s as corporations became more powerful. Large corporations often used their size and strength to drive smaller competitors out of business. Carnegie and Rockefeller, for example, pressured railroads to charge their companies lower shipping rates. Powerful trusts also arranged to sell goods and services below market value. Smaller competitors went out of business trying to match those prices. Then the trusts raised prices again.

Some people became concerned when a trust gained a **monopoly**, or total ownership of a product or service. Critics argued that monopolies reduced necessary competition. They believed competition in a free market economy kept prices low and the quality of goods and services high.

Some Americans also worried about the political power of wealthy trusts. Many citizens and small businesses wanted the government to help control monopolies and trusts. People who favored trusts responded that trusts were more efficient and gave the consumer dependable products or services.

"What a Funny Little Government"

This 1899 cartoon of John D. Rockefeller expressed a fear shared by many Americans—trusts, such as Standard Oil, had grown too powerful.

What do you think the smokestacks on the Capitol represent?

What does the position of the White House suggest?

Analyze Historical Sources
How does the cartoonist show Rockefeller's power?

Reading Check
Analyze How did concerns about trusts lead to the Sherman Antitrust Act?

Many members of Congress favored big business. However, elected officials could not ignore the concerns of voters. In July 1890 Congress passed the **Sherman Antitrust Act**, a law that made it illegal to create monopolies or trusts that restrained trade. It stated that any "attempt to monopolize . . . any part of the trade or commerce among the several States" was a crime. However, the act did not clearly define a trust in legal terms. The antitrust laws were therefore difficult to enforce. Corporations and trusts kept growing in size and power.

Summary and Preview In this lesson you learned how, in the late 1800s, some corporations became monopolies that dominated entire industries, such as oil. In the next lesson you will learn about how industrial workers organized to improve working conditions.

Lesson 2 Assessment

Review Ideas, Terms, and People

1. **a. Identify** What are horizontal and vertical integration?

   b. Explain What are the benefits of investing in corporations?

   c. Evaluate What do you think about the business methods of Carnegie, Rockefeller, and Stanford?

2. **a. Describe** What is social Darwinism?

   b. Summarize What concerns did critics of big business have regarding trusts?

   c. Evaluate Was the Sherman Antitrust Act successful? Why or why not?

Critical Thinking

3. **Contrast** In this lesson you learned about new business practices. Create a graphic organizer like the one below and identify examples of these new business practices.

New Practices	Example

Industrial Workers

The Big Idea

Changes in the workplace led to a rise in labor unions and workers' strikes.

Main Ideas

- The desire to maximize profits and become more efficient led to poor working conditions.

- Workers began to organize and demand improvements in working conditions and pay.

- Labor strikes often turned violent and failed to accomplish their goals.

Key Terms and People

Frederick W. Taylor
collective bargaining
Knights of Labor
Terence V. Powderly
American Federation of Labor (AFL)
Samuel Gompers
Mary Harris Jones
Haymarket Riot
Homestead strike
Pullman strike

Reading Check
Identify Cause and Effect Why did companies begin to use scientific management, and how did it affect workers?

If YOU were there . . .

You run a button machine in a clothing factory in the 1890s. You work from 7:00 in the morning until 6:00 at night, every day except Sunday. Your only break is 15 minutes for lunch. Now you hear about a movement to start a workers' union to bargain with your employer. Union members will ask for an eight-hour workday. But you think your employer might fire you if you join.

Would you join the union?

Maximizing Profits and Efficiency

During the late 1800s several factors led to a decline in the quality of working conditions. Skilled craftspeople found themselves replaced by machines operated by unskilled workers, who were low-paid and easily replaced. This was an unfortunate side effect of new technologies and increasing labor specialization, or the splitting of work into smaller and more specific tasks.

For workers, specialization often meant having to perform the same small task over and over again. This made workers tired, bored, and more likely to be injured. But, for factories, specialization reduced costs and greatly increased production. For example, specialization along Ford's moving assembly line sped the production and lowered the cost of making automobiles. As a result, automobiles became affordable to a wider segment of the population than ever before.

In 1909 **Frederick W. Taylor**, an efficiency engineer, published a popular book called *The Principles of Scientific Management*. He encouraged managers to view workers as interchangeable parts of the production process. In factories, managers influenced by Taylor paid less attention to working conditions. Injuries increased, and as conditions grew worse, workers looked for ways to bring about change.

Poor Working Conditions

Small, crowded rooms. Stuffy air. Unsafe workplaces. Long hours. Low pay. No job security. These were the facts of working life for millions of Americans during the Second Industrial Revolution.

What does this photograph suggest about working conditions?

Workers Organize

By the late 1800s working conditions and pay were so poor that workers began to join labor unions to improve their lot. By joining forces with others, they hoped to pressure employers into paying better wages and improving working conditions. With **collective bargaining**—all workers acting collectively, or together—workers had a much greater chance of success in negotiating with management. Most employers opposed collective bargaining. One company president said, "I shall never give in. I would rather go out of business."

Tailors who wanted to protect their interests founded the first national labor union, the **Knights of Labor**, in Philadelphia in 1869 as a secret society. In the 1880s, under the leadership of **Terence V. Powderly**, the Knights ended its policy of secrecy. It also began to accept unskilled workers, women, and African Americans as members. By 1886 the group had more than 700,000 members.

With the motto "An injury to one is a concern of all," the Knights of Labor campaigned for many reforms. It pushed for an eight-hour workday, equal pay for equal work, and an end to child labor. Union members also wanted the government to regulate trusts. In its early years, the Knights

Samuel Gompers 1850–1924

Samuel Gompers was born to Jewish parents in London. He immigrated to the United States with his parents in 1863 at age 13. He worked as a cigar maker and joined a local union, eventually becoming its president. In time, the cigar-makers' union was reorganized and later joined the American Federation of Labor. Gompers became the AFL's first president and remained so, except for the year 1895, until his death. He campaigned for basic trade-union rights, such as the right to picket and to organize boycotts and strikes. His efforts on behalf of workers helped organized labor to gain respect.

Summarize
How did Samuel Gompers help the labor movement?

discouraged strikes, preferring tactics such as boycotts and negotiations. Yet soon enough, strikes would become commonplace.

Another early labor union was the **American Federation of Labor (AFL)**, led by **Samuel Gompers**. The AFL was founded by members of craft unions who were unhappy with how the Knights of Labor represented their interests. While the Knights organized individual workers, the AFL organized unions, such as the mineworkers' and steelworkers' unions. The AFL also limited its membership to skilled workers. This gave the union great bargaining power but left out most workers. The AFL tried to get better wages, hours, and working conditions for laborers. By 1890 the AFL's membership was larger than that of the Knights. Using strikes and other tactics, the AFL won wage increases and shorter workweeks.

Many women took active roles in unions. For example, **Mary Harris Jones**, an Irish immigrant, dedicated herself to improving the lives of workers. "Mother Jones," as she was affectionately called, was a fiery speaker, who used her abilities to organize strikes and educate workers.

Reading Check
Contrast How did the Knights of Labor and the AFL differ?

Labor Strikes

By the late 1800s other unions were gaining strength. Major workers' strikes swept the country and included miners in Colorado, steelworkers in Pennsylvania, and railroad workers in Illinois and California. Some strikes involved violent clashes with police. One of the worst confrontations occurred in Chicago in 1886.

In May 1886 thousands of union members in Chicago went on strike because they wanted an eight-hour workday. Two strikers were killed in a fight with police. The next night, workers met at Haymarket Square to protest the killings. In what became known as the **Haymarket Riot**, an unidentified person threw a dynamite bomb at police, who were trying to

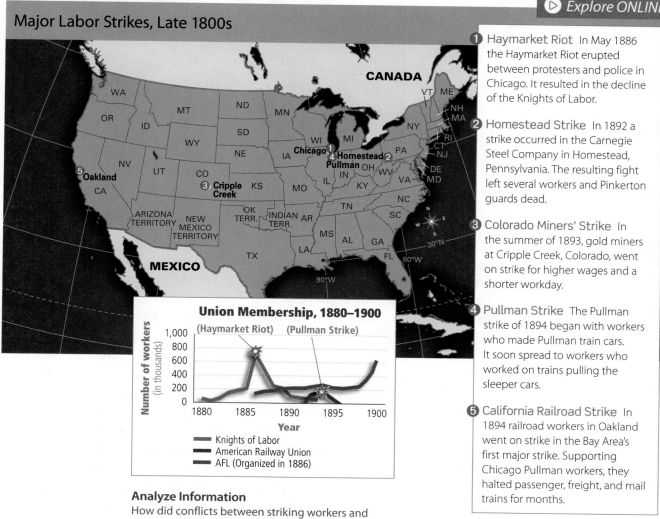

Major Labor Strikes, Late 1800s

Explore ONLINE!

1 Haymarket Riot In May 1886 the Haymarket Riot erupted between protesters and police in Chicago. It resulted in the decline of the Knights of Labor.

2 Homestead Strike In 1892 a strike occurred in the Carnegie Steel Company in Homestead, Pennsylvania. The resulting fight left several workers and Pinkerton guards dead.

3 Colorado Miners' Strike In the summer of 1893, gold miners at Cripple Creek, Colorado, went on strike for higher wages and a shorter workday.

4 Pullman Strike The Pullman strike of 1894 began with workers who made Pullman train cars. It soon spread to workers who worked on trains pulling the sleeper cars.

5 California Railroad Strike In 1894 railroad workers in Oakland went on strike in the Bay Area's first major strike. Supporting Chicago Pullman workers, they halted passenger, freight, and mail trains for months.

Union Membership, 1880–1900

(Haymarket Riot) (Pullman Strike)

Number of workers (in thousands)

1,000 800 600 400 200 0

1880 1885 1890 1895 1900

Year

— Knights of Labor
— American Railway Union
— AFL (Organized in 1886)

Analyze Information
How did conflicts between striking workers and authorities affect union membership?

break up the crowd. The police panicked and fired into the crowd. Before the situation calmed down, seven police officers and four workers were killed. More than 100 others suffered injuries.

Police arrested numerous suspects and eventually charged eight people with conspiracy and murder. No evidence existed to connect these men to the crime. In fact, five of them were not even in Haymarket Square when the bomb went off. Still, all eight were convicted and sentenced to death. Four were hanged and one killed himself in prison. In 1893 the new governor of Illinois pardoned the last three. He believed that their guilt had not been proven.

Sometimes, business owners succeeded in breaking up unions. In 1892 a violent strike called the **Homestead strike** took place at Andrew Carnegie's Homestead steel factory in Pennsylvania. Union members there protested a plan to buy new machinery and cut jobs. The company refused to negotiate with the union and locked workers out of the plant, hiring

The Pullman Strike
On July 6, 1894, during the Pullman Strike, a mob of frustrated strikers toppled and set fire to hundreds of railcars in South Chicago.

strikebreakers to perform their jobs. The workers responded by seizing control of the plant. Gunfire erupted on July 6, when Pinkerton detectives hired by the company tried to enter the plant. A fierce battle raged for 14 hours, leaving 16 people dead. The governor called out the state militia to restore order. Continuing for four more months, the union was eventually defeated.

Another major strike happened at George Pullman's Pullman Palace Car Company in the company town of Pullman, Illinois. Most of the company workers lived there, paying high rents. During a financial depression that began in 1893, Pullman laid off about half of the workers and cut pay for those who were left, without lowering their rents. On May 11, 1894, workers began the **Pullman strike**, which stopped traffic on many railroad lines until federal courts ordered the workers to return to their jobs. President Grover Cleveland sent federal troops to Chicago to stop the strike. Such defeats seriously damaged the labor movement for years.

Reading Check
Analyze What were the effects of early major strikes on workers?

Summary and Preview Workers formed unions to fight for better conditions and to keep their jobs. In the next module you will learn about a new wave of immigrants in the late 1800s.

Lesson 3 Assessment

Review Ideas, Terms, and People

1. a. Recall Why did conditions in factories begin to decline?

b. Draw Conclusions How were workers affected by specialization and scientific management?

c. Evaluate Do you think scientific management made businesses more successful? Explain.

2. a. Identify What role did Mary Harris Jones play in the labor movement?

b. Analyze Why did workers use collective bargaining, and why did business owners oppose it?

c. Explain What were the origins and accomplishments of the Knights of Labor and the American Federation of Labor?

d. Elaborate Do you think the demands made by labor unions were reasonable?

3. a. Describe What major labor strikes took place in the late 1800s?

b. Evaluate Do you think President Cleveland was right to use federal troops to end the Pullman strike? Explain.

Critical Thinking

4. Analyze In this lesson you learned about the problems workers faced. Create a table like the one below and show how workers tried to solve the problems they faced.

Problem	Solution

Social Studies Skills

Analyze Costs and Benefits

Define the Skill

Everything you do has both costs and benefits connected to it. *Benefits* are things that you gain from something. *Costs* are what you give up to obtain benefits. For example, if you buy a video game, the benefits of your action include the game itself and the enjoyment of playing it. The most clear cost is what you pay for the game. However, there are other costs that do not involve money. One is the time you spend playing the game. This is a cost because you give up something else, such as doing your homework or watching a TV show, when you choose to play the game.

The ability to analyze costs and benefits is a valuable life skill as well as a useful tool in the study of history. Weighing an action's benefits against its costs can help you decide whether or not to take it.

Learn the Skill

Analyzing the costs and benefits of historical events will help you to better understand and evaluate them. Follow these guidelines to do a cost-benefit analysis of an action or decision in history.

1. First determine what the action or decision was trying to accomplish. This step is needed in order to determine which of its effects were benefits and which were costs.

2. Then look for the positive or successful results of the action or decision. These are its benefits.

3. Consider the negative or unsuccessful effects of the action or decision. Also think about what positive things would have happened if it had *not* occurred. All these things are its costs.

4. Making a chart of the costs and benefits can be useful. By comparing the list of benefits to the list of costs, you can better understand the action or decision and evaluate it.

For example, you learned in Module 20 about the Second Industrial Revolution and its effects on the American economy. A cost-benefit analysis of the changes in American businesses might produce a chart like this one:

Benefits	Costs
New inventions made life easier.	New business methods ran smaller companies out of business.
Communication became easier with new technologies.	Workers received lower wages.
Efficient management reduced costs of products.	Strikes resulted in violence and deaths.
Workers began to organize for better conditions.	

Based on this chart, one might conclude that the Second Industrial Revolution was beneficial to the nation's economy.

Practice the Skill

Among the changes that occurred in the early 1900s was an increase in specialization and efficiency in the workplace. Use information from the module and the guidelines above to do a cost-benefit analysis of this development. Then write a paragraph explaining whether or not it was a wise one.

Module 20 Assessment

Review Vocabulary, Terms, and People

Identify the descriptions below with the correct term or person from the module.

1. Labor organization that represented both skilled and unskilled laborers and was the first national labor union in the United States

2. Inventor who patented the telephone in 1876

3. A way of making steel quickly and cheaply by blasting hot air through melted iron to quickly remove waste

4. A system of business in which one company owns businesses in each step of the manufacturing process

5. Powerful business leader who helped to found the Central Pacific Railroad

6. Union speaker who worked to better the lives of mine workers

7. A method of negotiating for better wages or working conditions in which all workers act together to ensure a better chance for success

---

Comprehension and Critical Thinking

Lesson 1

8. a. **Identify** What was the Second Industrial Revolution?
    b. **Draw Conclusions** Why were advances in transportation and communication important to the Second Industrial Revolution?
    c. **Elaborate** Which invention do you think had the greatest effect on people's lives in the late 1800s? Explain your answer.

Lesson 2

9. a. **Recall** What criticisms were made of business leaders and trusts?
    b. **Analyze** How did the rise of corporations and powerful business leaders lead to the growth of big business?
    c. **Evaluate** Do you think the growth of big business helped or hurt ordinary Americans? Explain your answer.

Lesson 3

10. a. **Recall** What led to poor working conditions in factories during the Second Industrial Revolution?
    b. **Make Inferences** Why did labor unions have a better chance of improving working conditions than laborers did on their own?
    c. **Evaluate** Did the strikes of the 1880s and 1890s hurt or help the labor movement in the long run? Explain your answer.

Review Themes

11. Economics How did the rise of big business affect consumers in the United States?

12. Society and Culture What changes in society were brought about by the organization of labor?

Reading Skills

Identify Patterns of Organization *Use the Reading Skills taught in this module to answer the question about the reading selection below.*

> Corporations provided several important advantages over earlier business forms. Stockholders in a corporation are not responsible for business debts. If a corporation fails financially, the stockholders lose only the money that they invested. Stockholders are also usually free to sell their stock to whomever they want, whenever they want.

13. By which structural pattern is the above passage organized?

    a. Listing

    b. Cause-effect

    c. Chronological order

    d. Comparison-contrast

Social Studies Skills

Analyze Costs and Benefits *Use the Social Studies Skills taught in this module to answer the question below.*

14. Write two costs and two benefits of the Pullman strike from the point of view of the workers who participated.

Focus on Writing

15. Write a Business Plan Consider what you learned in this module and determine a good product to sell during the late 1800s. Decide which business practices you would use and which you would not. Consider how you would encourage investors to support your plan. Write two or three paragraphs in which you explain why your product would sell, which business practices you can use to make your product, and how to avoid conflicts with workers. Remember to explain to the investors why your plan will work.

Henry Ford

Henry Ford was a brilliant inventor and industrialist and founder of the Ford Motor Company. He helped bring about a time of rapid growth and progress that forever changed how people worked and lived. Henry Ford grew up on his family's farm near Dearborn, Michigan. As a child, he disliked life on the farm. He found the clicks and whirs of machinery much more exciting. When Ford was 16, he went to nearby Detroit to work in a machine shop. From there, he turned his ideas for how to make affordable and well-built cars into one of the world's largest automobile companies.

Explore the amazing life and career of Henry Ford online. You can find a wealth of information, video clips, primary sources, activities, and more through your online textbook.

> "My 'gasoline buggy' was the first and for a long time the only automobile in Detroit. It was considered . . . a nuisance, for it made a racket and it scared horses."
>
> —Henry Ford

 My Life and Work

Read the document to learn more about Henry Ford's life and career in his own words.

Big Plans

Watch the video to learn more about Henry Ford's early career.

Taking the Low Road

Watch the video to explore Henry Ford's vision for his car company.

The Assembly Line

Watch the video to see how Henry Ford used the assembly line to produce cars more efficiently and cheaply.

Module 21

Immigrants and Urban Life

★

Essential Question

How did immigration and rapid urban growth shape life in the United States?

About the Photo: These immigrants to the United States entered through Ellis Island.

 Explore ONLINE!

HISTORY

VIDEOS, including...
- Arrival at Ellis Island
- Angel Island: Ellis Island of the West
- Chicago Fire
- Jacob Riis

☑ Document-Based Investigations

☑ Graphic Organizers

☑ Interactive Games

☑ Image Carousel: Coming to America

☑ Image with Hotspots: Steel Beam Skyscrapers

In this module you will learn about immigration and its effects on U.S. cities. You will also read about some of the challenges faced by these cities.

What You Will Learn ...

Lesson 1: A New Wave of Immigration **664**
The Big Idea A new wave of immigration in the late 1800s brought large numbers of immigrants to the United States.

Lesson 2: The Growth of Cities **670**
The Big Idea American cities experienced dramatic expansion and change in the late 1800s.

Lesson 3: City Life **674**
The Big Idea The rapid growth of cities in the late 1800s created both challenges and opportunities.

Timeline of Events 1870–1910

United States	World

1870

1873 Olmsted designs the U.S. Capitol grounds.

1876 The Centennial Exposition opens in Philadelphia.

1878 Electric streetlights are introduced in London.

1880

< **1886** Workers complete the Statue of Liberty.

1886 Impressionists' exhibit opens in Paris.

1889 Jane Addams founds Hull House in Chicago.

1890

1891 Construction begins on Russia's Trans-Siberian Railroad.

1893 The Ferris wheel is introduced at the 1893 Columbian Exposition in Chicago. ∨

1900

1901 The first Nobel Prizes are awarded in Stockholm, Sweden. >

1910

Reading Social Studies

THEME FOCUS:

Economics, Society and Culture

In this module you will read about the changes in society and culture in the late 1800s. Among these changes was an increase in immigration. New immigrants to America found a society full of economic opportunities and hardships. Immigration and technology combined to change the way of life in cities.

READING FOCUS:

Understand Historical Fact versus Historical Fiction

When you read a book like *The Red Badge of Courage* or see a movie about World War II, do you ever wonder how much is fiction and how much is fact?

Distinguish Fact from Fiction Historical fiction gives readers a chance to meet real historical people and real historical events in the framework of a made-up story. Some of what you read in historical fiction could be verified in an encyclopedia, but other parts existed only in the author's mind until he or she put it on paper. As a good reader of history, you should know the difference between facts, which can be proved or verified, and fiction.

Notice how one reader determined which details could be verified or proved.

> That was a *woman filling her pail by the hydrant* you just bumped against. The *sinks are in the hallway*, that all the tenants may have access—and all be poisoned alike by their summer stenches. Hear the pump squeak! It is the lullaby of tenement house babes. In summer, when *a thousand thirsty throats pant of a cooling drink in this block*, it is worked in vain . . .
>
> —from *How the Other Half Lives,* by Jacob Riis

The woman filling her pail isn't a fact I can check. He's just using her as an example of what women did.

We could probably check city records to see whether the buildings really had sinks in the hallways.

The writer is generalizing here. We probably can't prove 1,000 thirsty throats. We could find out whether the city's water pumps actually went dry in the summer. That's verifiable.

You Try It!

The following passage is from How the Other Half Lives *by Jacob Riis, a journalist and photographer who documented New York tenement life in the late 1800s. After you read it, answer the questions below.*

> This gap between dingy brick-walls is the yard. That strip of smoke-colored sky up there is the heaven of these people. Do you wonder the name does not attract them to the churches? That baby's parents live in the rear tenement here. She is at least as clean as the steps we are now climbing. There are plenty of houses with half a hundred such in. The tenement is much like the one in front we just left, only fouler, closer, darker—we will not say more cheerless. The word is a mockery. A hundred thousand people lived in rear tenements in New York last year. Here is a room neater than the rest. The woman, a stout matron with hard lines of care in her face, is at the wash-tub. "I try to keep the childer clean," she says, apologetically, but with a hopeless glance around.
> —Jacob Riis, *How the Other Half Lives*

1. Which facts from the paragraph above can be confirmed?
2. What sources might you check to confirm some of these facts?
3. List two things from the passage that could not be confirmed.
4. Why are these two things not able to be confirmed?

As you read Module 21, notice which facts you could easily confirm.

Key Terms and People

Lesson 1
old immigrants
new immigrants
steerage
benevolent societies
tenements
sweatshops
Chinese Exclusion Act

Lesson 2
mass transit
suburbs
mass culture
Joseph Pulitzer
William Randolph Hearst
department stores
Frederick Law Olmsted

Lesson 3
Jacob Riis
settlement houses
Jane Addams
Hull House
assimilation
Florence Kelley

A New Wave of Immigration

The Big Idea

A new wave of immigration in the late 1800s brought large numbers of immigrants to the United States.

Main Ideas

- U.S. immigration patterns changed during the late 1800s as new immigrants arrived from Europe, Asia, and Mexico.

- Immigrants worked hard to adjust to life in the United States.

- Some Americans opposed immigration and worked to restrict it.

Key Terms and People

old immigrants
new immigrants
steerage
benevolent societies
tenements
sweatshops
Chinese Exclusion Act

If YOU were there . . .

You live with your family on a small farm in Italy in the 1890s. You want to earn some money to help your parents, but there are not many jobs nearby. You have heard that jobs are easy to find in the booming factories of the United States. But you speak no English and know no one in America.

Would you travel to the United States in search of new opportunities?

Changing Patterns of Immigration

Millions of immigrants came to the United States from northern Europe in the mid-1800s. They came mainly from Great Britain, Germany, Ireland, and the countries of Scandinavia. Except for the Irish, who were Roman Catholics, most were Protestants. Many were skilled workers. Others settled in rural areas and became farmers. By the late 1800s immigrants from northern Europe were known as **old immigrants**. A newer and larger wave of immigration—from different parts of the world—was arriving in the United States.

New Immigrants During the 1880s more than 5 million immigrants arrived in the United States—about the same number of people as had arrived during the six decades from 1800 to 1860 combined. The majority of these **new immigrants** were from southern and eastern Europe. Thousands of Czechs, Greeks, Hungarians, Italians, Poles, Russians, and Slovaks came to the United States to find new opportunities and better lives. A young woman from Russia spoke for many of her fellow immigrants when she said she hoped "for all manner of miracles in a strange, wonderful land!"

New immigrants came from many different cultural and religious backgrounds. They included Orthodox Christians, Roman Catholics, and Jews. Some were escaping political or

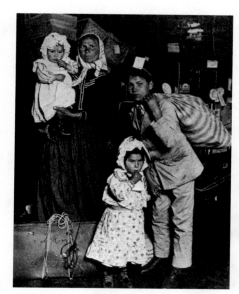

Immigrants often arrived at Ellis Island with few belongings. This Italian family is looking for lost baggage.

Reading Check
Contrast How was the experience of immigrants at Ellis Island different from that of immigrants at Angel Island?

religious persecution. They were eager for the job opportunities created by the U.S. industrial boom of the late 1800s.

Arriving in a New Land Immigrants usually faced a difficult journey by ship to America. Most traveled in **steerage**—an area below a ship's deck where steering mechanisms were located. Steerage tickets were inexpensive, but the cabins were hot, cramped, and foul-smelling. Many passengers were seasick for the entire journey. Some even died of diseases contracted along the way.

Once in the United States, new arrivals were processed through government-run immigration centers. The busiest center on the East Coast was Ellis Island, which opened in New York Harbor in 1892. The first immigrant processed through Ellis Island was Annie Moore Schayer, a 14-year-old from Ireland. Over the next 40 years, millions of European immigrants came through Ellis Island.

At immigration centers officials interviewed and examined immigrants to decide whether to let them enter the country. People with contagious diseases or legal problems could be turned away. "There was this terrible anxiety that one of us might be rejected," remembered one immigrant traveling with his family. "And if one of us was, what would the rest of the family do?" This rarely happened, however. Less than 2 percent of the people who arrived at Ellis Island were not allowed into the country.

On the West Coast, many Chinese immigrants entered the United States through Angel Island, which opened near San Francisco in 1910. Because laws limited immigration from China, only people whose fathers were U.S. citizens were allowed into the country. Chinese immigrants were often kept at Angel Island for weeks or months while officials investigated their families.

Mexican immigrants also came to the United States in large numbers in the late 1800s. The main processing center for immigrants from Mexico was in El Paso, Texas. Most settled in the Southwest. They found work in construction, steel mills, and mines, and on large commercial farms.

Adjusting to a New Life

Once they entered the United States, immigrants began the hard work of adjusting to life in a new country. They needed to find homes and jobs. They had to learn a new language and get used to new customs. This was all part of building a new life.

Immigrant Neighborhoods Many immigrants moved into neighborhoods with others from the same country. In these neighborhoods, they could speak their native language and eat foods that reminded them of home. Immigrants could also practice the customs that their families had passed down from generation to generation. An Italian immigrant remembered that in his new neighborhood, "cheeses from Italy, sausage, salamis were all hanging in the window."

In their newly adopted neighborhoods, many immigrant groups published newspapers in their own languages. They founded schools, clubs,

Coming to America

During the late 1800s the places people came from began to change. The charts below show the percentages of people who moved from different places. The total number of immigrants reached a peak in the 1880s, when about 5 million people came to the United States.

Analyze Information
By how much did the percentage of immigrants from northern and western Europe change from 1840 to 1900?

Swedish immigrant Swan August Swanson followed his father to Wisconsin to help with the family farm. Like many new Americans, he married within the immigrant community. ∨

Shifting Patterns of Immigration

Where Immigrants Came From, 1840–1860

93%
1%
1%
2%
3%

Where Immigrants Came From, 1880–1900

61%
.5%
1.5%
6%
31%

■ Northern and western Europe
■ Eastern and southern Europe
■ North and South America
■ Asia
■ All other areas

∧ Augustin and Maria Lozano and their two children are shown after moving from Mexico to California. Many Mexican immigrants moved into the Southwest.

The son of Italian immigrants, Amadeo Peter Giannini founded the Bank of Italy in San Francisco in 1904. Due to his guidance and perseverance, it became the largest privately owned bank in the world. ∨

∧ In this photo, Japanese men and Chinese women leave the detention center on Angel Island in San Francisco Bay. Angel Island was the processing center for many immigrants from Asia.

and places of worship to help preserve their customs. In New York City, for example, Jewish immigrants founded a theater that gave performances in Yiddish—the language spoken by Jews from central and eastern Europe.

Immigrants often opened local shops and small neighborhood banks. Business owners helped new arrivals by offering credit and giving small loans. Such aid was important for newcomers because there were few commercial banks in immigrant neighborhoods. In 1904 Italian immigrant Amadeo Peter Giannini started the Bank of Italy in San Francisco. This bank later grew and became the Bank of America.

Some immigrant communities formed **benevolent societies**. These aid organizations offered immigrants help in cases of sickness, unemployment, or death. At that time, few national government agencies provided such aid.

Even with neighborhood support, however, immigrants often found city life difficult. Many immigrants lived in **tenements**. These were poorly built, overcrowded apartment buildings. Lacking adequate light, ventilation, and sanitation, tenements were very unhealthy places to live. Disease spread rapidly in the crowded conditions.

The plight of tenement dwellers sparked preliminary efforts at reform. In some cities, local boards of health were established to set sanitation rules. Enforcement was often uneven, however, and the poorer neighborhoods received less attention than richer ones.

Immigrants worked hard to adjust to their new country. Children often learned American customs more quickly than their parents. In public schools, immigrant children learned English from McGuffey's Readers. The Readers were illustrated textbooks that taught reading and writing.

Finding Work Many new immigrants had worked on farms in their homelands. Few could afford to buy land in the United States, however. Instead, they found jobs in cities, where most of the country's manufacturing took place.

Having come from rural areas, few new immigrants were skilled in modern manufacturing or industrial work. They often had no choice but to take low-paying, unskilled jobs. They often worked in garment factories, steel mills, or construction. Long hours were common.

Not all industrial labor took place in large factories. Some immigrants worked for little pay in small shops or mills located in their own neighborhoods. Often associated with the clothing industry, these workplaces were called **sweatshops** because of long hours and hot, unhealthy working conditions. One young immigrant worker remembered:

"When the shirtwaists were finished at the machine . . . we were given scissors to cut the threads off. It wasn't heavy work, but it was monotonous [boring], because you did the same thing from seven-thirty in the morning till nine at night."

—Pauline Newman, quoted in *American Mosaic: The Immigrant Experience in the Words of Those Who Lived It*, by Joan Morrison and Charlotte Fox Zabusky

Asian Americans Today

Today, almost 15 million people in the United States are of Asian origin. They account for about 5 percent of the U.S. population—or about 1 in 20 Americans. Asian Americans trace their roots to various countries, including China, India, the Philippines, and, like this family, Vietnam. Many of these people left their homeland to escape oppression. They sought a life of freedom in the United States. Most Asian Americans live in the West. California has by far the largest Asian American population of any state.

Analyze Information
What push-pull factors do you think caused so many people to move to the United States?

Reading Check
Summarize
How did new immigrants help themselves and others to try to make successful lives in the United States?

Immigrants with skills that were in demand sometimes found work outside factories and sweatshops. Some worked as bakers, carpenters, masons, or skilled machinists. Others saved or borrowed money to open small businesses such as laundries, barbershops, or street vending carts. New immigrants often opened the same types of businesses in which other immigrants from the same country were already succeeding. They worked hard for long hours to become successful themselves.

Opposition to Immigration

Some Americans welcomed new immigrants. Many business leaders, for example, wanted immigrant workers who were willing to work for low pay. In general, however, anti-immigrant feelings grew as immigration increased in the late 1800s. Some labor unions opposed immigration because their members believed immigrants would take jobs away from native-born Americans.

Other Americans called nativists also feared that too many new immigrants were being allowed into the country. Many nativists held racial and ethnic prejudices. They thought that the new immigrants would not learn American customs, which might harm American society.

Academic Vocabulary
advocate to plead in favor of

Some nativists were violent toward immigrants. Others **advocated** laws and policies to stop or limit immigration. For example, in 1880 about 105,000 Chinese immigrants lived in the United States. Two years later, Congress passed the **Chinese Exclusion Act**. This law banned new immigrants to the United States from China for ten years. This was the first time a nationality was banned from entering the country. Although the law violated treaties with China, Congress continued to renew it for several decades. Other immigration policies included another law passed in 1892 that restricted convicts, immigrants with certain diseases, and those likely to need public assistance from entering the country.

Despite such opposition, immigrants continued to arrive in large numbers. They worked for low pay in factories. They built buildings, highways, and railroads. Their labor helped power the continuing industrial growth of the late 1800s and early 1900s. They did not always achieve their dreams as quickly as they had hoped. But most immigrants remained confident about the future for themselves and their families in the United States. A Jewish immigrant from Russia named Abraham Hyman expressed this idea, saying, "Your feeling is that a better time is coming, if not for yourself, for your families, for your children."

Summary and Preview Immigrants helped build the nation's economy and cities, but they met resistance from some native-born Americans. In the next lesson you will learn about what life was like in urban America.

Reading Check
Analyze Why did nativists oppose immigration?

Lesson 1 Assessment

Review Ideas, Terms, and People

1. **a. Identify** What was Ellis Island?

   b. Contrast What differences existed between the old immigrants and the new immigrants?

2. **a. Identify** What job opportunities were available to new immigrants?

   b. Summarize How did immigrants attempt to adapt to their new lives in the United States?

   c. Elaborate Why do you think many immigrants tolerated difficult living and working conditions?

3. **a. Recall** What was the purpose of the Chinese Exclusion Act?

   b. Explain Why did some labor unions oppose immigration?

   c. Predict How might the growing opposition to immigration lead to problems in the United States?

Critical Thinking

4. **Categorize** In this lesson you learned about the benefits and challenges new U.S. immigrants faced. Create a graphic organizer similar to the one below and categorize the challenges immigrants faced in different areas of life.

Education:

Work:

Challenges faced by new immigrants

Culture:

Living Conditions:

The Growth of Cities

The Big Idea

American cities experienced dramatic expansion and change in the late 1800s.

Main Ideas

- Both immigrants and native-born Americans moved to growing urban areas in record numbers in the late 1800s and early 1900s.

- New technology and ideas helped cities change and adapt to rapid population growth.

Key Terms and People

mass transit
suburbs
mass culture
Joseph Pulitzer
William Randolph Hearst
department stores
Frederick Law Olmsted

If YOU were there . . .

The year is 1905 and you have just come to the city of Chicago from the small town where you grew up. People rush past as you stop to stare up at the skyscrapers. Elevated trains roar overhead, and electric streetcars clatter along streets already crowded with pushcarts and horse-drawn wagons.

Will you stay and look for work in this big city?

Growth of Urban Areas

In 1850 New York City was the only U.S. city with a population of more than 500,000. By 1900 New York City, Chicago, Philadelphia, St. Louis, Boston, and Baltimore all had more than half a million residents. More than 35 U.S. cities had populations greater than 100,000. About 40 percent of Americans now lived in urban areas.

As you have read, new immigrants were responsible for a lot of this urban growth. So were families from rural areas in the United States. As farm equipment replaced workers in the countryside, large numbers of rural residents moved to the cities in search of work in manufacturing and related fields. This fundamental shift in the economy had far-reaching social effects. Previously, most Americans had worked on farms. People worked for themselves, kept the profits they earned, and made much of what they needed.

Americans who worked in factories faced a far different economic situation. They were wage earners. That is, instead of earning income from their own work, they were paid a set amount by business owners. Instead of making the things they needed, they had to buy them—using limited wages—from merchants in the city where they lived.

African Americans from the rural South also began moving to northern cities in the 1890s. They hoped to escape discrimination and find better educational and economic opportunities. Cities such as Chicago; Cleveland,

Ohio; Detroit, Michigan; and New York City saw large increases in their African American populations during the late 1800s and early 1900s.

Perhaps the most dramatic example of urban growth was the rise of Chicago. The city's population exploded from 30,000 in 1850 to 1.7 million in 1900. Chicago passed St. Louis as the biggest city in the Midwest. Along with the large numbers of African Americans moving to the city, many of Chicago's new residents were immigrants from southern and eastern Europe. In 1900 immigrants and their children made up three-quarters of Chicago's population.

Chicago's location was another **factor** in its rapid growth. Many of the new railroad lines connecting the East and West coasts ran through Chicago. This put Chicago at the heart of the nation's trade in lumber, grain, and meat. Thousands of new Chicago residents found work in the city's huge slaughterhouses and meatpacking plants. Here, meat from the West and Midwest was packed into refrigerated train cars and shipped to growing eastern cities, where it could be sold in shops to customers.

Changing Cities

American cities such as Chicago were ill-prepared for the rapid urban growth of the late 1800s and early 1900s. Where was everyone going to live? How were people going to get from home to work on crowded city streets? Several new technologies helped cities meet these challenges. These technologies forever changed the look and function of U.S. cities.

Building Skyscrapers With so many people moving to urban areas, cities quickly ran out of building space in downtown areas. One solution would be to build taller buildings. Typical city buildings in the mid-1800s were only five stories tall, but taller structures were impossible to construct because the building materials available were either too weak or too heavy.

This changed with the rise of the American steel industry in the late 1800s. Mills began producing tons of strong and inexpensive steel. Soon, architects such as Louis Sullivan of Chicago began designing multistory buildings called skyscrapers. Architects used steel beams to make sturdy frames that could support the weight of tall buildings. This allowed builders to use limited city space more efficiently.

The safety elevator, patented by Elisha Otis in the 1850s, helped make skyscrapers practical. Previous elevators had been unsafe because they would crash to the ground if the elevator cable snapped. Otis's safety elevator included a device to hold the elevator in place if the cable broke.

Getting Around Taller buildings made it possible for more people to live and work in city centers. This increased the need for **mass transit**, or public transportation designed to move many people. By the late 1860s New York City had elevated trains running on tracks above the streets. Chicago followed in the 1890s.

Some cities built underground railroads, known as subways. In 1897 the first subway in the United States opened in Boston. In 1904 the first line of the New York City subway system began operation. Cable cars and

Academic Vocabulary
factor cause

Reading Check
Identify Cause and Effect
What factors led to massive population growth in urban areas during the late 1800s and early 1900s?

In the late 1800s, cities like Chicago took bold steps to alleviate crowding by testing new forms of construction and transportation.

Frederick Law Olmsted

Connect to the Arts Frederick Law Olmsted designed Central Park to serve as a place where New York City residents could relax, exercise, and enjoy nature. Olmsted included areas for horseback riding, ice-skating, boating, and baseball. The Children's District was designed as a place where parents could bring children to stay cool in the summer.

Why do you think a city dweller might be attracted to Central Park?

Olmsted intentionally placed the pond near busy streets, hoping that it would attract walkers.

People can walk, ride, or roller-skate on the many trails through Central Park.

electric trolleys also became common. These streetcars cheaply and quickly carried people in the cities to and from work.

Many Americans who could afford it moved to **suburbs**, residential neighborhoods outside of downtown areas that had begun springing up before the Civil War. Mass transit networks made such moves possible. People could live in the suburbs and take trolleys, subways, or trains into the cities.

New Ideas In the late 1800s the United States also began to develop forms of **mass culture**, or leisure and cultural activities shared by many people. One factor contributing to mass culture was a boom in publishing. The invention of the Linotype, an automatic typesetting machine, greatly reduced the time and cost of printing. In 1850 there were fewer than 300 daily newspapers in the country. Because of the use of Linotype machines, by 1900 there were more than 2,000 newspapers.

Big cities often had many newspapers, so publishers had to compete for readers. In 1896 **Joseph Pulitzer** added a color comic to his *New York World* newspaper. More people started buying Pulitzer's paper. **William Randolph Hearst** was publisher of the *New York Journal*. He saw that comics helped sell newspapers. So he added a color comic strip to his paper. Soon, newspapers across the country were adding comic strips.

Mass culture affected how people shopped as well. Giant retail shops, or **department stores**, appeared in some cities during the late 1800s. One of the earliest was Marshall Field in Chicago. Field's offered low prices and large quantities of products. It also was the first department store to offer its customers a restaurant where they could eat while shopping. Newspaper and magazine advertising was used to bring in customers. Advertisers realized that women made most purchasing decisions about household goods, so they targeted their messages to them. The public was also attracted by fancy window displays.

Advertisers also tried new approaches to win customers. Food companies often used wholesome farm images to convey a sense of purity. Some companies came up with clever brand names, such as Uneeda Biscuit crackers, to help customers remember their products.

Rural dwellers did not have access to urban department stores. But they could purchase a huge variety of goods from mail-order companies. In 1897 Sears, Roebuck and Company produced a 507-page catalog. It offered everything from slippers to stoves to saddles. Mail-order customers simply made their selections, sent in their payments, and waited for the merchandise they ordered to arrive by rail or post.

World fairs were another example of mass culture. Fairs brought merchants together, which sometimes resulted in new ideas and products. At the 1904 St. Louis World's Fair, for example, a Syrian food vendor began making cones for a nearby ice cream vendor who had run out of dishes. Ice cream cones became popular throughout the country.

The demand for public entertainment also led to the creation of amusement parks, such as New York's Coney Island. The inexpensive entry tickets made Coney Island a favorite destination for children and families. For a nickel, visitors could ride a new invention called the Switchback Railway—the country's first roller coaster.

As cities grew, people became aware of the need for open public space. Landscape architect **Frederick Law Olmsted** became nationally famous. He designed Central Park in New York City, as well as many state and national parks. Some of his other well-known projects include Prospect Park in Brooklyn, New York, and the U.S. Capitol grounds, which he worked on between 1874 and 1895.

Summary and Preview Immigration and new technology helped cities grow in the late 1800s. In the next lesson you will learn about some of the problems caused by rapid urban growth.

Reading Check
Summarize
What forms of mass culture were available in urban areas?

Lesson 2 Assessment

Review Ideas, Terms, and People

1. **a. Identify** What groups of people began moving to cities in the late 1800s?
   b. Explain Why did African Americans begin to move to northern cities in the 1890s?
   c. Predict Do you think cities such as Chicago continued to grow in the 1900s? Why or why not?

2. **a. Define** What is mass transit? What made mass transit necessary?
   b. Explain How did new inventions make it possible for people to build skyscrapers?
   c. Evaluate Which improvement to urban living do you think had the greatest impact on people's lives? Explain your answer.

Critical Thinking

3. **Identify Cause and Effect** In this lesson you learned about the causes for the growth of cities. Create a graphic organizer similar to the one below and identify the effects of city growth. You may need to add more circles.

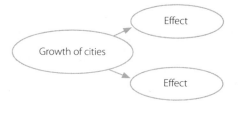

City Life

The Big Idea

The rapid growth of cities in the late 1800s created both challenges and opportunities.

Main Ideas

- Crowded urban areas faced a variety of social problems.
- People worked to improve the quality of life in U.S. cities.

Key Terms and People

Jacob Riis
settlement houses
Jane Addams
Hull House
assimilation
Florence Kelley

If YOU were there . . .

You live in a fast-growing city in 1895. When you walk the streets, you meet families who are packed into run-down apartments in crowded, filthy neighborhoods. You meet immigrants who want to study English but have no money for classes. You are determined to help these city residents improve their lives.

What would you do to help improve life in your city?

Urban Problems

In cities of the late 1800s and early 1900s, there was a shortage of affordable housing. This forced many poor families to squeeze into tiny tenement apartments, which were frequently unsafe and unsanitary. Journalist and photographer **Jacob Riis** became famous for exposing the horrible conditions in New York City tenements. Riis wrote about one typical tenement family:

> "There were nine in the family: husband, wife, an aged grandmother, and six children . . . All nine lived in two rooms, one about ten feet square that served as parlor, bedroom, and eating-room, the other a small hall-room made into a kitchen."
>
> —Jacob Riis, *How the Other Half Lives*

Overcrowding caused sanitation problems. Most cities did not have a good system for collecting trash, so garbage often piled up outside apartment buildings. An article in the *New York Tribune* described the garbage in front of one tenement as a "mass of air poisoning, death-breeding filth, reeking in the fierce sunshine."

Unsafe conditions were also common in tenements. Before 1900 most cities did not have laws requiring landlords to fix their tenements or to maintain safety standards. A fire on one floor could easily spread, and fire escapes were often blocked or broken.

Overcrowded city tenements caused problems such as disease, fire, and crime.

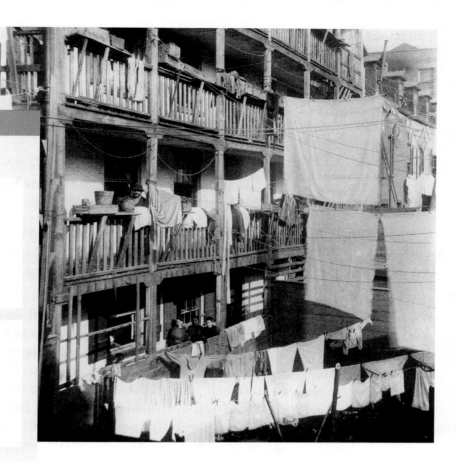

Tenement Life

Causes
- Overcrowding
- Unsafe buildings
- Unsanitary conditions
- Scarce running water
- Poor ventilation

▼

Effects
- Diseases such as tuberculosis and cholera
- High child death rates
- Fire
- Crime

Tenement rooms had few or no windows to let in fresh air and sunshine. Comfort was also scarce, with so many people crowded into such small spaces. Running water and indoor plumbing were also scarce. So was clean water. Cities often dumped garbage into local rivers that were used for drinking water.

Disease-causing bacteria grew easily in these conditions. Diseases such as cholera, typhoid, influenza, and tuberculosis spread quickly in crowded neighborhoods. Children were the most vulnerable to these diseases. For example, babies born in Chicago in 1870 had only a 50 percent chance of living to the age of five.

Air pollution was also a serious environmental problem in many growing cities. This was a time when many business leaders were building huge oil refineries, steel mills, and other factories. The steel mills of Andrew Carnegie, for example, helped make Pittsburgh the nation's steel-making center in the late 1800s. Steel mills brought jobs and wealth to Pittsburgh. But they also caused some of the nation's worst environmental issues. "Every street appears to end in a huge, black cloud," said one writer. "Pittsburgh is smoke, smoke, smoke—everywhere smoke." The air was so polluted at times that the city had to turn on outdoor lighting during the day.

The work of many city governments slowly helped to lessen some of these urban problems. By the late 1800s new sewage and water purification systems improved city sanitation. Many major cities began hiring full-time firefighters and police officers. Police officers in cities were typically placed in one neighborhood. They knew the local residents and were frequently involved in local activities. They could spot local problems and, in many cases, provide help to immigrants.

Improving City Life

Jacob Riis hoped his book *How the Other Half Lives* would shock many Americans—and it did. A reformer named Lawrence Veiller helped lead the effort to improve conditions in tenements. Describing the effects of tenement living on children, he wrote:

> "A child living its early years in dark rooms, without sunlight or fresh air, does not grow up to be a normal, healthy person . . . It is not of such material that strong nations are made."
> —Lawrence Veiller, quoted in *Readings in American History, Vol. 2*

Veiller worked with an organization called the Charity Organization Society (COS) to get changes made to New York laws. In 1900 he and the COS sponsored an exhibit of photographs and maps graphically showing the conditions of New York tenements. More than 10,000 people visited the exhibit, and they were shocked by what they saw. The work of Veiller and the COS helped pass the 1901 New York State Tenement House Act. This law required new buildings to have better ventilation and running water. It became a model for housing reform in other states.

Because there was little government aid available in the 1800s, private organizations generally took on the task of helping the urban poor. Some individuals set up **settlement houses**, or neighborhood centers in poor areas that offered education, recreation, and social activities.

Hull House
Neighborhood children attended kindergarten at Hull House. Their parents typically had low-paying jobs, and many were children of immigrants. Children like these had few other options for education.

How did Hull House try to improve the lives of children?

Jane Addams 1860–1935

Jane Addams was born in Cedarville, Illinois. Like many upper-class women of the era, she received a college education but found few jobs open to her. In 1888, on a visit to England with classmate Ellen Gates Starr, she visited a London settlement house. On their return to the United States, Addams and Starr opened a settlement house in Chicago. They started a kindergarten and a public playground. Addams also became involved in housing safety and sanitation issues, factory inspection, and immigrants' rights. In 1931 she shared the Nobel Peace Prize for her work with the Women's International League for Peace and Freedom.

Summarize
How did Jane Addams try to improve the lives of workers?

Settlement houses were staffed by professionals and volunteers. Many were educated women who came from wealthy families. In 1886 Charles B. Stover and Stanton Coit established the first settlement house in the United States. It was called Neighborhood Guild and was located on the Lower East Side in New York City. In 1889 **Jane Addams** and Ellen Gates Starr moved into a run-down building in a poor Chicago neighborhood and turned it into **Hull House**, the most famous settlement house of the period.

The Hull House staff focused on the needs of immigrant families. By 1893 Hull House was serving 2,000 people a week. Some families went through a process of **assimilation**, in which they adopted some American beliefs and aspects of American culture. The Hull House staff helped to assimilate the immigrants by providing English classes, day care, and cooking and sewing classes. Children and adults took part in club meetings, art classes, plays, and learned American sports.

Jane Addams and the staff at Hull House also worked for reforms. They studied the problems facing immigrants and poor city dwellers, then searched for ways to improve conditions. **Florence Kelley** was one important reformer at Hull House. She visited sweatshops and wrote about the problems there. Her work helped convince lawmakers to take action. Illinois passed a law in 1893 to limit working hours for women and to prevent child labor.

Kelley became the state's chief factory inspector and helped enforce the law. Although she believed more reforms were needed, she did report some improvements:

"Previous to the passage of the factory law of 1893, it was the rule of [a candy] factory to work the children . . . from 7 A.M. to 9 P.M., with twenty minutes for lunch, and no supper, a working week of eighty-two hours . . . Since the enactment of the factory law, their working week has consisted of six days of eight hours each, a reduction of thirty-four hours a week."

– Florence Kelley and Alzina P. Stevens, from *Hull House Maps and Papers*

Reading Check
Draw Conclusions
How did Hull House help improve city life?

As Hull House gained recognition, the settlement house movement spread to other cities. Most settlement houses continued to provide programs and services for city dwellers through the early 1900s. Some, such as Germantown Settlement in Pennsylvania, remain active today.

Summary and Preview Reformers in the late 1800s worked to solve urban problems. In the next module you will learn how Progressives pushed for further reforms.

Lesson 3 Assessment

Review Ideas, Terms, and People

1. a. **Describe** What were conditions like in tenements?

   b. **Summarize** What problems resulted from the rapid growth of cities?

   c. **Draw Conclusions** Why do you think people lived in tenements?

2. a. **Define** What is a settlement house?

   b. **Explain** How did settlement houses help city dwellers?

   c. **Evaluate** Do you think settlement houses were successful? Why or why not?

Critical Thinking

3. **Categorize** In this lesson you learned about urban problems. Create a chart similar to the one below and identify the responses to those problems.

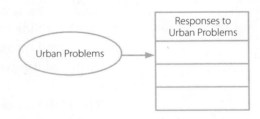

Urban Problems → Responses to Urban Problems

Social Studies Skills

Make Comparisons

Define the Skill

Understanding similarities is important when studying history. Comparing two or more people, things, events, or ideas highlights the similarities between them. Making comparisons can help clarify larger historical issues. This is true when comparing different time periods or when comparing different things from the same time period. Making comparisons is important in identifying historical connections.

Learn the Skill

When you encounter similar people, things, events, or ideas in history, use the following guidelines to make comparisons.

1. Identify who or what you are going to compare.

2. Look for similarities between them. Find examples of what makes them alike. Note any differences as well.

3. Use comparison words such as "like," "both," and "similar" to point out similarities.

    In this module you have learned about several reformers, including Lawrence Veiller and Florence Kelley. Veiller helped lead the effort to improve conditions in tenements. Kelley was a reformer who worked at Hull House.

Lawrence Veiller and Florence Kelley were alike in many ways. Although Veiller focused on tenements and Kelley concentrated on factory work, both were concerned with problems that affected children. Both did research about their issues. Both then wrote about the poor conditions they found.

Both Veiller and Kelley worked successfully for laws that would improve those conditions. Kelley's work helped convince Illinois lawmakers to pass a law to limit child labor. Similarly, Veiller helped to get the 1901 New York State Tenement House Act passed.

Practice the Skill

Review the module to find two people, things, events, or ideas that are similar. Then apply the guidelines to answer the following questions.

1. Which people, things, events, or ideas will you compare? Why is each of them important?

2. How are they alike? How are they different?

Module 21 Assessment

Review Vocabulary, Terms, and People

Identify the descriptions below with the correct term or person from the module.

1. Public transportation systems built to move many people and ease traffic in crowded cities

2. Founded Hull House with Ellen Gates Starr in 1889

3. Organizations created by immigrants to help each other in times of sickness, unemployment, or other troubles

4. Law banning Chinese people from moving to the United States

5. Neighborhood centers in poor urban areas that offered education, recreation, and social activities

6. Landscape architect who designed New York City's Central Park

7. Small shops or mills where immigrants worked for long hours in hot, unhealthy conditions

Comprehension and Critical Thinking

Lesson 1

8. a. **Identify** From what parts of the world did the wave of new immigrants come?

   b. **Analyze** In what ways did immigration patterns in the United States change in the late 1800s?

   c. **Elaborate** In your opinion, were the difficulties that immigrants faced worth the benefits of life in the United States? Explain.

Lesson 2

9. a. **Recall** Why did U.S. cities experience such rapid growth in the late 1800s?

   b. **Analyze** How did new technologies help cities deal with population growth?

   c. **Elaborate** Would you have preferred to live in a city or in a suburb? Why?

Lesson 3

10. a. **Recall** What were conditions like in tenements in the late 1800s?

    b. **Make Inferences** Why did rapid population growth cause problems in cities?

    c. **Elaborate** Why do you think the settlement house movement grew in the late 1800s and early 1900s?

Review Themes

11. **Economics** What role did economics play in the growth of cities?

12. **Society and Culture** How did the lives of city dwellers change with the rise of mass culture?

Reading Skills

Understand Historical Fact versus Historical Fiction *Use the Reading Skills taught in this module to answer the question about the reading selection below.*

> Mass culture affected how people shopped as well. Giant retail shops, or department stores, appeared in some cities during the late 1800s. One of the earliest was Marshall Field in Chicago. Field's offered low prices and large quantities of products. It also was the first department store to offer its customers a restaurant where they could eat while shopping. Newspaper and magazine advertising was used to bring in customers. Advertisers realized that women made most purchasing decisions about household goods. The public was also attracted by fancy window displays.

13. Which facts above can be verified? Where would you look to verify them?

Social Studies Skills

Make Comparisons *Use the Social Studies Skills taught in this module to complete the activity below.*

14. Choose two reforms that were discussed in this module. Make a comparison between the two.

Focus on Writing

15. **Write a Memo** In this module you learned about the people, places, and events of the late 1800s. Suppose you are a writer at a television network developing a story idea for a drama series set in this time period. Decide which people, places, and events you will include in your television drama series. Then draft a one- or two-paragraph memo to your boss describing the series. Remember to describe the basic plot, setting, and characters.

Ellis Island

For most European immigrants, Ellis Island was the first stop. Between 1892 and 1954, the immigration station processed over 12 million immigrants. These immigrants went through an inspection before they were allowed to enter the United States. Those with serious health problems were sent home, as were those who did not meet various legal requirements. Others were sent home because they exceeded immigration quotas.

However, if immigrants could clear these hurdles, they were free to enter the United States and begin their new lives.

Go online to explore some of the personal stories and recollections of immigrants who made the journey to America and passed through Ellis Island. You can find a wealth of information, video clips, primary sources, activities, and more through your online textbook.

Go online to view these and other **HISTORY®** resources.

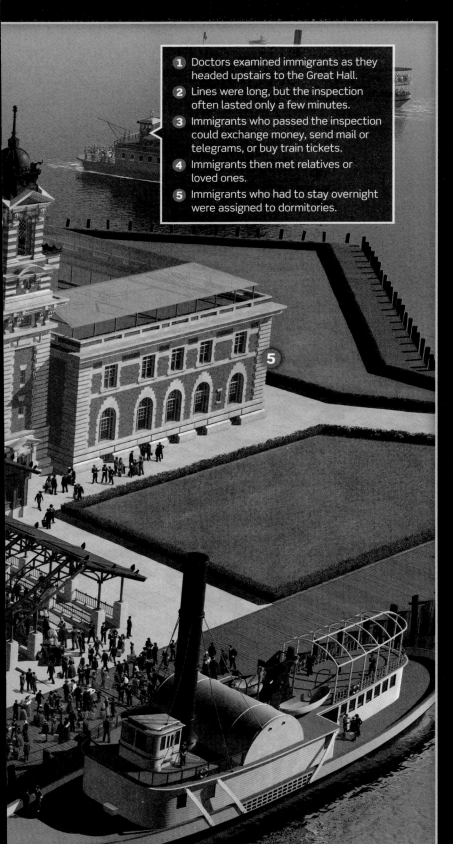

1. Doctors examined immigrants as they headed upstairs to the Great Hall.
2. Lines were long, but the inspection often lasted only a few minutes.
3. Immigrants who passed the inspection could exchange money, send mail or telegrams, or buy train tickets.
4. Immigrants then met relatives or loved ones.
5. Immigrants who had to stay overnight were assigned to dormitories.

The Golden Door

Watch the video to see how and why immigrants traveled to the United States.

Examination

Watch the video to see the physical examination that immigrants experienced at Ellis Island.

Quotas

Watch the video to see how immigration quotas affected immigrants trying to come to the United States.

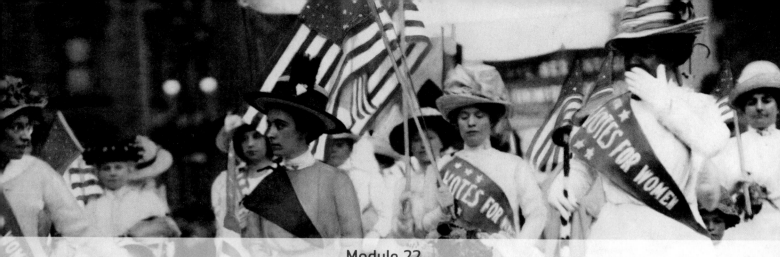

Module 22

The Progressive Spirit of Reform

Essential Question

How progressive were the Progressives?

About the Photo: The reform movements of the late 1800s and early 1900s were led by ordinary citizens such as these women, calling for their right to vote.

▷ *Explore ONLINE!*

HISTORY.

VIDEOS, including...
- Teddy Roosevelt vs. Corporate America
- James Garfield
- Triangle Shirtwaist Fire
- W.E.B. Du Bois

☑ Document-Based Investigations

☑ Graphic Organizers

☑ Interactive Games

☑ Image Carousel: Gilded Age Presidents

☑ Image with Hotspots: The Other Half

☑ Image with Hotspots: Working Conditions for Children, Early 1900s

In this module you will learn about the reform movements that swept across the United States in the late 1800s and early 1900s.

What You Will Learn ...

Lesson 1: The Gilded Age and the Progressive Movement 686
The Big Idea From the late 1800s through the early 1900s, the Progressive movement addressed problems in American society.

Lesson 2: Reforming the Workplace 695
The Big Idea In the early 1900s Progressives and other reformers focused on improving conditions for American workers.

Lesson 3: The Rights of Women and Minorities 701
The Big Idea The Progressive movement made advances for the rights of women and some minorities.

Lesson 4: The Progressive Presidents 707
The Big Idea American presidents in the early 1900s did a great deal to promote progressive reforms.

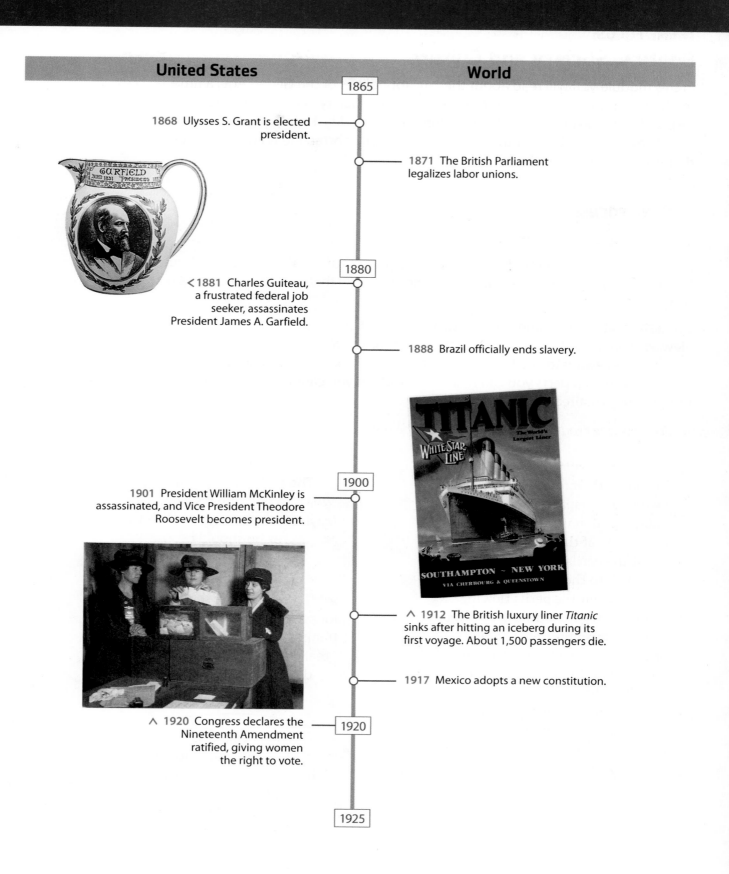

United States	World

1865

1868 Ulysses S. Grant is elected president.

1871 The British Parliament legalizes labor unions.

1880

< **1881** Charles Guiteau, a frustrated federal job seeker, assassinates President James A. Garfield.

1888 Brazil officially ends slavery.

1900

1901 President William McKinley is assassinated, and Vice President Theodore Roosevelt becomes president.

∧ **1912** The British luxury liner *Titanic* sinks after hitting an iceberg during its first voyage. About 1,500 passengers die.

1917 Mexico adopts a new constitution.

1920

∧ **1920** Congress declares the Nineteenth Amendment ratified, giving women the right to vote.

1925

Reading Social Studies

THEME FOCUS:

Politics, Society and Culture

In this module you will read about the corrupt politics of the Gilded Age, a time marked by attempts at reform. You will learn how society and culture reacted and responded to the problems of corruption and inequality. Finally, you will read about several presidents of the early 1900s who supported ideas and initiatives that promoted social reform.

READING FOCUS:

Evaluate Sources

Historical texts and current history books are good sources of information about the past. However, some sources can be more reliable than others to learn the truth.

Evaluate Texts Sometimes people write texts with a specific purpose or viewpoint in mind. Determining what the author's goal was in writing a passage can help you evaluate whether to believe all of the text, or merely some of it. Knowing which parts you can believe and which you cannot will help you understand what really happened in history.

Notice how one reader evaluated the source below.

> The man, therefore, who as the owner of newspapers, would corrupt public opinion is the most dangerous enemy of the State. We may talk about the perils incident [dangers attached] to the concentration of wealth, about the perils flowing from a disregard of fiduciary [financial] responsibility, about abuses of privilege, about exploiting the government for private advantage; but all of these menaces, great as they are, are nothing compared with a deliberate, persistent, artful, purchased endeavor to [change and direct] the public judgment.
>
> —*Harper's Weekly*, October 20, 1906

The author is using strong words to describe his viewpoint. Maybe he isn't being as objective as he should be.

The article lists several ideas that the author seems to think are bad. Are these things really bad? Can that help me determine the author's viewpoint?

This magazine was widely read when the article appeared. I think that makes the article a good source for some viewpoints of the time.

You Try It!

Read the passage below and evaluate whether you would use it as a source for a paper.

> Space is no intervention now between communication. [N]ot only do the wires of copper bind the world together in closer communication, but with the telephone it is possible to converse [talk] with friends a thousand miles away, hearing distinctly every word and recognizing the individual voice. Closer acquaintance has thus wrought [created] vast changes in public opinions and policies. The entire civilized world has been drawn more closely together, old ideas and prejudices have been wiped out.
>
> *—Cincinnati Times-Star*, January 1, 1900, quoted in *Yellow Journalism* by W. Joseph Campbell

1. What viewpoint of new technology is the author taking in this article? How can you tell?
2. Do you believe that the telephone brought about "changes in public opinions and policies"? Why or why not? Why might the author say this?
3. Can you trust the author when he says that "old ideas and prejudices have been wiped out"? Why or why not? Why might the author say this?
4. Did this article appear in a well-known newspaper? Does this make it more trustworthy or less?
5. Would you use this article as a source for writing a paper about how new inventions affected life in the early 1900s? Explain your answer.

As you read Module 22, evaluate the primary sources for their usefulness in understanding history.

Key Terms and People

Lesson 1
political machines
Progressives
muckrakers
Seventeenth Amendment
recall
initiative
referendum
Robert M. La Follette

Lesson 2
Triangle Shirtwaist Fire
workers' compensation laws
capitalism
socialism
William "Big Bill" Haywood
Industrial Workers of the World

Lesson 3
Eighteenth Amendment
National American Woman Suffrage Association
Alice Paul
Nineteenth Amendment
Booker T. Washington
Ida B. Wells
W. E. B. Du Bois
National Association for the Advancement of Colored People

Lesson 4
Theodore Roosevelt
Pure Food and Drug Act
conservation
William Howard Taft
Progressive Party
Woodrow Wilson
Sixteenth Amendment

The Gilded Age and the Progressive Movement

The Big Idea

From the late 1800s through the early 1900s, the Progressive movement addressed problems in American society.

Main Ideas

- Political corruption was common during the Gilded Age.

- Progressives pushed for reforms to improve living conditions.

- Progressive reforms expanded the voting power of citizens.

Key Terms and People

political machines
Progressives
muckrakers
Seventeenth Amendment
recall
initiative
referendum
Robert M. La Follette

If YOU were there . . .

You live in a big-city neighborhood in the 1890s. You and your brother are both looking for jobs. You know that the man down the street is the "ward boss." He can always get city jobs for his friends and neighbors. But in return you'll have to promise to vote the way he tells you to in the upcoming election.

Would you ask the ward boss for a job? Why or why not?

Political Corruption

The late 1800s in the United States are often called the Gilded Age. The term came from a novel by that name. *The Gilded Age* highlighted the inequality between wealthy business owners, who profited from the Industrial Revolution, and workers, who often labored under terrible conditions for little pay. Many people began to believe that the government should help fix this inequality. The first step was to get rid of corruption in politics.

Political Machines In the late 1800s **political machines** were powerful organizations of professional politicians that dominated city and county politics. Political machines sorted out some of the biggest urban issues of the time. However, they often resorted to corrupt methods.

For example, political machines were notorious for election fraud. Not only did they pay people to vote for their candidates, they also stuffed ballot boxes with extra votes for their candidates and bribed vote counters. Some political machines even hired men called "repeaters" to cast several votes in the same election. To avoid being caught, repeaters would change their coats and shave off their beards between votes. Hence the old Chicago saying "Vote early and vote often."

Political machines were run by leaders called bosses, who used their position to gain money and power. The boss

"Who Stole the People's Money? 'Twas Him"

This 1871 political cartoon shows "Boss" Tweed (bottom left) standing in a ring of corrupt politicians known as Tammany Hall. The cartoonist shows each person blaming the one next to him for government corruption. The labels on the men's backs show that they represent different interests.

Analyze Historical Sources
Why do you think the men are shown standing in a circle?

The men have labels on their backs that show they represent different interests.

would demand bribes and payoffs in exchange for contracts and jobs, as did other machine politicians. They also frequently traded favors for votes. For example, the boss might hand out city jobs to unqualified people in exchange for their political support.

New York City's political machine, Tammany Hall, was one of the most notorious political machines. After winning city elections in 1888, members of Tammany Hall rewarded their supporters with about 12,000 jobs. The leader of Tammany Hall was William Marcy Tweed. Along with his greedy friends, "Boss" Tweed stole enormous amounts of money—up to $200 million—from the city.

Despite such corruption, political machines did a number of good things. They built parks, sewers, schools, and roads in many cities. They also provided key social services, such as orphanages and fire brigades.

Machine politicians made a special effort to reach out to immigrants and poor families. They helped newcomers find jobs and homes, supplied coal in winter, and provided turkeys for holiday suppers. As one Boston politician said, the role of the machine boss was "to be . . . somebody that any bloke [man] can come to . . . and get help." In return, many poor families and immigrants gratefully supported political bosses and machines.

Cleaning Up Political Corruption Corruption was also a problem to the federal government. Many people thought that the corruption extended to the administration of President Ulysses S. Grant. During Grant's second term, federal officials were jailed for taking bribes from whiskey makers in exchange for allowing them to avoid paying taxes. Another scandal involved members of Congress who had taken bribes to allow the Union Pacific Railway to receive government funds. These scandals and others caused many Americans to question the honesty of national leaders.

Gilded Age Presidents

Rutherford B. Hayes

Republican; in office: 1877–1881
Hayes promised to reform the government with "thorough, radical, and complete" changes.

James A. Garfield

Republican; in office: 1881
Garfield attempted reforms before he was assassinated.

Chester A. Arthur

Republican; in office: 1881–1885
Arthur supported a system for awarding federal jobs based on merit, not party loyalty.

Grover Cleveland

*Democrat;
in office: 1885–1889, 1893–1897*
Cleveland was known for his honesty and for getting involved in the day-to-day details of government.

Benjamin Harrison

Republican; in office: 1889–1893
Harrison supported the Sherman Antitrust Act, which regulated business monopolies.

William McKinley

Republican; in office: 1897–1901
McKinley avoided scandals and helped win public trust in the government.

In response, Americans began calling for changes in the civil service, the government job system. They disliked the spoils system, the practice of giving jobs to the winning candidates' supporters. Thomas Jefferson was the first to reward supporters with jobs. After his administration, each time a new party took power, it replaced many government officials. Many new employees were unqualified and untrained.

By the late 1800s government corruption was widespread. Reformers demanded that only qualified people be given government jobs. In response, President Rutherford B. Hayes made minor reforms, such as firing a powerful member of the New York Republican political machine. President James A. Garfield also attempted reforms. But on July 2, 1881, Garfield was attacked and shot twice by a mentally unstable federal job seeker named Charles Guiteau. The president later died from his wounds. Vice President Chester A. Arthur became president.

Arthur continued the push for reforms by backing the Pendleton Civil Service Act, which was passed in 1883. This law set up a merit system for awarding federal jobs. Under the Pendleton Act, more than 10 percent of government job applicants had to pass an exam before they could be hired. It was a start to reforming other government practices.

Reading Check
Analyze Information
What factors led to civil-service reform?

Progressives Push for Reforms

A group of reformers known as **Progressives** also worked to improve society in the late 1800s. Progressives tried to solve problems caused by rapid industrial and urban growth. They wanted to eliminate the causes of problems such as crime, disease, and poverty. They fought for reforms ranging from better working conditions to education programs in poor neighborhoods.

Muckrakers at Work Some journalists urged Progressives to action by writing stories that vividly described problems in society. These journalists were nicknamed **muckrakers** because they "raked up" and exposed the muck, or filth, of society. Muckrakers wrote about troubling issues such as

Historical Source

The Other Half

In 1890 Jacob Riis published *How the Other Half Lives*. The book was a collection of photographs of residents and workers in New York City tenement buildings, including families and immigrants. Sweatshops, such as the one here, were located in tenements to avoid the labor laws that affected factories. Workers crowded into the small, stuffy spaces. The conditions of life that Riis showed in his photographs, like this one, shocked many wealthier Americans.

Sweatshops turned out large amounts of clothing at low prices.

This 12-year-old boy said he was 16 in order to keep his job of pulling threads.

Analyze Historical Sources
How might this photograph encourage people to become reformers?

child labor, racial discrimination, living conditions in housing slums, and corruption in business and politics.

In 1902 and 1903 Lincoln Steffens wrote a series of articles in *McClure's Magazine* exposing corruption in city government. In one article, he described how government officials in St. Louis, Missouri, used their positions to earn extra money illegally:

> "Men empowered to issue peddlers' licenses and permits to citizens who wished to erect awnings or use a portion of the sidewalk for storage purposes charged an amount in excess of the prices stipulated [set] by law, and pocketed the difference."
>
> —Lincoln Steffens, *The Shame of the Cities*

Another muckraker, Ida B. Tarbell, wrote articles criticizing the unfair business practices of the Standard Oil Company. Upton Sinclair exposed unsanitary practices in the meat-processing industry in his novel *The Jungle*.

Although such writing angered many politicians and business leaders, it also helped to unite Progressives. Muckrakers influenced voters, causing them to pressure politicians into backing reforms.

Reform Successes A major goal of Progressive reformers was to help the urban poor. You have read about the work of housing reformers, which led to the 1901 New York State Tenement House Act. Other Progressives started settlement houses similar to Jane Addams's Hull House. People usually started settlement houses in poor areas in order to improve education, housing, and sanitation there.

The movement for urban reform also led to new professions. City planners helped design safer building codes and opened new public parks. Civil engineers improved transportation by paving streets and building bridges. Sanitation engineers tried to solve problems concerning pollution, waste disposal, and impure water supplies. Death rates dropped dramatically in areas where planners and engineers addressed these problems.

Progressives also believed that improving education would lead to a better society. In response to their demands, states passed laws requiring all children to attend school. Some Progressives started kindergarten programs to help young city children learn basic social skills. In 1873 reformer Susan Blow opened the first American public kindergarten in St. Louis. By 1898 more than 4,000 kindergartens had opened in the United States.

John Dewey was a key supporter of early childhood education. His **motive** was to help children learn problem-solving skills, not just memorize facts. He thought this would help them in everyday life. Dewey's teaching methods became a model for progressive education across the country.

Progressives also worked to improve the education of doctors and nurses. In the late 1800s there were not enough well-trained and professionally organized doctors. Researchers knew the causes of diseases such

Academic Vocabulary
motive a reason for doing something

as pneumonia and tuberculosis. However, there were few medical organizations that could help spread this knowledge.

Under the leadership of Joseph McCormack, the American Medical Association (AMA) brought together local medical organizations in 1901. The AMA supported laws designed to protect public health and showed how Progressives could organize to help improve society. Other organizations followed the AMA's lead.

Reading Check
Find Main Ideas
How did progressive reforms improve society?

Expansion of Voting Power

Some Progressives worked to reduce the power of political machines in state and local governments. In many places, reformers replaced corrupt ballots that listed only one party's candidates with ballots prepared by the government that listed all candidates. Under pressure from reformers, many states adopted secret ballots. This ensured privacy for every voter.

Voting Reforms Progressives thought officials would be more responsive to voters if voters were directly involved in government. To help make this happen, reformers worked to expand voting power. For example, they favored the **Seventeenth Amendment**, which allowed Americans to vote directly for U.S. senators. Before the constitutional amendment was passed in 1913, state legislatures had elected senators.

Reformers also favored the direct primary, an election in which voters choose candidates to run for public office directly. In 1903 Wisconsin became the first state to have a direct primary. Previously, party leaders had selected which candidates would run for office.

Other reform measures allowed voters to take action against corrupt politicians. Some states and cities gave unhappy voters the right to sign a petition asking for a special vote. The purpose of that vote was to **recall**, or remove, an official before the end of his or her term. If enough voters signed the petition, the vote took place. The official could then be removed from office if there was a majority of recall votes.

— BIOGRAPHY —

Robert M. La Follette 1855–1925

Born in rural Wisconsin in 1855, Robert M. La Follette began his political career at a young age. He was elected to the U.S. House of Representatives in 1884, becoming the youngest member of Congress. He soon earned the nickname "Fighting Bob" for his energetic speaking style and his active support for progressive reforms.

After serving as Wisconsin's governor and as U.S. senator, La Follette ran for president as the Progressive Party candidate in 1924. He won his home state and received about 16 percent of the popular vote.

Draw Conclusions
Why might La Follette have been proud of the nickname "Fighting Bob"?

In California, Oregon, and states in the Midwest, Progressives worked on reforms to give voters direct influence over new laws. A procedure called the **initiative** allowed voters to propose a new law by collecting signatures on a petition. If enough signatures were collected, the proposed law was voted on at the next election. Another measure was called the **referendum**. It permitted voters to approve or reject a law that had already been proposed or passed by a government body. This process gave voters a chance to overrule laws that they opposed.

Government Reforms Progressives also tried to change the way city government operated. Some reformers wanted city government to be run like a business. As a result of their efforts, several cities changed to council-manager governments. Under this system, voters elect a city council. The council then appoints a professional manager to run the city. Other business-minded reformers supported the commission form of government. Under this system, the city is headed by a group of elected officials. Each official manages a major city agency, such as housing or transportation.

One of the leaders of the effort to reform state government was Wisconsin's Republican governor **Robert M. La Follette**. La Follette decreased the power of political machines. He used university professors and other experts to help write new laws and work in state agencies. He also made information on how politicians voted available to the public. That way, voters would know if leaders had kept their campaign promises. Called the Wisconsin Idea, La Follette's plan became a model for progressive reforms in other states.

Reading Check
Summarize
How did Progressives work to change voting procedures?

Summary and Preview Progressives worked to reform government and improve city life. In the next lesson you will learn about reforms in working conditions.

Lesson 1 Assessment

Review Ideas, Terms, and People

1. a. Recall What was the main goal of political machines during the Gilded Age?

b. Draw Conclusions Why do you think some immigrants supported political machines?

c. Predict Do you think the system of testing government job applicants created by the Pendleton Civil Service Act would work to reduce corruption in the spoils system? Why or why not?

2. a. Identify Who were muckrakers, and what effect did they have on reform?

b. Explain How did Progressives try to improve education?

c. Evaluate Which progressive reform do you think was most important? Why?

3. a. Describe What new ideas and practices were introduced to give voters more power?

b. Draw Conclusions How did progressive reforms limit the power of political machines?

Critical Thinking

4. Categorize In this lesson you learned about key progressive reforms and the problems they addressed. Create a chart similar to the one below and use it to categorize the various progressive reforms.

Progressive Reforms		
Social	Political	Urban

Reform Literature

Word Help

cuffs punches
utter complete
close stuffy
sole only
access right to use
stenches bad smells
in vain without success
galling causing pain; irritating
fetters chains
heaves rises and falls
avail help

❶ The writer wants you to imagine that he is taking you on a tour of the building. *Why do you think he chooses this way to describe the place?*

❷ Find one detail that appeals to each sense: sight, sound, smell, taste, and touch. *How would you sum up, in one sentence, the place that Riis describes?*

About the Reading *How the Other Half Lives* describes the tenement houses where immigrants lived in New York City. Its author, Jacob Riis, was a newspaper reporter. His nonfiction book made Americans aware of the extremes of poverty suffered by working people. Riis believed that every human being deserved a decent, safe place to live. *How the Other Half Lives* led to reforms and new laws that improved housing conditions.

As You Read Look for details that help you see, hear, and smell Cherry Street.

From *How the Other Half Lives*
by Jacob Riis (1849–1914)

Cherry Street. Be a little careful, please! ❶ The hall is dark and you might stumble over the children pitching pennies back there. Not that it would hurt them; kicks and cuffs are their daily diet. They have little else. Here where the hall turns and dives into utter darkness is a step, and another, another. A flight of stairs. You can feel your way, if you cannot see it. Close? Yes! What would you have? All the fresh air that ever enters these stairs comes from the hall door that is forever slamming, and from the windows of dark bedrooms that in turn receive from the stairs their sole supply of the elements God meant to be free . . . That was a woman filling her pail by the hydrant you just bumped against. The sinks are in the hallway, that all the tenants may have access—and all be poisoned alike by their summer stenches. Hear the pump squeak! It is the lullaby of tenement house babes. In summer, when a thousand thirsty throats pant for a cooling drink in this block, it is worked in vain. . . . ❷

The sea of a mighty population, held in galling fetters, heaves uneasily in the tenements. . . . If it rise once more, no human power may avail to check it. The gap between the classes in which it surges, unseen, unsuspected by the thoughtless, is widening day by day. . . . I know of but one bridge that will carry us over safe, a bridge founded upon justice and built of human hearts.

Word Help

borax white powder used in manufacturing and cleaning

glycerine sweet, sticky liquid

hoppers containers

consumption eating or drinking

consumption tuberculosis, a lung disease that was fatal at that time

ladled added with a large spoon

❶ *What overall effect or mood does Sinclair create?*

❷ *Based on the details in this passage, what were the packers most concerned about?*

❸ *Why do you think rats were considered nuisances?*

❹ *Find details that reveal how one improvement in working conditions might have resulted in healthier sausage.*

About the Reading *The Jungle* focused the nation's attention on immigrant workers in the meatpacking industry. Upton Sinclair's novel showed bosses forcing human beings to live and work like animals. He also described, in shocking detail, how meat was handled. Sinclair published his book in 1906. Later that same year, the U.S. government passed the Pure Food and Drug Act and the Meat Inspection Act. Many Americans even gave up eating meat for a while.

As You Read Look for details that create one overwhelming effect.

From *The Jungle*
by Upton Sinclair (1878–1968)

There was never the least attention paid to what was cut up for sausage; there would come back from Europe old sausage that had been rejected, and that was mouldy and white—it would be dosed with borax and glycerine, and dumped into hoppers, and made over again for home consumption. There would be meat that had tumbled out on the floor, in the dirt and sawdust, where the workers had tramped and spit uncounted billions of consumption germs. ❶ There would be meat stored in great piles in rooms and the water from leaky roofs would drip over it, and thousands of rats would race about on it. It was too dark in these storage places to see well, but a man would run his hand over these piles of meat and sweep off handfuls of the dried dung of rats. ❷ These rats were nuisances, and the packers would put poisoned bread out for them; they would die, and then rats, bread, and meat would go into the hoppers together. . . . ❸ There was no place for the men to wash their hands before they ate their dinner, and so they made a practice of washing them in the water that was to be ladled into the sausage. ❹

Connect Literature to History

1. **Identify Cause and Effect** Jacob Riis and Upton Sinclair were both muckraking journalists. Why do you think so much muck existed in the tenements and in the meatpacking business? Why had people ignored those conditions for so long?

2. **Identify Cause and Effect** Both Riis and Sinclair believed that improving conditions for immigrants would benefit all of society. Explain how one specific change in the tenements might have a favorable effect on everyone. Then explain how one specific change in meat handling might affect everyone.

3. **Compare and Contrast** Both *How the Other Half Lives* and *The Jungle* inspired Progressives to work for reform. Which work do you think had the greater effect on its readers? Use details from each passage to explain your answer.

Reforming the Workplace

The Big Idea

In the early 1900s Progressives and other reformers focused on improving conditions for American workers.

Main Ideas

- Reformers attempted to improve conditions for child laborers.
- Unions and reformers took steps to improve safety in the workplace and to limit working hours.

Key Terms and People

Triangle Shirtwaist Fire
workers' compensation laws
capitalism
socialism
William "Big Bill" Haywood
Industrial Workers of the World

If YOU were there . . .

You have been working in a hat factory since 1900, when you were eight years old. Now you are experienced enough to run one of the sewing machines. You don't earn as much as older workers, but your family needs every penny you bring home. Still, the long hours make you very tired. One day you hear that people are trying to stop children from doing factory work. They think that children should be at school or playing.

Would you be for or against this social reform? Why?

Improving Conditions for Children

In the early 1900s a reformer named Marie Van Vorst took a series of jobs in factories and clothing mills around the country. She wanted to investigate working conditions for children by living and working alongside them. In a South Carolina textile mill, Van Vorst met children as young as seven years old. She described working with one young child:

> "Through the looms I catch sight of . . . my landlord's little child. She is seven; so small that they have a box for her to stand on. . . . I can see only her fingers as they clutch at the flying spools."
>
> —Marie Van Vorst, *The Woman Who Toils: Being the Experiences of Two Ladies as Factory Girls*

This girl—and other children like her—provided cheap labor for manufacturers. Some children were paid as little as 40 cents per day. Marie Van Vorst helped focus attention on the problem of child labor. Eliminating the problems of child labor became a major issue for Progressives and other reformers.

Children at Work Children did many jobs in the late 1800s. Boys sold newspapers and shined shoes on the streets. Girls often cooked or cleaned for boarders staying with their families. Girls also worked at home with their mothers, sewing clothes or making handicrafts.

Like the child Van Vorst encountered, many children worked in industry. In 1900 more than 1.75 million children age 15 and under worked in factories, mines, and mills, earning very low wages.

Calls for Reform As reporters published shocking accounts of working conditions for children, more people became aware of the problem. Progressives began to call for new reforms. You have read about Florence Kelley's work against child labor in Illinois. Kelley also served as a board member of the National Consumers' League, the major lobbying group for women's and children's labor issues. A lobbying group works to influence legislators in favor of a cause.

During the early 1900s, reformers finally succeeded in getting some laws passed to ease the conditions of child laborers. In 1912 the state of Massachusetts passed the first minimum wage law, and a commission was created to establish rates for child workers.

In 1916 and 1919 Congress passed federal child labor laws. The laws banned products made with child labor from being shipped from one state to another. The Supreme Court, however, ruled that the laws were unconstitutional. The Court argued that the laws went beyond the federal government's legal power to regulate interstate commerce.

In any case, laws alone could not end child labor. Some parents ignored child labor laws so that their children could continue contributing to the family income. Children were often instructed to lie about their age to government inspectors and tell them they were older than they really were.

Reading Check
Find Main Ideas
How did reformers try to improve child labor conditions?

Child Labor
Young children did much of the work in the American factories of the late 1800s. They were paid less than adult workers.

Working Conditions for Children, Early 1900s

This illustration shows some of the jobs that children did in glass factories in the early 1900s. You can see that there were many ways for young workers to be injured on the job.

Hot air blew from the glass ovens into the working space.

Adult workers closely supervised child workers.

Workers wore no protection against the fires and machinery.

Temperatures in the ovens used to make glass were more than 2,000° Fahrenheit.

Bending and lifting often left young workers tired and sore after their long day's work.

Analyze Visuals
Using the illustration, what can you tell about the life and work of these boys?

Safety and Working Conditions

Child labor reform was only part of the progressive effort to help American workers. Many Progressives also favored laws to ensure workers' safety, limit working hours, and protect workers' rights.

Workplace Safety Workplace accidents were common in the 1800s and early 1900s. In 1900 some 35,000 people were killed in industrial accidents. About 500,000 suffered injuries. One child described how her sister was injured using a machine in a string factory. "You see you mustn't talk or look off a minute," she explained. "My sister was like me. She forgot and talked, and just that minute her finger was off, and she didn't even cry till she picked it up."

Accidents like this were not big news in the early 1900s, but in 1911 a much greater workplace tragedy shocked the nation. It took place at the Triangle Shirtwaist Company, a New York City clothing factory that employed mostly Jewish and Italian teenage immigrant women. On the afternoon of March 25, a fire started on the eighth floor of the factory. Workers tried to escape, but factory owners had locked the exit doors—to reduce theft of materials, they said.

Within moments, the eighth floor was ablaze. The fire spread quickly to

DOCUMENT-BASED INVESTIGATION   Historical Source

Triangle Shirtwaist Fire

Ethel Monick was one of the teenage factory workers at the Triangle Shirtwaist Company. In the trial that followed the disaster, she described her experience in the fire. Rose Freedman, pictured, was the longest-living survivor of the fire. She died in 2001.

I seen the fire and then I seen all the girls rushing down to the place to escape. So I tried to go through the Greene Street door, and there were quick girls there and I seen I can't get out there, so I went to the elevator, and then I heard the elevator fall down, so I ran through to the Washington Place side. . . . I tried the door and I could not open it, so I thought I was not strong enough to open it, so I hollered girls here is a door, and they all rushed over and they tried to open it, but it was locked and they hollered "the door is locked and we can't open it!"

—Testimony of Ethel Monick, age 16

Analyze Historical Sources
According to Monick, what is the feeling in the factory?

two other floors. With the doors locked, escape was nearly impossible. The building's only fire escape collapsed under the weight of panic-stricken workers, sending them tumbling to their deaths. With flames at their backs, dozens of other workers leaped from the windows.

By the time firefighters brought the fire under control, 146 workers had died. At a memorial service for the victims, union leader Rose Schneiderman called for action. "It is up to the working people to save themselves," she said. The **Triangle Shirtwaist Fire** and similar accidents led to the passage of laws improving factory safety standards.

Labor leaders and reformers also fought for **workers' compensation laws**, which guaranteed a portion of lost wages to workers injured on the job. In 1902 Maryland became the first state to pass such a law. However, new laws were not always strictly enforced. Working conditions remained poor in many places.

The Courts and Labor Not everyone supported the new workplace regulations. Some business leaders believed that the economy should operate without any government interference. They went to court to block new labor laws.

One important case began in New York in 1897, after the state passed a law limiting bakers to a ten-hour workday. Joseph Lochner, a bakery owner, challenged the law. The case eventually went to the U.S. Supreme Court in 1905. In *Lochner* v. *New York*, the Court ruled that states could not restrict the rights of employers and workers to enter into any type of labor agreement. The New York law was declared unconstitutional.

The Supreme Court did uphold some limits on working hours for women and children. In the 1908 *Muller* v. *Oregon* case, the Court upheld laws restricting women's work hours. The justices stated that such laws protected women's health, which was of public concern.

Labor Unions Throughout the Progressive Era, labor unions were a strong force for improving working conditions. During this time, union membership grew, rising from about 800,000 in 1900 to about 5 million in 1920.

Founded in 1896 and led by Samuel Gompers, the American Federation of Labor (AFL) continued to be one of the strongest labor unions. The AFL focused on better working conditions and pay for skilled workers. Gompers supported the American economic system of **capitalism**, in which private businesses run most industries and competition determines the price of goods. Still, using strikes and other methods, the AFL won wage increases and shorter workweeks.

Workers also joined energetic new labor unions to fight for reforms. The International Ladies' Garment Workers' Union (ILGWU) was founded in 1900. Unlike the AFL, which allowed only skilled workers, the ILGWU organized unskilled laborers. In 1909 the garment workers called for a mass strike known as the "Uprising of the 20,000." The strikers won a shorter workweek and higher wages. They also attracted thousands of workers to the union.

Workers faced long hours of grueling work after the Supreme Court struck down a New York law limiting bakery employee workdays to 10 hours a day and 60 hours a week.

Some union members, however, believed in **socialism**—a system in which the government owns and operates a country's means of production. Socialists, led by Eugene V. Debs, hoped that the government would protect workers.

In 1905 a group of socialists and union leaders founded a union that welcomed immigrants, women, African Americans, and others not welcome in the AFL. Led by **William "Big Bill" Haywood**, this socialist union was called the **Industrial Workers of the World** (IWW). Its goal was to organize all workers into one large union that would overthrow capitalism. Known as "Wobblies," IWW members used strikes and boycotts to advance their cause, as well as more radical strategies, such as industrial sabotage.

At the height of its strength in 1912, the IWW led about 20,000 textile workers on strike in Lawrence, Massachusetts, to protest pay cuts. After a bitter, well-publicized ten-week strike, the mill owners gave in and raised wages. The IWW's success, however, was short-lived. Several of their strikes were terrible failures. Fearing the union's revolutionary goals, the government cracked down on the IWW's activities. Strong opposition led to its decline by 1920.

Reading Check
Analyze Information
How did reforms change the workplace?

Summary and Preview Progressive reformers fought to improve working conditions. In the next lesson you will learn about how women and minorities struggled for their rights.

Lesson 2 Assessment

Review Ideas, Terms, and People

1. **a. Recall** What jobs did child laborers often hold?
   b. Explain Why did businesses employ children in factories?
   c. Elaborate Why do you think reformers began to demand improvements to child labor conditions?
2. **a. Identify** What events led to the movement to improve workplace safety?
   b. Make Inferences Why did the Industrial Workers of the World frighten some people?
   c. Predict What conflicts might arise between supporters of capitalism and socialism?

Critical Thinking

3. **Analyze** In this lesson you learned about important labor problems in the 1800s and the workers they affected. Create a graphic organizer similar to the one below to give specific examples of how Progressives tried to reform child labor, women's labor, and workplace conditions.

The Rights of Women and Minorities

The Big Idea
The Progressive movement made advances for the rights of women and some minorities.

Main Ideas
- Women fought for temperance and the right to vote.
- African American reformers challenged discrimination and called for equality.
- Progressive reforms failed to benefit all minorities.

Key Terms and People
Eighteenth Amendment
National American Woman Suffrage Association
Alice Paul
Nineteenth Amendment
Booker T. Washington
Ida B. Wells
W. E. B. Du Bois
National Association for the Advancement of Colored People

If YOU were there . . .

You are a member of the class of 1912 graduating from an excellent women's college. You have always been interested in science, especially biology. You would like to be a doctor, but you know that medical schools accept very few women. One career path for you is to go into social work. Yet that's not what you really want to do.

How would you want to use your education?

Women Fight for Temperance and Voting Rights

New educational opportunities drew more women into the Progressive movement. In the late 1800s women began attending women's colleges, such as Smith College in Massachusetts and Vassar College in New York, in record numbers. In 1870 only about 20 percent of college students were women. By 1910 that number had doubled. The goal of female students was "to develop as fully as may be the powers of womanhood," said Sophia Smith, founder of Smith College.

Many female graduates entered fields such as social work and teaching. They found it much harder to enter professions such as law and medicine, which were dominated by men. Denied access to such professions, women often put their education to use by becoming active in reform. Women's clubs campaigned for causes such as temperance, women's suffrage, child welfare, and political reform.

The Temperance Movement In the mid-1800s many of these reformers blamed social problems such as family violence and criminal behavior on a number of factors, including urbanization and immigration. They also blamed problems on alcohol consumption. As a result, many groups took up the cause of temperance, or avoidance of alcohol.

In 1874 reformers from many different backgrounds formed the Woman's Christian Temperance Union (WCTU), which fought for adoption of local and state laws restricting the sale of alcohol. Under the leadership of Frances Willard, the organization started 10,000 branches. More than 1,000 saloons were forced to shut down as a result of temperance supporters' efforts.

One especially radical temperance fighter chose more dramatic tactics to fight for her cause. In the 1890s Carry Nation became famous for storming into saloons with a hatchet and smashing liquor bottles. Nation described destroying a Kansas saloon with bricks and rocks:

"I threw as hard, and as fast as I could, smashing mirrors and bottles and glasses and it was astonishing how quickly this was done."

—Carry Nation, *The Use and Need of the Life of Carry A. Nation, 1909*

Tall and strong, Nation was often arrested for her protest actions. Still, the temperance movement was effective. In 1919 its efforts led to the passage of the **Eighteenth Amendment**, banning the production, sale, and transportation of alcoholic beverages throughout the United States.

The Right to Vote Women reformers also fought for suffrage, or the right to vote. Many people at this time opposed giving women the vote. Political bosses, for instance, worried about the anticorruption efforts of women. Some business leaders worried that women voters would support minimum wage and child labor laws. Other people believed that women should only be homemakers and mothers and not politically active citizens.

In spite of such opposition, the women's suffrage movement began to gain national support in the 1890s. Elizabeth Cady Stanton and Susan B. Anthony founded the **National American Woman Suffrage Association** (NAWSA) in 1890 to promote the cause of women's suffrage. That same year, women won the right to vote in Wyoming. Colorado, Idaho, and Utah soon followed.

In several western states, women had the right to vote. However, it did not become a national right until the ratification of the Nineteenth Amendment in 1920.

The Nineteenth Amendment

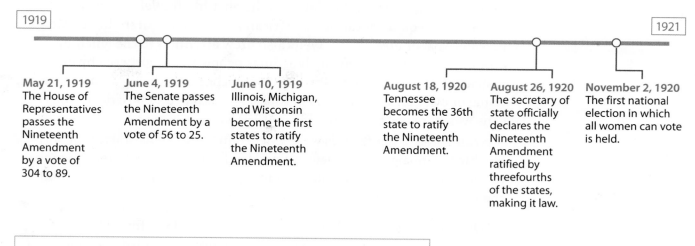

1919

May 21, 1919
The House of Representatives passes the Nineteenth Amendment by a vote of 304 to 89.

June 4, 1919
The Senate passes the Nineteenth Amendment by a vote of 56 to 25.

June 10, 1919
Illinois, Michigan, and Wisconsin become the first states to ratify the Nineteenth Amendment.

August 18, 1920
Tennessee becomes the 36th state to ratify the Nineteenth Amendment.

August 26, 1920
The secretary of state officially declares the Nineteenth Amendment ratified by threefourths of the states, making it law.

November 2, 1920
The first national election in which all women can vote is held.

1921

Interpret Timelines
After its passage in Congress, how long did it take for the Nineteenth Amendment to be ratified?

Reading Check
Analyze Information
How did reformers draw attention to the temperance and women's suffrage movements?

Carrie Chapman Catt became president of NAWSA in 1900. Catt mobilized more than 1 million volunteers for the movement. She argued that women should have a voice in creating laws that affected them. "We women demand an equal voice," she said. "We shall accept nothing less."

Some women believed that NAWSA did not go far enough. In 1913 **Alice Paul** founded what would become the National Woman's Party (NWP). The NWP used parades, public demonstrations, picketing, hunger strikes, and other means to draw attention to the suffrage cause. Paul even organized picketing in front of the White House. Paul and other NWP leaders were jailed for their actions.

Suffragists finally succeeded in gaining the vote. In 1919 the U.S. Congress passed the **Nineteenth Amendment**, granting American women the right to vote. The Nineteenth Amendment was ratified by the states the following year, making it law.

African Americans Challenge Discrimination

White reformers often overlooked issues such as racial discrimination and segregation. African American reformers found such issues inescapable. They took the lead in addressing these problems.

One of the most important African American leaders was **Booker T. Washington**. Born into slavery, Washington believed that African Americans should not openly challenge segregation. He thought that whites and blacks could work together yet live separate social lives. Over time, Washington believed that African Americans could gain equal social standing by becoming self-sufficient and economically secure. In 1881 he founded the Tuskegee Institute in Alabama to help African Americans learn trades as well as skills for self-sufficiency.

Other African Americans spoke out more directly against racial segregation, discrimination, and violence. Journalist **Ida B. Wells** wrote articles about the unequal education for African American children. In her Memphis newspaper *Free Speech*, Wells also drew attention to the lynching of African Americans. During lynchings people were murdered by mobs instead of receiving a trial. People were lynched after being accused of a crime or even for breaking social codes. More than 3,000 African Americans were lynched between 1885 and 1915.

After three of her friends were lynched in 1892, Wells started an anti-lynching campaign in her newspaper. Death threats forced Wells to move to the North. But she continued campaigning against lynching. In 1900 she wrote:

> "Our country's national crime is lynching . . . In fact, for all kinds of offenses—and, for no offenses—from murders to misdemeanors, men and women are put to death without judge or jury."
>
> —Ida B. Wells, from her article "Lynch Law in America"

DOCUMENT-BASED INVESTIGATION   Historical Source

Fighting Discrimination

Booker T. Washington and W. E. B. Du Bois had very different views on how African Americans could improve their social and economic standing.

> "Our greatest danger is that in the great leap from slavery to freedom we may overlook the fact that the masses of us are to live by the productions of our hands, and fail to keep in mind that we shall prosper in proportion as we learn to dignify and glorify common labour and put brains and skill into the common occupations of life. . . . It is at the bottom of life we must begin, and not at the top."
>
> —Booker T. Washington

> "Is it possible, and probable, that nine millions of men can make effective progress in economic lines if they are deprived of political rights, made a servile **caste**,[1] and allowed only the most meager chance for developing their exceptional men? If history and reason give any distinct answer to these questions, it is an emphatic No."
>
> —W. E. B. Du Bois

[1] *caste* lower social rank

Analyze Historical Sources
How do the views of Washington and Du Bois differ?

Like Wells, **W. E. B. Du Bois** took a direct approach to fighting racial injustice. Born in Massachusetts, Du Bois was an educator and civil rights activist. He earned a doctorate from Harvard University. As part of his research, he studied and publicized cases of racial prejudice.

Du Bois believed that African Americans should openly protest unjust treatment and demand equal rights immediately. He also promoted higher education for the most capable African Americans, who he called the "Talented Tenth." These were the teachers, ministers, and professionals that Du Bois believed should lead the struggle for equal rights.

Founding members of the Niagara Movement, including W.E.B. Du Bois (center), sat for this portrait in 1905.

In 1905 Du Bois launched the Niagara Movement to protest discrimination. Four years later, in 1909, he helped found an even more influential organization, **National Association for the Advancement of Colored People** (NAACP). Still active today, the NAACP is a civil rights organization that supports economic and educational equality for African Americans. In its early years, the NAACP worked to secure for African Americans the rights guaranteed by the Thirteenth, Fourteenth, and Fifteenth Amendments to the U.S. Constitution. These rights included equal protection under the law and voting rights for all adult men.

The NAACP fought discrimination against African Americans by using the courts. In 1915 it won the important case of *Guinn* v. *United States*, which made grandfather clauses illegal. These laws were used in the South to keep African Americans from voting. Grandfather clauses imposed strict qualifications on voters unless their grandfathers had been allowed to vote. Many white voters met this requirement and were automatically permitted to vote in elections. However, most African Americans' grandfathers had been enslaved and could not vote.

Another important organization was the National Urban League. It was formed in 1911 by Dr. George Edmund Haynes. This organization aided many African Americans moving from the South by helping them find jobs and housing in northern cities. The Urban League addressed many of the same problems faced by other Progressives, such as health, sanitation, and education.

Reading Check
Find Main Ideas
What was the purpose of the NAACP?

Limits of Reform

The Progressive movement achieved some remarkable successes. But Progressive efforts at reform had limits. In addition to overlooking the challenges faced by African Americans, white reformers also overlooked the discrimination faced by other ethnic groups. Native Americans, for example, were largely left behind by the Progressive movement. Some reformers tried to improve conditions for Native Americans by culturally **assimilating** them into, or having them adopt, white American culture. Unfortunately, these efforts often came at a high cost to Native American culture, religion, and language.

Academic Vocabulary
assimilation
adoption of another culture's way of life

In 1911 two Native American Progressives, Dr. Carlos Montezuma and Dr. Charles Eastman, founded the Society of American Indians. It was the first national organization that aimed to unite diverse Native American groups in an effort to promote American Indian rights. Many of its early leaders believed that integration into white society would help end Native American poverty. Many other Native Americans, however, wanted to preserve their traditional culture. They resisted the movement to adopt white culture and worked to preserve Native American culture.

Immigrants from non-European countries also formed groups to help support their members. Chinese immigrants, for example, organized associations in the communities in which they lived. District associations, cultural groups, churches, and temples provided public services that white reformers ignored. San Francisco's Chinese Hospital was built in 1925 by such a group. Anti-Chinese riots in some western towns and cities caused Chinese immigration to drop, however.

Immigrants from Mexico increased during this time. The borders between the United States and its neighbors were fairly easy to cross. Many Mexican immigrants moved to the South and Southwest. They became an important part of the societies and economies of these regions. Many Mexican immigrants found jobs in the mining and railroad industries. Others became farmers or migrant workers. Progressive labor laws and factory reforms did nothing to improve the poor living and working conditions of migrant farm workers.

Reading Check
Summarize What were the limitations of progressive reforms?

Summary and Preview Many U.S. citizens worked for progressive reforms. In the next lesson you will read about presidents who also worked for progressive goals.

Lesson 3 Assessment

Review Ideas, Terms, and People

1. a. Identify What did the Eighteenth and Nineteenth Amendments accomplish?

b. Summarize How did Alice Paul and the National Woman's Party try to draw attention to the issue of women's suffrage?

2. a. Identify What role did Ida B. Wells play in reform efforts for African Americans?

b. Contrast How did Booker T. Washington differ from other African American leaders?

c. Evaluate Do you think the National Association for the Advancement of Colored People was successful in fighting discrimination? Explain.

3. a. Describe What discrimination did Chinese Americans face?

b. Summarize How were some minority groups overlooked by the Progressive movement?

Critical Thinking

4. Analyze In this lesson you learned about the causes supported by different groups of progressive reformers. Create a graphic organizer similar to the one below to identify the progressive reforms introduced by the temperance movement, the women's suffrage movement, and African Americans.

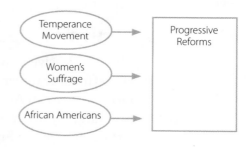

The Progressive Presidents

The Big Idea

American presidents in the early 1900s did a great deal to promote progressive reforms.

Main Ideas

- Theodore Roosevelt's progressive reforms tried to balance the interests of business, consumers, and laborers.

- William Howard Taft angered Progressives with his cautious reforms, while Woodrow Wilson enacted far-reaching banking and antitrust reforms.

Key Terms and People

Theodore Roosevelt
Pure Food and Drug Act
conservation
William Howard Taft
Progressive Party
Woodrow Wilson
Sixteenth Amendment

If YOU were there . . .

It is 1912 and you're voting in your first presidential election. This election is unusual—there are three major candidates. One is the popular former president Theodore Roosevelt, who is running as a third-party candidate. He thinks the Republican candidate will not make enough progressive reforms. But the Democratic candidate is a progressive reformer, too.

How will you decide which candidate to support?

Roosevelt's Progressive Reforms

During a summer tour after his second inauguration in 1901, President William McKinley met a friendly crowd in Buffalo, New York. Suddenly, anarchist Leon Czolgosz stepped forward and shot the president. A little more than a week later, McKinley died. Vice President **Theodore Roosevelt** took office.

Roosevelt's Square Deal Roosevelt believed that the interests of businesspeople, laborers, and consumers should be balanced for the public good. He called this policy the Square Deal. He put the policy to the test in 1902 when faced by a coal miners' strike. Roosevelt knew the strike might leave the country without heating fuel for the coming winter. He threatened to take over the mines unless managers and strikers agreed to arbitration—a formal process to settle disputes. He felt this was the only fair way to protect Americans.

> "The labor unions shall have a square deal, and the corporations shall have a square deal, and in addition all private citizens shall have a square deal."
>
> —President Theodore Roosevelt, quoted in *The Presidency of Theodore Roosevelt*, by Lewis L. Gould

Regulating Big Business Roosevelt made regulating big business a top goal of his administration. Muckrakers helped build support for this regulation. The public was shocked, for instance, after reading Upton Sinclair's description of the meatpacking industry in *The Jungle*. Roosevelt opened an investigation and later convinced Congress to pass a meat inspection law.

In 1906 Congress passed the **Pure Food and Drug Act**. This law prohibited the manufacture, sale, and transport of mislabeled or contaminated food and drugs. Roosevelt also was the first president to successfully use the 1890 Sherman Antitrust Act to break up a monopoly. He persuaded Congress to regulate railroad-shipping rates. The public largely supported this expansion of federal regulatory powers.

Conservation Roosevelt's love of the outdoors inspired him to join other Progressives in supporting **conservation**, or the protection of nature and its resources. Roosevelt was the first president to consider conservation an important national priority.

People believed in conservation for various reasons. Preservationists such as John Muir thought that nature should be left untouched so that people could enjoy its beauty:

> "Thousands of tired, nerve-shaken, over-civilized people are
> beginning to find out that going to the mountains is going
> home; that wildness is a necessity; and that mountain parks
> and reservations are useful not only as fountains of timber and
> irrigating rivers, but as fountains of life."
>
> —John Muir, *Our National Parks*

Other conservationists wanted to make sure the nation used its natural resources efficiently. Gifford Pinchot, the first head of the newly created

President Theodore Roosevelt and conservationist John Muir in Yosemite National Park in California

Forest Service, valued forests for the resources they provided to build "prosperous homes." The disagreement between the two ideals of conservation eventually widened.

While Roosevelt was in office, the Forest Service gained control of nearly 150 million acres of public land. Roosevelt doubled the number of national parks, created 18 national monuments, and started 51 bird sanctuaries.

Reading Check
Summarize What reforms did Roosevelt support?

Reforms of Taft and Wilson

Theodore Roosevelt hoped that his secretary of war, **William Howard Taft**, would take his place as president in 1908. Like Roosevelt, Taft favored business regulation and opposed socialism. With Roosevelt's assistance, Taft defeated William Jennings Bryan in the election of 1908.

Taft Angers Progressives Despite their friendship, Roosevelt and Taft held different ideas about how a president should act. Taft thought Roosevelt had claimed more power than was constitutional.

Academic Vocabulary
various of many types

As president, therefore, Taft moved cautiously with reform and regulation. This upset Roosevelt and **various** Progressives, who supported stricter regulation of big business. Taft's administration started twice as many antitrust lawsuits as Roosevelt's had. But Progressives were not satisfied.

Taft angered Progressives further by signing the Payne-Aldrich Tariff of 1909. This tariff reduced some rates on imported goods, but it raised others. Progressives wanted all tariffs to be lowered, in order to lower prices for consumers.

Furious with Taft, Roosevelt decided to run for president again in 1912. After Taft won the Republican nomination, Roosevelt and his followers formed the **Progressive Party**. It was nicknamed the Bull Moose Party because Roosevelt said he was "as strong as a bull moose." The split between Taft and Roosevelt divided the Republican vote, and Democratic candidate **Woodrow Wilson** won the electoral vote by a wide margin.

Wilson's Reforms In his inaugural address, Wilson spoke of the terrible social conditions of many working-class Americans. "We have been proud of our industrial achievements," he said, "but we have not hitherto [yet] stopped thoughtfully enough to count the human cost." Passing reform legislation was Wilson's top goal. He pushed for two measures soon after taking office: tariff revision and banking reform.

Wilson backed the Underwood Tariff Act of 1913, which lowered tariffs. The act also introduced a version of the modern income tax. The new tax was made possible in 1913 by the ratification of the **Sixteenth Amendment**. This amendment allows the federal government to impose direct taxes on citizens' incomes.

President Wilson next addressed banking reform. The 1913 Federal Reserve Act created the modern banking system. The Federal Reserve Board (the "Fed") oversees 12 regional Federal Reserve Banks. It makes sure that money is distributed where it is most needed. These are bankers'

The Progressive Amendments, 1909–1920

Number	Description	Proposed by Congress	Ratified by States
16th	Federal income tax	1909	1913
17th	Senators elected by the people rather than state legislatures	1912	1913
18th	Manufacture, sale, and transport of alcohol prohibited	1917	1919
19th	Women's suffrage	1919	1920

banks that serve consumer banks. The Federal Reserve Act created a more flexible currency system by allowing consumer banks to have more control over the money supply. To raise money, the Fed lowers the interest rate that it charges member banks. These banks then borrow more from the Fed, and thus have more money to lend to people and businesses.

Wilson also pushed for laws to regulate big business. The Clayton Antitrust Act of 1914 strengthened federal laws against monopolies. The Federal Trade Commission, created in 1914, had the power to investigate and punish unfair trade practices. Wilson's success in guiding reform programs through Congress helped him to win re-election in 1916.

Reading Check
Analyze Information
Why did Wilson win the election of 1912?

Summary and Preview The progressive presidents tried to change American society for the better. In the next module you will learn how they also helped the United States become a world power.

Lesson 4 Assessment

Review Ideas, Terms, and People

1. a. Describe How did Theodore Roosevelt support progressive reforms?

b. Analyze Why did many Americans support conservation?

c. Evaluate Do you think Roosevelt's reforms benefited the nation? Why or why not?

2. a. Identify What was the Progressive Party? Why was it created?

b. Compare and Contrast How were the administrations of William Howard Taft and Roosevelt similar, and how were they different?

c. Evaluate Which president do you think had the biggest influence on progressive reform—Roosevelt, Taft, or Woodrow Wilson? Explain your choice.

Critical Thinking

3. Compare and Contrast In this lesson you learned about the achievements of each of the progressive presidents. Create a Venn diagram similar to the one below and compare and contrast the reforms of the progressive presidents.

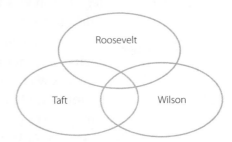

Short- and Long-term Causal Relationships

Define the Skill

Most historical events are the result of other events. When something happens as a result of other things that occur, it is an effect of those things. Some events take place soon after the things that cause them. Such events are called *short-term effects*. In contrast, *long-term effects* can occur years, decades, or even hundreds of years after the events that caused them. Being able to recognize short-term and long-term cause-and-effect relationships will help you to better understand historical events.

Learn the Skill

Clue words can sometimes reveal a cause-and-effect relationship between events. Often, however, such language clues may not be present. Therefore, when you study history, you should always look for other clues that might explain why an action or event occurred.

Short-term effects are usually fairly easy to identify. In historical writing they are often closely linked to the event that caused them. For example, consider this passage from Module 22.

"Some Progressives worked to change state and local governments in order to reduce the power of political machines. In many places, reformers replaced corrupt ballots that listed only one party's candidates with government-prepared ballots that listed all candidates. Under pressure from reformers, many states adopted secret ballots, giving every voter a private vote."

This passage contains no clue words. Yet it is clear that cause-and-effect relationships exist. The power of political machines created corrupt voting practices. Reformers wanted to change this. One effect of this situation was the government-prepared ballot, and another was the secret ballot.

Recognizing long-term causal relationships is often more difficult. Since long-term effects take place well after the event that caused them, they may not be discussed at the same time as their cause. This is why you should always question why an event occurred as you learn about it. For example, in 1971 Congress passed the first federal law to protect the health and safety of all workers. This law was a long-term result of efforts begun years earlier by the Progressives you read about in this module.

Many long-term effects result from major forces running through history that make things happen. They include economics, science and technology, expansion, conflict and cooperation among people, cultural clashes and differences, and moral and religious issues. Ask yourself if one of these forces is involved in the event being studied. If so, the event may have long-term effects that you should be on the lookout for when studying later events.

Practice the Skill

Review the information in Module 22 and answer these questions to practice recognizing short- and long-term causal relationships.

1. All packaged food today must have its contents listed on the container. This requirement is a long-term effect of what progressive reform?

2. Write a paragraph explaining the effects of the muckrakers on the news media today.

Module 22 Assessment

Review Vocabulary, Terms, and People

Complete each sentence by filling in the blank with the correct term or person from the module.

1. Some Americans supported a(n) _____ system, which proposed government ownership of the country's means of production.

2. Republican _____ began a program to reform state politics in Wisconsin.

3. The _____ granted women in the United States the right to vote.

4. The _____ prohibited the manufacture, sale, and transport of mislabeled or contaminated food and drugs.

5. During the Gilded Age, _____ often dominated local politics and used corruption to get their candidates elected.

6. _____ were journalists who wrote about troubling issues such as child labor, tenement housing, and political corruption.

Comprehension and Critical Thinking

Lesson 1

7. a. **Describe** What tactics did bosses and political machines use to gain control of local governments?

    b. **Analyze** What changes did Progressives make to city life?

    c. **Elaborate** Which progressive reform do you think had the greatest effect on Americans?

Lesson 2

8. a. **Identify** What reforms were made to improve working conditions, and who was affected by these reforms?

    b. **Contrast** What are the differences between capitalism and socialism?

    c. **Elaborate** If you were a business owner, would you have supported the progressive workplace reforms? Explain your answer.

Lesson 3

9. a. **Recall** What minority groups were overlooked by progressive reform efforts?

    b. **Analyze** How did women's involvement in the Progressive movement lead to constitutional change?

    c. **Elaborate** Do you agree with Booker T. Washington's approach to improving life for African Americans? Explain your answer.

Lesson 4

10. a. **Describe** How did William Howard Taft disappoint Progressives?

     b. **Compare** In what ways were the reforms of presidents Roosevelt, Taft, and Wilson similar?

     c. **Elaborate** Would you have supported Wilson's progressive reforms? Explain your answer.

Review Themes

11. **Politics** What role did political machines play in local politics during the Gilded Age?

12. **Society and Culture** How did the movement for workplace reforms affect children?

13. **Economics** How did the Federal Reserve influence the American economy?

Reading Skills

Evaluate Sources *Use the Reading Skills taught in this module to answer the question about the reading selection below.*

> The next day Rose went to town [Chicago] alone. The wind had veered [turned] to the south, the dust blew, and the whole terrifying panorama [view] of life in the street seemed some way blurred together, and forms of men and animals were like figures in tapestry. The grind and clang and clatter and hiss and howl of the traffic was all about her . . .
>
> —Hamlin Garland, from his novel
> *The Rose of Dutcher's Coolly*, 1895

14. Is this a good source for understanding the experiences of Chicago in the late 1800s? Why or why not?

Social Studies Skills

Short- and Long-Term Causal Relationships
Use the Social Studies Skills taught in this module to answer the question about the reading selection below.

> Despite their friendship, Roosevelt and Taft held different ideas about how a president should act. Taft thought Roosevelt had claimed more power than was constitutional.
>
> As president, therefore, Taft moved cautiously with reform and regulation.

15. According to the passage above, what was a long-term cause of Taft's cautious reforms?

Focus on Speaking

16. **Share Your Campaign Promises** Serious problems face the nation, and you must convince voters that you should be the one to tackle those problems. Create a list of campaign promises that you would make if you were a progressive politician running for office in the United States in the late 1800s or early 1900s. Which promises will be most helpful in getting you elected? Look at your promises to see whether they focus on issues important to voters. Then write a speech including your campaign promises that you can deliver to your class.

Module 23

America as a World Power

Essential Question
Why did the United States turn to empire in the late 1800s?

About the Photo: Through a combination of economic strength, military might, and aggressive foreign policy, the United States made its presence known in many parts of the world. One such place was Panama, where the United States built the Panama Canal, shown here.

▷ *Explore ONLINE!*

HISTORY

VIDEOS, including...
- Panama Canal Locks
- China: The Boxer Uprising
- The Battle of San Juan Hill
- Theodore Roosevelt: Big Stick Foreign Policies

☑ Document-Based Investigations

☑ Graphic Organizers

☑ Interactive Games

☑ Image with Hotspots: Perry Arrives in Japan

☑ Interactive Map: War in the Caribbean

☑ Animation: The Panama Canal

In this module you will learn about how the United States became a world power in the late 1800s and early 1900s.

What You Will Learn ...

Lesson 1: The United States Gains Overseas Territories 718
The Big Idea In the last half of the 1800s, the United States joined the race for control of overseas territories.

Lesson 2: The Spanish-American War 724
The Big Idea As a result of the Spanish- American War, the United States expanded its reach into new parts of the world.

Lesson 3: The United States and Latin America 732
The Big Idea The United States expanded its role in Latin America in the early 1900s with new foreign policy.

United States	World

1860

1867 The United States buys Alaska. ∨

1868 Japan begins a time of modernization known as the Meiji Restoration.

1880

∧ **1885** The Indian National Congress is formed in British-controlled India.

1890 Congress passes the McKinley Tariff, which gives a subsidy to U.S. sugar producers.

1895 Cubans rebel against Spanish rule.

1898 The United States wins the Spanish-American War, gaining the Philippine Islands and Puerto Rico. ∨

1900

1900 The Boxer Rebellion erupts in China.

1903 Panama declares itself an independent nation.

1910 The Mexican Revolution begins.

1914 The Panama Canal officially opens.

1920

Reading Social Studies

THEME FOCUS:

Geography and Politics

In this module you will learn about how the political geography of the United States changed as it acquired overseas territories. You will also read about how national and international politics affected foreign policy and brought new responsibilities to the government of the United States.

READING FOCUS:

Compare Historical Texts

A good way to learn what people in the past thought is to read what they wrote. However, most documents will only tell you one side of the story. By comparing writings by different people, you can learn a great deal about various sides of a historical issue or debate.

Compare Texts When you compare historical texts, you should consider two things: who wrote the documents and what the documents were meant to achieve. To do this, you need to find the writers' main point or points.

Document 1

"We have cherished the policy of noninterference with affairs of foreign governments wisely inaugurated [begun] by Washington, keeping ourselves free from entanglement, either as allies or foes, content to leave undisturbed with them the settlement of their own domestic concerns."

—*President William McKinley, First Inaugural Address, 1897*

Document 2

"Therefore, Mr. President, here is a war with terrible characteristics flagrant [obvious] at our very doors [in Cuba]. We have the power to bring it to an end. I believe that the whole American people would welcome steps in that direction."

—*Senator Henry Cabot Lodge, Speech in Congress, 1896*

Document 1	Document 2
Writer	
President William McKinley	Senator Henry Cabot Lodge
Main Point	
The United States should not involve itself in the affairs of other countries.	The United States should go to war in Cuba.
Both Sides of the Issue	
Americans were torn over the war in Cuba. Some thought the United States should remain uninvolved as it always had. Others thought it was time for a change in foreign policy.	

You Try It!

Read the following passages, both taken from presidential addresses to Congress. As you read, look for the main point each president makes in his address.

Foreign Policy

In treating of our foreign policy and of the attitude that this great Nation should assume in the world at large, it is absolutely necessary to consider the Army and the Navy, and the Congress, through which the thought of the Nation finds its expression, should keep ever vividly in mind the fundamental fact that it is impossible to treat our foreign policy, whether this policy takes shape in the effort to secure justice for others or justice for ourselves, save as conditioned upon the attitude we are willing to take toward our Army, and especially toward our Navy.

—President Theodore Roosevelt,
Message to Congress, 1904

The diplomacy of the present administration has sought to respond to modern ideas of commercial intercourse [involvement]. This policy has been characterized as substituting dollars for bullets. It is one that appeals alike to idealistic humanitarian sentiments [feelings], to the dictates [rules] of sound policy and strategy, and to legitimate [make real] commercial aims.

—President William Howard Taft,
Message to Congress, 1912

After you read the passages, answer the following questions.

1. What was the main point Roosevelt made in his address?

2. What was the main point Taft made in his address?

3. How can a comparison of Roosevelt's and Taft's addresses to Congress help you understand the issues that shaped U.S. foreign policy in the early 1900s?

As you read Module 23, organize your notes to help you point out the similarities and differences among events or policies.

Key Terms and People

Lesson 1
imperialism
isolationism
William H. Seward
Liliuokalani
spheres of influence
Open Door Policy
Boxer Rebellion

Lesson 2
yellow journalism
Teller Amendment
Emilio Aguinaldo
Anti-Imperialist League
Platt Amendment

Lesson 3
Panama Canal
Roosevelt Corollary
dollar diplomacy
Mexican Revolution
John J. Pershing
Francisco "Pancho" Villa

The United States Gains Overseas Territories

The Big Idea

In the last half of the 1800s, the United States joined the race for control of overseas territories.

Main Ideas

- The United States ended its policy of isolationism and began imperial expansion.

- Hawaii became a U.S. territory in 1898.

- The United States sought trade with Japan and China.

Key Terms and People

imperialism
isolationism
William H. Seward
Liliuokalani
spheres of influence
Open Door Policy
Boxer Rebellion

If YOU were there . . .

You are a Hawaiian living on Maui, one of the Hawaiian Islands, in 1890. Your parents work in a sugar mill owned by American planters. Although the mill supplies jobs, you don't trust the sugar planters. They have already made your king sign a treaty that gives them a lot of power in the islands. You are afraid they will take over the government.

What would you do if the planters took over your islands?

End of Isolation

In the 1800s powerful Western nations were busy building naval bases to protect their shipping routes around the world. This was an aspect of **imperialism**—building an empire by founding colonies or conquering other nations. Between 1870 and 1914, Europeans used this foreign policy to extend their colonial empires until they controlled most of Africa and Southeast Asia.

Roots of Imperialism Several forces drove this wave of European imperialism. Countries wanted sources of raw materials—such as copper, rubber, and tin—to fuel industrial growth. Businesspeople wanted new markets for their manufactured goods. And many Europeans saw colonies as a source of power and national pride.

In contrast, the United States followed a limited foreign policy of **isolationism**—avoiding involvement in the affairs of other countries. In 1789 President George Washington had warned Americans "to steer clear of permanent alliances" with other countries. American leaders tried to follow this advice by staying out of overseas conflicts.

By the late 1800s, however, some American leaders believed the United States needed to expand to keep its economy strong. They sought new sources for raw materials and new places to sell goods. To do so, they wanted the United

States to expand beyond North America and establish territories overseas. In 1890 Alfred T. Mahan wrote *The Influence of Sea Power upon History*. In this book he argued that the United States needed a strong navy to protect its economic interests. Such a navy would need overseas bases and coaling stations—places for ships to take on coal for fuel.

Mahan and others argued that it was in the nation's interest to shift its foreign policy. They supported imperial expansionism. This is a policy of gaining power by taking control of other lands. For the United States this meant acquiring new lands as U.S. territories. Advocates of expansionism claimed that it would increase the nation's financial prosperity, strengthen the nation's military, and help spread democratic ideals. In the late 1800s the U.S. foreign policy did indeed shift from isolationism to imperialism.

Seward's Folly The United States took its first steps in becoming a world power by acquiring Alaska. In 1867 the United States greatly expanded its North American territory. Secretary of State **William H. Seward** arranged the purchase of Alaska from Russia for $7.2 million. Some people thought Alaska was a frozen wasteland, calling the deal "Seward's Folly" [foolish act]. But Seward had purchased an area more than twice the size of Texas for two cents an acre. And as he had hoped, Alaska became a source of valuable natural resources such as fur, timber, and minerals. Gold was found in Alaska in the 1890s, bringing miners and settlers to the area.

▷ Explore ONLINE!

U.S. Territories in the Pacific, 1856–1899

Interpret Maps
Between 1856 and 1898, Alaska and many Pacific islands, including Hawaii, became U.S. territories.

1. **Location** What U.S. territory was located below the equator?

2. **Region** In what year did the United States acquire the most territories?

Reading Check
Analyze Why did U.S. leaders end isolationist policies in the late 1800s?

Based on Seward's belief that the United States "must continue to move on westward," the nation also annexed the Midway Islands in 1867. The islands' location about halfway between the U.S. West Coast and Japan made Midway an excellent coaling station for the U.S. Navy.

The United States wanted the island group of Samoa for similar reasons. The United States and Germany agreed to divide Samoa in 1899.

Hawaii Becomes a Territory

Even more appealing than Samoa were the Hawaiian Islands. The islands provided an economic opportunity for the United States and a chance to gain even more world power. Hawaiians first saw Europeans in 1778. Trading and whaling ships in the Pacific soon began stopping in Hawaii. In the early 1800s American missionaries came and attempted to convert Hawaiians to Christianity. Missionaries opened businesses and raised crops, such as sugarcane. Some Americans became rich sugar planters.

By the 1840s most shops and shipyards in Hawaii were owned by Americans. Sugar became a leading export of the Hawaiian economy. An 1875 treaty allowed Hawaiian sugar to be shipped duty-free to the United States. (A duty is a tax on imported items.) This agreement helped the Hawaiian sugar industry prosper.

The American planters used their power to force the Hawaiian king to sign a new constitution in 1887. It became known as the Bayonet Constitution because the king was forced to sign it at gunpoint. The constitution granted more power to the planter-controlled legislature. Many Hawaiians feared the foreigners' increase in power.

In 1891 the king died, and his sister, **Liliuokalani** (li-LEE-uh-woh-kuh-LAHN-ee), became queen. She proposed a new constitution that would return power to the monarchy. American planters in Hawaii saw these plans as threats to their political and economic interests. The planters

--- BIOGRAPHY ---

Liliuokalani 1838–1917

Born in Honolulu, Queen Liliuokalani was the first and only queen of Hawaii. She was a defender of Hawaiian traditions and territory. Even after being driven from power in 1893, she continued speaking out on behalf of native-born Hawaiians. In 1897 she traveled to Washington, DC. She met with President Grover Cleveland to argue against the annexation of Hawaii by the United States. Today her reign is a proud reminder of the islands' history as an independent nation.

Draw Conclusions

Why do you think Liliuokalani was a symbol of Hawaiian pride?

revolted. John L. Stevens, U.S. minister to Hawaii, called 150 marines ashore to support the revolt. It succeeded without a battle. The planters formed a new government. They asked the U.S. government to annex Hawaii to become part of the United States.

U.S. leaders already understood the value of the islands. It was in their interest to gain control. In 1887 they had negotiated with Hawaii's king to allow a U.S. base at Pearl Harbor. It was one of the best natural harbors in the eastern Pacific. The base became an important refueling station for American merchant and military ships bound for Asia. This helped the United States continue to gain world political power.

Congress voted to annex the Hawaiian Islands in 1898. Hawaii officially changed from an independent country to an American territory. As a territory, Hawaii would fall under the control of the United States.

With American territory now stretching between two oceans, America was well placed to extend its influence in the Pacific. Through purchase and annexation, the nation began expanding beyond its shores and becoming a world power.

Reading Check
Identify Cause and Effect Why did American planters in Hawaii stage a revolt?

United States Seeks Trade with Japan and China

Economic interest also drew the United States to Japan and China. The United States wanted to open and secure trade markets in both of these Asian countries.

Opening Trade with Japan By the mid-1800s European powers had formed strong trade ties with most East Asian countries. However, the island nation of Japan had isolated itself from the rest of the world for hundreds of years.

The United States wanted to open up trade with Japan before Europeans arrived. President Millard Fillmore sent Commodore Matthew Perry to Japan to secure "friendship, commerce, [and] a supply of coal and provisions." Perry attempted a peaceful alliance in 1853 to influence economic change, but he was not successful.

Perry returned to Japan in 1854 with seven warships. He gave Japanese leaders gifts and tried to show some of the benefits that Japanese-American trade would have. For instance, Perry presented them with a telegraph transmitter and a model train. This effort—and the presence of U.S. naval power—persuaded Japanese officials to open trade with the United States. The two countries signed a trade agreement in 1858.

Some Japanese leaders welcomed trade with the United States. In 1868 people who favored the industrialization **process** came to power in Japan. This began a 40-year period of modernization. By the 1890s Japan was becoming a major imperial power. It defeated China in the Sino-Japanese War from 1894 to 1895. As a result, Japan gained new territory and enjoyed the same trading privileges in China as European countries. In 1904 Japan attacked Russian forces stationed in China. President Theodore Roosevelt helped to negotiate a peace treaty to end the Russo-

Academic Vocabulary
process a series of steps by which a task is accomplished

Perry Arrives in Japan

Connect to the Arts This painting from 1854 shows Commodore Perry landing at Yokohama, Japan. He staged a parade to disembark and meet the imperial commissioners who represented the emperor. This meeting was the first official meeting between an agent of the United States and officials from Japan.

What impression do you think Commodore Perry intended to make?

How might the Japanese have felt seeing these ships arrive?

Japanese War a year later. Japan gained control of Korea, a lease on Port Arthur in China, and other rights. Japan had become a world power.

Foreign Powers in China After Japan defeated China, other countries took advantage of China's weakness. They did this by seizing **spheres of influence**—areas where foreign nations claimed special rights and economic privileges. Germany, Great Britain, France, Japan, and Russia all took control of areas within China.

Some U.S. leaders feared that the United States would be closed out of Chinese markets and resources. To promote its national interests, the United States took action. In 1899 Secretary of State John Hay sent notes to Japan and many European countries announcing the **Open Door Policy**. This policy stated that all nations should have equal access to trade in China. The policy was neither rejected nor accepted by European powers and Japan, but it made U.S. intentions clear.

As a result, many Chinese resented the power and control held by foreign nations. This hostility sparked the **Boxer Rebellion**. The Boxers were Chinese nationalists who were angered by foreign involvement in China. In their language, the group was called the Fists of Righteous Harmony. Westerners called them Boxers because they used a clenched fist as their symbol. Although officially denounced, they were secretly supported by the Chinese government.

In June 1900 the Boxers took to the streets of Beijing, China's capital. They laid siege to the walled settlement where foreigners lived. They killed more than 200 people.

The siege continued for two months. Foreign military forces, including United States Marines, fought their way from the port of Tianjin to Beijing. There they invaded the Forbidden City, the imperial palace complex. The Boxers were soon defeated. China was forced to make a cash payment of $333 million to foreign governments, $25 million of which went to the United States.

Foreign forces engage Chinese nationalists in battle at Tianjin, China, in this illustration of China's Boxer Rebellion.

Secretary of State Hay then sent another Open Door note to Japan and the European nations. The Open Door Policy remained in effect until World War II again closed China's borders to foreign influence.

Reading Check
Identify Cause and Effect What factors led to the Boxer Rebellion, and what was the result?

Summary and Preview The United States greatly expanded its territory and influence in the Pacific. In the next lesson you will learn about the causes and effects of the Spanish-American War.

Lesson 1 Assessment

Review Ideas, Terms, and People

1. a. **Describe** What policy had the United States followed regarding other countries before the late 1800s?

   b. **Analyze** Why did the United States expand to Alaska and to islands in the Pacific?

   c. **Evaluate** Why did the United States change its foreign policy from one of isolationism to imperialism?

2. a. **Sequence** What events led to Hawaii's annexation as a U.S. territory?

   b. **Elaborate** Explain why the planters revolted against Queen Liliuokalani.

   c. **Compare and Contrast** In what way did Hawaii change when it became a territory of the United States?

3. a. **Describe** What was the purpose of the Open Door Policy?

   b. **Contrast** How was the U.S. experience establishing trade with China different from U.S. attempts to open trade with Japan?

   c. **Evaluate** Do you think Japan made the right decision in agreeing to open trade with the United States? Explain your answer.

Critical Thinking

4. **Generalize** In this lesson you learned about the areas or trade rights gained by the United States. Create a chart similar to the one below and identify the benefits of these areas and trade rights. Describe how these helped the United States become a world power.

American Expansion	
Areas or Trade Rights Gained	Benefits for United States

The Spanish-American War

The Big Idea

As a result of the Spanish-American War, the United States expanded its reach into new parts of the world.

Main Ideas

- In 1898 the United States went to war with Spain in the Spanish-American War.
- The United States gained territories in the Caribbean and Pacific.

Key Terms and People

yellow journalism
Teller Amendment
Emilio Aguinaldo
Anti-Imperialist League
Platt Amendment

If YOU were there . . .

You live in New York City in 1898. Newspaper headlines are screaming about the start of war in Cuba. You hear that Theodore Roosevelt wants volunteers for a cavalry troop called the Rough Riders. You know how to ride a horse, and you've admired Roosevelt ever since he was New York's police commissioner. You know it will be dangerous, but it also sounds like a great adventure.

Would you join the Rough Riders? Why?

War with Spain

You read earlier that newspaper publishers Joseph Pulitzer and William Randolph Hearst were in a fierce competition for readers. In the late 1890s their newspapers published stories from Cuba, where Cuban rebels were fighting for independence from Spain. To attract readers, Pulitzer and Hearst printed sensational, often exaggerated, news stories. This technique is called **yellow journalism**. Vivid stories about Spanish brutality in Cuba convinced many Americans that the U.S. military should support the Cuban rebels.

Newspapers such as this one used yellow journalism to encourage Americans to seek war with Spain.

Despite growing support for military action in Cuba, President Grover Cleveland was opposed to U.S. involvement. In 1896 William McKinley, a supporter of Cuban independence, was elected president. At first, he was against war, but American public opinion forced him to take action. Several events soon led to war.

In February 1898, Hearst's newspaper published a letter written by the Spanish minister to the United States, Enrique Dupuy de Lôme. In it, de Lôme called McKinley "weak and a bidder for the admiration of the crowd." Many Americans were outraged.

In January 1898, even before de Lôme's letter became public, the United States sent the battleship USS *Maine* to Havana Harbor. Riots had broken out in Havana, the Cuban capital. The *Maine*'s mission was to protect U.S. citizens and economic interests in Cuba from the violence. On February 15 the *Maine* exploded and sank, with a loss of 266 men. Although the cause of the explosion was unclear, the American press immediately blamed Spain. "Remember the *Maine*!" became a rallying cry for angry Americans.

President McKinley requested $50 million to prepare for war. Congress approved the money. Although Cuba was not a U.S. territory, Congress issued a resolution on April 20 declaring Cuba independent and demanding that Spain leave the island within three days. Attached to the resolution was the **Teller Amendment**, which stated that the United States had no interest in taking control of Cuba. In response to the resolution, Spain declared war on the United States. The next day, Congress passed, and McKinley signed, a declaration of war against Spain.

"Remember the *Maine*!"

Most of the men aboard the USS *Maine* were sleeping when a terrible explosion demolished the forward third of the ship at 9:40 p.m. on February 15, 1898. The rest of the ship sank quickly. Some 266 men were killed.

How do you think such images of the Maine *might have affected Americans?*

War in the Philippines While attention was focused on Cuba, the U.S. Navy won a quick victory nearly halfway around the world in the Philippines, a Spanish colony in the Pacific. Filipinos, like Cubans, were rebelling against Spanish rule.

As soon as the Spanish-American War began, American commodore George Dewey raced to the Philippines with four large warships and two small gunboats. On May 1, ignoring reports that mines beneath the water barred his way, Dewey sailed into Manila Bay and destroyed the Spanish Pacific fleet stationed there. Dewey's forces sank or captured ten ships. The Spanish lost 381 lives, but none of Dewey's men were killed.

Dewey had defeated the Spanish, but he did not have enough troops to occupy and secure the Philippines. Troops eventually arrived, and on August 13, U.S. troops and Filipino rebels led by **Emilio Aguinaldo** (ahg-ee-NAHL-doh) took control of the Philippine capital, Manila.

War in the Caribbean In contrast to the navy, the U.S. Army was unprepared for war. At the start of the Spanish-American War, the entire U.S. Army had only 28,000 soldiers. New volunteers raised that figure to more than 280,000 within months. The army did not have enough rifles or bullets for these soldiers. It did not even have appropriate clothing for the troops. Many soldiers received warm woolen uniforms even though Cuba had a warm, tropical climate.

The soldiers faced harsh living conditions in Cuba. They ate canned meat that one general called "embalmed beef." Many were stricken with yellow fever and other deadly diseases. More than 2,000 Americans died from diseases they contracted in Cuba. Fewer than 400 were killed in battle.

BIOGRAPHY

Theodore Roosevelt 1858–1919

Theodore Roosevelt was born into a wealthy family in New York City. As a young man, following the tragic deaths of his mother and wife, Roosevelt set out for a new life in the Dakota Territory. For two years he lived as a cattle rancher and cowboy. In 1886 he returned to New York to pursue politics.

In 1898 Roosevelt became a national hero for leading the Rough Riders in the Spanish-American War. Soon after, he was elected governor of New York. In 1901, while Roosevelt was serving as vice president, President McKinley was assassinated. At age 42, Roosevelt was the youngest man in U.S. history to assume the presidency. As president, Roosevelt fought for progressive reforms and set aside millions of acres as national parks and forests. Roosevelt's aggressive foreign policy expanded American power in the world.

Draw Conclusions
What characteristics made Theodore Roosevelt a successful leader?

The most colorful group of U.S. soldiers was the 1st Volunteer Cavalry, nicknamed the Rough Riders. Second in command of this group was Lieutenant Colonel Theodore Roosevelt. Roosevelt had organized the Rough Riders to fight in Cuba. Volunteers included Native Americans, college athletes, cowboys, miners, and ranchers. Newspaper stories of their heroism earned the Rough Riders Americans' admiration. Four privates of the African American 10th Cavalry, who served with the Rough Riders, received the Congressional Medal of Honor.

Landing on June 22, 1898, the U.S. troops captured the hills around the main Spanish forces at Santiago. At the village of El Caney on July 1, some 7,000 U.S. soldiers, aided by Cuban rebels, overwhelmed about 600 Spanish defenders.

The main U.S. force then attacked and captured San Juan Hill. The Rough Riders and the African American 9th and 10th cavalries captured nearby Kettle Hill. The many accounts of the battle became popular with the American public back home. A journalist on the scene described the soldiers' charge:

"It was a miracle of self-sacrifice, a triumph of bulldog courage. . . . The fire of the Spanish riflemen . . . doubled and trebled [tripled] in fierceness, the crests of the hills crackled and burst in amazed roars and rippled with waves of tiny flame. But the blue line [of United States soldiers] crept steadily up and on."

—Richard Harding Davis, quoted in *The American Reader*, edited by Paul M. Angle

On July 3 the commander of the Spanish fleet decided to try breaking through the U.S. blockade. Though every Spanish ship was destroyed in the battle, American forces suffered only two casualties. Santiago surrendered two weeks later. President McKinley began peace negotiations with Spain, which was assured of defeat. A few days later, U.S. troops invaded Spanish-held Puerto Rico, which surrendered with little resistance. Spain signed a cease-fire agreement on August 12, 1898.

United States Gains Territories

Although Americans had declared war to secure Cuba's independence, U.S. leaders began demanding that Spain also give up other colonies. As a result of the Spanish-American War, the peace treaty placed Cuba, Guam, Puerto Rico, and the Philippines under U.S. control. The United States was developing as a strong world political power.

In reaction, some Americans formed the **Anti-Imperialist League**. This group opposed the treaty and the creation of an American colonial empire. They argued that the treaty threatened democracy because it denied self-government to the people living in the newly acquired territories. The Senate approved the peace treaty by a vote of 57 to 27—just one vote more than the two-thirds majority needed to ratify treaties.

Cuba The Teller Amendment had declared that the United States would not annex Cuba and it would have independence. However, McKinley wanted to create stability and increase U.S. economic activity there. He set

Reading Check
Compare How was fighting in the Pacific and the Caribbean similar?

War in the Caribbean

▶ Explore ONLINE!

Legend:
→ U.S. forces
✶ U.S. victories
⚡ U.S. blockade
■ Spanish possessions

0 — 200 — 400 Miles
0 — 200 — 400 Kilometers

UNITED STATES

Tampa
FLORIDA
Gulf of Mexico
USS *Maine* sunk, February, 1898
ATLANTIC OCEAN
30°N
BAHAMAS (BR.)
Tropic of Cancer
Havana
Santiago
CUBA
San Juan Hill, July, 1898
DOMINICAN REPUBLIC
HAITI
PUERTO RICO
20°N
JAMAICA (BR.)

The Battle of San Juan Hill, shown in this painting, became a symbol of American courage in the Spanish-American War.

Interpret Maps
1. **Location** What is significant about the location of the U.S. naval blockade?

up a military government—a government controlled by the U.S. military. He appointed Leonard Wood, who had commanded the Rough Riders during the war, as governor. Wood quickly began building schools and a sanitation system.

Even with the new sanitation system, disease remained a major problem. Dr. Walter Reed, head of the army's Yellow Fever Commission, was sent to Cuba in 1900 to help fight the disease. He and his volunteers conducted experiments, including allowing themselves to be bitten by infected insects. They soon proved that yellow fever was transmitted by mosquitoes. Getting rid of the standing water where mosquitoes lived helped health officials to control the disease.

Governor Wood also oversaw the writing of a Cuban constitution. The document included the **Platt Amendment**. This amendment limited Cuba's right to make treaties and allowed the United States to intervene in Cuban affairs. It also required Cuba to sell or lease land to the United States. Cuban leaders compared the Platt Amendment to "handing over the keys to our house so that they [the Americans] can enter it at any time, whenever the desire seizes them." The Cubans reluctantly accepted the amendment, and U.S. troops withdrew. The amendment remained in force until 1934. The U.S. government stayed actively involved in Cuban affairs until the late 1950s.

Puerto Rico Like Cubans, Puerto Ricans had hoped for independence after the war. Instead, the U.S. government made the island an American territory. The United States set up a government and appointed top officials. Puerto Ricans were allowed little say in their own affairs. On April 12, 1900, the Foraker Act established a civil government in Puerto Rico. It was headed by a governor and included a two-house legislature.

This 1901 illustration shows the capture of Filipino rebel leader, Emilio Aguinaldo.

A debate over the new territory soon arose. People who lived in Puerto Rico were considered citizens of the island but not of the United States. In 1917 the Jones Act gave Puerto Ricans U.S. citizenship and made Puerto Rico a self-governing territory. This act allowed Puerto Ricans to elect both houses of the legislature. However, another 30 years passed before Puerto Ricans could elect their own governor. Today the island has its own constitution and elected officials. However, it remains associated with the United States as a commonwealth under U.S. control.

The Philippines Spain had surrendered the Philippines in return for a $20 million payment from the United States. Americans agreed with President McKinley, who said that the United States would benefit from the islands' naval and commercial value. He also said that annexing the islands would keep Europeans from seizing them.

Filipino rebels, however, had expected to gain independence after the war. They had helped U.S. forces to capture Manila. When the United States decided instead to keep the islands, war broke out. Rebels led by Emilio Aguinaldo started a guerrilla war against the American forces. More than 4,200 U.S. soldiers and hundreds of thousands of Filipinos died before the conflict ended in 1902.

That same year, Congress passed the Philippine Government Act. It provided that an appointed governor and a two-house legislature would rule the Philippines. In 1946 the United States granted full independence to the Philippines.

Reading Check
Summarize What areas did the United States control as a result of the war?

Summary and Preview The United States fought a war with Spain and gained new territories in the Pacific and Caribbean regions. In the next lesson you will learn about U.S. interests in Latin America.

Lesson 2 Assessment

Review Ideas, Terms, and People

1. **a. Recall** What was the cause of the conflict between Cuba and Spain?

   b. Analyze How did yellow journalism affect public support for U.S. military action in Cuba?

   c. Elaborate In what way did the sinking of the USS *Maine* help cause the Spanish-American War?

2. **a. Identify** What territories did the United States gain as a result of the war?

   b. Analyze Why did some Americans oppose the annexation of the Philippines?

   c. Elaborate Explain how the Spanish-American War affected the relations between the United States and other countries.

Critical Thinking

3. **Categorize** Review your notes on the results of the Spanish-American War. Then copy the graphic organizer shown below. Use your notes to identify arguments for and against taking control of foreign territories.

Arguments against Imperialism		Arguments for Imperialism
	vs.	

History and Geography

America's Global Influence by 1900

By 1900 most of the current boundaries of the United States had been established. But the world had become a much smaller place. American inventions were spreading, changing daily life in countries around the world. In addition, U.S. troops stationed in China were displaying the increasing importance of the United States in global affairs.

ASIA

Beijing

PACIFIC OCEAN

Beijing Before 1898 U.S. troops had never fought outside of the Western Hemisphere. But in 1900, U.S. troops joined an international force to put down the Boxer Rebellion in Beijing.

On July 5, 1900, William Jennings Bryan spoke out against U.S. involvement in China, saying "Imperialism is the most dangerous of the evils now menacing [threatening] our country."

New York City Nearly 500,000 people immigrated to the United States in 1900. By 1920 more than 16 million had come. Many arrived in New York City.

Paris The Paris Exposition of 1900 showcased many U.S. inventions. One British writer claimed the exposition displayed "the Americanization of the world."

London

EUROPE

Paris

ATLANTIC OCEAN

UNITED STATES

New York

London In August 1900 English farmers protested in London against new farm equipment introduced from the United States that they feared would cause farmers to lose their jobs.

AFRICA

SOUTH AMERICA

Interpret Maps

1. **Region** By 1900 what role was the U.S. military playing in China?

2. **Movement** In what ways did the U.S. role in world affairs change in the late 1800s and early 1900s?

The United States and Latin America

The Big Idea

The United States expanded its role in Latin America in the early 1900s with new foreign policy.

Main Ideas

- The United States built the Panama Canal in the early 1900s.
- Theodore Roosevelt changed U.S. foreign policy toward Latin America.
- Presidents Taft and Wilson promoted U.S. interests in Latin America.

Key Terms and People

Panama Canal
Roosevelt Corollary
dollar diplomacy
Mexican Revolution
John J. Pershing
Francisco "Pancho" Villa

If YOU were there . . .

You are an engineer, and you've been working on the Panama Canal for almost eight years. Your work crews used huge steam shovels to slice through a ridge of mountains and built a large artificial lake. You planned a system to move ships through different water levels. Now your work is done. You can watch massive ships travel from the Atlantic to the Pacific.

Which part of the work on the canal was the most challenging?

Building the Panama Canal

A canal across the narrow neck of Central America would link the Atlantic and Pacific oceans and cut some 8,000 miles off the voyage by ship from the West to the East coasts of the United States. It would also allow the U.S. Navy to link its Atlantic and Pacific naval fleets quickly.

Revolution in Panama No one was a stronger supporter of a Central American canal than President Theodore Roosevelt. He knew it made good economic and political sense to build the canal. It would reduce travel time for commercial and military transport. The Spanish-American War, fought in both oceans, also made clear the need for such a shortcut.

Roosevelt knew that the best spot for the canal was the Isthmus of Panama. At the time, this area was part of the nation of Colombia. Roosevelt was unable to convince the Colombian senate to lease a strip of land across Panama to the United States.

Roosevelt considered other ways to gain control of the land. He learned that Panamanian revolutionaries were planning a revolt against Colombia. On November 2, 1903, a U.S. warship arrived outside Colón, Panama. The next day the revolt began. Blocked by the U.S. warship, Colombian forces could not reach Panama to stop the rebellion. Panama declared itself an independent country. The United States then recognized the new nation.

The new government of Panama supported the idea of a canal across its land. The United States agreed to pay Panama $10 million plus $250,000 a year for a 99-year lease on a ten-mile-wide strip of land across the isthmus.

Building the Canal Canal construction began in 1904. Building the canal was a huge challenge. The first obstacle to overcome was tropical disease. The canal route ran through 51 miles of forests and swamps filled with mosquitoes, many of which carried the deadly diseases malaria and yellow fever.

Dr. William C. Gorgas, who had helped Dr. Walter Reed stamp out yellow fever in Cuba, organized a successful effort to rid the canal route of disease-carrying mosquitoes. If Gorgas had not been successful, the canal's construction would have taken much longer. It also would have cost much more in terms of both lives and money.

Even with the reduced risk of disease, the work was very dangerous. Most of the canal had to be blasted out of solid rock with explosives. Workers used dozens of steam shovels to cut a narrow, eight-mile-long channel through the mountains of central Panama. Sometimes workers died when their shovels struck explosive charges. "The flesh of men flew in the air like birds every day," recalled one worker from the West Indies.

More than 44,000 workers, including many black West Indians, labored on the canal. Some 6,000 lives were lost during the American construction of the **Panama Canal**. It was finally opened to ships on August 15, 1914, linking the Atlantic and Pacific oceans. An opening ceremony was held the next year. It had taken ten years to complete, and the cost was $375 million. It was probably the most expensive construction project in the world at that time. In the end, however, the world had its "highway between the oceans." Building the canal also began to change the relationship between the United States and Latin American nations.

Reading Check
Draw Conclusions
Why did building the canal cost so many lives?

The massive Gatun Locks, shown here under construction in 1914, raise ships 85 feet onto Gatun Lake, an inland waterway on the Panama Canal.

Explore ONLINE!

Increasing Exports The Panama Canal did not just increase trade between the East and West coasts of the United States. By shortening the trip from many U.S. ports to other parts of the world, the canal also led to increased exports of agricultural and manufactured goods. It helped the U.S. economy continue to grow.

By how many miles did the Panama Canal shorten the shipping distance between New York City and San Francisco?

NORTH AMERICA

UNITED STATES

San Francisco

New York City

Gulf of Mexico

CENTRAL AMERICA

5,200 Miles

13,000 Miles

PACIFIC OCEAN

Caribbean Sea

Panama Canal

ATLANTIC OCEAN

SOUTH AMERICA

Tropic of Cancer

50°N

40°N

30°N

20°N

10°N

0° Equator

10°S

20°S

Tropic of Capricorn

30°S

40°S

50°S

Canal zone
Canal route
Railroad
Locks

0   10   20 Miles
0   10   20 Kilometers

Colón   Cristobal
Caribbean Sea
Gatun Locks
Gatun Lake
Gaillard Cut
Pedro Miguel Locks
Miraflores Locks
PANAMA
Panama City
Balboa
Bay of Panama

0   400   800 Miles
0   400   800 Kilometers

120°W   110°W   100°W   90°W   80°W   70°W   60°W   50°W   40°W   30°W

Interpret Maps

1. **Place** Why was Panama chosen as the site for a canal?

2. **Movement** How many locks did ships have to travel through from Balboa to Colón?

U.S. Policy Toward Latin America

As president, Theodore Roosevelt actively pursued progressive reforms at home. He also believed the United States should play a more active role in the Western Hemisphere. In 1900 Roosevelt said, "I have always been fond of the West African proverb: 'Speak softly and carry a big stick; you will go far.'" Roosevelt wanted everyone to know he would use a "big stick"—meaning U.S. military force—to protect economic and strategic interests of the United States in Latin America.

Roosevelt's foreign policy was a change from the policies of previous presidents. In the 1823 Monroe Doctrine, President James Monroe had warned European nations not to interfere in the Western Hemisphere. And, while the Monroe Doctrine became a major principle of U.S. foreign policy, the United States did not have the military strength to enforce it. By the time of Roosevelt's presidency, this situation was changing. The United States was growing stronger and expanding its influence as a world power.

How should the United States use its new power in Latin America? This question came up often in the early 1900s. In the late 1800s Europeans and Americans had invested large sums of money in Latin America. Much of this investment had come in the form of bank loans. Venezuela, for example, fell deeply in debt to British and German lenders. In 1902 Venezuela refused to repay these debts. A similar situation arose in the Caribbean nation of the Dominican Republic in 1904. European powers prepared to use military force to collect the debts.

Roosevelt insisted the countries repay their debts. But he did not want to allow Europeans to intervene in Latin America. The presence of

Historical Source

Roosevelt's Imperialism

Theodore Roosevelt's foreign policy is shown visually in this cartoon. Roosevelt is the giant leading a group of ships that represent debt collection. The U.S. president is patrolling the Caribbean Sea and Latin American countries, trying to enforce the payment of debts to European countries.

What do you think this stick represents?

Why are these vessels warships?

Analyze Historical Sources
What is the cartoonist trying to tell viewers about the Roosevelt Corollary?

European forces there would violate the Monroe Doctrine and threaten U.S. power in the region.

Roosevelt knew that U.S. officials would have to force debtor nations to repay their loans in order to keep European nations from directly intervening in Latin America. In December 1904 he announced what became known as the **Roosevelt Corollary** to the Monroe Doctrine. This addition warned that in cases of "wrongdoing" by Latin American countries, the United States might exercise "international police power." The Roosevelt Corollary expanded the Monroe Doctrine and increased United States involvement in the affairs of Latin America.

The Roosevelt Corollary asserted a new <u>role</u> for the United States as an "international police power" in the Western Hemisphere. Roosevelt actively enforced the corollary throughout the rest of his presidency. This led to great resentment from Latin American countries.

Academic Vocabulary
role assigned behavior

Reading Check
Find Main Ideas
Why did Roosevelt announce the Roosevelt Corollary?

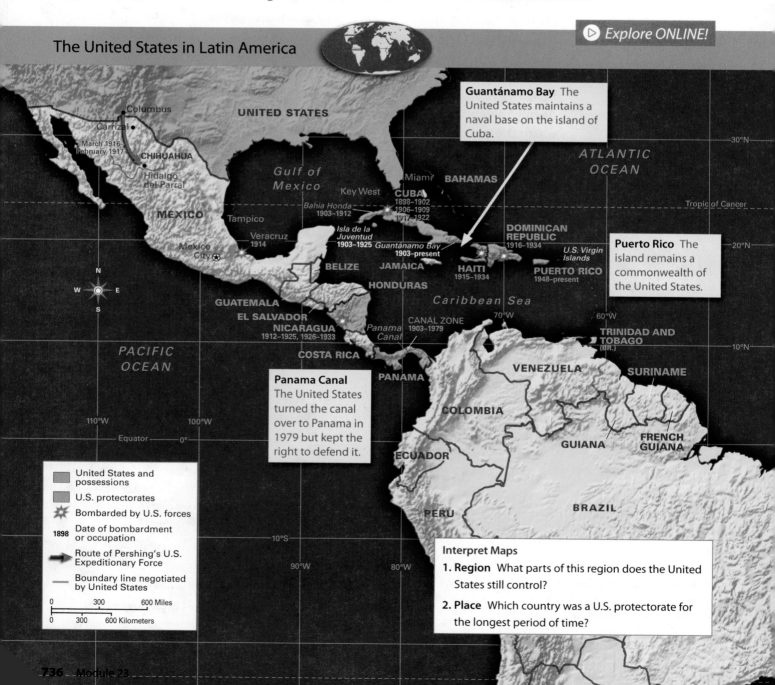

Explore ONLINE!

The United States in Latin America

Guantánamo Bay The United States maintains a naval base on the island of Cuba.

Puerto Rico The island remains a commonwealth of the United States.

Panama Canal The United States turned the canal over to Panama in 1979 but kept the right to defend it.

UNITED STATES
Columbus
Carrizal
March 1916–February 1917
CHIHUAHUA
Hidalgo del Parral
MEXICO
Mexico City
Tampico
Veracruz 1914
Gulf of Mexico
Key West
Miami
BAHAMAS
CUBA
1898–1902
1906–1909
1917–1922
Bahia Honda 1903–1912
Isla de la Juventud 1903–1925
Guantánamo Bay 1903–present
BELIZE
JAMAICA
HAITI 1915–1934
DOMINICAN REPUBLIC 1916–1934
U.S. Virgin Islands
PUERTO RICO 1948–present
HONDURAS
GUATEMALA
EL SALVADOR
NICARAGUA 1912–1925, 1926–1933
COSTA RICA
PANAMA
Panama Canal
CANAL ZONE 1903–1979
Caribbean Sea
TRINIDAD AND TOBAGO (BR.)
VENEZUELA
COLOMBIA
ECUADOR
GUIANA
SURINAME
FRENCH GUIANA
PERU
BRAZIL
ATLANTIC OCEAN
PACIFIC OCEAN
Tropic of Cancer
Equator
30°N
20°N
10°N
10°S
110°W
100°W
90°W
80°W
70°W
60°W

N W E S

Legend:
- United States and possessions
- U.S. protectorates
- ✴ Bombarded by U.S. forces
- **1898** Date of bombardment or occupation
- → Route of Pershing's U.S. Expeditionary Force
- — Boundary line negotiated by United States

0   300   600 Miles
0   300   600 Kilometers

Interpret Maps
1. **Region** What parts of this region does the United States still control?
2. **Place** Which country was a U.S. protectorate for the longest period of time?

U.S. Foreign Policy

Departing from the example set by the nation's first president, George Washington, future presidents increased U.S. involvement around the world, particularly in Latin America.

Washington's Farewell Address

The United States will not become involved in European affairs.

Monroe Doctrine

The United States will defend its interests in the Western Hemisphere and keep European powers out.

Roosevelt Corollary

The United States will police wrongdoing by nations in the Western Hemisphere.

Taft's Dollar Diplomacy

The United States will use economic means to aid its interests in Latin America.

Wilson and Democracy

The United States will promote and protect democracy in the Western Hemisphere.

U.S. Interests in Latin America

William Howard Taft, who became president in 1909, also acted to protect U.S. economic interests in Latin America. Taft used a foreign policy called **dollar diplomacy**—influencing governments through economic, not military, intervention.

President Taft described dollar diplomacy as "substituting dollars for bullets. It is . . . directed to the increase of American trade." He wanted to encourage stability and keep Europeans out of Latin America by expanding U.S. business interests there.

For example, in 1911 Nicaragua failed to repay a loan from British investors. American bankers lent Nicaragua $1.5 billion in return for control of the National Bank of Nicaragua and the government-owned railway. When local anger over this deal led to revolt in Nicaragua, Taft sent U.S. Marines to protect American interests.

When President Woodrow Wilson took office in 1913, he rejected Taft's dollar diplomacy. He believed the United States had a moral obligation to promote democracy in Latin America. This, he believed, would advance American interests abroad. Nonetheless, Wilson was willing to use military force to protect U.S. interests. When civil unrest shook Haiti in 1915 and the Dominican Republic in 1916, Wilson sent in military troops. In both cases, U.S. Marines occupied the countries for years.

In 1910 many Mexicans revolted against the harsh rule of Mexican dictator Porfirio Díaz. This was the start of the **Mexican Revolution**, a long, violent struggle for power in Mexico. The war affected U.S. interests because Americans had invested more than $1 billion in Mexican land, mining, oil, and railways. American business leaders feared they would lose their investments.

Though U.S. troops pursued Mexican revolutionary Pancho Villa (above) for nearly a year, they were unable to capture him.

In 1914 President Wilson learned that a German ship carrying weapons was headed to the port of Veracruz, Mexico. To keep the weapons from reaching the rebels, Wilson ordered the navy to seize Veracruz. Wilson acted again in 1916, sending General **John J. Pershing** and 15,000 U.S. soldiers into Mexico. Pershing's mission was to catch the rebel leader **Francisco "Pancho" Villa**, who had killed 17 Americans in New Mexico. The farther Pershing pushed into Mexico, the more the Mexicans resented the Americans. After 11 months of searching, Pershing failed to capture Villa and Wilson recalled the troops. For the rest of Wilson's presidency, relations between the United States and Mexico remained tense.

In 1917 a new constitution promised to bring order to Mexico. The constitution contained ideas of Mexico's revolutionary leaders, and it protected the liberties and rights of citizens. Despite the new constitution, however, fighting continued. Mexico's economy suffered terribly. Agriculture was disrupted, mines were abandoned, and factories were destroyed. Many Mexican men and women immigrated to the United States in search of work and a more stable life.

Reading Check
Summarize How did Wilson respond to events in Mexico?

Summary and Review In the early 1900s the United States changed its foreign policy and expanded its involvement in Latin America in order to secure its strategic and economic interests.

Lesson 3 Assessment

Review Ideas, Terms, and People

1. a. Recall Why did the United States want to build a canal?

b. Analyze What challenges did the builders of the Panama Canal face, and how did they overcome them?

c. Explain How did Roosevelt's efforts to build the Panama Canal affect the economy of the United States?

2. a. Describe What problem was causing conflict between European and Latin American nations?

b. Summarize How and why did Theodore Roosevelt change U.S. policy toward Latin America?

c. Evaluate How did the Roosevelt Corollary affect the relationship between the United States and Latin American nations?

3. a. Recall What did Woodrow Wilson believe was the United States's obligation to Latin America?

b. Compare and Contrast How were the foreign policies of Taft and Wilson toward Latin America similar, and how were they different?

Critical Thinking

4. Categorize Review your notes on U.S. policies toward Latin America. Then copy the web diagram below. Use it to analyze how national interest influenced American policies toward Latin America.

Social Studies Skills

Understand Continuity and Change

Define the Skill

A well-known saying claims that "the more things change, the more they stay the same." Nowhere does this observation apply better than to the study of history. Any examination of the past will show many changes—nations expanding or shrinking, empires rising and falling, changes in leadership, or people on the move, for example.

The reasons for change have not changed, however. The same general forces have driven the actions of people and nations across time. These forces are the threads that run through history and give it continuity, or connectedness. They are the "sameness" in a world of continuous change.

Learn the Skill

You can find the causes of all events of the past in one or more of these major forces or themes that connect all history.

1. **Cooperation and Conflict** Throughout time, people and groups have worked together to achieve goals. They have also opposed others who stood in the way of their goals.

2. **Cultural Invention and Interaction** The values and ideas expressed in art, literature, customs, and religion have enriched the world. But the spread of cultures and their contact with other cultures have produced conflict as well.

3. **Geography and Environment** Physical environment and natural resources have shaped how people live. Efforts to gain, protect, or make good use of land and resources have been major causes of cooperation and conflict in history.

4. **Science and Technology** *Technology,* or the development and use of tools, has helped humans across time make better use of their environment. Science has changed their knowledge of the world, and changed their lives, too.

5. **Economic Opportunity and Development** From hunting and gathering to herding, farming, manufacturing, and trade, people have tried to make the most of their resources. The desire for a better life has also been a major reason people have moved from one place to another.

6. **The Impact of Individuals** Political, religious, military, business, and other leaders have been a major influence in history. The actions of many ordinary people have also shaped history.

7. **Nationalism and Imperialism** *Nationalism* is the desire of a people to have their own country. *Imperialism* is the desire of a nation to influence or control other nations. Both have existed across time.

8. **Political and Social Systems** People have always been part of groups—families, villages, nations, or religious groups, for example. The groups to which people belong shape how they relate to others around them.

Practice the Skill

Check your understanding of continuity and change in history by answering the following questions.

1. What forces of history are illustrated by the events in the module you just studied? Explain with examples.

2. How do the events in this module show continuity with earlier periods in U.S. history?

Module 23 Assessment

Review Vocabulary, Terms, and People

1. In which of the following did the United States declare that it had no interest in taking control of Cuba?
   a. Roosevelt Corollary
   b. Monroe Doctrine
   c. Open Door Policy
   d. Teller Amendment

2. Which leader upset sugar planters in Hawaii by proposing a plan to return power to the monarchy?
   a. Liliuokalani
   b. John L. Stevens
   c. Millard Fillmore
   d. Woodrow Wilson

3. Which president supported Panama's revolt against Colombia in 1903?
   a. Woodrow Wilson
   b. William McKinley
   c. William Howard Taft
   d. Theodore Roosevelt

4. Who led U.S. forces into Mexico after attacks against U.S. citizens by Mexican rebels?
   a. John Hay
   b. William H. Seward
   c. John J. Pershing
   d. Theodore Roosevelt

Comprehension and Critical Thinking

Lesson 1

5. a. Identify Into what areas did the United States expand in the late 1800s?
   b. Draw Conclusions How did the United States benefit from contact with foreign nations and territories?
   c. Elaborate Which policy would you have supported—isolationism or imperialism? Explain your answer.

Lesson 2

6. a. Describe What events led the United States to declare war on Spain?
   b. Draw Conclusions How did winning the Spanish-American War help the U.S. develop as a world power?
   c. Predict How might foreign countries have viewed the actions of the United States in the Spanish-American War?

Lesson 3

7. a. Identify In what ways did the United States become involved in Latin American affairs?
   b. Draw Conclusions Why did the United States expand its role in Latin America in the early 1900s?
   c. Evaluate Do you think the United States should have been as actively involved in Latin America as it was? Explain your answer.

Module 23 Assessment, continued

Review Themes

8. **Geography** How did the geography of the United States change after the end of its policy of isolationism?

9. **Politics** How did the policy of imperialism affect American politics in the late 1800s and early 1900s?

Reading Skills

Compare Historical Texts *Use the Reading Skills taught in this module to answer the question about the reading selections below.*

> A. "Sad to say, this most precious and sublime feature of the Yosemite National Park (Hetch Hetchy Valley), one of the greatest of all our natural resources for the uplifting joy and peace and health of the people, is in danger of being dammed and made into a reservoir to help supply San Francisco with water and light. . . ."
>
> —John Muir, *The Yosemite*, 1912

> B. "As we all know, there is no use of water that is higher than the domestic use. Then, if there is, as the engineers tell us, no other source of supply that is anything like so reasonably available as this one; if this is the best, and, within reasonable limits of cost, the only means of supplying San Francisco with water, we come straight to the question of whether the advantage of leaving this valley in a state of nature is greater than the advantage of using it for the benefit of the city of San Francisco."
>
> —Gifford Pinchot, address to Congress, 1913

10. How do the two men quoted above differ on the issue of building a dam in the Hetch Hetchy Valley?

Social Studies Skills

Understand Continuity and Change *Use the Social Studies Skills taught in this module to complete the activity below.*

11. Pick three of the themes listed in the Social Studies Skills. Then, using the building of the Panama Canal as a case study, identify instances of continuity and change for each theme. Summarize your findings in a paragraph.

Focus on Writing

12. **Write a List of Pros and Cons** In this module you learned how the United States increased its role in international affairs. Create a list of the pros and cons of U.S. involvement with other nations in the late 1800s and early 1900s. Decide whether you want to include in your lists only facts, only opinions, or some of each. Consider how your analysis of history can help guide U.S. foreign policy in the future. When you have finished your list, use it as the basis for a paragraph recommending either that the United States continue to involve itself in the affairs of other nations or that it pull back from such involvement.

Module 24

World War I

★

Essential Question

How did World War I impact America and transform Europe?

About the Photo: Soldiers faced terrible conditions as they fought the enemy from their trench positions.

 Explore ONLINE!

VIDEOS, including...
- The Challenge
- Armistice
- The Flu
- Wilson Works for Peace

HISTORY

☑ Document-Based Investigations

☑ Graphic Organizers

☑ Interactive Games

☑ Image with Hotspots: Trench Warfare

☑ Image Carousel: The United States Mobilizes for War

☑ Interactive Map: World War I, 1914–1918

In this module you will learn how an assassination in Europe sparked the deadliest war the world had ever seen. You will find out how the United States was drawn into the war and will read about new battle strategies.

What You Will Learn ...

Lesson 1: The Road to War 746
The Big Idea In 1914 tensions in Europe exploded into the deadliest war the world had ever seen.

Lesson 2: Americans Prepare for War 751
The Big Idea After entering World War I in 1917, Americans began the massive effort of preparing for war.

Lesson 3: Americans in World War I. 757
The Big Idea American troops helped the Allies achieve victory in World War I.

Lesson 4: Establishing Peace. 763
The Big Idea The United States and the victorious Allied powers clashed over postwar plans.

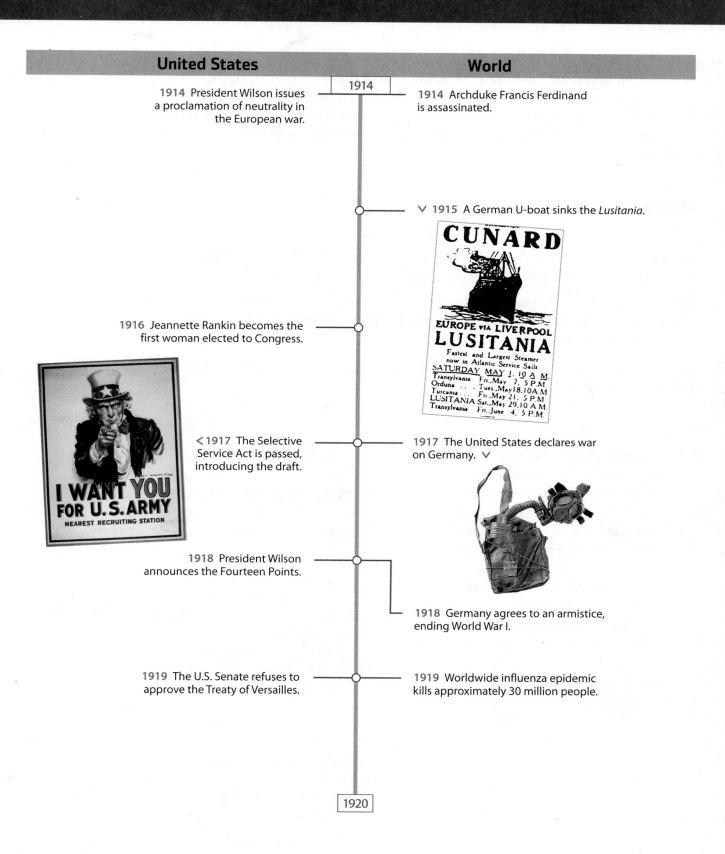

United States	World

1914

1914 President Wilson issues a proclamation of neutrality in the European war.

1914 Archduke Francis Ferdinand is assassinated.

∨ **1915** A German U-boat sinks the *Lusitania*.

1916 Jeannette Rankin becomes the first woman elected to Congress.

< **1917** The Selective Service Act is passed, introducing the draft.

1917 The United States declares war on Germany. ∨

1918 President Wilson announces the Fourteen Points.

1918 Germany agrees to an armistice, ending World War I.

1919 The U.S. Senate refuses to approve the Treaty of Versailles.

1919 Worldwide influenza epidemic kills approximately 30 million people.

1920

Reading Social Studies

THEME FOCUS:
Politics and Economics

In this module you will read about World War I and the changes it brought to the United States and the world. Many of the political tensions that led to the war were caused by the rise of nationalism in European countries. You will read about how the war devastated European economies and how peace affected European countries.

READING FOCUS:
Recognize Fallacies in Reasoning

As part of evaluating a historical argument, you can judge whether the reasoning is sound. A *fallacy* is a false or mistaken idea.

Recognize Fallacies As you identify a main idea, judge its soundness. Look for cause-and-effect relationships that support the idea. Decide whether you think the argument is logical.

Notice how a reader explained the logical reasoning behind the main idea in the following paragraph.

Three main factors led to a shortage of labor in the United States during the war. First, American factories were working nonstop to produce weapons and supplies for the Allied forces. Factories needed new workers to meet this huge demand. Second, the war almost completely cut off immigration. As you know, immigrants had provided a steady source of labor to American industry. And third, many of the young men who would normally take factory jobs were off fighting in Europe.

If factories were working overtime, they would need more workers. This supports the main idea of a labor shortage.

If factories were used to having immigrants to hire, and there were fewer immigrants, it would make sense that there was a labor shortage.

Here's a third reason for a labor shortage: many men became soldiers. It makes sense that there was a labor shortage during the war.

You Try It!

The man who assassinated Archduke Francis Ferdinand was a Serb.

↓

All Serbians wanted war with Austria-Hungary.

Wilson wanted to establish the League of Nations.

↓

because he thought it would help ensure peace.

Trench warfare was a new kind of warfare.

↓

Therefore, trench warfare was more horrible than any other kind of warfare.

Key Terms and People

Lesson 1
militarism
Archduke Francis Ferdinand
mobilize
Central powers
Allied powers
trench warfare
stalemate
U-boats

Lesson 2
Lusitania
Zimmermann Note
Selective Service Act
Liberty bonds
National War Labor Board

Lesson 3
American Expeditionary Force
Communists
armistice

Lesson 4
League of Nations.
reparations
Treaty of Versailles
Henry Cabot Lodge

1. Is the first conclusion reasonable? Why or why not? How can you tell?
2. Do you think the second conclusion is logical or illogical? What makes you think so?
3. Is the third conclusion a fallacy of reason? What reasonable conclusions can you draw from the statement?

As you read Module 24, notice how the authors use logical reasoning to support their main ideas.

The Road to War

The Big Idea

In 1914 tensions in Europe exploded into the deadliest war the world had ever seen.

Main Ideas

- Many factors contributed to the outbreak of World War I.
- European nations suffered massive casualties in the war's early battles.

Key Terms and People

militarism
Archduke Francis Ferdinand
mobilize
Central powers
Allied powers
trench warfare
stalemate
U-boats

If YOU were there . . .

You are walking past a newspaper stand when a headline catches your eye: "Austria-Hungary's Archduke Francis Ferdinand Assassinated in Sarajevo." Your first thought is, "Who's he?" You pick up the paper and read about the archduke and about the rising tensions in Europe related to his death. The article makes it sound like Europe is about to explode into war.

At this point, do you think the assassination will affect the United States? Why or why not?

Outbreak of War

Though Europe was at peace in the early 1900s, relations between European nations were not necessarily friendly. In fact, feelings of fear and distrust were growing among European powers such as Germany, France, Great Britain, Russia, and Austria-Hungary. This dangerous tension had several important causes.

Tensions in Europe One cause of tension was the rise of nationalism in the 1800s. Nationalism is a strong sense of pride and loyalty to one's nation or culture. Nationalism inspired people who shared a language or culture to want to unite politically. In 1871, for example, Chancellor Otto von Bismarck and Kaiser Wilhelm I brought together several German states to form the nation of Germany.

While nationalism helped bring stability to Germany, it caused instability in other places. The empire of Austria-Hungary included people from many different cultural groups. One of these groups was the Slavs. Slavic nationalists wanted to break away from Austria-Hungary and join the independent Slavic country of Serbia on the Balkan Peninsula. Leaders of Austria-Hungary reacted angrily, seeing this movement as a threat to their empire.

Another source of tension in Europe was imperialism. Britain's huge empire, stretching from Africa to Asia, brought it wealth and power. Eager to share in such benefits, other European powers competed for control of overseas territories. Fierce competition for territory took place within Europe as well. For example, Germany had taken the Alsace-Lorraine region from France in the Franco-Prussian War in 1871. France wanted it back.

In this competitive atmosphere, nations focused their resources on **militarism**—the aggressive strengthening of armed forces. European nations raced to build armies and navies that were larger than ever before.

As nations became more powerful, they sought to protect themselves by forming new alliances. Germany formed an alliance with Austria-Hungary in 1879. In this alliance system, each promised to defend the other in case of enemy attack. Concerned with Germany's growing power, France and Russia created their own alliance in 1893. Britain joined France and Russia in 1907.

The assassination of Archduke Francis Ferdinand and his wife, Sophie, by a Serb nationalist sparked the beginning of World War I.

The Spark With so much hostility dividing the nations of Europe, a German general felt that "a European war is bound to come sooner or later." All that was needed was a spark to set Europe on fire. That spark flew from the Balkan province of Bosnia and Herzegovina.

Bosnia and Herzegovina had gained independence from Turkish rule in 1878. In 1908, however, Austria-Hungary annexed the province. Slavic nationalists resisted violently—they wanted the region to be part of Serbia.

On June 28, 1914, **Archduke Francis Ferdinand**, heir to the throne of Austria-Hungary, visited the province's capital of Sarajevo with his wife, Sophie. While riding through the streets, they were shot and killed by a 19-year-old Serb nationalist named Gavrilo Princip.

The assassination shattered Europe's fragile peace. Determined to crush Serbia and the Slavic nationalists, Austria-Hungary declared war on Serbia. Very quickly, other countries were pulled into the fighting. Russia had promised to support Serbia in case of war. It began to **mobilize**, or prepare its military for war. On August 1 Germany, Austria-Hungary's ally, declared war on Russia. Two days later, Germany also declared war on France, Russia's ally. To reach France quickly, the German army marched into Belgium on August 4. Britain, which had promised to support Belgium, then declared war on Germany.

As the fighting started, the alliance between Austria-Hungary and Germany came to be known as the **Central powers**. Bulgaria and the Ottoman Empire later sided with the Central Powers. France, Russia, and Britain were known as the **Allied powers**. Italy joined them in 1915. Over the next several years, soldiers from 30 nations and six continents would fight in what was then called the Great War. The conflict later became known as World War I.

Reading Check
Identify Cause and Effect How did nationalism contribute to political tensions in Europe?

Early Battles of the War

Both sides expected the war to be over in a few months. German leaders planned to defeat France quickly, before Russia could join the fighting. But as the Germans marched toward France, they met fierce resistance from Belgian soldiers. This gave Britain and France time to mobilize their own troops. New military technologies changed military strategy and resulted in an unprecedented number of casualties.

The First Battle of the Marne Belgian resistance slowed the German advance but could not stop it. On September 3 the German army was just 25 miles from Paris, the capital of France. The French army blocked the German advance at the Marne River, east of Paris. The First Battle of the Marne raged for several days before the Germans were pushed back.

By mid-September French and German troops faced each other along a long battle line called the western front. The western front stretched from the North Sea all the way to Switzerland. Meanwhile, the Russian and German armies were struggling back and forth along the eastern front. The eastern front reached from the Black Sea to the Baltic Sea. It quickly became clear that this war would be longer and deadlier than anyone had expected.

A New Kind of War Part of what made World War I so long and deadly was a new technique called **trench warfare**. In trench warfare soldiers defended a position by fighting from the protection of deep ditches. When the French defeated the Germans in the First Battle of the Marne, the Germans did not retreat far. Instead, they dug trenches nearby. Opposite them, the French dug their own trenches. A 400-mile-long network of trenches soon stretched across the western front.

Trench Warfare

Trenches were dug in a zigzag pattern so that the enemy could not stand at one end and fire down the length of a trench.

Airplanes could scout enemy positions and drop bombs into trenches.

Tanks were not damaged by either machine-gun or rifle fire. Their use marked the beginning of the end for trench warfare.

No-man's-land was the area between opposing trenches. It was about 250 yards wide and full of barbed wire and abandoned military equipment.

Some trenches served as first-aid posts.

Analyze Information
How does this picture help you understand why World War I was so deadly for soldiers?

Soldiers fought in these cold, wet, and muddy ditches, sometimes for months at a time. The filthy trenches were perfect breeding grounds for germs. Soldiers on both sides died from disease. An American in the French army described life in the trenches:

> "The impossibility of the simplest kind of personal cleanliness makes vermin [bugs] a universal ill, against which there is no remedy. Cold, dirt, discomfort, are the ever present conditions, and the soldier's life comes to mean . . . the most misery that the human organism [body] can support."
>
> —Alan Seeger, *Letters and Diary of Alan Seeger*

The empty patch of ground between enemy trenches came to be known as "no-man's-land." This area was quickly stripped of trees and blasted full of holes by artillery shells. Anyone who ventured into no-man's-land was likely to be killed by enemy fire.

Another factor that made World War I deadlier than previous wars was the use of modern technology. New machine guns, for example, could fire 400 to 600 bullets a minute. Enormous artillery guns fired shells over the trenches. The shells exploded and sent speeding scraps of metal onto the soldiers below. Other shells spread poisonous gases. If soldiers were not wearing gas masks, the gas destroyed their lungs, causing slow, painful deaths. Poisonous gases were originally banned but came back into use by both sides by the end of the war. This was called chemical warfare.

Other new weapons included tanks and aircraft, including airplanes. Tanks are armored combat vehicles that can cause heavy damage but cannot be destroyed easily. Airplanes were used to fire down on soldiers in trenches and to gather information about enemy locations. Airplanes also battled each other in fights called "dogfights."

Many of the weapons first used in World War I, such as tanks and airplanes, are still used in warfare today. The use of poison gas, however, has been outlawed by international treaties.

This image shows British soldiers firing a machine gun and wearing early gas masks to protect against a gas attack.

Land and Sea Battles After a year of vicious fighting, the war had become a **stalemate**—a situation in which neither side can win a decisive victory. Determined to break the stalemate, both sides launched massive attacks in 1916. In February 1916 the Germans attacked the French city of Verdun, at the southern end of the western front. That summer, the Allies staged an attack along the Somme River, in northeastern France. Both battles raged for months, as the armies attacked and counterattacked.

By the end of the year, the Germans had failed to take Verdun. At the Somme River, the Allies had advanced just seven miles. Almost nothing had changed on the western front. But nearly 1 million men had been killed at Verdun and the Somme River.

As the stalemate on land dragged on, sea battles in the Atlantic Ocean and the North Sea became even more important. The powerful British navy blockaded the ports of the Central powers. They also laid explosive mines in the North Sea. These could blow a huge hole in a ship, sinking

German U-boats
Germany developed small submarines called U-boats as part of its war strategy. U-boats could strike Allied ships without being seen. They destroyed around 10 million tons of Allied and neutral ships and cargo from 1914 to 1918.

Reading Check
Categorize What new technologies did armies in World War I use?

Academic Vocabulary
neutral unbiased, not favoring either side in a conflict

it in minutes. The tactic effectively stopped ships from reaching German ports with needed supplies.

The Germans responded by using submarines called **U-boats**. U-boats launched torpedoes against Allied supply ships, causing heavy losses. The Germans also attacked ships belonging to **neutral** countries they believed were helping the Allies. This would soon pull the United States into World War I.

Summary and Preview World War I became a stalemate by 1916 as countries battled for control. In the next lesson you will find out why the United States decided to join the fighting.

Lesson 1 Assessment

Review Ideas, Terms, and People

1. **a. Describe** What factors contributed to the outbreak of World War I?
   b. Contrast How did nationalism affect Germany and Austria-Hungary differently?
   c. Predict What might have happened if Russia had not honored its agreement to defend Serbia?
   d. Evaluate What were the impacts of changes in military technologies used during World War I?

2. **a. Identify** What were the outcomes of the early battles of the war?
   b. Explain How did Belgian resistance affect the German war plan?
   c. Evaluate How successful was trench warfare as a strategy?

Critical Thinking

3. **Identify Cause and Effect** In this lesson you learned about major battles of World War I. Create a graphic organizer similar to the one below and use it to show the outcomes of these early battles and how they affected the war.

Battle	Outcome	Results

★ Americans Prepare for War

The Big Idea

After entering World War I in 1917, Americans began the massive effort of preparing for war.

Main Ideas

- The United States entered the war after repeated crises with Germany.

- The United States mobilized for war by training troops and stepping up production of supplies.

- Labor shortages created new wartime opportunities for women and other Americans.

Key Terms and People

Lusitania
Zimmermann Note
Selective Service Act
Liberty bonds
National War Labor Board

If YOU were there . . .

Everywhere you go, people are talking about the war in Europe. The United States has just joined the fighting on the side of the Allied powers. Many young men you know are volunteering to fight. Women are signing up to drive ambulances or work as nurses. You know that the situation in Europe is dangerous, but you want to serve your country.

Will you volunteer for service in World War I?

The United States Enters World War I

Millions of Americans at this time were immigrants or children of immigrants. Many came from countries belonging to the Allied or Central powers. They naturally sympathized with their former homelands. This did not change the fact that most Americans viewed World War I as a European conflict. They did not want American soldiers sent to the bloody battlefields of Europe. Shortly after World War I began, President Woodrow Wilson announced that the United States would remain neutral. Most Americans agreed that America should stay out of the war. However, international, economic, and military developments swayed opinion in the United States siding with the Allies and entering World War I.

American Neutrality Threatened Although the United States had a policy of neutrality, its merchants continued to trade with European nations. American ships carried supplies and war materials to the Allies. U.S. banks invested $2 billion in European war bonds, nearly all of it in Allied countries.

The Germans used U-boat attacks to try to stop supplies from reaching the Allies. Sometimes they attacked ships without warning. In May 1915 a German U-boat sank the *Lusitania*, a British passenger liner. Nearly 1,200 people, including 128 Americans, were killed. The incident

Sinking of the *Lusitania*

In 1915 German U-boats sank the *Lusitania*, an event that pushed the United States toward entry into World War I. Newspapers quickly spread news of the disaster.

The ship was treated as an enemy warship.

"The accounts which have so far been received are fragmentary, and give no clear idea of the disaster. There is, however, no doubt that two torpedoes were fired without warning into the starboard side of the ship soon after 2 o'clock yesterday afternoon. There were conflicting accounts of the period during which the Lusitania remained afloat, but the Cunard Company states that she sunk 40 minutes after being struck."

—*The Register*, quoted in the *Times of London*

The ship sank before enough rescue ships could arrive.

Analyze Historical Sources
How might this disaster draw the United States into war with Germany?

fueled anti-German feeling in the United States. Throughout the coming war, German Americans faced nativist attacks, including anti-German speeches, discrimination, and physical attacks.

Secretary of State William Jennings Bryan resigned over President Wilson's handling of the affair. Bryan thought that Wilson's protest note to the Germans was designed to bring the United States into the war.

In March 1916 a German U-boat attacked the *Sussex*, a French passenger ship. Several of the 80 casualties were Americans. Wilson demanded that the Germans stop attacking nonmilitary ships. German leaders responded with the Sussex pledge, agreeing not to attack merchant ships without warning.

Congress Declares War When Wilson ran for reelection in 1916, the promise to remain neutral helped him win the election. Nearly a year after the Sussex pledge, however, the Germans again began launching attacks on ships, including American vessels. In response, Wilson broke off diplomatic relations with Germany.

The United States stepped closer to war when Americans found out about the **Zimmermann Note**, sometimes called the Zimmermann telegram. This secret telegram to Mexico sent by the German foreign minister, Arthur Zimmermann, was decoded and then published by American newspapers in March 1917. In the note, Zimmermann proposed an alliance against the United States. He promised that Germany would help Mexico recapture areas that Mexico had lost during the Mexican-American War.

The American public was outraged by the telegram. President Wilson asked Congress to declare war on Germany. "The world must be made safe for democracy," he proclaimed. Congress declared war on April 6, 1917. The American entrance into this military conflict influenced the development of the United States.

Mobilizing for War

In order to persuade the public to support the war effort, President Wilson formed the Committee on Public Information (CPI). The CPI organized rallies and parades. They published posters and pamphlets. Speakers known as "four-minute men" gave short patriotic speeches delivered in movie theaters and churches.

I WANT YOU FOR U.S. ARMY
NEAREST RECRUITING STATION

Shortly after the U.S. entered the war, illustrator James Montgomery Flagg created this famous recruitment poster featuring Uncle Sam. More than four million copies were printed.

The U.S. government's war effort also involved limiting some freedoms in the United States. The Espionage Act of 1917 and the Sedition Act of 1918 restricted free speech and allowed the government to arrest opponents of the war. Antiwar mail was prohibited and seized. About 900 opponents of the war were jailed for violating these laws. The Sedition Act was later repealed, but the Espionage Act is still in effect today.

To prepare the U.S. military, Congress passed the **Selective Service Act** in 1917. The act required men between the ages of 21 and 30 to register to be drafted. Almost 3 million Americans were drafted into service in World War I. A number of the draftees were African Americans. Altogether, about 400,000 African Americans served in the war. Their units were segregated from white forces and were commanded by white officers. Eventually, African Americans were trained as officers. During World War I, however, they were never placed in command of white troops.

Preparations for war were very expensive. Troops had to be trained, supplied, transported, and fed. Ships and airplanes had to be built and fueled. The government raised taxes and issued war bonds. Money from the sale of these **Liberty bonds** provided billions of dollars in loans to the Allies.

The government took other actions to supply the troops. The War Industries Board (WIB) oversaw the production and distribution of steel, copper, cement, and rubber. The Food Administration worked to increase food supplies and distribution for the troops. It guaranteed farmers high prices for their crops. To conserve food at home, citizens were encouraged to practice "meatless Mondays" and "wheatless Wednesdays." Many people also grew their own vegetables in "victory gardens" at home.

Another proposal to conserve food supplies was a prohibition, or ban, on alcoholic beverages. Most alcoholic beverages are made with food crops such as grapes and wheat. Soon after the United States entered the war, Congress granted the president powers to limit the alcohol content of wine and beer so that these crops could be used for food production instead. Some tried to discourage Americans from drinking beer by linking German Americans to the brewing industry. These people hoped that anti-German feelings would lead Americans to stop drinking beer.

In addition, the Fuel Administration was established to set production goals and prices for fuels. Its purpose was to make sure that fuel

Schenck v. United States (1919)

Background of the Case

Charles Schenck was arrested for violating the Espionage Act. He had printed and distributed pamphlets urging resistance to the draft. Schenck argued that the First Amendment, which guarantees freedom of speech and freedom of the press, gave him the right to criticize the government.

The Court's Ruling

The Supreme Court ruled that the pamphlet was not protected by the First Amendment and that the Espionage Act was constitutional.

The Court's Reasoning

The Supreme Court decided that under certain circumstances, such as a state of war, Congress could limit free speech. The Court created a test to distinguish between protected and unprotected speech. Unprotected speech would have to present "a clear and present danger" to national security. For example, the First Amendment would not protect a person who created a panic by yelling "Fire!" in a crowded theater.

Why It Matters

Schenck v. *United States* was important because it was the first case in which the Supreme Court interpreted the First Amendment. The Court concluded that certain constitutional rights, such as free speech, could be limited under extraordinary conditions, such as war. Later rulings by the Court narrowed the test of "clear and present danger" to speech advocating violence. The nonviolent expression of ideas and opinions—however unpopular—was thereby protected.

Analyze Information
1. According to the Supreme Court, when could free speech be limited?
2. How do you think this case affected other people who opposed the war?

Reading Check
Analyze Information How did the U.S. government gain public support for the war?

distribution needs for the military could always be met. To encourage fuel conservation, daylight saving time was introduced in March 1918 to extend daylight hours for those who worked long shifts in factories. Fuel conservation was promoted in other ways, such as through publicity campaigns calling for "gasless Sundays."

New Wartime Opportunities

Three main factors led to a shortage of labor in the United States during the war. First, American factories were working nonstop to produce weapons and supplies for the Allied forces. Factories needed new workers to meet this huge demand. Second, the war almost completely cut off immigration. As you know, immigrants had provided a steady source of labor to American industry. And third, many of the young men who would normally take factory jobs were off fighting in Europe.

Women's War Efforts This labor shortage created new opportunities for many workers. American women took on new roles to help the war effort. Some 1 million women joined the U.S. workforce during the war years. Women replaced male workers in steel mills, ammunition factories, and assembly lines. Women served as street car conductors and elevator operators. For many, this was their first experience working outside the home.

Women also worked for the war effort in Europe. About 25,000 American women worked as nurses, telephone operators, signalers, typists, and interpreters in France. Many women worked as volunteers, serving at Red Cross facilities and encouraging the sale of bonds and planting of victory gardens. Women were not given jobs in combat, but they braved gunfire at the front lines as nurses and ambulance drivers.

Other women, meanwhile, spoke out against U.S. participation in the war. Social reformer Jane Addams was against U.S. entry into the war. Jeannette Rankin of Montana, the first female member of Congress, was 1 of 50 House members to cast a vote against declaring war in 1917. "I want to stand by my country," she said, "but I cannot vote for war."

Labor and the War Even with so many women joining the workforce, factories needed additional workers. New job opportunities encouraged Mexican Americans from the West and African Americans from the South to move to northern industrial cities.

Because labor was scarce, workers were in a good position to demand better wages and conditions. Union membership increased. More than 4 million unionized workers went on strike during the war. Because factory owners could not easily replace workers, they often agreed to demands.

President Wilson set up the **National War Labor Board** in April 1918. The board helped workers and management avoid strikes and reach agreements. The board settled more than 1,000 labor disputes. Its members were generally sympathetic to workers. They helped establish a minimum wage and limited work hours. They also required fair pay for women.

Winning Support Many Americans had been in favor of the U.S. position of neutrality. Now, Americans had to be convinced that it was their duty

In World War I, women drove ambulances and entered the battlefield as nurses and medics. Red Cross volunteers were often responsible for the first stage of treatment of the wounded.

Patriotic Posters

Posters like this one encouraged American citizens to participate in the effort to provide weapons and food to soldiers fighting in World War I.

Analyze Visuals
How does this poster inspire patriotism?

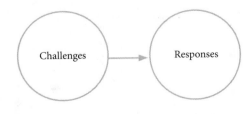

TEAMWORK WINS
UNITED STATES SHIPPING BOARD EMERGENCY FLEET CORPORATION

Reading Check
Find Main Ideas
How did war mobilization benefit American workers?

to support the war. A nationwide campaign of propaganda, or posters, newspaper stories, speeches, and other materials, was started to influence people's opinions. Popular movie stars were hired to speak on behalf of the war effort. Artists were hired to create patriotic posters and pamphlets. Propaganda helped build American support for the war.

Summary and Preview The war effort created new opportunities for women and other Americans. In the next lesson you will learn about what life was like for soldiers overseas.

Lesson 2 Assessment

Review Ideas, Terms, and People

1. **a. Explain** Why did the United States enter World War I?
   b. Evaluate Do you think the United States was right to stay neutral for so long? Why or why not?

2. **a. Recall** What was the purpose of the Committee on Public Information?
   b. Explain How did the United States prepare for war?
   c. Summarize How did the government exercise control over the economy during the war?

3. **a. Describe** How did women help the war effort abroad?
   b. Explain How do you think the end of the war affected labor unions? Explain your answer.
   c. Analyze How was daily life in the United States affected by World War I?

Critical Thinking

4. **Problem Solving** In this lesson you learned about new laws and government programs during World War I. Create a graphic organizer similar to the one below and use it to identify the challenges the United States faced when mobilizing for World War I. List which new laws, government programs, and other changes responded to those challenges.

Challenges → Responses

Americans in World War I

The Big Idea

American troops helped the Allies achieve victory in World War I.

Main Ideas

- American soldiers started to arrive in Europe in 1917.
- The Americans helped the Allies win the war.
- Germany agreed to an armistice after suffering heavy losses.

Key Terms and People

American Expeditionary Force
Communists
armistice

If YOU were there . . .

It is April 1918. You are marching into Paris with your army unit on your way to the front lines. Women and children throw flowers from windows and balconies as you pass through the city. You want to do whatever it takes to defend this city and its residents. You know that defeating Germany will be difficult and very dangerous.

Do you think American forces can help the Allies win the war?

American Soldiers Arrive

By the time U.S. troops started to arrive in Europe in 1917, the Allies were dangerously near defeat. German forces were advancing in France, once again driving toward Paris. The German navy was destroying Allied ships at sea. And on the eastern front, the Russians were desperately struggling to hold back the Germans.

Joining the Fight French and British generals called for immediate help on the front lines. They wanted the U.S. troops, known as the **American Expeditionary Force** (AEF), to join French and British units. But General John J. Pershing, leader of the American troops, insisted that the Americans join the fight as a separate force. He refused to have the AEF "scattered among the Allied forces where it will not be an American army at all."

Pershing also demanded that his troops be thoroughly trained for combat before rushing to the front lines. The AEF included many well-trained regular army and National Guard troops. But it also included a large number of inexperienced volunteers and draftees. Pershing gave the men three months of intense training in army discipline and trench warfare. He believed that taking the time to train his soldiers would help the Allies achieve victory.

World War I U.S. Soldier

You can learn a lot about what life was like for a U.S. soldier in World War I by studying the clothing and equipment that was used. Historians evaluate artifacts, such as these, to learn about U.S. history.

The appearance of the Springfield rifles fooled the Germans into thinking the Americans had machine guns.

Gas masks were carried in a pouch around the neck.

Soldiers carried a pack called a haversack, which held food, personal items, and extra socks.

A wool tunic was worn over a wool shirt and wool breeches.

A blanket could be carried at the bottom of the haversack with a special attachment.

Wool cloth strips called puttees were wrapped around the legs and tops of shoes for protection.

Analyze Historical Sources
What can you learn about life for U.S. soldiers by studying these artifacts?

Russia Leaves the War While Pershing trained his troops, the Allies' position became even more dangerous. In November 1917 a group of Russians called the Bolsheviks overthrew the Russian government and seized power. The Bolsheviks were **Communists**—people who favor the equal distribution of wealth and the end of all forms of private property.

Led by Vladimir Lenin, the new Russian government faced a desperate situation. Around 8 million Russians had been killed or wounded during the war. Soldiers were deserting from the eastern front, and sailors were leaving naval bases. Food riots raged in the cities. The Russians could not keep fighting under these conditions. In March 1918 Russia signed the Treaty of Brest-Litovsk, a peace agreement with the Central powers. A civil war then broke out in Russia between the Communists and forces loyal to the czar (ZAHR), Russia's emperor. The United States and other Allied countries sent aid to the czarist forces. Russia, however, one of the main Allied powers, was out of World War I.

Reading Check
Make Inferences
Why do you think General Pershing refused to put American troops in foreign units?

Winning the War

With Russia out of the fighting, German generals saw a chance to win the war. In the spring of 1918 Germany transferred many of its divisions of troops from the eastern front to the western front. Germany planned to smash the stalemate.

The Final Battles At the same time, American soldiers arrived. Even training had not prepared them for the realities of war. The troops lived on dried beef, hard biscuits, and canned emergency rations. The men shared the trenches with rats, lice, and sometimes the bodies of dead soldiers. A soldiers' song of the time described the situation:

> "Sing me to sleep where bullets fall,
>   Let me forget the war and all;
>   Damp is my dug-out [trench], cold my feet,
>   Nothing but bully [canned meat] and biscuits to eat."
>
> —Quoted in *Great Push: An Episode of the Great War*, by Patrick MacGill

On March 21, 1918, the Germans began blasting more than 6,000 heavy guns at Allied troops along the Somme River in northern France. The German advance, helped by a morning fog, surprised the Allies. German forces drove 40 miles into Allied lines before the advance stalled. Some 250,000 Germans had been killed or wounded. British and French casualties totaled 133,000.

The Germans then attacked farther south, advancing to the Marne River and pushing the French line back toward Paris. At this critical moment, General Pershing promised Allied commander Ferdinand Foch: "Infantry, artillery, aviation—all that we have . . . The American people would be proud to be engaged in the greatest battle of history." Two divisions of the AEF joined French forces.

The Germans were unprepared for the fresh energy and fighting skills of the Americans. The U.S. soldiers succeeded in stopping the German advance less than 50 miles from Paris. Then, at Belleau Wood, the Allies attacked and gradually drove the Germans back.

The German generals became desperate. In July 1918 they launched their final offensive—one last attempt to cross the Marne River. Terrible losses on the German side during this push stopped the German offensive. These losses also protected Paris from invasion. Although American troops suffered about 12,000 casualties, they had helped force a major turning point in the war.

Driving the Germans Back Now the Allies drove toward victory. There were more than 1 million U.S. troops in France, and they played a key role in the later battles of the war. In September 1918 Allied forces attacked and defeated the Germans at the town of Saint-Mihiel on the border of France and Germany. Along the Meuse River and in the Argonne Forest, near the French-Belgian border, American and Allied troops again attacked German forces.

Explore ONLINE!

Legend:
- Allied powers, 1916
- Central powers, 1916
- Neutral Countries
- Allied powers troop movements
- Central powers troop movements
- British naval blockade
- Farthest Russian advance (1914)
- Farthest Central powers advance
- Trench line, western front
- Armistice line, Nov. 11, 1918
- Allied victory
- Central powers victory
- Undecided battle
- German submarine activity

0   200   400 Miles
0   200   400 Kilometers

ATLANTIC OCEAN

NORWAY

SWEDEN

FINLAND

Petrograd

GREAT BRITAIN

North Sea

DENMARK

Baltic Sea

RUSSIA

Lusitania sunk May 1915

London

Sussex torpedoed March 1916

English Channel

Berlin

Stebark Aug. 1914

EASTERN FRONT DEC. 1917

Ypres Oct.–Nov. 1914 Apr.–May 1915

NETHERLANDS

BELGIUM

GERMANY

LUXEMBOURG

Somme July–Nov. 1916

Paris

ALSACE-LORRAINE

Battle of the Marne Sept. 1914, July 1918

Château-Thierry June 1918

Verdun Feb.–Dec. 1916

WESTERN FRONT

Argonne Forest Sept.–Oct. 1918

SWITZERLAND

Vienna

AUSTRIA-HUNGARY

Budapest

Bay of Biscay

FRANCE

Kobarid Oct.–Nov. 1917

SERBIA

BOSNIA and HERZEGOVINA

Sarajevo

ROMANIA

Black Sea

PORTUGAL

SPAIN

ITALY

Rome

Adriatic Sea

BULGARIA

Bosporus

MONTENEGRO

BALKANS

Constantinople

ALBANIA

Dardanelles Gallipoli April 1915–Jan. 1916

Mediterranean Sea

GREECE (Joined Allied Powers 1917)

OTTOMAN EMPIRE

Interpret Maps

1. **Human-Environment Interaction** Why was the British naval blockade located where it was?

2. **Location** In which country were the most battles fought, according to this map?

The 369th Infantry spent 191 days in combat, longer than any other American force sent to Europe during World War I. The "Harlem Hellfighters" became famous throughout Europe and America for their valor.

Among the many heroes of these battles was a young man from Tennessee named Alvin York. In October 1918 York killed 25 German gunners and captured 132 prisoners. His heroism earned him fame and many awards, including the Congressional Medal of Honor. His life story even became the basis for a popular movie in 1941.

Also among the brave American troops were the African American soldiers of the 369th Infantry. Known as the "Harlem Hellfighters," the 369th spent more time in combat than any other American unit. Its members were the first to reach the Rhine River on the German border. They aided French forces at Château-Theirry and Belleau Wood. France awarded them the prized Croix de Guerre (Cross of War) medal for their bravery.

The Allies were also winning the war at sea. Allied war planners used a new **strategy** called the convoy system to protect their ships. This meant that destroyers capable of sinking U-boats escorted and protected groups of Allied merchant ships.

By November 1918 American soldiers were making rapid advances toward Germany. "For the first time the enemy lines were completely broken through," reported General Pershing.

Armistice

At home and on the battlefield, Germans were tired of war. Food was so scarce in Germany that more than 800 German civilians were dying of starvation every day. In Germany and other nations of the Central powers, food riots and strikes occurred. Germany was also running out of soldiers. In addition to those killed or wounded in 1918, one-quarter of Germany's fighting men had been captured by the Allies.

Academic Vocabulary
strategy a plan for fighting a battle or war

Reading Check
Sequence Identify significant events leading to the turning of the tide in the war.

Germany's allies were also eager to end the war. Bulgaria and the Ottoman Empire quit the war in the fall of 1918. Austria-Hungary reached a peace agreement with the Allies on November 3. Seeing that his country was beaten, the German leader, Kaiser Wilhelm II, gave up his throne and fled to the Netherlands.

The Germans then agreed to a cease-fire. The Allies demanded that Germany pull back from all its conquered territory. They insisted that Germany destroy its aircraft, tanks, and big guns and surrender its U-boats. The Germans had no choice but to accept these demands to disarm. The **armistice**, or truce, went into effect on the 11th hour of the 11th day of the 11th month of 1918. "At eleven o'clock everything got so quiet that the silence was nearly unbearable," remembered an American soldier. Then the silence was broken with shouts like "I've lived through the war!"

Summary and Preview America's entry into World War I helped the Allies achieve victory. In the next lesson you will learn about the effort to work out a permanent peace agreement.

Reading Check
Identify Which circumstances led Kaiser Wilhelm II to give up his throne?

Lesson 3 Assessment

Review Ideas, Terms, and People

1. **a. Recall** What was the American Expeditionary Force?

   b. Analyze How did the Russian Revolution change the course of the war?

   c. Evaluate Why did Russia leave the war?

2. **a. Recall** How was the Second Battle of the Marne a turning point in the war?

   b. Analyze How did U.S. troops make a difference in the final battles of the war?

3. **a. Describe** What was Germany required to surrender in the armistice?

   b. Explain Were the terms of the armistice fair? Explain your answer.

Critical Thinking

4. **Categorize** In this lesson you learned about the victories of the American Expeditionary Force. Create a graphic organizer similar to the one below and use it to list challenges the Allies faced from 1917 to 1918. List the Allies' achievements during the same time period.

Allied Challenges	
Allied Achievements	

★ Establishing Peace

The Big Idea

The United States and the victorious Allied powers clashed over postwar plans.

Main Ideas

- The costs of war included millions of human lives as well as financial burdens.
- President Woodrow Wilson and European leaders met to work out a peace agreement.
- The U.S. Senate rejected the Treaty of Versailles.

Key Terms and People

League of Nations
reparations
Treaty of Versailles
Henry Cabot Lodge

If YOU were there . . .

Your older brother was drafted in 1917 and sent to fight on the western front in Europe. He has written home about the terrible conditions in the trenches and the horror of seeing men killed in battle. Now the war is over. You read in the newspaper that a peace treaty is being negotiated in Paris, France.

What do you hope the peace treaty will say?

The Costs of War

While soldiers and civilians around the world celebrated the end of World War I in November 1918, the tragedy of war was never far from people's minds. When asked what the armistice meant, one British soldier simply said, "Time to bury the dead."

War Dead The number of soldiers killed in World War I was beyond anything the world had ever experienced. About 5 million Allied soldiers and 3.5 million soldiers from the Central powers died in combat. More than 20 million soldiers on both sides were wounded. The war devastated an entire generation of young men in many European nations. In France, for example, 90 percent of the healthy young men had served in World War I. More than seven out of ten of these men were killed or wounded. While the United States

Memorials to soldiers killed in World War I, like this one at Somme, France, are located throughout Europe.

Deaths in World War I

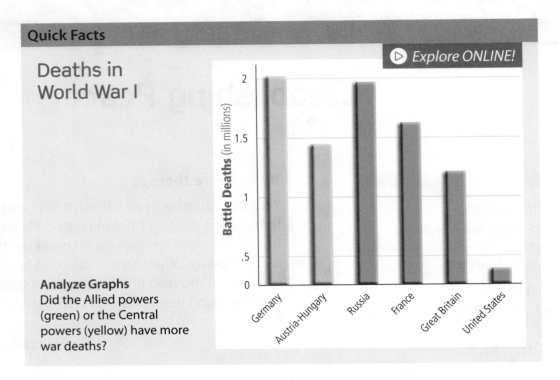

Explore ONLINE!

Analyze Graphs
Did the Allied powers (green) or the Central powers (yellow) have more war deaths?

escaped this extreme level of devastation, American forces did suffer heavy losses. Some 116,000 U.S. troops died and about 200,000 were wounded.

Financial Losses Along with the shocking human losses, the war brought financial disaster to many parts of Europe. Factories and farms were left in ruins. "For mile after mile nothing was left," said one British visitor about the French countryside. "No building was habitable [livable] and no field fit for the plow." With farmers unable to raise crops, severe food shortages occurred.

The overall economic cost of the war was huge. Property worth $30 billion had been destroyed. The Allies had spent $145 billion on the war effort, and the Central powers had spent $63 billion. France and Britain had borrowed large amounts of money to fight the war, and now they were deeply in debt to American banks. Germany was also in debt, and its people faced starvation.

The Influenza Epidemic The world was in for another shock in 1918 when a worldwide epidemic of influenza, or flu, broke out. The virus was extremely contagious and deadly. Over the next two years, it spread around the world, killing approximately 30 million people—even more than the war itself.

The epidemic started in an army training camp in Kansas. Because the flu is transmitted through the air, it spread rapidly. American soldiers unknowingly spread the disease to other army camps, to American civilians, and eventually to soldiers and civilians in Europe. One American doctor said that seeing stacks of bodies at an army camp in Massachusetts "beats any sight they ever had in France after a battle." Half of the Americans who died during this period died from influenza.

The epidemic changed life everywhere in the United States. In Chicago, for example, the flu more than doubled the normal death rate in the fall of 1918. Many of those killed were young and strong. State and local governments took measures to prevent the spread of the disease. Kearney, Nebraska, imposed a quarantine, forbidding people who were ill from leaving their homes. Many cities banned public gatherings, including school classes. A man named Dan Tonkel remembered what life was like for children in his hometown of Goldsboro, North Carolina:

> "I felt like I was walking on eggshells. I was afraid to go out, to play with my playmates, my classmates, my neighbors . . . I remember I was actually afraid to breathe. People were afraid to talk to each other. It was like—don't breathe in my face, don't even look at me, because you might give me germs that will kill me."
>
> —Dan Tonkel, quoted in *Influenza 1918: The Worst Epidemic in American History*, by Lynette Lezzoni

Although there was no cure for the flu, people would try anything. One woman surrounded her daughter with raw onions. Another remembered, "We hung bags of . . . garlic about our necks. We smelled awful, but it was okay, because everyone smelled bad." By the time the influenza epidemic ended in 1919, it had killed 800,000 Americans at home and abroad. Today, vaccinations help prevent major outbreaks of the flu and other contagious diseases.

Reading Check
Find Main Ideas
What made the influenza epidemic of 1918 so deadly?

The Peace Agreement

Even before the United States entered World War I, President Woodrow Wilson began making plans for a peace agreement. This peace agreement was one example of the United States leadership role at the conclusion of the war. Wilson was determined to do everything possible to prevent another world war. On January 8, 1918, he outlined his vision for the postwar world in a plan known as the Fourteen Points.

Wilson's Fourteen Points Wilson's Fourteen Points was a list of specific proposals for postwar peace. Several of the points would settle national border disputes. Others called for military cutbacks, proposed lower tariffs, and banned secret agreements between nations. Another proposed settlements for colonial peoples who wished to be independent. This reflected Wilson's strong belief in self-determination—the right of people to choose their own political status. The final point called for the creation of an international assembly of nations called the **League of Nations**. The league's mission would be to work to settle international disputes and encourage democracy.

European leaders disagreed with Wilson's vision for the peace settlement. They wanted it to clearly punish Germany for

Quick Facts

Key Goals of the Fourteen Points

- End secret alliances
- Encourage free shipping
- Remove barriers to trade
- Reduce armies and navies
- Resolve colonial claims
- Support the right of people to choose their own government
- Settle border disputes
- Establish the League of Nations

its role in the war. European leaders wanted to prevent Germany from ever again becoming a world power.

The Treaty of Versailles President Wilson traveled to Europe to attend the Paris Peace Conference, which was held at the palace of Versailles (ver-SY), outside of Paris. Wilson felt it was his duty to "play my full part in making good what [our soldiers] offered their lives to obtain."

The leaders, called the Big Four, were President Wilson, British prime minister David Lloyd George, French premier Georges Clemenceau, and Italian prime minister Vittorio Orlando. They took control of the conference. No representatives from Russia or the Central powers attended.

Many Allied leaders defended their own country's interests and insisted on severe punishment for Germany. They wanted Germany to accept complete blame for the war and pay for the damage it had caused. These **reparations**, or payments for war damages, were set at $33 billion. France and the other Allies also wanted to take control of large parts of German territory.

▷ Explore ONLINE!

Europe after World War I, 1914–1918

Legend:
- Countries created after World War I
- Occupied by Allies
- British mandate
- French mandate
- Lost by Austria–Hungary
- Lost by Bulgaria
- Lost by Germany
- Lost by Ottoman Empire
- Lost by Russia
- Area unchanged

*Becomes Republic of Turkey, 1923
**Becomes USSR, 1922

0   250   500 Miles
0   250   500 Kilometers

Interpret Maps

1. **Location** Poland was created from territories lost by which countries?

2. **Human-Environment Interaction** How did World War I change the map of Europe?

Woodrow Wilson
1856–1924

Woodrow Wilson was born in Virginia in 1856. The terrible destruction he saw as a child during the Civil War would later influence his response to World War I. As president, he backed reforms such as child-labor restrictions and an eight-hour workday for railroad workers. Although he eventually abandoned American neutrality during World War I, Wilson was committed to world peace after the war. For his role in helping found the League of Nations, Wilson won the Nobel Peace Prize in 1919.

Make Inferences
How did Wilson's childhood experiences affect his reaction to World War I?

Reading Check
Analyze Information
Why did Allied leaders object to Wilson's plan?

Wilson reluctantly agreed to the **Treaty of Versailles**, the peace settlement of World War I. In it, the League of Nations was established. Estonia, Finland, Latvia, Lithuania, Czechoslovakia, and Yugoslavia became independent countries. Poland was restored as a nation. The Central powers turned over their colonies to the League of Nations. The league assigned their colonies to other European powers to rule. Though the Treaty of Versailles did not give Wilson everything he wanted, he hoped the League of Nations would solve remaining problems.

Treaty of Versailles Rejected

The U.S. Constitution states that treaties must be ratified by at least two-thirds of the members of the Senate. Wilson knew he was going to have a hard time convincing some senators to vote to ratify the Versailles Treaty. Republican senator **Henry Cabot Lodge** declared: "No peace that satisfied Germany in any degree can ever satisfy us." Lodge wanted the winners to set the terms of the peace.

Republicans insisted on changes to the treaty before they would ratify it. Their main objection was the League of Nations' power to use military force. They were worried that as a member of the League, the United States could be forced to send troops to war based on decisions made by the League of Nations. This, they argued, conflicted with Congress's constitutional power to declare war.

Wilson refused to compromise. He insisted that the treaty be ratified exactly as it was written. He traveled around the country, trying to convince the public to pressure Republican senators to vote for the treaty. Before he completed his tour, however, Wilson was weakened by a stroke.

Lodge announced that he was prepared to accept most of the treaty. He still wanted to limit U.S. military commitment to the League of Nations. Wilson demanded that Democrats in the Senate refuse to change

Causes and Effects of World War I

Causes
- Nationalism
- Militarism
- Competition for territory
- Alliance system in Europe

Effects
- U.S. entry into the war in 1917
- Millions of deaths and widespread destruction in Europe
- Treaty of Versailles
- Creation of several new nations
- League of Nations

Reading Check
Support Points of View
Do you think Wilson should have compromised with Republicans in the Senate on the Treaty of Versailles? Why or why not?

the treaty. When the vote was taken on November 19, 1919, neither the Democrats nor the Republicans would compromise. The Treaty of Versailles was defeated in the Senate. Following extensive political debate, the United States refused to ratify the Treaty of Versailles.

It was a bitter disappointment for President Wilson. The United States signed separate peace treaties with Austria, Hungary, and Germany. They never joined the League of Nations.

Summary and Preview World War I changed the world map and affected the lives of millions. But efforts to build a lasting peace in the years that followed failed.

Lesson 4 Assessment

Review Ideas, Terms, and People

1. a. **Recall** Approximately how many soldiers were killed or wounded in World War I?

   b. **Draw Conclusions** How did the war affect the European economy?

   c. **Summarize** How did Americans try to fight the influenza epidemic of 1918?

2. a. **Recall** What was the League of Nations?

   b. **Explain** How did the Treaty of Versailles change the map of Europe?

   c. **Elaborate** Which countries did not attend the Paris Peace Conference? How do you think this affected the outcome?

   d. **Evaluate** What were Wilson's Fourteen Points?

3. a. **Identify** Who was Henry Cabot Lodge?

   b. **Predict** How might Wilson have ensured that the U.S. Senate would ratify the Treaty of Versailles?

   c. **Evaluate** What were reasons why the U.S. Senate refused to support the Treaty of Versailles?

Critical Thinking

4. **Identify Points of View** In this lesson you learned about the Treaty of Versailles. Create a graphic organizer similar to the one below and use it to compare the positions of Woodrow Wilson, Allied leaders, and Senate Republicans. Fill in the results of each person's or group's goals.

	Goals	Results
Woodrow Wilson		
Allied Leaders		
Senate Republicans		

Social Studies Skills

Use Visual Resources

Define the Skill

A major part of history is understanding the events and ideas of the past. Visual resources are good sources of information about the past. Visual resources include paintings, drawings, cartoons, posters, and photographs. The symbols and images in these resources tell us about the ideas and values of a time period. They often provide different information and points of view than do written documents.

Learn the Skill

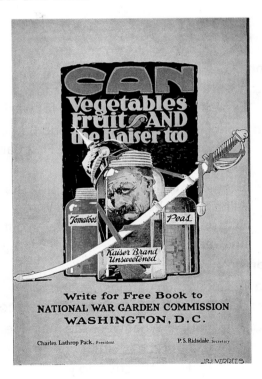

Visual resources can have special purposes. For example, the poster above was produced by the U.S. government to inspire patriotism and encourage support for the war effort. It uses symbols and images to suggest that all Americans can contribute to the war effort.

You know from reading the module that conserving food to provide supplies for troops was an important part of the war effort. This poster encourages Americans to can fruits and vegetables. The pictures show canned tomatoes and peas in glass jars.

The poster also shows the German kaiser in a jar. He cannot reach his sword, which is outside the jar. He is helpless. This suggests that, by canning fruit and vegetables, Americans can help defeat the German leader.

Practice the Skill

Study the World War I poster below. Like the other poster, it was produced by the U.S. government to encourage support for the war effort. Write a paragraph describing the poster. Your paragraph should include the specific purpose of the poster, the symbols it uses, and whether it conveys its message effectively. You can use the text above as a model.

Module 24 Assessment

Review Vocabulary, Terms, and People

Identify the descriptions below with the correct term or person from the module.

1. International assembly of nations designed to settle international disputes and encourage democracy

2. Strategy of defending a position by fighting from the protection of deep ditches

3. American fighting force trained and led by General John J. Pershing

4. Law that required men between the ages of 21 and 30 to register to be drafted into the armed forces

5. Senate leader who opposed the Treaty of Versailles

6. Truce between warring nations

7. Telegram from the German foreign minister proposing an alliance between Germany and Mexico against the United States

Comprehension and Critical Thinking

Lesson 1

8. a. **Identify** What event sparked World War I?

   b. **Explain** How did tensions in Europe lead to war?

   c. **Draw Conclusions** Why did the war in Europe become a stalemate?

Lesson 2

9. a. **Recall** What happened to the *Lusitania*? How did the American public react?

   b. **Analyze** How did the country's mobilization for war affect American women?

   c. **Evaluate** Do you think U.S. efforts to prepare for war were successful? Why or why not?

Lesson 3

10. a. **Identify** How did the American Expeditionary Force prepare for war?

    b. **Contrast** How was the Second Battle of the Marne different from the First Battle of the Marne?

    c. **Draw Conclusions** Do you think the Allies would have won World War I without American help? Explain your answer.

Lesson 4

11. a. **Recall** Which nations' leaders dominated the Paris Peace Conference?

    b. **Summarize** What were the main ideas of Wilson's Fourteen Points?

    c. **Predict** How effective do you think the League of Nations was? Why?

Review Themes

12. Economics How did World War I affect the economy of the United States?

13. Politics What lasting political changes were brought about by World War I?

Social Studies Skills

Use Visual Resources *Use the Social Studies Skills taught in this module to answer the question below.*

TEAMWORK WINS

UNITED STATES SHIPPING BOARD EMERGENCY FLEET CORPORATION

14. What parts of the U.S. war effort are shown in this poster?

Reading Skills

Recognize Fallacies in Reasoning *Use the Reading Skills taught in this module to answer the question about the reading selection below.*

> The number of soldiers killed in World War I was beyond anything the world had ever experienced. About 5 million Allied soldiers and 3.5 million soldiers from the Central powers died in combat. More than 20 million soldiers on both sides were wounded.

15. Which of the following is an example of a false conclusion drawn from the selection above?

   a. More soldiers were killed in World War I than in any war up to that point.

   b. World War I devastated the European population.

   c. Europe would never recover from World War I.

   d. The number of soldiers wounded was more than two times the number of soldiers killed.

Focus on Speaking

16. Present a Persuasive Speech You have learned that before the United States entered World War I, Americans debated joining the fight. Think about the arguments on both sides of the debate. Then form an opinion on whether the United States should have entered the war and prepare a speech presenting your point of view. You will have about five minutes to present your speech. Use note cards to organize your ideas. Begin by writing a one-sentence introduction clearly stating your opinion. Then write several sentences with details and examples from the module that support your point of view. Conclude your speech with a sentence that summarizes your ideas. Practice your speech and then present it to the class.

Dear home: LETTERS FROM WWI

When U.S. troops arrived in Europe in 1917 to fight in World War I, the war had been dragging on for nearly three years. The American soldiers suddenly found themselves in the midst of chaos. Each day, they faced the threats of machine-gun fire, poison gas, and aerial attacks. Still, the arrival of American reinforcements had sparked a new zeal among the Allies, who believed the new forces could finally turn the tide in their favor. The letters soldiers wrote to their families back home reveal the many emotions they felt on the battlefield: confusion about their surroundings, fear for their own safety, concern for friends and loved ones, and hope that the war would soon be over.

Explore World War I online through the eyes of the soldiers who fought in it. You can find a wealth of information, video clips, primary sources, activities, and more through your online textbook.

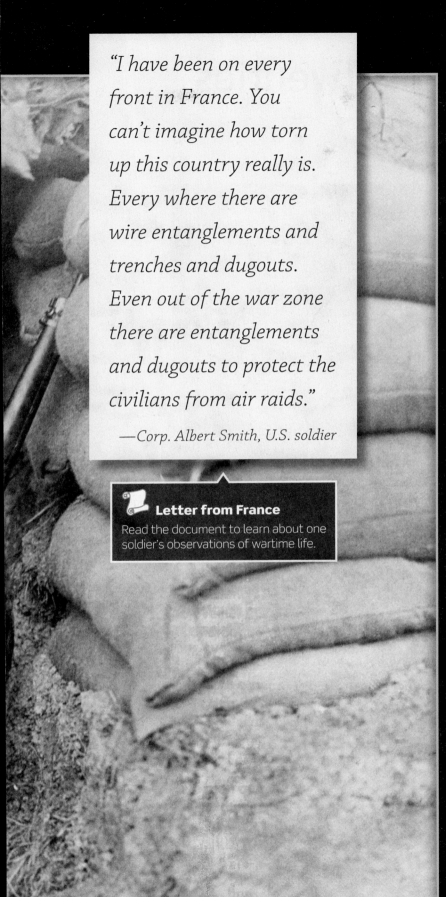

> "I have been on every front in France. You can't imagine how torn up this country really is. Every where there are wire entanglements and trenches and dugouts. Even out of the war zone there are entanglements and dugouts to protect the civilians from air raids."
>
> —Corp. Albert Smith, U.S. soldier

Letter from France
Read the document to learn about one soldier's observations of wartime life.

HISTORY. Go online to view these and other **HISTORY**® resources.

Over There
Watch the video to learn about the experiences of American soldiers on the way to Europe and upon their arrival.

War on the Western Front
Watch the video to hear one soldier's vivid account of battle and its aftermath.

Surrender!
Watch the video to experience soldiers' reactions to the news that the war was finally over.

The Roaring Twenties

Essential Question

How did American society change during the Roaring Twenties?

About the Photo: People flocked to bustling city centers like New York City's Times Square.

In this module you will learn about how American life changed in the years after World War I. You will also read about important artists of the Jazz Age.

What You Will Learn ...

Lesson 1: Boom Times **776**
The Big Idea American industries boomed in the 1920s, changing many Americans' way of life.

Lesson 2: Life during the 1920s **782**
The Big Idea Americans faced new opportunities, challenges, and fears as major changes swept the country in the 1920s.

Lesson 3: The Jazz Age. **790**
The Big Idea Musicians, artists, actors, and writers contributed to American popular culture in the 1920s.

▶ *Explore ONLINE!*

HISTORY

VIDEOS, including...
- America Goes Dry with Prohibition
- Warren G. Harding
- Growth of Radio

☑ Document-Based Investigations

☑ Graphic Organizers

☑ Interactive Games

☑ Image Carousel: Model T Assembly Line

☑ Image Slider: The 1928 Presidential Election

☑ Image Carousel: American Heroes

Timeline of Events 1918–1930

▶ Explore ONLINE!

United States		World
	1918	

∧ **1920** Warren Harding wins the presidency in a landslide victory.

1920 The League of Nations is established.

1922 The tomb of King Tutankhamen is discovered. >

1924 Native Americans are granted the right of U.S. citizenship. | **1924** | **1924** Joseph Stalin becomes dictator of Communist Russia.

THE SUN ALSO RISES
ERNEST HEMINGWAY
Author of "IN OUR TIME" and "THE TORRENTS OF SPRING"

< **1926** Ernest Hemingway publishes *The Sun Also Rises*.

1926 Prince Hirohito > becomes emperor of Japan.

1928 Alexander Fleming discovers penicillin.

< **1929** Construction begins on the Empire State Building.

1930

Reading Social Studies

THEME FOCUS:

Society and Culture, Science and Technology

In this module you will learn about the decade of the 1920s, a period called the Roaring Twenties. During this time, many in society thought that the Great War would be the last major war and that the future was bright. Also during this time, science and technology made leaps forward that would make life easier for millions of Americans.

READING FOCUS:

Synthesize Information

Learning about history means synthesizing, or combining, many different sources about the past. When you read these modules, you are reading a synthesis of other sources, accounts, and ideas about history.

Synthesize Once you have identified the subject you are studying, you should try to read as many different accounts of the story as you can. Be sure to investigate the author of a source to learn what his or her goals might be. Compare and contrast the different sources and evaluate which ones you believe. Finally, use all the various stories you have read to form your own interpretation of what happened in history.

You Try It!

Read these two accounts of the assassination of Archduke Francis Ferdinand and his wife, Sophie. Then write your own version of the story.

> "As the car came abreast he stepped forward from the curb, drew his automatic pistol from his coat and fired two shots. The first struck the wife of the Archduke, the Archduchess Sofia, in the abdomen. . . . She died instantly. The second bullet struck the Archduke close to the heart. He uttered only one word, 'Sofia'—a call to his stricken wife. Then his head fell back and he collapsed. He died almost instantly."
>
> —conspirator Borijove Jevtic

> "As I was pulling out my handkerchief to wipe the blood away from his mouth, the duchess cried out to him, 'In Heaven's name, what has happened to you?' At that she slid off the seat and lay on the floor of the car. . . . I had no idea that she too was hit and thought she had simply fainted with fright. Then I heard His Imperial Highness say, "Sopherl, Sopherl, don't die. Stay alive for the children!""
>
> —guard Count Franz von Harrach, quoted in "Assassination of an Archduke," *Eyewitness to History*

1. What differences do you notice between the two accounts?
2. Why might these different authors have a different view of the assassination?
3. How can you tell what each author's viewpoint is?
4. Write your own version of what might have happened. Use details that you believe from the sources above.

As you read Module 25, notice any differing views from different sources.

Key Terms and People

Lesson 1
Warren G. Harding
Calvin Coolidge
Teapot Dome scandal
Kellogg-Briand Pact
Model T
moving assembly line
Herbert Hoover

Lesson 2
flappers
Red Scare
Twenty-First Amendment
fundamentalism
Scopes trial
Great Migration
Marcus Garvey

Lesson 3
talkie
Jazz Age
Harlem Renaissance
Langston Hughes
Lost Generation
expatriates
Georgia O'Keeffe

Boom Times

The Big Idea

American industries boomed in the 1920s, changing many Americans' way of life.

Main Ideas

- President Harding promised a return to peace and prosperity.
- Calvin Coolidge supported a probusiness agenda.
- American business boomed in the 1920s.
- In 1928 Americans elected Herbert Hoover, hoping he would help good financial times continue.

Key Terms and People

Warren G. Harding
Calvin Coolidge
Teapot Dome scandal
Kellogg-Briand Pact
Model T
moving assembly line
Herbert Hoover

If YOU were there . . .

You have been working in a car factory for years, and now you have finally bought a car of your own—a shiny new 1920 Ford Model T. As you set out on your first drive, the car rattles and bounces over unpaved roads that were designed for horse-and-buggy travel. But you don't mind the rough ride. You now have the freedom to drive anywhere you want to go!

How will owning a car change your life?

Return to Peace and Prosperity

The end of World War I had an immediate impact on the economy. Because the government no longer needed war supplies, it canceled billions of dollars' worth of contracts with American factories. This meant that factories cut back on production at the very moment that millions of soldiers left the military and began looking for jobs. The result was a sharp rise in unemployment. Meanwhile, many people who did have jobs rushed to buy products they could not buy during the war. Prices soared. Wages could not keep up with the rising prices, and thus workers could no longer afford to buy the goods they needed and wanted. Many went on strike for higher wages—more than 4 million in 1919 alone.

As the 1920 presidential election approached, the economic difficulties were bad news for the party in power, Woodrow Wilson's Democratic Party. Many voters blamed the Democrats for the hard times. Sensing the public's anger, the Republicans looked for a candidate who would offer new hope for American voters. They chose **Warren G. Harding**, a senator from Ohio. Harding picked Governor **Calvin Coolidge** of Massachusetts as his running mate.

Harding based his campaign strategy on a promise to return the country to stability and prosperity, what he called "normalcy." His conservative policies contrasted with the reform-minded policies of the Progressive Era.

Academic
Vocabulary
incentive something
that encourages
people to behave a
certain way

Democrats believed there was still support for Wilson's ideas for reform. They ran Ohio governor James M. Cox for president, and New York's Franklin D. Roosevelt for vice president. But Harding's promise of a return to normalcy captured the public's mood in 1920. Harding won a landslide victory with about 60 percent of the popular vote.

Harding worked quickly to help strengthen the economy. He put together a cabinet of experts who believed in reducing money owed by the government and limiting government involvement in the economy. Secretary of the Treasury Andrew Mellon pushed for tax cuts for wealthy Americans. Mellon believed that this policy would give the wealthy an **incentive** to invest in new businesses and create new jobs for other Americans. Mellon's opponents called this idea the trickle-down theory, arguing that money would only "trickle down" in small drops to less-well-off Americans.

While Harding was president, businesses did in fact bounce back from the postwar recession. The economy created new, better-paying jobs, leading to an economic boom that lasted for most of the decade.

Harding faced problems in other areas, however. He had appointed many of his trusted friends to high positions. Some of these men used their positions to gain wealth through illegal means. "I have no trouble with my enemies," Harding once said. "But my . . . friends . . . keep me walking the floor nights."

What came to be known as the **Teapot Dome scandal** involved Secretary of the Interior Albert Fall, who accepted large sums of money and valuable gifts from private oil companies. In exchange, Fall allowed the companies to control government oil reserves in Elk Hills, California, and Teapot Dome, Wyoming. The U.S. Senate soon began investigating Fall, who was convicted of accepting bribes. He was the first cabinet member ever to be convicted of a crime for his actions while in office.

Coolidge's Probusiness Administration

Just before details of the Teapot Dome scandal became public, President Harding died of a heart attack. In August 1923 Vice President Calvin Coolidge took charge. Coolidge had a strong reputation as an honest and trustworthy leader. These qualities helped him restore confidence in the government.

Coolidge acted quickly to fire all officials who had been involved in the bribery scandals of Harding's administration. This helped him win the presidential election in 1924. He received nearly twice as many votes as the Democratic candidate, John W. Davis.

Coolidge proved to be even more probusiness than Harding had been. He once declared that "the business of America is business." He expanded the policies started under Harding, such as tax cuts for wealthier citizens. He also supported raising tariffs on foreign goods to decrease competition with domestic products. Despite higher tariffs, trade with other countries actually increased under Coolidge. This was mainly because many nations depended on trade with the United States to rebuild their economies after

Reading Check
Summarize What
did Harding mean
when he promised a
return to normalcy?

World War I. Not everyone profited from Coolidge's efforts, however. Coolidge vetoed congressional attempts to provide aid to farmers through the regulation of prices.

Like the United States, European nations wanted a return to prosperity. Europeans also wanted to avoid another devastating war. In 1928 the United States and 14 other nations signed the **Kellogg-Briand Pact**, an agreement that outlawed war. Eventually, 62 nations accepted the pact. There was no way to enforce the pact, however. One U.S. senator complained that the treaty would be "as effective to keep down war as a carpet would be to smother an earthquake." Still, it was a sign that most countries wanted to prevent another global conflict. Today, countries still try to prevent wars with international agreements. More than 180 nations have signed the Treaty on the Non-Proliferation of Nuclear Weapons, an agreement to prevent the spread of nuclear weapons.

Reading Check
Compare and Contrast How were Harding and Coolidge similar, and how were they different?

Business Booms

The 1920s were years of rapid economic growth in the United States. Between 1921 and 1929, U.S. manufacturing nearly doubled. As jobs and wages increased, so did people's ability to buy new products. Some of these products as well as developments in factory and labor productivity and transportation changed the way Americans lived. Their standard of living also changed.

Ford's Model T Today, we think of cars as a major part of American life. In the early 1900s, though, cars were seen as luxury items that only the wealthy could afford. Henry Ford, an inventor and business leader from Detroit, helped to change this. Ford dreamed of building a car that most Americans could afford:

> "I will build a motor car for the great multitude [most of the people]. It will be large enough for the family but small enough for the individual to run and care for. It . . . will be so low in price that no man making a good salary will be unable to own one."
>
> —Henry Ford, quoted in *My Life and Work*

Ford achieved his goal by building a sturdy and reliable car called the **Model T**, nicknamed the Tin Lizzie. In 1908 the Model T sold for $850. By 1925 it cost just $290. Ford was able to make his car affordable by cutting costs of production. For example, every car looked the same. The Model T came only in black for many years.

To decrease the time it took to make the cars, Ford also began using a **moving assembly line**. This system used conveyer belts to move parts and partly assembled cars from one group of workers to another. The workers stood in one place and specialized in one or two simple assembly tasks that they performed as parts moved past them. The moving assembly line greatly increased the efficiency of mass production.

In 1914 Ford raised the wages for his factory workers to $5 a day. This was good pay, compared with the $2 or $3 per day offered by many other factories. Ford believed the wage increase would keep his employees from

The Model T Assembly Line

These workers are building flywheel magnetos, a part of the ignition system of early engines. The workers perform the same action on each part as the part passes them. Ford's system reduced the time to build a flywheel from 20 minutes to 5 minutes.

The chassis, or frame, and the engine are assembled on separate lines. Workers on a third line then attach them.

The assembled chassis is then connected to the body of the car.

Completely assembled Ford Model T

Analyze Visuals
How does the moving assembly line reduce the time it takes to build a car?

quitting. He also lowered the workday to eight hours and employed people that other factories would not hire, such as African Americans and people with disabilities.

Even with the good wages, many workers had a hard time adjusting to the fast-paced and repetitive work on Ford's assembly line. One wife of an autoworker wrote to Ford saying, "My husband has come home and thrown himself down and won't eat his supper—so done out [tired]! . . . That $5 a day is a blessing—a bigger one than you know, but oh they earn it."

Ford wanted to help make his cars more affordable. He allowed customers to buy cars using an installment plan. Most people were used to saving up for years to buy items. Installment plans let people pay a small amount of the cost every month until the entire car was paid for. Ford's competitors also allowed customers to pay with installment plans. For a slightly higher price than the Model T, companies such as General Motors offered cars in a variety of colors and with more power.

The automobile changed, or impacted, the way Americans lived. With this advancement in transportation, they could now go on long drives or take jobs farther away from where they lived. Cars gave people a sense of freedom and adventure. As *Motor Car* magazine told drivers, "You are your master, the road is ahead . . . your freedom is complete."

Growing Industries The rise of the automobile affected the entire American economy. Millions of Americans found work. They made steel for car bodies, rubber for tires, or glass for windows. The government spent millions of dollars to improve road safety. The government hired workers to pave highways and build new bridges. People opened roadside businesses to serve travelers, such as gas stations, restaurants, and motels. The rising number of cars also created a demand for car repair shops and car insurance.

The Model T ▷ *Explore ONLINE!*

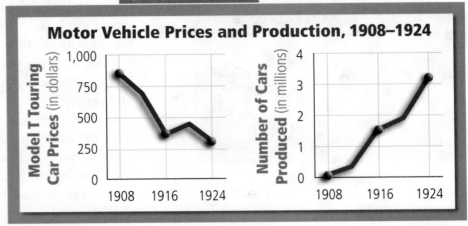

Motor Vehicle Prices and Production, 1908–1924

Analyze Graphs
Why did sales of the Model T increase?

Manufacturers of other types of products followed Ford's example. They began using assembly lines and allowing customers to pay on installment plans. Many companies also took advantage of the increasing number of homes with electricity. By 1929 about 85 percent of all Americans living in towns or cities had electricity. Companies responded by building new electrical appliances designed to make household chores easier. These companies made appliances such as washing machines, vacuum cleaners, and refrigerators.

As companies competed to sell these new goods, the advertising industry boomed. Companies advertised in magazines and on the radio to convince people that their lives would be improved if they owned a certain product. Many advertisers targeted women. They hoped to convince women that they needed the newest technological labor-saving products. For example, one advertisement for an electric dishwasher called its product "the greatest gift of electricity to the modern housewife."

Reading Check
Identify Cause and Effect How did the automobile change society?

Hoover Elected

With the economy booming, public support for the Republican Party remained strong. President Coolidge decided not to run for reelection in 1928. The Republican Party chose Coolidge's secretary of commerce, **Herbert Hoover**, as its nominee. The Democrats nominated New York governor Alfred E. Smith.

Hoover told voters that he was the right choice to maintain economic prosperity. Hoover boldly claimed that "we in America today are nearer to the final triumph over poverty than ever before in the history of any land."

Smith's campaign focused mainly on issues facing city dwellers. This concerned some rural voters. Smith's religious faith also became an issue. He was the first Catholic to run for president. His opponents stirred up fears that the pope and other church officials would control Smith. In the end, Hoover won easily, gaining 58 percent of the popular vote.

Reading Check
Draw Conclusions What helped Herbert Hoover win the presidency in 1928?

Republican Herbert Hoover defeated Democrat Alfred E. Smith in the 1928 presidential election.

Summary and Preview In this lesson you learned about politics and the economy in the 1920s. In the next lesson you will learn more about how society changed during the decade.

Lesson 1 Assessment

Review Ideas, Terms, and People

1. **a. Describe** What was the result of the 1920 presidential election, and why?

   b. Summarize What did the Teapot Dome scandal reveal about Warren G. Harding's administration?

2. **a. Identify** Who succeeded Harding as president, and what were his main policies?

   b. Analyze What was the main weakness of the Kellogg-Briand Pact?

3. **a. Recall** Why did American businesses grow during the 1920s?

   b. Explain Why were Model T prices low?

4. **a. Recall** Why was Herbert Hoover elected?

   b. Elaborate Whom would you have voted for in the 1928 election? Explain your answer.

Critical Thinking

5. **Summarize** In this lesson you learned about the U.S. presidents in the 1920s. Create a chart similar to the one below and expand on your notes by summarizing the main ideas or achievements of each president.

President	Ideas/Achievements

Life during the 1920s

The Big Idea

Americans faced new opportunities, challenges, and fears as major changes swept the country in the 1920s.

Main Ideas

- In the 1920s many young people found new independence in a changing society.

- Postwar tensions occasionally led to fear and violence.

- Competing ideals caused conflict between Americans with traditional beliefs and those with modern views.

- Following the war, minority groups organized to demand their civil rights.

Key Terms and People

flappers
Red Scare
Twenty-First Amendment
fundamentalism
Scopes trial
Great Migration
Marcus Garvey

If YOU were there . . .

The year is 1925. You have just finished school and you are visiting a big city for the first time. You and your friends go to a club and watch young people dancing energetically to popular music. The women have short hair and wear makeup, trying to copy the glamorous style of movie stars. Some of your friends start talking about finding an apartment and looking for jobs in the city.

Would you want to move to a big city in 1925? Why?

A Changing Society

The experience of living through World War I changed the way many young people saw the world around them and inspired social changes. Young men returning from Europe had visited far-off countries and learned about other cultures. Many of them came home with a desire to continue expanding their horizons. The title of one popular song in 1919 asked, "How 'Ya Gonna Keep' em Down on the Farm after They've Seen Paree [Paris]?"

Many young people moved away from farms and small towns to cities. By 1920, for the first time in American history, more than half of the country's population lived in urban areas. Young people took advantage of the economic opportunities of the 1920s to gain independence. In the past most young people had lived and worked at home until they got married. Now more young adults were experiencing a time of freedom before settling down. A new youth culture developed, which included going to parties and dance clubs, listening to popular music, and driving fast cars.

For many young Americans, access to education was an important part of this new independence. High school attendance doubled during the decade. The percentage of students going on to college was higher in the United States than in any other country. This included women, who were

Focus on Women

Bryn Mawr and other colleges provided education to women in new fields.

Bessie Coleman became the first African American woman to obtain her international pilot's license. She traveled the United States, performing stunts under the name "Brave Bessie."

Flappers challenged many of society's ideas about womanhood. They established new rules of speech, dress, and behavior.

Analyze Visuals
How do these images reflect new roles for women during the 1920s?

attending college in higher numbers than ever before.

The number of women in the workforce continued to grow as well. Women with college degrees worked as nurses, teachers, librarians, and social workers.

Women were also finding new opportunities in politics. In 1923 suffrage leader Alice Paul introduced the Equal Rights Amendment to Congress, calling for equality of rights regardless of a person's gender. The U.S. Senate passed the amendment 49 years later, but it was never ratified by the states. In 1925 Nellie Tayloe Ross (Wyoming) and Miriam "Ma" Ferguson (Texas) became the first women to serve as governors in the United States. Three years later, there were 145 women serving in state legislatures. Five women had won terms in the U.S. House of Representatives.

Still, women were discouraged from careers in medicine, law, and architecture. By the end of the 1920s, less than 5 percent of the country's doctors, lawyers, and architects were women. The percentage was small—but it was beginning to rise.

Some young women found other ways, including fashion, to express their freedom. Young women known as **flappers** cut their hair short and wore makeup and short dresses, openly challenging traditional ideas of how women were supposed to behave. Many older Americans considered this behavior scandalous. One 1920s writer expressed her admiration for flappers, by saying about her daughter:

> "I want my girl to do what she pleases, be what she pleases. . . . I want her to be a flapper, because flappers are brave."
>
> —Zelda Fitzgerald, quoted in *Zelda*, by Nancy Milford

Reading Check
Summarize How did women in the 1920s express their independence?

Fashion magazines, Hollywood movies, and advertising helped promote these new images and ideas of youthful freedom.

Fear and Violence

Not all social changes during the 1920s were peaceful. You have read about the hard times that hit the U.S. economy after World War I—unemployment, inflation, and labor disputes that resulted in large strikes.

These troubles worried many Americans. In this atmosphere, suspicion of foreigners and radicals, or people who believe in an extreme change in government, sometimes led to violence.

The Red Scare After the Communists took power in Russia in 1917, many Americans began to fear Communist ideas. They worried that Communists would soon try to gain power in the United States. This fear increased when millions of American workers went on strike in 1919. Many Americans blamed Communists and radicals for the upheaval.

These attitudes led to a **Red Scare**, a time of fear of Communists, or Reds. The Red Scare began in April 1919, when U.S. postal workers found bombs hidden in several packages addressed to famous Americans. Officials never found out who sent the bombs, but they suspected members of the Communist Party.

In June a bomb exploded outside the home of Attorney General A. Mitchell Palmer. Palmer responded by organizing police raids to break up Communists and other groups. In what became known as the Palmer raids, government agents arrested thousands of suspected radicals, often without evidence. Palmer frightened the public by warning that radicals were planning a revolution.

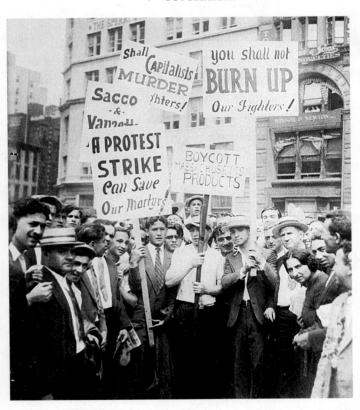

Sacco and Vanzetti

Supporters of Sacco and Vanzetti held rallies and raised money for the immigrants' defense. The men were found guilty and were executed in 1927.

Why did the Sacco and Vanzetti case become so famous?

The Red Scare led to one of the best-known criminal cases in American history. In 1920 police arrested Italian-born anarchists Nicola Sacco and Bartolomeo Vanzetti for the robbery and murder of a factory paymaster and his guard. (Anarchists are people opposed to organized government.) Though both men declared themselves innocent of the crime, Sacco and Vanzetti were found guilty. The American Civil Liberties Union (ACLU), founded in 1920 to defend people's civil rights, tried unsuccessfully to get the verdict overturned. Sacco and Vanzetti were convicted. They were executed in 1927.

Restricting Immigration Some people thought that a general fear of foreigners from different ethnic groups influenced the Sacco and Vanzetti case. Many recent immigrants were poor and did not speak English. Some Americans saw them as a threat to their jobs and culture. Immigrants "fill places that belong to the loyal wage-earning citizens of America," said Alabama senator James Thomas Heflin.

The government responded to these concerns with new laws. Immigration legislation, such as the Emergency Quota Act of 1921, limited the total number of immigrants

Reading Check
Draw Conclusions
Why were new immigration laws passed in the 1920s?

allowed into the country. It also favored immigrants from western Europe. The National Origins Act of 1924 banned immigration from East Asia entirely. It also further reduced the number of immigrants allowed to enter the country. These laws caused a dramatic drop in immigration to the United States.

Competing Ideals

Fear of radical ideas and foreigners was part of a larger clash over ideals and values in America. In these social conflicts, differences were growing between older, rural traditions and the beliefs and practices of modern urban society. Americans had very different ideas about what was best for the country's future.

Prohibition An issue that highlighted this conflict was prohibition. The Eighteenth Amendment went into effect in 1920. It outlawed the manufacture, sale, and transportation of alcoholic beverages. Support for prohibition was strongest in rural areas, while opposition was strongest in cities.

Government officials found it nearly impossible to enforce prohibition. Congress passed the Volstead Act. This act set fines and punishments for disobeying prohibition. Even respectable citizens, however, broke the law. Many people found ways to make alcohol at home using household products. Others bought alcohol at speakeasies, or illegal bars.

Organized criminals called bootleggers quickly seized control of the illegal alcohol business. They made their own alcohol or smuggled it in from Canada or Mexico. Gangsters bribed local police and politicians to avoid arrest. Competition between gangs often led to violent fighting. In Chicago, gangster Al "Scarface" Capone murdered his rivals to gain control of the alcohol trade. By 1927 Capone was earning more than $60 million a year from his illegal businesses.

Historical Source

Prohibition

Agents of federal and state governments tried to enforce the Eighteenth Amendment against great odds. They usually destroyed any liquor that they found. This photograph shows an illegal barrel of beer being broken with an ax. More illegal beer and liquor would soon turn up, however. Faced with a lack of public support and an impossible task of enforcing the ban on alcohol, prohibition was repealed with the Twenty-First Amendment in 1933.

Analyze Historical Sources
Why was enforcing prohibition such a hard task?

By the end of the decade, the nation was weary of the effects and impact of prohibition. The law had reduced alcohol consumption but had not stopped Americans from drinking. Prohibition had also created new ways for criminals to grow rich. Without government supervision of alcohol production, much of the alcohol consumed in speakeasies was more dangerous than what had been produced before prohibition. Many people came to believe that it would be better to have a legal alcohol trade that the government could monitor. In 1933 state and federal governments responded with the **Twenty-First Amendment**. This amendment ended prohibition. It made the manufacture and sale of alcohol legal again, but laws today still regulate drinking. The National Minimum Drinking Age Act of 1984 raised the minimum drinking age from 18 to 21 in every state.

Religious Ideals Youth culture of the 1920s and prohibition's failure concerned many religious leaders and religious groups. They saw these changes as movements away from **traditional** values. This led to a Protestant religious movement known as **fundamentalism**. Fundamentalism was characterized by the belief in a literal, or word-for-word, interpretation

Academic Vocabulary
traditional
customary, time-honored

Historical Sources

The Scopes Trial

The focus of the Scopes trial was whether or not John Scopes had broken the law. Prosecution witness **William Jennings Bryan**, however, saw the conflict as one between science and faith.

"*Science is a magnificent force, but it is not a teacher of morals. It can perfect machinery, but it adds no moral restraints to protect society from the misuse of the machine. . . . The [Scopes] case has assumed the proportions of a battle-royal [a struggle involving many people] between unbelief that attempts to speak through so-called science and the defenders of the Christian faith.*"

—William Jennings Bryan, from Bryan's Last Speech: *Undelivered Speech to the Jury in the Scopes Trial*

Clarence Darrow saw the conflict as a battle over free speech.

"*If today you can take a thing like evolution and make it a crime to teach it in the public school, tomorrow you can make it a crime to teach it in the private schools, and the next year you can make it a crime to teach it . . . in the church. At the next session you may ban books and the newspapers. Soon you may set Catholic against Protestant and Protestant against Protestant, and try to foist [force] your own religion upon the minds of men.*"

—Clarence Darrow, from the Scopes trial"

Analyze Historical Sources
Why did Darrow believe the Scopes trial was about free speech?

of the Bible. Popular preachers like Aimee Semple McPherson used the radio and modern marketing tools to draw followers. Fundamentalism was especially strong in rural areas and small towns. In these areas, people often blamed society's problems on the culture of urban areas.

Many fundamentalists believed that modern scientific theories conflicted with the teachings of the Bible. This included theories such as Charles Darwin's theory of evolution. Darwin's theory states that species evolve over time by adapting to their environment. To fundamentalists, this contradicted the biblical account of how the world was made. They opposed the teaching of evolution in public schools. Many cities and states passed laws to prevent the teaching of evolution.

In May 1925 a Dayton, Tennessee, high school science teacher named John T. Scopes was put on trial for teaching evolution. This became known as the **Scopes trial**. The fact that famous Americans represented each side heightened national interest in the event. Criminal attorney Clarence Darrow led the ACLU defense team. Three-time presidential candidate William Jennings Bryan assisted the prosecution.

Over live radio, Darrow and Bryan attacked each other's ideas. After more than a week on trial, Scopes was convicted and fined $100 for breaking the law. The state supreme court later overturned his conviction, but the debate over evolution continued.

Minority Rights

During World War I large numbers of African Americans began leaving the South to take jobs in northern factories. This movement, or migration, continued during the economic boom of the 1920s. It was called the **Great Migration**. While African Americans found jobs in the North, they did not escape racism. During the Great Migration, northern cities, such as New York City, grew.

Racial Tensions The economic recession that followed the war led to increased racial tensions. Many white laborers feared the competition for jobs. Several race riots broke out. In 1919, a race riot in Chicago left 38 dead. This riot was considered the worst of the approximately 25 riots that occurred during the Red Summer of 1919. In 1921 a group of whites attacked a community of African Americans in Tulsa, Oklahoma. This resulted in the businesses and homes of the Greenwood District being destroyed. At that time the Greenwood District was the wealthiest black community in the United States.

The Silent Parade, also called the Silent March or the Silent Protest Parade, happened on July 28, 1917, in New York City. The parade was partially a response to the East St. Louis riots in May and July 1917. White mobs killed between 40 and 250 blacks in these riots. In the Silent Parade between 8,000 and 10,000 African Americans marched. They protested lynching and anti-black violence. The National Association for the Advancement of Colored People, or NAACP, organized the parade. This was one of the first parades of this kind in New York City. It was also one of the first instances of blacks publicly demonstrating for civil rights.

Reading Check
Analyze Information
What cultural conflict did the Scopes trial represent?

The Great Migration

From 1940 to 1941, artist Jacob Lawrence created a series of paintings. They told the story of African Americans moving from the South to northern cities in search of jobs and equality. This is one of 60 paintings in the Migration Series. It shows African Americans about to begin their journey.

Draw Conclusions
Where are the people in the painting going?

Racial tensions and fear of foreigners helped give rise to a new form of the Ku Klux Klan. This racist group had terrorized African Americans during Reconstruction. The new Klan harassed Catholics, Jews, and immigrants, as well as African Americans. It also worked against urbanization, women's rights, and modern technology. By the mid-1920s the Klan had more than 5 million members. It had become an influential force in American politics. Its influence then began to decline as news of financial corruption became public.

Protecting Rights People who were the targets of the Klan's hatred found new ways to protect their rights. In 1922, for example, the NAACP began placing advertisements in newspapers. The ads presented the harsh facts about the large number of lynchings taking place across the South.

Another way minorities tried to protect their rights was to strengthen their culture. During the 1910s and 1920s, **Marcus Garvey** encouraged black people around the world to express pride in their culture. Garvey argued that black people should build their own businesses and communities to establish economic independence. These ideas were the basis of a movement known as black nationalism. The *New York Amsterdam News* praised Garvey's work, saying he "made black people proud of their race."

Hispanic Americans also organized to fight prejudice and promote civil rights. In 1929 Mexican American leaders met in Corpus Christi, Texas, to form the League of United Latin American Citizens (LULAC). This group worked to end unfair treatment such as segregation in schools and voting restrictions.

Most Native Americans lacked the legal protections of citizenship and the right to vote because they were not citizens of the United States. The

Marcus Garvey 1887–1940

Marcus Garvey grew up in Jamaica and moved to the United States in 1916. A talented speaker, he quickly became one of the country's most famous and controversial black leaders. His newspaper *Negro World* promoted the idea of building an independent black economy. To encourage worldwide trade among black people, he created the Black Star Steamship Line. Some black leaders, including W.E.B. Du Bois, considered Garvey's ideas dangerous and extremist. After a series of legal problems related to his steamship company, Garvey was arrested in 1922 and was later deported.

Make Inferences
How did Marcus Garvey try to help African Americans?

Reading Check
Find Main Ideas
How did minorities react to discrimination in the 1920s?

fact that thousands of Native Americans had performed military service in World War I helped bring about change. In 1924 Congress passed the Indian Citizenship Act. The act granted citizenship to all Native Americans. However, the federal government also attempted to buy or take back some of the reservation lands. Native Americans successfully organized to stop these attempts, which were part of a larger effort to encourage Indians to adopt the culture of white Americans.

Summary and Preview Americans saw many conflicts as their culture changed. In the next lesson you will learn about entertainment and the arts in the 1920s.

Lesson 2 Assessment

Review Ideas, Terms, and People

1. **a. Recall** How did flappers express their freedom?
   b. Elaborate How were young people of the 1920s more independent than their parents?

2. **a. Identify** What caused the Red Scare, and what was its result?
   b. Explain Describe the results of the immigration laws of the 1920s.

3. **a. Recall** What kinds of social conflicts developed during the 1920s?
   b. Describe What did the Twenty-First Amendment accomplish?
   c. Analyze How did fundamentalism influence the Scopes trial?

4. **a. Identify** How did minorities fight for their rights in the 1920s?

   b. Recall What was the Great Migration?
   c. Draw Conclusions Why did Marcus Garvey call for African Americans to build their own businesses?

Critical Thinking

5. **Identify Cause and Effect** In this lesson you learned about the social changes that took place in the 1920s. Create a chart similar to the one below and use it to identify the causes and effects of several changes in American society.

Cause		Effect
	→	
	→	
	→	

The Jazz Age

The Big Idea

Musicians, artists, actors, and writers contributed to American popular culture in the 1920s.

Main Ideas

- Radio and movies linked the country in a national culture.
- Jazz and blues music became popular nationwide.
- Writers and artists introduced new styles and artistic ideas.

Key Terms and People

talkie
Jazz Age
Harlem Renaissance
Langston Hughes
Lost Generation
expatriates
Georgia O'Keeffe

If YOU were there . . .

The year is 1924. The New York Giants are playing the Washington Senators in the World Series. You just bought your first radio, and you are listening to an announcer describe the tense action as the seventh and deciding game goes into extra innings. You used to have to wait to read about the games in the newspaper. Now you can follow your favorite team pitch by pitch!

What other forms of entertainment could the radio bring to you?

A National Culture

On November 2, 1920, KDKA, the first commercial radio station, announced that Warren Harding had won the presidential election held that day. Just one year later, stations broadcast the action from the 1921 World Series. One newspaper writer predicted, "It might not be too long before farmers at the four corners of the Union may sit in their own houses and hear the president of the United States." Such an event seemed amazing to Americans in the early 1900s. But it quickly became a reality. Soon, hundreds of radio stations began broadcasting all over the United States.

National radio networks, such as the National Broadcasting Company (NBC) and Columbia Broadcasting System (CBS), allowed people all over the country to listen to the same programs. People suddenly had access to music, news, weather reports, children's bedtime stories, sports broadcasts, and political speeches without leaving their homes. Business owners loved this technology. It allowed their advertisements to reach millions of listeners. Radio helped build a new national culture by allowing Americans everywhere to share common experiences.

Movies also became a major national passion in the 1920s. Early motion pictures had no sound. However, they opened a new world of exciting adventures for audiences. People packed theaters to see Westerns, romances, and stories about bootlegging gangsters. The 1927 movie *The Jazz Singer* thrilled movie fans. In the movie, actor Al Jolson shouted the line "You ain't heard nothin' yet!" This was the first **talkie**, or motion picture with sound.

The movies quickly became big business. By the end of the decade, Americans were buying 95 million movie tickets each week. This was an amazing figure, considering that the U.S. population was only 123 million.

Young movie fans copied hair and clothing styles of movie stars. Fans felt a personal connection to stars like Douglas Fairbanks, Charlie Chaplin, and Mary Pickford, who was known as "America's Sweetheart." Few fans at the time realized that Pickford was also a smart businesswoman. She was one of the highest paid actors in Hollywood and a founder of United Artists, one of the nation's most successful film companies.

Movie stars were not the only national heroes. Fans packed baseball stadiums to watch the great players of the 1920s, especially George Herman "Babe" Ruth. Ruth shattered home-run records, drawing thousands of new fans to the sport. Because baseball was segregated, African American players and business leaders started their own league. Negro League stars such as Satchel Paige and Josh Gibson are considered to be among the best baseball players in history.

Fans always loved to see athletes break records. In 1926 American swimmer Gertrude Ederle became the first woman to swim the English Channel between England and France. Ederle beat the men's world record by almost two hours.

Pilots also became national heroes in the 1920s. Charles Lindbergh dominated the national news in 1927. He completed the first nonstop solo flight across the Atlantic Ocean, traveling from New York to Paris. A few years later, Amelia Earhart became the first woman to fly solo across the Atlantic.

New ideas like psychoanalysis became more popular. Developed by physician Sigmund Freud, psychoanalysis is a method for examining human behavior to find out why people behave the way they do.

Charles Lindbergh specially modified his plane, the *Spirit of St. Louis,* for his transatlantic flight.

Reading Check
Summarize
How did American culture change during the 1920s?

Popular Music

With a booming economy and exciting forms of entertainment, the 1920s became known as the Roaring Twenties. An explosion in the popularity of jazz music gave the decade another nickname—the **Jazz Age**.

Jazz developed in New Orleans. African American musicians in this city blended spirituals with European harmonies and West African rhythms. When African Americans moved north during the Great Migration, they brought their music with them.

As with many new forms of popular culture, jazz sparked arguments between older and younger generations. "When my grandmother found out that I was playing jazz music . . . she told me that I had disgraced the family," remembered "Jelly Roll" Morton, an early jazz composer. But young Americans loved the music and the wild, fast-paced dances that went along with it. Dance crazes sweeping the nation included the Charleston, the Toddle, and the Shimmy. New magazines arose that taught dance steps to subscribers.

1920 — 1928

1920
Babe Ruth begins playing for the New York Yankees. >

1924 ∧
First Negro League World Series is played.

1925 ∧
Louis Armstrong begins recording with his band, the Hot Five.

1925
F. Scott Fitzgerald's *The Great Gatsby* is published.

1926
Gertrude Ederle becomes the first woman to swim across the English Channel.

1926
NBC, the first national radio network, begins broadcasting.

1927
Charles Lindbergh completes the first nonstop solo flight across the Atlantic Ocean.

1927
The Jazz Singer, the first full-length talkie, is released.

Interpret Timelines
Which events reflected people's interest in breaking records?

Jazz musicians such as Louis Armstrong experimented with various sounds and rhythms to create a new kind of music. Armstrong, who played the trumpet, was known for his solo numbers. His method of stepping out from the band to perform a solo was an **innovation** that is still copied by musicians today. Another major figure of the Jazz Age was conductor and composer Edward "Duke" Ellington. His "big band" sound blended many instruments together in songs such as "Take the A Train." Ellington described the exciting life of Jazz Age musicians in New York City:

"A lot of guys liked to play so much that in spite of being on a regular job, they'd still hire out to work matinees, or breakfast dances. . . . Nobody went to bed at nights and round three or four in the mornings you'd find everyone making the rounds bringing their horns with them."

—Duke Ellington, quoted in *Reminiscing in Tempo*, by Stuart Nicholson

Reading Check
Find Main Ideas Where did jazz originate, and what musical styles influenced it?

Blues music came from the rural South of the Mississippi delta. It also gained national popularity in the 1920s. Blues began as an expression of the suffering of African Americans during slavery. One of the leading blues singers of the 1920s was Bessie Smith, nicknamed the Empress of the Blues. "She had music in her soul," said Louis Armstrong.

Writers and Artists

As new forms of music were being created, writers and artists were also reshaping culture. Many works of the 1920s are still admired today.

The Harlem Renaissance Many of the African Americans who came north in the Great Migration built a thriving community in the Harlem neighborhood of New York City. This community became the center of the **Harlem Renaissance**, a period of African American artistic accomplishment. Artists of the Harlem Renaissance celebrated the cultural traditions and the life experiences of African Americans.

Harlem Renaissance writers included **Langston Hughes** and Claude McKay. Hughes produced poems, plays, and novels about African American life. His works often incorporated African American slang and jazz rhythms. McKay was a poet and activist. He spoke out against racial discrimination and called on African Americans to stand up against lynchings and other violence. Another important writer of the Harlem Renaissance was Zora Neale Hurston. Her novels, such as *Their Eyes Were Watching God*, reflected the experiences of African American women.

The Lost Generation Other Americans also wrote of their experiences living in the United States and in places around the world. Soon after he graduated from high school in Illinois, Ernest Hemingway volunteered as an ambulance driver in World War I. Hemingway called the war "the most colossal, murderous, mismanaged butchery that had ever taken place on earth." He began writing short stories and novels. Soon, he gained fame for his powerful and direct writing. Hemingway was among a group of young American writers who expressed disillusionment in the American society. They felt it denied them a voice in their own futures. Author Gertrude Stein called these writers "a lost generation." Writers who criticized American society in the 1920s thus became known as the **Lost Generation**.

Many members of the Lost Generation moved to Paris in the 1920s. They formed a community of **expatriates**—people who leave their home country to live elsewhere. Hemingway wrote about the expatriate community in his best-selling novel *The Sun Also Rises*. Another Lost Generation writer was F. Scott Fitzgerald, who wrote *The Great Gatsby*. His novel focused on what he saw as the loss of morality behind the seemingly fun and free-spirited times of the Jazz Age. Another writer of the time, Sinclair Lewis, became the first American to receive the Nobel Prize in literature.

Historical Sources

America

In one of his most celebrated poems, Claude McKay expressed his conflicted feelings about the United States. The poem describes how he feels resentment, love, and admiration for the country all at the same time.

Analyze Historical Sources
Who do you think McKay is referring to when he speaks of "her"?

"Although she feeds me bread of bitterness,
And sinks into my throat her tiger's tooth,
Stealing my breath of life, I will confess
I love this cultured hell that tests my youth!
Her vigor flows like tides into my blood,
Giving me strength erect against her hate.
Her bigness sweeps my being like a flood.
Yet as a rebel fronts a king in state,
I stand within her walls with not a shred
Of terror, malice, not a word of jeer.
Darkly I gaze into the days ahead,
And see her might and granite wonders there,
Beneath the touch of Time's unerring hand,
Like priceless treasures sinking in the sand."

Georgia O'Keeffe 1887–1986

Georgia O'Keeffe grew up in Wisconsin and studied art in Chicago and New York. While teaching art at a college in Canyon, Texas, she would sometimes hike in Palo Duro Canyon, where she sketched scenes of amazing colors and rock formations. This was the start of a lifelong fascination with the beauty of the desert landscape. O'Keeffe lived much of her life in rural New Mexico, where many of her paintings were created. Animal bones, rocks, and desert flowers fill her works. She would often paint these objects in close-up view, showing tiny details. O'Keeffe said, "Most people in the city rush around so, they have no time to look at a flower. I want them to see it whether they want to or not."

Find Main Ideas
How did Georgia O'Keeffe's life influence her painting?

New Directions in Art Painters were also experimenting with new artistic styles in the 1920s. Edward Hopper painted images of the loneliness of modern urban life. **Georgia O'Keeffe** was well known for her detailed paintings of flowers and of the Southwest.

Architects of the 1920s embraced a style they called art deco. Buildings constructed in this style had clean, sharp lines that resembled machines. Today, art deco skyscrapers still stand out in American skylines. New York City's Chrysler and Empire State Buildings are examples of art deco style.

In 1929, the Museum of Modern Art in New York City was founded. Photography was also being accepted as an art form during this time.

Summary and Preview Americans became interested in new forms of entertainment and art in the 1920s. In the next module you will learn about how life changed in the 1930s.

Reading Check
Compare and Contrast How were the artists of the Harlem Renaissance and the Lost Generation similar and different?

Lesson 3 Assessment

Review Ideas, Terms, and People

1. a. Recall What new forms of entertainment dominated American society during the 1920s?

b. Identify What was the first talkie?

2. a. Explain Why were the 1920s called the Jazz Age?

b. Make Inferences Why do you think jazz music became so popular?

3. a. Recall How did writers and artists express new ideas during the 1920s?

b. Describe What did the Lost Generation writers express in their works?

c. Predict How might the artists of the Harlem Renaissance influence African American artists of later generations?

Critical Thinking

4. Categorize In this lesson you learned about the popular culture in the 1920s. Create a chart similar to the one below and use it to categorize examples of popular culture in the 1920s.

Social Studies Skills

Compare Graphs

Define the Skill

Graphs are often a very useful way to organize historical information. They can present a large amount of detailed information clearly. Graphs can be an especially good way of showing how something like population or average income changed over time.

When information is organized in a graph, it is often easy to see patterns. Looking at two related graphs, you can compare patterns and make conclusions. For example, you can ask yourself, "Do the numbers in the graphs go up or down for the same reasons? What are the causes behind the changes shown by these graphs?"

Learn the Skill

These guidelines will help you to compare information in two or more graphs.

1. Use your basic graph-interpreting skills. Identify each graph's subject, purpose, and type. Study its parts and categories.

2. Analyze the data in each graph. Then compare any increases, decreases, changes, or patterns you find.

3. Finally, draw conclusions about the relationship between the information in each graph. Think about what could cause such relationships. It will probably help you to review what you know about related events at the same time.

Practice the Skill

Compare the graphs below to answer the following questions.

1. What are the topics of these graphs?

2. What percentage of American households had electricity in 1922? What was the first year when more than half of American households had electricity?

3. Based on the information in the graphs, draw a conclusion about how electricity changed American households.

Source: Historical Atlas of the United States

Module 25 Assessment

Review Vocabulary, Terms, and People

Complete each sentence by filling in the blank with the correct term or person from the module.

1. Harlem Renaissance writer _____ wrote poems, plays, and novels about African American life.

2. The United States and other nations signed the _____, which outlawed war.

3. In the _____, Clarence Darrow defended a high school teacher tried for teaching evolution.

4. The _____ repealed prohibition.

5. Writers who criticized American culture during the 1920s were known as the _____.

6. African Americans moved north for jobs during the _____.

Comprehension and Critical Thinking

Lesson 1

7. a. **Describe** What was President Warren Harding's plan for strengthening the U.S. economy?

    b. **Explain** What methods did Henry Ford's competitors use to attract customers?

    c. **Elaborate** What do you think might have made the Kellogg-Briand Pact more effective?

Lesson 2

8. a. **Recall** What was the Red Scare?

    b. **Analyze** What are some reasons women had more opportunities in the 1920s?

    c. **Evaluate** Would you have become involved in the youth culture if you had lived during the 1920s? Why or why not?

Lesson 3

9. a. **Identify** What were talkies?

    b. **Explain** How did African Americans play an important role in Jazz Age culture?

    c. **Predict** How do you think new aspects of American culture affected life after the 1920s?

Review Themes

10. **Society and Culture** How did the prosperity of the 1920s change American culture?

11. **Science and Technology** What new forms of technology emerged in the 1920s?

Social Studies Skills

Compare Graphs *Use the Social Studies Skills taught in this module to answer the question below.*

12. Look back at the line graphs in the Social Studies Skills. Do you think a graph showing the number of radio stations in the United States during the 1920s would look similar to these graphs? Explain your answer.

Reading Skills 21ST CENTURY

Synthesize Information *Use the Reading Skills taught in this module to answer the question below.*

> The number of women in the workforce continued to grow as well. Women with college degrees worked as nurses, teachers, librarians, and social workers. . . . Women were still discouraged from pursuing fields such as medicine, law, and architecture, however. By the end of the 1920s, less than 5 percent of the country's doctors, lawyers, and architects were women. The percentage was small—but it was beginning to rise.

13. Which of the following sources might have been used to synthesize the information above?
    a. a history of architecture
    b. an instructional manual for nurses
    c. a history of working women in the 1920s
    d. the list of graduates from a women's college in 1910

Focus on Writing

14. **Write a Radio Advertisement** Radio stations began to air regular broadcasts in the 1920s. Radios linked Americans from coast to coast, allowing them to hear the same programs and the same advertisements. In the 1920s Americans with means could afford to buy various products and could choose different entertainment, travel, fashion, and convenience. Choose one product that was popular in the 1920s that is mentioned in the module. Write a radio ad for that product. Think about these questions as you design your radio ad: Who is your audience? How will this product improve people's lives? What words or sounds will best describe your product? Write the dialogue for your ad, including directions for the actors. Also, include information about music or sound effects you want to use.

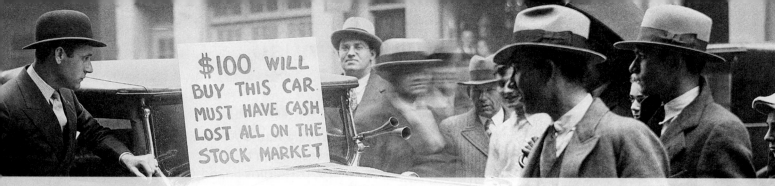

Module 26
The Great Depression

⭐

Essential Question
Was the Great Depression inevitable?

About the Photo: The Great Depression forced many people to sell everything they owned just to survive.

In this module you will learn about how Americans coped with the economic problems of the 1930s. You will also learn about the Dust Bowl and its effects.

What You Will Learn ...

Lesson 1: The End of Prosperity **802**
The Big Idea The collapse of the stock market in 1929 helped lead to the start of the Great Depression.

Lesson 2: Roosevelt's New Deal **809**
The Big Idea Franklin Roosevelt's New Deal included government programs designed to relieve unemployment and help the economy recover.

Lesson 3: Americans Face Hard Times **816**
The Big Idea All over the country, Americans struggled to survive the Great Depression.

▶ *Explore ONLINE!*

HISTORY.

VIDEOS, including...
- The Great Depression
- Run on Banks
- FDR's Fireside Chat
- Tennessee Valley Authority
- FDR's New Deal

☑ Document-Based Investigations

☑ Graphic Organizers

☑ Interactive Games

☑ Image with Hotspots: Blame It on Hoover

☑ Image with Hotspots: Packing the Supreme Court

☑ Interactive Map: The Dust Bowl, 1933–1936

United States | 1925 | **World**

1929 The U.S. stock market crashes on Black Tuesday.

1930 Mahatma Gandhi and a group of followers begin the Salt March.

∧ **1932** Franklin D. Roosevelt wins his first presidential election, beating Herbert Hoover.

1932 At least 30 million people worldwide are unemployed.

1933 Adolf Hitler becomes chancellor of Germany. >

1935 The CIO is organized.

1936 Jesse Owens wins four gold medals at the Berlin Olympics.

1937 The Social Security Act is ruled constitutional by the U.S. Supreme Court.

1937 War officially begins between Japan and China.

1938 Violence against German Jews erupts into *Kristallnacht* ("night of broken glass").

< **1939** The film *The Wizard of Oz* is released.

1940

Reading Social Studies

Economics, Politics

In this module you will learn about the Great Depression, one of the most serious economic crises in America's history. You will also learn about the politics that arose to try to deal with this crisis. Finally, you will read about how the Depression affected the global economy and how world leaders responded to it.

READING FOCUS:
Recognize Implied Main Ideas

When you read, you will notice that not every paragraph has a main idea sentence. Sometimes the main idea is implied.

Implied Main Ideas While main ideas give a basic structure to a paragraph, supporting details help convince the reader of the author's point. Main ideas can be presented in a sentence, or simply implied. Usually, a paragraph without a main idea sentence will still have an implied main idea that ties the sentences together.

Notice how one reader found the main idea of the following paragraph.

During the boom years of the 1920s, one General Motors executive boldly declared: "Anyone not only can be rich, but ought to be rich." For almost all of the Roaring Twenties, the stock market was a bull market, or one with rising stock values. It seemed easy to make money by investing in stocks. For example, you could have bought shares in the Radio Corporation of America for $85 each at the beginning of 1928. You could have sold them a year later for $549 each.

> This quote is about making money and being rich. Maybe the main idea is about money or economics.

> This sentence is about making money through the stock market. I guess the main idea has to do with investing.

> Here is a great example of how easy it was to make money in the 1920s. I think the main idea is something like "The stock market provided an easy way for many to become rich in the 1920s."

You Try It!

Read the following paragraph and then answer the questions below.

The action began when Roosevelt called Congress into a special session. Known as the Hundred Days, the session started just after the inauguration and lasted until the middle of June. During the Hundred Days, Roosevelt and Congress worked together to create new programs to battle the Depression and aid economic recovery. These programs became known as the New Deal.

1. List two ideas that this paragraph discusses.
2. How are these two ideas related to each other?
3. Write an example of the main idea of this paragraph.
4. Which details support your main idea?

As you read Module 26, think of a main idea for any paragraph that does not have a main idea sentence.

Key Terms and People

Lesson 1
buying on margin
Black Tuesday
business cycle
Great Depression
Bonus Army
Franklin D. Roosevelt

Lesson 2
New Deal
fireside chats
Tennessee Valley Authority
Frances Perkins
Eleanor Roosevelt
Social Security Act
Congress of Industrial Organizations
sit-down strike

Lesson 3
Dust Bowl
Mary McLeod Bethune
John Steinbeck
Woody Guthrie

The End of Prosperity

The Big Idea

The collapse of the stock market in 1929 helped lead to the start of the Great Depression.

Main Ideas

- The U.S. stock market crashed in 1929.
- The economy collapsed after the stock market crash.
- Many Americans were dissatisfied with Hoover's reaction to economic conditions.
- Roosevelt defeated Hoover in the election of 1932.

Key Terms and People

buying on margin
Black Tuesday
business cycle
Great Depression
Bonus Army
Franklin D. Roosevelt

If YOU were there . . .

For almost a year you've been working part-time at a neighborhood store. You earn money for your family and still have time to go to school. But when you arrive at work today, your boss says business has been so bad that he can't afford to pay you anymore. With your father out of work, your family had been counting on your income from this job.

How can you continue earning money to help your family?

The Stock Market Crashes

During the boom years of the 1920s, one General Motors executive boldly declared: "Anyone not only can be rich, but ought to be rich." Many people relied on the stock market to increase their wealth. The stock market is a market that people can use to buy or sell shares of ownership in a company. For almost all of the Roaring Twenties, the stock market was a bull market, or one with rising stock values. It seemed easy to make money by investing in stocks. For example, you could have bought shares in the Radio Corporation of America for $85 each at the beginning of 1928. You could have sold them a year later for $549 each.

The chance to make huge profits from small investments encouraged many people to buy stocks. Some people could not afford the stocks' full price. They began **buying on margin**—purchasing stocks on credit, or with borrowed money. These stockholders planned to sell the stocks at a higher price. Then they would pay back the loan and keep what remained as profit. But this plan was risky because it only worked if stock values went up. Few considered what would happen if the bull market turned into a bear market, or one with declining stock prices.

The Federal Reserve Board became concerned about the growing popularity of buying on margin. In the late 1920s the Board tried to make it more difficult and more costly for

Black Tuesday

More than 16 million shares were traded on Wall Street on Black Tuesday, a record that stood for 39 years. Just weeks later, roughly one-third of the value of the stock market had disappeared.

Stock Prices, March 1929–January 1930

Analyze Graphs
How are the events of Black Tuesday shown on the graph?

brokers to offer margin loans to investors. These actions helped decrease the amount that brokers borrowed from banks. However, soon, brokers began borrowing from large corporations and the risky investing practice continued.

Stock prices peaked in the late summer of 1929. Then prices started to drop. Frightened investors who had bought stocks on margin rushed to sell their stocks in order to pay off their loans. On Thursday, October 24, panic hit the stock market. Within three hours the market had lost $11 billion in value. The following Monday, prices dropped again. On Tuesday, October 29—a day that became known as **Black Tuesday**—the stock market crashed. So many people wanted to sell their stocks, and so few wanted to buy, that stock prices collapsed. One journalist described the nightmare:

"The wires to other cities were jammed with frantic orders to sell [stock]. So were the cables, radio, and telephones to Europe and the rest of the world. Buyers were few, sometimes wholly absent . . . This was real panic . . . When the closing bell rang, the great bull market was dead and buried."

—Jonathan Norton Leonard, from *Three Years Down*

In September 1929 the total value of all stocks was $87 billion. Less than two months later, more than $30 billion in stock value had disappeared. Investors who had bought stocks on margin became stuck with large debts.

Reading Check
Analyze Information
Why was buying on margin risky?

The Economy Collapses

President Herbert Hoover tried to calm public fears by assuring Americans that the economy was still strong. "The fundamental business of the country . . . is on a sound and prosperous basis," he said. But this was just the beginning of more than ten years of economic hard times.

The Banking Crisis One immediate effect of the stock market crash was a banking crisis. Banks had invested heavily in the stock market, so they lost heavily when the market crashed. Banks had also lent their customers money to buy stocks on margin. Now those customers were unable to pay back their loans. Some banks went out of business. People who had deposited their life savings in those banks lost everything.

This created a panic all over the country, as customers rushed to their banks to withdraw their money. But since banks usually do not keep enough cash on hand to cover all deposits, the banks soon ran out of money. Many had to close their doors. In 1931 alone, more than 2,200 banks closed. The banking crisis contributed to a business crisis. Some businesses lost their savings in failed banks and had to close. Others were forced to cut back production, which meant they needed fewer workers. Nearly 3 million people lost their jobs. In the last three months of 1929, U.S. unemployment soared from under half a million workers to more than 4 million.

Unemployment during the Depression

Connect to Economics People are considered unemployed if they are trying to find work but do not have a job. High rates of unemployment hurt the economy because unemployed people cannot buy many goods and services. This causes businesses to lose money.

Unemployment, 1929–1941

Analyze Graphs
During what year was unemployment the highest?

The Causes Throughout the history of the United States, the economy has followed a pattern of ups and downs. When businesses produce more than they can sell, unsold goods pile up. Businesses then cut back on their production and lay off workers. People who have lost their jobs, and others who are afraid they might soon lose their jobs, buy fewer goods. This causes more businesses to fail. This economic event is called a recession. Deep and long-lasting recessions are known as depressions.

As time passes, an economy will tend to bounce back. Consumers buy surplus goods, and companies increase production to meet the demand. Soon, more workers are hired and unemployment drops. This up-and-down pattern, known as the **business cycle**, continues in today's economy.

The United States had experienced recessions and depressions before 1929. Each time, the economy followed the business cycle and recovered. But the economy did not recover quickly from the downturn that began in 1929. Because of its severity and length, it was called the **Great Depression**.

Historians and economists still debate the exact causes of the Great Depression. Some believe that the government's monetary policy was a cause. Others believe that limited market competition and protectionism, or restriction of trade, played a part. However, most agree that a major factor was the overproduction of goods at a time when the market for those goods was shrinking. Companies built millions of cars and appliances during the 1920s. By the late 1920s, however, most people who could afford these products already had bought them. That meant that American businesses were producing far more goods than people were consuming.

Uneven distribution of wealth made this problem worse. In 1929 the wealthiest 5 percent of Americans earned one-third of all income, while the bottom 40 percent earned only one-eighth of all income. Millions of Americans simply did not earn enough money to buy expensive new products. Many of them lost their jobs, their wealth, and their homes.

Declining world trade also hurt American manufacturers. Europeans were still recovering from World War I and could not afford many American goods. At the same time, high tariffs made it difficult for European nations to sell products to the United States. As a result, Europeans had even less money to buy American goods.

Hoover's Reaction

As unemployment skyrocketed, more and more Americans struggled just to feed themselves and their families. Hungry people searched city dumps for scraps of food. One woman remembered taking off her glasses when she cooked so she could not see the maggots in the meat her family was about to eat. Private charities, as well as state and local governments, set up soup kitchens and breadlines in New York and across the country. But the need far exceeded the available resources. Many people turned to President Herbert Hoover and the federal government to lead the relief effort.

Reading Check
Make Predictions
Do you think the Great Depression could have been avoided? How?

"Blame It on Hoover"

Presidents can affect the economy to some degree through their policies. During the Great Depression, President Hoover was blamed for the financial crisis. Political cartoons like this one gave voice to those Americans who thought Hoover could have prevented the crisis or could have brought it to an end quickly through government programs.

How does the cartoonist show Hoover reacting to the crisis?

What kind of people are blaming Hoover?

Analyze Historical Sources
Why is this cartoon useful for showing the feelings of the American public during the Great Depression?

A Most Vicious Circle
—Costello in the Albany "News."

Academic Vocabulary
implement put in place

Hoover knew that many Americans needed help. He did not believe, however, that it was the federal government's role to provide direct relief to Americans. Hoover felt it was up to private individuals and institutions, not the government, to offer relief. Despite this belief, Hoover did **implement** some new government programs. In 1932 he created the Reconstruction Finance Corporation (RFC). That year, the RFC loaned $1.2 billion to 5,000 different financial institutions, including banks and farm mortgage companies. Hoover continued to resist giving direct assistance to individuals.

This angered Americans who believed the president should do more to fix the economy. People bitterly referred to empty pockets turned inside out as Hoover flags. Groups of tin and cardboard shacks built by homeless families were nicknamed Hoovervilles. These camps were built in cities and towns across the United States from New York to Los Angeles.

In 1932 a new Hooverville was built in Washington, DC. Its more than 17,000 residents were World War I veterans, some with their families. Called the **Bonus Army**, they had come to the capital to demand early payment of a military bonus. After the government denied the payment, most of the veterans returned home. About 2,000, however, stayed in their shantytown.

President Hoover authorized General Douglas MacArthur to use U.S. troops to evict the Bonus Army. MacArthur used force, including tear gas and tanks, to scatter the veterans. Several veterans were killed. The public reacted with outrage to the government's treatment of war veterans. Americans would have a chance to express this frustration in the upcoming election.

Reading Check
Make Generalizations
How would you describe President Hoover's response to the Depression?

Election of 1932

The Republican Party nominated Herbert Hoover again for president in 1932, but few people believed he could win. Regarding his chances of re-election, even Hoover realized that "the prospects are dark." Still, he began campaigning hard for a second term.

He called the election "a contest between two philosophies of government." He warned that the government aid programs Democrats were promising would weaken Americans' spirit of self-reliance.

By 1932, however, much of the public had lost confidence in Hoover. His insistence on limited government action earned him the reputation as a "do-nothing" president. Many even blamed him for the Depression. In contrast, as governor of New York during the first years of the Depression, Democratic presidential candidate **Franklin D. Roosevelt** had taken active steps to provide aid. He directed the state government to provide relief for the state's citizens, especially farmers. He also helped establish the Temporary Emergency Relief Administration, which gave unemployment assistance to many out-of-work New Yorkers. Roosevelt's programs provided help for one in every ten New York families.

BIOGRAPHY

Franklin Delano Roosevelt
1882–1945

Roosevelt lived much of his life in New York State, where he served in the state senate and as governor. He also lived in Washington, DC, while he was serving as assistant secretary of the navy and later as president.

As president, he began the New Deal, a set of government programs designed to help the country survive and recover from the Great Depression. He gave many Americans hope for the future when he spoke to them in his fireside chats.

Roosevelt led the United States during two of the most serious crises that our country has ever faced: the Great Depression and World War II. He served as president for 12 years, longer than any other president.

"The only thing we have to fear is fear itself, nameless, unreasoning, unjustified terror."

—Franklin Roosevelt,
1933 inaugural address

Make Predictions
How do you think Franklin Roosevelt's experience as president during the Depression might have helped him lead the country during World War II?

Reading Check
Analyze Information
How did Franklin
D. Roosevelt win the
1932 presidential
election?

Roosevelt's confident and optimistic personality appealed to many voters. At the Democratic Party convention, Roosevelt declared to Americans: "I pledge you, I pledge myself, to a new deal for the American people." Voters responded overwhelmingly to this message of hope. Roosevelt won the 1932 election in a landslide. He received 57 percent of the popular vote and swept the electoral vote in all but six states. In addition, the Democrats won strong majorities in both houses of Congress.

Summary and Preview Overproduction of goods, buying stocks on margin, and other economic practices in the 1920s contributed to the start of the Great Depression. After the stock market crash and the start of the Great Depression, Franklin Roosevelt offered hope for the future. In the next lesson you will learn about his programs for relief.

Lesson 1 Assessment

Review Ideas, Terms, and People

1. **a. Recall** Why did the stock market crash in 1929?

   b. Compare How is buying on margin similar to buying on an installment plan?

2. **a. Recall** What happened to the economy as a result of the stock market crash?

   b. Explain Why did many banks close in the late 1920s and early 1930s?

   c. Compare What similarities does the economy in the 1920s and 1930s share with the economy today?

   d. Draw Conclusions What do you think was the goal of U.S. tariffs?

3. **a. Make Inferences** Why did many Americans blame President Hoover for the Depression?

   b. Describe What did the Bonus Army want?

   c. Elaborate Do you think Americans were justified in blaming Hoover for the hard times?

4. **a. Identify** Which party was more successful in the 1932 elections?

   b. Make Inferences Why do you think voters did not listen to Hoover's ideas about government?

   c. Elaborate How do you think Franklin D. Roosevelt's experiences as governor of New York helped him appeal to voters?

Critical Thinking

5. **Identify Cause and Effect** In this lesson you learned about the American economy in the 1920s and 1930s. Create a chart similar to the one below and use it to identify the economic causes of the Depression and their effects.

★ Roosevelt's New Deal

The Big Idea

Franklin Roosevelt's New Deal included government programs designed to relieve unemployment and help the economy recover.

Main Ideas

- Congress approved many new programs during the Hundred Days.

- Critics expressed concerns about the New Deal.

- New Deal programs continued through Roosevelt's first term in what became known as the Second New Deal.

- Roosevelt clashed with the Supreme Court over the New Deal.

Key Terms and People

New Deal
fireside chats
Tennessee Valley Authority
Frances Perkins
Eleanor Roosevelt
Social Security Act
Congress of Industrial
   Organizations
sit-down strike

If YOU were there . . .

It has been five months since you lost your job. One of your friends has found work in a new government program that is hiring young people to work in national parks and forests. The pay is low, and you would have to leave home, but you would have enough food, a place to live, and a little money to send back to your family every month.

Would you take a job with the Civilian Conservation Corps? Why or why not?

The Hundred Days

Immediately after taking the oath of office in March 1933, President Franklin Roosevelt spoke to the nation. In his first inaugural address, Roosevelt told nervous Americans that economic recovery was possible. "The only thing we have to fear is fear itself," he said, "nameless, unreasoning, unjustified terror." It was only fear of the future, he argued, that could keep America from moving forward. Roosevelt spoke openly of the severe problems facing the American people—unemployment, failing banks, and products with no markets. He promised that the government would help. "This nation asks for action," he said, "and action now."

The action began when Roosevelt called Congress into a special session. Known as the Hundred Days, the session started just after the inauguration and lasted until the middle of June. During the Hundred Days, Roosevelt and Congress worked together to create new programs to battle the Depression and aid economic recovery. These programs became known as the **New Deal**.

Restoring Confidence One of Roosevelt's first goals was to restore confidence in American banks. The day after his inauguration, Roosevelt announced a "bank holiday." He ordered all banks to close temporarily. Three days later,

Congress's special session began. Congress quickly passed the Emergency Banking Relief Act. President Roosevelt signed it into law.

That Sunday, President Roosevelt gave the first of his **fireside chats**—radio addresses in which he spoke directly to the American people. In this first fireside chat, he explained the new bank relief law. The government would inspect the finances of every bank and allow only healthy banks to reopen. The Federal Deposit Insurance Corporation (FDIC) was established to help maintain stability in the United States financial system. It provided government insurance for deposits made into eligible banks. People no longer needed to fear losing their savings in the event of another bank failure. The new bank law and Roosevelt's fireside chat helped Americans trust banks with their money again. As banks reopened, there were no rushes to withdraw money. Over the next month Americans deposited almost $1 billion in banks.

Under Roosevelt's leadership, Congress also established the Securities and Exchange Commission (SEC). The SEC was an organization that would regulate operations within the stock market. Created to restore the confidence of investors in the market, the Securities and Exchange Commission established rules to prevent misleading sales practices.

Relief and Recovery Roosevelt next turned his attention to other serious problems. In 1933 some 13 million Americans were unemployed.

Historical Sources

Fireside Chats

An American family sits around the radio listening to President Roosevelt answer his critics in his first fireside chat.

"There is an element in . . . our financial system more important than currency [money], more important than gold, and that is the confidence of the people. Confidence and courage are the essentials of success in carrying out our plan. You people must have faith; you must not be stampeded by rumors or guesses. Let us unite in banishing [driving away] fear. We have provided the machinery to restore our financial system; it is up to you to support and make it work. It is your problem no less than it is mine. Together we cannot fail."

Analyze Historical Sources
According to Roosevelt, how should the American people help the government deal with the banking crisis?

Tennessee Valley Authority, 1933–1945

Explore ONLINE!

Legend:
- Tennessee Valley Authority
- Major dams
- △ Steam power plants

0   50   100 Miles
0   50   100 Kilometers

KENTUCKY

Nashville • Oak Ridge •
TENNESSEE   Knoxville • NORTH CAROLINA

Memphis •

Huntsville •
△ Decatur • Chattanooga •

MISSISSIPPI

ALABAMA   GEORGIA

Interpret Maps

1. **Human-Environment Interaction** What changes were made to the environment by the TVA?

2. **Place** Where were most of the dams built?

This represented about 25 percent of the nation's workforce. New Deal programs helped to get Americans back to work. The Civil Works Administration (CWA) employed more than 4 million Americans, building roads and airports. One grateful CWA worker expressed the feelings of many when he said, "I was working, and I could again hold my head up when I met people." The Civilian Conservation Corps (CCC) provided jobs for hundreds of thousands of people. They worked on projects such as planting trees and improving national parks.

Another federal project, the **Tennessee Valley Authority** (TVA), hired people to build dams and generators. This brought electricity and jobs to communities in the Tennessee River valley. The New Deal also included programs to help farmers. The Farm Credit Administration (FCA) helped farmers refinance their mortgages so they could keep their farms. The Agricultural Adjustment Act (AAA) helped stabilize agricultural prices.

The National Industrial Recovery Act (NIRA) addressed business concerns. It eliminated unfair competition among companies. This law was passed with support from Secretary of Labor **Frances Perkins**, the nation's first woman cabinet member.

Reading Check
Categorize Which New Deal programs employed people to build public projects?

New Deal Critics

While many Americans approved of the New Deal, others criticized President Roosevelt's programs. New Deal critics fell into two main groups—those who believed the New Deal went too far, and those who believed it did not go far enough.

Academic
Vocabulary
authority power,
right to rule

Those who felt the New Deal went too far criticized the enormous expansion of the federal government. For example, the American Liberty League, which drew members from both parties, charged that New Deal laws gave the president too much **authority**. Many business leaders were concerned that the high cost of new government programs would lead to new taxes, particularly on businesses.

One critic who thought the New Deal did not go far enough was Huey Long, a U.S. senator from Louisiana. Long proposed a program called Share Our Wealth, which would tax rich Americans and use the money to help the poor. Every family would receive $5,000 to buy a home, plus a guaranteed annual income of $2,500. Long's ideas, represented in the slogan "Every Man a King," proved very popular. As Long prepared to challenge Roosevelt in the 1936 presidential election, he announced his goal "to break up the swollen fortunes of America and to spread the wealth among all our people." Long's White House dreams ended when an assassin shot him in 1935.

Another fierce critic of Roosevelt's New Deal was Father Charles Edward Coughlin. Coughlin was a Roman Catholic priest in Detroit who developed a large following by broadcasting sermons over the radio. At the peak of Coughlin's popularity, one-third of the nation tuned into the weekly broadcasts of the "radio priest." Although he initially supported Roosevelt and his programs, Coughlin eventually decided that the New Deal helped only business interests. Coughlin wanted the government to nationalize, or take over, all of the country's wealth and natural resources.

Reading Check
Support a Point of View Do you agree with any of the New Deal critics? Why or why not?

Dr. Francis Townsend criticized the New Deal for not doing enough for older Americans. He proposed a plan providing for a monthly pension for people over the age of 60. Like Long and Coughlin, Townsend attracted many followers. Some of his ideas later would shape Roosevelt's thinking and policies.

The New Deal Continues

Despite criticism of the New Deal, Democrats increased their majorities in both houses of Congress in the 1934 election. With this show of support from the American people, Roosevelt continued to introduce additional New Deal legislation. These later laws were known as the Second New Deal.

The Second New Deal After the Civil Works Administration ended in 1934, Congress formed a new agency to provide jobs for unemployed Americans. Between 1935 and 1943, the Works Progress Administration (WPA) employed some 8.5 million people on tens of thousands of projects all over the country. WPA employees built more than 650,000 miles of roads; 75,000 bridges; 8,000 parks; and 800 airports. WPA workers built the Grand Coulee Dam in Washington and New York City's Lincoln Tunnel. They also built prisons, swimming pools, hospitals, and courthouses.

First Lady **Eleanor Roosevelt** was an active supporter of New Deal programs. She was concerned, however, that the WPA was not solving the problem of unemployment among young Americans in their teens and

Eleanor Roosevelt visits a WPA project to convert a city dump into a waterfront park.

National Youth Administration

A New Deal program called the National Youth Administration (NYA) helped thousands of young people continue their education while working to support their families. Eleanor Roosevelt was a strong supporter of the program, which aimed to teach young people the skills they would need to remain part of the workforce.

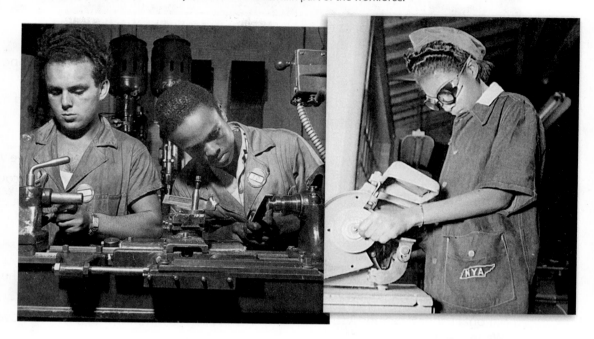

early twenties. "I live in real terror when I think we may be losing this generation," she said. "We have got to bring these young people into the active life of the community and make them feel that they are necessary." The First Lady helped convince the president to create the National Youth Administration (NYA). The NYA gave part-time jobs to many students. These jobs allowed young workers to stay in school and help their families. One NYA worker said, "I tell you, the first time I walked through the front door with my paycheck, I was somebody!"

President Roosevelt also wanted to help those who were "unable . . . to maintain themselves independently . . . through no fault of their own." The **Social Security Act**, passed in 1935, provided some financial security for the elderly, the disabled, children, and the unemployed. To help pay for these programs, the law placed a new tax on workers and employers. The passage of the Social Security Act marked the first time the federal government took direct responsibility for many citizens' economic well-being. In a national radio address, Secretary of Labor Perkins told Americans she believed Social Security was "a most significant step in our national development, a milestone in our progress toward the better-ordered society." Social Security is still an important financial safety net for many Americans. Nine out of ten individuals over the age of 65 receive benefits from the program.

New Deal Labor Programs The National Industrial Recovery Act of 1933 helped regulate business by requiring minimum wage and allowing collective bargaining. In 1935, however, the Supreme Court declared the NIRA unconstitutional.

Quick Facts

Selected New Deal Programs

Program	Purpose
Emergency Banking Relief Act	Gave the executive branch the right to regulate banks
Farm Credit Act (FCA)	Refinanced loans to keep farmers from losing their land
Civilian Conservation Corps (CCC)	Created jobs for single, unemployed young men
Agricultural Adjustment Act (AAA)	Paid farmers to grow less (declared unconstitutional)
Tennessee Valley Authority (TVA)	Built dams and power plants in the Tennessee Valley
Federal Deposit Insurance Corporation (FDIC)	Guaranteed deposits in individual bank accounts
National Industrial Recovery Act (NIRA)	Established fair competition laws (declared unconstitutional)
Civil Works Administration (CWA)	Provided jobs for the unemployed
Works Progress Administration (WPA)	Created jobs in construction, research, and the arts
National Youth Administration (NYA)	Provided part-time jobs to students
National Labor Relations Act (Wagner Act)	Recognized unions' right to bargain collectively
Social Security Act	Provided government aid to the retired and unemployed

In response to this setback, Congress passed the National Labor Relations Act (NLRA). This law is sometimes called the Wagner Act, after its sponsor, Senator Robert F. Wagner of New York. This law allowed workers to join labor unions and work together for better working conditions or salaries with collective bargaining. It also established the National Labor Relations Board to oversee union activities. Union membership grew after the passage of the Wagner Act. Organized labor became a powerful political force.

At the start of the Depression, many skilled workers belonged to craft unions. Such unions were often associated with the American Federation of Labor, which had existed since the 1880s. Unskilled workers, however, such as those who worked on assembly lines, did not qualify to belong to AFL unions. In 1935 a new union called the **Congress of Industrial Organizations** (CIO) organized workers into unions based on industry, not skill level. For example, all workers in the automobile industry would belong to the same union. The CIO also welcomed African American and Hispanic members, as well as women and immigrants.

Unions led a number of major strikes during the Depression. On New Year's Eve 1936, the CIO went on strike against General Motors for 44 days. Instead of leaving the buildings as strikers usually did, workers stayed in the factories so they could not be replaced by new workers. This strategy became known as the **sit-down strike**. The success of the General Motors strike attracted more workers to CIO unions.

Reading Check
Compare and Contrast How were the WPA and the Social Security Act similar, and how were they different?

Clashes with the Court

Roosevelt won re-election by a huge margin in 1936, carrying every state but Maine and Vermont. Democrats expanded their dominant control of Congress. But Roosevelt and the Democrats in Congress could not control the Supreme Court.

In 1935 the Supreme Court issued a series of rulings declaring several New Deal programs, including the AAA, unconstitutional. Roosevelt and his advisers felt that the entire New Deal was in danger. "Mr. President, they mean to destroy us," said Attorney General Homer Cummings.

Roosevelt decided to propose a plan for reorganizing the federal judiciary that was soon to be labeled the "court-packing" bill. This bill would allow the president to appoint a new Supreme Court justice for every justice who was 70 years old or older. If the bill passed, Roosevelt would be able to appoint six new justices immediately.

Roosevelt's judiciary plan drew harsh criticism from Congress and the public. Critics charged that Roosevelt was trying to change the balance of power so carefully defined in the U.S. Constitution. After a heated debate, Congress rejected the bill. The Supreme Court, however, did not overturn any more New Deal legislation. Roosevelt eventually had the opportunity to nominate nine new Supreme Court justices to replace those who had retired or died.

Reading Check
Analyze Information
Why did Roosevelt try to alter the Supreme Court?

Summary and Preview Roosevelt's New Deal programs brought economic relief to many Americans; however, the reforms did not resolve all of the hardships that people faced. In the next lesson you will read about how the country continued to suffer the effects of the Depression.

Lesson 2 Assessment

Review Ideas, Terms, and People

1. a. Recall What were the Hundred Days?

   b. Make Inferences What was the purpose of the bank holiday Roosevelt declared?

   c. Evaluate Which of the New Deal programs that passed during the Hundred Days was most effective? Why?

2. a. Describe Who were some of the critics of the New Deal?

   b. Contrast How were the ideas of Huey Long and the American Liberty League different?

   c. Elaborate Why do you think people supported New Deal critics such as Huey Long and Father Coughlin?

3. a. Identify What programs were part of the Second New Deal?

   b. Make Inferences Why did the Wagner Act encourage people to join unions?

4. a. Recall What happened to some of the New Deal programs when they were challenged in court?

   b. Make Inferences What was the purpose of Roosevelt's judiciary reorganization bill?

Critical Thinking

5. Problem Solving In this lesson you learned about the challenges faced by the nation and the president during the Depression. Create a chart similar to the one below and use it to identify Depression problems and New Deal solutions.

Depression Problems	New Deal Solutions

Americans Face Hard Times

The Big Idea

The Big Idea

All over the country, Americans struggled to survive the Great Depression.

Main Ideas

- Parts of the Great Plains came to be known as the Dust Bowl as severe drought destroyed farms there.

- Families all over the United States faced hard times.

- Depression-era culture helped lift people's spirits.

- The New Deal had lasting effects on American society.

Key Terms and People

Dust Bowl
Mary McLeod Bethune
John Steinbeck
Woody Guthrie

If YOU were there . . .

You own a wheat farm on the Great Plains, where you and your family live and work. Wheat prices have been low for years, and you have managed to get by only by borrowing thousands of dollars. Now the region is suffering through a terrible drought. Without water, you have been unable to grow any wheat at all. But if you do not start paying your debts, you will lose your farm.

Would you stay on your farm or leave and start a new life somewhere else?

The Dust Bowl

For American farmers, hard times began well before the start of the Great Depression. Despite the widespread prosperity of the 1920s, prices for farm products remained low. Many farmers went into debt or lost their farms. The Depression worsened this already bad situation. Conditions worsened again when a severe drought hit the Great Plains in the early 1930s and lasted most of the decade. From North Dakota to Texas, crops withered away. With no roots to hold it in place, topsoil began to blow away.

Massive dust storms swept the region, turning parts of the Great Plains into the **Dust Bowl**. "These storms were like rolling black smoke," recalled one Texas schoolboy. "We had to keep the lights on all day. We went to school with the headlights on, and with dust masks on." A woman from Kansas remembered dust storms "covering everything—including ourselves—in a thick, brownish gray blanket . . . Our faces were as dirty as if we had rolled in the dirt; our hair was gray and stiff and we ground dirt between our teeth."

Unable to raise crops, farmers in the Dust Bowl region could not pay their mortgages. Many lost their farms. Several New Deal programs tried to assist farmers by offering loans and by working to stabilize prices for farm products. Scientists also began thinking of ways to prevent dust storms during future droughts. Soil

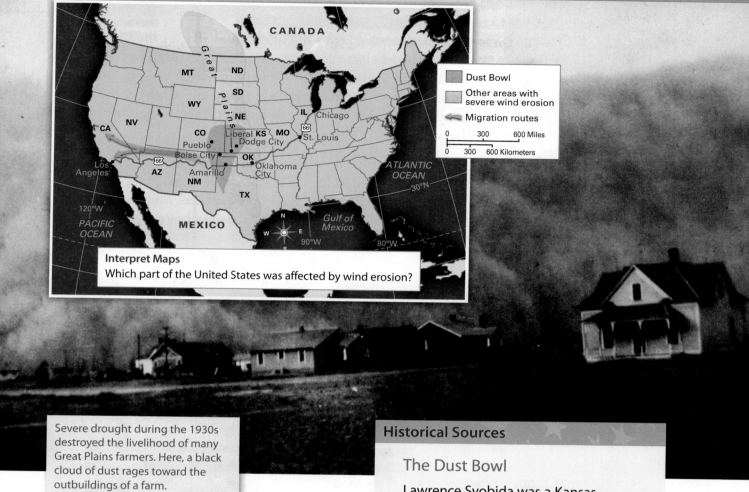

Interpret Maps
Which part of the United States was affected by wind erosion?

Severe drought during the 1930s destroyed the livelihood of many Great Plains farmers. Here, a black cloud of dust rages toward the outbuildings of a farm.

conservation experts encouraged farmers to adopt new farming methods to protect the soil. Grass was planted to hold soil in place, and rows of trees were planted to help break the wind. These changes have helped prevent another Dust Bowl in the years since the Great Depression.

For many farmers in the 1930s, however, the new programs came too late. After losing their crops and livestock to dust storms, about 2.5 million people left the area. Many packed up whatever they could fit in the family car or truck and drove to

Historical Sources

The Dust Bowl

Lawrence Svobida was a Kansas wheat farmer who saw his life's work destroyed in the 1930s.

"When I knew that my crop was irrevocably [forever] gone I experienced a deathly feeling which, I hope, can affect a man only once in a lifetime. My dreams and ambitions . . . and my shattered ideals seemed gone forever. The very desire to make a success of my life was gone, the spirit and urge to strive were dead within me. Fate had dealt me a cruel blow above which I felt utterly unable to rise."

Analyze Historical Sources
How did Svobida feel after his crop was destroyed?

Reading Check
Identify Cause and Effect How did the Dust Bowl affect farmers?

California to look for any kind of work they could find. Once there, they often found that there were already more workers than available jobs.

Hard Times

The Great Depression took a heavy toll on families all over the United States. Since many people lost their jobs, families were often forced to split up, as individual members roamed the country in search of work. To help their families buy food, children often had to drop out of school and take very low-paying jobs. Others left home to fend for themselves. One boy wrote this diary entry in 1932:

"Slept in paper box. Bummed swell breakfast three eggs and four pieces meat . . . Rode freight [train] to Roessville. Small burg [town], but got dinner. Walked Bronson . . . Couple a houses. Rode to Sidell . . . Hit homes for meals and turned down. Had to buy supper 20 cents. Raining."

—Anonymous, quoted in *The Great Depression*, by Thomas Minehan

The Great Depression was especially hard on minority groups. As white families moved West in search of jobs, Mexican Americans found it harder to get work. In California local leaders and unions convinced the government to deport many Mexican-born workers. Some of the workers' children were American-born, which made them U.S. citizens, but they were deported anyway.

DOCUMENT-BASED INVESTIGATION   Historical Sources

Migrant Mother

Photographer Dorothea Lange gained fame in the 1930s for documenting the conditions of the poor during the Depression. Lange took this famous photograph of a widowed migrant worker and two of her seven children. The woman worked in the pea fields of Nipomo, California. Her family survived by eating frozen peas and birds the children caught. The woman had just sold her car's tires for money to buy food.

Analyze Historical Sources
How would you describe the expression on the face of the woman in the photograph?

African Americans also faced discrimination. Many lost jobs to unemployed white workers. By 1932 unemployment had reached 50 percent in the African American neighborhood of Harlem in New York City. One man recalled traveling around Michigan in search of work. He went into a factory that was hiring workers:

"They didn't hire me because I didn't belong to the right kind of race. Another time I went into Saginaw, it was two white fellas and myself made three. The fella there hired the two men and didn't hire me. I was back out on the streets. That hurt me pretty bad, the race part."
—Louis Banks, quoted in *Hard Times: An Oral History of the Great Depression*, by Studs Terkel

In spite of this type of discrimination, hundreds of thousands of African Americans were able to find work through relief programs such as the CCC and WPA. President Roosevelt also consulted with African American leaders, including educator **Mary McLeod Bethune**. Bethune was one of several African Americans who Roosevelt appointed to his administration. Other members included Walter White, Robert C. Weaver, and William Henry Hastie. These advisers became known as the Black Cabinet. Their role was to advance the concerns of African Americans in the Roosevelt White House. They stood out as a powerful symbol of rising African American influence in government.

First Lady Eleanor Roosevelt was a strong supporter of equal rights. She encouraged the president to include African Americans in his recovery programs. In 1939 the Daughters of the American Revolution (DAR) refused to rent their auditorium to the African American opera singer Marian Anderson. In protest, Eleanor Roosevelt resigned her membership in the DAR. She then helped Anderson arrange a concert at the base of the Lincoln Memorial. Some 75,000 people attended. Millions more heard the national radio broadcast of the concert. Anderson later gave a private performance at the White House.

Marian Anderson singing at the Lincoln Memorial in Washington, DC, in 1939

Reading Check
Draw Inferences
What weakened families during the Depression?

Depression-Era Culture

Starting in 1935, new Works Progress Administration projects began to put the country's painters, sculptors, writers, and actors to work. When he was criticized for hiring artists, WPA director Henry Hopkins said, "They've got to eat just like other people."

Some of the work done by WPA artists has become an important part of American culture. For example, WPA musicians went into the nation's rural areas to record cowboy ballads, folk songs, and African American spirituals. This music might have been lost without these recordings. Artists employed by the WPA made more than 2,500 murals and 17,000 pieces of sculpture for public spaces. WPA writers created a permanent record of American life by interviewing Americans of many different backgrounds about their lives and memories. Today many of the thousands of interviews conducted by WPA writers are available on the Internet. You can read the stories of former slaves, pioneers, Native American leaders, and others in their own words.

Escape to the Movies

Weekly Movie Attendance, 1929–1939

Movie attendance (in millions)

120, 80, 40, 0

1929 1931 1933 1935 1937 1939

Analyze Information
How many Americans attended movies in 1931?

The movies of child-star Shirley Temple, "America's Little Darling," were among Hollywood's top moneymakers in the late 1930s.

Like many people at the time, author **John Steinbeck** was deeply affected by the Great Depression. Depression life became a main theme of Steinbeck's most famous novel, *The Grapes of Wrath*. The novel tells the story of the Joads, a family of farmers who are forced to move to California for work.

Some of the music of the day expressed themes similar to Steinbeck's. Oklahoma-born folk singer **Woody Guthrie** crisscrossed the country singing his songs of loss and struggle. One contained the line, "All along your green valley I'll work till I die"—a grim reality for some Americans.

Swing music, meanwhile, became popular for a different reason. Instead of focusing on the sadness of the Depression, swing helped people forget their troubles. Big-band leaders such as Duke Ellington, Benny Goodman, and Count Basie helped make swing wildly popular in the 1930s. People tuned into swing-music shows on inexpensive radios and danced to the fast-paced rhythms. Radios provided people with other forms of entertainment as well. Every week millions of Americans put aside their worries to listen to radio shows such as *Little Orphan Annie* and *The Lone Ranger*.

Movies offered Americans another welcome escape from reality. One boy remembered how he and his friends would save their pennies for movie tickets. "[It] was two for a nickel," he said. "You'd come to the movie in the summer like 8:30 in the mornin' and you'd see about 200 kids." For 25 cents or less, adults, too, could forget their troubles as they watched historical dramas, gangster films, comedies, and musicals.

Reading Check
Evaluate How was the work of writers and musicians affected by the Great Depression?

Causes and Effects of the New Deal

Causes	Effects
• Stock market crash	• Expanded role of federal government
• Banking crisis	• Created major programs such as Social Security and the FDIC
• Soaring unemployment	• Provided hope and relief to many Americans but did not end the Great Depression
• Farmers' troubles	
• Widespread poverty	

Effects of the New Deal

People are still debating the effects of the New Deal today. New Deal critics point out that Roosevelt's programs did not end the Great Depression. Full recovery occurred in the early 1940s, after the United States entered World War II. Roosevelt's supporters, however, believe that the New Deal gave Americans help and hope in a time of severe economic crisis.

People today do agree that the New Deal greatly expanded the role of the federal government. Some of the programs and agencies created as part of the New Deal, such as Social Security and the Federal Deposit Insurance Corporation (FDIC), remain part of our lives. Social Security still provides economic relief to the elderly, children, and those with disabilities. The FDIC protects the savings of bank customers.

Reading Check
Find the Main Idea
What are some current government programs that began during the New Deal?

Summary and Preview The New Deal helped Americans but did not end the Great Depression. The Depression finally ended after the United States entered World War II, which you will learn about in the next module.

Lesson 3 Assessment

Review Ideas, Terms, and People

1. **a. Identify** What was the Dust Bowl?
   b. Explain What factors contributed to farmers' difficulties in the 1920s and 1930s?
2. **a. Recall** What were some of the problems people faced during the Depression?
   b. Compare How was the experience of African Americans and Mexican Americans in the Depression similar?
   c. Evaluate Do you think President Roosevelt did enough to help African Americans? Explain your answer.
3. **a. Draw Conclusions** Why do you think swing music, radio shows, and movies were popular during the Great Depression?
   b. Identify How did the WPA help the arts?
4. **a. Recall** What are the different viewpoints on the success of the New Deal?
   b. Identify How did the New Deal change the involvement of the federal government in the economy?
   c. Elaborate How are Social Security and the FDIC still important today?

Critical Thinking

5. **Categorize** In this lesson you learned about life during the Great Depression. Create a chart similar to the one below and use it to identify challenges people faced during the Depression and the ways they coped.

Challenges people faced	Ways people coped with challenges

Literature in History

Depression-Era Literature

Word Help

migrant a person who moves regularly

Divide The Continental Divide separates rivers that flow east from those that flow west.

tributary a stream that feeds into a larger river or lake (Steinbeck applies the word to the road system.)

❶ From what are people on Highway 66 fleeing?

❷ How does Steinbeck describe what people are running from?

About the Reading Published in 1939, *The Grapes of Wrath* described the impact of the Great Depression on the nation. In this passage, John Steinbeck describes a journey of Dust Bowl families to California.

As You Read Look for details that appeal to the five senses.

From *The Grapes of Wrath*
by John Steinbeck (1902–1968)

Highway 66 is the main migrant road. 66—the long, concrete path across the country, waving gently up and down the map, from the Mississippi [River] to Bakersfield [California]—over the red lands and the gray lands, twisting up into the mountains, crossing the Divide and down into the bright and terrible desert to the mountains again, and into the rich California valleys.

66 is the path of people in flight, ❶ refugees from dust and shrinking land, from the thunder of tractors and shrinking ownership, from the desert's slow northward invasion, from the twisting winds that howl up out of Texas, from the floods that bring no richness to the land and steal what little richness is there. ❷ From all of these the people are in flight, and they come into 66 from the tributary side roads, from the wagon tracks and the rutted country roads. 66 is the mother road, the road of flight.

Connect Literature to History

1. **Analyze** According to this passage, why might driving between towns be a terror? What does this tell you about the migrants?

2. **Draw Conclusions** Based on Steinbeck's description and on what you already know, how might people traveling on Route 66 have felt? Why?

Social Studies Skills

Conduct a Debate

Define the Skill

The First Amendment to the U.S. Constitution guarantees freedom of speech, assembly, and the press. These freedoms have become a key part of American democracy. They guarantee that both government officials and citizens can express their opinions. People also have the right to express disagreement with leaders or the government.

The ability to discuss opposing points of view is key to a democratic society. In the United States, citizens vote for their leaders. Having access to different points of view helps people decide which candidates to support in elections.

One way to express opposing points of view is to have a debate. Debates are organized to present two sides of an issue. Debate rules make sure that both sides are treated fairly. By learning about the strengths and weaknesses of two positions on an issue, people can decide which position is more convincing.

Learn the Skill

Think about the opposition President Franklin D. Roosevelt faced when he tried to begin new programs during the Great Depression. He had to convince people to support his ideas. Roosevelt and members of his administration used radio programs and newspaper articles to promote their point of view and answer questions from their critics.

In a debate, it is important to make your point of view clear. Explain why you support a certain position or give specific reasons why you oppose it. The more detailed the argument, the more persuasive it will be. When you are in a debate, make sure to prepare plenty of evidence and examples to support your case.

Debaters have the chance not only to present a case but also to argue against the opposite point of view. One way to get ready for this is to think of possible arguments against your position. Prepare responses to each of these arguments in advance. Having good answers to criticism makes your position stronger.

In a debate, it is important to follow any rules that have been set up. Not all debates have the same rules. They do share some basic guidelines, however. Only one person is allowed to speak at once, and speaking time is limited. The two sides take turns presenting their arguments. Debates may have additional rules as well.

Practice the Skill

Suppose that your class is the Senate in 1933. President Roosevelt has already begun several new government programs. Now he is asking you to pass more new laws, which he believes will help the economy. Follow the guidelines above to have a debate about the New Deal. One group should support expanding the New Deal, and one group should oppose it. When the debate is over, answer the following questions.

1. Did your group make its point of view clear? Did it explain the reasons for taking that position? What do you think was your group's most persuasive supporting detail or example?

2. Did your group prepare arguments against the other side in advance? Were any of these arguments particularly effective?

Module 26 Assessment

Review Vocabulary, Terms, and People

Read each question and write the letter of the best response.

1. Which of the following refers to a severe economic downturn that lasted for more than ten years?
   a. the Bonus Army
   b. the Great Depression
   c. the bull market
   d. the business cycle

2. Who was Franklin Roosevelt's secretary of labor and the first woman cabinet member?
   a. Frances Perkins
   b. Mary McLeod Bethune
   c. Eleanor Roosevelt
   d. Dorothea Lange

3. Parts of the Great Plains where a severe drought struck were known as the
   a. Tennessee Valley.
   b. New Deal.
   c. Dust Bowl.
   d. Hoovervilles.

4. Which of the following means purchasing stocks on credit with a loan?
   a. the installment plan
   b. buying on margin
   c. the banking crisis
   d. bear market

Comprehension and Critical Thinking

Lesson 1

5. a. **Describe** What happened on Black Tuesday—October 29, 1929?
   b. **Summarize** How did President Hoover respond to the Depression?
   c. **Elaborate** Why do you think Americans were so unprepared for difficult times?

Lesson 2

6. a. **Recall** What New Deal programs did lawmakers create during the Hundred Days?
   b. **Explain** How did the Works Progress Administration help Americans?
   c. **Evaluate** Do you think the New Deal was successful? Explain your answer.

Lesson 3

7. a. **Recall** How did the Great Depression affect Mexican Americans?
   b. **Contrast** How did Depression-era culture show both hope and the difficulties of everyday life?
   c. **Draw Conclusions** Why do you think many African Americans supported President Roosevelt, even though they continued to face discrimination and segregation?

Review Themes

8. **Economics** How did the economy of the country change during the Great Depression?

9. **Politics** What role did politics play in easing the Great Depression?

Reading Skills

Recognize Implied Main Ideas *Use the Reading Skills taught in this module to complete the activity about the reading selection below.*

> Banks had invested heavily in the stock market, so they lost heavily when the market crashed. Banks had also lent their customers money to buy stocks on margin. Now those customers were unable to pay back their loans. Some banks went out of business. People who had deposited their life savings in those banks lost everything.

10. Write a main idea for the paragraph above.

Social Studies Skills

Conduct a Debate *Use the Social Studies Skills taught in this module to complete the activity below.*

11. Suppose you have been invited to participate in a debate on Franklin Roosevelt's plan to "pack" the Supreme Court by adding extra justices. First decide on your position. Then prepare several supporting arguments. Summarize the main points of your arguments in a paragraph.

Focus on Writing

12. **Write a Journal Entry** Think about what it was like to live during the Great Depression and how it affected the everyday lives, feelings, and thoughts of people. Then create a fictional character who lived during the Depression. Decide on the age of your character and a set of circumstances for your character. Choose one event from the Great Depression for your character to write about in a one-page journal entry. Include in your entry what your character's feelings and thoughts are about that event and about living during the Great Depression. Also include what your character's hopes and fears are for the future. Begin by placing a date from the 1930s at the top of the page.

Module 27
World War II

★

Essential Question
How did World War II impact the lives of Americans and the nation's role in the world?

About the Photo: The D-Day invasion at Normandy, France, was one of the most successful Allied invasions of the war.

▶ Explore ONLINE!

HISTORY.

VIDEOS, including...
- D-Day Invasion of Europe
- Winston Churchill
- U.S. Victory at the Battle of Midway

☑ Document-Based Investigations

☑ Graphic Organizers

☑ Interactive Games

☑ Interactive Map: World War II in Europe, 1942–1945

☑ Interactive Map: War in the Pacific, 1942–1945

☑ Image with Hotspots: Navaho Code Talkers

In this module you will read about U.S. involvement in World War II. You will also learn about how this involvement changed the society and economy of the United States.

What You Will Learn ...

Lesson 1: The War Begins 830
The Big Idea The rise of aggressive totalitarian governments led to the start of World War II.

Lesson 2: The Home Front 837
The Big Idea American involvement in World War II helped the U.S. economy and changed the lives of many Americans.

Lesson 3: War in Europe and North Africa 843
The Big Idea After fierce fighting in North Africa and Europe, the Allies stopped the German advance and slowly began driving back German forces.

Lesson 4: War in the Pacific 849
The Big Idea Allied forces reversed Japan's expansion in the Pacific and battled toward the main Japanese islands.

Lesson 5: Victory and Consequences 855
The Big Idea The Allies won World War II, the most devastating war in world history.

Timeline of Events 1935–1950

▶ *Explore ONLINE!*

United States

World

1935

1938 Orson Welles broadcasts "War of the Worlds."

∧ **1940** Alan Turing devises a way to break the code of the German Enigma machine.

∧ **1941** On December 7, the Japanese attack the U.S. fleet at Pearl Harbor, Hawaii.

1942 German submarines begin attacking the United States.

1943 Mussolini is overthrown and executed in Italy.

1944 U.S. forces participate in the D-Day invasion.

1944 The Allies enter Paris.

1945 The United States drops atomic bombs on Hiroshima and Nagasaki, Japan. ∨

1945 Hideki Tojo, prime minister of Japan, attempts suicide after atomic bombs are dropped on Japan. >

1950

Reading Social Studies

THEME FOCUS:

Geography, Society and Culture

In this module you will read about the causes and consequences of World War II. You will learn about how geography played an important role in the fighting of the war. You will also read about how society and culture reacted to the Second World War.

READING FOCUS:

Categorize

Have you ever read a schoolbook and been overwhelmed by the amount of information it contained? Categorizing events, people, and ideas can help you make sense of the facts you learn in this book.

Understand Categorizing Ideas, people, events, and things can all be categorized in many different ways. For the study of history, some of the most useful ways are by time period and by similarity between events. Categorizing events by the people involved can also be helpful. Within a category, you can make subcategories to further organize the information.

People Involved in WWII	Events of WWII
• Winston Churchill • Franklin D. Roosevelt • Adolf Hitler • Benito Mussolini • Hideki Tojo • Soldiers • Civilians	• Key battles • Treaties • Invasions ↓ **Invasions** • China • Rhineland • Czechoslovakia • Poland • Dunkirk • French Indochina • D-Day

You Try It!

The following passage is from the module you are getting ready to read. As you read the passage, look for ways to organize the information.

Japan Advances American and Filipino forces under the command of American general Douglas MacArthur could not stop Japan's advance in the Philippines. MacArthur left the islands in March 1942, vowing to return. More than 70,000 American and Filipino soldiers surrendered to the Japanese. The atrocities that followed were clear violations of human rights. The exhausted soldiers were forced to march 63 miles up the Bataan Peninsula to prison camps. Many prisoners were starved and beaten by Japanese soldiers. More than 600 Americans and about 10,000 Filipinos died in the Bataan Death March.

After you read the passage, answer the following questions.

1. What are two categories you could use to organize the information in this passage?
2. How many different kinds of people are mentioned in this passage?
3. What different places are mentioned in this passage?
4. Complete the chart below using the information from the passage above.

People involved	Countries involved	Places mentioned

As you read Module 27, remember to look for categories that can help you organize the information you read.

Key Terms and People

Lesson 1
totalitarianism
Benito Mussolini
fascism
Adolf Hitler
Nazis
Joseph Stalin
Axis Powers
appeasement
Winston Churchill
Allied Powers
Lend-Lease Act
Pearl Harbor

Lesson 2
War Production Board
A. Philip Randolph
Tuskegee Airmen
Benjamin O. Davis Jr.
zoot-suit riots
internment

Lesson 3
Battle of El Alamein
Dwight D. Eisenhower
Battle of Stalingrad
D-Day

Lesson 4
Douglas MacArthur
Bataan Death March
Chester Nimitz
Battle of the Coral Sea
Battle of Midway
island hopping
Battle of Leyte Gulf
kamikaze

Lesson 5
Battle of the Bulge
Harry S. Truman
Holocaust
genocide
Manhattan Project
atomic bomb

The War Begins

The Big Idea

The rise of aggressive totalitarian governments led to the start of World War II.

Main Ideas

- During the 1930s, totalitarian governments rose to power in Europe and Japan.

- German expansion led to the start of World War II in Europe in 1939.

- The United States joined the war after Japan attacked Pearl Harbor in 1941.

Key Terms and People

totalitarianism
Benito Mussolini
fascism
Adolf Hitler
Nazis
Joseph Stalin
Axis Powers
appeasement
Winston Churchill
Allied Powers
Lend-Lease Act
Pearl Harbor

If YOU were there . . .

The year is 1933, and your family is struggling through the Great Depression along with millions of others. Sometimes your parents wonder if they should have left Italy to come to the United States. But conditions in Italy are far from ideal. A dictator rules the country, and the people have little personal freedom.

What would you say to your parents?

The Rise of Totalitarianism

Desperate to end the hard times, many people were willing to give up their individual rights to leaders who promised to deliver prosperity and national glory. As a result, in the 1920s and 1930s, several European countries moved toward **totalitarianism**, a political system in which the government controls every aspect of citizens' lives. These governments were inspired by militant nationalism to expand their territory and power.

Italy In the years after World War I, the people of Italy suffered through economic depression, unemployment, strikes, and riots. Many Italians looked for a strong leader who could bring stability to the country. They found such a leader in **Benito Mussolini**, who gained complete control of Italy in 1922. Mussolini's rule was based on **fascism**, a political system in which the "state"—or government—is seen as more important than individuals. Fascist systems are typically militaristic and headed by a strong leader.

Mussolini restored order to Italy and improved the economy through public works projects. But the fascist government violently crushed all opposition, destroying basic individual rights such as freedom of speech. In 1935 Mussolini tried to expand Italy's territory by attacking the nation of Ethiopia, making it a colony. Haile Selassie, Ethiopia's overthrown emperor, warned the world, "It is us today. It will be you tomorrow."

Germany Germany was also suffering the effects of the global depression. In addition, many Germans were furious about the Treaty of Versailles, which forced Germany to make crippling reparation payments for its role in World War I. Politician, World War I veteran, and militant nationalist **Adolf Hitler** took advantage of public anger to gain power. A fiery speaker, he inspired huge audiences by vowing to restore Germany to prosperity and a position of international power.

Hitler also offered Germans a scapegoat, or someone to blame for their problems. He accused intellectuals, Communists, and especially Jews of causing Germany's defeat in World War I and its economic problems after the war. Only by ridding itself of Jews, Hitler declared, would Germany again rise to greatness. Hitler's National Socialist Party, or **Nazis**, gained a large following. Hitler became chancellor in 1933 and quickly seized all government power.

The Soviet Union Hitler spoke with fury of his hatred of communism. But he had something in common with the Communist ruler of the Soviet Union—both ruled as ruthless dictators. By 1928 **Joseph Stalin** had become dictator of the Soviet Union. In the 1930s Stalin terrorized those he saw as political enemies, killing or imprisoning millions of Soviet citizens. As one Soviet artist put it, "There isn't a single thinking adult in this country who hasn't thought that he might get shot."

The Third Reich

Hitler gained much of his power through the use of propaganda. Films and photographs like the one shown here showed Hitler and the Nazi Party as the best leaders for Germany. The propaganda often ignored or lied about aspects Hitler wanted hidden from the public.

How did propaganda help Hitler rise to power?

Japan Though Japan never had one single dictator, a group of nationalist military leaders slowly gained complete control over the government during the early 1900s. By the early 1930s this group had more influence than the Japanese emperor. The military leaders wanted to build a large Japanese empire in East Asia. In 1931 Japan invaded and conquered a region in northern China and called it Manchukuo. China's capital, Nanjing, was the site of massacres that claimed up to 300,000 Chinese victims. (Between 1937 and 1945 Japan's invasion of China would cost some 20 million lives.) The United States protested the invasion. Fearful of another world war, however, most Americans opposed using force to help China. The League of Nations also condemned Japan for the attack but was unable to take forceful action.

Germany Expands

Hitler dreamed of avenging Germany's defeat in World War I. "The lost land will never be won back by solemn appeals to God," he told Germans, "nor by hopes in any League of Nations, but only by force of arms." Hitler wanted to build an empire, uniting all German-speaking people in Europe. He also wanted "living space" for the growing German population.

In violation of the Treaty of Versailles, Hitler began to rebuild the German military. In 1936 Nazi troops invaded the Rhineland, a former German territory lost during World War I. That year he also signed an alliance with Mussolini, forming the **Axis Powers**. Japan later joined this pact. In 1938 Hitler forced Austria to unite with Germany. Then he demanded control of the Sudetenland, a region in Czechoslovakia where many Germans lived. When the Czechs refused, Hitler threatened war.

Appeasement Fails Czech leaders looked to their allies in France and Great Britain for help. But neither country wanted to be pulled into an armed conflict. British prime minister Neville Chamberlain organized a meeting with Hitler to work out a peaceful solution. At the 1938 Munich Conference, Germany was given control over the Sudetenland in return for a promise not to demand more land. This approach was known as **appeasement**—a policy of avoiding war with an aggressive nation by giving in to its demands. British admiral **Winston Churchill** was convinced that this strategy would not stop Hitler. "The government had to choose between shame and war," Churchill warned. "They have chosen shame. They will get war."

Churchill was right. In March 1939 German troops seized the rest of Czechoslovakia and began demanding territory from Poland. Great Britain and France pledged to defend Poland if Hitler attacked. To keep the Soviets out of the conflict, Hitler signed a nonaggression pact with Joseph Stalin in August 1939. In addition to promising not to attack each other, the two countries secretly agreed to divide Poland between them.

On September 1, 1939, Hitler's troops and tanks rushed into Poland. This was the start of World War II. Two days later, Britain and France, known as the **Allied Powers**, declared war on Germany. Neville

Reading Check
Compare and Contrast
What did the leaders of totalitarian governments have in common?

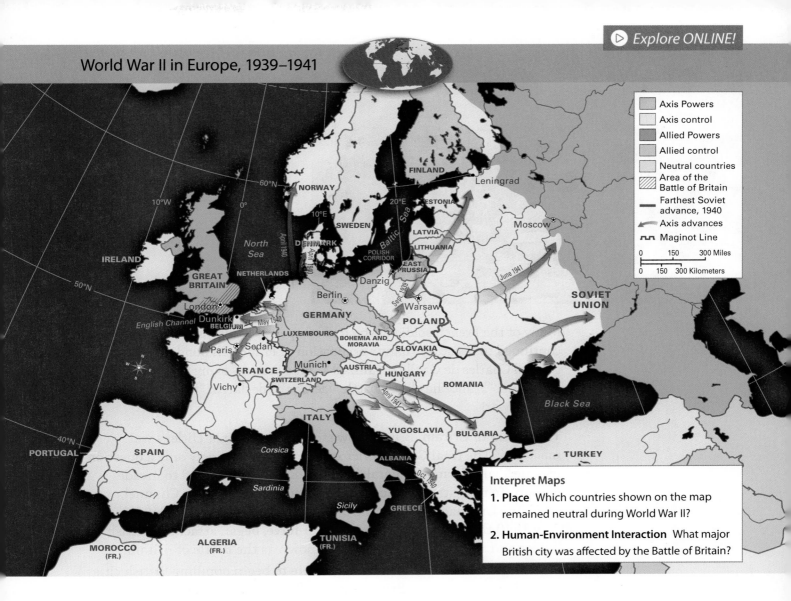

World War II in Europe, 1939–1941

Explore ONLINE!

Legend:
- Axis Powers
- Axis control
- Allied Powers
- Allied control
- Neutral countries
- Area of the Battle of Britain
- Farthest Soviet advance, 1940
- Axis advances
- Maginot Line

0   150   300 Miles
0   150   300 Kilometers

Interpret Maps

1. **Place** Which countries shown on the map remained neutral during World War II?

2. **Human-Environment Interaction** What major British city was affected by the Battle of Britain?

Chamberlain spoke bitterly of the failure of appeasement, saying, "Everything that I believed in during my public life has crashed into ruins."

Hitler Moves West The Allied Powers had little time to organize their forces to protect Poland. Using a strategy called *blitzkrieg*, or "lightning war," German tanks and airplanes broke through Polish defenses. As German forces drove into Poland from the west, the Soviets attacked from the east. Within a month, the two powers had taken control of Poland.

With Poland secure, Hitler turned toward western Europe. In the spring of 1940, Germany quickly conquered the countries of Denmark, Norway, Belgium, Luxembourg, and the Netherlands. German troops then invaded France, trapping hundreds of thousands of Belgian, British, and French soldiers in the French port city of Dunkirk. British ships and boats of all kinds raced to Dunkirk and carried the soldiers across the English Channel to safety in Britain.

German forces, meanwhile, continued their march through France. As the Germans approached the French capital of Paris, Italy declared war on the Allied Powers. France surrendered to Germany on June 22, 1940.

Nazi planes bombed London from September 1940 to May 1941. During that time, residents of London sought shelter wherever they could, including subway stations. Here, a merchant is open for business after a bombing raid.

Many of the French soldiers who had escaped at Dunkirk, however, continued to resist Germany's occupation of France. In London, French general Charles de Gaulle organized a "Free French" army to fight alongside the Allies. "France has lost a battle," de Gaulle declared, "but France has not lost the war!"

The Battle of Britain Britain now stood alone against Hitler's war machine. "The final German victory over England is now only a question of time," said German general Alfred Jodl. Hitler prepared to invade Britain. To move troops and equipment across the English Channel, Germany first had to defeat the British Royal Air Force (RAF). In July 1940 the Luftwaffe, or German air force, began attacking British planes and airfields in what became known as the Battle of Britain.

In August Hitler ordered the Luftwaffe to begin bombing British cities in the hope of crushing British morale. But Winston Churchill, the new prime minister, refused to give in. "We shall fight on the beaches," he vowed. "We shall fight in the fields and in the streets, we shall never surrender." Using the new technology of radar, the RAF was able to detect and destroy some 2,300 of the Luftwaffe's aircraft. Hitler canceled the invasion of Britain.

Reading Check
Sequence What event sparked World War II?

The United States Joins the War

Most Americans opposed Hitler's actions, but they did not want to join the war. When President Franklin Roosevelt ran for re-election in 1940, he told voters that "your boys are not going to be sent into any foreign wars." Privately, however, Roosevelt was convinced that the United States would soon be at war.

Helping the Allies In 1941 Roosevelt proposed new programs to assist the Allies. "We must be the great arsenal [arms supply] of democracy," he told Congress. In March 1941 Congress passed the **Lend-Lease Act**, allowing the president to aid any nation believed vital to U.S. defense. Under Lend-Lease, the United States sent billions of dollars' worth of aid in the form of weapons, tanks, airplanes, and food to Britain, the Nationalists in

China, and other Allied countries. In June 1941 Hitler violated his nonaggression pact with Stalin and invaded the Soviet Union. The Soviets then joined the Allies in the fight against Germany. In November the United States extended the Lend-Lease program to the Soviet Union, though many Americans worried about giving aid to a Communist country.

Japan Attacks Pearl Harbor Like Germany and Italy, Japan was quickly building an empire. After conquering much of China in the 1930s, Japanese forces moved into Southeast Asia. Japan's leaders wanted control of oil and other resources there.

When Japanese forces captured French Indochina in July 1941, Roosevelt protested. He demanded that Japan withdraw. Then the United States froze Japanese funds in its banks and cut off exports to Japan.

Japanese military leaders had already begun planning a large-scale attack to destroy the U.S. naval fleet stationed at **Pearl Harbor**, in Hawaii. This would give Japan time to secure control of East Asia before the U.S. military could respond.

Pearl Harbor, 1941

Explore ONLINE!

Japanese territory

Route of Japanese aircraft carriers

Japanese submarines deployed on December 6.

The first Japanese aircraft take off at 6 a.m. on December 7.

Interpret Maps

1. **Place** How many miles is it from Pearl Harbor to Tokyo?

2. **Movement** From where did the Japanese fleet leave on November 26?

Japanese forces bombarded the American naval fleet for several hours in the attack on Pearl Harbor. Eighteen ships were hit, and more than 2,400 Americans were killed.

At 7:55 a.m. on Sunday, December 7, 1941, Japanese airplanes dove from the sky and attacked Pearl Harbor. In just a few hours, the Japanese sank or damaged all of the battleships anchored at Pearl Harbor. More than 2,400 Americans were killed. Almost 200 airplanes were destroyed.

Speaking to Congress the next day, President Roosevelt called December 7, 1941, "a date which will live in infamy [disgrace]." Congress voted to declare war on Japan. Germany then declared war on the United States. Less than 25 years after entering World War I, the United States joined the Allies in another global war. This one would be even more devastating.

Summary and Preview Military aggression in Europe and Asia drew the United States into war. In the next lesson you will learn how the war affected the home front.

Reading Check
Identify Cause and Effect
What did Japan hope to gain by attacking Pearl Harbor?

Lesson 1 Assessment

Review Ideas, Terms, and People

1. a. Identify What types of leaders came to power in Italy, Germany, and the Soviet Union before World War II?

b. Explain Why did some Europeans have faith in these leaders?

2. a. Recall Which countries formed the Axis Powers and the Allied Powers?

b. Summarize What did Adolf Hitler promise the German people, and how did he act on this promise?

c. Elaborate Do you think Winston Churchill was a good choice for Britain's prime minister? Explain your answer.

3. a. Describe How did the Lend-Lease Act help the Allies?

b. Explain What event brought the United States into World War II?

Critical Thinking

4. Identify Cause and Effect In this lesson you learned about totalitarian countries and their leaders prior to World War II. Create a graphic organizer similar to the one below and use it to give details on the causes of World War II.

Causes of WWII

The Home Front

The Big Idea

American involvement in World War II helped the U.S. economy and changed the lives of many Americans.

Main Ideas

- Businesses, soldiers, and citizens worked to prepare the United States for war.

- The war brought new opportunities for many women and minorities.

- Japanese Americans faced internment during the war.

Key Terms and People

War Production Board
A. Philip Randolph
Tuskegee Airmen
Benjamin O. Davis Jr.
zoot-suit riots
internment

If YOU were there . . .

Shopping for food has become a whole new experience since the United States entered World War II. When your mother sends you to the grocery store these days, she gives you government-issued ration stamps. These stamps limit the amount of sugar, butter, and meat each family can buy. The sacrifice is difficult, but you know it will help the soldiers fighting overseas.

In what other ways can you help the war effort?

Preparing for War

The United States was still experiencing the effects of the Great Depression when the Japanese attacked Pearl Harbor in December 1941. The enormous effort of mobilizing for war finally brought the Depression to an end. The economy was converted to war production. Factories ran 24 hours a day, producing ships, tanks, jeeps, guns, and ammunition. Americans turned their knowledge of mass production toward the production of war supplies. One remarkable example was the building of Liberty ships—transport vessels for troops and supplies. Workers could build an entire 441-foot-long Liberty ship in as little as four days.

American workers were soon doubling the war production of Germany, Japan, and all other Axis Power countries combined. Unemployment fell to 1 percent in 1944. Agricultural production increased as well, as farmers sent food overseas to feed Allied soldiers. On the home front, one could buy only limited amounts of many foods, from coffee to canned goods. To organize the war effort, the government created the **War Production Board** (WPB) to oversee the conversion of factories to war production. In 1942, for example, the WPB banned the production of cars so that auto plants could produce military equipment. Essential resources, such as rubber for tires and gasoline, were rationed to ensure adequate supplies for military use.

In addition to metal, Americans collected old tires and recycled the rubber to make gas masks, lifeboats, and wheels for military vehicles.

The United States also needed millions of soldiers. Congress had begun to prepare for war by passing the Selective Training and Service Act in 1940. This was the first peacetime draft in the country's history. Men from the ages of 21 to 35 (later 18 to 38) were required to register for the draft. More than 16 million Americans served during the war.

To finance the war effort, the government increased taxes and sold war bonds. War bonds were essentially loans that people made to the government. People who bought war bonds in 1942, for example, would get their money back ten years later, with interest.

Americans also contributed to the war effort by collecting scrap metal that could be used in weapons factories. People learned to adjust to government rations limiting the supply of gasoline, rubber, shoes, and some foods. Posters urged Americans to "Use it up, wear it out, make it do, or do without."

Reading Check
Identify Cause and Effect How did the war affect the U.S. economy?

Wartime Opportunities

You read that wartime production during World War I created new opportunities for many women and minorities. The same thing happened on an even larger scale during World War II.

New Roles for Women With so many men leaving home to fight in World War II, factories badly needed new workers. The government urged women to fill these positions. Women found themselves doing work that had traditionally been considered "unladylike." One female riveter (a person who fastens parts on a machine) recalled her experiences building airplanes:

"[I] learned to use an electric drill . . . and I soon became an outstanding riveter. . . . The war really created opportunities for women. It was the first time we got a chance to show that we could do a lot of things that only men had done before."

—Winona Espinosa, quoted in "Rosie the Riveter Remembers"
American Heritage, February/March 1984

Women also filled new roles in military service. About 300,000 women served in the armed forces through special divisions such as the Women's Auxiliary Army Corps (WAAC) and Women's Airforce Service Pilots (WASP). WASP pilots flew test flights and ferried planes between factories and air bases. Army and navy nurses served in combat areas.

African Americans The Great Migration continued as African Americans moved to northern cities to find factory jobs. In most cases, however, black workers received lower pay than did white workers. They also were restricted in what kinds of jobs they were hired to perform.

To protest this unfair treatment, African American labor leader **A. Philip Randolph** began to organize a march to Washington, DC, in 1941. "If freedom and equality are not [granted for] the peoples of color, the war for democracy will not be won," he argued. Randolph canceled the march, however, after President Roosevelt issued an order prohibiting racial discrimination in the government and in companies producing war goods.

Supporting the War

Posters like these encouraged Americans to support their troops in a variety of ways. Building weaponry, growing food, saving scrap metal, and rationing all helped the war effort and allowed soldiers to have necessary supplies.

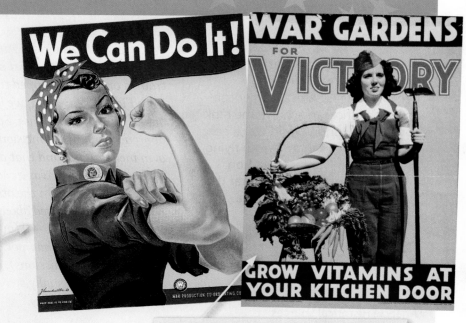

"Rosie the Riveter" became a symbol of women's work to support the war.

Victory gardens planted at home allowed more commercially produced food to be sent from farms to troops overseas.

Analyze Historical Sources
How did posters like these aim to help troops overseas?

About 1 million African Americans served in the armed forces during the war, mostly in segregated units. In the Navy, African Americans were assigned only to support positions and denied the right to participate in combat. Despite this, many black soldiers became national heroes during the war. One was Doris "Dorie" Miller, who displayed great courage during the attack on Pearl Harbor. Leaving his post as ship's cook, Miller manned a machine gun on the deck of the USS *West Virginia* until he was ordered to abandon the ship because it was sinking.

The **Tuskegee Airmen** were African American pilots who trained at the Tuskegee Army Air Field in Alabama. **Benjamin O. Davis Jr.**, who later became the first African American general in the U.S. Air Force, led the group. Davis and his pilots had to overcome prejudice in the military as well as the hazards of war. He later described the pilots as "outstanding Americans who served their country unselfishly. Despite treatment that would have demoralized men of lesser strength and character, they persisted through humiliations and dangers to earn the respect of their fellows." The Tuskegee Airmen flew thousands of successful combat missions in North Africa and Italy.

Mexican Americans About 300,000 Mexican Americans served in the military during the war. Many Mexican Americans also found wartime jobs on the West Coast and in the Midwest. Because of a shortage of farm workers, the federal government asked Mexico to provide agricultural workers. The workers, called *braceros*, were guaranteed a minimum wage, food, shelter, and clean living conditions. About 200,000 Mexicans worked in the *bracero* program.

Tuskegee Airmen

Benjamin O. Davis Jr. was a graduate of West Point who became the first African American Air Force officer to achieve the rank of general. During World War II he led the first African American flying unit, the 99th Fighter Squadron. These men had been trained at the Tuskegee Institute in Alabama.

"While no AAF [American Air Force] unit had gone into combat better trained or better equipped than the 99th Fighter Squadron, we lacked actual combat experience. So as we approached our first missions, my own inexperience and that of my flight commanders was a major source of concern. On the other hand, we had averaged about 250 hours per man in a P-40 (quite a lot for pilots who had not yet flown their first missions), and we possessed an unusually strong sense of purpose and solidarity."

—Benjamin O. Davis, *Benjamin O. Davis, American: An Autobiography*

Analyze Historical Sources
What advantages did the Tuskegee Airmen bring to battle?

Reading Check
Analyze Information
How did the war create both opportunities and challenges for minorities?

Young Mexican Americans of the time created their own culture by blending different music styles and clothing styles. Some men wore zoot suits—fancy, loose-fitting outfits with oversized hats. Despite their aiding of the war effort, many faced discrimination. In Los Angeles in June 1943, groups of sailors attacked Mexican Americans wearing zoot suits, beginning the **zoot-suit riots**. During the ten-day period, white mobs attacked many Mexican Americans.

Struggles at Home

Although members of every race participated in the war as American soldiers, life for minorities at home changed very little. African Americans were still subject to segregation, and Mexican Americans continued to have very little economic opportunity.

Japanese American Internment

Japanese Americans faced a different form of prejudice during World War II. After the Japanese attack on Pearl Harbor, some Americans began to look at Americans of Japanese descent with fear and suspicion. Most Japanese Americans lived on the West Coast at this time. It was feared that they would serve as secret agents for Japan and help Japan prepare an invasion of the West Coast or try to sabotage U.S. war efforts.

The U.S. government had no evidence to support these fears. In spite of this fact, President Roosevelt issued Executive Order 9066. This order allowed the government to begin the process of **internment**, or forced relocation and imprisonment, of Japanese Americans. About 115,000 Japanese Americans were evacuated from their homes and held in isolated internment camps. Half of those held in the camps were children. A smaller number of Americans of German and Italian ancestry were also held in internment camps during the war.

Fred Korematsu, a Japanese American citizen, refused to go to the camps and was arrested as a result. Saying that the internment order was unlawful and racist, Korematsu took his case all the way to the Supreme Court. In *Korematsu* v. *United States* (1944), the Supreme Court ruled against him, arguing that the unusual demands of wartime security justified the order.

At this time, some Japanese Americans were *Issei*, or immigrants born in Japan. But most were *Nisei*, American citizens born in the United States to Japanese immigrant parents. Whether they were U.S. citizens or not, Japanese Americans lost their jobs, homes, and belongings when they were

Japanese Americans

After the attack on Pearl Harbor, Japanese Americans were removed from their communities and ordered into internment camps far away from the West Coast.

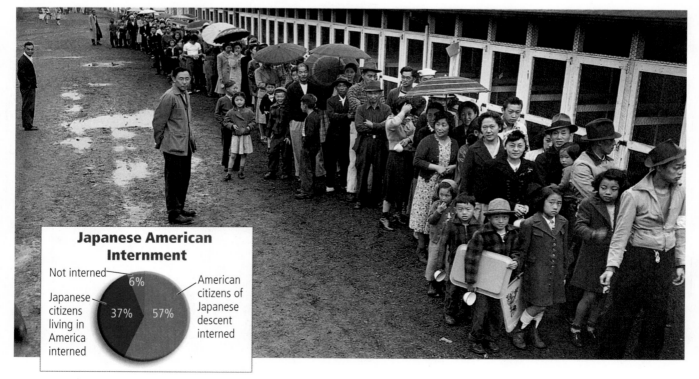

Japanese American Internment

Not interned 6%

Japanese citizens living in America interned 37%

American citizens of Japanese descent interned 57%

forced to move to internment camps. A farm owner named Yuri Tateishi spoke of feeling betrayed by his government. "You hurt," he said. "You give up everything that you worked for that far, and I think everybody was at the point of just having gotten out of the Depression and was just getting on his feet. And then all that happens! You have to throw everything away." After the Pearl Harbor attack, the government banned young Japanese American men from serving in the military. But Roosevelt reversed this policy in 1943. Daniel Inouye remembered the excitement he and his fellow Japanese Americans in Hawaii felt when they heard that the government was going to form an all-Nisei combat team. An army recruiter had prepared a pep talk for the young Japanese Americans, but this proved to be unnecessary:

> "As soon as he said that we were now eligible to volunteer, that room exploded into a fury of yells and motion. We went bursting out of there and ran—ran!—the three miles to the draft board . . . jostling for position, like a bunch of marathoners gone berserk."
>
> —Daniel Inouye, from *Journey to Washington*
> by Daniel Inouye and Lawrence Elliott

Reading Check
Analyze Information
Why were Japanese Americans interned?

Inouye was one of about 33,000 Nisei who served in World War II. The Japanese American 100th/442nd Regimental Combat Team received more than 18,000 decorations for bravery—more than any other unit of its size in U.S. military history. Many of the soldiers of the 100th/442nd served while their families were held in internment camps back home.

Summary and Preview The war effort changed life on the home front. In the next lesson you will learn about the fighting in Europe and North Africa.

Lesson 2 Assessment

Review Ideas, Terms, and People

1. a. **Describe** How did people on the home front support the war effort?

   b. **Identify** What government agency oversaw factory production during the war?

2. a. **Recall** What were the WAAC and the WASP?

   b. **Explain** Why did A. Philip Randolph organize a march on Washington and then cancel it?

   c. **Elaborate** How did the *bracero* program benefit both Mexicans and Americans?

3. a. **Define** What was the internment program?

   b. **Contrast** How did the U.S. government change its policy toward Japanese Americans serving in the military? How did many respond?

Critical Thinking

4. **Categorize** In this lesson you learned about the challenges and opportunities for different groups of people in America during World War II. Create a graphic organizer similar to the one below and use it to list opportunities that women, African Americans, and Mexican Americans found during the war.

Wartime Opportunities

Women	African Americans	Mexican Americans

War in Europe and North Africa

The Big Idea

After fierce fighting in North Africa and Europe, the Allies stopped the German advance and slowly began driving back German forces.

Main Ideas

- The Allies fought back against the Axis Powers in North Africa and Europe.
- Key Allied victories halted the German advance.
- In the D-Day invasion, Allied forces attacked German-controlled France.

Key Terms and People

Battle of El Alamein
Dwight D. Eisenhower
Battle of Stalingrad
D-Day

If YOU were there . . .

The year is 1943, and you are a senior in high school. You know that you will be drafted into the armed forces as soon as you graduate. Every day after school you listen to radio reports about the battles being fought around the world. Your future, and the future of the whole world, seem so uncertain.

How do you feel about fighting in this war?

The Allies Fight Back

In December 1941, soon after the United States entered the war, President Roosevelt met with British prime minister Winston Churchill to work out a plan to defeat the Axis Powers. Roosevelt agreed that the United States would place "Europe first" in its plans to defeat the Axis, while still aiding China in the fight against Japan in the Pacific. In addition, Roosevelt and Churchill agreed on two initial strategies: a buildup of troops in Britain to be used to invade France, and an assault on German forces in North Africa.

Meanwhile, the Soviets had been demanding Allied help on the eastern front, where they had borne the brunt of the European war for months after Hitler's invasion. Stalin wanted the Allies to attack in Europe immediately, to take some of the pressure off of the Soviet forces in the east. In July 1942, however, the Allies decided to put a European invasion on hold and launch an initial offensive in North Africa. Stalin was angry. The Soviets would have to continue to fight the war on the eastern front without a western European assault to distract the Germans.

As they prepared their battle plans, the Allies faced many obstacles. One major threat the Allies had to combat was U-boat attacks. In 1942 alone German U-boats sank more than 6 million tons of Allied materials. To prevent further damage, the Allies used the convoy system of multiple ships traveling at once, along with new sonar technology. Sonar,

The Allies began using sonar to destroy German U-boats, shown here in a German harbor.

Reading Check
Sequence What battle plan did the Allies agree to pursue after U.S. entry into the war?

which uses sound waves to detect objects underwater, helped Allied ships find and destroy German U-boats. In addition, new long-range Allied planes protected the convoys from the air. Long-range planes could also fly into German territory to drop bombs on factories, railroads, and cities, inflicting tremendous damage on German targets.

Halting the German Advance

Churchill predicted that the road to victory would be long and difficult. By winning several key battles, however, Allied forces finally stopped the German advance.

North Africa and Italy As you have read, a main focus for the Allies when the United States entered the war was North Africa. The Germans and British were battling for control there because Axis leaders wanted to grab control of the Suez Canal, a crucial supply route in Egypt. Germany's Afrika Korps was led by General Erwin Rommel, nicknamed the Desert Fox for his bold, surprise attacks.

In the summer of 1942, Rommel began an offensive to take Egypt. General Bernard Montgomery led the British forces to stop the Germans. The British stopped the Afrika Korps in July at the **Battle of El Alamein**. At the same time, U.S. and British troops, led by American general **Dwight D. Eisenhower**, came ashore in Morocco and Algeria, west of Egypt. Caught between two Allied forces, the Afrika Korps surrendered in May 1943.

With North Africa under their control, the Allies prepared to attack the Axis Powers in Europe. Churchill identified Italy as the "soft underbelly" of the Axis. Allied forces invaded the island of Sicily in July 1943 and moved from there to the Italian mainland. Italian leaders overthrew Mussolini and surrendered to the Allies. But Hitler refused to recognize the Axis defeat. He sent German troops to Italy to block the Allied advance.

Major Allied Leaders in Europe

Winston Churchill Prime Minister of Great Britain

Franklin Roosevelt President of the United States

Joseph Stalin Premier of the Soviet Union

Major Axis Leaders in Europe

Adolf Hitler Chancellor of Germany

Benito Mussolini Prime Minister of Italy

In January 1944, Allied forces tried to get behind the Germans with a surprise attack at Anzio, on the western coast of Italy. American and British troops landed at Anzio but were pinned down on the beach for several months. The "soft underbelly" proved to be much tougher than expected. Finally, the Allied forces in southern Italy battled north to Anzio. The combined forces captured Rome, the capital of Italy, in June 1944. Early in 1945, German forces were driven out of Italy. Italian freedom fighters executed Mussolini.

The Battle of Stalingrad Meanwhile, massive German and Soviet armies were battling on the eastern front. By the middle of 1942, Axis armies had driven deep into Soviet territory. Millions of Soviet soldiers had been killed or captured.

German forces then advanced to the key industrial city of Stalingrad, now called Volgograd. German firebombs set much of the city on fire. But Soviet leader Joseph Stalin was determined to hold on to Stalingrad at all costs. At one point in the fighting, the Soviet forces occupied only a small strip of land along the Volga River. Savage street fighting dragged on for months. The city's remaining buildings were destroyed. Soviet snipers used the ruined buildings to their advantage, firing at German soldiers from behind piles of stone and brick.

German supplies began to run desperately low as the harsh Russian winter began. Hitler remained obsessed with capturing Stalingrad,

Tanks thundered across Europe, destroying much of what lay in their paths.

Airplanes dropped millions of bombs on opposing forces. They were also used for moving troops and for spying on the enemy.

Reading Check
Sequence What events led to the Allied victories in Italy and the Soviet Union?

however. He ordered his troops to keep fighting, though he did not send enough new supplies or soldiers. Thousands of Germans froze or starved to death. In late January 1943 the German commander at Stalingrad defied Hitler and surrendered to save his remaining troops. The **Battle of Stalingrad** thus became a key turning point of the war.

The Soviet victory came at an enormous cost—more than 1 million Soviet soldiers died at Stalingrad. About 800,000 Axis soldiers were killed. After Stalingrad, the Soviets won another victory in the city of Kursk, in the biggest tank battle ever fought. The Axis Powers now began to retreat from the Soviet Union. The tide of the war in the east had turned.

The D-Day Invasion

After hard-fought victories in North Africa and Italy, the Allies were ready for an even tougher task—the invasion of German-occupied France. This was the first step toward the goal of liberating Europe and forcing Hitler to surrender.

Dwight Eisenhower was in charge of planning what would be the largest sea-to-land invasion ever attempted. Eisenhower knew that German forces were expecting an invasion of France. The Germans had planted mines and stretched barbed wire along the French coastline. Heavily armed German soldiers waited on the beaches in bombproof bunkers. Eisenhower warned his troops of the danger but expressed confidence in their ability to succeed. "The hopes and prayers of liberty-loving people everywhere march with you," he told them.

American, British, and Canadian troops invaded France on June 6, 1944—known as **D-Day**, or "designated day." They crossed the choppy waters of the English Channel and landed on five beaches in Normandy. More than 6,000 ships, 11,000 planes, and 156,000 men were part of the invasion. Soldiers jumped from boats and waded ashore, often under heavy fire.

World War II in Europe, 1942–1945

Legend

- Axis controlled, June 1944
- Allied controlled, June 1944
- Neutral country
- Farthest Axis advance, 1942
- Allied advance
- Major battle
- Allied air attack

0   150   300 Miles

0   150   300 Kilometers

FINLAND

Leningrad

NORWAY

SWEDEN

Baltic Sea

DENMARK

Stalingrad
Nov. 1942–
Feb. 1943

IRELAND

North Sea

SOVIET
UNION

GREAT
BRITAIN

NETHERLANDS

Elbe

Berlin
Apr.–May 1945

Oder River

Vistula River

London

Antwerp

50°N

BELGIUM

River

English
Channel

Battle of the Bulge
Dec. 1944

GERMANY

D-Day
June 1944

Paris

SLOVAKIA

ATLANTIC
OCEAN

FRANCE

Rhine River

Danube River

HUNGARY

SWITZERLAND

AUSTRIA

AUG. 1944

VICHY
FRANCE

ROMANIA

Black Sea

PORTUGAL

CROATIA

SERBIA

30°E

40°E

ITALY

Adriatic Sea

BULGARIA

SPAIN

Corsica

Rome

Anzio
Jan. 1944

MONTENEGRO

ALBANIA

TURKEY

40°N

Sardinia

Aegean
Sea

GIBRALTAR
(BR)

GREECE

NOV. 1942

SEPT. 1943

NOV. 1942

SPANISH
MOROCCO

NOV. 1942

Sicily

Malta

Crete

Mediterranean
Sea

MOROCCO

ALGERIA

JULY 1943

TUNISIA

El Alamein
Oct.–Nov. 1942

EGYPT

Interpret Maps

Location In which country shown on the map did most of the major battles take place?

American soldiers landed on the beaches of Normandy during the D-Day invasion.

Timeline: World War II in Europe, 1942–1945

1942

1945

November 1942
Allies win the Battle of El Alamein.

February 1943
Final German troops surrender at Stalingrad.

May 1943
Axis forces in North Africa surrender.

July 1943
Allies begin an invasion of Sicily.

June 5, 1944
Allies capture Rome.

June 6, 1944
Allied forces invade France on D-Day.

Analyze Timelines
Which event was a key turning point of the war on the eastern front?

Reading Check
Summarize
What was the goal of the D-Day invasion?

The Americans landed on two beaches, codenamed Utah and Omaha. Fighting was especially fierce on Omaha Beach, where almost 3,000 men were killed or wounded. "The entire beach was strewn with mines," wrote one U.S. soldier to his wife. "With a stream of lead coming towards us, we were at the mercy of the Germans."

By the end of D-Day, all five beaches were secured. The Allies then began driving east through French villages and countryside toward Germany.

Summary and Preview Allied victories led to the D-Day invasion. In the next lesson you will read about the Pacific war.

Lesson 3 Assessment

Review Ideas, Terms, and People

1. **a. Describe** What new strategies did the Allies use in the fight in Europe and North Africa?
   b. Draw Conclusions Why was it important for no individual Allied Power to make peace with the Axis countries?

2. **a. Recall** What role did Dwight D. Eisenhower play in the North Africa campaign?
   b. Analyze Why did the Allies decide to invade North Africa and Italy?
   c. Evaluate Why is the Battle of Stalingrad often called a turning point in the war?

3. **a. Identify** What was D-Day?
   b. Elaborate What did Eisenhower mean when he said, "The hopes and prayers of liberty-loving people everywhere march with you"?

Critical Thinking

4. **Categorize** In this lesson you learned about the major World War II battles and campaigns in different areas of the world. Create a graphic organizer similar to the one below and use it to explain the significance of each event shown.

Event	Significance
Battle of El Alamein	
Capture of Rome	
Battle of Stalingrad	
D-Day invasion	

War in the Pacific

The Big Idea

Allied forces reversed Japan's expansion in the Pacific and battled toward the main Japanese islands.

Main Ideas

- The Japanese continued advancing across the Pacific in 1942.
- The Allies stopped Japan's advance with key victories over the Japanese navy.
- The Allies began battling toward Japan.

Key Terms and People

Douglas MacArthur
Bataan Death March
Chester Nimitz
Battle of the Coral Sea
Battle of Midway
island hopping
Battle of Leyte Gulf
kamikaze

If YOU were there . . .

It is spring of 1945, and your older brother is fighting the Japanese in the Pacific. You've been following the news reports closely, and you know that fighting in the Pacific is terribly fierce. You hear that the Japanese soldiers often refuse to surrender, fighting to the death instead. Your brother reveals in his letters that he is lonely and suffering many hardships. Now you are writing to him.

What would you say to encourage him?

Japan Advances

Japan's attack on Pearl Harbor left the U.S. Pacific Fleet so weakened that it could not immediately respond to the Japanese advance. In addition, President Roosevelt had agreed to concentrate U.S. resources in Europe first. So, while the United States recovered from Pearl Harbor, Japan conquered Thailand, Burma, the British colonies of Hong Kong and Singapore, and the U.S. territories of Guam and Wake Island. The same day as the attack on Pearl Harbor, Japan invaded Hong Kong. British, Canadian, and Indian forces attempting to stop the invasion were outnumbered. Japan attacked the American-controlled Philippines the same day.

American and Filipino forces under the command of American general **Douglas MacArthur** could not stop Japan's advance in the Philippines. MacArthur left the islands in March 1942, vowing to return. More than 70,000 American and Filipino soldiers surrendered to the Japanese. The atrocities that followed were clear violations of human rights. The exhausted soldiers were forced to march 63 miles up the Bataan Peninsula to prison camps. Many prisoners were starved and beaten by Japanese soldiers. More than 600 Americans and about 10,000 Filipinos died in the **Bataan Death March**.

Reading Check
Identify Cause and Effect Why could the U.S. Pacific Fleet not immediately stop the Japanese advance?

Key Allied Victories

The Allies feared the Japanese might next attack India, Australia, or even the United States mainland. Admiral **Chester Nimitz** led the U.S. Pacific Fleet. Nimitz was determined to stop the Japanese advance, and he had an important advantage—the ability to crack secret Japanese codes.

American code breakers helped the Allies in two key naval battles in the Pacific. Nimitz learned that the Japanese were planning an attack on Port Moresby, New Guinea, an island just north of Australia. If the Japanese took New Guinea, they would have a base from which to invade Australia. In May 1942 Nimitz sent Allied forces to stop the Japanese fleet. American and Japanese aircraft carriers and fighter planes clashed in the **Battle of the Coral Sea**. In this battle both sides used a new kind of strategy. The opposing ships did not fire a single shot. In fact, they often were not in view of each other. Instead, airplanes taking off from the huge aircraft carriers attacked the ships. Although each side suffered heavy losses, neither won a clear victory. Still, the Japanese assault on Port Moresby was stopped.

Allied leaders then learned that the Japanese planned a surprise attack on the Midway Islands. Nimitz was prepared. The **Battle of Midway** began

Code Talkers

More than 40,000 Native Americans served in the U.S. armed forces during the war. About 400 Navajo Native Americans served as "code talkers," relaying coded messages based on the complex Navajo language. Japan's expert code breakers were never able to crack the Navajo code.

Why might the Japanese have been unable to break the Navajo code?

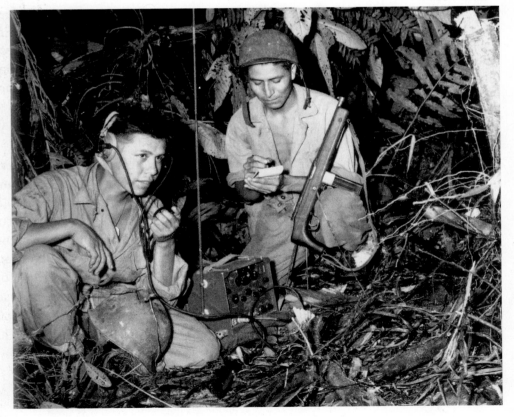

on June 4, 1942, when Japan started bombing the islands. American aircraft carriers launched their planes, catching the Japanese aircraft carriers while many of their planes were refueling on deck. American dive bombers destroyed four of Japan's aircraft carriers, severely weakening Japanese naval power. "Pearl Harbor has now been partially avenged," said Nimitz.

The Allies then began the enormous and difficult task of recapturing territory from Japan. In August 1942 American marines invaded Guadalcanal, one of the Solomon Islands northeast of Australia. Intense fighting raged for nearly six months. Marine Louis Ortega remembered that enemy bombs and bullets were only part of the danger in the hot, rainy jungles of Guadalcanal. Soldiers also suffered from diseases, such as malaria, and from hunger due to lack of supplies. "I had gone to Guadalcanal weighing about 150," Ortega said. "I left weighing about 110." American forces finally took control of the island in February 1943.

Battling toward Japan

Allied victories at Midway and Guadalcanal helped change the course of the war in the Pacific. The Allies now saw their chance to go on the offensive, with the goal of reaching Japan itself.

Island Hopping To fight their way toward Japan, Allied war planners developed a strategy called **island hopping**, where Allied forces took only the most strategically important islands, instead of each Japanese-held island. They could use each captured island as a base for the next attack, while isolating the Japanese forces on the bypassed islands.

Island hopping proved to be a successful strategy, though very costly to **execute**. Japanese forces fortified key islands and fought fiercely to hold on to them. In November 1943, U.S. Marines leapt off their boats and waded toward Tarawa, one of the Gilbert Islands. They advanced into ferocious fire from Japanese machine guns. "The water seemed never clear of . . . men," one marine said. "They kept falling, falling, falling." Both sides sustained heavy casualties at Tarawa, but the marines captured the island. The Allies won similar victories in the Marshall, Mariana, Volcano, and Bonin islands.

In October 1944 General MacArthur led a mission to retake the Philippines. The Japanese navy confronted the Allies at the **Battle of Leyte Gulf**, the largest naval battle in history. The Allies crushed the Japanese fleet, crippling Japan's naval power for the remainder of the war. It also gave the Allies a base from which to attack the main shipping routes that supplied Japan. After splashing ashore on Leyte, MacArthur proudly declared: "People of the Philippines: I have returned." Securing the Philippines took many more months of fighting. Allied forces and Filipino guerrillas finally drove out or captured all of the Japanese defenders by the summer of 1945.

Final Battles With key islands close to Japan secured, Allied planes began bombing targets in Japan in November 1944. A recently developed airplane, the B-29, played a major role in the effort. These planes, which

Reading Check
Draw Conclusions
How did the Allied victory at Midway change the course of the war in the Pacific?

Academic Vocabulary
execute perform, carry out

War in the Pacific, 1941–1945

Legend:
- Japan (Axis Power)
- Controlled by Japan, July 1942
- Allied
- Allied control
- ☆ Major battle
- ← Allied advance
- ◄- - Allied air attack
- 🍄 Atomic bombing

Scale: 0 — 500 — 1,000 Miles
0 — 500 — 1,000 Kilometers

**Labels on map:**

ALASKA
Bering Sea
Aleutian Islands 1943
SOVIET UNION
60°N
45°N
MONGOLIA
MANCHUKUO 1945
Beijing
KOREA
1945
1945
CHINA
1944
Chengdu
Hiroshima Aug. 6, 1945
JAPAN
Tokyo
PACIFIC OCEAN
30°N
Midway June 1942
Midway Islands
1943
Nagasaki Aug. 9, 1945
Okinawa April–June, 1945
Volcano Islands
1944–1945
1945
Iwo Jima (Iwo To) Feb.–Mar. 1945
Hawaiian Islands
Taiwan
BURMA
Hong Kong
1945
BATAAN PENINSULA
Mariana Islands
Tinian
Japanese attack Pearl Harbor Dec. 7, 1941
15°N
FRENCH INDOCHINA
PHILIPPINE ISLANDS
Philippine Sea June 1944
Guam
NIMITZ 1944
Marshall Islands
THAILAND
MALAYA
Leyte Gulf Oct. 1944
1944
Gilbert Islands
1943
0° Equator
DUTCH EAST INDIES
MACARTHUR
Bismarck Sea March 1943
Guadalcanal Aug. 1942–Feb. 1943
Solomon Islands
1942–1943
Port Moresby
Coral Sea May 1942
15°S
INDIAN OCEAN
150°E
AUSTRALIA
165°W
105°E
120°E
135°E

Interpret Maps

1. **Location** Did the area controlled by Japan by July 1942 include the Hawaiian Islands? How can you tell?

2. **Human-Environment Interaction** Which major battles occurred south of the equator?

Raising the Flag on Iwo Jima

Six marines are shown raising the American flag atop Mount Suribachi on the island of Iwo Jima after an important battle there. They were instructed to raise the flag on the highest point of the island so that all the men still fighting could see it.

could carry 20,000 pounds of explosives each, led bombing raids on more than 60 major Japanese cities. A March 1945 raid set Japan's capital city of Tokyo on fire, leaving 1 million people homeless. Japanese factories were destroyed, and food became so scarce that many people neared starvation. Even with the widespread loss of life and damage to the environment, Japan refused to surrender.

Two of the war's fiercest battles occurred on Japan's outer islands early in 1945. In February U.S. Marines stormed the beaches of Iwo Jima, now known as Iwo To. Japanese defenders were dug into caves, with orders to fight to the death. "On Iwo, we hardly ever saw the enemy," recalled one marine. After the marines raised the American flag on Iwo Jima, a month of bloody fighting followed. Of more than 20,000 Japanese defenders on Iwo Jima, about a thousand were taken prisoner—the rest were killed or wounded in battle. About 6,800 Americans had died.

Beginning in April an even deadlier battle was fought for the island of Okinawa. There were an estimated 100,000 Japanese soldiers on the island when U.S. forces began their attack. One U.S. Marine officer described the hard fighting at the Battle of Okinawa:

> "We poured a tremendous amount of metal in on those positions. . . . It seemed nothing could possibly be living in that churning mass where the shells were falling and roaring but when we next advanced, [Japanese troops] would still be there and madder than ever."
>
> —Colonel Wilburt S. Brown, quoted in *The Final Campaign: Marines in the Victory on Okinawa* by Colonel Joseph H. Alexander

Kamikaze pilots, some as young as 17, flew their airplanes directly into enemy targets, committing suicide to fulfill their duty.

In the waters near the island, Japanese planes struck U.S. ships with the tactic of **kamikaze**—purposely crashing piloted planes into enemy ships. In wave after wave, kamikaze pilots flew planes loaded with explosives straight down onto the decks of Allied ships. An American sailor who was on the deck of an aircraft carrier when a kamikaze attacked the ship described the scene. The plane "cartwheeled the length of the carrier and plowed into the planes we had on the [flight deck]. We were burning bow to stern . . . All the guys manning the guns were dead. Standing up. Pointing their guns. They never left their posts."

More than 2,500 kamikaze missions were flown, killing more than 4,000 Allied sailors. The fighting on Okinawa lasted nearly three months and led to terrible casualties. By the time the island was secure, some 12,000 Allied troops were dead and 36,000 wounded. The Japanese losses were staggering—some 110,000 troops and 80,000 civilians had been killed.

After their victories at Iwo Jima and Okinawa, the Allies were one step closer to final victory. Allied leaders began to plan for an all-out assault on the main Japanese islands.

Summary and Preview The Allies made major gains in the Pacific war, moving closer to Japan. In the next lesson you will learn how the Allies achieved full victory.

Reading Check
Analyze Information How did the Allied strategy in the Pacific change starting in 1943?

Lesson 4 Assessment

Review Ideas, Terms, and People

1. **a. Identify** Why were the Japanese able to advance in the Pacific in 1942?
   b. Explain Why did so many prisoners die on the Bataan Death March?

2. **a. Recall** What Allied victories halted Japan's advance?
   b. Analyze Why was the Battle of the Coral Sea important?
   c. Elaborate How do you think the war might have been different if the Allies had lost the Battle of Midway?

3. **a. Identify** What was island hopping?
   b. Explain What event led to the retaking of the Philippines?
   c. Evaluate Why do you think someone would serve as a kamikaze pilot?

Critical Thinking

4. **Sequence** In this lesson you learned about the main events of the Pacific war. Create a graphic organizer similar to the one below and use it to put the main events of the Pacific war in the correct sequence.

| 1942 | → | 1943 | → | 1944 | → | 1945 |

Victory and Consequences

The Big Idea

The Allies won World War II, the most devastating war in world history.

Main Ideas

- The Allies gained victory in Europe with Germany's surrender.
- Nazis murdered millions of Jews and other people in the Holocaust.
- Victory in the Pacific came after the United States dropped atomic bombs on Japan.

Key Terms and People

Battle of the Bulge
Harry S. Truman
Holocaust
genocide
Manhattan Project
atomic bomb

If YOU were there . . .

It is August 1944. You are an American soldier in France. You have seen the horrors of battle up close, but today is a day to rejoice. You and other Allied soldiers are marching through the streets of Paris, celebrating its liberation from Nazi control. It seems as if the whole city has come out to greet the Americans. People rush up to shake your hand. Children cheer and hand you flowers.

How does it feel to be part of this moment in history?

Germany Surrenders

In the weeks after the successful D-Day invasion, hundreds of thousands of Allied troops landed in France. Led by American general Omar Bradley, Allied forces began fighting their way across France toward Germany. At the same time, the Soviets were closing in on Germany from the east. Although Germany's defeat seemed certain to the Allies, Hitler refused to surrender.

In July 1944 Allied tank forces led by American general George Patton broke through German lines on the western front. While Patton drove forward, more Allied forces invaded southern France. Both groups of Allied forces fought their way toward Paris. Encouraged by the Allies' success, the citizens of Paris rebelled against the German-occupying forces. By the end of August, General Bradley was leading Allied troops through the streets of the freed city. "All Paris surged out to meet the Allied columns and welcome their liberators," remembered one witness. After securing Paris, the Allies continued driving through Belgium and Luxembourg, making their way toward Germany. Hitler drafted every able-bodied German man from the age of 16 to 60 and planned one last desperate attack.

Hitler's goal was for German forces to drive through a weak spot in the Allied lines and capture the city of Antwerp,

In the Battle of the Bulge, American soldiers faced a strong German attack in snowy forests during the coldest winter northern Europe had in 40 years.

Belgium. On December 16 the Germans seized a moment when Allied planes were grounded due to bad weather. In heavy snow some 25 German divisions attacked the Ardennes (ahr-DEN), a densely forested region defended by just a few American divisions. The Germans quickly pushed the Allied forces back about 65 miles, creating a huge bulge in the Allied lines. This gave the battle its name—the **Battle of the Bulge**.

Allied forces recovered rapidly and stopped the German advance. When the skies cleared in late December, Allied planes began pounding German troops. In early January 1945 the Germans began to retreat. American losses were heavy—between 70,000 and 81,000 casualties. Germany's losses were even greater, and Hitler's ability to wage offensive war was now completely crushed.

In the final months of the war, Allied bombing raids devastated major German cities such as Berlin and Hamburg. Both sides in World War II had used these kinds of bombing raids against the enemy's cities. German raids, for example, killed about 30,000 civilians in the British capital of London. In February 1945 Allied bombers attacked the German city of Dresden, igniting a firestorm that destroyed the city and killed more than 35,000 civilians. "Dresden was an inferno," recalled one U.S. soldier. "I have nightmares, even today."

As Allied forces surrounded Berlin, Hitler retreated to an underground bunker in the heart of the ruined city. On April 30, as Soviet troops entered Berlin, Hitler committed suicide. A week later, the Germans surrendered. The war in Europe had finally come to an end. The Allies celebrated May 8, 1945, as V-E (Victory in Europe) Day.

President Franklin Roosevelt, who had led the United States throughout World War II, did not live to see V-E Day. He died of a stroke on April 12. **Harry S. Truman** became president and immediately faced the challenge of winning the war in the Pacific.

Reading Check
Sequence What events led to Germany's surrender?

Horrors of the Holocaust

When Allied forces liberated Europe, they uncovered evidence of horrifying Nazi crimes against humanity. In a program of mass murder that became known as the **Holocaust**, Hitler and the Nazis had attempted to exterminate the entire Jewish population of Europe in the name of Aryan supremacy.

The Final Solution Soon after gaining power in Germany, Hitler began his campaign of terror against the Jews. The Nazis stripped German Jews of their citizenship and seized their property. On the "night of broken glass," or *Kristallnacht*, many Jewish homes and businesses were destroyed. Many Jews who did not escape the country were imprisoned in concentration camps such as Dachau (DAH-kow), near Munich.

When Germany conquered huge sections of Europe and the Soviet Union early in World War II, nearly 10 million Jews came under Hitler's control. The Nazis forced many Jews into urban centers called ghettos. Others were sent to concentration camps and used as slave labor. Many died from hunger or disease. The Nazis also formed special killing squads that rounded up groups of Jews, shot them, and buried them in mass graves. When the Germans invaded the Soviet Union, these squads murdered more than 33,000 Soviet Jews near Kiev in three days. By the end of 1941 the death squads had executed nearly 1 million people.

The Death Camps In January 1942 senior Nazi officials met to plan what they called "a final solution to the Jewish question." Hitler's "final solution" was **genocide**, or the extermination of an entire group of people. The Nazi plan was to kill the Jews in specially built death camps, mainly in German-occupied Poland. The camps were equipped with gas chambers designed to kill large numbers of people, and furnaces were used to cremate the bodies of victims.

By mid-1942 the Nazis had begun to ship Jews from throughout German-occupied Europe to the camps. Several hundred thousand Jews, for example, were transported by train from the ghetto in the Polish capital of Warsaw to a death camp called Treblinka. In April 1943 Jews in the Warsaw ghetto staged a violent uprising, attacking the Germans with guns and homemade bombs. It took German troops nearly a month to crush the revolt. Survivors were sent to Treblinka.

At the death camps most children, the elderly, and the sick were immediately executed. Those strong enough to work were used as laborers. When they became too weak to work, they too were sent to the gas chambers. Moritz Vegh was 13 when his family was sent from Czechoslovakia to Auschwitz, one of the most notorious of the death camps. He later described what happened to his mother and sister.

Buchenwald

Jews, Roma (also known as Gypsies), and other victims of Hitler and the Nazis were sent to concentration camps. Many were killed immediately upon arrival at the camps, while others were executed later. Families were forced apart, and prisoners were poorly fed and clothed. Some were used as subjects for medical experiments. This photo shows survivors of the Buchenwald concentration camp after their liberation.

How did Hitler use the concentration camps to fulfill part of his goals for Germany?

"When we got off the cattle truck, they ordered, 'Men, right; women, left.' . . . I went with my father. My little sister, Esther, she went with my mother. Esther was only eleven. She was holding my mother's hand. When they made a selection of the women, Esther clung to my mother. My mother wouldn't give her up. . . . They went straight to the gas chamber."

—Moritz Vegh, quoted in *The Boys: The Untold Story of 732 Young Concentration Camp Survivors*

Reading Check
Summarize What was the purpose of the Nazis' Final Solution?

Moritz survived the war, working as a laborer at Auschwitz.

The Allied soldiers who liberated the death camps were horrified by what they found. About 6 million Jews—some two-thirds of Europe's pre-war Jewish population—had been killed in the Holocaust. The Nazis had also murdered millions of others, including Roma (often known as Gypsies), Slavs, political opponents, and people with physical or mental disabilities.

Victory in the Pacific

In the Pacific, Allied planners prepared to invade Japan. They estimated that the invasion could result in more than 1 million Allied casualties.

The Allies had another option. Since 1942 Allied scientists had been working on a secret program known as the **Manhattan Project**. The goal was to develop an **atomic bomb**, a weapon that produces tremendous power by splitting atoms. (Germany had started trying to develop atomic weapons since before the war began. The Allies were determined to achieve that goal before the Nazis.) On July 16, 1945, the Allies successfully tested the first atomic bomb in the New Mexico desert. The massive explosion melted the desert sand into glass for 800 yards in all directions.

When Japanese leaders refused the Allies' demand for an unconditional surrender, President Truman gave the order to use the atomic bomb. On August 6, 1945, the B-29 bomber *Enola Gay* dropped an atomic bomb above the city of Hiroshima. "When I saw a very strong light, a flash, I put my arms over my face unconsciously," said one Japanese survivor. "Almost instantly I felt my face was inflating . . . I saw people looking for water and they died soon after they drank it . . . The whole city was destroyed and burning. There was no place to go." The explosion killed almost 80,000 people instantly. Thousands more died later from burns and radiation poisoning.

The atomic blast over Hiroshima destroyed the city. Almost 80,000 people were killed instantly, and thousands more died later from the effects of radiation.

Reading Check
Draw Conclusions
Why did Japan surrender?

Japanese leaders still refused to surrender. On August 9 U.S. forces dropped a second atomic bomb on the city of Nagasaki. About one-third of the city was destroyed, and approximately 22,000 people died immediately. The Japanese announced their surrender on August 15, 1945.

After the War

After six years, World War II was finally over. More than 50 million people had been killed—more than half of them civilians. National economies in Europe and Asia were devastated, and millions of people were left without food, water, or shelter. Since the war had been fought far from American soil, the United States escaped this level of destruction. As the strongest power left in the world, much of the responsibility for postwar rebuilding fell to the United States, which sent billions of dollars to its European allies and even its defeated enemies.

Japan was in ruins. Bombing raids had almost destroyed Tokyo, and the atomic bombs had flattened Hiroshima and Nagasaki. Japan had lost its empire. A legitimate government had to be established. General Douglas MacArthur took charge of rebuilding Japan. He disbanded the military and brought war criminals to trial. MacArthur and his team drew up a new constitution built on democratic principles, and it was quickly adopted. Although reviving the country's economy was not really part of his job, MacArthur also pushed through a plan for land reform. Other reforms gave workers the right to create labor unions. By the early 1950s Japan was well on the road to recovery. Once bitter enemies, the United States and Japan became allies.

Reading Check
Summarize How did Japan go from being an enemy to being an ally?

Summary and Preview In this lesson you learned how World War II ended. In the next module you will learn how the world recovered from the war and worked to prevent such wars in the future.

Lesson 5 Assessment

Review Ideas, Terms, and People

1. **a. Identify** What was the last major battle of the war in Europe?

   b. Evaluate What was the biggest task facing Harry S. Truman when he became president?

2. **a. Identify** What was the Holocaust?

   b. Elaborate How did the oppression of Jews increase during the war?

3. **a. Recall** What was the purpose of the Manhattan Project, and how did it result in the end of the war against Japan?

   b. Explain What was the status of the United States after the war?

   c. Predict How do you think the invention of the atomic bomb changed people's views of war?

Critical Thinking

4. **Identify Causes** In this lesson you learned about the final days of the war in both Europe and the Pacific. Create a graphic organizer similar to the one below and use it to show the short-term causes of Germany's and Japan's surrenders.

Literature of the Holocaust

Word Help

molten melted

phylacteries wooden prayer boxes strapped to the forehead and arm

ghetto neighborhood set aside for Jews

indiscriminately without care

surreptitiously secretly

convoy military escort

❶ The Hungarian police used physical force to gather people together.

About the Reading Elie Wiesel was taken to Auschwitz when he was age 15. Though he survived the camp, not all of his family did. Years after the war, Wiesel wrote about his time spent imprisoned at Auschwitz.

As You Read Look for ways that Wiesel describes the trauma of being taken away.

From **Night**
by Elie Wiesel (1928–2016), translated by Marion Wiesel

By eight o'clock in the morning, weariness had settled into our veins, our limbs, our brains, like molten lead. I was in the midst of prayer when suddenly there was shouting in the streets. I quickly unwound my phylacteries and ran to the window. Hungarian police had entered the ghetto and were yelling in the street nearby:

"All Jews, outside! Hurry!"

They were followed by Jewish police, who, their voices breaking, told us:

"The time has come . . . you must leave all this . . ."

The Hungarian police used their rifle butts, their clubs to indiscriminately strike old men and women, children and cripples. ❶

One by one, the houses emptied and the street filled with people carrying bundles. By ten o'clock, everyone was outside. The police were taking roll calls, once, twice, twenty times. The heat was oppressive. Sweat streamed from people's faces and bodies.

Children were crying for water.

Water! There was water close by in the houses, the backyards, but it was forbidden to break rank.

"Water, Mother, I am thirsty!"

Some of the Jewish police surreptitiously went to fill a few jugs. My sisters and I were still allowed to move about, as we were destined for the last convoy, and so we helped as best we could.

Connect Literature to History

1. **Analyze** During the early years of World War II, European Jews faced oppression. In time oppression changed to removal. How does Wiesel describe the removal of the Jews from his hometown?

2. **Describe** Jews were treated with physical violence by Nazi supporters. Give an example of violence against Jews found in this passage.

Social Studies Skills

Construct Timelines

Define the Skill

Timelines are a good way to organize historical information. Timelines clearly show a sequence of historical events over a certain period of time. Many timelines focus on a specific theme within a time period.

When you construct a timeline, it often makes the sequence of events easier to follow. Timelines show events in the order they happened and the amount of time between events. Constructing a timeline can therefore help you better understand events' context. For example, organizing events on a timeline can help you determine their causes and effects.

Learn the Skill

When you construct a timeline, you need to make some basic decisions. First, the timeline needs a topic. This topic can be general or specific. One example of a general topic is the 1940s. A more specific topic might be major battles of World War II. The timeline should cover a time period that includes the main events related to the topic. For example, it would make sense for a timeline on American battles in World War II to cover the period 1941 to 1945.

The next step in constructing a timeline is gathering information. This includes taking notes on events from the chosen time period related to the topic. It is important to write down the date when each event happened. Putting the events in order before making the timeline is often helpful. If there are too many events, it is a good idea to include only the most important ones.

The first step in actually constructing the timeline is to draw a straight line using a ruler. The next step is to mark even intervals on the timeline. Intervals are dates that divide the timeline into smaller, equal time periods. For example, a timeline of the 1940s might include two-year intervals: 1940, 1942, 1944, and so on. Then add events in the correct places on the timeline. The beginning and end of the timeline, each interval, and each event should be labeled with dates. The finished timeline should include at least six events. As a final touch, the timeline needs a title. The title tells what the entries in the timeline are about and may include the dates the timeline covers.

Practice the Skill

Follow these instructions to construct a timeline.

1. Using your textbook, choose a topic related to World War II for your timeline. Decide on the dates your timeline will need to cover.

2. Use your textbook to take notes on events to include in your timeline and their dates. Put the events in order.

3. Following the steps described above, construct your timeline. The finished timeline should include clearly labeled dates, at least six events, and a title.

Module 27 Assessment

Review Vocabulary, Terms, and People

Identify the term or person from the module that best fits each of the following descriptions.

1. The first African American flying unit in the U.S. military
2. American general who retreated from and then retook the Philippines
3. The dictator of the Soviet Union
4. A weapon that produces a massive explosion by splitting atoms
5. Battle at which British troops stopped the German Afrika Korps
6. Policy of avoiding war with an aggressive nation by giving in to its demands
7. Extermination of an entire group of people

Comprehension and Critical Thinking

Lesson 1

8. a. Identify What is fascism?
   b. Make Inferences Before Pearl Harbor, what U.S. policies suggested that the United States would join the Allies?
   c. Evaluate How well did the policy of appeasement work? Explain your answer.

Lesson 2

9. a. Recall What happened during the zoot-suit riots?
   b. Analyze Why was the War Production Board important to the war effort?
   c. Elaborate How do you think Japanese Americans felt about internment?

Lesson 3

10. a. Identify What led the Axis Powers to retreat from the Soviet Union?
    b. Summarize In which regions and countries did the Allies win major victories against Germany?
    c. Draw Conclusions Why do you think D-Day succeeded?

Lesson 4

11. a. Describe What did kamikaze pilots do?
    b. Explain How did cracking Japanese codes help the Allies in the Pacific?
    c. Draw Conclusions Why do you think Japan was determined to continue fighting?

Lesson 5

12. a. Recall What were the effects of the atomic bombs on Hiroshima and Nagasaki?
    b. Contrast How was the Holocaust different from other wartime tragedies?
    c. Evaluate Do you think the strategy of bombing civilian centers was fair? Why or why not?

Module 27 Assessment, continued

Review Themes

13. Geography How did geography affect the course of World War II?

14. Society and Culture What changes in society did World War II bring about?

Reading Skills

Categorize *Use the Reading Skills taught in this module to answer the question from the reading selection below.*

> American, British, and Canadian troops invaded France on June 6, 1944—known as D-Day, or "designated day." They crossed the choppy waters of the English Channel and landed on five beaches in Normandy. More than 6,000 ships, 11,000 planes, and 156,000 men were part of the invasion. Soldiers jumped from boats and waded ashore, often under heavy fire.

15. Which of the following general categories could help you organize this information?
  a. generals of the American forces
  b. types of ammunition used
  c. resources of invading forces
  d. leaders of Allied nations

Social Studies Skills

Construct Timelines *Use the Social Studies Skills taught in this module to answer the question below.*

16. Make a timeline about the end of World War II, covering the events of 1945.

Focus on Writing

17. Write Your Radio News Broadcast During World War II, millions of Americans had relatives fighting overseas. They relied on radio broadcasts for up-to-date news from the battlefronts around the world. Choose one event or story from World War II as the focus of your radio broadcast. You can include quotes from soldiers or national leaders. Remember that people cannot see your broadcast, so use descriptive language. Be sure to answer the following questions: Who? What? Where? When? Why? and How?

Memories of
WORLD WAR II

A global conflict, World War II shaped the history of both the United States and the world. Americans contributed to the war effort in numerous ways. Many enlisted in the military and served in Africa, Europe, and the Pacific. Others contributed by working in factories to produce the massive amounts of ships, planes, guns, and other supplies necessary to win the war. In the process, these Americans left behind firsthand accounts of their experiences during the war, both at home and abroad. Explore some of the personal stories and recollections of World War II online. You can find a wealth of information, video clips, primary sources, activities, and more through your online textbook.

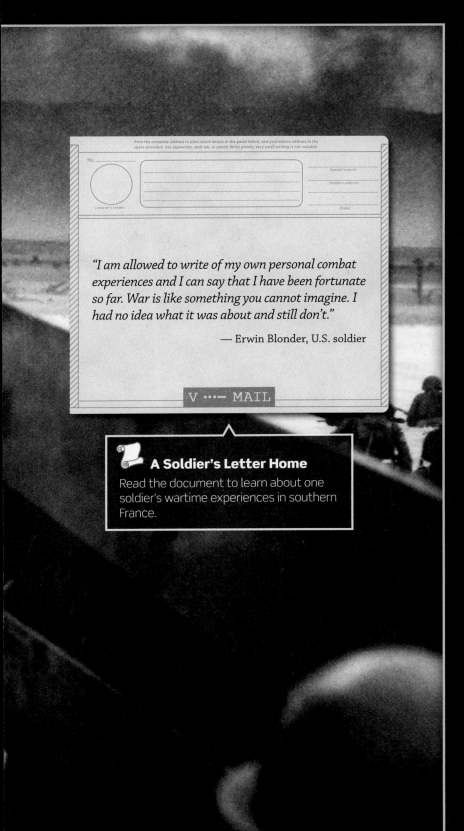

Print the complete address in plain block letters in the panel below, and your return address in the space provided. Use typewriter, dark ink, or pencil. Write plainly. Very small writing is not suitable.

No.

(Sender's name)

(Sender's address)

CENSOR'S STAMP

(Date)

"*I am allowed to write of my own personal combat experiences and I can say that I have been fortunate so far. War is like something you cannot imagine. I had no idea what it was about and still don't.*"

— Erwin Blonder, U.S. soldier

V ···– MAIL

A Soldier's Letter Home

Read the document to learn about one soldier's wartime experiences in southern France.

■◄ America Mobilizes for War

Watch the video to see how the United States mobilized its citizens for war and how society changed as a result.

■◄ Air War Over Germany

Watch the video to see how the P-51 Mustang helped the Allies win the air war over Germany.

■◄ The Pacific Islands

Watch the video to hear veterans describe their experiences fighting in the Pacific theater.

Module 28
The Cold War

★

Essential Question
How might the Cold War have been prevented?

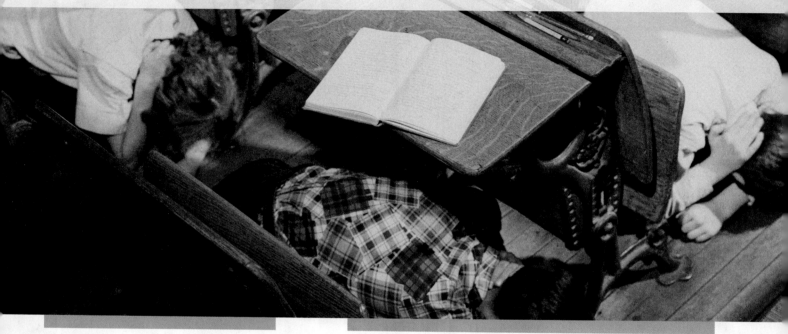

About the Photo: After World War II, the United States and the Soviet Union engaged in a nuclear arms race. Here, American students practice a "duck-and-cover" drill, designed to protect them from a nuclear bomb blast.

▶ Explore ONLINE!

HISTORY

VIDEOS, including...
• The Arms Race
• The Berlin Airlift
• Korean War Begins
• Suburbia and the Baby Boom

☑ Document-Based Investigations

☑ Graphic Organizers

☑ Interactive Games

☑ Interactive Map: Postwar Germany

☑ Image with Hotspots: Fear of Communism

☑ The Korean War Begins

☑ Image Carousel: Major Spy Cases

☑ Interactive Graphs: Postwar Boom, 1945–1960

In this module you will learn how American life changed as a result of the Cold War.

What You Will Learn ...

Lesson 1: Adjusting to Peace. 868
The Big Idea After World War II, Americans adjusted to new challenges both at home and around the world.

Lesson 2: War in Korea and a New Red Scare. 876
The Big Idea During the Cold War, the U.S. government confronted communism globally and within the United States.

Lesson 3: The Nation Prospers. 882
The Big Idea An expanding economy led to new ways of life for many Americans in the 1950s.

Timeline of Events 1945–1960

▶ *Explore ONLINE!*

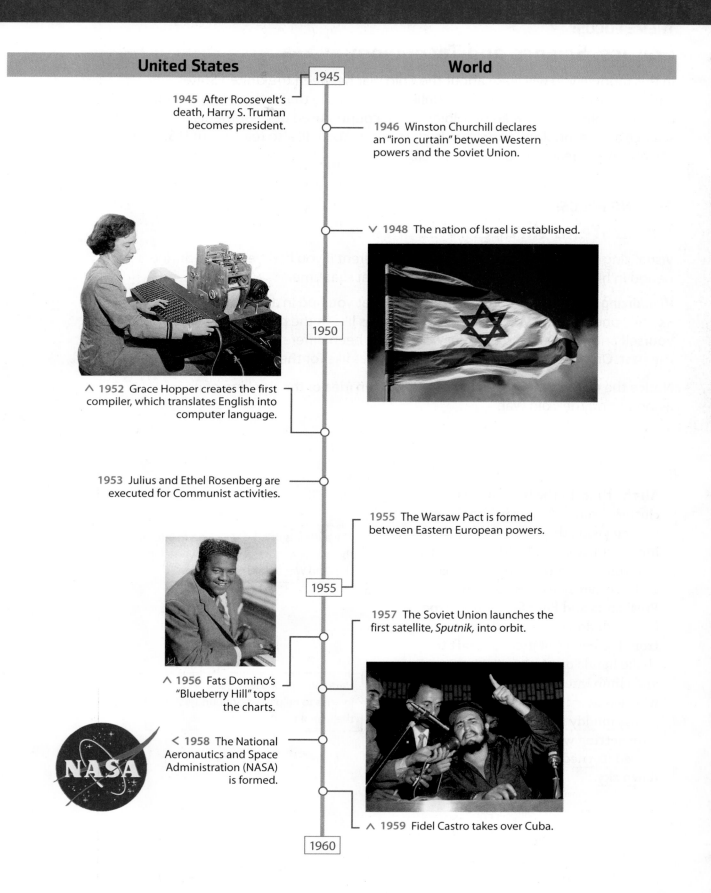

United States	World

1945

1945 After Roosevelt's death, Harry S. Truman becomes president.

1946 Winston Churchill declares an "iron curtain" between Western powers and the Soviet Union.

∨ **1948** The nation of Israel is established.

1950

∧ **1952** Grace Hopper creates the first compiler, which translates English into computer language.

1953 Julius and Ethel Rosenberg are executed for Communist activities.

1955 The Warsaw Pact is formed between Eastern European powers.

1955

1957 The Soviet Union launches the first satellite, *Sputnik,* into orbit.

∧ **1956** Fats Domino's "Blueberry Hill" tops the charts.

< **1958** The National Aeronautics and Space Administration (NASA) is formed.

∧ **1959** Fidel Castro takes over Cuba.

1960

Reading Social Studies

Politics, Science and Technology

In this module you will learn about the Cold War between the United States and the Soviet Union. This war was unlike other wars in that it was often fought between politicians instead of soldiers. Each country used developments in science and technology to declare itself superior. You will also read about U.S. society and its reaction to the Cold War.

READING FOCUS:
Understand through Visualizing

Visualizing how your life might have been different if you had been alive during a period in history can help you understand life at that time.

Visualizing Using clues about everyday life that you find in a history module like this one can help you imagine what life was like in the past. You can imagine yourself and your life, and how life would have been different if you had lived in the past. Or, you can try to imagine what life was like for the people then.

Notice the clues in this passage that give you an idea of the thinking of people living during the Cold War.

All the time, in the homely [plain], cluttered rooms of our private lives the television displayed the continuing spectacle of public life—all of it still going on in the windless places on the other side of the screen. Presidents and First Secretaries trod [climbed] down the metal staircases from the bellies of great aircraft to shake hands on the tarmac [runway] and climb into big black cars. Tanks wheeled down blind streets and across muddy fields. Rolls of heavy wire netting were unwound and veered [turned] upwards against a dawn sky.

—From *The Cruel Peace*, by Fred Inglis

> The author is using description to inform the reader about the feeling of watching the Cold War unfold on television.

> Here the author uses frightening images to help the reader understand the fear of the Cold War.

You Try It!

The following passage is from the module you are getting ready to read. As you read the passage, look for details that help you visualize the past.

> In 1946 Winston Churchill described how Soviet control cut these countries off from the Western world. "An iron curtain has descended [fallen] across the [European] Continent," he said. The term *iron curtain* thus came to be used to describe this division. Presidential adviser Bernard Baruch warned of the seriousness of the Soviet threat, saying, "Let us not be deceived—we are today in the midst of a cold war." The phrase *Cold War* came to be used to describe the struggle for global power between the United States and the Soviet Union.

After you read the passage, answer the following questions.

1. Which visual description helps you understand the attitude existing between the United States and the Soviet Union?
2. How does the quote by Winston Churchill help you visualize the political atmosphere of the time?
3. How does the phrase *Cold War* help you visualize the political atmosphere of the time?

As you read Module 28, look for details that help you visualize the past.

Key Terms and People

Lesson 1
Yalta Conference
Nuremberg trials
United Nations
superpowers
Cold War
containment
Truman Doctrine
Marshall Plan
North Atlantic Treaty Organization
GI Bill of Rights
Fair Deal

Lesson 2
Mao Zedong
38th parallel
Joseph McCarthy
hydrogen bomb
arms race
Sputnik
brinkmanship

Lesson 3
baby boom
Sun Belt
urban renewal
beats

Adjusting to Peace

The Big Idea

After World War II, Americans adjusted to new challenges both at home and around the world.

Main Ideas

- As World War II ended, leaders began planning the future of the postwar world.

- The United States and the Soviet Union went from being allies to enemies after World War II.

- Americans adjusted to postwar life.

Key Terms and People

Yalta Conference
Nuremberg trials
United Nations
superpowers
Cold War
containment
Truman Doctrine
Marshall Plan
North Atlantic Treaty Organization
GI Bill of Rights
Fair Deal

If YOU were there . . .

You are an adviser to President Harry S. Truman in July 1945. You have traveled with him to Potsdam, outside the ruined city of Berlin, where Allied leaders are discussing postwar plans. Everyone agrees that steps must be taken to prevent another world war. But you are worried that Soviet leader Joseph Stalin cannot be trusted.

What advice would you give to President Truman?

The Future of the Postwar World

As 1945 began, it was becoming clear that the Allies were going to win World War II. In February Allied leaders known as the Big Three—Franklin D. Roosevelt of the United States, Winston Churchill of Great Britain, and Joseph Stalin of the Soviet Union—met in the Soviet city of Yalta to discuss plans for peace.

In February, at the **Yalta Conference**, the three leaders made important decisions about the future of European governments. They expressed support for the creation of an international peacekeeping organization. They also agreed that nations freed from Germany should have the right "to create democratic institutions of their own choice." Stalin promised to allow free elections in the Soviet-occupied countries in Eastern Europe. However, after driving German troops out of Poland, Soviet forces set up a pro-Soviet Communist government.

In July 1945 President Truman met with the new British prime minister Clement Atlee and Soviet leader Joseph Stalin near Berlin, Germany, at the Potsdam Conference. The Allied leaders divided conquered Germany into four zones. Britain, France, the United States, and the Soviet Union would each occupy one zone. The capital city of Berlin—located deep inside the Soviet zone—was also divided into four zones.

Winston Churchill, Franklin Roosevelt, and Joseph Stalin (seated left to right) met at Yalta in 1945.

Clement Atlee, Harry Truman, and Joseph Stalin (seated left to right) met at Potsdam in 1945.

War Crimes Trials After World War II, Allied leaders formed a special court, called the International Military Tribunal, to try Axis leaders accused of war crimes. In November 1945 the tribunal put high-ranking Nazis on trial in the German city of Nuremberg in what became known as the **Nuremberg trials**. U.S. Supreme Court justice Robert H. Jackson served as the chief American attorney. In his opening statement, Jackson explained the importance of the trials:

> "The wrongs which we seek to condemn and punish have been so calculated [well planned], so malignant [evil] and devastating, that civilization cannot tolerate their being ignored because it cannot survive their being repeated."
>
> —Robert H. Jackson, quoted in *The Nuremberg Trial*, edited by Mitchell Bard

The court charged Nazi officials with "crimes against humanity." One defendant was Hermann Goering, a key planner of Hitler's "final solution." Another was Hans Frank, Poland's wartime governor, who had organized the killing of hundreds of thousands of Poles and Polish Jews. The tribunal found 19 Nazi leaders guilty. Of these, 12 leaders, including Goering and Frank, were sentenced to death.

The International Military Tribunal for the Far East held trials in Japan. Japan's wartime leader Hideki Tojo was convicted and executed. Seven other Japanese leaders were also sentenced to death. The trials in Germany and Japan helped establish the principle that individuals must be held responsible for committing war crimes, even when acting on behalf of a government.

The United Nations During the war, President Roosevelt had spoken of the need for a new international organization to promote world peace. Roosevelt did not believe the United States alone could bring peace to the whole world. "The structure of world peace," he said, "must be a peace which rests on the cooperative effort of the whole world."

In 1944 American, British, Soviet, and Chinese representatives met to draft a plan for the **United Nations** (UN)—an organization dedicated to

Today, the United Nations has more than 190 members and works to prevent war, provide disaster relief, prevent hunger and disease, and combat international terrorism.

resolving international conflicts. In 1945 representatives from 50 countries met to write the United Nations Charter. The UN Charter declared the organization's commitment "to unite our strength to maintain international peace and security." President Truman appointed Eleanor Roosevelt as one of the first U.S. delegates to the UN.

At the UN, Eleanor Roosevelt helped write and advocate for the Universal Declaration of Human Rights, which the UN adopted in 1948. During Franklin Roosevelt's presidency, she had changed the role of First Lady by holding her own press conferences, making speeches, and writing newspaper columns that actively promoted human rights, children's welfare, and equal rights for women and minorities.

One of the UN's first actions concerned Palestine, occupied by the British after World War I. The UN General Assembly voted to divide the area into separate Arab and Jewish states. Jews had begun moving to Palestine, an area important to the Jewish, Christian, and Islamic religions, after World War I. Many more moved there before and during World War II. On May 14, 1948, Jewish leaders announced the creation of the nation of Israel.

The United States quickly recognized the new Jewish state. Arab leaders refused to do so and claimed the land as their own. Armies from five Arab states attacked Israel. Israeli forces drove them back, and the two sides reached a truce in 1949. Israel then joined the UN. But tensions remained high.

Reading Check
Find Main Ideas
What steps did world leaders take to establish peace?

From Allies to Enemies

After World War II, the United States and the Soviet Union emerged as **superpowers**, or powerful countries who influenced events in their regions of the world. During World War II, the two countries had cooperated to win the war. Afterward, the differences between the two nations led to new hostility. The Soviet Union hoped to spread communism around the world. Americans remained committed to capitalism and democracy.

The Iron Curtain After Stalin created a Communist government in Poland, the Soviet Union expanded its control over Eastern Europe by creating "satellite states"—countries under complete Soviet control. In 1946 Winston Churchill described how Soviet control cut these countries off from the Western world. "An iron curtain has descended [fallen] across the [European] Continent," he said. The term *iron curtain* thus came to be used to describe this division. Presidential adviser Bernard Baruch warned of the seriousness of the Soviet threat, saying, "Let us not be deceived—we are today in the midst of a cold war." The phrase **Cold War** came to be used to describe the struggle for global power between the United States and the Soviet Union.

This cartoon shows Czechoslovakia's freedom being crushed by the Soviet Union.

Cold War Policies The United States quickly developed a new foreign policy to deal with the Cold War. It was based on the goal of **containment**, or preventing the Soviet Union from expanding its influence around the world.

In 1945 the Soviet Union began demanding control over areas in the Mediterranean Sea that were under Turkish authority. In 1946 Communist rebels in Greece threatened to topple the Greek monarchy. At Truman's request, Congress passed an aid package worth millions of dollars for Greece and Turkey. The money, the president said, would "support free peoples who are resisting attempted subjugation [conquest] by armed minorities or outside pressures." U.S. aid helped the Greek army defeat the Communist rebels and protected Turkey from Soviet expansion. This policy of providing aid to help foreign countries fight communism became known as the **Truman Doctrine**.

The nations of Europe, meanwhile, were still devastated from World War II. American secretary of state George C. Marshall saw this as a threat both to stability in Europe and to the U.S. economy, which depended on trade with Europe. Marshall called on European leaders to develop plans for economic recovery, which the United States would help fund. Under the **Marshall Plan**, Western Europe received more than $13 billion in U.S. loans and grants for European economic recovery between 1948 and 1952. Soviet leaders rejected Marshall Plan aid. They also kept Eastern European nations from participating.

Japan was also left devastated by World War II. With the end of the war, U.S. forces under General Douglas MacArthur occupied Japan and began a series of reforms to help rebuild the country and to keep communism from taking hold. As part of the reform, Japan's emperor lost most of his authority. Power was given instead to an elected parliament. The Americans also helped strengthen and modernize the Japanese economy.

Cold War tensions rose further in 1948 when France, Britain, and the United States decided to join their occupation zones of Germany into one unit. The Soviet Union had good reason to fear the creation of a strong West German state. On June 24, the Soviet Union suddenly blocked all rail, highway, and water traffic between western Germany and the city of Berlin. West Berlin's 2 million residents were trapped behind the iron curtain.

To respond to this crisis without using military force, U.S. and British planes began airlifting supplies into West Berlin. For more than a year, planes delivered lifesaving food, fuel, and machinery to West Berliners. The Soviet Union made no determined effort to stop the airlift, fearing a war. It then lifted the blockade in May 1949.

That same year, the United States joined nine Western European countries, along with Iceland and Canada, to form the **North Atlantic Treaty Organization** (NATO). NATO members promised to defend each other if attacked. In 1955 the Soviet Union created the Warsaw Pact, which provided a unified system of military command between the Soviet Union and its Eastern European satellite countries for their mutual defense. When the Cold War ended, many former Warsaw Pact nations joined NATO. Today, NATO has 28 member nations.

Reading Check
Compare
How were NATO and the Warsaw Pact similar?

Cold War Europe, 1955

Explore ONLINE!

NATO member, 1955
Warsaw Pact member, 1955
Nonaligned Communist nation
Nonaligned nation
The United States, Canada, and Iceland were also NATO members.

0   250   500 Miles
0   250   500 Kilometers

Interpret Maps
1. **Place** Which countries remained nonaligned during the Cold War?
2. **Location** What is the northern-most NATO member country shown on the map?

In the aftermath of World War II, President Truman was charged with transitioning the nation's economy and people to peacetime.

Postwar America

You have read about the economic depression that followed the end of World War I. As World War II ended, President Truman was worried about a similar downturn. More than 16 million Americans had served in the armed forces during the war. Now they were coming home, and most would be looking for work.

President Truman, who was sworn in as president when Roosevelt died in 1945, led the country through the end of World War II and the start of the Cold War. He had been an artillery officer in France during World War I, and he was familiar with the issues veterans faced returning from war.

The Postwar Economy To provide jobs for returning veterans, the government urged the millions of women who had gone to work during the war to give up their jobs. New laws also eased the transition for returning soldiers. The Servicemen's Readjustment Act, or **GI Bill of Rights**, offered veterans money for school as well as loans for houses, farms, and businesses. The GI Bill's home loans enabled veterans to buy about 20 percent of the new houses built right after the war. Some 8 million veterans used the GI Bill's educational benefits to attend colleges and technical schools to receive training for jobs. Thousands more took out loans to open their own businesses. Bob Dole, former U.S. senator from Kansas, described how the GI Bill changed his life:

> "In my case, I went from a couple of nondescript [ordinary] years in college before the war, and came back and made excellent grades. I went on to law school and got involved in politics. None of that would have happened without the GI Bill."
>
> —Bob Dole, quoted in *GI Bill: The Law That Changed America*, by Milton Greenberg

Another major postwar change was Truman's decision to end the rationing of scarce products. Prices skyrocketed as people rushed to buy gasoline and other products that had been limited during the war. The inflation rate in 1946 rose above 18 percent. The U.S. economy remained strong, however.

Labor Unrest More than 35 percent of all nonfarm workers were members of unions in 1946, more than ever before. With prices rising quickly, workers went on strike to demand higher wages. In 1946 alone, 4.5 million workers participated in nearly 5,000 strikes.

The strikes became a major political problem for President Truman. Many people began to wonder if he could handle the presidency. In April 1946 the 400,000-member United Mine Workers of America union went on strike. When Truman was unable to negotiate a settlement, he placed the mines under government control. In May Truman ended a railroad strike by threatening to draft all the striking workers into the army.

To reduce the power of labor unions, Congress passed the Taft-Hartley Act in 1947. This act outlawed closed shops—businesses that could hire only union members. It also allowed the president to order an 80-day "cooling-off" period before a strike began. In addition, union leaders had to swear they were not Communists. In spite of his clashes with unions, Truman thought this bill went too far to weaken unions. He vetoed the bill, but Congress overrode his veto.

Civil Rights After serving their country in World War II, many African Americans faced prejudice and segregation at home. "Black servicemen were overseas dying for this country," said civil rights lawyer Constance Baker Motley. "And . . . they would be coming home to a situation that said, in effect, You're a second-class citizen." African American veterans helped lead a major effort to gain equal rights.

Truman responded in 1946 by appointing the Committee on Civil Rights to investigate discrimination and suggest solutions. As a result of the committee's report, Truman recommended that Congress pass anti-lynching laws, outlaw segregation, and protect civil rights. Congress failed to act on Truman's ideas. But in 1948, under pressure from African American groups, Truman issued an executive order ending segregation in the armed forces. He also banned discrimination in the hiring of federal employees.

The Election of 1948 As the election of 1948 drew near, President Truman's chances of re-election looked bleak. The Republicans had gained control of Congress in 1946. They felt confident that their presidential candidate, New York governor Thomas Dewey, could beat Truman.

Truman faced challenges from within the Democratic Party as well. Some southern Democrats protested Truman's support for civil rights laws by walking out of the 1948 Democratic National Convention. Many joined the States' Rights Party, or Dixiecrats, which favored racial segregation. The Dixiecrats nominated their own presidential candidate—South Carolina governor Strom Thurmond.

Truman took his case for re-election directly to the American people. He traveled more than 30,000 miles by train and delivered hundreds of speeches. He attacked what he called the "do-nothing, good-for-nothing" Congress for refusing to pass his legislation.

Jackie Robinson

On April 15, 1947, Jackie Robinson played his first game for the Brooklyn Dodgers. Robinson became a hero to millions by ending segregation in major league baseball. He went on to be a Hall of Fame player—and an outspoken supporter of equal rights. "The right of every American to first-class citizenship is the most important issue of our time," Robinson said.

How did Robinson show his support for equal rights for all Americans?

"I spoke I believe altogether to between fifteen and twenty million people," he later said. "I met them face to face, and I convinced them, and they voted for me." Truman won a surprise victory. The Democratic Party also regained control of both houses of Congress.

In his 1949 State of the Union Address, Truman urged Congress to support his plans for the nation. Truman's domestic program, called the **Fair Deal**, included a higher minimum wage, the creation of a national health insurance plan for all Americans, and expanded Social Security benefits for the elderly. It also asked for federal protection of civil rights and an end to racial discrimination in hiring.

Congress approved some parts of the Fair Deal, such as a higher minimum wage and expanded Social Security benefits. Congress rejected other Fair Deal proposals. These included civil rights legislation that would have created a permanent Fair Employment Practices Committee.

Summary and Preview The United States faced a series of new challenges after World War II. In the next lesson you will learn how the fear of communism grew in the 1950s.

Reading Check
Analyze Information
How did the GI Bill help returning soldiers?

Lesson 1 Assessment

Review Ideas, Terms, and People

1. a. **Describe** How did the Allies divide Germany at the Potsdam Conference?

   b. **Explain** Why were the Nuremberg trials important?

   c. **Predict** Based on its founding and early years, do you think the United Nations would be an effective organization?

2. a. **Identify** What was the Truman Doctrine?

   b. **Analyze** How did the Marshall Plan help stabilize Western Europe?

   c. **Elaborate** Why do you think the United States and Western European countries were concerned about Soviet expansion?

3. a. **Recall** What kinds of programs were included in President Truman's Fair Deal?

   b. **Explain** What was the purpose of the Taft-Hartley Act?

   c. **Evaluate** Do you think President Truman did enough to promote civil rights? Why or why not?

Critical Thinking

6. **Categorize** In this lesson you learned about the westward expansion of the United States. Create a graphic organizer like the one below to rank the three most important effects of the Louisiana Purchase, from most important to least important, and explain why you chose that order.

Results of World War II	
In the United States	In the World

War in Korea and a New Red Scare

The Big Idea

During the Cold War, the U.S. government confronted communism globally and within the United States.

Main Ideas

- The United States fought Communist North Korea in the Korean War.

- Fear of Communists led to a new Red Scare at home.

- President Eisenhower faced Cold War crises around the world.

Key Terms and People

Mao Zedong
38th parallel
Joseph McCarthy
hydrogen bomb
arms race
Sputnik
brinkmanship

If YOU were there . . .

A radio broadcast on June 26, 1950, delivers a shocking announcement. Communist forces from North Korea have just invaded South Korea. President Truman has demanded that the North Koreans halt their invasion, but they seem to be ignoring this demand. Now Truman has to decide whether to use American military force to stop the North Koreans.

Do you think the United States should send troops to Korea? Why or why not?

The Korean War

The Cold War began in Europe but quickly spread to the Asian nations of China and Korea. In China the Communist Party and the Nationalist Party had been struggling for control of the country since the early 1900s. The two rivals joined forces against Japan during World War II but then resumed their civil war after Japan's defeat. The United States, as part of its commitment to stop the spread of communism, backed the Nationalists. The Nationalists were defeated, however, and were forced to flee to the island of Taiwan. Led by **Mao Zedong**, the Communists officially established the People's Republic of China on October 1, 1949. Many Americans saw this as a disastrous failure of U.S. foreign policy. They feared that all of Asia might soon fall to communism.

These fears were heightened by a crisis in Korea. Japan had controlled Korea from 1910 to the end of World War II. After the war, the Allies divided Korea at the **38th parallel**. The Soviet Union controlled the northern part of Korea, and the United States occupied the south. Both sides set up governments, neither of which recognized the other as legitimate.

Fighting in Korea On June 25, 1950, North Korea's Soviet-trained and -equipped army stormed across the 38th parallel and invaded South Korea. The United Nations called for a cease-fire. But the North Koreans continued their attack.

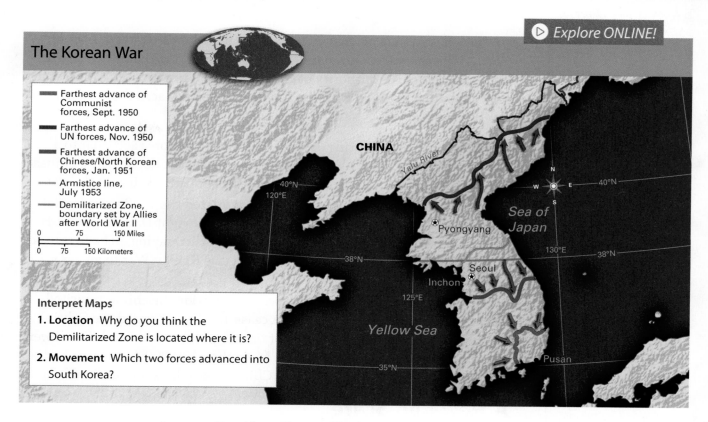

Legend:
- Farthest advance of Communist forces, Sept. 1950
- Farthest advance of UN forces, Nov. 1950
- Farthest advance of Chinese/North Korean forces, Jan. 1951
- Armistice line, July 1953
- Demilitarized Zone, boundary set by Allies after World War II

0   75   150 Miles
0   75   150 Kilometers

CHINA

Yalu River

Sea of Japan

Pyongyang

Seoul

Inchon

Yellow Sea

Pusan

40°N 120°E
38°N
125°E
35°N
40°N
130°E 38°N

Interpret Maps

1. **Location** Why do you think the Demilitarized Zone is located where it is?

2. **Movement** Which two forces advanced into South Korea?

President Truman had to make an immediate decision: Should the United States use force to try to stop the North Korean invasion? On June 27 Truman announced: "I have ordered United States air and sea forces to give the [South] Korean government troops cover and support." That same day, the UN decided to help South Korea "to repel the armed attack." American general Douglas MacArthur was put in command of the UN forces, which included troops from the United States and 15 other countries. The majority of the troops were from the United States and South Korea.

Douglas MacArthur graduated first in his class at West Point, and then began an army career that would last more than 50 years. He reached the rank of general in 1918 and commanded troops in World War I, World War II, and the Korean War.

In the early battles in the Korean War, MacArthur's forces were driven back to the southeastern tip of the Korean Peninsula, near the city of Pusan. Fierce fighting raged for six weeks before the UN troops turned the tide of the war with a surprise attack. Landing at the port city of Inchon on September 15, UN forces attacked the North Koreans from behind. About a month later, MacArthur's troops captured Pyongyang, North Korea's capital. They then advanced north to the Yalu River, the border between North Korea and China. MacArthur told Truman he would "have the boys home by Christmas."

Then China suddenly sent hundreds of thousands of soldiers across the border to join the North Koreans. They drove UN forces south again, back below the 38th parallel. MacArthur suggested air strikes on Chinese cities and an attack on mainland China. Truman refused permission. He was determined to contain the war in Korea.

When MacArthur publicly criticized the president's strategy, Truman relieved the general of command. "I fired General MacArthur because he wouldn't respect the authority of the president," Truman said. This was a very unpopular decision with the American public. MacArthur came home to a hero's welcome.

The War Ends By the spring of 1951 the fighting in Korea settled into a violent stalemate. The UN forces had driven the North Koreans and Chinese back across the 38th parallel. But neither side seemed able to win the war.

Americans' frustration with the war dominated the 1952 presidential election. The Republicans nominated war hero Dwight D. Eisenhower. He promised to end the increasingly unpopular conflict, saying, "The first task of a new administration will be to . . . bring the Korean War to an early and honorable end."

This promise helped Eisenhower win the election. Eisenhower visited Korea, but the conflict dragged on. A cease-fire finally ended the fighting on July 27, 1953. After three years of fighting, North and South Korea were again divided near the 38th parallel. More than 130,000 Americans had been killed or wounded. Korean and Chinese casualties topped 2 million.

Reading Check
Summarize
What were the effects of the Korean War?

A New Red Scare

The first Red Scare swept America after the Russian Revolution in 1917. Cold War fears led to another Red Scare in the late 1940s and 1950s. Attorney General J. Howard McGrath summed up these fears when he said, "There are today many Communists in America. They are everywhere—in factories, offices, butcher shops, on street corners."

Fear of Communists A congressional committee called the House Un-American Activities Committee (HUAC) investigated Communist influence in America. In 1947 HUAC launched a series of hearings to expose what it believed was Communist influence in the Hollywood movie industry. The committee branded as "red," or Communist, actors and writers who would not answer questions or who refused to reveal the names of suspected Communists. People suspected of Communist sympathies were often blacklisted, or denied work. Some of these people never worked in movies again.

Explosive spy cases also fed the fears that Communists were at work in the United States. In 1950 a German-born physicist was convicted of providing the Soviets information about the atomic bomb project at Los Alamos, New Mexico, that allowed them to develop an atomic bomb at least one year earlier than they would have. In 1951 Julius and Ethel Rosenberg also were tried for providing Soviet spies with secret details about atomic bomb design. The Rosenbergs denied the charges but were found guilty and executed in 1953.

Ethel and Julius Rosenberg passed military secrets related to the atomic bomb to the Soviets in the late 1940s. They were accused and convicted in 1951.

The Rise of McCarthy Wisconsin senator **Joseph McCarthy** contributed to fears in the early 1950s by charging that Communists were working inside the State Department. He claimed to have the names of 57 people

Fear of Communism

In the 1950s the fear of communism caused some government leaders to ignore the civil liberties of suspected Communists. Some critics, like this cartoonist, believed these tactics threatened the freedom of all Americans. Here, a frightened man climbs the arm of the Statue of Liberty to put out her torch.

Analyze Historical Sources
Why is the man shown to be putting out Liberty's torch?

"FIRE!"

The frightened man carries water to put out the fire.

The Statue of Liberty's burning torch symbolizes freedom.

Hysteria means "senseless excitement."

"FIRE!" from *Herblock: A Cartoonist's Life* (Times Books 1998)

who were "either card-carrying members or certainly loyal to the Communist Party."

McCarthy produced no **concrete** proof of crimes. Many people spoke out about McCarthy's accusations. When challenged, he made up new charges, labeling those who questioned him as "soft on communism." This method of making aggressive accusations without proof became known as McCarthyism.

Edward R. Murrow, a prominent journalist of the time, frequently criticized Senator McCarthy's tactics.

"If none of us ever read a book that was 'dangerous,' nor had a friend who was 'different,' or never joined an organization that advocated 'change,' we would all be just the kind of people Joe McCarthy wants. Whose fault is that? Not really [McCarthy's]. He didn't create this situation of fear. He merely exploited [took advantage of] it, and rather successfully."

"Murrow is a symbol—the leader and the cleverest of the jackal [wild dog] pack which is always found at the throat of anyone who dares to expose individual Communists and traitors. I am compelled by the facts to say to you that Mr. Edward R. Murrow, as far back as twenty years ago, was engaged in propaganda for Communist causes."

McCarthy finally went too far in 1954. In televised Senate hearings he charged that there were Communists in the U.S. Army. For five weeks Americans watched McCarthy's bullying tactics. At one point McCarthy tried to discredit Joseph Welch, the army's attorney, by attacking a young assistant in Welch's law firm. This shocked Welch—and the nation

Academic Vocabulary
concrete specific, real

watching the hearings on television. "Let us not assassinate this lad further, Senator," Welch said. "Have you left no sense of decency?" A later Senate vote condemned McCarthy's actions, but it came too late for those whose careers had been ruined by his attacks.

Eisenhower and the Cold War

Cold War tensions increased around the world during the presidency of Dwight Eisenhower. In this hostile atmosphere, Americans adjusted to the reality of living with the constant threat of nuclear war.

The Arms Race In 1950 President Truman approved work on the **hydrogen bomb**, a weapon far more powerful than the atomic bombs used in World War II. American scientists tested the first hydrogen bomb in the South Pacific in 1952. "The fireball expanded to three miles in diameter," said a test observer. He soon saw that the entire island on which the bomb exploded "had vanished, vaporized."

The Soviet Union tested its first atomic bomb in 1949 and its first hydrogen bomb in 1953. With these tests, the Soviet Union became the world's second nuclear superpower, or powerful country in possession of nuclear weapons. In what became a nuclear **arms race**, both the United States and the Soviet Union rushed to build more and more weapons. American school children practiced "duck-and-cover" drills, in which they were taught to crouch under their desks in case of nuclear attack. Some families built underground bomb shelters in their backyards for use in a nuclear emergency. The shelters were stocked with essentials.

In October 1957 the Soviets launched *Sputnik*, the world's first artificial satellite. Americans feared that if the Soviet Union could launch a satellite, it could launch missiles to attack the United States. In January 1958 the

Families kept essentials in their bomb shelters such as food, water, first aid supplies, and clothing.

United States responded by launching its own satellite. Later that year, the U.S. government established the National Aeronautics and Space Administration (NASA) to conduct space research.

Cold War Crises President Eisenhower modified Truman's policy of containment. He and Secretary of State John Foster Dulles supported **brinkmanship**—a willingness to go to the brink of war to oppose communism. "The ability to get to the verge [edge] without getting into war is the necessary art," Dulles explained. The president and Dulles also threatened the Soviet Union with "massive retaliation" against Soviet advances.

As part of his effort, Eisenhower used covert, or secret, operations around the world. In 1953, for example, the Central Intelligence Agency (CIA) helped overthrow the premier of Iran. American officials had feared he was a Communist. In 1954 the CIA helped organize the removal of the Guatemalan president for similar reasons.

In 1956 a crisis in Egypt seemed to push the world to the brink of a third world war. Egyptian leader Gamal Abdel Nasser nationalized the Suez Canal, a vital waterway connecting the Mediterranean and Red seas, in an attempt to collect tolls from the canal to finance a major dam project. Britain and France, which relied on the canal for trade, allied with Israel, a longtime enemy of Egypt, and invaded the area around the canal. The Soviet Union, an ally of Egypt, threatened to crush the invaders. This would force the United States to defend its allies. Finally, the Americans and the Soviet Union agreed to condemn the invasion, and the Suez crisis ended. After the brief moment of cooperation, the Cold War continued.

Summary and Preview After World War II, Americans responded to Communist threats at home and abroad. In the next lesson you will read about how America prospered during these challenging times.

Reading Check
Analyze
Information
How was the arms race a display of brinkmanship?

Lesson 2 Assessment

Review Ideas, Terms, and People

1. **a. Identify** What is the 38th parallel, and why was it important in the Korean War?

   b. Analyze How did the outcome of China's civil war affect the U.S. response to North Korea's attack?

   c. Evaluate Do you think President Truman should have fired MacArthur? Explain your answer.

2. **a. Describe** Why did a second Red Scare occur in the late 1940s and 1950s?

   b. Explain How did television affect Joseph McCarthy's power?

   c. Elaborate Why do you think the Red Scare lasted so long?

3. **a. Recall** How did Eisenhower deal with Cold War crises during his administration?

   b. Make Inferences How can you tell that the U.S. government took the launch of *Sputnik* seriously?

   c. Elaborate Why do you think the United States and the Soviet Union were able to cooperate during the Suez crisis?

Critical Thinking

4. **Categorize** In this lesson you learned about Cold War conflicts and crises. Create four boxes similar to the ones below and use each box to list each event under its appropriate location.

| Asia | Soviet Union | United States | Others |

The Nation Prospers

The Big Idea

An expanding economy led to new ways of life for many Americans in the 1950s.

Main Ideas

- America's economy boomed in the 1950s.
- Americans enjoyed new forms of popular culture.
- Social critics found fault with 1950s society.

Key Terms and People

baby boom
Sun Belt
urban renewal
beats

If YOU were there . . .

You live with your parents in an apartment building in 1954. You have grown up in the city, and you are used to walking or taking the subway everywhere you need to go. But your parents are talking about moving out to the suburbs. They like the idea of having a house of their own, with a driveway and a backyard. They ask what you think about moving to the suburbs.

How would you respond?

America's Economy in the 1950s

The American economy boomed during the 1950s. Millions of Americans earned more money than ever before and, therefore, had more money to spend on homes, cars, vacations, and large appliances. Feeling better off than they had during the Depression and World War II, many young Americans were getting married and starting families. This led to a **baby boom**, or a significant increase in the number of babies born.

A Nation on the Move Americans were also on the move in the 1950s, as people relocated to new parts of the country to take jobs and improve the quality of their lives. Many businesses and workers moved to the **Sun Belt**—southern and western states that offered a warm climate year-round and low tax rates. As a result, the region's population doubled in the 30 years after World War II.

The 1956 Highway Act also encouraged travel. This new law provided billions of dollars for the construction of a 41,000-mile interstate highway system. New highways helped to greatly increase both business and personal travel between cities throughout the country. The roads also made it easier for people to move to suburbs and commute to jobs in cities.

Suburbs and Cities The rising demand for homes in the suburbs encouraged developers to build new suburban neighborhoods. On Long Island, New York, William Levitt

Postwar Boom, 1945-1960

New Housing Construction

Amount Spent (in billions)

$40
$30
$20
$10
$0

1945   1960

Live Births

Births (in millions)

5
4
3
2

1945   1960

National Income

Total (in billions)

$450
$350
$250
$150
$50

1945   1960

Analyze Visuals
How did rising wealth affect families in the 1950s?

created Levittown, one of the nation's first preplanned suburbs. Between 1946 and 1951, Levitt built more than 17,000 low-priced, mass-produced houses. Like Henry Ford's Model T, Levitt's homes were designed to be simple and affordable. By the mid-1950s, builders were constructing similar suburban homes all over the country. By 1970 more Americans lived in suburbs than in cities.

Many families welcomed the comfort and convenience of suburban living. Suburban homes usually had driveways, large lawns, and labor-saving appliances. New schools were built in suburbs across the country to accommodate the increased number of students. Suburban children could participate in a wide variety of sports and other activities. Many mothers spent so much time driving their children from one activity to another that one commentator referred to the task as "motherhood on wheels."

Some critics of suburbs complained that suburban life was too heavily based on consumer culture. They also criticized the suburbs for encouraging conformity, or sameness. Most of the people living in the suburbs were white and middle class. In fact, some communities— including Levittown— refused to sell homes to black families.

Many American families used their newfound wealth to buy consumer products like houses, automobiles, and appliances. Advertisements like this one used an idealized version of an American family to sell products.

Some critics also complained that Levitt and other developers turned productive farmland into less productive residential areas. As more suburbs were built surrounding major cities—a process known as urban sprawl—less land was available to farmers. In the late 1970s and 1980s, many states, fearing that the country's most productive farmland would all be lost, passed laws to protect and preserve local farms.

As middle-class families moved to the suburbs, cities collected fewer tax dollars. This led to a decline in city services. Those who were unable to afford a move to the suburbs lived in increasingly decaying urban areas. As conditions worsened, the federal government began an **urban renewal** program—a plan to improve life in cities. Urban renewal projects focused on improving city services and urban housing. In reality, however, the programs sometimes led to more problems for urban residents.

American Pop Culture

American life was changing quickly in the 1950s as new technology developed. More money was available to buy a wider variety of products, and technological advances made life safer and easier for many.

Reading Check
Contrast
How was life different in suburbs and cities?

Life in the 1950s

Life for the average citizen in the United States changed dramatically in the prosperous years after World War II. More money was available to buy a wider variety of products, and technological advances made life safer and easier for many.

In 1952 Dr. Jonas Salk developed a vaccine for the paralyzing disease of polio.

Teenagers enjoyed the music of Elvis Presley and other rock 'n' roll stars.

Drive-in movie theaters became increasingly popular during the 1950s. Movies were shown on large outdoor screens as patrons watched from their cars. The largest drive-ins could accommodate 3,000 cars.

Many people began shopping in malls and eating at new fast-food restaurants. By the end of the decade, nearly 90 percent of all American families owned at least one television set. On average, American families watched about six hours of television a day.

Americans all over the country shared the experience of watching the same news, comedies, and sports programs. Many shows, such as *The Lone Ranger,* were versions of shows that began on the radio. Early hits included Milton Berle's variety show *Texaco Star Theater* and the Western drama *Gunsmoke.* But the most popular show was *I Love Lucy,* a situation comedy (or sitcom) starring Lucille Ball and her real-life husband, Cuban American bandleader Desi Arnaz. About 44 million Americans tuned in to one episode of *I Love Lucy* in 1953 to see the birth of their son—twice the number that watched President Eisenhower's inauguration the next day.

New styles of music also helped reshape American culture in the 1950s. African American jazz greats Charlie Parker and Dizzy Gillespie became known as the Fathers of Bebop, a complex jazz style often played at a rapid pace. Meanwhile, musicians like Elvis Presley, Buddy Holly, Chuck Berry, and Little Richard helped rock 'n' roll sweep the nation. Teenage music fans powered the rock 'n' roll revolution, buying more than 70 percent of all records sold in the late 1950s. Just like jazz in the 1920s, rock music drew criticism from some adults. One journalist even labeled rock 'n' roll "a menace to morals." An Arizona teenager responded to this type of criticism by saying, "Man, I believe the older generation just doesn't want the younger generation to have any fun."

Reading Check
Find Main Ideas
What changes took place in American pop culture during the 1950s?

Social Critics

Though the postwar years were happy and productive for many Americans, not everyone was happy with American society in the 1950s. Some women, for instance, were frustrated that they could only find work in a limited number of fields such as teaching, nursing, or office work. Others were discouraged by the expectation that they would give up their jobs when they got married. One woman recalled,

"There was always the assumption, even when I was getting my graduate degree in education, that any work I did was temporary, something to do until I assumed [began] my principal role in life which was to be the perfect wife and mother, supported by my husband."
—Sally Ann Carter, quoted in *The Fifties: A Women's Oral History,* by Brett Harvey

Ralph Ellison began his writing career with the Federal Writers' Project during the Great Depression. He eventually became famous for writing about discrimination against African Americans.

Many writers commented on 1950s society in their work. In 1951 J. D. Salinger published *The Catcher in the Rye.* The novel's teenage narrator, Holden Caulfield, criticizes the "phoniness" of the adults around him, who he believed loved only money and wanted everyone to be the same. In his 1952 novel *Invisible Man,* Ralph Ellison wrote about how African Americans felt left out by American society. "I am an invisible man," Ellison wrote. "I am invisible, understand, simply because people refuse to see me."

Young people known as beatniks, or **beats**, criticized society with unusual writing styles and rebellious behavior. The works of beat poet Allen Ginsberg and novelist Jack Kerouac inspired many young people to question the rules of mainstream American society. Many young people also identified with rebellious characters in popular movies of the 1950s. In the 1953 film *The Wild One,* actor Marlon Brando plays Johnny, a wild biker who challenges the rules of society. When asked, "Hey Johnny, what are you rebelling against?" Johnny replies, "Whadda ya got?"

Reading Check
Find Main Ideas
Why did people criticize 1950s society?

Summary and Preview In the 1950s, suburban life, television, and pop culture changed American society. In the next module you will learn how the civil rights movement affected the United States.

Lesson 3 Assessment

Review Ideas, Terms, and People

1. a. Recall How did a booming economy affect life in the United States in the 1950s?

b. Explain How did the growth of suburbs affect cities?

c. Elaborate How do you think the baby boom affected 1950s society?

2. a. Identify How did American pop culture change in the 1950s?

b. Make Inferences Based on what you have read, how was teenage culture in the 1950s different from adult culture?

3. a. Describe What was the novel *Invisible Man* about?

b. Compare What did J. D. Salinger and Jack Kerouac have in common?

c. Predict How do you think some women in the 1950s might have wanted to change their lives?

Critical Thinking

4. Analyze Information In this lesson you learned about 1950s suburban life and culture. Create a chart similar to the one below and use it to list the benefits and challenges of suburban life and culture.

Benefits   Challenges

Social Studies Skills

Interpret Battle Maps

Define the Skill

Battle maps show events during a battle or war. They may show army movements or locations of battles. A single battle map often shows events that occurred at different times. Reading the map key is very important when you interpret battle maps. Battle maps usually include many different symbols. The map key explains the symbols used on the map.

Learn the Skill

Follow these steps to interpret battle maps.

1. Read the title to determine what the map is about.

2. Study the map key to understand what the symbols on the map mean. Locate the symbols from the key on the map.

3. Look for labels and other information on the map. Use what you already know about the time period to determine the importance of these features.

4. Use the map to make a generalization about a battle or war, such as which side won.

Practice the Skill

1. What is this map about?

2. What does the solid blue line on this map represent? What does the solid red line represent?

3. What does the green line on the 38th parallel show? Why is this important? Based on this map, make a generalization about the Korean War.

The Korean War

- Farthest advance of Communist forces, Sept. 1950
- Farthest advance of UN forces, Nov. 1950
- Farthest advance of Chinese/North Korean forces, Jan. 1951
- Armistice line, July 1953
- Demilitarized Zone, boundary set by Allies after World War II

0   75   150 Miles
0   75   150 Kilometers

CHINA
Yalu River
Pyongyang
Sea of Japan
Seoul
Inchon
Yellow Sea
Pusan

Module 28 Assessment

Review Vocabulary, Terms, and People

Match the numbered person or term with the correct lettered definition.

1. GI Bill of Rights
2. Yalta Conference
3. Truman Doctrine
4. Joseph McCarthy
5. Fair Deal

a. U.S. senator who unfairly accused many citizens of being Communists
b. meeting at which Franklin Roosevelt, Winston Churchill, and Joseph Stalin discussed strategy for postwar peace
c. package of domestic reforms proposed by President Truman
d. U.S. policy of containing communism through economic aid
e. program that offered veterans money for school after World War II

Comprehension and Critical Thinking

Lesson 1

6. a. **Recall** What is the United Nations?
    b. **Explain** Why did Franklin Roosevelt support the formation of the UN?
    c. **Elaborate** Would you have supported the policy of containment? Why or why not?

Lesson 2

7. a. **Identify** How did the United States battle communism in Asia in the 1950s?
    b. **Explain** What effect did the launch of *Sputnik* have on the United States?
    c. **Evaluate** What were some risks and advantages of the strategy of brinkmanship?

Lesson 3

8. a. **Describe** How did life in the United States change in the 1950s?
    b. **Summarize** Why were some women frustrated with 1950s society?
    c. **Elaborate** How has American popular culture changed since the 1950s? How has it stayed the same?

Review Themes

9. **Politics** How did the Cold War affect political relations between the United States and the Soviet Union?

10. **Economics** What steps did the United States take to help rebuild Europe and Japan after World War II?

11. **Science and Technology** How did science and technology advance during the 1950s?

Reading Skills

Understand through Visualizing *Use the Reading Skills taught in this module to answer the question below.*

Wisconsin senator Joseph McCarthy contributed to fears in the early 1950s by charging that Communists were working inside the State Department. He claimed to have the names of 57 people who were "either card-carrying members or certainly loyal to the Communist Party."

12. What elements of the selection above help you visualize the feelings created by the Red Scare?

Social Studies Skills

Interpret Battle Maps *Use the Social Studies Skills taught in this module to answer the question below.*

13. Look back at the battle map in Lesson 2. In what year did North Korean forces make their farthest advance?

Focus on Writing

14. **Write Song Lyrics** To begin to write a song about the 1950s, first decide on a theme for your song. That theme can focus either on one event or idea or on several events. The lyrics should address something specific about what it was like to live in the United States in the 1950s. You may even want to write the song from the point of view of a young person living in the 1950s. What would that person think about? What would be his or her hopes and fears?

Module 29

The Vietnam War Years

★

Essential Question

Why did some Americans oppose the Vietnam War?

About the Photo: Soldiers from the U.S. 173rd Airborne Brigade take part in the Iron Triangle assault.

In this module you will learn how the U.S. commitment to stop the spread of communism worldwide led the United States into a long and costly war in Vietnam.

What You Will Learn ...

Lesson 1: Kennedy and Foreign Policy 894
The Big Idea The United States confronted Communist nations in Cold War conflicts around the world.

Lesson 2: Escalation in Vietnam 902
The Big Idea Johnson quickly expanded U.S. involvement in Vietnam, but American soldiers faced a determined enemy.

Lesson 3: The End of the War 910
The Big Idea Growing antiwar feelings in the United States helped convince the government to end U.S. involvement in the Vietnam War.

▶ *Explore ONLINE!*

HISTORY

VIDEOS, including...
- Causes of the Vietnam War
- Reaction to the Crisis
- Gulf of Tonkin Incident
- Kent State

☑ Document-Based Investigations

☑ Graphic Organizers

☑ Interactive Games

☑ Interactive Map: Crises in Cuba

☑ Image with Hotspots: The Apollo Space Program

☑ Interactive Map: The Vietnam War, 1968

☑ Image Slider: A Society Divided

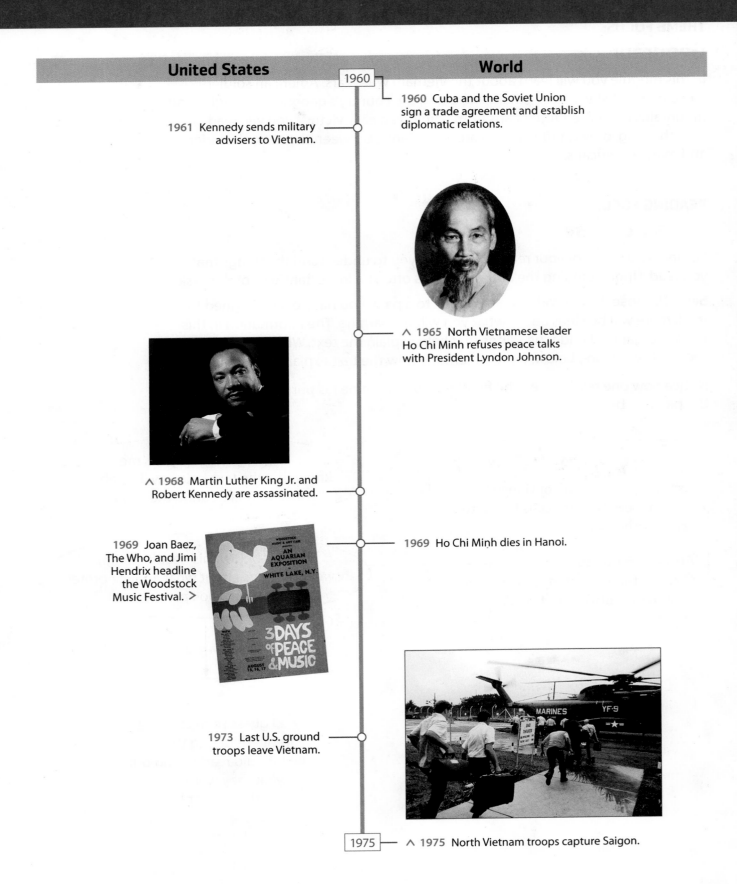

United States	World

1960

1960 Cuba and the Soviet Union sign a trade agreement and establish diplomatic relations.

1961 Kennedy sends military advisers to Vietnam.

∧ **1965** North Vietnamese leader Ho Chi Minh refuses peace talks with President Lyndon Johnson.

∧ **1968** Martin Luther King Jr. and Robert Kennedy are assassinated.

1969 Joan Baez, The Who, and Jimi Hendrix headline the Woodstock Music Festival. >

1969 Ho Chi Minh dies in Hanoi.

1973 Last U.S. ground troops leave Vietnam.

1975 ∧ **1975** North Vietnam troops capture Saigon.

Reading Social Studies

Geography

In this module you will learn about the Vietnam War years. American soldiers faced many obstacles in Vietnam, including the country's geography. Jungles and mountains prevented Americans from gaining an easy victory. You will read about how the long, drawn-out conflict caused divisions between the nation's leaders and many Americans.

READING FOCUS:

Set a Purpose

Setting a purpose for your reading can help you to understand the things that you read. Understanding the author's goal is often an important part of this task.

Set a Purpose When you open this book to a page you have been assigned to read, there will be clues about what you will be learning. The information in this book is organized under headings that help explain the text. When you read a section like the one below, try to determine how the text explains the heading.

Notice how one reader used the headings to determine his purpose for reading the passage below.

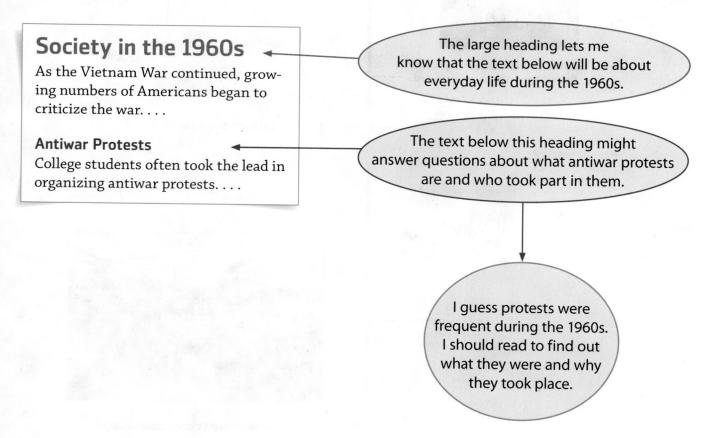

Society in the 1960s

As the Vietnam War continued, growing numbers of Americans began to criticize the war. . . .

Antiwar Protests

College students often took the lead in organizing antiwar protests. . . .

The large heading lets me know that the text below will be about everyday life during the 1960s.

The text below this heading might answer questions about what antiwar protests are and who took part in them.

I guess protests were frequent during the 1960s. I should read to find out what they were and why they took place.

You Try It!

The following passage is from the module you are getting ready to read. As you read the passage, look for information in the headings that tell you what to look for.

The Vietnam War Ends

While Nixon was running for re-election in 1972, Henry Kissinger continued peace negotiations with the North Vietnamese. . . .

The Impact in Southeast Asia

The war ended when North Vietnamese forces captured Saigon in April 1975. . . .

The Impact at Home

The Vietnam War carried heavy costs for the United States as well. . . .

After you read the passage, answer the following questions.

1. After reading the headings, what do you think this section is going to be about?
2. What are some questions you might ask before reading this section?
3. What information do you think you will learn from the section?

As you read Module 29, set a purpose before you read each section.

Lesson 1
Peace Corps
Fidel Castro
Berlin Wall
Cuban missile crisis
Neil Armstrong
Edwin "Buzz" Aldrin
Ho Chi Minh
domino theory
Vietcong

Lesson 2
Tonkin Gulf Resolution
Ho Chi Minh Trail
escalation
William Westmoreland
search-and-destroy missions
Tet Offensive
doves
hawks

Lesson 3
Students for a Democratic Society
hippies
Richard M. Nixon
Henry Kissinger
Vietnamization
Twenty-Sixth Amendment
War Powers Act
Vietnam Veterans Memorial

Kennedy and Foreign Policy

The Big Idea

The United States confronted Communist nations in Cold War conflicts around the world.

Main Ideas

- President Kennedy confronted Communist threats around the world.

- The United States and the Soviet Union raced to send a person to the moon.

- The Cold War conflict in Vietnam led the United States into war.

Key Terms and People

Peace Corps
Fidel Castro
Berlin Wall
Cuban missile crisis
Neil Armstrong
Edwin "Buzz" Aldrin
Ho Chi Minh
domino theory
Vietcong

If YOU were there . . .

You are a student in 1960. Whenever you discuss current events in class, students talk nervously about the ongoing nuclear arms race between the United States and the Soviet Union. If Cold War tensions ever spark an all-out nuclear war, entire cities and populations could be destroyed in just a matter of minutes.

Do you think Cold War tensions will lead to a nuclear war?

Kennedy Confronts Communism

As president, John F. Kennedy was committed to the Cold War policy of stopping the spread of communism worldwide. He maintained strong military forces and expanded the nation's supply of nuclear weapons. He also sought nonmilitary ways to defeat communism. For example, in a program called the Alliance for Progress, the United States pledged $20 billion in aid to countries in Latin America. This assistance did little to improve conditions in Latin America or U.S.–Latin American relations, however. Another nonmilitary program was more successful. Beginning in 1961, the **Peace Corps** sent volunteers to developing countries to help with projects such as digging wells and building schools.

Bay of Pigs In his early days as president, much of Kennedy's attention involved confronting communism with U.S. military forces. The first Cold War crisis during his administration took place in Cuba. In the late 1950s Cuban rebel **Fidel Castro** had led a revolution against an unpopular dictator. In 1959 he overthrew the dictator. Castro soon established a Communist government allied to the Soviet Union. Many Cubans who had opposed Castro fled to the United States.

Castro's close ties with the Soviet Union worried Kennedy, especially since Cuba is only about 90 miles from Florida. Soviet leaders could use Cuba as a base from which to attack the United States.

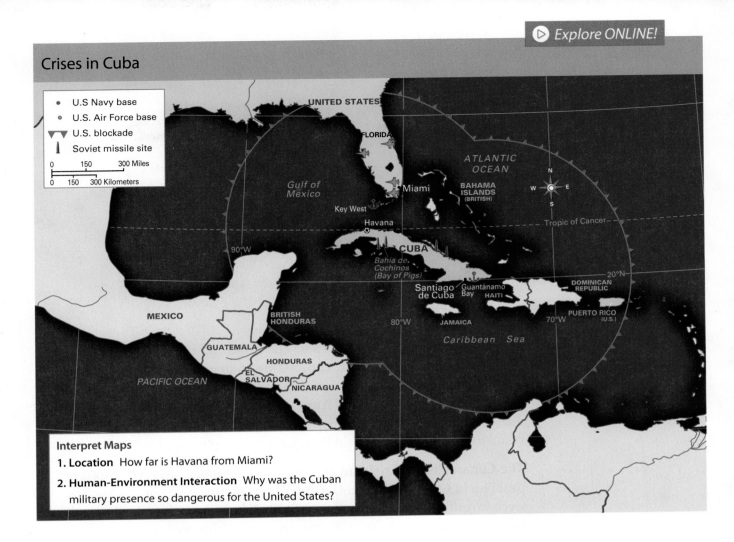

Crises in Cuba

Explore ONLINE!

Legend:
- U.S Navy base
- U.S. Air Force base
- U.S. blockade
- Soviet missile site

0 150 300 Miles
0 150 300 Kilometers

UNITED STATES
FLORIDA
ATLANTIC OCEAN
Gulf of Mexico
Miami
BAHAMA ISLANDS (BRITISH)
Key West
Havana
Tropic of Cancer
90°W
CUBA
Bahia de Cochinos (Bay of Pigs)
Santiago de Cuba
Guantánamo Bay
HAITI
DOMINICAN REPUBLIC
20°N
PUERTO RICO (U.S.)
MEXICO
BRITISH HONDURAS
80°W
JAMAICA
70°W
GUATEMALA
HONDURAS
Caribbean Sea
PACIFIC OCEAN
EL SALVADOR
NICARAGUA

Interpret Maps

1. **Location** How far is Havana from Miami?

2. **Human-Environment Interaction** Why was the Cuban military presence so dangerous for the United States?

While president, Dwight Eisenhower had developed a plan to remove Castro from power. The Central Intelligence Agency began training Cuban exiles to invade the island and overthrow Castro. Kennedy learned of the plan when he became president. He approved the operation.

On April 17, 1961, about 1,500 Cuban exiles landed by boat at Cuba's Bay of Pigs. Castro's forces quickly responded, killing about 300 of the invaders and capturing the rest. Many Americans criticized Kennedy for the disastrous invasion attempt. His administration was off to a shaky start.

The Berlin Wall Located behind the Iron Curtain in East Germany, the city of Berlin was the site of Kennedy's second crisis. East Berlin was part of Communist East Germany. West Berlin remained a part of democratic West Germany. It stood as a model of prosperity and freedom. About 2.5 million East Germans fled to West Berlin between 1949 and 1961. They were desperate for freedom and better economic opportunities. The steady loss of skilled workers alarmed Communist officials. Calling the open border between East and West Berlin a "handy escape route," Soviet premier Nikita Khrushchev demanded that the border be closed.

Khrushchev threatened to take over West Berlin. President Kennedy responded by vowing to defend the free city. "We cannot and will not

This map of Cuba was marked by President Kennedy during a cabinet briefing on the Cuban missile crisis.

permit the Communists to drive us out of Berlin," he warned. Then, on the night of August 12–13, 1961, the East German government began building the **Berlin Wall**, a barrier of concrete and barbed wire between East and West Berlin. Kennedy rushed American troops to West Berlin. But he was unwilling to go to war with the Soviet Union over the Berlin Wall. The wall stood as a symbol of the Cold War for nearly three decades.

The Cuban Missile Crisis In October 1962 Kennedy faced yet another problem in Cuba. American U-2 spy planes discovered that the Soviets were installing nuclear missiles in Cuba. If launched, the missiles could reach, and possibly destroy, American cities within minutes.

At a press conference on October 22, Kennedy demanded that the Soviet Union remove the missiles. During the **Cuban missile crisis**, the U.S. Navy formed a blockade around Cuba. The blockade was designed to prevent Soviet ships from bringing in more weapons. As Soviet ships approached the blockade, terrified Americans waited tensely for news updates. Then came some welcome news—the Soviet ships had turned back.

After the crisis ended, Khrushchev agreed to remove the nuclear missiles from Cuba. In return, Kennedy promised not to invade Cuba. He also agreed to remove some missiles in Italy and Turkey. To improve future communication, Kennedy and Khrushchev set up a telephone "hotline" so the leaders could talk directly to each other at a moment's notice. They also signed the Limited Nuclear Test Ban Treaty, which banned the testing of new nuclear weapons aboveground.

Race to the Moon

Although Kennedy and Khrushchev had taken some steps to prevent conflicts, the Cold War continued. One **aspect** of the Cold War that heated up in the 1960s was the space race—the competition between the United States and the Soviet Union to explore space. The Soviet Union pulled ahead in April 1961 when Soviet cosmonaut Yuri Gagarin became the first person to travel into space, orbiting Earth once.

Reading Check
Sequence When did Kennedy's three Cold War crises occur?

Academic Vocabulary
aspect part

The United States was determined to catch up to and surpass the Soviet Union in the space race. Kennedy outlined a bold plan in a 1961 speech to Congress:

> "I believe that this nation should commit itself to achieving the goal, before this decade is out, of landing a man on the moon and returning him safely to the earth."
>
> —John F. Kennedy, speech to Congress, May 25, 1961

It is difficult for us to imagine what it was like for Kennedy's audience to hear these words. Space travel seems normal to us today. But to people in the early 1960s, the idea of humans landing on the moon seemed like something out of a science fiction novel. Still, Americans supported the project. Congress provided NASA with billions of dollars to fund the development of new space-travel technology.

In May 1961 astronaut Alan Shepard Jr. became the first U.S. astronaut in space. The next year, John Glenn became the first American to orbit Earth. Then NASA pushed ahead with Project Apollo, with the goal of landing an astronaut on the moon. Even with careful planning, Apollo astronauts faced great danger. Three astronauts died in a fire during a prelaunch test in 1967.

On July 20, 1969, while millions of people around the world watched on television, the lunar module *Eagle* landed on the surface of the moon. American astronauts **Neil Armstrong** and **Edwin "Buzz" Aldrin** climbed out and became the first people to walk on the moon. "That's one small step for [a] man, one giant leap for mankind," said Armstrong as he touched the lunar surface. Armstrong and Aldrin planted the American flag on the moon's surface and collected samples of moon rocks. The Apollo program continued, achieving five more successful moon landings by 1972.

A vehicle known as the moon lander took two astronauts to the moon and returned them to the orbiting spacecraft.

Mission to the Moon

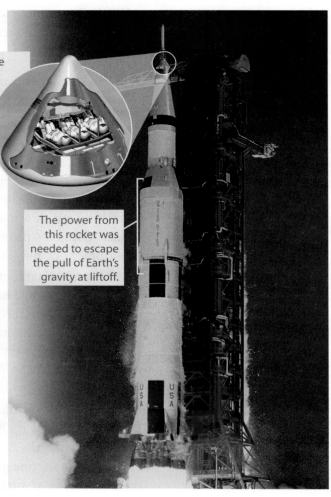

The astronauts guided the spacecraft from a capsule perched on the nose of the rocket. This capsule was the only part that returned to Earth.

The power from this rocket was needed to escape the pull of Earth's gravity at liftoff.

Connect to Science and Technology
The Apollo space program led to the creation of new technology to land people on the moon and bring them safely back to Earth. The design of the *Apollo 11* spacecraft involved separate pieces that played a role in different stages of the voyage. These included a rocket that could escape Earth's gravity, a spacecraft that orbited the moon, and a craft that could land on the moon and return to the orbiting spacecraft.

Analyze Visuals
What were some of the challenges of landing humans on the moon?

Reading Check
Analyze How did the events of July 20, 1969, fulfill the hope Kennedy had expressed in 1961?

The technology NASA developed enabled people to land on the moon and return safely back to Earth. The design of the *Apollo 11* spacecraft that first took astronauts to the moon involved separate pieces that played a role in different stages of the voyage. These included a rocket that could escape Earth's gravity, a spacecraft that orbited the moon, and a craft that could land on the moon and return to the orbiting spacecraft.

Conflict in Vietnam

The most serious and deadly event of the Cold War took place in Vietnam, a country in Southeast Asia. The Vietnamese struggled against the domination of China for centuries. By the early 1880s all of Vietnam was conquered by France. The French combined Vietnam with neighboring Laos and Cambodia to create a colony called French Indochina. French leaders imposed harsh taxes and put limits on political freedoms. Vietnamese nationalists began a struggle for independence in the early 1900s.

France and Vietnam One of the leading Vietnamese nationalists was **Ho Chi Minh**. Ho believed that only a Communist revolution could free the Vietnamese people.

During World War II, Japan drove the French out of Indochina. Ho Chi Minh did not want Vietnam to be controlled by yet another foreign power.

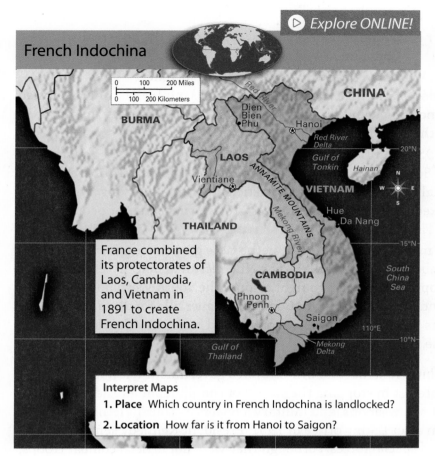

French Indochina

Explore ONLINE!

France combined its protectorates of Laos, Cambodia, and Vietnam in 1891 to create French Indochina.

Interpret Maps

1. **Place** Which country in French Indochina is landlocked?

2. **Location** How far is it from Hanoi to Saigon?

He organized a group called the Vietminh to resist Japanese occupation. When Japan was defeated by the Allies in 1945, Ho declared Vietnamese independence. Using words echoing those of the American Declaration of Independence, he said, "All men are born equal: the Creator has given us inviolable rights, life, liberty, and happiness." In reality, Ho did not believe in the democratic principles outlined in the American document.

Vietnam was still not free of foreign rule. France insisted that Vietnam was a French colony. French forces moved to regain control of Vietnam, leading to new fighting between the two sides.

Presidents Truman and Eisenhower both supported France with military aid. Military aid is often used by countries as a tool of foreign policy. In this case, American leaders were concerned that a Vietminh victory would lead to the spread of communism in Asia. They feared that if one country became Communist, nearby countries would also fall to communism. This was called the **domino theory**. Americans had already watched Communist victories in China and North Korea. They did not want Vietnam to be next.

The Vietminh had fewer weapons and supplies than the French, but they used hit-and-run guerrilla tactics to gradually weaken French forces. In May 1954 the Vietminh trapped a French army at Dien Bien Phu, where the French surrendered. In July French and Vietnamese leaders worked out an agreement called the Geneva Accords. This compromise temporarily divided Vietnam into North and South. It also called for democratic elections in July 1956 that would unite the two countries under one government.

North and South Vietnam North Vietnam became a Communist dictatorship led by Ho Chi Minh. South Vietnam had a Western-style government led by Ngo Dinh Diem (en-GOH DIN de-EM) and supported by the United States. U.S. officials hoped Diem would win control of the country in the 1956 elections.

Diem, however, quickly proved to be a disappointing leader. He put his own family members in top government positions and used his security forces to imprison and torture his political enemies. President Eisenhower was concerned, but he and his advisers saw Diem as the only realistic alternative to a Communist Vietnam.

In North Vietnam, meanwhile, Ho Chi Minh introduced land redistribution plans. Like Diem, Ho and the Vietminh violently persecuted their opponents. During the land redistribution process, they imprisoned and killed thousands of landowners.

As the 1956 reunification elections approached, however, a growing number of South Vietnamese supported Ho and the Vietminh. Diem refused to allow South Vietnam to participate in the elections. The United States backed this decision. Diem also arrested thousands of people who supported Ho.

In 1960 members of the North Vietnamese government formed the National Liberation Front (NLF). The NLF recruited South Vietnamese who were opposed to Diem to fight against the South Vietnamese government. The NLF relied on Communist guerrilla forces called the **Vietcong** as its army, which was supplied and funded by the North Vietnamese.

American Involvement The United States government felt it had a national interest in stopping the spread of communism. President Eisenhower sent aid, weapons, and military advisers to South Vietnam to aid Diem. Soon after taking office in 1961, President Kennedy sent more advisers and special forces. Although they were not official combat troops, the U.S. military advisers often accompanied the South Vietnamese army on combat missions. Some were killed in action. By late 1963 about 16,000 U.S. military personnel were serving in Vietnam.

South Vietnamese soldiers plot a firing pattern under the guidance of American military personnel.

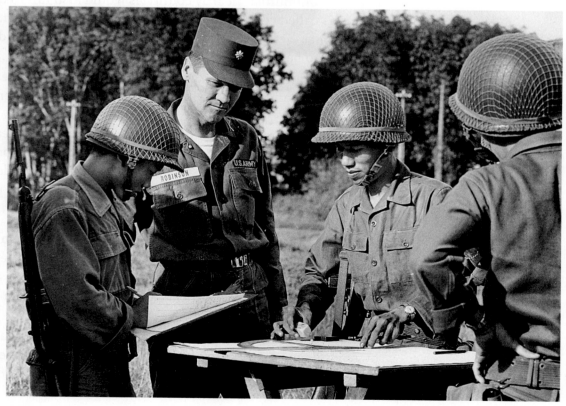

The Beginning of the Vietnam War

Causes
- French lose control of Vietnam
- Cold War tensions
- Civil war in Vietnam
- Assassination of President Diem

Effects
- Eisenhower and Kennedy send military advisers
- Gulf of Tonkin Resolution

The increased U.S. support did not help Diem, who was becoming less and less popular in South Vietnam. Several attempts were made to overthrow his government, all of which failed. Diem would not hold elections, and his opponents began to consider violence as their only option. He lost more support when he ordered his troops to fire on Buddhist demonstrators.

Some Buddhist monks protested by setting themselves on fire. Horrifying images of these protests helped turn U.S. public opinion against Diem.

In November 1963 a group of South Vietnamese army officers seized power and killed Diem and his brother. Only weeks later, Kennedy was assassinated, and Vice President Lyndon Johnson became president. Johnson immediately faced tough decisions about how to handle an increasingly unstable South Vietnam.

Summary and Preview In the 1950s and early 1960s, Cold War tensions caused conflicts around the world. In the next lesson you will read about increased U.S. involvement in Vietnam.

Reading Check
Evaluate Why did the United States see the Vietnam conflict as a Cold War struggle?

Lesson 1 Assessment

Review Ideas, Terms, and People

1. a. Describe What nonmilitary tactics did President Kennedy use to confront communism?

b. Explain How was the Cuban missile crisis resolved?

c. Evaluate In which Cold War crisis do you think President Kennedy showed the strongest leadership? Explain your answer.

2. a. Recall How did the Soviet Union take the lead in the space race in 1961?

b. Predict How do you think the Soviet Union responded to the successful U.S. landing of a man on the moon?

3. a. Identify Who was Ho Chi Minh?

b. Describe According to the domino theory, what did U.S. leaders think might happen if Vietnam became a Communist country?

c. Analyze Do you think the United States was justified in supporting Ngo Dinh Diem? Why or why not?

Critical Thinking

4. Identify Cause and Effect In this lesson you learned about the Cold War crises during the Kennedy administration. Create a chart similar to the one below and use it to list the causes and effects of each crisis.

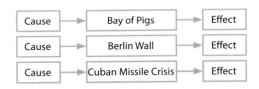

Cause	→	Bay of Pigs	→	Effect
Cause	→	Berlin Wall	→	Effect
Cause	→	Cuban Missile Crisis	→	Effect

Escalation in Vietnam

The Big Idea

Johnson quickly expanded U.S. involvement in Vietnam, but American soldiers faced a determined enemy.

Main Ideas

- President Johnson committed the United States to victory in Vietnam by expanding U.S. involvement.

- American soldiers faced new challenges fighting the Vietnam War.

- The Tet Offensive was an important turning point in the war.

Key Terms and People

Tonkin Gulf Resolution
Ho Chi Minh Trail
escalation
William Westmoreland
search-and-destroy missions
Tet Offensive
doves
hawks

If YOU were there . . .

It is 1965, and you have just been elected to Congress. You know voters are concerned about events in Vietnam, and you are carefully following the progress of the war. No one knows what will happen if the United States gets more deeply involved in the conflict. It might turn back the tide of communism. On the other hand, thousands of young soldiers might die.

Would you support sending U.S. troops to Vietnam? Why or why not?

Johnson Commits to Victory

Lyndon Johnson was determined to prevent Communists from taking over in South Vietnam. "We have the resources and the will to follow this course as long as it may take," Johnson said. He waited for a spark that might allow him to take action.

The Tonkin Gulf Resolution In the summer of 1964, a naval skirmish led to a rapid expansion of U.S. involvement in Vietnam. On August 2, 1964, the USS *Maddox* reportedly exchanged gunfire with North Vietnamese torpedo boats in the Gulf of Tonkin, off the North Vietnamese coast. Two days later, during a night of thunderstorms, U.S. ships reported a second attack. The captain of the *Maddox* was not sure his ship had actually been attacked, but the USS *Turner Joy* claimed to have picked up high-speed vessels on its radar. Despite the conflicting stories, President Johnson declared the incident an act of war.

Johnson asked Congress to give him the authority to take military action. Congress passed the **Tonkin Gulf Resolution**. The resolution gave the president the authority "to take all necessary measures to repel any armed attack against the forces of the United States." Johnson used the Tonkin Gulf Resolution to greatly expand the U.S. role in Vietnam.

Air Strikes Begin Johnson sent the first U.S. combat troops to South Vietnam in March 1965. At the same time, he ordered Operation Rolling Thunder, a series of air strikes on war industries in North Vietnam. The air strikes were also designed to disrupt the **Ho Chi Minh Trail**, a supply route the North Vietnamese used. The trail was a network of paths and tunnels that led from North Vietnam, through Laos and Cambodia, and into South Vietnam.

Because some of the Ho Chi Minh Trail was located in neutral countries, U.S. soldiers could not surround it on the ground. Instead, U.S. airplanes bombed the route. Sometimes planes bombed with napalm, or jellied gasoline, to kill troops and destroy supplies. Planes also released chemicals such as Agent Orange to kill the dense forests on the trail and to increase visibility from the air. American veterans and Vietnamese civilians later suffered serious health problems from exposure to these chemicals.

By late 1968 more than a million tons of explosives had been dropped on North and South Vietnam. Many Vietnamese soldiers and civilians were killed. The Communists' ability to wage war, however, was not destroyed.

Reading Check
Summarize
What authority did the Tonkin Gulf Resolution give to President Johnson?

U.S. Soldiers in Vietnam

From 1965 to 1968, President Johnson pursued a policy of **escalation**, or increased involvement, in the war. By 1968 more than 500,000 U.S. troops were serving in Vietnam. Backed by superior military technology, U.S. generals expected to win a quick victory. But the Vietnam War proved to be different from previous wars.

--- BIOGRAPHY ---

John McCain 1936–

John McCain's father and grandfather were both U.S. Navy admirals. The younger McCain also attended the Naval Academy and served in Vietnam as a combat pilot. On a bombing mission over Hanoi in 1967, his plane was shot down. McCain was held as a prisoner of war (POW) for more than five years. He was often tortured and kept in solitary confinement. McCain entered politics after the war. In 2010 he was elected to his fifth term as U.S. senator from Arizona. One of his priorities as a senator has been to help repair and strengthen U.S. relations with Vietnam. McCain was the Republican nominee for president in 2008.

As a lieutenant, John McCain served as a flight instructor.

Draw Inferences
If you were John McCain, would you want to establish good relations with Vietnam? Why or why not?

Strategies and Tactics In Vietnam there was rarely a front line where armies met face to face. Much of the war was fought in the jungles and villages of South Vietnam. General **William Westmoreland** commanded the U.S. ground forces involved in Vietnam. He developed a strategy based on **search-and-destroy missions**. During these missions U.S. patrols searched for hidden enemy camps, then destroyed them with massive firepower and air raids.

To make up for their disadvantage in firepower, Vietcong and North Vietnamese Army (NVA) troops used guerrilla warfare tactics. Moving quickly, they set deadly traps and land mines. They also knew the local geography. This allowed them to make quick surprise assaults on small groups of U.S. soldiers. Though the Vietcong and NVA suffered high casualty rates, they were able to match U.S. escalation by continuing to send new troops into combat. They also received supplies and weapons from Communist China and the Soviet Union.

The civilians of South Vietnam were often caught in the middle of the fighting. Vietcong forces entered villages at night. The forces killed people they believed were cooperating with the South Vietnamese government. South Vietnamese and American troops attacked villages they suspected of assisting the Vietcong. About 4 million South Vietnamese were driven from their homes. This undermined the crucial U.S. goal of winning the support and loyalty of South Vietnamese civilians.

Soldiers' Stories More than 2 million American soldiers served in the Vietnam War. Their average age was 18–21, several years younger than in previous American wars. About one-quarter of the soldiers were drafted, many from minority groups and poor families. College students—most

Historical Sources

Vietnam War

Charley Trujillo was a soldier in the Vietnam War. He later became a writer and filmmaker, focusing on the experiences of Latinos and Chicanos in the Vietnam War. Here he describes a day in Vietnam.

"Throughout the day we received mortar and sniper fire. By that evening we had suffered more casualties. The one I remember most was a guy we called the yippie. He was totally against the war and usually tried to avoid any violence. He was even thinking, for a while, of not carrying a rifle. It didn't help him much because the dude lost his leg that afternoon."

—Charley Trujillo, quoted in *Soldados: Chicanos In Viêt Nam*

Analyze Historical Sources
Why might Trujillo have remembered this casualty the most?

of whom were white and from wealthier families—were able to get draft releases called deferments.

American troops patrolled jungles and rice paddies, carrying 75–90 pounds of equipment through 100-degree heat and rainstorms that could last for days. They never knew when they might run into enemy fire. Soldiers also faced the constant danger of land mines and booby traps. "We required this kind of instant hair-trigger alertness," said marine officer Philip Caputo. "You simply trusted absolutely no one. I mean, from a 5-year-old kid to a 75-year-old woman."

While American troops were often able to win individual battles, they were rarely able to control the territory they had won for long. "You were just constantly walking out over the same ground," Caputo explained. "The enemy you were supposed to be defeating statistically kept coming back for more."

Reading Check
Compare and Contrast
How was Vietnam different from previous wars for U.S. soldiers?

Turning Points in Vietnam

By the end of 1967, U.S. military leaders argued that they were nearing victory in Vietnam. General Westmoreland said that he saw "a light at the end of the tunnel." But events in 1968 weakened the American public's confidence in this claim.

The Tet Offensive On January 30, 1968, the Vietnamese celebrated their New Year, called Tet. In previous years, a cease-fire had halted fighting on this holiday. In 1968, however, Vietcong and North Vietnamese forces launched the **Tet Offensive**—surprise attacks all over South Vietnam, including an attack on the U.S. Embassy in Saigon, South Vietnam's capital.

This Vietcong propaganda poster reads, "Vietnam will surely be victorious and America will surely be defeated."

South Vietnamese and U.S. forces successfully fought off the enemy strikes. Still, the massive size of the Tet Offensive shocked Americans. They had been told that the war would soon be over. Now they saw that the enemy was still strong and determined. Many began to wonder if government officials were being honest about the war. One poll taken after the Tet Offensive showed that only 33 percent of Americans believed that the United States was winning the war in Vietnam. About 49 percent said that the United States should never have become involved in the war.

In February 1968 Westmoreland asked for some 200,000 more troops. Many Americans questioned the wisdom of further escalation in Vietnam. President Johnson denied the general's request.

Hawks and Doves Television reports had an important impact on public opinion about the war. Americans could watch action from the battlefield and see real images of the war's brutality on nightly news broadcasts. Many were dismayed by what they saw.

Gradually, some Americans who had been supporters of the Vietnam War began to call for an end to U.S. involvement. Opponents of the war were called **doves**—named after the birds that symbolize peace. Many doves believed that the war was draining money that should be spent on

Explore ONLINE!

The Vietnam War, 1968

CHINA

NORTH VIETNAM

Red River

Dien Bien Phu
Xam Nua
Hanoi
BURMA
Red River Delta
20°N
Lach Chao Estuary
Gulf of Tonkin
LAOS
Muang Ngat
Vientiane
U.S. Seventh Fleet
Demilitarized Zone (DMZ)
THAILAND
Ho Chi Minh Trail
15°N
My Lai
South China Sea
Mekong River
CAMBODIA
SOUTH VIETNAM
Da Lat
Cam Rahn Bay
U.S. Seventh Fleet
Phnom Penh
Saigon
Gulf of Thailand
10°N
Ben Tre
Mekong Delta
100°E

Map Legend:
- Major U.S. air strikes
- Major U.S. bases
- Areas under attack in Tet Offensive, 1968
- Base areas/war zone
- Areas of prolonged fighting

0   100   200 Miles
0   100   200 Kilometers

105°E

Interpret Maps
1. **Place** In which countries did major U.S. air strikes occur?
2. **Human-Environment Interaction** Which country experienced most of the fighting in the Vietnam War?

social programs at home. Supporters of the war were called **hawks**. Hawks called for increased military spending, based on the belief that winning the Cold War took priority over domestic programs.

The bitter divisions between hawks and doves deepened as the Vietnam War continued. On March 16, 1968, a company of U.S. soldiers under the command of Lieutenant William Calley entered the South Vietnamese village of My Lai. Calley and his men expected to find Vietcong forces in My Lai. Their search-and-destroy mission turned into a massacre when American soldiers opened fire, killing about 500 unarmed villagers, including women and children.

Millions of Americans watched correspondent Walter Cronkite report the Vietnam War from the field. When Cronkite called the war a stalemate, or tie, President Johnson said, "I've lost middle America."

Reading Check
Summarize
What events made some Americans oppose the war?

At first, U.S. military officials tried to cover up news of the massacre. But former soldiers eventually made details of the events public. Lieutenant Calley was tried by the military and convicted of murder. As with the Tet Offensive, the My Lai massacre caused many Americans to question U.S. involvement in Vietnam.

Summary and Preview The Vietnam War escalated steadily under President Johnson. In the next lesson you will learn about the final years of the war.

Lesson 2 Assessment

Review Ideas, Terms, and People

1. **a. Recall** What events led Johnson to ask Congress for authority to take military action in Vietnam?

   b. Explain Why was the Ho Chi Minh Trail the target of U.S. air strikes?

   c. Predict What problems might arise from giving a president powers such as those defined in the Tonkin Gulf Resolution?

2. **a. Define** What was escalation?

   b. Contrast How did strategies and tactics of U.S. troops differ from those of the NVA and Vietcong?

3. **a. Describe** What were the goals of the doves and the hawks during the Vietnam War?

   b. Analyze How did television influence public opinion during the Vietnam War?

   c. Elaborate Why was the Tet Offensive such a surprise to U.S. forces?

Critical Thinking

4. **Sequence** In this lesson you have learned about the events that led to increased U.S. involvement in the Vietnam War. Create a chart similar to the one below and use it to put the events in the correct order.

The Vietcong Tunnels

Besides knowing the geography and terrain much better than U.S. forces, the Vietcong had the advantage of an underground system of tunnels. One large system of tunnels was installed some 47 miles north of Saigon in the Cu Chi district of South Vietnam. The picture on these pages is a re-created representation of these tunnels. The tunnels provided a place from which to fight that the Americans could not attack. A tunnel complex included special rooms in which to sleep, eat, plan, store weapons and supplies, and tend wounded soldiers.

The Vietcong used the tunnel meeting rooms to plan attacks on U.S. soldiers.

Firing post

Dormitory

Special doors were installed that could withstand bomb blasts and poisonous gases.

Hospital

Generators powered by bicycles provided electricity where needed.

American soldiers had trouble finding the hidden tunnel entrances, like the one in this photograph.

Air vents

Kitchen

Bomb shelter

Some tunnels contained traps that would harm invaders.

Some tunnel complexes like this one were connected to others through longer tunnels.

Weapons storage

The Vietcong dug wells so that they could have freshwater without leaving the tunnel system.

Analyze Visuals
How did the Vietcong's tunnel system help their soldiers fight U.S. forces?

The End of the War

The Big Idea

Growing antiwar feelings in the United States helped convince the government to end U.S. involvement in the Vietnam War.

Main Ideas

- Opinions about the Vietnam War divided American society in the 1960s.

- The war under Nixon expanded from Vietnam to Laos and Cambodia.

- The Vietnam War ended in 1973, but it had lasting effects on Vietnam and the United States.

Key Terms and People

Students for a
  Democratic Society
hippies
Richard M. Nixon
Henry Kissinger
Vietnamization
Twenty-Sixth Amendment
War Powers Act
Vietnam Veterans Memorial

Academic Vocabulary
values ideas that people hold dear and try to live by

If YOU were there . . .

You are a high school student in 1969. You follow events in Vietnam very closely and often talk about the war with your friends. Some of your friends are active in the antiwar movement, but you also have friends who support the war. You think each group makes good points, but you are having a hard time deciding which position you support.

**Would you join the antiwar protests?
Why or why not?**

Society in the 1960s

As the Vietnam War continued, growing numbers of Americans began to criticize the war. "The peaceniks [war protesters] these days are legion [many]," said Charlotte Keyes, who helped organize a group called Women Strike for Peace. "They are ninety-years-old and fifteen, heads of families and housewives with babies, students, [and] young people."

Antiwar Protests College students often took the lead in organizing antiwar protests. One of the most active protest groups was **Students for a Democratic Society** (SDS). Members of SDS protested the draft as well as companies that made weapons used in Vietnam.

By the end of 1968, students had held antiwar demonstrations on nearly 75 percent of college campuses. Some young men protested by publicly burning their draft cards. Others avoided military service by moving to Canada. Many Americans, however, criticized the antiwar movement as anti-American. In 1970, for example, thousands of construction workers marched in New York City, shouting, "All the way with the U.S.A."

For some Americans, the antiwar movement was part of a rejection of traditional **values** and government authority. Some young people chose to "drop out" of mainstream

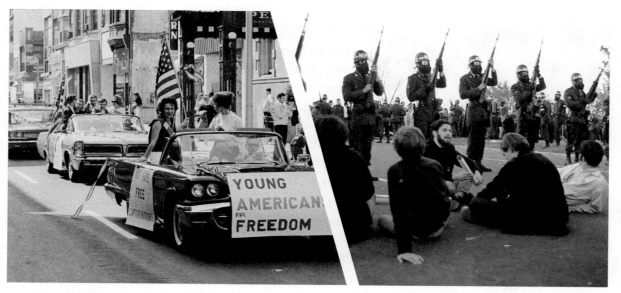

A Society Divided

Some young Americans supported the war in Vietnam. Many saw it as the only way to stop the spread of communism. Other young Americans protested the war. They believed the United States should not be involved in a violent conflict in Southeast Asia.

society and built a counterculture—a culture with its own values and ways of behaving. Members of this counterculture, called **hippies**, emphasized individual freedom, nonviolence, and communal sharing. Hippies expressed their rejection of traditional society by growing their hair long and wearing unusual clothes. They promoted openness and were sometimes called "flower children."

The views of hippies and war protesters upset many Americans. Commentators described a "generation gap," or division between older and younger Americans. "I know of no time in our history when the gap between the generations has been wider," said one university professor.

The Election of 1968 News of the Tet Offensive led to a sharp drop in the popularity of President Johnson. In early 1968 the percentage of Americans who approved of Johnson's performance as president fell from 48 to 36. The number of Americans who approved of the way Johnson was handling the war was even lower. As the 1968 presidential election approached, Johnson was even losing support within his own Democratic Party. On March 31 he went on live television and told Americans: "I shall not seek, and I will not accept, the nomination of my party for another term as president."

Several other candidates campaigned for the Democratic nomination. Johnson backed his vice president, Hubert Humphrey. Eugene McCarthy, a senator from Minnesota, ran as an outspoken antiwar candidate. Senator Robert F. Kennedy of New York argued that the United States should do everything possible to negotiate a quick and peaceful end to the war.

Kennedy won the California primary on June 5, 1968—an important step before the upcoming Democratic National Convention in Chicago. After giving his victory speech that night, he was assassinated by a man named Sirhan Sirhan.

National Guardsmen and antiwar protestors face off at the 1968 Democratic National Convention in Chicago.

Reading Check

Compare What did the expeditions of Lewis and Clark, Pike, and Frémont reveal about the West?

The Democrats were badly divided going into their party's convention in Chicago. Vice President Humphrey seemed certain to win the nomination. But many delegates disliked his close ties with President Johnson and the Vietnam War. Angry debates inside the convention hall were matched by antiwar protests on the streets. When police officers moved in to stop the demonstrations, a riot broke out. Television cameras broadcast live images of the violent chaos in Chicago. More than 100 police officers and 100 demonstrators were injured.

Humphrey won the Democratic nomination for president, but the events in Chicago damaged his chances of victory. Republican nominee **Richard M. Nixon** promised to restore order to American society and bring "peace with honor" to Vietnam. Nixon won the election, receiving 301 electoral votes to Humphrey's 191. Southern voters gave 46 electoral votes to George Wallace, a segregationist candidate of the American Independent Party.

The War under Nixon

President Nixon wanted to get U.S. troops out of Vietnam without creating the appearance of an American defeat. "I will not be the first president of the United States to lose a war," he told his fellow Republicans. With his national security adviser, **Henry Kissinger**, Nixon created a plan to pull U.S. troops from Vietnam and have the South Vietnamese Army take over all the fighting. This strategy was called **Vietnamization**.

Nixon began slowly withdrawing American troops from Vietnam. Without the knowledge of Congress or the American public, however, he approved bombing raids on Cambodia and Laos. The goal of these raids was to disrupt Vietcong supply lines. On April 30, 1970, Nixon announced that he had sent U.S. troops into Cambodia to attack Communist bases. "If, when the chips are down," he said, "the United States of America acts like a pitiful helpless giant, the forces of totalitarian anarchy will threaten free nations." Many Americans were furious. Rather than seeking peace, Nixon seemed to be expanding the war.

Student protests erupted on hundreds of college campuses. On May 4, at Kent State University in Ohio, the National Guard was called in to break up a demonstration. When the students refused to leave, guard troops used tear gas. Some students began throwing rocks at the National Guard. Several guard troops then opened fire into the crowd. Four students were killed. Horrified by the killings, antiwar activists expanded their protests all over the nation.

Antiwar feelings grew in June 1971, when the *New York Times* published secret government documents known as the Pentagon Papers. These documents revealed that U.S. officials had been lying to the American public about the progress of the war for years.

Public opinion was hardening against the war as the 1972 presidential race began. Democratic candidate George McGovern was an outspoken opponent of the war who promised voters an immediate U.S. troop withdrawal from Vietnam. "The doors of government will be opened, and that brutal war will be closed," he said.

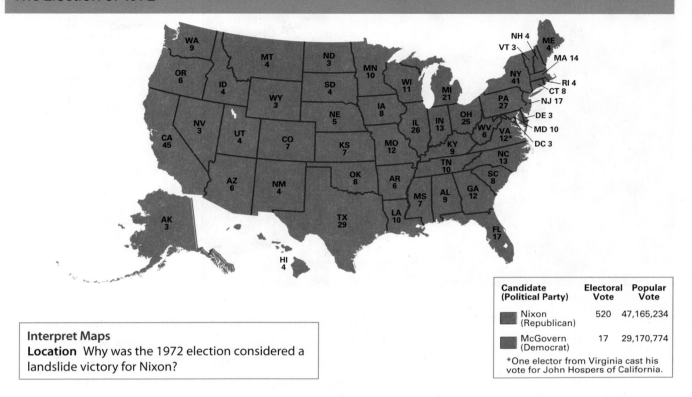

Candidate (Political Party)	Electoral Vote	Popular Vote
■ Nixon (Republican)	520	47,165,234
■ McGovern (Democrat)	17	29,170,774

*One elector from Virginia cast his vote for John Hospers of California.

Interpret Maps
Location Why was the 1972 election considered a landslide victory for Nixon?

Reading Check
Draw Conclusions
Why did McGovern lose in a landslide?

McGovern hoped to appeal to young voters, many of whom would be voting for the first time. The **Twenty-Sixth Amendment**, which was ratified in 1971, lowered the federal voting age from 21 to 18. McGovern did win a majority of these younger voters in 1972, but a majority of voters over 21 from both parties supported Nixon. Many of these voters feared that a McGovern victory would lead to greater disorder and protests. Nixon won by a landslide, receiving 520 electoral votes to McGovern's 17.

The Vietnam War Ends

While Nixon was running for re-election in 1972, Henry Kissinger continued peace negotiations with the North Vietnamese. On January 27, 1973, the United States signed a cease-fire called the Paris Peace Accords with representatives of North Vietnam, South Vietnam, and the Vietcong. The United States agreed to withdraw all its troops from Vietnam. North Vietnam agreed to return all American prisoners of war. Despite the peace agreement, fighting broke out between North and South Vietnam in 1974. The United States refused to send troops back to South Vietnam.

In 1975 North Vietnam invaded the South. Thousands of panic-stricken American Embassy workers and South Vietnamese scrambled to evacuate Saigon. "The city was in flames," remembered one American worker. "And the Communists had the city surrounded with missiles. . . . We realized that we were down to hours if not minutes." Helicopters lifted many people to ships waiting off the coast.

Today, relations between the United States and the united Vietnam have only slowly improved. In 1994 the United States lifted its long-standing trade embargo against Vietnam. In 1995 the former enemies officially established diplomatic relations. Many American veterans and tourists now visit Vietnam.

Quick Facts

Causes and Effects of the Vietnam War

Long-Term Causes

- Fear of Communist expansion
- U.S. support of South Vietnam's government

Immediate Causes

- Gulf of Tonkin incident
- Communist attacks against South Vietnam

Vietnam War

Effects

- Many thousands of Americans and millions of Vietnamese killed and injured
- Vietnam united as a Communist nation
- Political divisions created in the United States
- Increased Vietnamese immigration to the United States

The Impact in Southeast Asia The war ended when North Vietnamese forces captured Saigon in April 1975. Communist leaders created the Socialist Republic of Vietnam, uniting the former countries of North and South Vietnam. Hanoi became the capital, and Saigon was renamed Ho Chi Minh City.

Life remained extremely difficult in Vietnam after the war. Cities, villages, forests, and farms had been destroyed during the war. Some 250,000 South Vietnamese soldiers died in the war. About 1 million North Vietnamese and Vietcong soldiers were killed. The number of civilians killed is estimated at 2 million. Hundreds of thousands of former soldiers, officials, and other professionals were forced to live in "re-education camps." Another 1.5 million Vietnamese fled the country. About half of them settled in the United States. Thousands of other refugees from Southeast Asia joined them, such as the Hmong of Laos. The Hmong fought bravely alongside the U.S. military against the Communists during the war. Communist dictators took over Laos and Cambodia in 1975. The Cambodian Communist army, the Khmer Rouge, killed about 1.5 million people in a massive campaign to destroy supposed enemies of communism.

According to a 2007 U.S. Census survey, more than a million Vietnamese immigrants now live in the United States. Vietnamese, Laotian, and Cambodian immigrants to the United States have made significant contributions to the communities they join. Many of these communities are along the West and Gulf coasts.

The Impact at Home The Vietnam War carried heavy costs for the United States as well. Some 58,000 Americans were killed, and more than 300,000 were wounded.

Returning American soldiers were not always welcomed home as heroes as other war veterans had been. Some were insulted by antiwar protesters. As veterans struggled to readjust to civilian life, many suffered from post-traumatic stress disorder. This condition includes symptoms such as nightmares and flashbacks to traumatic experiences. Today, the U.S. government is more prepared to meet the needs of veterans with post-traumatic stress disorder. It offers counseling and information to vets and their families on how to deal with symptoms of trauma.

Another effect of the Vietnam War was that Americans had less trust in government officials, including the president. This led to the passage in 1973 of the **War Powers Act**. The act requires the president to get congressional approval before committing U.S. troops to an armed struggle.

The war also left a dismal economic legacy, affecting the development of the United States. Some estimates place the cost to American taxpayers at more than $150 billion. This cost added to the national debt and fueled inflation. The money spent on the war used funds that might have gone to domestic programs, such as those that help the poor.

Americans took a step toward healing the wounds of the war with the 1982 dedication of the **Vietnam Veterans Memorial**. Maya Ying Lin designed the black granite memorial. It lists the names of dead or missing American soldiers. Lin insisted that the names be listed in chronological order rather than in alphabetical order or by rank.

BIOGRAPHY

Maya Ying Lin
1959–

Ohio-born Maya Lin was a 21-year-old architecture student when she designed the Vietnam Veterans Memorial. Her design was chosen from more than 1,400 proposed memorial designs. The memorial is a V-shaped black granite wall that lists the names of more than 58,000 dead and missing Americans. Explaining the design, Lin said, "It was important to me to be extremely honest; not be concerned with the politics of war, but the results. I wanted to bring the visitor a concrete realization of the great loss."

The memorial is now one of the most-visited spots in Washington, DC. Many visitors leave letters, flowers, or other objects at the memorial to honor loved ones.

Draw Conclusions
How does Lin's design achieve the goal she describes?

The smooth, black-granite wall of the Vietnam Veterans Memorial, nearly 500 feet long, lists the 58,249 names of military men and women who died or were listed as missing in action.

Reading Check
Summarize What were the longterm effects of the Vietnam War?

The memorial has become a symbol of healing after a long and divisive war. Hundreds of people visit it daily. Some visitors leave flowers, personal mementos, or written messages. Others simply ponder the meaning of the memorial.

Summary and Preview The Vietnam War deeply divided American society. In the next module you will read about how American life changed in the 1970s and 1980s.

Lesson 3 Assessment

Review Ideas, Terms, and People

1. a. Identify What was Students for a Democratic Society?

b. Elaborate How did hippies express their disapproval of traditional culture?

c. Evaluate How did the Republicans win the presidential election of 1968?

2. a. Explain What was Vietnamization?

b. Summarize Why did the Pentagon Papers fuel antiwar feelings?

c. Elaborate How did the Twenty-Sixth Amendment affect the 1972 presidential election?

3. a. Recall How did the Vietnam War end?

b. Describe What was the experience of veterans returning home from Vietnam?

c. Analyze Do you think U.S. leaders made the right decision in signing the Paris Peace Accords? Why or why not?

Critical Thinking

4. Identify Effects In this lesson you learned about the causes of the end of the Vietnam War. Create a chart similar to the one below and use it to list the effects of the end of the war.

Social Studies Skills

Use Primary Sources: Oral Histories

Define the Skill

An important part of history is understanding the lives and experiences of people in the past. Oral histories and personal memoirs are primary sources that help historians understand how people in the past acted and felt.

Oral histories are interviews in which people talk about events they participated in or witnessed. In personal memoirs, people write about their memories of such events. Both oral histories and personal memoirs are different from other kinds of primary sources because they can be written long after an event takes place. However, they both include descriptions of firsthand experiences.

Learn the Skill

Follow these guidelines to analyze oral histories and personal memoirs.

1. Identify the situation that the oral history or memoir describes.

2. Find the emotions or events that stand out in the description.

3. Make a generalization about how the individual's experience helps us understand the time period or event. Do you think other people might have had similar experiences?

In the following quotation, Diana Dwan Poole describes her experience serving in the Army Nurse Corps in Vietnam.

"One of my rules was that nurses were not allowed to cry. The wounded and dying men in our care need our strength, I told them. We couldn't indulge in the luxury of our own feelings. . . . I was always straight with the soldiers. I would never say, 'Oh, you're going to be just fine,' if they were on their way out. I didn't lie."

Poole was a nurse in Vietnam. In this quotation, she describes working with wounded and dying patients. Her strength in the face of sadness and her honesty stand out.

Other nurses might have had experiences similar to Poole's. The nurses' situation—treating the wounded and the dying—also suggests the dangers soldiers faced.

Practice the Skill

Todd B. Walton was a sergeant in Iraq who found adjusting back to life at home challenging. Read the primary source quotation from Walton below.

"I would scan the overpasses for IEDs or something down on the bottom. Is there anybody on the top that is going to be trying to throw stuff in, obliviously I'm in truck mentality, you know, are they going to try to drop something into your truck. . . . Is there somebody manning a . . . weapon."

1. What situation does Walton describe?

2. Based on this description, how do you think Walton felt at the time?

3. How can Walton's experience help us better understand soldiers serving in Iraq?

Module 29 Assessment

Review Vocabulary, Terms, and People

Identify the descriptions below with the correct term or person from the module.

1. The Cuban rebel who overthrew an unpopular dictator and established a Communist government

2. A barrier made of concrete and barbed wire that separated East Berlin and West Berlin

3. The commander of U.S. ground forces in Vietnam who developed the strategy of search-and-destroy missions

4. Supporters of the Vietnam War who believed winning the Cold War took priority over domestic reform

5. The Republican nominee who won the 1968 election for president of the United States

6. The amendment that lowered the voting age from 21 to 18

Comprehension and Critical Thinking

Lesson 1

7. **a. Recall** What is the Peace Corps?

   b. Sequence Describe the sequence of events that led to American astronauts landing on the moon in 1969.

   c. Evaluate How do you think the Cuban missile crisis would have ended had the United States pursued air strikes or an invasion of Cuba?

Lesson 2

8. **a. Define** What is guerrilla warfare?

   b. Describe How did the American military try to disrupt the Ho Chi Minh Trail?

   c. Predict Do you think Americans' opinions about the war would have been different had there been no television reporting? Explain your answer.

Lesson 3

9. **a. Identify** What was the War Powers Act?

   b. Explain What was Henry Kissinger's role in the Vietnam War?

   c. Summarize What long-term effects did the Vietnam War have on the United States?

Module 29 Assessment, continued

Review Themes

10. **Geography** How did the geography of Vietnam help the Vietcong?

11. **Geography** How did the geography of Vietnam affect American forces?

Reading Skills

Set a Purpose *Use the Reading Skills taught in this module to answer the question about the reading selection below.*

> ### Johnson Commits to Victory
>
> Lyndon Johnson was determined to prevent Communists from taking over in South Vietnam. "We have the resources and the will to follow this course as long as it may take," Johnson said. . . .
>
> #### The Tonkin Gulf Resolution
> In the summer of 1964, a naval skirmish led to a rapid expansion of U.S. involvement in Vietnam. On August 2, 1964, the USS *Maddox* reportedly exchanged gunfire with North Vietnamese torpedo boats in the Gulf of Tonkin, off the North Vietnamese coast. . . .

12. Which of the following is an example of a purpose you could set for the passage above?

    a. Find out why the Vietnam War was fought.

    b. Find out Johnson's view of the Vietnam War.

    c. Find out when the Vietnam War ended.

    d. Find out what the Vietnam Veterans Memorial is.

Social Studies Skills

Use Primary Sources: Oral Histories *Read this passage from marine officer Philip Caputo. Then use the Social Studies Skills taught in this module to answer the question below.*

> "You simply trusted absolutely no one. I mean, from a 5-year-old kid to a 75-year-old woman."

13. How do you think Caputo felt about not being able to trust anyone? Do you think he felt safe? Why or why not?

Focus on Writing

14. **Present a Newscast** Newscasts during the Cold War were a big source of information that reported world and war events to the American people. You will present a five-minute newscast to your class about events in the Cold War. Make notes and include several segments on different topics from the module. One could be an interview with a friend in the role of a soldier back from Vietnam, a government official, or an antiwar protester. You can also use pictures to illustrate the events you are reporting. Write your script and practice reading it before your presentation.

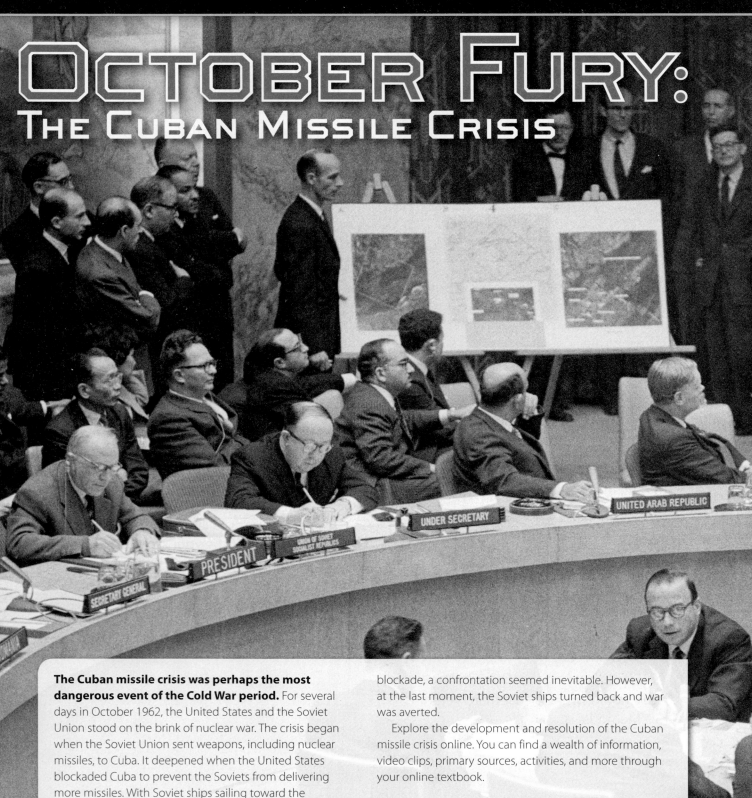

OCTOBER FURY:
THE CUBAN MISSILE CRISIS

The Cuban missile crisis was perhaps the most dangerous event of the Cold War period. For several days in October 1962, the United States and the Soviet Union stood on the brink of nuclear war. The crisis began when the Soviet Union sent weapons, including nuclear missiles, to Cuba. It deepened when the United States blockaded Cuba to prevent the Soviets from delivering more missiles. With Soviet ships sailing toward the blockade, a confrontation seemed inevitable. However, at the last moment, the Soviet ships turned back and war was averted.

Explore the development and resolution of the Cuban missile crisis online. You can find a wealth of information, video clips, primary sources, activities, and more through your online textbook.

Go online to view these and other **HISTORY**® resources.

📜 **Prelude to Crisis**

Watch the video to learn about the buildup to the Cuban missile crisis.

🎥 **Getting Ready for War**

Watch the video to see how the missiles in Cuba created tension between the United States and the Soviet Union.

FALLOUT SHELTER IN BASEMENT

🎥 **Crisis Averted?**

Watch the video to see how the Cuban missile crisis brought the United States and the Soviet Union to the brink of nuclear war.

🎥 **Lessons Learned**

Watch the video to learn about the impact of the Cuban missile crisis.

Module 30

The Civil Rights Movement

★

Essential Question

How successful was the civil rights movement?

About the Photo: African Americans launched a major civil rights movement in the years following World War II. Members of the movement organized demonstrations to protest unfair treatment, like the March on Washington shown here.

In this module you will learn about the efforts of African Americans and others to gain civil rights protections in the 1950s, 1960s, and 1970s.

What You Will Learn ...

Lesson 1: The Civil Rights Movement Takes Shape **924**
The Big Idea Civil rights activists used legal challenges and public protests to confront segregation.

Lesson 2: Kennedy, Johnson, and Civil Rights **931**
The Big Idea The civil rights movement made major advances during the presidencies of John F. Kennedy and Lyndon B. Johnson.

Lesson 3: Rights for Other Americans **938**
The Big Idea Encouraged by the success of the civil rights movement, many groups worked for equal rights in the 1960s.

▶ Explore ONLINE!

VIDEOS, including...
- Civil Rights Act of 1964
- Little Rock Nine
- March on Washington

HISTORY

- ☑ Document-Based Investigations
- ☑ Graphic Organizers
- ☑ Interactive Games
- ☑ Image Carousel: The Montgomery Bus Boycott
- ☑ Interactive map: Freedom Rides, 1961
- ☑ Image Carousel: Women and Equal Rights

United States

World

1950

1953 Soviet leader Joseph Stalin dies.

1954 Thurgood Marshall argues against segregation in the Supreme Court case *Brown* v. *Board of Education*. ∨

1957 The Soviets launch *Sputnik*, the first human-made satellite.

1960

1961 The Berlin Wall divides East and West Berlin.

1963 Lee Harvey Oswald assassinates President John F. Kennedy.

1966 The National Organization for Women is formed.

1966 Indira Gandhi becomes prime minister of India. ∨

1969 La Raza Unida is organized to support the rights of Mexican Americans.

∧ **1973** The American Indian Movement protests at Wounded Knee.

1975

Reading Social Studies

THEME FOCUS:

Politics, Society and Culture

In this module you will read about the important changes in American society during the period called the civil rights era. You will learn about how many people came to see politics as a way to correct social inequalities that existed for certain groups in the United States, such as African Americans, women, Mexican Americans, Native Americans, and people with disabilities. You will also read about life in the 1960s.

READING FOCUS:

Use Context Clues: Synonyms

Some words mean almost the same thing. Understanding the similarities can help you understand words whose meaning you may not know.

Understand Synonyms Words that have similar meanings are called synonyms. Often, a synonym is given as a definition. The synonym will probably be a word you already understand. This will help you learn the new word through context clues.

Notice how one reader uses synonyms to understand words she does not understand.

An AIM leader described the groups' goals, saying, "We don't want civil rights in the white man's society—we want our own sovereign [*self-governing*] rights."

This is a word I don't know the meaning of.

These brackets mean that the word inside is a synonym of the word or phrase that comes before. The word inside is a synonym of *sovereign*.

The word *sovereign* must mean to govern on one's own.

You Try It!

The following passage is from the module you are getting ready to read. As you read the passage, look for synonyms in the definitions of unfamiliar words.

On February 1, 1960, the students went into Woolworth and staged a sit-in—a demonstration in which protesters sit down and refuse to leave. They sat in the "whites-only" section of the lunch counter and ordered coffee. They were not served, but they stayed until the store closed. The next day, they returned with dozens more students to continue the sit-in. Soon, another sit-in began at the lunch counter of a nearby store.

After you read the passage, answer the following questions.

1. What word is a synonym of *sit-in* that is given in that word's definition?
2. What clue is given that helps you find the synonym in the above passage?
3. Can you think of another synonym for *sit-in* that might have been used?

As you read Module 30, look for synonyms that can help you define words you don't know.

Key Terms and People

Lesson 1
Thurgood Marshall
Brown v. *Board of Education*
Little Rock Nine
Emmett Till
Rosa Parks
Montgomery bus boycott
Martin Luther King Jr.
sit-in
Student Nonviolent
  Coordinating Committee

Lesson 2
John F. Kennedy
Freedom Rides
Medgar Evers
March on Washington
Lyndon B. Johnson
Civil Rights Act of 1964
Voting Rights Act of 1965
Great Society
Black Power
Malcolm X

Lesson 3
Cesar Chavez
Dolores Huerta
United Farm Workers
Betty Friedan
National Organization for
  Women
Shirley Chisholm
Equal Rights Amendment
Phyllis Schlafly
American Indian Movement
Earl Warren
Warren Court
Disabled in Action

The Civil Rights Movement Takes Shape

The Big Idea

Civil rights activists used legal challenges and public protests to confront segregation.

Main Ideas

- Civil rights leaders battled school segregation in court.

- The Montgomery bus boycott helped end segregation on buses.

- Students organized sit-ins to protest segregation.

Key Terms and People

Thurgood Marshall
Brown v. *Board of Education*
Little Rock Nine
Emmett Till
Rosa Parks
Montgomery bus boycott
Martin Luther King Jr.
sit-in
Student Nonviolent
    Coordinating Committee

If YOU were there . . .

You are an African American student in the 1950s. You get up early every day and take a long bus ride across the city to an African American public school. There is another school just three blocks from your home, but only white students are welcome there. You have heard, however, that this school will soon be opening its doors to black students as well.

> Would you want to be one of the first African Americans to attend this school? Why or why not?

Battling Segregation

The push for black civil rights in the United States gained new momentum after World War II. As black veterans came home, many of them were no longer willing to put up with discrimination. They and other African Americans began to call for an end to racial inequality and campaigned for change. As a result, African Americans made a number of key gains. In 1948 President Harry S. Truman desegregated the armed forces. That same year, Truman also banned discrimination in the hiring of federal employees. President Dwight D. Eisenhower, elected in 1952, took further steps to reduce racial discrimination in hiring practices. Meanwhile, at the state level, several northern and western states passed laws banning racial discrimination in public housing.

Despite these gains, many opportunities remained closed to African Americans in the 1950s. Although this period was a time of economic prosperity for many white Americans, few black Americans shared in this new wealth. Furthermore, white resistance to black equality remained strong. Such opposition was particularly evident in the South. White citizens continued to use unfair laws, fear, and violence to keep black citizens from voting or standing up for their rights.

The "separate-but-equal" doctrine legalized the racial segregation of public facilities, so long as the facilities were equal. However, separate facilities, such as these water fountains, were rarely equal.

One major barrier to equality for blacks was segregation. The 1896 Supreme Court case *Plessy* v. *Ferguson* established the "separate-but-equal" doctrine. This doctrine stated that federal, state, and local governments could allow segregation as long as separate facilities were equal. One result of this ruling was that states in both the North and South maintained separate schools for white and black students. Government officials often insisted that though these schools were separate, they were equal in quality.

In fact, however, schools for black children typically received far less funding. Early civil rights leaders focused on ending segregation in America's public schools. Leaders of the movement were members of the National Association for the Advancement of Colored People (NAACP).

Brown v. Board of Education The NAACP's strategy was to show that separate schools were unequal. The NAACP attorneys **Thurgood Marshall**, who went on to become Supreme Court justice, and Jack Greenberg led the courtroom battles against segregation. In the early 1950s, five school segregation cases from Delaware, Kansas, South Carolina, Virginia, and Washington, DC, came together under the title of **Brown v. Board of Education**. The "Brown" in the case title was a seven-year-old African American girl from Topeka, Kansas, named Linda Brown. Though she lived near a school for white children, Linda Brown had to travel across town to a school for black children. Linda's father and the NAACP sued to allow Linda to attend the school closer to her home.

On May 17, 1954, the Supreme Court issued a unanimous ruling on *Brown* v. *Board of Education*. Segregation in schools and other public facilities was illegal.

The next year, the Court ordered public schools to desegregate, or integrate, "with all deliberate speed." These rulings would prove difficult to enforce.

Little Rock Nine In the entire South, only three school districts began desegregating in 1954. Most others **implemented** gradual integration plans. In Little Rock, Arkansas, the school board started by integrating one high school. It allowed nine outstanding black students to attend Central High School. These students became known as the **Little Rock Nine**. Arkansas governor Orval Faubus worked to prevent desegregation at Central High School, however. He used National Guard troops to block the Little Rock Nine from entering the school.

On the morning of September 4, 1957, eight of the nine students arrived at the school together and were turned away by the National Guard. Then the ninth student, 15-year-old Elizabeth Eckford, arrived at the school by herself. She found the entrance blocked by the National Guard. Turning around, she faced a screaming mob. Someone began yelling, "*Lynch her! Lynch her!*" Finally, a white man and woman guided Eckford to safety.

Elizabeth Eckford and the rest of the Little Rock Nine went home. For weeks, Governor Faubus refused to allow them to attend the school. The

Academic Vocabulary
implemented put in place

Brown v. Board of Education (1954)

Background of the Case

In 1896 the Supreme Court had ruled in *Plessy* v. *Ferguson* that "separate-but-equal" facilities were constitutional. In 1951 the NAACP sued the Board of Education of Topeka, Kansas. It argued that segregated schools did not give equal opportunities to black and white children. After hearing many arguments, the Court made its ruling in 1954.

The Court's Ruling

The Supreme Court overturned the *Plessy* doctrine of "separate-but-equal." It ruled that racially segregated schools were not equal and were therefore unconstitutional. All of the justices agreed to the ruling, making it unanimous.

The Court's Reasoning

The Supreme Court decided that segregation violated the Fourteenth Amendment's guarantee of "equal protection of the laws." Its opinion stated, "We conclude that, in the field of public education, the doctrine of 'separate-but-equal' has no place. Separate educational facilities are inherently [naturally] unequal."

Why It Matters

The ruling in *Brown* v. *Board of Education* led to integrated public schools. It also opened the door to other successful challenges to segregation in public places.

Linda Brown, age 9

Analyze Information

1. How did the ruling in *Brown* v. *Board of Education* overturn the 1896 Supreme Court ruling in *Plessy* v. *Ferguson*?

2. How might parents of both black and white children at the time have reacted to the ruling in *Brown* v. *Board of Education*?

---

tense situation lasted until President Eisenhower sent federal troops to escort the students into the school.

The Little Rock Nine began attending classes, but resistance to integration continued. Some white students insulted, harassed, and attacked the black students. In spite of these obstacles, eight of the nine remained at the school. In May 1958 Ernest Green became the first African American student to graduate from Central High. When Green's name was called at the graduation ceremony, no one clapped. "But I figured they didn't have to," he later said. "After I got that diploma, that was it. I had accomplished what I had come there for."

The Murder of Emmett Till Despite early victories against segregation, blacks remained second-class citizens to many white Americans, particularly in the South. This situation gained nationwide attention in 1955 with the murder of **Emmett Till**, a 14-year-old boy from Chicago, Illinois. Till had gone to the town of Money, Mississippi, to visit relatives. Having

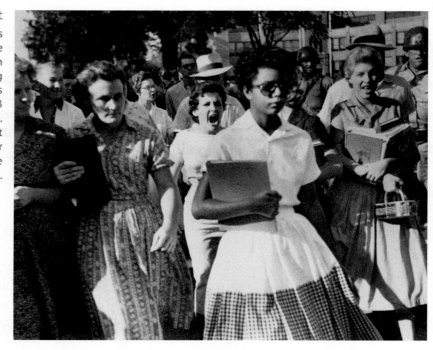

A Shared Past

This famous photograph shows Elizabeth Eckford walking to Little Rock's Central High School on September 4, 1957. The young woman shouting at Eckford is Hazel Bryan Massery. In 1963 Massery apologized to Eckford. Massery had decided she did not want to be, she said, the "poster child of the hate generation." The two women later became friends.

grown up in the North, the black teenager did not understand the South's strict racial etiquette. Shortly after arriving in Money, Till visited a local grocery store where he said something to the owner, a young white woman named Carolyn Bryant. She later claimed he asked her for a date and whistled at her, but there is some doubt that this was the case. Whatever Till said, she took offense. Her husband, Roy, soon found out about the incident.

Four days later, Roy Bryant and his half brother J. W. Milam kidnapped Till in the middle of the night. They brutally beat him, shot him, and tossed his body in the Tallahatchie River. National reports of Till's murder deeply moved many Americans.

Bryant and Milam stood trial for the crime, but a jury of 12 white men found them not guilty. Months later, the two men confessed to the killing to a reporter for *Look* magazine. Till's senseless murder—and his killers' acquittal—awakened more Americans to the racism that southern blacks faced and to the need for action.

Reading Check
Summarize
What obstacles faced supporters of desegregation?

Montgomery Bus Boycott

The victory in *Brown* v. *Board of Education* had a major impact on American society. However, segregation continued to be enforced in many other public places and facilities in the South. One major area that remained segregated was public transportation.

The NAACP decided to continue the battle against segregation in Montgomery, Alabama. Black passengers there were required to sit in the back of city buses. If the whites-only front section filled up, black passengers had to give up their seats.

On December 1, 1955, a seamstress and NAACP worker named **Rosa Parks** boarded a bus and sat in the front row of the section reserved for black passengers. When the bus became full, the driver told Parks and

Rosa Parks 1913–2005

Rosa Parks was born in Tuskegee, Alabama, and spent most of her childhood in Montgomery. While working as a seamstress, Parks became an active member of the NAACP.

She was fired from her seamstress job for her leading role in the Montgomery bus boycott. After the boycott succeeded, she and her husband moved to Detroit, Michigan. She continued working for fair treatment for all Americans and started a program to teach children about the Underground Railroad and the civil rights movement.

Find the Main Idea
How did Rosa Parks work for equal rights?

three others to give their seats to white passengers. Parks refused. The bus driver called the police, and Parks was taken to jail.

To protest Parks's arrest, African American professor Jo Ann Robinson organized a boycott of Montgomery buses. Local leaders formed the Montgomery Improvement Association (MIA) to help strengthen the boycott. In the **Montgomery bus boycott**, thousands of African Americans stopped riding the buses. Some white residents supported the boycott as well. Bus ridership fell by 70 percent.

To lead the MIA, African American leaders turned to **Martin Luther King Jr.**, a young Baptist minister. The 26-year-old King already had a reputation as a powerful speaker whose words could motivate and inspire listeners.

As the boycott continued, bus drivers guided nearly empty buses down the city streets. Leaders planned a carpool system that helped people find rides at more than 40 locations throughout Montgomery. For 381 days, boycotters carpooled, took taxis, rode bicycles, and walked. Still, Montgomery's leaders refused to integrate the bus system.

As in Little Rock during the school segregation fight, many white residents were angry about the attempt to end segregation. Some people resorted to violence. King's home was bombed, and he received hate mail and phone calls threatening him and his family. The police also harassed and arrested carpool drivers. In spite of this intimidation, the boycott gained national attention, sparking similar protests in other cities.

Finally, in November 1956 the Supreme Court ruled that segregation on public transportation was illegal. The next month, King joined other black and white ministers to ride the first integrated bus in Montgomery. "It . . . makes you feel that America is a great country and we're going to do more to make it greater," remembered Jo Ann Robinson.

The Montgomery bus boycott helped make Martin Luther King Jr. a nationally known civil rights leader. He formed the Southern Christian Leadership Conference (SCLC), which led campaigns for civil rights throughout the South.

Reading Check
Identify Cause and Effect
What event sparked the Montgomery bus boycott?

Sit-ins and the SNCC

Like public schools and buses, many private businesses in the South were segregated. In Greensboro, North Carolina, four students decided to challenge this form of segregation. They targeted a lunch counter at Woolworth, a popular department store. Black customers were supposed to eat standing up at one end of the counter. White customers sat down to eat at the other end.

On February 1, 1960, the students went into Woolworth and staged a **sit-in**—a demonstration in which protesters sit down and refuse to leave. They sat in the whites-only section of the lunch counter and ordered coffee. They were not served, but they stayed until the store closed. The next day, they returned with dozens more students to continue the sit-in. Soon, another sit-in began at the lunch counter of a nearby store.

People across the country read newspaper stories about the Greensboro sit-ins. Picket lines supporting the sit-ins began to appear outside of Woolworth stores in northern cities. Other black students in North Carolina and across the South began to hold similar protests at segregated facilities such as libraries, restaurants, and churches. The student protesters practiced the strategy of nonviolent resistance. No matter how much they were insulted or threatened, they refused to respond with violence. They were inspired by Martin Luther King Jr., who was a strong supporter of nonviolent action.

BIOGRAPHY

Martin Luther King Jr. 1929–1968

King grew up in Atlanta, Georgia, where his father was a pastor. He studied to become a minister in Pennsylvania. He received his doctorate in Massachusetts, then became pastor of a church in Alabama. He traveled throughout the country as a civil rights leader.

As a powerful and moving speaker, King became one of the leading voices of the civil rights movement. He was committed to achieving equality through nonviolent protest. He led a series of successful marches and protests, including the 1955 Montgomery bus boycott and the 1963 March on Washington.

His leadership helped make the civil rights movement a success. His belief in and passion for nonviolence led to the boycotts, sit-ins, and marches that helped African Americans gain equal treatment. King's work helped bring an end to legal segregation and led to new laws guaranteeing equal rights for all Americans.

Evaluate
Which of Martin Luther King Jr.'s contributions to the civil rights movement was most important? Why?

During this sit-in at a segregated lunch counter, young African Americans sat with their white friends and asked to be served. The activists reacted calmly as onlookers harassed them.

Reading Check
Compare
How were sit-ins similar to other civil rights protests?

These social conflicts led to change in North Carolina and the rest of the United States. Over time, some restaurants and businesses, including Woolworth, began the process of integration. To continue the struggle for civil rights, the leaders of the student protests formed the **Student Nonviolent Coordinating Committee** (SNCC) in the spring of 1960. The SNCC activists trained protesters and organized civil rights demonstrations. Bob Moses, a leader of the SNCC, helped organize sit-ins and voter registration drives.

Summary and Preview In the 1950s, court rulings and protests challenged segregation. In the next lesson you will learn how the civil rights movement continued the fight against inequality.

Lesson 1 Assessment

Review Ideas, Terms, and People

1. **a. Analyze** In what areas did early laws ban racial discrimination?

   b. Summarize How did the Supreme Court impact the desegregation of public schools?

   c. Identify Who were the Little Rock Nine?

2. **a. Recall** What was the purpose of the Montgomery bus boycott?

   b. Analyze Why was the arrest of Rosa Parks a turning point in the civil rights movement?

   c. Elaborate Why do you think the bus boycott lasted so long?

3. **a. Identify** What means did the Student Nonviolent Coordinating Committee use to protest segregation?

   b. Make Inferences What might have inspired the Greensboro students to stage a sit-in?

   c. Evaluate Do you think picketing and boycotts are an effective form of protest? Why or why not?

Critical Thinking

4. **Sequence** In this lesson you learned about events that challenged segregation. Create a graphic organizer similar to the one below and use it to show the sequence of major events in the civil rights movement described in this lesson.

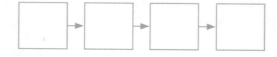

Kennedy, Johnson, and Civil Rights

The Big Idea

The civil rights movement made major advances during the presidencies of John F. Kennedy and Lyndon B. Johnson.

Main Ideas

- John F. Kennedy was elected president in 1960.
- Civil rights leaders continued to fight for equality.
- Lyndon B. Johnson became president when Kennedy was assassinated.
- Changes occurred in the civil rights movement in the late 1960s.

Key Terms and People

John F. Kennedy
Freedom Rides
Medgar Evers
March on Washington
Lyndon B. Johnson
Civil Rights Act of 1964
Voting Rights Act of 1965
Great Society
Black Power
Malcolm X

If YOU were there . . .

You are a civil rights activist living and working in the South. It is 1960, a presidential election year. The battle for fair treatment has been difficult, and you hope that the next president will support civil rights. Both major presidential candidates will be visiting your area soon. You might have a chance to meet them and ask some questions.

What questions would you ask the candidates?

Kennedy Elected

When **John F. Kennedy** won the election of 1960, he became the youngest person ever elected president of the United States. For many Americans, Kennedy and his wife, Jacqueline, brought a sense of style and excitement to the White House. Kennedy was also the first Roman Catholic to become president.

In his inaugural address, Kennedy spoke of the opportunities and dangers facing Americans. "Man holds in his mortal hands the power to abolish all forms of human poverty and all forms of human life," he said. He encouraged all Americans to support freedom throughout the world. He said, "And so, my fellow Americans, ask not what your country can do for you—ask what you can do for your country."

As president, Kennedy pursued a set of proposals he called the New Frontier. His plan included a higher minimum wage and tax cuts to help stimulate economic growth. It called for new spending on the military and on the space program, and new programs to help poor and unemployed Americans. Kennedy also proposed providing greater financial help to public schools. However, political conflicts slowed the development of these programs. Fearing a budget imbalance, Republicans and conservative southern Democrats blocked much of the legislation Kennedy introduced.

John F. Kennedy 1917–1963

John F. Kennedy was born to a politically powerful and wealthy family in Massachusetts. He graduated from Harvard University, then joined the U.S. Navy. He commanded a patrol boat in the South Pacific during World War II and was wounded in a sea battle. Kennedy was elected to the House of Representatives at the age of 29 and to the Senate six years later. He was elected president in 1960, bringing a youthful energy to the White House. He had served for fewer than three years when he was assassinated.

Identify
What experiences helped prepare Kennedy to lead the nation?

Reading Check
Draw Inferences
What do you think African American voters hoped for from the new president?

Kennedy also spoke of his support for the goals of the civil rights movement. This had helped convince many African Americans to vote for him in the election of 1960. As president, however, Kennedy moved slowly on civil rights legislation. He was reluctant to anger Republicans and conservative southern Democrats in Congress. He needed their support to pass other items on his agenda. Kennedy was also busy dealing with foreign policy crises.

The Fight for Rights Continues

Public schools and some businesses had begun to desegregate. But other facilities remained strictly segregated.

Freedom Rides In 1947 a civil rights group called the Congress of Racial Equality (CORE) began protests in which African Americans rode in the whites-only section of interstate buses. In 1960 the Court ruled that segregation of bus stations was illegal. CORE decided to put pressure on President Kennedy to enforce this ruling.

To accomplish this, CORE organized a series of protests called the **Freedom Rides**. On these rides black and white bus riders traveled together to segregated bus stations in the South. White riders planned to use facilities set aside for African Americans in bus stations. Black riders would use whites-only facilities.

The Freedom Rides began in May 1961, when 13 riders boarded a bus traveling from Washington, DC, to New Orleans, Louisiana. In one Alabama town, the riders were viciously attacked by a white mob. After more attacks, CORE leaders decided to stop the protest to protect the riders' lives.

The leaders of the SNCC decided to continue the Freedom Rides. The SNCC activists faced the same violence as the CORE riders. Arriving in Montgomery, Alabama, in late May, they were attacked by a furious mob.

Freedom Rides, 1961

▶ Explore ONLINE!

Freedom Riders were attacked by white mobs, who threw stones, slashed tires, and set buses on fire. One series of rides was discontinued to protect the safety of the riders.

PA
NJ
IA
OH
MD
IN
Washington, DC ☆
DE
May 4
WV
Richmond
IL
VA
KY
Greensboro
MO
Charlotte
May 8
NC
Nashville
Rock Hill
TN
May 9
Memphis
Winnsboro
May 10
Birmingham
Atlanta
SC
AR
May 14
May 17
Augusta
Anniston
May 14
GA
MS
Meridian
Montgomery
May 20
Jackson
Selma
May 24
AL
LA

New Orleans

→ Core route
→ SNCC route
✦ Arrests
✦ Violence

0   100   200 Miles
0 100 200 Kilometers

Interpret Maps

1. **Place** Where did the Freedom Riders attempt to travel?

2. **Location** According to this map, in which state did the Freedom Riders meet the most resistance?

Many Freedom Riders were jailed in Jackson, Mississippi. That same month, President Kennedy ordered the Interstate Commerce Commission to enforce strict bans on segregation in interstate bus terminals.

King in Birmingham In 1963 Martin Luther King Jr. organized marches in Birmingham, Alabama. King was arrested and jailed for marching without a permit. While jailed, he wrote a "Letter from Birmingham Jail," explaining his commitment to nonviolence. "We will reach the goal of freedom in Birmingham and all over the nation, because the goal of America is freedom."

King was released from jail and led a new round of marches. In May 1963 some 2,500 demonstrators marched through downtown Birmingham. Police commissioner Eugene "Bull" Connor ordered his officers to unleash their attack dogs and blast the marchers with high-pressure water hoses. Televised images of their tactics shocked Americans.

The Assassination of Medgar Evers Pressure for civil rights legislation continued to grow. President Kennedy called racial discrimination "a moral crisis." In June 1963 he announced support for a sweeping civil rights bill to end racial discrimination completely. Just hours later, the head of the NAACP in Mississippi, **Medgar Evers**, was murdered in front of his home in Jackson, Mississippi. Evers was one of the movement's most effective leaders. His slaying shocked many Americans.

Police quickly arrested a Ku Klux Klan member named Byron De La Beckwith. All-white juries failed to reach a verdict in two trials, and De La Beckwith went free. In 1994 he was tried again based on some comments he had made. He was convicted and died in prison in 2001.

The March on Washington To demonstrate support for the civil rights movement, African American leaders held the **March on Washington**—a massive demonstration for civil rights. On August 28, 1963, Martin Luther King Jr. stood at the Lincoln Memorial before a diverse crowd of more than 200,000 people. In his famous "I Have a Dream" speech, King expressed his hope for a future in which all Americans would enjoy equal rights and opportunities.

Reading Check Summarize How did the Birmingham marches affect public opinion?

Johnson Becomes President

In the months following the March on Washington, Congress debated Kennedy's civil rights legislation. In November 1963 Kennedy began a quick tour of Texas cities.

Kennedy Assassinated On November 22, 1963, Kennedy rode through Dallas in a convertible, waving to supporters in the streets. Suddenly, gunshots rang out. Kennedy had been shot twice, and he died soon afterward in a Dallas hospital. Vice President **Lyndon B. Johnson** was quickly sworn in as president. Dallas police arrested an alleged assassin, Lee Harvey Oswald.

The assassination stunned Americans, who grieved the young president's death. Many of Kennedy's goals were left unfinished. Vowing to continue Kennedy's work, President Johnson urged Congress to pass a civil rights bill.

Civil Rights Laws On July 2, 1964, President Johnson signed the **Civil Rights Act of 1964**. The act banned segregation in public places. It also outlawed discrimination in the workplace on the basis of color, gender, religion, or national origin.

BIOGRAPHY

Lyndon B. Johnson 1908–1973

Lyndon B. Johnson grew up in rural Texas. After working his way through college, Johnson taught school for a year. In 1937, at the age of 29, he was elected to the House of Representatives. He was elected to the Senate in 1948. Johnson was known for his ability to guide bills through Congress by convincing members from both political parties to support them. As one fellow member of Congress said, "Lyndon got me by the lapels [jacket collar] and put his face on top of mine and he talked and talked." Johnson was elected vice president in 1960 and became president in 1963.

Compare and Contrast
How was Johnson's career similar to Kennedy's, and how was it different?

Johnson and Civil Rights

After he became president, Lyndon Johnson promised to continue Kennedy's plans for civil rights legislation. Johnson worked with Congress and African American leaders to create and pass laws that would help ensure equality for all Americans. Here, Johnson is shown signing the Civil Rights Act of 1964 as Martin Luther King Jr. and other leaders look on.

That summer, activists began to push for equal voting rights for African Americans in the South. Legally, of course, African Americans had the right to vote. But in much of the South, threats and unfair election rules often kept them from the polls. During the "Freedom Summer" of 1964, hundreds of volunteers, including many white college students, came to Mississippi. Their goal was to help African Americans register to vote.

Volunteers were threatened and attacked. On June 21 three civil rights workers—James Chaney, a young black Mississippian plasterer's apprentice; Andrew Goodman, a Jewish Queens College student; and Michael Schwerner, a Jewish social worker from New York City—were murdered by members of the Ku Klux Klan. Martin Luther King Jr. organized a voting rights march from Selma, Alabama, to Montgomery, during which many marchers were beaten and jailed. Violence against civil rights workers convinced many people to support voter registration efforts.

Congress approved the **Voting Rights Act of 1965**, which Johnson signed into law in August. This law gave the federal government new powers to protect African Americans' voting rights. Within three years, more than half of all qualified African Americans in the South registered to vote.

Quick Facts

The Great Society

Great Society Legislation:

- Civil Rights Act of 1964
- Voting Rights Act of 1965
- Elementary and Secondary Education Act of 1965
- Medicare and Medicaid Bill, 1965
- Department of Housing and Urban Development Act of 1965

The Great Society President Johnson won the election of 1964 by a huge margin. He saw this as a vote of approval for his program of domestic reforms that he called the **Great Society**. "The Great Society rests on abundance and liberty for all," Johnson said.

Congress quickly passed most of Johnson's Great Society legislation. Great Society programs included Medicare, which helps senior citizens afford health care, and Medicaid, which gives health care aid to low-income citizens. Another act gave local schools more than $1 billion to help students

Timeline: Civil Rights Movement, Key Events

1950

1965

1955
Rosa Parks refuses to give up her seat on a Montgomery, Alabama, bus, sparking a citywide bus boycott. >

1960
The first sit-in at a segregated lunch counter occurs in Greensboro, North Carolina.

1963
Four young girls die in a bombing of a Birmingham, Alabama, church. The deaths lead to riots and civil unrest during which police attack African Americans. ∨

1964 ∧
Civil rights leader Martin Luther King Jr. receives the Nobel Peace Prize for his work in nonviolent demonstrations against segregation.

Interpret Timelines
Which events in the timeline are examples of nonviolent protest?

Reading Check
Summarize How did President Johnson support civil rights?

with special needs. The Department of Housing and Urban Development (HUD) was created to help low-income families get better housing. Robert Weaver served as HUD's secretary, becoming the first African American appointed to a presidential cabinet.

Changes in the Civil Rights Movement

Many young civil rights reformers found the pace of change too slow. Others entirely rejected the goal of racial integration.

New Directions One such activist was Stokely Carmichael, who had participated in the Freedom Rides and many marches. But in the mid-1960s, he broke with the goal of nonviolence. Carmichael was a founder of the **Black Power** movement, which called for African American independence. Black Power activists believed that blacks should reject integration, focusing instead on controlling their own communities.

Malcolm X helped inspire the Black Power movement. He was a leader of the Nation of Islam, an organization that combined ideas about African American independence with the teachings of Islam. Malcolm X argued that African Americans should work for social and political independence. He believed that African Americans had the right to defend themselves, using violence if necessary.

In 1964 Malcolm X traveled to the Muslim holy city of Mecca, where he met Muslims of many races. He began to hope that different races could coexist in peace, although he still supported freedom "by any means necessary." But in 1965 Malcolm X broke with the Nation of Islam and was killed by three of its members.

Violence in the Streets Slow progress in the civil rights movement frustrated many members of the black community. In some U.S. cities, tensions exploded into violent, sometimes deadly, riots. One such riot occurred in August 1965 in the Watts section of Los Angeles. Twenty-four people were killed, and much of Watts was destroyed.

In April 1968 Martin Luther King Jr. was shot and killed in Memphis, Tennessee. As televised reports spread the news of King's assassination, furious rioters took to the streets in more than 100 American cities. The movement had lost its most visible leader.

Summary and Preview Under Kennedy and Johnson, major civil rights legislation was passed. In the next lesson you will learn how more groups began to push for equal rights.

Reading Check
Contrast How did Malcolm X's goals differ from Martin Luther King Jr.'s?

Lesson 2 Assessment

Review Ideas, Terms, and People

1. **a. Describe** How was John F. Kennedy different from previous presidents?

   b. Analyze Why did many African Americans vote for Kennedy? Did his election to office bring the results they might have expected?

2. **a. Identify** What were the Freedom Rides?

   b. Explain How did television influence public opinion about the civil rights movement?

3. **a. Recall** What happened in Dallas, Texas, on November 22, 1963?

   b. Draw Conclusions Based on Johnson's plans for the Great Society, what do you think he believed was the purpose of government?

4. **a. Recall** What challenges did the civil rights movement face in the late 1960s?

   b. Elaborate Why did Malcolm X reject the goal of racial integration?

Critical Thinking

5. **Evaluate** In this lesson you learned about the goals and achievements of leaders who supported civil rights. Create a graphic organizer similar to the one below and use it to evaluate the leaders discussed in the section. Tell whether or not you think the leaders' actions were effective.

Leader	Evaluation

Rights for Other Americans

The Big Idea

Encouraged by the success of the civil rights movement, many groups worked for equal rights in the 1960s.

Main Ideas

- Hispanic Americans organized for civil rights and economic opportunities.

- The women's movement worked for equal rights.

- Other Americans also fought for change.

Key Terms and People

Cesar Chavez
Dolores Huerta
United Farm Workers
Betty Friedan
National Organization for Women
Shirley Chisholm
Equal Rights Amendment
Phyllis Schlafly
American Indian Movement
Earl Warren
Warren Court
Disabled in Action

If YOU were there . . .

Your parents came to the United States from Mexico, and you were born in California in the 1950s. You and your family work year-round picking crops—the work is hard, and the pay is low. You're trying to put aside some money for school, but your family barely makes enough to get by. Some farmworkers are talking about going on strike for better wages.

**Would you join the strike?
Why or why not?**

Hispanic Americans Organize for Change

The Hispanic population of the United States grew to 4 million by 1960 and to more than 10 million by 1970. Though people of Mexican descent made up the majority of this population, Hispanic Americans were a diverse group. Many people from Puerto Rico, Cuba, and other Latin American countries also lived in the United States.

The success of African Americans in battling segregation encouraged Hispanic Americans to fight for their own rights. **Cesar Chavez** was one of many Hispanic Americans who worked to improve conditions. In 1962, with help from **Dolores Huerta** and Gil Padilla, Chavez formed a union. It would later become the **United Farm Workers** (UFW). This union was committed to the goal of better pay and working conditions for migrant farmworkers—those who move seasonally from farm to farm for work. Chavez led the UFW in a five-year strike and boycott against California grape growers. Huerta worked by his side as the union's chief negotiator for contracts. They negotiated to guarantee farmworkers fair wages, benefits, and humane working conditions. The workers finally won better wages and benefits in 1970. The UFW became a national organization in 1976.

Chavez shared Martin Luther King Jr.'s commitment to nonviolent protest. To those who complained about the slow

Cesar Chavez 1927–1993

Cesar Chavez was born on a small family ranch in Arizona. After losing their land during the Great Depression, Chavez and his family began working as migrant farmworkers. Moving from town to town in search of work, Chavez went to more than 30 different schools. He served in the U.S. Navy during World War II, then returned to the fields to help migrant workers fight for better pay and working conditions. The soft-spoken Chavez seemed to many an unlikely leader of a protest movement. But Chavez quickly became an influential leader, continuing to lead the struggle for farmworkers' rights into the 1990s. Before his death, Chavez insisted, "It's not me who counts, it's the Movement."

Make Inferences
Why do you think Chavez began the farmworkers' movement?

Academic Vocabulary
consequences the effects of a particular event or events

Reading Check
Sequence What group helped inspire the Chicano movement?

pace of change, he pointed out that nonviolence takes time, and he urged them to be patient.

Chavez helped inspire young leaders in what became known as the Chicano movement. To fight discrimination and gain greater political influence, Chicano activists formed a political party called *La Raza Unida*, or the United Race. The Hispanic civil rights movement had important **consequences**. A 1968 amendment to the Elementary and Secondary Education Act required schools to teach students whose first language was not English in both languages until they learned English. The Voting Rights Act of 1975 required communities with large immigrant populations to print ballots in the voters' preferred language.

The Women's Movement

Activists also brought public attention to women's position in society. In 1963 a government commission reported that women had fewer job opportunities than men and were often paid less for the same work. President Kennedy responded by ordering an end to discrimination based on gender in civil service jobs. That same year Congress passed the Equal Pay Act. This act required many employers to pay men and women equal salaries for the same work. The Civil Rights Act of 1964 banned discrimination based on both gender and race.

Some women also began to question their traditional roles in society. In her 1963 book *The Feminine Mystique*, **Betty Friedan** described the dissatisfaction some women felt with their traditional roles of wife, mother, and homemaker.

Friedan became a leader of the modern women's rights movement. In 1966 she helped found the **National Organization for Women** (NOW)

In the 1960s women began to organize to demand equal rights. The movement became known as women's liberation. Many activists supported a woman's right to equal pay and equal protection under the law.

Shirley Chisholm became the first African American woman elected to Congress in 1968.

Betty Friedan authored *The Feminine Mystique*, a book declaring that many women wanted achievements beyond those of becoming a wife and mother.

to fight for equal educational and career opportunities for women. Other women worked for change by running for and holding public office. In 1968 **Shirley Chisholm** was elected to represent a New York City district in the House of Representatives. She was the first African American woman elected to the U.S. Congress.

In the early 1970s NOW and other women's rights activists supported and lobbied for an amendment to the Constitution. The **Equal Rights Amendment** (ERA) would outlaw all discrimination based on sex. The ERA was approved by Congress in 1972.

For an amendment to go into effect, it must be ratified by three-fourths of the states—or 38 out of 50 states. The ERA was ratified by 30 state legislatures by the end of 1973. But many opponents came forward to block the ERA. **Phyllis Schlafly**, a conservative activist, founded the group STOP ERA to prevent its ratification. Schlafly and her supporters argued that the ERA would hurt families by encouraging women to focus on careers rather than on motherhood. Such opposition weakened support for the ERA. In June 1982 the amendment fell three states short of ratification.

Despite this failure, the women's movement achieved many of its goals. Women found new opportunities in education and the workplace. For example, women began attending many formerly all-male universities. Increasing numbers of women pursued careers in traditionally all-male fields such as law and medicine. Many women also won political office at all levels of government.

Other Voices for Change

Other Americans also began to demand change in laws and other discriminating practices during the 1960s and 1970s. In 1974 the Asian American Legal Defense and Education Fund was founded. Its purpose was to build an "informed and active Asian America." The National Italian American Foundation (1975) advocated for Italian Americans. League of United Latin American Citizens was founded much earlier. It played an important

Reading Check
Find Main Ideas
What were some achievements of the women's movement of the 1960s?

Some activists worked to maintain what they saw as women's protected status under the law. Phyllis Schlafly argued against the Equal Rights Amendment, saying it would reduce the legal rights of wives and mothers.

activist role for Hispanic Americans during this period as well and continues to do so today. Native Americans and people with disabilities were also inspired by the civil rights movement.

Native Americans One major issue for Native Americans was their lack of control over tribal lands. Many worked through the National Congress of American Indians (NCAI) to gain more control over reservation lands from the federal government. They helped win passage of the Indian Civil Rights Act of 1968.

Other activists thought that groups like the NCAI worked too slowly. In November 1969 a group of young Native Americans occupied Alcatraz Island in San Francisco Bay. They did this to protest the government's takeover of Native American lands.

One of the groups that participated in the Alcatraz protest was the **American Indian Movement** (AIM). It was founded in 1968 to fight for Native Americans' rights. In February 1973 AIM activists seized a trading post and church at Wounded Knee, South Dakota. Wounded Knee is the site of the U.S. Army's massacre of Sioux Indians in 1890. Federal marshals surrounded Wounded Knee. The standoff ended with a gun battle killing two protesters and wounding one federal agent.

Such protests brought attention to issues facing Native Americans. In the early 1970s Congress began passing laws granting Native Americans greater self-government on tribal lands.

Rights for Individuals During the 1960s Supreme Court decisions brought major changes to American society. Under the leadership of Chief Justice **Earl Warren**, Court rulings greatly extended individual rights and freedoms. In *Escobedo* v. *Illinois* (1964), the justices decided that a person has the right to a lawyer during police questioning. In 1966 the Court extended these rights again in the case of *Miranda* v. *Arizona*. The Court ruled that accused persons must be informed of their rights at the time of their arrest. Today police in the United States carry cards with the Miranda warnings printed on them. They routinely "Mirandize" suspects by "reading them their rights."

The **Warren Court** issued many landmark decisions that further defined individual rights. One of these decisions was made in *Tinker* v. *Des Moines Independent Community School District* (1969). The Court established the right of public school students to express political opinions at school. The ruling stated that speech protected by the First Amendment includes not only spoken words but also "symbolic speech," or acts that express an opinion.

In this time of activism, some advocates felt that bringing cases before the Supreme Court might be a way to gain more rights for the LGBT (lesbian, gay, bisexual, and transgender) community. Their attempts, however, were not successful. During the 1970s and 1980s, members of the LGBT community began to fight openly for civil rights. Direct action groups sprang up throughout the country. They called for an end to antigay discrimination. Some people condemned this activism but were unable to slow the pace of change. By the early 1990s, several states and more than 100 local communities had outlawed such discrimination.

The Disability Rights Movement In 1970 Judy Heumann and other activists created **Disabled in Action** (DIA) to make people aware of challenges facing people with disabilities. People with disabilities often lacked access to both job opportunities and to public places. The DIA's work led to the passage of new laws. The Rehabilitation Act of 1973 banned federal agencies from discriminating against people with disabilities. The Education of Handicapped Children Act of 1975 required public schools to provide a quality education to children with disabilities. In 1990 the Americans with Disabilities Act (ADA) outlawed all discrimination against people with disabilities.

Judy Heumann and other activists formed Disabled in Action in 1970. The group promotes legislation and access to independent living for people with disabilities.

Reading Check
Contrast How were the tactics of AIM and DIA different?

Summary and Preview The fight for equal rights had far-reaching effects on American society. In the next module you will learn about world conflicts that also affected Americans.

Lesson 3 Assessment

Review Ideas, Terms, and People

1. **a. Evaluate** How did Hispanic Americans fight for civil rights?

   b. Describe Who benefited from laws like the Elementary and Secondary Education Act of 1968 and the Voting Rights Act of 1975?

2. **a. Analyze** What democratic rights and freedoms did women have to fight to obtain?

   b. Explain What happened during the ratification process of the Equal Rights Amendment?

   c. Evaluate Do you think holding elected office and lobbying are effective methods to cause change? Explain your answer.

3. **a. Analyze** In what way was the American Indian Movement similar to the Black Power movement?

   b. Identify What laws banned discrimination against people with disabilities?

Critical Thinking

4. **Categorize** In this lesson you learned about the achievements of groups that worked for equal rights. Create a graphic organizer similar to the one below and use it to identify the achievements of each group.

Hispanic Americans	Women	Native Americans	People with Disabilities

Social Studies Skills

Make Speeches

Define the Skill

In a democracy, activists, government leaders, and candidates for public office often need to address people directly. Speeches allow public figures to deliver a message to many people at once. People can use speeches to make their views known. They can use speeches to try to persuade people to support their ideas or programs.

Learn the Skill

Think about the role of speeches in the civil rights movement. Politicians and civil rights leaders used speeches to increase awareness of and support for the movement's goals. President John F. Kennedy is remembered as a powerful and effective speaker. On June 11, 1963, he gave a speech on civil rights that moved and inspired many listeners. Here is a brief excerpt from that speech, which he broadcast from the White House:

"The heart of the question is whether all Americans are to be afforded equal rights and equal opportunities, whether we are going to treat our fellow Americans as we want to be treated. If an American, because his skin is dark, cannot eat lunch in a restaurant open to the public, if he cannot send his children to the best public school available, if he cannot vote for the public officials who will represent him, if, in short, he cannot enjoy the full and free life which all of us want, then who among us would be content to have the color of his skin changed and stand in his place? Who among us would then be content with the counsels of patience and delay?"

Kennedy used repetition to express his message about the need for a civil rights bill. For example, notice that he included a series of phrases beginning with the word *if* to emphasize the injustices faced by African Americans. Not only do these phrases begin with the same word, but they also repeat the same grammatical pattern. Through this technique, Kennedy created a powerful rhythm that helped persuade his listeners.

The words of Kennedy's civil rights speech are powerful, but Kennedy's delivery made the speech even stronger. Kennedy spoke with confidence in a loud, clear voice. He also used direct eye contact and appropriate facial expressions to connect with his television audience.

Following these steps can help you make a persuasive speech.

1. Write the speech. Make sure it includes a clear main idea, good examples, and convincing language.

2. Practice. Practice reading your speech out loud to a friend. You can also practice at home in front of a mirror.

3. Give the speech. Remember to speak loudly and clearly and to look at your audience.

Practice the Skill

Suppose that you are a politician or civil rights leader in the 1960s. Following the steps above, write a short speech in favor of equal rights for African Americans, Hispanic Americans, women, Native Americans, or Americans with disabilities. After you have written and practiced your speech, give the speech to the class.

Module 30 Assessment

Review Vocabulary, Terms, and People

Complete each sentence by filling in the blank with the correct term or person from the module.

1. _____ was an African American civil rights leader and minister who believed in nonviolent, direct action.

2. In 1960 black students staged a(n) _____ at a Woolworth lunch counter in Greensboro, North Carolina.

3. The Congress of Racial Equality organized the _____ to protest segregation in bus stations throughout the South.

4. The _____ protected the voting rights of African Americans.

5. The _____ worked to get better pay and working conditions for migrant farmworkers.

6. _____ was the first African American woman elected to the U.S. Congress.

Comprehension and Critical Thinking

Lesson 1

7. **a. Describe** What was the Court's ruling in the *Brown* v. *Board of Education* case?

   b. Explain What did the Student Nonviolent Coordinating Committee do to fight segregation?

   c. Draw Conclusions Why do you think Martin Luther King Jr. was chosen to lead the MIA?

Lesson 2

8. **a. Recall** What was the New Frontier?

   b. Contrast What roles did leaders from CORE and SNCC play in the Freedom Rides?

   c. Compare and Contrast How were Malcolm X's ideas and strategies similar to those of Martin Luther King Jr.? How did they differ?

Lesson 3

9. **a. Identify** What is the National Organization for Women?

   b. Summarize How did Cesar Chavez help migrant farmworkers?

   c. Elaborate How did the Americans with Disabilities Act help disabled Americans?

Review Themes

10. Politics How did political changes help minorities achieve their goals?

11. Society and Culture How did society change during the civil rights era?

Reading Skills

Use Context Clues: Synonyms *Use the Reading Skills taught in this module to answer the question below.*

> The Little Rock Nine began attending classes, but resistance to integration continued. Some white students insulted, harassed, and attacked the black students. In spite of these obstacles, eight of the nine remained at the school.

12. Which of the following would be a good synonym for the word *harassed*?

   a. comforted

   b. assisted

   c. helped

   d. insulted

Social Studies Skills

Make Speeches *Use the Social Studies Skills taught in this module to answer the question below.*

13. What steps should you follow to make a persuasive speech?

Focus on Writing

14. Write a Bill In this module you learned about the civil rights movement and the passage of new civil rights laws. Imagine that you are a member of Congress during the 1950s and 1960s. You want to write a new civil rights bill to help people gain fair treatment under the law. What is its goal? How will it expand civil rights? Is it designed to help a certain group of people? Discuss the reasons you believe it is important to expand civil rights in this way. You may refer to problems or events the bill responds to as well as to earlier civil rights laws and legal decisions.

Module 31

Searching for Order

Essential Question

Did the United States mainly experience progress or decline in the late 20th century?

About the Photo: The nation's 200th birthday was celebrated on July 4, 1976.

In this module you will read about the economic and foreign policies of presidents in the late twentieth century. You will also learn about social issues in this period and about the Watergate scandal that led to President Nixon's resignation.

Explore ONLINE!

HISTORY

VIDEOS, including...
- Watergate
- Impeachment
- Carter Promotes Human Rights
- Reagan's Foreign Policy

✓ Document-Based Investigations

✓ Graphic Organizers

✓ Interactive Games

✓ Interactive Graph: Affirmative Action and Education

✓ Interactive Chart: Supply-Side Economics

✓ Interactive Map: Central American Conflicts in the 1980s

What You Will Learn ...

Lesson 1: Nixon's Presidency and Watergate 950
The Big Idea Richard Nixon's policies helped ease Cold War tensions before the Watergate scandal brought down his presidency.

Lesson 2: America in the 1970s 957
The Big Idea Americans faced major challenges both at home and around the world in the 1970s.

Lesson 3: The Reagan Presidency 964
The Big Idea President Reagan enacted conservative policies at home and took a strong anti-Communist stance in the Cold War.

Lesson 4: The End of the Twentieth Century 969
The Big Idea The United States and the world faced many new challenges at the end of the twentieth century.

Timeline of Events 1968–2000

United States | 1968 | **World**

1968 Richard Nixon is elected president.

1969 Golda Meir becomes prime minister of Israel. >

1970 America celebrates its first Earth Day.

< 1974 Nixon resigns the presidency. Gerald Ford is sworn in.

1973 Egypt and Syria attack Israel.

1975 South Vietnam surrenders to North Vietnam.

1976 Jimmy Carter is elected president.

1979 The Three Mile Island accident creates doubts about nuclear energy. >

1979 The Soviet Union invades Afghanistan. ∨

< 1981 After 444 days of captivity, the Iran hostage crisis ends.

1985 Ronald Reagan is sworn in to his second term as president.

1988 George H. W. Bush is elected president.

1989 Most of the Berlin Wall is dismantled. ∨

1990 U.S. and UN forces liberate Kuwait from Iraqi control in the Persian Gulf War. ∨

1994 Nelson Mandela is elected president of South Africa. >

1997 Hong Kong returns to Chinese control.

1995 Extremists bomb a federal building in Oklahoma.

2000

THEME FOCUS:

Economics, Politics

In this module you will learn about issues faced by several modern presidents. You will also read about crises in the economy and in politics that changed the way Americans viewed their role as a nation. Finally, you will learn about American society in the 1970s.

READING FOCUS:

Summarize

After reading a large amount of information, you can summarize it into a shorter amount that is easier for you to understand.

Understand Summarizing Using the ideas and information presented in a book can be easier if you summarize what the author is saying. When you summarize, you can use some of the key ideas and words to write your own sentences that explain the information. When you write a summary, some details can be left out.

Read the following passage and its summary. Notice which details the author chose to include and which to leave out.

The American population was changing in the 1970s. Throughout American history, most immigrants to the United States had come from Europe. Beginning in the 1970s, however, a majority of new immigrants came from the Americas and Asia. This pattern continues today.

Summary The population immigrating to the United States began changing during the 1970s. Now the majority of immigrants come from Latin America and Asia.

This passage contains most of the same information but is shorter. Not all of the information is included.

You Try It!

The following passage is from the module you are getting ready to read. As you read the passage, look for information that is important enough to go in a summary.

"Are you better off than you were four years ago?" That was the question Republican candidate Ronald Reagan asked voters during the 1980 presidential campaign. Millions of voters answered "No," giving Reagan an easy victory over President Carter. Reagan won 489 electoral votes to Carter's 49. On January 20, 1981—the day of Reagan's inauguration—Iran finally released the American hostages after 444 days in captivity.

After you read the passage, answer the following questions.

1. Do you think the campaign slogan from the passage above is essential information for a summary of the election?

2. Do you think the number of electoral votes should be included in your summary?

3. Write a two-sentence summary of the passage above.

As you read Module 31, practice summarizing the information from several paragraphs.

Key Terms and People

Lesson 1
stagflation
Organization of Petroleum
   Exporting Countries
realpolitik
Strategic Arms Limitation Talks
détente
Watergate
Gerald Ford
pardon

Lesson 2
affirmative action
Rachel Carson
Jimmy Carter
human rights
apartheid
sanctions
Camp David Accords
Iran hostage crisis

Lesson 3
Ronald Reagan
supply-side economics
deficit
Iran-Contra affair
Mikhail Gorbachev

Lesson 4
George H. W. Bush
Saddam Hussein
Operation Desert Storm
Colin Powell
Bill Clinton
North American Free Trade
   Agreement
Madeleine Albright
terrorism

Nixon's Presidency and Watergate

The Big Idea

Richard Nixon's policies helped ease Cold War tensions before the Watergate scandal brought down his presidency.

Main Ideas

- Americans faced domestic challenges, including an energy and economic crisis.

- Nixon's foreign policy led to improved relations with Communist powers.

- The Watergate scandal forced Nixon to resign.

- Gerald Ford became president upon Nixon's resignation and faced many challenges.

Key Terms and People

stagflation
Organization of Petroleum Exporting Countries
realpolitik
Strategic Arms Limitation Talks
détente
Watergate
Gerald Ford
pardon

If YOU were there . . .

You experienced a decade of conflict and change in the 1960s. You were a witness to major events in the civil rights movement, and you lived through frightening Cold War crises. You saw leaders assassinated and astronauts walk on the moon. You have some friends who fought in Vietnam and others who led antiwar protests.

Do you think the United States is now headed in the right direction? Why or why not?

Domestic Challenges

As president, Richard Nixon promised to work on behalf of Americans who opposed protests and supported his plan for ending the war. Nixon called these Americans the Silent Majority. He criticized student protesters and called on them to stop their activities. He did not believe Americans should leave Vietnam quickly.

New Federalism Nixon also had a new plan for government. Nixon knew that his supporters blamed the federal government for setting high taxes and interfering in citizens' lives. He proposed a plan called the New Federalism. The plan would limit the power of the federal government. His policies represented a major shift in direction from Lyndon Johnson's Great Society ideas. Under Nixon's plan, grants of money from the federal government went directly to state and local governments, who decided how to spend the money. This plan reflected Nixon's conservatism, or a belief in limiting the involvement of government in citizens' lives.

President Nixon promised to reduce welfare spending and to restore law and order. He supported policies that gave more power to police and to the courts.

His political philosophy affected the Supreme Court as well. As president, he appointed four new justices. Many Court decisions soon began to reflect a more conservative point of view.

Nixon did not push for new civil rights legislation. He believed that the government had done enough in the 1960s, saying, "The laws have caught up with our consciences."

Economic Troubles Nixon faced the difficult economic challenge of so-called **stagflation**—the economic condition of combined stagnant economic growth and high inflation. From 1967 to 1974, rising prices reduced the purchasing power of the U.S. dollar by more than 30 percent.

One cause of inflation was the rising cost of oil. By the early 1970s the United States was importing about one-third of its oil. Much of this oil was purchased from Middle Eastern nations that were members of the **Organization of Petroleum Exporting Countries**, or OPEC. This group worked to control the production and sale of oil to keep prices high.

Most OPEC countries were Arab countries that had been opposed to the creation of the Jewish state of Israel. On October 6, 1973, the Jewish holy day of Yom Kippur, Egypt and Syria attacked Israel. The attack started what would become known as the Yom Kippur War. The United States sent military supplies to help Israel.

The Energy Crisis

Connect to Economics Rising oil prices in the early 1970s had a major impact on the U.S. economy. Because oil was more expensive, the cost of everything made from oil—gasoline, heating oil, electricity, and other key products—also shot up. These higher prices led to rising inflation.

U.S. Inflation Rates, 1970–1985

Percent change from previous year

15 / 10 / 5 / 0

1970 1975 1980 1985

World Oil Prices, 1970–1985

Dollars per barrel

75 / 50 / 25 / 0

1970 1975 1980 1985

GAS SHORTAGE! Sales Limited to 10 GALS. OF GAS. PER CUSTOMER

Analyze Graphs
How were trends in oil prices and inflation similar during the 1970s?

Reading Check
Identify Cause and
Effect What was one
cause of inflation?

Arab members of OPEC responded angrily to support for Israel. They declared an embargo, or ban, on oil sales to the United States. The oil embargo and soaring oil prices caused an energy crisis. This worsened an already weak U.S. economy.

Nixon's Foreign Policy

As the energy crisis demonstrated, international events could have a serious impact on life in the United States. Henry Kissinger, a German American professor who became Nixon's senior foreign policy adviser, helped Nixon develop a new approach to foreign policy. Nixon's foreign policy decisions would be based on practical American interests, not on moral or political ideals. This approach was known as **realpolitik**, the German term meaning "actual politics."

Nixon credited his realpolitik strategies with bringing an end to the Vietnam War. These strategies used political pressure from the Soviet Union and China to convince the North Vietnamese to negotiate. Realpolitik was controversial, however. In several Latin American countries, for example, the United States backed harsh military governments because they were friendly to U.S. interests.

In the ongoing Cold War rivalries with China and the Soviet Union, the realpolitik approach led to important changes. American officials had long feared China and the Soviet Union would work together to spread communism. But by 1970 it was clear that these two Communist powers had become bitter rivals. One cause of this rivalry was the Cultural Revolution. Chinese leader Mao Zedong launched this campaign in 1966 to regain control of his country's government. Mao and his allies attempted to rid China of capitalist and traditional influences. Millions of Chinese people were persecuted during the Cultural Revolution. In addition to attacking his internal enemies, Mao accused Soviet leaders of betraying the ideals of communism by being too "soft" in their policies dealing with capitalist countries.

Nixon believed it was in America's interest to widen this split and to improve U.S. relations with both Communist powers. He first turned his attention to China. Nixon lifted restrictions on trade and travel and opened negotiations. In 1972 Nixon became the first U.S. president to make an official visit to China. His visit received wide acclaim in the media. Newscasts showed Nixon and Mao shaking hands and trading jokes during their meeting.

Nixon's trip led to improved U.S.-China relations. It also caught the attention of Soviet leaders. They became more open to talks with the United States. In May 1972 Nixon flew to Moscow, where he and Soviet leader Leonid Brezhnev participated in the **Strategic Arms Limitation Talks** (SALT). These talks led to a treaty limiting each country's nuclear weapons. The SALT agreement opened a period of **détente** (day-TAHNT), or less hostile relations, between the United States and the Soviet Union. Détente brought economic benefits, as the Soviets began buying millions of tons of grain from American farmers.

On his visit to China in 1972, Nixon visited many sites, including the Great Wall.

Reading Check
Draw Conclusions Do
you think realpolitik
was a good strategy?
Why or why not?

The Watergate Scandal

On June 17, 1972, five men were arrested while breaking into the Democratic National Committee's offices at the Watergate Hotel in Washington, DC. The burglars were carrying camera equipment and secret recording devices. Police soon discovered that some of them had ties to the Nixon administration. One had worked for the Committee to Reelect the President (CRP).

Nixon denied that anyone in his administration was involved in the Watergate break-in, and the White House public relations campaign was successful in keeping the trust of the American people. Nixon went on to win the 1972 election in a landslide. But early in Nixon's second term, the seemingly minor break-in exploded into a massive political scandal that became known as **Watergate**.

Watergate Scandal

On May 28, 1972, five men burglarized the Democratic National Committee headquarters in the Watergate Hotel, shown here. They bugged telephones and took pictures of files. The burglars returned for more information on June 17 and were arrested.

Washington Post reporters soon linked the break-in to the presidential re-election campaign. A White House cover-up began.

The Senate formed a committee to investigate the break-in and possible cover-up. Its hearings (shown right) were televised.

Faced with impeachment for an illegal cover-up of the break-in, Nixon resigned. President Gerald Ford later pardoned Nixon.

Analyze Information
Why was Nixon threatened with impeachment by the House?

Investigating the Break-in Did Nixon administration officials have anything to do with the Watergate break-in? Reporters Bob Woodward and Carl Bernstein investigated that question in a series of articles in the *Washington Post*. Key figures in the Nixon administration refused to talk to the reporters. Then a government official contacted Woodward. The official had inside information on the Watergate investigation. The informant was not revealed until 2005, more than 30 years later. W. Mark Felt, second-in-command at the FBI during Watergate, was the inside source. However, at the time, Woodward called Felt by a secret codename to protect his identity. With Felt's information, Woodward and Bernstein began publishing stories about Nixon administration officials and their illegal activities. The stories revealed that the CRP had hidden illegal campaign contributions and spread false rumors about Democratic candidates. They also presented evidence that officials in the Nixon White House were trying to cover up the facts of the Watergate break-in.

Senator Sam Ervin led a Senate committee that launched its own investigation of Watergate. When the committee began televised hearings in May 1973, millions of Americans tuned in. The most damaging witness was

United States v. Nixon (1974)

Background of the Case

During the Watergate investigation, a special prosecutor asked for the tapes of President Nixon's Oval Office conversations. Nixon claimed that he did not have to obey court orders to turn over the tapes because of executive privilege. On July 8, 1974, the case went before the Supreme Court.

The Court's Ruling

The Supreme Court announced its unanimous decision on July 24. It stated, "the legitimate [lawful] needs of the judicial process may outweigh presidential privilege." Nixon could not use executive privilege to avoid the subpoenas.

The Court's Reasoning

The Court decided to hear the case more quickly than most cases because of its importance to the functioning of government and the interest of the American public. The Supreme Court ruled that to claim executive privilege, a president would have to show a convincing national security reason. Nixon had no such reason for refusing to hand over the tapes.

Why It Matters

The Supreme Court ruling showed that, despite their unique and important position, presidents do have to obey the law. It also showed that the government could use the powers defined in the Constitution to prevent one branch from becoming too powerful. Less than a week later, the House Judiciary Committee voted to impeach Nixon.

Analyze Information

1. How is this case an example of the checks and balances system?

2. What do you think was the most important impact of this Supreme Court decision?

---

former White House attorney John Dean. He testified that Nixon was personally involved in the Watergate cover-up. Dean could not prove this, however. Then another witness, former White House staffer Alexander Butterfield, revealed that Nixon had tape-recorded almost all of his Oval Office conversations.

Committee members asked Nixon to allow them to listen to the tapes. Nixon refused to hand the tapes over to a special prosecutor. He claimed executive privilege—a president's right to keep information secret for reasons of national security. In July 1974 the Supreme Court ordered Nixon to turn over the tapes. The recordings proved that Nixon had directed the Watergate cover-up and lied about it to Congress and the public.

While this investigation was unfolding, Vice President Spiro Agnew resigned. He faced charges that he had taken bribes and failed to pay taxes. Nixon appointed Michigan congressman **Gerald Ford** as vice president.

Nixon Resigns After studying the case, the House Judiciary Committee recommended impeachment. Judiciary Committee member Barbara Jordan of Texas explained why she thought Nixon should be impeached:

> "My faith in the Constitution is whole, it is complete, it is total. And I am not going to sit here and be an idle spectator to the . . . destruction of the Constitution."
>
> —Barbara Jordan, in a speech before Congress, 1974

On July 27, 1974, the committee approved its first article of impeachment. This article charged Nixon with obstruction of justice. Within the next week, the committee approved two more articles. One article was for the abuse of power and one for contempt of Congress.

On August 8, 1974, Nixon appeared on national television. He announced, "I shall resign the presidency effective at noon tomorrow." Nixon became the first president in American history to resign from office. Gerald Ford was sworn in as president on August 9.

One of the **consequences** of Watergate was that many Americans lost faith in government officials. In a poll taken in 1974, just 36 percent of Americans said they trusted the government. Others, however, saw a more positive side of Watergate. Senator Sam Ervin viewed the hearings and Nixon's resignation as evidence that the government was able to rid itself of corruption. "Watergate . . . proved our Constitution works," he said.

Academic Vocabulary
consequences the effects of a particular event or events

Reading Check
Sequence
What events led to Nixon's resignation?

Ford as President

Vice President Gerald Ford became the first modern president to hold the office without being elected to it. Ford lost some public support when he granted Richard Nixon a **pardon**, or freedom from punishment. He declared it was best for the nation that Nixon not be tried for his crime. Ford stated that Nixon would be "cruelly and excessively penalized" and "ugly passions would again be aroused [stirred]."

A U.S. Marine changes the official presidential photograph from one of Nixon to one of Ford.

Other issues added to Ford's difficulties. Oil prices and unemployment remained high, and stagflation continued. The United States also had an increasing trade deficit, an imbalance in which a country imports more than it exports.

Ford argued that inflation was the main cause of the economic troubles. He began a campaign called Whip Inflation Now (WIN). WIN encouraged people to save money and businesses to hold down wages and prices. Ford's plan met with resistance from many members of Congress, who wanted to increase spending to help the poor and unemployed. In 1975 Ford and Congress began to compromise. Still, inflation and unemployment remained high.

Summary and Preview Gerald Ford became president after the Watergate scandal ended Nixon's presidency. In the next lesson you will learn about life in the 1970s.

Reading Check
Analyze Information
Do you think President Ford was right to pardon Nixon?

Lesson 1 Assessment

Review Ideas, Terms, and People

1. a. Describe What challenges did the United States face during President Nixon's terms of office?

   b. Summarize Why do rising oil prices have such a widespread effect on the economy?

   c. Make Inferences Why do you think the Organization of Petroleum Exporting Countries objected to U.S. support for Israel?

2. a. Identify Who was Henry Kissinger?

   b. Contrast How was realpolitik different from other foreign policy approaches?

   c. Draw Conclusions Why do you think improved U.S.-China relations made the Soviets more open to talks with the United States?

3. a. Recall What was the Watergate scandal?

   b. Explain Why were President Nixon's tapes important?

   c. Elaborate Why do you think President Nixon decided to resign?

4. a. Describe How did Gerald Ford become president of the United States?

   b. Predict Do you think WIN was effective in helping the economy?

Critical Thinking

5. Sequence In this lesson you learned about Nixon's domestic policy, foreign policy, and the Watergate scandal. Create a table similar to the one below and use it to list, in order, the key events that took place during Nixon's presidency.

Event	Date

America in the 1970s

The Big Idea

Americans faced major challenges both at home and around the world in the 1970s.

Main Ideas

- American society debated key social issues during the 1970s.
- Jimmy Carter was elected president in 1976.
- Carter had successes as well as failures in foreign policy during his administration.

Key Terms and People

affirmative action
Rachel Carson
Jimmy Carter
human rights
apartheid
sanctions
Camp David Accords
Iran hostage crisis

If YOU were there . . .

It is July 4, 1976. Today, the entire nation is celebrating the 200th anniversary of the signing of the Declaration of Independence. As you sit with your family watching a spectacular fireworks show, you think about the challenges this country has faced throughout its history. You think about the economic and foreign policy challenges facing Americans right now.

What are your hopes for the nation's future?

Social Issues of the 1970s

The American population was changing in the 1970s. Throughout American history, most immigrants to the United States had come from Europe. Beginning in the 1970s, however, a majority of new immigrants came from the Americas and Asia. This pattern continues today. Another change was that the birthrate, or number of births per 1,000 people, was declining. By 1970 Americans 65 and older became one of the fastest-growing population groups.

Debating Rights As the population grew and changed, American society faced challenges in trying to balance the views of all Americans. Some of these challenges involved women's issues. The Equal Rights Amendment caused nationwide debate in the 1970s. Although the ERA was not ratified, the women's movement did make important gains. A 1972 federal law known as Title IX banned discrimination on the basis of sex in educational programs that receive federal funds. The number of women admitted to medical and law schools climbed quickly. Title IX also opened the door for many more women to participate in college sports and earn athletic scholarships. In 1973 the Supreme Court legalized abortion in the case *Roe* v. *Wade*. Opponents of abortion began to form groups seeking to overturn the decision. Today, the issue of abortion remains highly controversial.

Issues of the 1970s

Environmental protection, women's rights, and affirmative action were among the major issues of the 1970s.

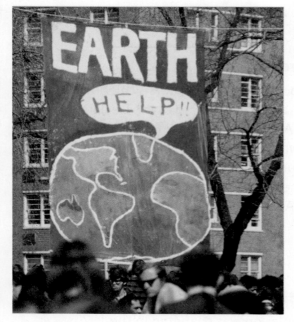

The environment became an important issue of national debate. Activists pushed for legislation and individual action to help protect the Earth.

Supporters of the Equal Rights Amendment urged states to ratify the amendment. They believed it would guarantee equal protection to women under the Constitution.

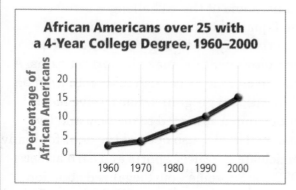

African Americans over 25 with a 4-Year College Degree, 1960–2000

Affirmative action helped African Americans and other minorities gain access to universities and certain jobs. The issue also created much debate.

In the 1970s Americans also debated **affirmative action**, the practice of giving special consideration to nonwhites or women to make up for past discrimination. Supporters argued that minorities and women needed affirmative action to improve their educational and job opportunities. Opponents insisted that any preferences based on race or gender were unfair.

Many African Americans benefited from new opportunities in the 1970s. For example, the number of African Americans attending college increased. In 1976 the number was four times higher than it had been a decade earlier. Many people credited affirmative action programs with this increase.

Environmental Battles The environment also became a major issue in the 1970s. In her book *Silent Spring*, biologist **Rachel Carson** brought attention to the dangers of pollution. She explained how chemicals used to kill insects travel through the food chain and affect people's health.

> "Man, however much he may like to pretend the contrary [opposite], is part of nature. Can he escape a pollution that is now so thoroughly distributed throughout our world?"
>
> —Rachel Carson, *Silent Spring*

Silent Spring was first published in 1962. It helped inspire a nationwide movement to improve the environment. Environmentalists in the United States celebrated the first Earth Day on April 22, 1970. "Earth Day is to remind each person of his [or her] . . . equal responsibility . . . to preserve and improve the Earth," explained activists.

Environmentalists brought attention to other issues in addition to pollution. These issues included the risks of nuclear power, the overuse of natural resources, and the loss of natural habitats due to human development. Many environmentalists linked these problems to population growth. From 1900 to 1975, there were major changes in population. The population of the United States nearly tripled. The world's population grew from roughly 1.6 billion to 4 billion.

Congress passed new laws to limit the release of pollutants. The Environmental Protection Agency (EPA) was established in 1970 to carry out these laws. The mission of the EPA is to protect human health and the environment. It conducts research and writes and enforces rules to provide this protection.

One of the EPA's major efforts has been to reduce acid rain. It can form when air pollution mixes with water in the atmosphere. Acid rain can fall hundreds of miles from the source of pollution, harming plants and wildlife. In 1976 a scientist found that many of the lakes in Adirondack Park in New York State no longer had any fish because the water had become too acidic. In 1990 the EPA created a program to reduce pollution that causes acid rain.

The government also took action to repair damage caused by pollution. In 1980 Congress passed a law to promote the cleanup of heavily contaminated sites. The Love Canal disaster in the town of Niagara Falls, New York, inspired the creation of the law. Chemical companies had dumped large quantities of toxic waste into the canal before it was closed and covered with earth. A school and rows of homes were built nearby. Residents began to report high rates of serious health problems. Eventually, more than 900 families were moved from the site.

The environmental movement has claimed many victories since the 1970s. Americans are increasingly aware of how their actions affect the environment. As protections increased, however, debates have grown about how to balance business interests with environmental concerns.

Urban Decay In the 1970s many American cities fell into crisis, especially in the Midwest and the Northeast. As middle-class families moved to new suburbs following World War II, businesses followed them. Cities were harmed by the loss of jobs and taxpayers as well as by social problems such as crime and drug abuse. These conditions, known as urban decay, drove even more families to leave.

At times the downward spiral of urban decay seemed hopeless to reverse. For example, in 1975 New York City was on the verge of bankruptcy. After President Ford gave a speech in which he refused to provide the city with federal assistance, the *Daily News* published a front-page headline that read: "FORD TO CITY: DROP DEAD." New York began to stabilize in the 1980s, but other cities such as Detroit and Cleveland have continued to struggle.

Carter Elected

To oppose Republican Gerald Ford in the 1976 presidential election, Democrats nominated **Jimmy Carter**, a little-known former governor of Georgia. The Democrats purposely chose a candidate who was untouched by recent government scandals. Carter knew that the Vietnam War and Watergate had badly shaken American voters' trust in government. "I will never lie to you," he told voters.

Reading Check
Compare and Contrast
How are Title IX and affirmative action similar and different?

The Election of 1976

Jimmy Carter

Gerald Ford

	Candidate	Party	Electoral Vote	Popular Vote	% Popular Vote
	Carter	Democrat	297	40,828,929	50.1
	Ford	Republican	240	39,148,940	48.0

*One electoral vote was cast for Ronald Reagan.

Source: *World Almanac and Book of Facts, 2004*

Interpret Maps

Place Which areas of the country did Carter win in 1976?

Carter defeated Ford in a close election. As president, Carter wanted to show a new spirit of informality and openness at the White House. On inauguration day, he and his family broke with tradition by walking to the inauguration rather than riding in a limousine.

Americans seemed to respond positively to his straightforward style. However, Carter faced serious challenges. High unemployment and inflation continued. The ongoing energy crisis also kept oil prices high. Many Americans became frustrated with the president's inability to solve these problems.

Although Democrats controlled Congress, Carter had a hard time convincing members to support his proposals. For example, Carter proposed a national energy plan. It called for conservation and the use of alternative energy sources such as solar energy. Congress demanded changes to the complex plan. The plan was never fully passed.

Carter also wanted to expand the use of nuclear power. This was one way he hoped to decrease the country's dependence on imported oil. But an accident at the Three Mile Island nuclear power plant in Pennsylvania caused new worries about the safety of nuclear energy. On March 28, 1979, a reactor core at Three Mile Island overheated. As a result, the plant released a small amount of radioactive gas into the air. This frightening incident damaged the nuclear power industry, and the federal government put in place a ban on building new reactors.

Reading Check

Draw Conclusions How did the Three Mile Island incident affect Carter's energy plan?

Carter and Foreign Policy

President Carter rejected Nixon's realpolitik approach to foreign policy. He argued that "fairness, not force, should lie at the heart of our dealings with the nations of the world."

Changing Policies Carter favored policies that promoted **human rights**—the basic rights and freedoms of all people. He reduced U.S. aid to several former allies that committed human rights violations. In South Africa, Carter hoped to pressure the government into ending **apartheid**, a system of laws requiring racial segregation. He called for **sanctions**, or economic penalties, to encourage reform.

Carter's approach to foreign policy had effects in Latin America as well. Many Latin Americans resented previous U.S. interference in their countries. American control of the Panama Canal stood as a symbol of power in the region. In 1977 Carter signed treaties that would transfer control of the canal to Panama by the year 2000.

Carter had less success improving relations with the Soviet Union. Détente broke down when he criticized the Soviet Union for committing human rights abuses. Then in 1979 the Soviet Union invaded

Historical Sources

The Camp David Accords

In 1978 President Carter invited Israel's prime minister Menachem Begin and Egypt's president Anwar el-Sadat to meet at Camp David. The goal was to end conflict between their two nations, but the negotiations were very difficult. Carter later wrote about one moment when the talks nearly broke down.

"*Within a few minutes Sadat announced angrily that a stalemate [standstill] had been reached. He saw no reason for the discussions to continue. As far as he was concerned, they were over . . . They [Sadat and Begin] were moving toward the door, but I got in front of them to partially block the way. I urged them not to break off their talks, to give me another chance to use my influence and analysis, to have confidence in me. Begin agreed readily. I looked straight at Sadat; finally, he nodded his head. They left without speaking to each other.*"

Leaders Anwar el-Sadat (left), Jimmy Carter, and Menachem Begin (right) reached a peace agreement for the Middle East in the Camp David Accords.

Analyze Historical Sources
Why do you think Begin and el-Sadat agreed to continue their negotiations?

Afghanistan. Carter responded by breaking off arms-control talks and refusing to allow U.S. athletes to participate in the 1980 Summer Olympics in Moscow.

The Middle East While Cold War tensions increased, Carter worked to ease tensions in the Middle East. Egypt and Israel had been in conflict for 30 years. In 1978 Carter invited Egyptian president Anwar el-Sadat and Israeli prime minister Menachem Begin (men-AHK-uhm BAY-guhn) to the presidential retreat at Camp David, Maryland. After 13 days of meetings, the two leaders reached a peace agreement called the **Camp David Accords**. Many consider the agreement to be Carter's greatest achievement.

Carter also experienced disaster in the Middle East. The United States had supported the pro-American shah, or king, of Iran since the 1950s. Many Iranians resented the shah's reform efforts. They also disliked the country's shift from a traditional and agricultural society to a more urban and industrial one. The government severely punished its opponents and controlled all political participation. Many members of the opposition supported the views of Islamic spiritual leader Ruhollah Khomeini. Khomeini had been forced to leave the country because of his criticisms of the shah's policies.

In 1979 Khomeini's supporters drove the shah out of Iran. A month later, Khomeini took control of the government. On November 4, a group

Hostages Released

Approximately 52 Americans were held hostage by Iranian militants during the Iran hostage crisis. The men and women were kept blindfolded by their captors. After 444 days in captivity, the Americans were released.

of Iranian students attacked the U.S. embassy in Tehran, the capital of Iran, seizing about 90 American hostages. The **Iran hostage crisis** lasted for more than a year.

In the early days of the crisis, some hostages were released. The Iranian captors often blindfolded and beat the remaining hostages. Carter ended Iranian oil imports and froze Iranian assets in American banks. After a failed rescue attempt in April 1980, many Americans lost confidence in Carter's leadership.

Summary and Preview President Carter's policies included both successes and failures. In the next lesson you will learn about the policies of Ronald Reagan.

Reading Check
Make Inferences
Overall, do you think President Carter's foreign policy was effective? Why or why not?

Lesson 2 Assessment

Review Ideas, Terms, and People

1. **a. Recall** What social issues did Americans debate during the 1970s?

   b. Contrast How had immigration patterns changed by the 1970s?

   c. Draw Conclusions Why do you think *Silent Spring* remained important in the 1970s?

   d. Elaborate How is the EPA's mission reflected in its response to Love Canal and acid rain?

2. **a. Describe** How did Jimmy Carter break with tradition at his inauguration?

   b. Analyze Why did Carter's promise of honesty appeal to voters?

   c. Elaborate How did the Three Mile Island accident affect the energy crisis?

3. **a. Recall** What idea guided President Carter's approach to foreign policy?

   b. Explain What agreement was made in the treaties that Carter signed with Panama?

   c. Analyze Why did Carter lose political support during the Iran hostage crisis?

   d. Draw Conclusions Why do you think many people consider the Camp David Accords Carter's greatest achievement?

Critical Thinking

4. **Evaluate** In this lesson you learned about the new government policies in the 1970s. Create a graphic organizer similar to the one below to show President Carter's successes and failures.

Successes

Failures

The Reagan Presidency

The Big Idea

President Reagan enacted conservative policies at home and took a strong anti-Communist stance in the Cold War.

Main Ideas

- President Reagan based his policies on conservative ideas.

- Reagan took a tough stand against communism in his foreign policy.

Key Terms and People

Ronald Reagan
supply-side economics
deficit
Iran-Contra affair
Mikhail Gorbachev

In July 1981, Reagan explained his plan to reduce taxes during a televised address to the nation from the Oval Office.

If YOU were there . . .

It is 1980, and you are a top adviser to the newly elected president, Ronald Reagan. You think about the challenges Reagan will face. High inflation and unemployment are plaguing the economy. Relations with the Soviet Union are falling apart. Also, 52 Americans are still being held hostage in Iran.

What would be your first recommendation to the president?

Reagan and Conservative Ideas

"Are you better off than you were four years ago?" That was the question Republican candidate **Ronald Reagan** asked voters during the 1980 presidential campaign. Millions of voters answered "No," giving Reagan an easy victory over President Carter. Reagan won 489 electoral votes to Carter's 49. On January 20, 1981—the day of Reagan's inauguration—Iran finally released the American hostages after 444 days in captivity.

Reagan's approach to government was based on conservative ideas. He wanted to cut taxes and reduce regulations on businesses. He promised to scale back the size of government, arguing that government involvement in business and society harmed individual ambition. "Government is not the solution to our problem; government is the problem," Reagan declared in his inaugural address.

Just two months into his presidency, Reagan was shot and severely wounded in an assassination attempt by John Hinckley Jr. Reagan was released from the hospital within two weeks and returned to work.

Reaganomics Reagan's economic policies, which some called Reaganomics, were based on a theory called **supply-side economics**. This theory calls for sharp tax cuts with the goal of increasing the amount of money people and businesses have to invest. This investment would lead to economic growth and the creation of new jobs. Over time, the expanding economic activity would produce increased tax revenues for the government.

Though many Democrats opposed this theory, Congress approved most of Reagan's plan for large cuts in business and personal taxes. To help balance the budget, Reagan called for spending cuts as well. Congress agreed to cut the rate of the growth of spending on social programs such as school lunches, low-income housing, and food stamps.

The economy experienced a brief recession early in Reagan's presidency. Then in 1983 the economy rebounded and began a long period of expansion. Business profits and tax revenues increased.

At the same time, spending on defense was increased dramatically, from $180 billion in 1981 to nearly $280 billion in 1985. The new spending outpaced the new tax revenues. The result was a rapidly rising **deficit**—the amount by which a government's spending exceeds its revenues.

Conservative Goals One of Reagan's conservative goals was to reduce government regulation of key industries. Reagan hoped fewer rules would encourage expansion in those industries, thereby improving the U.S. economy. Congress responded by reducing regulations on industries such as television, airlines, and banking.

Reagan was also able to move the Supreme Court in a more conservative direction by appointing politically conservative judges. In 1981 he appointed Sandra Day O'Connor to the Court. She became the first woman to serve as a Supreme Court justice. Reagan later appointed two more conservative justices: Antonin Scalia and Anthony M. Kennedy.

Election of 1984 President Reagan ran for re-election in 1984 against Democratic candidate Walter Mondale, who had served as Jimmy Carter's

——— BIOGRAPHY ———

Sandra Day O'Connor 1930–

Sandra Day O'Connor grew up on a ranch in Arizona and entered Stanford University at age 16. She graduated third in her class from Stanford Law School in 1952. When she applied for jobs as a lawyer, however, she found that law firms were not willing to hire women. She turned instead to public service in Arizona, holding jobs including assistant attorney general, state senator, and judge. She was serving on the Arizona Court of Appeals when she was nominated to the Supreme Court by Ronald Reagan. The Senate confirmed O'Connor's appointment by a vote of 99–0. O'Connor retired from the bench in 2005.

Analyze Information
Why did Sandra Day O'Connor begin working in public service?

vice president. Mondale chose Geraldine Ferraro as his running mate. Ferraro was the first woman to run for vice president on a major-party ticket. She spoke of the implications of her nomination:

> "By choosing an American woman to run for our nation's second-highest office, you send a powerful signal to all Americans. . . . We will place no limits on achievement. If we can do this, we can do anything."
>
> —Geraldine Ferraro, *Ferraro: My Story*

Reading Check
Summarize
What theories did
Reaganomics include?

The economy was booming as the election approached. Mondale argued that Reagan's economic policies unfairly favored the wealthy. Voters, however, gave Reagan a landslide victory. Reagan received 59 percent of the popular vote and captured 525 of the 538 electoral votes.

Reagan and Foreign Policy

President Reagan was an outspoken critic of communism and the Soviet Union, which he called an "evil empire." He saw the Cold War as a fight of "good versus evil, right versus wrong."

BIOGRAPHY

Ronald Reagan 1911–2004

Ronald Reagan grew up in Illinois. In 1937 he moved to California, where he became a well-known movie actor. He later entered politics and was elected governor of California. Then he served eight years as president.

Reagan worked to reshape the American government and economy based on conservative values. In foreign policy, he took an aggressive stand toward communism and the Soviet Union. Reagan challenged the Soviet leader to allow freedom in Eastern Europe. In a famous speech at the Berlin Wall, he said, "Mr. Gorbachev, tear down this wall!" Reagan and Gorbachev later signed the Intermediate-Range Nuclear Forces (INF) Treaty. It was the first treaty that reduced the number of nuclear weapons held by both countries.

Reagan was nicknamed the Great Communicator. He inspired many Americans with his sense of humor and his optimistic view of America's future. Many voters credited him with restoring their confidence after the difficulties of the 1970s. Many believe that Reagan's buildup of the U.S. military contributed to major changes in the Cold War and the eventual fall of Communist governments in the Soviet Union and Eastern Europe.

Find Main Ideas
What was Reagan's biggest foreign policy achievement? Use evidence from the reading to support your answer.

Central American Conflicts in the 1980s

Explore ONLINE!

Legend:
- Guerrilla activity or civil war
- U.S. base in continuous operation since 1903
- U.S. military presence or intervention

0   200   400 Miles
0   200   400 Kilometers

UNITED STATES

ATLANTIC OCEAN

Gulf of Mexico

Miami

THE BAHAMAS

MEXICO

Mexico City

Havana

CUBA

CAYMAN IS. (U.K.) — Guantánamo Bay

DOMINICAN REPUBLIC

PUERTO RICO (U.S.)

HAITI

JAMAICA   Port-au-   Santo
Kingston   Prince   Domingo

GUATEMALA   Belmopan
            BELIZE   HONDURAS
                     1983, 1988

Caribbean Sea

Guatemala City
EL SALVADOR   Tegucigalpa

1981   NICARAGUA

San   Managua   Panama
Salvador   Canal

PACIFIC
OCEAN   COSTA   Panama
            RICA   City

GRENADA
1983

San
José

1989   PANAMA   COLOMBIA

Caracas

VENEZUELA

Georgetown

GUYANA

Interpret Maps

1. **Location** In which two countries did the United States intervene in 1983?

2. **Human-Environment Interaction** Why might the United States have intervened in the countries where it did?

Conflicts in Central America Civil wars raged in several Central American countries in the 1980s as communism spread in the area. Reagan supported anti-Communist governments in El Salvador and Guatemala with financial aid. Critics of this policy charged that the aid went to military governments that committed major human rights violations.

In Nicaragua, a revolutionary group called the Sandinistas overthrew the country's pro-American dictator in 1979. U.S. leaders became concerned when the Sandinistas formed closer ties with Communist Cuba. Reagan cut all U.S. aid to Nicaragua and began supporting anti-Sandinista rebels known as the Contras. This led to fears that the United States could be drawn into war. In 1984 Congress passed a ban on more U.S. military aid to the Contras.

A group of Reagan administration officials secretly found a way to continue funding the Contras. One member of the group was Oliver North, a marine officer serving as a national security aide. North helped arrange the sale of U.S. missiles to Iran. In exchange, Iran released U.S. hostages who had been taken by terrorists loyal to Iran. Profits from this secret deal were sent to the Contras. These profits were in violation of the congressional ban. The so-called **Iran-Contra affair** became a national controversy when it was exposed in 1986. Congressional hearings concluded that President Reagan was not guilty of illegal activity. Several White House officials, however, were convicted of crimes related to the affair.

Reagan and Gorbachev During his first term, President Reagan took a tough stand against the Soviet Union. He stopped arms negotiations and quickly expanded the U.S. military.

The Soviet Union tried to keep up with American spending in the arms race. This contributed to desperate economic times in the Soviet Union during the 1980s. In 1985 **Mikhail Gorbachev** became the new Soviet leader. To deal with his country's economic problems, he began a process of political and economic reforms called *perestroika*. He also adopted a new policy of political openness called *glasnost*. The newfound freedoms introduced by Gorbachev's policies threatened other leaders of the Soviet Union. But most of its citizens and leaders in the West supported these freedoms.

Reagan became convinced of Gorbachev's desire for change. In 1987 the two leaders signed the Intermediate-Range Nuclear Forces Treaty. The treaty eliminated all medium-range nuclear weapons in Europe. Cold War tensions were decreasing for the first time since the early 1970s.

Summary and Preview Conservative ideas influenced many of Ronald Reagan's policies. In the next lesson you will learn about the policies of presidents in the 1990s.

Reading Check
Identify Cause and Effect Why did President Reagan change his tough stand toward the Soviet Union?

Lesson 3 Assessment

Review Ideas, Terms, and People

1. **a. Recall** What was Ronald Reagan's view of government?

   b. Analyze Why did the federal budget deficit rise during Reagan's presidency?

   c. Draw Conclusions Why do you think so many Americans voted for Reagan in the 1984 election?

2. **a. Recall** What changes did Mikhail Gorbachev make in the Soviet Union?

   b. Explain How did Reagan administration officials violate the law in the Iran-Contra affair?

   c. Predict Do you think Reagan's policies were effective in fighting communism?

Critical Thinking

3. **Summarize** In this lesson you learned about the domestic and foreign policies of President Reagan. Create a table similar to the one below to list each policy with its correct geographic focus.

United States	Central America	Soviet Union

The End of the Twentieth Century

The Big Idea

The United States and the world faced many new challenges at the end of the twentieth century.

Main Ideas

- Major global changes took place during the presidency of George H. W. Bush.

- During Bill Clinton's presidency, the nation experienced scandal, economic growth, and the rise of terrorist threats.

Key Terms and People

George H. W. Bush
Saddam Hussein
Operation Desert Storm
Colin Powell
Bill Clinton
North American Free Trade Agreement
Madeleine Albright
terrorism

If YOU were there . . .

You are visiting the city of West Berlin in 1989. Just after midnight on November 9, you see huge crowds of people pouring into the streets to celebrate. You rush outside to find out what's going on. "The wall is falling!" people shout. You run toward the Berlin Wall, and there you see East and West Germans working together to rip down the hated wall.

What might the fall of the Berlin Wall mean for the future?

George H. W. Bush

Ronald Reagan was popular with a majority of voters as his second term as president came to an end. Republicans hoped this would help Reagan's vice president, **George H. W. Bush**, win the election of 1988. Bush's Democratic opponent was Massachusetts governor Michael Dukakis. After a hard-fought campaign, Bush won the election with 426 electoral votes to Dukakis's 111.

The Cold War Ends As Bush began his presidency, Mikhail Gorbachev continued his reform programs in the Soviet Union. In the Soviet-controlled states of Eastern Europe, people demanded even faster change and more freedom. Pro-democracy movements in Hungary, Poland, and other nations put increasing pressure on Communist governments. This pressure produced world-changing results in 1989, as pro-Soviet governments across Eastern Europe began to fall.

In October 1989 massive protests in East Germany led to the resignation of Communist leader Erich Honecker. The new government agreed to open the borders of East Germany. This included the border guarded by the Berlin Wall. At midnight on November 9, a wild celebration broke out as East and West Berliners jumped onto the Berlin Wall, shouting and dancing. Some smashed through parts of the wall with hammers and chisels. The wall began crumbling to

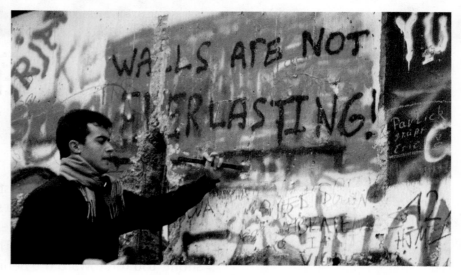

the ground. It had stood as a symbol of the Cold War since 1961. Within a year, the two Germanys reunited as one democratic country.

Several Soviet republics soon declared independence from the Soviet regime. Hard-line Communists were desperate to hold on to power. They took Gorbachev hostage in August 1991 and tried to seize the government. Thousands of Soviets took to the streets in protest. Ignoring orders to stop the protesters, many soldiers joined the crowds. Pro-democracy leader Boris Yeltsin encouraged the protesters to stand strong. Within a few months, Gorbachev resigned and the Soviet Union broke apart.

After Gorbachev's resignation, Bush worked with Russian president Yeltsin to improve relations between the United States and Russia. In February 1992 they issued a formal statement declaring an end to the Cold War. In January 1993 Yeltsin and Bush signed the START II pact. This treaty was supposed to reduce the number of nuclear weapons held by both nations, but it was never put into effect.

The Persian Gulf War President Bush called for all countries to work together, especially during times of crisis. A major crisis soon developed in the Middle East. In August 1990 Iraq's dictator, **Saddam Hussein**, invaded neighboring oil-rich Kuwait.

Members of the United Nations called for the immediate withdrawal of Iraqi troops. President Bush, with strong public support, began assembling a coalition, or alliance, of nations to drive Iraq from Kuwait by force.

Saddam refused to withdraw from Kuwait. In response, a U.S.-led multi-national coalition launched **Operation Desert Storm**. This air offensive was led by U.S. generals Norman Schwarzkopf and **Colin Powell**. Powell was the chair of the joint chiefs of staff and the highest-ranking African American ever to serve in the U.S. military. After a six-week bombing campaign, ground forces entered Kuwait. Within days, Iraq agreed to a cease-fire.

About 22,300 Iraqi soldiers and civilians were killed in the Persian Gulf War. The coalition forces lost around 223 soldiers, 148 of whom were American. More than 35,000 American women served in the war, though federal laws prevented them from serving in combat.

The Persian Gulf War, 1990–1991

▷ Explore ONLINE!

TURKEY

SYRIA

Mediterranean Sea

LEBANON

Haifa

ISRAEL

Jerusalem

Tel Aviv

JORDAN

EGYPT

Euphrates River

Tigris River

Baghdad

IRAQ

IRAN

KUWAIT

Kuwait City

Dhahran

Persian Gulf

BAHRAIN

QATAR

U.A.E.

Riyadh

SAUDI ARABIA

OMAN

Red Sea

YEMEN

Arabian Sea

→ Iraqi invasion, Aug. 2, 1990

✴ Scud missile attack

➔ UN ground forces, Feb. 23–27, 1991

✴ UN air attacks, Jan.–Feb. 1991

0   150   300 Miles
0   150   300 Kilometers

1 Allied air strikes against targets, including Baghdad, begin January 7th.

2 Iraq launches scud missile attacks unsuccessfully against targets in Israel and Saudi Arabia.

3 Allies' ground attack begins February 24th.

Interpret Maps

1. **Place** Where did Iraqi forces invade?

2. **Location** From which country did UN ground forces attack Iraq?

President Bush explained the importance of the war, telling Congress:

"Now, we can see a new world coming into view. A world in which there is the very real prospect of a new world order . . . A world in which freedom and respect for human rights find a home among all nations."

—George H. W. Bush, March 6, 1991

Economic Policy Bush had campaigned on a firm pledge not to raise taxes. Once he was in office, however, he faced pressure due to the high federal deficit and a weakening economy. Bush proposed a plan to lower the deficit with spending cuts. The Democrats in Congress rejected his plan. In 1990 he compromised by agreeing to tax increases, which angered many conservatives. This step did not prevent the economy from entering a recession. In the spring of 1992, the unemployment rate climbed above 7 percent—a six-year high. Americans began to think that Bush was good at foreign policy but ineffective at home.

Reading Check
Summarize How did the world change between 1989 and 1991?

Clinton's Presidency

An overwhelming majority of Americans supported President Bush's handling of the Gulf War. By the time of the 1992 election, however, the struggling U.S. economy had become a more important issue for most voters. Arkansas governor **Bill Clinton** was the Democratic nominee for president. He told voters he would focus on improving the economy. Clinton won a three-way race against Bush and H. Ross Perot, who ran as an independent candidate.

Clinton and Congress Under President Clinton's leadership, Congress passed a budget. It was designed to reduce the deficit by cutting spending and raising taxes. He also convinced Congress to support the **North American Free Trade Agreement** (NAFTA). This treaty eliminated trade barriers between the United States, Canada, and Mexico. The treaty was controversial. Supporters claimed that it would strengthen the economies of all three nations. Critics argued that the United States would lose jobs to Mexico, where wages were lower.

In the 1994 congressional elections, House minority leader Newt Gingrich of Georgia helped lead Republicans to an important victory. Gingrich and other Republicans promoted a set of policies called the Contract with

Historical Sources

NAFTA

Just before Congress voted on NAFTA in 1993, Vice President Al Gore and former presidential candidate H. Ross Perot debated the controversial issue on national television.

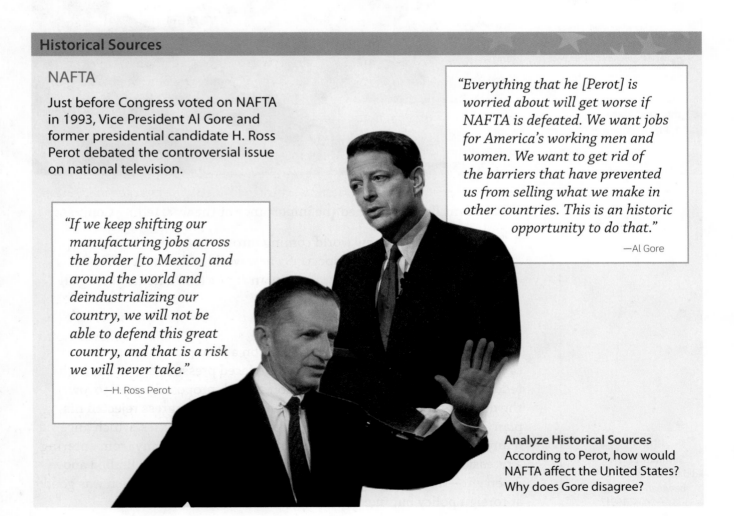

"If we keep shifting our manufacturing jobs across the border [to Mexico] and around the world and deindustrializing our country, we will not be able to defend this great country, and that is a risk we will never take."

—H. Ross Perot

"Everything that he [Perot] is worried about will get worse if NAFTA is defeated. We want jobs for America's working men and women. We want to get rid of the barriers that have prevented us from selling what we make in other countries. This is an historic opportunity to do that."

—Al Gore

Analyze Historical Sources
According to Perot, how would NAFTA affect the United States? Why does Gore disagree?

Bill Clinton 1946–

Bill Clinton was born in Hope, Arkansas. As a teenager he met and shook hands with President John Kennedy. This experience heightened his interest in becoming a politician. He became a Rhodes scholar at Oxford after graduating from college. After graduating from Yale Law School, Clinton returned to Arkansas. He was elected governor in 1978. He lost his bid for re-election in 1980. Clinton ran again in 1982 and won, serving ten more years as governor. Clinton was elected president in 1992 and re-elected in 1996. The country experienced the longest period of continued economic growth during his presidency. In 1998, however, Clinton became only the second president in U.S. history to be impeached.

Draw Conclusions
Why might meeting President Kennedy have influenced Clinton?

America. These policies promised lower taxes and smaller government. Republicans gained control of both houses of Congress for the first time since 1952.

A growing economy helped Clinton win a second term in 1996 over Senator Bob Dole of Kansas. By 1998 the U.S. government was taking in more money than it was spending. However, questions about Clinton's personal and official conduct dominated his second term. Government investigators charged that the president had conducted an improper relationship with a White House intern and then lied about it under oath. In 1998 the House of Representatives voted to impeach Clinton for obstruction of justice. The Senate acquitted him of the charges in 1999. The scandal damaged Clinton's public image, though his approval ratings remained high, due in part to the booming economy.

A Dangerous World The collapse of the Soviet Union left the United States as the world's only superpower. In 1997 President Clinton appointed **Madeleine Albright** as the first woman to be secretary of state. Albright had been born in Prague. Her family then moved to the United States, fleeing the Holocaust. She helped adapt U.S. foreign policy to this complex new world.

The United States worked to promote global peace and democracy. In the Balkan region of Europe, for example, civil war erupted in Yugoslavia. Several of its republics declared independence. In Bosnia, one of the former republics, fighting broke out in 1992 among three groups: Bosniaks

(Bosnian Muslims), Croats, and Serbs. Many Bosniak civilians were killed or forced out of Serb-controlled territory. These actions were known as "ethnic cleansing." After more than three years of bloody fighting, the United States helped negotiate a peace agreement. President Clinton then sent 20,000 U.S. troops to Bosnia to help maintain peace.

Clinton also took an active role in the Oslo peace process. The process started in 1993, when Israel and the Palestinian Authority agreed to take steps toward a negotiated settlement of their conflict. The process broke down in 2000, after the failure of talks aimed at a final agreement.

In the 1990s, **terrorism**—the use of violence by individuals or small groups to advance political goals—became a major issue. In April 1995 American terrorists bombed a federal government office building in Oklahoma City. The attack killed 168 people and injured hundreds of others. Timothy McVeigh led the terrorists. McVeigh was an ex-Army soldier who held extreme views against the government. The United States also faced increasingly deadly attacks by extremist Islamic groups. Hundreds were killed in bomb attacks on U.S. embassies in Africa in 1998.

Summary and Preview The Cold War ended in 1990. In the next module you will learn about the challenges the nation and the world are facing in the twenty-first century.

Reading Check
Identify Cause and Effect How did the end of the Cold War change the U.S. role in the world?

Lesson 4 Assessment

Review Ideas, Terms, and People

1. **a. Recall** What domestic challenges did George H. W. Bush face during his presidency?

   b. Summarize What were some of the major world events during Bush's presidency?

   c. Identify What was the purpose of Operation Desert Storm?

   d. Evaluate How did the Persian Gulf War test President Bush's vision of a new world order?

2. **a. Recall** What were some of the high points and low points of Bill Clinton's presidency?

   b. Contrast How is terrorism different from standard warfare?

   c. Elaborate Do you think Congress was right to pass the North American Free Trade Agreement? Explain your answer.

Critical Thinking

3. **Sequence** In this lesson you learned about key events that occurred during the presidencies of George H. W. Bush and Bill Clinton. Create a table similar to the one below to identify the major events described in the lesson and the year they occurred.

Year	Event

Social Studies Skills

Determine the Strength of an Argument

Define the Skill

Studying history often involves learning about different opinions. In order to understand these opinions, it is important to recognize strong arguments. Strong arguments are based on convincing supporting evidence. Examples and points should be true and should make sense in the context of the argument. For example, supporting points should relate to the main idea of the argument. It is also important to consider any evidence against the argument.

Many people in the past have made decisions based on the strength of an argument. Determining the strength of an argument is important for the present as well. Your judgments can help you decide whether or not to support a policy, idea, or candidate.

During the 1970s Americans had to determine the strength of arguments during the Watergate scandal. If Nixon had not resigned, for example, members of the House of Representatives would have had to decide whether or not to vote to impeach the president. They would have had to weigh the evidence and determine the strength of arguments for and against him.

Learn the Skill

In *Silent Spring*, Rachel Carson argued that environmental pollution was harmful and had to be stopped. Here is part of her argument:

"Man, however much he may like to pretend the contrary, is part of nature. Can he escape a pollution that is now so thoroughly distributed throughout our world?"

How strong is Carson's argument? In *Silent Spring*, she gives many examples of the harmful effects of pollutants and insect poisons. This makes her argument stronger. In the quotation, Carson points out that humans rely upon nature. As nature becomes polluted, she argues, humans will not be able to avoid the harmful health effects of that pollution.

Carson's argument was strong enough to convince the American people and Congress to take action. The environmental movement grew, and new laws were passed to protect the nation's air and water.

Practice the Skill

Suppose that you are a member of Congress during the Watergate scandal. You have to decide whether or not to impeach President Nixon. Your decision will depend on the strength of the arguments in favor of impeachment. Review the module and answer the following questions to help determine the strength of those arguments.

1. What is the evidence against President Nixon? How does this evidence strengthen or weaken the case against him?

2. Is there any evidence that President Nixon is innocent? How strong is this evidence?

3. Would you vote to impeach the president? Explain your answer.

Module 31 Assessment

Review Vocabulary, Terms, and People

Read each question and write the letter of the best response.

1. Which of the following refers to a period of less hostile U.S.-Soviet relations in the 1970s?
   a. détente
   b. stagflation
   c. realpolitik
   d. *perestroika*

2. Which of the following was a theory that influenced President Reagan's policies?
   a. Whip Inflation Now
   b. supply-side economics
   c. SALT
   d. *glasnost*

3. One of President Clinton's major achievements was getting Congress to pass
   a. the ERA.
   b. the Camp David Accords.
   c. NAFTA.
   d. Operation Desert Storm.

Comprehension and Critical Thinking

Lesson 1

4. a. Identify Who were the reporters who uncovered the Watergate scandal?
   b. Analyze What were some results of Nixon's visit to China?
   c. Elaborate Why do you think Nixon called his supporters the Silent Majority?

Lesson 2

5. a. Recall What happened at Three Mile Island?
   b. Analyze How were new rules and laws in the 1970s used to protect individuals and the public in general?
   c. Contrast How were the foreign policies of Nixon and Carter different?
   d. Draw Conclusions Why do you think many Americans responded to *Silent Spring*?

Lesson 3

6 a. Describe What happened in the election of 1980?
   b. Summarize What were some results of Reagan's conservative policies?

   c. Evaluate Do you think Congress was right to ban aid to the Contras in Nicaragua?

Lesson 4

7. a. Recall What events led to the breakup of the Soviet Union?
   b. Explain How did the Clinton administration attempt to end foreign conflicts?
   c. Evaluate Do you think NAFTA helped the U.S. economy? Explain.

Review Themes

8. Economics How did the energy crisis affect the economy of the United States?

9. Politics How did the politics of the presidents discussed in this module affect the foreign policy of the United States?

Reading Skills

Summarize *Use the Reading Skills taught in this module to complete the activity below.*

Carter also experienced disaster in the Middle East. The United States had supported the pro-American shah, or king, of Iran since the 1950s. Many Iranians resented the shah's reform efforts. They also disliked the country's shift from a traditional and agricultural society to a more urban and industrial one. The government severely punished its opponents and controlled all political participation. Many members of the opposition supported the views of Islamic spiritual leader Ruhollah Khomeini. Khomeini had been forced to leave the country because of his criticisms of the shah's policies.

In 1979 Khomeini's supporters drove the shah out of Iran. A month later, Khomeini took control of the government. On November 4, a group of Iranian students attacked the U.S. embassy in Tehran, the capital of Iran, seizing about 90 American hostages. The Iran hostage crisis lasted for more than a year.

10. Summarize the beginning of the Iran hostage crisis in three sentences.

Social Studies Skills

Determine the Strength of an Argument *Use the Social Studies Skills taught in this module to answer the question about the selection below.*

In this module you have read about the Supreme Court case *United States* v. *Nixon*. Nixon argued that executive privilege, a president's right to keep information secret for reasons of national security, protected him from having to give up tapes of his official conversations.

11. In your opinion, how strong was Nixon's argument?

Focus on Writing

12. **Write a Historical Novel** Suppose you have decided to write a historical novel set during the 1970s through the 1990s. You want your story to bring one or more of the major events of this time period to life for readers. Choose a subject that you would like to focus on in your novel. Think about the main events you will describe and the main characters your story will include. Then write the first page of your novel. Be sure to describe where and when your story is taking place. Since this is a novel, you should feel free to write dialogue for historical figures who appear in your story.

Module 32

The Twenty-First Century

Essential Question
How is the United States different today than in 1776?

About the Photo: Young people like these are helping to shape the future of the United States.

Explore ONLINE!

VIDEOS, including...
- Election 2008
- 9/11 Watershed Event
- Fighting the War on Terrorism
- Condoleezza Rice
- Computers

- ☑ Document-Based Investigations
- ☑ Graphic Organizers
- ☑ Interactive Games
- ☑ Image with Hotspots: The Global Automobile Industry
- ☑ Interactive Map: World Life Expectancy, 1990–2013
- ☑ Image Carousel: Factors in Climate Change

In this module you will read about the amazing events that have changed our world in recent years. You will also learn about the War on Terror and the development of new technologies.

What You Will Learn ...

Lesson 1: Challenges for a New Millennium **982**
The Big Idea George W. Bush and the United States responded to terrorist attacks and a changing economy.

Lesson 2: Domestic and Foreign Policy Issues **988**
The Big Idea Presidents George W. Bush and Barack Obama led the country through many domestic and foreign challenges.

Lesson 3: Rapid Changes **994**
The Big Idea The United States continues to grow and change as we move ahead in the twenty-first century.

Timeline of Events 1995–2015

▶ *Explore ONLINE!*

United States

World

1995

^ 2000 George W. Bush wins the disputed presidential election of 2000.

2000

< 2001 Terrorists attack the World Trade Center and the Pentagon on September 11.

^ 2001 The Taliban regime is driven from power in Afghanistan.

2002 The Department of Homeland Security is created to oversee domestic security.

2003 The Human Genome Project successfully completes the mapping of human genes.

2005 Hurricane Katrina hits several southern states, especially devastating the city of New Orleans.

2005

2005 Iraqis choose new leaders in a democratic election. >

2008 Barack Obama is elected the first African American president of the United States.

2008 For the first time in the world's history, more people live in cities than in rural areas.

2010

2010 Arab Spring, a political movement against oppressive and corrupt government, begins in parts of Africa and the Middle East.

2013 The Boston Marathon is bombed, leaving several dead and hundreds injured.

2013 Pope Francis is elected pope following the resignation of Pope Benedict XVI.

2014 New York City's new World Trade Center building opens, 13 years after 9/11.

2014 The largest Ebola epidemic spreads into several African countries, raising fears around the globe.

2015

Reading Social Studies

THEME FOCUS:

Economics, Politics

In this module you will read about the most recent presidents and their administrations. You will learn about the changing role the United States has gained in the global economy and global politics. You will also read about September 11, 2001, and learn how that tragedy helped shape the world you live in today.

READING FOCUS:

Predict

Often when you are reading, predicting what might come next can help you understand what is happening in the story of history.

Understand Predicting Predicting what may come next in the logical progression of a story relies on understanding what has happened in the past. You have learned many different responses to crises that have occurred throughout U.S. history. You can use this knowledge to predict what may come in the future.

Notice how one reader uses information from the past to predict what may happen in the future.

> The war in Iraq caused fierce debate at home. After months of searching, no weapons of mass destruction were uncovered. No concrete ties between Saddam and al Qaeda could be proven either. Critics began to accuse the Bush administration of exaggerating the danger Saddam posed to the United States. The continuing violence between Iraqi insurgents and U.S. soldiers led many Americans to call for an end to the war.

After reading this section, one reader thought:

> I have read about other wars in which the American public was divided over the action the country should take. In the War of 1812, there was a convention of delegates opposed to the war. In the 1960s and 1970s, many citizens publicly protested the Vietnam War. What happened in these past wars that might happen in the Iraq War? I predict that this war will not end with a clear victory because the American people do not fully support it.

You Try It!

The following passage is from the module you are getting ready to read. As you read the passage, look for the facts that can help you predict what might happen in the future.

The Internet was first developed in 1969 by scientists at the U.S. Department of Defense. Early computer networks were used mainly by government and university researchers. Then in the 1990s, computer programmers developed the World Wide Web, enabling people to access information from computers around the world. Internet use exploded in the 1990s. Computers and the Internet made it easier and faster for people at home, work, and school to access and share information. This important development was known as the Information Revolution.

After you read the passage, answer the following questions.

1. What other revolutions have you read about in the study of American history, and how have they affected American society?

2. Is the Information Revolution similar to any other revolution you have read about?

3. How might the Information Revolution affect American society in the future?

As you read Module 32, use the information given to predict what may happen in American society in the next ten years.

Key Terms and People

Lesson 1
Al Gore
George W. Bush
World Trade Center
Pentagon
al Qaeda
Osama bin Laden
weapons of mass destruction
service economy
globalization

Lesson 2
Department of Homeland Security
USA PATRIOT Act
Condoleezza Rice
Nancy Pelosi
Barack Obama
Patient Protection and Affordable Care Act

Lesson 3
Internet
Information Revolution
AIDS
ozone layer
global warming
Medicare
Social Security

Challenges for a New Millennium

The Big Idea

George W. Bush and the United States responded to terrorist attacks and a changing economy.

Main Ideas

- George W. Bush won the disputed 2000 presidential election.

- Americans debated the future of the War on Terror that began after terrorists attacked the United States.

- The American economy and job market rapidly changed and affected domestic policy.

Key Terms and People

Al Gore
George W. Bush
World Trade Center
Pentagon
al Qaeda
Osama bin Laden
weapons of mass destruction
service economy
globalization

If YOU were there . . .

It is the December after the presidential election between George W. Bush and Al Gore. For weeks, people have been talking about whether the votes can be recounted by hand. The race was too close to call on election night, and now the candidates are involved in a court case that will decide who the next president will be.

How would you solve the problem of recounting votes?

The 2000 Presidential Election

The United States was at peace and enjoying economic prosperity as the 2000 presidential election neared. The Democrats chose **Al Gore**, who had served as Bill Clinton's vice president, as their nominee. The Republican candidate was Texas governor **George W. Bush**, the son of former president George H. W. Bush.

Campaign Issues One major campaign issue was how to use the federal budget surplus, which totaled nearly $100 billion in 1999. Gore said he would put more money into education and health care, and use some of the surplus to pay off a part of the national debt. Bush promised to return the money to taxpayers through tax cuts. Bush and Gore also debated the role that the United States—now the world's only superpower—should play in global affairs. Campaign polls showed that the race was very close.

On election night, the voting in some states was so close that no winner could be declared right away. It was so close in Florida that the votes had to be recounted. A machine recount found that Bush had received a few hundred more votes than Gore. But Gore supporters wanted the votes in four counties to be counted by hand. They argued that this would ensure all votes were counted. The Bush campaign challenged this in court.

George W. Bush 1946–

George W. Bush was born in Connecticut and grew up mainly in Texas. His family has a long history in politics. His grandfather was a U.S. senator. His father served as president from 1989 to 1993. Bush was a member of the National Guard during the Vietnam War. Then he attended Harvard Business School. He was unsuccessful when he ran for Congress in 1978. He started several oil businesses in Texas. He also became part owner of the Texas Rangers baseball team. He was elected governor of Texas in 1994 and 1998. In 2000 he defeated Al Gore in one of the closest presidential races in American history.

Sequence
What did George W. Bush do before he was elected president?

After several weeks of suspense, the Supreme Court ruled. The Supreme Court said that the manual recounts could not ensure that all votes would be counted the same way. They ordered the recount to stop. Florida's 25 electoral votes went to Bush, making him the winner of the election. He was the first president in more than 100 years to win the electoral vote but lose the popular vote.

Bush's Early Days in Office The disputed election, however, caused lingering bitterness between Democrats and Republicans. Republicans held a small majority in the House of Representatives, while the Senate was split 50–50. When votes in the Senate are tied, the vice president casts the tie-breaking vote. This gave Vice President Dick Cheney an important role in helping to pass Republican legislation.

Bush appointed General Colin Powell to the key position of secretary of state. Powell became the first African American to hold this office. Bush carried through with his campaign promise to cut taxes. Six months after taking office, he signed into law a $1.35 trillion tax-cut plan. He also signed an education reform plan called No Child Left Behind. This created a national set of standards for every student and every school to meet. It also raised funding for schools.

Reading Check
Analyze Information
What was unusual about the outcome of the 2000 presidential election?

Fighting Terrorism

Despite many plans for educational and economic reform, President Bush was soon faced with the challenge of confronting terrorism. His administration became focused on developing a foreign policy to protect Americans from the growing threat of terrorist attacks after the events of September 11, 2001.

September 11, 2001 On September 11, 2001, terrorists took control of four commercial airliners. The hijackers used them as weapons to attack sites in Washington, DC, and New York City. They flew an airplane into each of the two towers of the **World Trade Center**, an important business center in New York City. The resulting fires caused the buildings, which had been the tallest in the nation, to crumble to the ground with many people inside. Another airplane was flown into the **Pentagon**, the headquarters of the Department of Defense located outside of Washington, DC. A fourth airplane crashed in a Pennsylvania field. About 3,000 people were killed in the attacks. These included the airplane passengers, workers and visitors in the World Trade Center and the Pentagon, and rescue workers aiding the victims.

The tragedy brought Americans together. The nation received support from foreign leaders and citizens. One French newspaper's headline read, "WE ARE ALL AMERICANS." President Bush promised to find and punish those responsible for the attacks.

United States officials determined that the hijackers were members of a fundamentalist Islamic terrorist group in Afghanistan called **al Qaeda**, or "the Base." The group was based in Afghanistan and was led by a wealthy Saudi Arabian exile, **Osama bin Laden**. The Taliban was an extreme Islamic group that ruled the country. After Taliban leaders refused to turn over bin Laden, the United States took military action. In October 2001 the United States attacked Afghanistan. It drove the Taliban from power but failed to find and capture bin Laden. The United States then began helping Afghanistan to rebuild and establish a democratic government.

War in Iraq After the attack on Afghanistan, attention turned to Iraq. President Bush argued that Saddam Hussein, the dictator of Iraq, posed an immediate threat to U.S. security. When the Persian Gulf War ended in 1991, Saddam had agreed to give up Iraq's **weapons of mass destruction**. These are chemical, biological, or nuclear weapons that can kill thousands. However, Saddam failed to fully cooperate with UN weapons inspectors.

Iraqis pull down a statue of Saddam Hussein in 2003, an act that symbolizes the toppling of his regime.

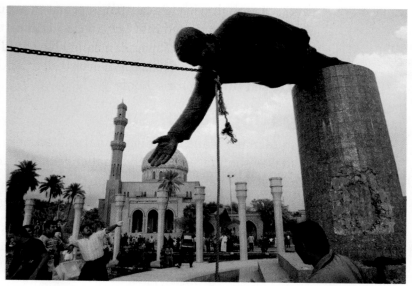

Leaders from France, Germany, and Russia argued that the UN inspectors should be given more time to search for weapons. President Bush and British prime minister Tony Blair disagreed. They said Iraq should be forced to comply with the weapons ban. On March 20, 2003, the United States and a coalition of allies launched a ground attack on Iraq. Saddam's government collapsed, and Saddam was eventually captured.

As in Afghanistan, U.S. officials began working with Iraqis to establish a democratic government. Violence continued, however. U.S. soldiers and Iraqis who were working to rebuild the country were attacked. Iraqi voters elected new government leaders and approved a new constitution in 2005. In 2006 an Iraqi court sentenced Saddam to death. He was executed a short time later. Deep divisions among Iraqis remained an issue, however, threatening the stability of the new government.

Reading Check
Summarize What led to the war in Iraq?

The New Global Economy

In addition to the issues the nation faced overseas, the Bush administration and later the administration of President Barack Obama confronted a variety of domestic problems. These challenges ranged from unemployment to the national debt.

In public opinion polls taken in 2010, Americans listed economic recovery and unemployment among the most important challenges facing the United States. Other major concerns included health insurance reform, terrorism, and immigration. The growing national debt was another key concern. After several years of surpluses, the government began running a deficit again in 2002. Slow economic growth, the cost of the war in Iraq, and tax cuts all contributed to the rising budget imbalance. Beginning with the 2010 budget, the deficit was expected to fall from previous years, but remain high as a percentage of Gross Domestic Product (GDP). The GDP is the value of all goods and services produced in a country each year.

Financial Crises Affect Americans The American economy has experienced important ups and downs in recent years. During the 1990s the stock market boomed, and unemployment fell to its lowest level in 30 years. Much of this economic growth was powered by Internet companies and other high-tech firms. When some high-tech firms failed to earn profits, their stocks lost value. Many went out of business. Unemployment began rising again. Large investment firms suffered huge losses due to their investments in risky mortgages. Amid controversy, the federal government provided money to help these firms recover.

Changes in American Industry In recent years, many traditional industries have declined in importance to the U.S. economy. Many textile companies, for example, have closed mills. They've shifted their operations to countries where labor is less expensive. There has also been an increased use of computer-driven robots to make manufactured goods. This has often eliminated many jobs. This is part of a larger trend in which the percentage of Americans working in manufacturing has steadily fallen. The U.S. economy has moved toward becoming a **service economy**. This

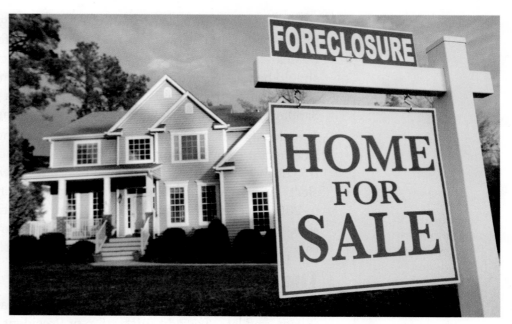

Financial Crisis

Slowing home sales and failed investments led to an economic downturn. The federal government helped with payments to several banks and manufacturing firms.

means that most people have jobs providing services, such as medical care or entertainment, rather than producing goods.

By the end of the 1990s, about 75 percent of American workers were employed in jobs in the service industry. By 2010 this number had risen to above 80 percent and keeps rising. Health care, computer engineering, and education are expected to be among the fastest-growing fields. Such predictions are based partly on population trends. As the number of older Americans increases, for example, so will the need for nurses and other health-care professionals.

Globalization and the U.S. Economy Another ongoing change in our modern economy is the process of **globalization**—growing connections among economies and cultures all over the world. Multinational corporations, or companies that do business in more than one country, play a large part in globalization. For example, you can find American fast-food restaurants in Russia and Japanese car factories in the United States. Increasing international trade has also contributed to globalization. The use of computerized manufacturing processes has sped up and increased productivity. This has improved the standard of living in many countries, providing more international trade opportunities. In 1995 more than 120 nations joined to form the World Trade Organization (WTO). The WTO's goal is to promote international trade by removing political and economic trade barriers between nations.

At the start of the twenty-first century, the global economy began to slow down. In 2001 the economies of more than a dozen countries were in recession. Many other countries reported lower growth rates. Foreign investment to developing countries declined, damaging their economies. The U.S. economy also weakened.

By 2004 both U.S. and world economies began to recover. However, several major banking firms collapsed and began a global financial crisis in late 2007. Even financially secure banks cut back on their lending. This meant that many businesses could not get the money to invest in new inventory. They could not hire new employees and sometimes had trouble paying their existing workers. The stock market dipped. Unemployment rose quickly. The United States was in an economic recession.

To pull the country out of the recession, the U.S. government passed legislation intended to boost investment in the public and private sectors. Approved by President Bush in 2008, the Troubled Asset Relief Program committed $475 billion to stabilize the U.S. banking and automobile industries. Later, President Obama signed into law the American Recovery and Reinvestment Act of 2009. This program distributed over $8 billion in funds to individuals through tax credits and programs such as Medicaid, food stamps, and unemployment benefits. ARRA also awarded grants and loans for government contracts to American businesses. These actions added jobs, increased GDP, and reduced unemployment in 2009. A slow economic recovery began.

Summary and Preview Terrorism became a major national and international concern after the events of September 11, 2001. At the same time, globalization had a profound effect on the U.S. economy. In the next lesson you will learn about other foreign and domestic policies and issues facing Americans today.

Reading Check
Identify Cause and Effect
What economic trend led to the creation of the World Trade Organization?

Lesson 1 Assessment

Review Ideas, Terms, and People

1. a. Describe What was the outcome of the 2000 presidential election?

b. Explain How did George W. Bush promise to use the government surplus?

c. Elaborate How do you think the election of 2000 shows the importance of voting?

2. a. Identify What is al Qaeda?

b. Explain Why did the United States enter into the war with Iraq?

c. Predict What do you think the future holds for the war on terror?

3. a. Recall How has the American economy changed in the past several decades?

b. Explain What caused government deficits to rise in the early 2000s?

c. Draw Conclusions How do you think globalization has changed the U.S. economy?

Critical Thinking

4. Identify Cause and Effect In this lesson you learned about the major events of George W. Bush's presidency. Create a cause-and-effect graphic organizer similar to the one below to describe events of the presidency of George W. Bush.

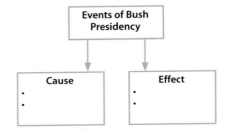

Domestic and Foreign Policy Issues

The Big Idea

Presidents George W. Bush and Barack Obama led the country through many domestic and foreign challenges.

Main Ideas

- The nation faced difficult challenges during President Bush's second term.

- Barack Obama became the first African American president of the United States.

- The Obama administration worked toward economic recovery and ending the Iraq War.

- Donald J. Trump won the 2016 presidential election.

Key Terms and People

Department of Homeland
   Security
USA PATRIOT Act
Condoleezza Rice
Nancy Pelosi
Barack Obama
Patient Protection and
   Affordable Care Act

If YOU were there . . .

The Department of Homeland Security has just been established to protect the United States from foreign and domestic threats. You are part of the department's leadership.

What do you think should be done first to safeguard the country?

George W. Bush

After the events of 9/11, President Bush declared that the United States was waging a War on Terror. The **Department of Homeland Security** was established in 2002 to manage the actions. The department was to analyze threats; guard the nation's borders, seaports, and airports; search for terrorists in the United States; and coordinate the country's response to terrorist attacks.

USA PATRIOT Act Responding to 9/11, Congress quickly passed the **USA PATRIOT Act** in late 2001 to give the government power to search and conduct electronic surveillance of suspected terrorists. This law gave the government expanded powers to protect the nation. It allowed the government to

- detain foreigners suspected of terrorism for a week without charging them with a crime,
- tap all phones used by suspects and monitor their email and Internet use,
- make search warrants valid across states,
- order U.S. banks to investigate sources of large foreign accounts, and
- prosecute terrorist crimes without any time restrictions.

Some people have questioned whether the USA PATRIOT Act is constitutional. Critics complained that it gave law enforcement too much power and posed a threat to basic American freedoms. To address these complaints, Congress

Timeline: 9/11 and Beyond

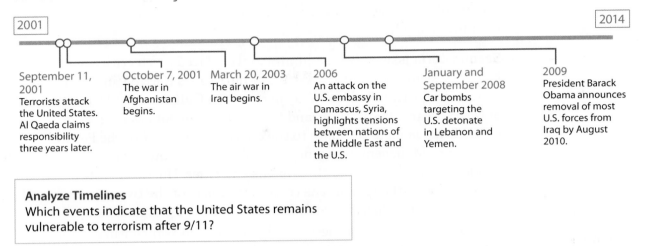

2001 — **2014**

September 11, 2001
Terrorists attack the United States. Al Qaeda claims responsibility three years later.

October 7, 2001
The war in Afghanistan begins.

March 20, 2003
The air war in Iraq begins.

2006
An attack on the U.S. embassy in Damascus, Syria, highlights tensions between nations of the Middle East and the U.S.

January and September 2008
Car bombs targeting the U.S. detonate in Lebanon and Yemen.

2009
President Barack Obama announces removal of most U.S. forces from Iraq by August 2010.

Analyze Timelines
Which events indicate that the United States remains vulnerable to terrorism after 9/11?

let some provisions of the law expire after a set period of time. Since then, some of the provisions have been extended for security purposes.

In response to 9/11, many states have also passed legislation specifying how and when electronic surveillance can be used by the government to monitor people. The debate over the constitutionality of many of these laws continues.

Debating the Iraq War The war in Iraq caused fierce debate at home. After months of searching, no weapons of mass destruction were uncovered. No concrete ties between Saddam Hussein and al Qaeda could be proven either. Critics began to accuse the Bush administration of exaggerating the danger that Saddam posed to the United States. The continuing violence between Iraqi insurgents and U.S. soldiers led many Americans to call for an end to the war. Meanwhile, growing concerns that Iraq's neighbor, Iran, was working to develop nuclear weapons caused additional tensions in the region.

Administration Changes George Bush was re-elected in the 2004 presidential election. Afterwards, Secretary of State Colin Powell resigned. Bush appointed **Condoleezza Rice** as his replacement. She became the first African American woman to hold the office. Bush's other new cabinet appointees included Alberto Gonzales, the first Hispanic attorney general.

In late 2005 Bush nominated two new Supreme Court justices, John Roberts and Samuel Alito. The Senate investigated each thoroughly before approving them. With the confirmation of Bush's nominees, the Court began making more conservative rulings.

Due to public discontent with his policies in the Middle East, President Bush lost much of his support among voters. Democrats gained a majority in both houses of Congress in the 2006 midterm elections. The new Congress elected **Nancy Pelosi** the first female Speaker of the House of Representatives. In response to the outcome of the election, Secretary of

Defense Donald Rumsfeld resigned and a new secretary, Robert Gates, was appointed. The newly elected Congress began calling for a plan to withdraw from Iraq.

Second-term Issues Bush's administration faced much criticism for its response to the natural disasters of hurricanes Katrina and Rita. Hurricane Katrina flooded many parts of the Gulf Coast and the city of New Orleans. Local, state, and federal governments were criticized for their inadequate response to the crisis. The director of the Federal Emergency Management Agency (FEMA) stepped down amid criticism. As victims tried to rebuild their towns and cities, Hurricane Rita struck a second blow to the region. The combined effects of the two storms caused many residents to permanently leave the Gulf Coast area.

President Bush became less popular as the Iraq War continued and the U.S. economy weakened. The financial markets collapsed in the fall of 2008, causing an economic recession. At this point, more than two-thirds of Americans disapproved of Bush administration policies.

Reading Check
Analyze Information What issues did Bush face in his second term?

Barack Obama

In the 2008 presidential election, Americans voted for a change by electing Democrat **Barack Obama**, a U.S. senator from Illinois. In defeating Republican senator John McCain of Arizona, Obama made history as the first African American to be elected president of the United States. Obama went on to be re-elected to the presidency in 2012.

Economic Recovery Soon after taking office, Obama pushed through an economic stimulus package in an effort to end the recession brought on by the crash of the financial markets in 2008. The $787 billion stimulus package law was intended to create 3.5 million American jobs within two

---

BIOGRAPHY

Barack Obama 1961–

In 2008 Barack Obama became the first African American president of the United States. Obama worked as a lawyer and community organizer in Chicago before entering politics. He won his first race for the Illinois State Senate in 1996 and was re-elected in 1998. He lost a 2000 bid for a seat in the U.S. House of Representatives. He was elected to the U.S. Senate in 2004. Obama came to national attention with his keynote address at the 2004 Democratic National Convention. He became the Democratic Party nominee for president four years later. In 2009 Obama won the Nobel Peace Prize, the fourth American president to win this honor.

Summarize
What political offices has Barack Obama held?

Speech on Health Care Reform

"In 2009 President Obama worked with members of Congress to create a health care reform plan, which became the basis for the Patient Protection and Affordable Care Act. His proposals were controversial, especially among Republicans. On September 9 Obama addressed a joint session of Congress to firm up support for the plan."

Analyze Historical Sources
According to Obama, how will the plan help those who already have insurance?

There are now more than 30 million American citizens who cannot get coverage. In just a two-year period, one in every three Americans goes without health care coverage at some point. And every day, 14,000 Americans lose their coverage. In other words, it can happen to anyone. . . .

Now is the time to deliver on health care. The plan I'm announcing tonight would meet three basic goals. It will provide more security and stability to those who have health insurance. It will provide insurance for those who don't. And it will slow the growth of health care costs for our families, our businesses, and our government. It's a plan that asks everyone to take responsibility for meeting this challenge—not just government, not just insurance companies, but everybody including employers and individuals. And it's a plan that incorporates ideas from senators and congressmen, from Democrats and Republicans—and yes, from some of my opponents in both the primary and general election.

years. By the end of 2009, the Federal Reserve reported that there were some signs that a slow economic recovery had begun.

Health Care Reform President Obama also tackled health care reform. A major issue facing the country was that many Americans did not have health insurance and were suffering for it. Some 17.4 percent of non-elderly Americans were uninsured in 2008. About 8 million of those were children.

In 2010 President Obama signed the **Patient Protection and Affordable Care Act** (PPACA) into law. The law aimed to make health care affordable to all Americans. It also specified that most Americans were required to get some level of health insurance. Beginning in 2013, uninsured Americans could buy health insurance plans set up in accordance with the PPACA. However, many people criticized aspects of Obama's health care reform. For instance, whether or not the government could mandate that citizens obtain health insurance is hotly debated.

Issues with health care reform combined with continuing high unemployment rates made some voters unhappy. Many Americans did not see any economic improvement in their lives. This discontent led to Republicans gaining a majority in the U.S. House of Representatives in the 2010 midterm elections.

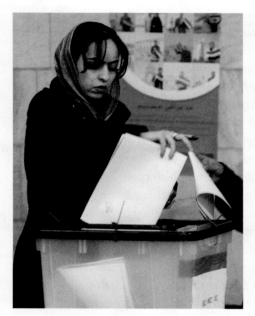

Though Iraq held free elections in 2005, American forces remained in the country through 2010 to help keep the peace.

War and Terrorism The Obama administration made specific plans to end combat operations in both Iraq and Afghanistan. In 2010 Operation Iraqi Freedom ended seven years after it began, with a withdrawal of combat troops. About 50,000 troops remained for smaller missions and to train Iraqi soldiers until the end of 2011. However, military operations in Afghanistan increased. Obama announced in 2009 that an additional 30,000 troops would be sent to Afghanistan to keep the Taliban from gaining ground. These soldiers joined about 70,000 already there.

Efforts to combat terrorism continued. In 2011 U.S. Special Forces tracked down and killed terrorist Osama bin Laden in Pakistan. This was a huge blow against al Qaeda. A terrorist group known as the Islamic State, or ISIS, gained strength and became a threat in 2014. ISIS quickly captured large areas of territory in Iraq and Syria. The Obama administration responded with military airstrikes against ISIS with the help of other allied countries. The United States also sent several thousand troops to Iraq to help train Iraqi forces.

Gun Violence Domestically, gun violence in schools and elsewhere was a growing problem that challenged presidents Clinton, Bush, and Obama. School shootings and other mass shootings happened in the United States about 67 times between 1996 and 2014. It became a top priority to Americans to stop gun violence everywhere. But how to solve the problem has been debated over and over again with differing opinions.

In 2010 the Supreme Court ruled that the Second Amendment's right to bear arms applies to local and state gun control laws. The Court held that the right to self-defense is fundamental to American civil liberties. This meant that laws banning handguns at state and local levels were unconstitutional. In 2013 President Obama responded to the killing of 20 first-graders in Newtown, Connecticut, with proposals to tighten federal gun-control laws. His plan included background checks for gun sales, an assault weapons ban, limiting ammunition magazine capacity, and other measures. The gun control debate is ongoing.

The 2016 Presidential Election

In 2016, as President Obama entered his final year in office, campaigns for the 2016 presidential election heated up. The election turned out to be one of the most surprising in U.S. history. The Democrats nominated former First Lady and Secretary of State Hillary Clinton as their candidate. The Republicans chose New York businessman and real estate developer Donald Trump.

Before Election Day, political surveys called polls predicted that Clinton would win. However, on November 8, 2016, Trump won the election. He secured 306 electoral votes, well over the 270 electoral votes needed to become President. However, he lost the popular vote to Clinton by nearly 3 million votes. On January 20, 2017, Donald Trump was sworn in as the 45th president of the United States.

Reading Check
Analyze
How was the election of President Barack Obama a first for the United States?

Reading Check
Identify
Who were the candidates for president in the 2016 election?

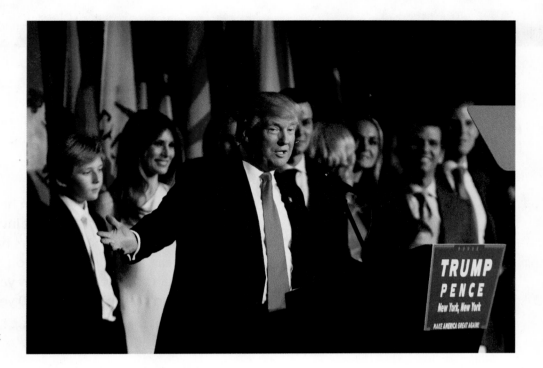

Surrounded by supporters and family, President-elect Donald Trump delivered his acceptance speech in New York on November 9, 2016.

Summary and Preview The new millennium brought many foreign and domestic challenges for our country's leaders. These challenges have been hotly debated by many Americans. In the next lesson you will learn about technological advances and population changes in the United States today.

Lesson 2 Assessment

Review Ideas, Terms, and People

1. a. Describe What power was given to the government by the USA PATRIOT Act?

b. Explain How did the war in Iraq become a source of strong debate?

c. Recall Who is Condoleezza Rice?

d. Interpret Based on Bush's choices for Supreme Court justice nominees, was his administration more politically liberal or conservative?

2. a. Describe What was the purpose of Obama's economic stimulus package?

b. Explain What was the major issue that health care reform was designed to solve?

c. Interpret Why do you think Obama at first reduced the amount of troops in Iraq rather than withdrawing all troops at one time?

d. Recall What 2010 ruling did the U.S. Supreme Court make regarding the Second Amendment's right to bear arms?

3. a. Identify How many electoral votes does a presidential candidate need to become president?

b. Summarize Why was the outcome of the 2016 election a surprise to voters?

Critical Thinking

4. Categorize In this lesson you learned about the foreign and domestic issues faced by presidents Bush and Obama. Create a table similar to the one below to categorize the presidential policies and actions taken by both presidents.

	International Issues	Domestic Issues
President Bush	• •	• •
President Obama	• •	• •

Rapid Changes

The Big Idea

The United States continues to grow and change as we move ahead in the twenty-first century.

Main Ideas

- Technological advances continue to solve everyday problems.

- The American population is aging and becoming more diverse than ever before.

Key Terms and People

Internet
Information Revolution
AIDS
ozone layer
global warming
Medicare
Social Security

If YOU were there . . .

You are a student studying American history. You have read about the dramatic impact that inventions, new industries, political changes, and wars have had on daily life over the years. In your own life, you have seen how much things can change in just a few years. Now picture yourself living in the United States 50 years from now.

What will be different about life in America?

Technology Moves Forward

As you have seen throughout this book, technological changes and new inventions have dramatic effects on life in the United States and around the world. This continues to be true of our lives today. Just think about all the ways you use technology every day.

One of the technologies that has changed everyday life is the **Internet**. This is a global system of computer networks that allows people anywhere in the world to communicate and share information. The Internet was first developed in 1969 by scientists at the U.S. Department of Defense. Early computer networks were used mainly by government and university researchers. Then in the 1990s, computer programmers developed the World Wide Web, enabling people to access information from computers around the world.

Internet use exploded in the 1990s. Computers and the Internet made it easier and faster for people at home, work, and school to access and share information. This important development was known as the **Information Revolution**.

The communication networks made possible by the Internet made economic interdependence among nations increase tremendously. Excitement about the Internet and the Information Revolution helped fuel the economic boom of the 1990s. Although not all Internet companies succeeded, the Internet has changed the way we find information and communicate with each other. Internet use continues to grow

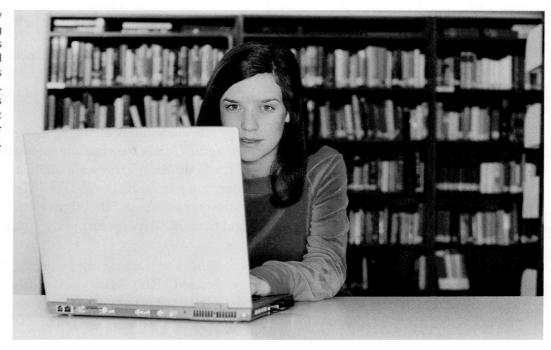

rapidly around the world today. Many companies capitalize on technological innovations by developing products for personal use. Consumers now want the most current technology in cell phones, laptop computers and tablets, and other personal electronic devices. It is a huge industry.

Cyberbullying A downside of the technological innovations now available to people is cyberbullying. Bullying is harassing a person with threats, lies, or embarrassment of some kind. Bullies intentionally try to hurt their victims. Cyberbullying is a type of bullying that is done online using cell phone text messages and voicemails or computer emails and instant messages. Cyberbullies can be people that one has met in person. They can also be online acquaintances or even strangers. Most often, cyberbullies know their targets.

The following types of cyberbullying are crimes in some states, but not in all:

- threats of violence
- a hate crime (harassment based on race, color, national origin, gender, disability, or religion)
- sexually explicit messages or photos
- stalking
- images of someone in a place where that person would expect privacy

The best defenses against this growing problem are to never give out personal information (such as passwords), to not respond to any threatening messages, to not send embarrassing pictures, and to be as polite as possible in messages. Police should be notified if there are state or local cyberbullying laws that apply. A cyberbullying instance that includes a hate crime may break federal civil rights laws.

Medical Advances Technology is also helping with new medical research. For example, researchers have made important breakthroughs in understanding connections between genetics and illness. In 2003 scientists completed the Human Genome Project. This identified more than 30,000 genes in human DNA. This information could be used to find treatments for a wide range of diseases, including cancer.

Improved technology has made medical diagnoses more successful as well. Magnetic resonance imaging (MRI), for example, produces cross-sectional images of any part of the body. As advances are made, the MRI procedure becomes faster, cheaper, and more widely available. Medical researchers foresee using tiny "nanosensors" about 50,000 times thinner than the width of a human hair to find tumors. They predict using "nanobots" to repair tissues and even genes.

Another ongoing challenge for medical researchers is fighting acquired immune deficiency syndrome (AIDS). **AIDS** is caused by the human immunodeficiency virus (HIV). It effectively shuts down the body's immune system. This makes it more likely that people with AIDS will contract other illnesses and die. As of 2015, as many as 36 million people worldwide had died from AIDS. Scientists have developed drugs that help control HIV. But they have not yet found a cure. Public health officials advocate abstinence and "safer sex" practices to help prevent the spread of HIV. In 2002 leaders from around the world founded the Global Fund to Fight AIDS, Tuberculosis, and Malaria. The Global Fund provides money to treat these deadly diseases and search for cures.

Environmental Damage and Protection Scientists are also searching for ways to help protect the environment. Because environmental quality affects every nation, international solutions are required. In the 1980s, for example, many people became concerned about the condition of the **ozone layer**. This is a thin layer of gas in the upper atmosphere that blocks harmful solar rays. The United States joined with more than 100 other nations

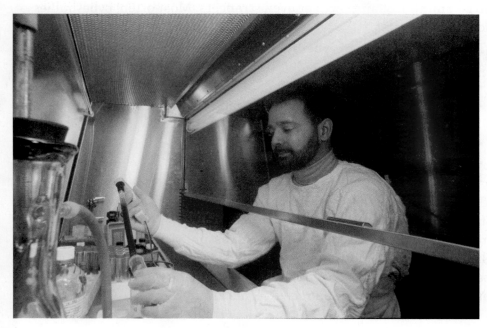

Medical Research
Medical research has improved the lives of millions, as new medicines combat old and new diseases.

Environmental Issues
The nation and the world face the issues of environmental damage and an increase in population.

to ban the use of chemicals that were harming the ozone layer. By 2004 some scientists reported that damage to the ozone layer was slowly being repaired.

Energy consumption in the United States has been increasing along with its population. Today, American transportation remains almost completely dependent on petroleum. In 2014 Americans consumed about 8.8 million barrels of petroleum in the form of gasoline per day. Americans are using more technologies requiring electricity in their homes and workplaces. These technologies include air conditioning, heating, appliances, and electronics. This has increased the use of coal, natural gas, and other energy sources. But while the total energy consumption is going up due to increased population, energy use per household has declined. This is the result of new, more energy-efficient technologies.

Scientists continue to look for ways to reduce American dependence on pollution-producing energy sources. One solution is to cut consumption of raw materials. Objects such as glass and plastic bottles and jars, newspapers, cardboard, and aluminum cans may be recycled. In 2007 recycling saved the energy equivalent of nearly 11 billion gallons of gasoline.

Another environmental issue facing the world is climate change, or **global warming**. Burning fossil fuels such as gasoline and coal releases carbon dioxide into Earth's atmosphere. Many scientists warn that rising levels of carbon dioxide are causing a greenhouse effect. Heat from the sun is trapped in Earth's atmosphere. This could cause temperatures to rise, which could trigger rising sea levels and more severe weather patterns. A 2001 United Nations scientific report predicted that Earth's average temperature could rise between 2 and 10 degrees by 2100. World leaders continue to meet to discuss ways to reduce the effects of global warming.

In October 2015 NASA's Curiosity rover took pictures of itself and sent them back to Earth, becoming one of the first Martian selfies.

Reading Check
Summarize In what key areas is technology changing modern life?

Concerns about global warming and high oil prices have encouraged development of new transportation technologies. In 2007 Americans bought record numbers of hybrid cars, which run partially on electricity. Scientists are also developing vehicles that will run entirely on hydrogen and release almost no pollution.

Space Exploration Some scientists take on issues facing our planet. Others look to the challenge of exploring space. In 2004 NASA landed two robotic vehicles on Mars. The rovers began exploring the Martian surface. They sent back images that people could see on NASA's website. In 2009 a probe discovered a significant amount of water on the moon's surface. More unmanned missions are planned.

Although shuttle accidents in 1986 and 2003 killed 14 astronauts, NASA's space shuttle program flew over 100 missions since its initial shuttle launch in 1981. In 2010 President Obama proposed a cut to NASA's budget for *Constellation*, a program that planned to send humans to the moon for the first time since 1972. In 2011 the *Atlantis* crew completed the final mission of NASA's 30-year shuttle program. However, human exploration of space continues on the International Space Station, a space laboratory that has been orbiting Earth and conducting research since 2010.

The Changing American Population

The American population will continue to grow in the twenty-first century. The population is changing and becoming more diverse.

Ethnic Diversity The U.S. Census Bureau reports that our population is more ethnically diverse than ever before. In 2013 the bureau reported that Hispanics made up about 17 percent of the country's total population, making them the country's largest minority group. African Americans made up just over 13 percent of the American population. Asian Americans were about 5 percent.

Not only is American society increasingly diverse. Individual Americans reflect this diversity as well. In the year 2000, the Census Bureau began allowing people to indicate in official surveys that they were of more than one race, and more than 6.8 million Americans did so. In 2008 American voters chose a man of mixed race, Barack Obama, as president for the first time.

These changes are greatly influenced by immigration patterns. Of the more than 40 million foreign-born residents, 53 percent were born in Latin America and 28 percent were born in Asia. Based on these trends, the Census Bureau predicts that the country's non-Hispanic white populations will become a minority by the year 2050. The settlement pattern of most immigrants is that they settle in a U.S. city heavily populated by people of a similar background.

Reasons for immigrating to a country are sometimes referred to as push-pull factors. Push factors are those that cause people to leave their homeland and migrate to another place. An example of a push factor is an environmental condition, such as drought or other natural disaster, that turns habitable land into uninhabitable land. Another example of a push factor is a political situation, such as war or the persecution of certain groups of people for ethnic or religious reasons. These and other push factors can motivate people to immigrate to another country in search of a better situation.

Pull factors draw or attract people to another location. Countries with good economic opportunities and high salaries are the destinations for immigrants attracted to those pull factors. Many immigrants to the United States are drawn by economic opportunities. Another example of a pull factor is a favorable climate that attracts immigrants to a country.

Religion Throughout American history, immigrants have added their religious beliefs to the cultural identity of the United States. Most first settlers in the original English colonies were Protestant Christians. Later, immigration increased the numbers of Catholics, Jews, and other religions. Today, immigrants continue to add to our nation's religious diversity. As more immigrants come from Asia and Africa, religions from those world regions have become a part of the American experience.

Currently, about 80 percent of Americans identify themselves as Christians. Among organized religions, the next largest group is Judaism, at about 2 percent of the population. Islam, Buddhism, and Hinduism continue to grow in the United States, although members of each of these faiths make up less than 1 percent of the total U.S. population.

Older Americans The U.S. Census Bureau found in 2010 that Americans were older than ever before. The median age was 37.2—six years older than in 1990. Increased longevity and the aging of the baby-boom generation were the reasons behind the rising median age. On average, Americans live to 78.2 years of age.

This older population places new demands on U.S. programs that provide elder care. These programs need to be reworked because millions of Americans will soon be affected. This includes health care programs such as **Medicare**, which pays medical expenses for senior citizens. The costs of providing Medicare are skyrocketing. By 2010 the costs exceeded $465 billion. The expense will continue to increase as the elderly population increases quickly.

The older population will also drain another U.S. program for the elderly—**Social Security**. It pays benefits to retired Americans. The Social Security system was designed to rely on continued funding from a vast number of younger workers who would contribute taxes to support a small number of retired workers. This worked well when there were many more workers than retirees to support. But in the near future, there will be so many retired people depending on the system that there will not be enough workers to supply the funding needed.

Reading Check
Draw Conclusions
How might the U.S. population change over the next 100 years?

This has led to many debates on how to reform the Social Security and Medicare systems, but no solutions have been decided upon yet. For Social Security, some solutions have been proposed, such as raising deductions for workers, taxing the benefits paid to wealthier Americans, and raising the age at which retirees can collect benefits. The debates are ongoing.

Summary Technological advances are happening quickly to solve problems but sometimes create new issues. The American population is aging and becoming more diverse than ever before. The United States continues to face challenges as well as create opportunities. How would you like to contribute to your country's future?

Lesson 3 Assessment

Review Ideas, Terms, and People

1. a. Identify What are some of the world's most recent technological advances?

b. Explain How did the Internet spark an Information Revolution?

c. Predict Do you think global warming will affect your life in the future? Why or why not?

2. a. Describe Describe the U.S. population today.

b. Make Inferences Why do you think the Census Bureau started allowing people to mark more than one race?

c. Elaborate How do you think diversity and shared ideals affect America?

Critical Thinking

3. Categorize In this lesson you learned about the changes taking place in the United States. Create a graphic organizer similar to the one below, adding circles as necessary, to describe major technological challenges for the future.

Social Studies Skills

Confront Controversial Issues

Define the Skill

The United States and the world face many challenges in the twenty-first century. People often have different opinions on how to deal with these challenges, which can lead to controversy. Some of the issues discussed in this book remain controversial.

As citizens of a democracy, Americans have a responsibility to confront controversial issues. This includes learning about different issues and why they are controversial. It also involves discussing the issues and forming opinions about them. Part of the democratic system is listening to other people's ideas about how to solve controversial issues and presenting your own ideas in a helpful way. In this way, everyone's ideas can be heard and discussed, so that the best course of action can be followed.

Learn the Skill

To confront controversial issues, it is important to understand them. You can start by identifying them. For example, one controversial issue in the twenty-first century is globalization—the process of economies and cultures becoming more closely connected. Some people think that globalization is a good way to improve the lives of all the world's citizens. Others think that globalization destroys what is unique about individual cultures.

Once the issue has been identified, you can learn more about it. Books, news reports, and articles are good sources of information on controversial issues. They can provide different points of view on an issue. Gathering different opinions about globalization, for example, can help you see why it is controversial. It can also help you determine your own point of view on the issue.

Follow these guidelines to confront other controversial issues.

1. Identify the issue.

2. Learn about the issue. Gather information on the subject from different sources. Determine why the issue is controversial.

3. Figure out your own point of view on the issue.

4. Discuss the issue with others. Because the issue is controversial and may lead to disagreements, it is important to be respectful of differences of opinion.

Practice the Skill

Follow these instructions to confront the controversial issue of how to deal with terrorism.

1. Find at least three articles showing different points of view about dealing with terrorism.

2. Read and take notes on the articles you have found. Based on what you have learned, determine your own point of view.

3. Have a class discussion about dealing with terrorism. Listen to opposing points of view. Share your own ideas and explain how you arrived at your point of view.

Immigration Today

America has always been a nation of immigrants. Today, people from every country move to the United States. In 2012 approximately 13 percent of the U.S. population was foreign born. Many of these people will eventually choose to become naturalized citizens.

Immigration has been a long-standing debate topic in the United States. Some Americans think that immigration should be open to any interested migrant. Others believe that it should be limited for the good of the country. With the threat of global terrorism, U.S. immigration policy is becoming more strict. People from certain countries must register with the Department of Homeland Security.

The issue of immigration has been complicated by illegal immigration. In 2009 the population of illegal immigrants living in the United States was estimated to be about 11 million. The U.S. Congress has been trying to address this problem for decades. It has passed laws attempting to bar illegal entry and limit benefits for illegal immigrants. Some states, such as those along the border between the United States and Mexico, have taken action to stop the illegal entry of people from Mexico and other nations in Central America. For example, Arizona passed a law giving state and local police more authority to enforce federal immigration laws. As of 2015, the debate over immigration and calls for reform continue.

Immigrants from Asia make up about 40 percent of all foreign-born U.S. residents. Chinese and Japanese immigrants have been coming to the United States for generations. Southeast Asians such as the Hmong, Laotians, Vietnamese, and Cambodians are among more recent arrivals.

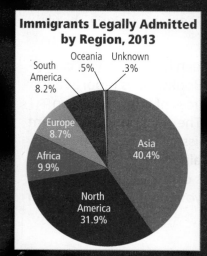

Immigrants Legally Admitted by Region, 2013

- South America 8.2%
- Oceania .5%
- Unknown .3%
- Europe 8.7%
- Africa 9.9%
- North America 31.9%
- Asia 40.4%

Many immigrants from Eastern and Western Europe come to the United States seeking a better life. They accounted for about 9 percent of the immigrants admitted in 2013.

Immigrants from around the world often choose to become naturalized U.S. citizens. The day they take the oath of American citizenship is often a day of celebration, as it was for this mother and daughter from Uganda.

Immigrants arrive in the United States searching for economic, educational, and political opportunities. Immigrants from Mexico and Central America made up about 20 percent of new permanent residents of the United States in 2013.

Interpret Maps

1. **Human-Environment Interaction** From which continent does the largest number of immigrants come?

2. **Movement** How do you think immigration affects U.S. society today?

Module 32 Assessment

Review Vocabulary, Terms, and People

Match the numbered person or term with the correct lettered definition.

1. World Trade Center
2. USA PATRIOT Act
3. Al Gore
4. global warming
5. Social Security
6. service economy
7. AIDS
8. Barack Obama

a. 2000 Democratic presidential candidate
b. the rise in average temperatures around the world
c. program that pays benefits to retired Americans
d. buildings attacked on September 11, 2001
e. deadly disease that shuts down the body's immune system
f. first African American president of the United States
g. in this situation, most jobs involve providing services rather than producing goods
h. gave the U.S. government power to search and conduct electronic surveillance of suspected terrorists

Comprehension and Critical Thinking

Lesson 1

9. a. Identify Who was responsible for the September 11, 2001, terrorist attacks on the United States?
   b. Explain Why was the 2000 U.S. presidential election controversial?
   c. Evaluate What happened in 2007 that contributed to an economic recession?

Lesson 2

10. a. Evaluate Do you think the United States was right to go to war with Iraq in 2003? Why?
    b. Recall What did the Patient Protection and Affordable Care Act require?
    c. Identify What events have made gun violence a current major issue?

Lesson 3

11. a. Identify What trend is responsible for increasing diversity in the United States?
    b. Explain What is the Information Revolution and how do we depend on it?
    c. Predict What aspects of life do you think will be most affected by new technology in the future?

Review Themes

12. **Economics** How have changes in the economy affected American society since 2000?

13. **Politics** How did international politics change over the course of George W. Bush's presidency?

Reading Skills

Predict *Use the Reading Skills taught in this module to answer the questions below.*

14. What might you predict for the future of society in the United States? What about the U.S. economy? How might American politics stay the same or change? What ideas in the module lead you to these conclusions?

Social Studies Skills

Confront Controversial Issues *Use the Social Studies Skills taught in this module to answer the question below.*

15. Name one controversial issue today. What are two different points of view on the issue?

Focus on Writing

16. **Design a Website** The popularity of the Internet dramatically increased in the 1990s, changing the way we communicate and share information. Review what you have learned in this module, and plan a website about America in the late twentieth and early twenty-first century. Decide whether it will be just one page or multiple linked pages. Include information on significant people, events, and ideas, as well as ideas for photos, audio, or video you would like to place on your site. You might also want to provide links to other websites where viewers can find more information. Make sure your links connect to reliable websites, such as government sites or those for newspapers or museums. Finally, choose the website address you would like to use.

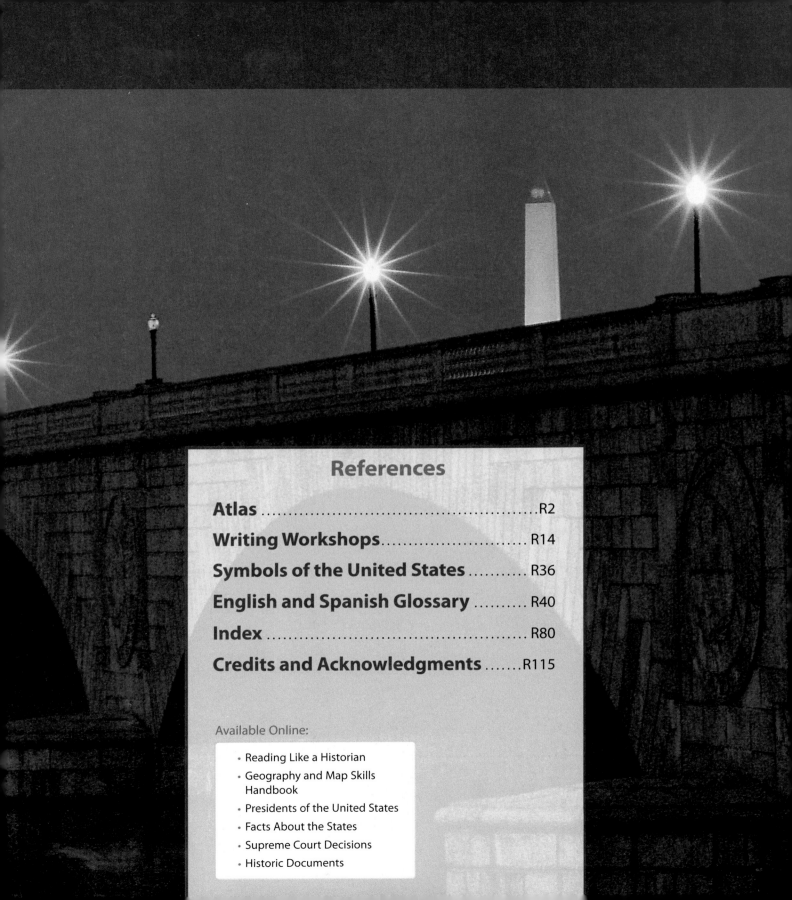

References

Atlas R2

Writing Workshops R14

Symbols of the United States R36

English and Spanish Glossary R40

Index R80

Credits and Acknowledgments R115

Available Online:

- Reading Like a Historian
- Geography and Map Skills Handbook
- Presidents of the United States
- Facts About the States
- Supreme Court Decisions
- Historic Documents

Strait of
Juan de Fuca
Puget
Sound
Seattle
Olympia ★ Tacoma
Spokane
WASHINGTON
Franklin D.
Roosevelt Lake
Pend
Oreille
Flathead
Lake
Portland
Columbia River
★ Salem
Eugene
OREGON
Cape
Mendocino
Goose
Lake
Shasta
Lake
Sacramento River
Pyramid
Lake
Reno
Carson City ★
Lake Tahoe
NEVADA
Berkeley
Oakland ★ Sacramento
San Francisco
San Francisco Bay
San Jose
Monterey
Bay
San Joaquin River
Fresno
CALIFORNIA
Santa Barbara
Ventura
Channel
Islands
Long
Beach
Los
Angeles
Anaheim
Santa Ana
San Diego
Riverside
Palm Springs
Salton
Sea
PACIFIC
OCEAN

IDAHO
Boise ★
Sun Valley
Snake
River
Pocatello
Great
Salt
Lake
Ogden
Salt Lake City ★
Provo
Utah
Lake
UTAH
Las
Vegas
Colorado River
Lake
Mead
Lake
Powell
ARIZONA
Flagstaff
Phoenix ★
Gila
River
Casa Grande
Tucson
Gulf of
California

MONTANA
Great Falls
Helena ★
Missouri River
Fort Peck
Lake
Yellowstone River
Billings
Yellowstone
Lake
WYOMING
Cheyenne ★
Green River
COLORADO
Boulder
Vail
Aspen
Denver ★
Colorado
Springs
Pueblo
Arkansas River
Taos
Santa Fe ★
Albuquerque
NEW MEXICO
Las Cruces
El Paso

NORTH DAKOTA
Lake
Sakakawea
Bismarck
Lake
Oahe
SOUTH DAKOTA
Pierre ★
Rapid City
NEBRASKA
Platte River
KANSAS
OKLAHOMA
Canadian River
Oklahoma City ★
Lawton
Amarillo
Lubbock
Brazos River
Abilene
Fort Worth
Midland
Odessa
Pecos River
TEXAS
Colorado River
Austin ★
Rio
Grande
Amistad
Reservoir
San Antonio
Corpus Christi
Laredo
Padre
Island

MEXICO

To understand the relative locations of Alaska and
Hawaii, as well as the vast distances separating them
from the rest of the United States, see the world map.

Kauai
Oahu
Niihau
Honolulu
HAWAII
Molokai
Maui
Lanai
PACIFIC
Kahoolawe
OCEAN
Hilo
Hawaii
0   75   150 Miles
0   75   150 Kilometers
Projection: Mercator

ARCTIC OCEAN
RUSSIA
Bering
Strait
Arctic Circle
Nome
Yukon River
CANADA
St. Lawrence
Island
St. Matthew
Island
Fairbanks
Nunivak
Island
ALASKA
Anchorage
Valdez
Skagway
Gulf of Alaska
Juneau
Kodiak Island
Alexander
Archipelago
0   250   500 Miles
0   250   500 Kilometers
Projection: Albers Equal Area

Bering Sea
Attu Island
PACIFIC
OCEAN
ALEUTIAN
ISLANDS

CANADA

MINNESOTA

Duluth

Superior   Marquette   Sault Ste. Marie

WISCONSIN

Lake Superior

MICHIGAN

MAINE

Augusta

Burlington   Montpelier   Portland
Lake
Champlain   VT   NH   Concord
Manchester

Minneapolis
★ St. Paul

Green Bay

Lake
Huron

Lake Michigan

Madison
★
Milwaukee

Saginaw

Grand
Rapids
Lansing ★   Detroit
Ann
Arbor

Lake Ontario

Rochester
Buffalo   Syracuse

Albany ★   Springfield   Boston
Worcester
Providence   Cape Cod

MA
Hartford   CT   RI

Hudson R.

Connecticut R.

Sioux Falls

IOWA

Sioux
City

Cedar
Rapids

Davenport
Des Moines

Rockford

Chicago   South
Gary   Bend
Fort Wayne

NEW YORK

Cleveland
Toledo   Youngstown
Akron

PENNSYLVANIA

Bridgeport   New Haven   Long Island Sound
Jersey City   Yonkers   Long Island
Newark   New York City

Allentown   Trenton   40°N

Lake Erie

OHIO

Columbus

Peoria

MISSOURI   Springfield

ILLINOIS
Indianapolis ★

INDIANA

Dayton
Cincinnati

WEST
VIRGINIA

Harrisburg
Pittsburgh   Philadelphia   Camden
Baltimore   NJ   Atlantic City
MD   ★ Dover   Delaware
Washington,   Annapolis   Bay
D.C.   DE
Chesapeake

70°W

Susquehanna
River

Kansas
City

Kansas
City

Jefferson
City

St. Louis
East St. Louis

Louisville
Evansville

Frankfort
★
Lexington

Charleston

VIRGINIA
Richmond ★   Bay

Newport News   Virginia Beach
Norfolk

ATLANTIC
OCEAN

Lake of the
Ozarks

Ohio River

KENTUCKY

Keystone
Lake

Lake
Barkley

35°N

Tulsa

Fayetteville

Kentucky
Lake

Nashville
Knoxville

Chattanooga

TENNESSEE

Greensboro
Winston-   Durham
Salem   Raleigh ★

Asheville   Charlotte

NORTH CAROLINA

Cape Hatteras

Memphis

ARKANSAS

Little Rock ★

Pine Bluff

Mississippi River

Huntsville

Greenville

SOUTH

Columbia ★

Savannah River

CAROLINA

Charleston

Shreveport

MISSISSIPPI

Vicksburg
★ Jackson

Birmingham

ALABAMA

Meridian

Montgomery ★

Atlanta
★

Columbus   Macon

GEORGIA

Savannah

Chattahoochee R.

Sea Islands

Red River

LOUISIANA

Beaumont
Houston

Baton Rouge

New Orleans

Mobile
Biloxi   Pensacola

Chandeleur
Islands

★ Tallahassee

Gainesville

Jacksonville

Galveston

Toledo
Bend
Reservoir

FLORIDA

Orlando

Cape
Canaveral

Gulf of Mexico

N
W   E
S

Tampa

St. Petersburg

Lake
Okeechobee

Fort
Myers

Fort
Lauderdale

BAHAMAS   25°N

Miami

Cape Sable

Florida Keys

Straits of Florida   75°W

National capital
★   State capitals
•   Other cities

0   100   200 Miles
0   100   200 Kilometers
Projection: Albers Equal Area

95°W   90°W   85°W   80°W

Strait of Juan de Fuca

Puget Sound

45°N

Mount Rainier
14,410 ft
(4,392 m)

Franklin D. Roosevelt Lake

Columbia River

COAST RANGES

CASCADE RANGE

Pend Oreille River

Clark Fork

Flathead Lake

Lewis Range

ROCKY

Milk River

Missouri River

Lake Sakakawea

Willamette River

Bitterroot Range

Salmon River

CONTINENTAL

Salmon River Mts.

Sawtooth Mts.

Snake River

Grand Tetons

Yellowstone Lake

Yellowstone River

Fort Peck Lake

Bighorn Mts.

Bighorn River

Powder River

Lake Oahe

GREAT

Klamath River

Goose Lake

Columbia Plateau

40°N

Cape Mendocino

Shasta Lake

Pyramid Lake

Wind River Range

Gannett Peak
13,804 ft
(4,207 m)

Wind River

Cheyenne River

Black Hills

White River

James River

INTERI

Wasatch Range

Niobrara River

North Platte River

Platte River

125°W

San Francisco Bay

Sacramento River

Central Valley

Lake Tahoe

GREAT

BASIN

Great Salt Lake

Utah Lake

Uinta Mts.

Green River

DIVIDE

Front Range

South Platte River

Republican River

PLAINS

Smoky Hill River

SIERRA NEVADA

35°N

Monterey Bay

San Joaquin River

Coast Ranges

Mount Whitney
14,494 ft
(4,419 m)

Death Valley

Mojave Desert

Colorado River

Lake Mead

Grand Canyon

Painted Desert

COLORADO

PLATEAU

Colorado River

Lake Powell

San Juan River

Mount Elbert
14,433 ft
(4,400 m)

Pikes Peak
14,110 ft
(4,301 m)

San Luis Valley

Sangre De Cristo Mts.

Rio Grande

DIVIDE

MOUNTAINS

Canadian River

PACIFIC

OCEAN

Channel Islands

Salton Sea

Imperial Valley

Gila River

Sonoran Desert

30°N

Gulf of California

CONTINENTAL

Pecos River

Colorado River

Amistad Reservoir

To understand the relative locations of Alaska and Hawaii, as well as the vast distances separating them from the rest of the United States, see the world map.

Rio Grande

Nueces River

Padre Island

MEXICO

Kauai

22°N

Niihau

Oahu

HAWAII

Molokai

Maui

PACIFIC OCEAN

Lanai

Kahoolawe

Mauna Kea
13,796 ft
(4,206 m)

Hawaii

N

W   E

S

19°N

ARCTIC OCEAN

RUSSIA

Arctic Circle

Bering Strait

BROOKS RANGE

CANADA

0   75   150 Miles

0   75   150 Kilometers

Projection: Mercator

Yukon River

Tanana River

ALASKA RANGE

Mount McKinley
20,320 ft
(6,194 m)

St. Lawrence Island

St. Matthew Island

Nunivak Island

Kuskokwim River

Bering Sea

Attu Island

55°N

50°N

N

W   E

S

0   250   500 Miles

0   250   500 Kilometers

Projection: Albers Equal Area

ALEUTIAN ISLANDS

Kodiak Island

Gulf of Alaska

Alexander Archipelago

55°N

PACIFIC OCEAN

CANADA

Red River

Isle Royale

Mesabi Range

Lake Superior

Lake Huron

Minnesota River

Mississippi River

Wisconsin River

Lake Michigan

St. Lawrence River

St. Lawrence Seaway

St. John River

Penobscot River

Long Fellow Mts.

Lake Champlain

White Mts.

Green Mts.

Adirondack Mts.

Connecticut River

Hudson River

Lake Ontario

Cape Cod

Missouri River

Des Moines River

Illinois River

Lake Erie

PLATEAU

Catskill Mts.

ALLEGHENY

APPALACHIAN MOUNTAINS

Susquehanna River

Long Island Sound

Long Island

40°N

O
R

P L A I N S

Kansas R.

Wabash River

Scioto River

River

Ohio

Monongahela R.

Kanawha River

Potomac River

Delaware River

James River

Delaware Bay

Chesapeake Bay

ATLANTIC OCEAN

70°W

Lake of the Ozarks

OZARK PLATEAU

Keystone Lake

Arkansas River

White River

River

Lake Barkley

Cumberland River

Kentucky Lake

Cumberland Plateau

Great Smoky Mts.

BLUE RIDGE MOUNTAINS

Roanoke River

Pamlico Sound

Cape Hatteras

35°N

Eufaula Lake

Ouachita Mts.

Lake Texoma

Tennessee River

Tombigbee River

P I E D M O N T

Oconee River

Savannah River

ELEVATION

Feet   Meters

13,120   4,000
6,560   2,000
1,640   500
656   200
(Sea level) 0   0 (Sea level)
Below   Below
sea level sea level

0   100   200 Miles
0   100   200 Kilometers

Projection: Albers Equal Area

Trinity River

Saline River

Red River

Mississippi

Pearl River

Alabama R.

Coosa River

COASTAL

PLAIN

Chattahoochee River

Altamaha River

Sea Islands

Brazos River

Toledo Bend Reservoir

GULF

Chandeleur Islands

Mississippi Delta

N
W   E
S

Okefenokee Swamp

Cape Canaveral

FLORIDA PENINSULA

80°W

95°W   90°W

85°W

Gulf of Mexico

Lake Okeechobee

BAHAMAS

25°N

75°W

The Everglades

Cape Sable

Florida Keys

Straits of Florida

ARCTIC OCEAN

Greenland
(DENMARK)

ALASKA
(U.S.)

60°N

Godtháb

ICELAND

Aleutian Islands

CANADA

NORTH
AMERICA

Vancouver

Winnipeg

Ottawa Montreal

40°N

Chicago Toronto

UNITED
STATES

New York City

ATLANTIC
OCEAN

Rabat

Casablanca

MOROCCO

Washington
D.C.

Los Angeles

Houston

Bermuda
(U.K.)

Tropic of Cancer

MEXICO

Western
Sahara
(Claimed by
Morocco)

20°N

Mexico
City

MAURITANIA

HAWAII
(U.S.)

Nouakchott

SENEGAL

CAPE VERDE

Dakar

GAMBIA

Bam

BI

Caracas

GUINEA-BISSAU

GUINEA

PACIFIC
OCEAN

VENEZUELA GUYANA

SIERRA
LEONE

CO
D'IV

Bogotá

Georgetown

SURINAME

Paramaribo

French Guiana
(FRANCE)

LIBERIA

COLOMBIA

0° Equator

Quito

KIRIBATI

Galápagos
Islands
(ECUADOR)

ECUADOR

N

W   E

S

PERU

SOUTH
AMERICA

BRAZIL

SAMOA

American
Samoa

Lima

Brasília

BOLIVIA

La Paz

20°S

TONGA

Sucre

Rio de Janeiro

Tropic of Capricorn

PARAGUAY

São Paulo

ATLANTIC
OCEAN

CHILE

Asunción

URUGUAY

Santiago

Buenos
Aires

Montevideo

ARGENTINA

○ National capital
• Other city

0   500   1,000 Miles

0   500 1,000 Kilometers

Projection: Mollweide

Falkland
Islands
(U.K.)

South
Georgia
(U.K.)

South Sandwich
Islands

90°W

80°W

60°S

160°W

140°W

120°W

SOUTHERN OCEAN

40°W

20°W

0   200   400 Miles

FLORIDA
(U.S.)

70°W

Antarctic Circle

0   200   400 Kilometers

Nassau

Projection: Mercator

Havana

BAHAMAS

Tropic of Cancer

60°W

Gulf of
Mexico

CUBA

Turks and Caicos Is.
(U.K.)

ATLANTIC OCEAN

20°N

Cayman Is.
(U.K.)

HAITI

DOMINICAN
REPUBLIC

Virgin Islands
(U.S. and U.K.)

1

MEXICO

BELIZE

JAMAICA

Port-au-Prince

Belmopan

Kingston

Santo
Domingo

Puerto Rico
(U.S.)

Guadeloupe (FRANCE)

2

GUATEMALA

HONDURAS

Caribbean Sea

Netherlands
Antilles
(NETHERLANDS)

3

Martinique (FRANCE)

Guatemala City

Tegucigalpa

San Salvador

NICARAGUA

Aruba
(NETHERLANDS)

4

EL SALVADOR

Managua

5

6

7

COSTA RICA

Panama
City

Port-of-
Spain

TRINIDAD AND
TOBAGO

San José

PANAMA

VENEZUELA

10°N

PACIFIC OCEAN

COLOMBIA

GUYANA

COUNTRY	CAPITAL
1 Antigua and Barbuda	St. Johns
2 St. Kitts and Nevis	Basseterre
3 Dominica	Roseau
4 St. Lucia	Castries
5 St. Vincent and the Grenadines	Kingstown
6 Barbados	Bridgetown
7 Grenada	St. George's

ARCTIC OCEAN

RUSSIA

EUROPE

Moscow

KAZAKHSTAN

Astana

Ulaanbaatar

MONGOLIA

ASIA

Harbin

GEORGIA

Istanbul

UZBEKISTAN

Almaty

KYRGYZSTAN

Beijing

NORTH
KOREA

JAPAN

Ankara

ARMENIA

Baku

Tashkent

TAJIKISTAN

Tianjin

Pyongyang

Seoul

Tokyo

TURKEY

AZERBAIJAN

TURKMENISTAN

Ashgabat

CHINA

SOUTH
KOREA

Nagoya

CYPRUS

Nicosia

SYRIA

Damascus

Tehran

Kabul

Islamabad

Wuhan

Shanghai

Osaka

Yokohama

TUNISIA

Beirut

Baghdad

AFGHANISTAN

Chongqing

Tunis

LEBANON

Jerusalem

IRAQ

IRAN

Delhi

Kathmandu

NEPAL

BHUTAN

Guangzhou

Taipei

gers

Tripoli

Amman

JORDAN

ISRAEL

KUWAIT

BAHRAIN

PAKISTAN

New
Delhi

Hong
Kong

TAIWAN

Tropic of Cancer

GERIA

LIBYA

Cairo

SAUDI

QATAR

OMAN

Karachi

INDIA

Dhaka

BANGLADESH

Northern
Mariana
(U.S.)

20°N

EGYPT

Riyadh

ARABIA

Muscat

Calcutta

MYANMAR
(BURMA)

LAOS

Hanoi

PACIFIC
OCEAN

AFRICA

UNITED ARAB
EMIRATES

Mumbai
(Bombay)

Yangon
(Rangoon)

THAILAND

VIETNAM

Manila

Guam (U.S.)

MARSHALL
ISLANDS

NIGER

CHAD

SUDAN

OMAN

ERITREA

YEMEN

Chennai
(Madras)

Bangkok

CAMBODIA

PHILIPPINES

Niamey

N'Djamena

Khartoum

Asmara

Sanaa

DJIBOUTI

Phnom
Penh

PALAU

NIGERIA

Abuja

CENTRAL
AFRICAN
REPUBLIC

SOUTH
SUDAN

Addis Ababa

ETHIOPIA

Colombo

SRI
LANKA

Ho Chi
Minh City

BRUNEI

FEDERATED STATES
OF MICRONESIA

ENIN

GO

Lagos

CAMEROON

Juba

UGANDA

SOMALIA

Kuala
Lumpur

MALAYSIA

ATORIAL
NEA

DEMOCRATIC
REPUBLIC
OF THE
CONGO

KENYA

Nairobi

MALDIVES

Singapore

SINGAPORE

NAURU

KIRIBATI

0° Equator

O TOMÉ
AND
NCIPE

GABON

REP.
OF THE
CONGO

RWANDA

BURUNDI

Kinshasa

TANZANIA

Dodoma

Dar es Salaam

SEYCHELLES

INDONESIA

PAPUA
NEW
GUINEA

Port Moresby

SOLOMON
ISLANDS

TUVALU

Cabinda
(ANGOLA)

Luanda

MALAWI

COMOROS

Jakarta

Surabaya

ANGOLA

ZAMBIA

MOZAMBIQUE

MADAGASCAR

Antananarivo

INDIAN OCEAN

TIMOR-LESTE

VANUATU

FIJI

NAMIBIA

Lusaka

ZIMBABWE

Harare

MAURITIUS

Réunion
(FRANCE)

New Caledonia
(FRANCE)

20°S

Windhoek

BOTSWANA

Gaborone

Pretoria

Maputo

SWAZILAND

AUSTRALIA

Tropic of Capricorn

Johannesburg

Bloemfontein

LESOTHO

SOUTH
AFRICA

Cape Town

Sydney

Canberra

Melbourne

NEW
ZEALAND

Wellington

60°E

SOUTHERN OCEAN

100°E

120°E

140°E

160°E

60°S

Tasmania

ANTARCTICA

20°E

40°E

COUNTRY / CAPITAL

	COUNTRY	CAPITAL
1	Czech Republic	Prague
2	Slovakia	Bratislava
3	Slovenia	Ljubljana
4	Croatia	Zagreb
5	Bosnia and Herzegovina	Sarajevo
6	Macedonia	Skopje
7	Serbia	Belgrade
8	Montenegro	Podgorica
9	Lithuania	Vilnius
10	Latvia	Riga
11	Estonia	Tallinn
12	Kosovo	Pristina

Inset map

0   250   500 Miles
0   250   500 Kilometers
Projection: Mollweide

ICELAND

Reykjavik

Arctic
Circle

SWEDEN

FINLAND

Helsinki

RUSSIA

NORWAY

60°N

Oslo

Stockholm

11

St. Petersburg

UNITED
KINGDOM

North
Sea

DENMARK

Copenhagen

10

Minsk

Moscow

Dublin

IRELAND

NETHERLANDS

Amsterdam

9

BELARUS

London

Brussels

BELGIUM

GERMANY

Berlin

Warsaw

POLAND

Kiev

UKRAINE

ATLANTIC
OCEAN

50°N

LUXEMBOURG

Paris

Prague 1

Vienna

2

Budapest

MOLDOVA

Chișinău

France

SWITZERLAND

Bern

AUSTRIA

3

HUNGARY

ROMANIA

MONACO

LIECHTENSTEIN

4

7

Bucharest

ITALY

5

12

BULGARIA

PORTUGAL

ANDORRA

Madrid

Corsica
(FRANCE)

SAN MARINO

VATICAN CITY

Rome

8

Sofia

Black Sea

ALBANIA

SPAIN

Balearic
Is. (SPAIN)

Sardinia
(ITALY)

6

Tiranë

GREECE

40°N

Lisbon

Gibraltar (U.K.)

Mediterranean

Sicily

Athens

MALTA

Sea

Crete

North America: Political

ASIA

ARCTIC OCEAN

+ North Pole

EUROPE

ICELAND

Greenland (DENMARK)

St. Lawrence Island

Nunivak Island

Bering Sea

Point Barrow

Beaufort Sea

Queen Elizabeth Islands

Ellesmere Island

Baffin Bay

Denmark Strait

Cape Farewell

ALASKA (U.S.)

Anchorage

Kodiak Island

Gulf of Alaska

Banks Island

Victoria Island

Great Bear Lake

Baffin Island

Davis Strait

Juneau

Alexander Archipelago

Queen Charlotte Islands

Great Slave Lake

Southampton Island

Coats Island

Mansel Island

Hudson Strait

Labrador Sea

PACIFIC OCEAN

Edmonton

Vancouver Island

Calgary

Vancouver

CANADA

Lake Winnipeg

Hudson Bay

Anticosti Island

Newfoundland

St. Pierre and Miquelon (FRANCE)

Seattle

Portland

Winnipeg

Lake Superior

Lake Huron

Prince Edward Island

Cape Breton Island

Gulf of St. Lawrence

Quebec

Montreal

Ottawa

Toronto

Lake Ontario

Lake Erie

Boston

Cape Cod

New York City

ATLANTIC OCEAN

San Francisco

San Jose

Great Salt Lake

Salt Lake City

Minneapolis

Milwaukee

Chicago

Lake Michigan

Detroit

Cleveland

Columbus

Philadelphia

Baltimore

Washington, D.C.

Denver

Kansas City

UNITED STATES

Indianapolis

St. Louis

Norfolk

Los Angeles

San Diego

Tijuana

Phoenix

Memphis

Atlanta

Birmingham

Jacksonville

Bermuda (U.K.)

Dallas

Austin

San Antonio

Houston

New Orleans

Miami

BAHAMAS

Turks and Caicos Islands (U.K.)

Tropic of Cancer

Monterrey

Gulf of Mexico

Florida Keys

Nassau

Straits of Florida

DOMINICAN REPUBLIC

Puerto Rico (U.S.)

San Juan

ST. KITTS & NEVIS

ANTIGUA & BARBUDA

MEXICO

Gulf of California

Havana

CUBA

HAITI

Santo Domingo

Virgin Is. (U.S., U.K.)

Guadeloupe (FRANCE)

DOMINICA

Guadalajara

Mexico City

Puebla

Mérida

Cayman Is. (U.K.)

Kingston

JAMAICA

Port-au-Prince

Martinique (FRANCE)

ST. LUCIA

BARBADOS

ST. VINCENT AND THE GRENADINES

GRENADA

Belmopan

BELIZE

Caribbean Sea

Netherlands Antilles (NETHERLANDS)

GUATEMALA

Guatemala City

HONDURAS

Tegucigalpa

San Salvador

NICARAGUA

EL SALVADOR

Managua

Aruba (NETHERLANDS)

TRINIDAD AND TOBAGO

San José

Panama Canal

Panama City

COSTA RICA

PANAMA

SOUTH AMERICA

Equator

National capital

● **Other city**

0   300   600 Miles

0   300   600 Kilometers

Projection: Azimuthal Equal-Area

South America: Political

CENTRAL
AMERICA

Caribbean Sea

Barranquilla
Cartagena
Caracas ✪
VENEZUELA
Lake Maracaibo

Medellín
Bogotá ✪
COLOMBIA
Cali

Georgetown ✪
Paramaribo ✪
GUYANA
Cayenne
SURINAME
French Guiana (FRANCE)

Malpelo Island
(COLOMBIA)

Quito ✪
ECUADOR
Guayaquil

0° Equator

Galápagos Islands (ECUADOR)

Belém

PERU

Trujillo

Recife

Callao ✪ Lima

Lake Titicaca
Arequipa

PACIFIC OCEAN

La Paz ✪
Lake Poopó
BOLIVIA
Sucre ✪

Brasília ✪

Salvador

Belo Horizonte

BRAZIL

PARAGUAY
Campinas
São Paulo
Asunción ✪

Rio de Janeiro
Tropic of Capricorn

Curitiba

San Ambrosio Island (CHILE)
San Félix Island (CHILE)

Tropic of Capricorn

Pôrto Alegre

CHILE

Juan Fernández Islands (CHILE)

Córdoba
Valparaíso
Santiago ✪

Rosario
URUGUAY

ATLANTIC OCEAN

Buenos Aires ✪
Montevideo ✪

ARGENTINA

✪ National capital
● Other city

0   250   500 Miles
0 250 500 Kilometers

Projection: Azimuthal Equal-Area

Strait of Magellan
Falkland Islands (U.K.)

Tierra del Fuego

South Georgia Island (U.K.)

ATLANTIC OCEAN

Europe: Political

ASIA

URAL MOUNTAINS

RUSSIA

Nizhny Novgorod

Moscow

Caspian Sea

SOUTHWEST ASIA

Barents Sea

White Sea

North Cape

St. Petersburg

ARCTIC OCEAN

FINLAND

Helsinki

Gulf of Finland

Tallinn
ESTONIA

LATVIA
Riga

LITHUANIA
Vilnius

RUSSIA

Minsk
BELARUS

Kiev

UKRAINE

MOLDOVA
Chisinau

Black Sea

SWEDEN

Stockholm

Gulf of Bothnia

Baltic Sea

Warsaw

POLAND

Krakow

Berlin

Dresden

CZECH REPUBLIC
Prague

SLOVAKIA
Bratislava

Vienna

Budapest

HUNGARY

ROMANIA

Bucharest

Sofia
BULGARIA

Belgrade
SERBIA

MONTENEGRO

KOSOVO
Pristina

MACEDONIA
Skopje

ALBANIA
Tirana

GREECE

Athens

Aegean Sea

Rhodes

Crete

NORWAY

Oslo

Bergen

DENMARK
Copenhagen

Hamburg

GERMANY

Cologne
Bonn

Amsterdam

THE NETHERLANDS

Munich

LIECHTENSTEIN
Vaduz

AUSTRIA

Bern

SWITZERLAND
Lake Geneva

SLOVENIA
Ljubljana

Zagreb
CROATIA

BOSNIA AND HERZEGOVINA
Sarajevo

Podgorica

Adriatic Sea

SAN MARINO
San Marino

ITALY

Rome

VATICAN CITY

Naples

Sea

Sicily

MALTA
Valletta

North Sea

Shetland Islands

Faeroe Islands
(DENMARK)

ICELAND

Reykjavik

Edinburgh

SCOTLAND

Belfast

NORTHERN IRELAND

Dublin

IRELAND

WALES

ENGLAND

UNITED KINGDOM

Liverpool

London

British Isles

Channel Islands
(U.K.)

English Channel

BELGIUM
Brussels

LUXEMBOURG
Luxembourg

Paris

FRANCE

Lyon

Marseille

MONACO
Monaco

Corsica
(FRANCE)

Sardinia
(ITALY)

ANDORRA
Andorra la Vella

PYRENEES

Barcelona

Balearic Islands
(SPAIN)

Bay of Biscay

ATLANTIC OCEAN

SPAIN

Madrid

Valencia

Seville

PORTUGAL

Lisbon

Gibraltar
(U.K.)

Strait of Gibraltar

Mediterranean

AFRICA

National capital
Other city

0   150   300 Miles
0   150   300 Kilometers

Projection: Azimuthal Equal-Area

70°N

60°N

50°N

40°N

10°W

20°W

30°W

0°

10°E

20°E

30°E

70°N
60°N
50°N
40°N
30°E
20°E
10°E
0°

Asia: Political

National capitals
Other cities

250 500 750 Miles
250 500 750 Kilometers

Projection: Two-Point Equidistant

AUSTRALIA

New Guinea

PACIFIC
OCEAN

Equator

TIMOR-LESTE

Dili

Aleutian Islands

Bering
Sea

Kuril Islands
(RUSSIA)

Sakhalin
Island

Sea of
Okhotsk

JAPAN

Sapporo

Yokohama

Tokyo

Kyoto

Osaka

Hiroshima

Nagasaki

RYUKYU
ISLANDS
(JAPAN)

Tropic of Cancer

TAIWAN

Taipei

PHILIPPINES

Manila

Celebes
Sea

INDONESIA

Ujung Pandang

Surabaya

Java Sea

Jakarta

Bandung

Vladivostok

NORTH KOREA

Pyongyang

Seoul

SOUTH
KOREA

Pusan

Dalian

Qingdao

Yellow
Sea

Shanghai

Nanjing

East
China
Sea

Hong Kong

South
China
Sea

VIETNAM

Hainan
(CHINA)

Macao

Guangzhou

Ho Chi Minh City

BRUNEI

Bandar Seri
Begawan

MALAYSIA

Kuala Lumpur

SINGAPORE

Singapore

Harbin

Fushun

Beijing

Wuhan

Chongqing

CHINA

Chengdu

Mandalay

LAOS

Vientiane

Hanoi

CAMBODIA

Phnom
Penh

THAILAND

Bangkok

Gulf of
Thailand

Andaman
Sea

Medan

Yakutsk

Ulaanbaatar

MONGOLIA

Irkutsk

Lake
Baykal

MYANMAR
(BURMA)

Yangon
(Rangoon)

BHUTAN

Thimphu

BANGLADESH

Dhaka

Andaman
Islands
(INDIA)

Nicobar Islands
(INDIA)

SRI LANKA

Colombo

Male

MALDIVES

INDIAN OCEAN

NEPAL

Kathmandu

Kolkata
(Calcutta)

Bay of
Bengal

Chennai
(Madras)

INDIA

Bangalore

RUSSIA

Novosibirsk

Omsk

URAL MOUNTAINS

Yekaterinburg

Chelyabinsk

Lake
Balkhash

Aral
Sea

KAZAKHSTAN

Astana

Almaty

Bishkek

KYRGYZSTAN

Tashkent

Dushanbe

TAJIKISTAN

Islamabad

New Delhi

Delhi

Jaipur

Ahmadabad

Lakshadweep
Islands
(INDIA)

Arabian
Sea

Mumbai
(Bombay)

North Pole

Arctic Circle

Moscow

RUSSIA

EUROPE

Barents
Sea

Kara
Sea

Laptev
Sea

Black Sea

GEORGIA

Tbilisi

ARMENIA

Yerevan

Ankara

TURKEY

Istanbul

Izmir

CYPRUS

Nicosia

LEBANON

Beirut

ISRAEL

Tel Aviv

Jerusalem

SYRIA

Damascus

Amman

JORDAN

Mediterranean Sea

AZERBAIJAN

Baku

Caspian Sea

TURKMENISTAN

Ashgabat

UZBEKISTAN

AFGHANISTAN

Kabul

Lahore

PAKISTAN

Karachi

Tehran

IRAN

Shiraz

Mosul

Baghdad

IRAQ

Basra

KUWAIT

Kuwait City

Persian Gulf

BAHRAIN

Manama

QATAR

Doha

Abu Dhabi

UNITED
ARAB
EMIRATES

Masqat
(Muscat)

OMAN

Riyadh

SAUDI
ARABIA

Mecca

Jidda

Red
Sea

YEMEN

Sanaa

Gulf of Aden

Socotra
(YEMEN)

AFRICA

Africa: Political

EUROPE

SOUTHWEST ASIA

Mediterranean Sea

Azores (PORTUGAL)

Madeira (PORTUGAL)

Strait of Gibraltar

Casablanca • Rabat

Algiers ⊛   Tunis

TUNISIA   Tripoli ⊛

MOROCCO

Canary Islands (SPAIN)

El Aaiún

WESTERN SAHARA (Claimed by Morocco)

Tropic of Cancer

ALGERIA

LIBYA

Alexandria •

Giza ⊛• Cairo

EGYPT

Red Sea

MAURITANIA   Nouakchott ⊛

CAPE VERDE ⊛   **MALI**

Praia •

SENEGAL   Dakar ⊛

GAMBIA   Banjul

Bissau   Bamako •

GUINEA-BISSAU   **GUINEA**

Conakry   Freetown

SIERRA LEONE   Monrovia

LIBERIA

NIGER   Niamey ⊛

BURKINA FASO   Ouagadougou ⊛

CÔTE D'IVOIRE   **GHANA**   Yamoussoukro   Abidjan   Accra

BENIN   **TOGO**   Lomé   Lagos • •

NIGERIA   • Abuja

Porto-Novo

Gulf of Guinea

CHAD   N'Djamena ⊛

Lake Chad

CAMEROON   Yaoundé ⊛

Malabo ⊛

EQUATORIAL GUINEA

SÃO TOMÉ AND PRÍNCIPE   São Tomé

CENTRAL AFRICAN REPUBLIC   Bangui •

SUDAN   Khartoum ⊛

ERITREA   Asmara ⊛

DJIBOUTI   Djibouti

Gulf of Aden

ETHIOPIA   • Addis Ababa

SOUTH SUDAN   • Juba

SOMALIA   Mogadishu •

Libreville ⊛   **REPUBLIC OF THE CONGO**

GABON   Brazzaville ⊛

CABINDA (ANGOLA)   Kinshasa

DEMOCRATIC REPUBLIC OF THE CONGO   Kisangani •

UGANDA   Kampala ⊛

RWANDA   Kigali ⊛

BURUNDI   Bujumbura ⊛

Lake Victoria

KENYA   Nairobi ⊛

TANZANIA   Dodoma ⊛

Lake Tanganyika   Dar es Salaam

Mombasa •   Pemba   Zanzibar

INDIAN OCEAN

Victoria •   **SEYCHELLES**

0° Equator

Luanda ⊛

ATLANTIC OCEAN

St. Helena (U.K.)

ANGOLA

• Lubumbashi

Lake Malawi (Nyasa)

ZAMBIA   Lusaka ⊛

MALAWI   Lilongwe ⊛

COMOROS   Moroni •

MOZAMBIQUE

Harare •   **ZIMBABWE**   Bulawayo •

Antananarivo •   **MAURITIUS**

MADAGASCAR   Port Louis ⊛

Réunion (FRANCE)

Tropic of Capricorn

NAMIBIA   Windhoek ⊛

BOTSWANA   Gaborone ⊛

Johannesburg •   Pretoria ⊛

Bloemfontein •   Maputo ⊛   Mbabane

SWAZILAND

Maseru ⊛

LESOTHO

SOUTH AFRICA

Cape Town •

Legend

⊛ National capital
• Other city

0   250   500 Miles
0   250   500 Kilometers

Projection: Azimuthal Equal-Area

N W E S

The Pacific: Political

NORTH AMERICA

ASIA

NORTH PACIFIC OCEAN

SOUTH PACIFIC OCEAN

Tropic of Cancer

0° Equator

Tropic of Capricorn

International Date Line

POLYNESIA

MICRONESIA

MELANESIA

Hawaiian Islands
Hawaii (U.S.)

Midway Island (U.S.)

Johnston Island (U.S.)

Palmyra Island (U.S.)
Fanning Island
Washington Island

Kingman Reef (U.S.)

Howland I. (U.S.)
Baker I. (U.S.)

Jarvis I. (U.S.)

Starbuck Island

Phoenix Islands

McKean I.
Gardner I.

KIRIBATI

Tokelau (N.Z.)

Manihiki Island

Cook Islands (NEW ZEALAND)
Rarotonga Island

American Samoa
Pago Pago

SAMOA
Apia

Niue (N.Z.)

TONGA
Nuku'alofa

Marquesas Islands (FRANCE)

Tuamotu Archipelago (FRANCE)

French Polynesia

Society Islands (FRANCE)
Papeete

Tahiti (FRANCE)

Tubuai Islands (FRANCE)

Rapa Island (FRANCE)

Easter Island (CHILE)

Pitcairn (U.K.)
Pitcairn Island

Ducie Island

Wallis & Futuna (FR.)

FIJI
Suva

Kermadec Islands (N.Z.)

Chatham Islands (N.Z.)

TUVALU
Funafuti

MARSHALL ISLANDS
Eniwetok I.
Kwajalein Island
Majuro

Tarawa

Gilbert Islands

Wake Island (U.S.)

NAURU

SOLOMON ISLANDS
Honiara

Guadalcanal I.

Port Vila

Espíritu Santo I.
Malekula I.
VANUATU

Loyalty Islands (FRANCE)

New Caledonia (FRANCE)
Noumea

Norfolk Island (AUSTRALIA)

North Island
Auckland
NEW ZEALAND
Wellington
Christchurch
South Island

Bounty Islands (N.Z.)

Auckland Islands (NEW ZEALAND)

MICRONESIA

Bonin Islands (JAPAN)

Volcano Islands (JAPAN)

Northern Marianas (U.S.)

Guam (U.S.)
Agana

Truk Is.

FEDERATED STATES OF MICRONESIA
Palikir

Bismarck Archipelago

PAPUA NEW GUINEA
Port Moresby

New Guinea

PALAU
Melekeok

Philippine Sea

South China Sea

Arafura Sea

Timor Sea

Darwin

Coral Sea

Tasman Sea

AUSTRALIA

Brisbane

Sydney
Canberra

Melbourne

Hobart

Adelaide

Perth

INDIAN OCEAN

Christmas Island (AUSTRALIA)

Legend:
⊕ National capital
● Other city

1,000 Miles
1,000 Kilometers
500
500
0

Projection: Azimuthal Equal-Area

Writing Workshop 1

A Biographical Narrative

ASSIGNMENT
Write a biographical narrative about a person who lived in the early Americas before or during the colonial period.

You have been listening to and telling narratives all your life. A biographical narrative, a form of historical writing, is a true story about an event or brief period in a person's life.

1. Prewrite

Get Started Consider the following questions as you begin to plan your narrative:

> *Think of all the people you read about in the first few modules. Which ones interested you most?*

> *What particular events and situations in these people's lives seem most exciting or significant?*

Pick one of these events or situations as the subject of your narrative.

TIP: ASK QUESTIONS
Try using the *5W-How?* questions (*Who? What? When? Where? Why? How?*) to help you think of descriptive details. Ask questions such as, **Who** was this person? **What** was he or she doing? Exactly **where** and **when** did the event occur? **How** did the person or other people react to the event?

Create an Interesting Narrative Make your narrative lively and interesting by including

physical descriptions *of people, places, and things, using details that appeal to the five senses (sight, hearing, touch, smell, taste).*

specific actions *that relate directly to the story you are telling.*

dialogue *between the people involved or direct quotations.*

background information *about the place, customs, and setting.*

all relevant details and information *needed to relate the events of the story and how they affected the person (and perhaps history).*

Organize the events in your narrative in chronological order, the order in which they occurred.

2. Write

You can use this framework to help you draft your narrative.

A WRITER'S FRAMEWORK

Introduction

- Grab your reader's attention with a striking detail or bit of dialogue.
- Introduce the historical person and setting, using specific details.
- Set the scene by telling how the event or situation began.

Body

- Present actions and details in the order in which they occurred.
- Connect actions with transition words like *first, then, next,* and *finally.*
- Provide specific details to make the person and the situation come alive.

Conclusion

- Wrap up the action of the narrative.
- Tell how the person was affected by what happened.
- Explain how the event or situation was important in the person's life and how it affected history.

3. Evaluate and Revise

Evaluate Read through your completed draft to make sure your narrative is complete, coherent, and clear. Then look for ways to improve it.

EVALUATION QUESTIONS FOR A BIOGRAPHICAL NARRATIVE

- Does your introduction grab the reader's attention? Do you introduce the historical person and tell how the event or situation began?
- Do you include details to make the person, place, and event seem real?

- Are the actions in the story in the order in which they occurred? Have you included all of the actions and details a reader would need to understand what happened?
- Does the conclusion tell how the event or situation affected the person and history?

A clear sense of the sequence of events is important in any narrative. Here is a list of words that show those relationships.

after	next
before	now
finally	soon
first	still
(second, etc.)	then
last	when
later	while

Revise When you revise your narrative, you may need to add transition words. Transition words help you link ideas between sentences and paragraphs. Notice the words in bold in the following sentences.

> **After** Cabeza de Vaca and the other adventurers left the beach and started inland, they separated into different groups. **Later**, Cabeza de Vaca heard that many of the others had died. **Still**, he never lost faith that he would reach his fellow Spaniards in Mexico.

4. Proofread and Publish

Proofread Throughout your narrative, you used transition words to link events. Make sure that you have spelled the words correctly and have not confused them with other words. For example, be sure to use two *l*'s in *finally* and not to mistake the transition word *then* for the comparative word *than*.

Publish One good way to share your biographical narrative is to exchange it with one or more classmates who have written about the same person you have. After reading each other's narratives, you can compare and contrast them. How are your stories similar? How do they differ?

5. Practice and Apply

Use the steps and strategies outlined in this workshop to write your biographical narrative.

Writing Workshop **R15**

Explaining a Political Process

ASSIGNMENT
Write a paper explaining how the federal system balances power among the legislative, executive, and judicial branches of government.

How do you register to vote? What is the difference between a civil court and a federal court? When we want to know about a process or system of our government, we often turn to written explanations.

1. Prewrite

Consider Purpose and Audience In this assignment, you will be writing for an audience of middle school students. You'll need to

- identify questions they might have about the process or system.
- identify factors or details that might confuse them.

As you plan your paper, keep your audience in mind.

TIP: USE A GRAPHIC ORGANIZER
A chart like the following can help you organize the body of your explanation.

Legislative	Executive	Judicial

Collect and Organize the Information The big idea, or thesis, of your explanation will be that the federal system balances the power among the three branches of government. To collect information about each branch and its powers, you can use a chart like the one shown here. Be sure to note the relationships among the parts. Also, note the important characteristics of each part. When you have completed the chart, you will have the basic organization of your paper.

2. Write

You can use this framework to help you write your first draft.

A WRITER'S FRAMEWORK

Introduction

- State the big idea of your paper.
- Explain briefly why this topic is important to the reader.

Body

- Identify the important characteristics of each part of the process or system.
- Explain any relationships between or among the parts.
- Define terms your readers might not know.
- Where appropriate, include graphics to illustrate your explanation.

Conclusion

- Restate your big idea in different words.
- Summarize your main points.

3. Evaluate and Revise

Evaluate Clear, straightforward language is important when explaining how things work. Use the following questions to discover ways to improve your paper.

> ### EVALUATION QUESTIONS FOR AN EXPLANATION OF A PROCESS OR SYSTEM
>
> - Does your big-idea statement accurately reflect your explanation of the process or system?
> - Do you discuss each part of the process or system in logical order?
> - Do you include details and information to explain each part of the process or system?
>
> - If you used bulleted or numbered lists, are the items parallel—that is, do they have the same grammatical forms or structures?
> - Does your conclusion restate your big idea and explain the importance of your topic?

TIP: USE BULLETED LISTS
The items in a bulleted list should be in the same grammatical forms or structures.

Not the same:

Duties of the judicial branch include

- interpret laws.
- overseeing lower courts.

The same:

Duties of the judicial branch include

- interpreting laws.
- overseeing lower courts.

Revise Sometimes a complex explanation sounds even more complex when you try to explain it in a paragraph. In those cases, a bulleted list of facts or examples may make it easier for your readers to understand the information you are presenting. As you revise your paper, consider whether you have any information you should put in a bulleted list.

4. Proofread and Publish

Proofread If you use special formatting in your paper, it is important to make sure that it is consistent. Here are some things to check:

- If you have used boldface or italic type, have you always used it in the same way—for important information, for a heading, for a technical term?
- If you have used a list of items, have you consistently used numbers or bullets?

Publish Since you are writing this paper for students, you might find a student in the sixth or seventh grade to read it. Find out whether your explanation seems clear and interesting.

5. Practice and Apply

Use the steps and strategies outlined in this workshop to write your explanation of a process or system.

Cause and Effect in History

ASSIGNMENT
Write a paper explaining the causes or the effects of the War of 1812.

Historians try to make sense of an event by considering why the event happened and what resulted from it. Exploring causes and effects can provide a deeper understanding of historical events and how they are connected to one another.

1. Prewrite

Identify Causes and Effects A **cause** is an action or a situation that makes something else happen. What happens is called an **effect**. For example, if you stay up too late watching TV (cause), you might find yourself nodding off in class (effect). Often an event or situation will have several causes as well as several effects. In those cases, we may look at the order in which the causes or effects occurred, or we may look at their relative importance.

TIP: USE A GRAPHIC ORGANIZER
Use a graphic organizer like this to organize your research.

Cause 1
↓
Cause 2
↓
Event or situation
↓
Effect
↓
Effect

Research and Organize For this paper, you will write about the causes or the effects of the event—the War of 1812. Gather information from the module in this textbook, an encyclopedia, or another source recommended by your teacher.

- Look for two or three reasons (causes) why the War of 1812 (the event or situation) occurred.
- At the same time, consider the war as a cause. Look for two or three effects of the war.

Then choose whether to write about the causes or the effects.

2. Write

You can use this framework to help you write your first draft.

A WRITER'S FRAMEWORK

Introduction

- Begin with a quote or interesting fact about the event.
- Identify the event you will discuss. [The War of 1812]
- Identify whether you will be discussing the causes or the effects.

Body

- Present the causes or effects in chronological (time) order or order of importance.
- Explain each cause or effect in its own paragraph, providing support with facts and examples.

Conclusion

- Summarize your ideas about the causes or the effects of the event [the war].

3. Evaluate and Revise

Evaluate Drawing clear, logical connections is the key to writing about causes and effects. Use these questions to evaluate and revise your paper.

> ### EVALUATION QUESTIONS FOR AN EXPLANATION OF CAUSES OR EFFECTS
>
> - Does your introduction begin with an interesting quotation or fact?
> - Does the introduction identify the event [the war] and the causes or events to be discussed?
> - Is each cause or effect explained in its own paragraph?
> - Do facts and examples help to explain each cause or effect and connect it to the event [the war]?
> - Are the causes or effects organized clearly—by chronological order or order of importance?
> - Does the conclusion summarize the causes or effects and their importance?

TIP: RECOGNIZE FALSE CAUSE-AND-EFFECT

In planning your essay, be careful to avoid false cause-and-effect relationships. The fact that one thing happened before or after another doesn't mean one caused the other. For example, the fact that James Madison was elected in 1808, just four years before the War of 1812, does not mean his election caused the War of 1812.

Revise Make sure the connections between the war and its causes or effects are clear by sharing your paper with a classmate. If your classmate is confused, add background information. If he or she disagrees with your conclusions, add evidence or rethink your reasoning.

4. Proofread and Publish

Proofread Some transitional words and phrases need to be set off from the sentence with commas. Here are two examples:

TIP: USE TRANSITIONS

Here are some transitional words and phrases that show cause or effect relationships: *because, as a result, therefore, for, since, so, consequently, for this reason.*

- The Louisiana Territory was a huge region of land. *As a result*, the size of the United States almost doubled when the land was purchased.

- Jefferson wanted to know more about the land he had purchased. *Therefore*, he asked Congress to fund an expedition.

Check your paper to see if you need to add commas after or around any transitional words or phrases.

Publish Get together with a classmate and share causes and/or effects. Compare your lists to see whether you have identified different causes or effects. Share your findings with your class.

5. Practice and Apply

Use the steps and strategies outlined in this workshop to write your explanation of the causes or effects of the War of 1812.

Writing Workshop 4

Comparing People or Events

ASSIGNMENT
Write a paper comparing and contrasting one of the following: (1) America before and after the Industrial Revolution, (2) the lives of free blacks in the North with the lives of free blacks in the South.

TIP: USE GRAPHIC ORGANIZERS
Venn diagrams help you focus on similarities and differences. Write details the subjects have in common in the overlapping area. Write details that make each subject different in the sections that do not overlap.

One way to learn more about historical figures or events is to compare and contrast them. By studying how the figures or events are alike and different, you can begin to see each one more clearly.

1. Prewrite

Get Started "How are they alike?" "How are they different?" Jot down answers to these questions as you research the lives of free blacks or the Industrial Revolution. Group your answers into points of comparison. For example, points of comparison for the lives of free blacks might be work, education, etc. Points of comparison for the Industrial Revolution might be factories or farming.

Organize Your Information There are two ways to organize a compare-and-contrast paper.

> **Block Style** *Say everything you have to say about one subject. Then say everything you have to say about the second subject. Discuss the points of comparison in the same order for each subject.*

> **Point-by-Point Style** *Discuss the points of comparison one at a time. Explain how the subjects are alike and different on one point of comparison, then another, and so on. Discuss the subjects in the same order for each point of comparison.*

2. Write

You can use this framework with your notes to help you write your first draft.

A WRITER'S FRAMEWORK

Introduction
- Identify the two subjects and give background information to help readers understand your comparisons.
- State your big idea, or main purpose, in comparing and contrasting them.

Body
- Use block or point-by-point organization.
- Use three points of comparison.
- Support your points with specific historical facts, details, and examples.

Conclusion
- Restate your big idea.
- Summarize the points you made.
- Expand on your big idea, perhaps by relating it to later historical events or other historical figures.

3. Evaluate and Revise

Evaluate Use these questions to discover ways to improve your paper.

EVALUATION QUESTIONS FOR A COMPARISON/ CONTRAST PAPER

- Do you introduce both subjects in the first paragraph?
- Do you provide relevant background information in a clear and concise manner?
- Do you state your big idea in the introduction?
- Do you include three points of comparison between the subjects?

- Do you use either the block style or point-by-point style to organize your points of comparison?
- Do you support your points of comparison with appropriate historical facts, details, and examples?
- Do you restate your big idea and summarize your points?

TIP: MAKE MEANING CLEAR

One way to make relationships between ideas clear is to repeat key or similar words and phrases in your writing. For example, you can use similar wording when comparing two historical figures on the same point of comparison.

EXAMPLE

Samuel Slater filled his labor needs by hiring entire families to work in the mills. Francis Lowell filled his labor needs by hiring young, unmarried women to work in the mills.

Revise As you reread your paper, look for sentences that start with *There was* or *There were*. Sentences beginning with *There was/There were* tend to be weak: The verbs *was* and *were* do not convey any action.

Weak
There was a decline in southern agriculture after the American Revolution.

Stronger
Southern agriculture declined after the American Revolution.

4. Proofread and Publish

Proofread In a research report, you may be referring to the titles of your sources of information. Check to see whether you have punctuated any titles according to these guidelines.

- Underlining (if you are writing) or italics (if you are using a computer) for books, movies, TV programs, Internet sites, and magazines or newspapers
- Quotation marks for magazine articles, newspaper articles, chapters in a book

Publish Share your paper with one or more classmates. After reading each other's papers, you can compare and contrast them.

5. Practice and Apply

Use the steps and strategies outlined in this workshop to write your paper comparing and contrasting two people or events.

A Social Studies Report

ASSIGNMENT
Collect information and write an informative report on a topic related to the Civil War.

TIP: NARROW THE TASK
The key to a successful research report is picking a topic that is broad enough that you can find information, but narrow enough that you can cover it in detail. To narrow a subject, focus on one aspect of the larger subject. Then think about whether that one aspect can be broken down into smaller parts. Here's an example of how to narrow a topic:

Too Broad: Civil War Leaders

Less Broad: Civil War Generals

Narrower: Robert E. Lee's Role in the Civil War

All research begins with a question. Why did the North win the Civil War? Why did Abraham Lincoln choose Ulysses S. Grant? In a research report, you find answers to questions like these and share what you learn with your reader.

1. Prewrite

Choose a Subject Since you will spend a lot of time researching and writing about your topic, pick one that interests you. First, think of several topics related to the Civil War. Narrow your list to one topic by thinking about what interests you and where you can find information about the topic.

Develop a Research Question A guiding question related to your topic will help focus your research. For example, here is a research question for the topic "Robert E. Lee's Role in the Civil War": How did Lee's decision to turn down the leadership of the Union army affect the Civil War? The answer to this question becomes the thesis, or the big idea of your report.

Find Historical Information Use at least three sources of historical information besides your textbook. Good sources include

- books, maps, magazines, and newspapers.
- television programs, movies, Internet sites, and CD-ROMs.

For each source, write down the kinds of information shown below. When taking notes, put a circled number next to each source.

Encyclopedia article
① "Title of Article." Name of Encyclopedia. Edition or year published.
Book
② Author. Title. City of Publication: Publisher, year published.
Magazine or newspaper article
③ Author. "Title of Article." Publication name. Date: page number(s).
Internet site
④ Author (if known). "Document title." Website. Date of electronic publication. Date information was accessed <url>.

Consult a variety of sources, including those with different points of view on the topic. Reading sources with different opinions will give you a more complete picture of your subject. For example, reading articles about Robert E. Lee written by a southern writer as well as a northern writer may give you a more balanced view of Lee.

TIP: RECORD OTHERS' IDEAS
You will be taking three types of notes:

Paraphrases Restatements of all the ideas in your own words

Summaries Brief restatements of only the most important parts

Direct quotations The writer's exact words inside quotation marks

Take Notes As you read the sources, take thorough notes. Take special care to spell names correctly and to record dates and facts accurately. If you use a direct quotation from a source, copy it word for word and enclose it in quotation marks. Along with each note, include the number of its source and its page number.

Organize Your Ideas and Information Informative research reports are usually organized in one of these ways:

- chronological order (the order in which events occurred)
- order of importance
- causes (actions that make something else happen) and effects (results of something else)

Use one of these orders to organize your notes in an outline. Here is a partial outline for a paper on Robert E. Lee.

The Thesis/Big Idea: Robert E. Lee's decision to decline the leadership of the Union army had serious consequences for the path of the Civil War.

I. Lee's Military Expertise
    A. Achievements at the U.S. Military Academy
    B. Achievements during the Mexican War

II. Lee's Personality and Character
    A. Intelligence and strength
    B. Honesty and fairness
    C. Daring and courage

III. Lee's Military Victories
    A. Battle of Fredericksburg
    B. Battle of Chancellorsville

---

2. Write

You can use this framework to help you write your first draft.

A WRITER'S FRAMEWORK

Introduction

- Start with a quote or an interesting historical detail to grab your reader's attention.
- State the main idea of your report.
- Provide any historical background readers need to understand your main idea.

Body

- Present your information under at least three main ideas, using logical order.
- Write at least one paragraph for each of these main ideas.
- Add supporting details, facts, or examples to each paragraph.

Conclusion

- Restate your main idea, using slightly different words.
- Include a general comment about your topic.
- You might comment on how the historical information in your report relates to later historical events.

Study a Model Here is a model of a research report. Study it to see how one student developed a paper. The first and the concluding paragraphs are shown in full. The paragraphs in the body of the paper are summarized.

INTRODUCTORY PARAGRAPH
Attention grabber

Statement of thesis

"I cannot raise my hand against my birthplace, my home, my children." With these words, Robert E. Lee changed the course of the Civil War. Abraham Lincoln had turned to Lee as his first choice for commander of the Union army. However, Lee turned Lincoln down, choosing instead to side with his home state of Virginia and take command of the Confederate army. Lee's decision to turn Lincoln down weakened the North and strengthened the Confederates, turning what might have been an easy victory for the North into a long, costly war.

BODY PARAGRAPHS

In the first part of the body of the report, the student points out that Lee graduated from the U.S. Military Academy at West Point, served in the Mexican War, and was a member of the Union army. She goes on to explain that he would have been a strong leader for the North, and his absence made the North weaker.

In the middle of the report, the writer discusses Lee's personality and character. She includes information about the strength of character he showed while in the military academy and while leading the Confederate army. She discusses and gives examples of his intelligence, his daring, his courage, and his honesty.

In the last part of the body of the report, the student provides examples of Lee leading the outnumbered Confederate army to a series of victories. The student provides details of the battles of Fredericksburg and Chancellorsville and explains how a lesser general than Lee may have lost both battles.

CONCLUDING PARAGRAPH
Summary of main points
Restatement of big idea

Lee's brilliant and resourceful leadership bedeviled a series of Union generals. He won battles that most generals would have lost. If Lee had used these skills to lead the larger and more powerful Union army, the Civil War might have ended in months instead of years.

3. Evaluate and Revise

Evaluate and Revise Your Draft Evaluate your first draft by carefully reading it twice. Ask the questions below to decide which parts of your first draft should be revised.

4. Proofread and Publish

Proofread To improve your report before sharing it, check the following:

- The spelling and capitalization of all proper names for people, places, things, and events.
- Punctuation marks around any direct quotation.
- Your list of sources (Works Cited or Bibliography) against a guide to writing research papers. Make sure you follow the examples in the guide when punctuating and capitalizing your source listings.

Publish Choose one or more of these ideas to publish your report:

- Share your report with your classmates by turning it into an informative speech.
- Submit your report to an online discussion group that focuses on the Civil War and ask for feedback.
- With your classmates, create a magazine that includes reports on several different topics or post the reports on your school website.

5. Practice and Apply

Use the steps and strategies outlined in this workshop to research and write an informative report on the Civil War.

Persuasion and History

ASSIGNMENT

ASSIGNMENT

Write a persuasive essay either for or against one of these statements.

1. New laws should have limited immigration in the late 1800s.
2. The government should have done more to improve conditions in tenements.

TIP: USE ORDER OF IMPORTANCE

How do you know whether to start or end with your most important or most convincing reason? If you are worried about getting your readers to read your entire paper, you might try to catch their attention by starting with the most convincing reason. If you are concerned that your readers remember one point after they finish reading, you may want to place that point, or reason, at the end of your paper.

You have probably heard people disagree about current political events—perhaps a new law or a government leader. People also disagree about events of the past. When we disagree about historical events, those of the past or those of the present, we can use persuasive arguments to convince others to agree with our opinion.

1. Prewrite

State Your Opinion Persuasion starts with an opinion or a position on a topic. Choose one of the statements in the assignment and decide on your opinion, either for or against. Write your opinion in a statement: it will be the big idea of your persuasive paper. For example, here is an opinion statement about the first topic:

> *The government should not have limited immigration in the late 1800s.*

Build and Organize a Logical Argument A strong persuasive essay includes a logical argument, sound reasoning, and proof in support of an opinion. Reasons tell why you have an opinion. Proof, or evidence, includes facts, examples, or expert opinions.

Opinion: *Reformers' work improved Americans' lives.*

Reason: *Reforms improved life in cities.*

Evidence: *Lawrence Veiller influenced the passage of the 1901 New York State Tenement House Act.*

Persuasive writing is usually organized by order of importance.

2. Write

Follow the framework below to help you write a first draft.

A WRITER'S FRAMEWORK

Introduction

- Start with an interesting opener, such as a quotation or a surprising fact.
- Include your opinion statement, or big idea, for the paper.

Body

- Present one reason and its supporting evidence in each body paragraph.
- Address your reasons by order of importance.

Conclusion

- Restate your opinion in different words.
- Summarize your reasons.
- Make a connection to a current event.

3. Evaluate and Revise

Evaluate Use these questions to discover ways to improve your draft.

EVALUATION QUESTIONS FOR A PERSUASIVE ESSAY

- Does your introduction include a clear statement of your opinion on the topic?
- Do you present your reasons by order of importance in the body paragraphs?
- Do you provide at least three reasons to support your opinion?

- Do you include facts, examples, or expert opinions to support each reason?
- Do you restate your opinion in different words in your conclusion?
- Does your conclusion include a summary of the reasons that support your opinion?

TIP: FACT VS. OPINION
Knowing the difference between a fact and an opinion is important for both writers and readers of persuasive essays.

- Facts are statements that can be proven true or false. *Jane Addams founded Hull House in 1889.*

- Opinions are statements of personal belief and cannot be proven. *Jane Addams was the greatest American woman of her time.*

Revise Your essay will be more forceful if you write in the active voice.

> **Passive voice:** *New parks were designed by Frederick Law Olmsted.*

> **Active voice:** *Frederick Law Olmsted designed new parks.*

Active voice is more forceful, and often clearer, because it makes a stronger connection between the action and the actor. However, we may use passive voice because we do not know, or do not want to say, who the actor is or was.

> **Example:** *New parks were designed in the late 1800s.*

4. Proofread and Publish

Proofread If you are writing your paper on a computer, you should use the spell-check feature to look for spelling errors. However, the spell-check feature will not help much if you have used the wrong word. Here are some examples to look for: *their/they're, its/it's, accept/except, affect/effect, advice/advise, altar/alter, capitol/capital.* When you spot one of these words in your paper, check your dictionary to make sure you have used the correct word.

Publish Share your essay with a classmate who took an opinion opposed to yours. Review each other's reasons. Can one of you persuade the other?

5. Practice and Apply

Use the steps and strategies in this workshop to write a persuasive essay.

Writing Workshop 7

Analyzing a Primary Source

ASSIGNMENT
Find a primary source from World War I and write an analysis of it.

Primary sources are often the best sources of information available to historians. Primary sources provide answers to questions about the past. They also provide a unique point of view from the past. Analyzing a primary source allows you to share that information.

1. Prewrite

TIP: USE THE INTERNET
If you find a primary source on the Internet, make sure it is accurate. You should be able to identify the person or institution that runs the website and make sure that person or institution is trustworthy. The website should include basic information about the source, such as its author, when it was written, and where it first appeared. University and library websites are excellent places to find primary sources.

Locate Primary Sources Many primary sources are available in libraries and on the Internet. Letters, diaries, autobiographies, memoirs, newspaper articles, public speeches, and legal documents are good examples of primary sources.

Read the Primary Source Take notes on these questions to better understand the document.

Who wrote the document?

What kind of document is it?

When was it written? Where did it originally appear?

What was the author's point of view? What was his or her experience during the war?

Why did the author write the document?

As you read the primary source, take notes on these questions.

Why is the document important? The answer to this question will be the main idea of your essay.

What questions about World War I does it answer? Answering this question will help you write your body paragraphs.

2. Write

You can use this framework to help you write your first draft.

A WRITER'S FRAMEWORK

Introduction	**Body**	**Conclusion**
• Introduce your primary source and its main purpose.	• Explain how the source answers at least two questions about World War I.	• Summarize the information in the source.
• Introduce the author of the source and include the date it was written.	• Include examples from the document.	• Restate why the document is important for historians.
• State your main idea, explaining why this source is important.		

3. Evaluate and Revise

Evaluate Use these questions to discover ways to improve your paper.

> ### EVALUATION QUESTIONS FOR ANALYZING A PRIMARY SOURCE
>
> - Do you introduce your primary source with its main purpose?
> - Do you introduce the author of the source and the document's date?
> - Do you state a main idea, explaining why this source is important?
> - Do you explain how the source answers at least two questions about World War I?
> - Do you include examples from the document?
> - Do you summarize the information in the source?

TIP: USE PRONOUNS EFFECTIVELY

Use pronouns such as *he, she,* and *it* to replace frequently used nouns and proper nouns. This will help you vary your sentences. Make sure that the person or thing to which each pronoun refers is clear. If it is not, repeat the original noun or name.

EXAMPLE

Woodrow Wilson proposed a peace plan called the Fourteen Points. He wanted to make sure the postwar peace would last.

Revise Make sure each paragraph has a topic sentence at the beginning. Then check the information in the paragraph. It should all relate to the topic sentence. If it does not, there are several ways to fix the paragraph. First, you can remove unrelated information. If the information is related but not clearly explained, add a more detailed explanation. You can also change the topic sentence to include all the information in the paragraph.

4. Proofread and Publish

Proofread Reread your paper carefully to make sure all the verbs are in the same tense. The past tense is usually best for history writing. Summaries of primary sources should also be in the past tense. A direct quotation from a primary source, however, should remain in its original tense.

Publish Share your paper with a classmate. Read each other's papers. Then write a one-paragraph summary of the new information you each learned.

5. Practice and Apply

Use the steps and strategies in this workshop to analyze your primary source.

Writing Workshop 8

A Descriptive Essay

ASSIGNMENT
Write an essay describing either Hoovervilles or the Dust Bowl during the Great Depression.

TIP: USE VISUAL IMAGES
Look at visual images such as photographs from the 1930s. What do they show about Hoovervilles or the Dust Bowl and the people who lived there? Use this information in your description.

Vivid descriptions of a place and time can help us understand history. Primary sources often provide such descriptions from one person's point of view. Historians provide a different point of view in descriptions based on many primary and secondary sources.

1. Prewrite

Get Started Descriptive essays depend on details that will help the reader create a mental picture. The quotes in Module 26 about the Dust Bowl are examples of vivid descriptions. The passage from *The Grapes of Wrath* is another good example. For your description, review the text on the Great Depression and look in the encyclopedia and other sources. Collect as many details as you can about Hoovervilles or the Dust Bowl. Try to find details that involve all of the five senses (sight, sound, smell, touch, and taste). Good description depends on strong details.

Organize Information Make one generalization that sums up all your details. This will be your main idea. Then organize the details and examples you have found into two, three, or four categories. These will become the body paragraphs of the essay. All of these categories should support the main idea.

For example, the main idea of an essay could be that the name *Dust Bowl* was an accurate description of the area. One detail might be that the gritty dirt often became caught in people's skin, hair, and clothing. This detail could fit into the category of people in the Dust Bowl.

2. Write

You can use this framework to help you write your first draft.

A WRITER'S FRAMEWORK

Introduction	**Body**	**Conclusion**
• Make a generalization about your topic. • List the categories that will be included in the body paragraphs.	• Separate details into paragraphs by category. • Use vivid details that involve the five senses. • Use details from different sources.	• Summarize your information. • Explain how your topic is related to larger issues.

3. Evaluate and Revise

Evaluate Use these questions to discover ways to improve your essay.

EVALUATION QUESTIONS FOR A DESCRIPTIVE ESSAY

- Do you begin with a generalization about your topic?
- Do you separate details into paragraphs by category?
- Do you use vivid details that involve the five senses?

- Do you use details from different sources?
- Do you explain how your topic is related to larger issues?

TIP: SHOW, DON'T TELL
Writers are often advised, "Show, don't tell." This phrase means that writers should use strong words, details, and examples to make a point. Choose vivid, clear examples for your description. They should not need much explanation.

Revise When you revise your essay, make examples and details as specific as possible. This will make your description more vivid.

> **General:** *People built flimsy houses in Hoovervilles.*
>
> **Specific:** *In Hoovervilles, people built shelters out of scraps of lumber, tin, and cardboard.*

4. Proofread and Publish

Proofread Check your sentences for fragments and run-ons. A fragment is an incomplete sentence. Adding a subject or a verb can often make a fragment into a complete sentence. A run-on has too many subjects and verbs for one sentence. It usually needs to be broken into two or more separate sentences.

Publish Share your essay with one or more classmates. Make illustrations based on the descriptions in each other's essays.

5. Practice and Apply

Use the steps and strategies in this workshop to write your descriptive essay.

A News Article

ASSIGNMENT
Write a news article about the anniversary of either (1) the Nuremberg trials, (2) the Supreme Court's *Brown* v. *Board of Education* decision, or (3) the opening of the Vietnam Veterans Memorial.

You have probably read many news articles in newspapers, magazines, or online. News articles keep people informed about events in their communities, the nation, and the world. Sometimes they also remind people about important events from the past.

1. Prewrite

Consider Purpose and Audience Remember that you are writing for people who have a choice about what to read. Your story must keep readers interested. How will you relate the topic of your story to their lives or emotions? At the same time, your story should give people information they need. In order to share information effectively, you must choose the most important details to include in your article.

TIP: BRAINSTORM
Brainstorm ways to interest people in the topic of your article. Take a few minutes to review what you know about the topic. Then write down as many questions, interesting points, and examples as you can.

Write a Compelling Article Make your article vivid and compelling by including

- a short headline showing what the article is about.
- a "hook"—an interesting fact or detail—to get the reader's attention at the beginning of the article.
- clear descriptions of people and events.
- specific examples and quotations.
- reasons why the event is important.

2. Write

You can use this framework to help you write the first draft of your article.

A WRITER'S FRAMEWORK

Introduction	Body	Conclusion
• Grab your reader's attention with a strong headline.	• Describe what happened, who was involved, and where, when, and why the event took place.	• Finish any incomplete thoughts.
• Begin with a striking detail or quotation for a hook.	• Explain the significance of the event.	• End with a quotation or example that sums up the main point of the article.
• Introduce the event and its importance to people today.	• Use details to connect the event to readers' lives or emotions.	

3. Evaluate and Revise

Evaluate Use these questions to discover ways to improve your news article.

> **EVALUATION QUESTIONS FOR A NEWS ARTICLE**
>
> - Do you begin with a strong headline and hook?
> - Do you introduce the event and its importance to people today?
> - Do you describe what happened, who was involved, and where, when, and why the event took place?
>
> - Do you explain the significance of the event?
> - Do you use details to connect the event to readers' lives or emotions?
> - Do you end with a quotation or example that sums up the main point of the article?

TIP: USE VIVID WRITING
Make sentences more interesting by using vivid words and images. Use strong words that help readers create a mental picture.

Revise Newspapers and magazines often have limited space. News articles must express a sharply focused idea briefly. To make sure that your article does this, read each sentence carefully. Each sentence should

- be clear and to the point.
- contain no unnecessary words or phrases.
- use only precise words. Eliminate words such as *very* unless they add meaning to the sentence.

4. Proofread and Publish

Proofread Read your essay aloud to catch any mistakes in your spelling or grammar. If something looks or sounds wrong, mark it. Come back to it later to correct the mistake. This is also a good strategy for identifying and fixing awkward sentences.

Publish Exchange articles with a classmate who wrote about a different topic. Did you learn from your classmate's article? Did you find it interesting? Put together a class newspaper that includes all the articles and headlines. Add pictures and display the newspaper on a bulletin board.

5. Practice and Apply

Use the steps and strategies in this workshop to write your news article.

Writing Workshop 10

An Oral History

ASSIGNMENT
Write an oral history, based on an interview with an adult you know, about one of the events in this module.

TIP: USE QUESTION WORDS
Use words like *Who? What? When? Where? Why?* and *How?* in your interview questions.

Oral histories can provide excellent sources of information about events in the recent past. An oral history is a report based on an interview with a person who experienced or remembers a historical event. Oral histories preserve personal experiences and memories for future generations.

1. Prewrite

Get Started Think about all the events you read about in this unit. Which ones interested you the most? Which ones do you think made the strongest impression on people at the time? Choose one as your subject.

Write Questions

- Focus on finding out how the person you are interviewing experienced the event you chose.
- Write at least ten questions.

Conduct an Interview

- Find an adult family member or friend to interview who remembers participating in or reacting to the event.
- Come prepared with your questions, paper, and something to write with.
- Take notes on the answers. Indicate direct quotations with quotation marks.
- Ask follow-up questions, even if you did not prepare them in advance.

2. Write

You can use this framework, along with your interview notes, to help you write your first draft.

A WRITER'S FRAMEWORK

Introduction

- Grab your reader's attention with an interesting quote from your interview.
- Introduce the event you chose and why it was important.
- Explain how the event affected the person you interviewed.

Body

- Describe the memories and experiences of the person you interviewed about the event.
- Summarize what you learned from the interview.
- Use quotes from the interview.

Conclusion

- Make a generalization about how people reacted to the event.
- Draw conclusions about how people's reactions to the event affected history.

3. Evaluate and Revise

Evaluate Use these questions to discover ways to improve your oral history.

EVALUATION QUESTIONS FOR AN ORAL HISTORY

- Do you introduce the event and the person you interviewed in the first paragraph?
- Do you focus on the event from a personal point of view?
- Do you describe the memories and experiences of the person you interviewed about the event?

- Do you summarize what you learned and use quotes from the interview?
- Do you make generalizations and draw conclusions about people's reactions to the event?

Revise When you revise your oral history, you may need to add background information. Check the material you have included from your interview. If anything is unclear, add more details about the event or time period. Make sure to explain clearly the connections between the personal experience and the event.

4. Proofread and Publish

Proofread In your oral history, you have been using quotations from the person you interviewed. Check the punctuation marks around these direct quotations. Also, check the spelling and capitalization of all proper names, such as the name of the person you interviewed.

Publish Share your oral history with classmates who wrote about the same event. How were the experiences of the people you interviewed similar and different? Share your oral history with the class. The person you interviewed would probably also like to see the finished project.

5. Practice and Apply

Use the steps and strategies in this workshop to write your oral history.

The American flag is a symbol of the nation. It is recognized instantly, whether as a big banner waving in the wind or a tiny emblem worn on a lapel. The flag is so important that it is a major theme of the national anthem, "The Star-Spangled Banner." One of the most popular names for the flag is the Stars and Stripes. It is also known as Old Glory.

The Meaning of the Flag

The American flag has 13 stripes—7 red and 6 white. In the upper-left corner of the flag is the union—50 white five-pointed stars against a blue background.

The 13 stripes stand for the original 13 American states, and the 50 stars represent the states of the nation today. According to the U.S. Department of State, the colors of the flag also are symbolic:

> **Red stands for courage.**
>
> **White symbolizes purity.**
>
> **Blue is the color of vigilance, perseverance, and justice.**

Displaying the Flag

It is customary not to display the American flag in bad weather. It is also customary for the flag to be displayed outdoors only from sunrise to sunset, except on certain occasions. In a few special places, however, the flag is always flown day and night. When flown at night, the flag should be illuminated.

Near a speaker's platform, the flag should occupy the place of honor at the speaker's right. When carried in a parade with other flags, the American flag should be on the marching right or in front at the center. When flying with the flags of the 50 states, the national flag must be at the center and the highest point. In a group of national flags, all should be of equal size and all should be flown from staffs, or flagpoles, of equal height.

The flag should never touch the ground or the floor. It should not be marked with any insignia, pictures, or words. Nor should it be used in any disrespectful way—as an advertising decoration, for instance. The flag should never be dipped to honor any person or thing.

Saluting the Flag

The United States, like other countries, has a flag code, or rules for displaying and honoring the flag. For example, all those present should stand at attention facing the flag and salute it when it is being raised or lowered or when it is carried past them in a parade or procession. A man wearing a hat should take it off and hold it with his right hand over his heart. All women and hatless men should stand with their right hands over their hearts to show their respect for the flag. The flag should also receive these honors during the playing of the national anthem and the reciting of the Pledge of Allegiance.

The Pledge of Allegiance

The Pledge of Allegiance was written in 1892 by Massachusetts magazine (*Youth's Companion*) editor Francis Bellamy. (Congress added the words "under God" in 1954.)

> *I pledge allegiance to the flag of the United States of America and to the republic for which it stands, one nation under God, indivisible, with liberty and justice for all.*

Civilians should say the Pledge of Allegiance with their right hands placed over their hearts. People in the armed forces give the military salute. By saying the Pledge of Allegiance, we promise loyalty ("pledge allegiance") to the United States and its ideals.

"The Star-Spangled Banner"

"The Star-Spangled Banner" is the national anthem of the United States. It was written by Francis Scott Key during the War of 1812. While being detained by the British aboard a ship on September 13–14, 1814, Key watched the British bombardment of Fort McHenry at Baltimore. The attack lasted 25 hours. The smoke was so thick that Key could not tell who had won. When the air cleared, Key saw the American flag that was still flying over the fort. "The Star-Spangled Banner" is sung to music written by British composer John Stafford Smith. In 1931 Congress designated "The Star-Spangled Banner" as the national anthem.

I

Oh, say, can you see, by the dawn's early light,
What so proudly we hailed at the twilight's last gleaming,
Whose broad stripes and bright stars through the perilous fight, O'er the ramparts we watched were so gallantly streaming? And the rockets' red glare, the bombs bursting in air, Gave proof through the night that our flag was still there. Oh, say, does that star-spangled banner yet wave O'er the land of the free, and the home of the brave?

II

On the shore, dimly seen through the mists of the deep,
Where the foe's haughty host in dread silence reposes,
What is that which the breeze, o'er the towering steep,
As it fitfully blows, half conceals, half discloses?
Now it catches the gleam of the morning's first beam,
In full glory reflected, now shines on the stream.
'Tis the star-spangled banner; oh, long may it wave
O'er the land of the free, and the home of the brave!

III

And where is that band who so vauntingly swore
That the havoc of war and the battle's confusion
A home and a country should leave us no more?
Their blood has washed out their foul footsteps' pollution.
No refuge could save the hireling and slave
From the terror of flight, or the gloom of the grave:
And the star-spangled banner in triumph doth wave
O'er the land of the free, and the home of the brave!

IV

Oh! thus be it ever when freemen shall stand
Between their loved homes and the war's desolation!
Blest with victory and peace, may the heaven-rescued land
Praise the Power that hath made and preserved us a nation!
Then conquer we must, for our cause it is just,
And this be our motto: "In God is our trust!"
And the star-spangled banner in triumph shall wave,
O'er the land of the free, and the home of the brave!

Sheet music to the national anthem

"America the Beautiful"

One of the most beloved songs celebrating our nation is "America, the Beautiful." Katharine Lee Bates first wrote the lyrics to the song in 1893 after visiting Colorado. The version of the song we know today is set to music by Samuel A. Ward. The first and last stanzas of "America, the Beautiful" are shown below.

O beautiful for spacious skies,
For amber waves of grain,
For purple mountain majesties
Above the fruited plain!
America! America!
God shed his grace on thee
And crown thy good with brotherhood
From sea to shining sea!

O beautiful for patriot dream
That sees beyond the years
Thine alabaster cities gleam
Undimmed by human tears!
America! America!
God shed his grace on thee
And crown thy good with brotherhood
From sea to shining sea!

Symbols of the United States

Mount Rushmore

Mount Rushmore, located in the Black Hills of South Dakota, is the world's largest sculpture. Known as the "Shrine of Democracy," it features the heads of four of the nation's greatest presidents—George Washington, Thomas Jefferson, Theodore Roosevelt, and Abraham Lincoln.

The original idea to carve massive figures into the mountainside came from South Dakota historian Doane Robinson. He thought that a giant sculpture of notable people in the history of the West would draw thousands of tourists to the Black Hills. Robinson chose sculptor Gutzon Borglum, who had worked on similar projects, to do the work. Borglum wanted to change the focus of the sculpture. He suggested that it should show four presidents who had played a major role in the country's development.

- George Washington—the commander of the Continental army during the American Revolution and the nation's first president
- Thomas Jefferson—the author of the Declaration of Independence who, as president, expanded the nation with the Louisiana Purchase
- Theodore Roosevelt—the president who oversaw the nation's rise to a world power
- Abraham Lincoln—the president who preserved the Union during the Civil War

After exploring the Black Hills, Borglum chose Mount Rushmore as the best site for the sculpture, and work began in 1927. A team of workers first used dynamite to blast away the rock. Then they used jackhammers to create facial features. Finally, they planed the surfaces smooth with hand tools.

Borglum's death in 1941 soon brought work on the sculpture to an end. During the 14 years of the project, his team had blasted some 450,000 tons of rock from the mountainside and created a monument of majestic proportions.

- The presidents' heads are some 60 feet high—about the distance from the pitcher's mound to home plate on a major league baseball diamond.
- The presidents' noses measure about 20 feet long.
- The presidents' eyes are 11 feet wide.
- The presidents' mouths are about 18 feet wide.

The 1927 Act of Congress that provided the initial funds for Borglum's sculpture declared Mount Rushmore a national memorial. Since the late 1930s, the National Park Service has managed the Mount Rushmore National Memorial, which hosts some 3 million visitors each year.

George Washington, Thomas Jefferson, Theodore Roosevelt, and Abraham Lincoln look down from the heights of Mount Rushmore.

Uncle Sam

One of the most recognizable symbols of the United States government is the character known as Uncle Sam. The origins of this symbol go back to the early 1800s. Samuel Wilson, a merchant from New York State, provided food for the army during the War of 1812. He marked the barrels of food "U.S." to indicate that they were government property. Over time, however, many soldiers began saying that the food was provided by "Uncle Sam."

During the mid-1800s, Uncle Sam began to take on a very distinct and recognizable appearance. This was largely due to the work of Thomas Nast, a cartoonist for the magazine *Harper's Weekly*. In his cartoons, Nast portrayed Sam as a tall, thin man with chin whiskers wearing a top hat, frock coat, and striped pants. Over the years, other artists adopted Nast's image of Uncle Sam, adding such features as a stars and stripes waistcoat.

Perhaps the most famous image of Uncle Sam was produced by artist James Montgomery Flagg during World War I. Originally drawn for a magazine cover warning Americans to be prepared for war, it was quickly adopted by the U.S. Army as a recruiting poster. More than 4 million copies of the poster were produced during 1917 and 1918. It was considered such a powerful recruiting tool that it was also used in the early years of World War II.

Flagg's stern-faced, finger-pointing Uncle Sam was a long way from Samuel Wilson, the food merchant from New York. Wilson, however, was not forgotten. In 1961 Congress recognized him as the origin of "America's national symbol of Uncle Sam."

Political Party Symbols

The symbols of the two major U.S. political parties—the Democratic donkey and the Republican elephant—are recognizable to many Americans. Both symbols have a colorful origin.

The use of the donkey as a symbol for Democrats dates to the presidential election of 1828. Supporters of John Quincy Adams declared that Democrat Andrew Jackson, Adams's opponent, was like a donkey—slow and not very bright. Jackson seized on this charge. He used the donkey on his campaign posters, noting that it was a simple, loyal, and hard-working animal. However, this image did not gain popularity until the mid-1800s—again through the work of Thomas Nast.

In his cartoons, Nast often used a donkey to represent supporters of the Democratic Party. In an 1874 cartoon, Nast showed the donkey, dressed in a lion skin, terrorizing other animals in a zoo. The elephant in the cartoon was labeled "The Republican Vote." In very short order, the two animals became the political party symbols.

This 1874 Thomas Nast cartoon is the first use of the Democratic donkey and the Republican elephant together.

Today, these animals remain the symbols of the two political parties. Images of the donkey and the elephant are used in campaign materials, usually decorated with stars and stripes.

Phonetic Respelling and Pronunciation Guide

Many of the key terms in this textbook have been respelled to help you pronounce them. The letter combinations used in the respelling throughout the narrative are explained in the following phonetic respelling and pronunciation guide. The guide is adapted from *Merriam-Webster's Collegiate Dictionary, 11th Edition; Merriam-Webster's Geographical Dictionary;* and *Merriam-Webster's Biographical Dictionary.*

MARK	AS IN	RESPELLING	EXAMPLE
a	alphabet	a	*AL-fuh-bet
ā	Asia	ay	AY-zhuh
ä	cart, top	ah	KAHRT, TAHP
e	let, ten	e	LET, TEN
ē	even, leaf	ee	EE-vuhn, LEEF
i	it, tip, British	i	IT, TIP, BRIT-ish
ī	site, buy, Ohio	y	SYT, BY, oh-HY-oh
	iris	eye	EYE-ris
k	card	k	KAHRD
ō	over, rainbow	oh	OH-vuhr, RAYN-boh
u̇	book, wood	ooh	BOOHK, WOOHD
ȯ	all, orchid	aw	AWL, AWR-kid
ȯi	foil, coin	oy	FOYL, KOYN
au̇	out	ow	OWT
ə	cup, butter	uh	KUHP, BUHT-uhr
ü	rule, food	oo	ROOL, FOOD
yü	few	yoo	FYOO
zh	vision	zh	VIZH-uhn

*A syllable printed in small capital letters receives heavier emphasis than the other syllable(s) in a word.

A

abolition an end to slavery (p. 489)
abolición fin de la esclavitud (pág. 489)

abolition movement a campaign to end slavery (p. 524)
movimiento abolicionista una campaña para poner fin a la esclavitud (pág. 524)

Adams-Onís Treaty (1819) an agreement in which Spain gave East Florida to the United States (p. 294)
Tratado de Adams y Onís (1819) acuerdo en el que España le dio el territorio del este de Florida a Estados Unidos (pág. 294)

affirmative action an active effort to improve the employment or educational opportunities of members of minority groups and women (p. 958)
acción afirmativa iniciativas para mejorar las oportunidades laborales o educativas de las minorías y de las mujeres (pág. 958)

African Diaspora the population of displaced Africans and their descendants around the world (p. 477)
diáspora africana población de africanos desplazados y sus descendientes en todo el mundo (pág. 477)

AIDS Acquired Immunodeficiency Syndrome, a disease that affects the immune system, making patients vulnerable to infections (p. 996)
SIDA síndrome de inmunodeficiencia adquirida; enfermedad que afecta al sistema inmunológico y hace que los pacientes sean vulnerables a infecciones (pág. 996)

Alamo Spanish mission in San Antonio, Texas, that was the site of a famous battle of the Texas Revolution in 1836 (p. 394)
El Álamo misión española en San Antonio, Texas; escenario de una famosa batalla durante la Revolución Texana de 1836 (pág. 394)

Alien and Sedition Acts (1798) laws passed by a Federalist-dominated Congress aimed at protecting the government from treasonous ideas, actions, and people (p. 266)
Leyes de Extranjeros y Sedición (1798) leyes aprobadas por un Congreso mayormente federalist para proteger al gobierno de la influencia de ideas, acciones y personas desleales (pág. 266)

Allied powers a group of nations that allied to fight the Central powers in World War I, and those countries in opposition to the Axis powers in World War II (pp. 747, 832)
potencias aliadas grupo de naciones que se aliaron para luchar contra las potencias centrales en la Primera Guerra Mundial, y los países que se oponían a las potencias del Eje en la Segunda Guerra Mundial (pág. 747, 832)

al Qaeda the name of the terrorist organization headed by Osama bin Laden and responsible for the September 11, 2001, attacks (p. 984)
al-Qaeda nombre de la organización terrorista encabezada por Osama bin Laden, responsable de los ataques del 11 de septiembre de 2001 (pág. 984)

amendment official change, correction, or addition to a law or constitution (pp. 173, 185)
enmienda cambio, corrección o adición oficial a una ley o constitución (pág. 173, 185)

American Anti-Slavery Society an organization started by William Lloyd Garrison whose members wanted immediate emancipation and racial equality for African Americans (pp. 490, 525)
Sociedad Americana contra la Esclavitud organización fundada por William Lloyd Garrison cuyos miembros pedían la emancipación inmediata y la igualdad racial de los afroamericanos (pág. 490, 525)

American Expeditionary Force the U.S. military forces sent to Europe during World War I and led by General John J. Pershing (p. 757)
Fuerza Expedicionaria Estadounidense fuerzas armadas de Estados Unidos bajo el mando del general John J. Pershing que fueron enviadas a Europa en la Primera Guerra Mundial (pág. 757)

American Federation of Labor (AFL) an organization that united skilled workers into national unions for specific industries (p. 654)
Federación Americana del Trabajo (AFL, por sus siglas en inglés) organización que unió a obreros especializados en sindicatos nacionales para industrias específicas (pág. 654)

American Indian Movement (AIM) a civil rights group organized to promote the interests of Native Americans (p. 941)
Movimiento de los Indígenas Americanos (AIM, por sus siglas en inglés) agrupación a favor de los derechos civiles que promueve los intereses de los indígenas norteamericanos (pág. 941)

American System Henry Clay's plan for raising tariffs to pay for internal improvements such as better roads and canals (p. 306)
Sistema Estadounidense plan de alza de aranceles creado por Henry Clay para hacer mejoras internas como la reparación de caminos y canales (pág. 306)

Antifederalists people who opposed ratification of the Constitution (pp. 170, 186)
antifederalistas personas que se oponían a la aprobación de la Constitución (pág. 170, 186)

Anti-Imperialist League a group of citizens opposed to imperialism and, specifically, to the peace treaty that gave the United States control of Cuba, Guam, Puerto Rico, and the Philippines (p. 727)
Liga Antiimperialista grupo de ciudadanos que se oponían al imperialismo y, más específi camente, al tratado de paz que daba a Estados Unidos el control de Cuba, Guam, Puerto Rico y Filipinas (pág. 727)

apartheid a system of segregation practiced in South Africa (p. 961)
apartheid sistema de segregación practicado en Sudáfrica (pág. 961)

appeasement the policy of giving into the demands of a nation in order to avoid war (p. 832)
apacigua miento contemporizacióno política de ceder ante las exigencias de una nación para evitar la Guerra (pág. 832)

English and Spanish Glossary

Appomattox Courthouse the location where General Robert E. Lee was forced to surrender, thus ending the Civil War (p. 605)
Appomattox Courthouse poblado de Virginia donde el general Robert E. Lee fue obligado a rendirse, dando fi n a la Guerra Civil (pág. 605)

armistice a truce or cease-fire agreement between warring nations (p. 762)
armisticio tregua o acuerdo de cese del fuego entre dos naciones en guerra (pág. 762)

arms race a growth in weapons based on the number of weapons an enemy country has (p. 880)
carrera armamentística aumento de armamentos según la cantidad de armas que tiene un país enemigo (pág. 880)

Articles of Confederation (1777) the document that created the first central government for the United States; was replaced by the Constitution in 1789 (p. 154)
Artículos de Confederación (1777) documento que creó el primer gobierno central en Estados Unidos; fue reemplazado por la Constitución en 1789 (pág. 154)

assimilate to give up traditional ways in favor of mainstream practices (p. 377)
asimilar renunciar a las formas tradicionales en favor de las prácticas generales (pág. 377)

assimilation a process of adopting American beliefs and aspects of American culture (p. 677)
asimilación un proceso de adopción de creencias y aspectos de la cultura americana (pág. 677)

astrolabe a device that enabled navigators to learn their ship's location by charting the position of the stars (p. 38)
astrolabio aparato que permitía a los navegantes saber la ubicación de su barco al trazar la posición de las estrellas (pág. 38)

atomic bomb a weapon that receives its explosive power from the splitting of atoms (p. 858)
bomba atómica arma cuyo poder explosivo es generado por la división de átomos (pág. 858)

Axis powers the coalition of nations in World War II that included Germany, Italy, and Japan (p. 832)
potencias del Eje coalición de naciones de la Segunda Guerra Mundial formada por Alemania, Italia y Japón (pág. 832)

B

baby boom a sharp increase in the number of American births during the 1950s and 1960s (p. 882)
boom de la natalidad gran aumento en la cantidad de nacimientos en Estados Unidos durante las décadas de 1950 y 1960 (pág. 882)

Bacon's Rebellion (1676) an atttack led by Nathaniel Bacon against American Indians and the colonial government in Virginia (p. 71)
Rebelión de Bacon (1676) ataque encabezado por Nathaniel Bacon contra los indígenas norteamericanos y el gobierno colonial en Virginia (pág. 71)

Bank of the United States a national bank chartered by Congress in 1791 to provide security for the U.S. economy (p. 254)
Banco de los Estados Unidos banco nacional formado por el Congreso en 1791 para dar seguridad a la economía de Estados Unidos (pág. 254)

Bataan Death March a forced march of American and Filipino soldiers captured by the Japanese along the Bataan Peninsula (p. 849)
marcha de la muerte de Bataán marcha forzada en la península de Bataán de soldados estadounidenses y filipinos capturados por los japoneses (pág. 849)

Battle of Antietam (1862) a Union victory in the Civil War that marked the bloodiest single-day battle in U.S. military history (p. 581)
batalla de Antieta (1862) victoria del ejército de la Unión durante la Guerra Civil en la batalla de un solo día más sangrienta de la historia militar de Estados Unidos (pág. 581)

Battle of Bunker Hill (1775) a Revolutionary War battle in Boston that demonstrated that the colonists could fight well against the British army (p. 117)
batalla de Bunker Hill (1775) batalla de la Guerra de Independencia estadounidense en Boston; en ésta se demostró que los colonos podían luchar bien contra el ejército británico (pág. 117)

Battle of El Alamein (1942) a turning point in World War II, in which Allied forces defeated the Afrika Korps of Germany (p. 844)
batalla del El Alamein (1942) momento decisivo en la Segunda Guerra Mundial, en el que las fuerzas aliadas derrotaron al *Afrika Korps* de Alemania (pág. 844)

Battle of Fallen Timbers (1794) a battle between U.S. troops and an American Indian confederation that ended Indian efforts to halt white settlement in the Northwest Territory (p. 259)
batalla de Fallen Timbers (1794) batalla entre las tropas estadounidenses y una confederación de indígenasnorteamericanos que puso fin a los intentos de los indígenas para detener la emigración de personas de raza blanca al Territorio del Noroeste (pág. 259)

Battle of Gettysburg (1863) a Union Civil War victory that turned the tide against the Confederates at Gettysburg, Pennsylvania (p. 600)
batalla de Gettysburg (1863) victoria del ejército de la Unión durante la Guerra Civil que cambió el curso de la guerra en contra de los confederados en Gettysburg, Pensilvania (pág. 600)

Battle of Lake Erie (1813) U.S. victory in the War of 1812, led by Oliver Hazard Perry; broke Britain's control of Lake Erie (p. 289)
batalla del lago Erie (1813) victoria en la Guerra de 1812 en la que el ejército estadounidense, comandado por Oliver Hazard Perry, puso fin al control británico del lago Erie (pág. 289)

Battle of Leyte Gulf (1944) the largest naval battle in history, during which the American fleet destroyed most of the Japanese fleet (p. 851)
batalla del golfo de Leyte (1944) la mayor batalla naval de la historia, durante la cual la flota estadounidense destruyó la mayor parte de la flota japonesa (pág. 851)

Battle of Midway (1942) battle of World War II that ended the Japanese advance in the Pacific (p. 850)
batalla de Midway (1942) batalla de la Segunda Guerra Mundial que puso fin al avance de los japoneses en el Pacífico (pág. 850)

Battle of New Orleans (1815) the greatest U.S. victory in the War of 1812; actually took place two weeks after a peace treaty had been signed ending the war (p. 291)
batalla de Nueva Orleáns (1815) la mayor victoria del ejército estadounidense en la Guerra de 1812; tuvo lugar dos semanas después de la firma de un tratado de paz en el que se declaraba el fi nal de la Guerra (pág. 291)

Battle of San Jacinto (1836) the final battle of the Texas Revolution; resulted in the defeat of the Mexican army and independence for Texas (p. 395)
batalla de San Jacinto (1836) batalla final de la Revolución Texana en la que el ejército mexicano fue derrotado y Texas obtuvo su independencia (pág. 395)

Battle of Saratoga (1777) a Revolutionary War battle in New York that resulted in a major defeat of British troops; marked the Patriots' greatest victory up to that point in the war (p. 132)
batalla de Saratoga (1777) batalla de la Guerra de Independencia estadounidense que tuvo lugar en Nueva York y en la que las fuerzas británicas sufrieron una de sus mayores derrotas; los patriotas obtuvieron su mayor victoria hasta ese momento (pág. 132)

Battle of Shiloh (1862) a Civil War battle in Tennessee in which the Union army gained greater control over the Mississippi River valley (p. 584)
batalla de Shiloh (1862) batalla de la Guerra Civil en Tennessee en la que el ejército de la Unión adquirió mayor control sobre el valle del río Mississippi (pág. 584)

Battle of Stalingrad (1942–1943) a major turning point in World War II; Soviet forces defeated Nazi forces after which the Nazis never recovered (p. 846)
batalla de Stalingrado (1942–1943) momento decisivo de la Segunda Guerra Mundial; las fuerzas soviéticas vencieron a las fuerzas nazis, que nunca más se recuperaron (pág. 846)

English and Spanish Glossary

Battle of the Bulge (1944–1945) the last German advance of World War II, which was stopped by Allied forces (p. 856)
batalla del Bulge (1944–1945) último avance alemán de la Segunda Guerra Mundial, que fue detenido por las fuerzas aliadas (pág. 856)

Battle of the Coral Sea (1942) the first strategic defeat of the Japanese Imperial Navy by American forces during World War II (p. 850)
batalla del mar del Coral (1942) primera derrota estratégica de la armada imperial japonesa ante las fuerzas estadounidenses en la Segunda Guerra Mundial (pág. 850)

Battle of the Little Big Horn (1876) "Custer's Last Stand"; battle between U.S. soldiers, led by George Armstrong Custer, and Sioux warriors, led by Crazy Horse and Sitting Bull, that resulted in the worst defeat for the U.S. Army in the West (p. 375)
batalla de Little Big Horn (1876) última batalla del general Custer; esta batalla entre las tropas de George Armstrong Custer y los guerreros siux al mando de Caballo Loco y Toro Sentado produjo la mayor derrota del ejército estadounidense en el Oeste (pág. 375)

Battle of Tippecanoe (1811) U.S. victory over an Indian confederation that wanted to stop white settlement in the Northwest Territory; increased tensions between Great Britain and the United States (p. 286)
batalla de Tippecanoe (1811) victoria del ejército estadounidense sobre la confederación indígena que intentaba evitar el establecimiento de poblaciones de blancos en el Territorio del Noroeste; esta batalla aumentó las hostilidades entre Gran Bretaña y Estados Unidos (pág. 286)

Battle of Trenton (1776) a Revolutionary War battle in New Jersey in which Patriot forces captured more than 900 Hessian troops (p. 132)
batalla de Trenton (1776) batalla de la Guerra de Independencia estadounidense que tuvo lugar en Nueva Jersey; en esta batalla las fuerzas de los patriotas capturaron a más de 900 soldados hessianos (pág. 132)

Battle of Yorktown (1781) the last major battle of the Revolutionary War; site of British general Charles Cornwallis's surrender to the Patriots in Virginia (p. 142)
batalla de Yorktown (1781) la última batalla importante de la Guerra de Independencia estadounidense; lugar donde se rindió el general británico Charles Cornwallis ante los patriotas en Virginia (pág. 142)

Bear Flag Revolt (1846) a revolt against Mexico by American settlers in California who declared the territory an independent republic (p. 403)
Revuelta de Bear Flag (1846) rebelión iniciada por colonos estadounidenses en contra de México para declarar al territorio de California una república independiente (pág. 403)

beats young people, many of whom were writers and artists, who discussed their dissatisfaction with the American society of the 1950s (p. 886)
beatniks jóvenes, en su mayoría escritores y artistas, que debatían acerca de su descontento con la sociedad estadounidense de la década de 1950 (pág. 886)

benevolent society an aid organization formed by immigrant communities (p. 667)
sociedad de benefi cencia organización de ayuda formada por comunidades de inmigrantes (pág. 667)

Berbers a group of people from northern Africa (p. 19)
bereberes grupo de habitantes del norte de África (pág. 19)

Bering Land Bridge a strip of land connecting Alaska with Russia that emerged from underwater around 38,000 BC (p. 6)
Puente de Tierra de Bering franja de tierra que conecta Alaska con Rusia y que surgió del agua alrededor del año 38,000 a.C. (pág. 6)

Berlin Wall a barrier of concrete and barbed wire between Communist East Berlin and West Berlin (p. 896)
Muro de Berlín barrera de concreto y alambre de púas que separaba la Berlín oriental comunista de la Berlín occidental (pág. 896)

Bessemer process a process developed in the 1850s that led to faster, cheaper steel production (p. 642)
proceso de Bessemer proceso de producción de acero más económico y rápido, desarrollado en la década de 1850 (pág. 642)

Bill of Rights the first 10 amendments to the Constitution; ratified in 1791 (pp. 174, 187)
Declaración de Derechos primeras 10 enmiendas a la Constitución; aprobada en 1791 (pág. 174, 187)

Black Codes laws passed in the southern states during Reconstruction that greatly limited the freedom and rights of African Americans (p. 620)
Códigos Negros decretos aprobados en los estados sureños en la época de la Reconstrucción que limitaron en gran medida la libertad y los derechos de los afroamericanos (pág. 620)

Black Death a series of plagues that killed about 25 million people in Europe starting in 1347 (p. 26)
Peste Negra serie de plagas que mataron a unos 25 millones de personas en Europa a partir de 1347 (pág. 26)

Black Power a social movement that called for African American power and independence (p. 936)
Black Power (Poder Negro) movimiento social que exigía el poder y la independencia de los afroamericanos (pág. 936)

Black Tuesday October 29, 1929, one of the largest U.S. stock market drops (p. 803)
martes negro 29 de octubre de 1929, una de las mayores caídas de la bolsa de valores de Estados Unidos (pág. 803)

bond a certificate that represents money the government has borrowed from private citizens (p. 250)
bono certificado que representa dinero que el gobierno toma prestado de los ciudadanos (pág. 250)

Bonus Army a group of World War I veterans that demanded their bonus payments early (p. 806)
Bonus Army grupo de veteranos de la Primera Guerra Mundial que exigía el pago de sus bonos por adelantado (pág. 806)

boomtown a Western community that grew quickly because of the mining boom and often disappeared when the boom ended (p. 365)
pueblo de rápido crecimiento comunidad del Oeste que se desarrolló con gran rapidez debido a la fiebre del oro, pero que desapareció cuando la fiebre terminó (pág. 365)

border states Delaware, Kentucky, Maryland, and Missouri; slave states that lay between the North and the South and did not join the Confederacy during the Civil War (p. 572)
estados fronterizos Delaware, Kentucky, Maryland y Missouri; estados esclavistas ubicados entre el Norte y el Sur y que no se unieron a la Confederación durante la Guerra Civil (pág. 572)

Boston Massacre (1770) an incident in which British soldiers fired into a crowd of colonists, killing five people (p. 109)
masacre de Boston (1770) incidente en el que los soldados británicos le dispararon a una multitud de colonos, dando muerte a cinco personas (pág. 109)

Boston Tea Party (1773) a protest against the Tea Act in which a group of colonists boarded British tea ships and dumped more than 340 chests of tea into Boston Harbor (p. 111)
Motín del Té de Boston (1773) protesta en contra de la Ley del Té en la que un grupo de colonos abordó barcos británicos que transportaban té y arrojó al mar alrededor de 340 baúles de té en el puerto de Boston (pág. 111)

Boxer Rebellion (1900) a siege of a foreign settlement in Beijing by Chinese nationalists who were angry at foreign involvement in China (p. 722)
rebelión de los boxers (1900) asedio a un asentamiento extranjero en Beijing por parte de un grupo de nacionalistas chinos que estaban enojados por la participación extranjera en China (pág. 722)

brinkmanship the Cold War foreign policy designed to "get to the verge without getting into the war" (p. 881)
política arriesgada política exterior durante la Guerra Fría diseñada para "llegar al borde de la guerra sin llegar a la guerra" (pág. 881)

English and Spanish Glossary

Brown v. *Board of Education* (1954) Supreme Court decision that ended segregation in public schools (p. 925)
Brown contra *la Junta Educativa* (1954) decisión de la Corte Suprema que puso fin a la segregación en las escuelas públicas (pág. 925)

buffalo soldiers African American soldiers who served in the cavalry during the wars for the west (p. 373)
soldados búfalo soldados afroamericanos que sirvieron en la caballería durante las guerras del oeste (pág. 373)

Bureau of Indian Affairs a government agency created in the 1800s to oversee federal policy toward Native Americans (p. 340)
Oficina de Asuntos Indígenas agencia creada por el gobierno en el siglo XIX para supervisar las políticas federales en cuanto a los indígenas norteamericanos (pág. 340)

business cycle the rhythm in which an economy expands and contracts its production (p. 805)
ciclo económico ritmo al que la producción de una economía se expande y se contrae (pág. 805)

buying on margin the process of purchasing stock with credit, hoping to sell at a high enough price to pay the loan and make a profit (p. 802)
compra a crédito proceso de comprar acciones con préstamos, con la esperanza de venderlas a un precio suficientemente alto para pagar el préstamo y obtener una ganancia (pág. 802)

C

Californios Spanish colonists in California in the 1800s (p. 400)
californios colonos españoles que vivían en California en el siglo XIX (pág. 400)

Camp David Accords (1978) an agreement between the heads of Israel and Egypt that began peace process in the Middle East (p. 962)
Acuerdos de Camp David (1978) acuerdo entre los líderes de Israel y Egipto que dio inicio a un proceso de paz en el Medio Oriente (pág. 962)

capitalism an economic system in which private businesses run most industries (p. 699)

capitalismo sistema económico en el que las empresas privadas controlan la mayoría de las industrias (pág. 699)

caravels ships that used triangular sails to sail against the wind, and had rudders to improve steering (p. 38)
carabelas barcos con velas triangulares usadas para navegar contra el viento y que tenían timones para mejorar la dirección (pág. 38)

cattle drive a long journey on which cowboys herded cattle to northern markets or better grazing lands (p. 366)
arreo de ganado viaje largo en el que los vaqueros arreaban ganado para llevarlo a los mercados del Norte o a mejores pastos (pág. 366)

Cattle Kingdom an area of the Great Plains on which many ranchers raised cattle in the late 1800s (p. 366)
Reino del Ganado área de las Grandes Planicies en la que muchos rancheros criaban ganado a fi nales de siglo XIX (pág. 366)

Central powers the coalition of nations in World War I that included the German, Austrio-Hungary, and Ottoman empires (p. 747)
Potencias Centrales coalición de naciones de la Primera Guerra Mundial formada por los imperios alemán, austrohúngaro y otomano (pág. 747)

charter an official document that gives a person the right to establish a colony (p. 56)
carta de constitución documento oficial que da a una persona el derecho de establecer una colonia (pág. 56)

checks and balances a system established by the Constitution that prevents any branch of government from becoming too powerful (pp. 167, 185)
equilibrio de poderes sistema establecido por la Constitución para evitar que cualquier poder del gobierno adquiera demasiada autoridad (pág. 167, 185)

Chinese Exclusion Act (1882) a law passed by Congress that banned Chinese from immigrating to the United States for 10 years (p. 668)
Ley de Exclusión de Chinos (1882) ley aprobada por el Congreso que prohibió la inmigración de chinos a Estados Unidos por 10 años (pág. 668)

Chisholm Trail a trail from San Antonio, Texas, to Abilene, Kansas, established by Jesse Chisholm in the late 1860s for cattle drives (p. 366)
Camino de Chisholm camino creado por Jesse Chisholm a finales de la década de 1860 que iba desde San Antonio, Texas hasta Abilene, Kansas, para arreos de ganado (pág. 366)

circumnavigate to travel all the way around the globe (p. 44)
circunnavegar darle la vuelta al planeta (pág. 44)

Civil Rights Act of 1866 a law that gave African Americans legal rights equal to those of white Americans (p. 622)
Ley de Derechos Civiles de 1866 ley que dio a los afroamericanos los mismos derechos legales que tenían los estadounidenses blancos (pág. 622)

Civil Rights Act of 1964 a law that ended discrimination based on race or gender (p. 934)
Ley de Derechos Civiles de 1964 ley que puso fin a la discriminación en base a la raza o al sexo (pág. 934)

Clermont the first full-sized U.S. commercial steamboat; developed by Robert Fulton and tested in 1807 (p. 435)
Clermont primer barco comercial de vapor de gran tamaño, diseñado por Robert Fulton y probado en 1807 (pág. 435)

Cold War a period of hostility between Western powers and Communist powers (p. 871)
Guerra Fría período de hostilidades entre las potencias de Occidente y las potencias comunistas (pág. 871)

collective bargaining a technique used by labor unions in which workers act collectively to change working conditions or wages (p. 653)
negociación colectiva método empleado por los sindicatos en el que los trabajadores actúan colectivamente para cambiar las condiciones laborales o los salarios (pág. 653)

Columbian Exchange the transfer of plants, animals, and diseases between the Americas and Europe, Asia, and Africa (p. 44)
intercambio colombino intercambio de plantas, animales y enfermedades entre las Américas y Europa, Asia y África (pág. 44)

Committees of Correspondence committees created by the Massachusetts House of Representatives in the 1760s to help towns and colonies share information about resisting British laws (p. 107)
comités de correspondencia comités creados por la Cámara de Representantes de Massachusetts en la década de 1760 para que lospueblos y colonias compartieran información sobra la resistencia a las leyes británicas (pág. 107)

common-school movement a social reform effort that began in the mid-1800s and promoted the idea of having all children educated in a common place regardless of social class or background (p. 521)
movimiento de escuelas comunes reforma social iniciada a mediados del siglo XIX para fomentar la idea de que todos los niños debían recibir educación en un mismo lugar sin importar su origen o clase social (pág. 521)

Common Sense (1776) a pamphlet written by Thomas Paine that criticized monarchies and convinced many American colonists of the need to break away from Britain (p. 119)
Sentido común (1776) escrito por Thomas Paine en el que criticaba a las monarquías y convenció a muchos colonos norteamericanos de la necesidad de independizarse de Gran Bretaña (pág. 119)

Communists people who believe in communism, or the political system in which all resources are shared equally (p. 758)
comunistas personas que creen en el comunismo, es decir, el sistema político en el que los recursos se distribuyen a todos por igual (pág. 758)

Compromise of 1850 Henry Clay's proposed agreement that allowed California to enter the Union as a free state and divided the rest of the Mexican Cession into two territories where slavery would be decided by popular sovereignty (pp. 498, 544)
Compromiso de 1850 acuerdo propuesto por Henry Clay en que se permitía a California entrar en la Unión como estado libre y se proponía la division del resto del territorio de la Cesión Mexicana en dos partes donde la esclavitud sería reglamentada por soberanía popular (pág. 498, 544)

English and Spanish Glossary

Compromise of 1877 an agreement to settle the disputed presidential election of 1876; Democrats agreed to accept Republican Rutherford B. Hayes as president in return for the removal of federal troops from the South (p. 630)
Compromiso de 1877 acuerdo en el que se resolvieron las disputadas elecciones presidenciales de 1876; los demócratas aceptaron al republican Rutherford B. Hayes como presidente a cambio del retiro de las tropas federales del Sur (pág. 630)

Comstock Lode Nevada gold and silver mine discovered by Henry Comstock in 1859 (p. 364)
veta de Comstock mina de oro y plata descubierta en Nevada por Henry Comstock en 1859 (pág. 364)

Confederate States of America the nation formed by the southern states when they seceded from the Union; also known as the Confederacy (p. 561)
Estados Confederados de América nación formada por los estados del Sur cuando se separaron de la Unión; también conocida como Confederación (pág. 561)

Congress of Industrial Organizations (CIO) a union that organized workers according to industry, not by skill (p. 814)
Congreso de Organizaciones Industriales (CIO, por sus siglas en inglés) sindicato que organizó a los trabajadores según la industria y no el nivel de especialización (pág. 814)

conquistador a Spanish soldier and explorer who led military expeditions in the Americas and captured land for Spain (p. 46)
conquistador soldado y explorador español que encabezó expediciones militares en América y capturó territorios en nombre de España (pág. 46)

conservation the planned management of natural resources to prevent their destruction (p. 708)
conservación administración planifi cada de los recursos naturales para evitar su destrucción (pág. 708)

constitution a set of basic principles that determines the powers and duties of a government (p. 153)

constitución conjunto de principios básicos que determina los poderes y las obligaciones de un gobierno (pág. 153)

Constitutional Convention (1787) a meeting held in Philadelphia at which delegates from the states wrote the Constitution (pp. 164, 183)
Convención Constitucional (1787) reunión en Filadelfia en la que delegados de los estados redactaron la Constitución (pág. 164, 183)

Constitutional Union Party a political party formed in 1860 by a group of northerners and southerners who supported the Union, its laws, and the Constitution (p. 560)
Partido Constitucional por la Unión partido politico formado en 1860 por habitantes del Norte y del Sur en apoyo de la Unión, sus leyes y la Constitución (pág. 560)

containment a foreign policy that attempts to stop the spread of communism without ending it in the countries in which it already exists (p. 871)
contención política exterior que intenta detener el avance del comunismo sin eliminarlo en los países en los que ya existe (pág. 871)

Continental army the army created by the Second Continental Congress in 1775 to defend the American colonies from Britain (p. 116)
Ejército Continental ejército creado por el Segundo Congreso Continental en 1775 para defender a las colonias norteamericanas del dominio británico (pág. 116)

contraband an escaped slave who joined the Union army during the Civil War (p. 593)
contrabando esclavo que escapó y se unió al ejército de la Unión durante la Guerra Civil (pág. 593)

Convention of 1818 an agreement between the United States and Great Britain that settled fishing rights and established new North American borders (p. 292)
Convención de 1818 acuerdo entre Estados Unidos y Gran Bretaña para definir los derechos de pesca y establecer las nuevas fronteras norteamericanas (pág. 292)

Copperheads a group of northern Democrats who opposed abolition and sympathized with the South during the Civil War (p. 595)

copperheads grupo de demócratas del Norte que se oponían a la abolición de la esclavitud y simpatizaban con las creencias sureñas durante la Guerra Civil (pág. 595)

corporation a business that sells portions of ownership called stock shares (p. 648)
corporación compañía que vende algunas partes en forma de acciones (pág. 648)

cotton belt a region stretching from South Carolina to east Texas where most U.S. cotton was produced during the mid-1800s (p. 454)
región algodonera zona que se extendía desde Carolina del Sur hasta el este de Texas, en la que se producía la mayor parte del algodón cosechado en Estados Unidos a mediados del siglo XIX (pág. 454)

cotton diplomacy Confederate efforts to use the importance of southern cotton to Britain's textile industry to persuade the British to support the Confederacy in the Civil War (p. 574)
diplomacia del algodón esfuerzos de la Confederación por aprovechar la importancia del algodón del Sur en la industria textil británica para convencer a Gran Bretaña de apoyar a la Confederación en la Guerra Civil (pág. 574)

cotton gin a machine invented by Eli Whitney in 1793 to remove seeds from short-staple cotton; revolutionized the cotton industry (p. 453)
desmotadora de algodón máquina inventada por Eli Whitney en 1793 para separar las fi bras de algodón de las semillas; revolucionó la industria del algodón (pág. 453)

Cuban missile crisis a threat to national security that occurred when the Soviet Union placed nuclear missiles in Cuba (p. 896)
crisis de los misiles de Cuba amenaza a la seguridad nacional que ocurrió cuando la Unión Soviética colocó misiles nucleares en Cuba (pág. 896)

culture the common values and traditions of a society, such as language, government, and family relationships (p. 7)
cultura valores y tradiciones comunes de una sociedad, como el lenguaje, la forma de gobierno y las relaciones familiares (pág. 7)

Cumberland Road the first federal road project, construction of which began in 1815; ran from Cumberland, Maryland, to present-day Wheeling, West Virginia (p. 307)
camino de Cumberland primer proyecto federal de construcción de carreteras, iniciado en 1815 para crear un camino entre Cumberland, Maryland y el poblado que actualmente lleva el nombre de Wheeling, en Virginia Occidental (pág. 307)

D

Dawes General Allotment Act (1887) legislation passed by Congress that split up Indian reservation lands among individual Indians and promised them citizenship (p. 377)
Ley de Adjudicación General de Dawes (1887) ley aprobada por el Congreso que dividía el terreno de las reservas indígenas entre sus habitantes y les prometía la ciudadanía (pág. 377)

D-Day (1944) an invasion of Nazi-occupied France by Allied forces (p. 846)
día D (1944) invasión de las fuerzas aliadas en Francia, ocupada por los nazis (pág. 846)

Declaration of Independence (1776) the document written to declare the colonies free from British rule (p. 120)
Declaración de Independencia (1776) document redactado para declarar la independencia de las colonias del dominio británico (pág. 120)

Declaration of Sentiments (1848) a statement written and signed by women's rights supporters at the Seneca Falls Convention; detailed their beliefs about social injustice against women (p. 532)
Declaración de Sentimientos (1848) declaración redactada y fi rmada por partidarios de los derechos de la mujer durante la Convención de Seneca Falls; se describía con detalle su punto de vista sobre las injusticias sociales que afectaban a las mujeres (pág. 532)

deficit the amount by which a government's spending exceeds its revenue (p. 965)
déficit cantidad en la que los gastos del gobierno superan sus ingresos (pág. 965)

English and Spanish Glossary

deflation a decrease in money supply and overall lower prices (p. 382)
deflación reducción de la disponibilidad del dinero y baja general en los precios (pág. 382)

democracy a government in which people rule themselves (p. 24)
democracia gobierno en el que el pueblo se gobierna a sí mismo (pág. 24)

Democratic Party a political party formed by supporters of Andrew Jackson after the presidential election of 1824 (p. 330)
Partido Demócrata partido político formado por partidarios de Andrew Jackson después de las elecciones presidenciales de 1824 (pág. 330)

Democratic-Republican Party a political party founded in the 1790s by Thomas Jefferson, James Madison, and other leaders who wanted to preserve the power of the state governments and promote agriculture (p. 264)
Partido Demócrata Republicano partido politico formado en la década de 1790 por Thomas Jefferson, James Madison y otros líderes políticos para preserver el poder de los gobiernos estatales y promover la agricultura (pág. 264)

Department of Homeland Security a federal agency set up in 2001 to coordinate national efforts to combat terrorism (p. 988)
Departamento de Seguridad Nacional una agencia federal creada en 2001 para coordinar los esfuerzos nacionales de lucha contra el terrorismo (pág. 988)

department store giant retail shop (p. 672)
tiendas por departamentos grandes comercios de venta al público (pág. 672)

deport to send an immigrant back to his or her country of origin (p. 234)
deportar enviar a un inmigrante de regreso a su país de origen (pág. 234)

depression a steep drop in economic activity combined with rising unemployment (p. 161)
depresión bajón considerable en la actividad económica, combinado con un alza en el desempleo (pág. 161)

détente a period of closer diplomatic relations between the United States and the Communist powers of China and the Soviet Union (p. 952)
distensión período de relaciones diplomáticas más estrechas entre Estados Unidos y las potencias comunistas de China y la Unión Soviética (pág. 952)

Disabled in Action (DIA) a group organized to promote the interests of people with disabilities (p. 942)
Discapacitados en Acción (DIA, por sus siglas en inglés) grupo organizado para promover los intereses de personas con discapacidades (pág. 942)

dollar diplomacy trying to influence foreign governments through economic, not military intervention (p. 737)
diplomacia del dólar modelo político que trata de influir en los gobiernos extranjeros a través del uso de su poder económico y no por la intervención militar (pág. 737)

domino theory the idea that Communism would spread rapidly throughout Southeast Asia (p. 899)
teoría del efecto dominó idea de que el comunismo se extendería rápidamente por el sureste de Asia (pág. 899)

Donner party a group of western travelers who were stranded in the Sierra Nevada during the winter of 1846–47; only 45 of the party's 87 members survived (p. 409)
grupo Donner grupo de viajeros del Oeste perdidos en la Sierra Nevada durante el invierno de 1846–47; sólo 45 de los 87 viajeros sobrevivieron (pág. 409)

double jeopardy the act of trying a person twice for the same crime (p. 226)
doble riesgo acto de juzgar a una persona dos veces por el mismo delito (pág. 226)

doves opponents of the Vietnam War (p. 905)
palomas opositores a la guerra de Vietnam (pág. 905)

draft a system of required service in the armed forces (p. 235)
conscripción sistema de servicio obligatorio en las fuerzas armadas (pág. 235)

dry farming a method of farming used by Plains farmers in the 1890s that shifted focus from water-dependent crops to more hardy crops (p. 380)
agricultura de secano método de cultivo que usaban los agricultores de las Planicies en la década de 1890 que provocó un cambio de los cultivos que dependían del agua a otros más resistentes (pág. 380)

due process the fair application of the law (p. 226)
  debido proceso aplicación justa de la ley (pág. 226)

Dust Bowl an area of the United States that suffered a severe drought during the 1930s (p. 816)
  Dust Bowl área de Estados Unidos que sufrió una grave sequía en la década de 1930 (pág. 816)

E

Eighteenth Amendment (1919) a constitutional amendment that outlawed the production and sale of alcoholic beverages in the United States; repealed in 1933 (p. 702)
  Decimoctava Enmienda (1919) enmienda constitucional que prohibió la producción y venta de bebidas alcohólicas en Estados Unidos; revocada en 1933 (pág. 702)

electoral college a group of people selected from each of the states to cast votes in presidential elections (p. 246)
  colegio electoral grupo de personas seleccionado en cada estado para votar en las elecciones presidenciales (pág. 246)

emancipation freeing of the slaves (p. 590)
  emancipación liberación de los esclavos (pág. 590)

Emancipation Proclamation (1862) an order issued by President Abraham Lincoln freeing the slaves in areas rebelling against the Union; took effect January 1, 1863 (p. 591)
  Proclamación de Emancipación (1862) orden emitida por el presidente Abraham Lincoln para liberar a los esclavos en las áreas que se rebelaban contra la Unión; entró en vigor el primero de enero de 1863 (pág. 591)

embargo the banning of trade with a country (p. 283)
  embargo prohibición del comercio con un país (pág. 283)

Embargo Act (1807) a law that prohibited American merchants from trading with other countries (p. 283)

Ley de Embargo (1807) ley que prohibía a los comerciantes norteamericanos comerciar con otros países (pág. 283)

eminent domain the government's power to take personal property to benefit the public (p. 226)
  derecho de expropiación poder otorgado al gobierno para tomar propiedades personales en beneficio del público (pág. 226)

empresarios agents who were contracted by the Mexican republic to bring settlers to Texas in the early 1800s (p. 393)
  empresarios agentes contratados por la República Mexicana para traer pobladores a Texas a principios del siglo XIX (pág. 393)

encomienda system a system in Spanish America that gave settlers the right to tax local Indians or to demand their labor in exchange for protecting them and converting them to Christianity (p. 51)
  sistema de encomienda sistema adoptado en la América española que permitía a los colonos cobrar impuestos a los indígenas o exigirles trabajo a cambio de su protección y de convertirlos al cristianismo (pág. 51)

Enforcement Acts (1870-1871) laws passed by Congress that made it a crime to interfere with elections or deny citizens equal protection under the law (p. 629)
  Actos de ejecución (1870-1871) leyes aprobadas por el Congreso que determinaron que era un crimen interferir con las elecciones o negar a los ciudadanos la igualdad ante la ley (pág. 629)

English Bill of Rights (1689) a shift of political power from the British monarchy to Parliament (p. 91)
  Declaración de Derechos inglesa (1689) cambio del poder político de la monarquía británica al Parlamento inglés (pág. 91)

Enlightenment the Age of Reason; movement that began in Europe in the 1700s as people began examining the natural world, society, and government (p. 95)
  Ilustración Era de la Razón; movimiento iniciado en Europa en el siglo XVIII cuando las personas empezaron a examinar la naturaleza, la sociedad y el gobierno (pág. 95)

English and Spanish Glossary

environment the climate and landscape that surrounds living things (p. 7)

medio ambiente clima y paisaje donde habitan seres vivos (pág. 7)

Equal Rights Amendment (ERA) a proposed amendment to the Constitution that would provide equal rights to women (p. 940)

Enmienda por la Igualdad de Derechos (ERA, por sus siglas en inglés) enmienda constitucional propuesta que otorgaría la igualdad de derechos a la mujer (pág. 940)

Era of Good Feelings a period of peace, pride, and progress for the United States from 1815 to 1825 (p. 302)

Era de los Buenos Sentimientos período de paz, orgullo y progreso en Estados Unidos de 1815 a 1825 (pág. 302)

Erie Canal the canal that runs from Albany to Buffalo, New York; completed in 1825 (p. 309)

canal de Erie canal que va de Albany a Buffalo, Nueva York; completado en 1825 (pág. 309)

escalation increased involvement in the Vietnam War (p. 903)

escalada mayor participación en la guerra de Vietnam (pág. 903)

executive branch the division of the federal government that includes the president and the administrative departments; enforces the nation's laws (pp. 167, 185)

poder ejecutivo división del gobierno federal que incluye al presidente y a los departamentos administrativos; hace cumplir las leyes de la nación (pág. 167, 185)

executive orders nonlegislative directives issued by the U.S. president in certain circumstances; executive orders have the force of congressional law (p. 192)

órdenes ejecutivas órdenes no legislativas dictadas por el presidente de Estados Unidos en circunstancias específicas; tienen la misma validez que las leyes del Congreso (pág. 192)

Exodusters African Americans who settled western lands in the late 1800s (p. 379)

Exodusters afroamericanos que se establecieron en el Oeste a fi nales del siglo XIX (pág. 379)

expatriates citizens who leave their country to live elsewhere (p. 793)

expatriados ciudadanos que abandonan su país para vivir en otro lugar (pág. 793)

F

factor a crop broker who managed the trade between southern planters and their customers (p. 457)

agente agrícola persona que administraba el comercio entre las plantaciones del Sur y sus clients (pág. 457)

Fair Deal President Truman's legislative plan for the nation that included antilynching laws (p. 875)

Fair Deal plan legislativo para la nación propuesto por el presidente Truman que incluía leyes en contra de los linchamientos (pág. 875)

fascism a political system in which the state or government is seen as more important than the individual (p. 830)

fascismo sistema político en el que se considera que el estado o gobierno es más importante que las personas (pág. 830)

federal system a system that divided powers between the states and the federal government (p. 188)

sistema federal sistema en el que se distribuye el poder entre los estados y el gobierno federal (pág. 188)

federalism U.S. system of government in which power is distributed between a central government and individual states (pp. 168, 185)

federalismo sistema de gobierno de Estados Unidos en el que el poder se divide entre una autoridad central y estados individuales (pág. 168, 185)

Federalist Papers a series of essays that defended and explained the Constitution and tried to reassure Americans that the states would not be overpowered by the proposed national government (pp. 171, 186)

Federalist Papers serie de ensayos que defendían y explicaban la Constitución para convencer a los estadounidenses de que el gobierno nacional propuesto no tendría más poder que los estados (pág. 171, 186)

Federalist Party a political party created in the 1790s and influenced by Alexander Hamilton that wanted to strengthen the federal government and promote industry and trade (p. 263)

Partido Federalista partido político creado en la década de 1790 e influenciado por las ideas de Alexander Hamilton para fortalecer al gobierno federal y fomentar la industria y el comercio (pág. 263)

Federalists people who supported ratification of the Constitution (pp. 170, 185)
federalistas personas que apoyaban la ratificación de la Constitución (pág. 170, 185)

Fifteenth Amendment (1870) a constitutional amendment that gave African American men the right to vote (p. 626)
Decimoquinta Enmienda (1870) enmienda constitucional que daba a los hombres afroamericanos el derecho al voto (pág. 626)

54th Massachusetts Infantry African American Civil War regiment that captured Fort Wagner in South Carolina (p. 593)
54to Batallón de Infantería de Massachusetts regimiento afroamericano de la Guerra Civil que tomó el fuerte Wagner en Carolina del Sur (pág. 593)

fireside chats radio programs in which Franklin Roosevelt explained his plan for recovery from the Great Depression (p. 810)
charlas junto a la chimenea programas de radio en los cuales Franklin Roosevelt explicaba su plan para que el país se recuperara de la Gran Depresión (pág. 810)

First Battle of Bull Run (1861) the first major battle of the Civil War, resulting in a Confederate victory; showed that the Civil War would not be won easily (p. 578)
primera batalla de Bull Run (1861) primera batalla importante de la Guerra Civil, en la cual ganó el ejército confederado; demostró que la guerra no se ganaría fácilmente (pág. 578)

First Continental Congress (1774) a meeting of colonial delegates in Philadelphia to decide how to respond to the closing of Boston Harbor, increased taxes, and abuses of authority by the British government; delegates petitioned King George III, listing the freedoms they believed colonists should enjoy (p. 113)

Primer Congreso Continental (1774) reunión de delegados de las colonias en Filadelfi a para decidir cómo responder al cierre del puerto de Boston, al alza de impuestos y a los abusos de la autoridad por parte del gobierno británico; los delegados hicieron peticiones al rey Jorge III, enumerando los derechos que consideraban justos para los colonos (pág. 113)

flappers young women who challenged traditional ideas of womanhood in the 1920s (p. 783)
flappers mujeres jóvenes que desafi aron las ideas tradicionales sobre la condición de la mujer en la década de 1920 (pág. 783)

folktale a story that often provides a moral lesson (pp. 466, 485)
cuento folclórico narración que con frecuencia ofrece una moraleja (pág. 466, 485)

Fort Sumter a federal outpost in Charleston, South Carolina, that was attacked by the Confederates in April 1861, sparking the Civil War (p. 570)
fuerte Sumter puesto de avanzada federal en Charleston, Carolina del Sur, cuyo ataque por parte de los confederados en abril de 1861 dio origen a la Guerra Civil (pág. 570)

forty-niner a gold-seeker who moved to California during the gold rush (p. 409)
del cuarenta y nueve buscador de oro que se mudó a California durante la fiebre del oro (pág. 409)

Fourteenth Amendment (1866) a constitutional amendment giving full rights of citizenship to all people born or naturalized in the United States, except for American Indians (p. 622)
Decimocuarta Enmienda (1866) enmienda constitucional que otorgaba derechos totales de ciudadanía a todas las personas nacidas en Estados Unidos o naturalizadas estadounidenses, con excepción de los indígenas americanos (pág. 622)

Freedmen's Bureau an agency established by Congress in 1865 to help poor people throughout the South (p. 617)
Oficina de los Libertos ofi cina creada por el Congreso en 1865 para ayudar a los pobres del Sur del país (pág. 617)

Freedom Rides a series of integrated bus rides through the South (p. 932)

Viajes de la Libertad serie de viajes en autobús por el Sur en los que se integraban las razas (pág. 932)

Freeport Doctrine (1858) a statement made by Stephen Douglas during the Lincoln-Douglas debates that pointed out how people could use popular sovereignty to determine if their state or territory should permit slavery (p. 557)

Doctrina de Freeport (1858) declaración hecha por Stephen Douglas durante los debates Lincoln-Douglas que señalaba que el pueblo podía usar la soberanía popular para decidir si su estado o territorio debía permitir la esclavitud (pág. 557)

Free-Soil Party a political party formed in 1848 by antislavery northerners who left the Whig and Democratic parties because neither addressed the slavery issue (pp. 497, 593)

Partido Tierra Libre partido político formado en 1848 por abolicionistas de los estados del Norte que habían abandonado el Partido Whig y el Partido Demócrata porque ninguno de los dos partidos tenía una postura sobre los esclavitud (pág. 497, 593)

French Revolution French rebellion that began in 1789 in which the French people overthrew the monarchy and made their country a republic (p. 255)

Revolución Francesa rebelión francesa iniciada en 1789 en la que la población francesa derrocó a la monarquía y convirtió el país en una república (pág. 255)

frontier an undeveloped area (p. 364)

frontera área que no está siendo utilizada por el ser humano (pág. 364)

Fugitive Slave Act (1850) a law that made it a crime to help runaway slaves; allowed for the arrest of escaped slaves in areas where slavery was illegal, and required their return to slaveholders (pp. 498, 545)

Ley de Esclavos Fugitivos (1850) ley que hacía que ayudar a un esclavo a escapar de su amo fuera un delito; permitía la captura de esclavos fugitivos en zonas donde la esclavitud era ilegal para devolverlos a sus dueños (pág. 498, 545)

fundamentalism a religious belief characterized by a literal interpretation of the Bible (p. 786)

fundamentalismo creencia religiosa caracterizada por una interpretación literal de la Biblia (pág. 786)

G

Gadsden Purchase (1853) U.S. purchase of land from Mexico that included the southern parts of present-day Arizona and New Mexico (p. 405)

Compra de Gadsden (1853) compra por parte del gobierno de Estados Unidos de territorio mexicano que incluía la región ocupada actualmente por el sur de Arizona y Nuevo México (pág. 405)

genocide the complete destruction of a racial or ethnic minority (p. 857)

genocidio destrucción total de una minoría racial o étnica (pág. 857)

Gettysburg Address (1863) a speech given by Abraham Lincoln in which he praised the bravery of Union soldiers and renewed his commitment to winning the Civil War (p. 602)

Discurso de Gettysburg (1863) discurso de Abraham Lincoln en el que alababa la valentía de las tropas de la Unión y renovaba su compromiso de triunfar en la Guerra Civil (pág. 602)

Ghost Dance a religious movement among Native Americans that spread across the Plains in the 1880s (p. 376)

Danza de los Espíritus movimiento religioso de los indígenas norteamericanos que se extendió por la región de las Planicies en la década de 1880 (pág. 376)

GI Bill of Rights (1944) a law that offered veterans money for school, houses, farms, and businesses (p. 873)

Declaración de Derechos de los Soldados (1944) ley que ofrecía a los veteranos de guerra dinero para su educación, vivienda, granjas y negocios (pág. 873)

Gibbons* v. *Ogden (1824) a Supreme Court ruling that reinforced the federal government's authority over the states (p. 437)

Gibbons contra *Ogden* (1824) decisión de la Corte Suprema que reforzó la autoridad del gobierno federal sobre los estados (pág. 437)

globalization the process in which the United States is becoming more interdependent with other nations (p. 986)
globalización proceso por el cual Estados Unidos empieza a tener más interdependencia con otras naciones (pág. 986)

global warming an environmental crisis in which the average temperature of the Earth is rising due to pollution (p. 997)
calentamiento global crisis del medio ambiente por la cual está aumentando la temperatura promedio de la Tierra debido a la contaminación (pág. 997)

Great Awakening a religious movement that became widespread in the American colonies in the 1730s and 1740s (p. 94)
Gran Despertar movimiento religioso que tuvo gran popularidad en las colonias norteamericanas en las décadas de 1730 y 1740 (pág. 94)

Great Compromise (1787) an agreement worked out at the Constitutional Convention establishing that a state's population would determine representation in the lower house of the legislature, while each state would have equal representation in the upper house of the legislature (pp. 166, 183)
Gran Compromiso (1787) acuerdo redactado durante la Convención Constitucional en el que se establece que la población de un estado debe determinar su representación en la cámara baja de la asamblea legislativa y que cada estado debe tener igual representación en la cámara alta de la asamblea (pág. 166, 183)

Great Depression a severe economic crisis that lasted for the entire decade of the 1930s (p. 805)
Gran Depresión grave crisis económica que duró toda la década de 1930 (pág. 805)

Great Migration a period of African American movement from the South to the North (p. 787)
Gran Migración período en que los afroamericanos del Sur se fueron a ciudades del Norte (pág. 787)

Great Society President Lyndon Johnson's legislative plan that included civil rights laws (p. 935)
Gran Sociedad plan legislativo del presidente Lyndon Johnson que incluía leyes a favor de los derechos civiles (pág. 935)

H

habeas corpus the constitutional protection against unlawful imprisonment (p. 595)
hábeas corpus protección constitucional contra el encarcelamiento ilegal (pág. 595)

hajj a pilgrimage to Mecca made by devout Muslims (p. 21)
hajj peregrinación a La Meca realizada por los musulmanes devotos (pág. 21)

Harlem Renaissance a period of artistic achievement during the 1920s (p. 792)
Renacimiento de Harlem período de logros artísticos durante la década de 1920 (pág. 792)

Hartford Convention (1815) a meeting of Federalists at Hartford, Connecticut, to protest the War of 1812 (p. 291)
Convención de Hartford (1815) reunión de federalistas en Hartford, Connecticut, para protestar por la Guerra de 1812 (pág. 291)

hawks supporters of the Vietnam War (p. 906)

halcones partidarios de la guerra de Vietnam (pág. 906) Haymarket Riot a riot that broke out at Haymarket Square in Chicago over the deaths of two strikers (p. 654)
Revuelta de Haymarket revuelta que se originó en la Plaza Haymarket de Chicago por la muerte de dos huelguistas (pág. 654)

hippies young people who rebelled against the mainstream culture of the 1960s (p. 911)
hippies jóvenes que se rebelaron contra la cultura convencional en la década de 1960 (pág. 911)

Ho Chi Minh Trail a series of jungle paths that allowed Communist forces to travel from North Vietnam to South Vietnam (p. 903)
Camino de Ho Chi Minh serie de caminos por la selva que permitía a las fuerzas comunistas ir desde Vietnam del Norte hacia Vietnam del Sur (pág. 903)

Holocaust a program of mass murder in which the Nazis tried to kill all Jews (p. 856)
Holocausto programa de asesinato en masa ideado por los nazis para exterminar a todos los judíos (pág. 856)

Homestead Act (1862) a law passed by Congress to encourage settlement in the West by giving government-owned land to small farmers (p. 378)

Ley de Heredad (1862) ley aprobada por el Congreso para fomentar la colonización del Oeste mediante la cesión de tierras del gobierno a pequeños agricultores (pág. 378)

Homestead strike (1892) a labor-union strike at Andrew Carnegie's Homestead Steel factory in Pennsylvania that erupted in violence between strikers and private detectives (p. 655)
huelga de Homestead (1892) huelga sindical en la fábrica de acero Homestead de Andrew Carnegie en Pensilvania, que produjo violencia entre huelguistas y detectives privados (pág. 655)

horizontal integration owning all the businesses in a certain field (p. 650)
integración horizontal posesión de todas las empresas en un campo específico (pág. 650)

Hudson River school a group of American artists in the mid-1800s whose paintings focused on the American landscape (p. 315)
Escuela del Río Hudson grupo de artistas estadounidenses de mediados del siglo XIX que pintaban diversos paisajes del territorio estadounidense (pág. 315)

Hull House a settlement house founded by Jane Addams and Ellen Gates Starr in 1889 (p. 677)
Casa Hull casa de asistencia a la comunidad fundada por Jane Addams y Ellen Gates Starr en 1889 (pág. 677)

human rights the basic rights of all people (p. 961)
derechos humanos derechos fundamentales de todas las personas (pág. 961)

hunter-gatherer a person who hunts animals and gathers wild plants to provide for his or her needs (p. 7)
cazador y recolector persona que caza animals y recolecta plantas para satisfacer sus necesidas (pág. 7)

hydrogen bomb a thermonuclear weapon that gets its power from splitting a hydrogen atom (p. 880)
bomba de hidrógeno arma termonuclear cuya potencia es generada por la división de un átomo de hidrógeno (pág. 880)

I

immigrant a person who moves to another country after leaving his or her homeland (p. 75)
inmigrante persona que abandona su país para establecerse en un país diferente (pág. 75)

immune having a natural resistance to disease (p. 476)
inmune la condición de tener resistencia natural contra la enfermedad (pág. 476)

impeach to bring charges against a public official (p. 191)
someter a juicio político presentar cargos en contra de un funcionario público (pág. 191)

impeachment the process used by a legislative body to bring charges of wrongdoing against a public official (p. 624)
juicio político proceso por el cual un cuerpo legislativo presenta cargos en contra de un funcionario público (pág. 624)

imperialism the practice of extending a nation's power by gaining territories for a colonial empire (p. 718)
imperialismo práctica en la que una nación amplía su poder adquiriendo territorios para un imperio colonial (pág. 718)

impressment the practice of forcing people to serve in the army or navy; led to increased tensions between Great Britain and the United States in the early 1800s (p. 282)
leva práctica que obligaba a las personas a servir en el ejército o la marina; aumentó las fricciones entre Gran Bretaña y Estados Unidos a principios del siglo XIX (pág. 282)

indentured servant a colonist who received free passage to North America in exchange for working without pay for a certain number of years (p. 70)
sirviente por contrato colono que recibía un pasaje gratuito a América del Norte a cambio de trabajar sin salario por varios años (pág. 70)

Indian Removal Act (1830) a congressional act that authorized the removal of Native Americans who lived east of the Mississippi River (p. 340)
Ley de Expulsión de Indígenas (1830) ley del Congreso que autorizaba la expulsión de los indígenas norteamericanos que vivían al este del río Mississippi (pág. 340)

Indian Territory an area covering most of present-day Oklahoma to which most Native Americans in the Southeast were forced to move in the 1830s (p. 340)

Territorio Indígena área que abarcaba la mayor parte del actual estado de Oklahoma a la que la mayoría de las tribus indígenas del sureste fueron obligadas a trasladarse durante la década de 1830 (pág. 340)

indict to formally accuse (p. 226)

acusar presentar cargos formales en contra de alguien (pág. 226)

Industrial Revolution a period of rapid growth in the use of machines in manufacturing and production that began in the mid-1700s (p. 424)

Revolución Industrial período de rápido desarrollo debido al uso de maquinaria en la fabricación y producción; comenzó a mediados del siglo XVIII (pág. 424)

Industrial Workers of the World (IWW) a union founded in 1905 by socialists and union leaders that included workers not welcomed in the AFL (p. 700)

Trabajadores Industriales del Mundo (IWW, por sus siglas en inglés) sindicato fundado en 1905 por socialistas y líderes sindicales que incluía a los trabajadores que no admitía la Federación Americana del Trabajo (pág. 700)

inflation increased prices for goods and services combined with the reduced value of money (p. 161)

inflación subida en los precios de los bienes al mismo tiempo que se reduce al valor del dinero (pág. 161)

Information Revolution an increase in the ability to share information between people and locations brought about by the Internet (p. 994)

Revolución de la Información aumento de la capacidad de compartir información entre personas y lugares producido por Internet (pág. 994)

initiative a method of allowing voters to propose a new law if enough signatures are collected on a petition (p. 692)

iniciativa método que permite a los votantes proponer una nueva ley si consiguen suficientes firmas para una petición (pág. 692)

interchangeable parts a process developed by Eli Whitney in the 1790s that called for making each part of a machine exactly the same (p. 426)

piezas intercambiables proceso desarrollado por Eli Whitney en la década de 1790 para que todas las piezas de una máquina fueran exactamente iguales (pág. 426)

interest group a group of people who share common interests for political action (p. 237)

grupo de interés grupo de personas que comparten intereses comunes en iniciativas políticas (pág. 237)

Internet a global system of computers that allows people across the world to communicate (p. 994)

Internet sistema global de computadoras que permite la comunicación entre personas de todo el mundo (pág. 994)

internment the imprisonment of Japanese Americans in special camps during World War II (p. 841)

internamiento encarcelamiento de japonesesamericanos en campos especiales durante la Segunda Guerra Mundial (pág. 841)

interstate commerce trade between two or more states (p. 160)

comercio interestatal intercambio comercial entre dos o más estados (pág. 160)

Intolerable Acts (1774) laws passed by Parliament to punish the colonists for the Boston Tea Party and to tighten government control of the colonies (p. 112)

Leyes Intolerables (1774) serie de leyes aprobadas por el Parlamento para castigar a los colonos que participaron en el Motín del Té de Boston y para aumentar su control sobre las colonias (pág. 112)

Iran-Contra affair a scandal during the Reagan administration in which government officials were accused of selling weapons to Iran and passing the profits to a revolutionary group known as the Contras (p. 968)

asunto Irán-Contras escándalo durante el gobierno de Reagan en el cual funcionarios del gobierno fueron acusados de vender armas a Irán y de entregar las ganancias a un grupo revolucionario conocido como los contras (pág. 968)

English and Spanish Glossary

Iran hostage crisis a crisis in which Americans were taken hostage by militants in Iran and held for over a year (p. 963)
crisis de los rehenes de Irán crisis en la cual varios estadounidenses fueron tomados como rehenes por militantes iraníes durante más de un año (pág. 963)

ironclad a warship that is heavily armored with iron (p. 582)
acorazado buque de guerra fuertemente protegido con hierro (pág. 582)

Iroquois League a political confederation of five northeastern Native American nations of the Seneca, Oneida, Mohawk, Cayuga, and Onondaga that made decisions concerning war and peace (p. 15)
Liga de Iroqueses confederación política formada por cinco naciones indígenas del noreste de Estados Unidos (los senecas, los oneidas, los mohawks, los cayugas y los onondagas) para tomar decisions relacionadas con asuntos de guerra y paz (pág. 15)

island-hopping the strategy used by U.S. forces in the Pacific during World War II that involved taking only strategically important islands (p. 851)
saltar de isla en isla estrategia de las fuerzas de Estados Unidos en el Pacífico durante la Segunda Guerra Mundial que consistía en tomar sólo las islas importantes desde el punto de vista estratégico (pág. 851)

isolationism a national policy of avoiding involvement in other countries' affairs (p. 718)
aislacionismo política nacional de evitar involucrarse en los asuntos de otras naciones (pág. 718)

J

Jacksonian Democracy an expansion of voting rights during the popular Andrew Jackson administration (p. 330)
democracia jacksoniana ampliación del derecho al voto durante el popular gobierno del president Andrew Jackson (pág. 330)

Jamestown the first colony in the U.S.; set up in 1607 along the James River in Virginia (p. 68)
Jamestown primera colonia en territorio estadounidense; fundada en 1607 a orillas del río James en Virginia (pág. 68)

Jay's Treaty (1794) an agreement negotiated by John Jay to work out problems between Britain and the United States over northwestern lands, British seizure of U.S. ships, and U.S. debts owed to the British (p. 257)
Tratado de Jay (1794) acuerdo negociado por John Jay para resolver los problemas entre Gran Bretaña y Estados Unidos por los territorios del noroeste, la confiscación británica de barcos estadounidenses, y las deudas que los estadounidenses les debían a los británicos (pág. 257)

Jazz Age a name for the decade of the 1920s based on the popularity of jazz music (p. 791)
Era del Jazz nombre que se le dio a la década de 1920 por la popularidad de la música de jazz (pág. 791)

Jim Crow law a law that enforced segregation in the southern states (p. 631)
ley de Jim Crow ley que imponía la segregación en los estados del Sur (pág. 631)

John Brown's raid (1859) an incident in which abolitionist John Brown and 21 other men captured a federal arsenal in Harpers Ferry, Virginia, in hope of starting a slave rebellion (p. 558)
ataque de John Brown (1859) incidente en el que el abolicionista John Brown y otros 21 hombres capturaron un arsenal federal en Harpers Ferry, Virginia, con la esperanza de iniciar una rebelión de esclavos (pág. 558)

joint-stock company a business formed by a group of people who jointly make an investment and share in the profits and losses (p. 28)
sociedad por acciones negocio formado por un grupo de personas que hacen una inversión juntos y comparten las ganancias y las pérdidas (pág. 28)

judicial branch the division of the federal government that is made up of the national courts; interprets laws, punishes criminals, and settles disputes between states (pp. 167, 185)
poder judicial división del gobierno federal formada por las cortes nacionales; interpreta las leyes, castiga a los delincuentes y resuelve las disputas entre estados (pág. 167, 185)

judicial review the Supreme Court's power to declare acts of Congress unconstitutional (p. 274) recurso de inconstitucionalidad (revision judicial) poder de la Corte Suprema para declarer inconstitucionales las leyes del Congreso (pág. 274)

Judiciary Act of 1789 legislation passed by Congress that created the federal court system (p. 248)

Ley de Judicatura de 1789 ley aprobada por el Congreso para crear el sistema federal de cortes (pág. 248)

K

kamikaze Japanese pilots who flew suicide missions during World War II (p. 854)

kamikaze piloto japonés que volaba en misiones suicidas durante la Segunda Guerra Mundial (pág. 854)

Kansas-Nebraska Act (1854) a law that allowed voters in Kansas and Nebraska to choose whether to allow slavery (p. 549)

Ley de Kansas y Nebraska (1854) ley que permitía a los votantes de Kansas y Nebraska decidir si permitían la esclavitud (pág. 549)

Kellogg-Briand Pact an agreement between nations proposing peaceful solutions to conflicts, signed after World War I (p. 778)

Pacto Kellogg-Briand acuerdo fi rmado entre naciones luego de la Primera Guerra Mundial que proponía soluciones pacíficas a los conflictos (pág. 778)

Kentucky and Virginia Resolutions (1798–1799) Republican documents that argued that the Alien and Sedition Acts were unconstitutional (p. 267)

Resoluciones de Kentucky y Virginia (1798–1799) documentos republicanos que argumentaban que las Leyes de No Intervención Extranjera y Sedición eran inconstitucionales (pág. 267)

Kitchen Cabinet Pres. Andrew Jackson's group of informal advisers; so called because they often met in the White House kitchen (p. 332)

gabinete de la cocina grupo informal de consejeros del presidente Andrew Jackson; llamado así porque solían reunirse en la cocina de la Casa Blanca (pág. 332)

kivas underground ceremonial chambers at the center of Anasazi communities (p. 12)

kivas cámaras ceremoniales subterráneas en el centro de las comunidades anasazi (pág. 12)

knights warriors who fought on horseback in return for land from nobles (p. 25)

caballeros guerreros que luchaban a caballo a cambio de tierras de los nobles (pág. 25)

Knights of Labor secret society that became the first truly national labor union in the United States (p. 653)

Caballeros del Trabajo sociedad secreta que se convirtió en el primer sindicato verdaderamente nacional en Estados Unidos (pág. 653)

Know-Nothing Party a political organization founded in 1849 by nativists who supported measures making it difficult for foreigners to become citizens and to hold office (p. 510)

Partido de los Ignorantes organización política fundada en 1849 por un grupo de nativistas; apoyaba medidas que dificultaban que los extranjeros obtuvieran la ciudadanía y que tuvieran cargos públicos (pág. 510)

Ku Klux Klan a secret society created by white southerners in 1866 that used terror and violence to keep African Americans from obtaining their civil rights (p. 629)

Ku Klux Klan sociedad secreta creada en 1866 por blancos del Sur que usaba el terror y la violencia para impedir que los afroamericanos obtuvieran derechos civiles (pág. 629)

L

Land Ordinance of 1785 legislation passed by Congress authorizing surveys and the division of public lands in the western region of the country (p. 155)

Ordenanza de Territorios de 1785 legislación aprobada por el Congreso en la que se autorizaban las mediciones de terreno y la división de territories públicos en el oeste del país (pág. 155)

League of Nations a coalition of governments designed to find peaceful solutions to disagreements, proposed by Woodrow Wilson (p. 765)

Liga de las Naciones coalición de gobiernos propuesta por Woodrow Wilson y diseñada para buscar soluciones pacíficas a los desacuerdos (pág. 765)

English and Spanish Glossary

legislative branch the division of the government that proposes bills and passes them into laws (pp. 167, 185)
    poder legislativo división del gobierno que propone proyectos de ley y los aprueba para convertirlos en leyes (pág. 167, 185)

Lend-Lease Act (1941) a law giving Franklin Roosevelt the power to sell, transfer, exchange, or lease military equipment to any country to help it defend itself against the Axis powers (p. 834)
    Ley de Préstamo y Arriendo (1941) ley que dio a Franklin Roosevelt el poder de vender, transferir, intercambiar o arrendar equipo militar a cualquier país para la defensa contra las potencias del Eje (pág. 834)

Lewis and Clark expedition an expedition led by Meriwether Lewis and William Clark that began in 1804 to explore the Louisiana Purchase (p. 356)
    expedición de Lewis y Clark expedición encabezada por Meriwether Lewis y William Clark que empezó en 1804 para explorar la Compra de Luisiana (pág. 356)

Liberty bonds loans to the government that aided its ability to prepare for World War I (p. 753)
    bonos de la Libertad préstamos hechos al gobierno que le permitieron prepararse para la Primera Guerra Mundial (pág. 753)

Lincoln-Douglas debates a series of debates between Republican Abraham Lincoln and Democrat Stephen Douglas during the 1858 U.S. Senate campaign in Illinois (p. 555)
    debates Lincoln-Douglas serie de debates entre el republicano Abraham Lincoln y el demócrata Stephen Douglas durante la campaña de 1858 para el Senado estadounidense en Illinois (pág. 555)

Line of Demarcation boundary between Spanish and Portuguese territories in the New World (p. 43)
    Línea de Demarcación límite entre los territorios españoles y portugueses en el Nuevo Mundo (pág. 43)

Little Rock Nine a group of nine African American students who began the integration of the Little Rock, Arkansas, public school system (p. 925)

los nueve de Little Rock grupo de nueve estudiantes afroamericanos que empezaron la integración del sistema de escuelas públicas de Little Rock, Arkansas (pág. 925)

Long Walk (1864) a 300-mile march made by Navajo captives to a reservation in Bosque Redondo, New Mexico, that led to the deaths of hundreds of Navajo (p. 375)
    Larga Marcha (1864) caminata de 300 millas que hizo un grupo de prisioneros navajos hasta una reserva indígena en Bosque Redondo, Nuevo México, en la que murieron cientos de ellos (pág. 375)

loose construction a way of interpreting the Constitution that allows the federal government to take actions that the Constitution does not specifically forbid it from taking (p. 254)
    interpretación flexible interpretación de la Constitución que permite al gobierno federal tomar acciones que la Constitución no prohíbe de manera específica (pág. 254)

Lost Generation the generation of young people who fought in World War I and eventually became disillusioned with the promise of American society (p. 793)
    generación perdida generación de jóvenes que lucharon en la Primera Guerra Mundial y terminaron desilusionados con las promesas de la sociedad estadounidense (pág. 793)

Louisiana Purchase (1803) the purchase of French land between the Mississippi River and the Rocky Mountains that doubled the size of the United States (pp. 271, 356)
    Compra de Luisiana (1803) adquisición del territorio francés localizado entre el río Mississippi y las montañas Rocallosas que duplicó el tamaño de Estados Unidos (pág. 271, 356)

Lowell system the use of waterpowered textile mills that employed young, unmarried women in the 1800s (p. 431)
    sistema de Lowell uso de molinos de agua en la industria textil, dando empleo a muchas mujeres jóvenes solteras en el siglo XIX (pág. 431)

Loyalists colonists who sided with Britain in the American Revolution (p. 120)
    leales colonos que apoyaron la causa británica durante la Guerra de Independencia estadounidense (pág. 120)

Lusitania a passenger ship bombed by Germany (p. 751)
Lusitania barco de pasajeros bombardeado por Alemania (pág. 751)

M

Magna Carta (1215) a charter of liberties agreed to by King John of England, it made the king obey the same laws as citizens (p. 152)
Carta Magna (1215) carta de libertades firmada por el rey Juan de Inglaterra que decía que el rey debía obedecer las mismas leyes que los ciudadanos (pág. 152)

majority rule the idea that policies are decided by the greatest number of people (p. 223)
gobierno de la mayoría idea de que las políticas se adoptan según lo que decida el mayor número de personas (pág. 223)

Manhattan Project the U.S. effort to build an atomic bomb (p. 858)
Proyecto Manhattan plan de Estados Unidos de fabricar una bomba atómica (pág. 858)

manifest destiny a belief shared by many Americans in the mid-1800s that the United States should expand across the continent to the Pacific Ocean (p. 397)
destino manifiesto creencia de muchos ciudadanos estadounidenses a mediados del siglo XIX de que Estados Unidos debía expandirse por todo el continente hasta el océano Pacífico (pág. 397)

Marbury v. Madison (1803) U.S. Supreme Court case that established the principle of judicial review (p. 273)
Marbury contra *Madison* (1803) caso de la Corte Suprema de Estados Unidos que estableció recurso de inconstitucionalidad (pág. 273)

March on Washington a huge demonstration organized by Martin Luther King Jr. to protest racial discrimination (p. 934)
Marcha en Washington manifestación enorme organizada por Martin Luther King, Jr. en protesta por la discriminación racial (pág. 934)

Marshall Plan the idea that the U.S. could help rebuild wartorn Europe with loans and other economic aid (p. 871)

Plan Marshall idea de que Estados Unidos podía contribuir con préstamos y otros tipos de ayuda económica a la reconstrucción de la Europa devastada por la guerra (pág. 871)

Massacre at Wounded Knee (1890) the U.S. Army's killing of approximately 150 Sioux at Wounded Knee Creek in South Dakota; ended U.S-Indian wars on the Plains (p. 375)
masacre de Wounded Knee (1890) matanza de aproximadamente 150 indios siux en Wounded Knee Creek, Dakota del Sur; dio por terminadas las guerras entre estadounidenses e indígenas en las Planicies (pág. 375)

mass culture leisure and cultural activities shared by many people (p. 672)
cultura de masas actividades culturales y del tiempo libre que les gustan a muchas personas (pág. 672)

mass production the efficient production of large numbers of identical goods (p. 427)
producción en masa producción eficiente de grandes cantidades de productos idénticos (pág. 427)

mass transit public transportation (p. 671)
transporte colectivo transporte público (pág. 671)

matrilineal related to ancestry traced through the maternal, or mother's, line (p. 15)
materno basado en linaje seguido por línea materna, o de la madre (pág. 15)

Mayflower Compact (1620) a document written by the Pilgrims establishing themselves as a political society and setting guidelines for self-government (p. 76)
Pacto del Mayflower (1620) documento redactado por los peregrinos en el que se establecían como sociedad política y establecían principios para gobernarse a sí mismos (pág. 76)

McCulloch v. Maryland (1819) U.S. Supreme Court case that declared the Second Bank of the United States was constitutional and that Maryland could not interfere with it (p. 337)
McCulloch contra *Maryland* (1819) caso de la Corte Suprema de Estados Unidos que declaraba que el Segundo Banco de la Nación era constitucional y que Maryland no podía intervenir en sus operaciones (pág. 337)

English and Spanish Glossary

Medicare a federal program, established in 1965, that provides hospital insurance and low-cost medical insurance to Americans aged 65 and over (p. 1000)
Medicare un programa federal, establecido en 1965, que ofrece seguro de hospital y seguro médico de bajo costo para los estadounidenses de 65 años y mayores (pág. 1000)

mercenaries hired foreign soldiers (p. 131)
mercenarios soldados extranjeros a sueldo (pág. 131)

Mexican Revolution a revolution led by Francisco Madero in 1910 that eventually forced the Mexican dictator Díaz to resign (p. 737)
Revolución Mexicana revolución iniciada en 1910 por Francisco Madero, que finalmente obligó al dictador mexicano Díaz a renunciar (pág. 737)

middle class the social and economic level between the wealthy and the poor (p. 511)
clase media nivel social y económico ubicado entre la clase rica y la clase pobre (pág. 511)

Middle Passage a voyage that brought enslaved Africans across the Atlantic Ocean to North America and the West Indies (p. 477)
Viaje Intermedio viaje a través del océano Atlántico para transportar esclavos africanos a América del Norte y a las Antillas (pág. 477)

migration the movement of people from one region to another (p. 7)
migración movimiento de personas de una región a otra (pág. 7)

militarism an increase in the importance of the military of a country (p. 747)
militarismo aumento de la importancia del ejército de un país (pág. 747)

minutemen American colonial militia members ready to fight at a minute's notice (p. 115)
minutemen milicanos norteamericanos en la época colonial que estaban preparados para combater en cualquier momento si la situación lo requería (pág. 115)

Missouri Compromise (1820) an agreement proposed by Henry Clay that allowed Missouri to enter the Union as a slave state and Maine to enter as a free state and outlawed slavery in any territories or states north of 36°30´ latitude (p. 310)

Compromiso de Missouri (1820) acuerdo propuesto por Henry Clay en el que se aceptaba a Missouri en la Unión como estado esclavista y a Maine como estado libre, además de prohibir la esclavitud en los territorios o estados al norte del paralelo 36°30´ (pág. 310)

mobilize to prepare for war (p. 747)
mobilizarse prepararse para la guerra (pág. 747)

Model T Henry Ford's automobile designed with the average American in mind (p. 778)
modelo T automóvil de Henry Ford diseñado para el estadounidense promedio (pág. 778)

monopoly a complete control over the entire supply of goods or a service in a particular market (p. 650)
monopolio control absoluto de toda la oferta de bienes o de un servicio en un mercado en particular (pág. 650)

Monroe Doctrine (1823) President James Monroe's statement forbidding further colonization in the Americas and declaring that any attempt by a foreign country to colonize would be considered an act of hostility (p. 304)
Doctrina Monroe (1823) declaración hecha por el presidente James Monroe en la que se prohibía la colonización adicional de las Américas y se declaraba que cualquier intento de colonización por parte de otro país se consideraría un acto hostil (pág. 304)

Montgomery bus boycott a boycott of the Montgomery, Alabama, public bus system to protest its policy of segregation (p. 928)
boicot a los autobuses de Montgomery boicot al sistema público de autobuses de Montgomery, Alabama, en protesta por su política de segregación (pág. 928)

Mormon a member of the Church of Jesus Christ of Latter-day Saints (p. 360)
mormón miembro de la Iglesia de Jesucristo de los Santos de los Últimos Días (pág. 360)

Morrill Act (1862) a federal law passed by Congress that gave land to western states to encourage them to build colleges (p. 378)
Ley de Morrill (1862) ley federal aprobada por el Congreso que otorgaba tierras a los estados del Oeste para fomentar la construcción de universidades (pág. 378)

Morse code a system developed by Alfred Lewis Vail for the telegraph that used a certain combination of dots and dashes to represent each letter of the alphabet (p. 441)
clave Morse sistema desarrollado por Alfred Lewis Vail para el telégrafo en el que una combinación de puntos y rayas representa cada letra del alfabeto (pág. 441)

mosques buildings used for Muslim prayer (p. 21)
mezquitas casas de oración musulmanas (pág. 21)

mountain men men hired by eastern companies to trap animals for fur in the Rocky Mountains and other western regions of the United States (p. 358)
montañeses hombres contratados por compañías del este para atrapar animales y obtener sus pieles en las montañas Rocallosas y en otras regiones del oeste de Estados Unidos (pág. 358)

moving assembly line an innovation of Henry Ford's that dramatically reduced the cost of production (p. 778)
cadena de montaje móvil innovación de Henry Ford que redujo signifi cativamente el costo de producción (pág. 778)

muckrakers a term coined for journalists who "raked up" and exposed corruption and problems of society (p. 689)
muckrakers término acuñado para nombrar a los periodistas que se dedicaban a investigar y exponer la corrupción y los problemas de la sociedad (pág. 689)

N

National American Woman Suffrage Association (NAWSA) an organization founded by Elizabeth Cady Stanton and Susan B. Anthony in 1890 to obtain women's right to vote (p. 702)
Asociación Nacional Americana para el Sufragio Femenino (NAWSA, por sus siglas en inglés) organización fundada en 1890 por Elizabeth Cady Stanton y Susan B. Anthony para obtener el derecho al voto de las mujeres (pág. 702)

National Association for the Advancement of Colored People (NAACP) an organization founded in 1909 by W.E.B. Du Bois and other reformers to bring attention to racial inequality (p. 705)
Asociación Nacional para el Progreso de la Gente de Color (NAACP, por sus siglas en inglés) organización fundada en 1909 por W.E.B. Du Bois y otros reformadores para llamar la atención sobre la desigualdad racial (pág. 705)

national debt the total amount of money owed by a country to its lenders (p. 250)
deuda nacional cantidad total de dinero que un país debe a quienes se lo prestaron (pág. 250)

National Grange a social and educational organization for farmers (p. 382)
National Grange organización social y educativa para los agricultores (pág. 382)

nationalism a sense of pride and devotion to a nation (p. 302)
nacionalismo sentimiento de orgullo y lealtad a una nación (pág. 302)

National Organization for Women (NOW) a group that organized to promote the interests of women (p. 939)
Organización Nacional de la Mujer (NOW, por sus siglas en inglés) grupo organizado para promover los intereses de la mujer (pág. 939)

National War Labor Board a government agency organized to help settle disputes between workers and employers in war industries (p. 755)
Junta Nacional del Trabajo en Tiempos de Guerra agencia del gobierno destinada a resolver disputas entre trabajadores y empleadores en las industrias relacionadas con la guerra (pág. 755)

nativists U.S. citizens who opposed immigration because they were suspicious of immigrants and feared losing jobs to them (p. 510)
nativistas ciudadanos estadounidenses que se oponían a la inmigración porque sospechaban de los inmigrantes y temían que se apropiaran de sus empleos (pág. 510)

Nat Turner's Rebellion (1831) a rebellion in which Nat Turner led a group of slaves in Virginia in an unsuccessful attempt to overthrow and kill planter families (p. 487)

English and Spanish Glossary

Rebelión de Nat Turner (1831) rebelión de un grupo de esclavos encabezados por Nat Turner en Virginia en un intento frustrado de derrocar y asesinar familias que eran dueñas de plantaciones (pág. 487)

naturalized citizen a person born in another country who has been granted citizenship in the United States (p. 234)
ciudadano naturalizado persona nacida en otro país que ha obtenido la ciudadanía estadounidense (pág. 234)

Nazis the National Socialist Party of Germany, headed by Adolf Hitler (p. 831)
nazis Partido Nacional de Alemania liderado por Adolf Hitler (pág. 831)

Neutrality Proclamation (1793) a statement made by President George Washington that the United States would not side with any of the nations at war in Europe following the French Revolution (p. 256)
Proclamación de Neutralidad (1793) declaración en la que el presidente George Washington anunció que Estados Unidos no sería aliado de ninguna de las naciones europeas en guerra después de la Revolución Francesa (pág. 256)

New Deal Franklin Roosevelt's legislative plan to end the Great Depression that included dramatic reforms of government agencies and powers (p. 809)
New Deal (Nuveo Trato) plan legislativo de Franklin Roosevelt para poner fin a la Gran Depresión; incluía profundas reformas en las agencias y poderes del gobierno (pág. 809)

new immigrant a term often used for an immigrant who arrived in the United States beginning in the 1880s (p. 664)
nuevo inmigrante término empleado a menudo para referirse a los inmigrantes que llegaron a Estados Unidos a partir de la década de 1880 (pág. 664)

New Jersey Plan a proposal to create a unicameral legislature with equal representation of states rather than representation by population; rejected at the Constitutional Convention (pp. 166, 183)
Plan de Nueva Jersey propuesta para la creación de un gobierno de una cámara con la misma representación para cada estado sin importer el tamaño de su población; fue rechazada en la Convención Constitucional (pág. 166, 183)

Nineteenth Amendment (1920) a constitutional amendment that gave women the vote (p. 703)
Decimonovena Enmienda (1920) enmienda constitucional que dio a la mujer el derecho al voto (pág. 703)

nominating conventions a meeting at which a political party selects its presidential and vice presidential candidate; first held in the 1820s (p. 330)
convenciones de nominación reunión en la que un partido político elige a sus candidatos a la presidencia y la vicepresidencia; se realizaron por primera vez en la década de 1820 (pág. 330)

Non-Intercourse Act (1809) a law that replaced the Embargo Act and restored trade with all nations except Britain, France, and their colonies (p. 284)
Ley de No Interacción (1809) ley que reemplazaba a la Ley de Embargo, restableciendo el comercio con todas las naciones, excepto Gran Bretaña, Francia y sus colonias (pág. 284)

North American Free Trade Agreement (NAFTA) a treaty that eliminated trade barriers between Canada, the United States, and Mexico (p. 972)
Tratado de Libre Comercio de América del Norte (TLCAN o NAFTA) tratado que eliminó las barreras comerciales entre Canadá, Estados Unidos y México (pág. 972)

North Atlantic Treaty Organization (NATO) an alliance of Western powers (p. 872)
Organización del Tratado del Atlántico Norte (OTAN) alianza de potencias occidentales (pág. 872)

Northwest Ordinance of 1787 legislation passed by Congress to establish a political structure for the Northwest Territory and create a system for the admission of new states (p. 155)
Ordenanza del Noroeste de 1787 legislación aprobada por el Congreso para establecer una estructura política en el Territorio del Noroeste y crear un proceso de admisión de nuevos estados (pág. 155)

Northwest Passage a nonexistent path through North America that early explorers searched for that would allow ships to sail from the Atlantic to the Pacific Ocean (p. 55)

Paso del Noroeste ruta inexistente buscada po muchos exploradores a lo largo de América del Norte para cruzar en barco del océano Atlántico al océano Pacífico (pág. 55)

Northwest Territory lands including present-day Illinois, Indiana, Michigan, Ohio, and Wisconsin; organized by the Northwest Ordinance of 1787 (p. 155)
Territorio del Noroeste región que incluía los actuals estados de Illinois, Indiana, Michigan, Ohio y Wisconsin; creado por la Ordenanza del Noroeste de 1787 (pág. 155)

nullification crisis a dispute led by John C. Calhoun that said that states could ignore federal laws if they believed those laws violated the Constitution (p. 335)
crisis de anulación controversia iniciada por John C. Calhoun que decía que los estados no tenían que hacer caso a las leyes federales si consideraban que desobedecían la Constitución (pág. 335)

Nuremberg trials the war crimes trials of Nazi leaders (p. 869)
juicios de Nuremberg juicios de los crímenes de guerra de los líderes Nazis (pág. 869)

O

old immigrant a term often used for an immigrant who arrived in the United States before the 1880s (p. 664)
antiguo inmigrante término empleado con frecuencia para referirse a los inmigrantes que llegaron a Estados Unidos antes de la década de 1880 (pág. 664)

Open Door Policy a policy established by the United States in 1899 to promote equal access for all nations to trade in China (p. 722)
política de puertas abiertas política establecida por Estados Unidos en 1899 para promover el acceso igualitario de todas las naciones al comercio con China (pág. 722)

Operation Desert Storm the military effort to free Kuwait from Saddam Hussein's invasion (p. 970)
Operación Tormenta del Desierto acción militar para liberar a Kuwait de la invasión de Saddam Hussein (pág. 970)

oral tradition passing down stories, poems, and songs by word of mouth (p. 466)

tradición oral transmitir verbalmente relatos, poemas y canciones de generación en generación (pág. 466)

Oregon Trail a 2,000-mile trail stretching through the Great Plains from western Missouri to the Oregon Territory (p. 359)
Camino de Oregón ruta de 2,000 millas que cruzaba las Grandes Planicies desde el oeste de Missouri hasta el Territorio de Oregón (pág. 359)

Organization of Petroleum Exporting Countries (OPEC) an alliance of oil rich countries that coordinates oil policies (p. 951)
Organización de Países Exportadores de Petróleo (OPEP) alianza de países ricos en petróleo que coordina las políticas petroleras (pág. 951)

overseer men hired by farmers and planters to oversee and direct the work of slaves on plantations (p. 464)
capataz hombres contratados por los agricultores y plantadores de supervisar y dirigir el trabajo de los esclavos en las plantaciones (pág. 464)

ozone layer a level of the Earth's atmosphere that is being depleted by pollution (p. 996)
capa de ozono nivel de la atmósfera de la Tierra que se está desgastando debido a la contaminación (pág. 996)

P

Paleo-Indians the first Americans who crossed from Asia into North America sometime between 38,000 and 10,000 BC (p. 7)
paleoindígenas primeros habitantes de América que cruzaron de Asia a América del Norte entre 38,000 y 10,000 a. C. (pág. 7)

Panama Canal an artificial waterway across the Isthmus of Panama; completed by the United States in 1914 (p. 733)
canal de Panamá canal artificial que atraviesa el istmo de Panamá; Estados Unidos completó su construcción en 1914 (pág. 733)

Panic of 1837 a financial crisis in the United States that led to an economic depression (p. 339)
Pánico de 1837 crisis financiera en Estados Unidos que provocó una depresión económica (pág. 339)

pardon freedom from punishment (pp. 192, 955)

indulto liberación de un castigo (pág. 192, 955)

patent an exclusive right to make or sell an invention (p. 645)

patente derecho exclusivo para fabricar o vender un invento (pág. 645)

Patient Protection and Affordable Care Act (PPACA) a law, passed in 2010, that required that health coverage be available to all Americans; it also specified that all individuals were required to get some level of health coverage (p. 991)

Ley de Protección al Paciente y Cuidado de Salud Asequible (PPACA) una ley, aprobada en 2010, que requiere que la cobertura de salud esté disponible para todos los estadounidenses; también especifica que todos los individuos deben tener un cierto nivel de cobertura de salud (pág. 991)

Patriots American colonists who fought for independence from Great Britain during the Revolutionary War (p. 114)

patriotas colonos que lucharon para independizarse de Gran Bretaña durante la Guerra de Independencia estadounidense (pág. 114)

Peace Corps a nonmilitary aid program introduced by John Kennedy (p. 894)

Cuerpos de Paz programa de ayuda no military introducido por John Kennedy (pág. 894)

Pearl Harbor a harbor in Hawaii that serves as the base of the U.S. Pacific fleet and was bombed in 1941 by Japan (p. 835)

Pearl Harbor puerto de Hawai que es la base de la flota del Pacífico de Estados Unidos; fue bombardeado por Japón en 1941 (pág. 835)

Pentagon the headquarters of the U.S. military, located outside of Washington, DC (p. 984)

Pentágono sede central del ejército de Estados Unidos, ubicado en las afueras de Washington, DC (pág. 984)

petition to make a formal request of the government (p. 225)

peticionar hacer una solicitud formal al gobierno (pág. 225)

Pickett's Charge (1863) a failed Confederate attack during the Civil War led by General George Pickett at the Battle of Gettysburg (p. 601)

ataque de Pickett (1863) ataque fallido del ejército confederado, al mando del general George Pickett, en la batalla de Gettysburg durante la Guerra Civil (pág. 601)

Pilgrim a member of a Puritan Separatist sect that left England in the early 1600s to settle in the Americas (p. 75)

peregrino miembro de una secta separatista puritan que se fue de Inglaterra a principios del siglo XVII para establecerse en América (pág. 75)

Pinckney's Treaty (1795) an agreement between the United States and Spain that changed Florida's border and made it easier for American ships to use the port of New Orleans (p. 257)

Tratado de Pinckney (1795) acuerdo entre Estados Unidos y España que modificó los límites de Florida y facilitó a los barcos estadounidenses el uso del Puerto de Nueva Orleáns (pág. 257)

placer miner a person who mines for gold by using pans or other devices to wash gold nuggets out of loose rock and gravel (p. 410)

buscador de oro con batea persona que busca oro con bateas u otros aparatos similares para lavar las pepitas de oro y separarlas de las piedras y la gravilla (pág. 410)

plantation a large farm that usually specialized in growing one kind of crop for profit (p. 52)

plantación gran finca que por lo general se especializaba en un cultivo específico para obtener ganancias (pág. 52)

planter a large-scale farmer who held more than 20 slaves (p. 454)

hacendado agricultor a gran escala que tenía más de 20 esclavos (pág. 454)

Platt Amendment a part of the Cuban constitution drafted under the supervision of the United States that limited Cuba's right to make treaties, gave the U.S. the right to intervene in Cuban affairs, and required Cuba to sell or lease land to the U.S. (p. 728)

Enmienda Platt parte de la constitución cubana redactada bajo la supervisión de Estados Unidos que limitaba el derecho de Cuba a fi rmar tratados, le daba a Estados Unidos el derecho de intervenir en los asuntos cubanos y le exigía a Cuba vender o arrendar tierras a Estados Unidos (pág. 728)

Plessy v. Ferguson (1896) U.S. Supreme Court case that established the "separate-but-equal" doctrine for public facilities (p. 631)
Plessy contra *Ferguson* (1896) caso en el que la Corte Suprema de Estados Unidos estableció la doctrina de "separados pero iguales" en los lugares públicos (pág. 631)

political action committee (PAC) an organization that collects money to distribute to candidates who support the same issues as the contributors (p. 237)
comité de acción política (PAC, por sus siglas en inglés) organización que recolecta dinero para distribuirlo a los candidatos que apoyen los mismos asuntos que los contribuyentes (pág. 237)

political machine a powerful organization that influenced city and county politics in the late 1800s (p. 686)
maquinaria política organización poderosa que influía en la política municipal y del condado a finales del siglo XIX (pág. 686)

political party a group of people who organize to help elect government officials and influence government policies (p. 263)
partido político grupo de personas que se organiza para facilitar la elección de los funcionarios del gobierno e influye en las políticas del gobierno (pág. 263)

poll tax a special tax that a person had to pay in order to vote (p. 631)
impuesto electoral impuesto especial que tenía que pagar una persona para poder votar (pág. 631)

Pony Express a system of messengers that carried mail between relay stations on a route 2,000 miles long in 1860 and 1861 (p. 367)
Pony Express sistema de mensajeros que llevaban el correo entre estaciones de relevo a lo largo de una ruta de 2,000 millas en 1860 y 1861 (pág. 367)

popular sovereignty the idea that political authority belongs to the people (pp. 185, 542)
soberanía popular idea de que la autoridad política pertenece al pueblo (pág. 185, 542)

Populist Party a political party formed in 1892 that supported free coinage of silver, work reforms, immigration restrictions, and government ownership of railroads and telegraph and telephone systems (p. 383)
Partido Populista partido político formado en 1892 que apoyaba la libre producción de monedas de plata, reformas laborales y restricciones de la inmigración, además de asignar al gobierno la propiedad de los sistemas ferroviario, telegráfico y telefónico (pág. 383)

Pottawatomie Massacre (1856) an incident in which abolitionist John Brown and seven other men murdered pro-slavery Kansans (p. 551)
masacre de Pottawatomie (1856) incidente en el que el abolicionista John Brown y siete hombres más asesinaron a habitantes esclavistas de Kansas (pág. 551)

precedent an action or decision that later serves as an example (p. 247)
precedente acción o decisión que más tarde sirve de ejemplo (pág. 247)

privateer a private ship authorized by a nation to attack its enemies (p. 256)
corsario barco privado autorizado por una nación para atacar a sus enemigos (pág. 256)

Progressives a group of reformers who worked to improve social and political problems in the late 1800s (p. 689)
progresistas grupo de reformistas que trabajaron para resolver problemas sociales y políticos a finales del siglo XIX (pág. 689)

Progressive Party a short-lived political party that attempted to institute social reforms (p. 709)
Partido Progresista partido político de poca duración que intentó establecer reformas sociales (pág. 709)

prospect to search for gold (p. 410)
prospectar buscar oro (pág. 410)

Protestant Reformation a religious movement begun by Martin Luther and others in 1517 to reform the Catholic Church (p. 53)
Reforma Protestante movimiento religioso iniciado por Martín Lutero y otros en 1517 para reformar la Iglesia católica (pág. 53)

Protestants reformers who protested certain practices of the Catholic Church (p. 54)
protestantes reformistas que protestaban por ciertas prácticas de la Iglesia católica (pág. 54)

English and Spanish Glossary

pueblos above-ground houses made of heavy clay called adobe that were built by Native Americans of the southwestern United States (p. 11)

pueblos casas de arcilla gruesa, llamada adobe, construidas más arriba de la superficie por indígenas del suroeste de Estados Unidos (pág. 11)

Pullman strike (1894) a railroad strike that ended when President Grover Cleveland sent in federal troops (p. 656)

huelga de Pullman (1894) huelga del ferrocarril que terminó cuando el presidente Grover Cleveland envió a tropas federales (pág. 656)

Pure Food and Drug Act (1906) a law that set regulatory standards for industries involved in preparing food (p. 708)

Ley de Alimentos y Medicamentos Puros (1906) ley que estableció normas regulatorias para las industrias de preparación de productos alimenticios (pág. 708)

Puritans Protestants who wanted to reform the Church of England (p. 75)

puritanos protestantes que querían reformar la Iglesia anglicana (pág. 75)

Q

Quakers Society of Friends; Protestant sect founded in 1640s in England whose members believed that salvation was available to all people (p. 85)

cuáqueros Sociedad de Amigos; secta protestante fundada en la década de 1640 en Inglaterra cuyos miembros creían que la salvación estaba al alcance de todos (pág. 85)

Quartering Act (1774) One of the Coercive or Intolerable Acts that helped fan the flames of revolution in the English colonies. It required each colonist to provide a place in their home, or quarter, for British soldiers. (p. 112)

Ley de Acuartelamiento (1774) Uno de los actos coersitivos o intolerables que ayudó a inspirar la revolución en las colonias inglesas. Requería que cada colono proveyera alojamiento en su casa para los soldados británicos. (pág. 112)

R

Radical Republicans members of Congress who felt that southern states needed to make great social changes before they could be readmitted to the Union (p. 622)

republicanos radicales miembros del Congreso convencidos de que los estados del Sur necesitaban hacer grandes cambios sociales antes de volver a ser admitidos en la Unión (pág. 622)

ratification an official approval (p. 154)

ratificación aprobación formal (pág. 154)

realpolitik a foreign policy in which U.S. interests are put over ethical or principled concerns (p. 952)

realpolitik política exterior según la cual los intereses de Estados Unidos están por encima de los asuntos éticos o de principios (pág. 952)

reason clear and ordered thinking; Greek philosopher Aristotle believed it was the basis of a good life (p. 23)

razón ideas claras y ordenadas; el fi lósofo griego Aristóteles pensaba que la razón era la base de una vida buena (pág. 23)

recall a vote to remove an official from office (p. 691)

destitución votación para sacar a un funcionario de su cargo (pág. 691)

Reconstruction (1865–1877) the period following the Civil War during which the U.S. government worked to reunite the nation and to rebuild the southern states (p. 614)

Reconstrucción (1865–1877) período posterior a la Guerra Civil en el que el gobierno de Estados Unidos trabajó por reunifi car de la nación y reconstruir los estados del Sur (pág. 614)

Reconstruction Acts (1867–1868) the laws that put the southern states under U.S. military control and required them to draft new constitutions upholding the Fourteenth Amendment (p. 623)

Leyes de Reconstrucción (1867–1868) leyes que declaraban a los estados del Sur territorio sujeto al control militar estadounidense y los obligaban a reformar sus constituciones de manera que defendieran la Decimocuarta Enmienda (pág. 623)

Redcoats British soldiers who fought against the colonists in the American Revolution; so called because of their bright red uniforms (p. 115)
casacas rojas soldados británicos que lucharon contra los colonos en la Guerra de Independencia estadounidense, llamados así por el color rojo fuerte de sus uniformes (pág. 115)

Red Scare a widespread fear of communism and Communists (p. 784)
Terror Rojo miedo ampliamente difundido al comunismo y los comunistas (pág. 784)

referendum a procedure that allows voters to approve or reject a law already proposed or passed by government (p. 692)
referéndum proceso que permite a los votantes aprobar o rechazar una ley previamente propuesta o aprobada por el gobierno (pág. 692)

reparations financial payments by the loser of a war (p. 766)
indemnizaciones compensación económica pagada por el bando que es vencido en la guerra (pág. 766)

Republican Party a political party formed in the 1850s to stop the spread of slavery in the West (p. 553)
Partido Republicano partido político formado en la década de 1850 para detener la expansión de la esclavitud en el Oeste (pág. 553)

reservations federal lands set aside for American Indians (p. 372)
reservas territorios federales reservados para los indígenas norteamericanos (pág. 372)

Rhode Island system a system developed by Samuel Slater in the mid-1800s in which whole families were hired as textile workers and factory work was divided into simple tasks (p. 431)
sistema de Rhode Island sistema desarrollado por Samuel Slater a mediados del siglo XIX mediante el cual se contrataba a familias completas para trabajar en la industria textil y en el que el trabajo de las fábricas estaba dividido en tareas sencillas (pág. 431)

Roosevelt Corollary (1904) Theodore Roosevelt's addition to the Monroe Doctrine warning nations in the Americas that if they didn't pay their debts, the United States would get involved (p. 736)
Corolario de Roosevelt (1904) agregado del presidente Theodore Roosevelt a la Doctrina Monroe advirtiendo a las naciones de América que si no pagaban sus deudas, el gobierno de Estados Unidos intervendría (pág. 736)

Rush-Bagot Agreement (1817) an agreement that limited naval power on the Great Lakes for both the United States and British Canada (p. 292)
Acuerdo de Rush-Bagot (1817) acuerdo que limitaba el poder naval de Estados Unidos y la Canadá británica en los Grandes Lagos (pág. 292)

S

salutary neglect an English policy of relaxing the enforcement of regulations in its colonies in return for the colonies' continued economic loyalty (p. 98)
negligencia saludable una política inglesa de regulaciones menos estrictas en sus colonias a cambio de la lealtad continua económica de las colonias (pág. 98)

sanctions economic restrictions placed on a country in an attempt to change its policy decisions (p. 961)
sanciones restricciones económicas aplicadas a un país en un intento de cambiar sus políticas (pág. 961)

Santa Fe Trail an important trade trail west from Independence, Missouri, to Santa Fe, New Mexico (p. 360)
Camino de Santa Fe importante ruta comercial que va desde Independence, Missouri, hasta Santa Fe, Nuevo México (pág. 360)

Scopes trial a trial in which John Scopes was accused of teaching evolution illegally (p. 787)
juicio de Scopes juicio en el cual John Scopes fue acusado de enseñar ilegalmente la teoría de la evolución (pág. 787)

search-and-destroy missions the strategy used in the Vietnam War in which enemy targets were located and attacked (p. 904)
misiones de búsqueda y destrucción estrategia de localización y ataque de objetivos enemigos usada en la guerra de Vietnam (pág. 904)

search warrant a judge's order authorizing the search of a person's home or property to look for evidence of a crime (p. 225)
orden de registro orden de un juez que permite registrar el hogar y las pertenencias de una persona en busca de pruebas de un delito (pág. 225)

secede to formally withdraw from the Union (pp. 497, 543)
separarse salirse formalmente de la Unión (pág. 497, 543)

Second Battle of Bull Run (1862) a Civil War battle in which the Confederate army forced most of the Union army out of Virginia (p. 579)
segunda batalla de Bull Run (1862) batalla de la Guerra Civil en la que el ejército confederado obligó a gran parte del ejército de la Unión a abandoner Virginia (pág. 579)

Second Continental Congress (1775) a meeting of colonial delegates in Philadelphia to decide how to react to fighting at Lexington and Concord (p. 116)
Segundo Congreso Continental (1775) reunión de delegados coloniales en Filadelfi a para decidir cómo reaccionar ante la lucha en Lexington y Concord (pág. 116)

Second Great Awakening a period of religious evangelism that began in the 1790s and became widespread in the United States by the 1830s (p. 518)
Segundo Gran Despertar período de evangelización religiosa iniciado en la década de 1790 que se extendió por Estados Unidos para la década de 1830 (pág. 518)

Second Industrial Revolution a period of rapid growth in manufacturing and industry in the late 1800s (p. 642)
Segunda Revolución Industrial período de gran crecimiento en la manufactura y en la industria a finales del siglo XIX (pág. 642)

sectionalism a devotion to the interests of one geographic region over the interests of the country as a whole (pp. 310, 497, 543)
regionalismo lealtad a los intereses de una region geográfica más que a los del país entero (pág. 310, 497, 543)

segregation the forced separation of people of different races in public places (p. 631)

segregación separación obligada de personas de diferentes razas en lugares públicos (pág. 631)

Selective Service Act (1917) a law that allowed the president to draft soldiers in times of war (p. 753)
Ley de Servicio Selectivo (1917) ley que permitía al presidente reclutar soldados en épocas de Guerra (pág. 753)

Seneca Falls Convention (1848) the first national women's rights convention at which the Declaration of Sentiments was written (p. 532)
Convención de Seneca Falls (1848) primera convención nacional a favor de los derechos de la mujer, en la cual se redactó la Declaración de Sentimientos (pág. 532)

service economy an economy in which most jobs involve providing services instead of producing goods (p. 985)
economía de servicios economía en la cual la mayoría de los trabajos consisten en ofrecer un servicio en lugar de producir bienes (pág. 985)

settlement houses neighborhood centers staffed by professionals and volunteers for education, recreation, and social activities in poor areas (p. 676)
organizaciones de servicio a la comunidad centros comunitarios atendidos por profesionales y voluntarios para ofrecer educación, recreación y actividades sociales en zonas pobres (pág. 676)

Seven Days' Battles (1862) a series of Civil War battles in which Confederate army successes forced the Union army to retreat from Richmond, Virginia, the Confederate capital (p. 579)
batallas de los Siete Días (1862) serie de batallas de la Guerra Civil en las que las victorias del ejército confederado obligaron a las tropas de la Unión a retirarse de Richmond, Virginia, la capital confederada (pág. 579)

Seventeenth Amendment (1913) a constitutional amendment allowing American voters to directly elect U.S. senators (p. 691)
Decimoséptima Enmienda (1913) enmienda constitucional que permite a los votantes estadounidenses elegir directamente a los senadores de Estados Unidos (pág. 691)

sharecropping a system used on southern farms after the Civil War in which farmers worked land owned by someone else in return for a small portion of the crops (p. 632)
cultivo de aparceros sistemausado en las granjas sureñas después de la Guerra Civil en el que los agricultores trabajaban las tierras de otra persona a cambio de una pequeña porción de la cosecha (pág. 632)

Shays's Rebellion (1786–87) an uprising of Massachusetts's farmers, led by Daniel Shays, to protest high taxes, heavy debt, and farm foreclosures (p. 161)
Rebelión de Shays (1786–87) rebelión de agricultores de Massachusetts, encabezados por Daniel Shays, para protestar por los altos impuestos, las grandes deudas y el embargo de las granjas (pág. 161)

Sherman Antitrust Act (1890) a law that made it illegal to create monopolies or trusts that restrained free trade (p. 651)
Ley Antimonopolio de Sherman (1890) ley que prohibía la creación de monopolios o consorcios que restringieran el libre comercio (pág. 651)

Siege of Vicksburg (1863) the Union army's six-week blockade of Vicksburg that led the city to surrender during the Civil War (p. 585)
Sitio de Vicksburg (1863) bloqueo de seis semanas realizado por el ejército de la Unión en Vicksburg para forzar la rendición de esa ciudad durante la Guerra Civil (pág. 585)

sit-down strike a strike in which workers stay at their work stations so that strikebreakers cannot replace them (p. 814)
huelga de brazos caídos huelga en la cual los trabajadores permanecen en el lugar de trabajo para que los rompehuelgas no los puedan reemplazar (pág. 814)

sit-in a form of protest in which African Americans sat at segregated lunch counters and requested service (p. 929)
sentada forma de protesta de los afroamericanos; se sentaban en los comedores que practicaban la segregación racial y pedían que les sirvieran (pág. 929)

Sixteenth Amendment (1913) an amendment to the Constitution that allows personal income to be taxed (p. 709)
Decimosexta Enmienda (1913) enmienda constitucional que permite los impuestos sobre los ingresos personales (pág. 709)

slave codes laws passed in the colonies to control slaves (p. 74)
códigos de esclavos leyes aprobadas por las colonias para controlar a los esclavos (pág. 74)

social Darwinism a view of society based on Charles Darwin's scientific theory of natural selection (p. 650)
darwinismo social visión de la sociedad basada en la teoría científi ca de la selección natural de Charles Darwin (pág. 650)

socialism economic system in which the government owns and operates a country's means of production (p. 700)
socialismo sistema económico en el que el gobierno controla y maneja los medios de producción de un país (pág. 700)

Social Security a program for providing pension benefits for many Americans aged 65 and older (p. 1000)
Seguridad Social un programa para proporcionar prestaciones de jubilación para muchos estadounidenses de 65 años y mayores (pág. 1000)

Social Security Act (1935) a law that instituted the pension plan Social Security (p. 813)
Ley del Seguro Social (1935) ley que estableció el plan de pensiones del Seguro Social (pág. 813)

sodbusters the name given to Plains farmers who worked hard to break up the region's tough sod (p. 380)
sodbusters nombre dado a los agricultores de las Planicies que se esforzaron mucho para trabajar el duro terreno de la región (pág. 380)

Spanish Armada a large Spanish fleet defeated by England in 1588 (p. 54)
Armada española gran flota española derrotada por las tropas de Inglaterra en 1588 (pág. 54)

speculator an investor who buys items at low prices in hope that their values will rise (p. 250)
especulador inversionista que compra artículos a precios bajos con la esperanza de que su valor aumente (pág. 250)

sphere of influence an area where foreign countries control trade or natural resources of another nation or area (p. 722)
esfera de influencia nación o lugar cuyos recursos naturales y comercio son controlados por otro país (pág. 722)

English and Spanish Glossary

spirituals emotional Christian songs sung by enslaved people in the South that mixed African and European elements and usually expressed slaves' religious beliefs (p. 466, 585)
espirituales canciones religiosas emotivas cantadas por los esclavos del Sur que combinaban elementos de origen africano y europeo y solían expresar sus creencias religiosas (pág. 466, 585)

spoils system a politician's practice of giving government jobs to his or her supporters (p. 332)
tráfico de influencias práctica de los políticos de ofrecer empleos a las personas que los apoyan (pág. 332)

Sputnik the first artificial satellite, launched by the Soviet Union in 1957 (p. 880)
Sputnik primer satélite artificial, lanzado por la Unión Soviética en 1957 (pág. 880)

stagflation a term describing a slowing economy mixed with high unemployment (p. 951)
estagflación término que describe una economía que disminuye su ritmo, acompañado de un desempleo alto (pág. 951)

stalemate a situation in which neither side can win a victory (p. 748)
punto muerto situación en la cual ninguna de las partes puede alcanzar la victoria (pág. 748)

Stamp Act of 1765 a law passed by Parliament that raised tax money by requiring colonists to pay for an official stamp whenever they bought paper items such as newspapers, licenses, and legal documents (p. 107)
Ley del Sello de 1765 ley aprobada por el Parlamento para recaudar impuestos en la que se obligaba a los colonos a pagar un sello oficial cada vez que compraran artículos de papel, como periódicos, licencias y documentos legales (pág. 107)

standard time the system set up by the railroad companies that divided the country into four time zones (p. 370)
hora estándar el sistema establecido por las compañías de ferrocarriles que dividieron al país en cuatro zonas de tiempo (pág. 370)

staple crop a crop that is continuously in demand (p. 86)
cultivo básico cultivo de demanda constante (pág. 86)

states' rights doctrine the belief that the power of the states should be greater than the power of the federal government (p. 335)
doctrina de los derechos estatales creencia de que el poder de los estados debe ser mayor que el del gobierno federal (pág. 335)

steerage the area on a ship in the lower levels where the steering mechanisms were located and where cramped quarters were provided for people who could only afford cheap passage (p. 665)
tercera clase nivel inferior un barco en el que se encontraban los mecanismos del timón y se ofrecían habitaciones reducidas para las personas que solo podían comprar un pasaje barato (pág. 665)

Strategic Arms Limitation Talks (SALT) negotiations between the United States and the Soviet Union designed to limit nuclear weapons (p. 952)
Tratados de Limitación de Armas Estratégicas (SALT, por sus siglas en inglés) negociaciones entre Estados Unidos y la Unión Soviética diseñadas para limitar el número de armas nucleares (pág. 952)

strict construction a way of interpreting the Constitution that allows the federal government to take only those actions the Constitution specifically says it can take (p. 254)
interpretación estricta interpretación de la Constitución que sólo permite al gobierno federal hacer las acciones mencionadas específicamente en ella (pág. 254)

strike the refusal of workers to perform their jobs until employers meet their demands (p. 433)
huelga negativa de los empleados a trabajar hasta que sus empleadores satisfagan sus demandas (pág. 433)

Student Nonviolent Coordinating Committee (SNCC) a group organized to promote civil rights for African Americans through nonviolent protests (p. 930)
Comité Coordinador Estudiantil No Violento (SNCC, por sus siglas en inglés) grupo organizado para promover los derechos civiles de los afroamericanos con protestas no violentas (pág. 930)

Students for a Democratic Society (SDS) a group organized to protest U.S. involvement in the Vietnam War (p. 910)
Estudiantes por una Sociedad Democrática (SDS, por sus siglas en inglés) grupo organizado para protestar por la participación de Estados Unidos en la guerra de Vietnam (pág. 910)

suburb a neighborhood outside of a downtown area (p. 672)
suburbio vecindario en las afueras de una ciudad (pág. 672)

suffrage voting rights (p. 153)
sufragio derecho al voto (pág. 153)

Sun Belt the southern area of the United States from Florida to California that experienced an increase in population during the 1970s (p. 882)
Sun Belt área del sur de Estados Unidos, desde Florida hasta California, en la que hubo un aumento de la población durante la década de 1970 (pág. 882)

superpower powerful countries that influence events in their regions of the world (p. 870)
superpotencia países poderosos que influyen en los acontecimientos en sus regiones del mundo (pág. 870)

supply-side economics economic theory that focuses on influencing the supply of labor and goods; it usually involves sharp tax cuts (p. 964)
economía de la oferta teoría económica que pretende influenciar la oferta de mano de obra y de bienes; por lo general, implica grandes reducciones de impuestos (pág. 964)

sweatshops hot, stuffy workshops in which workers prepare materials for low wages (p. 667)
fábricas explotadoras talleres calurosos y con el aire cargado en los cuales los trabajadores preparan materiales por salarios reducidos (pág. 667)

T

talkie a film that includes sound (p. 791)
película sonora película que incluye sonido (pág. 791)

tariff a tax on imports or exports (p. 159)
arancel impuesto pagado por las importaciones o exportaciones (pág. 159)

Tariff of Abominations (1828) the nickname given to a tariff by southerners who opposed it (p. 334)
Arancel de Abominaciones (1828) sobrenombre dado a un arancel por los habitantes del Sur que se oponían a éste (pág. 334)

Tea Act (1773) a law passed by Parliament allowing the British East India Company to sell its low-cost tea directly to the colonies, undermining colonial tea merchants; led to the Boston Tea Party (p. 110)
Ley del Té (1773) ley aprobada por el Parlamento británico que le permitía a la British East India Company vender té a bajo costo a las colonias directamente, afectando a los comerciantes de té coloniales; dio origen al Motín del Té de Boston (pág. 110)

Teapot Dome scandal a scandal under the Harding adminstration in which government offi cials were accused of taking bribes to allow oil to be mined from federal lands (p. 777)
escándalo de Teapot Dome escándalo durante el gobierno de Harding en el que se acusó a funcionarios del gobierno de aceptar sobornos para permitir que se usaran tierras federales para extraer petróleo (pág. 777)

technology the tools used to produce goods or to do work (p. 426)
tecnología herramientas utilizadas para producer bienes o realizar un trabajo (pág. 426)

teepees cone-shaped shelters made of buffalo skins used by Native Americans in the Plains region (p. 14)
tipis viviendas en forma de cono hechas de piel de búfalo que usaban los indígenas norteamericanos en la región de las Planicies (pág. 14)

telegraph a machine perfected by Samuel F. B. Morse in 1832 that uses pulses of electric current to send messages across long distances through wires (p. 441)
telégrafo máquina perfeccionada por Samuel F. B. Morse en 1832 que emplea impulsos eléctricos transmitidos por cables para enviar mensajes a grandes distancias (pág. 441)

Teller Amendment (1898) a congressional resolution stating that the U.S. had no interest in taking control of Cuba (p. 725)
Enmienda Teller (1898) resolución del Congreso en la que Estados Unidos declaró que no tenía intención de tomar el control de Cuba (pág. 725)

temperance movement a social reform effort begun in the mid-1800s to encourage people to drink less alcohol (p. 520)
movimiento de abstinencia movimiento de reforma social iniciado a mediados del siglo XIX para promover el que las personas bebieran menos alcohol (pág. 520)

tenements poorly built, overcrowded housing where many immigrants lived (pp. 511, 667)
casas de vecindad viviendas mal construidas y llenas de gente donde vivían muchos inmigrantes (pág. 511, 667)

Tennessee Valley Authority (TVA) a governmental agency designed to bring jobs and electricity to rural areas of the Tennessee River valley (p. 811)
Autoridad del Valle del Tennessee (TVA, por sus siglas en inglés) agencia del gobierno destinada a proveer empleos y energía eléctrica a las áreas rurales del valle del río Tennessee (pág. 811)

Ten Percent Plan President Abraham Lincoln's plan for Reconstruction; once 10 percent of voters in a former Confederate state took a U.S. loyalty oath, they could form a new state government and be readmitted to the Union (p. 615)
Plan del Diez por Ciento plan de Reconstrucción del presidente Abraham Lincoln; si el 10 por ciento de los votantes de un estado que había sido confederado juraba lealtad a la nación, podían formar un Nuevo gobierno y ser readmitidos en la Unión (pág. 615)

terrorism the systematic use of fear or terror to gain goals (p. 974)
terrorismo uso sistemático del miedo o el terror para alcanzar objetivos (pág. 974)

Tet Offensive (1968) a series of attacks by Vietcong forces that proved to many Americans the Vietnam War was not being won (p. 905)
ofensiva del Tet (1968) serie de ataques de las fuerzas del Vietcong que demostró a muchos estadounidenses que no estaban ganando la Guerra de Vietnam (pág. 905)

textile cloth (p. 425)
textil tela (pág. 425)

Thirteenth Amendment (1865) a constitutional amendment that outlawed slavery (p. 615)

Decimotercera Enmienda (1865) enmienda constitucional que prohibió la esclavitud (pág. 615)

38th Parallel the boundary between North and South Korea before the Korean War (p. 876)
paralelo 38 límite entre Corea del Sur Corea del Norte antes de la Guerra de Corea (pág. 876)

Three-Fifths Compromise (1787) an agreement worked out at the Constitutional Convention stating that only three-fifths of the slaves in a state would count when determining a state's population for representation in the lower house of Congress (pp. 167, 184)
Compromiso de las Tres Quintas Partes (1787) acuerdo negociado durante la Convención Constitucional en el que se estableció que solamente tres quintas de los esclavos en un estado contarían para al determiner la representación de ese estado en la cámara baja del Congreso (pág. 167, 184)

Toleration Act of 1649 a Maryland law that made restricting the religious rights of Christians a crime; the first law guaranteeing religious freedom to be passed in America (p. 72)
Ley de Tolerancia de 1649 ley de Maryland que calificaba como delito la restricción de los derechos religiosos de los cristianos; fue la primera ley que garantizó la libertad religiosa en América (pág. 72)

Tonkin Gulf Resolution (1964) gave President Johnson the power to send combat troops to Vietnam (p. 902)
Resolución del Golfo de Tonkin (1964) otorgó al presidente Johnson la autoridad de enviar tropas de combate a Vietnam (pág. 902)

totalitarianism a form of government in which every aspect of citizens' lives are controlled by the government (p. 830)
totalitarismo forma de gobierno en la cual todos los aspectos de la vida de los ciudadanos están bajo el control del gobierno (pág. 830)

total war a type of war in which an army destroys its opponent's ability to fight by targeting civilian and economic as well as military resources (p. 604) guerra total tipo de guerra en la que un ejército destruye la capacidad de lucha de su oponente mediante ataques a la población civil y a la economía así como a los recursos militares (pág. 604)

totems images of ancestors or animal spirits; carved onto tall, wooden poles by Native American peoples of the Pacific Northwest (p. 13)
tótems imágenes de antepasados o espíritus de animales; a menudo talladas en altos troncos de madera por los indígenas americanos de la costa noroeste del Pacífico (pág. 13)

town meeting a political meeting at which people make decisions on local issues; used primarily in New England (p. 91)
reunión del pueblo reunión política en la que las personas toman decisiones sobre temas locales; se usan principalmente en Nueva Inglaterra (pág. 91)

trade unions workers' organizations that try to improve working conditions (p. 433)
sindicatos organizaciones de trabajadores que intentan mejorar sus condiciones laborales (pág. 433)

Trail of Tears (1838–39) an 800-mile forced march made by the Cherokee from their homeland in Georgia to Indian Territory; resulted in the deaths of almost one-fourth of the Cherokee people (p. 343)
Ruta de las Lágrimas (1838–39) marcha forzada de 800 millas que hicieron los cheroquíes desde su territorio natal en Georgia hasta el Territorio Indígena, y en la que perdió la vida casi una cuarta parte del pueblo cheroquí (pág. 343)

transcendentalism the idea that people could rise above the material things in life; a popular movement among New England writers and thinkers in the mid-1800s (p. 513)
trascendentalismo creencia de que las personas podían prescindir de los objetos materiales en la vida; movimiento popular entre los escritores y pensadores de Nueva Inglaterra a mediados del siglo XIX (pág. 513)

transcontinental railroad a railroad system that crossed the continental United States; construction began in 1863 (p. 368)
tren transcontinental línea que cruzaba Estados Unidos de un extremo a otro; su construcción se inició en 1863 (pág. 368)

Transportation Revolution the rapid growth in the speed and convenience of transportation (p. 435)
Revolución del Transporte rápido desarrollo de la velocidad y comodidad de los medios de transporte (pág. 435)

Treaty of Fort Jackson (1814) a treaty signed after the U.S. victory at the Battle of Horseshoe Bend; the Creek were forced to give up 23 million acres of their land (p. 290)
Tratado del Fuerte Jackson (1814) tratado que se firmó tras la victoria de Estados Unidos en la batalla de Horseshoe Bend; los indígenas creek se vieron obligados a ceder 23 millones de acres de su territorio (pág. 290)

Treaty of Fort Laramie (1851) a treaty signed in Wyoming by the United States and northern Plains nations (p. 372)
Tratado del Fuerte Laramie (1851) tratado firmado en Wyoming por Estados Unidos y las naciones indígenas de las Planicies del norte (pág. 372)

Treaty of Ghent (1814) a treaty signed by the United States and Britain ending the War of 1812 (p. 291)
Tratado de Gante (1814) tratado firmado por Estados Unidos y Gran Bretaña para dar fi n a la Guerra de 1812 (pág. 291)

Treaty of Greenville (1795) an agreement between Native American confederation leaders and the U.S. government that gave the United States Indian lands in the Northwest Territory and guaranteed that U.S. citizens could safely travel through the region (p. 259)
Tratado de Greenville (1795) acuerdo entre los líderes de la confederación de indígenas norteamericanos y el gobierno estadounidense que otorgó a Estados Unidos tierras indígenas en el Territorio del Noroeste y garantizó la seguridad a los ciudadanos estadounidenses que viajaran por la región (pág. 259)

Treaty of Guadalupe Hidalgo (1848) a treaty that ended the Mexican-American War and gave the United States much of Mexico's northern territory (p. 405)
Tratado de Guadalupe Hidalgo (1848) tratado que daba por terminada la Guerra contra México y daba a Estados Unidos gran parte del norte del territorio mexicano (pág. 405)

English and Spanish Glossary

Treaty of Medicine Lodge (1867) an agreement between the U.S. government and southern Plains Indians in which the Indians agreed to move onto reservations (p. 373)
Tratado de Medicine Lodge (1867) acuerdo entre el gobierno de Estados Unidos y los indígenas de las Planicies del sur en el que los indígenas aceptaron irse a las reservas (pág. 373)

Treaty of Paris of 1783 a peace agreement that officially ended the Revolutionary War and established British recognition of the independence of the United States (p. 144)
Tratado de París de 1783 acuerdo de paz que oficialmente dio por terminada la Guerra de Independencia estadounidense y en el que Gran Bretaña reconocía la independencia de Estados Unidos (pág. 144)

Treaty of Tordesillas (1494) a treaty between Spain and Portugal that moved the Line of Demarcation (p. 43)
Tratado de Tordesillas (1494) tratado entre España y Portugal que modifi có la Línea de Demarcación (pág. 43)

Treaty of Versailles (1919) brought an end to World War I, but was never ratified by the United States (p. 767)
Tratado de Versalles (1919) puso fin a la Primera Guerra Mundial, pero Estados Unidos nunca lo ratificó (pág. 767)

Tredegar Iron Works a large iron factory that operated in Richmond, Virginia, in the early to mid-1800s (p. 458)
Tredegar Iron Works gran fábrica de acero que operaba a mediados del siglo XIX en Richmond, Virginia (pág. 458)

trench warfare a new kind of warfare in World War I that involved troops digging and fighting from deep trenches (p. 748)
guerra de trincheras nuevo tipo de guerra utilizado en la Primera Guerra Mundial en el cual las tropas cavaban trincheras profundas y luchaban desde ellas (pág. 748)

Triangle Shirtwaist Fire a factory fire that killed 146 workers trapped in the building; led to new safety standard laws (p. 699)
incendio de Triangle Shirtwaist incendio de una fábrica en el que murieron 146 trabajadores atrapados en el edificio; este suceso obligó a crear nuevas leyes de seguridad (pág. 699)

triangular trade trading networks in which goods and slaves moved among England, the American colonies, and Africa (p. 93)
comercio triangular redes comerciales en las que los bienes y los esclavos se intercambiaban entre Inglaterra, las colonias americanas y África (pág. 93)

Truman Doctrine a policy attempting to contain the spread of communism, beginning with military aid to the monarchies of Turkey and Greece (p. 871)
Doctrina Truman política que intentaba contener el avance del comunismo, ofreciendo inicialmente ayuda militar a las monarquías de Turquía y Grecia (pág. 871)

trust a number of companies legally grouped under a single board of directors (p. 650)
consorcio varias compañías agrupadas legalmente bajo el mando de una sola junta directiva (pág. 650)

Tuskegee Airmen a group of African American pilots who flew missions in World War I; they were the first African American military pilots (p. 839)
Aviadores de Tuskegee grupo de pilotos afroamericanos que volaron en misiones de la Primera Guerra Mundial; fueron los primeros pilotos afroamericanos del ejército (pág. 839)

Twenty-First Amendment (1933) an amendment to the Constitution that ended Prohibition (p. 786)
Vigésimoprimera Enmienda (1933) enmienda constitucional que puso fin a la Ley Seca (pág. 786)

Twenty-Sixth Amendment (1971) an amendment to the Constitution that lowered the voting age to 18 (p. 913)
Vigésimosexta Enmienda (1971) enmienda constitucional que redujo la edad mínima para votar a 18 años (pág. 913)

U

U-boats German submarines or "untersee boats" (p. 750)
U-boats submarinos alemanes o "barcos untersee" (pág. 750)

Uncle Tom's Cabin (1852) an antislavery novel written by Harriet Beecher Stowe that showed northerners the violent reality of slavery and drew many people to the abolitionists' cause (pp. 499, 546)
La cabaña del tío Tom (1852) novela abolicionista escrita por Harriet Beecher Stowe que mostró a los habitantes del norte del país la violenta realidad de la esclavitud e hizo que muchos se unieran a la causa abolicionista (pág. 499, 546)

Underground Railroad a network of people who helped thousands of enslaved people escape to the North by providing transportation and hiding places (p. 492, 526)
Tren Clandestino red de personas que ayudó a miles de esclavos a escapar al Norte ofreciéndoles transporte y lugares para esconderse (pág. 492, 526)

United Farm Workers a group organized to promote the interests of migrant farm workers, it eventually led to the Chicano movement (p. 939)
Trabajadores Agrícolas Unidos grupo organizado para promover los intereses de los trabajadores agrícolas migratorios; con el tiempo, dio origen al movimiento chicano (pág. 939)

United Nations an alliance of nations that attempts to end disputes between countries peacefully (p. 869)
Naciones Unidas alianza de naciones que intent resolver de manera pacífica las disputas entre los países (pág. 869)

urban renewal a governmental program that attempted to rid innercities of slums and replace them with lowand middle-income housing (p. 884)
renovación urbana programa gubernamental que intentó eliminar las barriadas de los centros urbanos y reemplazarlos con viviendas para personas de recursos bajos y medios (pág. 884)

USA PATRIOT Act (2001) a law that makes it easier for federal law enforcement agencies to collect information on suspected terrorists (p. 988)
Ley Patriota de EE.UU (2001) una ley que le facilita a las agencias federales recolectar información sobre los terroristas sospechosos (pág. 988)

USS *Constitution* a large warship (p. 282)
USS *Constitution* gran buque de guerra (pág. 282)

utopian communities places where people worked to establish a perfect society; such communities were popular in the United States during the late 1700s and early to mid-1800s (p. 514)
comunidades utópicas lugares en los que un grupo de personas trabajaba para establecer una sociedad perfecta; se popularizaron en Estados Unidos a finales del siglo XVIII y principios y mediados del XIX (pág. 514)

V

vaqueros Mexican cowboys in the West who tended cattle and horses (p. 399)
vaqueros arrieros mexicanos que vivían en el Oeste y se ganaban la vida ocupándose del ganado y los caballos (pág. 399)

vertical integration the business practice of owning all of the businesses involved in each step of a manufacturing process (p. 649)
integración vertical práctica empresarial de poseer todas las empresas que participan en cada paso de un proceso de manufactura (pág. 649)

veto to cancel a law (p. 192)
vetar cancelar una ley (pág. 192)

Vietcong the South Vietnam forces that were supported by North Vietnamese Communists (p. 900)
Vietcong fuerzas de Vietnam del Sur apoyadas por los comunistas de Vietnam del Norte (pág. 900)

Vietnamization a policy introduced in an attempt to leave the Vietnam War, in which Vietnamese forces would take over the fighting (p. 912)
vietnamización política introducida en un intento de salir de la guerra de Vietnam, según la cual las fuerzas vietnamitas se harían cargo de la lucha (pág. 912)

Vietnam Veterans Memorial a war memorial in Washington, DC, dedicated to the veterans of Vietnam (p. 915)
Monumento a los Veteranos de Vietnam monument conmemorativo de la guerra en Washington, DC dedicado a los veteranos de Vietnam (pág. 915)

English and Spanish Glossary

Virginia Plan (1787) the plan for government proposed at the Constitutional Convention in which the national government would have supreme power and a legislative branch would have two houses with representation determined by state population (pp. 165, 183)
Plan de Virginia (1787) plan de gobierno propuesto en la Convención Constitucional por el que el gobierno nacional tendría poder supremo y habría un poder legislativo con dos cámaras en las que la representación de cada estado sería determinada por su población (pág. 165, 183)

Virginia Statute for Religious Freedom (1786) a document that gave people in Virginia freedom of worship and prohibited tax money from being used to fund churches (p. 153)
Estatuto de Virginia para la Libertad Religiosa (1786) documento que reconocía a los habitantes de Virginia la libertad de culto y prohibía utilizar los impuestos para financiar iglesias (pág. 153)

Voting Rights Act of 1965 provided new powers to the federal government to protect African Americans' voting rights (p. 935)
Ley de Derecho al Voto de 1965 dio nueva autoridad al gobierno federal para proteger el derecho al voto de los afroamericanos (pág. 935)

W

War Hawks members of Congress who wanted to declare war against Britain after the Battle of Tippecanoe (p. 286)
halcones de guerra miembros del Congreso que querían declarar la guerra a Gran Bretaña tras la batalla de Tippecanoe (pág. 286)

War Powers Act (1973) a law that requires a president to get Congressional approval before sending troops into combat (p. 915)
Ley de Poderes de Guerra (1973) ley que requiere la aprobación del Congreso para que el presidente pueda enviar tropas a la guerra (pág. 915)

War Production Board a government agency set up to oversee production of war materials during World War II (p. 837)
Junta de Producción de Guerra agencia creada por el gobierno para supervisar la producción de materiales de guerra durante la Segunda Guerra Mundial (pág. 837)

Warren Court a Supreme Court headed by Chief Justice Earl Warren that issued many rulings that extended individual rights and freedoms (p. 941)
Corte Warren Corte Suprema presidida por el Magistrado Earl Warren que emitió muchas resoluciones que extendían los derechos y las libertades individuales (pág. 941)

Watergate a scandal in which President Nixon resigned over accusations of illegal activity (p. 953)
Watergate escándalo que provocó la renuncia del presidente Nixon por acusaciones de actividades ilegales (pág. 953)

weapons of mass destruction chemical, biological, or nuclear weapons that can kill thousands (p. 984)
armas de destrucción masiva armas químicas, biológicas o nucleares que pueden matar a miles de personas (pág. 984)

Whig Party a political party formed in 1834 by opponents of Andrew Jackson and who supported a strong legislature (p. 339)
Partido Whig partido político formado en 1834 por oponentes de Andrew Jackson que apoyaba una asamblea legislativa con mucha autoridad (pág. 339)

Whiskey Rebellion (1794) a protest of small farmers in Pennsylvania against new taxes on whiskey (p. 260)
Rebelión del Whisky (1794) protesta de pequeños agricultores de Pensilvania contra los nuevos impuestos sobre el whisky (pág. 260)

Wilderness Campaign (1864) a series of battles between Union and Confederate forces in northern and central Virginia that delayed the Union capture of Richmond (p. 603)
Campaña de Wilderness (1864) serie de batallas entre la Unión y los confederados en el norte y el centro de Virginia que retrasaron la captura de Richmond por parte de la Unión (pág. 603)

Wilmot Proviso (1846) a proposal to outlaw slavery in the territory added to the United States by the Mexican Cession; passed in the House of Representatives but was defeated in the Senate (pp. 496, 542)

Condición de Wilmot (1846) propuesta de prohibir la esclavitud en el territorio anexado a Estados Unidos por la Cesión Mexicana; aprobada por la Cámara de Representantes, pero rechazada por el Senado (pág. 496, 542)

Worcester v. Georgia (1832) the Supreme Court ruling that stated that the Cherokee nation was a distinct territory over which only the federal government had authority; ignored by both President Andrew Jackson and the state of Georgia (p. 342)
Worcester contra *Georgia* (1832) decisión de la Corte Suprema que establecía que la nación cheroquí era un territorio distinto sobre el que sólo el gobierno federal tenía autoridad; fue ignorada por el presidente Andrew Jackson y por el estado de Georgia (pág. 342)

workers' compensation laws laws that guarantee a portion of lost wages to workers who are injured on the job (p. 699)
leyes de compensación laboral leyes que garantizan una parte de los salarios caídos a los trabajadores que se lesionan en el trabajo (pág. 699)

World Trade Center a complex of several office buildings that were attacked by terrorists (p. 984)
World Trade Center complejo de varios edificios de oficinas que fue atacado por terroristas (pág. 984)

X

XYZ affair (1797) an incident in which French agents attempted to get a bribe and loans from U.S. diplomats in exchange for an agreement that French privateers would no longer attack American ships; it led to an undeclared naval war between the two countries (p. 265)
asunto XYZ (1797) incidente en el que funcionarios franceses intentaron obtener sobornos y préstamos de diplomáticos estadounidenses a cambio de un acuerdo por el cual sus corsarios no atacarían más a los barcos estadounidenses; provocó una guerra no declarada entre las fuerzas navales de ambas naciones (pág. 265)

Y

Yalta Conference a meeting between the leaders of the Allied powers that resulted in a plan for peace after World War II (p. 868)
Conferencia de Yalta reunión de los líderes de las fuerzas aliadas que produjo un plan de paz después de la Segunda Guerra Mundial (pág. 868)

yellow journalism the reporting of exaggerated stories in newspapers to increase sales (p. 724)
prensa amarillista publicación de noticias exageradas en los periódicos para aumentar las ventas (pág. 724)

yeomen owners of small farms (p. 461)
pequeños terratenientes dueños de granjas pequeñas (pág. 461)

Z

Zimmermann note a telegram from Germany to Mexico offering Mexico a return of territory in exchange for declaring war on the United States (p. 752)
telegrama Zimmermann telegrama de Alemania a México en el cual se ofrecía a México una devolución de territorios si le declaraba la guerra a Estados Unidos (pág. 752)

zoot-suit riots a series of riots during which Mexican Americans were attacked by whites (p. 840)
disturbios *zoot-suit* serie de disturbios durante los cuales personas de raza blanca atacaron a mexicanoamericanos (pág. 840)

Index

KEY TO INDEX

c = chart	*p* = photo
f = feature	*R* = Reference
m = map	*t* = table

A

AAA (Agricultural Adjustment Act), 811

abolitionists, 489–495; anti-abolitionist rally, 494*f*; anti-slavery literature, 480–481; in "Bleeding Kansas," 551, 551*p*; defined, 489; differences among, 489–491; *Dred Scott* decision and, 554; Fugitive Slave Act and, 546; John Brown's Raid and, 558–559; leaders of, 525–526; opposition to movement, 494–495, 527; overview, 475; religious roots of, 524–525; Republican Party and, 553; spreading the message of, 490–492; Underground Railroad and, 492–494, 493*m*, 526–527; *See also* slavery

abortion legalization, 957

accused, rights of, 226–228

acid rain, 959

ACLU (American Civil Liberties Union), 784, 787

Adams, Abigail, 247

Adams, Henry, 617

Adams, James, 183

Adams, John: Boston Massacre and, 109–110; not at Constitutional Convention, 164; as second president, 243*p*, 265–266; Whitney's interchangeable parts and, 427

Adams, John Quincy, Adams-Onís Treaty of 1819, 294; gag rule on slavery overturned by, 495; Jackson's defeat of, 326, 329–330; Monroe Doctrine supported by, 303–304; as president, 299*p*, 311

Adams, Samuel, 107, 109, 114, 170

Adams-Onís Treaty, 294

Addams, Jane, 661, 677, 677*f*, 690, 755

AEF (American Expeditionary Force), in World War I, 757

affirmative action, 958

Africa: African Diaspora, 477–478; Cape of Good Hope, 39–40; World War II in North, 843–848; *See also* slavery.

African Americans: as abolitionists, 491–492; affirmative action benefits for, 958, 958*c*; in American Revolution, 128; Banneker, Benjamin, 252*f*; baseball league of, 791; Beckwourth, Jim, 358, 358*p*; Bruce, Blanche K., 628; as "buffalo soldiers," 373; bus boycotts, 927–928; Charles H. Wright Museum of African American History, 538*p*; Cheswell, Wentworth, 120; Chisholm, Shirley, 940; Civil Rights Act of 1964, 934–935; in Civil War, 593–595; Coleman, Bessie, 783*p*; in Congress of Industrial Organizations union, 814; as cowboys, 367, 367*p*; culture of, in South, 465–466; discrimination challenged by, 703–705; *Dred Scott* decision, 554–555; Du Bois, W.E.B., 705; in early automotive industry, 779; education of, 522*p*, 522–523, 617–618; election of 1868, 625; Ellison, Ralph, 885*p*, 886; Emancipation Proclamation, 590–593; in First Seminole War (1817), 293; free, in the South, 461–462; Freedmen's Bureau, 617; Freedom Rides, 932–933; Fugitive Slave Act, 545–546; in Gold Rush (California), 411; in Great Depression, 812–815; Great Migration north of, 616–617, 670–671, 787–789; Great Society reforms, 935–936; increased activism of, 936–937; in Industrial Workers of the World union, 700; jazz music of, 791–792, 885; in Knights of Labor union, 653; Ku Klux Klan and, 628–629; Love, Nat, 367*p*; March on Washington, 934; Marshall, Thurgood, 194; minority rights in 1920s, 787–789; movement to northern cities by, 670–671; not addressed in Constitutional Convention of 1787, 164, 183; not addressed in Declaration of Independence, 122–123, 230; Obama, Barack, 979, 990–991, 991*f*; opportunities of 1970s, 958; poll tax banned, 221; postwar civil rights activism of, 874; Powell, Colin, 970, 983; Reconstruction Amendments and, 214*f*, 214–215, 615–617, 624*f*, 626; reconstruction and freedom for, 615–618; Reconstruction in North, 633–634; reform in communities of, 522–523; religion of, 466; Revels, Hiram, 611*p*, 628; Rice, Condoleezza, 989; Robinson, Jackie, 874*p*; school segregation battles, 924–927; as slave labor on plantations, 328, 334; slave rebellions, 467–468; as social critics, 885–886; in Spanish-American War, 727; spirituals (music) of, 316, 466, 819; Student Non-Violent Coordinating Committee, 929–930; in 2013 census, 998; voting rights restricted in South, 620–622, 631–632; voting rights under British, 153; in War of 1812, 291; Washington, Booker T., 703, 704*f*; Wells, Ida B., 704; westward movement of, 379, 379*p*; in World War I, 753, 761; in World War II, 838–839, 840*p*

African Methodist Episcopal (AME) Church, 519, 522

Agent Orange, in Vietnam War, 903

age of U.S. population, 999–1000

Agnew, Spiro, 954

Agricultural Adjustment Act (AAA), 811

agriculture: in ancient Greece, 23; of ancient Indians, 11–13; in California, 413; closed markets impact of, 159–160; Columbian Exchange and, 45; cotton industry, 452–457; equipment improvements for, 443; Erie Canal impact on, 309; German immigrants in, 509; of Ghana, 19; Jackson, Andrew, and, 328; Manifest Destiny and, 397; in Middle Ages, 25; Morrill Act of 1862, 378; National Grange, 382; of Native Americans, 14; poor land in Indian Territory and, 346*f*; Shays's Rebellion (1786), 161–162; slavery and, 476–477; Southern economy dependence on, 73–74, 333–334, 335*f*, 426; in Spanish America, 399; supply and demand, 381*c*; tariffs and, 335; utopian communities and, 514; water rights and, 407; in West, 334

Aguinaldo, Emilio, 726

AIDS (acquired immune deficiency syndrome), 996

AIM (American Indian Movement), 921*p*, 941

Ain't I a Woman (Truth), 526

airplanes, 646–647, 647*p*, 748*p*, 749

Alamo, battle of, 394

Alaska, 715*p*, 719–720

Albany Plan of Union, 96

Albright, Madeleine, 235, 973

Alcorn University, 628

Alcott, Louisa May, 517

Aldrin, Edwin "Buzz," 897

Aleut (Native American culture), 13

Algonquian Indians, 15, 95

Alien and Sedition Acts of 1798, 266–267, 271

Alighieri, Dante, 27

Allen, Richard, 522

Alliance for Progress, 894

Allied powers: in World War I ; financial losses, 764; France, Russia, Britain, and Italy, 747; peace agreement, 765–766; Russia's separate peace, 758; war dead, 763–764. *See also* World War I

Allied powers: in World War II,. Battle of Britain, 834; France surrender, 833–834; war declared by, 832–833. *See also* World War II

Almoravids (Islamic group), 20

Almy, William, 425

al Qaeda, 984

AMA (American Medical Association), 691

AME (African Methodist Episcopal) **Church,** 519, 522

amending Constitution, 168–169, 173, 185. *See also* Constitution, U.S.

America, empires in. See European empires in the Americas

America as world power. *See* United States, as world power

American Anti-Slavery Society, 490, 525, 615

American Civil Liberties Union (ACLU), 784, 787

American Colonization Society, 490

American Crisis, The (Paine), 131

American Expeditionary Force (AEF), in World War I, 757

American Federation of Labor, 639, 654, 654*f*, 699

American Fur Company, 358

American Independent Party, 912

American Indian Movement (AIM), 921*p*, 941

American Medical Association (AMA), 691

American Missionary Association, 617

American Party of 1854, 553

American Progress (Gast), 398*p*

American Recovery and Reinvestment Act of 2009, 987

American Red Cross, 597

American Revolution, 102–147, 147 MC1–147 MC2; Boston Massacre, 109–110; Boston Tea Party, 110–111; *Common Sense* (Paine), 119; Declaration of Independence, 120–127; defeats and victories, 130–133; early battles of, 117–118; European help, 133–134; First Continental Congress, 113–114; Great Britain tax raises, 106–109; historical interpretation skills, 142–144; Intolerable Acts, 112; reenactments, 102*p*; sea battles, 136–137; Second Continental Congress, 116; "shot heard 'round the world," 114–115; in South, 139–140; timeline for 1760 to 1785, 103; Treaty of Paris, 142–144; Valley Forge, winter at, 135–136; war effort, 128–130; in West, 137–138; Yorktown, battle of, 141–142

Americans, earliest, Mesoamerican and South American societies, 8–10, migrations, 6–8

American Slavery As It Is (Weld and Grimké), 491, 525

Americans with Disabilities Act of 1990, 179, 942

American System, 306

American Temperance Society, 520

American Temperance Union, 520

amnesty, for southerners, 615

Amsterdam News, 788

amusement parks, 673

Anaconda plan, in Civil War, 581

Anasazi (Native American culture), 11–12

Anderson, Joseph R., 449*p*, 458

Anderson, Marian, 819

Anderson, Robert, 571

Andros, Sir Edmund, 91

Angel Island, as immigrant entry point, 665, 666*p*

Anglican Church of England, 54

Annapolis Convention of 1786, 162–163

annexation of land, 390, 398

Anthony, Susan B., 531*f*, 533, 533*p*, 702

anti-abolitionist rallies, 494*f*

Antietam, battle of, in Civil War, 580*p*, 580–581

Antifederalists, 170–173, 185–186

anti-immigration movements, 509–510

Index

Anti-Imperialist League, 727
Antioch College, 521*f*
antislavery literature, 500, 546–547
antisuffragists, 530*p*
antitrust movement, 650–651
anti-Vietnam War protests, 910–911, 911*p*
Apache Indians, 14, 375
apartheid, 961
Apollo 11 space craft, 898, 898*p*
Appalachian Mountains, 88*p*
Appeal to the Christian Women of the South (Grimké), 491
Appeal to the Colored Citizens of the World (Walker), 490
appeasement, of Hitler in 1938, 832–833
Appomattox Courthouse, 605, 605*p*
Apprentice Laws, 620–621
apprentices, in New England colonies, 81–82
appropriation of lands, 125
Arab Spring (2010), 979
Arapaho Indians, 14
architecture, 317–318, 794
Argonne Forest, battle of, in World War I, 759
arguments, strength of, 975
Aristotle, of ancient Greece, 23
Arkwright, Richard, 425
Armistead, James, 142
armistice, at end of World War I, 761–762
arms, keeping and bearing, 225
arms race, nuclear, 880
Armstrong, Louis, 792, 792*f*
Armstrong, Neil, 897
Arnaz, Desi, 885
Arnold, Benedict, 117, 130, 141
art deco design, 794
Arthur, Chester A., 688*f*, 689
Arthur, T. S., 530
Articles of Confederation, 149, 152–155, 157
artists, American, 315–320
ascertained by law, crimes, 212
Ashley, William, 358
Asia, sea route to, 39–40
Asian American Legal Defense and Education Fund, 940

Asian Americans, 668*p*, 940
Askia the Great, of the Songhai empire, 22
aspects of slave communities, 485
assembly, freedom of, 212*p*, 224*p*, 225
assembly line, in manufacturing, 428*p*, 646, 778, 779*p*
assimilation, 377, 677
Association Test of 1776, 120
Astor, John Jacob, 358–359
astrolabe navigation instruments, 38
Atahualpa (Inca leader), 33*p*
Atlanta, GA, after Civil War, 633*p*
Atlee, Clement, 868
atomic bomb, 827*p*, 858*p*, 858–859, 878
Audubon, John James, 316, 316*p*
Austin, Stephen F., 393, 393*p*, 395
authority, in colonial Virginia, 70; presidential, during Great Depression, 812; rejection of government, 910
automobiles, Model T Ford, 778–779, price *versus* production, 780*c*
Avery College, 523
Axis powers, in World War II, 832
Aztec culture of Mesoamerica, 8–10, 9*m*, 46–47

B

baby boom, post-World War II, 882
Bache, Sarah Franklin, 143*f*
background checks for gun sales, 993
Bacon, Nathaniel, 71
Bacon's Rebellion of 1676, 71
Baez, Joan, 891
Bagley, Sarah G., 433–434
bail, right to, 227
Balboa, Vasco Núñez de, 44, 48*m*
Ball, Lucille, 885
bandwagon technique, in

propaganda, 506
banking crisis, in Great Depression, 804
Bank of Italy, in San Francisco, 667
Bank of the United States (national bank), Clay support for, 306, 309; establishment of, 254; Jackson's attacks on, 336–338, 338*f*; Jackson vetoes charter renewal of, 325; Jefferson's view of, 271
bankruptcy, laws of, 200
banks, in recession of 2007–2009, 986–987
Banneker, Benjamin, 252*f*
Baquaqua, Mahommah G., 481*f*
Barbary pirates, 282
bar graphs, 469
Barton, Clara, 597, 597*p*
baseball, 511, 791
Bataan Death March, 829, 849
battle maps, interpretation of, 887
Battle of Britain, in World War II, 834, 834*p*
Baumfree, Isabella, 529
Bay of Pigs (Cuba), invasion of 1961, 894–895
Bayonet Constitution, of Hawaii, 720
Bear Flag Revolt, 403, 403*p*
beatniks, 886
Beauregard, Pierre G. T., 577
Beckwourth, Jim, 358, 358*p*
Beecher, Catharine, 521
Beecher, Lyman, 518, 520, 547
Begin, Menachem, 961*f*, 962
Bell, Alexander Graham, 639, 644*f*, 645, 645*p*
Bell, John, 560
Belleau Wood, battle of, in World War I, 759
Bellows, Henry, 575
benevolent societies, in immigrant communities, 667
Berbers, 19
Bering Land Bridge, 6–7
Berkeley, Lord John, 85
Berle, Milton, 885
Berlin Conference of 1884, 351
Berlin Wall, 895–896, 921, 947*p*, 969–970, 970*p*

Bernstein, Carl, 953
Berry, Chuck, 885
Bessemer, Henry, 642, 644*f*
Bessemer steel process, 642
Bethune, Mary McLeod, 819
Bett, Mum, 125*p*
bias, 300, 445
bicameral legislature, in Constitution, 165–166
Biddle, Nicholas, 337
Bidwell, Annie, 353, 380
big business, dominance of, 648–651
Bill of Attainder (forbidden by Constitution), 202
Bill of Rights, accused, rights of, 226–228; English, 91, 152, 157, 174; First Amendment, 223–225; overview, 233*c*; protecting citizens by, 225; ratification of, 179, 186–187; states and citizens' rights, 228–229; text of, 211–213; in U.S. Constitution, 173–174
bills, laws from, 199–200
Billy Budd (Melville), 515
Bingham, George Caleb, 316
biographies: Addams, Jane, 677; Banneker, Benjamin, 252; Bryan, William Jennings, 383; Bush, George W., 983; Chavez, Cesar, 939; Chief Joseph, 376; Clay, Henry, 307; Clinton, Bill, 973; Douglass, Frederick, 491; Equiano, Olaudah, 93; Garvey, Marcus, 789; Gompers, Samuel, 654; Grant, Ulysses S., 589; Hutchinson, Anne, 80; Jackson, Andrew, 330; Jefferson, Thomas, 272; Johnson, Lyndon B., 934; Kennedy, John F., 932; King, Martin Luther, Jr., 929; La Follette, Robert M., 691; Lee, Robert E., 579; Liliuokalani, Queen of Hawaii, 720; Lin, Maya Ying, 915; Lincoln, Abraham, 592; McCain, John, 903; Morse, Samuel F. B., 442; Obama, Barack, 991; O'Connor, Sandra Day, 965; O'Keefe, Georgia, 794; Parks,

Rosa, 928; Penn, William, 86; Pontiac, 97; Roosevelt, Franklin Delano, 807; Roosevelt, Theodore, 726; Turner, Nat, 467; Washington, George, 116; Wilson, Woodrow, 767
Birds of America, The (Audubon), 316, 316*p*
Birmingham, AL, church bombings (1963), 936*f*
Bismarck, Otto von, 611, 746
"Black Cabinet," of Franklin Roosevelt, 819
Black Codes, 620–622
Black Death, in Middle Ages, 26
Blackfoot Indians, 14
Black Hawk (Sauk chief), 342
black nationalism movement, 788
Black Power movement, 936
Black Star Steamship Line, 789
Blackstone, William, 120
Black Tuesday (October 29, 1929), 803, 803*c*, 803*p*
Blackwell, Elizabeth, 575
"bleeding Kansas," 551*p*, 551–552
Blow, Susan, 690
Bolívar, Simon, 103*p*, 303
bomb shelters, 880*p*
bonds, 250
Bonus Army, in Great Depression, 806
boomtowns, in west, 365
Boone, Daniel, 354
Booth, John Wilkes, 618
bootleggers, 785
Borden, Gail, 421*p*
border states, in Civil War, 572
"Boss" Tweed, 687, 687*f*
Boston, MA American Revolutionary battles for, 117*m*
Boston Gazette and County Journal, 110*f*
Boston Manufacturing Company, 431
Boston Marathon bombing (2013), 979
Boston Massacre, 109*p*, 109–110, 110*f*, 111*c*
Boston Tea Party, 65, 110–111, 111*p*
Bowie, Jim, 394

Boxer Rebellion, in China, 715, 722–723, 723*p*, 730*m*
boycotts, 107
Bozeman Trail, 372
bracero **program,** 839, 840*p*
Bradford, William, 77
Bradley, Omar, 859
Bragg, Braxton, 614
Braille, Louis, 325, 505
Brando, Marlon, 886
Breckinridge, John C., 560
Breckinridge, Lucy, 460
Brezhnev, Leonid, 952
Bridger, Jim, 358
brinkmanship strategy, 881
Britain. *See* Great Britain
British East India Company, 110
Brooks, Preston, 552, 552*p*
Brown, John, 551, 558–559, 559*p*
Brown, Linda, 926*f*
Brown, Moses, 425
Brown, Smith, 425
Brown, William Wells, 492
Brown University, 521*f*
Brown v. *Board of Education* (1954), 179, 921*p*, 925, 926*f*
Bruce, Blanche K., 628
Bryan, William Jennings: anti-World War I view of, 752; Free Silver movement supported by, 382–383, 383*f*; against imperialism, 730*m*; in Scopes trial, 786*f*, 787; Taft defeat of, 709
Bryant, Roy, 927
Bryn Mawr College, 783*p*
Buchanan, James, 553, 561
Buena Vista, battle of (1847), 404*p*
buffalo: Cody, William "Buffalo Bill" and, 369; photograph of, 2*p*; Plains Indians dependency on, 371–372, 372*p*
buffalo soldiers, 373
Bulge, battle of, in World War II, 856, 856*p*
Bull Run/Manassas, battles of, in Civil War, 577–580
Bunker Hill, battle of, 117
Bureau of Indian Affairs, 340
Burgoyne, John, 132
Burnet, David, 394

Burns, Anthony, 498–499, 546
Burnside, Ambrose E., 598
Burr, Aaron, 264
Bush, George H. W., Cold War end, 969–970; economic policy, 971; election of, 947; Persian Gulf War, 970–971
Bush, George W., 979p, 982, 983f, 988–990
business, booms of Roaring Twenties, 778–780; cycles in, 804; dominance of big, 648–651; probusiness administration of Coolidge, 777–778
Butler, Andrew Pickens, 552
Butterfield, Alexander, 954
buying on margin, in stock market, 802
Byzantine Empire, 26

C

Cabeza de Vaca, Álvar Núñez, 49–50
cabinet of George Washington, 247p
Cabot, John, 55–56
Cahokia (Mississippian mound builders city), 12
Calhoun, John C., secession views of, 497, 543, 544f, 545p; on states' rights, 337p; Tariff of Abominations (1827), 334–335; as vice president, 330; as War Hawk in 1812, 286
California, in America's growth in 1850, 416m; Bear Flag Revolt, 403; boomtowns of, 365; conservation efforts in, 708p; early settlers in, 392, 399–400; gold rush, 389, 408–414; in Great Depression, 818–819; immigration to, 804p, 806p; labor strikes in, 654–655, 655c; Mexican American population, 406t; Mexican-American War and, 401; in Mexican Cession, 405; Native Americans in, 14; slavery question and, 497m, 497–498,

543; Stanford, Leland, as business leader, 650; Teapot Dome scandal, 777; telegraph line to, 367; United Farm Workers union in, 938; as western trail destination, 359
California Railroad strike of 1894, 655f
Calley, William, 906–907
Calvert, Cecilius, 71
Calvert, George, 71
Camp David Accords (1978), 961f, 962
Canada, American Revolution battles in, 130; to avoid Vietnam War military service, 910; in Cattle Kingdom, 366; early exploration of, 36, 56, 57m; Loyalists flee to, before American Revolution, 120; in NAFTA, 972; in NATO, 872; Paleo-Indian movements through, 7; Rush-Bagot Agreement signed by (1817), 292, 293m; slaves escaping to, 379, 526, 546; smuggling during Prohibition in U.S., 785; Tecumseh flight to, 286; Treaty of Paris of 1759 and, 97; War Hawks' desire to invade, 286; War of 1812 battles on border of, 288–290
canals, in early U.S., 308m
candid world, 124
capital, moving to Washington, DC, 251
capitalism, 338f, 699
capitation-based taxes (forbidden by Constitution), 202
Capone, Al "Scarface," 785
Caputo, Philip, 905
caravel ships, 38, 38p
Carmichael, Stokely, 936
Carnegie, Andrew, 649, 655, 675
Carnegie Steel Company, Homestead strike of 1892, 639
Carolinas, as English colonies, 73
carpetbaggers, in Reconstructionist South, 627
Carson, Rachel, 958

Carter, Jimmy, election, 947, 959–960, 960m; foreign policy, 961–963
Carteret, Sir George, 85
Cartier, Jacques, 56, 58
cartoons, political, 607, 806f
Cass, Lewis, 497, 542–543
Castro, Fidel, 865p, 894–895
Catcher in the Rye, The (Salinger), 885–886
categorizing skills, 828
Catholic religion, Catholic Reformation, 54; Maryland colony for, 71–72; in Spanish colonies, 52
Catlin, George, 316p
Catt, Carrie Chapman, 703
cattle drives, 366
Cattle Kingdom, 366–367
cattle ranching, westward expansion and, 366–367
causal relationships, identifying, 711
cause-effect chains, 422, 640
Cayuga Indians, 15
CBS (Columbia Broadcasting System), 790
CCC (Civilian Conservation Corps), 811
Centennial Exposition, Philadelphia (1876), 661
Central American conflicts in 1980s, 967m, 967–968
Central Intelligence Agency (CIA), 881, 895
central issues, identification of, 321
Central Pacific Railroad, 368, 650
Central Park, New York City, 672p, 673
Central Powers, in World War I, 747
Century of Dishonor, A (Jackson), 377
Chamberlain, Joshua, 600
Chamberlain, Neville, 832–833
Champlain, Samuel de, 58
chance, oversight, and error in history, 635
Chancellorsville battle, in Civil War, 598–599
Chaney, James, 935

Chaplin, Charlie, 791
Charity Organization Society (COS), 676
Charles H. Wright Museum of African American History, 538p
charter (permission to start colonies), 56
Chavez, Cesar, 938–939, 939f
checks and balances, in Constitution, 167–168, 185, 191f
Cheney, Dick, 983
Cherokee Indians, 15, 18, 325, 341–343, 347m
Cherokee Nation v. Georgia (1831), 342
Chestnut, Mary Boykin, 572, 614
Cheswell, Wentworth, 120
Chevalier, Michel, 437
Chicago, IL, Capone, Al "Scarface," in, 785; Democratic National Convention of 1968 in, 911–912; diseases in, 675; Erie Canal impact on, 313; growth of, 670–671; Hull House, 661, 677–678; influenza epidemic of 1918, 764–765; McCormick reaper manufactured in, 443; Obama, Barack, and, 991; political machines in, 686; race riots in 1919, 787; railroads, impact on, 440, 549, 643; Till, Emmett, from, 926; World's Columbian Exposition (1893), 644f, 661
Chickasaw Indians, 341, 347m
Chief Joseph, of Nez Percé Indians, 375, 376f
children, child labor, 430, 432f, 695–697, 696p–697p; in colonial Virginia, 71
China, Boxer Rebellion in, 715; immigrants from, in gold rush, 412; Nixon visit to, 952; U.S. trade with, 722–723
Chinese Exclusion Act of 1880, 668–669
Chisholm, Jesse, 366
Chisholm, Shirley, 940, 940p
Chisholm Trail, 366
Choctaw Indians, 18, 340–341, 347m

cholera epidemics, in cities, 511
Christy, David, 456
chronological order, 150, 640
Chrysler Building, New York, 794
Churchill, Winston, 832, 834, 843, 845p, 868
Church of England, 54
Church of Jesus Christ of Latter-day Saints (Mormons), 360
CIA (Central Intelligence Agency), 881, 895
Cigar Makers Union, 654f
CIO (Congress of Industrial Organizations), 814
circle graphs, 469
circuit riding judges, 192f
circumnavigating the globe, 44
circumstances, political, 303
citizenship, 234–238. See also Bill of Rights; Constitution, U.S.
city life, growth in 1900, 670–671; growth of, 511–512; improving, 676–678; problems in, 674–676; skyscrapers in, 671
Civilian Conservation Corps (CCC), 811
Civil Rights Act of 1866, 622
Civil Rights Act of 1875, 630–631
Civil Rights Act of 1964, 934, 935p, 939
civil rights movement, 920–945; for Asian Americans, 940; changes in, 936–937; disability rights movement, 942; Freedom Rides, 932–933; for Hispanic Americans, 938–939; individuals, rights for, 941–942; John F. Kennedy, 931–932; League of United Latin American Citizens, 940–941; Lyndon B. Johnson, 934–936; March on Washington of 1963, 934; Martin Luther King Jr. in Birmingham, 933; Medgar Evers assassinated, 933–934; Montgomery bus boycott,

927–928; National Italian American Foundation, 940; for Native Americans, 941; post-World War II, 874; segregation, battling, 924–927; sit-ins and SNCC, 929–930; speech-making skills, 943; timeline for 1950 to 1975, 921; women's movement, 939–940
civil service system, 688–689
Civil War, 566–609; reconstruction, after Civil War; African Americans in, 593–594; Antietam, battle of, 580–581; blockade breaking, 581–582; choosing sides in, 570–574, 573m; Emancipation Proclamation, 590–593; far west struggles, 584m, 586–587; Fredericksburg and Chancellorsville battles, 598–599; Gettysburg, battle of, 599–603; New Orleans, fall of, 584–585; opposition to, 594–595; political cartoons, 607; preparing for, 575–576; Sherman's strikes in the South, 603–605; soldiers' and civilians' lives in, 595–597; South surrenders, 567p, 605–606; in Tennessee, 583–584; timeline for 1861 to 1865, 567; Vicksburg, siege of, 585–586, 588m–589m; in Virginia, 577–580; Wilderness Campaign, 603; Civil Works Administration (CWA), 811. See also nation divided
Clark, George Rogers, 137
Clark, William, 271–272, 356
Classical Period, of ancient Greece, 23–24
Clay, Henry, American System for economic self-sufficiency, 306–307; biography of, 307p; Compromise of 1850, 543, 545p; election of 1824 and, 311, 329; Missouri Compromise and, 310; slavery compromises proposed by, 497, 498p; tariff reduction

proposals of, 336; as War Hawk in 1812, 286; as Whig Party candidate in 1844, 390, 398

Clayton Antitrust Act of 1914, 710

Clemenceau, George, 766

Clermont steamboat, 421, 435

Cleveland, Grover, 656, 688*f*, 720*f*, 725

cliff dwellings of Anasazi, 12*p*

Clinton, Bill, Congress and, 972–973, 973*f*; global issues, 973–974; impeachment of (1998), 191

Clinton, DeWitt, 173

Clinton, Henry, 139–140

closed markets, impact of, 160

Clotel (Brown), 492

coal mining, 438–439

"Code Talkers," Navajo, in World War II, 850*p*

Cody, William "Buffalo Bill," 369

Coercive Acts of 1774, 112

Coit, Stanton, 677

Cold War, 864–869; allies become enemies, 870–871; 1950s economy, 882–884; pop culture of, 884–885; postwar, 873–874; social critics, 885–886; battle map interpretation, 887; Bush, George H. W., and, 969–970; Eisenhower, Dwight D. and, 880–881; Europe in, 872*m*; Korean War, 876–878; postwar world, 868–870; Red Scares, 878–880; space exploration and, 896–898; timeline for 1945 to 1959, 865

Cole, Thomas, 315*p*, 316, 514

Coleman, Bessie, 783*p*

collective bargaining, 653

College of William and Mary, 83

Colorado Miners' strike of 1893, 655*f*

Columbia Broadcasting System (CBS), 790

Columbian Exchange, 44–45

Columbian Exposition (Chicago, 1893), 661

Columbus, Christopher, 3, 33*p*, 41–44, 42*m*, 43*f*

Comanche Indians, 373

Commerce Compromises, in Constitution, 167

Committee on Civil Rights (1946), 874

Committee on Public Information (CPI), 753

Committees of Correspondence, 107

Committee to Reelect the President (CRP), Watergate and, 953

common-school movement, 521

Common Sense (Paine), 119

communism: Bolsheviks in 1917 Russia, 758; fear of (Red Scares), 874–880; Kennedy confronting, 894–898. *See also* Vietnam War years

community service, 234*p*, 237–238

comparison-contrast patterns, 474, 640

comparison-making skills, 679

complex judicial cases, 554

component diagrams, 29

Compromise of 1820, 550*m*

Compromise of 1850, 498, 543–544, 550*m*

Compromise of 1877, 611

Comstock Lode (Nevada gold deposits), 364–365

conclusions, drawing, 326

Concord, battle of, 115

concrete legal victories, of labor unions, 434

concrete proof, 879

Confederate States of America, 561–562. *See also* Civil War

Congress, U.S.: U.S.; Alien and Sedition Acts of 1798, 266–267; Articles of Confederation, 153–154, 160–161; Bank of the United States established, 254; Bill of Rights, 173–174; "Bleeding Kansas" and, 551–552; child labor laws, 696; Chinese Exclusion Act of 1882, 668–669; Civil Rights Act of 1964, 934; Civil War military service draft, 595; Clinton impeached by, 973; communism and, 871, 878; in Constitution, 156*f*, 166–167; elastic clause in Constitution and, 188–189, 254; Embargo Act passed by, 283; Enforcement Acts, 629; environmental protection laws passed by, 959; Fugitive Slave Act of 1850, 545–546; Hawaii annexed, 1898, 721; Homestead Act of 1862, 378; impeachment powers of, 191; Indian Citizenship Act of 1924, 782; Indian Removal Act of 1830, 340; Interstate Commerce Act of 1887, 382; Judiciary Act of 1789, 248; Land Ordinance of 1785, 155; as legislative branch of government, 189–191; Lend-Lease Act of 1941, 834; Lewis and Clark Expedition funded by, 356; Missouri Compromise, 310; Morrill Act of 1862, 378; NASA supported by, in 1960s, 897; national bank established by, 306; navy creation by, 283*f*; Nixon impeached by, 955; Non-Intercourse Act passed by, 284; Pelosi, Nancy, as first female Speaker of the House, 989; Philippine Government Act, 729; presidential selection in 1824, 329; Progressive amendments, 1909–1920, 710*t*; Prohibition, 785; Pure Food and Drug Act of 1906, 708; readmission of southern states to union, 625; Reagan tax cuts and spending cuts approved by, 965; Reconstruction Amendments, 615–618, 620, 622; Roosevelt's special session of, 809–810; Sherman Antitrust Act, 651; Sherman Silver Purchase Act of 1888, 382; slave importation banned in 1808, 455; slavery issues avoided by, 494–495, 527; Spanish-American War declared, 725; Taft-Hartley Act of 1947, 873–874; tariffs passed by, 306, 334–336; Texas annexation, 399; Tonkin Gulf Resolution, 902; Treaty of Versailles rejected by, 759; Truman versus, 874–875; Twelfth Amendment on ballots, 269; USA PATRIOT Act of 2001, 988; veto override power of, 168; Voting Rights Act of 1965, 935; War of 1812 declared by, 286–287; War Powers Act of 1973, 915; Wilmot Proviso defeated in, 405; women's suffrage (Nineteenth Amendment), 703, 783;World War I declared, 752–753; World War II declaration, 836. *See also* Constitution

Congressional Medal of Honor, 727, 761

Congress of Industrial Organizations (CIO), 814

Congress of Racial Equality (CORE), 932

Connecticut, as English colony, 79

Connor, Eugene "Bull," 933

conquistadors (Spanish) **in Americas,** 46–48

consequences, of Hispanic civil rights movement, 939; of War of 1812, 291; of Watergate scandal, 955; conservation, 708p

Constitution, U.S., 178–222, citizenship rights and responsibilities, 234–238; Constitutional Convention (1787), 149, 164, 182–183; context skills, 239; creation of, 164–169; executive branch, 191–193; federalists and antifederalists, 185–186; federal system, 188–189; government system in, 185; Great Compromise, 183; judicial branch, 192–194; key facts about, 233t; legislative branch, 189–190, 196–203; loose construction of, 254; Nineteenth Amendment (women's suffrage) to, 533f; origins of, 156–157;

overview, 232–233; ratification of, 170–174, 186–187; slavery compromises, 183–184; strict construction of, 254; timeline for 1785 to 1995, 149, 179

Constitution, U.S., Bill of Rights, 223–229; accused, rights of, 226–228; First Amendment, 223–225; protecting citizens by, 225; states' and citizens' rights, 228–229

Constitution, U.S., text of, 195–222; amending process, 208; Amendments 11 to 27, 211–222; Amendments 1 to 10 (Bill of Rights), 211–213; executive branch, 203–205; judicial branch, 205–207; legislature, 196–203; national government supremacy, 209; preamble, 195; ratification, 210; states, relations among, 207–208

Constitutional Union Party, 560

Constitution Day (September 17), 230–233

containment, as Cold War policy, 871

contemporary culture, 341

context skills, 66, 239

Continental Army, 116

Continental Congress, 153–154

continuance, of federal office, 198

continuity and change, 739

contrabands (escaped slaves in Civil War), 593

controversial issues, identifying, 1001

Convention of 1818, 292

convictions versus bias, 445

convoy system, 761

Cook, James, 65p

Cooke, Jay, 370, 630

Coolidge, Calvin, 776, 777–778

Cooper, James Fenimore, 314–315, 319

Cooper, Peter, 437

Copeland, John A., 558–559

Copperheads (Civil War opposition in North), 595

Coral Sea, battle of (1942), 850

CORE (Congress of Racial Equality), 932

corn cultivation, 3p

Cornwallis, Charles, 132, 141

Coronado, Francisco Vásquez de, 50

corporations, 648–649

Corps of Discovery, 272, 354, 356

corruption, political, 686–689

corruption of blood (forbidden by Constitution), 207

Cortés, Hernán, 46

COS (Charity Organization Society), 676

cost-and-benefit analysis, 657

Costilla, Father Miguel Hidalgo y, 393

cotton, cotton belt, 454–455, 455m; cotton gin, 449p, 453–454; profitability of, 452; trade in, 455–457

cotton diplomacy, in Civil War, 574

Coughlin, Father Charles Edward, 812

Count Basie, 820

counterculture, 911

counterfeiting, 200

"court-packing" bill, 815

courts, colonial, 91–92

courts of appeals, 193

cowboys, work of, 366

Cox, James M., 777

CPI (Committee on Public Information), 753

craftspeople, in New England colonies, 81–82

Crawford, William, 329

Crazy Horse (Oglala Sioux chief), 372, 375

Creek Indians, 15, 341, 347m

Creek War of 1814, 290

Crimean War, 539

criminal activity, in cities, 511–512

criteria, 334

Crittenden, John J., 561

Crockett, Davy, 394

Cronkite, Walter, 907p

crop rotation, 454

crossbreeding cotton, 454

CRP (Committee to Reelect the President), Watergate and, 953

cruel and unusual punishment, 227

Crummel, Alexander, 522

Crusades, in Middle Ages, 25

Cuba, 726–728, 894–896, 895m–896m

Cuban missile crisis, 919 MC1–919 MC2

culture, contemporary, 341; of Great Depression of 1930s, 819–820; mass, 672–673; Mexican-American, 406; national identity and, 314–318; of Native Americans, 7–8, 13–17; of slaves in America, 465–467, 479, 485–486; in South, 459–461

Cumberland Road, 307–308

Cummings, Homer, 815

currency, dollar, 149

Custer, Armstrong, 374

cutaway diagrams, 29, 29p

Cuzco (Inca city), 10

CWA (Civil Works Administration), 811

cyberbullying, 995

D

Da Gama, Vasco, 39

Dana, Richard Henry, Jr., 400

Dare, Virginia, 58

Darrow, Clarence, 786f, 787

Dartmouth College **v.** *Woodward* (1819), 338f

Darwin, Charles, 650, 787

Daughters of the American Revolution (DAR), 819

da Vinci, Leonardo, 27

Davis, Benjamin O., Jr., 839, 840f

Davis, Henry, 615

Davis, Jefferson, 543, 561, 571, 574, 597, 628

Davis, John W., 777

Dawes, William, 114

Dawes Act of 1887, 351

Dawes General Allotment Act, 377

daylight savings time, 754

D-Day invasion, in World War II, 826p, 827, 846–848, 847p

Dean, John, 954

debating skills, 823

Debs, Eugene V., 700

decision-making skills, 295

Declaration of Independence, facts on, 230–231; signing, 122p; text of, 124–127; unfinished business in, 121–123; writing of, 120–121

Declaration of Sentiments (equal rights for women), 531f–532f, 532

Declaratory Act, of 1766, 108

Deere, John, 380, 443, 443f

deficits, 965, 985

deflation, 382

De La Beckwith, Byron, 934

Delano, Alonzo, 411

Delaware, in English colonies, 86

democracy, in ancient Greece, 24; Jacksonian, 328–330; Jeffersonian versus Jacksonian, 331c; in Latin America, 737, 737f

Democracy in America (de Tocqueville), 449

Democratic National Committee, Watergate scandal and, 953

Democratic Party, 330, 553

Democratic-Republican Party, 264

de Narváez, Pánfilo, 49

department stores, development of, 672

deportation, 234

depression, after Revolutionary War, 161

deregulation policies of Reagan, 965

de Soto, Hernando, 49

détente, 952, 961

Dewey, George, 726

Dewey, John, 690

Dewey, Thomas, 874

diagrams, interpreting, 29, 29p

Dial, The, 514

Dias, Bartolomeu, 39

Dickinson, Emily, 515

Diem, Ngo Dinh, 898–899, 901

direct democracy, in ancient Greece, 24

disability rights movement, 942

Disabled in Action (DIA), 942

discrimination, against African Americans, 703–705, 704f; banned in war industries, 838; against free African Americans in 1860, 461–462; reduced by Eisenhower, 924; Title IX (1972) ban on sexual, 957. *See also* civil rights movement

distinct responsibilities, of government branches, 189

district courts, 193

Dix, Dorothy, 520

Dogrib Indians, 13

Dole, Bob, 873, 973

dollar diplomacy, as foreign policy, 737, 737f

Dominican Republic, 737

Dominion of New England, 91

Domino, Fats, 865p

domino theory, of Communist expansion, 898

Donner party, 409

Dorchester Heights, battle of, 118

double jeopardy, 226

Douglas, Stephen, 549, 554–557, 557p, 572

Douglass, Frederick, 465, 491p, 491–492, 526, 532, 546p, 592, 616

doves and hawks, in Vietnam War years, 905–907

draft (required military service), 235–236, 236p, 595, 838

Drake, Edwin L., 644

Drake, Sir Francis, 54

drawing conclusions, 326

Dred Scott **decision,** 554–555

drive-in movie theaters, 884p

dry farming, by Plains farmers, 380

Du Bois, W.E.B., 704f, 705, 789

"duck-and-cover" drills, in American schools, 864p, 880

due process, 226

Dukakis, Michael, 969

Dulles, John Foster, 881

Dunny, Patrick, 509

Durand, Asher, 514p

Duryea, J. Frank and Charles, 644f, 646, 646p

Dust Bowl of 1930s, 816–818, 817m, 817p

Dutch presence in the Americas, 59–60, 84–85

Dutch West India Company, 85

duties, 200. *See also* tariffs

Index

E

Earhart, Amelia, 791
early childhood education, 690
Earp, Wyatt, 367p
Eastman, Charles, 705
Ebola epidemic of 2014, 979
Eckford, Elizabeth, 925, 927p
economy, after Revolution-
    ary War, 160–161; Bush,
    George H. W., and, 971; in
    California after gold rush,
    400–401; global, in twenty-
    first century, 985–987; Great
    Depression of 1930s collapse,
    804–805; Hamilton versus
    Jefferson's views of, 252;
    of middle English colonies,
    86–87; of New England colo-
    nies, 81–82; plantation labor
    force, 476–477; recession of
    2007–2009, 985–987; recov-
    ery of, after 2009, 990–991;
    service, 985–986; of southern
    English colonies, 73–74; stag-
    flation of 1967 to 1974, 951,
    951c, 951p; supply-side eco-
    nomics of Reagan, 964–965;
    Vietnam War impact on, 915
Ederley, Gertrude, 791, 792f
Edison, Thomas, 639, 644f,
    644–645
education, of African Americans
    after Civil War, 617–618,
    618p; early childhood, 690;
    increase in Roaring Twen-
    ties, 782; in New Eng-
    land colonies, 82–83; not
    addressed in Constitution,
    228–229; reform movements
    in, 520–522; state-funded,
    public, 301, 317–318
**Education of Handicapped
    Children Act of 1975,** 942
Edwards, Jonathan, 94
effect of sea exploration, 39
efficiency of machines, 424
Eiffel Tower, 639p
**Eighteenth Amendment to U.S.
    Constitution** (Prohibition),
    702, 785
Einstein, Albert, 235
Eisenhower, Dwight D., Cold
    War tensions and, 880–881;
    D-Day invasion led by, 846;

Fidel Castro and, 895; in
    North Africa World War II
    battles, 844; as president,
    878; racial discrimination
    reduced by, 924; Vietnam
    and, 899
El Alamein, battle of, 844
elastic clause of Constitution,
    189, 201
El Camino Real ("Royal Road"),
    in Spanish colonies, 48
elections, 1796, 263–265; 1800,
    268–269, 269f; 1828, 326,
    330–332; 1834, 327; 1852,
    548; 1860, 560m, 560–561;
    1866, 623; 1868, 625; 1876,
    630; 1920, 776–777; 1928,
    780–781; 1932, 807–808;
    1948, 874–875; 1960,
    931–932; 1968, 911–912;
    1972, 912–913, 913m; 1976,
    960; 1984, 965–966; 2000,
    982–983
Electoral College, 203m, 246
electricity, 644–645
**Elementary and Secondary
    Education Act of 1968,** 939
elements of life, 400
Ellington, Edward "Duke," 792,
    820
Ellis Island, as immigrant entry
    point, 660p, 665,
    681 MC1–681 MC2
Ellison, Ralph, 885p, 886
Ellison, William, 483
el-Sadat, Anwar, 961f, 962
Emancipation Proclamation,
    567p, 590–593, 591m, 615
Emancipator, The (newspaper),
    489
Embargo Act of 1807, 279,
    283–284, 299
Embree, Elihu, 475, 489
**Emergency Banking Relief Act
    of 1933,** 810
Emergency Quota Act of 1921,
    784–785
Emerson, Ralph Waldo,
    513–514
eminent domain, 226
emoluments, of federal office,
    198
empires in the Americas. *See*
    European empires in the
    Americas

Empire State Building, 773p,
    794
empresarios, in Texas, 393
encomienda system, in Spanish
    colonies, 51
energy consumption, 997
energy crisis, 951p
**Enforcement Acts of 1870 and
    1871,** 629
English Bill of Rights of 1689,
    91, 120, 152, 157
English colonies, 64–101;
    economy of middle colonies,
    86–87; French and Indian
    War, 95–98; governments
    in, 90–92; Great Awakening
    and Enlightenment, 93–94;
    growth in 1760, 88–89m;
    map of, 91m; New York and
    New Jersey, 84–85; Penn's
    colony, 85–86; timeline for
    1605 to 1770, 65; timelines,
    interpreting, 99; trade laws,
    92–94
English colonies, New England:
    economy of, 81–82; educa-
    tion in, 82–83; Pilgrims and
    Puritans, 75–77; religion and
    government in, 79–81
English colonies, southern:
    Carolinas and Georgia, 73;
    economies of, 73–74; James-
    town, 68–70; map of, 72m;
    Maryland, 71–72; Virginia,
    70–71
English laws, U.S. government
    and, 152
**English presence in the Ameri-
    cas,** 56–58. *See also* English
    colonies
Enigma code machine, 827p
Enlightenment movement,
    93–94, 152, 157
enumeration, for House of
    Representatives, 196
environmental issues, 958p,
    958–959, 996–998
**environments at end of Ice
    Age,** 7
EPA (U.S. Environmental Protec-
    tion Agency), 959
epidemics, in cities, 511
Equal Pay Act of 1963, 939
Equal Rights Amendment
    (ERA), 783, 940, 941p, 957

Equiano, Olaudah, 74, 93*f*
"Era of Good Feelings," 302
Ericsson, John, 582
Erie Canal, 298*p*, 309, 312*m*–313*m*
Eriksson, Leif (Viking explorer), 36–37
Erik the Red (Viking explorer), 36
error, oversight, and chance in history, 635
Ervin, Sam, 953, 955
escalation, 903
Escobedo v. *Illinois* (1964), 941
Espionage Act of 1917, 753, 754*f*
"ethnic cleansing," 974
ethnic diversity in Twenty-First century U.S., 998
Europe after World War I, 766*m*; American Revolution helped by, 133–134; in Cold War, 872*m*; before 1500, 23–27; militarism in, before World War I, 746; nationalism in before World War I, 746; World War II in, 833*m*, 843–848
European empires in the Americas, 32–63; Christopher Columbus, 41–44; Columbian Exchange, 44–45; Dutch presence, 59–60; English presence, 56–58; Ferdinand Magellan, 44; French presence, 58–59; historical question framing skills, 61; map of, 57*m*, 96*m*; Native Americans in Spanish colonies, 51–52; northwest passage search, 55–56; Protestant Reformation impact on, 53–54; sea voyages and, 37–40; southeastern Spanish colonies, 48–49; southwestern Spanish colonies, 49–51; Spain and England war impact on, 54–55; Spanish conquistadors, 46–48; timeline for 1400 to 1700, 33; of Vikings, 36–37
Evers, Medgar, 933–934
evolution, theory of, 787
excise taxes, 200
execution of strategies, 603, 851

executive branch of government, 167, 191–193, 203–205
executive orders, 192–193
executive privilege, 954*f*
Exodusters (African Americans moving west), 379
expatriates, 793
ex post facto law (forbidden by Constitution), 202

F

facilitated community growth, by women, 380
factors (crop brokers), 457
factors supporting slavery, 71
facts, opinions versus, 540
Fairbanks, Douglas, 791
Fairchild, George, 580
Fair Deal program, of Truman, 875
Fair Employment Act of 1942, 179
Fair Employment Practices Committee, 875
Fall, Albert, 777
fallacies in reasoning, 744
Fallen Timbers, battle of, 259
Farm Credit Administration (FCA), 811
Farmers' Alliances, 382
farmers' politics, 381–383
farming. *See* agriculture
Farragut, David, 585, 585*f*
fascism, 830
Fathers of Bebop (music), 885
Faubus, Orval, 925
FBI (Federal Bureau of Investigation), 953
FCA (Farm Credit Administration), 811
FDIC (Federal Deposit Insurance Corporation), 810*f*, 821
Federal Emergency Management Agency (FEMA), 990
federal form of government, national, state, and shared powers in, 208*f*
federalism system, 168, 170–173, 185, 188–189
Federalist Papers, 171–173, 186
Federalist Party, 185–186, 263, 284, 291

federal office terms and requirements, 197*c*
Federal Reserve Act of 1913, 709–710
Federal Reserve Board, 802–803
Federal Trade Commission, 710
Federal Writers' Project, 885*p*
Felt, W. Mark, 953
FEMA (Federal Emergency Management Agency), 990
Feminine Mystique, The (Friedan), 939
Ferguson, Miriam "Ma," 783
Ferraro, Geraldine, 965
Ferris, George, 644*f*
Ferris Wheel, at Columbian Exposition (Chicago, 1893), 661*p*
feudalism, in Middle Ages, 24–26
Fifteenth Amendment to Constitution, 624*f*, 625*p*, 626
54th Massachusetts Infantry, 593, 594*p*
Fillmore, Millard, 548, 553, 721
Finley, Robert, 490
Finney, Charles Grandison, 518
fireside chats, of Franklin D. Roosevelt, 810, 810*f*
First Amendment to U.S. Constitution, 223–225
First Continental Congress, 113–114
First Harvest in the Wilderness, The (Durand), 514*p*
First Seminole War of 1817, 293
First Virginia Charter, 68
fishing, in New England colonies, 81
Fisk University, 618
Fitzgerald, F. Scott, 792*f*, 793
"flappers" in Roaring Twenties, 783
flax, 457
Fleming, Alexander, 773
Fletcher v. *Peck* (1810), 338*f*
Florida: Adams-Onís Treaty, 293–294, 302, 362*m*; as Confederate state in Civil War, 561, 572; Cuban missile crisis near, 894, 895*m*; in election of 2000, 982–983; Hernando de Soto exploration of, 49;

Mexican American population in, 406c; Ponce de Leon exploration of, 48–49; readmitted to Union, 625; Second Seminole War, 344, 346m; slaves escaping to Spanish, 478; as slave state, 497m; in Treaty of Paris of 1783, 144

Foch, Ferdinand, 759

folktales, of slaves in South, 466, 485

Food Administration, in World War I, 753

food crops of South, 457

Foraker Act of 1900, 728

Ford, Gerald, 954, 955–956, 959, 960m

Ford, Henry, 646, 659 MC1–659 MC2, 778

Ford Motor Co., 778

foreign mercenaries, 126

foreign policy; 1807 to 1829, 302–305; of Jimmy Carter, 961–963; of Richard M. Nixon, 952; of Ronald Reagan, 966–968; of United States, 737f, 737–738

Fort Sumter, battle of, in Civil War, 567, 570–571, 571m

Fort Ticonderoga, 132

forty-niners (California gold rush), 409–410

Fourteen Points (Wilson), 765–766

Fourteenth Amendment to Constitution, 622–623, 624f

France: Alsace-Lorraine region of, 747; in American Revolution, 133–134, 134p, 136; in Cold War, 881; D-Day, June 6, 1944, in, 846–848; French Revolution, 254; Germany in zones after World War II, 868; Indochina (Vietnam) colony of, 898–899, 899m; John Adams and, 265; Louisiana Purchase by U.S., 271–272, 356–357; Louisiana traded by Spain to, 355; in Middle Ages, 24–25; neutrality of U.S. in 1793, 255–256; Northwest Passage sought by, 56; presence in the Americas, 58–59; refusal to assist

Confederacy, 602; as sphere of influence in China, 722; in Treaty of Paris of 1763, 88, 97; World War I, 748–750; World War I death toll, 763, 764c; World War I financial losses, 764; World War II, 832–834; XYZ Affair of 1793, 265, 266f

Francis Ferdinand, Archduke of Austria-Hungary, 743, 747, 747p

Frank, Hans, 869

Franklin, Benjamin: Albany Plan of Union of, 96; at Constitutional Convention of 1787, 164, 165p; as Federalist, 170; French assistance procured by, 134; *Poor Richard's Almanac*, 136; separation from Loyalist son, 120, 121f

Franklin, John Hope, 490

Franklin, William, 121, 121f

Frazier, William, 432–433

Fredericksburg battle, in Civil War, 598–599

free African Americans, 461–462, 462p

Free African Religious Society, 522

Freedmen's Bureau, 617–618, 622

Freedom Rides, 932–933, 933m

Freeport Doctrine, 557

Free Silver Movement, 382

Free-Soil Party, 497, 539, 543

Free Speech (Wells), 704

free states versus slave states, 497m

Frémont, John C., 358, 403, 417p, 554

French and Indian War, 95–98, 315

French Revolution, 243p, 255–256

Freud, Sigmund, 791

Friedan, Betty, 939, 940p

From Slavery to Freedom (Franklin and Moss), 490

frontier literature, 319–320

frontier's end, 383–384. *See also* southwest expansion; westward expansion

Fuel Administration, in World War I, 753–754

Fugitive Slave Act of 1850, 473, 498–499, 539, 545–547

Fuller, Margaret, 513–514, 529

Fulton, Robert, 421p, 435

functions of federal government, 271

fundamentalism, in religion, 786–787

Fundamental Orders of Connecticut (Hooker), 79

Futrell, Mary Hatwood, 229

G

Gadsden, James, 405

Gadsden Purchase, 405

Gagarin, Yuri, 896

Gage, Matilda Joslyn, 533–534

Gage, Thomas, 112

gag rule, 495

Galilei, Galileo, 33p

Gallatin, Albert, 271, 427

Gallaudet, Thomas, 505, 522

Galle, Johann, 421p

Gálvez, Bernardo de, 134, 134f

gam saan haak (Chinese immigrants in gold rush), 412

Gandhi, Indira, 921p

gang-labor system, on plantations, 482

Garfield, James A., 683, 688f, 689

Garrison, William Lloyd, 490–491, 505, 525, 531, 592, 615, 626

Garvey, Marcus, 788, 789f

gasoline-powered engine, 639

gasoline shortages of 1970s, 951p

Gast, John, 398p

Gates, Horatio, 140

Gaulle, Charles de, 834

General Amnesty Act of 1872, 629

General Motors Corporation, 802, 814

Genet, Edmond, 256

genocide, in World War II Germany, 857

George, David Lloyd, 766

Georgia: British defeat of, in Revolution, 139; Cherokee Indian removal from (1838), 342–343; in Confederacy, 561, 572; Constitution ratified by, 186; cotton trade and, 456–457; *Dred Scott* decision and, 554; as English colony, 73; Mexican American population in, 406*t*; Oglethorpe's settlement rules in pre-Revolutionary, 73; readmission to Union, 625; Sherman's attack of Atlanta, 603–604, 604*m*; slave codes of, 485; as slave state, 497*m*; Three-Fifths Compromise, 184

German, Obadiah, 287

Germantown Settlement (Pennsylvania), 678

Germany: Berlin Wall, 895–896, 969–970; divided, after World War II, 868; Holocaust genocide of Jewish people by, 856–858; immigrants from, 509; *Lusitania* sunk by, 751–752, 752*f*; Protestant Reformation of 1517 in, 53, 53*p*; Russia's separate peace with, in World War I, 758; sphere of influence in China of, 722; surrender of, in World War II, 855–856; totalitarianism in, 831, 831*p*; war crimes trials, after World War II, 869; World War I armistice, 761–762; World War I battles, 748–750, 759–761, 760*m*; World War I death toll, 763–764, 764*c*; World War I financial losses, 764; World War I reparations, 766; World War I U-boats, 750, 750*p*, 751, 752*f*; World War II defeat of, 844–848; World War II expansion of, 832–834; World War II surrender of, 855–856; Zimmermann Note, 752–753

Geronimo (Chiricahua Apache Indian leader), 375

Gettysburg, battle of, in Civil War, 599*p*–600*p*, 599–603; civilians at, 609 MC1–609 MC2

Gettysburg Address (Lincoln), 602*p*, 602–603

Ghana, 19–20, 20*p*

Ghost Dance religion, of Indians, 376

Giannini, Amadeo Peter, 666*p*, 667

Gibbons* v. *Ogden (1824), 309, 338*f*, 436–437

GI Bill of Rights, 873

Gibson, Josh, 791

Gilded Age, 686

Gillespie, Dizzy, 885

Gingrich, Newt, 972

Ginings, Gabriel, 81–82

Ginsberg, Allen, 886

global economy, of twenty-first century, 985–987

Global Fund to Fight AIDS, Tuberculosis, and Malaria, 996

globalization, 986

global warming, 997–998

Goering, Hermann, 869

golden spike, on transcontinental railroad, 369

"gold fever" (California gold rush), 409*p*–410*p*

gold rush, 419 MC1–419 MC2

gold standard, 382

gold trade, of Ghana, 19–20

Gompers, Samuel, 654, 654*f*, 699

Gonzales, Alberto, 989

Goodman, Andrew, 935

Goodman, Benny, 820

Gorbachev, Mikhail, 968–969

Gore, Al, 972*f*, 982

Gorgas, William C., 733

government: of ancient Greece, 23–24; of ancient Rome, 24; in English colonies, 90–92; in New England colonies, 79–81; organizing early, 247–248; terms about, 4*c*

government, forming, 148–177; Articles of Confederation, 152–155; challenges of, 158–163; points of view, determining, 175; timeline for 1777 to 1791, 149; *See also* Constitution, U.S.; English colonies

Grady, Henry, 631, 632, 633*p*

Grant, Ulysses S.: biography of, 589*f*; financial and political scandals in administration of, 629–630; Lee surrender to, 567*p*; as president, 625, 683; Siege of Vicksburg, 585; in Union western campaign, 583

Grapes of Wrath, The (Steinbeck), 820, 822

graphic organizers, 640

graph interpretation skills, 469, 764*c*, 795

Great Awakening, 93–94

Great Britain: Battle of Britain, in World War II, 834; English presence in the Americas, 56–58; Intolerable Acts of, 112; Parliamentary structure, 156; slave trade abolished in, 351; Spain's war with, 54–55; tax raises from, 106–109; trade with after Revolutionary War, 158–159; War of 1812 and, 290–292. *See also* English colonies

Great Compromise, in Constitution, 165–166, 166*f*, 183

Great Depression of 1930s, 798–825; culture of, 819–820; debating skills, 823; Dust Bowl, 816–818; economic collapse, 804–805; election of 1932, 807–808; hard times, 818–819; Hoover's reaction, 805–806; literature of, 822; Roosevelt's New Deal, 809–815, 821; stock market crash of 1929, 802–803; timeline for 1925 to 1940, 799

Great Exhibition of London, 1851, 421*p*

Great Gatsby, The (Fitzgerald), 792*f*, 793

Great Lakes, demilitarization of borders of, 292

Great Law of Peace, of Iroquois Confederation, 16

Great Migration: of African Americans to northern cities, 787, 788*p*, 792, 838; to English colonies, 78–79

Great Plains culture area, of Native Americans, 13*p*, 14–15

Great Pyramid of Giza, Egypt, 3*p*

Index

Great Society, of Lyndon B. Johnson, 935–936, 950

Greece, ancient, 23–24

Green, Ernest, 926

Greenberg, Jack, 925

Green Corn Ceremony, 77

Greene, Catherine, 453

Greene, Nathanael, 140–141

Grenville, George, 106–107

Grimké, Angelina and Sarah, 490–491, 495, 525, 528*p*, 528–529

group decision skills, 275

Grundy, Felix, 286

guerrilla warfare, in American Revolution, 140

Guinn v. *United States* (1915), 705

Guiteau, Charles, 683, 689

gun violence, in twenty-first century, 992–993

Gutenberg, Johannes, 27*p*, 28, 54*p*

Guthrie, Woody, 820

H

Habeas Corpus, Writ of, 202, 595

Haiti, 461, 737

hajj (pilgrimage to Mecca), 21

Hale, Nathan, 130

Half Penny Stamp Act, 103*p*

Hamilton, Alexander: at Battle of Yorktown, 142; Constitutional Convention of 1787, 163, 165*p*; as Federalist, 170, 171*p*; *Federalist Papers* written by, 171–173, 186; as Federalist Party founder, 263; opinion about average citizens, 253*f*; as secretary of the treasury, 247, 250–251; Thomas Jefferson *versus,* 252–253

Hamilton, Andrew, 92

Hamlet, James, 546

Hammond, James Henry, 455–456

Hancock, John, 114

Harding, Warren, 773*p*, 776–777, 790

Harlan, Marshall, 632

"Harlem Hellfighters," (369th Infantry) in World War I, 761, 761*p*

Harlem Renaissance, 792–793

Harpers Ferry, John Brown's raid on (1858), 539, 558–559

Harrison, Benjamin, 688*f*

Harrison, William Henry, 285, 286*p*, 289–290, 339

Hartford Convention, 291

Harvard, John, 83

Harvard University, 83, 326, 523

Hastie, William Henry, 819

Haudenosaunee Indians, 15

Haun, Catherine, 411

Hawaii, 720–721

hawks and doves, in Vietnam War years, 905–907

Hawthorne, Nathaniel, 505, 515

Hay, John, 722–723

Hayes, Rutherford B., 630, 688*f*, 689

Haymarket Riots, 654, 655*f*

Hayne, Robert Y., 336

Haynes, George Edmund, 705

Hayne-Webster debate, 335–336

Hays, Mary Ludwig, 130

Haywood, William "Big Bill," 700

headright system, plantations and, 70

health care reform, of 2010, 991, 992*f*

hearing impairment, 505, 522

Hearst, William Randolph, 672, 724–725

Heflin, James Thomas, 784

Helper, Hinton Rowan, 457

Hemingway, Ernest, 773, 793

hemp, 457

Hendrix, Jimi, 891

Henry, Patrick, 107*p*, 108, 113–114, 164, 170, 183

Henry the Navigator, of Portugal, 37

Henson, Josiah, 485

Heumann, Judy, 942, 942*p*

Highway Act of 1956, 882

hippies, 911

Hirohito, emperor of Japan, 773*p*

Hispanic Americans, civil rights of, 938–939

historical interpretation skills, 142–144

historical question framing skills, 61

Historical Source feature:
  African Americans in Union Army, 593; *America* (McKay), 793; Anaconda Plan, 581; Anti-Abolitionist Rally, 494; Blame It on Hoover, 806; Boston Massacre, 110; Camp David Accords (1978), 961; Choosing Sides (in American Revolution), 121; Christopher Columbus's Letter of 1494, 43; Compromise and the Slave Trade, 184; Declaration of Sentiments, 532; Devastation of the Indies, 51; Dust Bowl, 817; Embargo Act of 1807, 284; *Federalist Papers* Nos. 10 and 51, 172; Fighting Discrimination, 704; Fireside Chats, 810; Great Plains, September 17, 1804, 357; House Divided (Lincoln), 556; Jackson against the Bank, 338; Jefferson's Inaugural Address (1801), 270; John Brown's Last Speech, 559; Johnson vs. Stevens, 621; Letter from the Plains, 1863, 380; Mayflower Compact of 1620, 76; Migrant Mother, 818; Monroe Doctrine, 304; NAFTA, 972; Nat Turner's Rebellion, 488; The Other Half, 689; People's President (Jackson), 331; Prohibition, 785; Role of a Citizen, 253; Roosevelt's Imperialism, 735; Scopes Trial, 786; Sentiments of an American Woman (in American Revolution), 143; Seventh of March Speech (Webster), 544; Sinking of the *Lusitania*, 752; Southern View of the Compromise of 1850, 544; Speech on Health Care Reform, 992; State's Rights vs. the Union, 337; Supporting the War (posters), 839; Trail of Tears, 342; Triangle Shirtwaist Fire, 698; Tuskegee Airmen, 840; Valley Forge (in American Revolution),

135; Vietnam War, 904; war, views of, 286; Washington's Farewell Address (1796), 261; *We Owe Allegiance to No Crown* (Woodside, 1814), 303; "What a Funny Little Government," 651; "Who Stole the People's Money?," 687; World War I U.S. Soldier, 758; XYZ Affair, 266

historical texts, comparing, 716

History of Woman Suffrage (Gage, Stanton, and Anthony), 534

HISTORY Parntership, xviii-xix; Multimedia Connections, 31 MC1–31 MC2, 63 MC1–63 MC2, 147 MC1–147 MC2, 387 MC1–387 MC2, 419 MC1–419 MC2, 609 MC1–609 MC2, 659 MC1–659 MC2, 681 MC1–681 MC2, 771 MC1–771 MC2, 863 MC1–863 MC2, 919 MC1–919 MC2

Hitler, Adolf, 799*p*, 831*p*, 831–832, 845*p*

HIV (human immunodeficiency virus), 996

HMS *Leopard* (British warship), 283

Ho Chi Minh (Vietnamese leader), 891*p*, 898–899

Ho Chi Minh Trail (Vietnam War supply route), 903

Holly, Buddy, 885

Holmes, Oliver Wendell, 224–225

Holocaust, 856–858, 857*p*, 860

Homestead Act of 1862, 351, 378–379

Homestead steel mill, 642*p*

Homestead strike of 1892, 639, 655*f*, 655–656

Honecker, Erich, 969

Hong Kong, 351, 389, 449

Hood, John, 603

Hooker, Joseph, 598–599

Hooker, Thomas, 79

Hoover, Herbert, 780, 781*p*, 804–806

"Hoovervilles," in Great Depression, 806

Hope Leslie (Sedgwick), 315

Hopewell mound builders (Native American culture), 12

Hopi Indians, 14, 16

Hopkins, Henry, 819

Hopper, Grace, 865*p*

horizontal integration, 650

Horton, James, 430

House of Representatives, U.S. See Congress, U.S.; Constitution, U.S.

House Un-American Activities Committee (HUAC), 878

Houston, Sam, 394–395

Howard, Oliver O., 617

Howard University, 618

Howe, William, 130

How the Other Half Lives (Riis), 674, 676, 689*p*, 693

HUAC (House Un-American Activities Committee), 878

HUD (U.S. Department of Housing and Urban Development), 936

Hudson, Henry, 33*p*, 56

Hudson River school of art, 315–320

Huerta, Delores, 938

Hughes, Langston, 793

Huguenots, 54

Hull House (Chicago), 661, 676*p*, 677*f*, 677*p*, 677–678, 690

Human Genome Project, 979, 996

human rights, promotion of, 961

Humphrey, H., 430–431

Humphrey, Hubert, 911–912

Hundred Days (first 100 days of Roosevelt's first term as president), 809

100/442nd Regimental Combat Team (Japanese American), 842

Hunt, Walter, 443*f*

hunter-gatherers, 7

Huron Indians, 95

Hurricane Katrina, 979, 990, 990*p*

Hurricane Rita, 990

Hurston, Zora Neale, 793

Hussein, Saddam, 970, 984*p*, 984–985

Hutchinson, Anne, 80, 80*f*

hydrogen bomb, 880

Hyman, Abraham, 669

hypothetical questions, asking, 352

Ice Ages, 6

"I Have a Dream" speech (King), 934

ILGWU (International Ladies Garment Workers Union), 699

Illinois: abolitionist Lovejoy killed in (1837), 494; coal mining in, 438; In *Escobedo* v. *Illinois* (1964), 941; Exodusters move to, 379; Fox and Sauk Indians in, 342–344; as free state, 497*m*; labor strikes in Chicago, 654–655; Lincoln as senator from, 554–556; Lincoln vs. Douglas debates in, 592*f*; Mexican American population in, 406*c*; National Road to, 308; Nineteenth Amendment ratified by, 703*f*; in Northwest Territory, 155; Obama, Barack, as senator from, 990; Pullman strike of 1894, 656; settlement houses in, 677*f*, 677–678; Till, Emmett, from, 926–927. *See also* Chicago, IL

immigrants, 660–681; changing patterns of, 664–665; Chinese, 706; comparison-making skills, 679; 1865 to 1873, 634; Ellis Island entry of, 660*p*; to English colonies, 89*f*; from German revolution of 1848, 509; improving city life, 676–678; from Irish potato famine, 505*p*, 508–509; mass culture, 672–673; mass transit, 671–672; Mexican, 706; neighborhoods of, 665–667; 1900 to 1920, 731*p*; opposition to, 509–510, 668–669; Pilgrims, 75; push-pull factors of immigration, 510*f*; quotas on, 784–785; skyscraper building, 671; timeline for 1870 to 1910, 661; in twenty-first century, 998–999, 1002*c*, 1002*m*–1003*m*; urban growth in 1900, 670–671; urban problems, 674–676; work of, 667–668; World War I and, 754

impeachment: of Andrew Johnson, 611, 624–625; of Bill Clinton, 973; in Constitution, 191, 196–197, 205; of Richard Nixon, 955

imperialism, 718–719, 730*m*

implementation: of assembly line, 646; of government programs, 806; of school desegregation, 925

implications of Geraldine Ferraro nomination, 966

implications of Kansas-Nebraska Act, 549

implicit threats, from immigration, 510

imposts (taxes), 200

impressment, 282

Inca culture of Mesoamerica, 9*m*, 10, 33*p*, 47–48

incentives, 309, 777

Incidents in the Life of a Slave Girl (Jacobs), 492

indentured servants, in English colonies, 70

Indian Citizenship Act, 789

Indian Citizenship Act of 1968, 789

Indian Civil Rights Act of 1968, 941

Indian National Congress of 1885, 715*p*

Indian Removal Act of 1830, 340–344, 346*m*–347*m*

Indian reservations, 372, 376–377

Indians, Plains, 371–375; *See* Native Americans

Indian Territory, 340

Indian treaties, 346*c*

indictments, 211, 226

individuals, rights for, 941–942. *See also* Bill of Rights

industrial age, 638–659; big business dominance, 648–651; cost-and-benefit analysis, 657; Second Industrial Revolution, 642–647; timeline for 1870 to 1900, 639; workers in, 652–656

Industrial Revolution, 424–425, 511

Industrial Workers of the World (IWW), 700

infamous crimes, indictments required for, 211

inflation, 55, 161, 337

influence, spheres of, 722

Influence of Sea Power upon History, The (Mahan), 719

influencing government, 237

influenza epidemic, after World War I, 764–765

information, identifying, 612

Information Revolution, 994–995

initiatives, 692

innovation, 582, 792

Inouye, Daniel, 842

Institute for Colored Youth, 523

interchangeable parts, 426, 646

interest groups, 237

Intermediate-Rand Nuclear Forces (INF) **Treaty,** 966*f*, 968

International Ladies Garment Workers Union (ILGWU), 699

International Military Tribunal, 869

International Space Station (ISS), 998

Internet, 501, 994–995

internment of Japanese Americans in World War II, 841*p*, 841–842

interstate commerce: *Gibbons v. Ogden* (1824) decision on, 309; Interstate Commerce Act of 1887, 382; Interstate Commerce Commission, 382; regulation of, 160–161

Intolerable Acts of 1774, 111*c*, 112

Inuit (Native American culture), 13

inventions: agricultural, 443; airplane, 644*f*; automobile, 644*f*; barbed wire, 367; Bessemer steel making process, 644*f*; communications, 441–442, 645–646, 885; cotton gin, 453*p*, 453–454; dam and reservoir construction, 644*f*; Edison's "invention factory" in Menlo Park, 644–645; elevator safety

brake, 644*f*; Ferris wheel, 644*f*; ice box, 444; ice cream cones, 673; Internet, 501, 994–995; lightbulbs, 639, 644*f*; Linotype, 672; machine engine oiling, 644*f*; matches, 444; at Paris Exposition of 1900, 731*f*; safety pins, 444; sewing machine, 444; sonar, 843–844; spinning machine, 425, 425*p*; telegraph, 367; telephone, 644*f*, 645; water screw, 23. *See also* technology

investing in corporations, 648–649, 649*p*

Invisible Man (Ellison), 886

involuntary servitude, ban on, 213

Iran-Contra affair (1986), 968

Iran hostage crisis (1981), 947*p*, 962*p*, 962–963

Iraq, war in, 984–985, 989

Irish potato famine, 505, 508

ironclad warships, in Civil War, 582, 589*f*

iron curtain, 871

Iron Triangle assault, in Vietnam War, 890*p*

Iroquois Indians, 15*p*, 15–18, 95–96

Irving, Washington, 314, 320

Islamic State (ISIS) **terrorist group,** 992

Islam religion, 20

island hopping strategy, in World War II, 851

isolationism, in U.S., 718

Israel, 865*p*, 870

ISS (International Space Station), 998

Italy: banking in Renaissance, 28; Columbus from, 41; immigrants from, 665–666, 666*p*; Renaissance in, 26; totalitarianism in, 830; in World War II, 833, 844–845

Iwo Jima, battle of, 853*p*, 853–854

IWW (Industrial Workers of the World), 700

J

Jackson, Andrew, 324*p*, 324–328; democracy expansion, 328–330; in election of 1824, 311; election of 1828, 330–332; Indian Removal Act of 1830, 340–344, 346*m*–347*m*; national bank attacked by, 336–338; panic of 1837, 338–339; problem-solving skills, 345; sectional differences, 333–334; states' rights debate, 334–336; Texas annexation and, 396; timeline for 1825 to 1845, 324–349; in War of 1812, 278*p*, 279*p*, 290–291, 293–294, 294*p*

Jackson, Helen Hunt, 377

Jackson, Robert H., 869

Jackson, Thomas "Stonewall," 578–579, 599

Jacobs, Harriet, 492

Jamestown, as English colony, 68–70, 69*m*

Japan: atomic bomb and, 858*p*, 858–859; Meiji Restoration in, 715; Pearl Harbor attacked by (1941), 835*m*, 835–836, 836*p*; totalitarianism in, 832; U.S. trade with, 721–722; World War II in Pacific against, 849–854

Japanese Americans, internment of in World War II, 841*p*, 841–842

Jay, John, 171, 173, 186, 257

Jay's Treaty, 257

Jazz Age, 790–794

Jazz Singer, The (movie, 1927), 791, 792*f*

Jefferson, Thomas: Alexander Hamilton versus, 251–253; on architecture, 317; on Bill of Rights, 170; biography of, 272*f*; *Declaration of Independence* written by, 120; as Democratic-Republican Party candidate, 264; as diplomat, 183; Embargo Act, 283–284, 284*f*; manufacturing in U.S. and, 429; not able to attend Constitutional Convention, 164; opinion about average citizens, 253*f*; as secretary of state, 247; Spanish control of New Orleans and, 355; state claims to western lands, 154; as third president, 270–271

Jeffersonian democracy, 331*c*

Jewish religion: in America in 1850, 416*m*; in colonial New York and New Jersey, 84; as Hitler's scapegoat, 831; Holocaust and, 856–858, 869; immigrants of, 509, 667; Israel, establishment of, 870; Ku Klux Klan harassment, 788; religious diversity of U.S. and, 999; Yom Kippur War in Israel (1973), 951–952.07

Jim Crow laws, 631

Jodl, Alfred, 834

John, King of England, 157*p*

John Brown's raid on Harpers Ferry (1858), 539, 558–559

Johnson, Andrew, 191, 611, 618–622, 621*p*

Johnson, Eastman, 472*p*

Johnson, Lyndon B.: biography of, 934*f*; Civil Rights Act of 1965, 935*p*; civil rights movement and, 934–936; election of 1968 and, 911–912; Great Society reforms, 935–936; Vietnam War and, 902–903

Johnson, William, 461

Johnston, Joseph E., 577

joint-stock companies, in Renaissance, 28

Jolliet, Louis, 58–59

Jolson, Al, 791

Jones, John Paul, 136

Jones, Mary Harris, 654

Jones Act of 1917, 728

Jordan, Barbara, 235, 955

judicial branch of government, 167, 192–194, 205–207. *See also* U.S. Supreme Court

judicial review, 274

Judiciary Act of 1789, 193, 248, 273, 273*f*

Jungle, The (Sinclair), 690, 694, 708

K

kamikaze (suicide) pilots, in World War II, 854

Kansas: in *Brown v. Board of Education* (1954), 925, 926*f*; in Cattle Kingdom, 366; Dole, Bob, as senator from, 873, 973; Dust Bowl in, 816–817; Exodusters move to, 379; influenza epidemic of 1918 start in, 764; Nation, Carrie, and saloons in, 702; slavery issues in, 548–552

Kansas-Nebraska Act of 1854, 549–550, 550*m*, 554, 560

Kansas Pacific Railroad, 366

KDKA radio station, 790

Kearny, Stephen, 401, 403

Kelley, Florence, 677–678, 696

Kelley, Oliver Hudson, 382

Kellogg-Briand Pact of 1928, 778

Kennedy, Anthony M., 965

Kennedy, John F.: assassination of, 921, 934; Berlin Wall, 895–896; biography of, 932*f*; civil rights movement and, 931–932; Cuban missile crisis, 894–895; space exploration, 896–898; Vietnam War and, 899

Kennedy, Robert F., 891, 911

Kent State University, National Guard and (1970), 912

Kentucky and Virginia Resolutions, 266*f*

Kerouac, Jack, 886

Key to Uncle Tom's Cabin, A (Stowe), 547

Khomeini, Ruhollah, 962–963

Khrushchev, Nikita, 895–896

King, Martin Luther Jr., 891*p*; assassination of (1968), 937; biography of, 929*f*; in Birmingham, 933; March on Selma, AL, 935; March on Washington, 934; Montgomery Improvement Association (MIA), 928; Nobel Peace Prize, 936*f*

Kings Mountain, battle of, 140

Kissinger, Henry, 912, 952

Kitchen Cabinet, of Jackson, 332

kivas of Anasazi, 12
knights, in Middle Ages, 25
Knights of Labor, 653–654
knowledge, in Renaissance, 26–27
Know-Nothing Party (1854), 510, 553
Knox, Henry, as secretary of war, 247
Korean War, 874–876, 877*m*, 887*m*
Korematsu, Fred, 841
Korematsu v. *United States* (1944), 841
Kristallnacht, in Germany, 799
Ku Klux Klan, 379, 628–629, 629*p*, 788, 935

L

labor force, slaves as, 476–477
labor programs. *See* New Deal
labor shortages, in World War I, 755
labor unions: Congress of Industrial Organizations (CIO), 814; development of, 433–434; immigration opposed by, 668; in Progressive Era, 699–700; strikes of, 653–655, 655*m*, 873–874
Laden, Osama bin, 984, 992
Lady at Home, The (magazine), 530
Lafayette, Marquis de, 133, 134*f*, 142
Lafitte, Jean, 291
La Follette, Robert M., 691*f*, 692
Lai chun-chuen, 412
Lake Erie, battle of (1813), 289
land, conflict over, 284–285
landmark documents, comparison of, 189*f*
land ordinances of 1785 and 1787, 154*m*, 155
Lange, Dorothea, 818*f*
language, 16, 939
La Raza Unida, 921, 939
Larcom, Lucy, 432–433
La Salle, René-Robert, 59
Las Casas, Bartolomé de, 51*f*, 52, 477
Last of the Mohicans, The

(Cooper), 315, 319
Latin America policy of United States, 735–736, 736*m*
Lawrence, Jacob, 788*p*
Lawrence, KS, attack on (1856), 539, 551
League of Nations, 765–768, 773, 832
League of United Latin American Citizens (LULAC), 788, 940–941
Leaves of Grass (Whitman), 515
Lee, Robert E., 558, 567*p*, 579*f*, 579–580
"Legend of Sleepy Hollow, The" (Irving), 314, 320
legislative branch of government, 167, 189–190, 196–203. *See also* Congress, U.S.; Constitution, U.S.
Lend-Lease Act of 1941, 834
Lenin, Vladimir, 758
Lerner, Gerda, 491
lesbian, gay, bisexual, and transgender (LGBT) community, 942
"Letter from Birmingham Jail" (King), 933
Letters of Marque and Reprisal (arms for merchant ships), 201
Letters on the Equality of the Sexes and the Condition of Women (Grimké, Sarah), 529
Levitt, William, 882–884
Lewis, Meriwether, 271–272, 356
Lewis, Sinclair, 793
Lewis and Clark expedition of 1804–1806, 351, 356–357, 387 MC1–387 MC2
Lexington, battle of, 115, 115*p*
Leyte Gulf, battle of, 851
LGBT (lesbian, gay, bisexual, and transgender) community, 942
Liberator, The (newspaper), 490, 505*p*
Liberia, Africa, 299*p*, 490
Liberty bonds, 753
Life Among the Paiutes (Winnemucca), 376
Liliuokalani, Queen of Hawaii, 720, 720*f*
Limited Nuclear Test Ban Treaty, 896

Lin, May Ying, 915, 915*f*
Lincoln, Abraham: assassination of, 611, 618–619; biography of, 592*f*; debates with Stephen Douglas, 554–557, 556*c*, 556*p*; on *Dred Scott* decision, 554; election of 1860 of, 560–561; Harriet Beecher Stowe meeting with, 547; inaugural address of, 562; on John Brown's raid, 559; Ten Percent Plan of, 615. *See also* Civil War
Lincoln, Benjamin, 175
Lincoln, Mary Todd, 572
Lincoln-Douglas debates, 554–557
Lindbergh, Charles, 791, 792*f*
line graphs, 469
line of demarcation, for European empires in the Americas, 43
Lisa, Manuel, 358
listing, information presented by, 640
literature: antislavery, 500, 546–547; frontier, 319–320; of Great Depression of 1930s, 822; Holocaust, 860; reform, 693–694; romantic and realistic, 516–517
Little Bighorn, battle of, 351*p*, 374*p*, 374–375
Little Richard, 885
Little Rock Nine, in school desegregation, 925–926
Little Turtle (Miami chief), 258
Little Women (Alcott), 517
Livingston, Robert R., 356
lobbying groups, 696
Lochner, Joseph, 699
Lochner v. *New York* (1897), 699
Locke, John, 85, 120, 152, 157*p*
Lodge, Henry Cabot, 767
logging industry, 440
Lôme, Enrique Dupuy de, 725
Lone Star Republic (Texas) **flag,** 396*p*
Long, Huey, 812
Longfellow, Henry Wadsworth, 515–516
Longstreet, James, 600, 605
Long Walk, 375
Look magazine, 927

loose construction of Constitution (Hamilton), 254

Lost Generation, 793

Louisiana: African Americans in Union Army in, 593; in Confederacy, 560, 572, 583; Freedom Rides of 1960s in, 932, 933m; Grant's Civil War strategy in, 588m; Jefferson purchase of, 356; La Salle exploration of, 59; Long, Huey, as senator from, 812; in Missouri Compromise of 1850, 542; New Orleans importance in cotton trade, 456–457; readmission to Union, 615, 625; Separate Car Act of 1890, 631; Spanish difficulties in controlling, 355; steam-powered sawmill invented in, 457; in *Uncle Tom's Cabin* (Stowe), 547; White League in, 629

Louisiana Purchase, 271–272, 351, 355m, 356–358

Louis-Napoléon (emperor of France), 539

Louverture, Toussaint, 351, 461

Love, Nat, 367p

Love Canal disaster (1980), 959

Lovejoy, Elijah, 494

Lowell, Francis Cabot, 431, 457

Lowell Female Labor Reform Association, 433

Lowell system, for mill work, 431–433

Loyalists (to Britain), in American Revolution, 120

Lozano, Augustin and Maria, 666p

LULAC (League of United Latin American Citizens), 788, 940–941

lunar landing (1969), 897p–898p

Lusitania, 743p, 751, 752f

Luther, Martin, 53, 53p

lynchings, 704

M

MacArthur, Douglas: Bonus Army eviction by (1932), 806; Japan rebuilding, 859, 871; in Korean War, 877–878; Philippines, battles in, 849, 851

machine guns, in World War I, 749

machine-tool industry, 442

Macon, Nathaniel, 310

Madison, Dolley, 290p

Madison, James: Alien and Sedition Acts opposed by, 266–267; Bill of Rights priority of, 173–174, 186, 195; Capital move, 251; on closed market impacts, 160; Constitutional Convention of 1787, 163, 164, 164p, 165p, 183; Democratic-Republican Party founded by, 264; as Federalist, 170, 185–186, 287; *Federalist Papers* written by, 171–173, 186; in *Marbury* v. *Madison* (1803), 273f; national bank opposed by, 254; as president during War of 1812, 287, 290; as secretary of state, 271; states' right to disagree with federal government supported by, 336

Magellan, Ferdinand, 44

Magna Carta, 152, 157

magnetic resonance imaging (MRI), 996

Mahan, Alfred T., 719

Mahican (Mohican) **Indian tribe,** 59

main ideas, recognizing, 800

majority rule, 223

Malcolm X, 936

Mali, 20–21

mammoths, 6p

Mandan (Native American culture), 15

Mandela, Nelson, 947p

Manhattan Project, 858

manifest destiny, 397–400, 398p, 417p

Mann, Horace, 521, 521f

Mans Musa, of Mali, 21

Manuel of Portugal, 39

manufacturing growth: city growth and, 511; modern, 428p; in north in 1800s, 427–429

Mao Zedong, 876, 952

map interpretation skills, 415

Marbury, William, 273

Marbury v. *Madison* (1803), 273, 273f

March on Washington (1963), 920p, 934

margin, buying on, in stock market, 802

Marion, Francis, 140

Marion's Brigade, 140

Marne, first battle of, in World War I, 748

Marquette, Jacques, 58–59

marriages of African Americans after Civil War, 616–617

Marshall, George C., 871

Marshall, James, 409

Marshall, John, 273–274, 342, 437

Marshall, Thurgood, 194, 921p, 925

Marshall Field department stores, 672

Marshall Plan, 871

Maryland, as English colony, 71–72

Mason, Biddy, 411–412

Mason, George, 170, 171p

Massachusetts: American Revolutionary battles for Boston, 114m, 114–115, 115p, 117m; Boston Marathon bombing (2013), 979; Boston Massacre, 109p, 109–110, 110f, 111t; Boston Tea Party, 65, 110–111, 111p; Constitution of 1780, 153; economy in, 81–82; education in, 82, 318; Embargo Act of 1807 effect on, 283–284; 54th Massachusetts Infantry (African American) in Civil War, 593; as free state, 497m; on Fugitive Slave Act, 498; influenza epidemic of 1918 in, 764; labor reform in, 433; Mann, Horace, as first secretary of education in, 521, 521f; mentally ill, facilities for, 520; minimum wage law in, 696; Perkins School for the Blind in, 522; Radical Republicans in, 622; Shays's Rebellion in (1786), 161–162,

162*p*; Smith College in, 701; state board of education in, 318; textile mills in, 431; U.S. Constitution ratified by, 186; utopian groups in, 514; witch trials in Salem (1690s), 80–81

Massachusetts Bay Colony, 79–80

Massacre at Wounded Knee, 375

Massasoit (Wampanoag Indian chief), 77

mass culture, 672–673

Massery, Hazel Bryan, 927*p*

mass production, 426–427, 427*p*

mass transit, 671–672, 928, 932

matrilineal Native American cultures, 15

Maximilian of Austria, Archduke, 567*p*

Maya culture of Mesoamerica, 8, 8*p*, 31 MC1–31 MC2

Mayflower Compact, 65, 76, 76*f*, 152, 156

McCain, John, 903*f*, 990

McCarthy, Eugene, 911

McCarthy, Joseph, 874–880

McClellan, George B., 578–579, 595

McClure's Magazine, 690

McCormack, Joseph, 691

McCormick, Cyrus, 443, 443*f*

McCoy, Elijah, 644*f*

McCoy, Joseph, 366

McCulloch, James, 337

McCulloch v. *Maryland* (1819), 309, 337, 338*f*

McDowell, Irvin, 577

McGovern, George, 912–913

McGrath, Howard, 878

McGuffey, William Holmes, 521

McGuffey's Readers, 521

McKay, Claude, 793, 793*f*

McKinley, William, 383, 683, 688*f*, 725

McMillan, Harry, 482, 485

McPherson, Aimee Semple, 787

McVeigh, Timothy, 974

Meade, George G., 600–601

medical advances, 996

Medicare, 935, 1000

Meiji Restoration, in Japan, 715

Meir, Golda, 947*p*

Mellon, Andrew, 777

Melville, Herman, 515

mercantilism, 28, 92

mercenaries, 131

merchants in New England colonies, 81

Mesoamerican and South American societies, 3*p*, 8–10

Metacomet (Wampanoag Indian leader), 95

Mexican Americans: in Great Depression, 818; top ten states by population of, 406*c*; Treaty of Guadalupe Hidalgo, 405–406; in World War II, 839–840

Mexican-American War, 389, 401–404, 402*m*

Mexican Cession (California, Arizona, New Mexico, Nevada): American settlement in, 391, 405–407; map of, 416*m*–417*m*; slavery in, 498

Mexico: braceros from, 839; freedom from Spain (1821), 303, 393; immigrants from, 665, 666*p*, 706, 1002*f*–1003*f*; Mesoamerican cultures in, 9*m*; Mesoamerican societies in, 8–10; Mexican Revolution (1910), 715, 737–738; in NAFTA, 972; Spanish conquistadors in, 46–47; Texans revolt against (1835), 394–396; Zimmermann Note from Germany to (1917), 752

MIA (Montgomery Improvement Association), 928

Michelangelo, 27

Middle Ages, in Europe, 24–26, 26*p*

middle class, 26, 511

Middle colonies, Revolutionary War battles in, 129*m*

Middle Passage, of slaves, 93–94, 477, 480*m*

Midway, battle of (1942), 850–851

Midway Islands, 720

migrations: of African Americans after Civil War,

616–617, 838–839; of earliest Americans, 6–8, 7*m*; to English colonies, 78–79; maps of, 385, 385*m*

Migration Series paintings (Lawrence), 788*p*

Milam, J. W., 927

militarism, before World War I, 746

military control of South, in reconstruction, 623

Miller, Alfred Jacob, 316

Miller, Doris "Dorie," 839

mill work, 420*p*, 430–433, 632–633

mining, westward expansion and, 364–365

minority rights, 787–789

Minuit, Peter, 59

minutemen, in American Revolution, 115

Miranda v. *Arizona* (1966), 941

mission settlements, 47, 392, 399

Mississippi: Black Codes in, 620–621; in Confederacy, 561, 572; Evers, Medgar, killed in, 933; Indian Removal Act of 1830, 340–341; Red Shirts in, 629; Siege of Vickburg, in Civil War, 585–586, 588*m*–589*m*; as slave state, 497*m*; Till, Emmett, killed in, 926–927

Mississippian mound builders (Native American culture), 12

Mississippi River, 159*m*, 436*p*

Mississippi Valley, 59, 363*m*. *See also* Louisiana Purchase; westward expansion

Missouri Compromise of 1820, 299, 310*m*, 310–311, 496, 542

mobilization, for World War I, 747

Moby-Dick (Melville), 515

Moctezuma (Aztec leader), 46–47

Model T Ford, 778

Mohawk Indians, 15

Molasses Act of 1733, 93

Mondale, Walter, 965–966

Monick, Ethel, 698*p*

monopolies, 650–651

Monroe, James: as Antifederalist, 170; Louisiana Purchase by, 271, 356; Monroe Doctrine of, 299, 303–305, 735, 737; as president, 279*p*, 292, 299*p*, 302, 303*p*, 304
Montagnais (Native American culture), 13
Montesquieu, Baron de, 152
Montezuma, Carlos, 705
Montgomery, Bernard, 844
Montgomery, Richard, 130
Montgomery bus boycott, in civil rights movement, 927–928
Montgomery Improvement Association (MIA), 928
moon landing (1969), 897*p*–898*p*, 897–898
Morgan, John T., 631
Mormons, 360–361, 361*p*, 407
Morrill Act of 1862, 378
Morris, Gouverneur, 183–184, 246
Morrow, Edwin R., 879
Morse, Samuel F. B., 441–442, 442*f*, 443*f*
Morse code, 441
Morton, "Jelly Roll," 791
mosques, 21
Moss, Alfred A., Jr., 490
motion pictures, 790–791
motives, for early childhood education, 690
Motor Car **magazine,** 779
Mott, Lucretia, 525, 531
mound builders (Native American culture), 12–13
mountain men, 358–359
Mount Holyoke College, 521
movie attendance, 1929 to 1939, 820*c*
movie theaters, drive-in, 884*p*
moving assembly line, 778
MRI (magnetic resonance imaging), 996
muckrakers, 689
Muhammad, founder of Islam, 20
Muir, John, 708, 708*p*
Muller **v.** *Oregon* (1908), 699
multinational corporations, 986

Munetada, Kurozumi, 279
Munich Conference of 1938, 832
Murray, Judith Sargent, 246
Museum of Modern Art, New York, 794
music, 316–317
Mussolini, Benito, 827, 830, 832, 844, 845*p*
My Lai massacre (1968), 906–907

N

NAACP (National Association for the Advancement of Colored People), 705, 787–788, 925, 927
NAFTA (North American Free Trade Agreement), 972, 972*f*
name calling, in propaganda, 506
Napoleon, 279, 299
Narrative of the Life of Frederick Douglass (Douglass), 526
Nasser, Abdel, 881
Natchez Trace, 354
Nation, Carry, 702
National Aeronautics and Space Administration (NASA), 865*p*, 881, 897–898, 998
National American Woman Suffrage Association (NAWSA), 702–703
National Association for the Advancement of Colored People (NAACP), 705, 787–788, 925, 927
National Association Opposed to Women's Suffrage, 533*f*
national bank, 253–254
National Broadcasting Company (NBC), 790, 792*f*
National Citizen and Ballot Box, 534
National Congress of American Indians (NCAI), 941
National Consumer's League, 696
national debt, 250–251, 251*f*
national government, supremacy of, 209

National Grange of the Patrons of Husbandry, 381–382
national identity, 298–323; central issue identification, 321; culture, 314–318; Erie Canal, 312–313; foreign policy, 302–305; literature of the frontier, 319–320; nationalism and sectionalism, 306–311; timeline for 1807 to 1829, 298–323
National Industrial Recovery Act (NIRA), 811, 813
nationalism in Europe before World War I, 746
Nationalist Socialist Party (Nazis, Germany), 831
National Italian American Foundation, 940
National Labor Relations Act (NLRA, Wagner Act), 814
National Liberation Front (NLF), in Vietnam, 899
National Minimum Drinking Age Act of 1984, 786
National Organization for Women (NOW), 921, 939–940
National Origins Act of 1924, 785
National Road, 308, 308*m*
National War Labor Board, 755
National Woman Suffrage Association, 531*f*, 534
National Women's Party (NWP), 703
National Youth Administration (NYA), 812–813, 813*p*
nation divided, 538–565; election of 1860, 560–561; John Brown's raid on Harpers Ferry (1858), 558–559; Kansas, troubles in, 548–552; political divisions, 553–557; primary and secondary information sources, 563; slavery, 542–547; south, secession of, 561–562; timeline for 1848 to 1860, 539. *See also* Civil War
Nation of Islam, 936

Index

Native Americans: Battle of Little Bighorn, 351*p*; beliefs and practices, 16–18; as British Loyalists in American Revolution, 121; Catlin's paintings of, 316*p*; civil rights of, 941; in Civil War, 587; commerce clause of Constitution and, 200*f*; culture areas, 13–17, 16*m*; Doctrine of Discovery impact on, 44; early, 11–13; in English colonies, 95–98; environment influence on, 7–8; European diseases and, 44–45, 47, 476; in Florida, 293–294; French alliances with, 59; land losses of, 373*m*; languages, 16; Lewis and Clark expedition and, 357; in Mexican Cession, 405–406; Navajo "Code Talkers" in World War II, 850*p*; Northwest Territory conflicts, 258, 284–285; not addressed in Declaration of Independence, 122–123; Pilgrims and, 77, 81; Plains Indian conflicts, 371–375; as progressives, 705–706; reservations of, 372, 376–377; Sacagawea, 272; in Spanish colonies, 49–52, 51–52; Spanish mission settlements and, 392, 400; Treaty of Greenville, 243; U.S. citizenship granted to, 773, 788–789; War of 1812 impact on, 291. *See also* Indian Removal Act of 1830

nativists, 510, 668

NATO (North Atlantic Treaty Organization), 872

Nat Turner's Rebellion, 449, 473, 487, 487*m*, 487*p*, 488*f*

naturalized citizens, 125, 234–235

Navajo "Code Talkers" in World War II, 850*p*

Navajo Indians, 14, 375

naval power, 719

naval strategy, in Civil War, 581–582

Navigation Acts, 1650–1696, 92–93

NAWSA (National American Woman Suffrage Association), 702–703

Nazis (Nationalist Socialist Party, Germany), 831

NBC (National Broadcasting Company), 790

NCAI (National Congress of American Indians), 941

Negro World **newspaper,** 789

Neighborhood Guild (New York, 1886), 677

neighborhoods of immigrants, 665–667

neutrality: Neutrality Proclamation, 256, 256*f*; in War of 1812, 282–284; in World War I, 750–752

New Amsterdam (Dutch colony), 59*p*

New Deal (1930s): critics of, 811–812; effects of, 821, 821*c*; labor programs in, 813–814; programs of, 814*c*; relief and recovery, 810–811; restoring confidence, 809–810; second New Deal, 812–813; Supreme Court clashes, 815

New England Articles of Confederation, 80

New England colonies: economy of, 81–82; education in, 82–83; Pilgrims and Puritans, 75–77; religion and government in, 79–81

New England Primer, 82

New-England Tale, A (Sedgwick), 315

New Federalism, of Nixon, 950

New Hampshire: Association Test in (1776), 120; Constitution ratified by, 173, 179; economy of, 81–82; labor union achievements in, 434; Pierce, Franklin, from, 548

new immigrants, 664

New Jersey: American Revolution in, 131–132; as colony, 59–60, 84–85; Constitution ratified by, 186; Edison, Thomas, in Menlo Park, 644–645; New Jersey Plan, 166, 166*f*, 183; women's suffrage in, 153*p*

Newman, Robert, 114

New Orleans: battle of (1814), 278*p*, 279, 290–291; Civil War defeat of, 584–585; Pinckney's Treaty to open, 257

"New South," 633*p*

Newtown, Connecticut, killings of children (2013), 993

New York: American Revolution in, 130, 132, 133*m*; battle of, 130; as colony, 59*p*, 59–60, 84–85; Constitution ratified by, 173, 186; Erie Canal impact on, 309, 312*m*–313*m*; as free state, 497*m*; *Gibbons v. Ogden* (1824) on waterway use in, 435–436; Hudson, Henry, exploration of, 56; immigration to, 508, 667, 731*p*; Levittown suburban development, 882–883; *Lochner* v. *New York* (1905), 699; Love Canal disaster, 959; Mormon Church started in, 360; nativists in, 510; New York Slave Revolt of 1712, 85; Second Great Awakening in, 518; Seneca Falls Convention on women's rights (1848) in, 532; Temporary Emergency Relief Administration (1932), 807; Underground Railroad in, 491*f*; women given ownership of wages and property by (1860), 534

New York African Free School, 522

New York City: Brooklyn Bridge, 643; Central Park, 672*p*, 673; Charity Organization Society (SOC), 676; Chrysler Building, 794; Coney Island amusement park, 673; Empire State Building, 794; Lincoln Tunnel, 812; Museum of Modern Art, 794; New York Stock Exchange, 249, 649; police force, 519; in Roaring Twenties, 772*p*; September 11, 2001 attacks on World Trade Center in, 984; Silent Parade of July 1917, 787; subway system, 671–672; Tammany Hall political machine, 687

New York Journal **newspaper,** 672

New York Slave Revolt of 1712, 85

New York State Tenement House Act of 1901, 676, 690

New York Stock Exchange, 249, 649

New York Tribune **newspaper,** 674

New York World **newspaper,** 672

Nez Percé Indians, 357, 375

Night (Wiesel), 860

Nimitz, Chester, 850–851

Nineteenth Amendment to Constitution (voting rights for women), 179*p*, 218*p*, 533*f*, 683*p*, 702*p*, 703, 703*f*

NIRA (National Industrial Recovery Act), 811, 813

Nixon, Richard M.: domestic challenges, 950–952; election of, 947*p*; foreign policy, 952; Vietnam War and, 912–913; Watergate scandal, 953–955

NLF (National Liberation Front), in Vietnam, 899

NLRA (National Labor Relations Act, Wagner Act), 814

Nobel Prizes, 661*p*, 677*f*, 793

No Child Left Behind plan, 983

no-man's land, between trenches in World War I, 748*p*, 749

nominating conventions, 330. *See also* elections

Non-Intercourse Act of 1809, 284

North, Lord, 142

North Africa, World War II in, 843–848

North America after Treaty of Paris, 142*m*

North American Free Trade Agreement (NAFTA), 972, 972*f*

North Atlantic Treaty Organization (NATO), 872

Northeast culture area, of Native Americans, 15–16

Northern states in 1800s, 420–447; convictions versus bias, 445; farm equipment improvements, 443; home life improvements, 443–444;

Industrial Revolution, 424–425; Lowell system, 431–433; machines and processes, 425–427; manufacturing growth, 427–429; mill work, 430–431; reconstruction and, 633–634; steam power, 442–443; telegraph, 441–442; timeline for 1790 to 1860, 421; Transportation Revolution, 435–440; workers organizing, 433–434. *See also* Civil War; nation divided

North Star (Douglass), 491, 526, 526*p*

Northup, Solomon, 484

Northwest Coast culture area, of Native Americans, 13*p*, 13–14

Northwest Ordinances of 1787, 155

northwest passage, search for, 55*m*, 55–56

Northwest Territory, 155, 258–259, 259*m*, 259*p*, 284

NOW (National Organization for Women), 921, 939–940

nuclear arms race, 880

nullification crisis of 1828, 334–335

Nuremberg trials, after World War II, 869

NWP (National Women's Party), 703

NYA (National Youth Administration), 812–813

O

Oates, William, 601

Obama, Barack, 194, 979, 990–993, 991*f*

Oberlin College, 522*p*, 523

Observations on the New Constitution (Warren), 171

O'Connor, Sandra Day, 194, 965, 965*f*. *See also* U.S. Supreme Court

Oglethorpe, James, 73

Ohio: Erie Canal impact on, 312*m*–313*m*; as free state, 497*m*; Hopewell mound builders in, 12; Kent State University students killed by National Guard (1970), 912; labor union achievements in,

434; National Road in, 308, 308*m*; in Northwest Territory, 155; oil drilling in, 644; Peace Democrats against Civil War, 595, 912; Populist Party in, 382; Underground Railroad in, 499; urban growth in, 671

oil as power source, 643–644

oil prices of 1970s, 951*c*, 951*p*

O'Keefe, Georgia, 794, 794*f*

Okinawa, battle of, 853–854

Oklahoma land rush, 351, 383–384, 384*p*

old immigrants, 664

Old Three Hundred families (Texas settlers), 393

Olive Branch Petition of 1775, 116

Oliver, James, 380

Olmec culture of Mesoamerica, 3*p*, 8

Olmsted, Frederick Law, 661, 672*p*, 673

Oneida Indians, 15

Onís, Luis de, 294

Onondaga Indians, 15

OPEC (Organization of Petroleum Exporting Countries), 951–952

Open Door Policy, for China trade, 722–723

Operation Desert Storm, 970

opinions, facts *versus*, 540

Opium War, 325

oral history, 466, 917

Oregon territory, 351, 398–399

Oregon Trail, 359

organization, patterns of, 640

Organization of Petroleum Exporting Countries (OPEC), 951–952

Orient Express railroad, 351*p*

Orlando, Vittorio, 766

Ortega, Louis, 851

Osceola (Seminole chief), 342

Osgood, Samuel, 247

O'Sullivan, John, 397

Oswald, Lee Harvey, 921, 934

Otis, Elisha, 644*f*, 671

Otis, James, 107

Ottawa Indians, 97

Otto, Nikolaus A., 639

outlining skills, 34

Over Mountain Men, 137

overseers, 464

oversight, chance, and error in history, 635

oversimplification, in propaganda, 506

Oviedo, Fernández de, 476

Owens, Jesse, 799

Oxbow, The (Cole), 315*p*

ozone depletion, 996–997

P

Pacific: U.S. territories in (1856–1899), 719*m*, 720–721; World War II in, 849–854, 852*m*

Pacific Northwest, Convention of 1818 and, 292

Pacific Railway Acts of 1862 and 1864, 368

PACs (political action committees), 237

Padilla, Gil, 938

Paige, Satchel, 791

Paine, Thomas, 119, 131, 397

Paiute Indians, 376

Paleo-Indians, 7

Palmer, A. Mitchell, 784

Panama Canal, 714*p*, 715, 732–734, 733*p*, 734*m*, 961

Panic of 1837, 338–339, 433

Panic of 1873, 370, 630

Panic of 1893, 383

pardons, 192, 205, 955–956

Paris Exposition of 1900, 731*p*

Paris Peace Conference, 766

Parker, Charlie, 885

Parker, James, 487*m*

Parker, John, 115

Parks, Rosa, 927–928, 928*f*, 936*f*

Pasteur, Louis, 351*p*

patents, of Edison, 645

Paterson, William, 166, 183

Patient Protection and Affordable Care Act (PPACA) of 2010, 991, 992*f*

patriotic posters, in World War I, 756*p*, 769*p*

Patriots, in American Revolution, 114

patroon system, in New Netherland, 84

patterns of organization, 640

Patterson, John H., 648*p*

Patton, George, 859

Patuxet Indians, 77

Paul, Alice, 703, 783

Paul Revere's Ride (Longfellow), 516

Pawnee Indians, 15

Payne-Aldrich Tariff, 709

Peace Corps, 894

Pearl Harbor, Hawaii, Japanese attack on, 827*p*, 835*m*, 835–836, 836*p*

Pearson, Richard, 137

Pelosi, Nancy, 148*p*, 989

Pendleton Civil Service Act, 689

penicillin, 773

peninsulares (Spanish settlers), 51

Penn, William, 65, 86, 86*f*

Pennsylvania: abolitionist activity in, 524; African American colleges in, 523; Battle of Gettysburg in Civil War, 599*p*, 599–603, 600*p*, 601*m*, 602*p*; coal mining in, 438; Constitution ratified by, 186; as free state, 497*m*; labor strikes in, 654–656; labor union achievements in, 434; oil drilling in, 644; as Penn's colony, 85–87; Radical Republicans in, 621*f*, 622; September 11, 2001 attacks, 984; settlement houses in, 678; steel industry in, 643*p*; Three-Mile Island nuclear power plant incident, 960; Whiskey Rebellion (1791), 259–260

Pennsylvania Abolition Society, 524

Pentagon, September 11, 2001 attacks on, 979*p*, 984

Pentagon Papers, 912

Perkins, Frances, 811, 813

Perot, H. Ross, 972, 972*f*

Perry, Benjamin F., 620

Perry, Matthew, 351, 389, 721, 722*p*

Perry, Oliver Hazard, 289

Pershing, John J., 738, 757, 759, 761

Persian Gulf War, 947*p*, 970–971, 971*m*

Peter the Great, 65*p*

petition, right to, 212*p*, 225

petition for redress, 126

Philadelphia: African Americans educated in, 522–523; American Revolution in, 132, 135–136, 141; Constitutional Convention of 1787 in, 164, 182–183; growth of, 670; immigration to, 508; Independence Hall, 182*p*; Knights of Labor founded in, 653; lack of police force in mid-nineteenth century, 511; as largest British colonial city (1760), 86; population in 1790, 249; population in 1900, 670; trade in colonial, 86–87, 88*m*

Philadelphia Female Anti-Slavery Society, 525

Philippine Government Act of 1902, 729

Philippine Islands, 726–727, 729

photography, as accepted art form, 794

Pickett, George, 602

Pickett's Charge, in Battle of Gettysburg, 602*m*, 602–603

Pickford, Mary, 791

pictorial diagrams, 29, 29*p*

pie graphs, 469

Pierce, Edward L., 593

Pierce, Franklin, 548

Pike, Zebulon, 357–58

Pilgrims and Puritans, 75–77

Pinchot, Gifford, 708

Pinckney, Thomas, 257

Pinckney's Treaty, 257, 258*m*

Pioneers, The (Cooper), 315

Pitcher, Molly, 130

Pizarro, Francisco, 33*p*, 47–48

placer mining (California gold rush), 410

Plains Indians, 371–375

plantations, 52, 460*p*

planters, in cotton industry, 454, 459–460

Plato, of ancient Greece, 23, 26

Platt Amendment, 728

Index

Plessy v. *Ferguson* (1896), 631–632, 925, 926*f*
Plymouth colony, 78*m*
Plymouth colony re-creation, 64*p*
Pocahontas, 70
Poe, Edgar Allan, 515
points of view, 171, 175
police force, New York City, 519
political action committees (PACs), 237
political cartoons, 607, 806*f*
political parties: American Independent Party, 912; American Party of 1854, 553; Constitutional Union Party, 560; Democratic Party, 330, 553; Democratic-Republican Party, 264; Federalist Party, 185–186, 263, 284, 291; Free-Soil Party, 497, 539, 543; Know-Nothing Party (1854), 510, 553; National Women's Party (NWP), 703; overview, 263, 264*m*; Populist Party, 351, 382–383; Progressive Party, 709; Republican Party, 553, 625; Whig Party, 327, 339, 390, 398, 553
politics: of ancient Greece, 23–24; corruption, 686–689; of farmers, 381–383; machines, 686–687; nation divided by, 553–557
Polk, James K., 390, 398, 401, 542
poll taxes, 221, 221*p*, 631
Polo, Marco, 25, 37
Ponce de León, Juan, 48, 63 MC1–63 MC2
Pontiac (Indian leader), 65*p*
Pontiac's Rebellion, 97, 97*f*
Pony Express, 367
Poor Richard's Almanac (Franklin), 136
Pope, John, 579–580
Pope Francis, 979
popular sovereignty, 167, 185, 542
population in twenty-first century, 997–999
Populist Party, 351, 382–383
Portugal, exploration by, 37–40, 40*m*

postage rates in 1815, 281
postwar boom, 883*c*
potlatches, of Pacific Northwest Native American cultures, 13
Potsdam Conference, 868, 869*p*
Pottawatomie Massacre (1856), 551
Powderly, Terence V., 653
Powell, Colin, 970, 983
Powhatan Confederacy, 69–70
PPACA (Patient Protection and Affordable Care Act) **of 2010,** 991
precedent, 247
predictions, 980
prejudice, 445
Prescott, Samuel, 115
presidencies of 1970s–1990s, 946–977; Bush, George H. W., 969–971; Carter, Jimmy, 959–963; Clinton, Bill, 972–974; Ford, Gerald, 955–956; Nixon, Richard M., 950–955; Reagan, Ronald, 964–968; social issues of 1970s, 957–959; strength of arguments, 975; timeline for 1968 to 2000, 947
president, U.S.: campaigns of, 330; as Commander in Chief, 193; court appointments made by, 193; in executive branch of government, 167, 191; party preferences in, 339; popular vs. electoral college vote for, 311; requirements of, 197*c*; salary of, 204; separation of powers and, 190*c*; slavery issue and, 398; veto power of, 168, 334; working with Congress, 192. *See also* Constitution, U.S.; and *entries for individual presidents*
presidios (Spanish forts), 47, 392
Presley, Elvis, 884*p*, 885
press, freedom of, 92, 212*p*, 224
Preston, Thomas, 109–110
primary and secondary information sources, 563
primary food crops, of South, 457
Princip, Gavrilo, 747
principles, 622

Principles of Scientific Management, The (Taylor), 652
printing press, 27*p*, 28, 53, 54*p*
prison reform, 520
privateers, 256
problem-solving skills, 345
procedures, in Wade-Davis bill, 615
process of industrialization, 721
Proclamation of 1763 of King George III, 97–98
Progressive Party, 709
progressive reforms, 682–713; African American discrimination, 703–705; causal relationships, identifying, 711; child labor, 695–697; limits of, 705–706; political corruption, 686–689; push for, 689–691; reform literature, 693–694; safety and working conditions, 698–700; Theodore Roosevelt and, 707–709; timeline for 1865 to 1925, 683; voting power expansion, 691–692; William Howard Taft and, 709; women's fight for temperance and voting rights, 701–703; Woodrow Wilson and, 709–710
Progressives, 689–691
prohibition, 785, 785*f*
propaganda, information versus, 506
property rights for women, 533–534
proprietary colonies, 72–73
prospecting for gold (California gold rush), 410
Prospect Park, Brooklyn, New York, 673
Prosser, Gabriel, 467, 486
pro tempore, Senate President, 197
Protestant Reformation, impact on America, 53–54
public documents, 280
Publius, 171
Pueblo Indians, 14
pueblos: Native American, 11–12, 12*p*; Spanish towns as, 47, 392
Puerto Rico, 727–729

Pulitzer, Joseph, 672
pull factors, for immigration, 510, 999
Pullman, George, 656
Pullman strike of 1894, 655*f*, 656
Pure Food and Drug Act, 708
Puritans and Pilgrims, 75–77
push factors, for immigration, 510, 998–999

Q

Qing dynasty (China), 33
Quakers, 85, 475, 489, 522, 524, 531
Quartering Act of 1774, 112
quartering of soldiers, 126, 211
Quincy, Josiah, 109–110, 283, 520
quipu (Inca record keeping method), 11
quorum, 198
Qur'an of Islam, 20–21

R

racial discrimination. *See* civil rights movement; discrimination
Radical Republicans, 619, 621–622, 626, 633
Radio Corporation of America (RCA), 802
radios, 820
RAF (Royal Air Force, Great Britain), 834
railroads: Central Pacific, 650; 1830 to 1850, 437; Kansas Pacific, 366; Orient Express, 351*p*; Panic of 1873 and, 630; regulation of, 382; steel industry and, 643; Stephen Douglas and, 549; time zones set up by, 370; transcontinental, 367–370, 414
Raleigh, Sir Walter, 56
Randolph, A. Philip, 838
Randolph, Edmund, 183
Rankin, Jeannette, 743, 755
ratification: of Articles of Confederation, 154; of U. S. Constitution, 170–174, 186–187, 210

"Raven, The" (Poe), 515
RCA (Radio Corporation of America), 802
Reagan, Ronald: biography of, 966*f*; conservative ideas of, 964–966; foreign policy, 966–968; Sandra Day O'Connor appointed to Supreme Court by, 194
realistic literature, 516–517
realpolitik, 952
reason, in ancient Greek philosophy, 23
reasoning, fallacies in, 744
rebellions, slave, 467–468
recalling officials, 691
reconstruction, after Civil War, 610–637; African Americans, freedom for, 615–618; Andrew Johnson's plan, 618–622; beginning of, 614–615; chance, oversight, and error in history, 635; Congressional control of, 623–625; end of, 629–632; Fifteenth Amendment to Constitution, 626; Fourteenth Amendment to Constitution, 622–623; governments in, 627–628; Ku Klux Klan, 628–629; in North, 633–634; rebuilding southern industry, 632–633; timeline for 1865 to 1880, 611. *See also* Civil War
Reconstruction Acts of 1867, 623
Reconstruction Amendments (Thirteenth, Fourteenth, and Fifteenth) of Constitution, 214*p*, 622–623, 626
Reconstruction Finance Corporation (RFC), 806
recycling, 997
Redcoats, British soldiers as, 115
Red Cross, 755, 755*p*
redeemers, after Civil War, 631
Red Scares (fear of communism in U.S.), 784, 874–880
Red Summer of 1919, 787
Reed, Esther DeBerdt, 143*f*
Reed, Walter, 728, 733
referendums, 692

reform movements, 504–537; abolition of slavery, 524–527; African American communities, 522–523; city growth and urban problems, 511–512; education, 520–522; immigrants, 508–510; prison reform, 520; romantic and realistic literature, 516–517; romanticism, 514–515; second great awakening, 518–519; social responsibility skills, 535; temperance movement, 519–520; timeline for 1815 to 1855, 505; transcendentalists, 513–514; women's rights: opposition to, 530–531; Seneca Falls Convention, 531–534; struggle for, 528–530
reforms, progressive. *See* progressive reforms
reform schools, 520
regions of United States in early 1800s, 335*c*
Rehabilitation Act of 1973, 942
religion: of African Americans in South, 466; in English colonies, 88*c*; freedom of, 212*p*, 224; as immigration reason, 509; in New England colonies, 79–81; revivalist meetings, 316–317; in Roaring Twenties, 786–787; Second Great Awakening, 518–519; of slaves, 485–486, 486*p*; in South, 461; in twenty-first century, 999
Renaissance, 3*p*, 26–28
rendezvous, in fur trade, 358–359
reparations for war damages, 766
reprieves, presidential power to grant, 205
Republican Motherhood, 247
Republican Party, 553, 625
reservations, Indian, 372, 376–377. *See also* Native Americans
resources, North *versus* South, in Civil War, 574*c*
restraint of trade, 650–651
Revels, Hiram, 611*p*, 628

Revere, Paul, 109, 114, 114*m*, 173, 283

revival meetings, 518–519, 519*p*

RFC (Reconstruction Finance Corporation), 806

Rhode Island, as English colony, 79–80

Rhode Island system, 431

Rice, Condoleezza, 989

Ride for Liberty—The Fugitive Slaves, A (Johnson), 472*p*

Riis, Jacob, 674, 676, 689*p*, 693*p*

Rip Van Winkle (Irving), 314

roads in early U.S., 307–309, 308*m*

Roanoke, "lost colony" at, 57–58

Roaring Twenties, 772–797: bull stock market in, 802; business booms, 778–780; competing ideals, 784–786; fear and violence, 783–784; graph comparisons, 795; Hoover elected, 780–781; Jazz Age, 790–794; minority rights, 787–789; peace and prosperity, 776–777; probusiness administration of Coolidge, 777–778; societal changes, 782–783; timeline for 1918 to 1930, 773

Robinson, Jackie, 874*p*

Robinson, Jo Ann, 928

Rochambeau, Comte de, 142

Rockefeller, John D., 649–650, 651*f*

Rocky Mountains, 417*p*

Roebling, John, 644*f*

Roe v. *Wade* (1973), 957

Rolfe, John, 69–70

Roman Catholic Church. *See* Catholic religion

romanticism, 514*p*, 514–517

romantic literature, 516–517

Rome, 3*p*, 24, 24*p*

Rommel, Erwin ("Desert Fox"), 844

Roosevelt, Eleanor: as equal rights supporter, 819; National Youth Administration and, 812–813; Universal Declaration of Human Rights, 870

Roosevelt, Franklin D., 191; as Allied powers leader, 845*p*; allowing Japanese Americans to serve in military, 842; biography of, 807*f*; death of, 856; election of, 808; European strategy in World War II, 842; in 1920 election, 776–777; Temporary Emergency Relief Administration of New York, 807; term limits in Constitution, 220*p*; on United Nations, 868; U.S. entry into World War II, 834–836. *See also* Great Depression of 1930s

Roosevelt, Theodore: biography of, 726*f*; imperialism of, 735*f*; McKinley's assassination and, 683; Panama Canal and, 732; reforms of, 707–709; as Rough Rider in Spanish-American War, 727; Russo-Japanese War negotiations by, 721

Roosevelt corollary, to Monroe Doctrine, 737*f*

Rosenberg, Julius and Ethel, 865, 878

Rosetta Stone, 243*p*

"Rosie the Riveter," 839*f*

Ross, Nellie Tayloe, 783

Rough Riders, in Spanish-American War, 727

Royal Air Force (RAF, Great Britain), 834

Rule of Naturalization, 200

Rural nation, United States as, 248*p*

Rush-Bagot Agreement of 1817, 292

Russia: Alaska purchase from, 719; immigrants from, 379, 664; North American northwest coast and, 303, 359; Red Scares in U.S. from, 784, 878; Russo-Japanese War (1896), 721–722; in World War I, 747, 758. *See also* Soviet Union

Ruth, George Herman "Babe," 791, 792*f*

Rutledge, John, 184*f*

S

Sacagawea, 272, 357

Sacco, Nicola, 784, 784*p*

Sack of Lawrence, Kansas (1856), 539

safety and working conditions, 698–700

Saint-Mihiel, battle of, in World War I, 759

sales techniques, 648*p*

Salinger, J. D., 885–886

Salk, Jonas, 884*p*

Salomon, Haym, 130

SALT (Strategic Arms Limitation Talks) **of 1972,** 952

salt trade, of Ghana, 19, 20*p*

salutary neglect (British non-interference in English colonies), 98

Samoa, 720

Samoset, Pilgrims and, 77

Sampson, Deborah, 130

sanctions, to encourage reform, 961

San Francisco, growth of, 414*p*

San Jacinto, Battle of, 395

San Juan Hill, battle of, in Spanish-American War, 728*p*

Santa Anna, Antonio López de, 394

Sante Fe Trail, 360

Saratoga, battle of, 132, 133*m*, 134

scalawags, in Reconstructionist South, 627

Scalia, Antonin, 965

Scarlet Letter, The (Hawthorne), 505, 515

Schayer, Annie Moore, 665

schematic drawings, 29

Schenck v. *United States* (1919), 754*f*

Schlafly, Phyllis, 940, 941*p*

schools, in New England colonies, 82, 82*p*

Schwarzkopf, Norman, 970

Schwerner, Michael, 935

science, 27. *See also* inventions; technology

SCLC (Southern Christian Leadership Conference), 928

Scopes, John T., 787

Index

Scopes trial, 786f, 787
Scott, Dred, 554p, 554–555
Scott, Winfield, 404, 548, 573
SDS (Students for a Democratic Society), 910
"sea dogs," 54
search-and-destroy missions, in Vietnam War, 904
search warrants, 225
Sears, Roebuck and Company, 673
secession, 497, 539p, 561–562. *See also* Civil War; nation divided
Second Continental Congress, 116
second great awakening, 518–519
Second Industrial Revolution, 642–647
second New Deal, 812–813
Second Seminole War, 342m, 342–344
sectionalism: Jackson and, 333–334; in national identity, 306–311; Wilmot Proviso and, 497m, 542–543
securities, in Constitution, 200
Securities and Exchange Commission (SEC), 810
Sedgwick, Catharine Maria, 315
segregation: ban on, in military, 874; battling, 924–927; Jim Crow laws, 631–632; Progressive challenges to, 703–704; in World War II period, 840p. *See also* civil rights movement; discrimination
Selassie, Haile, 830
Selective Service Act of 1917, 743, 753
Selective Training and Service Act of 1940, 838
self-government, models of, 152–153. *See also* government, forming
Seminole Indians, 15, 293–294, 342m, 342–344, 347m
Senate, U.S. *See* Congress, U.S.; Constitution, U.S.
Seneca Falls Convention, 505p, 531–534
Seneca Indians, 15

Separate Car Act of 1890 (Louisiana), 631
separation of powers, in U.S. Constitution, 190f
Sepoy Mutiny of 1857, 539
September 11, 2001 attacks, 979p, 984
sequence chain, for events, 150
Sequoya (Indian leader), 325p, 342
Serviceman's Readjustment Act, 873
servitude, involuntary, ban on, 213
settlement houses: Addams, Jane, 677f, 677p; Hull House founded, 661, 677; Hull House kindergarten, 676p; Hull House services, 677–678; private organizations and, 676; Progressive reformers and, 690
Seven Days' Battles, in Civil War, 579
Seventeenth Amendment to U.S. Constitution (direct voting for senators), 691
Seward, William H., 543, 549, 560, 719–720
Seymour, Horatio, 625
sharecropping, 632
shared powers, in federal form of government, 208f
Shawnee Indians, 18, 285
Shays, Daniel, 161
Shays's Rebellion, 149, 151, 161–162, 162p, 175
Sherman, Roger, 165p, 166, 166p, 183
Sherman, William Tecumseh, 603–605, 617
Sherman Antitrust Act of 1890, 639, 651, 708
Sherman Silver Purchase Act of 1888, 382
Shiloh, battle of, in Civil War, 584
Shinto religion, 279
shipbuilding, in New England colonies, 81
Shoshone Indians, 16, 272, 357
"shot heard 'round the world" (in American Revolution), 114–115

Silent Parade of July, 1917, 787
Silent Spring (Carson), 958
Silk Road, 25
silver standard, 382
Silvester, Naomi, 77
Sinclair, Upton, 690, 694, 708
Singer, Isaac, 443f, 444
Singleton, Benjamin "Pap," 379
Sino-Japanese War (1894–1895), 721
Sioux Indians, 14–15, 16, 372
Sirhan, Sirhan, 912
sit-down strikes, 814
sit-ins, in civil rights movement, 929–930, 930p, 936f
Sitting Bull (Lakota Sioux chief), 351p, 374–375
Sixteenth Amendment to U.S. Constitution (income taxes), 709
skyscrapers, building, 671
Slater, Samuel, 425–426, 430–431
slave codes, 74, 485
slavery, 472–503; abolitionist message, 490–492; antislavery literature, 500; banned in Northwest Territory, 155; British abolishment of slave trade, 279; compromises on, 183–184, 497–498; culture, 465–467, 479, 485–486; education forbidden, 523; in English colonies, 70–71, 73, 93–94; French and British bans on, 351, 449; Fugitive Slave Act, 498–499; Internet research skills, 501; in Jamestown (1619), 33; labor force needs, 476–477; living under, 463–465, 483–485; in Mexican Cession, 405; in middle English colonies, 86; nation divided over, 542–547; in New Netherland, 85; opposition to, 489–490; opposition to ending, 494–495; Portugal's involvement in, 39–40; rebellions, 467–468, 486–488; in Republic of Texas, 394, 398; sectionalism based on, 334;

territorial expansion and, 496–497; Thirteenth Amendment to U.S. Constitution ban on, 214; Three-Fifths Compromise in Constitution, 166–167, 184*f*; timeline for 1619 to 1852, 472–503; trade in, 477–479, 480*m*–481*m*; Underground Railroad, 492–494; work of, 482–483. *See also* African Americans

Slidell, John, 401

Smith, Alfred E., 780

Smith, Bessie, 792

Smith, Jedidiah, 351, 358

Smith, John, 69

Smith, Joseph, 360

Smith, Margaret Bayard, 331*f*

Smith, Margaret Chase, 224

Smith, Sophia, 701

Smith College, 701

SNCC (Student Non-Violent Coordinating Committee), 929–930, 932–933

social Darwinism, 650

socialism in labor unions, 700

social responsibility skills, 535

Social Security, 799, 1000

Social Security Act of 1935, 813, 821

society, terms about, 4*c*

Society of American Indians, 705

Society of Friends, 85. *See also* Quakers

Socrates, of ancient Greece, 23

sodbusters, 380

Somme, battle of, in World War I, 749

sonar technology, 843–844, 844*p*

Songhai empire, of West Africa, 22

Song of Hiawatha, The (Longfellow), 515

Soninke, of Ghana, 19

Sons of Liberty, 109–110. *See also* American Revolution

Sotomayor, Sonia, 193*p*, 194. *See also* U.S. Supreme Court

sources of information, evaluating, 684

South, 448–471; American Revolution in, 139–140; cotton, 453–457; food crops, 457; free African Americans, 461–462; graph interpretation skills, 469; industries, 457–458; secession of, 539*p*, 561–562; society and culture, 459–461; timeline for 1790 to 1860, 449. *See also* Civil War; reconstruction, after Civil War

South, slavery in: culture, 465–467; living under, 448*p*, 463–465, 464*p*; rebellions of, 467–468

South American societies, 8–10

South Carolina; Nullification Act of 1832, 336; as slave state, 497*m*

South Carolina Exposition and Protest (Calhoun), 335

southeast culture area, of Native Americans, 15–16

Southern Christian Leadership Conference (SCLC), 928

southwest culture area, of Native Americans, 14

southwest expansion, 388–419; American settlement in Mexican Cession, 405–407; California gold rush, 408–414; into early Spanish colonies, 49–51; manifest destiny, 397–400; map interpretation skills, 415; Mexican-American War, 401–404; Texas revolution, 392–396; timeline for 1820 to 1855, 389; United States growth in 1850, 416*m*–417*m*. *See also* westward expansion

sovereignty, popular, 167, 185, 542

Soviet Union: Bolsheviks in 1917 Russia, 758; Cuba diplomatic relations with, 891; globalization and, 986; Kennedy confronting, 894–898; *Sputnik* space satellite, 865, 880, 921; in World War II, 831, 835; Yeltsin and Bush discussions, 970

space exploration by U.S., 896–898, 998

Spain: in American Revolution, 103*p*; conquistadors in Americas, 46–48; England's war with, 54–55; explorations of, 48*m*; Florida ownership negotiations, 293; Louisiana traded to France by, 355; Native Americans' treatment by, 51–52; Pinckney's Treaty with, 257; southeastern Spanish colonies, 48–49; southwestern Spanish colonies, 49–51; trade with after Revolutionary War, 159–160; viceroyalties in America of, 50*m*

Spanish-American War, 715*p*, 724–729, 728*p*

Spanish Armada, 54*p*, 54–55

special needs, education for people with, 522

speculators, 250

speech, freedom of, 212*p*, 224

speech-making skills, 943

spheres of influence, 722

spirituality, 514

spirituals (music), 466, 485–486

spoils system, 332

Sputnik (Soviet satellite), 865, 880, 921

Spy, The (Cooper), 315

Squanto, Pilgrims and, 77

Square Deal, of Theodore Roosevelt, 707

stalemate, in World War I, 749

Stalin, Joseph, 773, 831–832, 845*p*, 868

Stalingrad, battle of, 845–846

Stamp Act of 1765, 107–108, 111*t*

Standard Oil Company, 649, 649*p*, 690

standard time, 370

Stand Watie (Cherokee Indian leader), 587

Stanford, Leland, 413, 650

Stanford University, 650, 965*f*

Stanton, Elizabeth Cady, 531, 531*f*, 533–534, 702

staple crops, in English colonies, 86

Starr, Ellen Gates, 677, 677*f*

state powers, in federal form of government, 208*f*

states, debts of, 251

states' rights, 334–336. *See also* Constitution, U.S.

Statue of Liberty, 661*p*

St. Clair, Arthur, 258

steamboats, 421, 435–436, 436*p*

steam power, impact of, 442–443

steel industry, 439, 642–643

steerage, immigrants traveling in, 665

Steffens, Lincoln, 690

Stein, Gertrude, 793

Steinbeck, John, 820, 822

Stephens, Alexander, 460

Stephens, Ann Sophia, 515

stereotypes, 445

Steuben, Baron Friedrich von, 134, 134*f*

Stevens, John L., 721

Stevens, Thaddeus, 621*p*, 621–623

St. Louis World's Fair (1904), 673

stock market crash of 1929, 799*p*, 802–803

Stockton, Robert, 403

Stone, Lucy, 533*p*, 533–534

Stono Rebellion of 1739, 478–479

Stover, Charles B., 677

Stowe, Harriet Beecher, 499–500, 529, 539, 546–547

Strategic Arms Limitation Talks (SALT) **of 1972,** 952

strategies for sea battles in World War I, 761

Strauss, Levi, 412, 414

strength of arguments, 975

Strict construction of Constitution (Jefferson), 254

strikes, labor, 433, 654–655, 814

Strong, George Templeton, 437–438

Strong, Harriet, 644*f*

structure, economic, 476–477

Stuart, "Jeb," 599

Student Non-Violent Coordinating Committee (SNCC), 929–930, 932–933

Students for a Democratic Society (SDS), 910

Stuyvesant, Peter, 59, 84, 84*p*

suburban growth, postwar, 882–884, 883*p*

suburbs, growth of, 672

Suez Canal, 611*p*

Suez crisis of 1956, 881

suffrage. *See* voting rights

Sugar Act of 1764, 106, 111*t*

Sullivan, Louis, 671

summarizing, skill of, 180, 948

Sumner, Charles, 552, 552*p*, 622

Sun Also Rises, The (Hemingway), 773*p*, 793

Sun Belt, relocation to, 882

superpowers, U.S. and Soviet Union as, 870

supply and demand, agricultural, 381*c*

supply-side economics, 964–965

"survival of the fittest" theory (social Darwinism), 650

Sutter, John, 408–409

Svendsen, Gro, 380*f*

"Swamp Fox" (Francis Marion), 140, 140*p*

Swanson, Swan August, 666*p*

sweatshops, 667, 677, 689*p*

T

Taft, William Howard, 709, 737

Taft-Hartley Act of 1947, 873–874

Taino Indians, on Hispaniola, 41

Taiping Rebellion, in China, 567

"Talented Tenth," of African Americans, 705

Tales of a Wayside Inn (Longfellow), 516

Taliban, 984

"talkies" (movies), 791

Talleyrand, Charles, 356

Tammany Hall (NY political machine), 687

Taney, Roger B., 554–555

tanks, in World War I, 748*p*, 749

Tarbell, Ida B., 690

tariffs: agriculture and, 335; American System of protective, 306–307; Clay, Henry, reduction proposals of, 336; in Commerce Compromises of Constitution, 167;

Congress passage of, 306; as export barrier, 159; Payne-Aldrich Tariff, 709; Tariff of Abominations (1827), 334–335; Underwood Tariff Act of 1913, 709

Tarleton, Banastre, 139

Tateishi, Yuri, 842

taxation without representation, 106–107

taxes, Congressional power on, 200

Taylor, Frederick W., 652

Taylor, Zachary, 401, 403–404, 497, 543

Tea Act of 1773, 110, 111*t*

Teapot Dome scandal, 777

technology: city life changed by, 638*p*; communications, 441–442, 645–646, 885; cotton gin, 453–454; Internet, 501, 994–995; for mass production, 426; sonar, 843–844, 844*p*; twenty-first century, 994–998. *See also* industrial age; inventions

Tecumseh (Indian leader), 285–286, 286*p*

teepees, of Native Americans, 14

telegraph, 441–442, 645

telephone, 645–646

television, 885

Teller Amendment, 725

temperance movement, 519–520, 701–703

Temple, Shirley, 820*p*

tenements, 511, 667, 675, 675*p*

Tennessee: Civil War in, 583–584, 584*m*, 603; in Creek War (1814), 290; Jackson as first U.S. representative from, 330*f*; King, Martin Luther, Jr., killed in Memphis, 937; Nineteenth Amendment ratified by, 703*f*; Over Mountain Men from, 137; Scopes trial in (1925), 787; Second Great Awakening in, 518; as slave state, 497*m*; steamboats in Memphis, 436*p*

Tennessee Valley Authority (TVA), 811, 811*m*, 814*t*

Index

Tenochtitlán (Aztec city), 8

Ten Percent Plan, of southern reconstruction, 615

terrorism: Boston Marathon bombing (2013), 979; Islamic State (ISIS), 991–992; Oklahoma federal office building bombing (1995), 974; in twenty-first century, 983–985

Tet Offensive, in Vietnam War, 905

Texas: empresarios in, 393; Lone Star Republic flag, 396p; Old Three Hundred families in, 393; revolution in, 392–396, 395m; settlers ignoring laws in, 393; slavery in Republic of, 394, 398; U.S. annexation of, 396, 399

textile industry, 425, 425p

Thacher, James, 132

Thames River, battle of (1813), 289

Thanksgiving, 77

Their Eyes Were Watching God (Hurston), 793

Third Reich (Germany in World War II), 831p

Thirteenth Amendment to Constitution (slavery abolished), 615, 624f

38th parallel, 876

31st Pennsylvania Infantry, in Civil War, 596p

Thoreau, Henry David, 513p, 513–514

Three-Fifths Compromise, in Constitution, 166–167, 184

Three Mile Island (PA) **nuclear accident** (1979), 947p, 960

Thurmond, Strom, 874

Tilden, Samuel J., 630

Till, Emmett, 926–927

time, 4c, 370

timelines, 99, 861. *See also* timelines in each module

Tinker* v. *Des Moines Independent Community School District (1969), 941

Tippecanoe, battle of, 285–286

Tisquantum, Pilgrims and, 77

***Titanic* sinking,** 683p

Title IX (1972) **ban on sexual discrimination,** 957

tobacco, 457

Tocqueville, Alexis de, 237, 443, 449

Tojo, Hideki, 827p, 869

Toleration Act of 1649, 72

Tompkins, Sally Louisa, 597

***Tom Thumb* locomotive,** 421p, 437

Tonkel, Dan, 765

Tonkin Gulf Resolution, in Vietnam War, 902

Toponce, Alexander, 369

totalitarianism, 830–832

total war, 604

totems, of Pacific Northwest Native American cultures, 13

town meetings, in New England colonies, 91

Townsend, Francis, 812

Townshend Acts, of 1767, 108–109

trade: antitrust movement and, 650–651; under Articles of Confederation, 158–159; barriers to, 159m; in cotton, 455–457, 456f; in early European empires in the Americas, 45; in English colonies, 92–94; Great Depression impact on, 805; interstate, 160; in Middle Ages, 25–26; in middle English colonies, 86–87; in New England colonies, 81; in Renaissance, 28; slave, 477–479, 480m–481m; southwestern expansion and, 406–407

trade unions: beginning of, 433–434; Congress of Industrial Organizations (CIO), 814; in Great Britain, 505; immigration opposed by, 668; postwar strikes of, 873–874; in Progressive Era, 699–700

Tragle, Henry I., 488f

Trail of Tears, 325, 341p, 342, 342f. *See also* Indian Removal Act of 1830

trails of westward expansion, 359–361, 360m, 368m

transcendentalist movement, 513–514

transcontinental railroad, 367–370, 369p

Transportation Revolution, 435–440, 439m

transportation systems, improvement of, 306–309

Trans-Siberian Railroad (Russia), 661f

Travis, William, 394

Treaties of Fort Laramie, 372

Treaty at Holston River, 346c

Treaty at St. Louis, 346c

Treaty of Brest-Litovsk, 758

Treaty of Dancing Rabbit Creek, 340–341, 346c

Treaty of Fort Jackson (1814), 290, 346c

Treaty of Ghent (1814), 291

Treaty of Greenville of 1795, 243, 259, 284–285, 346c

Treaty of Guadalupe Hidalgo of 1848, 392, 405

Treaty of Medicine Lodge, 373

Treaty of Paris of 1759, 96–97, 142m, 142–144

Treaty of Paris of 1763, 88m

Treaty of Paris of 1783, 158

Treaty of Tordesillas of 1493, 43

Treaty of Versailles of 1918, 767–768, 831–832

Treaty on the Non-Proliferation of Nuclear Weapons, 778

Tredegar Iron Works, 449p, 458

trench warfare, in World War I, 742p, 748, 748p

Trenton, battle of, 131p, 132

trial by jury, right to, 236

Triangle Shirtwaist Company fire of 1911, 698p, 698–699

triangular trade, in colonies, 92m, 93

Troubled Asset Relief Program of 2008, 987

Troy Female Seminary, 521

Trujillo, Charley, 904f

Truman, Harry S.: desegregation of armed services by, 924; Eleanor Roosevelt appointed to UN by, 870; on hydrogen bomb, 880; Korean War and, 877–879; postwar strikes and, 873; at Potsdam Conference, 868; as president, 865; winning election of 1948, 874–875; in World War II, 856, 858

Index

Truman Doctrine, 871

trusts, 650

Truth, Sojourner, 492, 492*p*, 526, 529

Tubman, Harriet, 494, 526*p*, 527

Turing, Alan, 827

Turner, Nat, 467*f*, 467–468, 487

Tuscarora Indians, 16

Tuskegee Airmen, 839, 840*f*

Tuskegee Institute, 703

Tutankhamen tomb, discovery of, 773*p*

Tweed, William Marcy, 687

Twelfth Amendment to Constitution (presidential election procedure), 269

Twenty-First Amendment to Constitution (repeal of prohibition), 785*f*, 786

Twenty-First century, 978–1005; Bush, George W., 988–990; controversial issues, identifying, 1001; election of 2000, 982–983; global economy, 985–987; immigration, 1002*m*–1003*m*; Obama, Barack, 990–993; population changes, 998–999; religious changes, 999–1000; technological changes, 994–998; terrorism, 983–985; timeline for 2000 to present, 979

Twenty-Second Amendment to U.S. Constitution (two-term presidential limit), 191

Twenty-Sixth Amendment to Constitution (voting age lowered to 18), 179, 913

Two Years Before the Mast (Dana), 400

Tyler, John, 398

U

UFW (United Farm Workers), 938

Uncle Tom's Cabin (Stowe), 473, 499–500, 539, 546–547

Underground Railroad, 492–494, 493*m*, 499, 526–527

Underwood Tariff Act of 1913, 709

unemployment, 804*p*, 804–805. *See also* New Deal

Union army, in Civil War, 566*p*. *See also* Civil War

Union Pacific Railroad, 368

unions. *See* labor unions

United Colonies of New England, 80

United Farm Workers (UFW), 938

United Mine Workers, 873

United Nations, 869–870

United States: in 1760, 88–89*m*; in 1818–1819, 293*m*; in 1850, 416*m*–417*m*; in 1853, 415*m*; in Cold War, 873–875, 882–886; ethnic diversity in twenty-first century, 998; as postwar superpower, 870; Red Scares (fear of communism) in, 878–880; slavery and growth of, 496–497; in World War I, 751–753, 757–758, 758*f*; in World War II, 834–836. *See also* English colonies

United States, as world power, 714–741; Alaska purchase, 719–720; China, trade with, 722–723; continuity and change, 739; foreign policy, 737–738; Hawaii as territory, 720–721; imperialism in, 718–719; influence of, 730*m*–731*m*; Japan, trade with, 721–722; Latin America policy, 735–736; Panama Canal, 732–734; Spanish-American War, 724–729; timeline for 1867 to 1920, 715

United States, launching of, 242–277; Adams as second president, 265–266; Alien and Sedition Acts of 1798, 266–267; debt settlement, 250–252; election of 1800, 268–269; election of 1796, 263–265; expectations, 248–249; government, organizing, 247–248; group decision skills, 275; Jefferson as third president, 270–271; Jefferson versus Hamilton, 252–253; Louisiana Purchase,

271–272; national bank, 253–254; neutrality of, 255–258; Northwest Territory conflict, 258–259; Supreme Court, 272–274; timeline for 1785 to 1805, 243; Washington as first president, 246–247; Washington's farewell, 260–262; Whiskey Rebellion, 259–260

United States **v. Nixon** (1974), 954*f*

unreasonable searches and seizures, freedom from, 225

unwarrantable jurisdiction, 126

urban areas: in antebellum South, 461; decay of, 959; growth of, 511–512; reform of services in, 690; renewal of, 884

Urban League, 705

urban population, in early United States, 248*p*

USA PATRIOT Act of 2001, 988

U.S. Capitol grounds, 673

U.S. Census Bureau, 384, 998–999

U.S. Department of Agriculture, 382

U.S. Department of Defense, 994

U.S. Department of Homeland Security, 192*f*, 979, 988

U.S. Department of Housing and Urban Development (HUD), 936

U.S. Environmental Protection Agency (EPA), 959

U.S. Forest Service, 708–709

U.S. Sanitary Commission, 575

USS *Chesapeake* (warship), 283

USS *Constitution* (warship), 282, 283*p*, 288

USS *Maine* (warship), 725, 725*p*

USS *Monitor* **Center,** 582

U.S. Supreme Court: *Brown* v. *Board of Education* (1954), 179, 921*p*, 925, 926*f*; *Bush* v. *Gore election of 2000,* 983; capitalism and, 338*f*; *Cherokee Nation* v. *Georgia* (1831), 342; child labor laws and, 696; Civil Rights Act of 1875

declared unconstitutional by, 631; Constitutional establishment of, 168, 193–194; *Dartmouth College* v. *Woodward* (1819), 338*f*; decisions of, 192*f*; *Dred Scott* decision (1857), 554–555; election of 1876 decided by, 630; *Escobedo* v. *Illinois* (1964), 941; establishment of, 272–274; *Fletcher* v. *Peck* (1810), 338*f*; *Gibbons* v. *Ogden* (1824), 309, 338*f*, 436–437; *Guinn* v. *United States* (1915), 705; *Korematsu* v. *United States* (1944), 841; *Lochner* v. *New York* (1897), 699; *Marbury* v. *Madison* (1803), 273, 273*f*; *McCulloch* v. *Maryland* (1819), 309, 337, 338*f*; *Miranda* v. *Arizona* (1966), 941; *Muller* v. *Oregon* (1908), 699; National Industrial Recovery Act (NIRA) declared unconstitutional by, 813; New Deal programs declared unconstitutional by, 815; Nixon and, 950; O'Connor, Sandra Day as first woman on, 965*f*; *Plessy* v. *Ferguson* (1896), 631–632, 925, 926*f*; on railroad regulation, 382; *Roe* v. *Wade* (1973), 957; *Schenck* v. *United States* (1919), 754*f*; on Second Amendment, 992–993; segregation on public transportation ruled illegal by, 928, 932; *Tinker* v. *Des Moines Independent Community School District* (1969), 941; *United States* v. *Nixon* (1974), 954*f*; *Worcester* v. *Georgia* (1832), 342
Uto-Aztecan language family, 16
utopian communities, 514

V

Vail, Alfred Lewis, 441
Vallandigham, Clement L., 595
Vallejo, Mariano Guadalupe, 399, 403

Valley Forge, winter at, in American Revolution, 135–136
values, rejection of traditional, 910
Van Buren, Martin: elected president, 325*p*, 327; as Free-Soil Party candidate (1848), 497; as secretary of state under Jackson, 332; ten-hour workday for federal employees, 433; as vice president, 338
Van Vorst, Marie, 695
Vanzetti, Bartolomeo, 784, 784*p*
vaqueros (Mexican cowboys), 366, 399
Vassar College, 701
Vegh, Moritz, 857
Veiller, Lawrence, 676
Verdun, battle of, in World War I, 749
Verrazano, Giovanni da, 56
Versailles Treaty (World War I), 743, 767–768
vertical integration, in steel industry, 649
Vesey, Denmark, 467, 486
Vespucci, Amerigo, 44
veto power, of president, 192
Vicksburg, siege of, in Civil War, 585–586, 588*m*–589*m*
Victoria, Queen of Great Britain, 449*p*
Vietcong, 899
Vietnamization strategy, 912
Vietnam Veterans Memorial, 915–916, 916*p*
Vietnam War years, 890–919; antiwar protests, 910–911; conflict in, 898–901; election of 1968, 911–912; hawks and doves in, 905–907; Johnson commitment, 902–903; Kennedy and communism, 894–898; in 1968, 906*m*; Nixon and, 912–913; oral history, 917; Tet Offensive, 905; timeline for 1960 to 1975, 891; U.S. soldiers in, 899*p*, 903–905; Vietcong tunnels, 908*p*–909*p*; Vietnam War end, 891*p*, 913–916
Viking explorers, 36–37
Villa, Francisco "Pancho," 738

Virginia: Civil War in, 577–580, 578*m*; as English colony, 70–71; Virginia Declaration of Rights, 174; Virginia House of Burgesses, 152; Virginia Statute for Religious Freedom, 153, 156
Virginia Plan, in Constitution, 165, 166*f*, 183
visualization, understanding through, 866
visual resources skills, 769
vocabulary of social studies, 4–5
Volstead Act, 785
voting rights: of African Americans, 625*p*, 631–632; under British rule, 153; to 18 year olds in Twenty-sixth Amendment to Constitution, 179, 913; expansion of, 691–692; popular sovereignty from, 167; responsibility to vote, 236*p*, 236–237; to women in Nineteenth Amendment to Constitution, 218*p*, 633–634, 701–703
Voting Rights Act of 1965, 935
Voting Rights Act of 1975, 939

W

WAAC (Women's Auxiliary Army Corps), 838
Wabanaki Indians, 17
Wade, Benjamin, 615, 625
Wade-Davis bill, 615
wage earners, 670
Wagner, Robert F., 814
Wagner Act (National Labor Relations Act), 814
wagon trains, 350*p*. *See also* westward expansion
Walker, David, 490
Wallace, George, 912
Wampanoag Indians, 77, 81, 95
wampum (Native American money), 15
War Hawks, in War of 1812, 286–287
War Industries Board (WIB), 753
War of 1812, 278–297; British offensive, 290–291; call for,

286–287; decision-making process skill, 295; early battles in, 288–290; effects of, 291; Florida, gain of, 293–294; map of, 289*m*; settling British disputes, 292; timeline for 1807 to 1816, 279; violations of neutrality, 282–284; western conflicts, 284–286

War Powers Act of 1973, 915

War Production Board (WPB), in World War II, 837

warrants, probable cause needed for, 211

Warren, Earl, 941

Warren, Mercy Otis, 108, 171

Warsaw Pact of 1955, 865, 872

Washington, Booker T., 703, 704*f*

Washington, George: as American Revolution commander, 116, 128; at Battle of Yorktown, 142; biography of, 116*f*; at Constitutional Convention of 1787, 164, 165*p*, 182; Farewell Address after presidency, 260–262, 261*f*; farewell to troops, 144; as Federalist, 170; as first president, 243*p*, 246–247; in French and Indian War, 96

Washington, Martha, 246–247

Washington and Lee University, 579*f*

Washington Crossing the Delaware (Leutze), 131*p*

Washington, DC: in *Brown* v. *Board of Education* (1954), 925; Civil War isolation of, 572; free African Americans kidnapped in, 484; "Hooverville" in (1932), 806; Jackson statue in, 324*p*; Jefferson, Thomas, inaugurated in, 270; Lincoln assassinated in, 618; September 11, 2001 attacks on, 984; Vietnam Veterans Memorial in, 915*f*; War of 1812 attack on, 290, 290*p*; Washington, George, choice of, 252; Washington Monument in, 242*p*; Watergate scandal in, 953

Washington Post, 953

WASP (Women's Airforce Service Pilots), 838

Watergate scandal, 953–954, 953*p*

Waterloo, battle of, 279, 299

water rights in southwest, 407, 417*p*

Wayne, Anthony, 258

WCTU (Women's Christian Temperance Union), 702

weapons of mass destruction, 984

Weaver, Robert C., 819

Webber, Thomas, 575

Webster, Daniel, 336, 337*p*, 438, 544, 544*f*, 545*p*

Webster, Noah, 318

Welch, Joseph, 879–880

Weld, Charles Richard, 438

Weld, Theodore, 475, 489, 529

Welles, Orson, 827

Wells, Ida B., 704

west, American Revolution in, 137–138

West Africa, trading kingdoms of, 19–22, 21*m*

West Berlin airlift of 1949, 872

west culture area, of Native Americans, 14

Westinghouse, George, 645

Westmoreland, William, 904–905

westward expansion, 350–387; cattle kingdom, 366–367; farmers' politics, 381–383; first westerners, 354–355; frontier's end, 383–384; Indian reservations, 376–377; living on the plains, 378–381; Louisiana Purchase and, 356–358; maps of, 362*m*–363*m*; migration map reading, 385; mining boom, 364–365; mountain men, 358–359; Plains Indians, conflicts with, 371–375; timeline for 1800 to 1900, 351; trails for, 359–361; transcontinental railroad, 367–370. *See also* southwest expansion

Whig Party, 327, 339, 553

Whip Inflation Now (WIN) **program,** of Gerald Ford, 956

Whiskey Rebellion, 243, 259–260

White, John, 58

White, Walter, 819

Whitefield, George, 94

Whitman, Walt, 515

Whitney, Eli, 426*p*, 426–427, 453–454, 456*f*

Whittier, John Greenleaf, 490

Who, the, 891

WIB (War Industries Board), 753

Wiesel, Elie, 860

Wilder, Laura Ingalls, 381

Wilderness Campaign, in Civil War, 603

Wilderness Road, 354

Wild One, The (film), 886

Wilhelm I, Kaiser of Germany, 611, 746

Willard, Emma, 521

Willard, Frances, 702

William and Mary, College of, 83

William and Mary, King and Queen of England, 157*p*

Williams, Joseph E., 593*f*

Williams, Roger, 79–80

Wilmot, David, 405, 496, 542

Wilmot Proviso, 405, 496–497, 542–543

Wilson, James, 165*p*, 166, 166*p*, 183

Wilson, Woodrow: biography of, 767*f*; as Democratic candidate in 1912, 709; Fourteen Points, 765; Latin American democracy support from, 737–738; National War Labor Board set up by, 755; neutrality in World War I proclamation of, 743, 751–752; reforms of, 709–710; U.S. entry into World War I, 752–753

Winnemucca, Sarah, 376–377, 377*p*

Winthrop, John, 79–80

Wisconsin Idea, 692

witchcraft trials of 1690s New England, 80–81

Wizard of Oz (film), 799

Wolfe, James, 96

Woman in the Nineteenth Century (Fuller), 529

women: in American Revolutionary War, 129–130; antislavery movements and, 525p; in Civil War, 596–597; in colonial Virginia, 71; education for, 521, 522p; Equal Rights Amendment (ERA), 957, 958p; facilitating community growth, 380; limited employment opportunities for, 885; in middle English colonies, 87; not addressed in Declaration of Independence, 122; opposition to rights for, 530–531; in Plymouth Colony, 77; in Roaring Twenties, 782–783, 783p; Sandra Day O'Connor as first woman on Supreme Court, 965f; Seneca Falls Convention, 531–534; struggle for rights for, 528–530; temperance efforts of, 701–703; voting rights for, 153p, 179, 218p, 633–634, 682p, 683p, 701–703; women's movement of mid-twentieth century, 939–940; in World War I, 755; in World War II, 838, 839f

Women's Airforce Service Pilots (WASP), 838

Women's Auxiliary Army Corps (WAAC), 838

Women's Christian Temperance Union (WCTU), 702

Women's International League for Peace and Freedom, 677f

Wood, Leonard, 728

Woodside, John Archibald, 303

Woodstock Music Festival, 891p

Woodward, Bob, 953

Woodward, Charlotte, 532

Worcester v. *Georgia* (1832), 342

workers' compensation laws, 699

working conditions, safety of, 698–700

Works Progress Administration (WPA), 812, 819

World Anti-Slavery Convention of 1840, 531

world power, United States as. *See* United States, as world power

World's Columbian Exposition (Chicago, 1893), 644f

World Trade Center, September 11, 2001 attacks on, 979p, 984

World Trade Organization (WTO), 986

World War I, 742–771, 771 MC1– 771 MC2; armistice of, 761–762; costs of, 763–765, 764c; early battles of, 748–750; final battles of, 759–761; map of, 760m; mobilizing for, 753–754; opportunities, 754–756; outbreak of, 746–747; peace agreement after, 765–767; timeline for 1914 to 1920, 743; United States in, 751–753, 757–758; Versailles treaty rejected by U.S., 767–768; visual resources skills, 769

World War II, 826–863, 863 MC1–863 MC2; African Americans in, 838–839; in Europe and North Africa, 833m, 843–848; Germany expansion, 832–834; Holocaust literature, 860; Japanese American internment, 841–842; Mexican Americans in, 839–840; in Pacific, 849–854; preparing for, 837–838; timeline construction, 861; timeline for 1935 to 1950, 827; totalitarianism rise, 830–832; United States joins, 834–836; victory and consequences, 855–859; women in, 838

World Wide Web, 994

Wounded Knee, Massacre at, 375

Wovoka (Paiute Indian leader), 376

WPA (Works Progress Administration), 812, 819

WPB (War Production Board), in World War II, 837

Wright, Orville, 644f

Wright, Wilbur, 646

writers, American, 314–315

WTO (World Trade Organization), 986

X

XYZ affair of 1798, 265, 266f

Y

Yalta Conference of 1945, 868, 869p

yellow fever, 726, 733

Yellow Fever Commission, 728

yellow journalism, 724p, 724–725

Yeltsin, Boris, 970

yeomen, in South, 461

Yom Kippur War (1973), 951

York, Alvin, 761p

Yorktown, battle of, 103p, 141m, 141–142

Yosemite National Park, 708p

Young, Brigham, 361, 407

Z

Zavala, Lorenzo de, 394

Zenger, John Peter, 92

Zimmermann, Arthur, 752

Zimmermann Note, 752

zones, time, 370

zoot-suit riots of 1943, 840

Zuni (Native American culture), 14

For permission to reproduce copyrighted material, grateful acknowledgment is made to the following sources:

Excerpt from *The Grapes of Wrath* by John Steinbeck. Text copyright 1939 and renewed © 1967 by John Steinbeck. Reprinted by permission of Viking Penguin, a division of Penguin Group (USA) Inc., and Penguin Books Ltd.

Excerpt from *Night* by Elie Wiesel. Text copyright © 1972, 1985 by Elie Wiesel. English translation copyright © 2006 by Marion Wiesel. Originally published as *La Nuit* by Les Editions de Minuit. Text copyright © 1958 by Les Editions de Minuit. Reprinted by permission of Farrar Straus and Giroux, Georges Borchardt, Inc. for Les Editions de Minuit and Recorded Books.

Excerpt from "Now I Lay Me Down to Sleep" by Diana Dwan Poole, from *Chicken Soup for the Veteran's Soul* by Jack Canfield, Mark Victor Hansen, and Sidney R. Slagter. Copyright © by Diana Dwan Poole. Reprinted by permission of The Permissions Company.

Excerpt from "Interview with Todd B. Walton" from The Library of Congress *Veterans History Project*. Reprinted by permission of the Library of Congress.

Art and Photography Credits

Video reference screens © 2010 A&E Television Networks, LLC. All rights reserved.

Cover: *Cannon* Malcolm MacGregor/Getty Images; *paper texture* Tolga Tezcan Getty Images

Front Matter: *Signing the Declaration of Independence* ©Bettmann/Corbis; *Independence Hall* ©Dennis Degnan/Corbis; *Migrant Mother* Library of Congress Prints and Photographs Division, Washington, D.C. [LC-DIG-fsa-8b29516]; *Dust Bowl* NOAA George E. Marsh Album; *people with flags* ©Moodboard/Superstock.

Module 1: *Buffalo* ©Annie Griffiths/Corbis; *mammoth skeleton* ©Richard Cummins/Corbis; *Egyptian pyramids* ©Jupiterimages; *Olmec head* ©Yoshio Tomii/SuperStock; *Michelangelo David* ©Rabatti-Dominige/AKG Images; *Roman columns* ©Christopher Groenhout/Lonely Planet Images; *maize* Picture Research Consultants, Inc.; *Tikal* ©Getty Images; *Mesa Verde Cliff Palace* ©Photodisc/Getty Images; *bird shaped pipe* akg-images/Werner Forman; *sewing awl* ©Werner Forman/AKG Images; *painted effigy jar* Courtesy National Museum of the American Indian, Smithsonian Institution. 3/9547; 115 (t) *Iroquois longhouse* ©Marilyn Angel Wynn/Getty Images; *Iroquois longhouse illustration* The Granger Collection, NYC; *Mali salt market* ©John Elk III; *Ashante gold jewelry* ©Robert Estall photo agency/Alamy;

Roman Senate ©PRISMA/Ancient Art & Architecture Collection Ltd; *Charlemagne* ©INTERFOTO/Alamy; *Crusades painting* Iberfoto/Photoaisa; *rat* ©GK Hart/Vikki Hart/Photodisc/Getty Images; *Johann Gutenberg* The Granger Collection, NYC; *signing Magna Carta* ©Bettmann/Corbis.

Module 2: *Ships* © Rebecca Marvil/Index Stock Imagery/photolibrary.com; *Christopher Columbus* ©SuperStock, Inc./SuperStock; *Henry Hudson* © Tate Gallery, London/Art Resource, NY; *1570 compass* National Maritime Museum, Greenwich, London; *Galileo telescope* ©G. Tortoli/Ancient Art and Architecture Collection; *Francisco Pizarro* ©Time Life Pictures/Getty Images; *Christopher Columbus* ©SuperStock, Inc./SuperStock; *Estevanico* The Granger Collection, NYC; *de Las Casas* PRC Picture Research Consultants, Inc.; *Martin Luther* ©AKG Images; *printing press* Saint Bride Printing Library; *Spanish Armada* ©Mary Evans Picture Library; *Spanish coin* Bridgeman Art Library.

Module 3: *Plymouth Colony garden* ©Superstock; *Taj Mahal* ©David Ball/Corbis; *Peter the Great* ©Superstock; *Chief Pontiac* The Granger Collection, NYC; *Sandwich Islander* ©Culver Pictures, Inc.; *Virginia landscape* Colonial Williamsburg Foundation; *Fall of New Amsterdam* ©Superstock; *Appalachian Mountains* ©Superstock; *Boston satellite photo* NASA; *Port of Marseille* ©Superstock; *slave ship* Bridgeman Art Library.

Module 4: *War re-enactment* © James Lemass/Index Stock Imagery/photolibrary.com; *tax stamp act 1765* ©Everett Collection Inc./Superstock; *Declaration of Independence* The Granger Collection, NYC; *ships in battle* Falmouth Art Gallery, Cornwall, UK/The Bridgeman Art Library; *Simon Bolivar* ©North Wind Picture Archives/Alamy; *Patrick Henry* Virginia Historical Society; *tax stamp act 1765* ©Everett Collection Inc./Superstock; *Boston Massacre engraving* Peter Newark's American Pictures; *Boston Massacre* ©Bettmann/Corbis; *Boston Tea Party* American Antiquarian Society; *Battle of Lexington* The Granger Collection, NYC; *William Franklin* The Granger Collection, New York; *Benjamin Franklin* ©clipart.com; *Signing the Declaration of Independence* ©Bettmann/Corbis; *American flag (detail)* ©Getty Images/PhotoDisc; *Mum Bett* The Granger Collection, NYC; *British Soldier* ©Collection of The New-York Historical Society, neg. 31665; *Colonial Soldier #1921.101*, ©Collection of The New-York Historical; *Crossing the Delaware* ©Superstock; *Marquis de Lafayette* Chateau de Versailles, France/Giraudon/Bridgeman; *Bernardo de Galvez* ©Hotel Galvez; *Battle of Saratoga pistol* Saratoga National Historic Park; *Valley Forge* ©SuperStock/SuperStock; *Francis Marion ship* The Granger Collection, NYC.

Module 5: *Nancy Pelosi swears in Congress* ©2009 Jay Mallin; *James Madison miniature* Library of Congress Prints & Photographs Division, Washington, D.C. [LC-USZC4-4097]; *Continental bills* ©North Wind Picture Archives/Alamy; *Castillo de San Marcos* ©Nik Wheeler/Corbis; *Kremlin* ©Andrea Jemolo/Corbis; *women voting* The Granger Collection, NYC; *Mayflower reconstruction* ©Bettmann/Corbis; *Thomas Jefferson* ©Bettmann/Corbis; *signing Magna Carta* ©Bettmann/Corbis; *King William & Queen Mary* ©Michael Nicholson/Corbis; *John Locke* AISA/World Illustrated/Photoshot; *U.S. Constitution* National Archives (London); *Shays's Rebellion* The Granger Collection, NYC; *James Madison* ©Stock Montage/Getty Images; *Signing the Constitution* ©Hall of Representatives, Washington, DC/Bridgeman Art Library; cl) *Roger Sherman* ©Independence National Historical Park; *James Wilson* ©North Wind Picture Archives/Alamy.

Module 6: *Students* ©Sam Dudgeon/Houghton Mifflin Harcourt; *Woman Suffrage poster* Picture Research Consultants, Inc.; *teen voting* ©Tony Freeman/PhotoEdit, Inc.; *Brown v. Board of Education* ©Bettmann/Corbis; *Independence Hall* ©Dennis Degnan/Corbis; *John Rutledge* ©North Wind Picture Archives/Alamy; *Gouverneur Morris* ©Bridgeman Images; *photo of U.S. Constitution* ©Houghton Mifflin Harcourt; *Supreme Court* ©Jurgen Vogt/The Image Bank/Getty Images; *Sonia Sotomayor* AP Photo/Collection of the Supreme Court of the United States, Steve Petteway; *American flag (detail)* ©Getty Images/PhotoDisc; *John Thune* ©Michael Reynolds/epa/Corbis; *Congress* ©Mark Wilson/Getty Images; *signing document* ©Brooks Kraft/Corbis; *US Capitol building* ©Barry Howe/Corbis; *woman's hands* © Yang Liu/CORBIS; *smiling girl* ©Norm Detlaff/AP Images; *suffragette with banner* ©Bettmann/Corbis; *reading Nixon headline* ©Bettmann/CORBIS; *woman with megaphone* David Young-Wolff/PhotoEdit, Inc.; *African American voting* Library of Congress Prints and Photographs Division, Washington, D.C. [LC-USZ62-100971]; *suffragettes petition* Library of Congress Prints and Photographs Division, Washington, D.C. [LC-USZ62-78691]; *FDR portrait* © Oscar White/CORBIS; *FDR button* ©Bettmann/Corbis; *African American woman voting* ©1978 Matt Herron/TakeStock; *NYC union* ©New York Daily News Archive/Getty Images; *man addressing jury* ©Moodboard/Alamy; *female student raising hand* ©Ariel Skelley/Corbis; *Declaration of Independence photo* ©Houghton Mifflin Harcourt; *Constitution* National Archives (London); *swearing in US citizen* ©David Butow/Corbis; *U.S. Marine* ©Brownie Harris/Corbis; *election day* ©kleo67/Alamy; *teen volunteers* ©Ariel Skelley/Corbis.

Module 15: *Ride for Liberty* The Granger Collection, New York; *lower deck slave ship* ©Bettmann/Corbis; Uncle Tom's Cabin Picture Research Consultants, Inc.; *King Afonso* ©The New York Public Library/Schomburg Center for Research in Black Culture/Manuscripts, Archives and Rare Books Division; *crusher squeezes juice* British Library, London, UK/The Bridgeman Art Library; *lower deck slave ship* ©Bettmann/Corbis; *Elmina Castle* ©Michael Dwyer/Alamy; *slaves picking cotton* ©North Wind Picture Archives/Alamy; *slave with owner's child* The Granger Collection, New York; *African American church* South Carolina Historical Society; *William Lloyd Garrison* Trustees of the Boston Public Library; *Sojourner Truth* Courtesy of the Massachusetts Historical Society; *"Outrage," February 2, 1837 Handbill* Rare Book and Special Collections Division, Library of Congress, Washington, D.C. (41); *Henry Clay* National Portrait Gallery, Smithsonian Institution / Art Resource, NY; Uncle Tom's Cabin Picture Research Consultants, Inc.

Module 16: *Busy Port* ©Superstock; *proclaim liberty banner* Courtesy of the Massachusetts Historical Society; *Women Rights report* Picture Research Consultants, Inc.; *Braille typewriter* Photo © David Modica, courtesy American Printing House for the Blind Museum; *immigrants at Battery* Peter Newark's American Pictures; *"Outrage," February 2, 1837 Handbill* Rare Book and Special Collections Division, Library of Congress, Washington, D.C. (41); *Irish immigrant family* Wm. B. Becker Collection/American Museum of Photography; *Walden Pond* ©Corbis; *The First Harvest in the Wilderness*, 1855 (oil on canvas), Durand, Asher Brown (1796–1886) / Brooklyn Museum of Art, New York, USA / Gift of the Brooklyn Institute of Arts and Sciences / The Bridgeman Art Library; *Revival camp* The Granger Collection, New York; *temperance pledge* ©Getty Images; *Oberlin College students* Courtesy of Oberlin Archives; *Am I Not a Woman* The Granger Collection, New York; *Harriet Tubman* Library of Congress Prints and Photographs Division, Washington, D.C. [LC-USZ62-7816]; *North Star*, June 2, 1848. Edited by Frederick Douglass and Martin Delany. Newspaper. Library of Congress, Serial and Government Publications Division, Washington, D.C. (2-10); *Angelina Grimke* The Granger Collection, New York; *Sarah Grimke* The Granger Collection, New York; *National Anti-Suffrage Headquarters* ©Stock Montage, Inc.; *Declaration of Sentiments from Report of the Woman's Rights Convention, Held at Seneca Falls, New York July 19 and 20, 1848. Rochester: North Star Office, 1848.* Elizabeth Cady Stanton Papers, Library of Congress, Manuscript Division, Washington, D.C. (111.01.01)

[Digital ID# us0111_01a]; *Lucy Stone* ©Bettmann/Corbis; *Susan B. Anthony* ©Bettmann/Corbis; *Abigail Adams* Courtesy of the Massachusetts Historical Society; *Suffrage car* Library of Congress Prints and Photographs Division, Washington, D.C. [LC-DIG-ggbain-12924].

Module 17: *Women in museum* © Dave G. Houser; Uncle Tom's Cabin Picture Research Consultants, Inc.; *Napoleon III* The Art Archive/Private Collection/Dagli Orti; *Sepoy Mutiny* India Office Library & Records, The British Library; *Charleston Mercury* Library of Congress, Rare Book and Special Collections Division, Alfred Whital Stern Collection of Lincolniana [Digital ID# lprbscsm scsm0241]; *Henry Clay addressing Senate* Picture Research Consultants, Inc.; *Fugitive Slave Law convention* The Granger Collection, New York; *John Doy abolitionists* Kansas State Historical Society, Topeka, Kansas; *Brooks attacking Sumner* The Granger Collection, New York; *Abraham Lincoln* Library of Congress Prints and Photographs Division, Washington, D.C. [LC-DIG-ppmsca-19204]; *Stephen A. Douglas* Library of Congress Prints and Photographs Division, Washington, D.C. [LC-DIG-cwpbh-00882]; *John Brown* Fotosearch/Getty Images.

Module 18: *Union drummer boys* Library of Congress Prints and Photographs Division, Washington, D.C. [LC-B8171-7514]; *Emancipation poster* ©Superstock; *Kaiser Maximillian* ©Hulton-Deutsch Collection/Corbis; *Surrender at Appomattox* ©Superstock; *Scott's Great Snake* Library of Congress Geography and Map Division, Washington, D.C. [Digital ID # g3701 scw0011000]; *Union gunboats* ©North Wind Picture Archives/Alamy; *ironclad* Naval Historical Center; *4th U.S. Colored Infantry* Library of Congress, Prints and Photographs Division, Washington, D.C. [LC-DIG-cwpb-04294]; *recruitment poster (inset)* Courtesy of the Massachusetts Historical Society; *infantry family* ©Bettmann/Corbis; *Clara Barton* American Antiquarian Society; *Lincoln giving speech* Library of Congress Prints and Photographs Division, Washington, D.C. [LC-DIG-ppmsca-19926]; *Surrender at Appomattox* ©Superstock; *copperheads cartoon* The Granger Collection, New York; *Lincoln cartoon* ©Hulton Archive/Getty Images; *copperheads cartoon* The Granger Collection, New York.

Module 19: *Charleston Ruins* Still Picture Records Section, Special Media Archives Services Division (NWCS-S), National Archives [111-B-744]; *Lincoln assassination* © Kean Collection/Getty Images; *Johnson impeachment* The Granger Collection, New York; *Hiram Revels* Herbert F. Johnson Museum of Art, Cornell University; *Suez Canal* ©Michael Maslan Historic Photographs/CORBIS; *barge leaving Richmond* Library of Congress Prints

and Photographs Division, Washington, D.C. [LC-DIG-cwpb-04079]; *African American couple* University of Texas at El Paso Library, Special Collections; *Freedmen's Bureau school* ©Corbis; *Andrew Johnson* Library of Congress Prints and Photographs Division, Washington, D.C. [LC-BH83-171]; *Thaddeus Stevens* ©Corbis; *first vote* © North Wind/North Wind Picture Archives—All rights reserved; *Ku Klux Klan* ©Bettmann/Corbis; *visit from Ku Klux Klan* The Granger Collection, New York; *Henry Grady* ©Bettmann/Corbis; *Atlanta Georgia 1887* Courtesy of the Charleston Renaissance Gallery, Robert M. Hicklin Jr., Inc., Charleston, South Carolina.

Module 20: *Cable cars in San Francisco* Picture Research Consultants, Inc.; *Alexander Graham Bell* ©Bettmann/Corbis; *AFL lapel pin* George Meany Memorial Archives; *Eiffel Tower* © Bettmann/CORBIS; *Pierre and Marie Curie* Archives Larousse, Paris, France/Bridgeman Art Library; *steel mill* Library of Congress Prints and Photographs Division, Washington, D.C. [LC-D401-10924LC]; *Alexander Graham Bell* ©Bettmann/Corbis; *Duryea car* ©Hulton Archive/Getty Images; *Wright Brothers* Library of Congress Prints and Photographs Division, Washington, D.C. [LC-USZ62-6166-A]; *John Patterson* Montgomery County Historical Society; *oil refinery* ©Corbis; *stock certificate* ©INTERFOTO/Alamy; *Rockefeller cartoon* ©Snark/Art Resource, NY; *poor working conditions* Courtesy of Brown Brothers.

Module 21: *Immigrants arrive Ellis Island* ©Bettmann/Corbis; *Statue of Liberty* © Joseph Sohm/Visions of America/Corbis; *Ferris Wheel* ©Corbis; *Nobel Prize* ©Ted Spiegel/Corbis; *Mexican immigrants* Shades of L.A. Archives/Los Angeles Public Library; *Scandinavian immigrants* Col. Ernest Swanson Papers, Swenson Swedish Immigration Research Center, Augustana College, Rock Island, IL; *Asian immigrants* National Archives, #90-G-152-2038; *Italian immigrants* ©Corbis; *Asian American celebration* ©A. Ramey/PhotoEdit; *map of Central Park* ©Collection of The New-York Historical Society; *Central Park* © David Ball/CORBIS; *tenements* The Granger Collection, New York; *Hull House children* ©Wallace Kirkland/Getty Images.

Module 22: *Suffrage Parade* ©Bettmann/Corbis; *James Garfield pitcher* Collection of Janice L. and David J. Frent; *Titanic poster* The Granger Collection, New York; *women voting* Library of Congress Prints and Photographs Division, Washington, D.C. [LC-USZ62-75334]; *Boss Tweed cartoon* The Granger Collection, New York; *portraits of presidents Hayes, Garfield, Arthur, Cleveland, Harrison, McKinley* PRC Picture Research Consultants, Inc.; *boy working in sweatshop* ©Bettmann/

Corbis; *Jacob Riis* Library of Congress Prints and Photographs Division, Washington, D.C. [LC-USZ62-5511]; *The Jungle* Library of Congress Prints and Photographs Division, Washington, D.C. [LC-DIG-ppmsca-13488]; *child laborers* Library of Congress Prints and Photographs Division, Washington, D.C. [LC-DIG-nclc-01441]; *Rose Freedman* Courtesy of Steve Latham/PRC Picture Research Consultants; *suffragette protest* ©Bettmann/Corbis; *Roosevelt and Muir* ©Bettmann/Corbis.

Module 23: *Panama Canal* ©Corbis; *Mt. McKinley* ©Charles Sleicher; *Indian National Congress* Press Information Bureau of India; *Buffalo soldier* Denver Public Library, Western History Collection; *Queen Liliuokalani* ©Douglas Peebles/Corbis; *Perry arrives in Japan* National Portrait Gallery, Smithsonian Institution/Art Resource, NY; *Boxer Rebellion* Trustees of The British Library; *Maine Explosion headline* ©Bettmann/Corbis; *sunken USS* Maine ©Bettmann/Corbis; *Maine Explosion* PRC Picture Research Consultants; *Battle of Quasimas* Library of Congress Prints and Photographs Division, Washington, D.C. [LC-DIG-pga-01889]; *U.S. Marines in China* ©Bettmann/Corbis; *William Jennings Bryan* ©Bettmann/Corbis; *Ellis Island immigrants* ©Bettmann/Corbis; *Paris Exhibition* ©Bettmann/Corbis; *Panama Canal construction* Library of Congress Prints and Photographs Division, Washington, D.C. [Digital ID# pan6a24297]; *Roosevelt Big Stick cartoon* The Granger Collection, New York.

Module 24: *Soldiers in trench* ©Bettmann/CORBIS; cl) *Uncle Sam recruitment poster* Library of Congress Prints and Photographs Division, Washington, D.C. [LC-USZC4-3859]; *Lusitania poster* ©Stock Montage, Inc.; *gas mask* Collection of Colonel Stuart S. Corning/Courtesy of Picture Research Consultants, Inc.; *Ferdinand assassination* The Granger Collection, New York; *German U-Boat* ©Corbis; *Lusitania sinks* ©SuperStock/SuperStock; *Supreme Court* ©Jurgen Vogt/The Image Bank/Getty Images; *WWI Women* ©Underwood & Underwood/Corbis; *Teamwork Wins poster* ©K.J.Historical/Corbis; *gas mask* Sam Dungeon/Houghton Mifflin Harcourt; *Harlem Hellfighters* ©Hulton Archive/Getty Images; *Tyne Cot Cemetery* ©Michael St. Maur Sheil/Corbis; *War Garden Commission* Library of Congress Prints and Photographs Division, Washington, D.C. [LC-USZC4-10671]; *US Bonds poster* Library of Congress Prints and Photographs Division [LC-USZC4-9850]; *Teamwork Wins poster* ©K.J.Historical/Corbis.

Module 25: *Times Square 1925* Bridgeman Art Library; *Harding campaign button* ©Lance Schriner/Houghton Mifflin Harcourt; *King Tut* ©Egyptian National Museum, Cairo, Egypt/SuperStock; *The Sun Also Rises* The Granger Collection, New York; *Emperor Hirohito* ©Bettmann/Corbis; *Empire State Building* Courtesy Brown Brothers; *Model T assembly line* Courtesy Ford Motor Company; *Model T* © Science & Society Picture Library/Getty Images; *Hoover campaign poster* Janice L. and David J. Frent Collection of Political Americana; *Smith campaign poster* Janice L. and David J. Frent Collection of Political Americana; *M. Carey Thomas* Library of Congress Prints and Photographs Division, Washington, D.C. [LC-USZ62-133870]; *Bessie Coleman* ©Bettmann/Corbis; *Life Magazine cover* The Granger Collection, New York; *Sacco Vanzetti rally* Library of Congress Prints and Photographs Division, Washington, D.C. [LC-USZ62-136881]; *prohibition* ©Bettmann/Corbis; *The Great Migration* ©The Museum of Modern Art/Licensed by SCALA/Art Resource, NY; *baseball team* ©NewsCom; *Babe Ruth* ©Bettmann/Corbis; *Louis Armstrong* ©Hulton Archive/Getty Images; *Georgia O'Keeffe* ©Georgia O'Keeffe Museum, Santa Fe/Art Resource.

Module 26: *Car for sale* © Bettmann/CORBIS; *Variety headline* The Granger Collection, New York; *FDR campaign button* Janice L. and David J. Frent Collection of Political Americana; *Hitler* ©Bettmann/Corbis; *Wizard of Oz ruby slippers* Courtesy Everett Collection; *Black Tuesday* The Granger Collection, New York; *unemployed man with sign* Milton (Pete) Brooks/The Detroit News Archives; *Blame it On Hoover cartoon* Courtesy Brown Brothers; *family listening to radio* ©Bettmann/Corbis; *WPA teens working* Library of Congress Prints & Photographs Division, Washington, D.C. [LC-DIG-fsa-8d12548]; *WPA teen girl working* Library of Congress Prints & Photographs Division, Washington, D.C. [LC-DIG-fsa-8d12548]; *Dust Bowl* NOAA George E. Marsh Album; *Migrant Mother* Library of Congress Prints and Photographs Division, Washington, D.C. [LC-DIG-fsa-8b29516]; *Stowaway movie poster* ©Swim Ink 2 LLC/Corbis; *Grapes of Wrath* The Granger Collection, New York.

Module 27: *Landing craft in Philippines* © CORBIS; *Enigma machine* AKG-Images, London; *mushroom cloud* ©Hulton Archive/Getty Images; *Hideki Tojo* ©MPI/Getty Images; *Hitler saluting crowd* © Hugo Jaeger/Timepix/Time Life Pictures/Getty Images; *bombed London street* ©Corbis; *Pearl Harbor attack* ©Corbis; *Rosie Riveter poster* Picture Research Consultants, Inc.; *Victory Garden poster* Library of Congress Prints and Photographs Division, Washington, D.C. [LC-USZC4-4436]; *Tuskegee Airmen* U.S. Air Force/Collection of David Ethell; *segregated drinking fountains* ©Bettmann/Corbis; *Japanese internment camp* ©Seattle Post-Intelligencer Collection, Museum of History and Industry/Corbis; *German U-Boats* ©Everett Collection, Inc.; *Winston Churchill, Franklin D. Roosevelt, Joseph Stalin, Adolf Hitler, Benito Mussolini (all)* ©Bettmann/CORBIS; *plane* Library of Congress Prints & Photographs Division, Washington, D.C. [LC-DIG-fsac-1a35398]; *tanks* ©Corbis; *invasion of Normandy* ©Keystone/Getty Images; *Navajo code talkers* National Archives (NARA); *raising flag at Iwo Jima* ©Superstock; *Battle of the Bulge* ©Corbis; *prisoners at Buchenwald* ©H. Miller/Hulton Archive/Getty Images; *Hiroshima ruins* ©Bettmann/Corbis; *Auschwitz (barbed wire)* ©R H Productions/Getty Images.

Module 28: *Duck and cover drill* ©Bettmann/CORBIS; *woman using early computer* ©Bettmann/Corbis; *Israeli flag* © Carl & Ann Purcell/CORBIS; *Fats Domino* © Hulton Archive/Getty Images; *NASA logo* ©AP Images; *Fidel Castro* ©Bettmann/CORBIS; *Yalta Conference* ©Hulton-Deutsch Collection/Corbis; *Potsdam Conference* ©Bettmann/Corbis; *UN aid workers* ©AP Images; *Czechoslovakia cartoon* Editorial cartoon by Tom Little, 1948, Courtesy of The Tennessean; *Jackie Robinson card* ©The Granger Collection, NYC; *FIRE! cartoon* ©HERBLOCK, The Herb Block Foundation; *1950s American family* Image courtesy of The Advertising Archives; *Jonas Salk vaccine* ©Bettmann/Corbis; *drive-in theater* ©Bettmann/Corbis; (c) *Elvis Presley* Courtesy Elvis Presley Enterprises; *Ralph Ellison* ©Ben Martin/Time Life Pictures/Getty Images.

Module 29: *Helicopters in Vietnam* AP/Wide World Photos; *Ho Chi Minh* ©Hulton Archive/Getty Images; *MLK* ©Flip Schulke/Corbis; *Woodstock poster* ©Blank Archives/Getty Images; *evacuating Saigon* ©Dirck Halstead/Getty Images; *Buzz Aldrin on moon* ©Corbis; *Apollo 11 lift off* NASA S69-39525; *South Vietnamese soldiers* ©AP Images; *Lieutenant John McCain* ©Ron Sachs/Sygma/Corbis; *Charley Trujillo* Karin Higgins/Daily Staff/083102; *Walter Cronkite Vietnam* ©CBS Photo Archive/Getty Images; *soldiers in tunnel* National Archives (NARA); *pro-war parade* ©Leif Skoogfors/Corbis; *peace protest* ©Dick Swanson/Time Life Pictures/Getty Images; *Vietnam celebration* ©Paula Bronstein/Getty Images; *Maya Ying Lin* © Richard Howard/Time Life Pictures/Getty Images; *Vietnam Memorial* ©James P. Blair/Corbis.